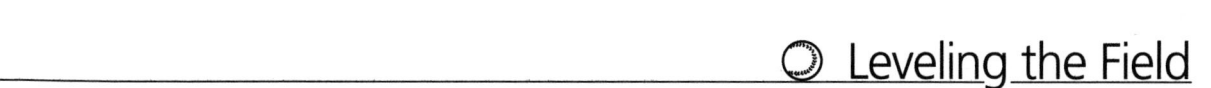 Leveling the Field

Leveling the Field

An Encyclopedia of Baseball's All-Time Great Performances

as Revealed Through Adjusted Statistics

G. SCOTT THOMAS

BLACK DOG
& LEVENTHAL
PUBLISHERS
NEW YORK

PUBLISHED BY

Black Dog & Leventhal Publishers, Inc.
151 West 19th Street
New York, NY 10011

DISTRIBUTED BY

Workman Publishing Company
708 Broadway
New York, NY 10003

Manufactured in the USA

Cover design by 27.12 Design Ltd.

Jacket art by Shasti O'Leary Soudant

Interior design by Martin Lubin Graphic Design

Cover photograph: Left to right (top row) Babe Ruth, Nap Lajoie, Honus Wagner, Randy Johnson, Sandy Koufax, Rich Gossage, Christy Mathewson, Eddie Mathews, Ty Cobb (middle row) Barry Bonds, Ernie Banks, Hoyt Wilhelm, Walter Johnson, Mike Schmidt, Lefty Grove, Roger Clemens, Willie Stargell, Rogers Hornsby (bottom row) Johnny Bench, Hank Aaron, Jimmie Foxx, Lou Gehrig, Mickey Cochrane, Willie Mays.

Cover photographs courtesy AP/Wide World Photos, Major League Baseball and Transcendental Graphics.

ISBN: 1-57912-255-8

h g f e d c b a

Library of Congress Cataloging-in-Publication Data available on file.

Contents

For my dad, who played the game and played it well

Acknowledgments

Many people helped with *Leveling the Field*. I offer my thanks to them all:

O To my parents, for nurturing an interest in baseball that has been severely tested by the rampant greed and incompetent leadership that curse the game today, but that still flickers, nonetheless.

O To Mike Kallay and Scott Smith of Street & Smith's Sports Annuals, for offering a forum for my first articles about adjusted statistics.

O To Bob Costas, Ralph Kiner, Pete Palmer, and Mike Veeck, for their constructive comments and much-appreciated encouragement during the early stages of this project.

O To my agents, Scott Mendel, Nikolai Vargas, and Jane Jordan Browne of Multimedia Product Development Inc., for their diligent efforts to find this book its best possible home.

O To Becky Koh and her colleagues at Black Dog & Leventhal, for their patience and professionalism in transforming my original manuscript into the final product that you're holding.

O And, last but not least, to my wife, Laura, and my daughter, Lindsay, for their unfailing support, good humor, and sense of fun, as well as their polite willingness to feign interest in a sport that clearly bores them both.

1 ⚾ Creating a Level Field

The past and the present are destined to quarrel. That's true in many walks of life, but especially true in baseball. Old-timers are often contemptuous of the modern game; they consider its players unskilled and its salaries exorbitant. One ex-player scoffs, "Baseball today is not what it should be. It makes me weep to think of the men of the old days and the boys of today. It's positively a shame – and they are getting big money for it, too." Another says: "The great trouble with baseball today is that most of the players are in the game for the money."

Comments like these about players' salaries are common in an era when Alex Rodriguez, a 25-year-old shortstop who has never appeared in a World Series, can attract a 10-year, $252-million contract. But these two critics aren't disgruntled, underpaid stars from the 1960s or 1970s ridiculing today's big-league ballplayers. They're two men who never heard of Alex Rodriguez and never saw the current century – Bill Joyce and Ty Cobb, sounding off in 1916 and 1925, respectively.

Joyce is long forgotten, a third baseman who knocked around the National League during the 1890s. He was a decent hitter, with a lifetime batting average of .294, but he was certainly no wizard in the field. He committed 509 errors in just 904 major-league games, a shaky record even in that era of tiny gloves and rocky infields.

Cobb, on the other hand, is one of the game's greatest legends, a lifetime .366 hitter, 12-time American League batting champion, the first player with 4,000 hits, and the first to be inducted into the Hall of Fame. The baseball world listened whenever he spoke, which was frequently. Cobb's unmatched skill at the plate was packaged with a cantankerous personality, maniacal obsession with money, and icy disdain for those who followed in his footsteps. Major-league ball, he insisted, had deteriorated steadily since his heyday.

Life magazine offered the 65-year-old Georgia Peach a forum for his invective in 1952. Its editors tossed the literary equivalent of a hanging curve, asking Cobb to write an article comparing the stars of his era and those of the present. "There are only two players in the major leagues who can be mentioned in the same breath with the oldtime greats," he wrote. Not the immortal Joe DiMaggio, who had retired the previous fall. Not Mickey Mantle or Willie Mays, then beginning illustrious careers. Not Richie Ashburn, Yogi Berra, Roy Campanella, Nellie Fox, George Kell, Ralph Kiner, Jackie Robinson, Duke Snider, or Ted Williams, all then in their prime and all destined for the Hall of Fame.

None of these all-time greats earned Cobb's applause. Phil Rizzuto and Stan Musial, he pronounced, were the only players of 1952 who would have been stars in his day. No one else. Case closed.

Cobb seemed to thaw a few years later, but it was merely a ruse, another way for him to mock the big-league descendants he considered so tremendously unworthy. The man who had topped

Ty Cobb (l.) and Stan Musial (r.) compare bat grips for NL president Ford Frick. Musial is one of the only two players who "can be mentioned in the same breath with the old time greats," according to Cobb in 1952.

Who's the greatest slugger of all? Gehrig? DiMaggio? The Babe? According to Jose Canseco it's Mark McGwire. "No one can even stand in his shoes."

.400 in 1911, 1912, and 1922 admitted that he couldn't hope to put up the same numbers against the pitchers of 1959. He guessed he might hit only .300, low indeed for a batter of his uncommon skills. Then came the clincher. "You've got to remember," he sneered, "I'm 73."

It works both ways, of course. Current players aren't always impressed with their predecessors, either. The colorful Jose Canseco, who has unleashed his powerful swing for several teams since 1985, was asked a couple of years ago to name the greatest slugger of all. Who was it: Ruth, Gehrig, DiMaggio, Aaron? None of them, said Canseco, opting instead for a contemporary, Mark McGwire. "No one can even stand in his shoes," Canseco insisted. "Not close to it. Not Babe Ruth. Not anyone."

Fighting words, indeed. So who is right?

Common sense suggests that the answer lies between the two extremes, somewhere to the left of Cobb and to the right of Canseco. Somewhere, perhaps, in the opinions of Jimmy Lanier.

Lanier was a bat boy in the 1920s for the Detroit Tigers, a team managed by none other than Cobb, who, though nearly 40, still roamed center field and hit for an impressive average (.378 in 1925). Lanier later moved to Atlanta, becoming such a devoted Braves fan that he regularly watched them on television well into his nineties. "All these young stars today are so wonderful, and the playing conditions are so much better now," he told an Atlanta reporter. "But the players in Mr. Cobb's day had all the abilities they have now, all of the same basic abilities. I think if you would take the 2000 Braves and put them in Detroit in 1925, with all the conditions of that day, and if you would take the 1925 Tigers and switch them over to today's equipment and conditions, there wouldn't be much difference, in my opinion."

The best way to test Lanier's theory, you might think, would be to compare statistics from the two seasons in question. Baseball, after all, is the most quantified of sports. Scorekeepers chart every pitch and every at bat, and they've been doing so for 130 years, ever since the major leagues were born. It seems all we need is to find the appropriate numbers for the 1925 Tigers and 2000 Braves and match them up.

But, of course, it's not that easy. Baseball's mass of statistics has its limitations, largely because the game has evolved so dramatically. Most teams in 1925 scratched for a run at a time, hoping to string enough singles together to win 3-2 or 2-1. The game we know is drastically different. Today's typical team aims for a big inning, swinging for the fences, willing to win 6-5 or 8-6 or even 11-10.

Is it realistic to compare statistics from two years that have so little in common? Is it fair? Not at all.

Consider the case of Babe Ruth and Hank Aaron. Ruth played from 1914 to 1935, pounding 714 home runs, a record generally considered unbreakable. But Aaron broke it, smashing 755 homers between 1954 and 1976. Which was the greater accomplishment? It's difficult to say, because the two men competed under starkly different conditions. Ruth played only in the daytime, Aaron mostly at night. Ruth played only on grass, Aaron sometimes on artificial turf. Ruth played only against whites, Aaron against players of all races, therefore competing against a much larger pool of players. Ruth traveled by train, Aaron by jet. Ruth rarely faced relief pitchers, Aaron often did. "This is the talk in every era," Aaron chuckled long after his career was over. "When I was chasing Babe's record, that's all I heard – the difference between the eras."

The Generation Gap

Philosophers and poets have been telling us for centuries that the universe is in constant flux. Heraclitus, one of Greece's early big-leaguers, wrote, "Nothing endures but change." Edmund Spenser, the great slugger of English prose, agreed: "Times do change and move continually." But it remained for one of the deepest of thinkers, Dizzy Dean, to sum up this eternal phenomenon in a single sentence. "I ain't what I used to be," he conceded, "but who the hell is?"

The question now facing us is this: Is there a way to account for the impact of change, allowing us to compare baseball statistics from different eras fairly and accurately?

The answer, based on evidence from other fields, is yes.

Take economics, for instance. The federal government long ago developed the consumer price index (CPI) to determine the rate of inflation. Economists head out each month to learn the current prices of consumer goods. They use a mathematical formula to convert their data to a single number, based on a 1982-1984 score of 100. A CPI higher than 100 is a sign that goods cost more than they did in those benchmark years. An index below 100 shows that prices are lower than they were in 1982–1984.

The beauty of the CPI is that it can be used to calculate the change in the cost of living over any given period since 1913, when the government began tracking prices. Consider this 20-year comparison: The CPI climbed from 77.8 in January 1980 to 168.8 in January 2000. That's an increase of 117 percent, which means the cost of living grew 117 percent during those two decades.

The practical application is clear. If you earned $20,000 at your job in 1980, your salary 20 years later would need to be 117 percent higher – $43,400 – to give you exactly the same purchasing power. If you were paid more than $43,400 in 2000, you were ahead of the curve. If you were making less than that, you were just another victim of inflation.

Baseball, of course, has been hit with its own version of inflation, with home runs being a case in point. The grand total for all National League hitters in 1901 was 227 home runs, which works out to 28 per team. The league-wide figure soared to 2,565 homers by 1998, or 160 per team. The St. Louis Cardinals alone blasted 223 homers in 1998, nearly as many as the entire league 97 years earlier.

Other statistics, such as stolen bases, haven't increased or decreased in a straight line during the past century, but have gone through alternating periods of inflation and deflation. The typical National League team stole 175 bases in 1901, a number that plummeted to 47 per team in 1950, then rebounded to 154 per team by 1987.

If the CPI can be used to remove inflation as a factor in comparing prices or salaries, can't the same principle be applied to home runs or stolen bases or other baseball statistics? I don't see any reason why not.

So that's what I've done. I have developed several formulas and computer programs that eliminate statistical inflation, allowing honest comparisons of players and teams from all periods of baseball history. Everything from past seasons – standings, playoff results, individual statistics, even salaries – has been converted to today's standards, so you can look at figures from different years and instantly determine the best.

I have come up with these formulas on my own, but I don't pretend to be a trailblazer. I'm aware that others have done and continue to do similar work. There's a whole group of number crunchers – sabermetricians – who do fascinating things with baseball statistics. They turn out books and articles showing how the designated hitter has changed the strategy of the game, or whether Norm Cash belongs in the Hall of Fame, or how much a "hitter's park" like Wrigley Field inflates batting averages. You probably know some of their names: Bill James, Pete Palmer, Rob Neyer. Their research is often groundbreaking stuff, and it can be quite interesting.

But, as far as I'm concerned, sabermetricians usually go too far. They become too technical and too arcane. They deal in standard deviations and regression analyses and obscure statistics like "runs created per 27 at bats." Not me. I prefer the numbers we all grew up with, like wins, losses, batting averages, home runs, and strikeouts. They're easy to understand, they've stood the test of time, and they're the only statistics you'll find in *Leveling the Field.*

Baseball, after all, isn't a research project. It's a game.

Or, to put it another way, I had no desire to write a mathematics textbook. So I didn't.

The rest of this chapter will offer step-by-step explanations of the formulas I used to adjust statistics from baseball's past. (Some of the explanations are pretty dry and studded with decimals, despite all my brave talk about not writing a math book. I think it's only fair that I go into considerable detail about my methods, but that doesn't mean you have to read all the fine print. Skim the rest of this chapter, if you can, to get a better idea of what I set out to do. If you really don't care, I think you can skip ahead without much harm.

There are six types of formulas:

○ Regular season standings
○ Playoff results
○ Individual statistics
○ Player salaries
○ Best players of all time
○ Best teams of all time

All of these formulas, of course, require numerical fuel. Several books and websites provide raw statistics for the major leagues, but my primary source was the best of all, the sixth edition of *Total Baseball,* the official encyclopedia of major league baseball. Two annual publications of *The Sporting News* – the *Baseball Register* and the *Complete Baseball Record Book* – also were useful. If these sources disagreed on a player's statistics, as they sometimes did, *Total Baseball* had the final word.

1. Regular Season Standings

Every major-league team plays a 162-game season in a league split into divisions. That's what we're accustomed to. That's what we've seen for more than 30 years. But most of baseball's history was different. Schedules were shorter, and divisions were nowhere to be seen.

The first big-leaguers, 1876's eight National League squads, played anywhere from 57 to 70 games. The length of the season ballooned to 126 games within a decade, and reached 140 by the dawn of the modern era in 1901. Stability was achieved three years later when both major leagues unveiled the 154-game slate they would use for more than half a century. The current schedule of 162 games debuted in the American League in 1961 and the National League the following season.

It wasn't until the end of the sixties that divisions first appeared, long after they had been adopted by professional football and basketball. Both leagues split into two divisions of six teams in 1969, bumping them up to seven teams after subsequent expansion. The current lineup of three divisions in both leagues has existed since 1994, with sizes ranging from four to six teams.

This book converts each season to the structure used today. I have adjusted every franchise's win–loss record to add up to 162 games every year, and I have created divisions for every season that lacked them. Year-by-year standings are expressed in a way that current fans can appreciate, allowing us to view any team's accomplishments, no matter when they occurred, in a modern light.

Here's my recipe for adjusting regular-season standings, with the 1946 St. Louis Cardinals serving as an example:

Step 1 Determine a team's actual winning percentage for the regular season. Subtract any extra games that were played to break ties for first place in a league or division. The Cardinals' record for 1946 is listed as 98 wins and 58 losses, but it includes their two-game sweep of a tiebreaker series with the Brooklyn Dodgers, who were deadlocked with St. Louis for the National League title. That means the Cards' regular-season record was 96-58, which yields a winning percentage of .623.

Step 2 Multiply the actual winning percentage by 162 to determine the adjusted number of wins, then truncate that figure. The formula for the Cards (.623 times 162) equals 100.926 wins, which gives us, for the moment, a truncated number of 100 and a remainder of .926.

Step 3 Bring the records of all teams within a league into balance, with total adjusted wins and losses being the same. Begin this process by adding the truncated adjusted wins for all teams. Determine the shortfall from the *required sum,* which is total number of games played by the entire league. National League teams in 1946 had a truncated total of 643 adjusted wins, 5 short of the required 648. That means the five franchises with the largest remainders receive an additional adjusted win. St. Louis, with a remainder of .926, is among the lucky ones, pushing its total to 101.

The other teams – those whose remainders aren't big enough – stay at their truncated number of adjusted wins.

Step 4 This step is used only in highly unusual circumstances where a league has one additional adjusted win to distribute, but has two eligible teams with identical remainders. Each has an equal claim on the extra win, but only one can have it. Which team should it be? Use a simple best-of-five formula to choose. Give one point to the team that scored more runs, hit more homers, had a higher batting average, allowed fewer runs, and delivered more strikeouts in the given season. The team with the most points gets the additional win. This step is necessary in only four cases since 1901: in the National League in 1916, 1922, and 1936, and in the American League in 1967.

Step 5 Subtract a team's adjusted wins from 162 to get its adjusted losses. That's 162 minus 101 for the 1946 Cardinals, yielding 61 losses.

Step 6 Determine a team's adjusted winning percentage. St. Louis has an adjusted record of 101-61, which is .623.

This process brings every team's record to 162 games. It effectively adjusts not only the shorter seasons prior to the sixties, but also those subsequent years when strikes interrupted the schedule, like in 1972, 1981, and 1994. And it even fills in the gaps for teams that missed a game here and there because of rainouts that were never made up.

My second major adjustment to regular-season standings is nowhere as precise as the steps above; imposing a divisional structure on every year since 1901 is inevitably arbitrary. But I did establish three rules to guide the process:

○ Divisions can have no more than five teams, and no fewer than three.

○ Geography is the determining factor for divisional lineups. The National League West, for example, must consist of the league's westernmost teams. (This is a rule the majors ignored in real life. Remember when Atlanta and Cincinnati were part of the NL West?) If franchises move, as so many did in the fifties, divisions must be altered to reflect new geographic realities. That's why I shift the Braves from the NL East in 1952, when they were based in Boston, to the NL West in 1953, when they arrived in Milwaukee. They slide back to the East in 1958 after the Dodgers and Giants moved to California.

○ A league's adjusted number of divisions must be higher than its actual number in a given year. If baseball had adopted a divisional structure as early as 1901, I believe it would have increased the number of divisions more rapidly than it actually did. (Look at the National Football League — it shot from two divisions in 1933 to six in 1970.) So I divided each league into two divisions from 1901 to 1968, three from 1969 to 1992, and four since 1993.

That leaves one tricky matter to consider. Should I change the number of games a team plays against divisional and other opponents, and then reconfigure each season's win-loss records accordingly? I decided not to, for three reasons.

The first (let's be honest) is that it would be a ton of work. Consider any season during that long period from 1904 to 1960, when each league had eight franchises and a 154-game schedule. Every team played every other team within its league 22 times each year. But let's say I decided to adjust the standings to an unbalanced slate of 162 games. A team might play each divisional rival 30 times and every team in the other division 18 times.

It's possible to make those adjustments, of course. I would need to find every team's record against every other team for every year, and then set my computer to work using those winning percentages to predict the outcomes of the adjusted match-ups. I can't say I would be eager to get started.

That's where the second reason comes in handy. It turns out that win–loss records don't change very much with an unbalanced schedule. I experimented on more than a dozen teams from different seasons. Most ended up with exactly the same win totals after the computer stopped whirring. The rest changed by only a game or two.

I thought I might have found an exception in the 1916 Philadelphia Athletics, who put together the worst winning percentage in the modern era. The A's, for whatever reason, played considerably better against nearby teams. Their winning percentages were .292 vs. the hypothetical AL East and .193 vs. the West. I assumed an unbalanced slate would improve Philadelphia's record substantially, because its number of games against East Division foes would grow from 66 in real life to 90 in the adjusted standings. I was wrong. The A's gained exactly two adjusted wins.

The final reason, to be blunt, is that baseball doesn't seem overly concerned about schedule equilibrium, so why should I be?

Teams within a division played all teams the same number of times at home and away until 1977, when the balancing act started coming unraveled in the American League. The same happened in 1993 in the National League. Interleague play (in 1997) and expansion (in 1998) created further imbalances. "It hasn't been a perfect schedule for a while," said Katy Feeney, the vice president in the commissioner's office in charge of the schedule, to which I can only add: No kidding.

2. Playoff Results

The New York Yankees won 20 World Series between 1923 and 1962. They took half of the titles awarded in that entire period – 20 of 40 – an amazing record that will never be duplicated.

Why not? Because it's so much harder to win a championship these days, that's why.

A season prior to 1969 was capped simply by the World Series pitting the American and National League champions. The 1923–1962 Yankees, great as they were, had to win just four games to add another prize to their trophy case. But the advent of divisional play intoduced a second round of playoffs, later joined by a third. Eight teams now qualify for postseason play that spans the month of October. A champion these days must string together eleven wins – three in the division series, four in the league championship series, and four in the World Series.

That's obviously more difficult. The longer the playoffs, the more likely an upset, as I found when comparing the final 30 World Series before the playoffs were extended (1939–1968) and the first 30 after extension (1969–1999, minus the strike year of 1994). I wanted to see how often the team with the highest winning percentage in a given season also took that year's championship. It happened 17 of 30 times when the World Series was the only postseason matchup, but just 8 of 30 times after extra rounds were added.

That set me wondering: If they had been forced to endure extended playoffs, how well would the great teams of the past have done? I developed a computer program to simulate postseason results for every year since 1901. Playoff participants were selected according to each season's adjusted standings:

○ Each league's divisional titlists were matched in a best-of-seven championship series from 1901 to 1968. The winners advanced to the World Series.

○ The simulated playoffs were expanded in 1969, with three divisional champs and a wild-card team meeting in two best-of-five series in each league. The winners went on to the league championship series, followed by the World Series.

○ The number of divisions in each league was expanded to four in 1993, spelling the end of the wild card. (This change kept the Florida Marlins out of the simulated playoffs in 1997, even though they were that year's world champs in real life.) The four divisional winners played in two division series, followed by the league championship series and the World Series.

Here, for the technically minded, is how my simulation program works, using the computerized 1996 World Series between Cleveland and Montreal as an example.

Step 1 Determine the average number of runs scored per game in a given year. Compare it to the average for the 2000 season, finding the multiplier that will change 2000's figure to the selected year's. The 1996 average was 10.07 runs by both teams in a single game, 2 percent less than 2000's average of 10.28. If 2000's figure is multiplied by 0.980, it will equal the 1996 average.

Step 2 Compare each team's number of runs scored to the major-league average for the given year. Then find the multiplier, using a process similar to the previous step. Montreal scored 4.57 runs per game in 1996, 9 percent below that year's single-team average of 5.04. A multiplier of 0.907 will change the big-league average to the Expos' average.

Step 3 Repeat Step 2 for each team's number of runs allowed. Montreal gave up 4.12 runs per game in 1996, resulting in a multiplier of 0.817.

Step 4 Square the multipliers that were generated by the previous two steps. Montreal ends up with a squared runs-scored multiplier of 0.823 and a squared runs-allowed multiplier of 0.667. (I take this step because sabermetricians have shown that a team's winning percentage can be predicted with surprising accuracy by a formula in which its runs scored and runs allowed are nearly squared. The actual factor is 1.83.)

Step 5 Use the computer to generate game-by-game scores for both teams. My computer used a database of scores from all 2,429 games played in 2000, randomly selecting a run total for the first team in each hypothetical contest, then repeating the process for the second team.

Step 6 Adjust the random scores to the given year's level, using the multiplier from Step 1. All raw scores for the simulated 1996 World Series are multiplied by 0.980.

Step 7 Multiply each team's scores by the two additional factors from Step 4: (1) its squared multiplier for runs scored, and (2) its opponent's squared multiplier for runs allowed. Montreal's scores are multiplied by 0.823 and 0.899, the latter being Cleveland's factor for runs allowed.

Step 8 Break any ties, having the computer generate extra-innings results for both teams, using a process similar to Step 5.

I used this program to play each series 100 times. Cleveland won 1996's computerized World Series 56 times, Montreal 44. That makes sense. The Indians racked up 100 adjusted wins that season, while the Expos had only 88. I'm sure most fans would agree that Cleveland was better.

But that's not the way baseball works. The better team doesn't always win. Think back to the 1969 World Series. The Orioles were hailed as one of the greatest teams of all time, while the "Miracle Mets" were considered to be way over their heads. I had them play 100 times in the computer, and Baltimore won 65 series. But real

life was different. New York, suddenly invincible, took the title in five games. It wasn't even close.

My program obviously needed to allow for upsets, so I had the computer randomly choose one series from each 100 simulations. The scores in the selected series became the official results in this book. The computer agreed with the odds-makers in 1996, picking Cleveland over Montreal in seven games, but it wasn't afraid of the occasional upset. The most shocking occurred in 1968, when Cincinnati took the simulated World Series despite winning just 18 of 100 matchups with Detroit.

I saw no reason to simulate a series if it actually occurred. The Orioles and Mets qualified for both the actual and computerized World Series in 1969, so I used the actual results. You'll find an asterisk (*) denoting every case where all the scores are from real games.

More rare is the double asterisk (**), which indicates that some, but not all, of the scores are real. The double asterisk usually means a series had to be extended. The actual league championship series, for example, were best-of-five affairs until 1985, but the simulated versions were always best-of-seven, occasionally requiring me to tack on a few computerized games. The 1983 American League series is a case in point. The Orioles beat the White Sox for the real AL title, three games to one, so the scores for the first four games are real. The fifth game, also an Oriole win, is simulated. An unusual double asterisk can be found in 1920, when the World Series was best of nine. I reduced it to best of seven, truncating the real results after Cleveland's fourth win.

One point should be stressed. I played every series 100 times in the computer, even if I used actual results in the book. You'll find each team's number of computerized victories in the righthand column, following the game-by-game scores.

And a final note: I use current team nicknames in the playoff results. I know they've changed over time. I know the Red Sox once were the Pilgrims, the Yankees were the Highlanders, the Phillies were the Blue Jays, the Braves were the Bees, and the Indians had a whole slew of names. But why confuse the issue? I'm sticking with the nicknames that are familiar today.

3. Individual Statistics

I've been talking, up to now, about the methods I have used to adjust or simulate team statistics. But the heart of *Leveling the Field* isn't the team; it's the individual. Most of this book is devoted to the statistics of individual players.

My theory is simple. If John Doe was 10-percent better than the average player in 1910, the reincarnation of John Doe would be 10-percent better than the average player today. The game has changed greatly during the intervening 90-odd years, as you know, and so have its statistical standards. What we need – and what this book presents – are ways to translate Doe's numbers from 1910 to their current equivalents.

Here's the basic way these formulas work, as shown in two rough examples. (Very rough, as you'll soon see. The numbers in these hypothetical cases are approximations, and certain nuances have been removed from the calculations. My aim here is to explain the thinking behind the mathematics detailed on the next few pages.)

○ A home run was a rare event in 1910, when a typical batter hit, let's say, three homers all season. Doe belted six home runs that year, 100 percent more than an average player. How does that translate to 2000? Conditions were drastically different by then, with the average batter blasting fifteen homers. Doe's adjusted number of homers from 1910 should be 100 percent better than 2000's average. That puts him at 30 home runs.

○ It works the other way, too. Players were much more likely to steal in baseball's early days. The average runner, for purposes of this example, had 20 stolen bases in 1910, but only 5 in 2000. Doe's total of 32 stolen bases was 60 percent above 1910's average. Its equivalent would be an adjusted total of just eight stolen bases in 2000.

What I'm saying, then, is that a player who hit 6 homers and stole 32 bases in 1910 performed at exactly the same level as his counterpart with 30 home runs and 8 stolen bases in 2000. What matters is how an individual player's statistics compare to the average statistics for the same season – and how that season's brand of baseball compares to the game we know today.

The beauty of this system is that all external factors are accounted for. If expansion makes it easier to belt the long ball, the average number of homers will soar, and a batter will have to slug more homers to obtain the same adjusted number. We saw that in the case of John Doe. His 6 homers in the dead-ball year of 1910 would be the same as 30 in 2000.

Or if jet travel or artificial turf or a change in strategy or something else makes conditions tougher for base runners, the number of stolen bases will plummet, and a specific player will need fewer stolen bases to reach the same adjusted figure. Doe had to swipe 32 bases in 1910 to be 60 percent above average, but a player in 2000's slower game would need just 8 steals to reach the same level.

What we have is baseball's version of the consumer price index, designed to counter the impact of statistical inflation or deflation. I have chosen a five-year period for my benchmark, so that all statistics from all seasons are converted to their 1996–2000 equivalents.

I need to touch on a couple of other points before taking you step by step through the formulas for hitters and pitchers.

You'll see in Chapter 2 that I adjusted the statistics for every Most Valuable Player and Cy Young Award winner since 1901. The catch, of course, is that no version of the MVP existed until 1911; the current award (controlled by baseball writers) didn't debut until 1931. The Cy Young was launched even later, 1956, with just one honoree per season. Separate awards for the best pitcher in each league didn't come until 1967.

I wanted to list the top players and pitchers for every season since 1901, so I chose to fill in the gaps with hypothetical winners selected by baseball historian Bill Deane. (You can find his entertaining venture in alternate history in *Total Baseball*.) I think it's fitting that the first winner of the American League Cy Young Award, back in 1901, would have been Cy Young.

Chapter 2 also shows each season's individual leaders in 19 statistical categories. The players listed are the real-life leaders in each category; my aim is to show what happened to their statistics after they were adjusted. It often happens that individual players with the same actual numbers end up with different adjusted numbers, sometimes substantially different, after the steps below are followed. (See the American League triples category in 1904 or the NL home run race in 1948, among many others.) It's also possible that the actual leader can be passed by someone else after adjustment. Lave Cross, for example, wasn't first in the American League in actual doubles in 1902, but he was first in adjusted doubles. Chapter 2, however, lists the names of the real co-leaders, along with their actual and adjusted numbers.

HITTERS (PART ONE)

Here's how hitters' records are adjusted, using Robin Yount's performance in the strike-shortened season of 1981 as an example:

Step 1 Adjust a batter's number of games played so that it conforms to a 162-game schedule. Divide actual games played (96 for Yount in 1981) by the total number of games in which his team competed (109 for Milwaukee), then multiply by 162. Round to the nearest whole number. Yount's adjusted number of games for 1981 is 143.

Step 2 Calculate a batter's adjusted number of at bats (ABs). Determine how many at bats he averaged per actual game, then multiply that figure by his adjusted number of games. Round to the nearest whole number. Yount had 377 at bats in his 96 actual games in 1981, which equals 3.927 ABs per game. That yields a total of 562 adjusted at bats in 143 adjusted games.

Step 3 Calculate a ratio that compares the actual performance of a single player to the actual performances of all other players in the same category. I'll use hits as an example. Yount had 103 hits in 377 at bats in 1981, equaling 0.27321 hits per at bat. (I'm sure you recognize that as Yount's batting average carried to two extra decimal places. But we can compute the same kind of average for any other statistic, such as runs scored per at bat or runs batted in per AB.) Then subtract the player's numbers from the major-league totals for the same season, which gives you the combined statistics for all other players. Everyone but Yount had 24,054 hits in 94,090 at bats in 1981, equaling 0.25565 hits per at bat. Match the player's average (0.27321 for Yount) to the average for all other players (0.25565) to determine the ratio. Yount's average is 1.06869 times larger than the figure for the rest of the majors, which means Yount was about 6.9 percent more likely than his typical competitor to get a hit in any given at bat in 1981.

Step 4 Determine a player's adjusted number (in this case, his adjusted number of hits). Multiply the player's ratio by the category's 1996-2000 standard and then by his adjusted number of at bats. Round to the nearest whole number. Yount's ratio of 1.06869 is multiplied by the major-league average for 1996 through 2000 (0.26893 hits per at bat) and his number of adjusted at bats in 1981 (562). This formula yields an adjusted total of 162 hits for Yount in 1981. (Steps 3 and 4 can be used to compute adjusted totals of runs scored, runs batted in, or stolen bases, while a player's adjusted batting average is calculated by dividing adjusted hits by adjusted at bats.)

HITTERS (PART TWO)

Extra-base hits are trickier. A player's number of doubles, triples, and home runs must yield the correct batting and slugging averages simultaneously, a tall order unless you follow the steps below. Yount again is the example:

Step 1 Same as the previous Step 1.

Step 2 Same as the previous Step 2.

Step 3 Calculate a player's ratios for doubles, triples, and homers, following the procedures in Step 3 above. Yount's ratios are 0.93943 for doubles (indicating that his number of doubles per at bat is below the average for all other players), 1.90807 for triples (nearly twice the average for everyone else), and 1.40924 for homers.

Step 4 Adjust a player's extra-base hits, using the procedures in Step 4 above. Yount ends up with adjusted totals of 28 doubles, 6 triples, and 25 home runs. These are raw numbers, not final figures, as we shall see.

Step 5 Add up the number of extra bases generated by a player's adjusted extra-base hits. Yount's total is 115 extra bases: 28 from doubles, 12 from triples, and 75 from homers.

Step 6 Determine a player's ideal adjusted slugging average. (It may not precisely match the figure we end up with in Step 9.) Take his actual slugging average (.41910 for Yount in 1981) and match it against the slugging average for all other major-leaguers the same year (.36837). Multiply the resulting ratio (1.13771) by 1996–2000's standard slugging average of .42750. The result for Yount is an adjusted figure of .486.

Step 7 Determine how many adjusted extra bases the player should have. Multiply his adjusted slugging average (.486 for Yount) by his adjusted at bats (562), then subtract his adjusted number of hits (162). Yount ideally should have 111 extra bases, according to this step.

Step 8 Recalibrate the raw number of doubles, triples, and homers generated in Step 4. Take the extra-base target from Step 7 (111) and divide it by the total from Step 5 (115). Multiply the resulting ratio (0.96522), in turn, by each of the figures from Step 4. Round off to the nearest whole number. Yount finishes with 27 doubles, 6 triples, and 24 homers.

Step 9 Calculate the final adjusted slugging average. Add up a player's adjusted total bases (273 for Yount: 105 singles, 27 doubles, 6 triples, 24 home runs) and divide the total by his adjusted at bats (562). Yount's adjusted slugging average for 1981 is .486.

PITCHERS

Our example here is Tom Seaver's performance in 1972, a slightly shortened season because of labor problems:

Step 1 Adjust a pitcher's number of appearances so that it fits a 162-game schedule. Divide actual games pitched (35 for Seaver in 1972) by the total number of games in which his team competed

(156 for the Mets), then multiply by 162. Round to the nearest whole number. Seaver's adjusted number of games for 1972 is 36.

Step 2 Calculate a pitcher's adjusted number of innings pitched (IPs). Determine how many innings he averaged per actual game, then multiply that figure by his adjusted number of games. Round to the nearest whole number. Seaver had 262 innings in his 35 actual games in 1972, which equals 7.486 IPs per game. That yields a rounded total of 269 adjusted innings in 36 adjusted games.

Step 3 Adjust a pitcher's wins. Divide his actual wins (21 for Seaver) by actual games (35) to determine his number of wins per game. It's exactly 0.6 for Seaver. Multiply that ratio by his adjusted games (36). Round to the nearest whole number. The result is 22 adjusted wins.

Step 4 Repeat Step 3 to adjust a pitcher's losses. Seaver's actual total of 12 is unchanged by the adjustment process.

Step 5 Calculate a ratio that compares the actual performance of a single pitcher to the actual performances of all other pitchers in the same category. Let's use earned runs as an example. Seaver allowed 85 earned runs in 262 innings in 1972, equaling 0.32443 earned runs per inning. Subtract the pitcher's numbers from the major-league totals for the same season, which provides the combined statistics for all other pitchers. Everyone but Seaver allowed 12,016 earned runs in 33,188.33 innings in 1972, equaling 0.36205 earned runs per inning. Match the pitcher's average (0.32443 for Seaver) to the average for all other pitchers (0.36205) to determine the ratio. Seaver's average is 0.89609 times the figure for the rest of the majors, which means he was about 10.4 percent less likely than a typical pitcher to give up an earned run in any given inning in 1972.

Step 6 Determine a pitcher's adjusted number (in this case, his adjusted number of earned runs). Multiply the pitcher's ratio by the category's 1996-2000 standard and then by his adjusted number of innings pitched. Round to the nearest whole number. Seaver's ratio of 0.89609 is multiplied by the major-league average for 1996 through 2000 (0.50834 earned runs per inning) and his number of adjusted innings in 1972 (269). This formula yields an adjusted total of 123 earned runs for Seaver in 1972. (Steps 5 and 6 also can be used to compute adjusted totals of hits or walks allowed, while a pitcher's adjusted earned run average is calculated by dividing adjusted earned runs by adjusted innings, then multiplying by nine.)

Two pitching statistics require a bit of extra care. Adjustments for saves and strikeouts generally follow the guidelines in Steps 5 and 6, but with a twist in each case.

My computer program doesn't allow a pitcher's adjusted number of saves to exceed his adjusted number of games minus his adjusted wins and losses. That's common sense, I know, but it's an essential part of the formula. If it didn't exist, several pitchers from the early years of the 20th century would boast outrageously (and impossibly) high adjusted save totals. Saves were so rare back then that each one would be the equivalent of several saves today.

The formula for strikeouts actually works on parallel tracks. It calculates strikeouts per inning, comparing a pitcher's average to the average for all other pitchers during the same season. It produces the same calculation and comparison for all outs resulting from batted balls (grounders, flies, foul outs). These two figures are brought into balance, much as we did above for extra-base hits, yielding a pitcher's adjusted strikeouts. Extra-base hits and strikeouts both are direct components of other statistics, which is why these additional steps are needed. Extra-base hits must conform with a hitter's adjusted slugging average, as we have seen. Strikeouts must do the same with innings pitched, since each strikeout equals one-third of an inning.

4. Player Salaries

Old-timers would have us believe that they played only for the love of the game. Money, they say, was meaningless. Don't listen to them. The truth is that major-leaguers have always been intensely concerned about money:

○ Christy Mathewson was considered to be self-less, a man seemingly without ego, but he also knew the value of a buck. He demanded a raise to $5,000, a huge salary at the time, after winning 20 games for the New York Giants in 1901. "When I opened my mouth to say $5,000, the words just refused to come," he admitted. "I felt in my soul that no such sum of money existed." He did, of course, manage to ask for the $5,000. He got $3,500, roughly equivalent to $100,000 today.

○ Walter Johnson, whose blazing fastball intimidated a generation of hitters, was remarkably mild-mannered off the mound, yet he turned bitter on financial matters. He earned $6,500 (approximately $120,000 today) after winning 32 games in 1912. "The employer tries to starve out the laborer," he complained.

○ Sandy Koufax and Don Drysdale used a similar analogy in 1966, when they staged a joint holdout during spring training. Koufax signed with the Dodgers for $130,000 a few days before the season started; Drysdale got $115,000. Koufax's attorney, J. William Hayes, said the Dodgers capitulated after he threatened a lawsuit against baseball's reserve clause, which bound a player to a team for life. "If we won the case," he

Kevin Brown, the highest paid pitcher in baseball.

said, "Koufax and Drysdale would be the Abraham Lincolns of baseball. They would have freed baseball players from slavery."

Emancipation, of course, came with the advent of free agency a decade later. Rapid inflation eventually yielded such contracts as Kevin Brown's 1999 deal with the Dodgers for $15 million a year, the most ever earned by a pitcher, and Alex Rodriguez's 2001 agreement with the Rangers for $25 million per season, the richest contract for any player.

I was curious what baseball would have been like if its stars had always been paid at today's

Alex Rodriguez's 2001 agreement with the Rangers for $25 million per season yielded the richest contract for any player.

wage scale. Or, to put it another way, how much would Mathewson, Johnson, Koufax, Drysdale, and other Hall of Famers earn if they were playing right now?

I took my first stab in 1999 at developing a formula to estimate the current market value of the 20th century's best players. My first step was to analyze the reported values of the contracts signed by 56 free-agent hitters and 27 free-agent pitchers after the 1998 season.

I compared each batter's annual pay to 25 statistical indicators. The dollar value of a hitter's contract, I discovered, was affected most heavily by three fairly equal factors: (1) his number of plate appearances in the past season, (2) his total runs scored in the past four years, and (3) his number of runs batted in during the past four seasons. Batting averages and fielding statistics had surprisingly little influence on pay levels.

I then compared each pitcher's annual pay to 35 sets of statistics. The size of a pitcher's deal, I found, was also determined by three factors: (1) his number of strikeouts in the past year, (2) his total innings pitched during the same season, and (3) his

number of wins and saves in the past four years, under a point system that gave wins three times the value of saves. Earned run average was among the statistics that had little impact on salary.

One additional factor turned out to be equally important for batters and pitchers – age. If two free agents had comparable statistics, the younger player almost always received higher pay.

I used this information to develop two computer models. The first estimated the yearly salary that any free-agent batter would have received in the winter of 1999; the second did the same for pitchers. I then tested my formulas by applying them to my study group of 83 free agents. The results were encouraging:

◯ The highest annual pay for any batter in the group was estimated by my first model to be $13.2 million, while the average pay for all 56 free-agent batters was pegged at $3.8 million. The actual figures were $13.3 million and $3.5 million, respectively.

◯ The top salary for any pitcher in the group was estimated to be $14.7 million, just short of Brown's actual $15 million. My second model predicted that the average pay for all 27 pitchers would be $4 million, slightly higher than the correct figure of $3.8 million.

It's impossible to be perfectly accurate in estimating free-agent salaries, given the irrationality of the current market. But I felt I had come as close as possible. I was ready to plug any player's adjusted statistics into either of my models to determine his value in the current marketplace.

Baseball's salary structure spiraled higher the next two years, culminating in Rodriguez's mammoth contract, and I updated my calculations to keep pace. This book's models reflect each player's estimated value in 2001 dollars, based on statistics adjusted to 1996-2000 performance levels and a 162-game schedule. (You can find season-by-season estimated salaries for 254 hitters in Chapter 6 and for 177 pitchers in Chapter 7. All are expressed in millions of dollars.)

Each computer model works the same way, comparing any player (or pitcher) from any season to the corresponding pool of free agents from 1999 to 2001. It matches ages and adjusted statistics, determining the approximate salary that an old-timer would earn today. A 28-year-old hitter who went to the plate 698 times in a season, scored an average of 113 runs per year over four seasons, and drove in 141 runs per year in the same four-season stretch would be worth $25.2 million, for example, while a pitcher of the same age with 17 wins per year over four seasons, 257 innings pitched, and 329 strikeouts would be valued at $25.5 million.

Keep in mind that the largest salaries don't automatically go to the best players. Rodriguez may be the highest-paid major leaguer, but he isn't supreme on the field. He has never been named Most Valuable Player. Brown, likewise, is paid more than any other pitcher, but he isn't the best. He has never picked up a Cy Young Award. Today's pay structure is irrational, as I say, and those irrationalities are reflected in my computer programs.

Also be aware that pitchers tend to have higher estimated values than batters, for two reasons:

The current market, on the one hand, is predisposed toward pitchers. The highest pay for a free-agent pitcher in my 1999 study group was 12.5 percent higher than the highest salary for a batter. The gap grew even broader in the middle range, with the median pay for all free-agent pitchers being 25 percent higher than the median for batters.

The second reason is that starting pitchers truly were workhorses in baseball's early years, pushing their estimated value sky high, because a key component of my formula is innings pitched. Joe McGinnity, for example, tossed an adjusted total of 497 innings in 1903, the record for the modern era. That's nearly twice as many as the major-league leader in 2000, Jon Lieber, at 251. If McGinnity was around today, I'm sure he would be limited to 250 innings or so, as well. But that's not the point. My goal is to estimate the current value of past performances, whatever they were. McGinnity's iron-man stint in 1903 would be worth $64.2 million in 2001.

I have tried to be as precise as possible, but to be honest, I've included this category primarily for fun. It should, if nothing else, give old-time ballplayers plenty to think about. And I know they think about it. Bob Gibson was asked recently if he would ever like to match skills with today's players. "Yeah, for just one reason," he replied. "I think I'd feel real comfortable making $15 million to $20 million a year." It actually would have been much more, Bob. You would have peaked at $32.3 million. You can look it up.

5. Best Players of All Time

We've been concerned, up to now, with objective statistics – wins, losses, runs, hits, strikeouts, batting averages, earned run averages, even salaries. Things that can be measured with precision. But now it's time to leap into the world of the subjective.

I've been stressing (perhaps overstressing) the point that this book levels the playing field, making it possible to compare the statistics of history's greatest players. Well, then, let's compare them.

Below are two formulas that rank the best batters and pitchers of the modern era (1901-2001). You might disagree with the way I've structured them – I'd be surprised if you didn't have a quibble or two – but that's the nature of subjective measures. I can think of dozens of legitimate ways to quantify player quality, and I'm sure you can, too. My goal here was to develop simple, straightforward formulas that use only the most important indicators. They base half of each player's score on his performance throughout his career, and the other half on how well he played during his very best seasons.

HITTERS

Batters first. These ratings are broken down by position. A player must have fielded a position for at least 1,000 games (actual games, not adjusted ones) and had at least 5,000 adjusted at bats to be eligible. That leaves out a few excellent hitters who didn't reach the games threshold at a single position (Dick Allen, Harmon Killebrew, Jackie Robinson) or didn't go to the plate enough (Roy Campanella, Al Rosen), but I think it's generally a fair measure of durability and longevity. It requires six or seven seasons as an everyday starter and a few more as a part-timer, not an

especially rigorous standard when we're talking about the greatest players of all time.

And there's a second eligibility requirement. A player must meet any one of the six criteria for inclusion in Chapter 6 (using actual, not adjusted, career totals). Among them:

○ Hall of Fame member
○ Most Valuable Player in any season since 1901
○ 2,500 games played
○ 2,500 hits
○ 400 home runs
○ .320 career batting average

The following formula uses only adjusted numbers, allowing direct comparisons of players throughout the modern era. You'll notice that I'm using only batting statistics. What about fielding? A fair question. My best answer is that the selection processes for All-Star teams and the Hall of Fame seem to focus almost entirely on hitting, just as I'm doing. Nothing makes critics howl louder, it seems, than the rare occasion when an old-timer with a relatively mediocre batting average enters the Hall of Fame primarily because of his glove. (Can you say Bill Mazeroski?)

So I'm looking for three qualities, with the relevant statistics in parentheses:

○ Run production (runs scored and runs batted in)
○ Hitting for average (batting average)
○ Hitting for power (slugging average)

Here's the way the formula actually works, using Hank Greenberg as an example:

Step 1 Calculate these adjusted statistics for an average season during a player's career: (1) at bats, (2) runs scored, (3) runs batted in, (4) batting average, and (5) slugging average. (Figures for a batter's average season are calculated by dividing career totals by his number of seasons.) Greenberg's average statistics are 419 at bats, 91 runs scored, 111 runs batted in, a batting average of .311, and a slugging average of .667.

Step 2 Calculate the same five adjusted statistics for a typical "summit" season during a player's career, showing what he was like at his peak. (To determine a player's summit years, I added the adjusted batting and slugging averages for each season in which a hitter had at least 324 adjusted at bats, the equivalent of two at bats per game in a 162-game season. The five years with the highest combined batting-slugging averages are the summit years. Figures for a batter's typical summit season are calculated by dividing summit totals by five.) Greenberg's summit statistics are 601 at bats, 140 runs scored, 175 runs batted in, a .319 batting average, and a .715 slugging average.

Step 3 Convert the player's runs and RBIs into rates per 500 at bats. Round off each answer to the nearest whole number. Greenberg scored 91 runs in 419 at bats in an average season. That's the same as 109 runs per 500 at bats.

Step 4 Compare the player's average season to the average seasons of all other eligible players who fielded the same position. Make comparisons in four areas: (1) runs scored per 500 at bats, (2) runs batted in per 500 at bats, (3) batting average, and (4) slugging average. Give 100 points to the player at each position who puts up the best number in a category. Determine the score for any other player by dividing his number by the category's best number, then multiplying by 100. Lou Gehrig leads all first basemen with 121 runs per 500 at bats, earning 100 points in that category. Greenberg, with 109 runs per 500 at bats, receives 90.08 points, the result of 109 divided by 121.

Step 5 Compare the player's summit season to the summit seasons of all other eligible players at the same position. Use the four statistics and the scoring system detailed in Step 4.

Step 6 Add the scores from the four categories in Step 4 and the four categories in Step 5. The maximum for any player is 800 points.

Step 7 Take the resulting total (746.72 points for Greenberg), divide it by the highest score received by any player at the same position (781.30), and multiply by 100. (This doesn't change the final rankings, but it does fit every player into a 100-point scale.) Greenberg ends up with 95.57 points. Keep in mind that each position's scale is weighted separately, with the top player receiving a score of 100. Final scores for players at different positions, as a result, are not directly comparable.

PITCHERS

Now on to the pitchers. There are three rankings: left-handed starters, right-handed starters, and relievers. (The scoring systems for starters and relievers are a bit different, as explained below.) Anyone who averaged more than three innings per appearance in his summit years (defined below) is classified as a starter; the rest are relievers.

A starting pitcher must have pitched an adjusted total of at least 2,000 innings during his career to be eligible, while a relief pitcher must have appeared in an adjusted total of at least 600 games. All pitchers also must meet any one of the seven criteria for Chapter 7 (using actual, not adjusted, career totals), including:

○ Hall of Fame member
○ Most Valuable Player in any season since 1901
○ Cy Young Award–winner in any season since 1901
○ 1,000 games pitched

- 600 games started
- 250 wins
- 300 saves

The pitchers' formula uses only adjusted statistics. It takes three qualities into account for starting pitchers, as reflected by the statistics listed in parentheses:

- Winning (wins and winning percentage)
- Keeping runners off the bases (combined total of hits and walks allowed)
- Run prevention (earned run average)

The ratings for relief pitchers are a bit simpler. Relievers, just like starters, are supposed to keep runners off the bases and prevent runs, so those factors are still considered. But you can't measure a reliever's effectiveness by his number of wins or his winning percentage. And I'm not crazy about using saves as a yardstick, either. A closer can pick up a save for pitching an inning or less, even if his team's victory was never directly threatened. That doesn't mean much to me.

Here, then, is a step-by-step rundown of the formula for pitchers, using Sandy Koufax as an example.

Step 1 Calculate these adjusted statistics for an average season during a pitcher's career: (1) innings pitched, (2) wins, (3) losses, (4) hits allowed, (5) walks allowed, and (6) earned run average (ERA). (Figures for a pitcher's average season are calculated by dividing career totals by his number of seasons.) This is Koufax's average season: 197 innings, 14 wins, 8 losses, 161 hits, 77 walks, and an ERA of 3.38.

Step 2 Calculate the same six adjusted statistics for a typical "summit" season during a pitcher's career, showing what he was like at his very best. (I developed a point system that takes into account a pitcher's adjusted wins, saves, and ERA in each

season when he had at least 54 adjusted innings pitched, the equivalent of one-third of an inning per game in a 162-game season. The five years with the highest point totals are defined as his summit years. Figures for a pitcher's typical summit season are calculated by dividing summit totals by five.) Here are Koufax's summit numbers: 292 innings, a 23–8 win–loss record, 230 hits, 83 walks, and an earned run average of 2.71.

Step 3 Convert a starting pitcher's wins to a rate per 250 innings. Round off each answer to the nearest whole number. (Ignore this step for relievers.) Koufax had 23 wins in 292 innings in his summit season. That's the same as 20 wins in 250 innings.

Step 4 Determine a starting pitcher's adjusted winning percentages. (Skip this step for relief pitchers.) Koufax's 23-8 mark in his summit year translates to a .742 winning percentage.

Step 5 Add the number of hits and walks that a pitcher allowed in a given season. Then convert to a rate per 250 innings for starters or 100 innings for relievers. Round off. Koufax gave up 238 hits and walks in 197 innings during his average season, which works out to 302 per 250 innings.

Step 6 If a pitcher is a starter, compare his average season to the average seasons of all other eligible left-handed or right-handed starters. Make comparisons in four areas: (1) wins per 250 innings, (2) winning percentage, (3) hits and walks allowed per 250 innings, and (4) earned run average. If a pitcher is a reliever, compare his average season to those of other eligible relievers in two areas: (1) hits and walks allowed per 100 innings and (2) earned run average. Give 100 points to the pitcher in each group (lefties, righties, or relievers) who has the best number in a category. Determine the score for any other pitcher by comparing his number to the category's best number. Always divide the smaller number by the bigger one. Carl

Hubbell leads all lefthanded starters with 286 hits and walks per 250 innings in his average season, earning 100 points in that category. Koufax, with 302 hits and walks per 250 innings, receives 94.70 points, the result of 286 divided by 302.

Step 7 Compare the pitcher's summit season to the summit seasons of all other eligible pitchers in the same group. Use the scoring system detailed in Step 6, with four categories for starters and two for relievers.

Step 8 Add the scores from all categories in Steps 6 and 7. Maximums are 800 points for a starter and 400 points for a reliever.

Step 9 Take the resulting total (745.32 points for Koufax), divide it by the highest score received by any pitcher in the same group (765.74), and multiply by 100. (Again, this doesn't alter the final rankings, but it does reduce all scores to a 100-point scale.) Koufax ends up with 97.33 points. It's worth reminding that each group's scale puts its top pitcher at 100 points. Final scores for pitchers in different groups cannot be compared.

6. Best Teams of All Time

If we can rank the best players of all time, why not do the same for the best teams? Why not, indeed?

Hundreds of teams have enjoyed great success since 1901. A total of 228 have posted single-season adjusted winning percentages higher than .600. That means their records, when converted to a 162-game schedule, have been 98–64 or better.

But a winning record isn't enough. A truly great team has a powerful offense, stingy pitching staff, and airtight defense. It doesn't just win; it wins big. It triumphs over tough competition. And

it is generally acknowledged by most fans to be the outstanding team in recent memory.

I have come up with a formula that takes all of these factors into account. The relevant statistics are in parentheses:

○ Record (winning percentage)

○ Offense (runs scored)

○ Pitching and defense (runs allowed)

○ Ability to win big (margin of victory)

○ Ability to beat tough opponents (statistical competition factor)

○ Best team of its season (World Series and league titles)

○ Best team of its decade or extended period (bonus points)

I chose an adjusted winning percentage of .600 as my threshold, giving me the pool of 228 eligible teams mentioned above. I figured that if a team couldn't win at least 60 percent of its games, it was not worthy of consideration among the greatest teams of all time.

My formula is necessarily elaborate, given all the factors to be considered. Here's how it works, using the 1939 New York Yankees as an example:

Step 1 Convert a team's regular-season record to fit a 162-game schedule, then calculate its adjusted winning percentage. The 1939 Yankees had 106 wins and 45 losses, the same as a 114–48 record in 162 games. That's an adjusted winning percentage of .704.

Step 2 Determine the adjusted number of runs a team scored per game. The process of converting the actual average (6.36 per game for the '39 Yanks) to its 2000 equivalent is complicated. Begin by subtracting the team's number of games, runs scored, and runs allowed from the major-league totals for a given year, yielding totals for the rest of the majors. Add the runs scored and runs allowed for the latter group, divide by its number of games played, and divide again by two, producing a per-game average for any team but the one in question (4.81 per game for any team but the Yankees in 1939). Divide this figure into the average output of a single team in 2000 (5.14 runs per game). Multiply the resulting ratio (1.07) by the team's actual average (6.36) to determine its adjusted number of runs per game (6.81 for the Yanks).

Step 3 Repeat the previous step to determine the adjusted number of runs that a team allowed per game. The figure for the 1939 Yankees is 3.91.

Step 4 Calculate the team's adjusted margin of victory, subtracting adjusted runs allowed from adjusted runs scored. The formula for the Yanks: 6.81 minus 3.91 equals a margin of 2.90 runs per game.

Step 5 Assign a numerical value to the level of competition that a team faced. The process of calculating this competition factor (CF) is so complex that I don't see much reason to describe it in detail. Perhaps a half-dozen people would be interested, and I'm not one of them. Suffice it to say that a team's CF is determined by the records of every other team in its league, specifically how far each team is above or below .500. If everyone finished the season at exactly .500, the league would be extremely competitive, and a team would have the highest possible CF, 1.10. (What's the special significance of a strange maximum like 1.10? There isn't any. It's just the highest score my calculations turned out.) The number decreases as the gap between good and bad teams widens. The 1941 Yankees had the highest CF of any team in history, 1.08, a sign that its opponents were evenly matched. The '39 Yanks earned a fairly low CF, 0.90.

Step 6 Calculate a team's raw score for adjusted winning percentage. The maximum score is 20 points. There are four components: (1) Give five points to the team with the highest adjusted winning percentage in the modern era (1901–2001). Other teams are scored according to a sliding scale that falls to zero points for the eligible team with the lowest winning percentage. (2) Give bonus points to the 50 teams with the highest percentages in the modern era, ranging from five points for 1st place to one-tenth of a point for 50th place. (3) Give bonus points to the 25 teams with the highest percentages in an extended period (either the pre-expansion period of 1901–1961 or the expansion period of 1962–2001), ranging from five points for first place to two-tenths of a point for 25th place. (4) Give bonus points to the five teams with the highest percentages in a decade, ranging from five points for 1st place to one point for fifth place.

Step 7 Repeat Step 6 to calculate a team's raw score for adjusted runs scored.

Step 8 Repeat Step 6 to calculate a team's raw score for adjusted runs allowed.

Step 9 Repeat Step 6 to calculate a team's raw score for adjusted margin of victory.

Step 10 Award a team 30 bonus points for winning the World Series, or 20 bonus points for winning its league championship, but not the World Series. (I'm talking about the actual league and World Series titles, not the simulated ones in Chapter 2.)

Step 11 Give extra weight to the raw score for adjusted winning percentage (generated in Step 6), multiplying it by 1.5. Then add that figure to the raw scores from Steps 7 through 10.

Step 12 Take Step 11's total and multiply it by the team's competition factor. The 1939 Yankees, as a result of all the calculations from Steps 6 through 12, receive an unadjusted final score of 92.88 points.

Step 13 Add another round of bonus points, based on a team's unadjusted final score. There are two components: (1) Give bonus points to the top 25 teams in an extended period (1901–1961 or 1962–2001), ranging from 25 points for 1st place to one point for 25th place. (2) Give bonus points to the top five teams in a decade, ranging from 25 points for first place to five points for fifth place.

Step 14 Take the resulting total (140.88 points for the 1939 Yankees), divide it by the highest score received by any team in the modern era

(158.22), and multiply by 100. (This doesn't change the final rankings, but it does fit every team into a 100-point scale.) The '39 Yanks end up with 89.04 points.

I used the same 14 steps, by the way, to rank the worst teams of all time – with one big change. The teams with the worst performances earned the highest scores. The pool of eligible teams consisted of all 241 franchises since 1901 with single-season adjusted winning percentages below .400.

2 ◯ The Modern Era

It's generally agreed that baseball's modern era began at the turn of the 20th century. Major-league ball is older than that – the National League dates back to 1876 – but it was considerably different in its early years. The pitcher, at the very start, stood only 45 feet from home plate (and a square home plate at that). Batters were allowed to request high or low pitches. Nine balls brought a walk, a number eventually reduced to eight, then seven, then six, then five. There was a brief experiment with four strikes for a strikeout. Major leagues such as the American Association, Union Association, and Players League came and went.

It took a quarter-century of evolution to develop the game we know today. The magical distance of 60 feet, 6 inches between pitcher and batter. The five-sided home plate. Four balls for a walk. Three strikes for a strikeout. The arrival of the American League to join the National.

The latter event – the AL's birth in 1901 – is acknowledged as the sunrise of the modern era. It's also the starting point for this chapter, which uses the techniques discussed in Chapter 1 to view baseball's past through a contemporary prism.

Here you'll find a two-page statistical summary for every season since 1901. There are four key elements:

◐ Regular-season standings have been adjusted, imposing a divisional structure on years that lacked one (those before 1969) and extending shorter seasons (those before 1961) to the current 162-game schedule.

◐ Playoff results for each season have been simulated.

◐ Most Valuable Player and Cy Young Award winners have been evaluated, featuring estimates of what their contracts would be worth in today's hyperinflated free-agent market.

◐ Statistics for each league's leading players in 19 categories have been converted to 1996–2000 performance levels.

Every season, in effect, has been mathematically adjusted to reflect current conditions. All teams belong to divisions, play the same number of games, and aim for their league's playoffs, the precursor to the World Series. All players are measured against today's standards, both on the field and in their paychecks. That means you can look at summaries for two different years, even two as widely separated as 1901 and 2001, and quickly and accurately compare the statistics of teams and players.

But first, a preview.

Let's take a quick trip through the era's ten decades, touching on the teams that fared best in the computerized playoffs and glancing at the players who put up the gaudiest adjusted numbers. Each decade's capsule begins with a chart of simulated and actual American League, National League, and World Series champions. And each ends with a year-by-year list of notable individual achievements. (If an adjusted number is among the 10 best in its category for the entire modern era, the player's rank is given in parentheses.)

1901–1909

The Chicago Cubs were the stars of the 20th century's first decade, taking two of the first six actual World Series. They should have won three titles, but collapsed inexplicably against the crosstown White Sox, the immortal Hitless Wonders, in 1906.

My computer wasn't quite so impressed with the Cubs, though, awarding them only a single championship in 1908. Pittsburgh and the New York Giants took top honors for the decade, winning two simulated titles each. The Pirates were champs in 1902 and 1909, with the '02

squad finishing 39 games ahead of the rest of the NL West. The Giants were back-to-back winners in 1904 and 1905. The '04 team could have printed playoff tickets in June; it ran away from the NL East by 53 games.

The decade's tightest divisional race occurred in 1908, when the Tigers and Indians tied for first place in the AL West and the White Sox finished a single game back. Detroit swept the best-of-three playoff from Cleveland and eventually moved on to the World Series, losing to the Cubs.

| | AL | | NL | | WS | |
	SIMULATED	ACTUAL	SIMULATED	ACTUAL	SIMULATED	ACTUAL
1901	White Sox	White Sox	Phillies	Pirates	Phillies	(no series)
1902	Browns	Athletics	Pirates	Pirates	Pirates	(no series)
1903	Red Sox	Red Sox	Giants	Pirates	Red Sox	Red Sox
1904	Red Sox	Red Sox	Giants	Giants	Giants	(no series)
1905	White Sox	Athletics	Giants	Giants	Giants	Giants
1906	White Sox	White Sox	Cubs	Cubs	White Sox	White Sox
1907	Athletics	Tigers	Cubs	Cubs	Athletics	Cubs
1908	Tigers	Tigers	Cubs	Cubs	Cubs	Cubs
1909	Athletics	Tigers	Pirates	Pirates	Pirates	Pirates

NOTABLE INDIVIDUAL ACHIEVEMENTS, 1901-1909

(all statistics are adjusted; current ranks on all-time lists are in parentheses):

1901 Nap Lajoie (Athletics) rapped 273 hits (first), batted .424 (second), had 493 total bases (fifth), and scored 174 runs (ninth). Jesse Burkett (Cardinals) had 256 hits (fifth). Cy Young (Red Sox) won 38 games (third).

1902 Lave Cross (Athletics) smashed 119 doubles (second). Young (Red Sox) again put up 38 wins (third).

1903 Joe McGinnity (Giants) pitched 497 innings (first) and won 36 games (seventh). Rube Waddell (Athletics) had 558 strikeouts (second). Ginger Beaumont (Pirates) scored 174 runs (ninth).

1904 Jack Chesbro (Yankees) won 42 games, the all-time single-season record. He pitched 471 innings (third). McGinnity (Giants) won 36 (seventh) for the second straight year. Waddell (Athletics) broke his previous record by striking out 559 (first). Lajoie (Indians) topped the .400 mark for a second time, batting .411 (tenth).

1905 Cy Seymour (Reds), at .410, became the only National Leaguer in the modern era to hit .400.

1906 Lajoie (Indians) set the single-season record for doubles, 138. Teammate Elmer Flick (Indians) chipped in another 89 doubles (fourth).

Mordecai Brown (Cubs) had an earned run average of 1.78 (seventh).

1907 Jimmy Collins (Red Sox-Athletics) hit 85 doubles (seventh).

1908 Ed Walsh (White Sox) tied Chesbro's modern-era record by winning 42 games. He also pitched 485 innings (second). Christy Mathewson (Giants) won 38 (third).

1909 Ty Cobb (Tigers) batted .417 (fourth). Tommy Leach (Pirates) scored 177 runs (eighth).

1910–1919

Most of this decade's champions were located in two cities. Boston earned five real-life titles: four by the Red Sox, one by the Braves. Philadelphia won three, all by the Athletics.

The simulated results weren't much different. The Red Sox took computerized championships in 1912, 1915, and 1916, just as they did in actual play. But they lost the simulated 1918

World Series to the New York Giants in six games. The A's couldn't duplicate their actual 1910 title, losing to Detroit by a single run in the seventh game of the AL Championship Series, but they did match their World Series wins in 1911 and 1913.

Imbalance was the rule in 1916, when the National League's four best teams were all in the

The infamous Black Sox never got a chance to fix the World Series in 1919. The Giants took the Yankees in six games.

Babe Ruth became the first player to crash the 70-home-run barrier, blasting 73 in 1919.

Eastern Division. New York finished last with a 92–70 mark. The Cubs, meanwhile, won the NL West at 71–91 before being swept by Brooklyn in the NLCS.

History truly was turned on its head in 1919.

The infamous Black Sox never got a chance to fix that year's World Series. Chicago entered the ALCS as a heavy favorite over the Yankees, yet lost in six contests. Is it possible to throw a computerized game?

	AL		NL		WS	
	SIMULATED	ACTUAL	SIMULATED	ACTUAL	SIMULATED	ACTUAL
1910	Tigers	Athletics	Cubs	Cubs	Tigers	Athletics
1911	Athletics	Athletics	Giants	Giants	Athletics	Athletics
1912	Red Sox	Red Sox	Giants	Giants	Red Sox	Red Sox
1913	Athletics	Athletics	Giants	Giants	Athletics	Athletics
1914	Athletics	Athletics	Braves	Braves	Braves	Braves
1915	Red Sox	Red Sox	Phillies	Phillies	Red Sox	Red Sox
1916	Red Sox	Red Sox	Dodgers	Dodgers	Red Sox	Red Sox
1917	White Sox	White Sox	Giants	Giants	White Sox	White Sox
1918	Red Sox	Red Sox	Giants	Cubs	Giants	Red Sox
1919	Yankees	White Sox	Giants	Reds	Giants	Reds

NOTABLE INDIVIDUAL ACHIEVEMENTS, 1910–1919

(all statistics are adjusted; current ranks on all-time lists are in parentheses):

1910 Ty Cobb (Tigers) and Nap Lajoie (Indians) both batted .415 (sixth). Cobb won the batting title when their averages were carried to an extra decimal place. Walter Johnson (Senators) struck out 489 (eighth).

1911 Cobb (Tigers) recorded the highest batting average of the modern era, .425. His 265 hits are second on the all-time list. Joe Jackson (Indians) batted .414 (ninth).

1912 Cobb (Tigers) crossed the .400 line for the fourth straight year, batting .411 (tenth). Joe Wood (Red Sox) had 36 wins (seventh), and Walter Johnson (Senators) had 35 (tenth). Johnson's ERA was 1.86 (ninth), and his strikeout total was 484 (ninth).

1913 Cobb (Tigers) made it five consecutive seasons. His average was .406. Johnson (Senators) won 38 games (third) and had an earned run average of 1.70 (fifth).

1914 Dutch Leonard (Red Sox) posted the lowest earned run average in the modern era, 1.52.

1915 Cobb (Tigers) scored 186 runs (third).

1916 Tris Speaker (Indians) hit for a .422 average (third). Cobb (Tigers) batted .405.

1917 Cobb (Tigers) batted .415 (sixth) on 257 hits (fourth).

1918 Cobb (Tigers) topped the .400 mark for the eighth and final time. His average was .407. Speaker (Indians) rapped 116 doubles (third).

1919 Babe Ruth (Red Sox) became the first player to break the 70-home-run barrier, blasting 73. He also was the first with a slugging average above .800, reaching .807 (ninth).

1920–1929

The Roaring Twenties saw the New York Yankees emerge as the greatest force in baseball. The decade began inauspiciously, with the Yanks falling short in three straight ALCS. They lost seven-game heartbreakers to Cleveland in 1920 and 1921 (both by a single run) and then were blown out by the St. Louis Browns in 1922.

But the tide turned the following year. History books and my computer agree that the Yanks won three world titles during the decade: 1923, 1927, and 1928. Those teams ran up a combined record of 24–6 in the simulated playoffs. The 1927 squad averaged nine runs a game while demolishing Detroit in the ALCS and Pittsburgh in the World Series.

Other teams of note included the Indians, winners of back-to-back computerized World Series in 1920–1921 and a third in 1926, and the Giants, who picked up simulated championships in 1922 and 1929.

The decade's hard-luck team was the St. Louis Cardinals, who grabbed the real-life title in 1926. They jumped to a 3-2 lead in that year's simulated NLCS, but lost the final two games to the Giants. The Cards finally made the World Series two years later, only to be swept by the Yankees.

	AL		NL		WS	
	SIMULATED	ACTUAL	SIMULATED	ACTUAL	SIMULATED	ACTUAL
1920	Indians	Indians	Dodgers	Dodgers	Indians	Indians
1921	Indians	Yankees	Pirates	Giants	Indians	Giants
1922	Browns	Yankees	Giants	Giants	Giants	Giants
1923	Yankees	Yankees	Giants	Giants	Yankees	Yankees
1924	Senators	Senators	Pirates	Giants	Pirates	Senators
1925	Senators	Senators	Giants	Pirates	Senators	Pirates
1926	Indians	Yankees	Giants	Cardinals	Indians	Cardinals
1927	Yankees	Yankees	Pirates	Pirates	Yankees	Yankees
1928	Yankees	Yankees	Cardinals	Cardinals	Yankees	Yankees
1929	Athletics	Athletics	Giants	Cubs	Giants	Athletics

The '20s saw the Yankees emerge as the greatest force in baseball. Here, Joe Dugan makes a play at third base.

NOTABLE INDIVIDUAL ACHIEVEMENTS, 1920–1929

(all statistics are adjusted; current ranks on all-time lists are in parentheses):

1920 Babe Ruth (Yankees) registered the highest slugging average in history, .971. He hit 91 home runs (second) and scored 189 runs (second). George Sisler (Browns) had 264 hits (third) and 483 total bases (eighth).

1921 Ruth (Yankees) did himself three better than the year before by blasting 94 homers, setting the record for the modern era. He scored 195 runs, the all-time record in that category. He also amassed 513 total bases (first), had a slugging average of .897 (second), and drove in 188 runs (seventh).

1922 Rogers Hornsby (Cardinals), with 72 homers, became the second player to hit at least 70 in a single year. His 504 total bases (third) were the most ever for a non-Yankee.

1923 Ruth (Yankees) rang up a slugging average of .835 (sixth).

1924 Dazzy Vance (Dodgers) struck out 525 batters (fourth). Ruth (Yankees) hit 75 homers (tenth) and slugged .800 (tenth).

1925 Hornsby (Cardinals) had 63 homers, 149 RBIs, and a .371 average.

1926 Ruth (Yankees) had a slugging average of .813 (eighth). Firpo Marberry (Senators) had 40 saves.

1927 Ruth (Yankees) hit 89 home runs (third). Lou Gehrig (Yankees) chipped in 83 (fourth), the highest total ever hit by anyone but Ruth. Gehrig also had 505 total bases (second) and 191 RBIs (fifth).

1928 Ruth (Yankees) hit another 78 homers (seventh) and scored 181 runs (sixth).

1929 Lefty O'Doul (Phillies) had 249 hits (ninth).

1930–1939

The Yankees were dominant throughout the thirties. New York won five World Series on the playing field and six in the computer during the decade.

The simulated playoffs yielded the Yanks an unprecedented five consecutive titles from 1935 to 1939. New York won 20 of 26 games in the American League Championship Series during those five years, then did even better in the World Series, winning 20 of 24. The only close call came when the White Sox extended the 1936 ALCS to a seventh game before falling. Both the 1938 and 1939 New York squads swept the American League series and World Series with eight straight wins.

The Yankees overshadowed both the neighboring New York Giants, who won computerized titles in 1931 and 1933, and the Philadelphia Athletics, who earned AL crowns in 1930 (with 107 wins) and 1931 (with 114). The A's also took the World Series in 1930.

Perhaps the most spirited club in the thirties was the Chicago Cubs, who fought their way to simulated National League titles in 1932 and every season from 1935 to 1938. It was the Cubs' bad luck that the Yankees were waiting for them in the World Series all five times.

	AL		NL		WS	
	SIMULATED	ACTUAL	SIMULATED	ACTUAL	SIMULATED	ACTUAL
1930	Athletics	Athletics	Cardinals	Cardinals	Athletics	Athletics
1931	Athletics	Athletics	Giants	Cardinals	Giants	Cardinals
1932	Yankees	Yankees	Cubs	Cubs	Yankees	Yankees
1933	Senators	Senators	Giants	Giants	Giants	Giants
1934	Tigers	Tigers	Cardinals	Cardinals	Cardinals	Cardinals
1935	Yankees	Tigers	Cubs	Cubs	Yankees	Tigers
1936	Yankees	Yankees	Cubs	Giants	Yankees	Yankees
1937	Yankees	Yankees	Cubs	Giants	Yankees	Yankees
1938	Yankees	Yankees	Cubs	Cubs	Yankees	Yankees
1939	Yankees	Yankees	Dodgers	Reds	Yankees	Yankees

NOTABLE INDIVIDUAL ACHIEVEMENTS, 1930–1939

(all statistics are adjusted; current ranks on all-time lists are in parentheses):

1930 Hack Wilson (Cubs) hit 70 home runs and drove in 181 runs (ninth). Lefty Grove (Athletics) won 30 games and struck out 394.

1931 Lou Gehrig (Yankees) drove in 204 runs (first), the only time a player has had more than 200 RBIs in a single season. Gehrig blasted 76 home runs (eighth). Ben Chapman (Yankees) stole 107 bases (tenth).

1932 Jimmie Foxx (Athletics) hit 82 homers (fifth), the most in a single season by a nonYankee. He reached 492 total bases (sixth) and had a slugging average of exactly .800 (tenth).

1933 Foxx (Athletics) hit 79 homers (sixth). He also had 196 RBIs (third) and 487 total bases (seventh).

1934 Gehrig (Yankees) drove in 181 runs (ninth). Dizzy Dean (Cardinals) won 32 games and struck out 361.

1935 Hank Greenberg (Tigers) had 189 runs batted in (sixth). Dean (Cardinals) struck out 373 on the way to another 30 wins.

Lou Gehrig drove in 204 runs in 1931, the only time a player has had more than 200 RBIs in a single season.

1936 Gehrig (Yankees) hit 70 homers. Woody Jensen (Pirates) had 723 at bats, the highest single-season total in the modern era.

1937 Greenberg (Tigers) drove in 198 runs (second).

1938 Greenberg (Tigers) hit 76 home runs (eighth). Foxx (Red Sox) hit 73 homers and drove in 196 runs (third).

1939 Bucky Walters (Reds) won 28 games on an earned run average of 2.44. Joe DiMaggio (Yankees) batted .373.

1940–1949

Parity returned to baseball in the forties. Six different teams won the decade's first six simulated World Series, quite a change from the Yankees' five straight championships to close out the 1930s. Among the revolving-door titleholders were two that had not been favored by the computer before, Cincinnati (1940) and Brooklyn (1942).

Two new powerhouses emerged in the latter half of the decade. The St. Louis Cardinals lost only six playoff games in taking back-to-back titles in 1946 and 1947, giving them three simulated championships for the decade, the same number as in real life. The Cleveland Indians stepped forward to duplicate their actual World Series triumph in 1948 and then added another in 1949. The latter came against the odds, because the Indians were underdogs both in the ALCS against the Yankees and in the World Series against the Cardinals.

Philadelphia fans could only wonder what such success was like. The Phillies finished last in the NL East seven times during the decade, climbing above .500 just once. The Athletics were nearly as bad, occupying last place in the AL East six out of ten years.

	AL		NL		WS	
	SIMULATED	ACTUAL	SIMULATED	ACTUAL	SIMULATED	ACTUAL
1940	Tigers	Tigers	Reds	Reds	Reds	Reds
1941	Yankees	Yankees	Dodgers	Dodgers	Yankees	Yankees
1942	Browns	Yankees	Dodgers	Cardinals	Dodgers	Cardinals
1943	Indians	Yankees	Dodgers	Cardinals	Indians	Yankees
1944	Browns	Browns	Cardinals	Cardinals	Cardinals	Cardinals
1945	Tigers	Tigers	Cubs	Cubs	Tigers	Tigers
1946	Tigers	Red Sox	Cardinals	Cardinals	Cardinals	Cardinals
1947	Yankees	Yankees	Cardinals	Dodgers	Cardinals	Yankees
1948	Indians	Indians	Braves	Braves	Indians	Indians
1949	Indians	Yankees	Cardinals	Dodgers	Indians	Yankees

NOTABLE INDIVIDUAL ACHIEVEMENTS, 1940–1949

(all statistics are adjusted; current ranks on all-time lists are in parentheses):

1940 Hank Greenberg (Tigers) had 60 home runs, 170 runs batted in, and a .343 batting average. Bob Feller (Indians) struck out 436.

1941 Ted Williams (Red Sox) batted .417 (fourth), the best average between 1917 and 2001. His slugging average of .838 (fifth) was the second-highest since 1933.

1942 Williams (Red Sox) scored 183 runs (fourth).

1943 George Case (Senators) stole 114 bases (seventh).

1944 Snuffy Stirnweiss (Yankees) had 113 stolen bases (eighth).

1945 Hal Newhouser (Tigers) won 26 games on a 2.30 earned run average. Stirnweiss (Yankees) led the American League with a .319 average. He also topped the league in at bats, runs, hits, triples, total bases, slugging average, and stolen bases.

1946 Feller (Indians) rang up 541 strikeouts (third), the most by any pitcher between 1905 and 2001. Williams (Red Sox) scored 182 runs (fifth), still the highest number by any player since World War II. Stan Musial (Cardinals) had 250 hits (seventh).

1947 Ralph Kiner (Pirates) and Johnny Mize (Giants) tied for the National League home-run title with 70 each.

1948 Musial (Cardinals), with 502 total bases (fourth), became the fourth player ever to top 500, and the only one to do so between 1928 and 2001.

1949 Kiner (Pirates) launched 72 home runs, still the most anyone has hit since World War II. Dale Mitchell (Indians) set the all-time single-season mark for triples, 23.

1950–1959

History tells us that the fifties belonged to the Yankees. They virtually owned the American League, representing it in eight of the decade's real-life World Series. Six ended in championships: 1950 through 1953, 1956, and 1958.

But it wasn't as easy in the computer, where the Yanks were limited to four world titles. Their nemesis was Cleveland, which upset New York in the ALCS three times (1951, 1952, 1955) despite being heavy underdogs. The Chicago White Sox also ousted the favored Yankees in the 1957 American League series.

The other New York teams filled the void.

The Giants won the simulated World Series in 1951 and 1954, and the Brooklyn Dodgers triumphed in 1955 and 1957. The latter was an event of great drama, as the Dodgers capped their final year in Brooklyn by sweeping the White Sox. (The Dodgers added a third title in 1959, their second year in Los Angeles.)

The Braves, who moved from Boston to Milwaukee in 1953, spoiled their new fans by winning seven straight divisional titles. But frustration was also part of the bargain. The Braves carried the 1953 World Series and five subsequent National League series to seven games – and lost them all.

The Yankees's Phil Rizzuto and Jerry Coleman double up Al Rosen in 1956.

	AL		NL		WS	
	SIMULATED	**ACTUAL**	**SIMULATED**	**ACTUAL**	**SIMULATED**	**ACTUAL**
1950	Yankees	Yankees	Phillies	Phillies	Yankees	Yankees
1951	Indians	Yankees	Giants	Giants	Giants	Yankees
1952	Indians	Yankees	Cardinals	Dodgers	Cardinals	Yankees
1953	Yankees	Yankees	Braves	Dodgers	Yankees	Yankees
1954	Indians	Indians	Giants	Giants	Giants	Giants
1955	Indians	Yankees	Dodgers	Dodgers	Dodgers	Dodgers
1956	Yankees	Yankees	Dodgers	Dodgers	Yankees	Yankees
1957	White Sox	Yankees	Dodgers	Braves	Dodgers	Braves
1958	Yankees	Yankees	Giants	Braves	Yankees	Yankees
1959	White Sox	White Sox	Dodgers	Dodgers	Dodgers	Dodgers

NOTABLE INDIVIDUAL ACHIEVEMENTS, 1950–1959

(all statistics are adjusted; current ranks on all-time lists are in parentheses):

1950 Jim Konstanty (Phillies) became the first reliever to be named Most Valuable Player. He won 16 games, saved 38, and had a 2.77 ERA. Sam Jethroe (Braves) stole 99 bases.

1951 Roy Campanella (Dodgers) batted .335 with 43 homers and 121 RBIs. Ned Garver (Browns) won 21 games for the team with the worst winning percentage in the majors.

1952 Robin Roberts (Phillies) won 29 games. Stan Musial (Cardinals) led the majors with a batting average of .359. He also tied Larry Doby (Indians) for the year's top slugging average, .623.

1953 Eddie Mathews (Braves) blasted 58 home runs. Al Rosen (Indians) hit 54 homers, drove in 164 runs, and batted .342. Roberts (Phillies) had another 24 wins with 318 strikeouts.

1954 Ted Kluszewski (Reds) hit 62 home runs.

Willie Mays (Giants) batted .356 with 56 homers and 130 RBIs. Bill Bruton (Braves) stole 90 bases.

1955 Herb Score (Indians) struck out 349. Ray Narleski (Indians) posted 32 saves.

1956 Mickey Mantle (Yankees) won the AL's triple crown with 62 homers, 151 runs batted in, and a .369 average.

1957 Ted Williams (Red Sox), with a .407 average, became the first player since Ty Cobb to hit .400 in two seasons. Hank Aaron (Braves) hit 54 homers and drove in 160 runs.

1958 Ernie Banks (Cubs) drilled 58 home runs. He also had 156 RBIs.

1959 Luis Aparicio (White Sox) stole 122 bases (fourth).

1960–1969

The Yankees showed a split personality during the sixties. They were typically efficient during the first half of the decade, advancing to the real-life World Series five straight times and winning it in 1961 and 1962. But in 1965 mediocrity suddenly became their hallmark. The Yankees spent four of the next five seasons below .500.

The computer detected New York's weaknesses even before they became apparent on the field. The Yankees won just two simulated American League crowns in the sixties, capped by a single world championship in 1961.

Chicago and Baltimore emerged as the AL's new powers. The White Sox took the

computerized World Series in 1960 and 1963, and the Orioles followed suit in 1965. Five National League teams split the remaining titles, led by the St. Louis Cardinals, who duplicated their actual victories in 1964 and 1967.

There was no shortage of excitement in the decade's simulated playoffs. Eleven series, including five World Series, went the full seven games. Six of the final contests were decided by a single run.

Postseason play grew even longer as the sixties came to an end. Expansion in 1969 inspired both leagues to switch from two to three divisions, adding an extra round of playoffs (and the concept of wild-card qualifiers) in the process.

	AL		NL		WS	
	SIMULATED	ACTUAL	SIMULATED	ACTUAL	SIMULATED	ACTUAL
1960	White Sox	Yankees	Pirates	Pirates	White Sox	Pirates
1961	Yankees	Yankees	Reds	Reds	Yankees	Yankees
1962	Twins	Yankees	Giants	Giants	Giants	Yankees
1963	White Sox	Yankees	Phillies	Dodgers	White Sox	Dodgers
1964	Yankees	Yankees	Cardinals	Cardinals	Cardinals	Cardinals
1965	Orioles	Twins	Dodgers	Dodgers	Orioles	Dodgers
1966	Orioles	Orioles	Pirates	Dodgers	Pirates	Orioles
1967	Red Sox	Red Sox	Cardinals	Cardinals	Cardinals	Cardinals
1968	Tigers	Tigers	Reds	Cardinals	Reds	Tigers
1969	Orioles	Orioles	Mets	Mets	Mets	Mets

NOTABLE INDIVIDUAL ACHIEVEMENTS, 1960–1969

(all statistics are adjusted; current ranks on all-time lists are in parentheses):

1960 Luis Aparicio (White Sox) stole 102 bases. Maury Wills (Dodgers) was right on his heels with 100.

1961 Roger Maris (Yankees) smashed 67 home runs and drove in 153 runs. Teammate Mickey Mantle (Yankees) was close behind with 60 HRs and 138 RBIs.

1962 Wills (Dodgers) stole 180 bases, the highest single-season total in the modern era.

1963 Sandy Koufax (Dodgers) won 25 games and struck out 341. Harmon Killebrew (Twins), Hank Aaron (Braves), and Willie McCovey (Giants) each hit 54 homers.

1964 Aparicio (Orioles) stole 111 bases (ninth). Dean Chance (Angels) registered an ERA of 2.10. Tony Oliva (Twins) rapped 232 hits for a .347 average.

1965 Wills (Dodgers) had 151 stolen bases (second). Koufax (Dodgers) had 416 strikeouts.

1966 Koufax (Dodgers) won 27 games with a 2.23 ERA. Lou Brock (Cardinals) stole 116 bases (sixth). Matty Alou (Pirates) batted .370.

1967 Carl Yastrzemski (Red Sox) won the AL's triple crown with 59 home runs, 157 RBIs, and a batting average of .363.

1968 Bob Gibson (Cardinals) had an earned run average of 1.71 (sixth). Denny McLain (Tigers) won 31 games.

1969 Alou (Pirates) had 251 hits (sixth), the most for any player between 1921 and 2001. Killebrew (Twins) launched 60 homers. Wayne Granger (Reds) made 89 pitching appearances (seventh).

1970–1979

The highlight of the seventies was the same in both of baseball's parallel universes: a single team winning three consecutive World Series from 1972 to 1974. But the champions were different.

The actual three-time titleholder was the Oakland Athletics, who knocked out the Reds, Mets, and Dodgers in successive years. The simulated champion was Los Angeles, which ousted the heavily favored A's in five games in 1972, then rolled over the Orioles and Yankees the next two seasons. Dodger pitchers yielded only 1.8 runs per game in the three World Series combined.

The National League dominated postseason play throughout the seventies, taking nine of the decade's ten simulated championships. The Dodgers grabbed a total of four (1970 plus the three already mentioned), and the Pittsburgh Pirates won three.

Boston was the only American League team to break through. The Red Sox were underdogs against all three playoff opponents in 1975, but they bounced the Orioles and Athletics to reach the World Series, where they stunned the Dodgers in six games, thrilling all of New England. It was the first computerized title for the Red Sox since 1916.

	AL		NL		WS	
	SIMULATED	ACTUAL	SIMULATED	ACTUAL	SIMULATED	ACTUAL
1970	Orioles	Orioles	Dodgers	Reds	Dodgers	Orioles
1971	Orioles	Orioles	Pirates	Pirates	Pirates	Pirates
1972	Athletics	Athletics	Dodgers	Reds	Dodgers	Athletics
1973	Orioles	Athletics	Dodgers	Mets	Dodgers	Athletics
1974	Yankees	Athletics	Dodgers	Dodgers	Dodgers	Athletics
1975	Red Sox	Red Sox	Dodgers	Reds	Red Sox	Reds
1976	Yankees	Yankees	Pirates	Reds	Pirates	Reds
1977	Yankees	Yankees	Reds	Dodgers	Reds	Yankees
1978	Angels	Yankees	Giants	Dodgers	Giants	Yankees
1979	Orioles	Orioles	Pirates	Pirates	Pirates	Pirates

NOTABLE INDIVIDUAL ACHIEVEMENTS, 1970–19792P6

(all statistics are adjusted; current ranks on all-time lists are in parentheses):

1970 Johnny Bench (Reds) hit 53 homers and drove in 168 runs. Sam McDowell (Indians) had 340 strikeouts.

1971 Mickey Lolich (Tigers) won 25 games and struck out 367 batters. Willie Stargell (Pirates) blasted 61 homers.

1972 Larry Bowa (Phillies) hit 18 triples (ninth). Billy Williams (Cubs) batted .367. Joe Morgan (Reds) scored 170 runs. Steve Carlton (Phillies) won 28 games for the team with the worst record in the National League.

1973 Roger Metzger (Astros) matched Bowa's 1972 feat with 18 triples (ninth). Mike Marshall (Expos) pitched in 92 games (third).

1974 Rod Carew (Twins) hit for a .382 average. Lou Brock (Cardinals) stole 131 bases (third).

Marshall (Dodgers), with 106 games pitched (first), became the only pitcher ever to top 93.

1975 Jim Palmer (Orioles) had 24 wins and a 2.58 earned run average. Mike Schmidt (Phillies) hit 50 homers.

1976 Joe Morgan (Reds) batted .337 with 136 runs batted in.

1977 Carew (Twins) hit for a .395 average. Nolan Ryan (Angels) allowed 225 walks (fourth), the most by any pitcher since 1917. Ryan also struck out 409.

1978 Jim Rice (Red Sox) smashed 62 homers with 164 runs batted in. Ron Guidry (Yankees) had a record of 25-3. Kent Tekulve (Pirates) pitched in 92 games (third).

1979 Tekulve (Pirates) upped his total by one, pitching in 93 games (second). Marshall (Twins) made 90 appearances (fifth), his third season above 89 during the decade.

1980–1989

The revolving door was in vogue throughout the eighties. No team was able to win back-to-back world titles in real life or in the simulated playoffs. Multiple champions were rare, limited to the Los Angeles Dodgers (two World Series wins in either scenario between 1980 and 1989) and the Oakland Athletics (two in simulation, one in actual play).

The computer was in a contrary mood for most of the decade. It duplicated only six real league champions: four in the American, two in the National. And it matched just two World Series winners: the 1984 Detroit Tigers and the 1989 A's.

Two expansion teams celebrated their first titles. The Milwaukee Brewers, born in 1969 as the Seattle Pilots, edged Atlanta in the seventh game of 1982's computerized World Series. It was an especially sweet victory because Atlanta had lured the Braves from Milwaukee 16 years earlier. The Toronto Blue Jays reached the top in 1987, becoming the first Canadian champions.

The three-division setup in each league generally led to close pennant races, especially in 1981 and 1983, when no team won a division by more than seven games. Oakland ran up the decade's biggest margin in 1988, 29 games in the AL West.

	AL		NL		WS	
	SIMULATED	ACTUAL	SIMULATED	ACTUAL	SIMULATED	ACTUAL
1980	Athletics	Royals	Dodgers	Phillies	Dodgers	Phillies
1981	Athletics	Yankees	Cardinals	Dodgers	Athletics	Dodgers
1982	Brewers	Brewers	Braves	Cardinals	Brewers	Cardinals
1983	Orioles	Orioles	Dodgers	Phillies	Dodgers	Orioles
1984	Tigers	Tigers	Cubs	Padres	Tigers	Tigers
1985	Blue Jays	Royals	Cardinals	Cardinals	Cardinals	Royals
1986	Tigers	Red Sox	Reds	Mets	Reds	Mets
1987	Blue Jays	Twins	Giants	Cardinals	Blue Jays	Twins
1988	Tigers	Athletics	Mets	Dodgers	Mets	Dodgers
1989	Athletics	Athletics	Giants	Giants	Athletics	Athletics

NOTABLE INDIVIDUAL ACHIEVEMENTS, 1980–1989

(all statistics are adjusted; current ranks on all-time lists are in parentheses):

1980 George Brett (Royals) batted .396 with 34 homers and 136 RBIs. Mike Schmidt (Phillies) hit 60 homers. Willie Wilson (Royals) had 705 at bats, the highest total between 1940 and 2001.

1981 Schmidt (Phillies) launched another 63 home runs. Gene Richards (Padres) hit 18 triples (ninth).

1982 Rickey Henderson (Athletics) stole 122 bases (fourth). Robin Yount (Brewers) batted .341 with 130 runs batted in.

1983 Wade Boggs (Red Sox) had a batting average of .373. Dan Quisenberry (Royals) saved 46 games (eighth), tying the highest total by any reliever before 1990.

1984 Bruce Sutter (Cardinals) matched Quisenberry's performance from the previous year, 46 saves (eighth).

1985 Dwight Gooden (Mets) had an earned run average of 1.79 (eighth). Boggs (Red Sox) had 250 hits (seventh), the best single-season total since 1970. His batting average was .385. Wilson (Royals) scampered to 21 triples (third).

1986 Don Mattingly (Yankees) rapped 249 hits (ninth). Boggs (Red Sox) batted .373. Dave Righetti (Yankees) had 46 saves (eighth).

1987 Tony Gwynn (Padres) batted .379. Kent Tekulve (Phillies) pitched in 90 games (fifth).

Wade Boggs had a batting average of .373 in 1983.

1988 Jose Canseco (Athletics) drilled 53 home runs and drove in 147 runs. Boggs (Red Sox) led the majors with a batting average of .389.

1989 Kevin Mitchell (Giants) had 60 homers. Kirby Puckett (Twins) had 228 hits.

1990–2001

Change has been the rule in recent years. The catalyst was expansion to Colorado and Florida in 1993, which triggered wholesale realignment. Each league ballooned to four divisions, and their winners would thereafter make up the entire playoff field. Gone was the wild card, which had produced five champions since 1969. Its swan song was the 1992 World Series win by Cincinnati, the second-place team in the NL Central.

The Yankees and Blue Jays enjoyed the most success in the World Series in real life, with New York grabbing four titles and Toronto two. But neither did as well in the simulated playoffs. The Yanks earned three computerized championships, while the Jays were unable to duplicate their 1992 and 1993 wins. Toronto fell in the first round in '92 and in the ALCS a year later.

Labor discord in 1994 forced cancellation of the World Series. But strikes don't exist in the simulated world, where the Yankees swept the White Sox in the ALCS and the Braves beat the Expos in a five-game NLCS. A closely matched World Series seemed in the offing, but New York took the Braves in four straight, allowing Atlanta a total of only nine runs.

	AL		NL		WS	
	SIMULATED	**ACTUAL**	**SIMULATED**	**ACTUAL**	**SIMULATED**	**ACTUAL**
1990	Athletics	Athletics	Mets	Reds	Mets	Reds
1991	Twins	Twins	Braves	Braves	Twins	Twins
1992	Brewers	Blue Jays	Reds	Braves	Reds	Blue Jays
1993	Rangers	Blue Jays	Phillies	Phillies	Phillies	Blue Jays
1994	Yankees	(none)	Braves	(none)	Yankees	(none)
1995	Indians	Indians	Braves	Braves	Braves	Braves
1996	Indians	Yankees	Expos	Braves	Indians	Yankees
1997	Indians	Indians	Braves	Marlins	Braves	Marlins
1998	Yankees	Yankees	Braves	Padres	Yankees	Yankees
1999	Indians	Yankees	Mets	Braves	Mets	Yankees
2000	White Sox	Yankees	Mets	Mets	Mets	Yankees
2001	Yankees	Yankees	Phillies	Diamondbacks	Yankees	Diamondbacks

NOTABLE INDIVIDUAL ACHIEVEMENTS, 1990–2001

(all statistics are adjusted; current ranks on all-time lists are in parentheses):

1990 Bobby Thigpen (White Sox) recorded 55 saves, the most by any pitcher in the modern era. Tony Fernandez (Blue Jays) had 19 triples (seventh).

1991 Cal Ripken Jr. (Orioles) hit 43 homers and drove in 130 runs.

1992 Dennis Eckersley (Athletics) had 50 saves (fifth).

1993 Randy Myers (Cubs) put up 52 saves (second).

1994 Greg Maddux (Braves) posted a 1.58

earned run average (second), the lowest since 1915. Lance Johnson (White Sox) rapped 19 triples (seventh). Lee Smith (Orioles) had 48 saves (seventh).

1995 Maddux (Braves) had an ERA of 1.69 (fourth). Jose Mesa (Indians) had 52 saves (second).

1996 Johnson (Mets) bettered his 1994 performance by hitting 22 triples (second), the highest single-season total since 1950. Kevin Brown (Marlins) had an ERA of 1.89 (tenth).

1997 Ken Griffey Jr. (Mariners) had 58 homers and 153 runs batted in. Pedro Martinez (Expos) fashioned an earned run average of 1.98.

1998 Mark McGwire (Cardinals) smashed 71 home runs. Trevor Hoffman (Padres) had 52 saves (second).

1999 McGwire (Cardinals) added another 64 homers. Martinez (Red Sox) had an ERA of 1.99.

2000 Martinez (Red Sox) registered an earned run average of 1.66 (third). Cristian Guzman (Twins) hit 20 triples (fifth).

2001 Barry Bonds (Giants) launched 72 home runs, the most since Ralph Kiner also hit 72 in 1949. Bonds' slugging average of .863 (third) was the highest by any batter in the modern era besides Babe Ruth. Mariano Rivera (Yankees) saved 50 games (fifth).

A Few Final Items

Now it's time for the numbers. The following 202 pages provide adjusted standings, simulated playoff results, and adjusted statistics for every season of the modern era.

The charts are self-explanatory, I think, and I'm sure you know most (if not all) of the abbreviations. But it never hurts to include a key, which I have done on the following page. I have also quickly reiterated three points. If you want further details about them (or anything else), you should find what you need in Chapter 1, where all of the technical explanations are outlined.

Three points:

○ I didn't bother to simulate any playoff series that occurred in real life. An asterisk indicates that every game listed actually took place. A double asterisk means that some of the games are real and some are simulated.

○ The Most Valuable Player and Cy Young awards were not presented in several seasons since 1901. I have filled the gaps with hypothetical winners selected by baseball historian Bill Deane.

○ Statistical leaders listed for each season are the actual leaders. It's possible that players who are tied in a given category won't have the same adjusted numbers. (An extreme example is the tie for most triples in the American League in 1904; Joe Cassidy's nineteen triples adjusts down to fifteen, and Buck Freeman's to five.) There also are a few cases where the actual leader was passed by another player when statistics were adjusted. (The AL's actual 1902 co-leaders in doubles, Harry Davis and Ed Delahanty, hit 51 and 42 adjusted doubles, respectively, but could not match Lave Cross's adjusted total of 119.)

REGULAR SEASON STANDINGS

GB	Games behind
L	Losses
Pct.	Winning percentage
Rk.	League rank
W	Wins
X	Qualifier for simulated playoffs

SIMULATED PLAYOFFS

*	Entire series as actually played
**	Part of series as actually played
%	Percentage of simulated series won (out of 100 played by computer)
(1-4)	First seed vs. fourth seed
(2-3)	Second seed vs. third seed
ALCS	American League Championship Series
ALDS	American League Division Series
Game results	Scores of games 1 through 7 are under the corresponding numbers
NLCS	National League Championship Series
NLDS	National League Division Series
Tiebreaker	Playoff to break a regular-season tie for a playoff slot
W	Wins
WS	World Series

OUTSTANDING PERFORMANCES

2B	Doubles
3B	Triples
AB	At bats
BA	Batting average
BB	Walks
ERA	Earned run average
G	Games pitched
H	Hits
HR	Home runs
IP	Innings pitched
L	Losses
MIL	Estimated value of player's performance (in millions of Year 2001 dollars)
R	Runs
RBI	Runs batted in
SA	Slugging average
SB	Stolen bases
SO	Strikeouts
SV	Saves
TB	Total bases
W	Wins
W-L	Win–loss record

The Modern Era
Season-by-Season Standings

1901 SEASON

REGULAR SEASON STANDINGS

AMERICAN LEAGUE

	ADJUSTED				ACTUAL			
	W	L	Pct.	GB	W	L	Pct.	Rk.
EAST								
X Boston	94	68	.580	0	79	57	.581	2
Philadelphia	88	74	.543	6	74	62	.544	4
Baltimore	83	79	.512	11	68	65	.511	5
Washington	74	88	.457	20	61	72	.459	6
WEST								
X Chicago	99	63	.611	0	83	53	.610	1
Detroit	89	73	.549	10	74	61	.548	3
Cleveland	64	98	.395	35	54	82	.397	7
Milwaukee	57	105	.352	42	48	89	.350	8

NATIONAL LEAGUE

	ADJUSTED				ACTUAL			
	W	L	Pct.	GB	W	L	Pct.	Rk.
EAST								
X Philadelphia	96	66	.593	0	83	57	.593	2
Brooklyn	94	68	.580	2	79	57	.581	3
Boston	81	81	.500	15	69	69	.500	5
New York	61	101	.377	35	52	85	.380	7
WEST								
X Pittsburgh	105	57	.648	0	90	49	.647	1
St. Louis	88	74	.543	17	76	64	.543	4
Chicago	62	100	.383	43	53	86	.381	6
Cincinnati	61	101	.377	44	52	87	.374	8

SIMULATED PLAYOFFS

AMERICAN LEAGUE

ALCS	W	1	2	3	4	5	%
Boston Red Sox	1	3	8	5	4	3	44
Chicago White Sox	4	7	13	8	1	6	56

NATIONAL LEAGUE

NLCS	W	1	2	3	4	5	6	%
Philadelphia Phillies	4	3	1	5	3	3	5	36
Pittsburgh Pirates	2	2	5	1	5	2	2	64

WORLD SERIES

WS	W	1	2	3	4	5	6	7	%
Chicago White Sox	3	1	3	5	1	0	3	2	62
Philadelphia Phillies	4	4	2	4	6	6	0	5	38

ACTUAL WINNERS

American League: Chicago White Sox
National League: Pittsburgh Pirates
World Series: (none)

OUTSTANDING PERFORMANCES

AWARD WINNERS

			STATS	
LG.	PLAYER	TEAM	ADJUSTED	ACTUAL
MOST VALUABLE PLAYERS				
AL	Nap Lajoie	Philadelphia	55 HR, 149 RBI, .424 BA, $25.9 MIL	14 HR, 125 RBI, .426 BA
NL	Honus Wagner	Pittsburgh	32 HR, 147 RBI, .350 BA, $25.3 MIL	6 HR, 126 RBI, .353 BA
CY YOUNG AWARDS				
AL	Cy Young	Boston	38-12 W-L, 0 SV, 2.10 ERA, $59.8 MIL	33-10 W-L, 0 SV, 1.62 ERA
NL	Noodles Hahn	Cincinnati	25-22 W-L, 0 SV, 3.55 ERA, $58.4 MIL	22-19 W-L, 0 SV, 2.71 ERA

AMERICAN LEAGUE LEADERS

			STATS	
CAT.	PLAYER	TEAM	ADJUSTED	ACTUAL
BATTING				
HR	Nap Lajoie	Philadelphia	55	14
RBI	Nap Lajoie	Philadelphia	149	125
BA	Nap Lajoie	Philadelphia	.424	.426
AB	Irv Waldron	Mil.-Wash.	696	598
R	Nap Lajoie	Philadelphia	174	145
H	Nap Lajoie	Philadelphia	273	232
2B	Nap Lajoie	Philadelphia	47	48
3B	Bill Keister	Baltimore	13	21
	Jimmy Williams	Baltimore	7	21
TB	Nap Lajoie	Philadelphia	493	350
SA	Nap Lajoie	Philadelphia	.766	.643
SB	Frank Isbell	Chicago	33	52
PITCHING				
W	Cy Young	Boston	38	33
L	Pete Dowling	Mil.-Cle.	29	25
SV	Bill Hoffer	Cleveland	4	3
ERA	Cy Young	Boston	2.10	1.62
G	Joe McGinnity	Baltimore	58	48
IP	Joe McGinnity	Baltimore	462	382
BB	Chick Fraser	Philadelphia	223	132
SO	Cy Young	Boston	366	158

NATIONAL LEAGUE LEADERS

			STATS	
CAT.	PLAYER	TEAM	ADJUSTED	ACTUAL
BATTING				
HR	Sam Crawford	Cincinnati	50	16
RBI	Honus Wagner	Pittsburgh	147	126
BA	Jesse Burkett	St. Louis	.373	.376
AB	Jesse Burkett	St. Louis	686	601
R	Jesse Burkett	St. Louis	164	142
H	Jesse Burkett	St. Louis	256	226
2B	Tom Daly	Brooklyn	64	38
	Ed Delahanty	Philadelphia	47	38
3B	Jimmy Sheckard	Brooklyn	5	19
TB	Jesse Burkett	St. Louis	414	306
SA	Jimmy Sheckard	Brooklyn	.635	.534
SB	Honus Wagner	Pittsburgh	31	49
PITCHING				
W	Bill Donovan	Brooklyn	29	25
L	Dummy Taylor	New York	31	27
SV	Jack Powell	St. Louis	6	3
	Bill Donovan	Brooklyn	5	3
ERA	Jesse Tannehill	Pittsburgh	2.84	2.18
G	Bill Donovan	Brooklyn	53	45
	Dummy Taylor	New York	52	45
	Jack Powell	St. Louis	51	45
IP	Noodles Hahn	Cincinnati	429	375.1
BB	Bill Donovan	Brooklyn	258	152
SO	Noodles Hahn	Cincinnati	507	239

1902 SEASON

REGULAR SEASON STANDINGS

AMERICAN LEAGUE

		ADJUSTED				ACTUAL			
	W	L	Pct.	GB	W	L	Pct.	Rk.
EAST									
X Philadelphia	99	63	.611	0	83	53	.610	1
Boston	91	71	.562	8	77	60	.562	3
Washington	73	89	.451	26	61	75	.449	6
Baltimore	59	103	.364	40	50	88	.362	8
WEST									
X St. Louis	93	69	.574	0	78	58	.574	2
Chicago	89	73	.549	4	74	60	.552	4
Cleveland	82	80	.506	11	69	67	.507	5
Detroit	62	100	.383	31	52	83	.385	7

NATIONAL LEAGUE

		ADJUSTED				ACTUAL			
	W	L	Pct.	GB	W	L	Pct.	Rk.
EAST									
X Brooklyn	88	74	.543	0	75	63	.543	2
Boston	87	75	.537	1	73	64	.533	3
Philadelphia	66	96	.407	22	56	81	.409	7
New York	57	105	.352	31	48	88	.353	8
WEST									
X Pittsburgh	120	42	.741	0	103	36	.741	1
Cincinnati	81	81	.500	39	70	70	.500	4
Chicago	81	81	.500	39	68	69	.496	5
St. Louis	68	94	.420	52	56	78	.418	6

SIMULATED PLAYOFFS

AMERICAN LEAGUE

ALCS	W	1	2	3	4	5	6	%
Philadelphia Athletics	2	1	3	9	5	9	1	72
St. Louis Browns	4	5	4	6	6	1	2	28

NATIONAL LEAGUE

NLCS	W	1	2	3	4		%
Brooklyn Dodgers	0	3	2	0	2		4
Pittsburgh Pirates	4	5	4	1	5		96

WORLD SERIES

WS	W	1	2	3	4		%
St. Louis Browns	0	0	3	1	2		6
Pittsburgh Pirates	4	4	8	4	17		94

ACTUAL WINNERS

American League: Philadelphia Athletics
National League: Pittsburgh Pirates
World Series: (none)

OUTSTANDING PERFORMANCES

AWARD WINNERS

			STATS	
LG.	PLAYER	TEAM	ADJUSTED	ACTUAL
MOST VALUABLE PLAYERS				
AL	Cy Young	Boston	38-13 W-L, 0 SV, 3.08 ERA, $62.8 MIL	32-11 W-L, 0 SV, 2.15 ERA
NL	Honus Wagner	Pittsburgh	25 HR, 116 RBI, .333 BA, $19.6 MIL	3 HR, 91 RBI, .330 BA
CY YOUNG AWARDS				
AL	Cy Young	Boston	38-13 W-L, 0 SV, 3.08 ERA, $62.8 MIL	32-11 W-L, 0 SV, 2.15 ERA
NL	Jack Taylor	Chicago	26-13 W-L, 1 SV, 1.90 ERA, $40.8 MIL	23-11 W-L, 1 SV, 1.33 ERA

AMERICAN LEAGUE LEADERS

			STATS	
CAT.	PLAYER	TEAM	ADJUSTED	ACTUAL
BATTING				
HR	Socks Seybold	Philadelphia	56	16
RBI	Buck Freeman	Boston	159	121
BA	Nap Lajoie	Phi.-Cle.	.381	.378
AB	Freddy Parent	Boston	666	567
R	Dave Fultz	Philadelphia	144	109
	Topsy Hartsel	Philadelphia	144	109
H	Charlie Hickman	Bos.-Cle.	229	193
2B	Harry Davis	Philadelphia	51	43
	Ed Delahanty	Washington	42	43
3B	Jimmy Williams	Baltimore	7	21
TB	Charlie Hickman	Bos.-Cle.	420	288
SA	Ed Delahanty	Washington	.731	.590
SB	Topsy Hartsel	Philadelphia	32	47
PITCHING				
W	Cy Young	Boston	38	32
L	Bill Dinneen	Boston	25	21
SV	Jack Powell	St. Louis	2	2
ERA	Ed Siever	Detroit	2.75	1.91
G	Cy Young	Boston	53	45
IP	Cy Young	Boston	453	384.2
BB	Earl Moore	Cleveland	175	101
SO	Rube Waddell	Philadelphia	459	210

NATIONAL LEAGUE LEADERS

			STATS	
CAT.	PLAYER	TEAM	ADJUSTED	ACTUAL
BATTING				
HR	Tommy Leach	Pittsburgh	37	6
RBI	Honus Wagner	Pittsburgh	116	91
BA	Ginger Beaumont	Pittsburgh	.360	.357
AB	Cozy Dolan	Brooklyn	680	592
R	Honus Wagner	Pittsburgh	134	105
H	Ginger Beaumont	Pittsburgh	222	193
2B	Honus Wagner	Pittsburgh	53	30
3B	Sam Crawford	Cincinnati	14	22
	Tommy Leach	Pittsburgh	9	22
TB	Sam Crawford	Cincinnati	366	256
SA	Honus Wagner	Pittsburgh	.573	.463
SB	Honus Wagner	Pittsburgh	27	42
PITCHING				
W	Jack Chesbro	Pittsburgh	32	28
L	Stan Yerkes	St. Louis	24	21
SV	Vic Willis	Boston	3	3
ERA	Jack Taylor	Chicago	1.90	1.33
G	Vic Willis	Boston	58	51
IP	Vic Willis	Boston	466	410
BB	Togie Pittinger	Boston	210	128
SO	Vic Willis	Boston	511	225

1903 SEASON

REGULAR SEASON STANDINGS

AMERICAN LEAGUE

		ADJUSTED				ACTUAL			
	W	L	Pct.	GB	W	L	Pct.	Rk.	
EAST									
X Boston	107	55	.660	0	91	47	.659	1	
Philadelphia	90	72	.556	17	75	60	.556	2	
New York	87	75	.537	20	72	62	.537	4	
Washington	51	111	.315	56	43	94	.314	8	
WEST									
X Cleveland	89	73	.549	0	77	63	.550	3	
Detroit	77	85	.475	12	65	71	.478	5	
St. Louis	76	86	.469	13	65	74	.468	6	
Chicago	71	91	.438	18	60	77	.438	7	

NATIONAL LEAGUE

		ADJUSTED				ACTUAL			
	W	L	Pct.	GB	W	L	Pct.	Rk.	
EAST									
X New York	98	64	.605	0	84	55	.604	2	
Brooklyn	84	78	.519	14	70	66	.515	5	
Boston	68	94	.420	30	58	80	.420	6	
Philadelphia	59	103	.364	39	49	86	.363	7	
WEST									
X Pittsburgh	106	56	.654	0	91	49	.650	1	
Chicago	96	66	.593	10	82	56	.594	3	
Cincinnati	86	76	.531	20	74	65	.532	4	
St. Louis	51	111	.315	55	43	94	.314	8	

SIMULATED PLAYOFFS

AMERICAN LEAGUE

ALCS	W	1	2	3	4				%
Boston Red Sox	4	8	3	7	6				76
Cleveland Indians	0	4	1	3	4				24

NATIONAL LEAGUE

NLCS	W	1	2	3	4	5	6	7	%
New York Giants	4	4	4	9	7	5	8	9	50
Pittsburgh Pirates	3	6	11	2	2	11	4	8	50

WORLD SERIES

WS	W	1	2	3	4	5		%
Boston Red Sox	4	3	9	9	4	7		65
New York Giants	1	2	10	2	0	2		35

ACTUAL WINNERS

American League: Boston Red Sox
National League: Pittsburgh Pirates
World Series: Boston Red Sox

OUTSTANDING PERFORMANCES

AWARD WINNERS

LG.	PLAYER	TEAM	STATS ADJUSTED	ACTUAL
MOST VALUABLE PLAYERS				
AL	Nap Lajoie	Cleveland	38 HR, 119 RBI, .353 BA, $12.7 MIL	7 HR, 93 RBI, .344 BA
NL	Honus Wagner	Pittsburgh	36 HR, 128 RBI, .366 BA, $16.5 MIL	5 HR, 101 RBI, .355 BA
CY YOUNG AWARDS				
AL	Cy Young	Boston	32-10 W-L, 3 SV, 3.05 ERA, $56.0 MIL	28-9 W-L, 2 SV, 2.08 ERA
NL	Christy Mathewson	New York	34-15 W-L, 2 SV, 3.30 ERA, $58.1 MIL	30-13 W-L, 2 SV, 2.26 ERA

AMERICAN LEAGUE LEADERS

CAT.	PLAYER	TEAM	STATS ADJUSTED	ACTUAL
BATTING				
HR	Buck Freeman	Boston	56	13
RBI	Buck Freeman	Boston	132	104
BA	Nap Lajoie	Cleveland	.353	.344
AB	Patsy Dougherty	Boston	679	590
R	Patsy Dougherty	Boston	136	107
H	Patsy Dougherty	Boston	231	195
2B	Socks Seybold	Philadelphia	40	45
3B	Sam Crawford	Detroit	12	25
TB	Buck Freeman	Boston	398	281
SA	Nap Lajoie	Cleveland	.638	.518
SB	Harry Bay	Cleveland	29	45
PITCHING				
W	Cy Young	Boston	32	28
L	Patsy Flaherty	Chicago	29	25
SV	George Mullin	Detroit	7	2
	Jack Powell	St. Louis	4	2
	Bill Dinneen	Boston	3	2
	Al Orth	Washington	3	2
	Cy Young	Boston	3	2
ERA	Earl Moore	Cleveland	2.54	1.74
G	Eddie Plank	Philadelphia	51	43
IP	Cy Young	Boston	393	341.2
BB	George Mullin	Detroit	182	106
SO	Rube Waddell	Philadelphia	558	302

NATIONAL LEAGUE LEADERS

CAT.	PLAYER	TEAM	STATS ADJUSTED	ACTUAL
BATTING				
HR	Jimmy Sheckard	Brooklyn	40	9
RBI	Sam Mertes	New York	131	104
BA	Honus Wagner	Pittsburgh	.366	.355
AB	Ginger Beaumont	Pittsburgh	704	613
R	Ginger Beaumont	Pittsburgh	174	137
H	Ginger Beaumont	Pittsburgh	247	209
2B	Fred Clarke	Pittsburgh	38	32
	Harry Steinfeldt	Cincinnati	32	32
	Sam Mertes	New York	30	32
3B	Honus Wagner	Pittsburgh	7	19
TB	Ginger Beaumont	Pittsburgh	385	272
SA	Fred Clarke	Pittsburgh	.656	.532
SB	Frank Chance	Chicago	44	67
	Jimmy Sheckard	Brooklyn	44	67
PITCHING				
W	Joe McGinnity	New York	36	31
L	Togie Pittinger	Boston	26	22
SV	Roscoe Miller	New York	8	3
	Carl Lundgren	Chicago	7	3
ERA	Sam Leever	Pittsburgh	3.00	2.06
G	Joe McGinnity	New York	63	55
IP	Joe McGinnity	New York	497	434
BB	Togie Pittinger	Boston	245	143
SO	Christy Mathewson	New York	500	267

1904 SEASON

REGULAR SEASON STANDINGS

AMERICAN LEAGUE

		ADJUSTED				ACTUAL		
	W	L	Pct.	GB	W	L	Pct.	Rk.
EAST								
X Boston	100	62	.617	0	95	59	.617	1
New York	99	63	.611	1	92	59	.609	2
Philadelphia	87	75	.537	13	81	70	.536	5
Washington	41	121	.253	59	38	113	.252	8
WEST								
X Chicago	94	68	.580	0	89	65	.578	3
Cleveland	92	70	.568	2	86	65	.570	4
St. Louis	69	93	.426	25	65	87	.428	6
Detroit	66	96	.407	28	62	90	.408	7

NATIONAL LEAGUE

		ADJUSTED				ACTUAL		
	W	L	Pct.	GB	W	L	Pct.	Rk.
EAST								
X New York	112	50	.691	0	106	47	.693	1
Brooklyn	59	103	.364	53	56	97	.366	6
Boston	58	104	.358	54	55	98	.359	7
Philadelphia	56	106	.346	56	52	100	.342	8
WEST								
X Chicago	99	63	.611	0	93	60	.608	2
Cincinnati	93	69	.574	6	88	65	.575	3
Pittsburgh	92	70	.568	7	87	66	.569	4
St. Louis	79	83	.488	20	75	79	.487	5

SIMULATED PLAYOFFS

AMERICAN LEAGUE

ALCS	W	1	2	3	4	5	6	7	%
Boston Red Sox	4	2	3	2	2	3	3	2	43
Chicago White Sox	3	4	2	0	3	2	4	1	57

NATIONAL LEAGUE

NLCS	W	1	2	3	4	5	6	7	%
New York Giants	4	5	0	6	2	5	2	7	87
Chicago Cubs	3	1	3	4	3	3	3	4	13

WORLD SERIES

WS	W	1	2	3	4	5	%
Boston Red Sox	1	4	1	1	4	1	38
New York Giants	4	5	9	5	0	5	62

ACTUAL WINNERS

American League: Boston Red Sox
National League: New York Giants
World Series: (none)

OUTSTANDING PERFORMANCES

AWARD WINNERS

LG.	PLAYER	TEAM	STATS ADJUSTED	ACTUAL
MOST VALUABLE PLAYERS				
AL	Jack Chesbro	New York	42-12 W-L, 0 SV, 3.11 ERA, $67.7 MIL	41-12 W-L, 0 SV, 1.82 ERA
NL	Joe McGinnity	New York	36-8 W-L, 7 SV, 2.75 ERA, $59.0 MIL	35-8 W-L, 5 SV, 1.61 ERA
CY YOUNG AWARDS				
AL	Jack Chesbro	New York	42-12 W-L, 0 SV, 3.11 ERA, $67.7 MIL	41-12 W-L, 0 SV, 1.82 ERA
NL	Joe McGinnity	New York	36-8 W-L, 7 SV, 2.75 ERA, $59.0 MIL	35-8 W-L, 5 SV, 1.61 ERA

AMERICAN LEAGUE LEADERS

CAT.	PLAYER	TEAM	STATS ADJUSTED	ACTUAL
BATTING				
HR	Harry Davis	Philadelphia	38	10
RBI	Nap Lajoie	Cleveland	138	102
BA	Nap Lajoie	Cleveland	.411	.376
AB	Patsy Dougherty	Bos.-N.Y.	668	647
R	Patsy Dougherty	Bos.-N.Y.	150	113
H	Nap Lajoie	Cleveland	239	208
2B	Nap Lajoie	Cleveland	66	49
3B	Joe Cassidy	Washington	15	19
	Chick Stahl	Boston	9	19
	Buck Freeman	Boston	5	19
TB	Nap Lajoie	Cleveland	423	305
SA	Nap Lajoie	Cleveland	.728	.552
SB	Harry Bay	Cleveland	24	38
	Elmer Flick	Cleveland	24	38
PITCHING				
W	Jack Chesbro	New York	42	41
L	Happy Townsend	Washington	27	26
SV	Case Patten	Washington	7	3
ERA	Addie Joss	Cleveland	2.70	1.59
G	Jack Chesbro	New York	57	55
IP	Jack Chesbro	New York	471	454.2
BB	George Mullin	Detroit	208	131
SO	Rube Waddell	Philadelphia	559	349

NATIONAL LEAGUE LEADERS

CAT.	PLAYER	TEAM	STATS ADJUSTED	ACTUAL
BATTING				
HR	Harry Lumley	Brooklyn	44	9
RBI	Bill Dahlen	New York	105	80
BA	Honus Wagner	Pittsburgh	.381	.349
AB	Ginger Beaumont	Pittsburgh	639	615
R	George Browne	New York	130	99
H	Ginger Beaumont	Pittsburgh	210	185
2B	Honus Wagner	Pittsburgh	61	44
3B	Harry Lumley	Brooklyn	5	18
TB	Honus Wagner	Pittsburgh	352	255
SA	Honus Wagner	Pittsburgh	.692	.520
SB	Honus Wagner	Pittsburgh	33	53
PITCHING				
W	Joe McGinnity	New York	36	35
L	Oscar Jones	Brooklyn	26	25
	Vic Willis	Boston	26	25
SV	Joe McGinnity	New York	7	5
ERA	Joe McGinnity	New York	2.75	1.61
G	Joe McGinnity	New York	52	51
IP	Joe McGinnity	New York	416	408
BB	Togie Pittinger	Boston	242	144
SO	Christy Mathewson	New York	359	212

1905 SEASON

REGULAR SEASON STANDINGS

AMERICAN LEAGUE

		ADJUSTED				ACTUAL		
	W	L	Pct.	GB	W	L	Pct.	Rk.
EAST								
X Philadelphia	101	61	.623	0	92	56	.622	1
Boston	83	79	.512	18	78	74	.513	4
New York	77	85	.475	24	71	78	.477	6
Washington	69	93	.426	32	64	87	.424	7
WEST								
X Chicago	98	64	.605	0	92	60	.605	2
Detroit	83	79	.512	15	79	74	.516	3
Cleveland	80	82	.494	18	76	78	.494	5
St. Louis	57	105	.352	41	54	99	.353	8

NATIONAL LEAGUE

		ADJUSTED				ACTUAL		
	W	L	Pct.	GB	W	L	Pct.	Rk.
EAST								
X New York	111	51	.685	0	105	48	.686	1
Philadelphia	88	74	.543	23	83	69	.546	4
Boston	54	108	.333	57	51	103	.331	7
Brooklyn	51	111	.315	60	48	104	.316	8
WEST								
X Pittsburgh	102	60	.630	0	96	57	.627	2
Chicago	97	65	.599	5	92	61	.601	3
Cincinnati	84	78	.519	18	79	74	.516	5
St. Louis	61	101	.377	41	58	96	.377	6

SIMULATED PLAYOFFS

AMERICAN LEAGUE

ALCS	W	1	2	3	4	5	%
Philadelphia Athletics	1	1	4	1	0	3	44
Chicago White Sox	4	3	3	6	3	4	56

NATIONAL LEAGUE

NLCS	W	1	2	3	4	%
New York Giants	4	9	7	6	7	84
Pittsburgh Pirates	0	3	0	3	4	16

WORLD SERIES

WS	W	1	2	3	4	5	6	%
Chicago White Sox	2	1	3	3	3	5	2	48
New York Giants	4	3	7	4	0	2	8	52

ACTUAL WINNERS

American League: Philadelphia Athletics
National League: New York Giants
World Series: New York Giants

OUTSTANDING PERFORMANCES

AWARD WINNERS

LG.	PLAYER	TEAM	STATS ADJUSTED	ACTUAL
MOST VALUABLE PLAYERS				
AL	Rube Waddell	Philadelphia	29-11 W-L, 0 SV, 2.39 ERA, $56.1 MIL	27-10 W-L, 0 SV, 1.48 ERA
NL	Christy Mathewson	New York	32-9 W-L, 4 SV, 2.06 ERA, $56.6 MIL	31-9 W-L, 3 SV, 1.28 ERA
CY YOUNG AWARDS				
AL	Rube Waddell	Philadelphia	29-11 W-L, 0 SV, 2.39 ERA, $56.1 MIL	27-10 W-L, 0 SV, 1.48 ERA
NL	Christy Mathewson	New York	32-9 W-L, 4 SV, 2.06 ERA, $56.6 MIL	31-9 W-L, 3 SV, 1.28 ERA

AMERICAN LEAGUE LEADERS

CAT.	PLAYER	TEAM	STATS ADJUSTED	ACTUAL
BATTING				
HR	Harry Davis	Philadelphia	38	8
RBI	Harry Davis	Philadelphia	109	83
BA	Elmer Flick	Cleveland	.335	.308
AB	George Stone	St. Louis	657	632
R	Harry Davis	Philadelphia	122	93
H	George Stone	St. Louis	211	187
2B	Harry Davis	Philadelphia	43	47
3B	Elmer Flick	Cleveland	7	18
TB	George Stone	St. Louis	356	259
SA	Elmer Flick	Cleveland	.614	.462
SB	Danny Hoffman	Philadelphia	28	46
PITCHING				
W	Rube Waddell	Philadelphia	29	27
L	Fred Glade	St. Louis	26	25
SV	Jim Buchanan	St. Louis	8	2
ERA	Rube Waddell	Philadelphia	2.39	1.48
G	Rube Waddell	Philadelphia	49	46
IP	George Mullin	Detroit	363	347.2
BB	George Mullin	Detroit	206	138
SO	Rube Waddell	Philadelphia	463	287

NATIONAL LEAGUE LEADERS

CAT.	PLAYER	TEAM	STATS ADJUSTED	ACTUAL
BATTING				
HR	Fred Odwell	Cincinnati	32	9
RBI	Cy Seymour	Cincinnati	156	121
BA	Cy Seymour	Cincinnati	.410	.377
AB	Ed Abbaticchio	Boston	634	610
R	Mike Donlin	New York	160	124
H	Cy Seymour	Cincinnati	249	219
2B	Cy Seymour	Cincinnati	45	40
3B	Cy Seymour	Cincinnati	6	21
TB	Cy Seymour	Cincinnati	450	325
SA	Cy Seymour	Cincinnati	.740	.559
SB	Art Devlin	New York	35	59
	Billy Maloney	Chicago	35	59
PITCHING				
W	Christy Mathewson	New York	32	31
L	Vic Willis	Boston	30	29
SV	Claud Elliott	New York	8	6
ERA	Christy Mathewson	New York	2.06	1.28
G	Joe McGinnity	New York	48	46
	Togie Pittinger	Philadelphia	48	46
IP	Irv Young	Boston	396	378
BB	Chick Fraser	Boston	224	149
SO	Christy Mathewson	New York	347	206

1906 SEASON

REGULAR SEASON STANDINGS

AMERICAN LEAGUE

	ADJUSTED				ACTUAL			
	W	L	Pct.	GB	W	L	Pct.	Rk.
EAST								
X New York	97	65	.599	0	90	61	.596	2
Philadelphia	87	75	.537	10	78	67	.538	4
Washington	59	103	.364	38	55	95	.367	7
Boston	51	111	.315	46	49	105	.318	8
WEST								
X Chicago	100	62	.617	0	93	58	.616	1
Cleveland	94	68	.580	6	89	64	.582	3
St. Louis	83	79	.512	17	76	73	.510	5
Detroit	77	85	.475	23	71	78	.477	6

NATIONAL LEAGUE

	ADJUSTED				ACTUAL			
	W	L	Pct.	GB	W	L	Pct.	Rk.
EAST								
X New York	102	60	.630	0	96	56	.632	2
Philadelphia	75	87	.463	27	71	82	.464	4
Brooklyn	70	92	.432	32	66	86	.434	5
Boston	53	109	.327	49	49	102	.325	8
WEST								
X Chicago	124	38	.765	0	116	36	.763	1
Pittsburgh	99	63	.611	25	93	60	.608	3
Cincinnati	69	93	.426	55	64	87	.424	6
St. Louis	56	106	.346	68	52	98	.347	7

SIMULATED PLAYOFFS

AMERICAN LEAGUE

ALCS	W	1	2	3	4	%
New York Yankees	0	3	3	1	3	51
Chicago White Sox	4	4	4	2	5	49

NATIONAL LEAGUE

NLCS	W	1	2	3	4	%
New York Giants	0	0	3	1	3	7
Chicago Cubs	4	2	10	4	5	93

WORLD SERIES

WS*	W	1	2	3	4	5	6	%
Chicago White Sox	4	2	1	3	0	8	8	6
Chicago Cubs	2	1	7	0	1	6	3	94

ACTUAL WINNERS

American League: Chicago White Sox
National League: Chicago Cubs
World Series: Chicago White Sox

OUTSTANDING PERFORMANCES

AWARD WINNERS

LG.	PLAYER	TEAM	STATS ADJUSTED	ACTUAL
MOST VALUABLE PLAYERS				
AL	Nap Lajoie	Cleveland	0 HR, 123 RBI, .389 BA, $10.1 MIL	0 HR, 91 RBI, .355 BA
NL	Frank Chance	Chicago	25 HR, 97 RBI, .347 BA, $12.4 MIL	3 HR, 71 RBI, .319 BA
CY YOUNG AWARDS				
AL	Al Orth	New York	28-18 W-L, 0 SV, 4.02 ERA, $39.3 MIL	27-17 W-L, 0 SV, 2.34 ERA
NL	Mordecai Brown	Chicago	27-6 W-L, 4 SV, 1.78 ERA, $32.9 MIL	26-6 W-L, 3 SV, 1.04 ERA

AMERICAN LEAGUE LEADERS

CAT.	PLAYER	TEAM	STATS ADJUSTED	ACTUAL
BATTING				
HR	Harry Davis	Philadelphia	51	12
RBI	Harry Davis	Philadelphia	136	96
BA	George Stone	St. Louis	.391	.358
AB	Elmer Flick	Cleveland	644	624
R	Elmer Flick	Cleveland	132	98
H	Nap Lajoie	Cleveland	242	214
2B	Nap Lajoie	Cleveland	138	48
3B	Elmer Flick	Cleveland	16	22
TB	George Stone	St. Louis	415	291
SA	George Stone	St. Louis	.679	.501
SB	John Anderson	Washington	22	39
	Elmer Flick	Cleveland	22	39
PITCHING				
W	Al Orth	New York	28	27
L	Joe Harris	Boston	22	21
	Cy Young	Boston	22	21
SV	Chief Bender	Philadelphia	9	3
	Otto Hess	Cleveland	6	3
ERA	Doc White	Chicago	2.62	1.52
G	Jack Chesbro	New York	51	49
IP	Al Orth	New York	354	338.2
BB	Cy Falkenberg	Washington	164	108
	George Mullin	Detroit	164	108
SO	Rube Waddell	Philadelphia	345	196

NATIONAL LEAGUE LEADERS

CAT.	PLAYER	TEAM	STATS ADJUSTED	ACTUAL
BATTING				
HR	Tim Jordan	Brooklyn	41	12
RBI	Jim Nealon	Pittsburgh	114	83
	Harry Steinfeldt	Chicago	113	83
BA	Honus Wagner	Pittsburgh	.372	.339
AB	Pug Bennett	St. Louis	626	595
R	Frank Chance	Chicago	141	103
	Honus Wagner	Pittsburgh	141	103
H	Harry Steinfeldt	Chicago	201	176
2B	Honus Wagner	Pittsburgh	66	38
3B	Fred Clarke	Pittsburgh	9	13
	Frank Schulte	Chicago	3	13
TB	Honus Wagner	Pittsburgh	338	237
SA	Harry Lumley	Brooklyn	.653	.477
SB	Frank Chance	Chicago	32	57
PITCHING				
W	Joe McGinnity	New York	29	27
L	Gus Dorner	Cin.-Bos.	27	26
SV	George Ferguson	New York	18	7
ERA	Mordecai Brown	Chicago	1.78	1.04
G	Joe McGinnity	New York	48	45
IP	Irv Young	Boston	383	358.1
BB	Doc Scanlan	Brooklyn	189	127
SO	Fred Beebe	Chi.-St.L.	290	171

1907 SEASON

REGULAR SEASON STANDINGS

AMERICAN LEAGUE

		ADJUSTED				ACTUAL			
	W	L	Pct.	GB	W	L	Pct.	Rk.
EAST								
X Philadelphia	98	64	.605	0	88	57	.607	2
New York	77	85	.475	21	70	78	.473	5
Boston	64	98	.395	34	59	90	.396	7
Washington	53	109	.327	45	49	102	.325	8
WEST								
X Detroit	99	63	.611	0	92	58	.613	1
Chicago	93	69	.574	6	87	64	.576	3
Cleveland	91	71	.562	8	85	67	.559	4
St. Louis	73	89	.451	26	69	83	.454	6

NATIONAL LEAGUE

		ADJUSTED				ACTUAL			
	W	L	Pct.	GB	W	L	Pct.	Rk.
EAST								
X Philadelphia	91	71	.562	0	83	64	.565	3
New York	87	75	.537	4	82	71	.536	4
Brooklyn	71	91	.438	20	65	83	.439	5
Boston	64	98	.395	27	58	90	.392	7
WEST								
X Chicago	114	48	.704	0	107	45	.704	1
Pittsburgh	96	66	.593	18	91	63	.591	2
Cincinnati	70	92	.432	44	66	87	.431	6
St. Louis	55	107	.340	59	52	101	.340	8

SIMULATED PLAYOFFS

AMERICAN LEAGUE

ALCS	W	1	2	3	4	5	6	%
Philadelphia Athletics	4	8	6	2	6	1	5	34
Detroit Tigers	2	7	3	4	5	6	0	66

NATIONAL LEAGUE

NLCS	W	1	2	3	4	5	6	%
Philadelphia Phillies	2	2	2	1	4	1	3	24
Chicago Cubs	4	1	4	2	2	6	5	76

WORLD SERIES

WS	W	1	2	3	4	5	6	7	%
Philadelphia Athletics	4	1	3	2	4	3	2	3	31
Chicago Cubs	3	9	1	5	3	2	5	2	69

ACTUAL WINNERS

American League: Detroit Tigers
National League: Chicago Cubs
World Series: Chicago Cubs

OUTSTANDING PERFORMANCES

AWARD WINNERS

LG.	PLAYER	TEAM	STATS ADJUSTED	ACTUAL
MOST VALUABLE PLAYERS				
AL	Ty Cobb	Detroit	41 HR, 169 RBI, .385 BA, $14.8 MIL	5 HR, 119 RBI, .350 BA
NL	Honus Wagner	Pittsburgh	41 HR, 113 RBI, .385 BA, $13.1 MIL	6 HR, 82 RBI, .350 BA
CY YOUNG AWARDS				
AL	Ed Walsh	Chicago	25-19 W-L, 11 SV, 2.90 ERA, $55.0 MIL	24-18 W-L, 4 SV, 1.60 ERA
NL	Christy Mathewson	New York	25-13 W-L, 4 SV, 3.65 ERA, $53.2 MIL	24-12 W-L, 2 SV, 2.00 ERA

AMERICAN LEAGUE LEADERS

CAT.	PLAYER	TEAM	STATS ADJUSTED	ACTUAL
BATTING				
HR	Harry Davis	Philadelphia	42	8
RBI	Ty Cobb	Detroit	169	119
BA	Ty Cobb	Detroit	.385	.350
AB	Jiggs Donahue	Chicago	628	609
R	Sam Crawford	Detroit	144	102
H	Ty Cobb	Detroit	247	212
2B	Harry Davis	Philadelphia	30	35
3B	Elmer Flick	Cleveland	9	18
TB	Ty Cobb	Detroit	416	283
SA	Ty Cobb	Detroit	.649	.468
SB	Ty Cobb	Detroit	30	49
PITCHING				
W	Addie Joss	Cleveland	28	27
	Doc White	Chicago	28	27
L	Al Orth	New York	22	21
	Barney Pelty	St. Louis	22	21
SV	Tom Hughes	Washington	12	4
	Ed Walsh	Chicago	11	4
	Bill Dinneen	Bos.-St.L.	8	4
ERA	Ed Walsh	Chicago	2.90	1.60
G	Ed Walsh	Chicago	58	56
IP	Ed Walsh	Chicago	437	422.1
BB	Frank Smith	Chicago	164	111
SO	Rube Waddell	Philadelphia	413	232

NATIONAL LEAGUE LEADERS

CAT.	PLAYER	TEAM	STATS ADJUSTED	ACTUAL
BATTING				
HR	Dave Brain	Boston	43	10
RBI	Sherry Magee	Philadelphia	123	85
BA	Honus Wagner	Pittsburgh	.385	.350
AB	Spike Shannon	New York	611	585
R	Spike Shannon	New York	145	104
H	Ginger Beaumont	Boston	219	187
2B	Honus Wagner	Pittsburgh	42	38
3B	Whitey Alperman	Brooklyn	8	16
	John Ganzel	Cincinnati	8	16
TB	Honus Wagner	Pittsburgh	378	264
SA	Honus Wagner	Pittsburgh	.709	.513
SB	Honus Wagner	Pittsburgh	37	61
PITCHING				
W	Christy Mathewson	New York	25	24
L	Stoney McGlynn	St. Louis	26	25
SV	Joe McGinnity	New York	9	4
ERA	Jack Pfiester	Chicago	2.09	1.15
G	Joe McGinnity	New York	49	47
IP	Stoney McGlynn	St. Louis	368	352.1
BB	Stoney McGlynn	St. Louis	168	112
SO	Christy Mathewson	New York	325	178

1908 SEASON

REGULAR SEASON STANDINGS

AMERICAN LEAGUE

	ADJUSTED				ACTUAL			
	W	L	Pct.	GB	W	L	Pct.	Rk.
EAST								
X Boston	79	83	.488	0	75	79	.487	5
Philadelphia	72	90	.444	7	68	85	.444	6
Washington	71	91	.438	8	67	85	.441	7
New York	54	108	.333	25	51	103	.331	8
WEST								
X Detroit	95	67	.586	0	90	63	.588	1
X Cleveland	95	67	.586	0	90	64	.584	2
Chicago	94	68	.580	1	88	64	.579	3
St. Louis	88	74	.543	7	83	69	.546	4

NATIONAL LEAGUE

	ADJUSTED				ACTUAL			
	W	L	Pct.	GB	W	L	Pct.	Rk.
EAST								
X New York	103	59	.636	0	98	56	.636	2
Philadelphia	87	75	.537	16	83	71	.539	4
Boston	66	96	.407	37	63	91	.409	6
Brooklyn	56	106	.346	47	53	101	.344	7
WEST								
X Chicago	104	58	.642	0	99	55	.643	1
Pittsburgh	103	59	.636	1	98	56	.636	2
Cincinnati	77	85	.475	27	73	81	.474	5
St. Louis	52	110	.321	52	49	105	.318	8

SIMULATED PLAYOFFS

AMERICAN LEAGUE

TIEBREAKER	W	1	2				%
Detroit Tigers	2	4	5				45
Cleveland Indians	0	2	4				55

ALCS	W	1	2	3	4	5	%
Boston Red Sox	1	6	2	4	0	2	44
Detroit Tigers	4	9	7	3	9	3	56

NATIONAL LEAGUE

NLCS	W	1	2	3	4	5	%
New York Giants	1	3	2	1	2	1	55
Chicago Cubs	4	1	4	4	4	3	45

WORLD SERIES

WS*	W	1	2	3	4	5	%
Detroit Tigers	1	6	1	8	0	0	33
Chicago Cubs	4	10	6	3	3	2	67

ACTUAL WINNERS

American League: Detroit Tigers
National League: Chicago Cubs
World Series: Chicago Cubs

OUTSTANDING PERFORMANCES

AWARD WINNERS

LG.	PLAYER	TEAM	STATS ADJUSTED	ACTUAL
MOST VALUABLE PLAYERS				
AL	Ed Walsh	Chicago	42-16 W-L, 10 SV, 2.71 ERA, $67.8 MIL	40-15 W-L, 6 SV, 1.42 ERA
NL	Christy Mathewson	New York	38-11 W-L, 8 SV, 2.73 ERA, $63.8 MIL	37-11 W-L, 5 SV, 1.43 ERA
CY YOUNG AWARDS				
AL	Ed Walsh	Chicago	42-16 W-L, 10 SV, 2.71 ERA, $67.8 MIL	40-15 W-L, 6 SV, 1.42 ERA
NL	Christy Mathewson	New York	38-11 W-L, 8 SV, 2.73 ERA, $63.8 MIL	37-11 W-L, 5 SV, 1.43 ERA

AMERICAN LEAGUE LEADERS

CAT.	PLAYER	TEAM	STATS ADJUSTED	ACTUAL
BATTING				
HR	Sam Crawford	Detroit	45	7
RBI	Ty Cobb	Detroit	158	108
BA	Ty Cobb	Detroit	.364	.324
AB	Sam Crawford	Detroit	622	591
R	Matty McIntyre	Detroit	154	105
H	Ty Cobb	Detroit	223	188
2B	Ty Cobb	Detroit	57	36
3B	Ty Cobb	Detroit	9	20
TB	Ty Cobb	Detroit	409	276
SA	Ty Cobb	Detroit	.668	.475
SB	Patsy Dougherty	Chicago	29	47
PITCHING				
W	Ed Walsh	Chicago	42	40
L	Joe Lake	New York	23	22
SV	Ed Walsh	Chicago	10	6
ERA	Addie Joss	Cleveland	2.22	1.16
G	Ed Walsh	Chicago	69	66
IP	Ed Walsh	Chicago	485	464
BB	Jimmy Dygert	Philadelphia	152	97
SO	Ed Walsh	Chicago	480	269

NATIONAL LEAGUE LEADERS

CAT.	PLAYER	TEAM	STATS ADJUSTED	ACTUAL
BATTING				
HR	Tim Jordan	Brooklyn	40	12
RBI	Honus Wagner	Pittsburgh	158	109
BA	Honus Wagner	Pittsburgh	.399	.354
AB	Eddie Grant	Philadelphia	626	598
R	Fred Tenney	New York	145	101
H	Honus Wagner	Pittsburgh	237	201
2B	Honus Wagner	Pittsburgh	37	39
3B	Honus Wagner	Pittsburgh	5	19
TB	Honus Wagner	Pittsburgh	452	308
SA	Honus Wagner	Pittsburgh	.761	.542
SB	Honus Wagner	Pittsburgh	33	53
PITCHING				
W	Christy Mathewson	New York	38	37
L	Bugs Raymond	St. Louis	26	25
SV	Joe McGinnity	New York	15	5
	Christy Mathewson	New York	8	5
	Mordecai Brown	Chicago	5	5
ERA	Christy Mathewson	New York	2.73	1.43
G	Christy Mathewson	New York	58	56
IP	Christy Mathewson	New York	405	390.2
BB	Nap Rucker	Brooklyn	201	125
SO	Christy Mathewson	New York	448	259

1909 SEASON

REGULAR SEASON STANDINGS

AMERICAN LEAGUE

	ADJUSTED				ACTUAL			
	W	L	Pct.	GB	W	L	Pct.	Rk.
EAST								
X Philadelphia	101	61	.623	0	95	58	.621	2
Boston	94	68	.580	7	88	63	.583	3
New York	79	83	.488	22	74	77	.490	5
Washington	45	117	.278	56	42	110	.276	8
WEST								
X Detroit	105	57	.648	0	98	54	.645	1
Chicago	83	79	.512	22	78	74	.513	4
Cleveland	75	87	.463	30	71	82	.464	6
St. Louis	66	96	.407	39	61	89	.407	7

NATIONAL LEAGUE

	ADJUSTED				ACTUAL			
	W	L	Pct.	GB	W	L	Pct.	Rk.
EAST								
X New York	97	65	.599	0	92	61	.601	3
Philadelphia	78	84	.481	19	74	79	.484	5
Brooklyn	58	104	.358	39	55	98	.359	6
Boston	48	114	.296	49	45	108	.294	8
WEST								
X Pittsburgh	117	45	.722	0	110	42	.724	1
Chicago	110	52	.679	7	104	49	.680	2
Cincinnati	82	80	.506	35	77	76	.503	4
St. Louis	58	104	.358	59	54	98	.355	7

SIMULATED PLAYOFFS

AMERICAN LEAGUE

ALCS	W	1	2	3	4	5	%
Philadelphia Athletics	4	6	2	3	3	3	58
Detroit Tigers	1	1	1	4	2	1	42

NATIONAL LEAGUE

NLCS	W	1	2	3	4	%
New York Giants	0	4	2	1	2	18
Pittsburgh Pirates	4	11	6	7	3	82

WORLD SERIES

WS	W	1	2	3	4	5	6	%
Philadelphia Athletics	2	3	2	2	2	2	1	49
Pittsburgh Pirates	4	7	1	1	4	5	2	51

ACTUAL WINNERS

American League: Detroit Tigers
National League: Pittsburgh Pirates
World Series: Pittsburgh Pirates

OUTSTANDING PERFORMANCES

AWARD WINNERS

LG.	PLAYER	TEAM	STATS ADJUSTED	ACTUAL
MOST VALUABLE PLAYERS				
AL	Ty Cobb	Detroit	47 HR, 146 RBI, .417 BA, $25.1 MIL	9 HR, 107 RBI, .377 BA
NL	Honus Wagner	Pittsburgh	35 HR, 140 RBI, .375 BA, $13.4 MIL	5 HR, 100 RBI, .339 BA
CY YOUNG AWARDS				
AL	Frank Smith	Chicago	25-17 W-L, 6 SV, 3.24 ERA, $43.0 MIL	25-17 W-L, 1 SV, 1.80 ERA
NL	Christy Mathewson	New York	26-6 W-L, 5 SV, 2.07 ERA, $42.1 MIL	25-6 W-L, 2 SV, 1.14 ERA

AMERICAN LEAGUE LEADERS

CAT.	PLAYER	TEAM	STATS ADJUSTED	ACTUAL
BATTING				
HR	Ty Cobb	Detroit	47	9
RBI	Ty Cobb	Detroit	146	107
BA	Ty Cobb	Detroit	.417	.377
AB	Roy Hartzell	St. Louis	626	595
R	Ty Cobb	Detroit	158	116
H	Ty Cobb	Detroit	245	216
2B	Sam Crawford	Detroit	37	35
3B	Frank Baker	Philadelphia	8	19
TB	Ty Cobb	Detroit	417	296
SA	Ty Cobb	Detroit	.709	.517
SB	Ty Cobb	Detroit	42	76
PITCHING				
W	George Mullin	Detroit	30	29
L	Bob Groom	Washington	27	26
SV	Frank Arellanes	Boston	16	8
ERA	Harry Krause	Philadelphia	2.51	1.39
G	Frank Smith	Chicago	52	51
IP	Frank Smith	Chicago	372	365
BB	Bob Groom	Washington	151	105
SO	Frank Smith	Chicago	307	177

NATIONAL LEAGUE LEADERS

CAT.	PLAYER	TEAM	STATS ADJUSTED	ACTUAL
BATTING				
HR	Red Murray	New York	36	7
RBI	Honus Wagner	Pittsburgh	140	100
BA	Honus Wagner	Pittsburgh	.375	.339
AB	Eddie Grant	Philadelphia	664	631
R	Tommy Leach	Pittsburgh	177	126
H	Larry Doyle	New York	195	172
2B	Honus Wagner	Pittsburgh	43	39
3B	Mike Mitchell	Cincinnati	6	17
TB	Honus Wagner	Pittsburgh	349	242
SA	Honus Wagner	Pittsburgh	.671	.489
SB	Bob Bescher	Cincinnati	30	54
PITCHING				
W	Mordecai Brown	Chicago	28	27
L	George Ferguson	Boston	24	23
SV	Mordecai Brown	Chicago	13	7
ERA	Christy Mathewson	New York	2.07	1.14
G	Mordecai Brown	Chicago	52	50
IP	Mordecai Brown	Chicago	356	342.2
BB	Earl Moore	Philadelphia	155	108
	Al Mattern	Boston	154	108
SO	Orval Overall	Chicago	347	205

1910 SEASON

REGULAR SEASON STANDINGS

AMERICAN LEAGUE

	ADJUSTED				ACTUAL			
	W	L	Pct.	GB	W	L	Pct.	Rk.
EAST								
X Philadelphia	110	52	.679	0	102	48	.680	1
New York	94	68	.580	16	88	63	.583	2
Boston	86	76	.531	24	81	72	.529	4
Washington	71	91	.438	39	66	85	.437	7
WEST								
X Detroit	90	72	.556	0	86	68	.558	3
Cleveland	76	86	.469	14	71	81	.467	5
Chicago	72	90	.444	18	68	85	.444	6
St. Louis	49	113	.302	41	47	107	.305	8

NATIONAL LEAGUE

	ADJUSTED				ACTUAL			
	W	L	Pct.	GB	W	L	Pct.	Rk.
EAST								
X New York	96	66	.593	0	91	63	.591	2
Philadelphia	83	79	.512	13	78	75	.510	4
Brooklyn	67	95	.414	29	64	90	.416	6
Boston	56	106	.346	40	53	100	.346	8
WEST								
X Chicago	109	53	.673	0	104	50	.675	1
Pittsburgh	91	71	.562	18	86	67	.562	3
Cincinnati	79	83	.488	30	75	79	.487	5
St. Louis	67	95	.414	42	63	90	.412	7

SIMULATED PLAYOFFS

AMERICAN LEAGUE

ALCS	W	1	2	3	4	5	6	7	%
Philadelphia Athletics	3	5	1	0	2	3	3	4	76
Detroit Tigers	4	6	2	2	1	2	1	5	24

NATIONAL LEAGUE

NLCS	W	1	2	3	4	5		%
New York Giants	1	5	7	0	3	3		36
Chicago Cubs	4	7	12	2	2	6		64

WORLD SERIES

WS	W	1	2	3	4	5	6	7	%
Detroit Tigers	4	1	4	1	10	5	0	4	25
Chicago Cubs	3	8	3	4	9	4	6	3	75

ACTUAL WINNERS

American League: Philadelphia Athletics
National League: Chicago Cubs
World Series: Philadelphia Athletics

OUTSTANDING PERFORMANCES

AWARD WINNERS

LG.	PLAYER	TEAM	STATS ADJUSTED	ACTUAL
MOST VALUABLE PLAYERS				
AL	Jack Coombs	Philadelphia	32-9 W-L, 4 SV, 2.12 ERA, $51.5 MIL	31-9 W-L, 1 SV, 1.30 ERA
NL	Sherry Magee	Philadelphia	35 HR, 157 RBI, .358 BA, $19.1 MIL	6 HR, 123 RBI, .331 BA
CY YOUNG AWARDS				
AL	Jack Coombs	Philadelphia	32-9 W-L, 4 SV, 2.12 ERA, $51.5 MIL	31-9 W-L, 1 SV, 1.30 ERA
NL	Christy Mathewson	New York	28-9 W-L, 0 SV, 3.12 ERA, $54.0 MIL	27-9 W-L, 0 SV, 1.89 ERA

AMERICAN LEAGUE LEADERS

CAT.	PLAYER	TEAM	STATS ADJUSTED	ACTUAL
BATTING				
HR	Jake Stahl	Boston	40	10
RBI	Sam Crawford	Detroit	155	120
BA	Ty Cobb	Detroit	.415	.383
AB	Nap Lajoie	Cleveland	595	591
R	Ty Cobb	Detroit	137	106
H	Nap Lajoie	Cleveland	247	227
2B	Nap Lajoie	Cleveland	70	51
3B	Sam Crawford	Detroit	7	19
TB	Nap Lajoie	Cleveland	401	304
SA	Ty Cobb	Detroit	.722	.551
SB	Eddie Collins	Philadelphia	43	81
PITCHING				
W	Jack Coombs	Philadelphia	32	31
L	Ed Walsh	Chicago	21	20
SV	Ed Walsh	Chicago	6	5
ERA	Ed Walsh	Chicago	2.08	1.27
G	Jack Coombs	Philadelphia	47	45
	Ed Walsh	Chicago	47	45
	Walter Johnson	Washington	46	45
IP	Walter Johnson	Washington	378	370
BB	Cy Morgan	Philadelphia	149	117
SO	Walter Johnson	Washington	489	313

NATIONAL LEAGUE LEADERS

CAT.	PLAYER	TEAM	STATS ADJUSTED	ACTUAL
BATTING				
HR	Frank Schulte	Chicago	44	10
	Fred Beck	Boston	39	10
RBI	Sherry Magee	Philadelphia	157	123
BA	Sherry Magee	Philadelphia	.358	.331
AB	Dick Hoblitzel	Cincinnati	635	611
R	Sherry Magee	Philadelphia	140	110
H	Bobby Byrne	Pittsburgh	203	178
	Honus Wagner	Pittsburgh	203	178
2B	Bobby Byrne	Pittsburgh	80	43
3B	Mike Mitchell	Cincinnati	6	18
TB	Sherry Magee	Philadelphia	355	263
SA	Sherry Magee	Philadelphia	.662	.507
SB	Bob Bescher	Cincinnati	37	70
PITCHING				
W	Christy Mathewson	New York	28	27
L	George Bell	Brooklyn	28	27
SV	Harry Gaspar	Cincinnati	14	7
	Mordecai Brown	Chicago	7	7
ERA	George McQuillan	Philadelphia	2.60	1.60
G	Al Mattern	Boston	53	51
IP	Nap Rucker	Brooklyn	336	320.1
BB	Bob Harmon	St. Louis	173	133
SO	Earl Moore	Philadelphia	302	185

1911 SEASON

REGULAR SEASON STANDINGS

AMERICAN LEAGUE

		ADJUSTED				ACTUAL			
	W	L	Pct.	GB	W	L	Pct.	Rk.
EAST								
X Philadelphia	108	54	.667	0	101	50	.669	1
Boston	82	80	.506	26	78	75	.510	4
New York	81	81	.500	27	76	76	.500	6
Washington	67	95	.414	41	64	90	.416	7
WEST								
X Detroit	94	68	.580	0	89	65	.578	2
Cleveland	85	77	.525	9	80	73	.523	3
Chicago	83	79	.512	11	77	74	.510	4
St. Louis	48	114	.296	46	45	107	.296	8

NATIONAL LEAGUE

		ADJUSTED				ACTUAL			
	W	L	Pct.	GB	W	L	Pct.	Rk.
EAST								
X New York	105	57	.648	0	99	54	.647	1
Philadelphia	84	78	.519	21	79	73	.520	4
Brooklyn	69	93	.426	36	64	86	.427	7
Boston	47	115	.290	58	44	107	.291	8
WEST								
X Chicago	97	65	.599	0	92	62	.597	2
Pittsburgh	90	72	.556	7	85	69	.552	3
St. Louis	82	80	.506	15	75	74	.503	5
Cincinnati	74	88	.457	23	70	83	.458	6

SIMULATED PLAYOFFS

AMERICAN LEAGUE

ALCS	W	1	2	3	4	5	6	%
Philadelphia Athletics	4	12	10	7	5	13	12	82
Detroit Tigers	2	7	5	8	6	2	1	18

NATIONAL LEAGUE

NLCS	W	1	2	3	4	5	6	7	%
New York Giants	4	5	2	2	0	3	2	5	57
Chicago Cubs	3	4	4	1	1	1	3	1	43

WORLD SERIES

WS*	W	1	2	3	4	5	6	%
Philadelphia Athletics	4	1	3	3	4	3	13	53
New York Giants	2	2	1	2	2	4	2	47

ACTUAL WINNERS

American League: Philadelphia Athletics
National League: New York Giants
World Series: Philadelphia Athletics

OUTSTANDING PERFORMANCES

AWARD WINNERS

LG.	PLAYER	TEAM	STATS ADJUSTED	ACTUAL
MOST VALUABLE PLAYERS				
AL	Ty Cobb	Detroit	40 HR, 143 RBI, .425 BA, $31.2 MIL	8 HR, 127 RBI, .420 BA
NL	Frank Schulte	Chicago	57 HR, 118 RBI, .304 BA, $12.6 MIL	21 HR, 107 RBI, .300 BA
CY YOUNG AWARDS				
AL	Walter Johnson	Washington	26-14 W-L, 1 SV, 2.56 ERA, $42.3 MIL	25-13 W-L, 1 SV, 1.90 ERA
NL	Christy Mathewson	New York	27-14 W-L, 5 SV, 2.69 ERA, $52.3 MIL	26-13 W-L, 3 SV, 1.99 ERA

AMERICAN LEAGUE LEADERS

CAT.	PLAYER	TEAM	STATS ADJUSTED	ACTUAL
BATTING				
HR	Frank Baker	Philadelphia	41	11
RBI	Ty Cobb	Detroit	143	127
BA	Ty Cobb	Detroit	.425	.420
AB	Clyde Milan	Washington	648	616
R	Ty Cobb	Detroit	166	147
H	Ty Cobb	Detroit	265	248
2B	Ty Cobb	Detroit	61	47
3B	Ty Cobb	Detroit	8	24
TB	Ty Cobb	Detroit	462	367
SA	Ty Cobb	Detroit	.742	.621
SB	Ty Cobb	Detroit	43	83
PITCHING				
W	Jack Coombs	Philadelphia	30	28
L	Jack Powell	St. Louis	20	19
SV	Charley Hall	Boston	12	4
	Ed Walsh	Chicago	10	4
	Eddie Plank	Philadelphia	7	4
ERA	Vean Gregg	Cleveland	2.43	1.80
G	Ed Walsh	Chicago	59	56
IP	Ed Walsh	Chicago	388	368.2
BB	Gene Krapp	Cleveland	161	138
SO	Ed Walsh	Chicago	414	255

NATIONAL LEAGUE LEADERS

CAT.	PLAYER	TEAM	STATS ADJUSTED	ACTUAL
BATTING				
HR	Frank Schulte	Chicago	57	21
RBI	Chief Wilson	Pittsburgh	120	107
	Frank Schulte	Chicago	118	107
BA	Honus Wagner	Pittsburgh	.337	.334
AB	Dick Hoblitzel	Cincinnati	634	622
R	Jimmy Sheckard	Chicago	133	121
H	Doc Miller	Boston	202	192
2B	Ed Konetchy	St. Louis	44	38
3B	Larry Doyle	New York	6	25
TB	Frank Schulte	Chicago	381	308
SA	Frank Schulte	Chicago	.639	.534
SB	Bob Bescher	Cincinnati	40	81
PITCHING				
W	Pete Alexander	Philadelphia	30	28
L	Earl Moore	Philadelphia	20	19
	Bill Steele	St. Louis	19	19
SV	Mordecai Brown	Chicago	20	13
ERA	Christy Mathewson	New York	2.69	1.99
G	Mordecai Brown	Chicago	55	53
IP	Pete Alexander	Philadelphia	390	367
BB	Bob Harmon	St. Louis	209	181
SO	Rube Marquard	New York	369	237

1912 SEASON

REGULAR SEASON STANDINGS

AMERICAN LEAGUE

		ADJUSTED				ACTUAL			
	W	L	Pct.	GB	W	L	Pct.	Rk.
EAST								
X Boston	112	50	.691	0	105	47	.691	1
Washington	97	65	.599	15	91	61	.599	2
Philadelphia	96	66	.593	16	90	62	.592	3
New York	53	109	.327	59	50	102	.329	8
WEST								
X Chicago	82	80	.506	0	78	76	.506	4
Cleveland	79	83	.488	3	75	78	.490	5
Detroit	73	89	.451	9	69	84	.451	6
St. Louis	56	106	.346	26	53	101	.344	7

NATIONAL LEAGUE

		ADJUSTED				ACTUAL			
	W	L	Pct.	GB	W	L	Pct.	Rk.
EAST								
X New York	110	52	.679	0	103	48	.682	1
Philadelphia	78	84	.481	32	73	79	.480	5
Brooklyn	61	101	.377	49	58	95	.379	7
Boston	55	107	.340	55	52	101	.340	8
WEST								
X Pittsburgh	100	62	.617	0	93	58	.616	2
Chicago	98	64	.605	2	91	59	.607	3
Cincinnati	79	83	.488	21	75	78	.490	4
St. Louis	67	95	.414	33	63	90	.412	6

SIMULATED PLAYOFFS

AMERICAN LEAGUE

ALCS	W	1	2	3	4	5		%
Boston Red Sox	4	2	3	11	1	8		91
Chicago White Sox	1	0	1	1	2	4		9

NATIONAL LEAGUE

NLCS	W	1	2	3	4	5	6	%
New York Giants	4	1	3	5	3	5	7	54
Pittsburgh Pirates	2	2	2	3	5	4	2	46

WORLD SERIES

WS*	W	1	2	3	4	5	6	7	%
Boston Red Sox	4	4	1	3	2	2	4	3	59
New York Giants	3	3	2	1	1	5	11	2	41

ACTUAL WINNERS

American League: Boston Red Sox
National League: New York Giants
World Series: Boston Red Sox

OUTSTANDING PERFORMANCES

AWARD WINNERS

LG.	PLAYER	TEAM	STATS ADJUSTED	ACTUAL
MOST VALUABLE PLAYERS				
AL	Tris Speaker	Boston	42 HR, 101 RBI, .384 BA, $20.0 MIL	10 HR, 90 RB, .383 BA
NL	Larry Doyle	New York	36 HR, 100 RBI, .330 BA, $15.1 MIL	10 HR, 90 RBI, .330 BA
CY YOUNG AWARDS				
AL	Joe Wood	Boston	36-5 W-L, 2 SV, 2.58 ERA, $55.1 MIL	34-5 W-L, 1 SV, 1.91 ERA
NL	Rube Marquard	New York	27-12 W-L, 3 SV, 3.48 ERA, $33.4 MIL	26-11 W-L, 1 SV, 2.57 ERA

AMERICAN LEAGUE LEADERS

CAT.	PLAYER	TEAM	STATS ADJUSTED	ACTUAL
BATTING				
HR	Frank Baker	Philadelphia	44	10
	Tris Speaker	Boston	42	10
RBI	Frank Baker	Philadelphia	147	130
BA	Ty Cobb	Detroit	.411	.409
AB	Eddie Foster	Washington	650	618
R	Eddie Collins	Philadelphia	155	137
H	Ty Cobb	Detroit	239	226
	Joe Jackson	Cleveland	237	226
2B	Tris Speaker	Boston	48	53
3B	Joe Jackson	Cleveland	12	26
TB	Joe Jackson	Cleveland	412	331
SA	Ty Cobb	Detroit	.697	.584
SB	Clyde Milan	Washington	45	88
PITCHING				
W	Joe Wood	Boston	36	34
L	Russ Ford	New York	22	21
SV	Ed Walsh	Chicago	16	10
ERA	Walter Johnson	Washington	1.86	1.39
G	Ed Walsh	Chicago	64	62
IP	Ed Walsh	Chicago	406	393
BB	George Kahler	Cleveland	145	121
SO	Walter Johnson	Washington	484	303

NATIONAL LEAGUE LEADERS

CAT.	PLAYER	TEAM	STATS ADJUSTED	ACTUAL
BATTING				
HR	Heinie Zimmerman	Chicago	49	14
RBI	Honus Wagner	Pittsburgh	116	102
BA	Heinie Zimmerman	Chicago	.373	.372
AB	Vin Campbell	Boston	654	624
R	Bob Bescher	Cincinnati	134	120
H	Heinie Zimmerman	Chicago	222	207
2B	Heinie Zimmerman	Chicago	30	41
3B	Chief Wilson	Pittsburgh	10	36
TB	Heinie Zimmerman	Chicago	405	318
SA	Heinie Zimmerman	Chicago	.681	.571
SB	Bob Bescher	Cincinnati	34	67
PITCHING				
W	Larry Cheney	Chicago	28	26
	Rube Marquard	New York	27	26
L	Lefty Tyler	Boston	23	22
SV	Slim Sallee	St. Louis	13	6
ERA	Jeff Tesreau	New York	2.66	1.96
G	Rube Benton	Cincinnati	52	50
IP	Pete Alexander	Philadelphia	331	310.1
BB	Marty O'Toole	Pittsburgh	192	159
SO	Pete Alexander	Philadelphia	326	195

1913 SEASON

REGULAR SEASON STANDINGS

AMERICAN LEAGUE

	ADJUSTED				ACTUAL			
	W	L	Pct.	GB	W	L	Pct.	Rk.
EAST								
X Philadelphia	102	60	.630	0	96	57	.627	1
Washington	95	67	.586	7	90	64	.584	2
Boston	85	77	.525	17	79	71	.527	4
New York	61	101	.377	41	57	94	.377	7
WEST								
X Cleveland	92	70	.568	0	86	66	.566	3
Chicago	83	79	.512	9	78	74	.513	5
Detroit	70	92	.432	22	66	87	.431	6
St. Louis	60	102	.370	32	57	96	.373	8

NATIONAL LEAGUE

	ADJUSTED				ACTUAL			
	W	L	Pct.	GB	W	L	Pct.	Rk.
EAST								
X New York	108	54	.667	0	101	51	.664	1
Philadelphia	94	68	.580	14	88	63	.583	2
Boston	74	88	.457	34	69	82	.457	5
Brooklyn	71	91	.438	37	65	84	.436	6
WEST								
X Chicago	93	69	.574	0	88	65	.575	3
Pittsburgh	85	77	.525	8	78	71	.523	4
Cincinnati	68	94	.420	25	64	89	.418	7
St. Louis	55	107	.340	38	51	99	.340	8

SIMULATED PLAYOFFS

AMERICAN LEAGUE

ALCS	W	1	2	3	4	5	6	7	%
Philadelphia Athletics	4	4	5	7	2	1	2	6	69
Cleveland Indians	3	6	2	2	6	4	1	5	31

NATIONAL LEAGUE

NLCS	W	1	2	3	4	5	6	7	%
New York Giants	4	2	4	6	5	7	4	6	66
Chicago Cubs	3	4	5	2	2	2	5	0	34

WORLD SERIES

WS*	W	1	2	3	4	5	%
Philadelphia Athletics	4	6	0	8	6	3	50
New York Giants	1	4	3	2	5	1	50

ACTUAL WINNERS

American League: Philadelphia Athletics
National League: New York Giants
World Series: Philadelphia Athletics

OUTSTANDING PERFORMANCES

AWARD WINNERS

LG.	PLAYER	TEAM	STATS ADJUSTED	ACTUAL
MOST VALUABLE PLAYERS				
AL	Walter Johnson	Washington	38-7 W-L, 4 SV, 1.70 ERA, $60.7 MIL	36-7 W-L, 2 SV, 1.14 ERA
NL	Jake Daubert	Brooklyn	16 HR, 65 RBI, .364 BA, $7.2 MIL	2 HR, 52 RBI, .350 BA
CY YOUNG AWARDS				
AL	Walter Johnson	Washington	38-7 W-L, 4 SV, 1.70 ERA, $60.7 MIL	36-7 W-L, 2 SV, 1.14 ERA
NL	Christy Mathewson	New York	26-12 W-L, 3 SV, 3.06 ERA, $39.9 MIL	25-11 W-L, 2 SV, 2.06 ERA

AMERICAN LEAGUE LEADERS

CAT.	PLAYER	TEAM	STATS ADJUSTED	ACTUAL
BATTING				
HR	Frank Baker	Philadelphia	41	12
RBI	Frank Baker	Philadelphia	147	117
BA	Ty Cobb	Detroit	.406	.390
AB	Sam Crawford	Detroit	645	609
R	Eddie Collins	Philadelphia	157	125
H	Joe Jackson	Cleveland	215	197
2B	Joe Jackson	Cleveland	48	39
3B	Sam Crawford	Detroit	7	23
TB	Sam Crawford	Detroit	390	298
SA	Joe Jackson	Cleveland	.684	.551
SB	Clyde Milan	Washington	40	75
PITCHING				
W	Walter Johnson	Washington	38	36
L	Jim Scott	Chicago	22	21
SV	Chief Bender	Philadelphia	17	13
ERA	Walter Johnson	Washington	1.70	1.14
G	Reb Russell	Chicago	55	52
IP	Walter Johnson	Washington	360	346
BB	Vean Gregg	Cleveland	158	124
SO	Walter Johnson	Washington	409	243

NATIONAL LEAGUE LEADERS

CAT.	PLAYER	TEAM	STATS ADJUSTED	ACTUAL
BATTING				
HR	Gavvy Cravath	Philadelphia	53	19
RBI	Gavvy Cravath	Philadelphia	155	128
BA	Jake Daubert	Brooklyn	.364	.350
AB	Max Carey	Pittsburgh	648	620
R	Max Carey	Pittsburgh	122	99
	Tommy Leach	Chicago	122	99
H	Gavvy Cravath	Philadelphia	190	179
2B	Red Smith	Brooklyn	47	40
3B	Vic Saier	Chicago	4	21
TB	Gavvy Cravath	Philadelphia	376	298
SA	Gavvy Cravath	Philadelphia	.701	.568
SB	Max Carey	Pittsburgh	32	61
PITCHING				
W	Tom Seaton	Philadelphia	28	27
L	Dan Griner	St. Louis	23	22
SV	Larry Cheney	Chicago	17	11
ERA	Christy Mathewson	New York	3.06	2.06
G	Larry Cheney	Chicago	56	54
IP	Tom Seaton	Philadelphia	329	322.1
BB	Tom Seaton	Philadelphia	169	136
SO	Tom Seaton	Philadelphia	289	168

1914 SEASON

REGULAR SEASON STANDINGS

AMERICAN LEAGUE

		ADJUSTED				ACTUAL			
	W	L	Pct.	GB	W	L	Pct.	Rk.
EAST								
X Philadelphia	105	57	.648	0	99	53	.651	1
Boston	96	66	.593	9	91	62	.595	2
Washington	85	77	.525	20	81	73	.526	3
New York	74	88	.457	31	70	84	.455	6
WEST								
X Detroit	85	77	.525	0	80	73	.523	4
St. Louis	75	87	.463	10	71	82	.464	5
Chicago	74	88	.457	11	70	84	.455	6
Cleveland	54	108	.333	31	51	102	.333	8

NATIONAL LEAGUE

		ADJUSTED				ACTUAL			
	W	L	Pct.	GB	W	L	Pct.	Rk.
EAST								
X Boston	99	63	.611	0	94	59	.614	1
New York	88	74	.543	11	84	70	.545	2
Brooklyn	79	83	.488	20	75	79	.487	5
Philadelphia	78	84	.481	21	74	80	.481	6
WEST								
X St. Louis	86	76	.531	0	81	72	.529	3
Chicago	82	80	.506	4	78	76	.506	4
Pittsburgh	73	89	.451	13	69	85	.448	7
Cincinnati	63	99	.389	23	60	94	.390	8

SIMULATED PLAYOFFS

AMERICAN LEAGUE

ALCS	W	1	2	3	4	5	6	%
Philadelphia Athletics	4	11	12	0	3	12	5	86
Detroit Tigers	2	2	2	4	4	5	2	14

NATIONAL LEAGUE

NLCS	W	1	2	3	4	5	6	7	%
Boston Braves	4	5	3	6	3	2	2	7	70
St. Louis Cardinals	3	6	1	1	2	4	4	4	30

WORLD SERIES

WS*	W	1	2	3	4	%
Philadelphia Athletics	0	1	0	4	1	61
Boston Braves	4	7	1	5	3	39

ACTUAL WINNERS

American League: Philadelphia Athletics
National League: Boston Braves
World Series: Boston Braves

OUTSTANDING PERFORMANCES

AWARD WINNERS

LG.	PLAYER	TEAM	STATS ADJUSTED	ACTUAL
MOST VALUABLE PLAYERS				
AL	Eddie Collins	Philadelphia	16 HR, 106 RBI, .365 BA, $19.7 MIL	2 HR, 85 RBI, .344 BA
NL	Johnny Evers	Boston	8 HR, 50 RBI, .295 BA, $4.6 MIL	1 HR, 40 RBI, .279 BA
CY YOUNG AWARDS				
AL	Walter Johnson	Washington	29-18 W-L, 3 SV, 2.71 ERA, $59.1 MIL	28-18 W-L, 1 SV, 1.72 ERA
NL	Bill James	Boston	27-7 W-L, 8 SV, 2.99 ERA, $33.1 MIL	26-7 W-L, 3 SV, 1.90 ERA

AMERICAN LEAGUE LEADERS

CAT.	PLAYER	TEAM	STATS ADJUSTED	ACTUAL
BATTING				
HR	Frank Baker	Philadelphia	34	9
RBI	Sam Crawford	Detroit	131	104
BA	Ty Cobb	Detroit	.390	.368
AB	Eddie Foster	Washington	632	616
R	Eddie Collins	Philadelphia	153	122
H	Tris Speaker	Boston	209	193
2B	Tris Speaker	Boston	73	46
3B	Sam Crawford	Detroit	10	26
TB	Tris Speaker	Boston	373	287
SA	Ty Cobb	Detroit	.649	.513
SB	Fritz Maisel	New York	41	74
PITCHING				
W	Walter Johnson	Washington	29	28
L	Joe Benz	Chicago	20	19
SV	Red Faber	Chicago	13	4
	Jack Bentley	Washington	12	4
	Roy Mitchell	St. Louis	12	4
	Jim Shaw	Washington	11	4
	Hooks Dauss	Detroit	9	4
ERA	Dutch Leonard	Boston	1.52	0.96
G	Walter Johnson	Washington	52	51
IP	Walter Johnson	Washington	379	371.2
BB	Jim Shaw	Washington	169	137
SO	Walter Johnson	Washington	361	225

NATIONAL LEAGUE LEADERS

CAT.	PLAYER	TEAM	STATS ADJUSTED	ACTUAL
BATTING				
HR	Gavvy Cravath	Philadelphia	49	19
RBI	Sherry Magee	Philadelphia	133	103
BA	Jake Daubert	Brooklyn	.348	.329
AB	Max Carey	Pittsburgh	608	593
R	George Burns	New York	127	100
H	Sherry Magee	Philadelphia	191	171
2B	Sherry Magee	Philadelphia	31	39
3B	Max Carey	Pittsburgh	12	17
TB	Sherry Magee	Philadelphia	372	277
SA	Sherry Magee	Philadelphia	.648	.509
SB	George Burns	New York	35	62
PITCHING				
W	Pete Alexander	Philadelphia	28	27
L	Red Ames	Cincinnati	23	23
SV	Slim Sallee	St. Louis	10	6
	Red Ames	Cincinnati	9	6
ERA	Bill Doak	St. Louis	2.70	1.72
G	Larry Cheney	Chicago	52	50
IP	Pete Alexander	Philadelphia	370	355
BB	Larry Cheney	Chicago	176	140
SO	Pete Alexander	Philadelphia	351	214

REGULAR SEASON STANDINGS

AMERICAN LEAGUE

	ADJUSTED				ACTUAL			
	W	L	Pct.	GB	W	L	Pct.	Rk.
EAST								
X Boston	108	54	.667	0	101	50	.669	1
Washington	90	72	.556	18	85	68	.556	4
New York	74	88	.457	34	69	83	.454	5
Philadelphia	46	116	.284	62	43	109	.283	8
WEST								
X Detroit	105	57	.648	0	100	54	.649	2
Chicago	98	64	.605	7	93	61	.604	3
St. Louis	66	96	.407	39	63	91	.409	6
Cleveland	61	101	.377	44	57	95	.375	7

NATIONAL LEAGUE

	ADJUSTED				ACTUAL			
	W	L	Pct.	GB	W	L	Pct.	Rk.
EAST								
X Philadelphia	96	66	.593	0	90	62	.592	1
Boston	88	74	.543	8	83	69	.546	2
Brooklyn	85	77	.525	11	80	72	.526	3
New York	74	88	.457	22	69	83	.454	8
WEST								
X Chicago	77	85	.475	0	73	80	.477	4
X Pittsburgh	77	85	.475	0	73	81	.474	5
St. Louis	76	86	.469	1	72	81	.471	6
Cincinnati	75	87	.463	2	71	83	.461	7

SIMULATED PLAYOFFS

AMERICAN LEAGUE

ALCS	W	1	2	3	4	5	6	%
Boston Red Sox	4	4	7	3	5	3	7	54
Detroit Tigers	2	5	4	4	1	0	3	46

NATIONAL LEAGUE

TIEBREAKER	W	1	2	3				%
Chicago Cubs	2	4	3	5				47
Pittsburgh Pirates	1	7	0	4				53

NLCS	W	1	2	3	4	5	6	7	%
Philadelphia Phillies	4	2	2	7	6	5	1	6	83
Chicago Cubs	3	3	3	0	0	3	3	1	17

WORLD SERIES

WS*	W	1	2	3	4	5	%
Boston Red Sox	4	1	2	2	2	5	47
Philadelphia Phillies	1	3	1	1	1	4	53

ACTUAL WINNERS

American League: Boston Red Sox
National League: Philadelphia Phillies
World Series: Boston Red Sox

OUTSTANDING PERFORMANCES

AWARD WINNERS

LG.	PLAYER	TEAM	STATS ADJUSTED	ACTUAL
MOST VALUABLE PLAYERS				
AL	Eddie Collins	Chicago	24 HR, 100 RBI, .358 BA, $26.1 MIL	4 HR, 77 RBI, .332 BA
NL	Pete Alexander	Philadelphia	33-11 W-L, 6 SV, 1.92 ERA, $60.1 MIL	31-10 W-L, 3 SV, 1.22 ERA
CY YOUNG AWARDS				
AL	Walter Johnson	Washington	28-14 W-L, 6 SV, 2.44 ERA, $57.6 MIL	27-13 W-L, 4 SV, 1.55 ERA
NL	Pete Alexander	Philadelphia	33-11 W-L, 6 SV, 1.92 ERA, $60.1 MIL	31-10 W-L, 3 SV, 1.22 ERA

AMERICAN LEAGUE LEADERS

CAT.	PLAYER	TEAM	STATS ADJUSTED	ACTUAL
BATTING				
HR	Braggo Roth	Chi.-Cle.	30	7
RBI	Sam Crawford	Detroit	144	112
	Bobby Veach	Detroit	144	112
BA	Ty Cobb	Detroit	.398	.369
AB	Eddie Foster	Washington	646	618
R	Ty Cobb	Detroit	186	144
H	Ty Cobb	Detroit	233	208
2B	Bobby Veach	Detroit	62	40
3B	Sam Crawford	Detroit	9	19
TB	Ty Cobb	Detroit	368	274
SA	Jack Fournier	Chicago	.629	.491
SB	Ty Cobb	Detroit	60	96
PITCHING				
W	Walter Johnson	Washington	28	27
L	Weldon Wyckoff	Philadelphia	23	22
SV	Carl Mays	Boston	20	7
ERA	Joe Wood	Boston	2.36	1.49
G	Harry Coveleski	Detroit	52	50
	Red Faber	Chicago	52	50
IP	Walter Johnson	Washington	351	336.2
BB	Weldon Wyckoff	Philadelphia	208	165
SO	Walter Johnson	Washington	347	203

NATIONAL LEAGUE LEADERS

CAT.	PLAYER	TEAM	STATS ADJUSTED	ACTUAL
BATTING				
HR	Gavvy Cravath	Philadelphia	58	24
RBI	Gavvy Cravath	Philadelphia	151	115
BA	Larry Doyle	New York	.344	.320
AB	George Burns	New York	650	622
R	Gavvy Cravath	Philadelphia	117	89
H	Larry Doyle	New York	213	189
2B	Larry Doyle	New York	57	40
3B	Tom Long	St. Louis	15	25
TB	Gavvy Cravath	Philadelphia	363	266
SA	Gavvy Cravath	Philadelphia	.656	.510
SB	Max Carey	Pittsburgh	22	36
PITCHING				
W	Pete Alexander	Philadelphia	33	31
L	Dick Rudolph	Boston	19	19
	Pete Schneider	Cincinnati	19	19
SV	Tom Hughes	Boston	16	9
ERA	Pete Alexander	Philadelphia	1.92	1.22
G	Tom Hughes	Boston	52	50
IP	Pete Alexander	Philadelphia	399	376.1
BB	Gene Dale	Cincinnati	131	107
SO	Pete Alexander	Philadelphia	415	241

1916 SEASON

REGULAR SEASON STANDINGS

AMERICAN LEAGUE

		ADJUSTED				ACTUAL		
	W	L	Pct.	GB	W	L	Pct.	Rk.
EAST								
X Boston	96	66	.593	0	91	63	.591	1
New York	84	78	.519	12	80	74	.519	4
Washington	80	82	.494	16	76	77	.497	7
Philadelphia	38	124	.235	58	36	117	.235	8
WEST								
X Chicago	94	68	.580	0	89	65	.578	2
Detroit	92	70	.568	2	87	67	.565	3
St. Louis	83	79	.512	11	79	75	.513	5
Cleveland	81	81	.500	13	77	77	.500	6

NATIONAL LEAGUE

		ADJUSTED				ACTUAL		
	W	L	Pct.	GB	W	L	Pct.	Rk.
EAST								
X Brooklyn	99	63	.611	0	94	60	.610	1
Philadelphia	96	66	.593	3	91	62	.595	2
Boston	95	67	.586	4	89	63	.586	3
New York	92	70	.568	7	86	66	.566	4
WEST								
X Chicago	71	91	.438	0	67	86	.438	5
Pittsburgh	68	94	.420	3	65	89	.422	6
Cincinnati	64	98	.395	7	60	93	.392	7
St. Louis	63	99	.389	8	60	93	.392	7

SIMULATED PLAYOFFS

AMERICAN LEAGUE

ALCS	W	1	2	3	4	5	%
Boston Red Sox	4	4	5	2	2	1	57
Chicago White Sox	1	1	1	3	0	0	43

NATIONAL LEAGUE

NLCS	W	1	2	3	4	%
Brooklyn Dodgers	4	3	5	2	4	68
Chicago Cubs	0	2	3	0	2	32

WORLD SERIES

WS*	W	1	2	3	4	5	%
Boston Red Sox	4	6	2	3	6	4	46
Brooklyn Dodgers	1	5	1	4	2	1	54

ACTUAL WINNERS

American League: Boston Red Sox
National League: Brooklyn Dodgers
World Series: Boston Red Sox

OUTSTANDING PERFORMANCES

AWARD WINNERS

LG.	PLAYER	TEAM	STATS ADJUSTED	ACTUAL
MOST VALUABLE PLAYERS				
AL	Tris Speaker	Cleveland	17 HR, 109 RBI, .422 BA, $19.6 MIL	2 HR, 79 RBI, .386 BA
NL	Pete Alexander	Philadelphia	34-13 W-L, 3 SV, 2.60 ERA, $59.7 MIL	33-12 W-L, 3 SV, 1.55 ERA
CY YOUNG AWARDS				
AL	Babe Ruth	Boston	24-13 W-L, 4 SV, 2.93 ERA, $33.5 MIL	23-12 W-L, 1 SV, 1.75 ERA
NL	Pete Alexander	Philadelphia	34-13 W-L, 3 SV, 2.60 ERA, $59.7 MIL	33-12 W-L, 3 SV, 1.55 ERA

AMERICAN LEAGUE LEADERS

CAT.	PLAYER	TEAM	STATS ADJUSTED	ACTUAL
BATTING				
HR	Wally Pipp	New York	43	12
RBI	Del Pratt	St. Louis	141	103
BA	Tris Speaker	Cleveland	.422	.386
AB	Burt Shotton	St. Louis	630	614
R	Ty Cobb	Detroit	158	113
H	Tris Speaker	Cleveland	238	211
2B	Tris Speaker	Cleveland	75	41
	Jack Graney	Cleveland	50	41
3B	Joe Jackson	Chicago	11	21
TB	Joe Jackson	Chicago	403	293
SA	Tris Speaker	Cleveland	.660	.502
SB	Ty Cobb	Detroit	43	68
PITCHING				
W	Walter Johnson	Washington	26	25
L	Joe Bush	Philadelphia	25	24
SV	Bob Shawkey	New York	13	8
ERA	Babe Ruth	Boston	2.93	1.75
G	Dave Davenport	St. Louis	60	59
IP	Walter Johnson	Washington	377	369.2
BB	Elmer Myers	Philadelphia	225	168
SO	Walter Johnson	Washington	382	228

NATIONAL LEAGUE LEADERS

CAT.	PLAYER	TEAM	STATS ADJUSTED	ACTUAL
BATTING				
HR	Dave Robertson	New York	41	12
	Cy Williams	Chicago	37	12
RBI	Heinie Zimmerman	Chi.-N.Y.	115	83
BA	Hal Chase	Cincinnati	.370	.339
AB	George Burns	New York	651	623
R	George Burns	New York	147	105
H	Hal Chase	Cincinnati	209	184
2B	Bert Niehoff	Philadelphia	49	42
3B	Bill Hinchman	Pittsburgh	7	16
TB	Zack Wheat	Brooklyn	356	262
SA	Zack Wheat	Brooklyn	.602	.461
SB	Max Carey	Pittsburgh	39	63
PITCHING				
W	Pete Alexander	Philadelphia	34	33
L	Lee Meadows	St. Louis	24	23
SV	Red Ames	St. Louis	15	8
ERA	Pete Alexander	Philadelphia	2.60	1.55
G	Lee Meadows	St. Louis	54	51
IP	Pete Alexander	Philadelphia	405	389
BB	Al Mamaux	Pittsburgh	178	136
SO	Pete Alexander	Philadelphia	299	167

1917 SEASON

REGULAR SEASON STANDINGS

AMERICAN LEAGUE

		ADJUSTED				ACTUAL			
	W	L	Pct.	GB	W	L	Pct.	Rk.
EAST								
X Boston	96	66	.593	0	90	62	.592	2
Washington	78	84	.481	18	74	79	.484	5
New York	75	87	.463	21	71	82	.464	6
Philadelphia	58	104	.358	38	55	98	.359	8
WEST								
X Chicago	105	57	.648	0	100	54	.649	1
Cleveland	93	69	.574	12	88	66	.571	3
Detroit	83	79	.512	22	78	75	.510	4
St. Louis	60	102	.370	45	57	97	.370	7

NATIONAL LEAGUE

		ADJUSTED				ACTUAL			
	W	L	Pct.	GB	W	L	Pct.	Rk.
EAST								
X New York	103	59	.636	0	98	56	.636	1
Philadelphia	93	69	.574	10	87	65	.572	2
Boston	76	86	.469	27	72	81	.471	6
Brooklyn	75	87	.463	28	70	81	.464	7
WEST								
X St. Louis	87	75	.537	0	82	70	.539	3
Cincinnati	82	80	.506	5	78	76	.506	4
Chicago	78	84	.481	9	74	80	.481	5
Pittsburgh	54	108	.333	33	51	103	.331	8

SIMULATED PLAYOFFS

AMERICAN LEAGUE

ALCS	W	1	2	3	4	5	%
Boston Red Sox	1	2	1	4	3	1	28
Chicago White Sox	4	5	3	1	5	6	72

NATIONAL LEAGUE

NLCS	W	1	2	3	4	5	%
New York Giants	4	9	3	3	3	7	90
St. Louis Cardinals	1	2	1	4	2	4	10

WORLD SERIES

WS*	W	1	2	3	4	5	6	%
Chicago White Sox	4	2	7	0	0	8	4	58
New York Giants	2	1	2	2	5	5	2	42

ACTUAL WINNERS

American League: Chicago White Sox
National League: New York Giants
World Series: Chicago White Sox

OUTSTANDING PERFORMANCES

AWARD WINNERS

LG.	PLAYER	TEAM	STATS ADJUSTED	ACTUAL
MOST VALUABLE PLAYERS				
AL	Eddie Cicotte	Chicago	29-12 W-L, 8 SV, 2.59 ERA, $49.5 MIL	28-12 W-L, 4 SV, 1.53 ERA
NL	Pete Alexander	Philadelphia	31-14 W-L, 0 SV, 3.11 ERA, $61.0 MIL	30-13 W-L, 0 SV, 1.83 ERA
CY YOUNG AWARDS				
AL	Eddie Cicotte	Chicago	29-12 W-L, 8 SV, 2.59 ERA, $49.5 MIL	28-12 W-L, 4 SV, 1.53 ERA
NL	Pete Alexander	Philadelphia	31-14 W-L, 0 SV, 3.11 ERA, $61.0 MIL	30-13 W-L, 0 SV, 1.83 ERA

AMERICAN LEAGUE LEADERS

CAT.	PLAYER	TEAM	STATS ADJUSTED	ACTUAL
BATTING				
HR	Wally Pipp	New York	39	9
RBI	Bobby Veach	Detroit	144	103
BA	Ty Cobb	Detroit	.415	.383
AB	Ty Cobb	Detroit	619	588
R	Donie Bush	Detroit	157	112
H	Ty Cobb	Detroit	257	225
2B	Ty Cobb	Detroit	60	44
3B	Ty Cobb	Detroit	9	24
TB	Ty Cobb	Detroit	467	335
SA	Ty Cobb	Detroit	.754	.570
SB	Ty Cobb	Detroit	40	55
PITCHING				
W	Eddie Cicotte	Chicago	29	28
L	Bob Groom	St. Louis	20	19
	Allen Sothoron	St. Louis	20	19
SV	Dave Danforth	Chicago	25	9
ERA	Eddie Cicotte	Chicago	2.59	1.53
G	Dave Danforth	Chicago	52	50
IP	Eddie Cicotte	Chicago	361	346.2
BB	Jim Shaw	Washington	165	123
SO	Walter Johnson	Washington	342	188

NATIONAL LEAGUE LEADERS

CAT.	PLAYER	TEAM	STATS ADJUSTED	ACTUAL
BATTING				
HR	Gavvy Cravath	Philadelphia	47	12
	Dave Robertson	New York	39	12
RBI	Heinie Zimmerman	New York	139	102
BA	Edd Roush	Cincinnati	.371	.341
AB	Hal Chase	Cincinnati	622	602
R	George Burns	New York	141	103
H	Heinie Groh	Cincinnati	204	182
2B	Heinie Groh	Cincinnati	83	39
3B	Rogers Hornsby	St. Louis	4	17
TB	Rogers Hornsby	St. Louis	353	253
SA	Rogers Hornsby	St. Louis	.639	.484
SB	Max Carey	Pittsburgh	33	46
PITCHING				
W	Pete Alexander	Philadelphia	31	30
L	Jesse Barnes	Boston	22	21
	Eppa Rixey	Philadelphia	22	21
SV	Slim Sallee	New York	7	4
ERA	Pete Alexander	Philadelphia	3.11	1.83
G	Phil Douglas	Chicago	53	51
IP	Pete Alexander	Philadelphia	405	388
BB	Pete Schneider	Cincinnati	156	117
SO	Pete Alexander	Philadelphia	380	200

1918 SEASON

REGULAR SEASON STANDINGS

AMERICAN LEAGUE

		ADJUSTED				ACTUAL			
	W	L	Pct.	GB	W	L	Pct.	Rk.
EAST								
X Boston	96	66	.593	0	75	51	.595	1
Washington	91	71	.562	5	72	56	.563	3
New York	79	83	.488	17	60	63	.488	4
Philadelphia	66	96	.407	30	52	76	.406	8
WEST								
X Cleveland	93	69	.574	0	73	54	.575	2
St. Louis	77	85	.475	16	58	64	.475	5
Chicago	75	87	.463	18	57	67	.460	6
Detroit	71	91	.438	22	55	71	.437	7

NATIONAL LEAGUE

		ADJUSTED				ACTUAL			
	W	L	Pct.	GB	W	L	Pct.	Rk.
EAST								
X New York	93	69	.574	0	71	53	.573	2
Brooklyn	73	89	.451	20	57	69	.452	5
Philadelphia	73	89	.451	20	55	68	.447	6
Boston	69	93	.426	24	53	71	.427	7
WEST								
X Chicago	106	56	.654	0	84	45	.651	1
Cincinnati	86	76	.531	20	68	60	.531	3
Pittsburgh	84	78	.519	22	65	60	.520	4
St. Louis	64	98	.395	42	51	78	.395	8

SIMULATED PLAYOFFS

AMERICAN LEAGUE

ALCS	W	1	2	3	4	5	6	7	%
Boston Red Sox	4	4	4	4	4	1	6	5	54
Cleveland Indians	3	3	0	2	5	4	7	2	46

NATIONAL LEAGUE

NLCS	W	1	2	3	4	5		%
New York Giants	4	3	2	5	3	4		43
Chicago Cubs	1	2	0	6	2	3		57

WORLD SERIES

WS	W	1	2	3	4	5	6	%
Boston Red Sox	2	2	2	4	5	1	1	54
New York Giants	4	3	6	0	0	2	2	46

ACTUAL WINNERS

American League: Boston Red Sox
National League: Chicago Cubs
World Series: Boston Red Sox

OUTSTANDING PERFORMANCES

AWARD WINNERS

LG.	PLAYER	TEAM	STATS ADJUSTED	ACTUAL
MOST VALUABLE PLAYERS				
AL	Babe Ruth	Boston	48 HR, 112 RBI, .317 BA, $5.9 MIL	11 HR, 66 RBI, .300 BA
NL	Hippo Vaughn	Chicago	27-12 W-L, 0 SV, 2.85 ERA, $52.8 MIL	22-10 W-L, 0 SV, 1.74 ERA
CY YOUNG AWARDS				
AL	Walter Johnson	Washington	29-16 W-L, 4 SV, 2.09 ERA, $60.0 MIL	23-13 W-L, 3 SV, 1.27 ERA
NL	Hippo Vaughn	Chicago	27-12 W-L, 0 SV, 2.85 ERA, $52.8 MIL	22-10 W-L, 0 SV, 1.74 ERA

AMERICAN LEAGUE LEADERS

CAT.	PLAYER	TEAM	STATS ADJUSTED	ACTUAL
BATTING				
HR	Babe Ruth	Boston	48	11
	Tilly Walker	Philadelphia	38	11
RBI	Bobby Veach	Detroit	131	78
BA	Ty Cobb	Detroit	.407	.382
AB	Eddie Foster	Washington	648	519
R	Ray Chapman	Cleveland	140	84
H	George Burns	Philadelphia	236	178
2B	Tris Speaker	Cleveland	116	33
3B	Ty Cobb	Detroit	7	14
TB	George Burns	Philadelphia	386	236
SA	Babe Ruth	Boston	.725	.555
SB	George Sisler	St. Louis	41	45
PITCHING				
W	Walter Johnson	Washington	29	23
L	Eddie Cicotte	Chicago	25	19
	Scott Perry	Philadelphia	24	19
SV	George Mogridge	New York	17	7
ERA	Walter Johnson	Washington	2.09	1.27
G	George Mogridge	New York	58	45
	Jim Bagby	Cleveland	57	45
IP	Scott Perry	Philadelphia	415	332.1
BB	Slim Love	New York	193	116
SO	Walter Johnson	Washington	428	162

NATIONAL LEAGUE LEADERS

CAT.	PLAYER	TEAM	STATS ADJUSTED	ACTUAL
BATTING				
HR	Gavvy Cravath	Philadelphia	38	8
RBI	Sherry Magee	Cincinnati	126	76
BA	Zack Wheat	Brooklyn	.356	.335
AB	Charlie Hollocher	Chicago	629	509
R	Heinie Groh	Cincinnati	142	86
H	Charlie Hollocher	Chicago	211	161
2B	Heinie Groh	Cincinnati	66	28
3B	Jake Daubert	Brooklyn	9	15
TB	Charlie Hollocher	Chicago	329	202
SA	Edd Roush	Cincinnati	.596	.455
SB	Max Carey	Pittsburgh	51	58
PITCHING				
W	Hippo Vaughn	Chicago	27	22
L	Rube Marquard	Brooklyn	23	18
	Joe Oeschger	Philadelphia	23	18
SV	Fred Anderson	New York	11	3
	Fred Toney	Cin.-N.Y.	8	3
	Joe Oeschger	Philadelphia	7	3
	Wilbur Cooper	Pittsburgh	5	3
ERA	Hippo Vaughn	Chicago	2.85	1.74
G	Burleigh Grimes	Brooklyn	51	40
IP	Hippo Vaughn	Chicago	357	290.1
BB	Pete Schneider	Cincinnati	188	117
SO	Hippo Vaughn	Chicago	381	148

1919 SEASON

REGULAR SEASON STANDINGS

AMERICAN LEAGUE

		ADJUSTED				ACTUAL			
	W	L	Pct.	GB	W	L	Pct.	Rk.
EAST								
X New York	93	69	.574	0	80	59	.576	3
Boston	78	84	.481	15	66	71	.482	5
Washington	65	97	.401	28	56	84	.400	7
Philadelphia	42	120	.259	51	36	104	.257	8
WEST								
X Chicago	102	60	.630	0	88	52	.629	1
Cleveland	98	64	.605	4	84	55	.604	2
Detroit	92	70	.568	10	80	60	.571	4
St. Louis	78	84	.481	24	67	72	.482	5

NATIONAL LEAGUE

		ADJUSTED				ACTUAL			
	W	L	Pct.	GB	W	L	Pct.	Rk.
EAST								
X New York	101	61	.623	0	87	53	.621	2
Brooklyn	80	82	.494	21	69	71	.493	5
Boston	66	96	.407	35	57	82	.410	6
Philadelphia	56	106	.346	45	47	90	.343	8
WEST								
X Cincinnati	111	51	.685	0	96	44	.686	1
Chicago	87	75	.537	24	75	65	.536	3
Pittsburgh	83	79	.512	28	71	68	.511	4
St. Louis	64	98	.395	47	54	83	.394	7

SIMULATED PLAYOFFS

AMERICAN LEAGUE

ALCS	W	1	2	3	4	5	6	%
New York Yankees	4	2	5	7	1	3	3	43
Chicago White Sox	2	3	4	6	9	2	1	57

NATIONAL LEAGUE

NLCS	W	1	2	3	4		%
New York Giants	4	3	2	3	5		47
Cincinnati Reds	0	0	1	1	0		53

WORLD SERIES

WS	W	1	2	3	4	5	6	%
New York Yankees	2	3	3	5	7	4	0	48
New York Giants	4	9	5	4	5	9	1	52

ACTUAL WINNERS

American League: Chicago White Sox
National League: Cincinnati Reds
World Series: Cincinnati Reds

OUTSTANDING PERFORMANCES

AWARD WINNERS

LG.	PLAYER	TEAM	STATS ADJUSTED	ACTUAL
MOST VALUABLE PLAYERS				
AL	Joe Jackson	Chicago	35 HR, 139 RBI, .360 BA, $15.8 MIL	7 HR, 96 RBI, .351 BA
NL	Edd Roush	Cincinnati	25 HR, 103 RBI, .329 BA, $14.3 MIL	4 HR, 71 RBI, .321 BA
CY YOUNG AWARDS				
AL	Walter Johnson	Washington	23-16 W-L, 4 SV, 2.20 ERA, $49.4 MIL	20-14 W-L, 2 SV, 1.49 ERA
NL	Hippo Vaughn	Chicago	24-16 W-L, 3 SV, 2.66 ERA, $51.8 MIL	21-14 W-L, 1 SV, 1.79 ERA

AMERICAN LEAGUE LEADERS

CAT.	PLAYER	TEAM	STATS ADJUSTED	ACTUAL
BATTING				
HR	Babe Ruth	Boston	73	29
RBI	Babe Ruth	Boston	168	114
BA	Ty Cobb	Detroit	.394	.384
AB	Buck Weaver	Chicago	661	571
R	Babe Ruth	Boston	152	103
H	Bobby Veach	Detroit	227	191
	Ty Cobb	Detroit	226	191
2B	Bobby Veach	Detroit	85	45
3B	Bobby Veach	Detroit	10	17
TB	Babe Ruth	Boston	410	284
SA	Babe Ruth	Boston	.807	.657
SB	Eddie Collins	Chicago	28	33
PITCHING				
W	Eddie Cicotte	Chicago	33	29
L	Harry Harper	Washington	24	21
SV	Allan Russell	N.Y.-Bos.	18	5
	Jim Shaw	Washington	11	5
	Bob Shawkey	New York	10	5
ERA	Walter Johnson	Washington	2.20	1.49
G	Jim Shaw	Washington	51	45
IP	Eddie Cicotte	Chicago	353	306.2
	Jim Shaw	Washington	348	306.2
BB	Howard Ehmke	Detroit	166	107
SO	Walter Johnson	Washington	334	147

NATIONAL LEAGUE LEADERS

CAT.	PLAYER	TEAM	STATS ADJUSTED	ACTUAL
BATTING				
HR	Gavvy Cravath	Philadelphia	32	12
RBI	Hy Myers	Brooklyn	105	73
BA	Edd Roush	Cincinnati	.329	.321
AB	Ivy Olson	Brooklyn	679	590
R	George Burns	New York	124	86
H	Ivy Olson	Brooklyn	193	164
2B	Ross Youngs	New York	57	31
3B	Billy Southworth	Pittsburgh	7	14
	Hy Myers	Brooklyn	6	14
TB	Hy Myers	Brooklyn	317	223
SA	Hy Myers	Brooklyn	.538	.436
SB	George Burns	New York	34	40
PITCHING				
W	Jesse Barnes	New York	29	25
L	Lee Meadows	St.L.-Phi.	24	20
SV	Oscar Tuero	St. Louis	22	4
ERA	Pete Alexander	Chicago	2.56	1.72
G	Oscar Tuero	St. Louis	53	45
IP	Hippo Vaughn	Chicago	355	306.2
BB	Jakie May	St. Louis	139	87
SO	Hippo Vaughn	Chicago	333	141

1920 SEASON

REGULAR SEASON STANDINGS

AMERICAN LEAGUE

		ADJUSTED			ACTUAL			
	W	L	Pct.	GB	W	L	Pct.	Rk.
EAST								
X New York	100	62	.617	0	95	59	.617	3
Boston	76	86	.469	24	72	81	.471	5
Washington	73	89	.451	27	68	84	.447	6
Philadelphia	51	111	.315	49	48	106	.312	8
WEST								
X Cleveland	103	59	.636	0	98	56	.636	1
Chicago	101	61	.623	2	96	58	.623	2
St. Louis	80	82	.494	23	76	77	.497	4
Detroit	64	98	.395	39	61	93	.396	7

NATIONAL LEAGUE

		ADJUSTED			ACTUAL			
	W	L	Pct.	GB	W	L	Pct.	Rk.
EAST								
X Brooklyn	98	64	.605	0	93	61	.604	1
New York	90	72	.556	8	86	68	.558	2
Boston	66	96	.407	32	62	90	.408	7
Philadelphia	66	96	.407	32	62	91	.405	8
WEST								
X Cincinnati	87	75	.537	0	82	71	.536	3
Pittsburgh	83	79	.512	4	79	75	.513	4
Chicago	79	83	.488	8	75	79	.487	5
St. Louis	79	83	.488	8	75	79	.487	5

SIMULATED PLAYOFFS

AMERICAN LEAGUE

ALCS	W	1	2	3	4	5	6	7	%
New York Yankees	3	7	7	0	5	8	5	7	44
Cleveland Indians	4	6	2	7	6	1	6	8	56

NATIONAL LEAGUE

NLCS	W	1	2	3	4	5	%
Brooklyn Dodgers	4	1	5	5	2	2	63
Cincinnati Reds	1	2	1	1	1	0	37

WORLD SERIES

WS**	W	1	2	3	4	5	6	%
Cleveland Indians	4	3	0	1	5	8	1	67
Brooklyn Dodgers	2	1	3	2	1	1	0	33

ACTUAL WINNERS

American League: Cleveland Indians
National League: Brooklyn Dodgers
World Series: Cleveland Indians

OUTSTANDING PERFORMANCES

AWARD WINNERS

LG.	PLAYER	TEAM	STATS ADJUSTED	ACTUAL
MOST VALUABLE PLAYERS				
AL	Babe Ruth	New York	91 HR, 164 RBI, .366 BA, $26.1 MIL	54 HR, 137 RBI, .376 BA
NL	Rogers Hornsby	St. Louis	36 HR, 111 RBI, .361 BA, $18.9 MIL	9 HR, 94 RBI, .370 BA
CY YOUNG AWARDS				
AL	Jim Bagby	Cleveland	32-13 W-L, 0 SV, 3.81 ERA, $52.0 MIL	31-12 W-L, 0 SV, 2.89 ERA
NL	Pete Alexander	Chicago	28-15 W-L, 5 SV, 2.49 ERA, $51.6 MIL	27-14 W-L, 5 SV, 1.91 ERA

AMERICAN LEAGUE LEADERS

CAT.	PLAYER	TEAM	STATS ADJUSTED	ACTUAL
BATTING				
HR	Babe Ruth	New York	91	54
RBI	Babe Ruth	New York	164	137
BA	George Sisler	St. Louis	.398	.407
AB	George Sisler	St. Louis	664	631
R	Babe Ruth	New York	189	158
H	George Sisler	St. Louis	264	257
2B	Tris Speaker	Cleveland	55	50
3B	Joe Jackson	Chicago	6	20
TB	George Sisler	St. Louis	483	399
SA	Babe Ruth	New York	.971	.847
SB	Sam Rice	Washington	67	63
PITCHING				
W	Jim Bagby	Cleveland	32	31
L	Scott Perry	Philadelphia	26	25
SV	Dickie Kerr	Chicago	12	5
	Urban Shocker	St. Louis	7	5
ERA	Bob Shawkey	New York	3.22	2.45
G	Jim Bagby	Cleveland	50	48
IP	Jim Bagby	Cleveland	354	339.2
BB	Dixie Davis	St. Louis	207	149
SO	Stan Coveleski	Cleveland	298	133

NATIONAL LEAGUE LEADERS

CAT.	PLAYER	TEAM	STATS ADJUSTED	ACTUAL
BATTING				
HR	Cy Williams	Philadelphia	42	15
RBI	Rogers Hornsby	St. Louis	111	94
	George Kelly	New York	111	94
BA	Rogers Hornsby	St. Louis	.361	.370
AB	Milt Stock	St. Louis	668	639
R	George Burns	New York	136	115
H	Rogers Hornsby	St. Louis	223	218
2B	Rogers Hornsby	St. Louis	51	44
3B	Hy Myers	Brooklyn	11	22
TB	Rogers Hornsby	St. Louis	396	329
SA	Rogers Hornsby	St. Louis	.642	.559
SB	Max Carey	Pittsburgh	54	52
PITCHING				
W	Pete Alexander	Chicago	28	27
L	Eppa Rixey	Philadelphia	23	22
SV	Bill Sherdel	St. Louis	17	6
ERA	Pete Alexander	Chicago	2.49	1.91
G	Jesse Haines	St. Louis	49	47
IP	Pete Alexander	Chicago	379	363.1
BB	Ferdie Schupp	St. Louis	176	127
SO	Pete Alexander	Chicago	378	173

1921 SEASON

REGULAR SEASON STANDINGS

AMERICAN LEAGUE

	ADJUSTED				ACTUAL			
	W	L	Pct.	GB	W	L	Pct.	Rk.
EAST								
X New York	104	58	.642	0	98	55	.641	1
Washington	85	77	.525	19	80	73	.523	4
Boston	79	83	.488	25	75	79	.487	5
Philadelphia	56	106	.346	48	53	100	.346	8
WEST								
X Cleveland	99	63	.611	0	94	60	.610	2
St. Louis	85	77	.525	14	81	73	.526	3
Detroit	75	87	.463	24	71	82	.464	6
Chicago	65	97	.401	34	62	92	.403	7

NATIONAL LEAGUE

	ADJUSTED				ACTUAL			
	W	L	Pct.	GB	W	L	Pct.	Rk.
EAST								
X New York	99	63	.611	0	94	59	.614	1
Boston	84	78	.519	15	79	74	.516	4
Brooklyn	82	80	.506	17	77	75	.507	5
Philadelphia	54	108	.333	45	51	103	.331	8
WEST								
X Pittsburgh	95	67	.586	0	90	63	.588	2
St. Louis	92	70	.568	3	87	66	.569	3
Cincinnati	74	88	.457	21	70	83	.458	6
Chicago	68	94	.420	27	64	89	.418	7

SIMULATED PLAYOFFS

AMERICAN LEAGUE

ALCS	W	1	2	3	4	5	6	7	%
New York Yankees	3	11	3	0	8	8	8	6	52
Cleveland Indians	4	10	7	9	9	3	5	7	48

NATIONAL LEAGUE

NLCS	W	1	2	3	4	5	6	7	%
New York Giants	3	5	2	4	5	0	5	3	59
Pittsburgh Pirates	4	2	5	5	3	4	2	4	41

WORLD SERIES

WS	W	1	2	3	4	5	6	7	%
Cleveland Indians	4	2	3	2	6	6	4	4	65
Pittsburgh Pirates	3	4	2	5	5	0	5	1	35

ACTUAL WINNERS

American League: New York Yankees
National League: New York Giants
World Series: New York Giants

OUTSTANDING PERFORMANCES

AWARD WINNERS

			STATS	
LG.	PLAYER	TEAM	ADJUSTED	ACTUAL
MOST VALUABLE PLAYERS				
AL	Babe Ruth	New York	94 HR, 188 RBI, .350 BA, $47.9 MIL	59 HR, 171 RBI, .378 BA
NL	Rogers Hornsby	St. Louis	48 HR, 137 RBI, .368 BA, $25.2 MIL	21 HR, 126 RBI, .397 BA
CY YOUNG AWARDS				
AL	Red Faber	Chicago	26-16 W-L, 2 SV, 2.78 ERA, $39.1 MIL	25-15 W-L, 1 SV, 2.48 ERA
NL	Burleigh Grimes	Brooklyn	23-14 W-L, 0 SV, 3.19 ERA, $40.6 MIL	22-13 W-L, 0 SV, 2.83 ERA

AMERICAN LEAGUE LEADERS

			STATS	
CAT.	PLAYER	TEAM	ADJUSTED	ACTUAL
BATTING				
HR	Babe Ruth	New York	94	59
RBI	Babe Ruth	New York	188	171
BA	Harry Heilmann	Detroit	.364	.394
AB	Jack Tobin	St. Louis	707	671
R	Babe Ruth	New York	195	177
H	Harry Heilmann	Detroit	231	237
2B	Tris Speaker	Cleveland	79	52
3B	Howie Shanks	Washington	8	18
	Jack Tobin	St. Louis	8	18
	George Sisler	St. Louis	6	18
TB	Babe Ruth	New York	513	457
SA	Babe Ruth	New York	.897	.846
SB	George Sisler	St. Louis	43	35
PITCHING				
W	Carl Mays	New York	29	27
	Urban Shocker	St. Louis	28	27
L	Eddie Rommel	Philadelphia	24	23
SV	Jim Middleton	Detroit	16	7
	Carl Mays	New York	11	7
ERA	Red Faber	Chicago	2.78	2.48
G	Carl Mays	New York	52	49
IP	Carl Mays	New York	357	336.2
BB	Dixie Davis	St. Louis	167	123
SO	Walter Johnson	Washington	316	143

NATIONAL LEAGUE LEADERS

			STATS	
CAT.	PLAYER	TEAM	ADJUSTED	ACTUAL
BATTING				
HR	George Kelly	New York	45	23
RBI	Rogers Hornsby	St. Louis	137	126
BA	Rogers Hornsby	St. Louis	.368	.397
AB	Ivy Olson	Brooklyn	695	652
R	Rogers Hornsby	St. Louis	143	131
H	Rogers Hornsby	St. Louis	229	235
2B	Rogers Hornsby	St. Louis	39	44
3B	Ray Powell	Boston	6	18
	Rogers Hornsby	St. Louis	5	18
TB	Rogers Hornsby	St. Louis	422	378
SA	Rogers Hornsby	St. Louis	.677	.639
SB	Frankie Frisch	New York	61	49
PITCHING				
W	Wilbur Cooper	Pittsburgh	23	22
	Burleigh Grimes	Brooklyn	23	22
L	George Smith	Philadelphia	21	20
SV	Lou North	St. Louis	21	7
ERA	Bill Doak	St. Louis	2.92	2.59
G	Jack Scott	Boston	50	47
IP	Wilbur Cooper	Pittsburgh	344	327
BB	Joe Oeschger	Boston	133	97
SO	Burleigh Grimes	Brooklyn	311	136

1922 SEASON

REGULAR SEASON STANDINGS

AMERICAN LEAGUE

	ADJUSTED				ACTUAL			
	W	L	Pct.	GB	W	L	Pct.	Rk.
EAST								
X New York	99	63	.611	0	94	60	.610	1
Washington	73	89	.451	26	69	85	.448	6
Philadelphia	68	94	.420	31	65	89	.422	7
Boston	64	98	.395	35	61	93	.396	8
WEST								
X St. Louis	98	64	.605	0	93	61	.604	2
Detroit	83	79	.512	15	79	75	.513	3
Cleveland	82	80	.506	16	78	76	.506	4
Chicago	81	81	.500	17	77	77	.500	5

NATIONAL LEAGUE

	ADJUSTED				ACTUAL			
	W	L	Pct.	GB	W	L	Pct.	Rk.
EAST								
X New York	98	64	.605	0	93	61	.604	1
Brooklyn	80	82	.494	18	76	78	.494	6
Philadelphia	60	102	.370	38	57	96	.373	7
Boston	56	106	.346	42	53	100	.346	8
WEST								
X Cincinnati	91	71	.562	0	86	68	.558	2
Pittsburgh	90	72	.556	1	85	69	.552	3
St. Louis	89	73	.549	2	85	69	.552	3
Chicago	84	78	.519	7	80	74	.519	5

SIMULATED PLAYOFFS

AMERICAN LEAGUE

ALCS	W	1	2	3	4		%
New York Yankees	0	0	0	3	1		47
St. Louis Browns	4	1	3	4	7		53

NATIONAL LEAGUE

NLCS	W	1	2	3	4	5	6	7	%
New York Giants	4	4	4	7	2	7	8	11	62
Cincinnati Reds	3	6	1	4	6	8	7	4	38

WORLD SERIES

WS	W	1	2	3	4	5	6	%
St. Louis Browns	2	3	6	12	5	4	2	51
New York Giants	4	7	4	1	8	9	3	49

ACTUAL WINNERS

American League: New York Yankees
National League: New York Giants
World Series: New York Giants

OUTSTANDING PERFORMANCES

AWARD WINNERS

LG.	PLAYER	TEAM	STATS ADJUSTED	ACTUAL
MOST VALUABLE PLAYERS				
AL	George Sisler	St. Louis	25 HR, 113 RBI, .392 BA, $23.0 MIL	8 HR, 105 RBI, .420 BA
NL	Rogers Hornsby	St. Louis	72 HR, 164 RBI, .376 BA, $31.7 MIL	42 HR, 152 RBI, .401 BA
CY YOUNG AWARDS				
AL	Eddie Rommel	Philadelphia	28-14 W-L, 6 SV, 3.68 ERA, $27.5 MIL	27-13 W-L, 2 SV, 3.28 ERA
NL	Wilbur Cooper	Pittsburgh	24-15 W-L, 0 SV, 3.55 ERA, $41.0 MIL	23-14 W-L, 0 SV, 3.18 ERA

AMERICAN LEAGUE LEADERS

CAT.	PLAYER	TEAM	STATS ADJUSTED	ACTUAL
BATTING				
HR	Ken Williams	St. Louis	64	39
RBI	Ken Williams	St. Louis	168	155
BA	George Sisler	St. Louis	.392	.420
AB	Sam Rice	Washington	666	633
R	George Sisler	St. Louis	144	134
H	George Sisler	St. Louis	241	246
2B	Tris Speaker	Cleveland	49	48
3B	George Sisler	St. Louis	8	18
TB	Ken Williams	St. Louis	411	367
SA	Babe Ruth	New York	.720	.672
SB	George Sisler	St. Louis	64	51
PITCHING				
W	Eddie Rommel	Philadelphia	28	27
L	Slim Harriss	Philadelphia	21	20
SV	Sam Jones	New York	15	8
ERA	Red Faber	Chicago	3.15	2.81
G	Eddie Rommel	Philadelphia	53	51
IP	Red Faber	Chicago	368	352
BB	Rip Collins	Boston	134	103
SO	Urban Shocker	St. Louis	343	149

NATIONAL LEAGUE LEADERS

CAT.	PLAYER	TEAM	STATS ADJUSTED	ACTUAL
BATTING				
HR	Rogers Hornsby	St. Louis	72	42
RBI	Rogers Hornsby	St. Louis	164	152
BA	Rogers Hornsby	St. Louis	.376	.401
AB	Rabbit Maranville	Pittsburgh	702	672
R	Rogers Hornsby	St. Louis	152	141
H	Rogers Hornsby	St. Louis	246	250
2B	Rogers Hornsby	St. Louis	34	46
3B	Jake Daubert	Cincinnati	9	22
TB	Rogers Hornsby	St. Louis	504	450
SA	Rogers Hornsby	St. Louis	.769	.722
SB	Max Carey	Pittsburgh	64	51
PITCHING				
W	Eppa Rixey	Cincinnati	26	25
L	Dolf Luque	Cincinnati	24	23
SV	Claude Jonnard	New York	17	5
ERA	Phil Douglas	New York	2.96	2.63
G	Lou North	St. Louis	56	53
IP	Eppa Rixey	Cincinnati	329	313.1
BB	Jimmy Ring	Philadelphia	132	103
SO	Dazzy Vance	Brooklyn	296	134

1923 SEASON

REGULAR SEASON STANDINGS

AMERICAN LEAGUE

		ADJUSTED				ACTUAL			
	W	L	Pct.	GB	W	L	Pct.	Rk.
EAST								
X New York	104	58	.642	0	98	54	.645	1
Washington	79	83	.488	25	75	78	.490	4
Philadelphia	74	88	.457	30	69	83	.454	6
Boston	65	97	.401	39	61	91	.401	8
WEST								
X Detroit	87	75	.537	0	83	71	.539	2
X Cleveland	87	75	.537	0	82	71	.536	3
St. Louis	79	83	.488	8	74	78	.487	5
Chicago	73	89	.451	14	69	85	.448	7

NATIONAL LEAGUE

		ADJUSTED				ACTUAL			
	W	L	Pct.	GB	W	L	Pct.	Rk.
EAST								
X New York	100	62	.617	0	95	58	.621	1
Brooklyn	80	82	.494	20	76	78	.494	6
Boston	57	105	.352	43	54	100	.351	7
Philadelphia	53	109	.327	47	50	104	.325	8
WEST								
X Cincinnati	96	66	.593	0	91	63	.591	2
Pittsburgh	91	71	.562	5	87	67	.565	3
Chicago	87	75	.537	9	83	71	.539	4
St. Louis	84	78	.519	12	79	74	.516	5

SIMULATED PLAYOFFS

AMERICAN LEAGUE

TIEBREAKER	W	1	2	3				%
Detroit Tigers	1	6	2	4				57
Cleveland Indians	2	4	4	7				43

ALCS	W	1	2	3	4	5	6	%
New York Yankees	4	7	1	1	7	11	2	57
Cleveland Indians	2	2	7	2	6	8	1	43

NATIONAL LEAGUE

NLCS	W	1	2	3	4	5	6	%
New York Giants	4	4	2	3	3	5	7	59
Cincinnati Reds	2	3	0	4	6	4	1	41

WORLD SERIES

WS*	W	1	2	3	4	5	6	%
New York Yankees	4	4	4	0	8	8	6	60
New York Giants	2	5	2	1	4	1	4	40

ACTUAL WINNERS

American League: New York Yankees
National League: New York Giants
World Series: New York Yankees

OUTSTANDING PERFORMANCES

AWARD WINNERS

LG.	PLAYER	TEAM	STATS ADJUSTED	ACTUAL
MOST VALUABLE PLAYERS				
AL	Babe Ruth	New York	73 HR, 145 RBI, .372 BA, $40.3 MIL	41 HR, 131 RBI, .393 BA
NL	Dolf Luque	Cincinnati	28-8 W-L, 5 SV, 2.21 ERA, $40.7 MIL	27-8 W-L, 2 SV, 1.93 ERA
CY YOUNG AWARDS				
AL	George Uhle	Cleveland	27-17 W-L, 10 SV, 4.33 ERA, $51.5 MIL	26-16 W-L, 5 SV, 3.77 ERA
NL	Dolf Luque	Cincinnati	28-8 W-L, 5 SV, 2.21 ERA, $40.7 MIL	27-8 W-L, 2 SV, 1.93 ERA

AMERICAN LEAGUE LEADERS

CAT.	PLAYER	TEAM	STATS ADJUSTED	ACTUAL
BATTING				
HR	Babe Ruth	New York	73	41
RBI	Babe Ruth	New York	145	131
BA	Harry Heilmann	Detroit	.383	.403
AB	Joe Dugan	New York	688	644
	Charlie Jamieson	Cleveland	682	644
R	Babe Ruth	New York	168	151
H	Charlie Jamieson	Cleveland	223	222
2B	Tris Speaker	Cleveland	57	59
3B	Sam Rice	Washington	11	18
	Goose Goslin	Washington	8	18
TB	Babe Ruth	New York	464	399
SA	Babe Ruth	New York	.835	.764
SB	Eddie Collins	Chicago	56	48
PITCHING				
W	George Uhle	Cleveland	27	26
L	Herman Pillette	Detroit	20	19
	Eddie Rommel	Philadelphia	20	19
SV	Allan Russell	Washington	25	9
ERA	Stan Coveleski	Cleveland	3.16	2.76
G	Eddie Rommel	Philadelphia	59	56
IP	George Uhle	Cleveland	378	357.2
BB	Elam Vangilder	St. Louis	147	120
SO	Walter Johnson	Washington	288	130

NATIONAL LEAGUE LEADERS

CAT.	PLAYER	TEAM	STATS ADJUSTED	ACTUAL
BATTING				
HR	Cy Williams	Philadelphia	61	41
RBI	Irish Meusel	New York	138	125
BA	Rogers Hornsby	St. Louis	.364	.384
AB	Jigger Statz	Chicago	689	655
R	Ross Youngs	New York	133	121
H	Frankie Frisch	New York	224	223
2B	Edd Roush	Cincinnati	58	41
3B	Max Carey	Pittsburgh	10	19
	Pie Traynor	Pittsburgh	8	19
TB	Frankie Frisch	New York	362	311
SA	Rogers Hornsby	St. Louis	.688	.627
SB	Max Carey	Pittsburgh	60	51
PITCHING				
W	Dolf Luque	Cincinnati	28	27
L	Wilbur Cooper	Pittsburgh	20	19
SV	Claude Jonnard	New York	20	5
ERA	Dolf Luque	Cincinnati	2.21	1.93
G	Claude Jonnard	New York	48	45
	Rosy Ryan	New York	48	45
IP	Burleigh Grimes	Brooklyn	344	327
BB	Jimmy Ring	Philadelphia	141	115
SO	Dazzy Vance	Brooklyn	405	197

1924 SEASON

REGULAR SEASON STANDINGS

AMERICAN LEAGUE

	ADJUSTED				ACTUAL			
	W	L	Pct.	GB	W	L	Pct.	Rk.
EAST								
X Washington	97	65	.599	0	92	62	.597	1
New York	95	67	.586	2	89	63	.586	2
Philadelphia	76	86	.469	21	71	81	.467	5
Boston	70	92	.432	27	67	87	.435	7
WEST								
X Detroit	90	72	.556	0	86	68	.558	3
St. Louis	79	83	.488	11	74	78	.487	4
Cleveland	71	91	.438	19	67	86	.438	6
Chicago	70	92	.432	20	66	87	.431	8

NATIONAL LEAGUE

	ADJUSTED				ACTUAL			
	W	L	Pct.	GB	W	L	Pct.	Rk.
EAST								
X New York	99	63	.611	0	93	60	.608	1
Brooklyn	97	65	.599	2	92	62	.597	2
Philadelphia	59	103	.364	40	55	96	.364	7
Boston	56	106	.346	43	53	100	.346	8
WEST								
X Pittsburgh	95	67	.586	0	90	63	.588	3
Cincinnati	88	74	.543	7	83	70	.542	4
Chicago	86	76	.531	9	81	72	.529	5
St. Louis	68	94	.420	27	65	89	.422	6

SIMULATED PLAYOFFS

AMERICAN LEAGUE

ALCS	W	1	2	3	4	5	%
Washington Senators	4	5	3	3	9	8	70
Detroit Tigers	1	3	4	2	3	2	30

NATIONAL LEAGUE

NLCS	W	1	2	3	4	%
New York Giants	0	1	3	2	2	54
Pittsburgh Pirates	4	3	4	3	6	46

WORLD SERIES

WS	W	1	2	3	4	%
Washington Senators	0	2	3	1	2	43
Pittsburgh Pirates	4	3	4	3	3	57

ACTUAL WINNERS

American League: Washington Senators
National League: New York Giants
World Series: Washington Senators

OUTSTANDING PERFORMANCES

AWARD WINNERS

LG.	PLAYER	TEAM	STATS ADJUSTED	ACTUAL
MOST VALUABLE PLAYERS				
AL	Walter Johnson	Washington	24-7 W-L, 0 SV, 3.06 ERA, $30.3 MIL	23-7 W-L, 0 SV, 2.72 ERA
NL	Dazzy Vance	Brooklyn	30-6 W-L, 0 SV, 2.43 ERA, $49.5 MIL	28-6 W-L, 0 SV, 2.16 ERA
CY YOUNG AWARDS				
AL	Walter Johnson	Washington	24-7 W-L, 0 SV, 3.06 ERA, $30.3 MIL	23-7 W-L, 0 SV, 2.72 ERA
NL	Dazzy Vance	Brooklyn	30-6 W-L, 0 SV, 2.43 ERA, $49.5 MIL	28-6 W-L, 0 SV, 2.16 ERA

AMERICAN LEAGUE LEADERS

CAT.	PLAYER	TEAM	STATS ADJUSTED	ACTUAL
BATTING				
HR	Babe Ruth	New York	75	46
RBI	Goose Goslin	Washington	140	129
BA	Babe Ruth	New York	.355	.378
AB	Sam Rice	Washington	671	646
R	Babe Ruth	New York	159	143
H	Sam Rice	Washington	211	216
2B	Joe Sewell	Cleveland	58	45
	Harry Heilmann	Detroit	49	45
3B	Wally Pipp	New York	8	19
TB	Babe Ruth	New York	448	391
SA	Babe Ruth	New York	.800	.739
SB	Eddie Collins	Chicago	51	42
PITCHING				
W	Walter Johnson	Washington	24	23
L	Joe Shaute	Cleveland	18	17
	Howard Ehmke	Boston	17	17
	Alex Ferguson	Boston	17	17
SV	Firpo Marberry	Washington	25	15
ERA	Walter Johnson	Washington	3.06	2.72
G	Firpo Marberry	Washington	52	50
IP	Howard Ehmke	Boston	322	315
BB	Joe Bush	New York	137	109
SO	Walter Johnson	Washington	344	158

NATIONAL LEAGUE LEADERS

CAT.	PLAYER	TEAM	STATS ADJUSTED	ACTUAL
BATTING				
HR	Jack Fournier	Brooklyn	47	27
RBI	George Kelly	New York	150	136
BA	Rogers Hornsby	St. Louis	.399	.424
AB	Glenn Wright	Pittsburgh	652	616
R	Frankie Frisch	New York	134	121
	Rogers Hornsby	St. Louis	133	121
H	Rogers Hornsby	St. Louis	224	227
2B	Rogers Hornsby	St. Louis	32	43
3B	Edd Roush	Cincinnati	13	21
TB	Rogers Hornsby	St. Louis	423	373
SA	Rogers Hornsby	St. Louis	.753	.696
SB	Max Carey	Pittsburgh	60	49
PITCHING				
W	Dazzy Vance	Brooklyn	30	28
L	Jesse Barnes	Boston	21	20
SV	Jakie May	Cincinnati	20	6
ERA	Dazzy Vance	Brooklyn	2.43	2.16
G	Ray Kremer	Pittsburgh	43	41
	Johnny Morrison	Pittsburgh	43	41
IP	Burleigh Grimes	Brooklyn	327	310.2
BB	Jimmy Ring	Philadelphia	138	108
SO	Dazzy Vance	Brooklyn	525	262

1925 SEASON

REGULAR SEASON STANDINGS

AMERICAN LEAGUE

		ADJUSTED				ACTUAL			
	W	L	Pct.	GB	W	L	Pct.	Rk.
EAST								
X Washington	103	59	.636	0	96	55	.636	1
Philadelphia	94	68	.580	9	88	64	.579	2
New York	72	90	.444	31	69	85	.448	7
Boston	50	112	.309	53	47	105	.309	8
WEST								
X St. Louis	87	75	.537	0	82	71	.536	3
Detroit	85	77	.525	2	81	73	.526	4
Chicago	83	79	.512	4	79	75	.513	5
Cleveland	74	88	.457	13	70	84	.455	6

NATIONAL LEAGUE

		ADJUSTED				ACTUAL			
	W	L	Pct.	GB	W	L	Pct.	Rk.
EAST								
X New York	92	70	.568	0	86	66	.566	2
Boston	74	88	.457	18	70	83	.458	5
Brooklyn	72	90	.444	20	68	85	.444	6
Philadelphia	72	90	.444	20	68	85	.444	6
WEST								
X Pittsburgh	101	61	.623	0	95	58	.621	1
Cincinnati	85	77	.525	16	80	73	.523	3
St. Louis	81	81	.500	20	77	76	.503	4
Chicago	71	91	.438	30	68	86	.442	8

SIMULATED PLAYOFFS

AMERICAN LEAGUE

ALCS	W	1	2	3	4	5	6	%
Washington Senators	4	0	18	6	7	1	6	74
St. Louis Browns	2	2	7	3	3	5	3	26

NATIONAL LEAGUE

NLCS	W	1	2	3	4	5	6	7	%
New York Giants	4	1	4	8	5	1	5	3	29
Pittsburgh Pirates	3	4	8	5	3	4	4	1	71

WORLD SERIES

WS	W	1	2	3	4	5	6	%
Washington Senators	4	5	5	6	1	0	7	60
New York Giants	2	3	2	2	3	5	1	40

ACTUAL WINNERS

American League: Washington Senators
National League: Pittsburgh Pirates
World Series: Pittsburgh Pirates

OUTSTANDING PERFORMANCES

AWARD WINNERS

LG.	PLAYER	TEAM	STATS ADJUSTED	ACTUAL
MOST VALUABLE PLAYERS				
AL	Roger Peckinpaugh	Washington	11 HR, 67 RBI, .272 BA, $3.6 MIL	4 HR, 64 RBI, .294 BA
NL	Rogers Hornsby	St. Louis	63 HR, 149 RBI, .371 BA, $16.7 MIL	39 HR, 143 RBI, .403 BA
CY YOUNG AWARDS				
AL	Stan Coveleski	Washington	21-5 W-L, 0 SV, 2.99 ERA, $17.0 MIL	20-5 W-L, 0 SV, 2.84 ERA
NL	Dazzy Vance	Brooklyn	23-10 W-L, 0 SV, 3.73 ERA, $39.5 MIL	22-9 W-L, 0 SV, 3.53 ERA

AMERICAN LEAGUE LEADERS

CAT.	PLAYER	TEAM	STATS ADJUSTED	ACTUAL
BATTING				
HR	Bob Meusel	New York	54	33
RBI	Bob Meusel	New York	141	138
BA	Harry Heilmann	Detroit	.362	.393
AB	Al Simmons	Philadelphia	692	654
R	Johnny Mostil	Chicago	140	135
H	Al Simmons	Philadelphia	248	253
2B	Marty McManus	St. Louis	41	44
3B	Goose Goslin	Washington	8	20
TB	Al Simmons	Philadelphia	430	392
SA	Ken Williams	St. Louis	.638	.613
SB	Johnny Mostil	Chicago	57	43
PITCHING				
W	Ted Lyons	Chicago	22	21
	Eddie Rommel	Philadelphia	22	21
L	Sam Jones	New York	22	21
SV	Firpo Marberry	Washington	34	15
ERA	Stan Coveleski	Washington	2.99	2.84
G	Firpo Marberry	Washington	59	55
IP	Herb Pennock	New York	289	277
BB	Lefty Grove	Philadelphia	159	131
SO	Lefty Grove	Philadelphia	258	116

NATIONAL LEAGUE LEADERS

CAT.	PLAYER	TEAM	STATS ADJUSTED	ACTUAL
BATTING				
HR	Rogers Hornsby	St. Louis	63	39
RBI	Rogers Hornsby	St. Louis	149	143
BA	Rogers Hornsby	St. Louis	.371	.403
AB	Sparky Adams	Chicago	661	627
R	Kiki Cuyler	Pittsburgh	150	144
H	Jim Bottomley	St. Louis	222	227
2B	Jim Bottomley	St. Louis	39	44
3B	Kiki Cuyler	Pittsburgh	10	26
TB	Rogers Hornsby	St. Louis	421	381
SA	Rogers Hornsby	St. Louis	.790	.756
SB	Max Carey	Pittsburgh	61	46
PITCHING				
W	Dazzy Vance	Brooklyn	23	22
L	Burleigh Grimes	Brooklyn	20	19
SV	Guy Bush	Chicago	13	4
	Johnny Morrison	Pittsburgh	10	4
ERA	Dolf Luque	Cincinnati	2.76	2.63
G	Johnny Morrison	Pittsburgh	47	44
IP	Pete Donohue	Cincinnati	315	301
BB	Jimmy Ring	Philadelphia	141	119
SO	Dazzy Vance	Brooklyn	445	221

1926 SEASON

REGULAR SEASON STANDINGS

AMERICAN LEAGUE

		ADJUSTED			ACTUAL			
	W	L	Pct.	GB	W	L	Pct.	Rk.
EAST								
X New York	96	66	.593	0	91	63	.591	1
Philadelphia	90	72	.556	6	83	67	.553	3
Washington	87	75	.537	9	81	69	.540	4
Boston	49	113	.302	47	46	107	.301	8
WEST								
X Cleveland	92	70	.568	0	88	66	.571	2
Chicago	86	76	.531	6	81	72	.529	5
Detroit	83	79	.512	9	79	75	.513	6
St. Louis	65	97	.401	27	62	92	.403	7

NATIONAL LEAGUE

		ADJUSTED			ACTUAL			
	W	L	Pct.	GB	W	L	Pct.	Rk.
EAST								
X New York	80	82	.494	0	74	77	.490	5
Brooklyn	75	87	.463	5	71	82	.464	6
Boston	70	92	.432	10	66	86	.434	7
Philadelphia	62	100	.383	18	58	93	.384	8
WEST								
X St. Louis	94	68	.580	0	89	65	.578	1
Cincinnati	92	70	.568	2	87	67	.565	2
Pittsburgh	89	73	.549	5	84	69	.549	3
Chicago	86	76	.531	8	82	72	.532	4

SIMULATED PLAYOFFS

AMERICAN LEAGUE

ALCS	W	1	2	3	4	5	%
New York Yankees	1	0	0	0	8	4	48
Cleveland Indians	4	2	8	2	4	10	52

NATIONAL LEAGUE

NLCS	W	1	2	3	4	5	6	7	%
New York Giants	4	5	4	4	5	1	3	3	31
St. Louis Cardinals	3	3	13	2	7	2	1	2	69

WORLD SERIES

WS	W	1	2	3	4	5	6	%
Cleveland Indians	4	3	3	5	3	3	8	63
New York Giants	2	2	2	1	4	4	3	37

ACTUAL WINNERS

American League: New York Yankees
National League: St. Louis Cardinals
World Series: St. Louis Cardinals

OUTSTANDING PERFORMANCES

AWARD WINNERS

LG.	PLAYER	TEAM	STATS ADJUSTED	ACTUAL
MOST VALUABLE PLAYERS				
AL	George Burns	Cleveland	15 HR, 127 RBI, .343 BA, $9.7 MIL	4 HR, 114 RBI, .358 BA
NL	Bob O'Farrell	St. Louis	21 HR, 75 RBI, .281 BA, $5.3 MIL	7 HR, 68 RBI, .293 BA
CY YOUNG AWARDS				
AL	George Uhle	Cleveland	28-12 W-L, 1 SV, 3.28 ERA, $42.9 MIL	27-11 W-L, 1 SV, 2.83 ERA
NL	Ray Kremer	Pittsburgh	21-6 W-L, 8 SV, 3.03 ERA, $23.9 MIL	20-6 W-L, 5 SV, 2.61 ERA

AMERICAN LEAGUE LEADERS

CAT.	PLAYER	TEAM	STATS ADJUSTED	ACTUAL
BATTING				
HR	Babe Ruth	New York	73	47
RBI	Babe Ruth	New York	163	146
BA	Heinie Manush	Detroit	.363	.378
AB	Sam Rice	Washington	683	641
R	Babe Ruth	New York	155	139
H	Sam Rice	Washington	221	216
	George Burns	Cleveland	218	216
2B	George Burns	Cleveland	81	64
3B	Lou Gehrig	New York	7	20
TB	Babe Ruth	New York	421	365
SA	Babe Ruth	New York	.813	.737
SB	Johnny Mostil	Chicago	49	35
PITCHING				
W	George Uhle	Cleveland	28	27
L	Milt Gaston	St. Louis	19	18
	Paul Zahniser	Boston	19	18
SV	Firpo Marberry	Washington	40	22
ERA	Lefty Grove	Philadelphia	2.91	2.51
G	Firpo Marberry	Washington	68	64
IP	George Uhle	Cleveland	335	318.1
BB	George Uhle	Cleveland	141	118
SO	Lefty Grove	Philadelphia	409	194

NATIONAL LEAGUE LEADERS

CAT.	PLAYER	TEAM	STATS ADJUSTED	ACTUAL
BATTING				
HR	Hack Wilson	Chicago	43	21
RBI	Jim Bottomley	St. Louis	132	120
BA	Bubbles Hargrave	Cincinnati	.337	.353
AB	Sparky Adams	Chicago	652	624
R	Kiki Cuyler	Pittsburgh	124	113
H	Eddie Brown	Boston	204	201
2B	Jim Bottomley	St. Louis	31	40
3B	Paul Waner	Pittsburgh	10	22
TB	Jim Bottomley	St. Louis	347	305
SA	Cy Williams	Philadelphia	.620	.568
SB	Kiki Cuyler	Pittsburgh	48	35
PITCHING				
W	Ray Kremer	Pittsburgh	21	20
	Lee Meadows	Pittsburgh	21	20
	Flint Rhem	St. Louis	21	20
	Pete Donohue	Cincinnati	20	20
L	Jesse Petty	Brooklyn	18	17
	Charlie Root	Chicago	18	17
SV	Chick Davies	New York	19	6
ERA	Ray Kremer	Pittsburgh	3.03	2.61
G	Jack Scott	New York	54	50
IP	Pete Donohue	Cincinnati	292	285.2
BB	Sheriff Blake	Chicago	110	92
SO	Dazzy Vance	Brooklyn	273	140

1927 SEASON

REGULAR SEASON STANDINGS

AMERICAN LEAGUE

	ADJUSTED				ACTUAL			
	W	L	Pct.	GB	W	L	Pct.	Rk.
EAST								
X New York	116	46	.716	0	110	44	.714	1
Philadelphia	96	66	.593	20	91	63	.591	2
Washington	89	73	.549	27	85	69	.552	3
Boston	54	108	.333	62	51	103	.331	8
WEST								
X Detroit	87	75	.537	0	82	71	.536	4
Chicago	74	88	.457	13	70	83	.458	5
Cleveland	70	92	.432	17	66	87	.431	6
St. Louis	62	100	.383	25	59	94	.386	7

NATIONAL LEAGUE

	ADJUSTED				ACTUAL			
	W	L	Pct.	GB	W	L	Pct.	Rk.
EAST								
X New York	97	65	.599	0	92	62	.597	3
Brooklyn	69	93	.426	28	65	88	.425	6
Boston	63	99	.389	34	60	94	.390	7
Philadelphia	54	108	.333	43	51	103	.331	8
WEST								
X Pittsburgh	99	63	.611	0	94	60	.610	1
St. Louis	97	65	.599	2	92	61	.601	2
Chicago	90	72	.556	9	85	68	.556	4
Cincinnati	79	83	.488	20	75	78	.490	5

SIMULATED PLAYOFFS

AMERICAN LEAGUE

ALCS	W	1	2	3	4	5	%
New York Yankees	4	14	2	12	16	16	92
Detroit Tigers	1	7	4	2	7	5	8

NATIONAL LEAGUE

NLCS	W	1	2	3	4	5	6	%
New York Giants	2	6	11	4	8	3	1	33
Pittsburgh Pirates	4	7	4	7	7	8	8	67

WORLD SERIES

WS*	W	1	2	3	4	%
New York Yankees	4	5	6	8	4	86
Pittsburgh Pirates	0	4	2	1	3	14

ACTUAL WINNERS

American League: New York Yankees
National League: Pittsburgh Pirates
World Series: New York Yankees

OUTSTANDING PERFORMANCES

AWARD WINNERS

LG.	PLAYER	TEAM	STATS ADJUSTED	ACTUAL
MOST VALUABLE PLAYERS				
AL	Lou Gehrig	New York	83 HR, 191 RBI, .354 BA, $26.5 MIL	47 HR, 175 RBI, .373 BA
NL	Paul Waner	Pittsburgh	29 HR, 142 RBI, .362 BA, $25.2 MIL	9 HR, 131 RBI, .380 BA
CY YOUNG AWARDS				
AL	Wilcy Moore	New York	20-7 W-L, 21 SV, 2.59 ERA, $27.0 MIL	19-7 W-L, 13 SV, 2.28 ERA
NL	Charlie Root	Chicago	28-16 W-L, 4 SV, 4.25 ERA, $34.5 MIL	26-15 W-L, 2 SV, 3.76 ERA

AMERICAN LEAGUE LEADERS

CAT.	PLAYER	TEAM	STATS ADJUSTED	ACTUAL
BATTING				
HR	Babe Ruth	New York	89	60
RBI	Lou Gehrig	New York	191	175
BA	Harry Heilmann	Detroit	.379	.398
AB	Earle Combs	New York	678	648
R	Babe Ruth	New York	173	158
H	Earle Combs	New York	230	231
2B	Lou Gehrig	New York	32	52
3B	Earle Combs	New York	13	23
TB	Lou Gehrig	New York	505	447
SA	Babe Ruth	New York	.841	.772
SB	George Sisler	St. Louis	33	27
PITCHING				
W	Waite Hoyt	New York	23	22
	Ted Lyons	Chicago	23	22
L	Slim Harriss	Boston	22	21
SV	Garland Braxton	Washington	30	13
	Wilcy Moore	New York	21	13
ERA	Wilcy Moore	New York	2.59	2.28
G	Garland Braxton	Washington	60	58
IP	Ted Lyons	Chicago	323	307.2
	Tommy Thomas	Chicago	323	307.2
BB	Earl Whitehill	Detroit	131	105
SO	Lefty Grove	Philadelphia	364	174

NATIONAL LEAGUE LEADERS

CAT.	PLAYER	TEAM	STATS ADJUSTED	ACTUAL
BATTING				
HR	Hack Wilson	Chicago	56	30
	Cy Williams	Philadelphia	46	30
RBI	Paul Waner	Pittsburgh	142	131
BA	Paul Waner	Pittsburgh	.362	.380
AB	Sparky Adams	Chicago	687	647
R	Rogers Hornsby	New York	145	133
	Lloyd Waner	Pittsburgh	144	133
H	Paul Waner	Pittsburgh	234	237
2B	Riggs Stephenson	Chicago	53	46
3B	Paul Waner	Pittsburgh	9	18
TB	Paul Waner	Pittsburgh	388	342
SA	Chick Hafey	St. Louis	.642	.590
SB	Frankie Frisch	St. Louis	61	48
PITCHING				
W	Charlie Root	Chicago	28	26
L	Jack Scott	Philadelphia	22	21
SV	Bill Sherdel	St. Louis	8	6
ERA	Ray Kremer	Pittsburgh	2.79	2.47
G	Charlie Root	Chicago	51	48
	Jack Scott	Philadelphia	50	48
IP	Charlie Root	Chicago	328	309
BB	Charlie Root	Chicago	147	117
SO	Dazzy Vance	Brooklyn	390	184

1928 SEASON

REGULAR SEASON STANDINGS

AMERICAN LEAGUE

		ADJUSTED				ACTUAL			
	W	L	Pct.	GB	W	L	Pct.	Rk.
EAST									
X New York	106	56	.654	0	101	53	.656	1
Philadelphia	104	58	.642	2	98	55	.641	2
Washington	79	83	.488	27	75	79	.487	4
Boston	60	102	.370	46	57	96	.373	8
WEST									
X St. Louis	86	76	.531	0	82	72	.532	3
Chicago	76	86	.469	10	72	82	.468	5
Detroit	72	90	.444	14	68	86	.442	6
Cleveland	65	97	.401	21	62	92	.403	7

NATIONAL LEAGUE

		ADJUSTED				ACTUAL			
	W	L	Pct.	GB	W	L	Pct.	Rk.
EAST									
X New York	98	64	.605	0	93	61	.604	2
Brooklyn	81	81	.500	17	77	76	.503	6
Boston	53	109	.327	45	50	103	.327	7
Philadelphia	46	116	.284	52	43	109	.283	8
WEST									
X St. Louis	100	62	.617	0	95	59	.617	1
Chicago	96	66	.593	4	91	63	.591	3
Pittsburgh	91	71	.562	9	85	67	.559	4
Cincinnati	83	79	.512	17	78	74	.513	5

SIMULATED PLAYOFFS

AMERICAN LEAGUE

ALCS	W	1	2	3	4	5		%
New York Yankees	4	4	0	9	13	12		81
St. Louis Browns	1	3	3	7	3	7		19

NATIONAL LEAGUE

NLCS	W	1	2	3	4	5	6	%
New York Giants	2	6	0	4	1	7	3	42
St. Louis Cardinals	4	1	5	8	3	5	5	58

WORLD SERIES

WS*	W	1	2	3	4		%
New York Yankees	4	4	9	7	7		52
St. Louis Cardinals	0	1	3	3	3		48

ACTUAL WINNERS

American League: New York Yankees
National League: St. Louis Cardinals
World Series: New York Yankees

OUTSTANDING PERFORMANCES

AWARD WINNERS

LG.	PLAYER	TEAM	STATS ADJUSTED	ACTUAL
MOST VALUABLE PLAYERS				
AL	Mickey Cochrane	Philadelphia	24 HR, 63 RBI, .280 BA, $9.2 MIL	10 HR, 57 RBI, .293 BA
NL	Jim Bottomley	St. Louis	59 HR, 151 RBI, .311 BA, $25.5 MIL	31 HR, 136 RBI, .325 BA
CY YOUNG AWARDS				
AL	Lefty Grove	Philadelphia	25-8 W-L, 6 SV, 2.91 ERA, $34.3 MIL	24-8 W-L, 4 SV, 2.58 ERA
NL	Burleigh Grimes	Pittsburgh	27-15 W-L, 6 SV, 3.41 ERA, $39.4 MIL	25-14 W-L, 3 SV, 2.99 ERA

AMERICAN LEAGUE LEADERS

CAT.	PLAYER	TEAM	STATS ADJUSTED	ACTUAL
BATTING				
HR	Babe Ruth	New York	78	54
RBI	Lou Gehrig	New York	157	142
	Babe Ruth	New York	157	142
BA	Goose Goslin	Washington	.363	.379
AB	Carl Lind	Cleveland	680	650
R	Babe Ruth	New York	181	163
H	Heinie Manush	St. Louis	243	241
2B	Heinie Manush	St. Louis	52	47
	Lou Gehrig	New York	38	47
3B	Earle Combs	New York	11	21
TB	Babe Ruth	New York	429	380
SA	Babe Ruth	New York	.761	.709
SB	Buddy Myer	Boston	43	30
PITCHING				
W	Lefty Grove	Philadelphia	25	24
	George Pipgras	New York	25	24
L	Red Ruffing	Boston	26	25
SV	Waite Hoyt	New York	11	8
ERA	Garland Braxton	Washington	2.86	2.51
G	Firpo Marberry	Washington	50	48
IP	George Pipgras	New York	314	300.2
BB	Hank Johnson	New York	128	104
SO	Lefty Grove	Philadelphia	371	183

NATIONAL LEAGUE LEADERS

CAT.	PLAYER	TEAM	STATS ADJUSTED	ACTUAL
BATTING				
HR	Jim Bottomley	St. Louis	59	31
	Hack Wilson	Chicago	52	31
RBI	Jim Bottomley	St. Louis	151	136
BA	Rogers Hornsby	Boston	.372	.387
AB	Lloyd Waner	Pittsburgh	702	659
R	Paul Waner	Pittsburgh	159	142
H	Freddie Lindstrom	New York	232	231
2B	Paul Waner	Pittsburgh	69	50
3B	Jim Bottomley	St. Louis	6	20
TB	Jim Bottomley	St. Louis	411	362
SA	Rogers Hornsby	Boston	.679	.632
SB	Kiki Cuyler	Chicago	53	37
PITCHING				
W	Burleigh Grimes	Pittsburgh	27	25
	Larry Benton	New York	26	25
L	Ed Brandt	Boston	22	21
SV	Hal Haid	St. Louis	13	5
	Bill Sherdel	St. Louis	6	5
ERA	Dazzy Vance	Brooklyn	2.35	2.09
G	Burleigh Grimes	Pittsburgh	51	48
IP	Burleigh Grimes	Pittsburgh	351	330.2
BB	Doug McWeeny	Brooklyn	138	114
SO	Dazzy Vance	Brooklyn	404	200

1929 SEASON

REGULAR SEASON STANDINGS

AMERICAN LEAGUE

	ADJUSTED				ACTUAL			
	W	L	Pct.	GB	W	L	Pct.	Rk.
EAST								
X Philadelphia	112	50	.691	0	104	46	.693	1
New York	92	70	.568	20	88	66	.571	2
Washington	76	86	.469	36	71	81	.467	5
Boston	61	101	.377	51	58	96	.377	8
WEST								
X Cleveland	86	76	.531	0	81	71	.533	3
St. Louis	84	78	.519	2	79	73	.520	4
Detroit	74	88	.457	12	70	84	.455	6
Chicago	63	99	.389	23	59	93	.388	7

NATIONAL LEAGUE

	ADJUSTED				ACTUAL			
	W	L	Pct.	GB	W	L	Pct.	Rk.
EAST								
X New York	90	72	.556	0	84	67	.556	3
Philadelphia	75	87	.463	15	71	82	.464	5
Brooklyn	74	88	.457	16	70	83	.458	6
Boston	59	103	.364	31	56	98	.364	8
WEST								
X Chicago	105	57	.648	0	98	54	.645	1
Pittsburgh	93	69	.574	12	88	65	.575	2
St. Louis	83	79	.512	22	78	74	.513	4
Cincinnati	69	93	.426	36	66	88	.429	7

SIMULATED PLAYOFFS

AMERICAN LEAGUE

ALCS	W	1	2	3	4	5	6	7	%
Philadelphia Athletics	4	3	1	10	9	4	4	2	94
Cleveland Indians	3	4	4	0	0	3	5	1	6

NATIONAL LEAGUE

NLCS	W	1	2	3	4	5	6	7	%
New York Giants	4	2	5	3	2	8	0	7	49
Chicago Cubs	3	7	4	2	9	6	2	2	51

WORLD SERIES

WS	W	1	2	3	4	5		%
Philadelphia Athletics	1	3	0	5	7	3		57
New York Giants	4	4	3	6	5	4		43

ACTUAL WINNERS

American League: Philadelphia Athletics
National League: Chicago Cubs
World Series: Philadelphia Athletics

OUTSTANDING PERFORMANCES

AWARD WINNERS

LG.	PLAYER	TEAM	STATS ADJUSTED	ACTUAL
MOST VALUABLE PLAYERS				
AL	Lew Fonseca	Cleveland	16 HR, 106 RBI, .344 BA, $9.6 MIL	6 HR, 103 RBI, .369 BA
NL	Rogers Hornsby	Chicago	58 HR, 150 RBI, .355 BA, $24.7 MIL	39 HR, 149 RBI, .380 BA
CY YOUNG AWARDS				
AL	Lefty Grove	Philadelphia	21-6 W-L, 10 SV, 2.87 ERA, $41.5 MIL	20-6 W-L, 4 SV, 2.81 ERA
NL	Burleigh Grimes	Pittsburgh	18-7 W-L, 5 SV, 3.21 ERA, $17.2 MIL	17-7 W-L, 2 SV, 3.13 ERA

AMERICAN LEAGUE LEADERS

CAT.	PLAYER	TEAM	STATS ADJUSTED	ACTUAL
BATTING				
HR	Babe Ruth	New York	62	46
RBI	Al Simmons	Philadelphia	163	157
BA	Lew Fonseca	Cleveland	.344	.369
AB	Roy Johnson	Detroit	670	640
R	Charlie Gehringer	Detroit	133	131
H	Dale Alexander	Detroit	209	215
	Charlie Gehringer	Detroit	209	215
2B	Heinie Manush	St. Louis	55	45
	Charlie Gehringer	Detroit	50	45
	Roy Johnson	Detroit	50	45
3B	Charlie Gehringer	Detroit	8	19
TB	Al Simmons	Philadelphia	411	373
SA	Babe Ruth	New York	.714	.697
SB	Charlie Gehringer	Detroit	37	27
PITCHING				
W	George Earnshaw	Philadelphia	26	24
L	Red Ruffing	Boston	23	22
SV	Firpo Marberry	Washington	16	11
ERA	Lefty Grove	Philadelphia	2.87	2.81
G	Firpo Marberry	Washington	52	49
IP	Dolly Gray	St. Louis	319	305
BB	George Earnshaw	Philadelphia	146	125
SO	Lefty Grove	Philadelphia	365	170

NATIONAL LEAGUE LEADERS

CAT.	PLAYER	TEAM	STATS ADJUSTED	ACTUAL
BATTING				
HR	Chuck Klein	Philadelphia	62	43
RBI	Hack Wilson	Chicago	160	159
BA	Lefty O'Doul	Philadelphia	.371	.398
AB	Lloyd Waner	Pittsburgh	697	662
R	Rogers Hornsby	Chicago	157	156
H	Lefty O'Doul	Philadelphia	249	254
2B	Johnny Frederick	Brooklyn	43	52
3B	Lloyd Waner	Pittsburgh	13	20
TB	Rogers Hornsby	Chicago	434	409
SA	Rogers Hornsby	St. Louis	.694	.679
SB	Kiki Cuyler	Chicago	58	43
PITCHING				
W	Pat Malone	Chicago	23	22
L	Watty Clark	Brooklyn	20	19
SV	Guy Bush	Chicago	18	8
	Johnny Morrison	Brooklyn	15	8
ERA	Bill Walker	New York	3.17	3.09
G	Guy Bush	Chicago	52	50
IP	Watty Clark	Brooklyn	293	279
BB	Claude Willoughby	Philadelphia	125	108
SO	Pat Malone	Chicago	348	166

1930 SEASON

REGULAR SEASON STANDINGS

AMERICAN LEAGUE

		ADJUSTED				ACTUAL			
	W	L	Pct.	GB	W	L	Pct.	Rk.	
EAST									
X Philadelphia	107	55	.660	0	102	52	.662	1	
Washington	99	63	.611	8	94	60	.610	2	
New York	91	71	.562	16	86	68	.558	3	
Boston	55	107	.340	52	52	102	.338	8	
WEST									
X Cleveland	85	77	.525	0	81	73	.526	4	
Detroit	79	83	.488	6	75	79	.487	5	
St. Louis	67	95	.414	18	64	90	.416	6	
Chicago	65	97	.401	20	62	92	.403	7	

NATIONAL LEAGUE

		ADJUSTED				ACTUAL			
	W	L	Pct.	GB	W	L	Pct.	Rk.	
EAST									
X New York	91	71	.562	0	87	67	.565	3	
Brooklyn	90	72	.556	1	86	68	.558	4	
Boston	74	88	.457	17	70	84	.455	6	
Philadelphia	55	107	.340	36	52	102	.338	8	
WEST									
X St. Louis	97	65	.599	0	92	62	.597	1	
Chicago	95	67	.586	2	90	64	.584	2	
Pittsburgh	84	78	.519	13	80	74	.519	5	
Cincinnati	62	100	.383	35	59	95	.383	7	

SIMULATED PLAYOFFS

AMERICAN LEAGUE

ALCS	W	1	2	3	4	5	%
Philadelphia Athletics	4	9	2	12	3	12	87
Cleveland Indians	1	4	4	2	2	2	13

NATIONAL LEAGUE

NLCS	W	1	2	3	4	5	6	%
New York Giants	2	1	8	8	5	7	2	42
St. Louis Cardinals	4	9	7	0	8	12	9	58

WORLD SERIES

WS*	W	1	2	3	4	5	6	%
Philadelphia Athletics	4	5	6	0	1	2	7	46
St. Louis Cardinals	2	2	1	5	3	0	1	54

ACTUAL WINNERS

American League: Philadelphia Athletics
National League: St. Louis Cardinals
World Series: Philadelphia Athletics

OUTSTANDING PERFORMANCES

AWARD WINNERS

LG.	PLAYER	TEAM	STATS ADJUSTED	ACTUAL
MOST VALUABLE PLAYERS				
AL	Joe Cronin	Washington	23 HR, 121 RBI, .314 BA, $12.4 MIL	13 HR, 126 RBI, .346 BA
NL	Hack Wilson	Chicago	70 HR, 181 RBI, .324 BA, $28.8 MIL	56 HR, 190 RBI, .356 BA
CY YOUNG AWARDS				
AL	Lefty Grove	Philadelphia	30-5 W-L, 15 SV, 2.40 ERA, $54.3 MIL	28-5 W-L, 9 SV, 2.54 ERA
NL	Pat Malone	Chicago	21-9 W-L, 10 SV, 3.74 ERA, $33.7 MIL	20-9 W-L, 4 SV, 3.94 ERA

AMERICAN LEAGUE LEADERS

CAT.	PLAYER	TEAM	STATS ADJUSTED	ACTUAL
BATTING				
HR	Babe Ruth	New York	64	49
RBI	Lou Gehrig	New York	168	174
BA	Al Simmons	Philadelphia	.347	.381
AB	Tom Oliver	Boston	680	646
R	Al Simmons	Philadelphia	146	152
H	Johnny Hodapp	Cleveland	216	225
2B	Johnny Hodapp	Cleveland	54	51
3B	Earle Combs	New York	12	22
TB	Lou Gehrig	New York	434	419
SA	Babe Ruth	New York	.724	.732
SB	Marty McManus	Detroit	39	23
PITCHING				
W	Lefty Grove	Philadelphia	30	28
L	Milt Gaston	Boston	21	20
	Jack Russell	Boston	21	20
SV	Lefty Grove	Philadelphia	15	9
ERA	Lefty Grove	Philadelphia	2.40	2.54
G	Lefty Grove	Philadelphia	53	50
IP	Ted Lyons	Chicago	312	297.2
BB	George Earnshaw	Philadelphia	169	139
SO	Lefty Grove	Philadelphia	394	209

NATIONAL LEAGUE LEADERS

CAT.	PLAYER	TEAM	STATS ADJUSTED	ACTUAL
BATTING				
HR	Hack Wilson	Chicago	70	56
RBI	Hack Wilson	Chicago	181	190
BA	Bill Terry	New York	.366	.401
AB	Taylor Douthit	St. Louis	698	664
R	Chuck Klein	Philadelphia	150	158
H	Bill Terry	New York	244	254
2B	Chuck Klein	Philadelphia	44	59
3B	Adam Comorosky	Pittsburgh	10	23
TB	Chuck Klein	Philadelphia	456	445
SA	Hack Wilson	Chicago	.711	.723
SB	Kiki Cuyler	Chicago	63	37
PITCHING				
W	Ray Kremer	Pittsburgh	21	20
	Pat Malone	Chicago	21	20
L	Larry French	Pittsburgh	19	18
	Benny Frey	Cincinnati	19	18
SV	Hi Bell	St. Louis	21	8
ERA	Dazzy Vance	Brooklyn	2.47	2.61
G	Hal Elliott	Philadelphia	50	48
IP	Ray Kremer	Pittsburgh	290	276
BB	Bill Hallahan	St. Louis	153	126
SO	Bill Hallahan	St. Louis	330	177

REGULAR SEASON STANDINGS

AMERICAN LEAGUE

		ADJUSTED				ACTUAL			
	W	L	Pct.	GB	W	L	Pct.	Rk.
EAST								
X Philadelphia	114	48	.704	0	107	45	.704	1
New York	100	62	.617	14	94	59	.614	2
Washington	97	65	.599	17	92	62	.597	3
Boston	66	96	.407	48	62	90	.408	6
WEST								
X Cleveland	82	80	.506	0	78	76	.506	4
St. Louis	66	96	.407	16	63	91	.409	5
Detroit	64	98	.395	18	61	93	.396	7
Chicago	59	103	.364	23	56	97	.366	8

NATIONAL LEAGUE

		ADJUSTED				ACTUAL			
	W	L	Pct.	GB	W	L	Pct.	Rk.
EAST								
X New York	93	69	.574	0	87	65	.572	2
Brooklyn	84	78	.519	9	79	73	.520	4
Philadelphia	70	92	.432	23	66	88	.429	6
Boston	67	95	.414	26	64	90	.416	7
WEST								
X St. Louis	106	56	.654	0	101	53	.656	1
Chicago	88	74	.543	18	84	70	.545	3
Pittsburgh	79	83	.488	27	75	79	.487	5
Cincinnati	61	101	.377	45	58	96	.377	8

SIMULATED PLAYOFFS

AMERICAN LEAGUE

ALCS	W	1	2	3	4		%
Philadelphia Athletics	4	8	5	14	6		81
Cleveland Indians	0	5	3	7	0		19

NATIONAL LEAGUE

NLCS	W	1	2	3	4	5	%
New York Giants	4	2	5	4	2	3	43
St. Louis Cardinals	1	1	1	0	3	0	57

WORLD SERIES

WS	W	1	2	3	4	5	6	%
Philadelphia Athletics	2	6	6	7	5	1	2	56
New York Giants	4	7	4	3	6	4	4	44

ACTUAL WINNERS

American League: Philadelphia Athletics
National League: St. Louis Cardinals
World Series: St. Louis Cardinals

OUTSTANDING PERFORMANCES

AWARD WINNERS

LG.	PLAYER	TEAM	STATS ADJUSTED	ACTUAL
MOST VALUABLE PLAYERS				
AL	Lefty Grove	Philadelphia	33-4 W-L, 5 SV, 2.26 ERA, $54.0 MIL	31-4 W-L, 5 SV, 2.06 ERA
NL	Frankie Frisch	St. Louis	13 HR, 91 RBI, .302 BA, $7.5 MIL	4 HR, 82 RBI, .311 BA
CY YOUNG AWARDS				
AL	Lefty Grove	Philadelphia	33-4 W-L, 5 SV, 2.26 ERA, $54.0 MIL	31-4 W-L, 5 SV, 2.06 ERA
NL	Ed Brandt	Boston	19-11 W-L, 3 SV, 3.21 ERA, $16.3 MIL	18-11 W-L, 2 SV, 2.92 ERA

AMERICAN LEAGUE LEADERS

CAT.	PLAYER	TEAM	STATS ADJUSTED	ACTUAL
BATTING				
HR	Lou Gehrig	New York	76	46
	Babe Ruth	New York	69	46
RBI	Lou Gehrig	New York	204	184
BA	Al Simmons	Philadelphia	.378	.390
AB	Earl Averill	Cleveland	655	627
R	Lou Gehrig	New York	180	163
H	Lou Gehrig	New York	214	211
2B	Earl Webb	Boston	61	67
3B	Roy Johnson	Detroit	10	19
TB	Lou Gehrig	New York	469	410
SA	Babe Ruth	New York	.768	.700
SB	Ben Chapman	New York	107	61
PITCHING				
W	Lefty Grove	Philadelphia	33	31
L	Pat Caraway	Chicago	25	24
	Dolly Gray	St. Louis	25	24
SV	Wilcy Moore	Boston	22	10
ERA	Lefty Grove	Philadelphia	2.26	2.06
G	Bump Hadley	Washington	57	55
IP	Rube Walberg	Philadelphia	311	291
BB	Wes Ferrell	Cleveland	157	130
SO	Lefty Grove	Philadelphia	342	175

NATIONAL LEAGUE LEADERS

CAT.	PLAYER	TEAM	STATS ADJUSTED	ACTUAL
BATTING				
HR	Chuck Klein	Philadelphia	55	31
RBI	Chuck Klein	Philadelphia	134	121
BA	Chick Hafey	St. Louis	.339	.349
AB	Lloyd Waner	Pittsburgh	712	681
R	Bill Terry	New York	135	121
	Chuck Klein	Philadelphia	134	121
H	Lloyd Waner	Pittsburgh	217	214
2B	Sparky Adams	St. Louis	72	46
3B	Bill Terry	New York	11	20
TB	Chuck Klein	Philadelphia	397	347
SA	Chuck Klein	Philadelphia	.638	.584
SB	Frankie Frisch	St. Louis	48	28
PITCHING				
W	Jumbo Elliott	Philadelphia	20	19
	Bill Hallahan	St. Louis	20	19
	Heinie Meine	Pittsburgh	20	19
L	Si Johnson	Cincinnati	20	19
SV	Jack Quinn	Brooklyn	27	15
ERA	Bill Walker	New York	2.50	2.26
G	Jumbo Elliott	Philadelphia	54	52
IP	Heinie Meine	Pittsburgh	300	284
BB	Bill Hallahan	St. Louis	136	112
SO	Bill Hallahan	St. Louis	308	159

1932 SEASON

REGULAR SEASON STANDINGS

AMERICAN LEAGUE

	ADJUSTED				ACTUAL			
	W	L	Pct.	GB	W	L	Pct.	Rk.
EAST								
X New York	113	49	.698	0	107	47	.695	1
Philadelphia	99	63	.611	14	94	60	.610	2
Washington	98	64	.605	15	93	61	.604	3
Boston	45	117	.278	68	43	111	.279	8
WEST								
X Cleveland	93	69	.574	0	87	65	.572	4
Detroit	81	81	.500	12	76	75	.503	5
St. Louis	66	96	.407	27	63	91	.409	6
Chicago	53	109	.327	40	49	102	.325	7

NATIONAL LEAGUE

	ADJUSTED				ACTUAL			
	W	L	Pct.	GB	W	L	Pct.	Rk.
EAST								
X Brooklyn	85	77	.525	0	81	73	.526	3
Philadelphia	82	80	.506	3	78	76	.506	4
Boston	81	81	.500	4	77	77	.500	5
New York	76	86	.469	9	72	82	.468	6
WEST								
X Chicago	95	67	.586	0	90	64	.584	1
Pittsburgh	90	72	.556	5	86	68	.558	2
St. Louis	76	86	.469	19	72	82	.468	6
Cincinnati	63	99	.389	32	60	94	.390	8

SIMULATED PLAYOFFS

AMERICAN LEAGUE

ALCS	W	1	2	3	4		%
New York Yankees	4	13	7	10	8		76
Cleveland Indians	0	7	5	2	1		24

NATIONAL LEAGUE

NLCS	W	1	2	3	4	5	%
Brooklyn Dodgers	1	2	2	4	1	1	39
Chicago Cubs	4	9	8	3	7	4	61

WORLD SERIES

WS*	W	1	2	3	4		%
New York Yankees	4	12	5	7	13		80
Chicago Cubs	0	6	2	5	6		20

ACTUAL WINNERS

American League: New York Yankees
National League: Chicago Cubs
World Series: New York Yankees

OUTSTANDING PERFORMANCES

AWARD WINNERS

LG.	PLAYER	TEAM	STATS ADJUSTED	ACTUAL
MOST VALUABLE PLAYERS				
AL	Jimmie Foxx	Philadelphia	82 HR, 186 RBI, .354 BA, $38.6 MIL	58 HR, 169 RBI, .364 BA
NL	Chuck Klein	Philadelphia	63 HR, 150 RBI, .339 BA, $38.9 MIL	38 HR, 137 RBI, .348 BA
CY YOUNG AWARDS				
AL	Lefty Grove	Philadelphia	26-10 W-L, 9 SV, 3.10 ERA, $51.5 MIL	25-10 W-L, 7 SV, 2.84 ERA
NL	Lon Warneke	Chicago	23-6 W-L, 0 SV, 2.58 ERA, $19.2 MIL	22-6 W-L, 0 SV, 2.37 ERA

AMERICAN LEAGUE LEADERS

CAT.	PLAYER	TEAM	STATS ADJUSTED	ACTUAL
BATTING				
HR	Jimmie Foxx	Philadelphia	82	58
RBI	Jimmie Foxx	Philadelphia	186	169
BA	Dale Alexander	Det.-Bos.	.358	.367
AB	Al Simmons	Philadelphia	705	670
R	Jimmie Foxx	Philadelphia	166	151
H	Al Simmons	Philadelphia	221	216
2B	Eric McNair	Philadelphia	40	47
3B	Joe Cronin	Washington	11	18
TB	Jimmie Foxx	Philadelphia	492	438
SA	Jimmie Foxx	Philadelphia	.800	.749
SB	Ben Chapman	New York	72	38
PITCHING				
W	Alvin Crowder	Washington	28	26
L	Bump Hadley	Chi.-St.L.	22	21
SV	Firpo Marberry	Washington	32	13
ERA	Lefty Grove	Philadelphia	3.10	2.84
G	Firpo Marberry	Washington	57	54
IP	Alvin Crowder	Washington	347	327
BB	Bump Hadley	Chi.-St.L.	212	171
SO	Red Ruffing	New York	350	190

NATIONAL LEAGUE LEADERS

CAT.	PLAYER	TEAM	STATS ADJUSTED	ACTUAL
BATTING				
HR	Chuck Klein	Philadelphia	63	38
	Mel Ott	New York	57	38
RBI	Don Hurst	Philadelphia	157	143
BA	Lefty O'Doul	Brooklyn	.359	.368
AB	Hughie Critz	New York	694	659
R	Chuck Klein	Philadelphia	167	152
H	Chuck Klein	Philadelphia	232	226
2B	Paul Waner	Pittsburgh	73	62
3B	Billy Herman	Cincinnati	5	19
TB	Chuck Klein	Philadelphia	471	420
SA	Chuck Klein	Philadelphia	.689	.646
SB	Chuck Klein	Philadelphia	37	20
PITCHING				
W	Lon Warneke	Chicago	23	22
L	Ownie Carroll	Cincinnati	20	19
SV	Jack Quinn	Brooklyn	22	8
ERA	Lon Warneke	Chicago	2.58	2.37
G	Larry French	Pittsburgh	49	47
IP	Dizzy Dean	St. Louis	298	286
BB	Van Mungo	Brooklyn	143	115
SO	Dizzy Dean	St. Louis	365	191

1933 SEASON

AMERICAN LEAGUE

		ADJUSTED				ACTUAL			
		W	L	Pct.	GB	W	L	Pct.	Rk.
EAST									
X	Washington	106	56	.654	0	99	53	.651	1
	New York	98	64	.605	8	91	59	.607	2
	Philadelphia	85	77	.525	21	79	72	.523	3
	Boston	69	93	.426	37	63	86	.423	7
WEST									
X	Cleveland	80	82	.494	0	75	76	.497	4
	Detroit	79	83	.488	1	75	79	.487	5
	Chicago	72	90	.444	8	67	83	.447	6
	St. Louis	59	103	.364	21	55	96	.364	8

NATIONAL LEAGUE

		ADJUSTED				ACTUAL			
		W	L	Pct.	GB	W	L	Pct.	Rk.
EAST									
X	New York	97	65	.599	0	91	61	.599	1
	Boston	87	75	.537	10	83	71	.539	4
	Brooklyn	69	93	.426	28	65	88	.425	6
	Philadelphia	64	98	.395	33	60	92	.395	7
WEST									
X	Pittsburgh	92	70	.568	0	87	67	.565	2
	Chicago	90	72	.556	2	86	68	.558	3
	St. Louis	87	75	.537	5	82	71	.536	5
	Cincinnati	62	100	.383	30	58	94	.382	8

AMERICAN LEAGUE

ALCS	W	1	2	3	4	5	6	7	%
Washington Senators	4	9	6	17	5	3	1	10	87
Cleveland Indians	3	1	7	0	4	5	3	1	13

NATIONAL LEAGUE

NLCS	W	1	2	3	4	5	%
New York Giants	4	4	2	7	0	4	61
Pittsburgh Pirates	1	2	0	1	1	3	39

WORLD SERIES

WS*	W	1	2	3	4	5	%
Washington Senators	1	2	1	4	1	3	48
New York Giants	4	4	6	0	2	4	52

ACTUAL WINNERS

American League: Washington Senators
National League: New York Giants
World Series: New York Giants

OUTSTANDING PERFORMANCES

AWARD WINNERS

LG.	PLAYER	TEAM	STATS ADJUSTED	ACTUAL
MOST VALUABLE PLAYERS				
AL	Jimmie Foxx	Philadelphia	79 HR, 196 RBI, .357 BA, $33.3 MIL	48 HR, 163 RBI, .356 BA
NL	Carl Hubbell	New York	24-13 W-L, 8 SV, 1.98 ERA, $41.6 MIL	23-12 W-L, 5 SV, 1.66 ERA
CY YOUNG AWARDS				
AL	Lefty Grove	Philadelphia	26-9 W-L, 10 SV, 3.83 ERA, $49.5 MIL	24-8 W-L, 6 SV, 3.20 ERA
NL	Carl Hubbell	New York	24-13 W-L, 8 SV, 1.98 ERA, $41.6 MIL	23-12 W-L, 5 SV, 1.66 ERA

AMERICAN LEAGUE LEADERS

CAT.	PLAYER	TEAM	STATS ADJUSTED	ACTUAL
BATTING				
HR	Jimmie Foxx	Philadelphia	79	48
RBI	Jimmie Foxx	Philadelphia	196	163
BA	Jimmie Foxx	Philadelphia	.357	.356
AB	Doc Cramer	Philadelphia	704	661
R	Lou Gehrig	New York	166	138
H	Heinie Manush	Washington	234	221
2B	Joe Cronin	Washington	65	45
3B	Heinie Manush	Washington	12	17
TB	Jimmie Foxx	Philadelphia	487	403
SA	Jimmie Foxx	Philadelphia	.797	.703
SB	Ben Chapman	New York	58	27
PITCHING				
W	Lefty Grove	Philadelphia	26	24
	Alvin Crowder	Washington	25	24
L	Ted Lyons	Chicago	23	21
SV	Jack Russell	Washington	26	13
ERA	Monte Pearson	Cleveland	2.79	2.33
G	Alvin Crowder	Washington	55	52
IP	Bump Hadley	St. Louis	338	316.2
BB	Bump Hadley	St. Louis	180	141
SO	Lefty Gomez	New York	323	163

NATIONAL LEAGUE LEADERS

CAT.	PLAYER	TEAM	STATS ADJUSTED	ACTUAL
BATTING				
HR	Chuck Klein	Philadelphia	54	28
RBI	Chuck Klein	Philadelphia	144	120
BA	Chuck Klein	Philadelphia	.368	.368
AB	Chick Fullis	Philadelphia	690	647
R	Pepper Martin	St. Louis	145	122
H	Chuck Klein	Philadelphia	238	223
2B	Chuck Klein	Philadelphia	37	44
3B	Arky Vaughan	Pittsburgh	11	19
TB	Chuck Klein	Philadelphia	443	365
SA	Chuck Klein	Philadelphia	.686	.602
SB	Pepper Martin	St. Louis	55	26
PITCHING				
W	Carl Hubbell	New York	24	23
L	Paul Derringer	St.L.-Cin.	29	27
SV	Phil Collins	Philadelphia	14	6
ERA	Carl Hubbell	New York	1.98	1.66
G	Dizzy Dean	St. Louis	50	48
IP	Carl Hubbell	New York	322	308.2
BB	Bill Hallahan	St. Louis	124	98
SO	Dizzy Dean	St. Louis	392	199

1934 SEASON

REGULAR SEASON STANDINGS

AMERICAN LEAGUE

		ADJUSTED				ACTUAL			
	W	L	Pct.	GB	W	L	Pct.	Rk.
EAST								
X New York	99	63	.611	0	94	60	.610	2
Boston	81	81	.500	18	76	76	.500	4
Philadelphia	74	88	.457	25	68	82	.453	5
Washington	70	92	.432	29	66	86	.434	7
WEST								
X Detroit	106	56	.654	0	101	53	.656	1
Cleveland	90	72	.556	16	85	69	.552	3
St. Louis	71	91	.438	35	67	85	.441	6
Chicago	57	105	.352	49	53	99	.349	8

NATIONAL LEAGUE

		ADJUSTED				ACTUAL			
	W	L	Pct.	GB	W	L	Pct.	Rk.
EAST								
X New York	98	64	.605	0	93	60	.608	2
Boston	84	78	.519	14	78	73	.517	4
Brooklyn	76	86	.469	22	71	81	.467	6
Philadelphia	61	101	.377	37	56	93	.376	7
WEST								
X St. Louis	101	61	.623	0	95	58	.621	1
Chicago	92	70	.568	9	86	65	.570	3
Pittsburgh	80	82	.494	21	74	76	.493	5
Cincinnati	56	106	.346	45	52	99	.344	8

SIMULATED PLAYOFFS

AMERICAN LEAGUE

ALCS	W	1	2	3	4	5	6	7	%
New York Yankees	1	5	0	3	6	1			50
Detroit Tigers	4	2	6	5	7	2			50

NATIONAL LEAGUE

NLCS	W	1	2	3	4	5	6	7	%
New York Giants	2	2	1	4	4	3	4		46
St. Louis Cardinals	4	5	7	1	3	4	6		54

WORLD SERIES

WS*	W	1	2	3	4	5	6	7	%
Detroit Tigers	3	3	3	1	10	3	3	0	52
St. Louis Cardinals	4	8	2	4	4	1	4	11	48

ACTUAL WINNERS

American League: Detroit Tigers
National League: St. Louis Cardinals
World Series: St. Louis Cardinals

OUTSTANDING PERFORMANCES

AWARD WINNERS

LG.	PLAYER	TEAM	STATS ADJUSTED	ACTUAL
MOST VALUABLE PLAYERS				
AL	Mickey Cochrane	Detroit	5 HR, 83 RBI, .308 BA, $9.3 MIL	2 HR, 76 RBI, .320 BA
NL	Dizzy Dean	St. Louis	32-7 W-L, 11 SV, 2.84 ERA, $51.5 MIL	30-7 W-L, 7 SV, 2.66 ERA
CY YOUNG AWARDS				
AL	Lefty Gomez	New York	27-5 W-L, 3 SV, 2.46 ERA, $41.1 MIL	26-5 W-L, 1 SV, 2.33 ERA
NL	Dizzy Dean	St. Louis	32-7 W-L, 11 SV, 2.84 ERA, $51.5 MIL	30-7 W-L, 7 SV, 2.66 ERA

AMERICAN LEAGUE LEADERS

CAT.	PLAYER	TEAM	STATS ADJUSTED	ACTUAL
BATTING				
HR	Lou Gehrig	New York	72	49
RBI	Lou Gehrig	New York	181	165
BA	Lou Gehrig	New York	.350	.363
AB	Doc Cramer	Philadelphia	687	649
R	Charlie Gehringer	Detroit	146	134
H	Charlie Gehringer	Detroit	217	214
2B	Hank Greenberg	Detroit	56	63
3B	Ben Chapman	New York	10	13
TB	Lou Gehrig	New York	462	409
SA	Lou Gehrig	New York	.759	.706
SB	Billy Werber	Boston	82	40
PITCHING				
W	Lefty Gomez	New York	27	26
L	Bobo Newsom	St. Louis	21	20
SV	Jack Russell	Washington	20	7
ERA	Lefty Gomez	New York	2.46	2.33
G	Jack Russell	Washington	56	54
IP	Lefty Gomez	New York	296	281.2
BB	Bobo Newsom	St. Louis	172	149
SO	Lefty Gomez	New York	296	158

NATIONAL LEAGUE LEADERS

CAT.	PLAYER	TEAM	STATS ADJUSTED	ACTUAL
BATTING				
HR	Ripper Collins	St. Louis	57	35
	Mel Ott	New York	55	35
RBI	Mel Ott	New York	148	135
BA	Paul Waner	Pittsburgh	.349	.362
AB	Jack Rothrock	St. Louis	681	647
R	Paul Waner	Pittsburgh	136	122
H	Paul Waner	Pittsburgh	225	217
2B	Kiki Cuyler	Chicago	53	42
	Ethan Allen	Philadelphia	48	42
3B	Joe Medwick	St. Louis	9	18
TB	Ripper Collins	St. Louis	417	369
SA	Ripper Collins	St. Louis	.661	.615
SB	Pepper Martin	St. Louis	47	23
PITCHING				
W	Dizzy Dean	St. Louis	32	30
L	Si Johnson	Cincinnati	23	22
SV	Carl Hubbell	New York	13	8
ERA	Carl Hubbell	New York	2.44	2.30
G	Curt Davis	Philadelphia	55	51
IP	Van Mungo	Brooklyn	336	315.1
BB	Van Mungo	Brooklyn	122	104
SO	Dizzy Dean	St. Louis	361	195

1935 SEASON

REGULAR SEASON STANDINGS

AMERICAN LEAGUE

		ADJUSTED				ACTUAL			
	W	L	Pct.	GB	W	L	Pct.	Rk.
EAST								
X New York	97	65	.599	0	89	60	.597	2
Boston	82	80	.506	15	78	75	.510	4
Washington	71	91	.438	26	67	86	.438	6
Philadelphia	63	99	.389	34	58	91	.389	8
WEST								
X Detroit	100	62	.617	0	93	58	.616	1
Cleveland	87	75	.537	13	82	71	.536	3
Chicago	79	83	.488	21	74	78	.487	5
St. Louis	69	93	.426	31	65	87	.428	7

NATIONAL LEAGUE

		ADJUSTED				ACTUAL			
	W	L	Pct.	GB	W	L	Pct.	Rk.
EAST								
X New York	97	65	.599	0	91	62	.595	3
Brooklyn	74	88	.457	23	70	83	.458	5
Philadelphia	68	94	.420	29	64	89	.418	7
Boston	40	122	.247	57	38	115	.248	8
WEST								
X Chicago	105	57	.648	0	100	54	.649	1
St. Louis	101	61	.623	4	96	58	.623	2
Pittsburgh	91	71	.562	14	86	67	.562	4
Cincinnati	72	90	.444	33	68	85	.444	6

SIMULATED PLAYOFFS

AMERICAN LEAGUE

ALCS	W	1	2	3	4	5	6	%
New York Yankees	4	4	7	0	5	5	3	39
Detroit Tigers	2	3	3	5	10	4	2	61

NATIONAL LEAGUE

NLCS	W	1	2	3	4	5		%
New York Giants	1	5	4	2	1	1		16
Chicago Cubs	4	1	7	5	9	6		84

WORLD SERIES

WS	W	1	2	3	4	5	6	%
New York Yankees	4	1	0	4	5	4	3	41
Chicago Cubs	2	8	5	3	2	3	0	59

ACTUAL WINNERS

American League: Detroit Tigers
National League: Chicago Cubs
World Series: Detroit Tigers

OUTSTANDING PERFORMANCES

AWARD WINNERS

LG.	PLAYER	TEAM	STATS ADJUSTED	ACTUAL
MOST VALUABLE PLAYERS				
AL	Hank Greenberg	Detroit	62 HR, 189 RBI, .317 BA, $26.1 MIL	36 HR, 170 RBI, .328 BA
NL	Gabby Hartnett	Chicago	25 HR, 99 RBI, .332 BA, $3.7 MIL	13 HR, 91 RBI, .344 BA
CY YOUNG AWARDS				
AL	Wes Ferrell	Boston	26-15 W-L, 0 SV, 3.78 ERA, $34.5 MIL	25-14 W-L, 0 SV, 3.52 ERA
NL	Dizzy Dean	St. Louis	30-13 W-L, 8 SV, 3.26 ERA, $55.6 MIL	28-12 W-L, 5 SV, 3.04 ERA

AMERICAN LEAGUE LEADERS

CAT.	PLAYER	TEAM	STATS ADJUSTED	ACTUAL
BATTING				
HR	Hank Greenberg	Detroit	62	36
	Jimmie Foxx	Philadelphia	57	36
RBI	Hank Greenberg	Detroit	189	170
BA	Buddy Myer	Washington	.337	.349
AB	Doc Cramer	Philadelphia	700	644
R	Lou Gehrig	New York	142	125
H	Joe Vosmik	Cleveland	217	216
2B	Joe Vosmik	Cleveland	59	47
3B	Joe Vosmik	Cleveland	11	20
TB	Hank Greenberg	Detroit	447	389
SA	Jimmie Foxx	Philadelphia	.684	.636
SB	Billy Werber	Boston	61	29
PITCHING				
W	Wes Ferrell	Boston	26	25
L	Bobo Newsom	St.L.-Wash.	19	18
SV	Jack Knott	St. Louis	18	7
ERA	Lefty Grove	Boston	2.90	2.70
G	Russ Van Atta	N.Y.-St.L.	61	58
IP	Wes Ferrell	Boston	338	322.1
BB	Sugar Cain	Phi.-St.L.	153	123
SO	Tommy Bridges	Detroit	318	163

NATIONAL LEAGUE LEADERS

CAT.	PLAYER	TEAM	STATS ADJUSTED	ACTUAL
BATTING				
HR	Wally Berger	Boston	52	34
RBI	Wally Berger	Boston	143	130
BA	Arky Vaughan	Pittsburgh	.373	.385
AB	Jo-Jo Moore	New York	707	681
R	Augie Galan	Chicago	146	133
H	Billy Herman	Chicago	231	227
2B	Billy Herman	Chicago	71	57
3B	Ival Goodman	Cincinnati	9	18
TB	Joe Medwick	St. Louis	412	365
SA	Arky Vaughan	Pittsburgh	.653	.607
SB	Augie Galan	Chicago	46	22
PITCHING				
W	Dizzy Dean	St. Louis	30	28
L	Ben Cantwell	Boston	26	25
SV	Dutch Leonard	Brooklyn	21	8
ERA	Cy Blanton	Pittsburgh	2.78	2.58
G	Orville Jorgens	Philadelphia	55	53
IP	Dizzy Dean	St. Louis	345	325.1
BB	Roy Parmelee	New York	112	97
SO	Dizzy Dean	St. Louis	373	190

1936 SEASON

REGULAR SEASON STANDINGS

AMERICAN LEAGUE

		ADJUSTED				ACTUAL			
	W	L	Pct.	GB	W	L	Pct.	Rk.	
EAST									
X New York	108	54	.667	0	102	51	.667	1	
Washington	87	75	.537	21	82	71	.536	3	
Boston	78	84	.481	30	74	80	.481	6	
Philadelphia	56	106	.346	52	53	100	.346	8	
WEST									
X Detroit	87	75	.537	0	83	71	.539	2	
X Chicago	87	75	.537	0	81	70	.536	3	
Cleveland	84	78	.519	3	80	74	.519	5	
St. Louis	61	101	.377	26	57	95	.375	7	

NATIONAL LEAGUE

		ADJUSTED				ACTUAL			
	W	L	Pct.	GB	W	L	Pct.	Rk.	
EAST									
X New York	97	65	.599	0	92	62	.597	1	
Boston	75	87	.463	22	71	83	.461	6	
Brooklyn	70	92	.432	27	67	87	.435	7	
Philadelphia	57	105	.352	40	54	100	.351	8	
WEST									
X Chicago	92	70	.568	0	87	67	.565	2	
St. Louis	91	71	.562	1	87	67	.565	2	
Pittsburgh	88	74	.543	4	84	70	.545	4	
Cincinnati	78	84	.481	14	74	80	.481	5	

SIMULATED PLAYOFFS

AMERICAN LEAGUE

TIEBREAKER	W	1	2	3					%
Detroit Tigers	1	9	8	3					49
Chicago White Sox	2	6	9	5					51

ALCS	W	1	2	3	4	5	6	7	%
New York Yankees	4	13	4	15	4	8	8	11	87
Chicago White Sox	3	1	3	6	5	9	10	6	13

NATIONAL LEAGUE

NLCS	W	1	2	3	4	5	%
New York Giants	1	1	1	2	1	0	40
Chicago Cubs	4	4	3	1	4	1	60

WORLD SERIES

WS	W	1	2	3	4	5	6	%
New York Yankees	4	2	3	3	7	3	6	68
Chicago Cubs	2	5	1	2	1	7	4	32

ACTUAL WINNERS

American League: New York Yankees
National League: New York Giants
World Series: New York Yankees

OUTSTANDING PERFORMANCES

AWARD WINNERS

LG.	PLAYER	TEAM	STATS ADJUSTED	ACTUAL
MOST VALUABLE PLAYERS				
AL	Lou Gehrig	New York	70 HR, 157 RBI, .336 BA, $32.6 MIL	49 HR, 152 RBI, .354 BA
NL	Carl Hubbell	New York	27-6 W-L, 6 SV, 2.32 ERA, $40.9 MIL	26-6 W-L, 3 SV, 2.31 ERA
CY YOUNG AWARDS				
AL	Tommy Bridges	Detroit	24-12 W-L, 0 SV, 3.63 ERA, $40.7 MIL	23-11 W-L, 0 SV, 3.60 ERA
NL	Carl Hubbell	New York	27-6 W-L, 6 SV, 2.32 ERA, $40.9 MIL	26-6 W-L, 3 SV, 2.31 ERA

AMERICAN LEAGUE LEADERS

CAT.	PLAYER	TEAM	STATS ADJUSTED	ACTUAL
BATTING				
HR	Lou Gehrig	New York	70	49
RBI	Hal Trosky	Cleveland	166	162
BA	Luke Appling	Chicago	.369	.388
AB	Lou Finney	Philadelphia	688	653
R	Lou Gehrig	New York	173	167
H	Earl Averill	Cleveland	228	232
2B	Charlie Gehringer	Detroit	63	60
3B	Red Rolfe	New York	9	15
	Earl Averill	Cleveland	7	15
	Joe DiMaggio	New York	6	15
TB	Hal Trosky	Cleveland	440	405
SA	Lou Gehrig	New York	.736	.696
SB	Lyn Lary	St. Louis	72	37
PITCHING				
W	Tommy Bridges	Detroit	24	23
L	Gordon Rhodes	Philadelphia	21	20
SV	Pat Malone	New York	15	9
ERA	Lefty Grove	Boston	2.82	2.81
G	Russ Van Atta	St. Louis	54	52
IP	Wes Ferrell	Boston	316	301
BB	Vern Kennedy	Chicago	164	147
SO	Tommy Bridges	Detroit	335	175

NATIONAL LEAGUE LEADERS

CAT.	PLAYER	TEAM	STATS ADJUSTED	ACTUAL
BATTING				
HR	Mel Ott	New York	50	33
RBI	Joe Medwick	St. Louis	143	138
BA	Paul Waner	Pittsburgh	.355	.373
AB	Woody Jensen	Pittsburgh	723	696
R	Arky Vaughan	Pittsburgh	125	122
H	Joe Medwick	St. Louis	221	223
2B	Joe Medwick	St. Louis	64	64
3B	Ival Goodman	Cincinnati	6	14
TB	Joe Medwick	St. Louis	405	367
SA	Mel Ott	New York	.623	.588
SB	Pepper Martin	St. Louis	44	23
PITCHING				
W	Carl Hubbell	New York	27	26
L	Bucky Walters	Philadelphia	22	21
SV	Dizzy Dean	St. Louis	13	11
ERA	Carl Hubbell	New York	2.32	2.31
G	Paul Derringer	Cincinnati	54	51
	Dizzy Dean	St. Louis	53	51
IP	Dizzy Dean	St. Louis	327	315
BB	Van Mungo	Brooklyn	129	118
SO	Van Mungo	Brooklyn	430	238

1937 SEASON

REGULAR SEASON STANDINGS

AMERICAN LEAGUE

		ADJUSTED				ACTUAL			
	W	L	Pct.	GB	W	L	Pct.	Rk.
EAST									
X New York	107	55	.660	0	102	52	.662	1
Boston	85	77	.525	22	80	72	.526	5
Washington	77	85	.475	30	73	80	.477	6
Philadelphia	58	104	.358	49	54	97	.358	7
WEST									
X Detroit	94	68	.580	0	89	65	.578	2
Chicago	91	71	.562	3	86	68	.558	3
Cleveland	87	75	.537	7	83	71	.539	4
St. Louis	49	113	.302	45	46	108	.299	8

NATIONAL LEAGUE

		ADJUSTED				ACTUAL			
	W	L	Pct.	GB	W	L	Pct.	Rk.
EAST									
X New York	101	61	.623	0	95	57	.625	1
Boston	84	78	.519	17	79	73	.520	5
Brooklyn	66	96	.407	35	62	91	.405	6
Philadelphia	65	97	.401	36	61	92	.399	7
WEST									
X Chicago	98	64	.605	0	93	61	.604	2
Pittsburgh	90	72	.556	8	86	68	.558	3
St. Louis	85	77	.525	13	81	73	.526	4
Cincinnati	59	103	.364	39	56	98	.364	8

SIMULATED PLAYOFFS

AMERICAN LEAGUE

ALCS	W	1	2	3	4	5	%
New York Yankees	4	10	8	12	6	8	90
Detroit Tigers	1	5	6	1	7	6	10

NATIONAL LEAGUE

NLCS	W	1	2	3	4	5	6	%
New York Giants	2	1	4	7	0	3	4	55
Chicago Cubs	4	2	3	6	5	4	5	45

WORLD SERIES

WS	W	1	2	3	4	%
New York Yankees	4	11	12	8	12	62
Chicago Cubs	0	4	1	3	3	38

ACTUAL WINNERS

American League: New York Yankees
National League: New York Giants
World Series: New York Yankees

OUTSTANDING PERFORMANCES

AWARD WINNERS

LG.	PLAYER	TEAM	STATS ADJUSTED	ACTUAL
MOST VALUABLE PLAYERS				
AL	Charlie Gehringer	Detroit	25 HR, 104 RBI, .360 BA, $20.0 MIL	14 HR, 96 RBI, .371 BA
NL	Joe Medwick	St. Louis	51 HR, 164 RBI, .364 BA, $26.1 MIL	31 HR, 154 RBI, .374 BA
CY YOUNG AWARDS				
AL	Lefty Gomez	New York	22-11 W-L, 0 SV, 2.48 ERA, $32.9 MIL	21-11 W-L, 0 SV, 2.33 ERA
NL	Carl Hubbell	New York	23-8 W-L, 7 SV, 3.43 ERA, $32.5 MIL	22-8 W-L, 4 SV, 3.20 ERA

AMERICAN LEAGUE LEADERS

CAT.	PLAYER	TEAM	STATS ADJUSTED	ACTUAL
BATTING				
HR	Joe DiMaggio	New York	69	46
RBI	Hank Greenberg	Detroit	198	183
BA	Charlie Gehringer	Detroit	.360	.371
AB	Buddy Lewis	Washington	685	668
R	Joe DiMaggio	New York	161	151
H	Beau Bell	St. Louis	221	218
2B	Beau Bell	St. Louis	55	51
3B	Dixie Walker	Chicago	9	16
	Mike Kreevich	Chicago	8	16
TB	Joe DiMaggio	New York	464	418
SA	Joe DiMaggio	New York	.723	.673
SB	Billy Werber	Philadelphia	64	35
	Ben Chapman	Wash.-Bos.	62	35
PITCHING				
W	Lefty Gomez	New York	22	21
L	Harry Kelley	Philadelphia	22	21
SV	Clint Brown	Chicago	34	18
ERA	Lefty Gomez	New York	2.48	2.1
G	Clint Brown	Chicago	56	53
IP	Wes Ferrell	Bos.-Wash.	289	281
BB	Bobo Newsom	Wash.-Bos.	179	167
SO	Lefty Gomez	New York	329	194

NATIONAL LEAGUE LEADERS

CAT.	PLAYER	TEAM	STATS ADJUSTED	ACTUAL
BATTING				
HR	Joe Medwick	St. Louis	51	31
	Mel Ott	New York	44	31
RBI	Joe Medwick	St. Louis	164	154
BA	Joe Medwick	St. Louis	.364	.374
AB	Joe Medwick	St. Louis	653	633
R	Joe Medwick	St. Louis	118	111
H	Joe Medwick	St. Louis	238	237
2B	Joe Medwick	St. Louis	51	56
3B	Arky Vaughan	Pittsburgh	12	17
TB	Joe Medwick	St. Louis	450	406
SA	Joe Medwick	St. Louis	.689	.641
SB	Augie Galan	Chicago	41	23
PITCHING				
W	Carl Hubbell	New York	23	22
L	Wayne LaMaster	Philadelphia	20	19
SV	Mace Brown	Pittsburgh	22	7
	Cliff Melton	New York	14	7
ERA	Jim Turner	Boston	2.55	2.38
G	Hugh Mulcahy	Philadelphia	59	56
IP	Claude Passeau	Philadelphia	304	292.1
BB	Hugh Mulcahy	Philadelphia	106	97
SO	Carl Hubbell	New York	274	159

1938 SEASON

REGULAR SEASON STANDINGS

AMERICAN LEAGUE

	ADJUSTED				ACTUAL			
	W	L	Pct.	GB	W	L	Pct.	Rk.
EAST								
X New York	106	56	.654	0	99	53	.651	1
Boston	96	66	.593	10	88	61	.591	2
Washington	80	82	.494	26	75	76	.497	5
Philadelphia	56	106	.346	50	53	99	.349	8
WEST								
X Cleveland	92	70	.568	0	86	66	.566	3
Detroit	88	74	.543	4	84	70	.545	4
Chicago	71	91	.438	21	65	83	.439	6
St. Louis	59	103	.364	33	55	97	.362	7

NATIONAL LEAGUE

	ADJUSTED				ACTUAL			
	W	L	Pct.	GB	W	L	Pct.	Rk.
EAST								
X New York	90	72	.556	0	83	67	.553	3
Boston	82	80	.506	8	77	75	.507	5
Brooklyn	75	87	.463	15	69	80	.463	7
Philadelphia	49	113	.302	41	45	105	.300	8
WEST								
X Chicago	95	67	.586	0	89	63	.586	1
Pittsburgh	93	69	.574	2	86	64	.573	2
Cincinnati	88	74	.543	7	82	68	.547	4
St. Louis	76	86	.469	19	71	80	.470	6

SIMULATED PLAYOFFS

AMERICAN LEAGUE

ALCS	W	1	2	3	4		%
New York Yankees	4	9	5	5	10		77
Cleveland Indians	0	6	4	3	7		23

NATIONAL LEAGUE

NLCS	W	1	2	3	4	5	6	7	%
New York Giants	3	3	1	5	3	3	6	0	42
Chicago Cubs	4	4	3	4	2	8	1	1	58

WORLD SERIES

WS*	W	1	2	3	4		%
New York Yankees	4	3	6	5	8		63
Chicago Cubs	0	1	3	2	3		37

ACTUAL WINNERS

American League: New York Yankees
National League: Chicago Cubs
World Series: New York Yankees

OUTSTANDING PERFORMANCES

AWARD WINNERS

LG.	PLAYER	TEAM	STATS ADJUSTED	ACTUAL
MOST VALUABLE PLAYERS				
AL	Jimmie Foxx	Boston	73 HR, 196 RBI, .342 BA, $29.8 MIL	50 HR, 175 RBI, .349 BA
NL	Ernie Lombardi	Cincinnati	30 HR, 104 RBI, .337 BA, $5.5 MIL	19 HR, 95 RBI, .342 BA
CY YOUNG AWARDS				
AL	Red Ruffing	New York	22-7 W-L, 0 SV, 3.53 ERA, $24.8 MIL	21-7 W-L, 0 SV, 3.31 ERA
NL	Bill Lee	Chicago	23-9 W-L, 6 SV, 2.84 ERA, $33.5 MIL	22-9 W-L, 2 SV, 2.66 ERA

AMERICAN LEAGUE LEADERS

CAT.	PLAYER	TEAM	STATS ADJUSTED	ACTUAL
BATTING				
HR	Hank Greenberg	Detroit	76	58
RBI	Jimmie Foxx	Boston	196	175
BA	Jimmie Foxx	Boston	.342	.349
AB	Doc Cramer	Boston	711	658
R	Hank Greenberg	Detroit	155	144
H	Joe Vosmik	Boston	214	201
2B	Joe Cronin	Boston	54	51
3B	Jeff Heath	Cleveland	9	18
TB	Jimmie Foxx	Boston	464	398
SA	Jimmie Foxx	Boston	.759	.704
SB	Frank Crosetti	New York	54	27
PITCHING				
W	Red Ruffing	New York	22	21
L	George Caster	Philadelphia	21	20
SV	Johnny Murphy	New York	19	11
ERA	Lefty Grove	Boston	3.31	3.08
G	Johnny Humphries	Cleveland	48	45
IP	Bobo Newsom	St. Louis	345	329.2
BB	Bob Feller	Cleveland	222	208
SO	Bob Feller	Cleveland	414	240

NATIONAL LEAGUE LEADERS

CAT.	PLAYER	TEAM	STATS ADJUSTED	ACTUAL
BATTING				
HR	Mel Ott	New York	53	36
RBI	Joe Medwick	St. Louis	131	122
BA	Ernie Lombardi	Cincinnati	.337	.342
AB	Frank McCormick	Cincinnati	687	640
R	Mel Ott	New York	127	116
H	Frank McCormick	Cincinnati	220	209
2B	Joe Medwick	St. Louis	48	47
3B	Johnny Mize	St. Louis	8	16
TB	Johnny Mize	St. Louis	367	326
SA	Johnny Mize	St. Louis	.665	.614
SB	Stan Hack	Chicago	32	16
PITCHING				
W	Bill Lee	Chicago	23	22
L	Hugh Mulcahy	Philadelphia	21	20
SV	Dick Coffman	New York	29	12
ERA	Bill Lee	Chicago	2.84	2.66
G	Mace Brown	Pittsburgh	54	51
	Dick Coffman	New York	54	51
IP	Paul Derringer	Cincinnati	329	307
BB	Clay Bryant	Chicago	132	125
SO	Clay Bryant	Chicago	258	135

1939 SEASON

REGULAR SEASON STANDINGS

AMERICAN LEAGUE

		ADJUSTED				ACTUAL			
	W	L	Pct.	GB	W	L	Pct.	Rk.
EAST								
X New York	114	48	.704	0	106	45	.702	1
Boston	95	67	.586	19	89	62	.589	2
Washington	69	93	.426	45	65	87	.428	6
Philadelphia	59	103	.364	55	55	97	.362	7
WEST								
X Cleveland	92	70	.568	0	87	67	.565	3
Chicago	89	73	.549	3	85	69	.552	4
Detroit	85	77	.525	7	81	73	.526	5
St. Louis	45	117	.278	47	43	111	.279	8

NATIONAL LEAGUE

		ADJUSTED				ACTUAL			
	W	L	Pct.	GB	W	L	Pct.	Rk.
EAST								
X Brooklyn	89	73	.549	0	84	69	.549	3
New York	83	79	.512	6	77	74	.510	5
Boston	68	94	.420	21	63	88	.417	7
Philadelphia	48	114	.296	41	45	106	.298	8
WEST								
X Cincinnati	102	60	.630	0	97	57	.630	1
St. Louis	98	64	.605	4	92	61	.601	2
Chicago	88	74	.543	14	84	70	.545	4
Pittsburgh	72	90	.444	30	68	85	.444	6

SIMULATED PLAYOFFS

AMERICAN LEAGUE

ALCS	W	1	2	3	4		%
New York Yankees	4	10	6	7	7		94
Cleveland Indians	0	2	3	2	1		6

NATIONAL LEAGUE

NLCS	W	1	2	3	4	5	6	%
Brooklyn Dodgers	4	2	4	1	5	4	5	38
Cincinnati Reds	2	5	2	5	1	3	4	62

WORLD SERIES

WS	W	1	2	3	4		%
New York Yankees	4	10	4	2	6		94
Brooklyn Dodgers	0	1	3	1	2		6

ACTUAL WINNERS

American League: New York Yankees
National League: Cincinnati Reds
World Series: New York Yankees

OUTSTANDING PERFORMANCES

AWARD WINNERS

LG.	PLAYER	TEAM	STATS ADJUSTED	ACTUAL
MOST VALUABLE PLAYERS				
AL	Joe DiMaggio	New York	46 HR, 139 RBI, .373 BA, $18.7 MIL	30 HR, 126 RBI, .381 BA
NL	Bucky Walters	Cincinnati	28-12 W-L, 0 SV, 2.44 ERA, $40.3 MIL	27-11 W-L, 0 SV, 2.29 ERA
CY YOUNG AWARDS				
AL	Bob Feller	Cleveland	25-9 W-L, 3 SV, 3.03 ERA, $40.2 MIL	24-9 W-L, 1 SV, 2.85 ERA
NL	Bucky Walters	Cincinnati	28-12 W-L, 0 SV, 2.44 ERA, $40.3 MIL	27-11 W-L, 0 SV, 2.29 ERA

AMERICAN LEAGUE LEADERS

CAT.	PLAYER	TEAM	STATS ADJUSTED	ACTUAL
BATTING				
HR	Jimmie Foxx	Boston	54	35
RBI	Ted Williams	Boston	160	145
BA	Joe DiMaggio	New York	.373	.381
AB	Frank Crosetti	New York	699	656
R	Red Rolfe	New York	153	139
H	Red Rolfe	New York	222	213
2B	Red Rolfe	New York	52	46
3B	Buddy Lewis	Washington	10	16
TB	Ted Williams	Boston	396	344
SA	Jimmie Foxx	Boston	.751	.694
SB	George Case	Washington	100	51
PITCHING				
W	Bob Feller	Cleveland	25	24
L	Vern Kennedy	Det.-St.L.	21	20
SV	Johnny Murphy	New York	28	19
ERA	Lefty Grove	Boston	2.73	2.54
G	Clint Brown	Chicago	64	61
IP	Bob Feller	Cleveland	312	296.2
BB	Bob Feller	Cleveland	154	142
SO	Bob Feller	Cleveland	426	246

NATIONAL LEAGUE LEADERS

CAT.	PLAYER	TEAM	STATS ADJUSTED	ACTUAL
BATTING				
HR	Johnny Mize	St. Louis	47	28
RBI	Frank McCormick	Cincinnati	138	128
BA	Johnny Mize	St. Louis	.342	.349
AB	Jimmy Brown	St. Louis	676	645
R	Billy Werber	Cincinnati	124	115
H	Frank McCormick	Cincinnati	212	209
2B	Enos Slaughter	St. Louis	57	52
3B	Billy Herman	Chicago	12	18
TB	Johnny Mize	St. Louis	399	353
SA	Johnny Mize	St. Louis	.676	.626
SB	Lee Handley	Pittsburgh	32	17
	Stan Hack	Chicago	31	17
PITCHING				
W	Bucky Walters	Cincinnati	28	27
L	Bob Klinger	Pittsburgh	18	17
	Max Butcher	Phi.-Pit.	18	17
SV	Clyde Shoun	St. Louis	24	9
	Bob Bowman	St. Louis	20	9
ERA	Bucky Walters	Cincinnati	2.44	2.29
G	Clyde Shoun	St. Louis	55	53
IP	Bucky Walters	Cincinnati	335	319
BB	Kirby Higbe	Chi.-Phi.	133	123
SO	Bucky Walters	Cincinnati	266	137
	Claude Passeau	Phi.-Chi.	259	137

1940 SEASON

REGULAR SEASON STANDINGS

AMERICAN LEAGUE

		ADJUSTED			ACTUAL			
	W	L	Pct.	GB	W	L	Pct.	Rk.
EAST								
X New York	93	69	.574	0	88	66	.571	3
Boston	86	76	.531	7	82	72	.532	4
Washington	67	95	.414	26	64	90	.416	7
Philadelphia	57	105	.352	36	54	100	.351	8
WEST								
X Detroit	95	67	.586	0	90	64	.584	1
Cleveland	94	68	.580	1	89	65	.578	2
Chicago	86	76	.531	9	82	72	.532	4
St. Louis	70	92	.432	25	67	87	.435	6

NATIONAL LEAGUE

		ADJUSTED			ACTUAL			
	W	L	Pct.	GB	W	L	Pct.	Rk.
EAST								
X Brooklyn	93	69	.574	0	88	65	.575	2
New York	77	85	.475	16	72	80	.474	6
Boston	69	93	.426	24	65	87	.428	7
Philadelphia	53	109	.327	40	50	103	.327	8
WEST								
X Cincinnati	106	56	.654	0	100	53	.654	1
St. Louis	89	73	.549	17	84	69	.549	3
Pittsburgh	82	80	.506	24	78	76	.506	4
Chicago	79	83	.488	27	75	79	.487	5

SIMULATED PLAYOFFS

AMERICAN LEAGUE

ALCS	W	1	2	3	4		%
New York Yankees	0	1	5	2	2		49
Detroit Tigers	4	10	6	7	8		51

NATIONAL LEAGUE

NLCS	W	1	2	3	4	5	6	7	%
Brooklyn Dodgers	3	4	2	1	1	4	1	0	22
Cincinnati Reds	4	3	1	6	4	3	2	1	78

WORLD SERIES

WS*	W	1	2	3	4	5	6	7	%
Detroit Tigers	3	7	3	7	2	8	0	1	37
Cincinnati Reds	4	2	5	4	5	0	4	2	63

ACTUAL WINNERS

American League: Detroit Tigers
National League: Cincinnati Reds
World Series: Cincinnati Reds

OUTSTANDING PERFORMANCES

AWARD WINNERS

LG.	PLAYER	TEAM	STATS ADJUSTED	ACTUAL
MOST VALUABLE PLAYERS				
AL	Hank Greenberg	Detroit	60 HR, 170 RBI, .343 BA, $28.8 MIL	41 HR, 150 RBI, .340 BA
NL	Frank McCormick	Cincinnati	31 HR, 143 RBI, .311 BA, $12.8 MIL	19 HR, 127 RBI, .309 BA
CY YOUNG AWARDS				
AL	Bob Feller	Cleveland	28-12 W-L, 4 SV, 2.90 ERA, $52.2 MIL	27-11 W-L, 4 SV, 2.61 ERA
NL	Bucky Walters	Cincinnati	23-11 W-L, 0 SV, 2.74 ERA, $33.6 MIL	22-10 W-L, 0 SV, 2.48 ERA

AMERICAN LEAGUE LEADERS

CAT.	PLAYER	TEAM	ADJUSTED	ACTUAL
BATTING				
HR	Hank Greenberg	Detroit	60	41
RBI	Hank Greenberg	Detroit	170	150
BA	Joe DiMaggio	New York	.354	.352
AB	Doc Cramer	Boston	696	661
R	Ted Williams	Boston	151	134
H	Doc Cramer	Boston	212	200
	Barney McCosky	Detroit	210	200
	Rip Radcliff	St. Louis	209	200
2B	Hank Greenberg	Detroit	46	50
3B	Barney McCosky	Detroit	14	19
TB	Hank Greenberg	Detroit	438	384
SA	Hank Greenberg	Detroit	.730	.670
SB	George Case	Washington	68	35
PITCHING				
W	Bob Feller	Cleveland	28	27
L	George Caster	Philadelphia	20	19
	Dutch Leonard	Washington	20	19
SV	Al Benton	Detroit	25	17
ERA	Bob Feller	Cleveland	2.90	2.61
G	Bob Feller	Cleveland	45	43
IP	Bob Feller	Cleveland	335	320.1
BB	Ken Chase	Washington	162	143
SO	Bob Feller	Cleveland	436	261

NATIONAL LEAGUE LEADERS

CAT.	PLAYER	TEAM	ADJUSTED	ACTUAL
BATTING				
HR	Johnny Mize	St. Louis	63	43
RBI	Johnny Mize	St. Louis	153	137
BA	Debs Garms	Pittsburgh	.358	.355
AB	Frank McCormick	Cincinnati	646	618
R	Arky Vaughan	Pittsburgh	126	113
H	Stan Hack	Chicago	202	191
	Frank McCormick	Cincinnati	201	191
2B	Frank McCormick	Cincinnati	44	44
3B	Arky Vaughan	Pittsburgh	9	15
TB	Johnny Mize	St. Louis	419	368
SA	Johnny Mize	St. Louis	.697	.636
SB	Lonny Frey	Cincinnati	42	22
PITCHING				
W	Bucky Walters	Cincinnati	23	22
L	Hugh Mulcahy	Philadelphia	23	22
SV	Jumbo Brown	New York	19	7
	Mace Brown	Pittsburgh	18	7
	Joe Beggs	Cincinnati	15	7
ERA	Bucky Walters	Cincinnati	2.74	2.48
G	Clyde Shoun	St. Louis	56	54
IP	Bucky Walters	Cincinnati	322	305
BB	Kirby Higbe	Philadelphia	136	121
SO	Kirby Higbe	Philadelphia	250	137

1941 SEASON

REGULAR SEASON STANDINGS

AMERICAN LEAGUE

		ADJUSTED				ACTUAL			
	W	L	Pct.	GB	W	L	Pct.	Rk.
EAST								
X New York	106	56	.654	0	101	53	.656	1
Boston	88	74	.543	18	84	70	.545	2
Washington	74	88	.457	32	70	84	.455	6
Philadelphia	67	95	.414	39	64	90	.416	8
WEST								
X Chicago	81	81	.500	0	77	77	.500	3
Cleveland	79	83	.488	2	75	79	.487	4
Detroit	79	83	.488	2	75	79	.487	4
St. Louis	74	88	.457	7	70	84	.455	6

NATIONAL LEAGUE

		ADJUSTED				ACTUAL			
	W	L	Pct.	GB	W	L	Pct.	Rk.
EAST								
X Brooklyn	105	57	.648	0	100	54	.649	1
New York	78	84	.481	27	74	79	.484	5
Boston	65	97	.401	40	62	92	.403	7
Philadelphia	45	117	.278	60	43	111	.279	8
WEST								
X St. Louis	103	59	.636	0	97	56	.634	2
Cincinnati	93	69	.574	10	88	66	.571	3
Pittsburgh	85	77	.525	18	81	73	.526	4
Chicago	74	88	.457	29	70	84	.455	6

SIMULATED PLAYOFFS

AMERICAN LEAGUE

ALCS	W	1	2	3	4		%
New York Yankees	4	2	5	4	5		84
Chicago White Sox	0	1	4	1	2		16

NATIONAL LEAGUE

NLCS	W	1	2	3	4	5	6	7	%
Brooklyn Dodgers	4	4	6	6	2	5	2	6	63
St. Louis Cardinals	3	5	3	5	3	3	5	4	37

WORLD SERIES

WS*	W	1	2	3	4	5		%
New York Yankees	4	3	2	2	7	3		45
Brooklyn Dodgers	1	2	3	1	4	1		55

ACTUAL WINNERS

American League: New York Yankees
National League: Brooklyn Dodgers
World Series: New York Yankees

OUTSTANDING PERFORMANCES

AWARD WINNERS

LG.	PLAYER	TEAM	STATS ADJUSTED	ACTUAL
MOST VALUABLE PLAYERS				
AL	Joe DiMaggio	New York	52 HR, 144 RBI, .366 BA, $19.9 MIL	30 HR, 125 RBI, .357 BA
NL	Dolph Camilli	Brooklyn	53 HR, 138 RBI, .293 BA, $13.0 MIL	34 HR, 120 RBI, .285 BA
CY YOUNG AWARDS				
AL	Bob Feller	Cleveland	26-14 W-L, 4 SV, 3.69 ERA, $55.3 MIL	25-13 W-L, 2 SV, 3.15 ERA
NL	Whit Wyatt	Brooklyn	23-10 W-L, 3 SV, 2.74 ERA, $25.1 MIL	22-10 W-L, 1 SV, 2.34 ERA

AMERICAN LEAGUE LEADERS

CAT.	PLAYER	TEAM	STATS ADJUSTED	ACTUAL
BATTING				
HR	Ted Williams	Boston	57	37
RBI	Joe DiMaggio	New York	144	125
BA	Ted Williams	Boston	.417	.406
AB	Doc Cramer	Washington	686	660
R	Ted Williams	Boston	157	135
H	Cecil Travis	Washington	233	218
2B	Lou Boudreau	Cleveland	53	45
3B	Jeff Heath	Cleveland	11	20
TB	Joe DiMaggio	New York	412	348
SA	Ted Williams	Boston	.838	.735
SB	George Case	Washington	68	33
PITCHING				
W	Bob Feller	Cleveland	26	25
L	Bobo Newsom	Detroit	21	20
SV	Johnny Murphy	New York	22	15
ERA	Thornton Lee	Chicago	2.77	2.37
G	Bob Feller	Cleveland	46	44
IP	Bob Feller	Cleveland	359	343
BB	Bob Feller	Cleveland	204	194
SO	Bob Feller	Cleveland	451	260

NATIONAL LEAGUE LEADERS

CAT.	PLAYER	TEAM	STATS ADJUSTED	ACTUAL
BATTING				
HR	Dolph Camilli	Brooklyn	53	34
RBI	Dolph Camilli	Brooklyn	138	120
BA	Pete Reiser	Brooklyn	.353	.343
AB	Johnny Rucker	New York	648	622
R	Pete Reiser	Brooklyn	134	117
H	Stan Hack	Chicago	200	186
2B	Pete Reiser	Brooklyn	46	39
	Johnny Mize	St. Louis	40	39
3B	Pete Reiser	Brooklyn	10	17
TB	Pete Reiser	Brooklyn	351	299
SA	Pete Reiser	Brooklyn	.636	.558
SB	Danny Murtaugh	Philadelphia	37	18
PITCHING				
W	Kirby Higbe	Brooklyn	23	22
	Whit Wyatt	Brooklyn	23	22
L	Rip Sewell	Pittsburgh	18	17
SV	Jumbo Brown	New York	17	8
ERA	Elmer Riddle	Cincinnati	2.62	2.24
G	Kirby Higbe	Brooklyn	50	48
IP	Bucky Walters	Cincinnati	318	302
BB	Kirby Higbe	Brooklyn	137	132
SO	Johnny Vander Meer	Cincinnati	341	202

1942 SEASON

REGULAR SEASON STANDINGS

AMERICAN LEAGUE

	ADJUSTED				ACTUAL			
	W	L	Pct.	GB	W	L	Pct.	Rk.
EAST								
X New York	108	54	.667	0	103	51	.669	1
Boston	99	63	.611	9	93	59	.612	2
Washington	67	95	.414	41	62	89	.411	7
Philadelphia	58	104	.358	50	55	99	.357	8
WEST								
X St. Louis	88	74	.543	0	82	69	.543	3
Cleveland	79	83	.488	9	75	79	.487	4
Detroit	77	85	.475	11	73	81	.474	5
Chicago	72	90	.444	16	66	82	.446	6

NATIONAL LEAGUE

	ADJUSTED				ACTUAL			
	W	L	Pct.	GB	W	L	Pct.	Rk.
EAST								
X Brooklyn	109	53	.673	0	104	50	.675	2
New York	91	71	.562	18	85	67	.559	3
Boston	65	97	.401	44	59	89	.399	7
Philadelphia	45	117	.278	64	42	109	.278	8
WEST								
X St. Louis	112	50	.691	0	106	48	.688	1
Cincinnati	81	81	.500	31	76	76	.500	4
Pittsburgh	73	89	.451	39	66	81	.449	5
Chicago	72	90	.444	40	68	86	.442	6

SIMULATED PLAYOFFS

AMERICAN LEAGUE

ALCS	W	1	2	3	4	5	6	7	%
New York Yankees	3	3	9	5	9	11	4	5	88
St. Louis Browns	4	4	4	6	7	5	6	6	12

NATIONAL LEAGUE

NLCS	W	1	2	3	4	%
Brooklyn Dodgers	4	3	5	5	3	44
St. Louis Cardinals	0	2	4	4	2	56

WORLD SERIES

WS	W	1	2	3	4	%
St. Louis Browns	0	0	6	1	1	26
Brooklyn Dodgers	4	2	7	9	14	74

ACTUAL WINNERS

American League: New York Yankees
National League: St. Louis Cardinals
World Series: St. Louis Cardinals

OUTSTANDING PERFORMANCES

AWARD WINNERS

LG.	PLAYER	TEAM	STATS ADJUSTED	ACTUAL
MOST VALUABLE PLAYERS				
AL	Joe Gordon	New York	37 HR, 132 RBI, .342 BA, $18.7 MIL	18 HR, 103 RBI, .322 BA
NL	Mort Cooper	St. Louis	23-7 W-L, 0 SV, 2.33 ERA, $27.0 MIL	22-7 W-L, 0 SV, 1.78 ERA
CY YOUNG AWARDS				
AL	Tex Hughson	Boston	24-6 W-L, 8 SV, 3.39 ERA, $25.8 MIL	22-6 W-L, 4 SV, 2.59 ERA
NL	Mort Cooper	St. Louis	23-7 W-L, 0 SV, 2.33 ERA, $27.0 MIL	22-7 W-L, 0 SV, 1.78 ERA

AMERICAN LEAGUE LEADERS

CAT.	PLAYER	TEAM	STATS ADJUSTED	ACTUAL
BATTING				
HR	Ted Williams	Boston	65	36
RBI	Ted Williams	Boston	178	137
BA	Ted Williams	Boston	.381	.356
AB	Doc Cramer	Detroit	655	630
R	Ted Williams	Boston	183	141
H	Johnny Pesky	Boston	233	205
2B	Don Kolloway	Chicago	68	40
3B	Stan Spence	Washington	15	15
TB	Ted Williams	Boston	441	338
SA	Ted Williams	Boston	.792	.648
SB	George Case	Washington	85	44
PITCHING				
W	Tex Hughson	Boston	24	22
L	Eddie Smith	Chicago	22	20
SV	Johnny Murphy	New York	16	11
ERA	Ted Lyons	Chicago	2.73	2.10
G	Joe Haynes	Chicago	44	40
IP	Tex Hughson	Boston	303	281
BB	Phil Marchildon	Philadelphia	155	140
SO	Tex Hughson	Boston	232	113
	Bobo Newsom	Washington	220	113

NATIONAL LEAGUE LEADERS

CAT.	PLAYER	TEAM	STATS ADJUSTED	ACTUAL
BATTING				
HR	Mel Ott	New York	50	30
RBI	Johnny Mize	New York	140	110
BA	Ernie Lombardi	Boston	.351	.330
AB	Jimmy Brown	St. Louis	631	606
R	Mel Ott	New York	151	118
H	Enos Slaughter	St. Louis	208	188
2B	Marty Marion	St. Louis	74	38
3B	Enos Slaughter	St. Louis	12	17
TB	Enos Slaughter	St. Louis	370	292
SA	Johnny Mize	New York	.637	.521
SB	Pete Reiser	Brooklyn	37	20
PITCHING				
W	Mort Cooper	St. Louis	23	22
L	Jim Tobin	Boston	23	21
SV	Hugh Casey	Brooklyn	31	13
ERA	Mort Cooper	St. Louis	2.33	1.78
G	Ace Adams	New York	64	61
IP	Jim Tobin	Boston	311	287.2
BB	Rube Melton	Philadelphia	128	114
SO	Johnny Vander Meer	Cincinnati	336	186

1943 SEASON

REGULAR SEASON STANDINGS

AMERICAN LEAGUE

	ADJUSTED				ACTUAL			
	W	L	Pct.	GB	W	L	Pct.	Rk.
EAST								
X New York	103	59	.636	0	98	56	.636	1
Washington	89	73	.549	14	84	69	.549	2
Boston	72	90	.444	31	68	84	.447	7
Philadelphia	52	110	.321	51	49	105	.318	8
WEST								
X Cleveland	87	75	.537	0	82	71	.536	3
Chicago	86	76	.531	1	82	72	.532	4
Detroit	82	80	.506	5	78	76	.506	5
St. Louis	77	85	.475	10	72	80	.474	6

NATIONAL LEAGUE

	ADJUSTED				ACTUAL			
	W	L	Pct.	GB	W	L	Pct.	Rk.
EAST								
X Brooklyn	86	76	.531	0	81	72	.529	3
Boston	72	90	.444	14	68	85	.444	6
Philadelphia	67	95	.414	19	64	90	.416	7
New York	58	104	.358	28	55	98	.359	8
WEST								
X St. Louis	111	51	.685	0	105	49	.682	1
Cincinnati	92	70	.568	19	87	67	.565	2
Pittsburgh	84	78	.519	27	80	74	.519	4
Chicago	78	84	.481	33	74	79	.484	5

SIMULATED PLAYOFFS

AMERICAN LEAGUE

ALCS	W	1	2	3	4	5	6	%
New York Yankees	2	8	4	3	2	0	2	67
Cleveland Indians	4	4	2	4	4	4	3	33

NATIONAL LEAGUE

NLCS	W	1	2	3	4	5	6	%
Brooklyn Dodgers	4	5	6	2	3	5	4	16
St. Louis Cardinals	2	0	1	10	6	4	2	84

WORLD SERIES

WS	W	1	2	3	4	5	6	%
Cleveland Indians	4	7	0	2	12	8	3	51
Brooklyn Dodgers	2	10	4	1	5	2	0	49

ACTUAL WINNERS

American League: New York Yankees
National League: St. Louis Cardinals
World Series: New York Yankees

OUTSTANDING PERFORMANCES

AWARD WINNERS

LG.	PLAYER	TEAM	STATS	
			ADJUSTED	ACTUAL
MOST VALUABLE PLAYERS				
AL	Spud Chandler	New York	21-4 W-L, 0 SV, 2.24 ERA, $17.3 MIL	20-4 W-L, 0 SV, 1.64 ERA
NL	Stan Musial	St. Louis	40 HR, 108 RBI, .379 BA, $18.6 MIL	13 HR, 81 RBI, .357 BA
CY YOUNG AWARDS				
AL	Spud Chandler	New York	21-4 W-L, 0 SV, 2.24 ERA, $17.3 MIL	20-4 W-L, 0 SV, 1.64 ERA
NL	Mort Cooper	St. Louis	22-8 W-L, 6 SV, 3.15 ERA, $32.2 MIL	21-8 W-L, 3 SV, 2.30 ERA

AMERICAN LEAGUE LEADERS

CAT.	PLAYER	TEAM	STATS	
			ADJUSTED	ACTUAL
BATTING				
HR	Rudy York	Detroit	65	34
RBI	Rudy York	Detroit	156	118
BA	Luke Appling	Chicago	.349	.328
AB	Dick Wakefield	Detroit	662	633
R	George Case	Washington	136	102
H	Dick Wakefield	Detroit	222	200
2B	Dick Wakefield	Detroit	54	38
3B	Wally Moses	Chicago	11	12
	Johnny Lindell	New York	10	12
TB	Rudy York	Detroit	392	301
SA	Rudy York	Detroit	.657	.527
SB	George Case	Washington	114	61
PITCHING				
W	Spud Chandler	New York	21	20
	Dizzy Trout	Detroit	21	20
L	Lum Harris	Philadelphia	22	21
SV	Gordon Maltzberger	Chicago	23	14
ERA	Spud Chandler	New York	2.24	1.64
G	Mace Brown	Boston	51	49
IP	Jim Bagby	Cleveland	288	273
BB	Hal Newhouser	Detroit	126	111
SO	Allie Reynolds	Cleveland	271	151

NATIONAL LEAGUE LEADERS

CAT.	PLAYER	TEAM	STATS	
			ADJUSTED	ACTUAL
BATTING				
HR	Bill Nicholson	Chicago	60	29
RBI	Bill Nicholson	Chicago	171	128
BA	Stan Musial	St. Louis	.379	.357
AB	Tommy Holmes	Boston	666	629
R	Arky Vaughan	Brooklyn	150	112
H	Stan Musial	St. Louis	247	220
2B	Stan Musial	St. Louis	63	48
3B	Stan Musial	St. Louis	14	20
TB	Stan Musial	St. Louis	458	347
SA	Stan Musial	St. Louis	.702	.562
SB	Arky Vaughan	Brooklyn	36	20
PITCHING				
W	Mort Cooper	St. Louis	22	21
	Elmer Riddle	Cincinnati	22	21
	Rip Sewell	Pittsburgh	22	21
L	Nate Andrews	Boston	21	20
SV	Les Webber	Brooklyn	26	10
ERA	Howie Pollet	St. Louis	2.36	1.75
G	Ace Adams	New York	73	70
IP	Al Javery	Boston	318	303
BB	Johnny Vander Meer	Cincinnati	184	162
SO	Johnny Vander Meer	Cincinnati	327	174

1944 SEASON

REGULAR SEASON STANDINGS

AMERICAN LEAGUE

	ADJUSTED				ACTUAL			
	W	L	Pct.	GB	W	L	Pct.	Rk.
EAST								
X New York	87	75	.537	0	83	71	.539	3
Boston	81	81	.500	6	77	77	.500	4
Philadelphia	76	86	.469	11	72	82	.468	5
Washington	67	95	.414	20	64	90	.416	8
WEST								
X St. Louis	94	68	.580	0	89	65	.578	1
Detroit	92	70	.568	2	88	66	.571	2
Cleveland	76	86	.469	18	72	82	.468	5
Chicago	75	87	.463	19	71	83	.461	7

NATIONAL LEAGUE

	ADJUSTED				ACTUAL			
	W	L	Pct.	GB	W	L	Pct.	Rk.
EAST								
X New York	71	91	.438	0	67	87	.435	5
Boston	68	94	.420	3	65	89	.422	6
Brooklyn	66	96	.407	5	63	91	.409	7
Philadelphia	65	97	.401	6	61	92	.399	8
WEST								
X St. Louis	110	52	.679	0	105	49	.682	1
Pittsburgh	95	67	.586	15	90	63	.588	2
Cincinnati	94	68	.580	16	89	65	.578	3
Chicago	79	83	.488	31	75	79	.487	4

SIMULATED PLAYOFFS

AMERICAN LEAGUE

ALCS	W	1	2	3	4	5	6	%
New York Yankees	2	2	4	5	5	1	4	36
St. Louis Browns	4	3	5	4	4	11	6	64

NATIONAL LEAGUE

NLCS	W	1	2	3	4		%
New York Giants	0	1	3	2	2		2
St. Louis Cardinals	4	5	8	3	13		98

WORLD SERIES

WS*	W	1	2	3	4	5	6	%
St. Louis Browns	2	2	2	6	1	0	1	19
St. Louis Cardinals	4	1	3	2	5	2	3	81

ACTUAL WINNERS

American League: St. Louis Browns
National League: St. Louis Cardinals
World Series: St. Louis Cardinals

OUTSTANDING PERFORMANCES

AWARD WINNERS

LG.	PLAYER	TEAM	STATS ADJUSTED	ACTUAL
MOST VALUABLE PLAYERS				
AL	Hal Newhouser	Detroit	30-9 W-L, 6 SV, 2.87 ERA, $41.0 MIL	29-9 W-L, 2 SV, 2.22 ERA
NL	Marty Marion	St. Louis	16 HR, 78 RBI, .275 BA, $7.4 MIL	6 HR, 63 RBI, .267 BA
CY YOUNG AWARDS				
AL	Dizzy Trout	Detroit	28-15 W-L, 0 SV, 2.75 ERA, $42.7 MIL	27-14 W-L, 0 SV, 2.12 ERA
NL	Bucky Walters	Cincinnati	24-8 W-L, 3 SV, 3.10 ERA, $25.8 MIL	23-8 W-L, 1 SV, 2.40 ERA

AMERICAN LEAGUE LEADERS

CAT.	PLAYER	TEAM	STATS ADJUSTED	ACTUAL
BATTING				
HR	Nick Etten	New York	43	22
RBI	Vern Stephens	St. Louis	138	109
BA	Lou Boudreau	Cleveland	.339	.327
AB	Mickey Rocco	Cleveland	682	653
R	Snuffy Stirnweiss	New York	158	125
H	Snuffy Stirnweiss	New York	223	205
2B	Lou Boudreau	Cleveland	74	45
3B	Snuffy Stirnweiss	New York	11	16
	Johnny Lindell	New York	8	16
TB	Johnny Lindell	New York	372	297
SA	Bobby Doerr	Boston	.630	.528
SB	Snuffy Stirnweiss	New York	113	55
PITCHING				
W	Hal Newhouser	Detroit	30	29
L	Bill Dietrich	Chicago	18	17
	Early Wynn	Washington	18	17
SV	Joe Berry	Philadelphia	26	12
	George Caster	St. Louis	24	12
	Gordon Maltzberger	Chicago	24	12
ERA	Dizzy Trout	Detroit	2.75	2.12
G	Joe Heving	Cleveland	66	63
IP	Dizzy Trout	Detroit	367	352.1
BB	Rufe Gentry	Detroit	125	108
SO	Hal Newhouser	Detroit	359	187

NATIONAL LEAGUE LEADERS

CAT.	PLAYER	TEAM	STATS ADJUSTED	ACTUAL
BATTING				
HR	Bill Nicholson	Chicago	59	33
RBI	Bill Nicholson	Chicago	151	122
BA	Dixie Walker	Brooklyn	.370	.357
AB	Woody Williams	Cincinnati	682	653
R	Bill Nicholson	Chicago	144	116
H	Stan Musial	St. Louis	211	197
	Phil Cavarretta	Chicago	210	197
2B	Stan Musial	St. Louis	62	51
3B	Johnny Barrett	Pittsburgh	14	19
TB	Bill Nicholson	Chicago	389	317
SA	Stan Musial	St. Louis	.659	.549
SB	Johnny Barrett	Pittsburgh	55	28
PITCHING				
W	Bucky Walters	Cincinnati	24	23
L	Ken Raffensberger	Philadelphia	21	20
SV	Ace Adams	New York	31	13
ERA	Ed Heusser	Cincinnati	3.08	2.38
G	Ace Adams	New York	68	65
IP	Bill Voiselle	New York	327	312.2
BB	Hal Gregg	Brooklyn	164	137
SO	Bill Voiselle	New York	318	161

1945 SEASON

REGULAR SEASON STANDINGS

AMERICAN LEAGUE

		ADJUSTED				ACTUAL			
	W	L	Pct.	GB	W	L	Pct.	Rk.
EAST								
X Washington	92	70	.568	0	87	67	.565	2
New York	86	76	.531	6	81	71	.533	4
Boston	75	87	.463	17	71	83	.461	7
Philadelphia	56	106	.346	36	52	98	.347	8
WEST								
X Detroit	93	69	.574	0	88	65	.575	1
St. Louis	87	75	.537	6	81	70	.536	3
Cleveland	82	80	.506	11	73	72	.503	5
Chicago	77	85	.475	16	71	78	.477	6

NATIONAL LEAGUE

		ADJUSTED				ACTUAL			
	W	L	Pct.	GB	W	L	Pct.	Rk.
EAST								
X Brooklyn	92	70	.568	0	87	67	.565	3
New York	83	79	.512	9	78	74	.513	5
Boston	72	90	.444	20	67	85	.441	6
Philadelphia	48	114	.296	44	46	108	.299	8
WEST								
X Chicago	103	59	.636	0	98	56	.636	1
St. Louis	100	62	.617	3	95	59	.617	2
Pittsburgh	86	76	.531	17	82	72	.532	4
Cincinnati	64	98	.395	39	61	93	.396	7

SIMULATED PLAYOFFS

AMERICAN LEAGUE

ALCS	W	1	2	3	4	5	6	7	%
Washington Senators	3	3	4	1	3	2	4	3	48
Detroit Tigers	4	2	5	7	2	5	2	4	52

NATIONAL LEAGUE

NLCS	W	1	2	3	4	5		%
Brooklyn Dodgers	1	5	7	6	0	6		21
Chicago Cubs	4	4	8	11	5	16		79

WORLD SERIES

WS*	W	1	2	3	4	5	6	7	%
Detroit Tigers	4	0	4	0	4	8	7	9	30
Chicago Cubs	3	9	1	3	1	4	8	3	70

ACTUAL WINNERS

American League: Detroit Tigers
National League: Chicago Cubs
World Series: Detroit Tigers

OUTSTANDING PERFORMANCES

AWARD WINNERS

			STATS	
LG.	PLAYER	TEAM	ADJUSTED	ACTUAL
MOST VALUABLE PLAYERS				
AL	Hal Newhouser	Detroit	26-9 W-L, 4 SV, 2.30 ERA, $42.6 MIL	25-9 W-L, 2 SV, 1.81 ERA
NL	Phil Cavarretta	Chicago	19 HR, 121 RBI, .369 BA, $12.2 MIL	6 HR, 97 RBI, .355 BA
CY YOUNG AWARDS				
AL	Hal Newhouser	Detroit	26-9 W-L, 4 SV, 2.30 ERA, $42.6 MIL	25-9 W-L, 2 SV, 1.81 ERA
NL	Red Barrett	Bos.-St.L.	24-13 W-L, 5 SV, 3.82 ERA, $20.5 MIL	23-12 W-L, 2 SV, 3.00 ERA

AMERICAN LEAGUE LEADERS

			STATS	
CAT.	PLAYER	TEAM	ADJUSTED	ACTUAL
BATTING				
HR	Vern Stephens	St. Louis	46	24
RBI	Nick Etten	New York	141	111
BA	Snuffy Stirnweiss	New York	.319	.309
AB	Snuffy Stirnweiss	New York	674	632
R	Snuffy Stirnweiss	New York	136	107
H	Snuffy Stirnweiss	New York	215	195
2B	Wally Moses	Chicago	67	35
3B	Snuffy Stirnweiss	New York	17	22
TB	Snuffy Stirnweiss	New York	387	301
SA	Snuffy Stirnweiss	New York	.574	.476
SB	Snuffy Stirnweiss	New York	62	33
PITCHING				
W	Hal Newhouser	Detroit	26	25
L	Bobo Newsom	Philadelphia	21	20
SV	Jim Turner	New York	19	10
ERA	Hal Newhouser	Detroit	2.30	1.81
G	Joe Berry	Philadelphia	55	52
IP	Hal Newhouser	Detroit	329	313.1
BB	Allie Reynolds	Cleveland	151	130
SO	Hal Newhouser	Detroit	400	212

NATIONAL LEAGUE LEADERS

			STATS	
CAT.	PLAYER	TEAM	ADJUSTED	ACTUAL
BATTING				
HR	Tommy Holmes	Boston	57	28
RBI	Dixie Walker	Brooklyn	154	124
BA	Phil Cavarretta	Chicago	.369	.355
AB	Dain Clay	Cincinnati	690	656
R	Eddie Stanky	Brooklyn	159	128
H	Tommy Holmes	Boston	244	224
2B	Tommy Holmes	Boston	45	47
3B	Luis Olmo	Brooklyn	9	13
TB	Tommy Holmes	Boston	466	367
SA	Tommy Holmes	Boston	.697	.577
SB	Red Schoendienst	St. Louis	48	26
PITCHING				
W	Red Barrett	Bos.-St.L.	24	23
L	Dick Barrett	Philadelphia	21	20
SV	Andy Karl	Philadelphia	36	15
	Ace Adams	New York	33	15
ERA	Hank Borowy	Chicago	2.70	2.13
G	Andy Karl	Philadelphia	70	67
IP	Red Barrett	Bos.-St.L.	297	284.2
BB	Hal Gregg	Brooklyn	133	120
SO	Preacher Roe	Pittsburgh	278	148

1946 SEASON

REGULAR SEASON STANDINGS

AMERICAN LEAGUE

	ADJUSTED				ACTUAL			
	W	L	Pct.	GB	W	L	Pct.	Rk.
EAST								
X Boston	109	53	.673	0	104	50	.675	1
New York	91	71	.562	18	87	67	.565	3
Washington	80	82	.494	29	76	78	.494	4
Philadelphia	52	110	.321	57	49	105	.318	8
WEST								
X Detroit	97	65	.599	0	92	62	.597	2
Chicago	78	84	.481	19	74	80	.481	5
Cleveland	72	90	.444	25	68	86	.442	6
St. Louis	69	93	.426	28	66	88	.429	7

NATIONAL LEAGUE

	ADJUSTED				ACTUAL			
	W	L	Pct.	GB	W	L	Pct.	Rk.
EAST								
X Brooklyn	101	61	.623	0	96	58	.623	1
Boston	86	76	.531	15	81	72	.529	4
Philadelphia	73	89	.451	28	69	85	.448	5
New York	64	98	.395	37	61	93	.396	8
WEST								
X St. Louis	101	61	.623	0	96	58	.623	1
Chicago	87	75	.537	14	82	71	.536	3
Cincinnati	70	92	.432	31	67	87	.435	6
Pittsburgh	66	96	.407	35	63	91	.409	7

SIMULATED PLAYOFFS

AMERICAN LEAGUE

ALCS	W	1	2	3	4	5	%
Boston Red Sox	1	11	4	1	3	3	49
Detroit Tigers	4	4	8	2	4	5	51

NATIONAL LEAGUE

NLCS**	W	1	2	3	4	5	%
Brooklyn Dodgers	1	2	4	4	2	2	42
St. Louis Cardinals	4	4	8	1	3	7	58

WORLD SERIES

WS	W	1	2	3	4	5	6	%
Detroit Tigers	2	6	1	3	2	5	2	40
St. Louis Cardinals	4	2	5	5	3	3	3	60

ACTUAL WINNERS

American League: Boston Red Sox
National League: St. Louis Cardinals
World Series: St. Louis Cardinals

OUTSTANDING PERFORMANCES

AWARD WINNERS

LG.	PLAYER	TEAM	STATS ADJUSTED	ACTUAL
MOST VALUABLE PLAYERS				
AL	Ted Williams	Boston	64 HR, 158 RBI, .361 BA, $38.7 MIL	38 HR, 123 RBI, .342 BA
NL	Stan Musial	St. Louis	37 HR, 131 RBI, .386 BA, $27.2 MIL	16 HR, 103 RBI, .365 BA
CY YOUNG AWARDS				
AL	Hal Newhouser	Detroit	27-9 W-L, 2 SV, 2.54 ERA, $51.4 MIL	26-9 W-L, 1 SV, 1.94 ERA
NL	Howie Pollet	St. Louis	22-11 W-L, 7 SV, 2.77 ERA, $19.7 MIL	21-10 W-L, 5 SV, 2.10 ERA

AMERICAN LEAGUE LEADERS

CAT.	PLAYER	TEAM	STATS ADJUSTED	ACTUAL
BATTING				
HR	Hank Greenberg	Detroit	68	44
RBI	Hank Greenberg	Detroit	163	127
BA	Mickey Vernon	Washington	.372	.353
AB	Johnny Pesky	Boston	645	621
R	Ted Williams	Boston	182	142
H	Johnny Pesky	Boston	228	208
2B	Mickey Vernon	Washington	72	51
3B	Hank Edwards	Cleveland	10	16
TB	Ted Williams	Boston	426	343
SA	Ted Williams	Boston	.796	.667
SB	George Case	Cleveland	57	28
PITCHING				
W	Bob Feller	Cleveland	27	26
	Hal Newhouser	Detroit	27	26
L	Dick Fowler	Philadelphia	17	16
	Lou Knerr	Philadelphia	17	16
	Phil Marchildon	Philadelphia	17	16
SV	Bob Klinger	Boston	17	9
ERA	Hal Newhouser	Detroit	2.54	1.94
G	Bob Feller	Cleveland	50	48
IP	Bob Feller	Cleveland	387	371.1
BB	Bob Feller	Cleveland	161	153
SO	Bob Feller	Cleveland	541	348

NATIONAL LEAGUE LEADERS

CAT.	PLAYER	TEAM	STATS ADJUSTED	ACTUAL
BATTING				
HR	Ralph Kiner	Pittsburgh	38	23
RBI	Enos Slaughter	St. Louis	166	130
BA	Stan Musial	St. Louis	.386	.365
AB	Stan Musial	St. Louis	648	624
R	Stan Musial	St. Louis	158	124
H	Stan Musial	St. Louis	250	228
2B	Stan Musial	St. Louis	64	50
3B	Stan Musial	St. Louis	13	20
TB	Stan Musial	St. Louis	451	366
SA	Stan Musial	St. Louis	.696	.587
SB	Pete Reiser	Brooklyn	69	34
PITCHING				
W	Howie Pollet	St. Louis	22	21
L	Dave Koslo	New York	20	19
SV	Ken Raffensberger	Philadelphia	12	6
ERA	Howie Pollet	St. Louis	2.77	2.10
G	Ken Trinkle	New York	50	48
IP	Howie Pollet	St. Louis	279	266
BB	Monte Kennedy	New York	123	116
SO	Johnny Schmitz	Chicago	226	135

1947 SEASON

REGULAR SEASON STANDINGS

AMERICAN LEAGUE

		ADJUSTED				ACTUAL		
	W	L	Pct.	GB	W	L	Pct.	Rk.
EAST								
X New York	102	60	.630	0	97	57	.630	1
Boston	87	75	.537	15	83	71	.539	3
Philadelphia	82	80	.506	20	78	76	.506	5
Washington	67	95	.414	35	64	90	.416	7
WEST								
X Detroit	90	72	.556	0	85	69	.552	2
Cleveland	84	78	.519	6	80	74	.519	4
Chicago	74	88	.457	16	70	84	.455	6
St. Louis	62	100	.383	28	59	95	.383	8

NATIONAL LEAGUE

		ADJUSTED				ACTUAL		
	W	L	Pct.	GB	W	L	Pct.	Rk.
EAST								
X Brooklyn	99	63	.611	0	94	60	.610	1
Boston	90	72	.556	9	86	68	.558	3
New York	85	77	.525	14	81	73	.526	4
Philadelphia	65	97	.401	34	62	92	.403	7
WEST								
X St. Louis	94	68	.580	0	89	65	.578	2
Cincinnati	77	85	.475	17	73	81	.474	5
Chicago	73	89	.451	21	69	85	.448	6
Pittsburgh	65	97	.401	29	62	92	.403	7

SIMULATED PLAYOFFS

AMERICAN LEAGUE

ALCS	W	1	2	3	4	5		%
New York Yankees	4	5	2	3	10	3		72
Detroit Tigers	1	3	4	1	1	1		28

NATIONAL LEAGUE

NLCS	W	1	2	3	4	5	6	%
Brooklyn Dodgers	2	8	2	0	6	1	5	45
St. Louis Cardinals	4	7	3	12	2	9	8	55

WORLD SERIES

WS	W	1	2	3	4	5		%
New York Yankees	1	4	5	4	5	7		60
St. Louis Cardinals	4	5	3	7	6	10		40

ACTUAL WINNERS

American League: New York Yankees
National League: Brooklyn Dodgers
World Series: New York Yankees

OUTSTANDING PERFORMANCES

AWARD WINNERS

LG.	PLAYER	TEAM	STATS ADJUSTED	ACTUAL
MOST VALUABLE PLAYERS				
AL	Joe DiMaggio	New York	33 HR, 114 RBI, .325 BA, $13.1 MIL	20 HR, 97 RBI, .315 BA
NL	Bob Elliott	Boston	35 HR, 135 RBI, .328 BA, $15.7 MIL	22 HR, 113 RBI, .317 BA
CY YOUNG AWARDS				
AL	Joe Page	New York	15-8 W-L, 27 SV, 2.90 ERA, $9.9 MIL	14-8 W-L, 17 SV, 2.48 ERA
NL	Ewell Blackwell	Cincinnati	23-8 W-L, 0 SV, 2.89 ERA, $25.5 MIL	22-8 W-L, 0 SV, 2.47 ERA

AMERICAN LEAGUE LEADERS

CAT.	PLAYER	TEAM	STATS ADJUSTED	ACTUAL
BATTING				
HR	Ted Williams	Boston	49	32
RBI	Ted Williams	Boston	133	114
BA	Ted Williams	Boston	.354	.343
AB	Johnny Pesky	Boston	659	638
R	Ted Williams	Boston	146	125
H	Johnny Pesky	Boston	221	207
2B	Lou Boudreau	Cleveland	64	45
3B	Tommy Henrich	New York	8	13
TB	Ted Williams	Boston	392	335
SA	Ted Williams	Boston	.719	.634
SB	Bob Dillinger	St. Louis	82	34
PITCHING				
W	Bob Feller	Cleveland	20	20
L	Hal Newhouser	Detroit	17	17
SV	Ed Klieman	Cleveland	32	17
	Joe Page	New York	27	17
ERA	Joe Haynes	Chicago	2.82	2.42
G	Ed Klieman	Cleveland	60	58
IP	Bob Feller	Cleveland	306	299
BB	Phil Marchildon	Philadelphia	139	141
SO	Bob Feller	Cleveland	330	196

NATIONAL LEAGUE LEADERS

CAT.	PLAYER	TEAM	STATS ADJUSTED	ACTUAL
BATTING				
HR	Ralph Kiner	Pittsburgh	70	51
	Johnny Mize	New York	70	51
RBI	Johnny Mize	New York	163	138
BA	Harry Walker	St.L.-Phi.	.375	.363
AB	Red Schoendienst	St. Louis	685	659
R	Johnny Mize	New York	162	137
H	Tommy Holmes	Boston	208	191
2B	Eddie Miller	Cincinnati	44	38
3B	Harry Walker	St.L.-Phi.	15	16
TB	Ralph Kiner	Pittsburgh	426	361
SA	Ralph Kiner	Pittsburgh	.726	.639
SB	Jackie Robinson	Brooklyn	69	29
PITCHING				
W	Ewell Blackwell	Cincinnati	23	22
L	Johnny Schmitz	Chicago	19	18
SV	Hugh Casey	Brooklyn	27	18
ERA	Warren Spahn	Boston	2.72	2.33
G	Ken Trinkle	New York	65	62
IP	Warren Spahn	Boston	304	289.2
BB	Kirby Higbe	Bkn.-Pit.	121	122
SO	Ewell Blackwell	Cincinnati	333	193

1948 SEASON

REGULAR SEASON STANDINGS

AMERICAN LEAGUE

	W	L	Pct.	GB	W	L	Pct.	Rk.
		ADJUSTED				ACTUAL		
EAST								
X Boston	101	61	.623	0	96	58	.623	1
New York	99	63	.611	2	94	60	.610	3
Philadelphia	89	73	.549	12	84	70	.545	4
Washington	59	103	.364	42	56	97	.366	7
WEST								
X Cleveland	101	61	.623	0	96	58	.623	1
Detroit	82	80	.506	19	78	76	.506	5
St. Louis	63	99	.389	38	59	94	.386	6
Chicago	54	108	.333	47	51	101	.336	8

NATIONAL LEAGUE

	W	L	Pct.	GB	W	L	Pct.	Rk.
		ADJUSTED				ACTUAL		
EAST								
X Boston	96	66	.593	0	91	62	.595	1
Brooklyn	88	74	.543	8	84	70	.545	3
New York	82	80	.506	14	78	76	.506	5
Philadelphia	70	92	.432	26	66	88	.429	6
WEST								
X St. Louis	90	72	.556	0	85	69	.552	2
Pittsburgh	87	75	.537	3	83	71	.539	4
Cincinnati	68	94	.420	22	64	89	.418	7
Chicago	67	95	.414	23	64	90	.416	8

SIMULATED PLAYOFFS

AMERICAN LEAGUE

ALCS**	W	1	2	3	4	5	6	%
Boston Red Sox	2	3	6	7	0	3	3	30
Cleveland Indians	4	8	4	0	4	8	9	70

NATIONAL LEAGUE

NLCS	W	1	2	3	4	5	6	%
Boston Braves	4	3	2	2	4	4	4	55
St. Louis Cardinals	2	2	4	3	3	2	1	45

WORLD SERIES

WS*	W	1	2	3	4	5	6	%
Cleveland Indians	4	0	4	2	2	5	4	58
Boston Braves	2	1	1	0	1	11	3	42

ACTUAL WINNERS

American League: Cleveland Indians
National League: Boston Braves
World Series: Cleveland Indians

OUTSTANDING PERFORMANCES

AWARD WINNERS

LG.	PLAYER	TEAM	STATS ADJUSTED	ACTUAL
MOST VALUABLE PLAYERS				
AL	Lou Boudreau	Cleveland	30 HR, 119 RBI, .364 BA, $12.5 MIL	18 HR, 106 RBI, .355 BA
NL	Stan Musial	St. Louis	62 HR, 148 RBI, .385 BA, $31.7 MIL	39 HR, 131 RBI, .376 BA
CY YOUNG AWARDS				
AL	Bob Lemon	Cleveland	21-15 W-L, 4 SV, 3.11 ERA, $26.4 MIL	20-14 W-L, 2 SV, 2.82 ERA
NL	Johnny Sain	Boston	25-16 W-L, 2 SV, 2.86 ERA, $40.2 MIL	24-15 W-L, 1 SV, 2.60 ERA

AMERICAN LEAGUE LEADERS

CAT.	PLAYER	TEAM	STATS ADJUSTED	ACTUAL
BATTING				
HR	Joe DiMaggio	New York	59	39
RBI	Joe DiMaggio	New York	177	155
BA	Ted Williams	Boston	.379	.369
AB	Dom DiMaggio	Boston	677	648
R	Tommy Henrich	New York	157	138
H	Bob Dillinger	St. Louis	221	207
2B	Ted Williams	Boston	47	44
3B	Tommy Henrich	New York	7	14
TB	Joe DiMaggio	New York	420	355
SA	Ted Williams	Boston	.689	.615
SB	Bob Dillinger	St. Louis	62	28
PITCHING				
W	Hal Newhouser	Detroit	22	21
L	Fred Sanford	St. Louis	22	21
SV	Russ Christopher	Cleveland	29	17
ERA	Gene Bearden	Cleveland	2.67	2.43
G	Joe Page	New York	58	55
IP	Bob Lemon	Cleveland	307	293.2
BB	Bill Wight	Chicago	130	135
SO	Bob Feller	Cleveland	290	164

NATIONAL LEAGUE LEADERS

CAT.	PLAYER	TEAM	STATS ADJUSTED	ACTUAL
BATTING				
HR	Johnny Mize	New York	56	40
	Ralph Kiner	Pittsburgh	55	40
RBI	Stan Musial	St. Louis	148	131
BA	Stan Musial	St. Louis	.385	.376
AB	Stan Rojek	Pittsburgh	666	641
R	Stan Musial	St. Louis	153	135
H	Stan Musial	St. Louis	246	230
2B	Stan Musial	St. Louis	50	46
3B	Stan Musial	St. Louis	10	18
TB	Stan Musial	St. Louis	502	429
SA	Stan Musial	St. Louis	.786	.702
SB	Richie Ashburn	Philadelphia	71	32
PITCHING				
W	Johnny Sain	Boston	25	24
L	Dutch Leonard	Philadelphia	18	17
SV	Harry Gumbert	Cincinnati	29	17
ERA	Harry Brecheen	St. Louis	2.48	2.24
G	Harry Gumbert	Cincinnati	65	61
IP	Johnny Sain	Boston	330	314.2
BB	Johnny Vander Meer	Cincinnati	120	124
SO	Harry Brecheen	St. Louis	255	149

1949 SEASON

REGULAR SEASON STANDINGS

AMERICAN LEAGUE

		ADJUSTED				ACTUAL			
	W	L	Pct.	GB	W	L	Pct.	Rk.
EAST								
X New York	102	60	.630	0	97	57	.630	1
Boston	101	61	.623	1	96	58	.623	2
Philadelphia	85	77	.525	17	81	73	.526	5
Washington	53	109	.327	49	50	104	.325	8
WEST								
X Cleveland	94	68	.580	0	89	65	.578	3
Detroit	91	71	.562	3	87	67	.565	4
Chicago	66	96	.407	28	63	91	.409	6
St. Louis	56	106	.346	38	53	101	.344	7

NATIONAL LEAGUE

		ADJUSTED				ACTUAL			
	W	L	Pct.	GB	W	L	Pct.	Rk.
EAST								
X Brooklyn	102	60	.630	0	97	57	.630	1
Philadelphia	85	77	.525	17	81	73	.526	3
Boston	79	83	.488	23	75	79	.487	4
New York	77	85	.475	25	73	81	.474	5
WEST								
X St. Louis	101	61	.623	0	96	58	.623	2
Pittsburgh	75	87	.463	26	71	83	.461	6
Cincinnati	65	97	.401	36	62	92	.403	7
Chicago	64	98	.395	37	61	93	.396	8

SIMULATED PLAYOFFS

AMERICAN LEAGUE

ALCS	W	1	2	3	4	5	%
New York Yankees	1	2	8	1	3	4	54
Cleveland Indians	4	3	2	3	4	5	46

NATIONAL LEAGUE

NLCS	W	1	2	3	4	5	6	7	%
Brooklyn Dodgers	3	0	6	6	6	5	6	1	54
St. Louis Cardinals	4	7	13	5	4	2	7	2	46

WORLD SERIES

WS	W	1	2	3	4	5	6	%
Cleveland Indians	4	2	3	1	3	7	2	44
St. Louis Cardinals	2	9	2	3	2	3	1	56

ACTUAL WINNERS

American League: New York Yankees
National League: Brooklyn Dodgers
World Series: New York Yankees

OUTSTANDING PERFORMANCES

AWARD WINNERS

LG.	PLAYER	TEAM	STATS ADJUSTED	ACTUAL
MOST VALUABLE PLAYERS				
AL	Ted Williams	Boston	59 HR, 179 RBI, .351 BA, $36.0 MIL	43 HR, 159 RBI, .343 BA
NL	Jackie Robinson	Brooklyn	27 HR, 138 RBI, .351 BA, $22.5 MIL	16 HR, 124 RBI, .342 BA
CY YOUNG AWARDS				
AL	Mel Parnell	Boston	26-7 W-L, 5 SV, 3.08 ERA, $27.1 MIL	25-7 W-L, 2 SV, 2.77 ERA
NL	Warren Spahn	Boston	22-14 W-L, 0 SV, 3.40 ERA, $32.6 MIL	21-14 W-L, 0 SV, 3.07 ERA

AMERICAN LEAGUE LEADERS

CAT.	PLAYER	TEAM	STATS ADJUSTED	ACTUAL
BATTING				
HR	Ted Williams	Boston	59	43
RBI	Ted Williams	Boston	179	159
	Vern Stephens	Boston	178	159
BA	George Kell	Detroit	.352	.343
AB	Dale Mitchell	Cleveland	674	640
R	Ted Williams	Boston	168	150
H	Dale Mitchell	Cleveland	219	203
2B	Ted Williams	Boston	41	39
3B	Dale Mitchell	Cleveland	23	23
TB	Ted Williams	Boston	430	368
SA	Ted Williams	Boston	.726	.650
SB	Bob Dillinger	St. Louis	49	20
PITCHING				
W	Mel Parnell	Boston	26	25
L	Paul Calvert	Washington	18	17
	Ned Garver	St. Louis	18	17
	Sid Hudson	Washington	18	17
SV	Joe Page	New York	37	27
ERA	Mike Garcia	Cleveland	2.59	2.36
G	Joe Page	New York	63	60
IP	Mel Parnell	Boston	310	295.1
BB	Tommy Byrne	New York	164	179
SO	Virgil Trucks	Detroit	276	153

NATIONAL LEAGUE LEADERS

CAT.	PLAYER	TEAM	STATS ADJUSTED	ACTUAL
BATTING				
HR	Ralph Kiner	Pittsburgh	72	54
RBI	Ralph Kiner	Pittsburgh	143	127
BA	Jackie Robinson	Brooklyn	.351	.342
AB	Richie Ashburn	Philadelphia	696	662
	Granny Hamner	Philadelphia	696	662
R	Pee Wee Reese	Brooklyn	147	132
H	Stan Musial	St. Louis	219	207
2B	Stan Musial	St. Louis	47	41
3B	Enos Slaughter	St. Louis	9	13
	Stan Musial	St. Louis	7	13
TB	Stan Musial	St. Louis	439	382
SA	Ralph Kiner	Pittsburgh	.730	.658
SB	Jackie Robinson	Brooklyn	92	37
PITCHING				
W	Warren Spahn	Boston	22	21
L	Howie Fox	Cincinnati	20	19
SV	Ted Wilks	St. Louis	24	9
ERA	Dave Koslo	New York	2.77	2.50
G	Ted Wilks	St. Louis	61	59
IP	Warren Spahn	Boston	310	302.1
BB	Herm Wehmeier	Cincinnati	106	117
SO	Warren Spahn	Boston	270	151

1950 SEASON

REGULAR SEASON STANDINGS

AMERICAN LEAGUE

		ADJUSTED				ACTUAL			
	W	L	Pct.	GB	W	L	Pct.	Rk.
EAST								
X New York	103	59	.636	0	98	56	.636	1
Boston	99	63	.611	4	94	60	.610	3
Washington	70	92	.432	33	67	87	.435	5
Philadelphia	55	107	.340	48	52	102	.338	8
WEST								
X Detroit	100	62	.617	0	95	59	.617	2
Cleveland	97	65	.599	3	92	62	.597	4
Chicago	63	99	.389	37	60	94	.390	6
St. Louis	61	101	.377	39	58	96	.377	7

NATIONAL LEAGUE

		ADJUSTED				ACTUAL			
	W	L	Pct.	GB	W	L	Pct.	Rk.
EAST								
X Philadelphia	96	66	.593	0	91	63	.591	1
Brooklyn	94	68	.580	2	89	65	.578	2
New York	90	72	.556	6	86	68	.558	3
Boston	87	75	.537	9	83	71	.539	4
WEST								
X St. Louis	83	79	.512	0	78	75	.510	5
Cincinnati	70	92	.432	13	66	87	.431	6
Chicago	68	94	.420	15	64	89	.418	7
Pittsburgh	60	102	.370	23	57	96	.373	8

SIMULATED PLAYOFFS

AMERICAN LEAGUE

ALCS	W	1	2	3	4	5	6	%
New York Yankees	4	5	1	9	3	9	5	62
Detroit Tigers	2	3	7	0	4	1	3	38

NATIONAL LEAGUE

NLCS	W	1	2	3	4	5	6	%
Philadelphia Phillies	4	6	2	3	5	1	4	55
St. Louis Cardinals	2	3	4	1	2	3	1	45

WORLD SERIES

WS*	W	1	2	3	4	%
New York Yankees	4	1	2	3	5	58
Philadelphia Phillies	0	0	1	2	2	42

ACTUAL WINNERS

American League: New York Yankees
National League: Philadelphia Phillies
World Series: New York Yankees

OUTSTANDING PERFORMANCES

AWARD WINNERS

LG.	PLAYER	TEAM	STATS ADJUSTED	ACTUAL
MOST VALUABLE PLAYERS				
AL	Phil Rizzuto	New York	10 HR, 70 RBI, .329 BA, $13.1 MIL	7 HR, 66 RBI, .324 BA
NL	Jim Konstanty	Philadelphia	16-7 W-L, 38 SV, 2.77 ERA, $8.3 MIL	16-7 W-L, 22 SV, 2.66 ERA
CY YOUNG AWARDS				
AL	Bob Lemon	Cleveland	24-12 W-L, 5 SV, 4.04 ERA, $34.1 MIL	23-11 W-L, 3 SV, 3.84 ERA
NL	Jim Konstanty	Philadelphia	16-7 W-L, 38 SV, 2.77 ERA, $8.3 MIL	16-7 W-L, 22 SV, 2.66 ERA

AMERICAN LEAGUE LEADERS

CAT.	PLAYER	TEAM	STATS ADJUSTED	ACTUAL
BATTING				
HR	Al Rosen	Cleveland	45	37
RBI	Walt Dropo	Boston	155	144
	Vern Stephens	Boston	155	144
BA	Billy Goodman	Boston	.358	.354
AB	George Kell	Detroit	661	641
R	Dom DiMaggio	Boston	141	131
H	George Kell	Detroit	228	218
2B	George Kell	Detroit	70	56
3B	Dom DiMaggio	Boston	8	11
	Bobby Doerr	Boston	7	11
	Hoot Evers	Detroit	7	11
TB	Walt Dropo	Boston	366	326
SA	Joe DiMaggio	New York	.622	.585
SB	Dom DiMaggio	Boston	42	15
PITCHING				
W	Bob Lemon	Cleveland	24	23
L	Alex Kellner	Philadelphia	21	20
SV	Mickey Harris	Washington	28	15
ERA	Early Wynn	Cleveland	3.35	3.20
G	Mickey Harris	Washington	55	53
IP	Bob Lemon	Cleveland	301	288
BB	Tommy Byrne	New York	147	160
SO	Bob Lemon	Cleveland	287	170

NATIONAL LEAGUE LEADERS

CAT.	PLAYER	TEAM	STATS ADJUSTED	ACTUAL
BATTING				
HR	Ralph Kiner	Pittsburgh	57	47
RBI	Del Ennis	Philadelphia	133	126
BA	Stan Musial	St. Louis	.350	.346
AB	Red Schoendienst	St. Louis	680	642
R	Earl Torgeson	Boston	127	120
H	Duke Snider	Brooklyn	211	199
2B	Red Schoendienst	St. Louis	57	43
3B	Richie Ashburn	Philadelphia	12	14
TB	Duke Snider	Brooklyn	383	343
SA	Stan Musial	St. Louis	.635	.596
SB	Sam Jethroe	Boston	99	35
PITCHING				
W	Warren Spahn	Boston	22	21
L	Bob Rush	Chicago	21	20
SV	Jim Konstanty	Philadelphia	38	22
ERA	Jim Hearn	St.L.-N.Y.	2.57	2.49
G	Jim Konstanty	Philadelphia	76	74
IP	Vern Bickford	Boston	327	311.2
BB	Herm Wehmeier	Cincinnati	125	135
SO	Warren Spahn	Boston	318	191

1951 SEASON

REGULAR SEASON STANDINGS

AMERICAN LEAGUE

		ADJUSTED				ACTUAL			
		W	L	Pct.	GB	W	L	Pct.	Rk.
EAST									
X	New York	103	59	.636	0	98	56	.636	1
	Boston	91	71	.562	12	87	67	.565	3
	Philadelphia	74	88	.457	29	70	84	.455	6
	Washington	65	97	.401	38	62	92	.403	7
WEST									
X	Cleveland	98	64	.605	0	93	61	.604	2
	Chicago	85	77	.525	13	81	73	.526	4
	Detroit	77	85	.475	21	73	81	.474	5
	St. Louis	55	107	.340	43	52	102	.338	8

NATIONAL LEAGUE

		ADJUSTED				ACTUAL			
		W	L	Pct.	GB	W	L	Pct.	Rk.
EAST									
X	New York	101	61	.623	0	96	58	.623	1
X	Brooklyn	101	61	.623	0	96	58	.623	1
	Boston	80	82	.494	21	76	78	.494	4
	Philadelphia	77	85	.475	24	73	81	.474	5
WEST									
X	St. Louis	85	77	.525	0	81	73	.526	3
	Cincinnati	72	90	.444	13	68	86	.442	6
	Pittsburgh	67	95	.414	18	64	90	.416	7
	Chicago	65	97	.401	20	62	92	.403	8

SIMULATED PLAYOFFS

AMERICAN LEAGUE

ALCS	W	1	2	3	4	5	6	%
New York Yankees	2	6	2	0	2	6	3	61
Cleveland Indians	4	3	6	2	3	4	5	39

NATIONAL LEAGUE

TIEBREAKER*	W	1	2	3			%
New York Giants	2	3	0	5			47
Brooklyn Dodgers	1	1	10	4			53

NLCS	W	1	2	3	4	5	%
New York Giants	4	7	5	3	5	6	72
St. Louis Cardinals	1	1	1	5	4	3	28

WORLD SERIES

WS	W	1	2	3	4	%
Cleveland Indians	0	1	1	1	1	35
New York Giants	4	4	5	2	2	65

ACTUAL WINNERS

American League: New York Yankees
National League: New York Giants
World Series: New York Yankees

OUTSTANDING PERFORMANCES

AWARD WINNERS

LG.	PLAYER	TEAM	STATS ADJUSTED	ACTUAL
MOST VALUABLE PLAYERS				
AL	Yogi Berra	New York	37 HR, 101 RBI, .303 BA, $14.2 MIL	27 HR, 88 RBI, .294 BA
NL	Roy Campanella	Brooklyn	43 HR, 121 RBI, .335 BA, $9.0 MIL	33 HR, 108 RBI, .325 BA
CY YOUNG AWARDS				
AL	Ned Garver	St. Louis	21-13 W-L, 0 SV, 4.21 ERA, $19.4 MIL	20-12 W-L, 0 SV, 3.73 ERA
NL	Sal Maglie	New York	24-6 W-L, 7 SV, 3.30 ERA, $30.6 MIL	23-6 W-L, 4 SV, 2.93 ERA

AMERICAN LEAGUE LEADERS

CAT.	PLAYER	TEAM	STATS ADJUSTED	ACTUAL
BATTING				
HR	Gus Zernial	Chi.-Phi.	44	33
RBI	Gus Zernial	Chi.-Phi.	147	129
BA	Ferris Fain	Philadelphia	.356	.344
AB	Dom DiMaggio	Boston	674	639
R	Dom DiMaggio	Boston	130	113
H	George Kell	Detroit	208	191
2B	George Kell	Detroit	56	36
	Sam Mele	Washington	51	36
	Eddie Yost	Washington	46	36
3B	Minnie Minoso	Cle.-Chi.	11	14
TB	Ted Williams	Boston	346	295
SA	Ted Williams	Boston	.618	.556
SB	Minnie Minoso	Cle.-Chi.	65	31
PITCHING				
W	Bob Feller	Cleveland	23	22
L	Ted Gray	Detroit	15	14
	Alex Kellner	Philadelphia	15	14
	Bob Lemon	Cleveland	15	14
	Billy Pierce	Chicago	15	14
	Duane Pillette	St. Louis	15	14
	Dizzy Trout	Detroit	15	14
SV	Ellis Kinder	Boston	30	14
ERA	Saul Rogovin	Det.-Chi.	3.16	2.78
G	Ellis Kinder	Boston	66	63
IP	Early Wynn	Cleveland	289	274.1
BB	Tommy Byrne	N.Y.-St.L.	151	150
SO	Vic Raschi	New York	284	164

NATIONAL LEAGUE LEADERS

CAT.	PLAYER	TEAM	STATS ADJUSTED	ACTUAL
BATTING				
HR	Ralph Kiner	Pittsburgh	56	42
RBI	Monte Irvin	New York	137	121
BA	Stan Musial	St. Louis	.367	.355
AB	Carl Furillo	Brooklyn	684	667
R	Ralph Kiner	Pittsburgh	142	124
	Stan Musial	St. Louis	142	124
H	Richie Ashburn	Philadelphia	240	221
2B	Alvin Dark	New York	53	41
3B	Gus Bell	Pittsburgh	8	12
	Stan Musial	St. Louis	8	12
TB	Stan Musial	St. Louis	413	355
SA	Ralph Kiner	Pittsburgh	.692	.627
SB	Sam Jethroe	Boston	74	35
PITCHING				
W	Larry Jansen	New York	24	23
	Sal Maglie	New York	24	23
L	Paul Minner	Chicago	18	17
	Ken Raffensberger	Cincinnati	18	17
	Willie Ramsdell	Cincinnati	18	17
SV	Ted Wilks	St.L.-Pit.	30	13
ERA	Chet Nichols	Boston	3.24	2.88
G	Ted Wilks	St.L.-Pit.	68	65
IP	Robin Roberts	Philadelphia	329	315
BB	Warren Spahn	Boston	110	109
SO	Warren Spahn	Boston	291	164
	Don Newcombe	Brooklyn	278	164

1952 SEASON

REGULAR SEASON STANDINGS

AMERICAN LEAGUE

		ADJUSTED				ACTUAL			
	W	L	Pct.	GB	W	L	Pct.	Rk.
EAST								
X New York	100	62	.617	0	95	59	.617	1
Philadelphia	83	79	.512	17	79	75	.513	4
Washington	82	80	.506	18	78	76	.506	5
Boston	80	82	.494	20	76	78	.494	6
WEST								
X Cleveland	98	64	.605	0	93	61	.604	2
Chicago	85	77	.525	13	81	73	.526	3
St. Louis	67	95	.414	31	64	90	.416	7
Detroit	53	109	.327	45	50	104	.325	8

NATIONAL LEAGUE

		ADJUSTED				ACTUAL			
	W	L	Pct.	GB	W	L	Pct.	Rk.
EAST								
X Brooklyn	102	60	.630	0	96	57	.627	1
New York	97	65	.599	5	92	62	.597	2
Philadelphia	91	71	.562	11	87	67	.565	4
Boston	68	94	.420	34	64	89	.418	7
WEST								
X St. Louis	92	70	.568	0	88	66	.571	3
Chicago	81	81	.500	11	77	77	.500	5
Cincinnati	73	89	.451	19	69	85	.448	6
Pittsburgh	44	118	.272	48	42	112	.273	8

SIMULATED PLAYOFFS

AMERICAN LEAGUE

ALCS	W	1	2	3	4		%
New York Yankees	0	5	5	3	1		59
Cleveland Indians	4	6	7	5	6		41

NATIONAL LEAGUE

NLCS	W	1	2	3	4	5	6	7	%
Brooklyn Dodgers	3	4	1	4	3	3	7	2	65
St. Louis Cardinals	4	3	6	2	4	4	0	5	35

WORLD SERIES

WS	W	1	2	3	4	5	6	%
Cleveland Indians	2	2	3	6	5	2	2	62
St. Louis Cardinals	4	1	4	7	3	4	5	38

ACTUAL WINNERS

American League: New York Yankees
National League: Brooklyn Dodgers
World Series: New York Yankees

OUTSTANDING PERFORMANCES

AWARD WINNERS

LG.	PLAYER	TEAM	STATS	
			ADJUSTED	ACTUAL
MOST VALUABLE PLAYERS				
AL	Bobby Shantz	Philadelphia	25-7 W-L, 0 SV, 3.06 ERA, $26.4 MIL	24-7 W-L, 0 SV, 2.48 ERA
NL	Hank Sauer	Chicago	52 HR, 149 RBI, .287 BA, $13.0 MIL	37 HR, 121 RBI, .270 BA
CY YOUNG AWARDS				
AL	Bobby Shantz	Philadelphia	25-7 W-L, 0 SV, 3.06 ERA, $26.4 MIL	24-7 W-L, 0 SV, 2.48 ERA
NL	Robin Roberts	Philadelphia	29-7 W-L, 4 SV, 3.19 ERA, $50.6 MIL	28-7 W-L, 2 SV, 2.59 ERA

AMERICAN LEAGUE LEADERS

CAT.	PLAYER	TEAM	STATS	
			ADJUSTED	ACTUAL
BATTING				
HR	Larry Doby	Cleveland	46	32
RBI	Al Rosen	Cleveland	130	105
BA	Ferris Fain	Philadelphia	.349	.327
AB	Nellie Fox	Chicago	674	648
R	Larry Doby	Cleveland	128	104
H	Nellie Fox	Chicago	213	192
2B	Ferris Fain	Philadelphia	68	43
3B	Bobby Avila	Cleveland	9	11
TB	Al Rosen	Cleveland	358	297
SA	Larry Doby	Cleveland	.623	.541
SB	Minnie Minoso	Chicago	51	22
PITCHING				
W	Bobby Shantz	Philadelphia	25	24
L	Art Houtteman	Detroit	21	20
SV	Harry Dorish	Chicago	19	11
ERA	Allie Reynolds	New York	2.55	2.06
G	Bill Kennedy	Chicago	49	47
IP	Bob Lemon	Cleveland	324	309.2
BB	Early Wynn	Cleveland	140	132
SO	Allie Reynolds	New York	254	160

NATIONAL LEAGUE LEADERS

CAT.	PLAYER	TEAM	STATS	
			ADJUSTED	ACTUAL
BATTING				
HR	Hank Sauer	Chicago	52	37
	Ralph Kiner	Pittsburgh	51	37
RBI	Hank Sauer	Chicago	149	121
BA	Stan Musial	St. Louis	.359	.336
AB	Bobby Adams	Cincinnati	670	637
R	Solly Hemus	St. Louis	130	105
	Stan Musial	St. Louis	130	105
H	Stan Musial	St. Louis	218	194
2B	Stan Musial	St. Louis	54	42
3B	Bobby Thomson	New York	10	14
TB	Stan Musial	St. Louis	379	311
SA	Stan Musial	St. Louis	.623	.538
SB	Pee Wee Reese	Brooklyn	71	30
PITCHING				
W	Robin Roberts	Philadelphia	29	28
L	Murry Dickson	Pittsburgh	22	21
SV	Al Brazle	St. Louis	23	16
ERA	Hoyt Wilhelm	New York	3	2.43
G	Hoyt Wilhelm	New York	75	71
IP	Robin Roberts	Philadelphia	347	330
BB	Vinegar Bend Mizell	St. Louis	112	103
	Herm Wehmeier	Cincinnati	111	103
SO	Warren Spahn	Boston	290	183

1953 SEASON

REGULAR SEASON STANDINGS

AMERICAN LEAGUE

		ADJUSTED				ACTUAL		
	W	L	Pct.	GB	W	L	Pct.	Rk.
EAST								
X New York	106	56	.654	0	99	52	.656	1
Boston	89	73	.549	17	84	69	.549	4
Washington	81	81	.500	25	76	76	.500	5
Philadelphia	62	100	.383	44	59	95	.383	7
WEST								
X Cleveland	97	65	.599	0	92	62	.597	2
Chicago	93	69	.574	4	89	65	.578	3
Detroit	63	99	.389	34	60	94	.390	6
St. Louis	57	105	.352	40	54	100	.351	8

NATIONAL LEAGUE

		ADJUSTED				ACTUAL		
	W	L	Pct.	GB	W	L	Pct.	Rk.
EAST								
X Brooklyn	110	52	.679	0	105	49	.682	1
Philadelphia	87	75	.537	23	83	71	.539	3
New York	74	88	.457	36	70	84	.455	5
Pittsburgh	53	109	.327	57	50	104	.325	8
WEST								
X Milwaukee	97	65	.599	0	92	62	.597	2
St. Louis	87	75	.537	10	83	71	.539	3
Cincinnati	72	90	.444	25	68	86	.442	6
Chicago	68	94	.420	29	65	89	.422	7

SIMULATED PLAYOFFS

AMERICAN LEAGUE

ALCS	W	1	2	3	4		%
New York Yankees	4	4	4	4	6		68
Cleveland Indians	0	3	1	2	3		32

NATIONAL LEAGUE

NLCS	W	1	2	3	4	5	6	7	%
Brooklyn Dodgers	3	7	3	10	7	3	2	4	58
Milwaukee Braves	4	1	5	2	5	4	5	5	42

WORLD SERIES

WS	W	1	2	3	4	5	6	7	%
New York Yankees	4	2	11	2	5	1	4	4	69
Milwaukee Braves	3	6	7	5	1	2	0	3	31

ACTUAL WINNERS

American League: New York Yankees
National League: Brooklyn Dodgers
World Series: New York Yankees

OUTSTANDING PERFORMANCES

AWARD WINNERS

LG.	PLAYER	TEAM	STATS ADJUSTED	ACTUAL
MOST VALUABLE PLAYERS				
AL	Al Rosen	Cleveland	54 HR, 164 RBI, .342 BA, $23.1 MIL	43 HR, 145 RBI, .336 BA
NL	Roy Campanella	Brooklyn	50 HR, 161 RBI, .318 BA, $9.8 MIL	41 HR, 142 RBI, .312 BA
CY YOUNG AWARDS				
AL	Billy Pierce	Chicago	19-13 W-L, 5 SV, 3.00 ERA, $26.7 MIL	18-12 W-L, 3 SV, 2.72 ERA
NL	Warren Spahn	Milwaukee	24-7 W-L, 4 SV, 2.31 ERA, $30.8 MIL	23-7 W-L, 3 SV, 2.10 ERA

AMERICAN LEAGUE LEADERS

CAT.	PLAYER	TEAM	STATS ADJUSTED	ACTUAL
BATTING				
HR	Al Rosen	Cleveland	54	43
RBI	Al Rosen	Cleveland	164	145
BA	Mickey Vernon	Washington	.344	.337
AB	Harvey Kuenn	Detroit	697	679
R	Al Rosen	Cleveland	129	115
H	Harvey Kuenn	Detroit	219	209
2B	Mickey Vernon	Washington	58	43
3B	Jim Rivera	Chicago	12	16
TB	Al Rosen	Cleveland	414	367
SA	Al Rosen	Cleveland	.661	.613
SB	Minnie Minoso	Chicago	68	25
PITCHING				
W	Bob Porterfield	Washington	23	22
L	Harry Byrd	Philadelphia	21	20
SV	Ellis Kinder	Boston	41	27
ERA	Ed Lopat	New York	2.66	2.42
G	Ellis Kinder	Boston	73	69
IP	Bob Lemon	Cleveland	301	286.2
BB	Mel Parnell	Boston	124	116
SO	Billy Pierce	Chicago	294	186

NATIONAL LEAGUE LEADERS

CAT.	PLAYER	TEAM	STATS ADJUSTED	ACTUAL
BATTING				
HR	Eddie Mathews	Milwaukee	58	47
RBI	Roy Campanella	Brooklyn	161	142
BA	Carl Furillo	Brooklyn	.351	.344
AB	Alvin Dark	New York	676	647
R	Duke Snider	Brooklyn	149	132
H	Richie Ashburn	Philadelphia	217	205
2B	Stan Musial	St. Louis	64	53
3B	Jim Gilliam	Brooklyn	14	17
TB	Duke Snider	Brooklyn	417	370
SA	Duke Snider	Brooklyn	.676	.627
SB	Bill Bruton	Milwaukee	70	26
PITCHING				
W	Robin Roberts	Philadelphia	24	23
	Warren Spahn	Milwaukee	24	23
L	Murry Dickson	Pittsburgh	20	19
	Warren Hacker	Chicago	20	19
SV	Al Brazle	St. Louis	30	18
ERA	Warren Spahn	Milwaukee	2.31	2.10
G	Hoyt Wilhelm	New York	71	68
IP	Robin Roberts	Philadelphia	362	346.2
BB	Johnny Lindell	Pit.-Phi.	146	139
SO	Robin Roberts	Philadelphia	318	198

1954 SEASON

REGULAR SEASON STANDINGS

AMERICAN LEAGUE

		ADJUSTED				ACTUAL		
	W	L	Pct.	GB	W	L	Pct.	Rk.
EAST								
X New York	108	54	.667	0	103	51	.669	2
Boston	73	89	.451	35	69	85	.448	4
Washington	69	93	.426	39	66	88	.429	6
Philadelphia	54	108	.333	54	51	103	.331	8
WEST								
X Cleveland	117	45	.722	0	111	43	.721	1
Chicago	99	63	.611	18	94	60	.610	3
Detroit	71	91	.438	46	68	86	.442	5
Baltimore	57	105	.352	60	54	100	.351	7

NATIONAL LEAGUE

		ADJUSTED				ACTUAL		
	W	L	Pct.	GB	W	L	Pct.	Rk.
EAST								
X New York	102	60	.630	0	97	57	.630	1
Brooklyn	97	65	.599	5	92	62	.597	2
Philadelphia	79	83	.488	23	75	79	.487	4
Pittsburgh	56	106	.346	46	53	101	.344	8
WEST								
X Milwaukee	93	69	.574	0	89	65	.578	3
Cincinnati	78	84	.481	15	74	80	.481	5
St. Louis	76	86	.469	17	72	82	.468	6
Chicago	67	95	.414	26	64	90	.416	7

SIMULATED PLAYOFFS

AMERICAN LEAGUE

ALCS	W	1	2	3	4	5	6	%
New York Yankees	2	5	1	4	3	5	2	46
Cleveland Indians	4	6	3	2	2	6	3	54

NATIONAL LEAGUE

NLCS	W	1	2	3	4	5	6	7	%
New York Giants	4	3	3	5	2	9	2	3	54
Milwaukee Braves	3	4	4	2	3	2	1	1	46

WORLD SERIES

WS*	W	1	2	3	4	%
Cleveland Indians	0	2	1	2	4	62
New York Giants	4	5	3	6	7	38

ACTUAL WINNERS

American League: Cleveland Indians
National League: New York Giants
World Series: New York Giants

OUTSTANDING PERFORMANCES

AWARD WINNERS

LG.	PLAYER	TEAM	STATS ADJUSTED	ACTUAL
MOST VALUABLE PLAYERS				
AL	Yogi Berra	New York	30 HR, 147 RBI, .316 BA, $15.9 MIL	22 HR, 125 RBI, .307 BA
NL	Willie Mays	New York	56 HR, 130 RBI, .356 BA, $14.4 MIL	41 HR, 110 RBI, .345 BA
CY YOUNG AWARDS				
AL	Bob Lemon	Cleveland	24-7 W-L, 0 SV, 3.18 ERA, $25.5 MIL	23-7 W-L, 0 SV, 2.72 ERA
NL	Johnny Antonelli	New York	22-7 W-L, 4 SV, 2.68 ERA, $19.7 MIL	21-7 W-L, 2 SV, 2.30 ERA

AMERICAN LEAGUE LEADERS

CAT.	PLAYER	TEAM	STATS ADJUSTED	ACTUAL
BATTING				
HR	Larry Doby	Cleveland	42	32
RBI	Larry Doby	Cleveland	147	126
BA	Bobby Avila	Cleveland	.351	.341
AB	Harvey Kuenn	Detroit	686	656
R	Mickey Mantle	New York	152	129
H	Nellie Fox	Chicago	217	201
	Harvey Kuenn	Detroit	217	201
2B	Mickey Vernon	Washington	44	33
3B	Minnie Minoso	Chicago	12	18
TB	Minnie Minoso	Chicago	348	304
SA	Ted Williams	Boston	.694	.635
SB	Jackie Jensen	Boston	56	22
PITCHING				
W	Bob Lemon	Cleveland	24	23
	Early Wynn	Cleveland	24	23
L	Don Larsen	Baltimore	22	21
SV	Johnny Sain	New York	29	22
ERA	Mike Garcia	Cleveland	3.10	2.64
G	Sonny Dixon	Wash.-Phi.	56	54
IP	Early Wynn	Cleveland	284	270.2
BB	Bob Turley	Baltimore	189	181
SO	Bob Turley	Baltimore	291	185

NATIONAL LEAGUE LEADERS

CAT.	PLAYER	TEAM	STATS ADJUSTED	ACTUAL
BATTING				
HR	Ted Kluszewski	Cincinnati	62	49
RBI	Ted Kluszewski	Cincinnati	167	141
BA	Willie Mays	New York	.356	.345
AB	Alvin Dark	New York	677	644
R	Stan Musial	St. Louis	142	120
	Duke Snider	Brooklyn	142	120
H	Don Mueller	New York	230	212
2B	Stan Musial	St. Louis	50	41
3B	Willie Mays	New York	7	13
TB	Duke Snider	Brooklyn	436	378
SA	Willie Mays	New York	.731	.667
SB	Bill Bruton	Milwaukee	90	34
PITCHING				
W	Robin Roberts	Philadelphia	24	23
L	Murry Dickson	Philadelphia	21	20
SV	Jim Hughes	Brooklyn	36	24
ERA	Johnny Antonelli	New York	2.68	2.30
G	Jim Hughes	Brooklyn	63	60
IP	Robin Roberts	Philadelphia	352	336.2
BB	Ruben Gomez	New York	113	109
SO	Robin Roberts	Philadelphia	300	185

1955 SEASON

REGULAR SEASON STANDINGS

AMERICAN LEAGUE

		ADJUSTED				ACTUAL			
	W	L	Pct.	GB	W	L	Pct.	Rk.
EAST								
X New York	101	61	.623	0	96	58	.623	1
Boston	88	74	.543	13	84	70	.545	4
Baltimore	60	102	.370	41	57	97	.370	7
Washington	56	106	.346	45	53	101	.344	8
WEST								
X Cleveland	98	64	.605	0	93	61	.604	2
Chicago	96	66	.593	2	91	63	.591	3
Detroit	83	79	.512	15	79	75	.513	5
Kansas City	66	96	.407	32	63	91	.409	6

NATIONAL LEAGUE

		ADJUSTED				ACTUAL			
	W	L	Pct.	GB	W	L	Pct.	Rk.
EAST								
X Brooklyn	104	58	.642	0	98	55	.641	1
New York	84	78	.519	20	80	74	.519	3
Philadelphia	81	81	.500	23	77	77	.500	4
Pittsburgh	63	99	.389	41	60	94	.390	8
WEST								
X Milwaukee	89	73	.549	0	85	69	.552	2
Cincinnati	79	83	.488	10	75	79	.487	5
Chicago	76	86	.469	13	72	81	.471	6
St. Louis	72	90	.444	17	68	86	.442	7

SIMULATED PLAYOFFS

AMERICAN LEAGUE

ALCS	W	1	2	3	4	5	6	7	%
New York Yankees	3	6	6	2	3	8	2	2	64
Cleveland Indians	4	4	2	4	4	1	4	5	36

NATIONAL LEAGUE

NLCS	W	1	2	3	4	5	6	7	%
Brooklyn Dodgers	4	9	1	2	4	10	1	4	67
Milwaukee Braves	3	7	3	3	3	3	7	3	33

WORLD SERIES

WS	W	1	2	3	4	%
Cleveland Indians	0	2	4	2	2	30
Brooklyn Dodgers	4	5	5	6	5	70

ACTUAL WINNERS

American League: New York Yankees
National League: Brooklyn Dodgers
World Series: Brooklyn Dodgers

OUTSTANDING PERFORMANCES

AWARD WINNERS

LG.	PLAYER	TEAM	STATS ADJUSTED	ACTUAL
MOST VALUABLE PLAYERS				
AL	Yogi Berra	New York	33 HR, 124 RBI, .282 BA, $12.4 MIL	27 HR, 108 RBI, .272 BA
NL	Roy Campanella	Brooklyn	38 HR, 123 RBI, .331 BA, $6.9 MIL	32 HR, 107 RBI, .318 BA
CY YOUNG AWARDS				
AL	Ray Narleski	Cleveland	9-1 W-L, 32 SV, 4.23 ERA, $8.4 MIL	9-1 W-L, 19 SV, 3.71 ERA
NL	Robin Roberts	Philadelphia	24-15 W-L, 3 SV, 3.74 ERA, $42.0 MIL	23-14 W-L, 3 SV, 3.28 ERA

AMERICAN LEAGUE LEADERS

CAT.	PLAYER	TEAM	ADJUSTED	ACTUAL
BATTING				
HR	Mickey Mantle	New York	46	37
RBI	Ray Boone	Detroit	134	116
	Jackie Jensen	Boston	133	116
BA	Al Kaline	Detroit	.354	.340
AB	Nellie Fox	Chicago	665	636
R	Al Smith	Cleveland	142	123
H	Al Kaline	Detroit	219	200
2B	Harvey Kuenn	Detroit	54	38
3B	Andy Carey	New York	9	11
	Mickey Mantle	New York	8	11
TB	Al Kaline	Detroit	367	321
SA	Mickey Mantle	New York	.662	.611
SB	Jim Rivera	Chicago	65	25
PITCHING				
W	Whitey Ford	New York	19	18
	Bob Lemon	Cleveland	19	18
	Frank Sullivan	Boston	19	18
L	Jim Wilson	Baltimore	19	18
SV	Ray Narleski	Cleveland	32	19
ERA	Billy Pierce	Chicago	2.25	1.97
G	Ray Narleski	Cleveland	63	60
IP	Frank Sullivan	Boston	275	260
BB	Bob Turley	New York	183	177
SO	Herb Score	Cleveland	349	245

NATIONAL LEAGUE LEADERS

CAT.	PLAYER	TEAM	ADJUSTED	ACTUAL
BATTING				
HR	Willie Mays	New York	64	51
RBI	Duke Snider	Brooklyn	157	136
BA	Richie Ashburn	Philadelphia	.352	.338
AB	Bill Bruton	Milwaukee	670	636
R	Duke Snider	Brooklyn	145	126
H	Ted Kluszewski	Cincinnati	210	192
2B	Hank Aaron	Milwaukee	51	37
	Johnny Logan	Milwaukee	51	37
3B	Dale Long	Pittsburgh	10	13
	Willie Mays	New York	9	13
TB	Willie Mays	New York	438	382
SA	Willie Mays	New York	.717	.659
SB	Bill Bruton	Milwaukee	65	25
PITCHING				
W	Robin Roberts	Philadelphia	24	23
L	Sam Jones	Chicago	21	20
SV	Jack Meyer	Philadelphia	24	16
ERA	Bob Friend	Pittsburgh	3.23	2.83
G	Clem Labine	Brooklyn	63	60
IP	Robin Roberts	Philadelphia	320	305
BB	Sam Jones	Chicago	192	185
SO	Sam Jones	Chicago	293	198

1956 SEASON

REGULAR SEASON STANDINGS

AMERICAN LEAGUE

	ADJUSTED				ACTUAL			
	W	L	Pct.	GB	W	L	Pct.	Rk.
EAST								
X New York	102	60	.630	0	97	57	.630	1
Boston	88	74	.543	14	84	70	.545	4
Baltimore	73	89	.451	29	69	85	.448	6
Washington	62	100	.383	40	59	95	.383	7
WEST								
X Cleveland	93	69	.574	0	88	66	.571	2
Chicago	89	73	.549	4	85	69	.552	3
Detroit	86	76	.531	7	82	72	.532	5
Kansas City	55	107	.340	38	52	102	.338	8

NATIONAL LEAGUE

	ADJUSTED				ACTUAL			
	W	L	Pct.	GB	W	L	Pct.	Rk.
EAST								
X Brooklyn	98	64	.605	0	93	61	.604	1
Philadelphia	75	87	.463	23	71	83	.461	5
New York	70	92	.432	28	67	87	.435	6
Pittsburgh	69	93	.426	29	66	88	.429	7
WEST								
X Milwaukee	97	65	.599	0	92	62	.597	2
Cincinnati	96	66	.593	1	91	63	.591	3
St. Louis	80	82	.494	17	76	78	.494	4
Chicago	63	99	.389	34	60	94	.390	8

SIMULATED PLAYOFFS

AMERICAN LEAGUE

ALCS	W	1	2	3	4	5		%
New York Yankees	4	13	7	4	6	4		71
Cleveland Indians	1	3	2	5	3	3		29

NATIONAL LEAGUE

NLCS	W	1	2	3	4	5	6	7	%
Brooklyn Dodgers	4	1	5	3	1	1	5	4	50
Milwaukee Braves	3	7	2	0	6	3	2	3	50

WORLD SERIES

WS*	W	1	2	3	4	5	6	7	%
New York Yankees	4	3	8	5	6	2	0	9	59
Brooklyn Dodgers	3	6	13	3	2	0	1	0	41

ACTUAL WINNERS

American League: New York Yankees
National League: Brooklyn Dodgers
World Series: New York Yankees

OUTSTANDING PERFORMANCES

AWARD WINNERS

LG.	PLAYER	TEAM	STATS ADJUSTED	ACTUAL
MOST VALUABLE PLAYERS				
AL	Mickey Mantle	New York	62 HR, 151 RBI, .369 BA, $26.4 MIL	52 HR, 130 RBI, .353 BA
NL	Don Newcombe	Brooklyn	28-7 W-L, 0 SV, 3.51 ERA, $32.2 MIL	27-7 W-L, 0 SV, 3.06 ERA
CY YOUNG AWARDS				
AL	Billy Pierce	Chicago	21-10 W-L, 2 SV, 3.82 ERA, $27.3 MIL	20-9 W-L, 1 SV, 3.32 ERA
NL	Don Newcombe	Brooklyn	28-7 W-L, 0 SV, 3.51 ERA, $32.2 MIL	27-7 W-L, 0 SV, 3.06 ERA

AMERICAN LEAGUE LEADERS

CAT.	PLAYER	TEAM	STATS ADJUSTED	ACTUAL
BATTING				
HR	Mickey Mantle	New York	62	52
RBI	Mickey Mantle	New York	151	130
BA	Mickey Mantle	New York	.369	.353
AB	Nellie Fox	Chicago	683	649
R	Mickey Mantle	New York	153	132
H	Harvey Kuenn	Detroit	214	196
2B	Jimmy Piersall	Boston	54	40
3B	Jackie Jensen	Boston	8	11
	Minnie Minoso	Chicago	8	11
	Jim Lemon	Washington	8	11
	Harry Simpson	Kansas City	8	11
TB	Mickey Mantle	New York	427	376
SA	Mickey Mantle	New York	.761	.705
SB	Luis Aparicio	Chicago	53	21
PITCHING				
W	Frank Lary	Detroit	22	21
L	Art Ditmar	Kansas City	23	22
SV	George Zuverink	Baltimore	27	16
ERA	Whitey Ford	New York	2.85	2.47
G	George Zuverink	Baltimore	65	62
IP	Frank Lary	Detroit	308	294
BB	Paul Foytack	Detroit	147	142
SO	Herb Score	Cleveland	362	263

NATIONAL LEAGUE LEADERS

CAT.	PLAYER	TEAM	STATS ADJUSTED	ACTUAL
BATTING				
HR	Duke Snider	Brooklyn	50	43
RBI	Stan Musial	St. Louis	125	109
BA	Hank Aaron	Milwaukee	.342	.328
AB	Johnny Temple	Cincinnati	661	632
R	Frank Robinson	Cincinnati	141	122
H	Hank Aaron	Milwaukee	218	200
2B	Hank Aaron	Milwaukee	48	34
3B	Bill Bruton	Milwaukee	11	15
TB	Hank Aaron	Milwaukee	382	340
SA	Duke Snider	Brooklyn	.644	.598
SB	Willie Mays	New York	103	40
PITCHING				
W	Don Newcombe	Brooklyn	28	27
L	Robin Roberts	Philadelphia	19	18
	Ron Kline	Pittsburgh	18	18
SV	Clem Labine	Brooklyn	31	19
ERA	Lew Burdette	Milwaukee	3.11	2.70
G	Elroy Face	Pittsburgh	70	68
IP	Bob Friend	Pittsburgh	327	314.1
BB	Sam Jones	Chicago	117	115
SO	Sam Jones	Chicago	239	176

1957 SEASON

REGULAR SEASON STANDINGS

AMERICAN LEAGUE

		ADJUSTED				ACTUAL			
	W	L	Pct.	GB	W	L	Pct.	Rk.
EAST								
X New York	103	59	.636	0	98	56	.636	1
Boston	86	76	.531	17	82	72	.532	3
Baltimore	81	81	.500	22	76	76	.500	5
Washington	58	104	.358	45	55	99	.357	8
WEST								
X Chicago	95	67	.586	0	90	64	.584	2
Detroit	82	80	.506	13	78	76	.506	4
Cleveland	80	82	.494	15	76	77	.497	6
Kansas City	63	99	.389	32	59	94	.386	7

NATIONAL LEAGUE

		ADJUSTED				ACTUAL			
	W	L	Pct.	GB	W	L	Pct.	Rk.
EAST								
X Brooklyn	88	74	.543	0	84	70	.545	3
Philadelphia	81	81	.500	7	77	77	.500	5
New York	73	89	.451	15	69	85	.448	6
Pittsburgh	65	97	.401	23	62	92	.403	7
WEST								
X Milwaukee	100	62	.617	0	95	59	.617	1
St. Louis	92	70	.568	8	87	67	.565	2
Cincinnati	84	78	.519	16	80	74	.519	4
Chicago	65	97	.401	35	62	92	.403	7

SIMULATED PLAYOFFS

AMERICAN LEAGUE

ALCS	W	1	2	3	4	%
New York Yankees	0	3	1	1	3	58
Chicago White Sox	4	4	2	3	4	42

NATIONAL LEAGUE

NLCS	W	1	2	3	4	%
Brooklyn Dodgers	4	5	3	7	4	42
Milwaukee Braves	0	4	2	1	3	58

WORLD SERIES

WS	W	1	2	3	4	%
Chicago White Sox	0	2	2	5	1	61
Brooklyn Dodgers	4	3	5	6	3	39

ACTUAL WINNERS

American League: New York Yankees
National League: Milwaukee Braves
World Series: Milwaukee Braves

OUTSTANDING PERFORMANCES

AWARD WINNERS

LG.	PLAYER	TEAM	STATS	
			ADJUSTED	ACTUAL
MOST VALUABLE PLAYERS				
AL	Mickey Mantle	New York	42 HR, 114 RBI, .382 BA, $25.9 MIL	34 HR, 94 RBI, .365 BA
NL	Hank Aaron	Milwaukee	54 HR, 160 RBI, .337 BA, $25.8 MIL	44 HR, 132 RBI, .322 BA
CY YOUNG AWARDS				
AL	Jim Bunning	Detroit	21-8 W-L, 2 SV, 3.19 ERA, $19.5 MIL	20-8 W-L, 1 SV, 2.69 ERA
NL	Warren Spahn	Milwaukee	22-12 W-L, 4 SV, 3.19 ERA, $24.0 MIL	21-11 W-L, 3 SV, 2.69 ERA

AMERICAN LEAGUE LEADERS

CAT.	PLAYER	TEAM	STATS	
			ADJUSTED	ACTUAL
BATTING				
HR	Roy Sievers	Washington	52	42
RBI	Roy Sievers	Washington	139	114
BA	Ted Williams	Boston	.407	.388
AB	Billy Gardner	Baltimore	677	644
R	Mickey Mantle	New York	147	121
H	Nellie Fox	Chicago	214	196
2B	Billy Gardner	Baltimore	49	36
	Minnie Minoso	Chicago	49	36
3B	Hank Bauer	New York	7	9
	Gil McDougald	New York	7	9
	Harry Simpson	K.C.-N.Y.	7	9
TB	Roy Sievers	Washington	383	331
SA	Ted Williams	Boston	.796	.731
SB	Luis Aparicio	Chicago	66	28
PITCHING				
W	Jim Bunning	Detroit	21	20
	Billy Pierce	Chicago	21	20
L	Chuck Stobbs	Washington	21	20
SV	Bob Grim	New York	23	19
ERA	Bobby Shantz	New York	2.92	2.45
G	George Zuverink	Baltimore	59	56
IP	Jim Bunning	Detroit	279	267.1
BB	Ray Moore	Baltimore	130	112
SO	Early Wynn	Cleveland	257	184

NATIONAL LEAGUE LEADERS

CAT.	PLAYER	TEAM	STATS	
			ADJUSTED	ACTUAL
BATTING				
HR	Hank Aaron	Milwaukee	54	44
RBI	Hank Aaron	Milwaukee	160	132
BA	Stan Musial	St. Louis	.367	.351
AB	Don Blasingame	St. Louis	684	650
R	Hank Aaron	Milwaukee	143	118
H	Red Schoendienst	N.Y.-Mil.	219	200
2B	Don Hoak	Cincinnati	51	39
3B	Willie Mays	New York	15	20
TB	Hank Aaron	Milwaukee	422	369
SA	Willie Mays	New York	.685	.626
SB	Willie Mays	New York	92	38
PITCHING				
W	Warren Spahn	Milwaukee	22	21
L	Robin Roberts	Philadelphia	23	22
SV	Clem Labine	Brooklyn	27	17
ERA	Johnny Podres	Brooklyn	3.19	2.66
G	Turk Lown	Chicago	70	67
IP	Bob Friend	Pittsburgh	291	277
BB	Dick Drott	Chicago	146	129
SO	Jack Sanford	Philadelphia	255	188

1958 SEASON

REGULAR SEASON STANDINGS

AMERICAN LEAGUE

	ADJUSTED				ACTUAL			
	W	L	Pct.	GB	W	L	Pct.	Rk.
EAST								
X New York	97	65	.599	0	92	62	.597	1
Boston	83	79	.512	14	79	75	.513	3
Baltimore	78	84	.481	19	74	79	.484	6
Washington	64	98	.395	33	61	93	.396	8
WEST								
X Chicago	86	76	.531	0	82	72	.532	2
Cleveland	82	80	.506	4	77	76	.503	4
Detroit	81	81	.500	5	77	77	.500	5
Kansas City	77	85	.475	9	73	81	.474	7

NATIONAL LEAGUE

	ADJUSTED				ACTUAL			
	W	L	Pct.	GB	W	L	Pct.	Rk.
EAST								
X Milwaukee	97	65	.599	0	92	62	.597	1
Pittsburgh	88	74	.543	9	84	70	.545	2
Cincinnati	80	82	.494	17	76	78	.494	4
Philadelphia	72	90	.444	25	69	85	.448	8
WEST								
X San Francisco	84	78	.519	0	80	74	.519	3
Chicago	76	86	.469	8	72	82	.468	5
St. Louis	76	86	.469	8	72	82	.468	5
Los Angeles	75	87	.463	9	71	83	.461	7

SIMULATED PLAYOFFS

AMERICAN LEAGUE

ALCS	W	1	2	3	4	5	6	%
New York Yankees	4	3	2	8	5	3	4	74
Chicago White Sox	2	1	4	3	7	1	2	26

NATIONAL LEAGUE

NLCS	W	1	2	3	4	5	6	7	%
Milwaukee Braves	3	1	9	3	3	1	5	6	67
San Francisco Giants	4	3	2	1	4	6	3	7	33

WORLD SERIES

WS	W	1	2	3	4	5	6	7	%
New York Yankees	4	4	7	1	4	5	7	7	73
San Francisco Giants	3	1	9	6	8	3	4	4	27

ACTUAL WINNERS

American League: New York Yankees
National League: Milwaukee Braves
World Series: New York Yankees

OUTSTANDING PERFORMANCES

AWARD WINNERS

LG.	PLAYER	TEAM	STATS ADJUSTED	ACTUAL
MOST VALUABLE PLAYERS				
AL	Jackie Jensen	Boston	41 HR, 147 RBI, .298 BA, $16.1 MIL	35 HR, 122 RBI, .286 BA
NL	Ernie Banks	Chicago	58 HR, 156 RBI, .327 BA, $26.4 MIL	47 HR, 129 RBI, .313 BA
CY YOUNG AWARDS				
AL	Bob Turley	New York	22-7 W-L, 2 SV, 3.52 ERA, $20.3 MIL	21-7 W-L, 1 SV, 2.97 ERA
NL	Warren Spahn	Milwaukee	23-12 W-L, 2 SV, 3.63 ERA, $29.9 MIL	22-11 W-L, 1 SV, 3.07 ERA

AMERICAN LEAGUE LEADERS

CAT.	PLAYER	TEAM	STATS ADJUSTED	ACTUAL
BATTING				
HR	Mickey Mantle	New York	49	42
RBI	Jackie Jensen	Boston	147	122
BA	Ted Williams	Boston	.342	.328
AB	Frank Malzone	Boston	655	627
R	Mickey Mantle	New York	153	127
H	Nellie Fox	Chicago	204	187
2B	Harvey Kuenn	Detroit	53	39
3B	Vic Power	K.C.-Cle.	8	10
TB	Mickey Mantle	New York	348	307
SA	Rocky Colavito	Cleveland	.672	.620
SB	Luis Aparicio	Chicago	71	29
PITCHING				
W	Bob Turley	New York	22	21
L	Pedro Ramos	Washington	19	18
SV	Ryne Duren	New York	27	20
ERA	Whitey Ford	New York	2.38	2.01
G	Tex Clevenger	Washington	57	55
IP	Frank Lary	Detroit	274	260.1
BB	Bob Turley	New York	144	128
SO	Early Wynn	Chicago	242	179

NATIONAL LEAGUE LEADERS

CAT.	PLAYER	TEAM	STATS ADJUSTED	ACTUAL
BATTING				
HR	Ernie Banks	Chicago	58	47
RBI	Ernie Banks	Chicago	156	129
BA	Richie Ashburn	Philadelphia	.365	.350
AB	Ernie Banks	Chicago	649	617
R	Willie Mays	San Francisco	146	121
H	Richie Ashburn	Philadelphia	236	215
2B	Orlando Cepeda	San Francisco	49	38
3B	Richie Ashburn	Philadelphia	12	13
TB	Ernie Banks	Chicago	432	379
SA	Ernie Banks	Chicago	.666	.614
SB	Willie Mays	San Francisco	76	31
PITCHING				
W	Bob Friend	Pittsburgh	23	22
	Warren Spahn	Milwaukee	23	22
L	Ron Kline	Pittsburgh	17	16
SV	Elroy Face	Pittsburgh	30	20
ERA	Stu Miller	San Francisco	2.92	2.47
G	Don Elston	Chicago	73	69
IP	Warren Spahn	Milwaukee	305	290
BB	Sam Jones	St. Louis	123	107
SO	Sam Jones	St. Louis	300	225

1959 SEASON

REGULAR SEASON STANDINGS

AMERICAN LEAGUE

	ADJUSTED				ACTUAL			
	W	L	Pct.	GB	W	L	Pct.	Rk.
EAST								
X New York	83	79	.512	0	79	75	.513	3
Boston	79	83	.488	4	75	79	.487	5
Baltimore	78	84	.481	5	74	80	.481	6
Washington	66	96	.407	17	63	91	.409	8
WEST								
X Chicago	99	63	.611	0	94	60	.610	1
Cleveland	94	68	.580	5	89	65	.578	2
Detroit	80	82	.494	19	76	78	.494	4
Kansas City	69	93	.426	30	66	88	.429	7

NATIONAL LEAGUE

	ADJUSTED				ACTUAL			
	W	L	Pct.	GB	W	L	Pct.	Rk.
EAST								
X Milwaukee	90	72	.556	0	86	68	.558	1
Pittsburgh	82	80	.506	8	78	76	.506	4
Cincinnati	78	84	.481	12	74	80	.481	5
Philadelphia	67	95	.414	23	64	90	.416	8
WEST								
X Los Angeles	91	71	.562	0	86	68	.558	1
San Francisco	87	75	.537	4	83	71	.539	3
Chicago	78	84	.481	13	74	80	.481	5
St. Louis	75	87	.463	16	71	83	.461	7

SIMULATED PLAYOFFS

AMERICAN LEAGUE

ALCS	W	1	2	3	4	5	6	7	%
New York Yankees	3	6	2	1	8	4	3	1	51
Chicago White Sox	4	5	4	6	7	8	2	2	49

NATIONAL LEAGUE

NLCS**	W	1	2	3	4	5	6	7	%
Milwaukee Braves	3	2	5	5	0	13	4	1	67
Los Angeles Dodgers	4	3	6	2	9	4	3	2	33

WORLD SERIES

WS*	W	1	2	3	4	5	6	%
Chicago White Sox	2	11	3	1	4	1	3	58
Los Angeles Dodgers	4	0	4	3	5	0	9	42

ACTUAL WINNERS

American League: Chicago White Sox
National League: Los Angeles Dodgers
World Series: Los Angeles Dodgers

OUTSTANDING PERFORMANCES

AWARD WINNERS

LG.	PLAYER	TEAM	STATS ADJUSTED	ACTUAL
MOST VALUABLE PLAYERS				
AL	Nellie Fox	Chicago	2 HR, 81 RBI, .321 BA, $13.0 MIL	2 HR, 70 RBI, .306 BA
NL	Ernie Banks	Chicago	54 HR, 169 RBI, .318 BA, $25.5 MIL	45 HR, 143 RBI, .304 BA
CY YOUNG AWARDS				
AL	Early Wynn	Chicago	23-10 W-L, 0 SV, 3.70 ERA, $23.3 MIL	22-10 W-L, 0 SV, 3.17 ERA
NL	Sam Jones	San Francisco	22-16 W-L, 7 SV, 3.29 ERA, $25.2 MIL	21-15 W-L, 4 SV, 2.83 ERA

AMERICAN LEAGUE LEADERS

CAT.	PLAYER	TEAM	STATS ADJUSTED	ACTUAL
BATTING				
HR	Rocky Colavito	Cleveland	50	42
	Harmon Killebrew	Washington	50	42
RBI	Jackie Jensen	Boston	133	112
BA	Harvey Kuenn	Detroit	.370	.353
AB	Nellie Fox	Chicago	648	624
R	Eddie Yost	Detroit	136	115
H	Harvey Kuenn	Detroit	218	198
2B	Harvey Kuenn	Detroit	58	42
3B	Bob Allison	Washington	8	9
TB	Rocky Colavito	Cleveland	347	301
SA	Al Kaline	Detroit	.579	.530
SB	Luis Aparicio	Chicago	122	56
PITCHING				
W	Early Wynn	Chicago	23	22
L	Pedro Ramos	Washington	20	19
SV	Turk Lown	Chicago	25	15
ERA	Hoyt Wilhelm	Baltimore	2.55	2.19
G	Gerry Staley	Chicago	70	67
IP	Early Wynn	Chicago	263	255.2
BB	Early Wynn	Chicago	133	119
SO	Jim Bunning	Detroit	264	201

NATIONAL LEAGUE LEADERS

CAT.	PLAYER	TEAM	STATS ADJUSTED	ACTUAL
BATTING				
HR	Eddie Mathews	Milwaukee	55	46
RBI	Ernie Banks	Chicago	169	143
BA	Hank Aaron	Milwaukee	.373	.355
AB	Vada Pinson	Cincinnati	682	648
R	Vada Pinson	Cincinnati	155	131
H	Hank Aaron	Milwaukee	242	223
2B	Vada Pinson	Cincinnati	62	47
3B	Wally Moon	Los Angeles	9	11
	Charlie Neal	Los Angeles	9	11
TB	Hank Aaron	Milwaukee	450	400
SA	Hank Aaron	Milwaukee	.693	.636
SB	Willie Mays	San Francisco	57	27
PITCHING				
W	Lew Burdette	Milwaukee	22	21
	Sam Jones	San Francisco	22	21
	Warren Spahn	Milwaukee	22	21
L	Bob Friend	Pittsburgh	20	19
SV	Don McMahon	Milwaukee	26	15
	Lindy McDaniel	St. Louis	22	15
ERA	Sam Jones	San Francisco	3.29	2.83
G	Don Elston	Chicago	68	65
	Bill Henry	Chicago	68	65
IP	Warren Spahn	Milwaukee	299	292
BB	Sam Jones	San Francisco	125	109
SO	Don Drysdale	Los Angeles	313	242

1960 SEASON

REGULAR SEASON STANDINGS

AMERICAN LEAGUE

	ADJUSTED				ACTUAL			
	W	L	Pct.	GB	W	L	Pct.	Rk.
EAST								
X New York	102	60	.630	0	97	57	.630	1
Baltimore	94	68	.580	8	89	65	.578	2
Washington	77	85	.475	25	73	81	.474	5
Boston	68	94	.420	34	65	89	.422	7
WEST								
X Chicago	91	71	.562	0	87	67	.565	3
Cleveland	80	82	.494	11	76	78	.494	4
Detroit	75	87	.463	16	71	83	.461	6
Kansas City	61	101	.377	30	58	96	.377	8

NATIONAL LEAGUE

	ADJUSTED				ACTUAL			
	W	L	Pct.	GB	W	L	Pct.	Rk.
EAST								
X Pittsburgh	100	62	.617	0	95	59	.617	1
Milwaukee	93	69	.574	7	88	66	.571	2
Cincinnati	71	91	.438	29	67	87	.435	6
Philadelphia	62	100	.383	38	59	95	.383	8
WEST								
X St. Louis	90	72	.556	0	86	68	.558	3
Los Angeles	86	76	.531	4	82	72	.532	4
San Francisco	83	79	.512	7	79	75	.513	5
Chicago	63	99	.389	27	60	94	.390	7

SIMULATED PLAYOFFS

AMERICAN LEAGUE

ALCS	W	1	2	3	4	5	6	%
New York Yankees	2	5	3	5	1	9	5	50
Chicago White Sox	4	0	6	6	3	3	6	50

NATIONAL LEAGUE

NLCS	W	1	2	3	4	5	6	7	%
Pittsburgh Pirates	4	4	3	6	4	2	2	2	74
St. Louis Cardinals	3	2	2	1	5	4	3	1	26

WORLD SERIES

WS	W	1	2	3	4	5	6	7	%
Chicago White Sox	4	5	6	2	4	6	3	5	55
Pittsburgh Pirates	3	2	1	3	5	3	6	4	45

ACTUAL WINNERS

American League: New York Yankees
National League: Pittsburgh Pirates
World Series: Pittsburgh Pirates

OUTSTANDING PERFORMANCES

AWARD WINNERS

LG.	PLAYER	TEAM	STATS ADJUSTED	ACTUAL
MOST VALUABLE PLAYERS				
AL	Roger Maris	New York	49 HR, 134 RBI, .298 BA, $14.2 MIL	39 HR, 112 RBI, .283 BA
NL	Dick Groat	Pittsburgh	3 HR, 59 RBI, .343 BA, $9.1 MIL	2 HR, 50 RBI, .325 BA
CY YOUNG AWARDS				
AL	Chuck Estrada	Baltimore	19-12 W-L, 3 SV, 4.30 ERA, $19.5 MIL	18-11 W-L, 2 SV, 3.58 ERA
NL	Vern Law	Pittsburgh	21-10 W-L, 0 SV, 3.70 ERA, $25.5 MIL	20-9 W-L, 0 SV, 3.08 ERA

AMERICAN LEAGUE LEADERS

CAT.	PLAYER	TEAM	STATS ADJUSTED	ACTUAL
BATTING				
HR	Mickey Mantle	New York	50	40
RBI	Roger Maris	New York	134	112
BA	Pete Runnels	Boston	.338	.320
AB	Nellie Fox	Chicago	637	605
R	Mickey Mantle	New York	142	119
H	Minnie Minoso	Chicago	204	184
2B	Tito Francona	Cleveland	45	36
3B	Nellie Fox	Chicago	9	10
TB	Mickey Mantle	New York	340	294
SA	Roger Maris	New York	.643	.581
SB	Luis Aparicio	Chicago	102	51
PITCHING				
W	Chuck Estrada	Baltimore	19	18
	Jim Perry	Cleveland	19	18
L	Pedro Ramos	Washington	19	18
SV	Mike Fornieles	Boston	22	14
	Johnny Klippstein	Cleveland	21	14
ERA	Frank Baumann	Chicago	3.22	2.67
G	Mike Fornieles	Boston	74	70
IP	Frank Lary	Detroit	289	274.1
BB	Steve Barber	Baltimore	127	113
SO	Jim Bunning	Detroit	262	201

NATIONAL LEAGUE LEADERS

CAT.	PLAYER	TEAM	STATS ADJUSTED	ACTUAL
BATTING				
HR	Ernie Banks	Chicago	51	41
RBI	Hank Aaron	Milwaukee	151	126
BA	Dick Groat	Pittsburgh	.343	.325
AB	Vada Pinson	Cincinnati	677	652
R	Bill Bruton	Milwaukee	134	112
H	Willie Mays	San Francisco	208	190
2B	Vada Pinson	Cincinnati	50	37
3B	Bill Bruton	Milwaukee	11	13
TB	Hank Aaron	Milwaukee	386	334
SA	Frank Robinson	Cincinnati	.659	.595
SB	Maury Wills	Los Angeles	100	50
PITCHING				
W	Ernie Broglio	St. Louis	22	21
	Warren Spahn	Milwaukee	22	21
L	Glen Hobbie	Chicago	21	20
SV	Lindy McDaniel	St. Louis	34	26
ERA	Mike McCormick	San Francisco	3.21	2.70
G	Elroy Face	Pittsburgh	71	68
IP	Larry Jackson	St. Louis	295	282
BB	Bob Buhl	Milwaukee	115	103
SO	Don Drysdale	Los Angeles	316	246

1961 SEASON

REGULAR SEASON STANDINGS

AMERICAN LEAGUE

	ADJUSTED				ACTUAL			
	W	L	Pct.	GB	W	L	Pct.	Rk.
EAST								
X New York	109	53	.673	0	109	53	.673	1
Baltimore	95	67	.586	14	95	67	.586	3
Cleveland	79	83	.488	30	78	83	.484	5
Boston	76	86	.469	33	76	86	.469	6
Washington	61	101	.377	48	61	100	.379	9
WEST								
X Detroit	101	61	.623	0	101	61	.623	2
Chicago	86	76	.531	15	86	76	.531	4
Los Angeles	71	91	.438	30	70	91	.435	8
Minnesota	71	91	.438	30	70	90	.438	7
Kansas City	61	101	.377	40	61	100	.379	9

NATIONAL LEAGUE

	ADJUSTED				ACTUAL			
	W	L	Pct.	GB	W	L	Pct.	Rk.
EAST								
X Cincinnati	98	64	.605	0	93	61	.604	1
Milwaukee	87	75	.537	11	83	71	.539	4
Pittsburgh	79	83	.488	19	75	79	.487	6
Philadelphia	50	112	.309	48	47	107	.305	8
WEST								
X Los Angeles	94	68	.580	0	89	65	.578	2
San Francisco	89	73	.549	5	85	69	.552	3
St. Louis	84	78	.519	10	80	74	.519	5
Chicago	67	95	.414	27	64	90	.416	7

SIMULATED PLAYOFFS

AMERICAN LEAGUE

ALCS	W	1	2	3	4	5	%
New York Yankees	4	4	4	11	6	7	65
Detroit Tigers	1	3	3	2	7	2	35

NATIONAL LEAGUE

NLCS	W	1	2	3	4	%
Cincinnati Reds	4	5	4	11	8	54
Los Angeles Dodgers	0	2	2	2	6	46

WORLD SERIES

WS*	W	1	2	3	4	5	%
New York Yankees	4	2	2	3	7	13	79
Cincinnati Reds	1	0	6	2	0	5	21

ACTUAL WINNERS

American League: New York Yankees
National League: Cincinnati Reds
World Series: New York Yankees

OUTSTANDING PERFORMANCES

AWARD WINNERS

LG.	PLAYER	TEAM	STATS ADJUSTED	ACTUAL
MOST VALUABLE PLAYERS				
AL	Roger Maris	New York	67 HR, 153 RBI, .280 BA, $19.8 MIL	61 HR, 142 RBI, .269 BA
NL	Frank Robinson	Cincinnati	43 HR, 142 RBI, .337 BA, $19.3 MIL	37 HR, 124 RBI, .323 BA
CY YOUNG AWARDS				
AL	Whitey Ford	New York	25-4 W-L, 0 SV, 3.66 ERA, $25.5 MIL	25-4 W-L, 0 SV, 3.21 ERA
NL	Warren Spahn	Milwaukee	22-14 W-L, 0 SV, 3.42 ERA, $23.6 MIL	21-13 W-L, 0 SV, 3.02 ERA

AMERICAN LEAGUE LEADERS

CAT.	PLAYER	TEAM	STATS ADJUSTED	ACTUAL
BATTING				
HR	Roger Maris	New York	67	61
RBI	Roger Maris	New York	153	142
BA	Norm Cash	Detroit	.376	.361
AB	Brooks Robinson	Baltimore	664	668
R	Mickey Mantle	New York	143	132
	Roger Maris	New York	142	132
H	Norm Cash	Detroit	200	193
2B	Al Kaline	Detroit	52	41
3B	Jake Wood	Detroit	11	14
TB	Roger Maris	New York	390	366
SA	Mickey Mantle	New York	.736	.687
SB	Luis Aparicio	Chicago	102	53
PITCHING				
W	Whitey Ford	New York	25	25
L	Pedro Ramos	Minnesota	20	20
SV	Luis Arroyo	New York	35	29
ERA	Dick Donovan	Washington	2.72	2.40
G	Luis Arroyo	New York	65	65
IP	Whitey Ford	New York	283	283
BB	Chuck Estrada	Baltimore	136	132
SO	Camilo Pascual	Minnesota	267	221

NATIONAL LEAGUE LEADERS

CAT.	PLAYER	TEAM	STATS ADJUSTED	ACTUAL
BATTING				
HR	Orlando Cepeda	San Francisco	53	46
RBI	Orlando Cepeda	San Francisco	162	142
BA	Roberto Clemente	Pittsburgh	.367	.351
AB	Maury Wills	Los Angeles	646	613
R	Willie Mays	San Francisco	147	129
H	Vada Pinson	Cincinnati	228	208
2B	Hank Aaron	Milwaukee	51	39
3B	George Altman	Chicago	9	12
TB	Hank Aaron	Milwaukee	402	358
SA	Frank Robinson	Cincinnati	.653	.611
SB	Maury Wills	Los Angeles	70	35
PITCHING				
W	Joey Jay	Cincinnati	22	21
	Warren Spahn	Milwaukee	22	21
L	Bob Friend	Pittsburgh	20	19
	Art Mahaffey	Philadelphia	20	19
SV	Elroy Face	Pittsburgh	24	17
	Stu Miller	San Francisco	24	17
ERA	Warren Spahn	Milwaukee	3.42	3.02
G	Jack Baldschun	Philadelphia	68	65
IP	Lew Burdette	Milwaukee	286	272.1
BB	Bob Gibson	St. Louis	130	119
SO	Sandy Koufax	Los Angeles	336	269

1962 SEASON

REGULAR SEASON STANDINGS

AMERICAN LEAGUE

	ADJUSTED				ACTUAL			
	W	L	Pct.	GB	W	L	Pct.	Rk.
EAST								
X New York	96	66	.593	0	96	66	.593	1
Cleveland	80	82	.494	16	80	82	.494	6
Baltimore	77	85	.475	19	77	85	.475	7
Boston	77	85	.475	19	76	84	.475	7
Washington	60	102	.370	36	60	101	.373	10
WEST								
X Minnesota	91	71	.562	0	91	71	.562	2
Los Angeles	86	76	.531	5	86	76	.531	3
Detroit	86	76	.531	5	85	76	.528	4
Chicago	85	77	.525	6	85	77	.525	5
Kansas City	72	90	.444	19	72	90	.444	9

NATIONAL LEAGUE

	ADJUSTED				ACTUAL			
	W	L	Pct.	GB	W	L	Pct.	Rk.
EAST								
X Cincinnati	98	64	.605	0	98	64	.605	3
Pittsburgh	94	68	.580	4	93	68	.578	4
Milwaukee	86	76	.531	12	86	76	.531	5
Philadelphia	82	80	.506	16	81	80	.503	7
New York	40	122	.247	58	40	120	.250	10
WEST								
X San Francisco	101	61	.623	0	101	61	.623	1
X Los Angeles	101	61	.623	0	101	61	.623	1
St. Louis	84	78	.519	17	84	78	.519	6
Houston	65	97	.401	36	64	96	.400	8
Chicago	59	103	.364	42	59	103	.364	9

SIMULATED PLAYOFFS

AMERICAN LEAGUE

ALCS	W	1	2	3	4	5	6	%
New York Yankees	2	6	2	2	9	4	3	49
Minnesota Twins	4	1	7	3	8	7	4	51

NATIONAL LEAGUE

TIEBREAKER*	W	1	2	3		%
San Francisco Giants	2	8	7	6		49
Los Angeles Dodgers	1	0	8	4		51

NLCS	W	1	2	3	4	5	6	7	%
Cincinnati Reds	3	5	4	6	9	6	5	7	48
San Francisco Giants	4	6	5	9	2	1	2	8	52

WORLD SERIES

WS	W	1	2	3	4	5	6	7	%
Minnesota Twins	3	7	4	7	8	4	2	3	44
San Francisco Giants	4	2	5	0	5	10	4	10	56

ACTUAL WINNERS

American League: New York Yankees
National League: San Francisco Giants
World Series: New York Yankees

OUTSTANDING PERFORMANCES

AWARD WINNERS

LG.	PLAYER	TEAM	STATS ADJUSTED	ACTUAL
MOST VALUABLE PLAYERS				
AL	Mickey Mantle	New York	34 HR, 99 RBI, .334 BA, $9.9 MIL	30 HR, 89 RBI, .321 BA
NL	Maury Wills	Los Angeles	9 HR, 52 RBI, .312 BA, $9.8 MIL	6 HR, 48 RBI, .299 BA
CY YOUNG AWARDS				
AL	Dick Donovan	Cleveland	20-10 W-L, 0 SV, 4.16 ERA, $13.9 MIL	20-10 W-L, 0 SV, 3.59 ERA
NL	Don Drysdale	Los Angeles	24-9 W-L, 1 SV, 3.25 ERA, $33.2 MIL	25-9 W-L, 1 SV, 2.83 ERA

AMERICAN LEAGUE LEADERS

CAT.	PLAYER	TEAM	STATS ADJUSTED	ACTUAL
BATTING				
HR	Harmon Killebrew	Minnesota	53	48
RBI	Harmon Killebrew	Minnesota	139	126
BA	Pete Runnels	Boston	.341	.326
AB	Bobby Richardson	New York	692	692
R	Albie Pearson	Los Angeles	127	115
H	Bobby Richardson	New York	218	209
2B	Floyd Robinson	Chicago	61	45
3B	Gino Cimoli	Kansas City	12	15
TB	Rocky Colavito	Detroit	338	309
SA	Mickey Mantle	New York	.660	.605
SB	Luis Aparicio	Chicago	52	31
PITCHING				
W	Ralph Terry	New York	23	23
L	Chuck Estrada	Baltimore	17	17
	Ed Rakow	Kansas City	17	17
SV	Dick Radatz	Boston	30	24
ERA	Hank Aguirre	Detroit	2.54	2.21
G	Dick Radatz	Boston	63	62
IP	Ralph Terry	New York	299	298.2
BB	Bo Belinsky	Los Angeles	130	122
SO	Camilo Pascual	Minnesota	245	206

NATIONAL LEAGUE LEADERS

CAT.	PLAYER	TEAM	STATS ADJUSTED	ACTUAL
BATTING				
HR	Willie Mays	San Francisco	54	49
RBI	Tommy Davis	Los Angeles	167	153
BA	Tommy Davis	Los Angeles	.361	.346
AB	Maury Wills	Los Angeles	682	695
R	Frank Robinson	Cincinnati	149	134
H	Tommy Davis	Los Angeles	236	230
2B	Frank Robinson	Cincinnati	65	51
3B	Maury Wills	Los Angeles	9	10
	Bill Virdon	Pittsburgh	8	10
	Johnny Callison	Philadelphia	7	10
	Willie Davis	Los Angeles	7	10
TB	Willie Mays	San Francisco	409	382
SA	Frank Robinson	Cincinnati	.678	.624
SB	Maury Wills	Los Angeles	180	104
PITCHING				
W	Don Drysdale	Los Angeles	24	25
L	Roger Craig	New York	24	24
SV	Elroy Face	Pittsburgh	33	28
ERA	Sandy Koufax	Los Angeles	2.93	2.54
G	Ron Perranoski	Los Angeles	69	70
IP	Don Drysdale	Los Angeles	307	314.1
BB	Jack Hamilton	Philadelphia	114	107
SO	Don Drysdale	Los Angeles	270	232

1963 SEASON

REGULAR SEASON STANDINGS

AMERICAN LEAGUE

		ADJUSTED			ACTUAL			
	W	L	Pct.	GB	W	L	Pct.	Rk.
EAST								
X New York	105	57	.648	0	104	57	.646	1
Baltimore	86	76	.531	19	86	76	.531	4
Cleveland	79	83	.488	26	79	83	.488	5
Boston	76	86	.469	29	76	85	.472	7
Washington	56	106	.346	49	56	106	.346	10
WEST								
X Chicago	94	68	.580	0	94	68	.580	2
Minnesota	92	70	.568	2	91	70	.565	3
Detroit	79	83	.488	15	79	83	.488	5
Kansas City	73	89	.451	21	73	89	.451	8
Los Angeles	70	92	.432	24	70	91	.435	9

NATIONAL LEAGUE

		ADJUSTED			ACTUAL			
	W	L	Pct.	GB	W	L	Pct.	Rk.
EAST								
X Philadelphia	87	75	.537	0	87	75	.537	4
Cincinnati	86	76	.531	1	86	76	.531	5
Milwaukee	84	78	.519	3	84	78	.519	6
Pittsburgh	74	88	.457	13	74	88	.457	8
New York	51	111	.315	36	51	111	.315	10
WEST								
X Los Angeles	99	63	.611	0	99	63	.611	1
St. Louis	93	69	.574	6	93	69	.574	2
San Francisco	88	74	.543	11	88	74	.543	3
Chicago	82	80	.506	17	82	80	.506	7
Houston	66	96	.407	33	66	96	.407	9

SIMULATED PLAYOFFS

AMERICAN LEAGUE

ALCS	W	1	2	3	4	5	6	7	%
New York Yankees	3	3	3	3	3	5	4	3	51
Chicago White Sox	4	4	4	1	2	3	5	4	49

NATIONAL LEAGUE

NLCS	W	1	2	3	4				%
Philadelphia Phillies	4	5	3	4	2				48
Los Angeles Dodgers	0	4	1	3	1				52

WORLD SERIES

WS	W	1	2	3	4	5			%
Chicago White Sox	4	2	3	4	3	4			63
Philadelphia Phillies	1	5	2	3	2	1			37

ACTUAL WINNERS

American League: New York Yankees
National League: Los Angeles Dodgers
World Series: Los Angeles Dodgers

OUTSTANDING PERFORMANCES

AWARD WINNERS

LG.	PLAYER	TEAM	STATS ADJUSTED	ACTUAL
MOST VALUABLE PLAYERS				
AL	Elston Howard	New York	35 HR, 106 RBI, .314 BA, $4.7 MIL	28 HR, 85 RBI, .287 BA
NL	Sandy Koufax	Los Angeles	25-5 W-L, 0 SV, 2.49 ERA, $33.8 MIL	25-5 W-L, 0 SV, 1.88 ERA
CY YOUNG AWARDS				
AL	Whitey Ford	New York	24-7 W-L, 1 SV, 3.61 ERA, $25.1 MIL	24-7 W-L, 1 SV, 2.74 ERA
NL	Sandy Koufax	Los Angeles	25-5 W-L, 0 SV, 2.49 ERA, $33.8 MIL	25-5 W-L, 0 SV, 1.88 ERA

AMERICAN LEAGUE LEADERS

CAT.	PLAYER	TEAM	ADJUSTED	ACTUAL
BATTING				
HR	Harmon Killebrew	Minnesota	54	45
RBI	Dick Stuart	Boston	148	118
BA	Carl Yastrzemski	Boston	.352	.321
AB	Bobby Richardson	New York	634	630
R	Bob Allison	Minnesota	124	99
H	Carl Yastrzemski	Boston	202	183
2B	Carl Yastrzemski	Boston	55	40
3B	Zoilo Versalles	Minnesota	11	13
TB	Dick Stuart	Boston	368	319
SA	Harmon Killebrew	Minnesota	.638	.555
SB	Luis Aparicio	Baltimore	73	40
PITCHING				
W	Whitey Ford	New York	24	24
L	Orlando Pena	Kansas City	20	20
SV	Stu Miller	Baltimore	34	27
ERA	Gary Peters	Chicago	3.07	2.33
G	Stu Miller	Baltimore	71	71
IP	Whitey Ford	New York	269	269.1
BB	Earl Wilson	Boston	128	105
SO	Camilo Pascual	Minnesota	226	202

NATIONAL LEAGUE LEADERS

CAT.	PLAYER	TEAM	ADJUSTED	ACTUAL
BATTING				
HR	Hank Aaron	Milwaukee	54	44
	Willie McCovey	San Francisco	54	44
RBI	Hank Aaron	Milwaukee	161	130
BA	Tommy Davis	Los Angeles	.357	.326
AB	Curt Flood	St. Louis	662	662
R	Hank Aaron	Milwaukee	150	121
H	Vada Pinson	Cincinnati	223	204
2B	Dick Groat	St. Louis	63	43
3B	Vada Pinson	Cincinnati	11	14
TB	Hank Aaron	Milwaukee	424	370
SA	Hank Aaron	Milwaukee	.676	.586
SB	Maury Wills	Los Angeles	72	40
PITCHING				
W	Sandy Koufax	Los Angeles	25	25
	Juan Marichal	San Francisco	25	25
L	Roger Craig	New York	22	22
SV	Lindy McDaniel	Chicago	26	22
ERA	Sandy Koufax	Los Angeles	2.49	1.88
G	Ron Perranoski	Los Angeles	69	69
IP	Juan Marichal	San Francisco	321	321.1
BB	Ray Culp	Philadelphia	124	102
SO	Sandy Koufax	Los Angeles	341	306

1964 SEASON

REGULAR SEASON STANDINGS

AMERICAN LEAGUE

		ADJUSTED				ACTUAL		
	W	L	Pct.	GB	W	L	Pct.	Rk.
EAST								
X New York	99	63	.611	0	99	63	.611	1
Baltimore	97	65	.599	2	97	65	.599	3
Cleveland	79	83	.488	20	79	83	.488	6
Boston	72	90	.444	27	72	90	.444	8
Washington	62	100	.383	37	62	100	.383	9
WEST								
X Chicago	98	64	.605	0	98	64	.605	2
Detroit	85	77	.525	13	85	77	.525	4
Los Angeles	82	80	.506	16	82	80	.506	5
Minnesota	79	83	.488	19	79	83	.488	6
Kansas City	57	105	.352	41	57	105	.352	10

NATIONAL LEAGUE

		ADJUSTED				ACTUAL		
	W	L	Pct.	GB	W	L	Pct.	Rk.
EAST								
X Cincinnati	92	70	.568	0	92	70	.568	2
X Philadelphia	92	70	.568	0	92	70	.568	2
Milwaukee	88	74	.543	4	88	74	.543	5
Pittsburgh	80	82	.494	12	80	82	.494	6
New York	53	109	.327	39	53	109	.327	10
WEST								
X St. Louis	93	69	.574	0	93	69	.574	1
San Francisco	90	72	.556	3	90	72	.556	4
Los Angeles	80	82	.494	13	80	82	.494	6
Chicago	76	86	.469	17	76	86	.469	8
Houston	66	96	.407	27	66	96	.407	9

SIMULATED PLAYOFFS

AMERICAN LEAGUE

ALCS	W	1	2	3	4		%
New York Yankees	4	6	2	4	5		43
Chicago White Sox	0	5	1	3	3		57

NATIONAL LEAGUE

TIEBREAKER	W	1	2				%
Cincinnati Reds	2	4	4				60
Philadelphia Phillies	0	1	1				40

NLCS	W	1	2	3	4	5	6	%
Cincinnati Reds	2	3	2	2	7	3	2	50
St. Louis Cardinals	4	6	6	0	6	6	6	50

WORLD SERIES

WS*	W	1	2	3	4	5	6	7	%
New York Yankees	3	5	8	2	3	2	8	5	67
St. Louis Cardinals	4	9	3	1	4	5	3	7	33

ACTUAL WINNERS

American League: New York Yankees
National League: St. Louis Cardinals
World Series: St. Louis Cardinals

OUTSTANDING PERFORMANCES

AWARD WINNERS

LG.	PLAYER	TEAM	STATS	
			ADJUSTED	ACTUAL
MOST VALUABLE PLAYERS				
AL	Brooks Robinson	Baltimore	34 HR, 143 RBI, .340 BA, $15.1 MIL	28 HR, 118 RBI, .317 BA
NL	Ken Boyer	St. Louis	31 HR, 145 RBI, .317 BA, $19.4 MIL	24 HR, 119 RBI, .295 BA
CY YOUNG AWARDS				
AL	Dean Chance	Los Angeles	20-9 W-L, 5 SV, 2.10 ERA, $20.3 MIL	20-9 W-L, 4 SV, 1.65 ERA
NL	Larry Jackson	Chicago	24-11 W-L, 0 SV, 4.02 ERA, $24.8 MIL	24-11 W-L, 0 SV, 3.14 ERA

AMERICAN LEAGUE LEADERS

CAT.	PLAYER	TEAM	STATS	
			ADJUSTED	ACTUAL
BATTING				
HR	Harmon Killebrew	Minnesota	58	49
RBI	Brooks Robinson	Baltimore	143	118
BA	Tony Oliva	Minnesota	.347	.323
AB	Bobby Richardson	New York	670	679
R	Tony Oliva	Minnesota	132	109
H	Tony Oliva	Minnesota	232	217
2B	Tony Oliva	Minnesota	56	43
3B	Rich Rollins	Minnesota	8	10
	Zoilo Versalles	Minnesota	8	10
TB	Tony Oliva	Minnesota	422	374
SA	Boog Powell	Baltimore	.689	.606
SB	Luis Aparicio	Baltimore	111	57
PITCHING				
W	Dean Chance	Los Angeles	20	20
	Gary Peters	Chicago	20	20
L	Diego Segui	Kansas City	17	17
SV	Dick Radatz	Boston	34	29
ERA	Dean Chance	Los Angeles	2.10	1.65
G	John Wyatt	Kansas City	81	81
IP	Dean Chance	Los Angeles	278	278.1
BB	Al Downing	New York	146	120
SO	Al Downing	New York	238	217

NATIONAL LEAGUE LEADERS

CAT.	PLAYER	TEAM	STATS	
			ADJUSTED	ACTUAL
BATTING				
HR	Willie Mays	San Francisco	58	47
RBI	Ken Boyer	St. Louis	145	119
BA	Roberto Clemente	Pittsburgh	.365	.339
AB	Curt Flood	St. Louis	679	679
R	Dick Allen	Philadelphia	152	125
H	Roberto Clemente	Pittsburgh	227	211
	Curt Flood	St. Louis	227	211
2B	Lee Maye	Milwaukee	59	44
3B	Dick Allen	Philadelphia	11	13
	Ron Santo	Chicago	11	13
TB	Dick Allen	Philadelphia	399	352
SA	Willie Mays	San Francisco	.690	.607
SB	Maury Wills	Los Angeles	102	53
PITCHING				
W	Larry Jackson	Chicago	24	24
L	Tracy Stallard	New York	20	20
SV	Hal Woodeshick	Houston	27	23
ERA	Sandy Koufax	Los Angeles	2.22	1.74
G	Bob Miller	Los Angeles	73	74
IP	Don Drysdale	Los Angeles	321	321.1
BB	Bob Veale	Pittsburgh	151	124
SO	Bob Veale	Pittsburgh	274	250

1965 SEASON

REGULAR SEASON STANDINGS

AMERICAN LEAGUE

		ADJUSTED				ACTUAL			
	W	L	Pct.	GB	W	L	Pct.	Rk.
EAST								
X Baltimore	94	68	.580	0	94	68	.580	3
Cleveland	87	75	.537	7	87	75	.537	5
New York	77	85	.475	17	77	85	.475	6
Washington	70	92	.432	24	70	92	.432	8
Boston	62	100	.383	32	62	100	.383	9
WEST								
X Minnesota	102	60	.630	0	102	60	.630	1
Chicago	95	67	.586	7	95	67	.586	2
Detroit	89	73	.549	13	89	73	.549	4
California	75	87	.463	27	75	87	.463	7
Kansas City	59	103	.364	43	59	103	.364	10

NATIONAL LEAGUE

		ADJUSTED				ACTUAL			
	W	L	Pct.	GB	W	L	Pct.	Rk.
EAST								
X Pittsburgh	90	72	.556	0	90	72	.556	3
Cincinnati	89	73	.549	1	89	73	.549	4
Milwaukee	86	76	.531	4	86	76	.531	5
Philadelphia	86	76	.531	4	85	76	.528	6
New York	50	112	.309	40	50	112	.309	10
WEST								
X Los Angeles	97	65	.599	0	97	65	.599	1
San Francisco	95	67	.586	2	95	67	.586	2
St. Louis	80	82	.494	17	80	81	.497	7
Chicago	72	90	.444	25	72	90	.444	8
Houston	65	97	.401	32	65	97	.401	9

SIMULATED PLAYOFFS

AMERICAN LEAGUE

ALCS	W	1	2	3	4	5	6	%
Baltimore Orioles	4	2	3	5	4	3	9	34
Minnesota Twins	2	5	2	4	1	7	5	66

NATIONAL LEAGUE

NLCS	W	1	2	3	4	5	6	%
Pittsburgh Pirates	2	2	2	3	3	2	1	45
Los Angeles Dodgers	4	3	3	2	2	4	3	55

WORLD SERIES

WS	W	1	2	3	4	5	6	%
Baltimore Orioles	4	0	4	2	4	3	5	40
Los Angeles Dodgers	2	3	3	1	2	4	1	60

ACTUAL WINNERS

American League: Minnesota Twins
National League: Los Angeles Dodgers
World Series: Los Angeles Dodgers

OUTSTANDING PERFORMANCES

AWARD WINNERS

LG.	PLAYER	TEAM	STATS ADJUSTED	ACTUAL
MOST VALUABLE PLAYERS				
AL	Zoilo Versalles	Minnesota	25 HR, 94 RBI, .299 BA, $19.5 MIL	19 HR, 77 RBI, .273 BA
NL	Willie Mays	San Francisco	63 HR, 137 RBI, .348 BA, $19.5 MIL	52 HR, 112 RBI, .317 BA
CY YOUNG AWARDS				
AL	Eddie Fisher	Chicago	15-7 W-L, 29 SV, 3.11 ERA, $9.5 MIL	15-7 W-L, 24 SV, 2.40 ERA
NL	Sandy Koufax	Los Angeles	26-8 W-L, 2 SV, 2.65 ERA, $51.2 MIL	26-8 W-L, 2 SV, 2.04 ERA

AMERICAN LEAGUE LEADERS

CAT.	PLAYER	TEAM	STATS ADJUSTED	ACTUAL
BATTING				
HR	Tony Conigliaro	Boston	40	32
RBI	Rocky Colavito	Cleveland	132	108
BA	Tony Oliva	Minnesota	.352	.321
AB	Zoilo Versalles	Minnesota	666	666
R	Zoilo Versalles	Minnesota	155	126
H	Tony Oliva	Minnesota	203	185
2B	Zoilo Versalles	Minnesota	62	45
	Carl Yastrzemski	Boston	58	45
3B	Bert Campaneris	Kansas City	10	12
	Zoilo Versalles	Minnesota	9	12
TB	Zoilo Versalles	Minnesota	354	308
SA	Carl Yastrzemski	Boston	.613	.536
SB	Bert Campaneris	Kansas City	79	51
PITCHING				
W	Mudcat Grant	Minnesota	21	21
L	Bill Monbouquette	Boston	18	18
	Dave Morehead	Boston	18	18
	John O'Donoghue	Kansas City	18	18
SV	Ron Kline	Washington	34	29
ERA	Sam McDowell	Cleveland	2.84	2.18
G	Eddie Fisher	Chicago	82	82
IP	Mel Stottlemyre	New York	291	291
BB	Sam McDowell	Cleveland	154	132
SO	Sam McDowell	Cleveland	352	325

NATIONAL LEAGUE LEADERS

CAT.	PLAYER	TEAM	STATS ADJUSTED	ACTUAL
BATTING				
HR	Willie Mays	San Francisco	63	52
RBI	Deron Johnson	Cincinnati	160	130
BA	Roberto Clemente	Pittsburgh	.361	.329
AB	Pete Rose	Cincinnati	670	670
R	Tommy Harper	Cincinnati	155	126
H	Pete Rose	Cincinnati	229	209
2B	Hank Aaron	Milwaukee	51	40
3B	Johnny Callison	Philadelphia	13	16
TB	Willie Mays	San Francisco	412	360
SA	Willie Mays	San Francisco	.744	.645
SB	Maury Wills	Los Angeles	151	94
PITCHING				
W	Sandy Koufax	Los Angeles	26	26
L	Jack Fisher	New York	23	24
SV	Ted Abernathy	Chicago	36	31
ERA	Sandy Koufax	Los Angeles	2.65	2.04
G	Ted Abernathy	Chicago	83	84
IP	Sandy Koufax	Los Angeles	336	335.2
BB	Tony Cloninger	Milwaukee	139	119
	Bob Veale	Pittsburgh	139	119
SO	Sandy Koufax	Los Angeles	416	382

1966 SEASON

REGULAR SEASON STANDINGS

AMERICAN LEAGUE

		ADJUSTED				ACTUAL			
	W	L	Pct.	GB	W	L	Pct.	Rk.
EAST								
X Baltimore	98	64	.605	0	97	63	.606	1
Cleveland	81	81	.500	17	81	81	.500	5
Washington	73	89	.451	25	71	88	.447	8
Boston	72	90	.444	26	72	90	.444	9
New York	71	91	.438	27	70	89	.440	10
WEST								
X Minnesota	89	73	.549	0	89	73	.549	2
Detroit	88	74	.543	1	88	74	.543	3
Chicago	83	79	.512	6	83	79	.512	4
California	80	82	.494	9	80	82	.494	6
Kansas City	75	87	.463	14	74	86	.463	7

NATIONAL LEAGUE

		ADJUSTED				ACTUAL			
	W	L	Pct.	GB	W	L	Pct.	Rk.
EAST								
X Pittsburgh	92	70	.568	0	92	70	.568	3
Philadelphia	87	75	.537	5	87	75	.537	4
Atlanta	85	77	.525	7	85	77	.525	5
Cincinnati	77	85	.475	15	76	84	.475	7
New York	66	96	.407	26	66	95	.410	9
WEST								
X Los Angeles	95	67	.586	0	95	67	.586	1
San Francisco	94	68	.580	1	93	68	.578	2
St. Louis	83	79	.512	12	83	79	.512	6
Houston	72	90	.444	23	72	90	.444	8
Chicago	59	103	.364	36	59	103	.364	10

SIMULATED PLAYOFFS

AMERICAN LEAGUE

ALCS	W	1	2	3	4	5	6	7	%
Baltimore Orioles	4	1	6	7	3	3	3	5	59
Minnesota Twins	3	5	3	2	2	4	6	2	41

NATIONAL LEAGUE

NLCS	W	1	2	3	4	5	6	7	%
Pittsburgh Pirates	4	1	2	3	2	5	1	2	45
Los Angeles Dodgers	3	2	1	2	4	2	5	1	55

WORLD SERIES

WS	W	1	2	3	4	5	6	7	%
Baltimore Orioles	0	1	3	2	6				44
Pittsburgh Pirates	4	7	8	6	7				56

ACTUAL WINNERS

American League: Baltimore Orioles
National League: Los Angeles Dodgers
World Series: Baltimore Orioles

OUTSTANDING PERFORMANCES

AWARD WINNERS

			STATS	
LG.	PLAYER	TEAM	ADJUSTED	ACTUAL
MOST VALUABLE PLAYERS				
AL	Frank Robinson	Baltimore	58 HR, 152 RBI, .343 BA, $23.2 MIL	49 HR, 122 RBI, .316 BA
NL	Roberto Clemente	Pittsburgh	37 HR, 146 RBI, .343 BA, $13.8 MIL	29 HR, 119 RBI, .317 BA
CY YOUNG AWARDS				
AL	Jim Kaat	Minnesota	25-13 W-L, 0 SV, 3.57 ERA, $32.4 MIL	25-13 W-L, 0 SV, 2.75 ERA
NL	Sandy Koufax	Los Angeles	27-9 W-L, 0 SV, 2.23 ERA, $50.9 MIL	27-9 W-L, 0 SV, 1.73 ERA

AMERICAN LEAGUE LEADERS

			STATS	
CAT.	PLAYER	TEAM	ADJUSTED	ACTUAL
BATTING				
HR	Frank Robinson	Baltimore	58	49
RBI	Frank Robinson	Baltimore	152	122
BA	Frank Robinson	Baltimore	.343	.316
AB	Luis Aparicio	Baltimore	668	659
R	Frank Robinson	Baltimore	152	122
H	Tony Oliva	Minnesota	207	191
2B	Carl Yastrzemski	Boston	52	39
3B	Bobby Knoop	California	8	11
TB	Frank Robinson	Baltimore	422	367
SA	Frank Robinson	Baltimore	.724	.637
SB	Bert Campaneris	Kansas City	81	52
PITCHING				
W	Jim Kaat	Minnesota	25	25
L	Mel Stottlemyre	New York	20	20
SV	Jack Aker	Kansas City	37	32
ERA	Gary Peters	Chicago	2.55	1.98
G	Eddie Fisher	Chi.-Balt.	67	67
IP	Jim Kaat	Minnesota	305	304.2
BB	Dean Chance	California	143	114
SO	Sam McDowell	Cleveland	247	225

NATIONAL LEAGUE LEADERS

			STATS	
CAT.	PLAYER	TEAM	ADJUSTED	ACTUAL
BATTING				
HR	Hank Aaron	Atlanta	52	44
RBI	Hank Aaron	Atlanta	155	127
BA	Matty Alou	Pittsburgh	.370	.342
AB	Felipe Alou	Atlanta	662	666
R	Felipe Alou	Atlanta	149	122
H	Felipe Alou	Atlanta	235	218
2B	Johnny Callison	Philadelphia	56	40
3B	Tim McCarver	St. Louis	11	13
TB	Felipe Alou	Atlanta	400	355
SA	Dick Allen	Philadelphia	.719	.632
SB	Lou Brock	St. Louis	116	74
PITCHING				
W	Sandy Koufax	Los Angeles	27	27
L	Dick Ellsworth	Chicago	22	22
SV	Phil Regan	Los Angeles	25	21
ERA	Sandy Koufax	Los Angeles	2.23	1.73
G	Clay Carroll	Atlanta	73	73
IP	Sandy Koufax	Los Angeles	323	323
BB	Tony Cloninger	Atlanta	145	116
SO	Sandy Koufax	Los Angeles	352	317

1967 SEASON

REGULAR SEASON STANDINGS

AMERICAN LEAGUE

		ADJUSTED				ACTUAL		
	W	L	Pct.	GB	W	L	Pct.	Rk.
EAST								
X Boston	92	70	.568	0	92	70	.568	1
Baltimore	77	85	.475	15	76	85	.472	6
Washington	76	86	.469	16	76	85	.472	6
Cleveland	75	87	.463	17	75	87	.463	8
New York	72	90	.444	20	72	90	.444	9
WEST								
X Detroit	91	71	.562	0	91	71	.562	2
X Minnesota	91	71	.562	0	91	71	.562	2
Chicago	89	73	.549	2	89	73	.549	4
California	85	77	.525	6	84	77	.522	5
Kansas City	62	100	.383	29	62	99	.385	10

NATIONAL LEAGUE

		ADJUSTED				ACTUAL		
	W	L	Pct.	GB	W	L	Pct.	Rk.
EAST								
X Cincinnati	87	75	.537	0	87	75	.537	4
Philadelphia	82	80	.506	5	82	80	.506	5
Pittsburgh	81	81	.500	6	81	81	.500	6
Atlanta	77	85	.475	10	77	85	.475	7
New York	61	101	.377	26	61	101	.377	10
WEST								
X St. Louis	102	60	.630	0	101	60	.627	1
San Francisco	91	71	.562	11	91	71	.562	2
Chicago	87	75	.537	15	87	74	.540	3
Los Angeles	73	89	.451	29	73	89	.451	8
Houston	69	93	.426	33	69	93	.426	9

SIMULATED PLAYOFFS

AMERICAN LEAGUE

TIEBREAKER	W	1	2						%
Detroit Tigers	0	3	2						53
Minnesota Twins	2	7	3						47

ALCS	W	1	2	3	4	5	6	7	%
Boston Red Sox	4	4	9	7	2	4	3	2	56
Minnesota Twins	3	5	7	10	1	3	4	1	44

NATIONAL LEAGUE

NLCS	W	1	2	3	4	5			%
Cincinnati Reds	1	1	4	1	1	1			36
St. Louis Cardinals	4	2	2	2	6	3			64

WORLD SERIES

WS*	W	1	2	3	4	5	6	7	%
Boston Red Sox	3	1	5	2	0	3	8	2	43
St. Louis Cardinals	4	2	0	5	6	1	4	7	57

ACTUAL WINNERS

American League: Boston Red Sox
National League: St. Louis Cardinals
World Series: St. Louis Cardinals

OUTSTANDING PERFORMANCES

AWARD WINNERS

LG.	PLAYER	TEAM	STATS ADJUSTED	ACTUAL
MOST VALUABLE PLAYERS				
AL	Carl Yastrzemski	Boston	59 HR, 157 RBI, .363 BA, $19.8 MIL	44 HR, 121 RBI, .326 BA
NL	Orlando Cepeda	St. Louis	35 HR, 145 RBI, .362 BA, $11.8 MIL	25 HR, 111 RBI, .325 BA
CY YOUNG AWARDS				
AL	Jim Lonborg	Boston	22-9 W-L, 0 SV, 4.38 ERA, $20.4 MIL	22-9 W-L, 0 SV, 3.16 ERA
NL	Mike McCormick	San Francisco	22-10 W-L, 0 SV, 3.95 ERA, $16.1 MIL	22-10 W-L, 0 SV, 2.85 ERA

AMERICAN LEAGUE LEADERS

CAT.	PLAYER	TEAM	STATS ADJUSTED	ACTUAL
BATTING				
HR	Carl Yastrzemski	Boston	59	44
	Harmon Killebrew	Minnesota	57	44
RBI	Carl Yastrzemski	Boston	157	121
BA	Carl Yastrzemski	Boston	.363	.326
AB	Cesar Tovar	Minnesota	641	649
R	Carl Yastrzemski	Boston	145	112
H	Carl Yastrzemski	Boston	210	189
2B	Tony Oliva	Minnesota	46	34
3B	Paul Blair	Baltimore	10	12
TB	Carl Yastrzemski	Boston	431	360
SA	Carl Yastrzemski	Boston	.744	.622
SB	Bert Campaneris	Kansas City	91	55
PITCHING				
W	Jim Lonborg	Boston	22	22
	Earl Wilson	Detroit	22	22
L	George Brunet	California	19	19
SV	Minnie Rojas	California	32	27
ERA	Joel Horlen	Chicago	2.83	2.06
G	Bob Locker	Chicago	77	77
IP	Dean Chance	Minnesota	284	283.2
BB	Sam McDowell	Cleveland	149	123
SO	Jim Lonborg	Boston	267	246

NATIONAL LEAGUE LEADERS

CAT.	PLAYER	TEAM	STATS ADJUSTED	ACTUAL
BATTING				
HR	Hank Aaron	Atlanta	53	39
RBI	Orlando Cepeda	St. Louis	145	111
BA	Roberto Clemente	Pittsburgh	.398	.357
AB	Lou Brock	St. Louis	693	689
R	Lou Brock	St. Louis	147	113
	Hank Aaron	Atlanta	146	113
H	Roberto Clemente	Pittsburgh	231	209
2B	Rusty Staub	Houston	61	44
3B	Vada Pinson	Cincinnati	10	13
TB	Hank Aaron	Atlanta	413	344
SA	Hank Aaron	Atlanta	.688	.573
SB	Lou Brock	St. Louis	85	52
PITCHING				
W	Mike McCormick	San Francisco	22	22
L	Jack Fisher	New York	18	18
SV	Ted Abernathy	Cincinnati	34	28
ERA	Phil Niekro	Atlanta	2.57	1.87
G	Ted Abernathy	Cincinnati	70	70
	Ron Perranoski	Los Angeles	70	70
IP	Jim Bunning	Philadelphia	302	302.1
BB	Bob Veale	Pittsburgh	144	119
SO	Jim Bunning	Philadelphia	275	253

1968 SEASON

REGULAR SEASON STANDINGS

AMERICAN LEAGUE

		ADJUSTED				ACTUAL			
	W	L	Pct.	GB	W	L	Pct.	Rk.
EAST								
X Baltimore	91	71	.562	0	91	71	.562	2
Cleveland	87	75	.537	4	86	75	.534	3
Boston	86	76	.531	5	86	76	.531	4
New York	83	79	.512	8	83	79	.512	5
Washington	65	97	.401	26	65	96	.404	10
WEST								
X Detroit	103	59	.636	0	103	59	.636	1
Oakland	82	80	.506	21	82	80	.506	6
Minnesota	79	83	.488	24	79	83	.488	7
California	67	95	.414	36	67	95	.414	8
Chicago	67	95	.414	36	67	95	.414	8

NATIONAL LEAGUE

		ADJUSTED				ACTUAL			
	W	L	Pct.	GB	W	L	Pct.	Rk.
EAST								
X Cincinnati	83	79	.512	0	83	79	.512	4
Atlanta	81	81	.500	2	81	81	.500	5
Pittsburgh	80	82	.494	3	80	82	.494	6
Philadelphia	76	86	.469	7	76	86	.469	7
New York	73	89	.451	10	73	89	.451	9
WEST								
X St. Louis	97	65	.599	0	97	65	.599	1
San Francisco	88	74	.543	9	88	74	.543	2
Chicago	84	78	.519	13	84	78	.519	3
Los Angeles	76	86	.469	21	76	86	.469	7
Houston	72	90	.444	25	72	90	.444	10

SIMULATED PLAYOFFS

AMERICAN LEAGUE

ALCS	W	1	2	3	4		%
Baltimore Orioles	0	2	3	0	1		36
Detroit Tigers	4	4	5	3	3		64

NATIONAL LEAGUE

NLCS	W	1	2	3	4	5	6	%
Cincinnati Reds	4	6	2	2	5	1	6	35
St. Louis Cardinals	2	0	9	1	4	8	2	65

WORLD SERIES

WS	W	1	2	3	4	5	6	7	%
Detroit Tigers	3	4	11	9	4	4	7	1	82
Cincinnati Reds	4	5	6	4	7	5	4	4	18

ACTUAL WINNERS

American League: Detroit Tigers
National League: St. Louis Cardinals
World Series: Detroit Tigers

OUTSTANDING PERFORMANCES

AWARD WINNERS

LG.	PLAYER	TEAM	STATS ADJUSTED	ACTUAL
MOST VALUABLE PLAYERS				
AL	Denny McLain	Detroit	31-6 W-L, 0 SV, 2.97 ERA, $42.8 MIL	31-6 W-L, 0 SV, 1.96 ERA
NL	Bob Gibson	St. Louis	22-9 W-L, 0 SV, 1.71 ERA, $31.4 MIL	22-9 W-L, 0 SV, 1.12 ERA
CY YOUNG AWARDS				
AL	Denny McLain	Detroit	31-6 W-L, 0 SV, 2.97 ERA, $42.8 MIL	31-6 W-L, 0 SV, 1.96 ERA
NL	Bob Gibson	St. Louis	22-9 W-L, 0 SV, 1.71 ERA, $31.4 MIL	22-9 W-L, 0 SV, 1.12 ERA

AMERICAN LEAGUE LEADERS

CAT.	PLAYER	TEAM	STATS ADJUSTED	ACTUAL
BATTING				
HR	Frank Howard	Washington	64	44
RBI	Ken Harrelson	Boston	155	109
BA	Carl Yastrzemski	Boston	.341	.301
AB	Bert Campaneris	Oakland	638	642
R	Dick McAuliffe	Detroit	133	95
H	Bert Campaneris	Oakland	200	177
2B	Reggie Smith	Boston	52	37
3B	Jim Fregosi	California	12	13
TB	Frank Howard	Washington	418	330
SA	Frank Howard	Washington	.694	.552
SB	Bert Campaneris	Oakland	91	62
PITCHING				
W	Denny McLain	Detroit	31	31
L	George Brunet	California	17	17
SV	Al Worthington	Minnesota	23	18
ERA	Luis Tiant	Cleveland	2.44	1.60
G	Wilbur Wood	Chicago	88	88
IP	Denny McLain	Detroit	336	336
BB	Sam McDowell	Cleveland	141	110
SO	Sam McDowell	Cleveland	310	283

NATIONAL LEAGUE LEADERS

CAT.	PLAYER	TEAM	STATS ADJUSTED	ACTUAL
BATTING				
HR	Willie McCovey	San Francisco	53	36
RBI	Willie McCovey	San Francisco	148	105
BA	Pete Rose	Cincinnati	.383	.335
AB	Felipe Alou	Atlanta	658	662
R	Glenn Beckert	Chicago	138	98
H	Felipe Alou	Atlanta	238	210
	Pete Rose	Cincinnati	238	210
2B	Lou Brock	St. Louis	77	46
3B	Lou Brock	St. Louis	14	14
TB	Billy Williams	Chicago	401	321
SA	Willie McCovey	San Francisco	.688	.545
SB	Lou Brock	St. Louis	92	62
PITCHING				
W	Juan Marichal	San Francisco	26	26
L	Claude Osteen	Los Angeles	18	18
	Ray Sadecki	San Francisco	18	18
SV	Phil Regan	L.A.-Chi.	32	25
ERA	Bob Gibson	St. Louis	1.71	1.12
G	Ted Abernathy	Cincinnati	78	78
IP	Juan Marichal	San Francisco	326	326
BB	Bob Veale	Pittsburgh	120	94
SO	Bob Gibson	St. Louis	296	268

1969 SEASON

REGULAR SEASON STANDINGS

AMERICAN LEAGUE

	ADJUSTED				ACTUAL			
	W	L	Pct.	GB	W	L	Pct.	Rk.
EAST								
X Baltimore	109	53	.673	0	109	53	.673	1
Boston	87	75	.537	22	87	75	.537	5
Washington	86	76	.531	23	86	76	.531	6
New York	81	81	.500	28	80	81	.497	7
CENTRAL								
X Minnesota	97	65	.599	0	97	65	.599	2
X Detroit	90	72	.556	7	90	72	.556	3
Chicago	68	94	.420	29	68	94	.420	10
Cleveland	62	100	.383	35	62	99	.385	12
WEST								
X Oakland	88	74	.543	0	88	74	.543	4
California	71	91	.438	17	71	91	.438	8
Kansas City	69	93	.426	19	69	93	.426	9
Seattle	64	98	.395	24	64	98	.395	11

NATIONAL LEAGUE

	ADJUSTED				ACTUAL			
	W	L	Pct.	GB	W	L	Pct.	Rk.
EAST								
X New York	100	62	.617	0	100	62	.617	1
X Atlanta	93	69	.574	7	93	69	.574	2
Philadelphia	63	99	.389	37	63	99	.389	10
Montreal	52	110	.321	48	52	110	.321	11
CENTRAL								
X Chicago	92	70	.568	0	92	70	.568	3
Cincinnati	89	73	.549	3	89	73	.549	5
Pittsburgh	88	74	.543	4	88	74	.543	6
St. Louis	87	75	.537	5	87	75	.537	7
WEST								
X San Francisco	90	72	.556	0	90	72	.556	4
Los Angeles	85	77	.525	5	85	77	.525	8
Houston	81	81	.500	9	81	81	.500	9
San Diego	52	110	.321	38	52	110	.321	11

SIMULATED PLAYOFFS

AMERICAN LEAGUE

ALDS (1-4)	W	1	2	3		%
Baltimore Orioles	3	7	8	6		82
Oakland Athletics	0	1	2	4		18

ALDS (2-3)	W	1	2	3		%
Minnesota Twins	3	6	1	8		58
Detroit Tigers	0	5	0	1		42

ALCS**	W	1	2	3	4	%
Baltimore Orioles	4	4	1	11	6	67
Minnesota Twins	0	3	0	2	3	33

NATIONAL LEAGUE

NLDS (1-4)	W	1	2	3	4	5	%
New York Mets	3	3	11	2	4	3	50
San Francisco Giants	2	2	4	4	6	2	50

NLDS (2-3)	W	1	2	3		%
Atlanta Braves	3	3	5	5		51
Chicago Cubs	0	2	4	3		49

NLCS**	W	1	2	3	4	%
New York Mets	4	9	11	7	2	44
Atlanta Braves	0	5	6	4	1	56

WORLD SERIES

WS*	W	1	2	3	4	5	%
Baltimore Orioles	1	4	1	0	1	3	65
New York Mets	4	1	2	5	2	5	35

ACTUAL WINNERS

American League: Baltimore Orioles
National League: New York Mets
World Series: New York Mets

OUTSTANDING PERFORMANCES

AWARD WINNERS

LG.	PLAYER	TEAM	STATS ADJUSTED	ACTUAL
MOST VALUABLE PLAYERS				
AL	Harmon Killebrew	Minnesota	60 HR, 168 RBI, .299 BA, $19.3 MIL	49 HR, 140 RBI, .276 BA
NL	Willie McCovey	San Francisco	55 HR, 151 RBI, .346 BA, $12.9 MIL	45 HR, 126 RBI, .320 BA
CY YOUNG AWARDS				
AL	Mike Cuellar	Baltimore	23-11 W-L, 0 SV, 3.03 ERA, $24.3 MIL	23-11 W-L, 0 SV, 2.38 ERA
AL	Denny McLain	Detroit	24-9 W-L, 0 SV, 3.54 ERA, $34.5 MIL	24-9 W-L, 0 SV, 2.80 ERA
NL	Tom Seaver	New York	25-7 W-L, 0 SV, 2.80 ERA, $26.8 MIL	25-7 W-L, 0 SV, 2.21 ERA

AMERICAN LEAGUE LEADERS

CAT.	PLAYER	TEAM	STATS ADJUSTED	ACTUAL
BATTING				
HR	Harmon Killebrew	Minnesota	60	49
RBI	Harmon Killebrew	Minnesota	168	140
BA	Rod Carew	Minnesota	.360	.332
AB	Horace Clarke	New York	641	641
R	Reggie Jackson	Oakland	148	123
H	Tony Oliva	Minnesota	214	197
2B	Tony Oliva	Minnesota	53	39
3B	Del Unser	Washington	8	8
TB	Frank Howard	Washington	393	340
SA	Reggie Jackson	Oakland	.705	.608
SB	Tommy Harper	Seattle	106	73
PITCHING				
W	Denny McLain	Detroit	24	24
L	Luis Tiant	Cleveland	20	20
SV	Ron Perranoski	Minnesota	37	31
ERA	Dick Bosman	Washington	2.80	2.19
G	Wilbur Wood	Chicago	76	76
IP	Denny McLain	Detroit	325	325
BB	Luis Tiant	Cleveland	135	129
SO	Sam McDowell	Cleveland	311	279

NATIONAL LEAGUE LEADERS

CAT.	PLAYER	TEAM	STATS ADJUSTED	ACTUAL
BATTING				
HR	Willie McCovey	San Francisco	55	45
RBI	Willie McCovey	San Francisco	151	126
BA	Pete Rose	Cincinnati	.377	.348
AB	Matty Alou	Pittsburgh	698	698
R	Bobby Bonds	San Francisco	144	120
	Pete Rose	Cincinnati	143	120
H	Matty Alou	Pittsburgh	251	231
2B	Matty Alou	Pittsburgh	66	41
3B	Roberto Clemente	Pittsburgh	11	12
TB	Hank Aaron	Atlanta	385	332
SA	Willie McCovey	San Francisco	.760	.656
SB	Lou Brock	St. Louis	77	53
PITCHING				
W	Tom Seaver	New York	25	25
L	Clay Kirby	San Diego	20	20
SV	Fred Gladding	Houston	33	29
ERA	Juan Marichal	San Francisco	2.67	2.10
G	Wayne Granger	Cincinnati	89	90
IP	Gaylord Perry	San Francisco	325	325.1
BB	Bill Stoneman	Montreal	128	123
SO	Fergie Jenkins	Chicago	305	273

1970 SEASON

REGULAR SEASON STANDINGS

AMERICAN LEAGUE

		ADJUSTED				ACTUAL		
	W	L	Pct.	GB	W	L	Pct.	Rk.
EAST								
X Baltimore	108	54	.667	0	108	54	.667	1
X New York	93	69	.574	15	93	69	.574	3
Boston	87	75	.537	21	87	75	.537	5
Washington	70	92	.432	38	70	92	.432	9
CENTRAL								
X Detroit	79	83	.488	0	79	83	.488	7
Cleveland	76	86	.469	3	76	86	.469	8
Milwaukee	65	97	.401	14	65	97	.401	10
Chicago	56	106	.346	23	56	106	.346	12
WEST								
X Minnesota	98	64	.605	0	98	64	.605	2
Oakland	89	73	.549	9	89	73	.549	4
California	86	76	.531	12	86	76	.531	6
Kansas City	65	97	.401	33	65	97	.401	10

NATIONAL LEAGUE

		ADJUSTED				ACTUAL		
	W	L	Pct.	GB	W	L	Pct.	Rk.
EAST								
X New York	83	79	.512	0	83	79	.512	6
Atlanta	76	86	.469	7	76	86	.469	8
Philadelphia	73	89	.451	10	73	88	.453	10
Montreal	73	89	.451	10	73	89	.451	11
CENTRAL								
X Cincinnati	102	60	.630	0	102	60	.630	1
X Pittsburgh	89	73	.549	13	89	73	.549	2
Chicago	84	78	.519	18	84	78	.519	5
St. Louis	76	86	.469	26	76	86	.469	8
WEST								
X Los Angeles	88	74	.543	0	87	74	.540	3
San Francisco	86	76	.531	2	86	76	.531	4
Houston	79	83	.488	9	79	83	.488	7
San Diego	63	99	.389	25	63	99	.389	12

SIMULATED PLAYOFFS

AMERICAN LEAGUE

ALDS (1-4)	W	1	2	3	4	5		%
Baltimore Orioles	3	2	3	6	7	5		90
Detroit Tigers	2	5	4	2	2	2		10

ALDS (2-3)	W	1	2	3	4	5		%
Minnesota Twins	3	4	3	1	6	6		55
New York Yankees	2	1	4	5	3	5		45

ALCS**	W	1	2	3	4	5	6	%
Baltimore Orioles	4	10	11	6	2	0	2	57
Minnesota Twins	2	6	3	1	4	1	1	43

NATIONAL LEAGUE

NLDS (1-4)	W	1	2	3		%
Cincinnati Reds	0	2	2	4		56
New York Mets	3	5	3	6		44

NLDS (2-3)	W	1	2	3	4	5	%
Pittsburgh Pirates	2	6	3	4	5	2	49
Los Angeles Dodgers	3	7	6	1	2	7	51

NLCS	W	1	2	3	4	5	6	%
New York Mets	2	5	5	2	5	2	2	47
Los Angeles Dodgers	4	6	2	3	1	3	4	53

WORLD SERIES

WS	W	1	2	3	4	5	6	%
Baltimore Orioles	2	5	2	5	3	3	1	72
Los Angeles Dodgers	4	3	3	3	4	4	5	28

ACTUAL WINNERS

American League: Baltimore Orioles
National League: Cincinnati Reds
World Series: Baltimore Orioles

OUTSTANDING PERFORMANCES

AWARD WINNERS

LG.	PLAYER	TEAM	STATS	
			ADJUSTED	ACTUAL
MOST VALUABLE PLAYERS				
AL	Boog Powell	Baltimore	40 HR, 129 RBI, .314 BA, $11.8 MIL	35 HR, 114 RBI, .297 BA
NL	Johnny Bench	Cincinnati	53 HR, 168 RBI, .311 BA, $14.9 MIL	45 HR, 148 RBI, .293 BA
CY YOUNG AWARDS				
AL	Jim Perry	Minnesota	24-12 W-L, 0 SV, 3.58 ERA, $19.1 MIL	24-12 W-L, 0 SV, 3.04 ERA
NL	Bob Gibson	St. Louis	23-7 W-L, 0 SV, 3.67 ERA, $31.4 MIL	23-7 W-L, 0 SV, 3.12 ERA

AMERICAN LEAGUE LEADERS

CAT.	PLAYER	TEAM	STATS	
			ADJUSTED	ACTUAL
BATTING				
HR	Frank Howard	Washington	51	44
RBI	Frank Howard	Washington	143	126
BA	Alex Johnson	California	.349	.329
AB	Horace Clarke	New York	682	686
R	Carl Yastrzemski	Boston	142	125
H	Tony Oliva	Minnesota	216	204
2B	Cesar Tovar	Minnesota	51	36
	Amos Otis	Kansas City	50	36
	Tony Oliva	Minnesota	47	36
3B	Cesar Tovar	Minnesota	11	13
TB	Carl Yastrzemski	Boston	371	335
SA	Carl Yastrzemski	Boston	.655	.592
SB	Bert Campaneris	Oakland	59	42
PITCHING				
W	Mike Cuellar	Baltimore	24	24
	Dave McNally	Baltimore	24	24
	Jim Perry	Minnesota	24	24
L	Mickey Lolich	Detroit	19	19
SV	Ron Perranoski	Minnesota	35	34
ERA	Diego Segui	Oakland	3.00	2.56
G	Wilbur Wood	Chicago	77	77
IP	Sam McDowell	Cleveland	305	305
	Jim Palmer	Baltimore	305	305
BB	Sam McDowell	Cleveland	133	131
SO	Sam McDowell	Cleveland	340	304

NATIONAL LEAGUE LEADERS

CAT.	PLAYER	TEAM	STATS	
			ADJUSTED	ACTUAL
BATTING				
HR	Johnny Bench	Cincinnati	53	45
RBI	Johnny Bench	Cincinnati	168	148
BA	Rico Carty	Atlanta	.389	.366
AB	Matty Alou	Pittsburgh	677	677
R	Billy Williams	Chicago	155	137
H	Pete Rose	Cincinnati	217	205
	Billy Williams	Chicago	217	205
2B	Wes Parker	Los Angeles	63	47
3B	Willie Davis	Los Angeles	15	16
TB	Billy Williams	Chicago	413	373
SA	Willie McCovey	San Francisco	.677	.612
SB	Bobby Tolan	Cincinnati	81	57
PITCHING				
W	Bob Gibson	St. Louis	23	23
	Gaylord Perry	San Francisco	23	23
L	Steve Carlton	St. Louis	19	19
SV	Wayne Granger	Cincinnati	37	35
ERA	Tom Seaver	New York	3.31	2.82
G	Ron Herbel	S.D.-N.Y.	76	76
IP	Gaylord Perry	San Francisco	329	328.2
BB	Carl Morton	Montreal	127	125
SO	Tom Seaver	New York	317	283

1971 SEASON

REGULAR SEASON STANDINGS

AMERICAN LEAGUE

		ADJUSTED				ACTUAL		
	W	L	Pct.	GB	W	L	Pct.	Rk.
EAST								
X Baltimore	104	58	.642	0	101	57	.639	1
X Boston	85	77	.525	19	85	77	.525	5
New York	82	80	.506	22	82	80	.506	6
Washington	64	98	.395	40	63	96	.396	11
CENTRAL								
X Detroit	91	71	.562	0	91	71	.562	3
Chicago	79	83	.488	12	79	83	.488	7
Milwaukee	69	93	.426	22	69	92	.429	10
Cleveland	60	102	.370	31	60	102	.370	12
WEST								
X Oakland	102	60	.630	0	101	60	.627	2
X Kansas City	85	77	.525	17	85	76	.528	4
California	76	86	.469	26	76	86	.469	8
Minnesota	75	87	.463	27	74	86	.463	9

NATIONAL LEAGUE

		ADJUSTED				ACTUAL		
	W	L	Pct.	GB	W	L	Pct.	Rk.
EAST								
X New York	83	79	.512	0	83	79	.512	5
Atlanta	82	80	.506	1	82	80	.506	7
Montreal	72	90	.444	11	71	90	.441	10
Philadelphia	67	95	.414	16	67	95	.414	11
CENTRAL								
X Pittsburgh	97	65	.599	0	97	65	.599	1
X St. Louis	90	72	.556	7	90	72	.556	2
Chicago	83	79	.512	14	83	79	.512	5
Cincinnati	79	83	.488	18	79	83	.488	8
WEST								
X San Francisco	90	72	.556	0	90	72	.556	2
Los Angeles	89	73	.549	1	89	73	.549	4
Houston	79	83	.488	11	79	83	.488	8
San Diego	61	101	.377	29	61	100	.379	12

SIMULATED PLAYOFFS

AMERICAN LEAGUE

TIEBREAKER	W	1	2				%
Boston Red Sox	0	0	1				42
Kansas City Royals	2	2	4				58

ALDS (1-4)	W	1	2	3	4	5	%
Baltimore Orioles	3	1	1	3	8	5	79
Kansas City Royals	2	2	2	2	3	3	21

ALDS (2-3)	W	1	2	3			%
Oakland Athletics	3	8	4	8			56
Detroit Tigers	0	5	2	3			44

ALCS**	W	1	2	3	4		%
Baltimore Orioles	4	5	5	5	5		63
Oakland Athletics	0	3	1	3	3		37

NATIONAL LEAGUE

NLDS (1-4)	W	1	2	3		%
Pittsburgh Pirates	3	4	5	8		79
New York Mets	0	3	4	1		21

NLDS (2-3)	W	1	2	3	4	5	%
San Francisco Giants	3	5	5	8	2	8	45
St. Louis Cardinals	2	1	4	9	3	4	55

NLCS**	W	1	2	3	4	5	%
Pittsburgh Pirates	4	4	9	2	9	9	77
San Francisco Giants	1	5	4	1	5	3	23

WORLD SERIES

WS*	W	1	2	3	4	5	6	7	%
Baltimore Orioles	3	5	11	1	3	0	3	1	58
Pittsburgh Pirates	4	3	3	5	4	4	2	2	42

ACTUAL WINNERS

American League: Baltimore Orioles
National League: Pittsburgh Pirates
World Series: Pittsburgh Pirates

OUTSTANDING PERFORMANCES

AWARD WINNERS

LG.	PLAYER	TEAM	STATS ADJUSTED	ACTUAL
MOST VALUABLE PLAYERS				
AL	Vida Blue	Oakland	24-8 W-L, 0 SV, 2.39 ERA, $26.2 MIL	24-8 W-L, 0 SV, 1.82 ERA
NL	Joe Torre	St. Louis	34 HR, 171 RBI, .392 BA, $16.5 MIL	24 HR, 137 RBI, .363 BA
CY YOUNG AWARDS				
AL	Vida Blue	Oakland	24-8 W-L, 0 SV, 2.39 ERA, $26.2 MIL	24-8 W-L, 0 SV, 1.82 ERA
NL	Fergie Jenkins	Chicago	24-13 W-L, 0 SV, 3.66 ERA, $41.3 MIL	24-13 W-L, 0 SV, 2.77 ERA

AMERICAN LEAGUE LEADERS

CAT.	PLAYER	TEAM	STATS ADJUSTED	ACTUAL
BATTING				
HR	Bill Melton	Chicago	43	33
RBI	Harmon Killebrew	Minnesota	151	119
BA	Tony Oliva	Minnesota	.364	.337
AB	Sandy Alomar	California	689	689
R	Don Buford	Baltimore	127	99
H	Cesar Tovar	Minnesota	223	204
2B	Reggie Smith	Boston	42	33
3B	Freddie Patek	Kansas City	11	11
TB	Reggie Smith	Boston	355	302
SA	Tony Oliva	Minnesota	.642	.546
SB	Amos Otis	Kansas City	79	52
PITCHING				
W	Mickey Lolich	Detroit	25	25
L	Denny McLain	Washington	23	22
SV	Ken Sanders	Milwaukee	41	31
ERA	Vida Blue	Oakland	2.39	1.82
G	Ken Sanders	Milwaukee	84	83
IP	Mickey Lolich	Detroit	376	376
BB	Sam McDowell	Cleveland	171	153
SO	Mickey Lolich	Detroit	367	308

NATIONAL LEAGUE LEADERS

CAT.	PLAYER	TEAM	STATS ADJUSTED	ACTUAL
BATTING				
HR	Willie Stargell	Pittsburgh	61	48
RBI	Joe Torre	St. Louis	171	137
BA	Joe Torre	St. Louis	.392	.363
AB	Larry Bowa	Philadelphia	650	650
R	Lou Brock	St. Louis	157	126
H	Joe Torre	St. Louis	247	230
2B	Cesar Cedeno	Houston	57	40
3B	Roger Metzger	Houston	14	11
	Joe Morgan	Houston	10	11
TB	Joe Torre	St. Louis	409	352
SA	Hank Aaron	Atlanta	.782	.669
SB	Lou Brock	St. Louis	97	64
PITCHING				
W	Fergie Jenkins	Chicago	24	24
L	Steve Arlin	San Diego	19	19
SV	Dave Giusti	Pittsburgh	36	30
ERA	Tom Seaver	New York	2.33	1.76
G	Wayne Granger	Cincinnati	70	70
IP	Fergie Jenkins	Chicago	325	325
BB	Bill Stoneman	Montreal	163	146
SO	Tom Seaver	New York	338	289

1972 SEASON

REGULAR SEASON STANDINGS

AMERICAN LEAGUE

		ADJUSTED				ACTUAL		
	W	L	Pct.	GB	W	L	Pct.	Rk.
EAST								
X Boston	89	73	.549	0	85	70	.548	4
Baltimore	84	78	.519	5	80	74	.519	5
New York	83	79	.512	6	79	76	.510	6
Cleveland	75	87	.463	14	72	84	.462	10
CENTRAL								
X Chicago	92	70	.568	0	87	67	.565	2
X Detroit	89	73	.549	3	86	70	.551	3
Minnesota	81	81	.500	11	77	77	.500	7
Milwaukee	67	95	.414	25	65	91	.417	11
WEST								
X Oakland	97	65	.599	0	93	62	.600	1
Kansas City	80	82	.494	17	76	78	.494	8
California	78	84	.481	19	75	80	.484	9
Texas	57	105	.352	40	54	100	.351	12

NATIONAL LEAGUE

		ADJUSTED				ACTUAL		
	W	L	Pct.	GB	W	L	Pct.	Rk.
EAST								
X New York	86	76	.531	0	83	73	.532	6
Atlanta	74	88	.457	12	70	84	.455	8
Montreal	73	89	.451	13	70	86	.449	9
Philadelphia	61	101	.377	25	59	97	.378	12
CENTRAL								
X Pittsburgh	100	62	.617	0	96	59	.619	1
X Cincinnati	100	62	.617	0	95	59	.617	2
Chicago	89	73	.549	11	85	70	.548	4
St. Louis	78	84	.481	22	75	81	.481	7
WEST								
X Los Angeles	89	73	.549	0	85	70	.548	4
X Houston	89	73	.549	0	84	69	.549	3
San Francisco	72	90	.444	17	69	86	.445	10
San Diego	61	101	.377	28	58	95	.379	11

SIMULATED PLAYOFFS

AMERICAN LEAGUE

ALDS (1-4)*	W	1	2	3	4	5		%
Oakland Athletics	3	3	5	0	3	2		72
Detroit Tigers	2	2	0	3	4	1		28

ALDS (2-3)	W	1	2	3	4		%
Chicago White Sox	1	3	2	1	3		46
Boston Red Sox	3	2	7	5	6		54

ALCS	W	1	2	3	4	5	6	%
Boston Red Sox	2	2	2	3	10	2	3	17
Oakland Athletics	4	3	6	1	1	5	4	83

NATIONAL LEAGUE

TIEBREAKER	W	1	2		%
Los Angeles Dodgers	2	7	5		48
Houston Astros	0	3	1		52

NLDS (1-4)	W	1	2	3	%
Cincinnati Reds	3	6	3	5	85
New York Mets	0	3	2	3	15

NLDS (2-3)	W	1	2	3	4	5	%
Pittsburgh Pirates	2	4	7	4	2	2	66
Los Angeles Dodgers	3	2	3	5	3	3	34

NLCS	W	1	2	3	4	5	6	%
Cincinnati Reds	2	4	6	5	1	1	3	65
Los Angeles Dodgers	4	5	3	2	11	4	4	35

WORLD SERIES

WS	W	1	2	3	4	5	%
Oakland Athletics	1	0	3	0	2	2	71
Los Angeles Dodgers	4	3	0	3	3	3	29

ACTUAL WINNERS

American League: Oakland Athletics
National League: Cincinnati Reds
World Series: Oakland Athletics

OUTSTANDING PERFORMANCES

AWARD WINNERS

LG.	PLAYER	TEAM	STATS ADJUSTED	ACTUAL
MOST VALUABLE PLAYERS				
AL	Dick Allen	Chicago	54 HR, 157 RBI, .340 BA, $16.0 MIL	37 HR, 113 RBI, .308 BA
NL	Johnny Bench	Cincinnati	57 HR, 174 RBI, .298 BA, $19.9 MIL	40 HR, 125 RBI, .270 BA
CY YOUNG AWARDS				
AL	Gaylord Perry	Cleveland	25-17 W-L, 1 SV, 2.68 ERA, $40.6 MIL	24-16 W-L, 1 SV, 1.92 ERA
NL	Steve Carlton	Philadelphia	28-10 W-L, 0 SV, 2.75 ERA, $51.4 MIL	27-10 W-L, 0 SV, 1.97 ERA

AMERICAN LEAGUE LEADERS

CAT.	PLAYER	TEAM	STATS ADJUSTED	ACTUAL
BATTING				
HR	Dick Allen	Chicago	54	37
RBI	Dick Allen	Chicago	157	113
BA	Rod Carew	Minnesota	.351	.318
AB	Bert Campaneris	Oakland	654	625
R	Bobby Murcer	New York	141	102
H	Joe Rudi	Oakland	209	181
2B	Lou Piniella	Kansas City	50	33
3B	Joe Rudi	Oakland	9	9
	Carlton Fisk	Boston	8	9
TB	Bobby Murcer	New York	395	314
SA	Dick Allen	Chicago	.726	.603
SB	Bert Campaneris	Oakland	77	52
PITCHING				
W	Gaylord Perry	Cleveland	25	24
	Wilbur Wood	Chicago	25	24
L	Pat Dobson	Baltimore	19	18
	Mel Stottlemyre	New York	19	18
SV	Sparky Lyle	New York	40	35
ERA	Luis Tiant	Boston	2.70	1.91
G	Paul Lindblad	Texas	69	66
IP	Wilbur Wood	Chicago	400	376.2
BB	Nolan Ryan	California	189	157
SO	Nolan Ryan	California	394	329

NATIONAL LEAGUE LEADERS

CAT.	PLAYER	TEAM	STATS ADJUSTED	ACTUAL
BATTING				
HR	Johnny Bench	Cincinnati	57	40
RBI	Johnny Bench	Cincinnati	174	125
BA	Billy Williams	Chicago	.367	.333
AB	Pete Rose	Cincinnati	679	645
R	Joe Morgan	Cincinnati	170	122
H	Pete Rose	Cincinnati	230	198
2B	Cesar Cedeno	Houston	55	39
	Willie Montanez	Philadelphia	54	39
3B	Larry Bowa	Philadelphia	18	13
TB	Billy Williams	Chicago	435	348
SA	Billy Williams	Chicago	.729	.606
SB	Lou Brock	St. Louis	93	63
PITCHING				
W	Steve Carlton	Philadelphia	28	27
L	Steve Arlin	San Diego	22	21
SV	Clay Carroll	Cincinnati	44	37
ERA	Steve Carlton	Philadelphia	2.75	1.97
G	Mike Marshall	Montreal	68	65
	Clay Carroll	Cincinnati	68	65
IP	Steve Carlton	Philadelphia	363	346.1
BB	Steve Arlin	San Diego	147	122
SO	Steve Carlton	Philadelphia	376	310

1973 SEASON

REGULAR SEASON STANDINGS

AMERICAN LEAGUE

	ADJUSTED				ACTUAL			
	W	L	Pct.	GB	W	L	Pct.	Rk.
EAST								
X Baltimore	97	65	.599	0	97	65	.599	1
X Boston	89	73	.549	8	89	73	.549	3
New York	80	82	.494	17	80	82	.494	7
Cleveland	71	91	.438	26	71	91	.438	11
CENTRAL								
X Detroit	85	77	.525	0	85	77	.525	5
Minnesota	81	81	.500	4	81	81	.500	6
Chicago	77	85	.475	8	77	85	.475	9
Milwaukee	74	88	.457	11	74	88	.457	10
WEST								
X Oakland	94	68	.580	0	94	68	.580	2
Kansas City	88	74	.543	6	88	74	.543	4
California	79	83	.488	15	79	83	.488	8
Texas	57	105	.352	37	57	105	.352	12

NATIONAL LEAGUE

	ADJUSTED				ACTUAL			
	W	L	Pct.	GB	W	L	Pct.	Rk.
EAST								
X New York	83	79	.512	0	82	79	.509	4
Montreal	79	83	.488	4	79	83	.488	8
Atlanta	76	86	.469	7	76	85	.472	10
Philadelphia	71	91	.438	12	71	91	.438	11
CENTRAL								
X Cincinnati	99	63	.611	0	99	63	.611	1
St. Louis	81	81	.500	18	81	81	.500	6
Pittsburgh	80	82	.494	19	80	82	.494	7
Chicago	77	85	.475	22	77	84	.478	9
WEST								
X Los Angeles	96	66	.593	0	95	66	.590	2
X San Francisco	88	74	.543	8	88	74	.543	3
Houston	82	80	.506	14	82	80	.506	5
San Diego	60	102	.370	36	60	102	.370	12

SIMULATED PLAYOFFS

AMERICAN LEAGUE

ALDS (1-4)	W	1	2	3	4	5	%
Baltimore Orioles	3	2	5	6	0	3	93
Detroit Tigers	2	3	2	2	1	2	7

ALDS (2-3)	W	1	2	3	4		%
Oakland Athletics	1	5	8	2	3		50
Boston Red Sox	3	6	2	3	4		50

ALCS	W	1	2	3	4		%
Baltimore Orioles	4	5	5	5	8		65
Boston Red Sox	0	3	1	2	1		35

NATIONAL LEAGUE

NLDS (1-4)*	W	1	2	3	4	5	%
Cincinnati Reds	2	2	0	2	2	2	61
New York Mets	3	1	5	9	1	7	39

NLDS (2-3)	W	1	2	3	4		%
Los Angeles Dodgers	3	7	3	8	3		67
San Francisco Giants	1	3	5	6	1		33

NLCS	W	1	2	3	4	5	6	%
New York Mets	2	5	1	2	1	2	2	38
Los Angeles Dodgers	4	4	5	3	3	0	5	62

WORLD SERIES

WS	W	1	2	3	4	%
Baltimore Orioles	0	4	1	1	1	48
Los Angeles Dodgers	4	5	2	3	2	52

ACTUAL WINNERS

American League: Oakland Athletics
National League: New York Mets
World Series: Oakland Athletics

OUTSTANDING PERFORMANCES

AWARD WINNERS

LG.	PLAYER	TEAM	STATS ADJUSTED	ACTUAL
MOST VALUABLE PLAYERS				
AL	Reggie Jackson	Oakland	40 HR, 137 RBI, .306 BA, $14.7 MIL	32 HR, 117 RBI, .293 BA
NL	Pete Rose	Cincinnati	8 HR, 75 RBI, .354 BA, $19.2 MIL	5 HR, 64 RBI, .338 BA
CY YOUNG AWARDS				
AL	Jim Palmer	Baltimore	22-9 W-L, 1 SV, 2.92 ERA, $32.2 MIL	22-9 W-L, 1 SV, 2.40 ERA
NL	Tom Seaver	New York	19-10 W-L, 0 SV, 2.54 ERA, $32.4 MIL	19-10 W-L, 0 SV, 2.08 ERA

AMERICAN LEAGUE LEADERS

CAT.	PLAYER	TEAM	STATS ADJUSTED	ACTUAL
BATTING				
HR	Reggie Jackson	Oakland	40	32
RBI	Reggie Jackson	Oakland	137	117
BA	Rod Carew	Minnesota	.367	.350
AB	Roy White	New York	639	639
R	Reggie Jackson	Oakland	116	99
H	Rod Carew	Minnesota	213	203
2B	Pedro Garcia	Milwaukee	41	32
	Sal Bando	Oakland	39	32
3B	Al Bumbry	Baltimore	11	11
	Rod Carew	Minnesota	11	11
TB	Sal Bando	Oakland	334	295
	Dave May	Milwaukee	334	295
	George Scott	Milwaukee	333	295
SA	Reggie Jackson	Oakland	.599	.531
SB	Tommy Harper	Boston	72	54
PITCHING				
W	Wilbur Wood	Chicago	24	24
L	Stan Bahnsen	Chicago	21	21
SV	John Hiller	Detroit	41	38
ERA	Jim Palmer	Baltimore	2.92	2.40
G	John Hiller	Detroit	65	65
IP	Wilbur Wood	Chicago	359	359.1
BB	Nolan Ryan	California	173	162
SO	Nolan Ryan	California	454	383

NATIONAL LEAGUE LEADERS

CAT.	PLAYER	TEAM	STATS ADJUSTED	ACTUAL
BATTING				
HR	Willie Stargell	Pittsburgh	54	44
RBI	Willie Stargell	Pittsburgh	139	119
BA	Pete Rose	Cincinnati	.354	.338
AB	Pete Rose	Cincinnati	680	680
R	Bobby Bonds	San Francisco	153	131
H	Pete Rose	Cincinnati	241	230
2B	Willie Stargell	Pittsburgh	51	43
3B	Roger Metzger	Houston	18	14
TB	Bobby Bonds	San Francisco	384	341
SA	Willie Stargell	Pittsburgh	.732	.646
SB	Lou Brock	St. Louis	93	70
PITCHING				
W	Ron Bryant	San Francisco	24	24
L	Steve Carlton	Philadelphia	20	20
SV	Mike Marshall	Montreal	36	31
ERA	Tom Seaver	New York	2.54	2.08
G	Mike Marshall	Montreal	92	92
IP	Jack Billingham	Cincinnati	293	293.1
	Steve Carlton	Philadelphia	293	293.1
BB	Jerry Reuss	Houston	125	117
SO	Tom Seaver	New York	306	251

1974 SEASON

REGULAR SEASON STANDINGS

AMERICAN LEAGUE

	ADJUSTED				ACTUAL			
	W	L	Pct.	GB	W	L	Pct.	Rk.
EAST								
X Baltimore	91	71	.562	0	91	71	.562	1
X New York	89	73	.549	2	89	73	.549	3
Boston	84	78	.519	7	84	78	.519	5
Cleveland	77	85	.475	14	77	85	.475	8
CENTRAL								
X Minnesota	82	80	.506	0	82	80	.506	6
Chicago	81	81	.500	1	80	80	.500	7
Milwaukee	76	86	.469	6	76	86	.469	10
Detroit	72	90	.444	10	72	90	.444	11
WEST								
X Oakland	90	72	.556	0	90	72	.556	2
Texas	85	77	.525	5	84	76	.525	4
Kansas City	77	85	.475	13	77	85	.475	8
California	68	94	.420	22	68	94	.420	12

NATIONAL LEAGUE

	ADJUSTED				ACTUAL			
	W	L	Pct.	GB	W	L	Pct.	Rk.
EAST								
X Atlanta	88	74	.543	0	88	74	.543	3
Philadelphia	80	82	.494	8	80	82	.494	7
Montreal	79	83	.488	9	79	82	.491	8
New York	71	91	.438	17	71	91	.438	10
CENTRAL								
X Cincinnati	98	64	.605	0	98	64	.605	2
X Pittsburgh	88	74	.543	10	88	74	.543	3
St. Louis	87	75	.537	11	86	75	.534	5
Chicago	66	96	.407	32	66	96	.407	11
WEST								
X Los Angeles	102	60	.630	0	102	60	.630	1
Houston	81	81	.500	21	81	81	.500	6
San Francisco	72	90	.444	30	72	90	.444	9
San Diego	60	102	.370	42	60	102	.370	12

SIMULATED PLAYOFFS

AMERICAN LEAGUE

ALDS (1-4)	W	1	2	3	4	5		%
Baltimore Orioles	3	3	3	7	4	5		52
Minnesota Twins	2	4	6	1	3	3		48

ALDS (2-3)	W	1	2	3	4	5		%
Oakland Athletics	2	1	4	1	4	1		59
New York Yankees	3	2	2	3	2	2		41

ALCS	W	1	2	3	4	5		%
Baltimore Orioles	1	0	3	5	3	2		61
New York Yankees	4	3	4	4	4	3		39

NATIONAL LEAGUE

NLDS (1-4)*	W	1	2	3	4		%
Los Angeles Dodgers	3	3	5	0	12		69
Pittsburgh Pirates	1	0	2	7	1		31

NLDS (2-3)	W	1	2	3	4	5		%
Cincinnati Reds	2	1	3	3	3	5		54
Atlanta Braves	3	4	2	1	5	8		46

NLCS	W	1	2	3	4	5	6	%
Los Angeles Dodgers	4	6	1	6	0	2	4	67
Atlanta Braves	2	2	2	5	3	1	1	33

WORLD SERIES

WS	W	1	2	3	4	5		%
New York Yankees	1	1	1	7	1	1		8
Los Angeles Dodgers	4	3	4	6	2	8		92

ACTUAL WINNERS

American League: Oakland Athletics
National League: Los Angeles Dodgers
World Series: Oakland Athletics

OUTSTANDING PERFORMANCES

AWARD WINNERS

LG.	PLAYER	TEAM	STATS ADJUSTED	ACTUAL
MOST VALUABLE PLAYERS				
AL	Jeff Burroughs	Texas	36 HR, 142 RBI, .315 BA, $9.6 MIL	25 HR, 118 RBI, .301 BA
NL	Steve Garvey	Los Angeles	31 HR, 132 RBI, .327 BA, $12.1 MIL	21 HR, 111 RBI, .312 BA
CY YOUNG AWARDS				
AL	Catfish Hunter	Oakland	25-12 W-L, 0 SV, 3.14 ERA, $33.9 MIL	25-12 W-L, 0 SV, 2.49 ERA
NL	Mike Marshall	Los Angeles	15-12 W-L, 39 SV, 3.07 ERA, $25.5 MIL	15-12 W-L, 21 SV, 2.42 ERA

AMERICAN LEAGUE LEADERS

CAT.	PLAYER	TEAM	STATS ADJUSTED	ACTUAL
BATTING				
HR	Dick Allen	Chicago	43	32
RBI	Jeff Burroughs	Texas	142	118
BA	Rod Carew	Minnesota	.382	.364
AB	Don Money	Milwaukee	629	629
R	Carl Yastrzemski	Boston	111	93
H	Rod Carew	Minnesota	227	218
2B	Joe Rudi	Oakland	48	39
3B	Mickey Rivers	California	12	11
TB	Joe Rudi	Oakland	332	287
SA	Dick Allen	Chicago	.655	.563
SB	Billy North	Oakland	58	54
PITCHING				
W	Catfish Hunter	Oakland	25	25
	Fergie Jenkins	Texas	25	25
L	Mickey Lolich	Detroit	21	21
SV	Terry Forster	Chicago	33	24
ERA	Catfish Hunter	Oakland	3.14	2.49
G	Rollie Fingers	Oakland	76	76
IP	Nolan Ryan	California	333	332.2
BB	Nolan Ryan	California	219	202
SO	Nolan Ryan	California	452	367

NATIONAL LEAGUE LEADERS

CAT.	PLAYER	TEAM	STATS ADJUSTED	ACTUAL
BATTING				
HR	Mike Schmidt	Philadelphia	50	36
RBI	Johnny Bench	Cincinnati	153	129
BA	Ralph Garr	Atlanta	.370	.353
AB	Dave Cash	Philadelphia	687	687
R	Pete Rose	Cincinnati	130	110
H	Ralph Garr	Atlanta	223	214
2B	Pete Rose	Cincinnati	67	45
3B	Ralph Garr	Atlanta	17	17
TB	Johnny Bench	Cincinnati	363	315
SA	Mike Schmidt	Philadelphia	.634	.546
SB	Lou Brock	St. Louis	131	118
PITCHING				
W	Andy Messersmith	Los Angeles	20	20
	Phil Niekro	Atlanta	20	20
L	Bill Bonham	Chicago	22	22
	Randy Jones	San Diego	22	22
	Steve Rogers	Montreal	22	22
SV	Mike Marshall	Los Angeles	39	21
ERA	Buzz Capra	Atlanta	2.86	2.28
G	Mike Marshall	Los Angeles	106	106
IP	Phil Niekro	Atlanta	302	302.1
BB	Steve Carlton	Philadelphia	147	136
SO	Steve Carlton	Philadelphia	305	240

1975 SEASON

REGULAR SEASON STANDINGS

AMERICAN LEAGUE

		ADJUSTED				ACTUAL		
	W	L	Pct.	GB	W	L	Pct.	Rk.
EAST								
X Boston	96	66	.593	0	95	65	.594	2
X Baltimore	92	70	.568	4	90	69	.566	3
New York	84	78	.519	12	83	77	.519	5
Cleveland	81	81	.500	15	79	80	.497	6
CENTRAL								
X Minnesota	77	85	.475	0	76	83	.478	8
Chicago	76	86	.469	1	75	86	.466	9
Milwaukee	68	94	.420	9	68	94	.420	11
Detroit	58	104	.358	19	57	102	.358	12
WEST								
X Oakland	98	64	.605	0	98	64	.605	1
Kansas City	91	71	.562	7	91	71	.562	4
Texas	79	83	.488	19	79	83	.488	7
California	72	90	.444	26	72	89	.447	10

NATIONAL LEAGUE

		ADJUSTED				ACTUAL		
	W	L	Pct.	GB	W	L	Pct.	Rk.
EAST								
X Philadelphia	86	76	.531	0	86	76	.531	4
New York	82	80	.506	4	82	80	.506	5
Montreal	75	87	.463	11	75	87	.463	8
Atlanta	67	95	.414	19	67	94	.416	11
CENTRAL								
X Cincinnati	108	54	.667	0	108	54	.667	1
X Pittsburgh	93	69	.574	15	92	69	.571	2
St. Louis	82	80	.506	26	82	80	.506	5
Chicago	75	87	.463	33	75	87	.463	8
WEST								
X Los Angeles	88	74	.543	0	88	74	.543	3
San Francisco	81	81	.500	7	80	81	.497	7
San Diego	71	91	.438	17	71	91	.438	10
Houston	64	98	.395	24	64	97	.398	12

SIMULATED PLAYOFFS

AMERICAN LEAGUE

ALDS (1-4)	W	1	2	3	4		%
Oakland Athletics	3	12	4	5	8		80
Minnesota Twins	1	4	3	6	1		20

ALDS (2-3)	W	1	2	3	4	5	%
Boston Red Sox	3	7	3	4	4	5	36
Baltimore Orioles	2	0	5	1	8	4	64

ALCS**	W	1	2	3	4		%
Oakland Athletics	0	1	3	3	1		61
Boston Red Sox	4	7	6	5	4		39

NATIONAL LEAGUE

NLDS (1-4)	W	1	2	3		%
Cincinnati Reds	3	9	8	8		81
Philadelphia Phillies	0	5	1	2		19

NLDS (2-3)	W	1	2	3	4		%
Pittsburgh Pirates	1	2	0	2	0		51
Los Angeles Dodgers	3	1	4	3	2		49

NLCS	W	1	2	3	4	5	6	%
Cincinnati Reds	2	0	0	4	6	4	3	62
Los Angeles Dodgers	4	2	4	5	2	2	4	38

WORLD SERIES

WS	W	1	2	3	4	5	6	%
Boston Red Sox	4	1	6	2	6	5	5	44
Los Angeles Dodgers	2	6	5	6	2	4	2	56

ACTUAL WINNERS

American League: Boston Red Sox
National League: Cincinnati Reds
World Series: Cincinnati Reds

OUTSTANDING PERFORMANCES ·

AWARD WINNERS

LG.	PLAYER	TEAM	STATS ADJUSTED	ACTUAL
MOST VALUABLE PLAYERS				
AL	Fred Lynn	Boston	31 HR, 124 RBI, .346 BA, $7.5 MIL	21 HR, 105 RBI, .331 BA
NL	Joe Morgan	Cincinnati	25 HR, 110 RBI, .341 BA, $13.2 MIL	17 HR, 94 RBI, .327 BA
CY YOUNG AWARDS				
AL	Jim Palmer	Baltimore	24-11 W-L, 1 SV, 2.58 ERA, $34.1 MIL	23-11 W-L, 1 SV, 2.09 ERA
NL	Tom Seaver	New York	22-9 W-L, 0 SV, 2.93 ERA, $27.4 MIL	22-9 W-L, 0 SV, 2.38 ERA

AMERICAN LEAGUE LEADERS

CAT.	PLAYER	TEAM	STATS ADJUSTED	ACTUAL
BATTING				
HR	Reggie Jackson	Oakland	48	36
	George Scott	Milwaukee	48	36
RBI	George Scott	Milwaukee	127	109
BA	Rod Carew	Minnesota	.375	.359
AB	George Brett	Kansas City	634	634
R	Fred Lynn	Boston	122	103
H	George Brett	Kansas City	204	195
2B	Fred Lynn	Boston	57	47
3B	Mickey Rivers	California	16	13
	George Brett	Kansas City	12	13
TB	George Scott	Milwaukee	363	318
SA	Fred Lynn	Boston	.649	.566
SB	Mickey Rivers	California	75	70
PITCHING				
W	Jim Palmer	Baltimore	24	23
	Catfish Hunter	New York	23	23
L	Wilbur Wood	Chicago	20	20
SV	Rich Gossage	Chicago	32	26
ERA	Jim Palmer	Baltimore	2.58	2.09
G	Rollie Fingers	Oakland	75	75
IP	Catfish Hunter	New York	328	328
BB	Mike Torrez	Baltimore	142	133
SO	Frank Tanana	California	333	269

NATIONAL LEAGUE LEADERS

CAT.	PLAYER	TEAM	STATS ADJUSTED	ACTUAL
BATTING				
HR	Mike Schmidt	Philadelphia	50	38
RBI	Greg Luzinski	Philadelphia	140	120
BA	Bill Madlock	Chicago	.370	.354
AB	Dave Cash	Philadelphia	699	699
R	Pete Rose	Cincinnati	131	112
H	Dave Cash	Philadelphia	223	213
2B	Pete Rose	Cincinnati	65	47
3B	Ralph Garr	Atlanta	11	11
TB	Greg Luzinski	Philadelphia	367	322
SA	Dave Parker	Pittsburgh	.621	.541
SB	Davey Lopes	Los Angeles	82	77
PITCHING				
W	Tom Seaver	New York	22	22
L	Rick Reuschel	Chicago	17	17
SV	Rawly Eastwick	Cincinnati	30	22
	Al Hrabosky	St. Louis	29	22
ERA	Randy Jones	San Diego	2.78	2.24
G	Gene Garber	Philadelphia	71	71
IP	Andy Messersmith	Los Angeles	322	321.2
BB	J.R. Richard	Houston	144	138
SO	Tom Seaver	New York	308	243

1976 SEASON

REGULAR SEASON STANDINGS

AMERICAN LEAGUE

	ADJUSTED				ACTUAL			
	W	L	Pct.	GB	W	L	Pct.	Rk.
EAST								
X New York	99	63	.611	0	97	62	.610	1
X Baltimore	88	74	.543	11	88	74	.543	3
Boston	83	79	.512	16	83	79	.512	6
Cleveland	83	79	.512	16	81	78	.509	7
CENTRAL								
X Minnesota	85	77	.525	0	85	77	.525	5
Detroit	74	88	.457	11	74	87	.460	10
Milwaukee	66	96	.407	19	66	95	.410	11
Chicago	64	98	.395	21	64	97	.398	12
WEST								
X Kansas City	90	72	.556	0	90	72	.556	2
X Oakland	88	74	.543	2	87	74	.540	4
California	76	86	.469	14	76	86	.469	8
Texas	76	86	.469	14	76	86	.469	8

NATIONAL LEAGUE

	ADJUSTED				ACTUAL			
	W	L	Pct.	GB	W	L	Pct.	Rk.
EAST								
X Philadelphia	101	61	.623	0	101	61	.623	2
New York	86	76	.531	15	86	76	.531	5
Atlanta	70	92	.432	31	70	92	.432	11
Montreal	55	107	.340	46	55	107	.340	12
CENTRAL								
X Cincinnati	102	60	.630	0	102	60	.630	1
X Pittsburgh	92	70	.568	10	92	70	.568	3
Chicago	75	87	.463	27	75	87	.463	7
St. Louis	72	90	.444	30	72	90	.444	10
WEST								
X Los Angeles	92	70	.568	0	92	70	.568	3
Houston	80	82	.494	12	80	82	.494	6
San Francisco	74	88	.457	18	74	88	.457	8
San Diego	73	89	.451	19	73	89	.451	9

SIMULATED PLAYOFFS

AMERICAN LEAGUE

TIEBREAKER	W	1	2	3			%
Baltimore Orioles	2	2	5	3			53
Oakland Athletics	1	0	6	2			47

ALDS (1-4)	W	1	2	3	4		%
New York Yankees	3	8	2	4	9		64
Minnesota Twins	1	4	3	2	4		36

ALDS (2-3)	W	1	2	3	4	5	%
Kansas City Royals	2	6	6	4	5	3	70
Baltimore Orioles	3	3	0	5	6	4	30

ALCS	W	1	2	3	4	5	6	%
New York Yankees	4	3	2	4	3	4	6	72
Baltimore Orioles	2	4	3	3	2	3	2	28

NATIONAL LEAGUE

NLDS (1-4)	W	1	2	3	4	5	%
Cincinnati Reds	2	8	5	10	3	3	71
Pittsburgh Pirates	3	4	7	3	4	6	29

NLDS (2-3)	W	1	2	3			%
Philadelphia Phillies	3	6	3	3			61
Los Angeles Dodgers	0	4	1	1			39

NLCS	W	1	2	3	4	5	6	%
Philadelphia Phillies	2	4	7	3	2	3	4	74
Pittsburgh Pirates	4	3	5	4	3	7	5	26

WORLD SERIES

WS	W	1	2	3	4	5	%
New York Yankees	1	1	2	3	3	3	60
Pittsburgh Pirates	4	2	5	5	1	4	40

ACTUAL WINNERS

American League: New York Yankees
National League: Cincinnati Reds
World Series: Cincinnati Reds

OUTSTANDING PERFORMANCES

AWARD WINNERS

LG.	PLAYER	TEAM	STATS ADJUSTED	ACTUAL
MOST VALUABLE PLAYERS				
AL	Thurman Munson	New York	29 HR, 131 RBI, .318 BA, $12.3 MIL	17 HR, 105 RBI, .302 BA
NL	Joe Morgan	Cincinnati	42 HR, 136 RBI, .337 BA, $13.1 MIL	27 HR, 111 RBI, .320 BA
CY YOUNG AWARDS				
AL	Jim Palmer	Baltimore	22-13 W-L, 0 SV, 3.26 ERA, $32.5 MIL	22-13 W-L, 0 SV, 2.51 ERA
NL	Randy Jones	San Diego	22-14 W-L, 0 SV, 3.57 ERA, $25.4 MIL	22-14 W-L, 0 SV, 2.74 ERA

AMERICAN LEAGUE LEADERS

CAT.	PLAYER	TEAM	STATS ADJUSTED	ACTUAL
BATTING				
HR	Graig Nettles	New York	47	32
RBI	Lee May	Baltimore	134	109
BA	George Brett	Kansas City	.352	.333
AB	George Brett	Kansas City	645	645
R	Roy White	New York	130	104
H	George Brett	Kansas City	227	215
2B	Amos Otis	Kansas City	45	40
3B	George Brett	Kansas City	13	14
TB	George Brett	Kansas City	351	298
SA	Reggie Jackson	Baltimore	.596	.502
SB	Billy North	Oakland	66	75
PITCHING				
W	Jim Palmer	Baltimore	22	22
L	Nolan Ryan	California	18	18
SV	Sparky Lyle	New York	30	23
ERA	Mark Fidrych	Detroit	3.02	2.34
G	Bill Campbell	Minnesota	78	78
IP	Jim Palmer	Baltimore	315	315
BB	Nolan Ryan	California	207	183
SO	Nolan Ryan	California	409	327

NATIONAL LEAGUE LEADERS

CAT.	PLAYER	TEAM	STATS ADJUSTED	ACTUAL
BATTING				
HR	Mike Schmidt	Philadelphia	55	38
RBI	George Foster	Cincinnati	149	121
BA	Bill Madlock	Chicago	.356	.339
AB	Dave Cash	Philadelphia	666	666
R	Pete Rose	Cincinnati	160	130
H	Pete Rose	Cincinnati	227	215
2B	Pete Rose	Cincinnati	57	42
3B	Dave Cash	Philadelphia	16	12
TB	Mike Schmidt	Philadelphia	361	306
SA	Joe Morgan	Cincinnati	.684	.576
SB	Davey Lopes	Los Angeles	55	63
PITCHING				
W	Randy Jones	San Diego	22	22
L	Steve Rogers	Montreal	17	17
	Dick Ruthven	Atlanta	17	17
SV	Rawly Eastwick	Cincinnati	34	26
ERA	John Denny	St. Louis	3.26	2.52
G	Dale Murray	Montreal	81	81
IP	Randy Jones	San Diego	315	315.1
BB	J.R. Richard	Houston	171	151
SO	Tom Seaver	New York	305	235

1977 SEASON

REGULAR SEASON STANDINGS

AMERICAN LEAGUE

	ADJUSTED				ACTUAL			
	W	L	Pct.	GB	W	L	Pct.	Rk.
EAST								
X New York	100	62	.617	0	100	62	.617	2
X Baltimore	98	64	.605	2	97	64	.602	3
X Boston	98	64	.605	2	97	64	.602	3
Cleveland	71	91	.438	29	71	90	.441	10
Toronto	54	108	.333	46	54	107	.335	14
CENTRAL								
X Kansas City	102	60	.630	0	102	60	.630	1
Chicago	90	72	.556	12	90	72	.556	6
Minnesota	85	77	.525	17	84	77	.522	7
Detroit	74	88	.457	28	74	88	.457	8
Milwaukee	67	95	.414	35	67	95	.414	11
WEST								
X Texas	94	68	.580	0	94	68	.580	5
California	74	88	.457	20	74	88	.457	8
Seattle	64	98	.395	30	64	98	.395	12
Oakland	63	99	.389	31	63	98	.391	13

NATIONAL LEAGUE

	ADJUSTED				ACTUAL			
	W	L	Pct.	GB	W	L	Pct.	Rk.
EAST								
X Philadelphia	101	61	.623	0	101	61	.623	1
Montreal	75	87	.463	26	75	87	.463	8
New York	64	98	.395	37	64	98	.395	11
Atlanta	61	101	.377	40	61	101	.377	12
CENTRAL								
X Pittsburgh	96	66	.593	0	96	66	.593	3
X Cincinnati	88	74	.543	8	88	74	.543	4
St. Louis	83	79	.512	13	83	79	.512	5
Chicago	81	81	.500	15	81	81	.500	6
WEST								
X Los Angeles	98	64	.605	0	98	64	.605	2
Houston	81	81	.500	17	81	81	.500	6
San Francisco	75	87	.463	23	75	87	.463	8
San Diego	69	93	.426	29	69	93	.426	10

SIMULATED PLAYOFFS

AMERICAN LEAGUE

TIEBREAKER	W	1	2				%
Baltimore Orioles	0	2	1				52
Boston Red Sox	2	5	2				48

ALDS (1-4)	W	1	2	3			%
Kansas City Royals	3	3	15	5			58
Texas Rangers	0	2	6	1			42

ALDS (2-3)	W	1	2	3	4		%
New York Yankees	3	8	6	2	4		61
Boston Red Sox	1	2	7	0	3		39

ALCS**	W	1	2	3	4	5	6	%
Kansas City Royals	2	7	2	6	4	3	4	44
New York Yankees	4	2	6	2	6	5	6	56

NATIONAL LEAGUE

NLDS (1-4)	W	1	2	3	4	5	%
Philadelphia Phillies	2	6	6	8	6	2	59
Cincinnati Reds	3	7	5	5	7	4	41

NLDS (2-3)	W	1	2	3	4	5	%
Los Angeles Dodgers	2	3	2	2	7	0	72
Pittsburgh Pirates	3	2	3	4	1	2	28

NLCS	W	1	2	3	4	%
Pittsburgh Pirates	0	3	1	1	5	46
Cincinnati Reds	4	4	7	2	6	54

WORLD SERIES

WS	W	1	2	3	4	5	6	%
New York Yankees	2	2	3	2	13	9	5	79
Cincinnati Reds	4	3	5	4	3	3	6	21

ACTUAL WINNERS

American League: New York Yankees
National League: Los Angeles Dodgers
World Series: New York Yankees

OUTSTANDING PERFORMANCES

AWARD WINNERS

LG.	PLAYER	TEAM	STATS ADJUSTED	ACTUAL
MOST VALUABLE PLAYERS				
AL	Rod Carew	Minnesota	20 HR, 111 RBI, .395 BA, $13.8 MIL	14 HR, 100 RBI, .388 BA
NL	George Foster	Cincinnati	59 HR, 165 RBI, .327 BA, $16.3 MIL	52 HR, 149 RBI, .320 BA
CY YOUNG AWARDS				
AL	Sparky Lyle	New York	13-5 W-L, 31 SV, 2.50 ERA, $8.3 MIL	13-5 W-L, 26 SV, 2.17 ERA
NL	Steve Carlton	Philadelphia	23-10 W-L, 0 SV, 3.02 ERA, $25.4 MIL	23-10 W-L, 0 SV, 2.64 ERA

AMERICAN LEAGUE LEADERS

CAT.	PLAYER	TEAM	STATS ADJUSTED	ACTUAL
BATTING				
HR	Jim Rice	Boston	49	39
RBI	Larry Hisle	Minnesota	133	119
BA	Rod Carew	Minnesota	.395	.388
AB	Rick Burleson	Boston	667	663
R	Rod Carew	Minnesota	143	128
H	Rod Carew	Minnesota	245	239
2B	Hal McRae	Kansas City	63	54
3B	Rod Carew	Minnesota	12	16
TB	Jim Rice	Boston	411	382
SA	Jim Rice	Boston	.634	.593
SB	Freddie Patek	Kansas City	51	53
PITCHING				
W	Dave Goltz	Minnesota	20	20
	Dennis Leonard	Kansas City	20	20
	Jim Palmer	Baltimore	20	20
L	Vida Blue	Oakland	19	19
	Wayne Garland	Cleveland	19	19
	Rick Langford	Oakland	19	19
SV	Bill Campbell	Boston	35	31
ERA	Frank Tanana	California	2.91	2.54
G	Sparky Lyle	New York	72	72
IP	Jim Palmer	Baltimore	319	319
BB	Nolan Ryan	California	225	204
SO	Nolan Ryan	California	409	341

NATIONAL LEAGUE LEADERS

CAT.	PLAYER	TEAM	STATS ADJUSTED	ACTUAL
BATTING				
HR	George Foster	Cincinnati	59	52
RBI	George Foster	Cincinnati	165	149
BA	Dave Parker	Pittsburgh	.344	.338
AB	Pete Rose	Cincinnati	655	655
R	George Foster	Cincinnati	137	124
H	Dave Parker	Pittsburgh	219	215
2B	Dave Parker	Pittsburgh	51	44
3B	Garry Templeton	St. Louis	16	18
TB	George Foster	Cincinnati	412	388
SA	George Foster	Cincinnati	.670	.631
SB	Frank Taveras	Pittsburgh	68	70
PITCHING				
W	Steve Carlton	Philadelphia	23	23
L	Jerry Koosman	New York	20	20
	Phil Niekro	Atlanta	20	20
SV	Rollie Fingers	San Diego	40	35
ERA	John Candelaria	Pittsburgh	2.69	2.34
G	Rollie Fingers	San Diego	78	78
IP	Phil Niekro	Atlanta	330	330.1
BB	Phil Niekro	Atlanta	180	164
SO	Phil Niekro	Atlanta	324	262

1978 SEASON

REGULAR SEASON STANDINGS

AMERICAN LEAGUE

		ADJUSTED				ACTUAL		
	W	L	Pct.	GB	W	L	Pct.	Rk.
EAST								
X New York	99	63	.611	0	99	63	.611	1
X Boston	99	63	.611	0	99	63	.611	1
Baltimore	91	71	.562	8	90	71	.559	5
Cleveland	70	92	.432	29	69	90	.434	11
Toronto	59	103	.364	40	59	102	.366	13
CENTRAL								
X Milwaukee	93	69	.574	0	93	69	.574	3
Kansas City	92	70	.568	1	92	70	.568	4
Detroit	86	76	.531	7	86	76	.531	8
Minnesota	73	89	.451	20	73	89	.451	9
Chicago	72	90	.444	21	71	90	.441	10
WEST								
X California	87	75	.537	0	87	75	.537	6
X Texas	87	75	.537	0	87	75	.537	6
Oakland	69	93	.426	18	69	93	.426	12
Seattle	57	105	.352	30	56	104	.350	14

NATIONAL LEAGUE

		ADJUSTED				ACTUAL		
	W	L	Pct.	GB	W	L	Pct.	Rk.
EAST								
X Philadelphia	90	72	.556	0	90	72	.556	3
Montreal	76	86	.469	14	76	86	.469	8
Atlanta	69	93	.426	21	69	93	.426	10
New York	66	96	.407	24	66	96	.407	12
CENTRAL								
X Cincinnati	93	69	.574	0	92	69	.571	2
Pittsburgh	88	74	.543	5	88	73	.547	5
Chicago	79	83	.488	14	79	83	.488	7
St. Louis	69	93	.426	24	69	93	.426	10
WEST								
X Los Angeles	95	67	.586	0	95	67	.586	1
X San Francisco	89	73	.549	6	89	73	.549	4
San Diego	84	78	.519	11	84	78	.519	6
Houston	74	88	.457	21	74	88	.457	9

SIMULATED PLAYOFFS

AMERICAN LEAGUE

TIEBREAKER	W	1	2	3			%
California Angels	2	0	3	2			39
Texas Rangers	1	6	2	0			61

ALDS (1-4)	W	1	2	3	4	5	%
New York Yankees	2	4	2	4	5	3	67
California Angels	3	5	5	3	3	6	33

ALDS (2-3)	W	1	2	3	4		%
Boston Red Sox	1	5	2	4	7		43
Milwaukee Brewers	3	7	9	2	9		57

ALCS	W	1	2	3	4		%
Milwaukee Brewers	0	2	5	2	1		69
California Angels	4	3	7	4	4		31

NATIONAL LEAGUE

NLDS (1-4)	W	1	2	3	4	5	%
Los Angeles Dodgers	2	5	4	2	3	2	65
San Francisco Giants	3	2	5	0	4	3	35

NLDS (2-3)	W	1	2	3					%
Cincinnati Reds	3	3	4	2					28
Philadelphia Phillies	0	2	3	1					72

NLCS	W	1	2	3	4	5	6	7	%
Cincinnati Reds	3	1	3	2	0	5	2	4	51
San Francisco Giants	4	2	4	1	1	4	1	6	49

WORLD SERIES

WS	W	1	2	3	4	%
California Angels	0	1	3	3	0	55
San Francisco Giants	4	5	4	4	3	45

ACTUAL WINNERS

American League: New York Yankees
National League: Los Angeles Dodgers
World Series: New York Yankees

OUTSTANDING PERFORMANCES

AWARD WINNERS

			STATS	
LG.	PLAYER	TEAM	ADJUSTED	ACTUAL
MOST VALUABLE PLAYERS				
AL	Jim Rice	Boston	62 HR, 164 RBI, .328 BA, $26.9 MIL	46 HR, 139 RBI, .315 BA
NL	Dave Parker	Pittsburgh	43 HR, 140 RBI, .349 BA, $18.5 MIL	30 HR, 117 RBI, .334 BA
CY YOUNG AWARDS				
AL	Ron Guidry	New York	25-3 W-L, 0 SV, 2.17 ERA, $25.5 MIL	25-3 W-L, 0 SV, 1.74 ERA
NL	Gaylord Perry	San Diego	21-6 W-L, 0 SV, 3.38 ERA, $17.5 MIL	21-6 W-L, 0 SV, 2.73 ERA

AMERICAN LEAGUE LEADERS

			STATS	
CAT.	PLAYER	TEAM	ADJUSTED	ACTUAL
BATTING				
HR	Jim Rice	Boston	62	46
RBI	Jim Rice	Boston	164	139
BA	Rod Carew	Minnesota	.348	.333
AB	Jim Rice	Boston	673	677
R	Ron LeFlore	Detroit	150	126
H	Jim Rice	Boston	221	213
2B	George Brett	Kansas City	56	45
3B	Jim Rice	Boston	11	15
TB	Jim Rice	Boston	456	406
SA	Jim Rice	Boston	.678	.600
SB	Ron LeFlore	Detroit	65	68
PITCHING				
W	Ron Guidry	New York	25	25
L	Rick Wise	Cleveland	20	19
SV	Rich Gossage	New York	31	27
ERA	Ron Guidry	New York	2.17	1.74
G	Bob Lacey	Oakland	74	74
IP	Jim Palmer	Baltimore	296	296
BB	Nolan Ryan	California	165	148
SO	Nolan Ryan	California	329	260

NATIONAL LEAGUE LEADERS

			STATS	
CAT.	PLAYER	TEAM	ADJUSTED	ACTUAL
BATTING				
HR	George Foster	Cincinnati	53	40
RBI	George Foster	Cincinnati	143	120
BA	Dave Parker	Pittsburgh	.349	.334
AB	Enos Cabell	Houston	660	660
R	Ivan DeJesus	Chicago	123	104
H	Steve Garvey	Los Angeles	211	202
2B	Pete Rose	Cincinnati	65	51
3B	Garry Templeton	St. Louis	13	13
TB	Dave Parker	Pittsburgh	385	340
SA	Dave Parker	Pittsburgh	.658	.585
SB	Omar Moreno	Pittsburgh	68	71
PITCHING				
W	Gaylord Perry	San Diego	21	21
L	Phil Niekro	Atlanta	18	18
SV	Rollie Fingers	San Diego	40	37
ERA	Craig Swan	New York	3.04	2.43
G	Kent Tekulve	Pittsburgh	92	91
IP	Phil Niekro	Atlanta	334	334.1
BB	J.R. Richard	Houston	156	141
SO	J.R. Richard	Houston	382	303

1979 SEASON

AMERICAN LEAGUE

		ADJUSTED				ACTUAL		
	W	L	Pct.	GB	W	L	Pct.	Rk.
EAST								
X Baltimore	104	58	.642	0	102	57	.642	1
X Boston	92	70	.568	12	91	69	.569	3
New York	90	72	.556	14	89	71	.556	4
Cleveland	81	81	.500	23	81	80	.503	10
Toronto	53	109	.327	51	53	109	.327	14
CENTRAL								
X Milwaukee	96	66	.593	0	95	66	.590	2
Detroit	85	77	.525	11	85	76	.528	6
Kansas City	85	77	.525	11	85	77	.525	7
Minnesota	82	80	.506	14	82	80	.506	9
Chicago	74	88	.457	22	73	87	.456	11
WEST								
X California	88	74	.543	0	88	74	.543	5
Texas	83	79	.512	5	83	79	.512	8
Seattle	67	95	.414	21	67	95	.414	12
Oakland	54	108	.333	34	54	108	.333	13

NATIONAL LEAGUE

		ADJUSTED				ACTUAL		
	W	L	Pct.	GB	W	L	Pct.	Rk.
EAST								
X Montreal	96	66	.593	0	95	65	.594	2
Philadelphia	84	78	.519	12	84	78	.519	6
Atlanta	67	95	.414	29	66	94	.413	11
New York	63	99	.389	33	63	99	.389	12
CENTRAL								
X Pittsburgh	98	64	.605	0	98	64	.605	1
X Cincinnati	91	71	.562	7	90	71	.559	3
St. Louis	86	76	.531	12	86	76	.531	5
Chicago	80	82	.494	18	80	82	.494	7
WEST								
X Houston	89	73	.549	0	89	73	.549	4
Los Angeles	79	83	.488	10	79	83	.488	8
San Francisco	71	91	.438	18	71	91	.438	9
San Diego	68	94	.420	21	68	93	.422	10

AMERICAN LEAGUE

ALDS (1-4)*	W	1	2	3	4		%
Baltimore Orioles	3	6	9	3	8		63
California Angels	1	3	8	4	0		37

ALDS (2-3)	W	1	2	3		
Milwaukee Brewers	0	2	2	4		50
Boston Red Sox	3	11	4	5		50

ALCS	W	1	2	3	4	%
Baltimore Orioles	4	5	5	6	6	65
Boston Red Sox	0	3	2	5	1	35

NATIONAL LEAGUE

NLDS (1-4)	W	1	2	3		%
Pittsburgh Pirates	3	3	5	5		72
Houston Astros	0	2	1	1		28

NLDS (2-3)	W	1	2	3	4	5		%
Montreal Expos	3	1	3	0	7	7		51
Cincinnati Reds	2	5	1	2	2	5		49

NLCS	W	1	2	3	4	5	6	%
Montreal Expos	2	4	1	1	1	4	1	49
Pittsburgh Pirates	4	2	2	3	3	3	3	51

WORLD SERIES

WS*	W	1	2	3	4	5	6	7	%
Baltimore Orioles	3	5	2	8	9	1	0	1	63
Pittsburgh Pirates	4	4	3	4	6	7	4	4	37

ACTUAL WINNERS

American League: Baltimore Orioles
National League: Pittsburgh Pirates
World Series: Pittsburgh Pirates

OUTSTANDING PERFORMANCES

AWARD WINNERS

LG.	PLAYER	TEAM	STATS ADJUSTED	ACTUAL
MOST VALUABLE PLAYERS				
AL	Don Baylor	California	44 HR, 154 RBI, .299 BA, $22.3 MIL	36 HR, 139 RBI, .296 BA
NL	Keith Hernandez	St. Louis	15 HR, 115 RBI, .350 BA, $18.6 MIL	11 HR, 105 RBI, .344 BA
NL	Willie Stargell	Pittsburgh	37 HR, 90 RBI, .285 BA, $2.7 MIL	32 HR, 82 RBI, .281 BA
CY YOUNG AWARDS				
AL	Mike Flanagan	Baltimore	24-9 W-L, 0 SV, 3.54 ERA, $26.0 MIL	23-9 W-L, 0 SV, 3.08 ERA
NL	Bruce Sutter	Chicago	6-6 W-L, 40 SV, 2.58 ERA, $9.5 MIL	6-6 W-L, 37 SV, 2.22 ERA

AMERICAN LEAGUE LEADERS

CAT.	PLAYER	TEAM	STATS ADJUSTED	ACTUAL
BATTING				
HR	Gorman Thomas	Milwaukee	52	45
RBI	Don Baylor	California	154	139
BA	Fred Lynn	Boston	.338	.333
AB	Buddy Bell	Texas	670	670
R	Don Baylor	California	132	120
H	George Brett	Kansas City	215	212
2B	Chet Lemon	Chicago	50	44
	Cecil Cooper	Milwaukee	48	44
3B	George Brett	Kansas City	16	20
TB	Jim Rice	Boston	402	369
SA	Fred Lynn	Boston	.686	.637
SB	Willie Wilson	Kansas City	81	83
PITCHING				
W	Mike Flanagan	Baltimore	24	23
L	Phil Huffman	Toronto	18	18
SV	Mike Marshall	Minnesota	38	32
ERA	Ron Guidry	New York	3.17	2.78
G	Mike Marshall	Minnesota	90	90
IP	Dennis Martinez	Baltimore	300	292.1
BB	Mike Torrez	Boston	133	121
SO	Nolan Ryan	California	286	223

NATIONAL LEAGUE LEADERS

CAT.	PLAYER	TEAM	STATS ADJUSTED	ACTUAL
BATTING				
HR	Dave Kingman	Chicago	57	48
RBI	Dave Winfield	San Diego	131	118
BA	Keith Hernandez	St. Louis	.350	.344
AB	Omar Moreno	Pittsburgh	691	695
R	Keith Hernandez	St. Louis	127	116
H	Garry Templeton	St. Louis	213	211
2B	Keith Hernandez	St. Louis	60	48
3B	Garry Templeton	St. Louis	16	19
TB	Dave Winfield	San Diego	361	333
SA	Dave Kingman	Chicago	.664	.613
SB	Omar Moreno	Pittsburgh	74	77
PITCHING				
W	Joe Niekro	Houston	21	21
	Phil Niekro	Atlanta	21	21
L	Phil Niekro	Atlanta	20	20
SV	Bruce Sutter	Chicago	40	37
ERA	J.R. Richard	Houston	3.08	2.71
G	Kent Tekulve	Pittsburgh	93	94
IP	Phil Niekro	Atlanta	350	342
BB	Phil Niekro	Atlanta	127	113
SO	J.R. Richard	Houston	397	313

1980 SEASON

REGULAR SEASON STANDINGS

AMERICAN LEAGUE

		ADJUSTED				ACTUAL		
	W	L	Pct.	GB	W	L	Pct.	Rk.
EAST								
X New York	103	59	.636	0	103	59	.636	1
X Baltimore	100	62	.617	3	100	62	.617	2
Boston	84	78	.519	19	83	77	.519	5
Cleveland	80	82	.494	23	79	81	.494	8
Toronto	67	95	.414	36	67	95	.414	12
CENTRAL								
X Kansas City	97	65	.599	0	97	65	.599	3
Milwaukee	86	76	.531	11	86	76	.531	4
Detroit	84	78	.519	13	84	78	.519	5
Minnesota	78	84	.481	19	77	84	.478	9
Chicago	71	91	.438	26	70	90	.438	11
WEST								
X Oakland	83	79	.512	0	83	79	.512	7
Texas	76	86	.469	7	76	85	.472	10
California	66	96	.407	17	65	95	.406	13
Seattle	59	103	.364	24	59	103	.364	14

NATIONAL LEAGUE

		ADJUSTED				ACTUAL		
	W	L	Pct.	GB	W	L	Pct.	Rk.
EAST								
X Philadelphia	91	71	.562	0	91	71	.562	3
Montreal	90	72	.556	1	90	72	.556	4
Atlanta	82	80	.506	9	81	80	.503	7
New York	67	95	.414	24	67	95	.414	11
CENTRAL								
X Cincinnati	89	73	.549	0	89	73	.549	5
Pittsburgh	83	79	.512	6	83	79	.512	6
St. Louis	74	88	.457	15	74	88	.457	9
Chicago	64	98	.395	25	64	98	.395	12
WEST								
X Houston	92	70	.568	0	92	70	.568	1
X Los Angeles	92	70	.568	0	92	70	.568	1
San Francisco	75	87	.463	17	75	86	.466	8
San Diego	73	89	.451	19	73	89	.451	10

SIMULATED PLAYOFFS

AMERICAN LEAGUE

ALDS (1-4)	W	1	2	3	4			%
New York Yankees	1	2	5	0	1			60
Oakland Athletics	3	5	4	1	4			40

ALDS (2-3)	W	1	2	3	4	5		%
Baltimore Orioles	2	7	7	7	4	4		48
Kansas City Royals	3	4	1	9	7	6		52

ALCS	W	1	2	3	4	5	6	%
Kansas City Royals	2	5	2	5	3	3	1	58
Oakland Athletics	4	3	3	3	4	5	7	42

NATIONAL LEAGUE

NLDS (1-4)	W	1	2	3				%
Houston Astros	3	3	3	5				54
Cincinnati Reds	0	0	2	1				46

NLDS (2-3)	W	1	2	3	4	5		%
Los Angeles Dodgers	3	1	4	3	2	1		55
Philadelphia Phillies	2	2	3	0	6	0		45

NLCS**	W	1	2	3	4	5	6	%
Houston Astros	2	7	1	1	3	2	2	48
Los Angeles Dodgers	4	1	4	4	2	4	3	52

WORLD SERIES

WS	W	1	2	3	4	5		%
Oakland Athletics	1	1	2	3	3	1		44
Los Angeles Dodgers	4	3	3	2	5	5		56

ACTUAL WINNERS

American League: Kansas City Royals
National League: Philadelphia Phillies
World Series: Philadelphia Phillies

OUTSTANDING PERFORMANCES

AWARD WINNERS

LG.	PLAYER	TEAM	STATS ADJUSTED	ACTUAL
MOST VALUABLE PLAYERS				
AL	George Brett	Kansas City	34 HR, 136 RBI, .396 BA, $12.1 MIL	24 HR, 118 RBI, .390 BA
NL	Mike Schmidt	Philadelphia	60 HR, 140 RBI, .292 BA, $16.1 MIL	48 HR, 121 RBI, .286 BA
CY YOUNG AWARDS				
AL	Steve Stone	Baltimore	25-7 W-L, 0 SV, 3.87 ERA, $18.7 MIL	25-7 W-L, 0 SV, 3.23 ERA
NL	Steve Carlton	Philadelphia	24-9 W-L, 0 SV, 2.78 ERA, $37.0 MIL	24-9 W-L, 0 SV, 2.34 ERA

AMERICAN LEAGUE LEADERS

CAT.	PLAYER	TEAM	ADJUSTED	ACTUAL
BATTING				
HR	Ben Oglivie	Milwaukee	52	41
	Reggie Jackson	New York	51	41
RBI	Cecil Cooper	Milwaukee	141	122
BA	George Brett	Kansas City	.396	.390
AB	Willie Wilson	Kansas City	705	705
R	Willie Wilson	Kansas City	154	133
H	Willie Wilson	Kansas City	234	230
2B	Robin Yount	Milwaukee	55	49
3B	Alfredo Griffin	Toronto	15	15
	Willie Wilson	Kansas City	15	15
TB	Cecil Cooper	Milwaukee	371	335
SA	George Brett	Kansas City	.735	.664
SB	Rickey Henderson	Oakland	89	100
PITCHING				
W	Steve Stone	Baltimore	25	25
L	Brian Kingman	Oakland	20	20
SV	Rich Gossage	New York	37	33
	Dan Quisenberry	Kansas City	37	33
ERA	Rudy May	New York	2.93	2.46
G	Dan Quisenberry	Kansas City	75	75
IP	Rick Langford	Oakland	290	290
BB	Jim Clancy	Toronto	148	128
SO	Len Barker	Cleveland	248	187

NATIONAL LEAGUE LEADERS

CAT.	PLAYER	TEAM	ADJUSTED	ACTUAL
BATTING				
HR	Mike Schmidt	Philadelphia	60	48
RBI	Mike Schmidt	Philadelphia	140	121
BA	Bill Buckner	Chicago	.329	.324
AB	Omar Moreno	Pittsburgh	676	676
R	Keith Hernandez	St. Louis	128	111
H	Steve Garvey	Los Angeles	202	200
2B	Pete Rose	Philadelphia	61	42
3B	Rodney Scott	Montreal	15	13
	Omar Moreno	Pittsburgh	13	13
TB	Mike Schmidt	Philadelphia	375	342
SA	Mike Schmidt	Philadelphia	.684	.624
SB	Ron LeFlore	Montreal	87	97
PITCHING				
W	Steve Carlton	Philadelphia	24	24
L	Phil Niekro	Atlanta	18	18
SV	Bruce Sutter	Chicago	31	28
ERA	Don Sutton	Los Angeles	2.63	2.20
G	Dick Tidrow	Chicago	84	84
IP	Steve Carlton	Philadelphia	304	304
BB	Nolan Ryan	Houston	113	98
SO	Steve Carlton	Philadelphia	370	286

1981 SEASON

REGULAR SEASON STANDINGS

AMERICAN LEAGUE

		ADJUSTED				ACTUAL		
	W	L	Pct.	GB	W	L	Pct.	Rk.
EAST								
X Baltimore	91	71	.562	0	59	46	.562	3
X New York	89	73	.549	2	59	48	.551	4
Boston	88	74	.543	3	59	49	.546	6
Cleveland	82	80	.506	9	52	51	.505	9
Toronto	57	105	.352	34	37	69	.349	14
CENTRAL								
X Milwaukee	92	70	.568	0	62	47	.569	2
X Detroit	89	73	.549	3	60	49	.550	5
Chicago	83	79	.512	9	54	52	.509	8
Kansas City	79	83	.488	13	50	53	.485	10
Minnesota	61	101	.377	31	41	68	.376	13
WEST								
X Oakland	95	67	.586	0	64	45	.587	1
Texas	88	74	.543	7	57	48	.543	7
California	75	87	.463	20	51	59	.464	11
Seattle	65	97	.401	30	44	65	.404	12

NATIONAL LEAGUE

		ADJUSTED				ACTUAL		
	W	L	Pct.	GB	W	L	Pct.	Rk.
EAST								
X Montreal	90	72	.556	0	60	48	.556	4
Philadelphia	89	73	.549	1	59	48	.551	6
Atlanta	77	85	.475	13	50	56	.472	8
New York	65	97	.401	25	41	62	.398	10
CENTRAL								
X Cincinnati	99	63	.611	0	66	42	.611	1
X St. Louis	94	68	.580	5	59	43	.578	2
Pittsburgh	73	89	.451	26	46	56	.451	9
Chicago	60	102	.370	39	38	65	.369	12
WEST								
X Los Angeles	93	69	.574	0	63	47	.573	3
Houston	90	72	.556	3	61	49	.555	5
San Francisco	82	80	.506	11	56	55	.505	7
San Diego	60	102	.370	33	41	69	.373	11

SIMULATED PLAYOFFS

AMERICAN LEAGUE

TIEBREAKER	W	1	2						%
New York Yankees	0	3	1						57
Detroit Tigers	2	4	3						43

ALDS (1-4)	W	1	2	3	4	5			%
Oakland Athletics	3	2	3	5	4	3			50
Detroit Tigers	2	4	1	2	5	2			50

ALDS (2-3)	W	1	2	3					%
Milwaukee Brewers	0	2	2	2					60
Baltimore Orioles	3	4	4	6					40

ALCS	W	1	2	3	4	5	6	7	%
Oakland Athletics	4	0	0	5	2	5	5	3	67
Baltimore Orioles	3	3	5	0	3	1	0	2	33

NATIONAL LEAGUE

NLDS (1-4)	W	1	2	3	4	5			%
Cincinnati Reds	2	2	6	0	4	2			46
Montreal Expos	3	5	4	3	3	3			54

NLDS (2-3)	W	1	2	3	4	5			%
St. Louis Cardinals	3	4	2	1	4	3			39
Los Angeles Dodgers	2	2	7	3	3	2			61

NLCS	W	1	2	3	4	5	6		%
St. Louis Cardinals	4	0	5	2	5	6	3		51
Montreal Expos	2	2	1	3	3	3	1		49

WORLD SERIES

WS	W	1	2	3	4	5			%
Oakland Athletics	4	5	2	3	3	3			46
St. Louis Cardinals	1	2	8	2	2	1			54

ACTUAL WINNERS

American League: New York Yankees
National League: Los Angeles Dodgers
World Series: Los Angeles Dodgers

OUTSTANDING PERFORMANCES

AWARD WINNERS

LG.	PLAYER	TEAM	STATS ADJUSTED	ACTUAL
MOST VALUABLE PLAYERS				
AL	Rollie Fingers	Milwaukee	9-4 W-L, 45 SV, 1.32 ERA, $8.9 MIL	6-3 W-L, 28 SV, 1.04 ERA
NL	Mike Schmidt	Philadelphia	63 HR, 169 RBI, .333 BA, $19.3 MIL	31 HR, 91 RBI, .316 BA
CY YOUNG AWARDS				
AL	Rollie Fingers	Milwaukee	9-4 W-L, 45 SV, 1.32 ERA, $8.9 MIL	6-3 W-L, 28 SV, 1.04 ERA
NL	Fernando Valenzuela	Los Angeles	19-10 W-L, 0 SV, 3.16 ERA, $19.5 MIL	13-7 W-L, 0 SV, 2.48 ERA

AMERICAN LEAGUE LEADERS

CAT.	PLAYER	TEAM	STATS ADJUSTED	ACTUAL
BATTING				
HR	Dwight Evans	Boston	48	22
	Eddie Murray	Baltimore	48	22
	Tony Armas	Oakland	47	22
	Bobby Grich	California	45	22
RBI	Eddie Murray	Baltimore	148	78
BA	Carney Lansford	Boston	.354	.336
AB	Jim Rice	Boston	677	451
R	Rickey Henderson	Oakland	163	89
H	Rickey Henderson	Oakland	212	135
2B	Cecil Cooper	Milwaukee	60	35
3B	John Castino	Minnesota	12	9
TB	Dwight Evans	Boston	375	215
SA	Bobby Grich	California	.629	.543
SB	Rickey Henderson	Oakland	80	56
PITCHING				
W	Dennis Martinez	Baltimore	22	14
	Steve McCatty	Oakland	21	14
	Jack Morris	Detroit	21	14
	Pete Vuckovich	Milwaukee	21	14
L	Luis Leal	Toronto	20	13
	Juan Berenguer	K.C.-Tor.	20	13
	Jerry Koosman	Minn.-Chi.	19	13
SV	Rollie Fingers	Milwaukee	45	28
ERA	Steve McCatty	Oakland	2.97	2.33
G	Doug Corbett	Minnesota	80	54
IP	Dennis Leonard	Kansas City	318	201.2
BB	Jack Morris	Detroit	131	78
SO	Len Barker	Cleveland	268	127

NATIONAL LEAGUE LEADERS

CAT.	PLAYER	TEAM	STATS ADJUSTED	ACTUAL
BATTING				
HR	Mike Schmidt	Philadelphia	63	31
RBI	Mike Schmidt	Philadelphia	169	91
BA	Bill Madlock	Pittsburgh	.358	.341
AB	Ozzie Smith	San Diego	663	450
R	Mike Schmidt	Philadelphia	144	78
H	Pete Rose	Philadelphia	223	140
2B	Bill Buckner	Chicago	64	35
3B	Gene Richards	San Diego	18	12
	Craig Reynolds	Houston	17	12
TB	Mike Schmidt	Philadelphia	399	228
SA	Mike Schmidt	Philadelphia	.747	.644
SB	Tim Raines	Montreal	102	71
PITCHING				
W	Tom Seaver	Cincinnati	21	14
L	Pat Zachry	New York	22	14
	Steve Mura	San Diego	21	14
SV	Bruce Sutter	St. Louis	42	25
ERA	Nolan Ryan	Houston	2.17	1.69
G	Gary Lucas	San Diego	84	57
IP	Fernando Valenzuela	Los Angeles	285	192.1
BB	Bruce Berenyi	Cincinnati	133	77
SO	Fernando Valenzuela	Los Angeles	348	180

1982 SEASON

REGULAR SEASON STANDINGS

AMERICAN LEAGUE

		ADJUSTED				ACTUAL			
	W	L	Pct.	GB	W	L	Pct.	Rk.
EAST								
X Baltimore	94	68	.580	0	94	68	.580	2
Boston	89	73	.549	5	89	73	.549	5
New York	79	83	.488	15	79	83	.488	8
Cleveland	78	84	.481	16	78	84	.481	9
Toronto	78	84	.481	16	78	84	.481	9
CENTRAL								
X Milwaukee	95	67	.586	0	95	67	.586	1
X Kansas City	90	72	.556	5	90	72	.556	4
Chicago	87	75	.537	8	87	75	.537	6
Detroit	83	79	.512	12	83	79	.512	7
Minnesota	60	102	.370	35	60	102	.370	14
WEST								
X California	93	69	.574	0	93	69	.574	3
Seattle	76	86	.469	17	76	86	.469	11
Oakland	68	94	.420	25	68	94	.420	12
Texas	64	98	.395	29	64	98	.395	13

NATIONAL LEAGUE

		ADJUSTED				ACTUAL			
	W	L	Pct.	GB	W	L	Pct.	Rk.
EAST								
X Atlanta	89	73	.549	0	89	73	.549	2
X Philadelphia	89	73	.549	0	89	73	.549	2
Montreal	86	76	.531	3	86	76	.531	6
New York	65	97	.401	24	65	97	.401	11
CENTRAL								
X St. Louis	92	70	.568	0	92	70	.568	1
Pittsburgh	84	78	.519	8	84	78	.519	7
Chicago	73	89	.451	19	73	89	.451	10
Cincinnati	61	101	.377	31	61	101	.377	12
WEST								
X Los Angeles	88	74	.543	0	88	74	.543	4
San Francisco	87	75	.537	1	87	75	.537	5
San Diego	81	81	.500	7	81	81	.500	8
Houston	77	85	.475	11	77	85	.475	9

SIMULATED PLAYOFFS

AMERICAN LEAGUE

ALDS (1-4)	W	1	2	3	4		%
Milwaukee Brewers	3	10	4	3	4		61
Kansas City Royals	1	8	10	1	3		39

ALDS (2-3)	W	1	2	3	4	5	%
Baltimore Orioles	2	3	6	4	6	5	46
California Angels	3	2	9	7	0	9	54

ALCS**	W	1	2	3	4	5	6	%
Milwaukee Brewers	4	3	2	5	9	4	6	43
California Angels	2	8	4	3	5	3	4	57

NATIONAL LEAGUE

NLDS (1-4)	W	1	2	3	4	5	%
St. Louis Cardinals	2	4	0	4	1	2	42
Los Angeles Dodgers	3	0	2	2	2	3	58

NLDS (2-3)	W	1	2	3	4	5	%
Atlanta Braves	3	6	2	2	5	3	57
Philadelphia Phillies	2	4	3	4	2	2	43

NLCS	W	1	2	3	4	5	%
Atlanta Braves	4	1	6	8	4	3	47
Los Angeles Dodgers	1	2	3	4	3	2	53

WORLD SERIES

WS	W	1	2	3	4	5	6	7	%
Milwaukee Brewers	4	1	3	12	18	4	0	6	70
Atlanta Braves	3	2	2	3	5	7	2	3	30

ACTUAL WINNERS

American League: Milwaukee Brewers
National League: St. Louis Cardinals
World Series: St. Louis Cardinals

OUTSTANDING PERFORMANCES

AWARD WINNERS

LG.	PLAYER	TEAM	STATS ADJUSTED	ACTUAL
MOST VALUABLE PLAYERS				
AL	Robin Yount	Milwaukee	38 HR, 130 RBI, .341 BA, $19.7 MIL	29 HR, 114 RBI, .331 BA
NL	Dale Murphy	Atlanta	44 HR, 125 RBI, .289 BA, $19.0 MIL	36 HR, 109 RBI, .281 BA
CY YOUNG AWARDS				
AL	Pete Vuckovich	Milwaukee	18-6 W-L, 0 SV, 3.98 ERA, $15.7 MIL	18-6 W-L, 0 SV, 3.34 ERA
NL	Steve Carlton	Philadelphia	23-11 W-L, 0 SV, 3.68 ERA, $31.0 MIL	23-11 W-L, 0 SV, 3.10 ERA

AMERICAN LEAGUE LEADERS

CAT.	PLAYER	TEAM	STATS ADJUSTED	ACTUAL
BATTING				
HR	Reggie Jackson	California	47	39
	Gorman Thomas	Milwaukee	46	39
RBI	Hal McRae	Kansas City	153	133
BA	Willie Wilson	Kansas City	.342	.332
AB	Paul Molitor	Milwaukee	662	666
R	Paul Molitor	Milwaukee	156	136
H	Robin Yount	Milwaukee	215	210
2B	Robin Yount	Milwaukee	53	46
	Hal McRae	Kansas City	52	46
3B	Willie Wilson	Kansas City	16	15
TB	Robin Yount	Milwaukee	402	367
SA	Robin Yount	Milwaukee	.637	.578
SB	Rickey Henderson	Oakland	122	130
PITCHING				
W	LaMarr Hoyt	Chicago	19	19
L	Matt Keough	Oakland	18	18
	Frank Tanana	Texas	18	18
SV	Dan Quisenberry	Kansas City	37	35
ERA	Rick Sutcliffe	Cleveland	3.50	2.96
G	Ed Vande Berg	Seattle	78	78
IP	Dave Stieb	Toronto	288	288.1
BB	Dave Righetti	New York	123	108
SO	Floyd Bannister	Seattle	263	209

NATIONAL LEAGUE LEADERS

CAT.	PLAYER	TEAM	STATS ADJUSTED	ACTUAL
BATTING				
HR	Dave Kingman	New York	44	37
RBI	Dale Murphy	Atlanta	125	109
	Al Oliver	Montreal	125	109
BA	Al Oliver	Montreal	.340	.331
AB	Bill Buckner	Chicago	657	657
R	Lonnie Smith	St. Louis	138	120
H	Al Oliver	Montreal	210	204
2B	Al Oliver	Montreal	49	43
3B	Dickie Thon	Houston	9	10
TB	Al Oliver	Montreal	350	317
SA	Mike Schmidt	Philadelphia	.605	.547
SB	Tim Raines	Montreal	72	78
PITCHING				
W	Steve Carlton	Philadelphia	23	23
L	Bruce Berenyi	Cincinnati	18	18
SV	Bruce Sutter	St. Louis	39	36
ERA	Steve Rogers	Montreal	2.86	2.40
G	Kent Tekulve	Pittsburgh	85	85
IP	Steve Carlton	Philadelphia	296	295.2
BB	Nolan Ryan	Houston	124	109
SO	Steve Carlton	Philadelphia	356	286

1983 SEASON

REGULAR SEASON STANDINGS

AMERICAN LEAGUE

		ADJUSTED				ACTUAL			
	W	L	Pct.	GB	W	L	Pct.	Rk.
EAST								
X Baltimore	98	64	.605	0	98	64	.605	2
New York	91	71	.562	7	91	71	.562	4
Toronto	89	73	.549	9	89	73	.549	5
Boston	78	84	.481	20	78	84	.481	8
Cleveland	70	92	.432	28	70	92	.432	11
CENTRAL								
X Chicago	99	63	.611	0	99	63	.611	1
X Detroit	92	70	.568	7	92	70	.568	3
Milwaukee	87	75	.537	12	87	75	.537	6
Kansas City	79	83	.488	20	79	83	.488	7
Minnesota	70	92	.432	29	70	92	.432	11
WEST								
X Texas	77	85	.475	0	77	85	.475	9
Oakland	74	88	.457	3	74	88	.457	10
California	70	92	.432	7	70	92	.432	11
Seattle	60	102	.370	17	60	102	.370	14

NATIONAL LEAGUE

		ADJUSTED				ACTUAL			
	W	L	Pct.	GB	W	L	Pct.	Rk.
EAST								
X Philadelphia	90	72	.556	0	90	72	.556	2
X Atlanta	88	74	.543	2	88	74	.543	3
Montreal	82	80	.506	8	82	80	.506	6
New York	68	94	.420	22	68	94	.420	12
CENTRAL								
X Pittsburgh	84	78	.519	0	84	78	.519	5
St. Louis	79	83	.488	5	79	83	.488	8
Cincinnati	74	88	.457	10	74	88	.457	10
Chicago	71	91	.438	13	71	91	.438	11
WEST								
X Los Angeles	91	71	.562	0	91	71	.562	1
Houston	85	77	.525	6	85	77	.525	4
San Diego	81	81	.500	10	81	81	.500	7
San Francisco	79	83	.488	12	79	83	.488	8

SIMULATED PLAYOFFS

AMERICAN LEAGUE

ALDS (1-4)	W	1	2	3	4	5	%
Chicago White Sox	3	1	7	2	2	4	70
Texas Rangers	2	3	5	3	1	2	30

ALDS (2-3)	W	1	2	3	4	5	%
Baltimore Orioles	3	6	0	8	4	5	51
Detroit Tigers	2	7	3	5	3	4	49

ALCS**	W	1	2	3	4	5	%
Baltimore Orioles	4	1	4	11	3	11	47
Chicago White Sox	1	2	0	1	0	6	53

NATIONAL LEAGUE

NLDS (1-4)	W	1	2	3	4	5	%
Los Angeles Dodgers	3	0	4	5	1	4	56
Pittsburgh Pirates	2	5	2	3	5	2	44

NLDS (2-3)	W	1	2	3	4		%
Philadelphia Phillies	3	0	3	6	3		48
Atlanta Braves	1	3	2	5	0		52

NLCS**	W	1	2	3	4	5	6	7	%
Philadelphia Phillies	3	1	1	7	7	1	1	4	62
Los Angeles Dodgers	4	0	4	2	2	2	2	5	38

WORLD SERIES

WS	W	1	2	3	4		%
Baltimore Orioles	0	2	6	3	2		63
Los Angeles Dodgers	4	4	7	4	6		37

ACTUAL WINNERS

American League: Baltimore Orioles
National League: Philadelphia Phillies
World Series: Baltimore Orioles

OUTSTANDING PERFORMANCES

AWARD WINNERS

LG.	PLAYER	TEAM	STATS ADJUSTED	ACTUAL
MOST VALUABLE PLAYERS				
AL	Cal Ripken Jr.	Baltimore	35 HR, 116 RBI, .329 BA, $15.6 MIL	27 HR, 102 RBI, .318 BA
NL	Dale Murphy	Atlanta	45 HR, 138 RBI, .312 BA, $25.4 MIL	36 HR, 121 RBI, .302 BA
CY YOUNG AWARDS				
AL	LaMarr Hoyt	Chicago	24-10 W-L, 0 SV, 4.34 ERA, $25.5 MIL	24-10 W-L, 0 SV, 3.66 ERA
NL	John Denny	Philadelphia	19-6 W-L, 0 SV, 2.81 ERA, $15.8 MIL	19-6 W-L, 0 SV, 2.37 ERA

AMERICAN LEAGUE LEADERS

CAT.	PLAYER	TEAM	STATS ADJUSTED	ACTUAL
BATTING				
HR	Jim Rice	Boston	48	39
RBI	Cecil Cooper	Milwaukee	145	126
	Jim Rice	Boston	144	126
BA	Wade Boggs	Boston	.373	.361
AB	Cal Ripken Jr.	Baltimore	663	663
R	Cal Ripken Jr.	Baltimore	138	121
H	Cal Ripken Jr.	Baltimore	218	211
2B	Cal Ripken Jr.	Baltimore	51	47
3B	Robin Yount	Milwaukee	8	10
TB	Jim Rice	Boston	378	344
SA	George Brett	Kansas City	.617	.563
SB	Rickey Henderson	Oakland	96	108
PITCHING				
W	LaMarr Hoyt	Chicago	24	24
L	Larry Gura	Kansas City	18	18
SV	Dan Quisenberry	Kansas City	46	45
ERA	Rick Honeycutt	Texas	2.88	2.42
G	Dan Quisenberry	Kansas City	69	69
IP	Jack Morris	Detroit	294	293.2
BB	Richard Dotson	Chicago	119	106
SO	Jack Morris	Detroit	288	232

NATIONAL LEAGUE LEADERS

CAT.	PLAYER	TEAM	STATS ADJUSTED	ACTUAL
BATTING				
HR	Mike Schmidt	Philadelphia	49	40
RBI	Dale Murphy	Atlanta	138	121
BA	Bill Madlock	Pittsburgh	.334	.323
AB	Mookie Wilson	New York	638	638
R	Tim Raines	Montreal	151	133
H	Jose Cruz	Houston	195	189
	Andre Dawson	Montreal	194	189
2B	Johnny Ray	Pittsburgh	50	38
	Al Oliver	Montreal	47	38
	Bill Buckner	Chicago	44	38
3B	Brett Butler	Atlanta	12	13
TB	Andre Dawson	Montreal	375	341
SA	Dale Murphy	Atlanta	.594	.540
SB	Tim Raines	Montreal	79	90
PITCHING				
W	John Denny	Philadelphia	19	19
L	Mike Torrez	New York	17	17
SV	Lee Smith	Chicago	30	29
ERA	Atlee Hammaker	San Francisco	2.67	2.25
G	Bill Campbell	Chicago	82	82
IP	Steve Carlton	Philadelphia	284	283.2
BB	Mike Torrez	New York	126	113
SO	Steve Carlton	Philadelphia	335	275

REGULAR SEASON STANDINGS

AMERICAN LEAGUE

		ADJUSTED			ACTUAL			
	W	L	Pct.	GB	W	L	Pct.	Rk.
EAST								
X Toronto	89	73	.549	0	89	73	.549	2
X New York	87	75	.537	2	87	75	.537	3
Boston	86	76	.531	3	86	76	.531	4
Baltimore	85	77	.525	4	85	77	.525	5
Cleveland	75	87	.463	14	75	87	.463	10
CENTRAL								
X Detroit	104	58	.642	0	104	58	.642	1
Kansas City	84	78	.519	20	84	78	.519	6
Minnesota	81	81	.500	23	81	81	.500	7
Chicago	74	88	.457	30	74	88	.457	11
Milwaukee	67	95	.414	37	67	94	.416	14
WEST								
X California	81	81	.500	0	81	81	.500	7
Oakland	77	85	.475	4	77	85	.475	9
Seattle	74	88	.457	7	74	88	.457	11
Texas	70	92	.432	11	69	92	.429	13

NATIONAL LEAGUE

		ADJUSTED			ACTUAL			
	W	L	Pct.	GB	W	L	Pct.	Rk.
EAST								
X New York	90	72	.556	0	90	72	.556	3
Philadelphia	81	81	.500	9	81	81	.500	5
Atlanta	80	82	.494	10	80	82	.494	6
Montreal	78	84	.481	12	78	83	.484	9
CENTRAL								
X Chicago	97	65	.599	0	96	65	.596	1
X St. Louis	84	78	.519	13	84	78	.519	4
Pittsburgh	75	87	.463	22	75	87	.463	10
Cincinnati	70	92	.432	27	70	92	.432	11
WEST								
X San Diego	92	70	.568	0	92	70	.568	2
Houston	80	82	.494	12	80	82	.494	6
Los Angeles	79	83	.488	13	79	83	.488	8
San Francisco	66	96	.407	26	66	96	.407	12

SIMULATED PLAYOFFS

AMERICAN LEAGUE

ALDS (1-4)	W	1	2	3	4	5		%
Detroit Tigers	3	1	10	2	1	10		86
California Angels	2	4	6	1	4	1		14

ALDS (2-3)	W	1	2	3	4		%
Toronto Blue Jays	1	7	1	3	1		35
New York Yankees	3	3	4	6	15		65

ALCS	W	1	2	3	4	5	6	7	%
Detroit Tigers	4	6	3	1	6	1	1	8	68
New York Yankees	3	5	5	3	3	8	0	5	32

NATIONAL LEAGUE

NLDS (1-4)	W	1	2	3		%
Chicago Cubs	3	6	5	4		65
St. Louis Cardinals	0	2	1	2		35

NLDS (2-3)	W	1	2	3	4	5		%
San Diego Padres	2	2	6	6	1	2		65
New York Mets	3	3	3	4	2	3		35

NLCS	W	1	2	3	4		%
Chicago Cubs	4	6	8	5	2		73
New York Mets	0	3	3	2	1		27

WORLD SERIES

WS	W	1	2	3	4	5	6	7	%
Detroit Tigers	4	5	5	3	2	3	3	7	66
Chicago Cubs	3	6	1	5	4	0	0	3	34

ACTUAL WINNERS

American League: Detroit Tigers
National League: San Diego Padres
World Series: Detroit Tigers

OUTSTANDING PERFORMANCES

AWARD WINNERS

LG.	PLAYER	TEAM	STATS ADJUSTED	ACTUAL
MOST VALUABLE PLAYERS				
AL	Willie Hernandez	Detroit	9-3 W-L, 34 SV, 2.31 ERA, $8.3 MIL	9-3 W-L, 32 SV, 1.92 ERA
NL	Ryne Sandberg	Chicago	28 HR, 98 RBI, .325 BA, $14.9 MIL	19 HR, 84 RBI, .314 BA
CY YOUNG AWARDS				
AL	Willie Hernandez	Detroit	9-3 W-L, 34 SV, 2.31 ERA, $8.3 MIL	9-3 W-L, 32 SV, 1.92 ERA
NL	Rick Sutcliffe	Cle. (A)-Chi. (N)	20-6 W-L, 0 SV, 4.37 ERA, $19.3 MIL	20-6 W-L, 0 SV, 3.64 ERA

AMERICAN LEAGUE LEADERS

CAT.	PLAYER	TEAM	STATS ADJUSTED	ACTUAL
BATTING				
HR	Tony Armas	Boston	54	43
RBI	Tony Armas	Boston	143	123
BA	Don Mattingly	New York	.355	.343
AB	Julio Franco	Cleveland	654	658
R	Dwight Evans	Boston	140	121
H	Don Mattingly	New York	214	207
2B	Don Mattingly	New York	50	44
3B	Dave Collins	Toronto	15	15
	Lloyd Moseby	Toronto	12	15
TB	Tony Armas	Boston	378	339
SA	Harold Baines	Chicago	.605	.541
SB	Rickey Henderson	Oakland	63	66
PITCHING				
W	Mike Boddicker	Baltimore	20	20
L	LaMarr Hoyt	Chicago	18	18
SV	Dan Quisenberry	Kansas City	45	44
ERA	Mike Boddicker	Baltimore	3.34	2.79
G	Willie Hernandez	Detroit	80	80
IP	Dave Stieb	Toronto	267	267
BB	Mark Langston	Seattle	134	118
SO	Mark Langston	Seattle	243	204

NATIONAL LEAGUE LEADERS

CAT.	PLAYER	TEAM	STATS ADJUSTED	ACTUAL
BATTING				
HR	Dale Murphy	Atlanta	46	36
	Mike Schmidt	Philadelphia	45	36
RBI	Gary Carter	Montreal	124	106
	Mike Schmidt	Philadelphia	123	106
BA	Tony Gwynn	San Diego	.365	.351
AB	Juan Samuel	Philadelphia	701	701
R	Ryne Sandberg	Chicago	133	114
H	Tony Gwynn	San Diego	221	213
2B	Tim Raines	Montreal	51	38
	Johnny Ray	Pittsburgh	51	38
3B	Juan Samuel	Philadelphia	17	19
	Ryne Sandberg	Chicago	16	19
TB	Dale Murphy	Atlanta	367	332
SA	Dale Murphy	Atlanta	.605	.547
SB	Tim Raines	Montreal	73	75
PITCHING				
W	Joaquin Andujar	St. Louis	20	20
L	Jeff Russell	Cincinnati	18	18
SV	Bruce Sutter	St. Louis	46	45
ERA	Alejandro Pena	Los Angeles	2.98	2.48
G	Ted Power	Cincinnati	78	78
IP	Joaquin Andujar	St. Louis	261	261.1
BB	Fernando Valenzuela	Los Angeles	120	106
SO	Dwight Gooden	New York	319	276

1985 SEASON

REGULAR SEASON STANDINGS

AMERICAN LEAGUE

	ADJUSTED				ACTUAL			
	W	L	Pct.	GB	W	L	Pct.	Rk.
EAST								
X Toronto	100	62	.617	0	99	62	.615	1
X New York	98	64	.605	2	97	64	.602	2
Baltimore	83	79	.512	17	83	78	.516	7
Boston	81	81	.500	19	81	81	.500	8
Cleveland	60	102	.370	40	60	102	.370	14
CENTRAL								
X Kansas City	91	71	.562	0	91	71	.562	3
Chicago	85	77	.525	6	85	77	.525	5
Detroit	85	77	.525	6	84	77	.522	6
Minnesota	77	85	.475	14	77	85	.475	9
Milwaukee	71	91	.438	20	71	90	.441	12
WEST								
X California	90	72	.556	0	90	72	.556	4
Oakland	77	85	.475	13	77	85	.475	9
Seattle	74	88	.457	16	74	88	.457	11
Texas	62	100	.383	28	62	99	.385	13

NATIONAL LEAGUE

	ADJUSTED				ACTUAL			
	W	L	Pct.	GB	W	L	Pct.	Rk.
EAST								
X New York	98	64	.605	0	98	64	.605	2
Montreal	85	77	.525	13	84	77	.522	5
Philadelphia	75	87	.463	23	75	87	.463	9
Atlanta	66	96	.407	32	66	96	.407	10
CENTRAL								
X St. Louis	101	61	.623	0	101	61	.623	1
X Cincinnati	90	72	.556	11	89	72	.553	4
Chicago	77	85	.475	24	77	84	.478	8
Pittsburgh	57	105	.352	44	57	104	.354	12
WEST								
X Los Angeles	95	67	.586	0	95	67	.586	3
Houston	83	79	.512	12	83	79	.512	6
San Diego	83	79	.512	12	83	79	.512	6
San Francisco	62	100	.383	33	62	100	.383	11

SIMULATED PLAYOFFS

AMERICAN LEAGUE

ALDS (1-4)	W	1	2	3	4	5		%
Toronto Blue Jays	3	6	6	1	2	8		71
California Angels	2	4	4	3	5	5		29

ALDS (2-3)	W	1	2	3	4	5		%
New York Yankees	3	2	5	2	10	7		69
Kansas City Royals	2	3	3	3	1	4		31

ALCS	W	1	2	3	4	5		%
Toronto Blue Jays	4	4	9	4	2	4		54
New York Yankees	1	2	6	5	0	2		46

NATIONAL LEAGUE

NLDS (1-4)	W	1	2	3	4	5		%
St. Louis Cardinals	3	4	2	1	7	2		67
Cincinnati Reds	2	3	3	2	2	1		33

NLDS (2-3)	W	1	2	3	4	5		%
New York Mets	2	4	2	5	1	2		55
Los Angeles Dodgers	3	3	4	1	4	4		45

NLCS*	W	1	2	3	4	5	6	%
St. Louis Cardinals	4	1	2	4	12	3	7	56
Los Angeles Dodgers	2	4	8	2	2	2	5	44

WORLD SERIES

WS	W	1	2	3	4	5	6	%
Toronto Blue Jays	2	1	1	1	3	3	1	45
St. Louis Cardinals	4	3	2	5	1	1	5	55

ACTUAL WINNERS

American League: Kansas City Royals
National League: St. Louis Cardinals
World Series: Kansas City Royals

OUTSTANDING PERFORMANCES ·

AWARD WINNERS

			STATS	
LG.	PLAYER	TEAM	ADJUSTED	ACTUAL
MOST VALUABLE PLAYERS				
AL	Don Mattingly	New York	42 HR, 166 RBI, .338 BA, $15.5 MIL	35 HR, 145 RBI, .324 BA
NL	Willie McGee	St. Louis	15 HR, 93 RBI, .369 BA, $14.4 MIL	10 HR, 82 RBI, .353 BA
CY YOUNG AWARDS				
AL	Bret Saberhagen	Kansas City	20-6 W-L, 0 SV, 3.37 ERA, $15.9 MIL	20-6 W-L, 0 SV, 2.87 ERA
NL	Dwight Gooden	New York	24-4 W-L, 0 SV, 1.79 ERA, $32.5 MIL	24-4 W-L, 0 SV, 1.53 ERA

AMERICAN LEAGUE LEADERS

			STATS	
CAT.	PLAYER	TEAM	ADJUSTED	ACTUAL
BATTING				
HR	Darrell Evans	Detroit	46	40
RBI	Don Mattingly	New York	166	145
BA	Wade Boggs	Boston	.385	.368
AB	Kirby Puckett	Minnesota	691	691
R	Rickey Henderson	New York	167	146
H	Wade Boggs	Boston	250	240
2B	Don Mattingly	New York	52	48
3B	Willie Wilson	Kansas City	21	21
TB	Don Mattingly	New York	406	370
SA	George Brett	Kansas City	.638	.585
SB	Rickey Henderson	New York	76	80
PITCHING				
W	Ron Guidry	New York	22	22
L	Matt Young	Seattle	19	19
SV	Dan Quisenberry	Kansas City	39	37
ERA	Dave Stieb	Toronto	2.92	2.48
G	Dan Quisenberry	Kansas City	84	84
IP	Bert Blyleven	Cle.-Minn.	294	293.2
BB	Phil Niekro	New York	131	120
SO	Bert Blyleven	Cle.-Minn.	250	206

NATIONAL LEAGUE LEADERS

			STATS	
CAT.	PLAYER	TEAM	ADJUSTED	ACTUAL
BATTING				
HR	Dale Murphy	Atlanta	44	37
RBI	Dave Parker	Cincinnati	142	125
BA	Willie McGee	St. Louis	.369	.353
AB	Juan Samuel	Philadelphia	663	663
R	Dale Murphy	Atlanta	134	118
H	Willie McGee	St. Louis	226	216
2B	Dave Parker	Cincinnati	47	42
3B	Willie McGee	St. Louis	17	18
TB	Dave Parker	Cincinnati	383	350
SA	Pedro Guerrero	Los Angeles	.632	.577
SB	Vince Coleman	St. Louis	104	110
PITCHING				
W	Dwight Gooden	New York	24	24
L	Jose DeLeon	Pittsburgh	19	19
SV	Jeff Reardon	Montreal	42	41
ERA	Dwight Gooden	New York	1.79	1.53
G	Tim Burke	Montreal	78	78
IP	Dwight Gooden	New York	277	276.2
BB	Ron Darling	New York	124	114
SO	Dwight Gooden	New York	318	268

1986 SEASON

REGULAR SEASON STANDINGS

AMERICAN LEAGUE

		ADJUSTED				ACTUAL		
	W	L	Pct.	GB	W	L	Pct.	Rk.
EAST								
X Boston	96	66	.593	0	95	66	.590	1
X New York	90	72	.556	6	90	72	.556	3
Toronto	86	76	.531	10	86	76	.531	6
Cleveland	84	78	.519	12	84	78	.519	7
Baltimore	73	89	.451	23	73	89	.451	11
CENTRAL								
X Detroit	87	75	.537	0	87	75	.537	4
Milwaukee	77	85	.475	10	77	84	.478	8
Kansas City	76	86	.469	11	76	86	.469	9
Chicago	72	90	.444	15	72	90	.444	12
Minnesota	71	91	.438	16	71	91	.438	13
WEST								
X California	92	70	.568	0	92	70	.568	2
Texas	87	75	.537	5	87	75	.537	4
Oakland	76	86	.469	16	76	86	.469	9
Seattle	67	95	.414	25	67	95	.414	14

NATIONAL LEAGUE

		ADJUSTED				ACTUAL		
	W	L	Pct.	GB	W	L	Pct.	Rk.
EAST								
X New York	108	54	.667	0	108	54	.667	1
X Philadelphia	87	75	.537	21	86	75	.534	3
Montreal	78	84	.481	30	78	83	.484	7
Atlanta	72	90	.444	36	72	89	.447	10
CENTRAL								
X Cincinnati	86	76	.531	0	86	76	.531	4
St. Louis	80	82	.494	6	79	82	.491	6
Chicago	71	91	.438	15	70	90	.438	11
Pittsburgh	64	98	.395	22	64	98	.395	12
WEST								
X Houston	96	66	.593	0	96	66	.593	2
San Francisco	83	79	.512	13	83	79	.512	5
San Diego	74	88	.457	22	74	88	.457	8
Los Angeles	73	89	.451	23	73	89	.451	9

SIMULATED PLAYOFFS

AMERICAN LEAGUE

ALDS (1-4)	W	1	2	3			%
Boston Red Sox	0	3	7	1			51
Detroit Tigers	3	5	9	2			49

ALDS (2-3)	W	1	2	3	4	5	%
California Angels	3	3	12	2	4	2	46
New York Yankees	2	6	4	1	5	1	54

ALCS	W	1	2	3	4	5	6	7	%
California Angels	3	2	0	4	4	6	7	4	50
Detroit Tigers	4	3	2	2	6	3	4	6	50

NATIONAL LEAGUE

NLDS (1-4)	W	1	2	3	4	5	%
New York Mets	2	7	1	4	7	3	77
Cincinnati Reds	3	2	4	6	2	5	23

NLDS (2-3)	W	1	2	3			%
Houston Astros	3	4	6	3			51
Philadelphia Phillies	0	1	1	2			49

NLCS	W	1	2	3	4	5	6	7	%
Houston Astros	3	1	4	3	1	0	3	1	61
Cincinnati Reds	4	4	2	1	3	2	2	2	39

WORLD SERIES

WS	W	1	2	3	4	5	%
Detroit Tigers	1	8	8	2	1	3	63
Cincinnati Reds	4	9	0	11	6	10	37

ACTUAL WINNERS

American League: Boston Red Sox
National League: New York Mets
World Series: New York Mets

OUTSTANDING PERFORMANCES

AWARD WINNERS

LG.	PLAYER	TEAM	STATS ADJUSTED	ACTUAL
MOST VALUABLE PLAYERS				
AL	Roger Clemens	Boston	24-4 W-L, 0 SV, 2.87 ERA, $19.8 MIL	24-4 W-L, 0 SV, 2.48 ERA
NL	Mike Schmidt	Philadelphia	43 HR, 134 RBI, .303 BA, $12.4 MIL	37 HR, 119 RBI, .290 BA
CY YOUNG AWARDS				
AL	Roger Clemens	Boston	24-4 W-L, 0 SV, 2.87 ERA, $19.8 MIL	24-4 W-L, 0 SV, 2.48 ERA
NL	Mike Scott	Houston	18-10 W-L, 0 SV, 2.55 ERA, $20.6 MIL	18-10 W-L, 0 SV, 2.22 ERA

AMERICAN LEAGUE LEADERS

CAT.	PLAYER	TEAM	STATS ADJUSTED	ACTUAL
BATTING				
HR	Jesse Barfield	Toronto	45	40
RBI	Joe Carter	Cleveland	134	121
BA	Wade Boggs	Boston	.373	.357
AB	Tony Fernandez	Toronto	683	687
R	Rickey Henderson	New York	145	130
H	Don Mattingly	New York	249	238
2B	Don Mattingly	New York	59	53
3B	Brett Butler	Cleveland	15	14
TB	Don Mattingly	New York	420	388
SA	Don Mattingly	New York	.620	.573
SB	Rickey Henderson	New York	76	87
PITCHING				
W	Roger Clemens	Boston	24	24
L	Richard Dotson	Chicago	17	17
	Mike Morgan	Seattle	17	17
SV	Dave Righetti	New York	46	46
ERA	Roger Clemens	Boston	2.87	2.48
G	Mitch Williams	Texas	80	80
IP	Bert Blyleven	Minnesota	272	271.2
BB	Bobby Witt	Texas	153	143
SO	Mark Langston	Seattle	268	245

NATIONAL LEAGUE LEADERS

CAT.	PLAYER	TEAM	STATS ADJUSTED	ACTUAL
BATTING				
HR	Mike Schmidt	Philadelphia	43	37
RBI	Mike Schmidt	Philadelphia	134	119
BA	Tim Raines	Montreal	.349	.334
AB	Tony Gwynn	San Diego	642	642
R	Von Hayes	Philadelphia	120	107
	Tony Gwynn	San Diego	119	107
H	Tony Gwynn	San Diego	220	211
2B	Von Hayes	Philadelphia	52	46
3B	Mitch Webster	Montreal	13	13
TB	Dave Parker	Cincinnati	331	304
SA	Mike Schmidt	Philadelphia	.595	.547
SB	Vince Coleman	St. Louis	95	107
PITCHING				
W	Fernando Valenzuela	Los Angeles	21	21
L	Rick Mahler	Atlanta	18	18
SV	Todd Worrell	St. Louis	37	36
ERA	Mike Scott	Houston	2.55	2.22
G	Craig Lefferts	San Diego	83	83
IP	Mike Scott	Houston	275	275.1
BB	Floyd Youmans	Montreal	125	118
SO	Mike Scott	Houston	333	306

1987 SEASON

REGULAR SEASON STANDINGS

AMERICAN LEAGUE

		ADJUSTED				ACTUAL			
	W	L	Pct.	GB	W	L	Pct.	Rk.
EAST								
X Toronto	96	66	.593	0	96	66	.593	2
New York	89	73	.549	7	89	73	.549	4
Boston	78	84	.481	18	78	84	.481	8
Baltimore	67	95	.414	29	67	95	.414	13
Cleveland	61	101	.377	35	61	101	.377	14
CENTRAL								
X Detroit	98	64	.605	0	98	64	.605	1
X Milwaukee	91	71	.562	7	91	71	.562	3
Minnesota	85	77	.525	13	85	77	.525	5
Kansas City	83	79	.512	15	83	79	.512	6
Chicago	77	85	.475	21	77	85	.475	10
WEST								
X Oakland	81	81	.500	0	81	81	.500	7
Seattle	78	84	.481	3	78	84	.481	8
California	75	87	.463	6	75	87	.463	11
Texas	75	87	.463	6	75	87	.463	11

NATIONAL LEAGUE

		ADJUSTED				ACTUAL			
	W	L	Pct.	GB	W	L	Pct.	Rk.
EAST								
X New York	92	70	.568	0	92	70	.568	2
X Montreal	91	71	.562	1	91	71	.562	3
Philadelphia	80	82	.494	12	80	82	.494	6
Atlanta	69	93	.426	23	69	92	.429	11
CENTRAL								
X St. Louis	95	67	.586	0	95	67	.586	1
Cincinnati	84	78	.519	11	84	78	.519	5
Pittsburgh	80	82	.494	15	80	82	.494	6
Chicago	77	85	.475	18	76	85	.472	8
WEST								
X San Francisco	90	72	.556	0	90	72	.556	4
Houston	76	86	.469	14	76	86	.469	9
Los Angeles	73	89	.451	17	73	89	.451	10
San Diego	65	97	.401	25	65	97	.401	12

SIMULATED PLAYOFFS

AMERICAN LEAGUE

ALDS (1-4)	W	1	2	3	4		%
Detroit Tigers	1	1	12	3	0		65
Oakland Athletics	3	8	0	4	1		35

ALDS (2-3)	W	1	2	3	4		%
Toronto Blue Jays	3	6	3	9	12		74
Milwaukee Brewers	1	4	5	4	4		26

ALCS	W	1	2	3	4	5	%
Toronto Blue Jays	4	5	6	0	8	13	86
Oakland Athletics	1	3	1	4	4	6	14

NATIONAL LEAGUE

NLDS (1-4)**	W	1	2	3	4	5	%
St. Louis Cardinals	2	5	0	6	2	3	47
San Francisco Giants	3	3	5	5	4	6	53

NLDS (2-3)	W	1	2	3			%
New York Mets	0	3	4	1			68
Montreal Expos	3	4	5	6			32

NLCS	W	1	2	3	4	5	6	%
Montreal Expos	2	4	3	5	4	2	1	38
San Francisco Giants	4	3	10	8	3	6	4	62

WORLD SERIES

WS	W	1	2	3	4	5	6	7	%
Toronto Blue Jays	4	7	3	3	6	1	3	7	60
San Francisco Giants	3	0	1	0	7	3	4	2	40

ACTUAL WINNERS

American League: Minnesota Twins
National League: St. Louis Cardinals
World Series: Minnesota Twins

OUTSTANDING PERFORMANCES

AWARD WINNERS

LG.	PLAYER	TEAM	STATS ADJUSTED	ACTUAL
MOST VALUABLE PLAYERS				
AL	George Bell	Toronto	49 HR, 140 RBI, .315 BA, $18.5 MIL	47 HR, 134 RBI, .308 BA
NL	Andre Dawson	Chicago	51 HR, 145 RBI, .293 BA, $9.6 MIL	49 HR, 137 RBI, .287 BA
CY YOUNG AWARDS				
AL	Roger Clemens	Boston	20-9 W-L, 0 SV, 3.16 ERA, $25.9 MIL	20-9 W-L, 0 SV, 2.97 ERA
NL	Steve Bedrosian	Philadelphia	5-3 W-L, 41 SV, 3.03 ERA, $7.6 MIL	5-3 W-L, 40 SV, 2.83 ERA

AMERICAN LEAGUE LEADERS

CAT.	PLAYER	TEAM	STATS ADJUSTED	ACTUAL
BATTING				
HR	Mark McGwire	Oakland	50	49
RBI	George Bell	Toronto	140	134
BA	Wade Boggs	Boston	.372	.363
AB	Ruben Sierra	Texas	643	643
R	Paul Molitor	Milwaukee	120	114
H	Kirby Puckett	Minnesota	212	207
	Kevin Seitzer	Kansas City	212	207
2B	Paul Molitor	Milwaukee	45	41
3B	Willie Wilson	Kansas City	15	15
TB	George Bell	Toronto	382	369
SA	Mark McGwire	Oakland	.636	.618
SB	Harold Reynolds	Seattle	49	60
PITCHING				
W	Roger Clemens	Boston	20	20
	Dave Stewart	Oakland	20	20
L	Mike Moore	Seattle	19	19
SV	Tom Henke	Toronto	36	34
ERA	Jimmy Key	Toronto	2.93	2.76
G	Mark Eichhorn	Toronto	89	89
IP	Charlie Hough	Texas	285	285.1
BB	Bobby Witt	Texas	147	140
SO	Mark Langston	Seattle	284	262

NATIONAL LEAGUE LEADERS

CAT.	PLAYER	TEAM	STATS ADJUSTED	ACTUAL
BATTING				
HR	Andre Dawson	Chicago	51	49
RBI	Andre Dawson	Chicago	145	137
BA	Tony Gwynn	San Diego	.379	.370
AB	Juan Samuel	Philadelphia	655	655
R	Tim Raines	Montreal	129	123
H	Tony Gwynn	San Diego	223	218
2B	Tim Wallach	Montreal	46	42
3B	Juan Samuel	Philadelphia	14	15
TB	Andre Dawson	Chicago	367	353
SA	Jack Clark	St. Louis	.616	.597
SB	Vince Coleman	St. Louis	90	109
PITCHING				
W	Rick Sutcliffe	Chicago	18	18
L	Bob Knepper	Houston	17	17
SV	Steve Bedrosian	Philadelphia	41	40
ERA	Nolan Ryan	Houston	2.93	2.76
G	Kent Tekulve	Philadelphia	90	90
IP	Orel Hershiser	Los Angeles	265	264.2
BB	Fernando Valenzuela	Los Angeles	130	124
SO	Nolan Ryan	Houston	289	270

1988 SEASON

REGULAR SEASON STANDINGS

AMERICAN LEAGUE

		ADJUSTED				ACTUAL		
	W	L	Pct.	GB	W	L	Pct.	Rk.
EAST								
X Boston	89	73	.549	0	89	73	.549	3
Toronto	87	75	.537	2	87	75	.537	5
New York	86	76	.531	3	85	76	.528	7
Cleveland	78	84	.481	11	78	84	.481	9
Baltimore	54	108	.333	35	54	107	.335	14
CENTRAL								
X Minnesota	91	71	.562	0	91	71	.562	2
X Detroit	88	74	.543	3	88	74	.543	4
Milwaukee	87	75	.537	4	87	75	.537	5
Kansas City	85	77	.525	6	84	77	.522	8
Chicago	72	90	.444	19	71	90	.441	11
WEST								
X Oakland	104	58	.642	0	104	58	.642	1
California	75	87	.463	29	75	87	.463	10
Texas	70	92	.432	34	70	91	.435	12
Seattle	68	94	.420	36	68	93	.422	13

NATIONAL LEAGUE

		ADJUSTED				ACTUAL		
	W	L	Pct.	GB	W	L	Pct.	Rk.
EAST								
X New York	101	61	.623	0	100	60	.625	1
Montreal	81	81	.500	20	81	81	.500	8
Philadelphia	65	97	.401	36	65	96	.404	11
Atlanta	55	107	.340	46	54	106	.338	12
CENTRAL								
X Cincinnati	88	74	.543	0	87	74	.540	3
X Pittsburgh	86	76	.531	2	85	75	.531	4
Chicago	77	85	.475	11	77	85	.475	9
St. Louis	76	86	.469	12	76	86	.469	10
WEST								
X Los Angeles	95	67	.586	0	94	67	.584	2
San Diego	83	79	.512	12	83	78	.516	5
San Francisco	83	79	.512	12	83	79	.512	6
Houston	82	80	.506	13	82	80	.506	7

SIMULATED PLAYOFFS

AMERICAN LEAGUE

ALDS (1-4)	W	1	2	3	4		%
Oakland Athletics	1	1	7	2	3		65
Detroit Tigers	3	2	3	5	5		35

ALDS (2-3)	W	1	2	3	4		%
Minnesota Twins	3	6	9	3	2		38
Boston Red Sox	1	0	5	6	1		62

ALCS	W	1	2	3	4	5	%
Minnesota Twins	1	1	4	3	3	4	55
Detroit Tigers	4	2	3	6	6	6	45

NATIONAL LEAGUE

NLDS (1-4)	W	1	2	3	4	5	%
New York Mets	3	2	1	5	2	2	74
Pittsburgh Pirates	2	3	0	3	3	1	26

NLDS (2-3)	W	1	2	3			%
Los Angeles Dodgers	0	3	4	3			53
Cincinnati Reds	3	5	5	4			47

NLCS	W	1	2	3	4	5	6	%
New York Mets	4	6	4	1	0	3	4	74
Cincinnati Reds	2	0	1	2	1	0	2	26

WORLD SERIES

WS	W	1	2	3	4	5	6	7	%
Detroit Tigers	3	5	1	7	1	1	2	1	36
New York Mets	4	1	2	6	6	7	1	7	64

ACTUAL WINNERS

American League: Oakland Athletics
National League: Los Angeles Dodgers
World Series: Los Angeles Dodgers

OUTSTANDING PERFORMANCES

AWARD WINNERS

LG.	PLAYER	TEAM	STATS ADJUSTED	ACTUAL
MOST VALUABLE PLAYERS				
AL	Jose Canseco	Oakland	53 HR, 147 RBI, .325 BA, $19.1 MIL	42 HR, 124 RBI, .307 BA
NL	Kirk Gibson	Los Angeles	33 HR, 90 RBI, .306 BA, $12.2 MIL	25 HR, 76 RBI, .290 BA
CY YOUNG AWARDS				
AL	Frank Viola	Minnesota	24-7 W-L, 0 SV, 3.25 ERA, $26.0 MIL	24-7 W-L, 0 SV, 2.64 ERA
NL	Orel Hershiser	Los Angeles	23-8 W-L, 1 SV, 2.76 ERA, $26.0 MIL	23-8 W-L, 1 SV, 2.26 ERA

AMERICAN LEAGUE LEADERS

CAT.	PLAYER	TEAM	STATS ADJUSTED	ACTUAL
BATTING				
HR	Jose Canseco	Oakland	53	42
RBI	Jose Canseco	Oakland	147	124
BA	Wade Boggs	Boston	.389	.366
AB	Kirby Puckett	Minnesota	657	657
R	Wade Boggs	Boston	152	128
H	Kirby Puckett	Minnesota	248	234
2B	Wade Boggs	Boston	59	45
3B	Willie Wilson	Kansas City	14	11
	Harold Reynolds	Seattle	13	11
	Robin Yount	Milwaukee	11	11
TB	Kirby Puckett	Minnesota	405	358
SA	Jose Canseco	Oakland	.643	.569
SB	Rickey Henderson	New York	83	93
PITCHING				
W	Frank Viola	Minnesota	24	24
L	Bert Blyleven	Minnesota	17	17
SV	Dennis Eckersley	Oakland	45	45
ERA	Allan Anderson	Minnesota	2.99	2.45
G	Chuck Crim	Milwaukee	70	70
IP	Dave Stewart	Oakland	276	275.2
BB	Charlie Hough	Texas	147	126
SO	Roger Clemens	Boston	331	291

NATIONAL LEAGUE LEADERS

CAT.	PLAYER	TEAM	STATS ADJUSTED	ACTUAL
BATTING				
HR	Darryl Strawberry	New York	50	39
RBI	Will Clark	San Francisco	129	109
BA	Tony Gwynn	San Diego	.331	.313
AB	Steve Sax	Los Angeles	632	632
R	Brett Butler	San Francisco	129	109
H	Andres Galarraga	Montreal	194	184
2B	Andres Galarraga	Montreal	46	42
3B	Andy Van Slyke	Pittsburgh	14	15
TB	Andres Galarraga	Montreal	368	329
SA	Darryl Strawberry	New York	.618	.545
SB	Vince Coleman	St. Louis	71	81
PITCHING				
W	Orel Hershiser	Los Angeles	23	23
	Danny Jackson	Cincinnati	23	23
L	Tom Glavine	Atlanta	17	17
SV	John Franco	Cincinnati	39	39
ERA	Joe Magrane	St. Louis	2.67	2.18
G	Rob Murphy	Cincinnati	76	76
IP	Orel Hershiser	Los Angeles	267	267
BB	Kevin Gross	Philadelphia	103	89
SO	Nolan Ryan	Houston	261	228

1989 SEASON

REGULAR SEASON STANDINGS

AMERICAN LEAGUE

		ADJUSTED			ACTUAL			
	W	L	Pct.	GB	W	L	Pct.	Rk.
EAST								
X Toronto	89	73	.549	0	89	73	.549	4
Baltimore	87	75	.537	2	87	75	.537	5
Boston	83	79	.512	6	83	79	.512	6
New York	75	87	.463	14	74	87	.460	10
Cleveland	73	89	.451	16	73	89	.451	11
CENTRAL								
X Kansas City	92	70	.568	0	92	70	.568	2
Milwaukee	81	81	.500	11	81	81	.500	8
Minnesota	80	82	.494	12	80	82	.494	9
Chicago	69	93	.426	23	69	92	.429	13
Detroit	59	103	.364	33	59	103	.364	14
WEST								
X Oakland	99	63	.611	0	99	63	.611	1
X California	91	71	.562	8	91	71	.562	3
Texas	83	79	.512	16	83	79	.512	6
Seattle	73	89	.451	26	73	89	.451	11

NATIONAL LEAGUE

		ADJUSTED			ACTUAL			
	W	L	Pct.	GB	W	L	Pct.	Rk.
EAST								
X New York	87	75	.537	0	87	75	.537	4
Montreal	81	81	.500	6	81	81	.500	7
Philadelphia	67	95	.414	20	67	95	.414	11
Atlanta	64	98	.395	23	63	97	.394	12
CENTRAL								
X Chicago	93	69	.574	0	93	69	.574	1
St. Louis	86	76	.531	7	86	76	.531	5
Cincinnati	75	87	.463	18	75	87	.463	9
Pittsburgh	74	88	.457	19	74	88	.457	10
WEST								
X San Francisco	92	70	.568	0	92	70	.568	2
X San Diego	89	73	.549	3	89	73	.549	3
Houston	86	76	.531	6	86	76	.531	5
Los Angeles	78	84	.481	14	77	83	.481	8

SIMULATED PLAYOFFS

AMERICAN LEAGUE

ALDS (1-4)**	W	1	2	3	4		%
Oakland Athletics	3	7	6	3	6		54
Toronto Blue Jays	1	3	3	7	5		46

ALDS (2-3)	W	1	2	3	4	5	%
Kansas City Royals	3	4	4	3	5	4	42
California Angels	2	6	6	2	4	1	58

ALCS	W	1	2	3	4	5	6	7	%
Oakland Athletics	4	3	3	1	7	4	2	6	57
Kansas City Royals	3	1	6	2	1	3	4	3	43

NATIONAL LEAGUE

NLDS (1-4)	W	1	2	3			%
Chicago Cubs	0	3	2	4			41
New York Mets	3	7	7	11			59

NLDS (2-3)	W	1	2	3			%
San Francisco Giants	3	2	8	8			57
San Diego Padres	0	1	0	0			43

NLCS	W	1	2	3	4	5	%
San Francisco Giants	4	0	7	7	6	2	46
New York Mets	1	5	1	1	4	1	54

WORLD SERIES

WS*	W	1	2	3	4	%
Oakland Athletics	4	5	5	13	9	62
San Francisco Giants	0	0	1	7	6	38

ACTUAL WINNERS

American League: Oakland Athletics
National League: San Francisco Giants
World Series: Oakland Athletics

OUTSTANDING PERFORMANCES

AWARD WINNERS

LG.	PLAYER	TEAM	STATS ADJUSTED	ACTUAL
MOST VALUABLE PLAYERS				
AL	Robin Yount	Milwaukee	30 HR, 122 RBI, .337 BA, $13.2 MIL	21 HR, 103 RBI, .318 BA
NL	Kevin Mitchell	San Francisco	60 HR, 149 RBI, .308 BA, $14.5 MIL	47 HR, 125 RBI, .291 BA
CY YOUNG AWARDS				
AL	Bret Saberhagen	Kansas City	23-6 W-L, 0 SV, 2.68 ERA, $20.3 MIL	23-6 W-L, 0 SV, 2.16 ERA
NL	Mark Davis	San Diego	4-3 W-L, 44 SV, 2.32 ERA, $7.7 MIL	4-3 W-L, 44 SV, 1.85 ERA

AMERICAN LEAGUE LEADERS

CAT.	PLAYER	TEAM	STATS ADJUSTED	ACTUAL
BATTING				
HR	Fred McGriff	Toronto	46	36
RBI	Ruben Sierra	Texas	141	119
BA	Kirby Puckett	Minnesota	.359	.339
AB	Steve Sax	New York	655	651
	Joe Carter	Cleveland	651	651
R	Wade Boggs	Boston	134	113
	Rickey Henderson	N.Y.-Oak.	134	113
H	Kirby Puckett	Minnesota	228	215
2B	Wade Boggs	Boston	72	51
3B	Ruben Sierra	Texas	12	14
TB	Ruben Sierra	Texas	391	344
SA	Ruben Sierra	Texas	.617	.543
SB	Rickey Henderson	N.Y.-Oak.	72	77
PITCHING				
W	Bret Saberhagen	Kansas City	23	23
L	Doyle Alexander	Detroit	18	18
SV	Jeff Russell	Texas	37	38
ERA	Bret Saberhagen	Kansas City	2.68	2.16
G	Chuck Crim	Milwaukee	76	76
IP	Bret Saberhagen	Kansas City	262	262.1
BB	Bobby Witt	Texas	127	114
SO	Nolan Ryan	Texas	336	301

NATIONAL LEAGUE LEADERS

CAT.	PLAYER	TEAM	STATS ADJUSTED	ACTUAL
BATTING				
HR	Kevin Mitchell	San Francisco	60	47
RBI	Kevin Mitchell	San Francisco	149	125
BA	Tony Gwynn	San Diego	.356	.336
AB	Todd Benzinger	Cincinnati	628	628
R	Will Clark	San Francisco	123	104
	Howard Johnson	New York	123	104
	Ryne Sandberg	Chicago	123	104
H	Tony Gwynn	San Diego	215	203
2B	Tim Wallach	Montreal	49	42
	Pedro Guerrero	St. Louis	47	42
3B	Robby Thompson	San Francisco	10	11
TB	Kevin Mitchell	San Francisco	392	345
SA	Kevin Mitchell	San Francisco	.722	.635
SB	Vince Coleman	St. Louis	59	65
PITCHING				
W	Mike Scott	Houston	20	20
L	Don Carman	Philadelphia	15	15
	Orel Hershiser	Los Angeles	15	15
	Ken Hill	St. Louis	15	15
SV	Mark Davis	San Diego	44	44
ERA	Scott Garrelts	San Francisco	2.80	2.28
G	Mitch Williams	Chicago	76	76
IP	Orel Hershiser	Los Angeles	257	256.2
BB	Ken Hill	St. Louis	111	99
SO	Jose DeLeon	St. Louis	231	201

REGULAR SEASON STANDINGS

AMERICAN LEAGUE

	ADJUSTED				ACTUAL			
	W	L	Pct.	GB	W	L	Pct.	Rk.
EAST								
X Boston	88	74	.543	0	88	74	.543	3
X Toronto	86	76	.531	2	86	76	.531	4
Cleveland	77	85	.475	11	77	85	.475	8
Baltimore	77	85	.475	11	76	85	.472	10
New York	67	95	.414	21	67	95	.414	14
CENTRAL								
X Chicago	94	68	.580	0	94	68	.580	2
Detroit	79	83	.488	15	79	83	.488	7
Kansas City	75	87	.463	19	75	86	.466	11
Milwaukee	74	88	.457	20	74	88	.457	12
Minnesota	74	88	.457	20	74	88	.457	12
WEST								
X Oakland	103	59	.636	0	103	59	.636	1
Texas	83	79	.512	20	83	79	.512	5
California	80	82	.494	23	80	82	.494	6
Seattle	77	85	.475	26	77	85	.475	8

NATIONAL LEAGUE

	ADJUSTED				ACTUAL			
	W	L	Pct.	GB	W	L	Pct.	Rk.
EAST								
X New York	91	71	.562	0	91	71	.562	2
Montreal	85	77	.525	6	85	77	.525	5
Philadelphia	77	85	.475	14	77	85	.475	7
Atlanta	65	97	.401	26	65	97	.401	12
CENTRAL								
X Pittsburgh	95	67	.586	0	95	67	.586	1
X Cincinnati	91	71	.562	4	91	71	.562	2
Chicago	77	85	.475	18	77	85	.475	7
St. Louis	70	92	.432	25	70	92	.432	11
WEST								
X Los Angeles	86	76	.531	0	86	76	.531	4
San Francisco	85	77	.525	1	85	77	.525	5
Houston	75	87	.463	11	75	87	.463	9
San Diego	75	87	.463	11	75	87	.463	9

SIMULATED PLAYOFFS

AMERICAN LEAGUE

ALDS (1-4)	W	1	2	3	4		%
Oakland Athletics	3	3	1	4	2		52
Toronto Blue Jays	1	1	6	2	1		48

ALDS (2-3)	W	1	2	3	4		%
Chicago White Sox	3	10	3	1	2		53
Boston Red Sox	1	5	2	6	1		47

ALCS	W	1	2	3	4	5	6	%
Oakland Athletics	4	4	3	2	7	3	6	68
Chicago White Sox	2	2	4	3	4	1	2	32

NATIONAL LEAGUE

NLDS (1-4)	W	1	2	3	4		%
Pittsburgh Pirates	3	6	1	7	4		60
Los Angeles Dodgers	1	4	4	3	3		40

NLDS (2-3)	W	1	2	3	4		%
New York Mets	3	5	5	2	5		55
Cincinnati Reds	1	3	2	3	1		45

NLCS	W	1	2	3	4	5	6	7	%
Pittsburgh Pirates	3	3	5	6	3	2	2	3	49
New York Mets	4	5	1	5	1	3	4	8	51

WORLD SERIES

WS	W	1	2	3	4	5	6	%
Oakland Athletics	2	0	2	1	4	1	1	52
New York Mets	4	1	1	2	1	4	2	48

ACTUAL WINNERS

American League: Oakland Athletics
National League: Cincinnati Reds
World Series: Cincinnati Reds

OUTSTANDING PERFORMANCES

AWARD WINNERS

LG.	PLAYER	TEAM	STATS ADJUSTED	ACTUAL
MOST VALUABLE PLAYERS				
AL	Rickey Henderson	Oakland	36 HR, 70 RBI, .339 BA, $7.3 MIL	28 HR, 61 RBI, .325 BA
NL	Barry Bonds	Pittsburgh	41 HR, 131 RBI, .314 BA, $14.9 MIL	33 HR, 114 RBI, .301 BA
CY YOUNG AWARDS				
AL	Bob Welch	Oakland	27-6 W-L, 0 SV, 3.48 ERA, $18.8 MIL	27-6 W-L, 0 SV, 2.95 ERA
NL	Doug Drabek	Pittsburgh	22-6 W-L, 0 SV, 3.27 ERA, $16.2 MIL	22-6 W-L, 0 SV, 2.76 ERA

AMERICAN LEAGUE LEADERS

CAT.	PLAYER	TEAM	STATS ADJUSTED	ACTUAL
BATTING				
HR	Cecil Fielder	Detroit	62	51
RBI	Cecil Fielder	Detroit	152	132
BA	George Brett	Kansas City	.343	.329
AB	Harold Reynolds	Seattle	642	642
R	Rickey Henderson	Oakland	137	119
H	Rafael Palmeiro	Texas	199	191
2B	Jody Reed	Boston	56	45
	George Brett	Kansas City	53	45
3B	Tony Fernandez	Toronto	19	17
TB	Cecil Fielder	Detroit	378	339
SA	Cecil Fielder	Detroit	.660	.592
SB	Rickey Henderson	Oakland	57	65
PITCHING				
W	Bob Welch	Oakland	27	27
L	Tim Leary	New York	19	19
SV	Bobby Thigpen	Chicago	55	57
ERA	Roger Clemens	Boston	2.29	1.93
G	Bobby Thigpen	Chicago	77	77
IP	Dave Stewart	Oakland	267	267
BB	Randy Johnson	Seattle	131	120
SO	Nolan Ryan	Texas	259	232

NATIONAL LEAGUE LEADERS

CAT.	PLAYER	TEAM	STATS ADJUSTED	ACTUAL
BATTING				
HR	Ryne Sandberg	Chicago	50	40
RBI	Matt Williams	San Francisco	141	122
BA	Willie McGee	St. Louis	.339	.335
AB	Joe Carter	San Diego	634	634
R	Ryne Sandberg	Chicago	134	116
H	Brett Butler	San Francisco	200	192
	Lenny Dykstra	Philadelphia	200	192
2B	Gregg Jefferies	New York	45	40
3B	Mariano Duncan	Cincinnati	10	11
TB	Ryne Sandberg	Chicago	383	344
SA	Barry Bonds	Pittsburgh	.628	.565
SB	Vince Coleman	St. Louis	68	77
PITCHING				
W	Doug Drabek	Pittsburgh	22	22
L	Jose DeLeon	St. Louis	19	19
SV	John Franco	New York	32	33
ERA	Danny Darwin	Houston	2.60	2.21
G	Juan Agosto	Houston	82	82
IP	Frank Viola	New York	250	249.2
BB	John Smoltz	Atlanta	97	90
SO	David Cone	New York	261	233

1991 SEASON

REGULAR SEASON STANDINGS

AMERICAN LEAGUE

	ADJUSTED				ACTUAL			
	W	L	Pct.	GB	W	L	Pct.	Rk.
EAST								
X Toronto	91	71	.562	0	91	71	.562	2
Boston	84	78	.519	7	84	78	.519	5
New York	71	91	.438	20	71	91	.438	12
Baltimore	67	95	.414	24	67	95	.414	13
Cleveland	57	105	.352	34	57	105	.352	14
CENTRAL								
X Minnesota	95	67	.586	0.	95	67	.586	1
X Chicago	87	75	.537	8	87	75	.537	3
Detroit	84	78	.519	11	84	78	.519	5
Milwaukee	83	79	.512	12	83	79	.512	8
Kansas City	82	80	.506	13	82	80	.506	10
WEST								
X Texas	85	77	.525	0	85	77	.525	4
Oakland	84	78	.519	1	84	78	.519	5
Seattle	83	79	.512	2	83	79	.512	8
California	81	81	.500	4	81	81	.500	11

NATIONAL LEAGUE

	ADJUSTED				ACTUAL			
	W	L	Pct.	GB	W	L	Pct.	Rk.
EAST								
X Atlanta	94	68	.580	0	94	68	.580	2
Philadelphia	78	84	.481	16	78	84	.481	6
New York	78	84	.481	16	77	84	.478	8
Montreal	71	91	.438	23	71	90	.441	11
CENTRAL								
X Pittsburgh	98	64	.605	0	98	64	.605	1
X St. Louis	84	78	.519	14	84	78	.519	4
Chicago	78	84	.481	20	77	83	.481	6
Cincinnati	74	88	.457	24	74	88	.457	10
WEST								
X Los Angeles	93	69	.574	0	93	69	.574	3
X San Diego	84	78	.519	9	84	78	.519	4
San Francisco	75	87	.463	18	75	87	.463	9
Houston	65	97	.401	28	65	97	.401	12

SIMULATED PLAYOFFS

AMERICAN LEAGUE

ALDS (1-4)	W	1	2	3	4		%
Minnesota Twins	3	7	10	4	6		68
Texas Rangers	1	3	4	7	1		32

ALDS (2-3)	W	1	2	3	4		%
Toronto Blue Jays	3	0	3	5	6		49
Chicago White Sox	1	2	2	2	2		51

ALCS*	W	1	2	3	4	5	%
Minnesota Twins	4	5	2	3	9	8	56
Toronto Blue Jays	1	4	5	2	3	5	44

NATIONAL LEAGUE

TIEBREAKER	W	1	2				%
St. Louis Cardinals	2	3	6				43
San Diego Padres	0	1	5				57

NLDS (1-4)	W	1	2	3	4	5	%
Pittsburgh Pirates	3	4	2	3	4	6	74
St. Louis Cardinals	2	2	4	4	2	2	26

NLDS (2-3)	W	1	2	3	4		%
Atlanta Braves	3	3	2	6	3		46
Los Angeles Dodgers	1	2	3	4	2		54

NLCS*	W	1	2	3	4	5	6	7	%
Pittsburgh Pirates	3	5	0	3	3	1	0	0	61
Atlanta Braves	4	1	1	10	2	0	1	4	39

WORLD SERIES

WS*	W	1	2	3	4	5	6	7	%
Minnesota Twins	4	5	3	4	2	5	4	1	54
Atlanta Braves	3	2	2	5	3	14	3	0	46

ACTUAL WINNERS

American League: Minnesota Twins
National League: Atlanta Braves
World Series: Minnesota Twins

OUTSTANDING PERFORMANCES

AWARD WINNERS

LG.	PLAYER	TEAM	STATS ADJUSTED	ACTUAL
MOST VALUABLE PLAYERS				
AL	Cal Ripken Jr.	Baltimore	43 HR, 130 RBI, .340 BA, $16.3 MIL	34 HR, 114 RBI, .323 BA
NL	Terry Pendleton	Atlanta	29 HR, 98 RBI, .336 BA, $9.5 MIL	22 HR, 86 RBI, .319 BA
CY YOUNG AWARDS				
AL	Roger Clemens	Boston	18-10 W-L, 0 SV, 3.06 ERA, $26.1 MIL	18-10 W-L, 0 SV, 2.62 ERA
NL	Tom Glavine	Atlanta	20-11 W-L, 0 SV, 2.99 ERA, $16.4 MIL	20-11 W-L, 0 SV, 2.55 ERA

AMERICAN LEAGUE LEADERS

CAT.	PLAYER	TEAM	STATS ADJUSTED	ACTUAL
BATTING				
HR	Jose Canseco	Oakland	53	44
	Cecil Fielder	Detroit	53	44
RBI	Cecil Fielder	Detroit	152	133
BA	Julio Franco	Texas	.360	.341
AB	Paul Molitor	Milwaukee	665	665
R	Paul Molitor	Milwaukee	152	133
H	Paul Molitor	Milwaukee	227	216
2B	Rafael Palmeiro	Texas	53	49
3B	Lance Johnson	Chicago	16	13
	Paul Molitor	Milwaukee	12	13
TB	Cal Ripken Jr.	Baltimore	408	368
SA	Danny Tartabull	Kansas City	.663	.593
SB	Rickey Henderson	Oakland	54	58
PITCHING				
W	Scott Erickson	Minnesota	20	20
	Bill Gullickson	Detroit	20	20
L	Kirk McCaskill	California	19	19
SV	Bryan Harvey	California	44	46
ERA	Roger Clemens	Boston	3.06	2.62
G	Duane Ward	Toronto	81	81
IP	Roger Clemens	Boston	271	271.1
BB	Randy Johnson	Seattle	165	152
SO	Roger Clemens	Boston	268	241

NATIONAL LEAGUE LEADERS

CAT.	PLAYER	TEAM	STATS ADJUSTED	ACTUAL
BATTING				
HR	Howard Johnson	New York	47	38
RBI	Howard Johnson	New York	134	117
BA	Terry Pendleton	Atlanta	.336	.319
AB	Mark Grace	Chicago	627	619
R	Brett Butler	Los Angeles	128	112
H	Terry Pendleton	Atlanta	197	187
2B	Bobby Bonilla	Pittsburgh	51	44
3B	Ray Lankford	St. Louis	15	15
TB	Will Clark	San Francisco	337	303
	Terry Pendleton	Atlanta	336	303
SA	Will Clark	San Francisco	.596	.536
SB	Marquis Grissom	Montreal	71	76
PITCHING				
W	Tom Glavine	Atlanta	20	20
	John Smiley	Pittsburgh	20	20
L	Bud Black	San Francisco	16	16
SV	Lee Smith	St. Louis	45	47
ERA	Dennis Martinez	Montreal	2.80	2.39
G	Barry Jones	Montreal	77	77
IP	Greg Maddux	Chicago	263	263
BB	Jose DeJesus	Philadelphia	139	128
SO	David Cone	New York	267	241

1992 SEASON

AMERICAN LEAGUE

	ADJUSTED				ACTUAL			
	W	L	Pct.	GB	W	L	Pct.	Rk.
EAST								
X Toronto	96	66	.593	0	96	66	.593	1
Baltimore	89	73	.549	7	89	73	.549	5
Cleveland	76	86	.469	20	76	86	.469	8
New York	76	86	.469	20	76	86	.469	8
Boston	73	89	.451	23	73	89	.451	11
CENTRAL								
X Milwaukee	92	70	.568	0	92	70	.568	3
X Minnesota	90	72	.556	2	90	72	.556	4
Chicago	86	76	.531	6	86	76	.531	6
Detroit	75	87	.463	17	75	87	.463	10
Kansas City	72	90	.444	20	72	90	.444	12
WEST								
X Oakland	96	66	.593	0	96	66	.593	1
Texas	77	85	.475	19	77	85	.475	7
California	72	90	.444	24	72	90	.444	12
Seattle	64	98	.395	32	64	98	.395	14

NATIONAL LEAGUE

	ADJUSTED				ACTUAL			
	W	L	Pct.	GB	W	L	Pct.	Rk.
EAST								
X Atlanta	98	64	.605	0	98	64	.605	1
Montreal	87	75	.537	11	87	75	.537	4
New York	72	90	.444	26	72	90	.444	9
Philadelphia	70	92	.432	28	70	92	.432	11
CENTRAL								
X Pittsburgh	96	66	.593	0	96	66	.593	2
X Cincinnati	90	72	.556	6	90	72	.556	3
St. Louis	83	79	.512	13	83	79	.512	5
Chicago	78	84	.481	18	78	84	.481	8
WEST								
X San Diego	82	80	.506	0	82	80	.506	6
Houston	81	81	.500	1	81	81	.500	7
San Francisco	72	90	.444	10	72	90	.444	9
Los Angeles	63	99	.389	19	63	99	.389	12

AMERICAN LEAGUE

ALDS (1-4)	W	1	2	3	4			%
Oakland Athletics	3	7	6	3	8			52
Minnesota Twins	1	2	3	5	5			48

ALDS (2-3)	W	1	2	3	4			%
Toronto Blue Jays	1	0	6	4	2			43
Milwaukee Brewers	3	8	5	7	4			57

ALCS	W	1	2	3	4	5	6	%
Oakland Athletics	2	1	4	1	6	0	2	44
Milwaukee Brewers	4	5	3	6	5	7	4	56

NATIONAL LEAGUE

NLDS (1-4)	W	1	2	3		%
Atlanta Braves	3	7	10	4		82
San Diego Padres	0	3	0	3		18

NLDS (2-3)	W	1	2	3	4	5	%
Pittsburgh Pirates	2	5	2	0	4	1	62
Cincinnati Reds	3	4	4	4	3	4	38

NLCS	W	1	2	3	4	5	6	7	%
Atlanta Braves	3	3	1	3	4	3	4	2	56
Cincinnati Reds	4	4	2	2	2	1	5	4	44

WORLD SERIES

WS	W	1	2	3	4	5	6	%
Milwaukee Brewers	2	3	7	2	1	2	2	55
Cincinnati Reds	4	1	4	4	3	4	3	45

ACTUAL WINNERS

American League: Toronto Blue Jays
National League: Atlanta Braves
World Series: Toronto Blue Jays

OUTSTANDING PERFORMANCES

AWARD WINNERS

LG.	PLAYER	TEAM	STATS ADJUSTED	ACTUAL
MOST VALUABLE PLAYERS				
AL	Dennis Eckersley	Oakland	7-1 W-L, 50 SV, 2.36 ERA, $7.0 MIL	7-1 W-L, 51 SV, 1.91 ERA
NL	Barry Bonds	Pittsburgh	45 HR, 123 RBI, .328 BA, $15.5 MIL	34 HR, 103 RBI, .311 BA
CY YOUNG AWARDS				
AL	Dennis Eckersley	Oakland	7-1 W-L, 50 SV, 2.36 ERA, $7.0 MIL	7-1 W-L, 51 SV, 1.91 ERA
NL	Greg Maddux	Chicago	20-11 W-L, 0 SV, 2.65 ERA, $25.5 MIL	20-11 W-L, 0 SV, 2.18 ERA

AMERICAN LEAGUE LEADERS

CAT.	PLAYER	TEAM	STATS ADJUSTED	ACTUAL
BATTING				
HR	Juan Gonzalez	Texas	55	43
RBI	Cecil Fielder	Detroit	148	124
BA	Edgar Martinez	Seattle	.362	.343
AB	Travis Fryman	Detroit	659	659
R	Tony Phillips	Detroit	136	114
H	Kirby Puckett	Minnesota	221	210
2B	Edgar Martinez	Seattle	50	46
	Frank Thomas	Chicago	49	46
3B	Lance Johnson	Chicago	15	12
TB	Kirby Puckett	Minnesota	356	313
SA	Mark McGwire	Oakland	.666	.585
SB	Kenny Lofton	Cleveland	58	66
PITCHING				
W	Kevin Brown	Texas	21	21
	Jack Morris	Toronto	21	21
L	Erik Hanson	Seattle	17	17
SV	Dennis Eckersley	Oakland	50	51
ERA	Roger Clemens	Boston	2.95	2.41
G	Kenny Rogers	Texas	81	81
IP	Kevin Brown	Texas	266	265.2
BB	Randy Johnson	Seattle	160	144
SO	Randy Johnson	Seattle	272	241

NATIONAL LEAGUE LEADERS

CAT.	PLAYER	TEAM	STATS ADJUSTED	ACTUAL
BATTING				
HR	Fred McGriff	San Diego	46	35
RBI	Darren Daulton	Philadelphia	130	109
BA	Gary Sheffield	San Diego	.348	.330
AB	Marquis Grissom	Montreal	653	653
R	Barry Bonds	Pittsburgh	130	109
H	Terry Pendleton	Atlanta	209	199
	Andy Van Slyke	Pittsburgh	209	199
2B	Andy Van Slyke	Pittsburgh	53	45
3B	Deion Sanders	Atlanta	14	14
TB	Gary Sheffield	San Diego	366	323
SA	Barry Bonds	Pittsburgh	.706	.624
SB	Marquis Grissom	Montreal	69	78
PITCHING				
W	Tom Glavine	Atlanta	20	20
	Greg Maddux	Chicago	20	20
L	Tom Candiotti	Los Angeles	15	15
	Orel Hershiser	Los Angeles	15	15
SV	Lee Smith	St. Louis	42	43
ERA	Bill Swift	San Francisco	2.56	2.08
G	Joe Boever	Houston	81	81
IP	Greg Maddux	Chicago	268	268
BB	David Cone	New York	123	82
SO	John Smoltz	Atlanta	248	215

REGULAR SEASON STANDINGS

AMERICAN LEAGUE

	ADJUSTED				ACTUAL			
	W	L	Pct.	GB	W	L	Pct.	Rk.
EAST								
X Toronto	95	67	.586	0	95	67	.586	1
New York	88	74	.543	7	88	74	.543	3
Baltimore	85	77	.525	10	85	77	.525	5
Boston	80	82	.494	15	80	82	.494	9
GREAT LAKES								
X Chicago	94	68	.580	0	94	68	.580	2
Detroit	85	77	.525	9	85	77	.525	5
Cleveland	76	86	.469	18	76	86	.469	10
Milwaukee	69	93	.426	25	69	93	.426	13
CENTRAL								
X Texas	86	76	.531	0	86	76	.531	4
Kansas City	84	78	.519	2	84	78	.519	7
Minnesota	71	91	.438	15	71	91	.438	11
WEST								
X Seattle	82	80	.506	0	82	80	.506	8
California	71	91	.438	11	71	91	.438	11
Oakland	68	94	.420	14	68	94	.420	14

NATIONAL LEAGUE

	ADJUSTED				ACTUAL			
	W	L	Pct.	GB	W	L	Pct.	Rk.
EAST								
X Philadelphia	97	65	.599	0	97	65	.599	3
Montreal	94	68	.580	3	94	68	.580	4
New York	59	103	.364	38	59	103	.364	14
CENTRAL								
X St. Louis	87	75	.537	0	87	75	.537	5
Chicago	84	78	.519	3	84	78	.519	7
Pittsburgh	75	87	.463	12	75	87	.463	9
Cincinnati	73	89	.451	14	73	89	.451	10
SOUTH								
X Atlanta	104	58	.642	0	104	58	.642	1
Houston	85	77	.525	19	85	77	.525	6
Florida	64	98	.395	40	64	98	.395	12
WEST								
X San Francisco	103	59	.636	0	103	59	.636	2
Los Angeles	81	81	.500	22	81	81	.500	8
Colorado	67	95	.414	36	67	95	.414	11
San Diego	61	101	.377	42	61	101	.377	13

SIMULATED PLAYOFFS

AMERICAN LEAGUE

ALDS (1-4)	W	1	2	3	4				%
Toronto Blue Jays	3	6	6	4	6				59
Seattle Mariners	1	7	1	3	0				41

ALDS (2-3)	W	1	2	3	4	5			%
Chicago White Sox	2	6	1	4	4	5			43
Texas Rangers	3	0	4	2	5	6			57

ALCS	W	1	2	3	4	5	6	7	%
Toronto Blue Jays	3	5	1	5	8	1	6	7	55
Texas Rangers	4	6	7	4	2	2	3	15	45

NATIONAL LEAGUE

NLDS (1-4)	W	1	2	3		%
Atlanta Braves	3	2	6	5		74
St. Louis Cardinals	0	1	3	0		26

NLDS (2-3)	W	1	2	3		%
San Francisco Giants	0	0	2	6		53
Philadelphia Phillies	3	4	5	7		47

NLCS*	W	1	2	3	4	5	6	%
Atlanta Braves	2	3	14	9	1	3	3	78
Philadelphia Phillies	4	4	3	4	2	4	6	22

WORLD SERIES

WS	W	1	2	3	4		%
Texas Rangers	0	3	1	2	7		37
Philadelphia Phillies	4	5	8	4	8		63

ACTUAL WINNERS

American League: Toronto Blue Jays
National League: Philadelphia Phillies
World Series: Toronto Blue Jays

OUTSTANDING PERFORMANCES

AWARD WINNERS

LG.	PLAYER	TEAM	STATS ADJUSTED	ACTUAL
MOST VALUABLE PLAYERS				
AL	Frank Thomas	Chicago	47 HR, 138 RBI, .322 BA, $18.5 MIL	41 HR, 128 RBI, .317 BA
NL	Barry Bonds	San Francisco	53 HR, 132 RBI, .341 BA, $22.2 MIL	46 HR, 123 RBI, .336 BA
CY YOUNG AWARDS				
AL	Jack McDowell	Chicago	22-10 W-L, 0 SV, 3.68 ERA, $20.4 MIL	22-10 W-L, 0 SV, 3.37 ERA
NL	Greg Maddux	Atlanta	20-10 W-L, 0 SV, 2.56 ERA, $20.6 MIL	20-10 W-L, 0 SV, 2.36 ERA

AMERICAN LEAGUE LEADERS

CAT.	PLAYER	TEAM	STATS ADJUSTED	ACTUAL
BATTING				
HR	Juan Gonzalez	Texas	52	46
RBI	Albert Belle	Cleveland	139	129
BA	John Olerud	Toronto	.368	.363
AB	Cal Ripken Jr.	Baltimore	641	641
R	Rafael Palmeiro	Texas	133	124
H	Paul Molitor	Toronto	214	211
2B	John Olerud	Toronto	58	54
3B	Lance Johnson	Chicago	16	14
TB	Ken Griffey Jr.	Seattle	380	359
SA	Juan Gonzalez	Texas	.670	.632
SB	Kenny Lofton	Cleveland	67	70
PITCHING				
W	Jack McDowell	Chicago	22	22
L	Scott Erickson	Minnesota	19	19
SV	Jeff Montgomery	Kansas City	44	45
	Duane Ward	Toronto	44	45
ERA	Kevin Appier	Kansas City	2.79	2.56
G	Greg Harris	Boston	80	80
IP	Cal Eldred	Milwaukee	258	258
BB	Wilson Alvarez	Chicago	131	122
SO	Randy Johnson	Seattle	337	308

NATIONAL LEAGUE LEADERS

CAT.	PLAYER	TEAM	STATS ADJUSTED	ACTUAL
BATTING				
HR	Barry Bonds	San Francisco	53	46
RBI	Barry Bonds	San Francisco	132	123
BA	Andres Galarraga	Colorado	.377	.370
AB	Lenny Dykstra	Philadelphia	637	637
R	Lenny Dykstra	Philadelphia	154	143
H	Lenny Dykstra	Philadelphia	197	194
2B	Charlie Hayes	Colorado	47	45
3B	Steve Finley	Houston	13	13
TB	Barry Bonds	San Francisco	389	365
SA	Barry Bonds	San Francisco	.722	.677
SB	Chuck Carr	Florida	56	58
PITCHING				
W	John Burkett	San Francisco	22	22
	Tom Glavine	Atlanta	22	22
L	Doug Drabek	Houston	18	18
SV	Randy Myers	Chicago	52	53
ERA	Greg Maddux	Atlanta	2.56	2.36
G	Mike Jackson	San Francisco	81	81
IP	Greg Maddux	Atlanta	267	267
BB	Ramon Martinez	Los Angeles	112	104
SO	Jose Rijo	Cincinnati	252	227

1994 SEASON

REGULAR SEASON STANDINGS

AMERICAN LEAGUE

		ADJUSTED				ACTUAL		
	W	L	Pct.	GB	W	L	Pct.	Rk.
EAST								
X New York	100	62	.617	0	70	43	.619	1
Baltimore	91	71	.562	9	63	49	.563	4
Toronto	77	85	.475	23	55	60	.478	6
Boston	76	86	.469	24	54	61	.470	7
GREAT LAKES								
X Chicago	96	66	.593	0	67	46	.593	2
Cleveland	95	67	.586	1	66	47	.584	3
Detroit	75	87	.463	21	53	62	.461	9
Milwaukee	75	87	.463	21	53	62	.461	9
CENTRAL								
X Kansas City	90	72	.556	0	64	51	.557	5
Minnesota	76	86	.469	14	53	60	.469	8
Texas	74	88	.457	16	52	62	.456	11
WEST								
X Oakland	72	90	.444	0	51	63	.447	12
Seattle	71	91	.438	1	49	63	.438	13
California	66	96	.407	6	47	68	.409	14

NATIONAL LEAGUE

		ADJUSTED				ACTUAL		
	W	L	Pct.	GB	W	L	Pct.	Rk.
EAST								
X Montreal	105	57	.648	0	74	40	.649	1
New York	79	83	.488	26	55	58	.487	6
Philadelphia	76	86	.469	29	54	61	.470	8
CENTRAL								
X Cincinnati	94	68	.580	0	66	48	.579	3
Pittsburgh	75	87	.463	19	53	61	.465	9
St. Louis	75	87	.463	19	53	61	.465	9
Chicago	70	92	.432	24	49	64	.434	13
SOUTH								
X Atlanta	97	65	.599	0	68	46	.596	2
Houston	93	69	.574	4	66	49	.574	4
Florida	72	90	.444	25	51	64	.443	12
WEST								
X Los Angeles	82	80	.506	0	58	56	.509	5
San Francisco	78	84	.481	4	55	60	.478	7
Colorado	73	89	.451	9	53	64	.453	11
San Diego	65	97	.401	17	47	70	.402	14

SIMULATED PLAYOFFS

AMERICAN LEAGUE

ALDS (1-4)	W	1	2	3			%
New York Yankees	3	6	12	6			82
Oakland Athletics	0	2	7	5			18

ALDS (2-3)	W	1	2	3	4	5	%
Chicago White Sox	3	7	0	10	3	5	62
Kansas City Royals	2	1	5	4	5	3	38

ALCS	W	1	2	3	4		%
New York Yankees	4	9	10	5	7		52
Chicago White Sox	0	7	4	2	5		48

NATIONAL LEAGUE

NLDS (1-4)	W	1	2	3			%
Montreal Expos	3	6	3	6			68
Los Angeles Dodgers	0	3	2	3			32

NLDS (2-3)	W	1	2	3	4	5	%
Atlanta Braves	3	6	3	3	2	3	55
Cincinnati Reds	2	5	2	7	4	1	45

NLCS	W	1	2	3	4	5	%
Montreal Expos	1	1	2	1	2	2	47
Atlanta Braves	4	3	1	3	3	3	53

WORLD SERIES

WS	W	1	2	3	4	%
New York Yankees	4	2	6	3	3	51
Atlanta Braves	0	0	5	2	2	49

ACTUAL WINNERS

American League: (none)
National League: (none)
World Series: (none)

OUTSTANDING PERFORMANCES

AWARD WINNERS

			STATS	
LG.	**PLAYER**	**TEAM**	**ADJUSTED**	**ACTUAL**
MOST VALUABLE PLAYERS				
AL	Frank Thomas	Chicago	56 HR, 147 RBI, .353 BA, $31.6 MIL	38 HR, 101 RBI, .353 BA
NL	Jeff Bagwell	Houston	57 HR, 166 RBI, .367 BA, $19.4 MIL	39 HR, 116 RBI, .368 BA
CY YOUNG AWARDS				
AL	David Cone	Kansas City	22-7 W-L, 0 SV, 2.97 ERA, $19.4 MIL	16-5 W-L, 0 SV, 2.94 ERA
NL	Greg Maddux	Atlanta	23-9 W-L, 0 SV, 1.58 ERA, $27.5 MIL	16-6 W-L, 0 SV, 1.56 ERA

AMERICAN LEAGUE LEADERS

			STATS	
CAT.	**PLAYER**	**TEAM**	**ADJUSTED**	**ACTUAL**
BATTING				
HR	Ken Griffey Jr.	Seattle	60	40
RBI	Kirby Puckett	Minnesota	163	112
BA	Paul O'Neill	New York	.357	.359
AB	Travis Fryman	Detroit	655	464
R	Frank Thomas	Chicago	154	106
H	Kenny Lofton	Cleveland	230	160
2B	Chuck Knoblauch	Minnesota	66	45
3B	Lance Johnson	Chicago	19	14
TB	Albert Belle	Cleveland	424	294
SA	Frank Thomas	Chicago	.734	.729
SB	Kenny Lofton	Cleveland	86	60
PITCHING				
W	Jimmy Key	New York	24	17
L	Tim Belcher	Detroit	21	15
SV	Lee Smith	Baltimore	48	33
ERA	Steve Ontiveros	Oakland	2.67	2.65
G	Bob Wickman	New York	76	53
IP	Chuck Finley	California	257	183.1
BB	Todd Van Poppel	Oakland	131	89
	Mike Moore	Detroit	128	89
SO	Randy Johnson	Seattle	306	204

NATIONAL LEAGUE LEADERS

			STATS	
CAT.	**PLAYER**	**TEAM**	**ADJUSTED**	**ACTUAL**
BATTING				
HR	Matt Williams	San Francisco	63	43
RBI	Jeff Bagwell	Houston	166	116
BA	Tony Gwynn	San Diego	.394	.394
AB	Dante Bichette	Colorado	672	484
R	Jeff Bagwell	Houston	149	104
H	Tony Gwynn	San Diego	228	165
2B	Craig Biggio	Houston	65	44
	Larry Walker	Montreal	62	44
3B	Brett Butler	Los Angeles	12	9
	Darren Lewis	San Francisco	12	9
TB	Jeff Bagwell	Houston	426	300
SA	Jeff Bagwell	Houston	.755	.750
SB	Craig Biggio	Houston	54	39
PITCHING				
W	Ken Hill	Montreal	23	16
	Greg Maddux	Atlanta	23	16
L	Andy Benes	San Diego	20	14
SV	John Franco	New York	43	30
ERA	Greg Maddux	Atlanta	1.58	1.56
G	Steve Reed	Colorado	84	61
IP	Greg Maddux	Atlanta	291	202
BB	Darryl Kile	Houston	119	82
SO	Andy Benes	San Diego	276	189

1995 SEASON

AMERICAN LEAGUE

		ADJUSTED				ACTUAL			
	W	L	Pct.	GB	W	L	Pct.	Rk.
EAST								
X Boston	97	65	.599	0	86	58	.597	2
New York	89	73	.549	8	79	65	.549	3
Baltimore	80	82	.494	17	71	73	.493	7
Toronto	63	99	.389	34	56	88	.389	13
GREAT LAKES								
X Cleveland	112	50	.691	0	100	44	.694	1
Chicago	76	86	.469	36	68	76	.472	9
Milwaukee	73	89	.451	39	65	79	.451	11
Detroit	68	94	.420	44	60	84	.417	12
CENTRAL								
X Texas	83	79	.512	0	74	70	.514	6
Kansas City	79	83	.488	4	70	74	.486	8
Minnesota	63	99	.389	20	56	88	.389	13
WEST								
X Seattle	88	74	.543	0	78	66	.542	4
X California	88	74	.543	0	78	66	.542	4
Oakland	75	87	.463	13	67	77	.465	10

NATIONAL LEAGUE

		ADJUSTED				ACTUAL			
	W	L	Pct.	GB	W	L	Pct.	Rk.
EAST								
X New York	78	84	.481	0	69	75	.479	8
X Philadelphia	78	84	.481	0	69	75	.479	8
Montreal	74	88	.457	4	66	78	.458	12
CENTRAL								
X Cincinnati	96	66	.593	0	85	59	.590	2
Chicago	82	80	.506	14	73	71	.507	6
St. Louis	70	92	.432	26	62	81	.434	13
Pittsburgh	65	97	.401	31	58	86	.403	14
SOUTH								
X Atlanta	101	61	.623	0	90	54	.625	1
Houston	85	77	.525	16	76	68	.528	5
Florida	76	86	.469	25	67	76	.469	10
WEST								
X Los Angeles	88	74	.543	0	78	66	.542	3
Colorado	87	75	.537	1	77	67	.535	4
San Diego	79	83	.488	9	70	74	.486	7
San Francisco	75	87	.463	13	67	77	.465	11

AMERICAN LEAGUE

TIEBREAKER**	W	1	2			%
Seattle Mariners	2	9	4			48
California Angels	0	1	3			52

ALDS (1-4)	W	1	2	3		%
Cleveland Indians	3	6	7	4		82
Texas Rangers	0	5	1	3		18

ALDS (2-3)	W	1	2	3	4	5	%
Boston Red Sox	3	1	1	5	5	9	55
Seattle Mariners	2	2	4	4	4	2	45

ALCS**	W	1	2	3	4	5	%
Cleveland Indians	4	5	4	8	4	12	64
Boston Red Sox	1	4	0	2	5	3	36

NATIONAL LEAGUE

TIEBREAKER	W	1	2			%
New York Mets	0	5	1			56
Philadelphia Phillies	2	6	4			44

NLDS (1-4)	W	1	2	3	4		%
Atlanta Braves	3	3	0	2	3		72
Philadelphia Phillies	1	0	3	1	2		28

NLDS (2-3)*	W	1	2	3		%
Cincinnati Reds	3	7	5	10		65
Los Angeles Dodgers	0	2	4	1		35

NLCS*	W	1	2	3	4	%
Atlanta Braves	4	2	6	5	6	56
Cincinnati Reds	0	1	2	2	0	44

WORLD SERIES

WS*	W	1	2	3	4	5	6	%
Cleveland Indians	2	2	3	7	2	5	0	67
Atlanta Braves	4	3	4	6	5	4	1	33

ACTUAL WINNERS

American League: Cleveland Indians
National League: Atlanta Braves
World Series: Atlanta Braves

OUTSTANDING PERFORMANCES

AWARD WINNERS

LG.	PLAYER	TEAM	STATS ADJUSTED	ACTUAL
MOST VALUABLE PLAYERS				
AL	Mo Vaughn	Boston	47 HR, 146 RBI, .303 BA, $18.7 MIL	39 HR, 126 RBI, .300 BA
NL	Barry Larkin	Cincinnati	18 HR, 76 RBI, .321 BA, $9.6 MIL	15 HR, 66 RBI, .319 BA
CY YOUNG AWARDS				
AL	Randy Johnson	Seattle	20-2 W-L, 0 SV, 2.56 ERA, $24.3 MIL	18-2 W-L, 0 SV, 2.48 ERA
NL	Greg Maddux	Atlanta	22-2 W-L, 0 SV, 1.69 ERA, $25.8 MIL	19-2 W-L, 0 SV, 1.63 ERA

AMERICAN LEAGUE LEADERS

CAT.	PLAYER	TEAM	ADJUSTED	ACTUAL
BATTING				
HR	Albert Belle	Cleveland	59	50
RBI	Mo Vaughn	Boston	146	126
	Albert Belle	Cleveland	145	126
BA	Edgar Martinez	Seattle	.359	.356
AB	Lance Johnson	Chicago	680	607
R	Albert Belle	Cleveland	140	121
	Edgar Martinez	Seattle	139	121
H	Lance Johnson	Chicago	210	186
2B	Edgar Martinez	Seattle	60	52
	Albert Belle	Cleveland	59	52
3B	Kenny Lofton	Cleveland	14	13
TB	Albert Belle	Cleveland	435	377
SA	Albert Belle	Cleveland	.707	.690
SB	Kenny Lofton	Cleveland	58	54
PITCHING				
W	Mike Mussina	Baltimore	21	19
L	Jason Bere	Chicago	17	15
	Kevin Gross	Texas	17	15
	Mike Moore	Detroit	17	15
SV	Jose Mesa	Cleveland	52	46
ERA	Randy Johnson	Seattle	2.56	2.48
G	Jesse Orosco	Baltimore	73	65
IP	David Cone	Tor.-N.Y.	260	229.1
BB	Al Leiter	Toronto	125	108
SO	Randy Johnson	Seattle	342	294

NATIONAL LEAGUE LEADERS

CAT.	PLAYER	TEAM	ADJUSTED	ACTUAL
BATTING				
HR	Dante Bichette	Colorado	48	40
RBI	Dante Bichette	Colorado	147	128
BA	Tony Gwynn	San Diego	.372	.368
AB	Brian McRae	Chicago	652	580
R	Craig Biggio	Houston	142	123
H	Tony Gwynn	San Diego	224	197
	Dante Bichette	Colorado	223	197
2B	Mark Grace	Chicago	61	51
3B	Brett Butler	N.Y.-L.A.	11	9
	Eric Young	Colorado	10	9
TB	Dante Bichette	Colorado	414	359
SA	Dante Bichette	Colorado	.637	.620
SB	Quilvio Veras	Florida	60	56
PITCHING				
W	Greg Maddux	Atlanta	22	19
L	Paul Wagner	Pittsburgh	18	16
SV	Randy Myers	Chicago	43	38
ERA	Greg Maddux	Atlanta	1.69	1.63
G	Curt Leskanic	Colorado	86	76
IP	Greg Maddux	Atlanta	240	209.2
	Denny Neagle	Pittsburgh	237	209.2
BB	Ramon Martinez	Los Angeles	93	81
SO	Hideo Nomo	Los Angeles	277	236

1996 SEASON

REGULAR SEASON STANDINGS

AMERICAN LEAGUE

		ADJUSTED				ACTUAL			
		W	L	Pct.	GB	W	L	Pct.	Rk.
EAST									
X	New York	92	70	.568	0	92	70	.568	2
	Baltimore	88	74	.543	4	88	74	.543	4
	Boston	85	77	.525	7	85	77	.525	6
	Toronto	74	88	.457	18	74	88	.457	12
GREAT LAKES									
X	Cleveland	100	62	.617	0	99	62	.615	1
	Chicago	85	77	.525	15	85	77	.525	6
	Milwaukee	80	82	.494	20	80	82	.494	8
	Detroit	53	109	.327	47	53	109	.327	14
CENTRAL									
X	Texas	90	72	.556	0	90	72	.556	3
	Minnesota	78	84	.481	12	78	84	.481	9
	Kansas City	75	87	.463	15	75	86	.466	11
WEST									
X	Seattle	86	76	.531	0	85	76	.528	5
	Oakland	78	84	.481	8	78	84	.481	9
	California	70	92	.432	16	70	91	.435	13

NATIONAL LEAGUE

		ADJUSTED				ACTUAL			
		W	L	Pct.	GB	W	L	Pct.	Rk.
EAST									
X	Montreal	88	74	.543	0	88	74	.543	4
	New York	71	91	.438	17	71	91	.438	12
	Philadelphia	67	95	.414	21	67	95	.414	14
CENTRAL									
X	St. Louis	88	74	.543	0	88	74	.543	4
	Cincinnati	81	81	.500	7	81	81	.500	8
	Chicago	76	86	.469	12	76	86	.469	10
	Pittsburgh	73	89	.451	15	73	89	.451	11
SOUTH									
X	Atlanta	96	66	.593	0	96	66	.593	1
	Houston	82	80	.506	14	82	80	.506	7
	Florida	80	82	.494	16	80	82	.494	9
WEST									
X	San Diego	91	71	.562	0	91	71	.562	2
	Los Angeles	90	72	.556	1	90	72	.556	3
	Colorado	83	79	.512	8	83	79	.512	6
	San Francisco	68	94	.420	23	68	94	.420	13

SIMULATED PLAYOFFS

AMERICAN LEAGUE

ALDS (1-4)	W	1	2	3	4	5		%
Cleveland Indians	3	5	6	13	5	8		67
Seattle Mariners	2	8	0	10	10	3		33

ALDS (2-3)*	W	1	2	3	4		%
New York Yankees	3	2	5	3	6		34
Texas Rangers	1	6	4	2	4		66

ALCS	W	1	2	3	4	5	6	%
Cleveland Indians	4	4	2	0	14	7	6	55
New York Yankees	2	2	4	4	3	2	4	45

NATIONAL LEAGUE

NLDS (1-4)**	W	1	2	3	4		%
Atlanta Braves	1	4	3	2	3		60
St. Louis Cardinals	3	2	8	3	4		40

NLDS (2-3)	W	1	2	3	4		%
San Diego Padres	1	5	1	2	1		51
Montreal Expos	3	2	2	6	3		49

NLCS	W	1	2	3	4	5	6	7	%
Montreal Expos	4	3	2	2	5	0	7	7	49
St. Louis Cardinals	3	4	4	1	1	3	4	5	51

WORLD SERIES

WS	W	1	2	3	4	5	6	7	%
Cleveland Indians	4	4	5	4	3	2	4	2	56
Montreal Expos	3	5	1	1	4	3	2	1	44

ACTUAL WINNERS

American League: New York Yankees
National League: Atlanta Braves
World Series: New York Yankees

OUTSTANDING PERFORMANCES

AWARD WINNERS

LG.	PLAYER	TEAM	STATS ADJUSTED	ACTUAL
MOST VALUABLE PLAYERS				
AL	Juan Gonzalez	Texas	47 HR, 142 RBI, .313 BA, $12.1 MIL	47 HR, 144 RBI, .314 BA
NL	Ken Caminiti	San Diego	40 HR, 129 RBI, .324 BA, $9.4 MIL	40 HR, 130 RBI, .326 BA
CY YOUNG AWARDS				
AL	Pat Hentgen	Toronto	20-10 W-L, 0 SV, 3.18 ERA, $20.1 MIL	20-10 W-L, 0 SV, 3.22 ERA
NL	John Smoltz	Atlanta	24-8 W-L, 0 SV, 2.91 ERA, $25.6 MIL	24-8 W-L, 0 SV, 2.94 ERA

AMERICAN LEAGUE LEADERS

CAT.	PLAYER	TEAM	STATS ADJUSTED	ACTUAL
BATTING				
HR	Mark McGwire	Oakland	52	52
RBI	Albert Belle	Cleveland	148	148
BA	Alex Rodriguez	Seattle	.357	.358
AB	Kenny Lofton	Cleveland	666	662
R	Alex Rodriguez	Seattle	141	141
H	Paul Molitor	Minnesota	224	225
2B	Alex Rodriguez	Seattle	55	54
3B	Chuck Knoblauch	Minnesota	15	14
TB	Alex Rodriguez	Seattle	381	379
SA	Mark McGwire	Oakland	.730	.730
SB	Kenny Lofton	Cleveland	74	75
PITCHING				
W	Andy Pettitte	New York	21	21
L	Jim Abbott	California	18	18
SV	John Wetteland	New York	43	43
ERA	Juan Guzman	Toronto	2.92	2.93
G	Mike Myers	Detroit	83	83
	Eddie Guardado	Minnesota	83	83
IP	Pat Hentgen	Toronto	266	265.2
BB	Rich Robertson	Minnesota	117	116
SO	Roger Clemens	Boston	260	257

NATIONAL LEAGUE LEADERS

CAT.	PLAYER	TEAM	STATS ADJUSTED	ACTUAL
BATTING				
HR	Andres Galarraga	Colorado	47	47
RBI	Andres Galarraga	Colorado	149	150
BA	Tony Gwynn	San Diego	.353	.353
AB	Lance Johnson	New York	682	682
R	Ellis Burks	Colorado	141	142
H	Lance Johnson	New York	226	227
2B	Jeff Bagwell	Houston	49	48
3B	Lance Johnson	New York	22	21
TB	Ellis Burks	Colorado	392	392
SA	Ellis Burks	Colorado	.639	.639
SB	Eric Young	Colorado	52	53
PITCHING				
W	John Smoltz	Atlanta	24	24
L	Frank Castillo	Chicago	16	16
	Pat Rapp	Florida	16	16
SV	Jeff Brantley	Cincinnati	44	44
	Todd Worrell	Los Angeles	44	44
ERA	Kevin Brown	Florida	1.89	1.89
G	Brad Clontz	Atlanta	81	81
IP	John Smoltz	Atlanta	254	253.2
BB	Al Leiter	Florida	120	119
SO	John Smoltz	Atlanta	279	276

1997 SEASON

REGULAR SEASON STANDINGS

AMERICAN LEAGUE

	ADJUSTED				ACTUAL			
	W	L	Pct.	GB	W	L	Pct.	Rk.
EAST								
X Baltimore	98	64	.605	0	98	64	.605	1
New York	96	66	.593	2	96	66	.593	2
Boston	78	84	.481	20	78	84	.481	9
Toronto	76	86	.469	22	76	86	.469	11
GREAT LAKES								
X Cleveland	87	75	.537	0	86	75	.534	4
Chicago	81	81	.500	6	80	81	.497	6
Detroit	79	83	.488	8	79	83	.488	7
Milwaukee	78	84	.481	9	78	83	.484	8
CENTRAL								
X Texas	77	85	.475	0	77	85	.475	10
Minnesota	68	94	.420	9	68	94	.420	12
Kansas City	67	95	.414	10	67	94	.416	13
WEST								
X Seattle	90	72	.556	0	90	72	.556	3
Anaheim	84	78	.519	6	84	78	.519	5
Oakland	65	97	.401	25	65	97	.401	14

NATIONAL LEAGUE

	ADJUSTED				ACTUAL			
	W	L	Pct.	GB	W	L	Pct.	Rk.
EAST								
X New York	88	74	.543	0	88	74	.543	4
Montreal	78	84	.481	10	78	84	.481	9
Philadelphia	68	94	.420	20	68	94	.420	13
CENTRAL								
X Pittsburgh	79	83	.488	0	79	83	.488	8
Cincinnati	76	86	.469	3	76	86	.469	10
St. Louis	73	89	.451	6	73	89	.451	12
Chicago	68	94	.420	11	68	94	.420	13
SOUTH								
X Atlanta	101	61	.623	0	101	61	.623	1
Florida	92	70	.568	9	92	70	.568	2
Houston	84	78	.519	17	84	78	.519	6
WEST								
X San Francisco	90	72	.556	0	90	72	.556	3
Los Angeles	88	74	.543	2	88	74	.543	4
Colorado	83	79	.512	7	83	79	.512	7
San Diego	76	86	.469	14	76	86	.469	10

SIMULATED PLAYOFFS

AMERICAN LEAGUE

ALDS (1-4)	W	1	2	3			%
Baltimore Orioles	3	3	12	12			65
Texas Rangers	0	0	2	5			35

ALDS (2-3)	W	1	2	3	4	5	%
Seattle Mariners	2	0	7	6	4	9	51
Cleveland Indians	3	5	4	3	11	10	49

ALCS*	W	1	2	3	4	5	6	%
Baltimore Orioles	2	3	4	1	7	4	0	66
Cleveland Indians	4	0	5	2	8	2	1	34

NATIONAL LEAGUE

NLDS (1-4)	W	1	2	3			%
Atlanta Braves	3	7	3	4			87
Pittsburgh Pirates	0	3	1	2			13

NLDS (2-3)	W	1	2	3	4		%
San Francisco Giants	3	2	6	1	7		48
New York Mets	1	0	4	3	5		52

NLCS	W	1	2	3	4	5	6	7	%
Atlanta Braves	4	1	3	7	1	5	8	4	76
San Francisco Giants	3	2	2	2	4	6	4	0	24

WORLD SERIES

WS	W	1	2	3	4	5	6	7	%
Cleveland Indians	3	5	0	1	1	7	1	1	29
Atlanta Braves	4	0	2	3	0	5	8	3	71

ACTUAL WINNERS

American League: Cleveland Indians
National League: Florida Marlins
World Series: Florida Marlins

OUTSTANDING PERFORMANCES

AWARD WINNERS

LG.	PLAYER	TEAM	STATS ADJUSTED	ACTUAL
MOST VALUABLE PLAYERS				
AL	Ken Griffey Jr.	Seattle	58 HR, 153 RBI, .308 BA, $19.9 MIL	56 HR, 147 RBI, .304 BA
NL	Larry Walker	Colorado	51 HR, 135 RBI, .370 BA, $16.0 MIL	49 HR, 130 RBI, .366 BA
CY YOUNG AWARDS				
AL	Roger Clemens	Toronto	21-7 W-L, 0 SV, 2.11 ERA, $18.9 MIL	21-7 W-L, 0 SV, 2.05 ERA
NL	Pedro Martinez	Montreal	17-8 W-L, 0 SV, 1.98 ERA, $19.7 MIL	17-8 W-L, 0 SV, 1.90 ERA

AMERICAN LEAGUE LEADERS

CAT.	PLAYER	TEAM	STATS ADJUSTED	ACTUAL
BATTING				
HR	Ken Griffey Jr.	Seattle	58	56
RBI	Ken Griffey Jr.	Seattle	153	147
BA	Frank Thomas	Chicago	.350	.347
AB	Nomar Garciaparra	Boston	684	684
R	Ken Griffey Jr.	Seattle	130	125
H	Nomar Garciaparra	Boston	211	209
2B	John Valentin	Boston	48	47
3B	Nomar Garciaparra	Boston	11	11
TB	Ken Griffey Jr.	Seattle	400	393
SA	Ken Griffey Jr.	Seattle	.658	.646
SB	Brian Hunter	Detroit	70	74
PITCHING				
W	Roger Clemens	Toronto	21	21
L	James Baldwin	Chicago	15	15
	Cal Eldred	Milwaukee	15	15
	Tim Wakefield	Boston	15	15
SV	Randy Myers	Baltimore	45	45
ERA	Roger Clemens	Toronto	2.11	2.05
G	Mike Myers	Detroit	88	88
IP	Roger Clemens	Toronto	264	264
	Pat Hentgen	Toronto	264	264
BB	Ken Hill	Tex.-Ana.	98	95
SO	Roger Clemens	Toronto	289	292

NATIONAL LEAGUE LEADERS

CAT.	PLAYER	TEAM	STATS ADJUSTED	ACTUAL
BATTING				
HR	Larry Walker	Colorado	51	49
RBI	Andres Galarraga	Colorado	146	140
BA	Tony Gwynn	San Diego	.375	.372
AB	Mark Grudzielanek	Montreal	649	649
R	Craig Biggio	Houston	152	146
H	Tony Gwynn	San Diego	222	220
2B	Mark Grudzielanek	Montreal	57	54
3B	Delino DeShields	St. Louis	14	14
TB	Larry Walker	Colorado	417	409
SA	Larry Walker	Colorado	.734	.720
SB	Tony Womack	Pittsburgh	57	60
PITCHING				
W	Denny Neagle	Atlanta	20	20
L	Mark Leiter	Philadelphia	17	17
SV	Jeff Shaw	Cincinnati	41	42
ERA	Pedro Martinez	Montreal	1.98	1.90
G	Julian Tavarez	San Francisco	89	89
IP	John Smoltz	Atlanta	256	256
BB	Shawn Estes	San Francisco	103	100
SO	Curt Schilling	Philadelphia	316	319

1998 SEASON

REGULAR SEASON STANDINGS

AMERICAN LEAGUE

	ADJUSTED				ACTUAL			
	W	L	Pct.	GB	W	L	Pct.	Rk.
EAST								
X New York	114	48	.704	0	114	48	.704	1
Boston	92	70	.568	22	92	70	.568	2
Baltimore	79	83	.488	35	79	83	.488	8
Tampa Bay	63	99	.389	51	63	99	.389	14
GREAT LAKES								
X Cleveland	89	73	.549	0	89	73	.549	3
Toronto	88	74	.543	1	88	74	.543	4
Chicago	80	82	.494	9	80	82	.494	7
Detroit	65	97	.401	24	65	97	.401	13
CENTRAL								
X Texas	88	74	.543	0	88	74	.543	4
Kansas City	72	90	.444	16	72	89	.447	11
Minnesota	70	92	.432	18	70	92	.432	12
WEST								
X Anaheim	85	77	.525	0	85	77	.525	6
Seattle	77	85	.475	8	76	85	.472	9
Oakland	74	88	.457	11	74	88	.457	10

NATIONAL LEAGUE

	ADJUSTED				ACTUAL			
	W	L	Pct.	GB	W	L	Pct.	Rk.
EAST								
X New York	88	74	.543	0	88	74	.543	6
Philadelphia	75	87	.463	13	75	87	.463	11
Pittsburgh	69	93	.426	19	69	93	.426	13
Montreal	65	97	.401	23	65	97	.401	14
CENTRAL								
X Chicago	89	73	.549	0	89	73	.549	4
St. Louis	83	79	.512	6	83	79	.512	7
Colorado	77	85	.475	12	77	85	.475	9
Milwaukee	74	88	.457	15	74	88	.457	12
SOUTH								
X Atlanta	106	56	.654	0	106	56	.654	1
Houston	102	60	.630	4	102	60	.630	2
Cincinnati	77	85	.475	29	77	85	.475	9
Florida	54	108	.333	52	54	108	.333	16
WEST								
X San Diego	98	64	.605	0	98	64	.605	3
San Francisco	89	73	.549	9	89	73	.549	4
Los Angeles	83	79	.512	15	83	79	.512	7
Arizona	65	97	.401	33	65	97	.401	14

SIMULATED PLAYOFFS

AMERICAN LEAGUE

ALDS (1-4)	W	1	2	3				%
New York Yankees	3	6	9	9				89
Anaheim Angels	0	2	1	2				11

ALDS (2-3)	W	1	2	3				%
Cleveland Indians	3	10	13	6				64
Texas Rangers	0	7	7	0				36

ALCS*	W	1	2	3	4	5	6	%
New York Yankees	4	7	1	1	4	5	9	84
Cleveland Indians	2	2	4	6	0	3	5	16

NATIONAL LEAGUE

NLDS (1-4)	W	1	2	3	4	5	%
Atlanta Braves	3	2	3	2	4	7	74
New York Mets	2	3	1	3	0	1	26

NLDS (2-3)	W	1	2	3	4		%
San Diego Padres	1	6	3	1	4		61
Chicago Cubs	3	1	4	2	5		39

NLCS**	W	1	2	3	4	5	%
Atlanta Braves	4	7	2	6	3	4	83
Chicago Cubs	1	1	1	2	4	2	17

WORLD SERIES

WS	W	1	2	3	4	5	6	7	%
New York Yankees	4	5	3	6	6	2	2	6	57
Atlanta Braves	3	6	2	1	0	6	3	5	43

ACTUAL WINNERS

American League: New York Yankees
National League: San Diego Padres
World Series: New York Yankees

OUTSTANDING PERFORMANCES

AWARD WINNERS

LG.	PLAYER	TEAM	STATS ADJUSTED	ACTUAL
MOST VALUABLE PLAYERS				
AL	Juan Gonzalez	Texas	47 HR, 163 RBI, .322 BA, $15.7 MIL	45 HR, 157 RBI, .318 BA
NL	Sammy Sosa	Chicago	67 HR, 163 RBI, .311 BA, $22.8 MIL	66 HR, 158 RBI, .308 BA
CY YOUNG AWARDS				
AL	Roger Clemens	Toronto	20-6 W-L, 0 SV, 2.72 ERA, $16.8 MIL	20-6 W-L, 0 SV, 2.65 ERA
NL	Tom Glavine	Atlanta	20-6 W-L, 0 SV, 2.55 ERA, $14.9 MIL	20-6 W-L, 0 SV, 2.47 ERA

AMERICAN LEAGUE LEADERS

CAT.	PLAYER	TEAM	STATS ADJUSTED	ACTUAL
BATTING				
HR	Ken Griffey Jr.	Seattle	58	56
RBI	Juan Gonzalez	Texas	163	157
BA	Bernie Williams	New York	.343	.339
AB	Alex Rodriguez	Seattle	690	686
R	Derek Jeter	New York	132	127
H	Alex Rodriguez	Seattle	217	213
2B	Juan Gonzalez	Texas	50	50
3B	Jose Offerman	Kansas City	14	13
TB	Albert Belle	Chicago	402	399
SA	Albert Belle	Chicago	.664	.655
SB	Rickey Henderson	Oakland	68	66
PITCHING				
W	David Cone	New York	20	20
	Roger Clemens	Toronto	20	20
	Rick Helling	Texas	20	20
L	Tom Candiotti	Oakland	16	16
	Jaime Navarro	Chicago	16	16
	Juan Guzman	Tor.-Bal.	16	16
SV	Tom Gordon	Boston	45	46
ERA	Roger Clemens	Toronto	2.72	2.65
G	Sean Runyan	Detroit	88	88
IP	Scott Erickson	Baltimore	251	251.1
BB	Tony Saunders	Tampa Bay	117	111
SO	Roger Clemens	Toronto	270	271

NATIONAL LEAGUE LEADERS

CAT.	PLAYER	TEAM	STATS ADJUSTED	ACTUAL
BATTING				
HR	Mark McGwire	St. Louis	71	70
RBI	Sammy Sosa	Chicago	163	158
BA	Larry Walker	Colorado	.368	.363
AB	Doug Glanville	Philadelphia	678	678
R	Sammy Sosa	Chicago	138	134
H	Dante Bichette	Colorado	221	219
2B	Craig Biggio	Houston	51	51
3B	David Dellucci	Arizona	13	12
TB	Sammy Sosa	Chicago	420	416
SA	Mark McGwire	St. Louis	.763	.752
SB	Tony Womack	Pittsburgh	59	58
PITCHING				
W	Tom Glavine	Atlanta	20	20
L	Darryl Kile	Colorado	17	17
SV	Trevor Hoffman	San Diego	52	53
ERA	Greg Maddux	Atlanta	2.29	2.22
G	Rod Beck	Chicago	81	81
IP	Curt Schilling	Philadelphia	269	268.2
BB	Joey Hamilton	San Diego	112	106
SO	Curt Schilling	Philadelphia	299	300

1999 SEASON

REGULAR SEASON STANDINGS

AMERICAN LEAGUE

		ADJUSTED				ACTUAL		
	W	L	Pct.	GB	W	L	Pct.	Rk.
EAST								
X New York	98	64	.605	0	98	64	.605	1
Boston	94	68	.580	4	94	68	.580	4
Baltimore	78	84	.481	20	78	84	.481	8
Tampa Bay	69	93	.426	29	69	93	.426	12
GREAT LAKES								
X Cleveland	97	65	.599	0	97	65	.599	2
Toronto	84	78	.519	13	84	78	.519	6
Chicago	76	86	.469	21	75	86	.466	9
Detroit	69	93	.426	28	69	92	.429	11
CENTRAL								
X Texas	95	67	.586	0	95	67	.586	3
Kansas City	64	98	.395	31	64	97	.398	13
Minnesota	64	98	.395	31	63	97	.394	14
WEST								
X Oakland	87	75	.537	0	87	75	.537	5
Seattle	79	83	.488	8	79	83	.488	7
Anaheim	70	92	.432	17	70	92	.432	10

NATIONAL LEAGUE

		ADJUSTED				ACTUAL		
	W	L	Pct.	GB	W	L	Pct.	Rk.
EAST								
X New York	96	66	.593	0	96	66	.593	4
Pittsburgh	79	83	.488	17	78	83	.484	7
Philadelphia	77	85	.475	19	77	85	.475	8
Montreal	68	94	.420	28	68	94	.420	14
CENTRAL								
X St. Louis	76	86	.469	0	75	86	.466	10
Milwaukee	74	88	.457	2	74	87	.460	11
Colorado	72	90	.444	4	72	90	.444	13
Chicago	67	95	.414	9	67	95	.414	15
SOUTH								
X Atlanta	103	59	.636	0	103	59	.636	1
Houston	97	65	.599	6	97	65	.599	3
Cincinnati	96	66	.593	7	96	66	.593	4
Florida	64	98	.395	39	64	98	.395	16
WEST								
X Arizona	100	62	.617	0	100	62	.617	2
San Francisco	86	76	.531	14	86	76	.531	6
Los Angeles	77	85	.475	23	77	85	.475	8
San Diego	74	88	.457	26	74	88	.457	12

SIMULATED PLAYOFFS

AMERICAN LEAGUE

ALDS (1-4)	W	1	2	3	4	5		%
New York Yankees	3	2	4	6	7	5		71
Oakland Athletics	2	9	6	4	3	3		29

ALDS (2-3)	W	1	2	3	4	5		%
Cleveland Indians	3	5	10	5	0	10		63
Texas Rangers	2	1	1	6	1	1		37

ALCS	W	1	2	3	4	5	6	%
New York Yankees	2	5	5	1	1	5	12	54
Cleveland Indians	4	7	6	0	2	1	15	46

NATIONAL LEAGUE

NLDS (1-4)	W	1	2	3	4		%
Atlanta Braves	1	3	5	2	3		73
St. Louis Cardinals	3	4	0	5	4		27

NLDS (2-3)*	W	1	2	3	4		%
Arizona Diamondbacks	1	4	7	2	3		57
New York Mets	3	8	1	9	4		43

NLCS	W	1	2	3	4	5	%
New York Mets	4	7	8	5	0	4	68
St. Louis Cardinals	1	3	4	3	4	1	32

WORLD SERIES

WS	W	1	2	3	4	5	6	7	%
Cleveland Indians	3	3	1	6	6	1	8	3	50
New York Mets	4	6	2	5	3	2	1	5	50

ACTUAL WINNERS

American League: New York Yankees
National League: Atlanta Braves
World Series: New York Yankees

OUTSTANDING PERFORMANCES

AWARD WINNERS

LG.	PLAYER	TEAM	STATS ADJUSTED	ACTUAL
MOST VALUABLE PLAYERS				
AL	Ivan Rodriguez	Texas	34 HR, 110 RBI, .328 BA, $14.6 MIL	35 HR, 113 RBI, .332 BA
NL	Chipper Jones	Atlanta	43 HR, 108 RBI, .317 BA, $19.2 MIL	45 HR, 110 RBI, .319 BA
CY YOUNG AWARDS				
AL	Pedro Martinez	Boston	23-4 W-L, 0 SV, 1.99 ERA, $20.3 MIL	23-4 W-L, 0 SV, 2.07 ERA
NL	Randy Johnson	Arizona	17-9 W-L, 0 SV, 2.42 ERA, $23.1 MIL	17-9 W-L, 0 SV, 2.48 ERA

AMERICAN LEAGUE LEADERS

CAT.	PLAYER	TEAM	STATS ADJUSTED	ACTUAL
BATTING				
HR	Ken Griffey Jr.	Seattle	46	48
RBI	Manny Ramirez	Cleveland	162	165
BA	Nomar Garciaparra	Boston	.355	.357
AB	B.J. Surhoff	Baltimore	673	673
R	Roberto Alomar	Cleveland	135	138
H	Derek Jeter	New York	217	219
2B	Shawn Green	Toronto	45	45
3B	Jose Offerman	Boston	11	11
TB	Shawn Green	Toronto	356	361
SA	Manny Ramirez	Cleveland	.655	.663
SB	Brian Hunter	Det.-Sea.	43	44
PITCHING				
W	Pedro Martinez	Boston	23	23
L	Brian Moehler	Detroit	16	16
SV	Mariano Rivera	New York	45	45
ERA	Pedro Martinez	Boston	1.99	2.07
G	Buddy Groom	Oakland	76	76
	Bob Wells	Minnesota	76	76
IP	David Wells	Toronto	232	231.2
BB	Scott Erickson	Baltimore	95	99
SO	Pedro Martinez	Boston	316	313

NATIONAL LEAGUE LEADERS

CAT.	PLAYER	TEAM	STATS ADJUSTED	ACTUAL
BATTING				
HR	Mark McGwire	St. Louis	64	65
RBI	Mark McGwire	St. Louis	145	147
BA	Larry Walker	Colorado	.377	.379
AB	Neifi Perez	Colorado	690	690
R	Jeff Bagwell	Houston	140	143
H	Luis Gonzalez	Arizona	204	206
2B	Craig Biggio	Houston	56	56
3B	Bobby Abreu	Philadelphia	11	11
	Neifi Perez	Colorado	11	11
TB	Sammy Sosa	Chicago	390	397
SA	Larry Walker	Colorado	.701	.710
SB	Tony Womack	Arizona	71	72
PITCHING				
W	Mike Hampton	Houston	22	22
L	Steve Trachsel	Chicago	18	18
SV	Ugueth Urbina	Montreal	41	41
ERA	Randy Johnson	Arizona	2.42	2.48
G	Steve Kline	Montreal	82	82
IP	Randy Johnson	Arizona	272	271.2
BB	Russ Ortiz	San Francisco	121	125
SO	Randy Johnson	Arizona	369	364

REGULAR SEASON STANDINGS

AMERICAN LEAGUE

		ADJUSTED				ACTUAL		
	W	L	Pct.	GB	W	L	Pct.	Rk.
EAST								
X New York	88	74	.543	0	87	74	.540	5
Boston	85	77	.525	3	85	77	.525	6
Baltimore	74	88	.457	14	74	88	.457	11
Tampa Bay	69	93	.426	19	69	92	.429	13
GREAT LAKES								
X Chicago	95	67	.586	0	95	67	.586	1
Cleveland	90	72	.556	5	90	72	.556	4
Toronto	83	79	.512	12	83	79	.512	7
Detroit	79	83	.488	16	79	83	.488	9
CENTRAL								
X Kansas City	77	85	.475	0	77	85	.475	10
Texas	71	91	.438	6	71	91	.438	12
Minnesota	69	93	.426	8	69	93	.426	14
WEST								
X Oakland	92	70	.568	0	91	70	.565	2
Seattle	91	71	.562	1	91	71	.562	3
Anaheim	82	80	.506	10	82	80	.506	8

NATIONAL LEAGUE

		ADJUSTED				ACTUAL		
	W	L	Pct.	GB	W	L	Pct.	Rk.
EAST								
X New York	94	68	.580	0	94	68	.580	4
Pittsburgh	69	93	.426	25	69	93	.426	13
Montreal	67	95	.414	27	67	95	.414	14
Philadelphia	65	97	.401	29	65	97	.401	15
CENTRAL								
X St. Louis	95	67	.586	0	95	67	.586	2
Colorado	82	80	.506	13	82	80	.506	8
Milwaukee	73	89	.451	22	73	89	.451	11
Chicago	65	97	.401	30	65	97	.401	15
SOUTH								
X Atlanta	95	67	.586	0	95	67	.586	2
Cincinnati	85	77	.525	10	85	77	.525	6
Florida	79	83	.488	16	79	82	.491	9
Houston	72	90	.444	23	72	90	.444	12
WEST								
X San Francisco	97	65	.599	0	97	65	.599	1
Los Angeles	86	76	.531	11	86	76	.531	5
Arizona	85	77	.525	12	85	77	.525	6
San Diego	76	86	.469	21	76	86	.469	10

SIMULATED PLAYOFFS

AMERICAN LEAGUE

ALDS (1-4)	W	1	2	3	4	5		%
Chicago White Sox	3	12	7	3	16	7		68
Kansas City Royals	2	1	14	9	5	6		32

ALDS (2-3)*	W	1	2	3	4	5		%
Oakland Athletics	2	5	0	2	11	5		57
New York Yankees	3	3	4	4	1	7		43

ALCS	W	1	2	3	4	5	6	%
Chicago White Sox	4	4	7	7	8	7	11	52
New York Yankees	2	8	6	2	1	8	4	48

NATIONAL LEAGUE

NLDS (1-4)*	W	1	2	3	4		%
San Francisco Giants	1	5	4	2	0		57
New York Mets	3	1	5	3	4		43

NLDS (2-3)*	W	1	2	3			%
St. Louis Cardinals	3	7	10	7			53
Atlanta Braves	0	5	4	1			47

NLCS*	W	1	2	3	4	5	%
St. Louis Cardinals	1	2	5	8	6	0	55
New York Mets	4	6	6	2	10	7	45

WORLD SERIES

WS	W	1	2	3	4	5	6	%
Chicago White Sox	2	5	2	0	4	1	4	55
New York Mets	4	3	3	4	3	5	5	45

ACTUAL WINNERS

American League: New York Yankees
National League: New York Mets
World Series: New York Yankees

OUTSTANDING PERFORMANCES

AWARD WINNERS

LG.	PLAYER	TEAM	STATS ADJUSTED	ACTUAL
MOST VALUABLE PLAYERS				
AL	Jason Giambi	Oakland	41 HR, 134 RBI, .331 BA, $12.4 MIL	43 HR, 137 RBI, .333 BA
NL	Jeff Kent	San Francisco	31 HR, 121 RBI, .332 BA, $12.9 MIL	33 HR, 125 RBI, .334 BA
CY YOUNG AWARDS				
AL	Pedro Martinez	Boston	18-6 W-L, 0 SV, 1.66 ERA, $19.9 MIL	18-6 W-L, 0 SV, 1.74 ERA
NL	Randy Johnson	Arizona	19-7 W-L, 0 SV, 2.53 ERA, $23.3 MIL	19-7 W-L, 0 SV, 2.64 ERA

AMERICAN LEAGUE LEADERS

CAT.	PLAYER	TEAM	STATS ADJUSTED	ACTUAL
BATTING				
HR	Troy Glaus	Anaheim	45	47
RBI	Edgar Martinez	Seattle	141	145
BA	Nomar Garciaparra	Boston	.371	.372
AB	Darin Erstad	Anaheim	676	676
R	Johnny Damon	Kansas City	132	136
H	Darin Erstad	Anaheim	239	240
2B	Carlos Delgado	Toronto	57	57
3B	Cristian Guzman	Minnesota	20	20
TB	Carlos Delgado	Toronto	371	378
SA	Manny Ramirez	Cleveland	.679	.697
SB	Johnny Damon	Kansas City	53	46
PITCHING				
W	Tim Hudson	Oakland	20	20
	David Wells	Toronto	20	20
L	Brad Radke	Minnesota	16	16
SV	Todd Jones	Detroit	42	42
	Derek Lowe	Boston	42	42
ERA	Pedro Martinez	Boston	1.66	1.74
G	Kelly Wunsch	Chicago	83	83
IP	Mike Mussina	Baltimore	238	237.2
BB	Kevin Appier	Oakland	97	102
SO	Pedro Martinez	Boston	286	284

NATIONAL LEAGUE LEADERS

CAT.	PLAYER	TEAM	STATS ADJUSTED	ACTUAL
BATTING				
HR	Sammy Sosa	Chicago	48	50
RBI	Todd Helton	Colorado	142	147
BA	Todd Helton	Colorado	.371	.372
AB	Andruw Jones	Atlanta	656	656
R	Jeff Bagwell	Houston	147	152
H	Todd Helton	Colorado	215	216
2B	Todd Helton	Colorado	59	59
3B	Tony Womack	Arizona	13	14
TB	Todd Helton	Colorado	395	405
SA	Todd Helton	Colorado	.681	.698
SB	Luis Castillo	Florida	72	62
PITCHING				
W	Tom Glavine	Atlanta	21	21
L	Omar Daal	Ari.-Phi.	19	19
SV	Antonio Alfonseca	Florida	45	45
ERA	Kevin Brown	Los Angeles	2.47	2.58
G	Steve Kline	Montreal	83	83
IP	Jon Lieber	Chicago	251	251
BB	Matt Clement	San Diego	119	125
SO	Randy Johnson	Arizona	350	347

2001 SEASON

REGULAR SEASON STANDINGS

AMERICAN LEAGUE

		ADJUSTED				ACTUAL			
	W	L	Pct.	GB	W	L	Pct.	Rk.
EAST								
X New York	96	66	.593	0	95	65	.594	3
Boston	83	79	.512	13	82	79	.509	7
Baltimore	63	99	.389	33	63	98	.391	13
Tampa Bay	62	100	.383	34	62	100	.383	14
GREAT LAKES								
X Cleveland	91	71	.562	0	91	71	.562	4
Chicago	83	79	.512	8	83	79	.512	6
Toronto	80	82	.494	11	80	82	.494	8
Detroit	66	96	.407	25	66	96	.407	11
CENTRAL								
X Minnesota	85	77	.525	0	85	77	.525	5
Texas	73	89	.451	12	73	89	.451	10
Kansas City	65	97	.401	20	65	97	.401	12
WEST								
X Seattle	116	46	.716	0	116	46	.716	1
Oakland	102	60	.630	14	102	60	.630	2
Anaheim	75	87	.463	41	75	87	.463	9

NATIONAL LEAGUE

		ADJUSTED				ACTUAL			
	W	L	Pct.	GB	W	L	Pct.	Rk.
EAST								
X Philadelphia	86	76	.531	0	86	76	.531	7
New York	82	80	.506	4	82	80	.506	9
Montreal	68	94	.420	18	68	94	.420	13
Pittsburgh	62	100	.383	24	62	100	.383	16
CENTRAL								
X St. Louis	93	69	.574	0	93	69	.574	1
Chicago	88	74	.543	5	88	74	.543	5
Colorado	73	89	.451	20	73	89	.451	12
Milwaukee	68	94	.420	25	68	94	.420	13
SOUTH								
X Houston	93	69	.574	0	93	69	.574	1
Atlanta	88	74	.543	5	88	74	.543	5
Florida	76	86	.469	17	76	86	.469	11
Cincinnati	66	96	.407	27	66	96	.407	15
WEST								
X Arizona	92	70	.568	0	92	70	.568	3
San Francisco	90	72	.556	2	90	72	.556	4
Los Angeles	86	76	.531	6	86	76	.531	7
San Diego	79	83	.488	13	79	83	.488	10

SIMULATED PLAYOFFS

AMERICAN LEAGUE

ALDS (1-4)	W	1	2	3	4	5	%
Seattle Mariners	3	3	4	7	8	5	95
Minnesota Twins	2	6	5	2	2	2	5

ALDS (2-3)	W	1	2	3	4	5	%
New York Yankees	3	3	7	3	0	7	61
Cleveland Indians	2	1	1	4	1	1	39

ALCS*	W	1	2	3	4	5	%
Seattle Mariners	1	2	2	14	1	3	76
New York Yankees	4	4	3	3	3	12	24

NATIONAL LEAGUE

NLDS (1-4)	W	1	2	3	4	5	%
Houston Astros	2	0	8	4	1	2	56
Philadelphia Phillies	3	6	3	3	2	9	44

NLDS (2-3)*	W	1	2	3	4	5	%
St. Louis Cardinals	2	0	4	3	4	1	47
Arizona Diamondbacks	3	1	1	5	1	2	53

NLCS	W	1	2	3	4		%
Arizona Diamondbacks	0	4	3	1	4		65
Philadelphia Phillies	4	5	4	2	5		35

WORLD SERIES

WS	W	1	2	3	4		%
New York Yankees	4	4	5	5	5		57
Philadelphia Phillies	0	2	2	2	1		43

ACTUAL WINNERS

American League: New York Yankees
National League: Arizona Diamondbacks
World Series: Arizona Diamondbacks

OUTSTANDING PERFORMANCES

AWARD WINNERS

LG.	PLAYER	TEAM	STATS ADJUSTED	ACTUAL
MOST VALUABLE PLAYERS				
AL	Ichiro Suzuki	Seattle	8 HR, 71 RBI, .357 BA, $19.6 MIL	8 HR, 69 RBI, .350 BA
NL	Barry Bonds	San Francisco	72 HR, 142 RBI, .334 BA, $13.1 MIL	73 HR, 137 RBI, .328 BA
CY YOUNG AWARDS				
AL	Roger Clemens	New York	20-3 W-L, 0 SV, 3.64 ERA, $16.2 MIL	20-3 W-L, 0 SV, 3.51 ERA
NL	Randy Johnson	Arizona	21-6 W-L, 0 SV, 2.56 ERA, $23.8 MIL	21-6 W-L, 0 SV, 2.49 ERA

AMERICAN LEAGUE LEADERS

CAT.	PLAYER	TEAM	STATS ADJUSTED	ACTUAL
BATTING				
HR	Alex Rodriguez	Texas	51	52
RBI	Bret Boone	Seattle	146	141
BA	Ichiro Suzuki	Seattle	.357	.350
AB	Ichiro Suzuki	Seattle	692	692
R	Alex Rodriguez	Texas	138	133
H	Ichiro Suzuki	Seattle	247	242
2B	Jason Giambi	Oakland	46	47
3B	Cristian Guzman	Minnesota	14	14
TB	Alex Rodriguez	Texas	393	393
SA	Jason Giambi	Oakland	.660	.660
SB	Ichiro Suzuki	Seattle	61	56
PITCHING				
W	Mark Mulder	Oakland	21	21
L	Jose Mercedes	Baltimore	17	17
SV	Mariano Rivera	New York	50	50
ERA	Freddy Garcia	Seattle	3.16	3.05
G	Paul Quantrill	Toronto	80	80
IP	Freddy Garcia	Seattle	239	238.2
BB	Hideo Nomo	Boston	105	96
SO	Hideo Nomo	Boston	216	220

NATIONAL LEAGUE LEADERS

CAT.	PLAYER	TEAM	STATS ADJUSTED	ACTUAL
BATTING				
HR	Barry Bonds	San Francisco	72	73
RBI	Sammy Sosa	Chicago	166	160
BA	Larry Walker	Colorado	.356	.350
AB	Jimmy Rollins	Philadelphia	656	656
R	Sammy Sosa	Chicago	151	146
H	Rich Aurilia	San Francisco	210	206
2B	Lance Berkman	Houston	54	55
3B	Jimmy Rollins	Philadelphia	12	12
TB	Sammy Sosa	Chicago	425	425
SA	Barry Bonds	San Francisco	.863	.863
SB	Juan Pierre	Colorado	50	46
	Jimmy Rollins	Philadelphia	50	46
PITCHING				
W	Matt Morris	St. Louis	22	22
	Curt Schilling	Arizona	22	22
L	Bobby Jones	San Diego	19	19
SV	Robb Nen	San Francisco	45	45
ERA	Randy Johnson	Arizona	2.56	2.49
G	Steve Kline	St. Louis	89	89
IP	Curt Schilling	Arizona	257	256.2
BB	Ryan Dempster	Florida	123	112
SO	Randy Johnson	Arizona	367	372

3 ◯ The Best Performances

There are certain numbers so closely associated with baseball that they have become sacred. Mention the numbers 60, 61, 70, and 73 to a true fan, for instance, and he or she will instantly recognize them as the home-run records established, in turn, by Babe Ruth, Roger Maris, Mark McGwire, and Barry Bonds. Say 190, 511, or 755, and the same fan will envision Hack Wilson raising the bar for runs batted in, Cy Young piling up the most wins in history, or Hank Aaron setting the career standard for homers.

But these numbers, revered though they may be, are outmoded in the wake of the previous chapter. They have been replaced by a new series of adjusted numbers that are primed for immortality. Say goodbye to 73, 190, 511, and 755. Say hello to 94, 204, 579, and 1,157.

This chapter, in effect, is baseball's new record book, naming the top players in 20 categories – 12 for hitters, 8 for pitchers. You'll see rankings of the ten best single-season and career performances in each category, expressed in adjusted statistics. (Single-season records are confined to the modern era, 1901–2001. Career records cover everyone who has played in the majors since 1876.) You will also find a remnant of the old system, the ten career leaders in actual statistics.

The 20 categories flow in the same order as Chapter 2's annual summaries of individual leaders, beginning with home runs and ending with strikeouts. That means batters are up first, followed by pitchers. I'll conclude with a section on salaries, listing the players throughout history who would have warranted the highest pay in 2001 dollars.

BATTING RECORDS

The best place to start is to introduce the hitters who are baseball's new recordholders. Then we'll take a closer look at each category. Below are lists of the single-season batting records for the modern era and what I call the "expansion period." (I know the American League jumped the gun by expanding in 1961, but I date the expansion period to 1962, the first year that both leagues had new teams and a 162-game schedule.) The third list shows the career leaders in each category. All numbers, of course, have been adjusted to 1996–2000 performance levels.

SINGLE SEASON (MODERN ERA, 1901–2001)

Home runs: Babe Ruth (1921), 94
Runs batted in: Lou Gehrig (1931), 204
Batting average: Ty Cobb (1911), .425
Games played: Many players, 162
At bats: Woody Jensen (1936), 723
Runs scored: Babe Ruth (1921), 195
Hits: Nap Lajoie (1901), 273
Doubles: Nap Lajoie (1906), 138

Triples: Dale Mitchell (1949), 23
Total bases: Babe Ruth (1921), 513
Slugging average: Babe Ruth (1920), .971
Stolen bases: Maury Wills (1962), 180

Total bases: Jim Rice (1978), 456
Slugging average: Barry Bonds (2001), .863
Stolen bases: Maury Wills (1962), 180

SINGLE SEASON (EXPANSION PERIOD, 1962–2001)

Home runs: Barry Bonds (2001), 72
Runs batted in: Johnny Bench (1972), 174
Batting average: Roberto Clemente (1967), .398
Games played: Many players, 162
At bats: Willie Wilson (1980), 705
Runs scored: Joe Morgan (1972), 170
Hits: Matty Alou (1969), 251
Doubles: Lou Brock (1968), 77
Triples: Lance Johnson (1996), 22

CAREER

Home runs: Babe Ruth, 1,157
Runs batted in: Hank Aaron, 2,768
Batting average: Ty Cobb, .376
Games played: Pete Rose, 3,622
At bats: Pete Rose, 14,298
Runs scored: Ty Cobb, 2,792
Hits: Pete Rose, 4,606
Doubles: Cap Anson, 1,221
Triples: Roberto Clemente, 140
Total bases: Hank Aaron, 7,886
Slugging average: Babe Ruth, .757
Stolen bases: Rickey Henderson, 1,342

Home runs

Single season: America watched with interest in 2001 as Barry Bonds chased the single-season mark for home runs. That's all it was – interest. There wasn't the intensity that had existed three years earlier, when Mark McGwire and Sammy Sosa launched their joint attack on Roger Maris's seemingly immortal record of 61. McGwire hit 70 homers in 1998 – a temporary mark, as it turned out. Bonds passed him and pushed the actual record up to 73.

But Bonds isn't the dominant figure in this category. Nor is McGwire or Sosa or Maris. Babe Ruth is. Ruth smashed 59 home runs in 152 games in 1921, singlehandedly hitting one-eighth of the American League's 477 homers. (Bonds would have needed 369 to account for one-eighth of the National League's home runs in 2001.) Only two AL teams other than the Yankees topped Ruth's total in 1921. The Babe's output that season equals an adjusted figure of 94 home runs, the greatest performance by a slugger in a single year.

Ruth also ranks second with 91 adjusted homers in 1920, and third with 89 in 1927. He blasted at least 73 in eight different seasons between 1919 and 1928, an unprecedented decade of power.

Twenty-three batters have hit 70 adjusted home runs in a single season. They're all listed below.

Babe Ruth holds the record for home runs in a season with 94 in 1921. Bonds, McGwire, and Sosa have a long way to go.

HOME RUNS: SINGLE SEASON

PLAYER	YEAR	TEAM	ADJUSTED HR
Babe Ruth	1921	New York (A)	94
Babe Ruth	1920	New York (A)	91
Babe Ruth	1927	New York (A)	89
Lou Gehrig	1927	New York (A)	83
Jimmie Foxx	1932	Philadelphia (A)	82
Jimmie Foxx	1933	Philadelphia (A)	79
Babe Ruth	1928	New York (A)	78
Lou Gehrig	1931	New York (A)	76
Hank Greenberg	1938	Detroit (A)	76
Babe Ruth	1924	New York (A)	75
Babe Ruth	1919	Boston (A)	73
Babe Ruth	1923	New York (A)	73
Babe Ruth	1926	New York (A)	73
Jimmie Foxx	1938	Boston (A)	73
Rogers Hornsby	1922	St. Louis (N)	72
Lou Gehrig	1934	New York (A)	72
Ralph Kiner	1949	Pittsburgh (N)	72
Barry Bonds	2001	San Francisco (N)	72
Mark McGwire	1998	St. Louis (N)	71
Hack Wilson	1930	Chicago (N)	70
Lou Gehrig	1936	New York (A)	70
Ralph Kiner	1947	Pittsburgh (N)	70
Johnny Mize	1947	New York (N)	70

Career: Who else but the Babe? Ruth hit 734 adjusted home runs from 1919 through 1928, averaging an amazing 73 per season for a decade. Only five other players had more home runs in their lifetimes than Ruth did in that ten-year stretch. Toss in the rest of his career, and the Babe ended up with 1,157 adjusted homers, 210 ahead of anyone else. (His total in real life was 714.)

Second place belongs to Hank Aaron, holder of the actual record of 755 home runs. His 947 adjusted homers reflect the fact that he was an effective slugger during a period when pitchers generally had the upper hand. Four others are above 800 on the adjusted side: Willie Mays, Jimmie Foxx, Lou Gehrig, and Mel Ott.

The men who have hit at least 500 real-life home runs form an exclusive group. It has just 17 members, a number that balloons to 50 after career totals are adjusted. Everyone above the 500 threshold in adjusted or actual terms is listed below.

Hank Aaron plays second fiddle to the Bambino in career homers.

ADJUSTED HOME RUNS: CAREER

PLAYER	ADJUSTED HR	PLAYER	ADJUSTED HR
Babe Ruth	1,157	Andre Dawson	581
Hank Aaron	947	Honus Wagner	580
Willie Mays	834	Al Simmons	579
Jimmie Foxx	827	Joe DiMaggio	575
Lou Gehrig	810	Dan Brouthers	568
Mel Ott	802	Dave Kingman	567
Ted Williams	734	Billy Williams	563
Frank Robinson	731	Sam Crawford	558
Reggie Jackson	729	Johnny Mize	552
Mike Schmidt	709	Darrell Evans	537
Stan Musial	705	Jose Canseco	529
Harmon Killebrew	700	Tony Perez	528
Rogers Hornsby	670	Duke Snider	525
Mickey Mantle	666	Dwight Evans	520
Willie McCovey	654	Fred McGriff	520
Eddie Murray	651	Cal Ripken Jr.	520
Barry Bonds	643	Ken Griffey Jr.	518
Ernie Banks	639	Johnny Bench	517
Mark McGwire	639	Graig Nettles	516
Eddie Mathews	629	Hank Greenberg	515
Roger Connor	623	Jim Rice	514
Dave Winfield	618	Al Kaline	508
Willie Stargell	615	Goose Goslin	505
Carl Yastrzemski	599	Dale Murphy	504
Ty Cobb	587	Rafael Palmeiro	500

ACTUAL HOME RUNS: CAREER

PLAYER	ACTUAL HR
Hank Aaron	755
Babe Ruth	714
Willie Mays	660
Frank Robinson	586
Mark McGwire	583
Harmon Killebrew	573
Barry Bonds	567
Reggie Jackson	563
Mike Schmidt	548
Mickey Mantle	536
Jimmie Foxx	534
Ted Williams	521
Willie McCovey	521
Ernie Banks	512
Eddie Mathews	512
Mel Ott	511
Barry Bonds	643

Runs batted in

Single season: The ball was never livelier than in 1930. The combined batting average for all big leaguers was .296, the high-water mark in baseball history. Six National League teams posted averages above .300. It was the perfect year to set a hitting record, and that's what Hack Wilson did, driving in 190 runs for the Chicago Cubs. Five other players boasted more than 150 actual RBIs the same year.

The next season was a much different story. The game's brain trust apparently turned the intensity down a notch or two, taking away a bit of the ball's zip. The collective average slipped to .278, and the number of home runs dropped by almost 500. But Lou Gehrig seemed unaffected. The Yankee first baseman drove in 184 runs, nearly as many as Wilson the year before, even though conditions were considerably tougher. Gehrig's feat in 1931 translates to an adjusted total of 204 runs batted in, the only time a batter topped 200 adjusted RBIs in a single season.

Wilson remains among the top ten players on the list below. His 190 RBIs in 1930 equals 181 at current performance levels.

RUNS BATTED IN: SINGLE SEASON

PLAYER	YEAR	TEAM	ADJUSTED RBI
Lou Gehrig	1931	New York (A)	204
Hank Greenberg	1937	Detroit (A)	198
Jimmie Foxx	1933	Philadelphia (A)	196
Jimmie Foxx	1938	Boston (A)	196
Lou Gehrig	1927	New York (A)	191
Hank Greenberg	1935	Detroit (A)	189
Babe Ruth	1921	New York (A)	188
Jimmie Foxx	1932	Philadelphia (A)	186
Hack Wilson	1930	Chicago (N)	181
Babe Ruth	1931	New York (A)	181
Lou Gehrig	1934	New York (A)	181

Career: Adjustment makes no difference at the top of the career RBI standings. Hank Aaron holds first place with 2,297 actual runs batted in. He also leads the adjusted list with 2,768. Next comes Babe Ruth, second in both cases, trailing Aaron by 84 actual and 256 adjusted RBIs.

The top seven hitters in the adjusted rankings can also be found on the actual top ten list. Three players of fairly recent vintage move up to occupy eighth, ninth, and tenth places in adjusted RBIs: Carl Yastrzemski, Frank Robinson, and Dave Winfield.

Cap Anson slugged a career total of 2,498 RBIs. Gehrig, who had a great season in 1931, is nowhere to be found on the top-10 career list.

RUNS BATTED IN: CAREER

PLAYER	ADJUSTED RBI	PLAYER	ACTUAL RBI
Hank Aaron	2,768	Hank Aaron	2,297
Babe Ruth	2,512	Babe Ruth	2,213
Cap Anson	2,498	Lou Gehrig	1,995
Ty Cobb	2,407	Stan Musial	1,951
Stan Musial	2,294	Ty Cobb	1,937
Willie Mays	2,278	Jimmie Foxx	1,922
Eddie Murray	2,259	Eddie Murray	1,917
Carl Yastrzemski	2,245	Willie Mays	1,903
Frank Robinson	2,193	Cap Anson	1,879
Dave Winfield	2,163	Mel Ott	1,860

Batting average

Single season: Nap Lajoie set the bar extremely high at the dawn of the modern era. He rapped 232 hits in 544 at bats for the Philadelphia Athletics in 1901, giving him an actual batting average of .426. It remains the era's best real-life average a century later.

But Lajoie has to settle for second place on the adjusted single-season list. The edge goes to Ty Cobb, who batted .420 in 1911, a year not quite as congenial for hitters as 1901. (The combined batting average for all major leaguers was .266 in 1911, compared to .272 in 1901.) Cobb's adjusted average becomes .425, a tick ahead of Lajoie's .424.

Sixteen players (with more than 400 at bats) have posted adjusted batting averages of .400 or better since 1901. Cobb fills exactly half of those slots, eight. Ted Williams is the only hitter to qualify since 1920, with adjusted averages of .417 in 1941 and .407 in 1957.

BATTING AVERAGE: SINGLE SEASON

PLAYER	YEAR	TEAM	ADJUSTED BA
Ty Cobb	1911	Detroit (A)	.425
Nap Lajoie	1901	Philadelphia (A)	.424
Tris Speaker	1916	Cleveland (A)	.422
Ty Cobb	1909	Detroit (A)	.417
Ted Williams	1941	Boston (A)	.417
Ty Cobb	1910	Detroit (A)	.415
Nap Lajoie	1910	Cleveland (A)	.415
Ty Cobb	1917	Detroit (A)	.415
Joe Jackson	1911	Cleveland (A)	.414
Nap Lajoie	1904	Cleveland (A)	.411
Ty Cobb	1912	Detroit (A)	.411
Cy Seymour	1905	Cincinnati (N)	.410
Ty Cobb	1918	Detroit (A)	.407
Ted Williams	1957	Boston (A)	.407
Ty Cobb	1913	Detroit (A)	.406
Ty Cobb	1916	Detroit (A)	.405

Career: Ty Cobb is baseball's undisputed batting champion. His average for 24 seasons (1905–1928) was .366, climbing to .376 after adjustment. No one comes close to either number. Cobb is eight points ahead of the runner-

Ty Cobb is baseball's undisputed batting champion.

up in actual batting average and nineteen points ahead in adjusted average. (A player needed 7,500 actual or 8,000 adjusted at bats to be eligible for these rankings.)

The only other hitter above .350 in actual terms was Rogers Hornsby, who slips to an adjusted figure of .348. Three other batters crossed the .350 threshold on the adjusted list: Dan Brouthers, Ted Williams, and Nap Lajoie.

Two leading hitters of special interest to recent fans are Tony Gwynn, fifth with an adjusted lifetime average of .349, and Rod Carew, tied for eighth at .345. Neither qualified for the top ten in actual batting average.

BATTING AVERAGE: CAREER

PLAYER	ADJUSTED BA	PLAYER	ACTUAL BA
Ty Cobb	.376	Ty Cobb	.366
Dan Brouthers	.357	Rogers Hornsby	.358
Ted Williams	.355	Ed Delahanty	.346
Nap Lajoie	.351	Tris Speaker	.345
Tony Gwynn	.349	Ted Williams	.344
Tris Speaker	.348	Babe Ruth	.342
Rogers Hornsby	.348	Harry Heilmann	.342
Stan Musial	.345	Willie Keeler	.341
Rod Carew	.345	Lou Gehrig	.340
Cap Anson	.344	George Sisler	.340

Games played

Single season: The National League expanded from a 154-game schedule to a 162-game slate in 1962, but the Los Angeles Dodgers extended the season even further. They tied San Francisco for the National League title, forcing a three-game tiebreaker, which the Giants won. Shortstop Maury Wills played all 165 games for the Dodgers that year, setting the actual record for a single season.

There's no reason to list the adjusted leaders in this category. I converted every season to 162 games, so that's the maximum anyone could play. Wills, for example, is credited with 162 adjusted games in 1962.

Career: Pete Rose was a regular from the day that he joined the Cincinnati Reds in 1963 as a 22-year-old second baseman, appearing in 157 games that first season. He peaked at 163 games in 1974 and again in 1979, and he played 162 games six other years. The actual total at the end of his 24-year career was 3,562 games, the most in big-league history. The adjustment process tacked on another 60 games, mostly in seasons shortened by labor disputes, to boost Rose to 3,622.

The two runners-up, Carl Yastrzemski and Hank Aaron, hold the same positions in the actual and adjusted standings. The big gainer is Cap Anson, who starred for the Chicago Cubs, primarily at first base, from 1876 to 1897. Seasons ranged from 60 to 147 games during Anson's career. Converting each of those years to 162 games added 1,020 to his total. Anson appeared in 2,276 games in real life – well down in the rankings – but he soared to 3,296 on the adjusted list, good for fourth place.

GAMES PLAYED: CAREER

PLAYER	ADJUSTED GAMES	PLAYER	ACTUAL GAMES
Pete Rose	3,622	Pete Rose	3,562
Carl Yastrzemski	3,367	Carl Yastrzemski	3,308
Hank Aaron	3,357	Hank Aaron	3,298
Cap Anson	3,296	Ty Cobb	3,035
Ty Cobb	3,216	Eddie Murray	3,026
Stan Musial	3,151	Stan Musial	3,026
Eddie Murray	3,148	Cal Ripken Jr.	3,001
Rickey Henderson	3,084	Willie Mays	2,992
Cal Ripken Jr.	3,082	Rickey Henderson	2,979
Dave Winfield	3,068	Dave Winfield	2,973

At bats

Single season: A hitter needs three ingredients to get a large number of at bats: (1) He must play as many games as possible. (2) He can't draw many walks. (3) His team must hit well, affording him extra chances at the plate.

Willie Wilson, a left fielder with the Kansas City Royals, followed this recipe to perfection in 1980. He played all but one of his team's 162 games. He walked only 28 times all year, roughly once every six games. And the Royals posted a team batting average of .286, the highest in the majors that year. The result for Wilson was 705 at bats, which remains the actual big-league record.

But it's not the adjusted record. That belongs to Pittsburgh left fielder Woody Jensen, who racked up 696 at bats in 153 games (better than 4.5 per game) during the 1936 season, adjusting to 723 over a 162-game slate. Jensen had the necessary factors working in his favor. He missed just three games, he drew only sixteen walks, and the Pirates led the National League in runs scored and batting average.

Career: It's no surprise that nine of the ten lifetime leaders in actual games played are also among the ten leaders in actual career at bats.

Pete Rose holds the record in real life. He racked up 14,053 at bats in 3,562 games, the equivalent of 3.9 at bats per game for 24 years. Rose also heads the adjusted list, adding 245 to reach a total of 14,298 at bats.

Rose and Hank Aaron are the only players with more than 12,000 actual at bats. Five players are above 12,000 in the adjusted rankings: Rose, Cap Anson, Aaron, Carl Yastrzemski, and Ty Cobb.

AT BATS: SINGLE SEASON

PLAYER	YEAR	TEAM	ADJUSTED AB
Woody Jensen	1936	Pittsburgh (N)	723
Lloyd Waner	1931	Pittsburgh (N)	712
Doc Cramer	1938	Boston (A)	711
Jack Tobin	1921	St. Louis (A)	707
Jo-Jo Moore	1935	New York (N)	707
Al Simmons	1932	Philadelphia (A)	705
Willie Wilson	1980	Kansas City (A)	705
Willie Keeler	1901	Brooklyn (N)	704
Ginger Beaumont	1903	Pittsburgh (N)	704
Doc Cramer	1933	Philadelphia (A)	704

AT BATS: CAREER

PLAYER	ADJUSTED AB	PLAYER	ACTUAL AB
Pete Rose	14,298	Pete Rose	14,053
Cap Anson	13,359	Hank Aaron	12,364
Hank Aaron	12,593	Carl Yastrzemski	11,988
Carl Yastrzemski	12,206	Cal Ripken Jr.	11,551
Ty Cobb	12,123	Ty Cobb	11,434
Cal Ripken Jr.	11,842	Eddie Murray	11,336
Eddie Murray	11,810	Robin Yount	11,008
Jim O'Rourke	11,528	Dave Winfield	11,003
Stan Musial	11,432	Stan Musial	10,972
Dave Winfield	11,353	Willie Mays	10,881

Runs scored

Single season: A strong case could be made that no hitter has ever put up better numbers than Babe Ruth did in 1921. We already know that Ruth smashed 94 adjusted home runs that year, the single-season record, and had 188 adjusted RBIs, seventh-best on that list. He also set the all-time mark for total bases with 513, as we shall see later in this chapter.

The Babe dominated yet another category during that wondrous year. He scored 177 runs in 152 games, setting a real-life record that still stands more than eight decades later. It translates to 195 runs after adjustment, also a record. And right behind Ruth in the single-season rankings is … Ruth, who scored 189 adjusted runs the previous year, 1920. Ted Williams is again the only player since 1940 to qualify for the top ten, with 183 adjusted runs in 1942 and 182 in 1946.

RUNS SCORED: SINGLE SEASON

PLAYER	YEAR	TEAM	ADJUSTED R
Babe Ruth	1921	New York (A)	195
Babe Ruth	1920	New York (A)	189
Ty Cobb	1915	Detroit (A)	186
Ted Williams	1942	Boston (A)	183
Ted Williams	1946	Boston (A)	182
Babe Ruth	1928	New York (A)	181
Lou Gehrig	1931	New York (A)	180
Tommy Leach	1909	Pittsburgh (N)	177
Nap Lajoie	1901	Philadelphia (A)	174
Ginger Beaumont	1903	Pittsburgh (N)	174

Career: Sportswriters generally agreed that Rickey Henderson should have retired after the 2000 season. He was 42 years old, carrying the accumulated aches and pains from 22 seasons of big-league ball, and it seemed he had lost a step, maybe two. But Henderson persistently scouted for a new employer, landing in San Diego for his 23rd year in the majors. He came back for a simple reason. He was chasing records, including Ty Cobb's career mark for actual runs scored,

Rickey Henderson never really did break Cobb's career record for runs scored. With only 2,577 runs, he's still way behind the leaders.

which he passed in early October. The 2001 season ended with Henderson at 2,248 runs, Cobb at 2,246.

The adjusted list is an entirely different matter. Cobb, with 2,792 runs scored, is the unchallenged leader. He holds a solid margin of 133 over Pete Rose, who ranks second with 2,659. Then comes Hank Aaron at 2,620. Henderson is well back in fourth place, a distant 215 adjusted runs behind Cobb.

RUNS SCORED: CAREER

PLAYER	ADJUSTED R	PLAYER	ACTUAL R
Ty Cobb	2,792	Rickey Henderson	2,248
Pete Rose	2,659	Ty Cobb	2,246
Hank Aaron	2,620	Hank Aaron	2,174
Rickey Henderson	2,577	Babe Ruth	2,174
Willie Mays	2,477	Pete Rose	2,165
Babe Ruth	2,464	Willie Mays	2,062
Cap Anson	2,356	Stan Musial	1,949
Stan Musial	2,302	Lou Gehrig	1,888
Tris Speaker	2,298	Tris Speaker	1,882
Eddie Collins	2,243	Mel Ott	1,859

Hits

Single season: George Sisler hit everything that was pitched his way in 1920. He was in the zone, to use a current phrase, and he didn't leave it from April to September. The St. Louis Browns first baseman struck out just 19 times in 631 at bats. That was impressive enough, but even more amazing was Sisler's 257 hits, good for a .407 average. His hit total remains the actual single-season mark, and he accomplished it in just 154 games.

Sisler's feat is overshadowed by two others in the adjusted rankings. Nap Lajoie rapped out 232 hits for the Philadelphia A's in 1901. He appeared in 23 fewer games than Sisler, and he played under slightly tougher conditions, because the major-league batting average was .272 in 1901, compared to .277 in 1920. That's why Lajoie takes first place with an adjusted total of 273 hits. Ty Cobb edges into second place with 265 in 1911, followed by Sisler's adjusted figure for 1920, 264. Five other players had seasons at 250 or higher.

Two stars from the 1980s are among the leaders in this category. Wade Boggs sprayed 250 adjusted hits for the Red Sox in 1985, and Don Mattingly had 249 for the Yankees a year later.

HITS: SINGLE SEASON

PLAYER	YEAR	TEAM	ADJUSTED H
Nap Lajoie	1901	Philadelphia (A)	273
Ty Cobb	1911	Detroit (A)	265
George Sisler	1920	St. Louis (A)	264
Ty Cobb	1917	Detroit (A)	257
Jesse Burkett	1901	St. Louis (N)	256
Matty Alou	1969	Pittsburgh (N)	251
Stan Musial	1946	St. Louis (N)	250
Wade Boggs	1985	Boston (A)	250
Cy Seymour	1905	Cincinnati (N)	249
Lefty O'Doul	1929	Philadelphia (N)	249
Don Mattingly	1986	New York (A)	249

Career: Think back to 1985, when Pete Rose was closing in on Ty Cobb's career record for hits. Newspapers reminded us day after day that the magic number was 4,191, a mark that had stood since Cobb's retirement 57 years earlier. Rose broke it on September 11, 1985, slapping a single for hit 4,192. The game was stopped, and the Reds presented Rose with a red Corvette to mark the occasion. It bore the Ohio license plate PR 4192.

There's just one problem. Rose already held the real-life record that fateful night. Researchers

Pete Rose blows by Cap Anson's career record for hits.

4,606. Cobb (4,554) and Hank Aaron (4,097) are the only other batters above 4,000. Forty players rapped out at least 3,000 adjusted hits, and 24 did the same in actual play. All are listed below.

HITS: CAREER

PLAYER	ADJUSTED H	PLAYER	ACTUAL H
Pete Rose	4,606	Pete Rose	4,256
Cap Anson	4,593	Ty Cobb	4,189
Ty Cobb	4,554	Hank Aaron	3,771
Hank Aaron	4,097	Stan Musial	3,630
Stan Musial	3,940	Tris Speaker	3,514
Honus Wagner	3,820	Carl Yastrzemski	3,419
Jim O'Rourke	3,773	Honus Wagner	3,415
Tris Speaker	3,767	Paul Molitor	3,319
Carl Yastrzemski	3,692	Eddie Collins	3,315
Nap Lajoie	3,634	Willie Mays	3,283
Willie Mays	3,576	Eddie Murray	3,255
Eddie Collins	3,572	Nap Lajoie	3,242
Paul Molitor	3,534	Cal Ripken Jr.	3,184
Eddie Murray	3,493	George Brett	3,154
Roger Connor	3,479	Paul Waner	3,152
Jake Beckley	3,359	Robin Yount	3,142
Cal Ripken Jr.	3,358	Tony Gwynn	3,141
George Brett	3,345	Dave Winfield	3,110
Sam Crawford	3,338	Rod Carew	3,053
Robin Yount	3,323	Lou Brock	3,023
Tony Gwynn	3,322	Wade Boggs	3,010
Dave Winfield	3,321	Al Kaline	3,007
Willie Keeler	3,307	Roberto Clemente	3,000
Rod Carew	3,290	Rickey Henderson	3,000
Roberto Clemente	3,275		
Al Kaline	3,262		
Lou Brock	3,249		
Dan Brouthers	3,244		
Paul Waner	3,219		
Jesse Burkett	3,214		
Frank Robinson	3,207		
Rickey Henderson	3,204		
Wade Boggs	3,181		
Brooks Robinson	3,089		
Zack Wheat	3,083		
Harold Baines	3,051		
Sam Rice	3,033		
Rogers Hornsby	3,032		
John Ward	3,031		
Lave Cross	3,019		

have since revised Cobb's hit total to 4,189, the number now listed in *Total Baseball*. Rose is the only man ahead of him, with a final total of 4,256 actual hits.

Rose chased down a different leader on the adjusted list. Cap Anson held the record of 4,593 adjusted hits until Rose squeaked by him with

Doubles

Single season: The adjusted record in this category might be the hardest to believe in this book. Nap Lajoie, says the computer, drilled an adjusted total of 138 doubles for the Cleveland Indians in 1906. That's a two-base hit nearly every game, and it's more than double (pardon the weak pun) the actual record of 67, set by right fielder Earl Webb of the Boston Red Sox in 1931.

Let me explain. Lajoie hit an unusually large number of doubles in 1906, leading the majors with 48. Fully 22.4 percent of his 214 hits were two-baggers; the corresponding share for all other players that year was just 13.2 percent. Doubles occur more frequently in our lively era than in the dead-ball year of 1906, with 19.4 percent of all hits between 1996 and 2000 going for two bases. That means the number of doubles for a typical player from 1906 will climb considerably when adjusted to current standards. Lajoie's total, as you can imagine, soars sky-high.

A final quirk pushes Lajoie beyond the stratosphere. All extra-base hits are adjusted simultaneously, as explained in Chapter 1. Lajoie didn't hit any home runs in 1906, forcing the computer to split all of his extra-base hits between doubles and triples, slightly elevating each.

In 1906 Nap Lajoie hit an average of one double nearly every game he played

DOUBLES: SINGLE SEASON

PLAYER	YEAR	TEAM	ADJUSTED 2B
Nap Lajoie	1906	Cleveland (A)	138
Lave Cross	1902	Philadelphia (A)	119
Tris Speaker	1918	Cleveland (A)	116
Elmer Flick	1906	Cleveland (A)	89
Ty Cobb	1919	Detroit (A)	89
Lave Cross	1905	Philadelphia (A)	87
Jimmy Collins	1907	Bos.-Phi. (A)	85
Bobby Veach	1919	Detroit (A)	85
Dave Bancroft	1920	Phi.-N.Y. (N)	85
Ginger Beaumont	1902	Pittsburgh (N)	83
Tris Speaker	1915	Boston (A)	83
Sam Rice	1917	Washington (A)	83
Heinie Groh	1917	Cincinnati (N)	83

Career: Doubles are more common today than in the old days, as I noted above. The career totals for old-timers, as a result, are substantially higher on the adjusted side than on the actual ledger. The most extreme case is that of Cap Anson, who jumps from 528 actual two-base hits to 1,221 adjusted doubles. The latter is the highest figure in baseball history.

Six players blasted more than 1,000 adjusted doubles. All played in the 19th or early 20th century, except for Pete Rose, who ranks third with 1,094. No one in real life has hit more than the 792 doubles slapped by Tris Speaker from 1907 to 1928.

DOUBLES: CAREER

PLAYER	ADJUSTED 2B	PLAYER	ACTUAL 2B
Cap Anson	1,221	Tris Speaker	792
Tris Speaker	1,143	Pete Rose	746
Pete Rose	1,094	Stan Musial	725
Nap Lajoie	1,027	Ty Cobb	724
Ty Cobb	1,015	George Brett	665
Jim O'Rourke	1,001	Nap Lajoie	657
Stan Musial	903	Carl Yastrzemski	646
Sam Rice	876	Honus Wagner	640
Honus Wagner	872	Hank Aaron	624
Jake Beckley	843	Paul Molitor	605
		Paul Waner	605

Triples

Single season: Fans in the early 20th century usually saw a triple or two when they went to the ballpark. Their odds were best in 1912, when the average was 1.1 triples per game, with three-baggers accounting for 6.1 percent of all hits. The latter figure remains the highest in the modern era. It was fitting that Pittsburgh center fielder Chief Wilson set the actual single-season record the same year, 36 triples.

Times have changed. Fans hailed 1998 as the Year of the Homer, but it was also the worst season for triples in a century. The average was 0.4 per game in 1998, with just 2.0 percent of all hits being triples. It stands to reason, then, that adjusting old-timers' statistics to 1996–2000 performance levels will greatly reduce their totals in this category. Wilson's 1912 mark, for example, would be equal to just 10 three-base hits today.

The adjusted single-season mark belongs to Cleveland outfielder Dale Mitchell, who raced to 23 triples in 149 games for the 1949 Indians, playing in cavernous Municipal Stadium. Close on his heels was Lance Johnson, with 22 adjusted triples in 1996.

Career: Roberto Clemente had all the tools. The Pittsburgh right fielder hit for average (an adjusted .340 over eighteen seasons) and power (eight years with 20 or more adjusted homers), and he also had impressive speed. Proof of the latter was the 166 triples he hit from 1955 to 1972, 27th in the category's actual rankings.

But Clemente vaults all the way to first place when the list is converted to current standards. He winds up with 140 adjusted triples, 6 ahead of the runner-up, Sam Crawford, an outfielder for the Reds and Tigers between 1899 and 1917. Rounding out the top five are three stars from the

TRIPLES: SINGLE SEASON

PLAYER	YEAR	TEAM	ADJUSTED 3B
Dale Mitchell	1949	Cleveland (A)	23
Lance Johnson	1996	New York (N)	22
Eddie Collins	1916	Chicago (A)	21
Willie Wilson	1985	Kansas City (A)	21
Edd Roush	1916	N.Y.-Cin. (N)	20
Cristian Guzman	2000	Minnesota (A)	20
Tony Fernandez	1990	Toronto (A)	19
Lance Johnson	1994	Chicago (A)	19
Larry Bowa	1972	Philadelphia (N)	18
Roger Metzger	1973	Houston (N)	18
Gene Richards	1981	San Diego (N)	18

Roberto Clemente vaults to first place for career triples.

latter half of the 20th century: Pete Rose, Lou Brock, and George Brett.

Totals for players from the distant past were adjusted sharply downward, reflecting the declining frequency of the three-base hit. Crawford tops the actual list with 309 triples, the equivalent of just 134 today. Ty Cobb, second with 295 actual triples, falls to 121 in adjusted terms.

TRIPLES: CAREER

PLAYER	ADJUSTED 3B	PLAYER	ACTUAL 3B
Roberto Clemente	140	Sam Crawford	309
Sam Crawford	134	Ty Cobb	295
Pete Rose	129	Honus Wagner	252
Lou Brock	129	Jake Beckley	243
George Brett	124	Roger Connor	233
Willie Davis	123	Tris Speaker	222
Ty Cobb	121	Fred Clarke	220
Sam Rice	121	Dan Brouthers	205
Eddie Collins	121	Joe Kelley	194
Stan Musial	117	Paul Waner	191

Total bases

Single season: Babe Ruth again. The Bambino racked up 457 total bases for the Yankees during his unparalleled 1921 season, the product of 204 hits (including 59 home runs) in 152 games, setting an actual single-season record that remains today. His adjusted figures for 1921 are even better: 200 hits (94 homers among them) in 161 games. End result: 513 total bases, also a record.

Rogers Hornsby was the only other player with at least 450 actual total bases in a season. He reached precisely that many for the St. Louis Cardinals in 1922, ripping out 250 hits in 154 games, including 42 homers. His adjusted total climbed to 504, based on 246 hits (including 72 home runs). Two other batters topped 500 adjusted total bases in a single season: Lou Gehrig with 505 in 1927 and Stan Musial with 502 in 1948. Musial is the only player since 1940 to qualify for the adjusted top ten.

TOTAL BASES: SINGLE SEASON

PLAYER	YEAR	TEAM	ADJUSTED TB
Babe Ruth	1921	New York (A)	513
Lou Gehrig	1927	New York (A)	505
Rogers Hornsby	1922	St. Louis (N)	504
Stan Musial	1948	St. Louis (N)	502
Nap Lajoie	1901	Philadelphia (A)	493
Jimmie Foxx	1932	Philadelphia (A)	492
Jimmie Foxx	1933	Philadelphia (A)	487
George Sisler	1920	St. Louis (A)	483
Babe Ruth	1927	New York (A)	475
Chuck Klein	1932	Philadelphia (N)	471

Career: Hank Aaron endured intense media coverage as he chased Babe Ruth's lifetime home-run record in the early 1970s. All of America, it seemed, wanted to know if Aaron had the stuff to pass Ruth's mark of 714 homers, once considered unapproachable. The answer came on April 8, 1974, when Aaron lofted career homer 715 over the left-center-field fence in Atlanta.

That day stood in stark contrast to another event two years earlier. Aaron received scant publicity in 1972 when he passed Stan Musial for first place in career total bases, easily as impressive a feat as becoming the home-run king.

He ended his 23-year career with 6,856 actual total bases, 722 ahead of Musial's 6,134. Willie Mays, at 6,066, is the only other player above 6,000 on the actual list.

Aaron also tops the adjusted rankings with 7,886 total bases, coming from 2,277 singles, 798 doubles, 75 triples, and 947 home runs. Also above 7,000 are Ty Cobb, Cap Anson, and Musial.

TOTAL BASES: CAREER

PLAYER	ADJUSTED TB	PLAYER	ACTUAL TB
Hank Aaron	7,886	Hank Aaron	6,856
Ty Cobb	7,572	Stan Musial	6,134
Cap Anson	7,429	Willie Mays	6,066
Stan Musial	7,192	Ty Cobb	5,854
Willie Mays	6,965	Babe Ruth	5,793
Babe Ruth	6,790	Pete Rose	5,752
Pete Rose	6,690	Carl Yastrzemski	5,539
Honus Wagner	6,618	Eddie Murray	5,397
Tris Speaker	6,447	Frank Robinson	5,373
Carl Yastrzemski	6,397	Dave Winfield	5,221

Slugging average

Single season: The press made sure that fans were fully informed about Barry Bonds's assault on the single-season home-run record in 2001. Cable sports channels interrupted regular programming to cover each of his plate appearances live. Newspapers published daily boxes showing how he stacked up against Mark McGwire's 1998 pace. But no one noticed that the San Francisco left fielder was on his way to breaking another record that was considerably more durable than McGwire's 70 homers. Bonds finished the year with an actual slugging percentage of .863, based on 411 total bases in 476 at bats. He topped a mark that had stood for eight decades, Babe Ruth's .847 slugging average in 1920.

Ruth was the undisputed monarch in this category before Bonds came along. He not only set the 1920 mark, but also held the next two positions in the actual rankings, .846 in 1921 and .772 in 1927. No one (with 400 or more at bats) other than Ruth and Bonds has slugged higher than .765 in any season since 1901.

Ruth's adjusted numbers are even more amazing. His performance in 1920 translates to a slugging average of .971, based on 467 total bases

in 481 at bats. The Babe owns three of the five best performances on the adjusted list – and seven of the 10 best – affirming his status as the game's greatest power hitter. Bonds and Ted Williams, who slugged an adjusted .838 in 1941, are the only players to qualify for the top 10 after 1933.

SLUGGING AVERAGE: SINGLE SEASON

PLAYER	YEAR	TEAM	ADJUSTED SA
Babe Ruth	1920	New York (A)	.971
Babe Ruth	1921	New York (A)	.897
Barry Bonds	2001	San Francisco (N)	.863
Babe Ruth	1927	New York (A)	.841
Ted Williams	1941	Boston (A)	.838
Babe Ruth	1923	New York (A)	.835
Lou Gehrig	1927	New York (A)	.828
Babe Ruth	1926	New York (A)	.813
Babe Ruth	1919	Boston (A)	.807
Babe Ruth	1924	New York (A)	.800
Jimmie Foxx	1932	Philadelphia (A)	.800

Career: Only five individuals were responsible for the best single-season slugging averages on the list immediately above: Babe Ruth, Ted Williams, Lou Gehrig, Jimmie Foxx, and Barry Bonds. So it comes as no surprise that the same men hold the top five positions in the

Barry Bonds (above) and Ted Williams are the only players after 1933 to make the top 10 for single season slugging average.

actual career rankings. All but Bonds are at the head of the adjusted list, as well. (A player needed 7,500 actual at bats or 8,000 adjusted at bats to be eligible.)

At the top, naturally, is Ruth, who finished 56 points ahead of the runner-up on the actual list. The Babe reached 5,793 total bases in just 8,399 at bats, yielding a slugging average of .690. His adjusted figures are even more impressive, hinting at the havoc he would wreak against today's pitchers: 6,790 total bases in 8,964 at bats, equaling a .757 slugging average.

Williams ranks second on both sides, with actual and adjusted career averages of .634 and .707, respectively. The latter puts him with Ruth as the only members of baseball's .700 slugging club.

SLUGGING AVERAGE: CAREER

PLAYER	ADJUSTED SA	PLAYER	ACTUAL SA
Babe Ruth	.757	Babe Ruth	.690
Ted Williams	.707	Ted Williams	.634
Lou Gehrig	.676	Lou Gehrig	.632
Jimmie Foxx	.659	Jimmie Foxx	.609
Rogers Hornsby	.643	Barry Bonds	.585
Dan Brouthers	.641	Rogers Hornsby	.577
Stan Musial	.629	Stan Musial	.559
Hank Aaron	.626	Willie Mays	.557
Willie Mays	.626	Mickey Mantle	.557
Ty Cobb	.625	Hank Aaron	.555

Stolen bases

Single season: Maury Wills demonstrated a rare combination of blazing speed and baserunning savvy from the moment he joined the Los Angeles Dodgers in 1959. The fleet shortstop stole a total of 92 bases his first three years, leading the National League twice. But Wills turned on his afterburners in 1962, pilfering 104 bases, the first time anyone in the modern era had reached

triple digits in a single season. (No other team in baseball had more than 99 steals that year.) He was named the NL's Most Valuable Player. Wills's adjusted total in 1962 was an astounding 180 stolen bases, an average of more than one per game.

Wills's real-life record slipped into other hands long ago. The current single-season

Maury Wills still holds the record for stolen bases in a season with 180 (an average of over one per game) set in 1962.

Career: Rickey Henderson might best be compared to the Energizer bunny; he keeps running and running and running. Henderson crossed the 100-steal threshold in three different seasons, peaking at 130 in 1982, and he grabbed at least 50 stolen bases ten other times. He amassed 1,395 actual stolen bases while playing for seven teams during a 23-year career. That's an average of 61 steals each and every season.

Henderson, as a result, has an enormous lead in the actual rankings, 457 steals ahead of runner-up Lou Brock. But the gap nearly vanishes in the adjusted standings, where Henderson has 1,342 stolen bases and Brock has 1,285. Maury Wills didn't make the top ten in actual steals, primarily because he played just fourteen seasons, but his 988 adjusted stolen bases vault him into third place. Rounding out the top five are two other shortstops who helped bring basestealing back into vogue between the mid-fifties and the mid-seventies, Luis Aparicio and Bert Campaneris.

champ is Rickey Henderson, with 130 actual steals for Oakland in 1982. But no one has come close in the adjusted rankings. Wills not only stands first with 180, but he also ranks second with 151 steals in 1965. No other player has more than 131.

STOLEN BASES: SINGLE SEASON

PLAYER	YEAR	TEAM	ADJUSTED SB
Maury Wills	1962	Los Angeles (N)	180
Maury Wills	1965	Los Angeles (N)	151
Lou Brock	1974	St. Louis (N)	131
Luis Aparicio	1959	Chicago (A)	122
Rickey Henderson	1982	Oakland (A)	122
Lou Brock	1966	St. Louis (N)	116
George Case	1943	Washington (A)	114
Snuffy Stirnweiss	1944	New York (A)	113
Luis Aparicio	1964	Baltimore (A)	111
Ben Chapman	1931	New York (A)	107

STOLEN BASES: CAREER

PLAYER	ADJUSTED SB	PLAYER	ACTUAL SB
Rickey Henderson	1,342	Rickey Henderson	1,395
Lou Brock	1,285	Lou Brock	938
Maury Wills	988	Billy Hamilton	912
Luis Aparicio	958	Ty Cobb	892
Bert Campaneris	871	Tim Raines	808
Joe Morgan	826	Vince Coleman	752
Tim Raines	778	Eddie Collins	744
Vince Coleman	704	Arlie Latham	739
George Case	685	Max Carey	738
Max Carey	673	Honus Wagner	722

PITCHING RECORDS

It's time to turn our attention to the pitchers. Here are the single-season pitching recordholders for the modern era and the expansion period, followed by the career leaders in each category. All statistics have been adjusted to 1996–2000 performance levels.

SINGLE SEASON (MODERN ERA, 1901–2001)

Wins: Jack Chesbro (1904) and Ed Walsh (1908), 42

Losses: Dummy Taylor (1901), 31

Saves: Bobby Thigpen (1990), 55

Earned run average: Dutch Leonard (1914), 1.52

Games pitched: Mike Marshall (1974), 106

Innings pitched: Joe McGinnity (1903), 497

Walks allowed: Bill Donovan (1901), 258

Strikeouts: Rube Waddell (1904), 559

SINGLE SEASON (EXPANSION PERIOD, 1962–2001)

Wins: Denny McLain (1968), 31

Losses: Roger Craig (1962), 24

Saves: Bobby Thigpen (1990), 55

Earned run average: Greg Maddux (1994), 1.58

Games pitched: Mike Marshall (1974), 106

Innings pitched: Wilbur Wood (1972), 400

Walks allowed: Nolan Ryan (1977), 225

Strikeouts: Nolan Ryan (1973), 454

CAREER

Wins: Cy Young, 579

Losses: Jim Galvin, 477

Saves: Lee Smith, 498

Earned run average: Ed Walsh, 2.93

Games pitched: Jesse Orosco, 1,159

Innings pitched: Jim Galvin, 9,159

Walks allowed: Mickey Welch, 3,292

Strikeouts: Nolan Ryan, 6,870

Wins

Single season: If anyone had suggested a four-man rotation a century ago, most managers would have chuckled. The idea of a five-man rotation would have moved them to hysterical laughter. A big-league team relied on just two or three pitchers back then. Starters were supposed to finish what they began. And they were expected to pitch often, admittedly an easier task in the age of the dead ball than it would be today.

Jack Chesbro was considered a workhorse even in that heyday of workhorses. He started 51 games in 1904 – a third of the Yankees' entire schedule – and completed 48. He pitched almost 455 innings. This extra work, of course, allowed old-timers to figure in more decisions than today's pitchers can with their five-day schedules. Chesbro won 41 games for New York in 1904, making him the only pitcher in the modern era to register more than 40 actual wins in a single season. His adjusted total of 42 victories, also a record, was tied in 1908 by Ed Walsh of the Chicago White Sox.

Everyone on the list below pitched in the first two decades of the 20th century. The most recent was Walter Johnson, with 38 adjusted wins in 1913.

Career: The accepted standard for career excellence is 300 wins. Just 20 pitchers in history have reached that magic figure, and all are in the Hall of Fame. Two of today's star hurlers, Roger Clemens and Greg Maddux, have a shot at joining this elite group during the next couple of years. No one else is close.

That's why Cy Young's statistics are so amazing. Young picked up 300 victories with relative ease and just kept going, amassing 511 actual wins between 1890 and 1911. If a current pitcher were to win 22 games for 20 straight years, he would still fall 71 wins short of Young's mark. The odds against getting even that far, of course, are astronomical.

Young stands 94 victories ahead of the runner-up, fireballer Walter Johnson, who posted 417 actual wins for the Washington Senators. Then come two legends with 373 each, Pete Alexander and Christy Mathewson.

The adjusted standings are much closer, thanks to sharp upward revisions for several starters from the 19th century. (Schedules were considerably shorter in baseball's early years. Victory totals consequently soar when converted to a 162-game slate.) Young remains the leader with 579 adjusted wins, but Jim Galvin (1879–1892) is close behind with 556. Everyone with at least 300 wins, actual or adjusted, is listed below.

WINS: SINGLE SEASON

PLAYER	YEAR	TEAM	ADJUSTED W
Jack Chesbro	1904	New York (A)	42
Ed Walsh	1908	Chicago (A)	42
Cy Young	1901	Boston (A)	38
Cy Young	1902	Boston (A)	38
Christy Mathewson	1908	New York (N)	38
Walter Johnson	1913	Washington (A)	38
Joe McGinnity	1903	New York (N)	36
Joe McGinnity	1904	New York (N)	36
Joe Wood	1912	Boston (A)	36
Walter Johnson	1912	Washington (A)	35

Jim Galvin follows right on the heels of Cy Young for career wins with 556.

WINS: CAREER

PLAYER	ADJUSTED W	PLAYER	ACTUAL W
Cy Young	579	Cy Young	511
Jim Galvin	556	Walter Johnson	417
Tim Keefe	482	Pete Alexander	373
Charley Radbourn	464	Christy Mathewson	373
Mickey Welch	454	Warren Spahn	363
Jim McCormick	447	Jim Galvin	361
Walter Johnson	443	Kid Nichols	361
Kid Nichols	417	Tim Keefe	342
John Clarkson	412	Steve Carlton	329
Christy Mathewson	393	John Clarkson	328
Pete Alexander	392	Eddie Plank	326
Tony Mullane	387	Nolan Ryan	324
Warren Spahn	378	Don Sutton	324
Eddie Plank	350	Phil Niekro	318
Steve Carlton	337	Gaylord Perry	314
Nolan Ryan	330	Tom Seaver	311
Don Sutton	330	Charley Radbourn	309
Phil Niekro	323	Mickey Welch	307
Gaylord Perry	319	Lefty Grove	300
Tom Seaver	319	Early Wynn	300
Lefty Grove	317		
Early Wynn	314		
Gus Weyhing	306		

Losses

Single season: The modern era has had several 30-game winners (most recently Denny McLain with the 1968 Detroit Tigers), but it has never seen a 30-game loser. Vic Willis of the Boston Braves came closest, setting the real-life record for hard luck with 29 defeats in 1905. (Willis deserves credit for tenacity, if nothing else. He kept taking the mound despite the mounting losses. He started 41 games that season, completing 36.)

But the 30-loss threshold is unable to withstand the power of statistical adjustment. Luther Taylor, better known by the endearing nickname of Dummy, pitched 45 games for the 1901 New York Giants, winning 18 and losing 27. The latter translates to an adjusted total of 31

losses, the single-season record. Willis's 1905 mark works out to 30 adjusted defeats, making him the only other member of a rare, undesirable club.

LOSSES: SINGLE SEASON

PLAYER	YEAR	TEAM	ADJUSTED L
Dummy Taylor	1901	New York (N)	31
Vic Willis	1905	Boston (N)	30
Pete Dowling	1901	Mil.-Cle. (A)	29
Patsy Flaherty	1903	Chicago (A)	29
Paul Derringer	1933	St.L.-Cin. (N)	29
George Bell	1910	Brooklyn (N)	28
Happy Townsend	1904	Washington (A)	27
Gus Dorner	1906	Cin.-Bos. (N)	27
Irv Young	1906	Boston (N)	27
Bob Groom	1909	Washington (A)	27

Dummy Taylor pitched a heartbreaking 31 losses in 1901.

Career: Every dedicated fan knows that Cy Young holds the lifetime record for wins. But who owns the mark for losses? Probably some unfortunate soul who suffered through a painfully frustrating career, only to be condemned to perpetual obscurity.

Wrong. He was actually a successful, familiar star: Cy Young.

Young won 511 games, to be sure, but he appeared in 906, starting almost all of them. That left plenty of room for defeats, and he stacked up 316. The only other pitcher above 300 is Jim Galvin, who pitched for fourteen seasons before the modern era. Nolan Ryan is third with 292 actual defeats.

Galvin vaults into the lead after adjustment. He ends up with 477 adjusted losses, nearly 100 more than the runner-up, Jim McCormick, another veteran of baseball's prehistoric days. Young is third with 355 adjusted defeats.

LOSSES: CAREER

PLAYER	ADJUSTED L	PLAYER	ACTUAL L
Jim Galvin	477	Cy Young	316
Jim McCormick	378	Jim Galvin	308
Cy Young	355	Nolan Ryan	292
Tim Keefe	336	Walter Johnson	279
Mickey Welch	320	Phil Niekro	274
Tony Mullane	297	Gaylord Perry	265
Nolan Ryan	295	Don Sutton	256
Walter Johnson	294	Jack Powell	254
Charley Radbourn	284	Eppa Rixey	251
Phil Niekro	279	Bert Blyleven	250
Jack Powell	279		

Saves

Single season: Welcome to the newest category in this chapter. Baseball didn't adopt the save as an official statistic until 1969. Researchers subsequently filled in the blanks, calculating saves for every game back to the 19th century. Not that it mattered. All of the single-season leaders have pitched since 1980. These specialists, who rarely worked more than an inning a night, are known in today's vernacular as closers.

The all-time mark was set by Bobby Thigpen, who picked up 57 actual saves for the 1990 White Sox, which means he closed nearly 61 percent of Chicago's 94 wins. Thigpen's adjusted total for the same year was 55 saves, topping those standings as well.

The oldest performance among the top ten was Dan Quisenberry's 46 adjusted saves in 1983. Clay Carroll rang up the highest total before 1980: 44 adjusted saves for the Reds in

1972. The recordholder prior to 1950 was one of the pioneer relief specialists, Washington's Firpo Marberry, with 40 adjusted saves in 1926.

SAVES: SINGLE SEASON

PLAYER	YEAR	TEAM	ADJUSTED SV
Bobby Thigpen	1990	Chicago (A)	55
Randy Myers	1993	Chicago (N)	52
Jose Mesa	1995	Cleveland (A)	52
Trevor Hoffman	1998	San Diego (N)	52
Dennis Eckersley	1992	Oakland (A)	50
Mariano Rivera	2001	New York (A)	50
Lee Smith	1994	Baltimore (A)	48
Dan Quisenberry	1983	Kansas City (A)	46
Bruce Sutter	1984	St. Louis (N)	46
Dave Righetti	1986	New York (A)	46
Dennis Eckersley	1990	Oakland (A)	46

Career: Old-timers dominate the career rankings in most categories, but not here. All of the leaders in both actual and adjusted saves are still alive.

Topping both lists is Lee Smith, who worked out of the bullpen for eight teams from 1980 to 1997. He piled up 478 actual saves, translating to 498 after adjustment. Smith's frequent changes of venue didn't impair his ability to come through in the clutch. He picked up at least 30 adjusted saves in ten different seasons, peaking at 48 for the Orioles in 1994.

Two other relievers – John Franco and Rollie Fingers – are above 400 on the adjusted list. Fingers experienced the sharpest increase of any of the category's leaders, climbing 24 percent from 341 actual to 422 adjusted saves.

SAVES: CAREER

PLAYER	ADJUSTED SV	PLAYER	ACTUAL SV
Lee Smith	498	Lee Smith	478
John Franco	435	John Franco	422
Rollie Fingers	422	Dennis Eckersley	390
Dennis Eckersley	397	Jeff Reardon	367
Jeff Reardon	377	Randy Myers	347
Randy Myers	357	Rollie Fingers	341
Rich Gossage	347	John Wetteland	330
Bruce Sutter	343	Rick Aguilera	318
John Wetteland	340	Trevor Hoffman	314
Rick Aguilera	326	Tom Henke	311

Earned run average

Single season: Dutch Leonard was a decent pitcher. He managed to stick around for 11 years with the Red Sox and Tigers, picking up 139 wins. He wasn't a Hall of Famer by any means, but he did fit comfortably into the second or third slot in the rotation, keeping most games close and winning a few more than he lost.

But there was one golden season when Leonard transcended his usual station in life. He pitched 225 innings for the Red Sox in 1914, putting up a dazzling 19–5 record and an earned run average that could only be called superhuman: 0.96. No other pitcher who worked at least 150 innings in a single season has ever posted an actual ERA below 1.00. Leonard himself would never again get below 2.17.

Leonard's adjusted earned run average for 1914 is considerably higher, of course, because offensive firepower was weaker in that dead-ball season than in the baseline period of 1996–2000, yet it also ranks as the best ever. Leonard's adjusted 1.52 edges Greg Maddux's 1.58 for the Atlanta Braves in 1994. Two current pitchers hold third and fourth place: Pedro Martinez in 2000 and Maddux again in 1995.

EARNED RUN AVERAGE: SINGLE SEASON

PLAYER	YEAR	TEAM	ADJUSTED ERA
Dutch Leonard	1914	Boston (A)	1.52
Greg Maddux	1994	Atlanta (N)	1.58
Pedro Martinez	2000	Boston (A)	1.66
Greg Maddux	1995	Atlanta (N)	1.69
Walter Johnson	1913	Washington (A)	1.70
Bob Gibson	1968	St. Louis (N)	1.71
Mordecai Brown	1906	Chicago (N)	1.78
Dwight Gooden	1985	New York (N)	1.79
Walter Johnson	1912	Washington (A)	1.86
Kevin Brown	1996	Florida (N)	1.89

Career: Several of baseball's early pitching stars boasted earned run averages that were breathtaking. Foremost among them was Ed Walsh, one of the original iron men, who worked 1,765 innings for the White Sox in a five-year period, 1906 to 1910. His worst ERA for any season in that period was 1.88. His actual ERA for his entire career was in the same ballpark, 1.82, encompassing fourteen seasons and 430 games. It remains the lowest in history. (A pitcher needed 1,900 actual innings or 2,000 adjusted innings to be eligible for these rankings.)

But don't forget that baseball has changed drastically since Walsh's time. The typical big-league game in 1908 saw only 6.77 runs by both teams; the average for 2000 was half-again as high, 10.28 per game. The adjustment process, as a result, substantially elevates earned run averages from the early years of the modern era. Walsh's career ERA climbs more than a full point to 2.93, still very impressive and still, in fact, the best ever.

Rounding out the adjusted top five are two other pitchers from the early 20th century (Walter Johnson and Addie Joss), one of the greatest relievers of all time (Hoyt Wilhelm), and one of today's top starters (Greg Maddux).

EARNED RUN AVERAGE: CAREER

PLAYER	ADJUSTED ERA	PLAYER	ACTUAL ERA
Ed Walsh	2.93	Ed Walsh	1.82
Walter Johnson	3.00	Addie Joss	1.89
Greg Maddux	3.05	Mordecai Brown	2.06
Hoyt Wilhelm	3.08	John Ward	2.10
Addie Joss	3.14	Christy Mathewson	2.13
Carl Hubbell	3.25	Rube Waddell	2.16
Dizzy Dean	3.27	Walter Johnson	2.17
Whitey Ford	3.27	Tommy Bond	2.25
Mordecai Brown	3.30	Ed Reulbach	2.28
Pete Alexander	3.31	Will White	2.28

Games pitched

Single season: This is a category where adjusted and actual numbers rarely differ much, if at all. The workhorse reliever became common only after the debut of the 162-game schedule, so adjustment usually doesn't change a pitcher's number of games. (The rare exception is a strike year such as 1981 or 1994, when adjusted games are substantially higher than actual ones.)

Mike Marshall easily tops both the actual and adjusted rankings with 106 appearances for the Los Angeles Dodgers in 1974. Marshall worked 208 innings, running up a 15–12 record and an adjusted total of 39 saves. He won the National League's Cy Young Award that year.

GAMES PITCHED: SINGLE SEASON

PLAYER	YEAR	TEAM	ADJUSTED G
Mike Marshall	1974	Los Angeles (N)	106
Kent Tekulve	1979	Pittsburgh (N)	93
Mike Marshall	1973	Montreal (N)	92
Kent Tekulve	1978	Pittsburgh (N)	92
Mike Marshall	1979	Minnesota (A)	90
Kent Tekulve	1987	Philadelphia (N)	90
Wayne Granger	1969	Cincinnati (N)	89
Mark Eichhorn	1987	Toronto (A)	89
Julian Tavarez	1997	San Francisco (N)	89
Steve Kline	2001	St. Louis (N)	89

Career: The four leaders on the adjusted and actual lists are identical. Jesse Orosco, Dennis Eckersley, Hoyt Wilhelm, and Kent Tekulve won fame as relievers, though Eckersley also spent twelve years as a starter and Wilhelm handled a few dozen starts himself. Each of the four pitched at least 1,050 actual games.

Orosco tops both rankings with 1,131 actual and 1,159 adjusted appearances. He added 24 games when 1994 and 1995, both shortened by labor problems, were converted to 162-game slates. And he picked up four other adjusted appearances along the way in his 22-year career.

The sharpest increases were recorded by men who pitched in baseball's early years, when schedules were substantially shorter. Jim Galvin and Cy Young both vaulted past 1,000 games and into the top ten after adjustment.

GAMES PITCHED: CAREER

PLAYER	ADJUSTED G	PLAYER	ACTUAL G
Jesse Orosco	1,159	Jesse Orosco	1,131
Dennis Eckersley	1,111	Dennis Eckersley	1,071
Hoyt Wilhelm	1,094	Hoyt Wilhelm	1,070
Kent Tekulve	1,076	Kent Tekulve	1,050
Jim Galvin	1,073	Lee Smith	1,022
Lee Smith	1,068	Rich Gossage	1,002
Rich Gossage	1,036	John Franco	998
John Franco	1,024	Lindy McDaniel	987
Cy Young	1,021	Dan Plesac	946
Lindy McDaniel	1,001	Rollie Fingers	944

Innings pitched

Single season: It's easy to see why Joe McGinnity was known as "Iron Man" McGinnity. He started and won both ends of three different doubleheaders for the New York Giants in 1903, going the distance in all six of those games. McGinnity topped the majors that year by pitching 434 innings, more than one-third of all innings the Giants played. His adjusted total climbs to 497 innings, the all-time record, after the Giants' 142-game season is converted to a 162-game schedule.

White Sox ace Ed Walsh, no slouch himself in the workhorse department, set the real-life mark with 464 innings pitched in 1908. But Walsh had the luxury of several extra games to set the record; the Sox took the field 156 times that year. His adjusted total is 485 innings, 12 behind McGinnity.

It comes as no surprise that the top ten consists solely of hurlers from the first decade of the modern era, when starters routinely worked 100 to 150 innings more than they do today. Wilbur Wood, a White Sox knuckleballer, is the only pitcher to join the 400 club since 1918. He pitched precisely 400 adjusted innings in 1972.

INNINGS PITCHED: SINGLE SEASON

PLAYER	YEAR	TEAM	ADJUSTED IP
Joe McGinnity	1903	New York (N)	497
Ed Walsh	1908	Chicago (A)	485
Jack Chesbro	1904	New York (A)	471
Vic Willis	1902	Boston (N)	466
Joe McGinnity	1901	Baltimore (A)	462
Cy Young	1902	Boston (A)	453
Ed Walsh	1907	Chicago (A)	437
Cy Young	1901	Boston (A)	432
Noodles Hahn	1901	Cincinnati (N)	429
Joe McGinnity	1904	New York (N)	416

Career: Cy Young started more games (815) and completed more starts (749) than any pitcher in major-league history. It was virtually inevitable that he would also end up with the most innings

The appropriately nicknamed Joe "Iron Man" McGinnity pitched 497 innings in 1903.

The two leaders swap positions on the adjusted list. Galvin takes the lead with 9,159 innings, while Young is second with 8,281. Galvin was incredibly durable, to be sure, completing 639 of his 681 starts in real life. But his innings pitched grew 54 percent primarily because seasons were much shorter in his day (1879–1892) than they are now. Adjusting Galvin's career to conform with a 162-game schedule added more than 3,200 innings to his total.

INNINGS PITCHED: CAREER

PLAYER	ADJUSTED IP	PLAYER	ACTUAL IP
Jim Galvin	9,159	Cy Young	7,356
Cy Young	8,281	Jim Galvin	5,941
Jim McCormick	7,380	Walter Johnson	5,914
Tim Keefe	7,246	Phil Niekro	5,404
Mickey Welch	7,144	Nolan Ryan	5,386
Charley Radbourn	6,716	Gaylord Perry	5,350
Walter Johnson	6,261	Don Sutton	5,282
Tony Mullane	6,135	Warren Spahn	5,244
Kid Nichols	5,817	Steve Carlton	5,217
John Clarkson	5,675	Pete Alexander	5,190

pitched, which he did. Young's actual lifetime total of 7,356 puts him 1,415 innings (the equivalent of 157 games) ahead of the runner-up, Jim Galvin.

Walks allowed

Single season: Bob Feller intimidated hitters from the first pitch he fired in the major leagues. One reason was his blazing speed; the Cleveland righty deserved his nickname of "Rapid Robert." The other was his lack of familiarity with the strike zone, which kept opponents nice and loose in the batter's box.

Feller struck out 240 hitters for the Indians in 1938, leading the majors at the age of 19. But he walked almost as many, 208, which remains the actual record to this day. The typical big-league pitcher dealt 3.6 walks per nine innings that year. Feller's ratio was almost twice as high:

6.7 per nine innings. (Feller soon got himself under control. He was impressively efficient by 1946, striking out 348 batters, more than twice the 153 he walked.)

But Feller's 1938 performance is merely eighth on the adjusted list, where it translates to 222 walks. First place – and the distinction of being the pitcher with the worst control in a single year – goes to Bill Donovan, with 258 adjusted walks for Brooklyn in 1901. He, like Feller, carried an appropriate nickname: "Wild Bill," of course.

WALKS ALLOWED: SINGLE SEASON

PLAYER	YEAR	TEAM	ADJUSTED BB
Bill Donovan	1901	Brooklyn (N)	258
Togie Pittinger	1903	Boston (N)	245
Togie Pittinger	1904	Boston (N)	242
Elmer Myers	1916	Philadelphia (A)	225
Nolan Ryan	1977	California (A)	225
Chick Fraser	1905	Boston (N)	224
Chick Fraser	1901	Philadelphia (A)	223
Bob Feller	1938	Cleveland (A)	222
Nolan Ryan	1974	California (A)	219
Bump Hadley	1932	Chi.-St.L. (A)	212

Career: The parallels between Bob Feller and Nolan Ryan are obvious. Both arrived in the majors with outstanding speed and questionable control, though both eventually improved their strikeout-to-walk ratios. Feller owned the career record for walks (1,764) when he retired in 1956, but Ryan put that mark in the shadows with his final actual total of 2,795.

There were two reasons why Ryan passed Feller by such a large margin. He was slightly wilder, giving up 4.7 walks per nine innings over his career, compared to Feller's lifetime ratio of 4.1 per nine innings. And he stuck around much longer, pitching in 237 more games and 1,559 more innings than Feller did.

But Ryan and Feller give way to a couple of old-timers in the adjusted rankings. The leader is Mickey Welch, who delivered 3,292 adjusted walks for the Troy Trojans (remember them?) and New York Giants between 1880 and 1892. Next comes Jim McCormick, with 3,171 adjusted walks from 1878 to 1887.

WALKS ALLOWED: CAREER

PLAYER	ADJUSTED BB	PLAYER	ACTUAL BB
Mickey Welch	3,292	Nolan Ryan	2,795
Jim McCormick	3,171	Steve Carlton	1,833
Nolan Ryan	3,134	Phil Niekro	1,809
Tim Keefe	2,853	Early Wynn	1,775
Tony Mullane	2,531	Bob Feller	1,764
Steve Carlton	2,060	Bobo Newsom	1,732
Charley Radbourn	2,039	Amos Rusie	1,707
Phil Niekro	2,035	Charlie Hough	1,665
Amos Rusie	2,019	Gus Weyhing	1,566
Chick Fraser	2,011	Red Ruffing	1,541

Strikeouts

Single season: The 1973 season was a disappointment for the California Angels. They limped to the finish line four games below .500, well out of the pennant race. But Angels righty Nolan Ryan approached his final start of the year with typical intensity, fanning sixteen batters in eleven innings to set the actual single-season record for strikeouts, 383. He barely eclipsed the previous mark of 382 by Dodgers lefty Sandy Koufax in 1965.

Ryan and Koufax both threw smoke, no doubt about it. Ryan notched 10.6 strikeouts per nine innings during his record year, precisely twice the average of 5.3 for all pitchers in 1973.

Koufax's 10.2 per nine innings was 70 percent higher than 1965's standard.

But neither of these recent greats can be found on the adjusted list below. Top honors go to Rube Waddell, an eccentric left-hander who starred briefly for the Philadelphia Athletics early in the 20th century. Waddell topped the majors with 349 strikeouts in 1904. His ratio of 8.2 per nine innings is seemingly inferior to Ryan or Koufax, but what's important is that Waddell more than doubled 1904's overall average of 3.8. His adjusted total is 559 strikeouts, the all-time record, edging his 558 from the previous year.

Nolan Ryan remains the leader in career strikeouts with 6,870, including four seasons over 400.

Career: Nolan Ryan is the leader in career strikeouts, both actual and adjusted. The former title is his by a wide margin. Ryan pitched 27 years for the Mets, Angels, Astros, and Rangers, ringing up more than 300 strikeouts six times and finishing in the 200s nine times. His actual lifetime total of 5,714 is nearly 1,600 ahead of the runner-up, Steve Carlton.

Ryan's adjusted total is even more impressive, 6,870 strikeouts, including four seasons with over 400 and another four in the 300s. But these standings are considerably tighter, with two other renowned fireballers close behind, Cy Young at 6,667 and Walter Johnson at 6,631. A total of seven pitchers amassed more than 5,000 adjusted strikeouts in their careers, entering a realm occupied only by Ryan in real life.

STRIKEOUTS: SINGLE SEASON

PLAYER	YEAR	TEAM	ADJUSTED SO
Rube Waddell	1904	Philadelphia (A)	559
Rube Waddell	1903	Philadelphia (A)	558
Bob Feller	1946	Cleveland (A)	541
Dazzy Vance	1924	Brooklyn (N)	525
Vic Willis	1902	Boston (N)	511
Noodles Hahn	1901	Cincinnati (N)	507
Christy Mathewson	1903	New York (N)	500
Walter Johnson	1910	Washington (A)	489
Walter Johnson	1912	Washington (A)	484
Ed Walsh	1908	Chicago (A)	480

STRIKEOUTS: CAREER

PLAYER	ADJUSTED SO	PLAYER	ACTUAL SO
Nolan Ryan	6,870	Nolan Ryan	5,714
Cy Young	6,667	Steve Carlton	4,136
Walter Johnson	6,631	Roger Clemens	3,717
Tim Keefe	6,402	Bert Blyleven	3,701
Jim McCormick	5,735	Tom Seaver	3,640
Jim Galvin	5,469	Don Sutton	3,574
Steve Carlton	5,177	Gaylord Perry	3,534
Charley Radbourn	4,941	Walter Johnson	3,509
Kid Nichols	4,897	Randy Johnson	3,412
Amos Rusie	4,860	Phil Niekro	3,342

Pay

Precision has been the watchword of this chapter. All the real-life statistics — games, innings, at bats, right down the line — were carefully compiled by the major leagues and reliable sources like *Total Baseball.* All adjusted numbers were calculated according to formulas I explained in detail in Chapter 1. Everything has been strictly black and white up to this point.

Welcome to the gray area.

Baseball doesn't keep records of its highest annual salaries. Teams or players rarely announce contract terms. They usually leak them to the press, sometimes accurately, more often in embellished forms. It's not unusual for newspapers and websites to cite widely different figures for the same deal.

We do have a pretty good idea, though, of the pace of inflation during the past century, even if the numbers aren't precise. *Total Baseball* has identified the following players as the first to reach certain milestones. (I have converted each to its equivalent in 2001 dollars, shown in parentheses.)

$50,000: Babe Ruth, 1923 (same as $520,000 in 2001)

$100,000: Hank Greenberg, 1947 ($810,000)

$500,000: Mike Schmidt, 1977 ($1.5 million)

$1 million: Nolan Ryan, 1980 ($2.2 million)

$2 million: George Foster, 1982 ($3.7 million)

$3 million: Kirby Puckett, 1990 ($4.1 million)

$5 million: Roger Clemens, 1991 ($6.5 million)

$10 million: Albert Belle, 1997 ($11 million)

$15 million: Kevin Brown, 1999 ($16 million)

$25 million: Alex Rodriguez, 2001

Old-timers have viewed this dizzying escalation with a mixture of awe and disgust. Who could blame them for feeling shortchanged? "If I were sitting down with George Steinbrenner and based on what Dave Winfield got for his statistics," Joe DiMaggio once reflected, "I'd have to say, 'George, you and I are about to become partners.'"

I have developed two computer models to estimate what DiMaggio and other greats would have earned in 2001, as I explained in Chapter 1. These models simulate baseball's pay structure with reasonable accuracy, making it possible to translate past performances to current pay levels. The resulting dollar values are not my opinion of what selected players were worth; they are dispassionate estimates of what those players would have earned as free agents today.

That's an important distinction. We tend to equate pay with excellence. We somehow assume

Bobby Bonds, smiling because he's the highest paid hitter in an expansion period season.

that the best players get the most money, though today's irrational market doesn't work that way. Alex Rodriguez was the highest-paid position player in 2001, but he wasn't the MVP. Kevin Brown earned more money than any other pitcher, but he didn't win the Cy Young Award. Not everyone has a handle on this gap between quality and quantity, though Kirby Puckett certainly does. "I'm part of this family now," he said when he was inducted into the Hall of Fame. "Alex Rodriguez can't get in with $252 million. We won't let him in. You can't buy into this team."

Hitters in a single season: Two Yankees enjoyed seasons worth more than $40 million in 2001 dollars, dwarfing Rodriguez's actual record of $25 million a year. Leading the pack is Lou Gehrig, whose adjusted stats for 1931 included 76 home runs, 180 runs scored, 204 runs batted in, and a .331 batting average. What would those numbers bring today on the free-agent market? Try $48.3 million. Babe Ruth holds the next two slots: $47.9 million in 1921 and $40.3 million in 1923.

I have included a second list below, confined to the expansion period (1962–2001). The leader, to everyone's surprise, I'm sure, is Bobby Bonds. Bobby, not Barry. (Keep in mind what I said about the irrationality of the market.) The elder Bonds scored 153 adjusted runs and chipped in 112 adjusted RBIs for the Giants in 1973, translating to $31.7 million in 2001 dollars. It helped that Bobby Bonds was young (27) and durable, two factors that greatly enhance a player's value.

PAY: HITTERS (SINGLE SEASON) 1901–2001

PLAYER	YEAR	TEAM	ADJUSTED MILLIONS
Lou Gehrig	1931	New York (A)	$48.3
Babe Ruth	1921	New York (A)	$47.9
Babe Ruth	1923	New York (A)	$40.3
Ted Williams	1942	Boston (A)	$39.2
Chuck Klein	1932	Philadelphia (N)	$38.9
Ted Williams	1946	Boston (A)	$38.7
Jimmie Foxx	1932	Philadelphia (A)	$38.6
Lou Gehrig	1933	New York (A)	$36.6
Lou Gehrig	1934	New York (A)	$36.0
Ted Williams	1949	Boston (A)	$36.0

HITTERS (SINGLE SEASON) 1962–2001

PLAYER	YEAR	TEAM	ADJUSTED MILLIONS
Bobby Bonds	1973	San Francisco (N)	$31.7
Frank Thomas	1994	Chicago (A)	$31.6
Bobby Bonds	1972	San Francisco (N)	$31.5
Hank Aaron	1963	Milwaukee (N)	$28.6
Jim Rice	1978	Boston (A)	$26.9
Frank Robinson	1962	Cincinnati (N)	$26.4
Billy Williams	1966	Chicago (N)	$26.0
Cal Ripken Jr.	1985	Baltimore (A)	$25.9
Frank Thomas	1995	Chicago (A)	$25.9
Hank Aaron	1962	Milwaukee (N)	$25.7
Billy Williams	1965	Chicago (N)	$25.7
Bobby Bonds	1970	San Francisco (N)	$25.7

Pitchers in a single season: Estimated values are much higher for pitchers than hitters, as I noted in Chapter 1. The two reasons bear repeating: (1) Today's owners tend to fork over more money to pitchers, which is reflected in the computer model. (2) Old-timers often worked 100 to 150 innings more than today's starters do. That inflates their value, because a pitcher's total number of innings is a key factor considered by my computer.

Eleven old-timers, in fact, had seasons that would be worth more than $60 million today. That's four times the $15 million Kevin Brown was paid in 2001, the actual single-season record. The leader is Ed Walsh, who pitched 485 adjusted innings for the White Sox in 1908, putting together a 42–16 record, with 480 strikeouts and a 2.71 ERA (all figures adjusted, of course). His performance carries the incomprehensible value of $67.8 million in 2001 dollars.

Steve Carlton ranks first in the expansion period. His 1972 season for Philadelphia would be worth $51.4 million. These were Carlton's adjusted statistics that year: 363 innings, 28 wins, 376 strikeouts, 2.75 ERA. The only other pitcher above $50 million since 1962 was Sandy Koufax, who crossed the line in his final two seasons, 1965 and 1966.

PAY: PITCHERS (SINGLE SEASON) 1901–2001

PLAYER	YEAR	TEAM	ADJUSTED MILLIONS
Ed Walsh	1908	Chicago (A)	$67.8
Jack Chesbro	1904	New York (A)	$67.7
Joe McGinnity	1903	New York (N)	$64.2
Christy Mathewson	1908	New York (N)	$63.8
Vic Willis	1902	Boston (N)	$63.5
Cy Young	1902	Boston (A)	$62.8
Pete Alexander	1917	Philadelphia (N)	$61.0
Joe McGinnity	1901	Baltimore (A)	$60.8
Walter Johnson	1913	Washington (A)	$60.7
Walter Johnson	1912	Washington (A)	$60.1
Pete Alexander	1915	Philadelphia (N)	$60.1

Christy Mathewson, one of the highest earners in a single season.

PITCHERS (SINGLE SEASON) 1962–2001

PLAYER	YEAR	TEAM	ADJUSTED MILLIONS
Steve Carlton	1972	Philadelphia (N)	$51.4
Sandy Koufax	1965	Los Angeles (N)	$51.2
Sandy Koufax	1966	Los Angeles (N)	$50.9
Denny McLain	1968	Detroit (A)	$42.8
Nolan Ryan	1974	California (A)	$42.0
Fergie Jenkins	1971	Chicago (N)	$41.3
Fergie Jenkins	1974	Texas (A)	$40.9
Juan Marichal	1968	San Francisco (N)	$40.7
Gaylord Perry	1972	Cleveland (A)	$40.6
Catfish Hunter	1975	New York (A)	$40.4

Career: The imbalance between pitchers and hitters is especially striking on the career salary lists. Two hurlers – Jim Galvin and Cy Young – would have had total earnings of more than $1 billion if they had been paid according to today's scale. That's billion with a B.

Galvin heads the list at nearly $1.12 billion. He ranks first in the adjusted career standings for innings pitched, second in wins, fifth in games pitched, and sixth in strikeouts. Then comes Young at $1.05 billion. He also is among the adjusted leaders in all of the crucial categories: first in wins, second in strikeouts, second in innings, ninth in games. Another six pitchers are above $750 million.

Only two batters, on the other hand, put together careers that were worth more than $400 million in 2001 dollars: Cap Anson ($422 million) and Lou Gehrig (nearly $407 million). Anson ranks second all-time in adjusted hits and third in RBIs and total bases. Gehrig is third in slugging average and fifth in home runs on the adjusted lists. Rounding out the top five are two well-known stars, Babe Ruth and Hank Aaron, and a fairly obscure outfielder from the 19th century, Jim O'Rourke. (Ruth deserves an asterisk, indicating that he also had a career value of $104.4 million as a pitcher. His grand total: $492.1 million.)

PAY: HITTERS & PITCHERS (CAREER)

BATTERS	ADJUSTED MILLIONS	PITCHERS	ADJUSTED MILLIONS
Cap Anson	$422.0	Jim Galvin	$1,117.5
Lou Gehrig	$406.8	Cy Young	$1,053.7
Babe Ruth	$387.7	Mickey Welch	$926.2
Hank Aaron	$375.7	Jim McCormick	$906.2
Jim O'Rourke	$352.8	Tim Keefe	$905.5
Pete Rose	$329.1	Charley Radbourn	$857.0
Jimmie Foxx	$324.6	Kid Nichols	$795.3
King Kelly	$324.5	Walter Johnson	$768.2
Willie Mays	$321.1	Tony Mullane	$740.3
Ted Williams	$318.9	John Clarkson	$738.0

4 ○ The Best Players

The interesting thing about great teams is that they always have a weak link or two. The storied 1927 Yankees, for example, were feeble behind the plate, where Pat Collins and Johnny Grabowski split the catching duty. The left side of the infield was manned by a couple of journeymen, Mark Koenig at short and Joe Dugan at third. Folklore depicts the '27 Yanks as a team of supermen, led by the Sultan of Swat, Babe Ruth, and the Iron Horse, Lou Gehrig. But it was also a club of mere mortals like Collins and company.

The same disparity existed on more recent teams remembered by today's fans. The Big Red Machine, the Cincinnati Reds of the mid-seventies, was powered by Joe Morgan, Pete Rose, and Johnny Bench, but it also depended on role players like Dan Driessen and Cesar Geronimo. The '98 Yankees, winners of 114 games in the regular season, gave substantial playing time to the likes of Chad Curtis, Jorge Posada, and Joe Girardi. None is destined for Cooperstown.

And I haven't even mentioned pitchers. The '75 Reds had perhaps the worst starting rotation ever assembled by a truly great team. Gary Nolan, Jack Billingham, Fred Norman, Don Gullett, and Pat Darcy didn't exactly inspire fear in the hearts of National League hitters. None picked up more than fifteen wins, even though Cincinnati's record was a dazzling 108–54.

The point is that no one in the history of baseball has been able to put together a team without a weakness. Even all-star squads don't fill the bill. Look at the rosters for the 2001 All-Star Game in Seattle. Sean Casey was invited, as were Tony Clark, Ryan Klesko, Phil Nevin, Magglio Ordonez, Paul Quantrill, and Ben Sheets. Competent players, yes. Stars? I don't think so.

The only way to assemble a true all-star team is to broaden the pool of eligible players, which is what this chapter does. It draws from the entire modern era, selecting only the best of the best. I have devised a formula that compares the all-time greats at each position, evaluating each player's performance during his entire career, with special emphasis on his peak seasons. The details are explained in Chapter 1.

A few points bear repeating:

○ Each position is scored on a separate 100-point scale. The top player is pegged at exactly 100, with all other scores based on that benchmark. (That means you can't compare scores for different positions, since the scales are different. Ninety-five points for a second baseman isn't the same as 95 for a right fielder.)

○ A position player must have played that position for at least 1,000 actual games and must have a minimum of 5,000 adjusted at bats to be eligible for consideration. A starting pitcher needs to have pitched at least 2,000 adjusted innings, while a reliever must have appeared in 600 or more adjusted games.

○ A player also must have crossed at least one threshold of excellence during his career. The possibilities include making the Hall of Fame, winning a Most Valuable Player Award or Cy

Young Award, or reaching a statistical milestone. Full lists of the criteria for batters and pitchers can be found in Chapter 1.

The scoring formulas use only adjusted statistics. Half of a player's score is determined by his average performance throughout his entire career, while the other half depends on his summit years, defined as his five best seasons. Batters are graded on runs scored per 500 at bats, runs batted in per 500 at bats, batting average, and slugging average. Starting pitchers are scored on wins per 250 innings pitched, winning percentage, hits and walks allowed per 250 innings, and earned run average. Relievers are measured in just two categories: hits and walks per 100 innings and ERA.

I will use these rankings to put together a 26-man "dream team," made up of the greatest players since 1901. The top two players behind the plate and at each infield and outfield position will make the squad, along with six starting pitchers and four relievers. The runnersup will form our second team, again with 26 players. **Keep in mind that all of the statistics mentioned on the following pages are adjusted, unless otherwise noted.**

My rankings start below, going position by position. Each player is listed with his batting or throwing side (lefty, right, or both), his score on his position's 100-point scale, and eight sets of adjusted statistics. These are the columns from left to right:

BATTERS (ADJUSTED STATISTICS)

R^A: Runs scored per 500 at bats (average season throughout career)

RBI^A: Runs batted in per 500 at bats (average season)

BA^A: Batting average (average season)

SA^A: Slugging average (average season)

R^S: Runs scored per 500 at bats (summit season)

RBI^S: Runs batted in per 500 at bats (summit season)

BA^S: Batting average (summit season)

SA^S: Slugging average (summit season)

STARTING PITCHERS (ADJUSTED STATISTICS)

W^A: Wins per 250 innings pitched (average season throughout career)

$W\%^A$: Winning percentage (average season)

$H+BB^A$: Hits and walks allowed per 250 innings pitched (average season)

ERA^A: Earned run average (average season)

W^S: Wins per 250 innings pitched (summit season)

$W\%^S$: Winning percentage (summit season)

$H+BB^S$: Hits and walks allowed per 250 innings pitched (summit season)

ERA^S: Earned run average (summit season)

RELIEF PITCHERS (ADJUSTED STATISTICS)

W^A: Wins per 100 innings pitched (average season throughout career)

SV^A: Saves per 100 innings pitched (average season)

$H+BB^A$: Hits and walks allowed per 100 innings pitched (average season)

ERA^A: Earned run average (average season)

W^S: Wins per 100 innings pitched (summit season)

SV^S: Saves per 100 innings pitched (summit season)

$H+BB^S$: Hits and walks allowed per 100 innings pitched (summit season)

ERA^S: Earned run average (summit season)

Catchers

Johnny Bench wasn't a great contact hitter. He batted .300 just four times in his seventeen-year career with Cincinnati. His lifetime average was only .283. Several catchers have done better than that, including guys who aren't in the Hall of Fame, like Ted Simmons and Elston Howard.

But Bench was unsurpassed among catchers as a power hitter. He blasted 30 or more home runs in nine different seasons, peaking at 57 homers in 1972, the year he won his second Most Valuable Player Award. He topped 150 RBIs three times. No catcher in history has driven in more runs per 500 at bats (107 over his entire career, 128 at his summit) or registered a higher slugging average (.546 career, .613 summit).

It was this ability to produce runs that earned Bench the job as starting catcher on our dream team. His selection was buttressed by two qualities that weren't considered by the scoring system. Bench was an excellent fielder, winning ten straight Gold Glove Awards from 1968 to 1977. And he certainly knew how to win, anchoring two of the greatest teams in baseball history, the 1975 and 1976 Reds.

Backing up Bench is Bill Dickey, who batted .306 for the Yankees from 1928 to 1946, .317 in his five peak seasons. His power wasn't equal to Bench's, but he did top 20 homers every year from 1932 to 1939. And he averaged 122 RBIs

Johnny Bench is unsurpassed among catchers as a power hitter.

per 500 at bats in his summit years, better than any catcher but Bench.

Handling the duties behind the plate for the second team are Mickey Cochrane and Yogi Berra. Cochrane played only thirteen seasons, but he was a dependable hitter (.304 career, .318 summit) and a solid defensive performer. He was twice chosen MVP. Berra won three MVP trophies in the 1950s, when the Yankees were seemingly invincible. He drilled 30 or more homers every year from 1950 through 1957, and he had 100 or more RBIs in eleven straight seasons (1948–1958).

		BATS	SCORE	R[A]	RBI[A]	BA[A]	SA[A]	R[S]	RBI[S]	BA[S]	SA[S]
1	Johnny Bench	R	100.00	85	107	.283	.546	98	128	.304	.613
2	Bill Dickey	L	97.59	77	100	.306	.528	93	122	.317	.596
3	Mickey Cochrane	L	96.76	103	82	.304	.510	111	95	.318	.558
4	Yogi Berra	L	96.05	86	105	.295	.530	91	106	.311	.561
5	Carlton Fisk	R	92.85	84	88	.281	.508	99	98	.310	.571
6	Ted Simmons	B	91.27	72	93	.296	.491	85	103	.324	.557
7	Gabby Hartnett	R	90.86	70	95	.285	.525	78	104	.310	.582
8	Ernie Lombardi	R	88.25	55	93	.306	.515	65	102	.332	.572
9	Ivan Rodriguez	R	88.06	77	76	.307	.494	85	83	.326	.543
10	Gary Carter	R	87.54	73	88	.272	.486	85	96	.295	.548

First Basemen

Lou Gehrig was an amazingly strong hitter for an amazingly long time. The Yankee first baseman launched 50 or more home runs eleven straight times (1927–1937). He scored more than 120 runs and drove in another 120 for thirteen consecutive seasons (1926–1938). He scored more runs per 500 at bats (121 career, 129 summit) than any first baseman in history, and his lifetime slugging average of .676 is the highest ever for his position. He still holds the all-time record for RBIs by any player in a single season, 204 in 1931.

Is it any wonder that Gehrig is the dream team's starter at first base?

Right behind him on the depth chart is the tremendously strong Jimmie Foxx, the forerunner of today's muscular sluggers. Foxx hit at least 50 homers every year from 1929 through 1940, also scoring more than 100 runs and driving in a minimum of 116 in each of those seasons.

Second-team honors go to Hank Greenberg and Mark McGwire. Greenberg's career was relatively short, interrupted for service in World War II, but he was an unparalleled run producer during his prime. He generated more RBIs per 500 at bats than any first baseman in history (132 career, 146 summit), with at least 60 homers in five different seasons.

McGwire actually finished fifth in this category, but he qualified for the second team as a substitute for Stan Musial, the man ahead of

Lou Gehrig (r) is the dream team's starter at first base. Backing him up is the tremendously strong Jimmie Foxx (l).

him. Musial fared even better in the competition at left field, winning a roster spot there. (He played more than 1,000 games at each position.) McGwire, of course, is best known for breaking Roger Maris's actual home-run record in 1998, an accomplishment that tended to obscure his long-term excellence. He was one of only four first basemen ever to have at least 140 RBIs per 500 at bats during his summit years.

		BATS	SCORE	R^A	RBI^A	BA^A	SA^A	R^S	RBI^S	BA^S	SA^S
1	Lou Gehrig	L	100.00	121	129	.326	.676	129	146	.343	.752
2	Jimmie Foxx	R	97.89	113	123	.317	.659	128	144	.346	.761
3	Hank Greenberg	R	95.57	109	132	.311	.667	116	146	.319	.715
4	Stan Musial	L	90.19	101	100	.345	.629	117	102	.373	.713
5	Mark McGwire	R	90.01	101	122	.269	.616	120	140	.290	.708
6	Willie McCovey	L	87.86	91	114	.288	.588	113	134	.322	.687
7	Johnny Mize	L	87.51	95	112	.315	.625	105	115	.329	.684
8	Jeff Bagwell	R	86.87	105	108	.309	.573	116	118	.316	.623
9	Orlando Cepeda	R	83.15	85	103	.318	.565	96	117	.336	.629
10	Norm Cash	L	82.63	93	100	.292	.558	103	117	.317	.627

Second Basemen

Rogers Hornsby, by most accounts, was an insufferable human being, but the scoring system paid no attention to his personality defects, sizable though they might have been. What counted was his ability to hit consistently and with power, a rare combination indeed at second base, making him the clear choice to be the dream team's starter.

Hornsby batted over .350 nine times, climaxing at .399 in 1924. And he topped 50 homers four times, peaking at 72 in 1922. Hornsby was the only second baseman in history to average more than 100 RBIs per 500 at bats over an entire career, and he also enjoyed a wide lead over his counterparts in slugging average (.643 career, .738 summit). His wide range of skills earned him five Most Valuable Player Awards during his 23-year career.

Second place in the rankings belongs to Nap Lajoie. Accounts of his fielding ability vary wildly. Some contemporaries remembered him as sure-handed; others considered him a defensive liability. But there was no doubt about his skills at the plate. Lajoie batted .424 for the Philadelphia A's in 1901, the second-highest single-season average of the modern era. His lifetime average of .351 and summit average of .406 are the highest among all second basemen.

Playing second base for the second squad are Eddie Collins and Charlie Gehringer. Collins was certainly no power hitter, but he made solid contact and was fast on his feet. That's why he scored an average of 106 runs per 500 at bats, tying Joe Morgan for the lead in that category among second basemen. Between

Consistency and power, a rare combination in second baseman Rogers Hornsby.

1908 and 1927 Collins batted over .300 every season but one.

Gehringer, who played nineteen seasons for the Tigers, edged Morgan for fourth place by the barest of margins, one-hundredth of a rating point. The longer he played, the better Gehringer seemed to get. He scored the most runs in his career (150) during his thirteenth season, then reached his highest batting average (.360) the following year, 1937.

		BATS	SCORE	R^A	RBI^A	BA^A	SA^A	R^S	RBI^S	BA^S	SA^S
1	Rogers Hornsby	R	100.00	104	104	.348	.643	116	113	.376	.738
2	Nap Lajoie	R	94.65	88	94	.351	.590	112	103	.406	.701
3	Eddie Collins	L	87.54	106	76	.338	.516	122	78	.368	.584
4	Charlie Gehringer	R	86.32	103	83	.309	.516	111	94	.335	.563
5	Joe Morgan	L	86.31	106	72	.287	.485	132	99	.321	.577
6	Bobby Doerr	R	84.98	86	98	.295	.524	94	108	.309	.569
7	Joe Gordon	R	82.90	88	94	.274	.526	93	104	.293	.567
8	Rod Carew	L	81.94	91	64	.345	.487	102	81	.370	.559
9	Tony Lazzeri	R	81.79	81	97	.280	.500	88	104	.306	.552
10	Larry Doyle	L	80.18	90	74	.306	.520	100	71	.333	.582

Shortstops

Legend has it that Honus Wagner, the dream team's starting shortstop, was as pleasant and self-effacing as his keystone partner, Hornsby, was egotistical and overbearing. His sunny personality was melded with exceptional skills, winning him Most Valuable Player honors five times.

Wagner batted over .300 for fifteen straight seasons (1899–1913), resulting in a career average of .342, easily the best for any shortstop, as was his summit average of .388. He also led all shortstops in runs per 500 at bats (97 career, 125 summit) and slugging average (.593 career, .703 summit). His greatest season was 1908, when he smacked 56 homers and 158 RBIs and batted .399.

Wagner's backup is Ernie Banks, whom most fans remember as a first baseman. But Banks played short his first nine seasons with the Cubs, and he played it well, twice being named MVP, making him the first player from a losing team to win the award. He swatted 112 homers those two seasons (1958–1959), while scoring 258 runs and driving in 325. He was the only shortstop in history to average more than 100 RBIs per 500 at bats over the entire span of his career. And forget

Five-time MVP winner Honus Wagner earns a spot as shortstop on the dream team.

the talk that Banks was a poor fielder; he won the Gold Glove for NL shortstops in 1960.

The second team's shortstops are Joe Cronin and Arky Vaughan. Cronin rapped more than 100 RBIs eleven times between 1930 and 1941, and scored a minimum of 104 runs nine times during the same span. Banks was the only shortstop whose lifetime ratio of RBIs per 500 at bats was higher than Cronin's.

Vaughan, who played from 1932 to 1948, is obscure to today's fans, but his greatness can't be denied. He led the National League in runs scored and triples three times each, and held the season's best title once for stolen bases, batting average, and slugging average, as well. Vaughan scored more runs per 500 at bats and had a higher career batting average than any shortstop but Wagner.

		BATS	SCORE	R^A	RBI^A	BA^A	SA^A	R^S	RBI^S	BA^S	SA^S
1	Honus Wagner	R	100.00	97	96	.342	.593	125	117	.388	.703
2	Ernie Banks	R	89.60	81	102	.292	.560	99	115	.307	.644
3	Joe Cronin	R	85.65	85	99	.294	.506	97	104	.306	.554
4	Arky Vaughan	L	83.98	95	75	.316	.502	104	83	.331	.555
5	Robin Yount	R	82.05	85	73	.296	.476	104	90	.324	.576
6	Cal Ripken Jr.	R	80.60	78	80	.284	.478	95	90	.323	.572
7	Barry Larkin	R	79.60	90	67	.306	.477	97	80	.318	.533
8	Lou Boudreau	R	78.45	81	75	.304	.478	87	79	.330	.522
9	Alan Trammell	R	78.19	84	67	.294	.451	93	81	.335	.539
10	Luke Appling	R	77.24	80	69	.312	.446	84	82	.342	.502

Third Basemen

No third baseman has ever matched Mike Schmidt's ability to produce runs, which is why he is a starter for the dream team. Schmidt was a solid, consistent performer for the Phillies, scoring and driving in at least 100 runs every year but one from 1974 through 1987. (The exceptions weren't exactly bad seasons: 92 RBIs in 1978, 92 runs scored in 1987.) He drilled 40 or more homers twelve times, peaking at 63 in 1981.

Schmidt's lifetime numbers are equally impressive. He topped all third basemen in runs per 500 at bats (104 career, 115 summit), RBIs

No third baseman has ever matched Schmidt's ability to produce runs.

per 500 at bats (111 career, 127 summit), and slugging percentage (.590 career, .652 summit). It didn't hurt that he also was an excellent fielder, winning ten Gold Gloves.

Joining Schmidt on the first team is Eddie Mathews, generally underappreciated despite his Hall-of-Fame career. It didn't help that he played in Hank Aaron's shadow for the great Milwaukee Braves teams of the 1950s. Mathews never was named MVP (Schmidt won three awards), but he was a feared slugger, driving in 100 or more runs eleven times in thirteen seasons (1953–1965). Only Schmidt, among all third basemen, scored more runs per 500 at bats or posted a higher slugging percentage.

The second team's slots are filled by Frank Baker and George Brett. The former was known as "Home Run" Baker in his day (1908–1922), which shows how times have changed. His actual career total of 96 homers could be equaled by one of today's sluggers in a season and a half. What set Baker apart, his nickname to the contrary, was his skill as a contact hitter. His lifetime average of .320 is second to Wade Boggs in the position rankings.

Brett boasted a higher batting average in his summit years (.347) than any of the men ranked ahead of him at third base. He reached the .300 level 15 times in his 21 seasons with the Kansas City Royals. His best year was .396 in 1980.

		BATS	SCORE	R^A	RBI^A	BA^A	SA^A	R^S	RBI^S	BA^S	SA^S
1	Mike Schmidt	R	100.00	104	111	.279	.590	115	127	.299	.652
2	Eddie Mathews	L	96.73	102	98	.286	.565	111	119	.304	.648
3	Frank Baker	L	94.00	88	97	.320	.552	99	109	.343	.607
4	George Brett	L	93.77	88	88	.317	.541	104	110	.347	.626
5	Ron Santo	R	92.14	85	99	.299	.533	100	107	.330	.610
6	Ken Boyer	R	88.57	86	89	.306	.513	97	98	.325	.566
7	Bob Elliott	R	88.43	85	95	.298	.504	90	109	.319	.549
8	Wade Boggs	L	85.76	91	61	.339	.476	105	70	.378	.544
9	Darrell Evans	L	85.05	87	87	.258	.482	101	102	.277	.563
10	Pie Traynor	R	84.09	80	87	.304	.467	85	100	.327	.502

Left Fielders

The competition for the starting job in left field turned out to be no competition at all. Ted Williams outdistanced the pack by more than fifteen rating points, the widest margin at any position except right field.

It's hard to deny that Williams and Babe Ruth, the starter in right field, were the modern era's two greatest hitters. Ted's lifetime batting average was better than the Babe's (.355 to .329), and he was the only player to match Ruth's feat of posting a career slugging

percentage above .700. But Ruth gets the overall edge; his slugging average was 50 points higher than Williams', and he scored and drove in more runs per 500 at bats.

Williams, however, is the undisputed king in left field, leading seven of the eight statistical categories shown below. He batted over .350 ten times during his nineteen years with the Red Sox, topping .400 in 1941 (.417) and 1957 (.407), making him the only player at any position to reach that exalted level since 1920. And, for good measure, he blasted more than 50 homers in five seasons.

The only left fielder who comes close to Williams's scoring ability is Barry Bonds, who ranks second in runs per 500 at bats (116 career, 130 summit). Bonds also demonstrated considerable power, especially in 2001, when he set the actual records for home runs and slugging average in a single season.

Stan Musial and Willie Stargell patrol left field for the second team. Musial is the only player to finish among the top four at two different positions (see first base). He never batted below .322 for the Cardinals from 1942 through 1958, and he hit more than 30 homers every year from 1943 through 1957 (except for 1945, which he missed because of World War II).

Stargell is best remembered as the aging father figure who led the 1979 Pirates to a world title, but he was much more than that. He ranks second to Williams in RBIs per 500 at bats (118 career, 134 summit), twice topping 150 RBIs in a single season.

Ted Williams is the undisputed king in left field.

		BATS	SCORE	R^A	RBI^A	BA^A	SA^A	R^S	RBI^S	BA^S	SA^S
1	Ted Williams	L	100.00	131	133	.355	.707	155	144	.388	.802
2	Barry Bonds	L	84.95	116	104	.299	.615	130	122	.323	.720
3	Stan Musial	L	83.66	101	100	.345	.629	117	102	.373	.713
4	Willie Stargell	L	83.08	91	118	.301	.609	111	134	.327	.695
5	Joe Jackson	L	82.81	103	95	.369	.641	111	90	.388	.678
6	Ralph Kiner	R	80.33	103	107	.287	.609	113	118	.301	.675
7	Albert Belle	R	79.27	87	111	.301	.588	101	122	.325	.665
8	Billy Williams	L	78.10	92	96	.312	.567	107	111	.342	.645
9	Sherry Magee	R	77.90	92	98	.313	.556	113	109	.338	.619
10	Carl Yastrzemski	L	76.12	90	92	.302	.524	114	100	.349	.636

Center Fielders

No battle could have been tighter than the contest in center field. Ty Cobb snatched the starting job from Mickey Mantle by one hundredth of a rating point. Joe DiMaggio finished a close third, just 0.29 points off the pace. (All three men, by the way, are essentially even in another regard: each won Most Valuable Player honors three times.)

Cobb, of course, posted the best batting average for anyone with at least 8,000 career at bats, .376. His summit average was an amazing .417. He batted over .400 eight times for the Tigers (1909–1913 and 1916–1918) during his 24-year career. Perhaps equally impressive was the fact that he never fell below .317 in a full season. Cobb also had surprising power, as indicated by his slugging average for his summit years, .726, better than any other center fielder in history.

Mantle, relegated to the dream team's bench by the tiniest of margins, had all the tools. He was exceptionally fast, especially in his early seasons with the Yankees. He covered center field well, though he didn't share Willie Mays' reputation as a glove wizard. And his offensive ability was beyond dispute. Mantle scored at least 105 runs every year from 1952 through 1962, leading all center fielders in runs per 500 at bats (120 career, 137 summit). He blasted more than 40 homers seven times, while also reaching the .300 level eleven times during his eighteen-year career.

The depth at this position is demonstrated by the two stars who had to settle for the second team: DiMaggio and Mays. DiMaggio leads all center fielders in career slugging average (.642) and runs batted in per 500 at bats (121 career, 139 summit). He drove in more than 110 runs in all but two of his thirteen seasons with the Yankees.

Mays won twelve Gold Gloves in his career and would have had more, except the Gold Glove didn't debut until his sixth season in the bigs. He also had power (hitting as many as 64 homers in a season) and speed (scoring more than 140 runs in nine separate seasons with the Giants).

		BATS	SCORE	R^A	RBI^A	BA^A	SA^A	R^S	RBI^S	BA^S	SA^S
1	Ty Cobb	L	100.00	115	99	.376	.625	127	109	.417	.726
2	Mickey Mantle	B	99.99	120	107	.315	.619	137	132	.349	.717
3	Joe DiMaggio	R	99.71	110	121	.327	.642	114	139	.351	.711
4	Willie Mays	R	94.91	112	103	.321	.626	119	111	.345	.707
5	Tris Speaker	L	92.24	106	85	.348	.595	124	98	.384	.663
6	Al Simmons	R	91.38	87	107	.320	.572	106	126	.358	.674
7	Duke Snider	L	91.15	98	104	.307	.593	116	117	.322	.671
8	Ken Griffey Jr.	L	88.59	96	105	.302	.591	105	113	.314	.643
9	Earl Averill	L	86.57	98	94	.306	.570	108	104	.323	.619
10	Reggie Smith	B	85.79	96	94	.305	.561	104	107	.320	.612

Right Fielders

The Bambino. The Sultan of Swat. The Greatest Player Ever. All of those appellations fit Babe Ruth, the runaway winner in right field. His margin of victory, 17.37 rating points, was the widest at any position.

The phrase "larger than life" is often used to describe Ruth's personality, but it applies equally to his statistics. He hit more than 50 homers every season but one from 1919 through 1933. He is the all-time leader in home runs (1,157) and slugging average (.757). He holds the single-season marks for homers (94), runs scored (195), total bases (513), and slugging average (.971). And he tops all right fielders in six of the eight categories below. (The exceptions are career and summit batting averages, both led by Roberto Clemente.)

Ruth's backup is the only man who stands ahead of him in actual home runs over a career, Hank Aaron. A strong case can be made that Aaron was one of the ten greatest hitters in baseball history. He seemed to develop as a slugger as he got older, especially after the Braves moved to Atlanta. His best season for home runs was 1971, his eighteenth, when he drilled 60. Aaron's slugging averages (.626 career, .715 summit) topped everyone at the position but Ruth.

The second team's right fielders are Frank Robinson and Larry Walker. Robinson was the only player to win an MVP award in each league. He finished second to Ruth in the career rankings for runs per 500 at bats, with 108. He hit 30 or more homers in 15 of his 21 seasons.

There's no doubt that playing in Colorado's high altitude has elevated Walker's numbers, but he isn't the first player to benefit from a comfortable home park. (You don't think Ruth enjoyed having the right-field fence just 295 feet away in Yankee Stadium? Or that Aaron liked playing in a stadium nicknamed the Launching Pad?) The fact remains that Walker's numbers are competitive with the all-time greats in right field, especially his batting average (.320 career, .355 summit).

		BATS	SCORE	R^A	RBI^A	BA^A	SA^A	R^S	RBI^S	BA^S	SA^S
1	Babe Ruth	L	100.00	138	140	.329	.757	164	156	.357	.872
2	Hank Aaron	R	82.63	104	109	.325	.626	115	123	.345	.715
3	Frank Robinson	R	81.57	108	107	.314	.606	118	122	.341	.679
4	Larry Walker	L	80.10	103	100	.320	.593	119	112	.355	.671
5	Harry Heilmann	R	78.37	88	107	.330	.580	102	115	.364	.645
6	Mel Ott	L	78.15	105	104	.299	.586	116	121	.307	.637
7	Chuck Klein	L	76.75	92	95	.308	.578	107	113	.344	.672
8	Sam Crawford	L	75.31	86	95	.327	.580	104	99	.355	.628
9	Al Kaline	R	75.11	94	92	.316	.539	109	109	.341	.608
10	Roberto Clemente	R	74.70	90	82	.340	.537	100	101	.377	.617

Left-handed Starters

Lefty Grove was the greatest lefthander in baseball history, perhaps the greatest pitcher, period. He certainly was the game's dominant lefty in his prime, earning six consecutive Cy Young Awards (all hypothetical) from 1928 to 1933. He had 161 wins and just 42 losses during that span.

Grove registered a lifetime record of 317–148, the best ratio of wins to losses for anyone on the list of 300-game winners. He paced the American League in earned run average nine times and strikeouts seven times during his seventeen years with the A's and Red Sox. His summit figures of 24 wins per 250 innings and an .800 winning percentage are the best for any pitcher, lefty or righty, who worked at least 2,000 innings over his career.

Joining Grove on the dream team are Randy Johnson and Sandy Koufax, who picked up seven Cy Young trophies between them. Johnson, at six feet ten inches, literally towers over his staffmates. His summit ERA of 2.50 is the lowest ever by a lefty. He led the American League in strikeouts four times, the National League three times.

Koufax saved his best for last, winning 53 games and striking out 768 batters during his final two seasons (1965–1966). His ERA in his summit years (2.71) was lower than any lefthander but Johnson, and he allowed fewer baserunners over his career than any lefty but Carl Hubbell. His three Cy Youngs, by the way, were all awarded by unanimous votes.

The lefties on the second team come from three different periods of the modern era, Hubbell, Whitey Ford, and Ron Guidry. Hubbell won 266 games for the Giants over sixteen seasons (1928–1943), picking up two MVPs and three Cy Young Awards along the way. He was the stingiest lefty in history, allowing 286 hits

Lefty Grove was arguably the greatest pitcher in baseball history.

and walks per 250 innings. No one else was below 302.

Ford pitched for great teams in the fifties and sixties, to be sure, but he managed to outperform them. His winning percentage in an average season was .682, compared to .579 for all other Yankee pitchers. His career ERA of 3.27 is lower than any lefty but Hubbell.

There might be a few eyebrows raised at Guidry's selection, but there shouldn't be. His numbers are competitive with those of other great lefthanders. His career winning percentage was better than two men ahead of him in the rankings, and he allowed fewer baserunners than Grove did. His win–loss record for his three finest seasons with the Yankees (1978, 1983, 1985) was a combined 68–18.

		THROWS	SCORE	W[A]	W%[A]	H+BB[A]	ERA[A]	W[S]	W%[S]	H+BB[S]	ERA[S]
1	Lefty Grove	L	100.00	19	.679	315	3.32	24	.800	290	2.88
2	Randy Johnson	L	98.90	18	.682	308	3.40	19	.760	263	2.50
3	Sandy Koufax	L	97.33	18	.636	302	3.38	20	.742	268	2.71
4	Carl Hubbell	L	97.10	18	.630	286	3.25	19	.686	264	2.72
5	Whitey Ford	L	94.97	18	.682	324	3.27	20	.778	308	3.17
6	Ron Guidry	L	92.53	18	.650	313	3.88	20	.741	290	3.26
7	Lefty Gomez	L	92.29	19	.636	338	3.66	21	.719	312	3.19
8	Tom Glavine	L	91.50	17	.625	334	3.69	22	.724	314	3.13
9	Warren Spahn	L	90.73	17	.600	313	3.62	19	.667	294	2.97
10	Hal Newhouser	L	89.64	16	.571	336	3.62	20	.714	305	2.95

Right-handed Starters

Greg Maddux is the surprise winner in this category, outscoring two of the Hall of Fame's greatest legends, Walter Johnson and Christy Mathewson, as well as the righty with more victories than any other active pitcher, Roger Clemens.

His performance at his peak is what earned Maddux the title of best right-handed starter. No pitcher, lefty or righty, gave up fewer hits and walks per 250 innings (242) or posted a lower earned run average (2.15) during his summit years. Maddux kept his ERA below 2.70 for seven straight seasons (1992–1998), earning four consecutive Cy Young Awards to start that span, and running up a 137–56 record for the seven years combined. His ERA over his sixteen-year career with the Cubs and Braves, 3.05, is the third-lowest among all pitchers who worked at least 2,000 innings.

Johnson and Mathewson are the dream team's other righties. Johnson was one of the modern era's great fireballers, winning two Most Valuable Player Awards and seven hypothetical Cy Youngs. He struck out an average of 316 batters every season of the 21 he pitched for the Senators, topping 400 four times. The Big Train's

No pitcher can touch Greg Maddux during his summit years.

career ERA (3.00) and summit ERA (2.17) both rank second among all eligible starters.

Mathewson was famed as much for his gentlemanly demeanor as for his skill on the mound. He picked up two MVPs and eight Cy Young Awards during his seventeen years with the Giants. Matty won at least 23 games each season from 1903 through 1914, posting 23 wins per 250 innings at his peak, tops among all righties. His winning percentage of .657 was second-best among right-handed starters.

The second team's righthanders are Clemens, Mordecai Brown, and Pete Alexander. Nothing proves Clemens' durability more than his success with the voters. He won his first Cy Young in 1986 as a 24-year-old Red Sox neophyte. He picked up his sixth in 2001 as a 39-year-old

Yankee veteran. His winning percentages (.667 career, .778 summit) are the highest for any righty.

Brown is best known today for the physical deformity that brought him his nickname, "Three Finger." A childhood accident sliced off one finger and paralyzed another, giving him a natural knuckleball. He made the most of it, winning more than 20 games for the Cubs for six straight seasons (1906–1911).

Alexander was blessed with excellent control of his pitches, but not of himself. He was plagued with epilepsy and alcoholism, yet ripped off four 30-win seasons for the Phillies between 1911 and 1917. He swept the MVP and Cy Young Awards three straight years beginning in 1915, an unprecedented feat.

		THROWS	SCORE	W^A	$W\%^A$	$H+BB^A$	ERA^A	W^S	$W\%^S$	$H+BB^S$	ERA^S
1	Greg Maddux	R	100.00	19	.654	288	3.05	20	.750	242	2.15
2	Walter Johnson	R	97.38	18	.600	289	3.00	21	.696	254	2.17
3	Christy Mathewson	R	95.02	19	.657	303	3.35	23	.750	288	2.78
4	Roger Clemens	R	94.66	18	.667	305	3.38	21	.778	278	2.63
5	Mordecai Brown	R	93.98	19	.643	309	3.30	22	.730	286	2.75
6	Pete Alexander	R	92.69	18	.645	293	3.31	20	.705	281	2.73
7	Cy Young	R	92.55	17	.619	288	3.37	21	.741	272	2.87
8	Addie Joss	R	90.32	17	.633	283	3.14	18	.657	274	2.99
9	Ed Walsh	R	90.07	17	.625	288	2.93	17	.596	276	2.72
10	Tom Seaver	R	89.66	16	.615	304	3.56	19	.724	272	2.72

Relievers

Old-timers would have us believe that relievers weren't necessary during most of the modern era. Pitchers always finished what they started, or so goes the myth. The truth is that bullpen specialists have been around almost since the beginning. Firpo Marberry appeared in relief about 50 times a year for the Senators of the 1920s, racking up 40 saves in 1926. Joe Page amassed 113 saves in four seasons for the post-

war Yankees. Jim Konstanty was the National League's MVP in 1950, winning 16 games and saving 38 others for the champion Phillies.

But relievers didn't attain prominence until the past quarter-century, which is when most of this category's leaders pitched. No team today would go without a fully staffed bullpen, nor would our dream team. (Keep in mind that relievers were scored on just two categories, hits and walks allowed per 100 innings and earned run average. Wins and saves, both in ratios per 100 innings, are shown below, but had no impact on the scoring.)

John Wetteland, who split twelve seasons (1989–2000) among four teams, is ranked as the era's greatest relief pitcher. His hallmark was his control, an essential quality for a closer. Wetteland allowed the fewest base runners of any reliever in history, giving up just 116 hits and walks per 100 innings. His summit ERA (2.22) is the lowest for anyone in this category but Rich Gossage. Wetteland topped 40 saves four times, never pitching more than 103 innings in a season.

Filling out the first team's bullpen are Hoyt Wilhelm, Tom Henke, and Gossage. Wilhelm, a knuckleballer, was the first pitcher in baseball history to appear in 1,000 games. He worked so many innings (2,309) over 21 seasons that he became the first reliever eligible for the career ERA rankings, where his 3.08 remains fourth overall. He is the only Hall of Famer among the modern era's top ten relievers.

Henke pitched fourteen years, most notably for the Blue Jays, piling up at least 30 saves in six different seasons. He tied Wetteland for the fewest hits and walks allowed by a reliever over an entire career, 116 every 100 innings.

Gossage was well-traveled, playing for nine teams in 22 seasons, but perhaps is best

remembered as the Yankees' closer in the late seventies and early eighties. His ERA in his summit years (2.15) is the lowest ever for a bullpen specialist. He saved at least 20 games each year from 1977 through 1986.

The second team's relief squad consists of Bruce Sutter, Doug Jones, John Franco, and Dan Quisenberry. Sutter missed making the dream team by less than three-tenths of a rating point. He saved 40 games for a mediocre Cubs team in 1979, earning a Cy Young Award, the only reliever in the top ten to do so. He registered 40 or more saves three times in his twelve-year career.

Jones was another bullpen vagabond, pitching for seven teams between 1982 and 2000, including two separate stints in Milwaukee and Cleveland. His summit years were extraordinarily good. He allowed just 108 baserunners per 100 innings at his peak, fewer than anyone but Wetteland and Dennis Eckersley (who did not qualify for the top-ten list below).

The only lefty among the eight best relievers is Franco, who pitched eighteen years for the Reds and Mets, saving at least 30 games in half of them. His summit ERA (2.45) is better than those of anyone but Wetteland and Gossage.

Quisenberry closed the door for the great Kansas City Royals teams of the 1980s. He registered 31 or more saves for six consecutive seasons, peaking at 46 in 1983.

		THROWS	SCORE	W^A	W%^A	H+BB^A	ERA^A	W^S	W%^S	H+BB^S	ERA^S
1	John Wetteland	R	100.00	6	42	116	3.17	7	52	107	2.22
2	Hoyt Wilhelm	R	94.34	6	14	122	3.08	8	17	113	2.62
3	Tom Henke	R	93.40	5	40	116	3.06	7	43	114	2.92
4	Rich Gossage	R	92.94	7	19	132	3.65	9	27	114	2.15
5	Bruce Sutter	R	92.66	7	32	121	3.42	5	36	112	2.57
6	Doug Jones	R	92.04	6	26	128	3.57	7	41	108	2.48
7	John Franco	L	91.02	8	37	138	3.04	9	40	125	2.45
8	Dan Quisenberry	R	89.85	6	24	124	3.24	6	31	114	3.00
9	Jesse Orosco	L	89.02	7	10	131	3.42	9	21	120	2.59
10	Jeff Montgomery	R	88.35	6	35	129	3.59	6	34	118	2.63

Dream Team, Plus One

That's the end of my statistical tryouts. This chapter has now assembled two teams of the greatest players from the modern era. The first, my true "dream team," consists of the two best men at each position in the field, six superior starting pitchers (the top three from the separate rankings of lefties and righties), and the four relievers with the highest scores. The second team is nearly as good, containing the runners-up in every category. No weak links on either squad.

Here are the rosters:

POSITION	FIRST TEAM	SECOND TEAM
C	Johnny Bench Bill Dickey	Mickey Cochrane Yogi Berra
IB	Lou Gehrig Jimmie Foxx	Hank Greenberg Mark McGwire
2B	Rogers Hornsby Nap Lajoie	Eddie Collins Charlie Gehringer
SS	Honus Wagner Ernie Banks	Joe Cronin Arky Vaughan
3B	Mike Schmidt Eddie Mathews	Frank Baker George Brett
LF	Ted Williams Barry Bonds	Stan Musial Willie Stargell
CF	Ty Cobb Mickey Mantle	Joe DiMaggio Willie Mays
RF	Babe Ruth Hank Aaron	Frank Robinson Larry Walker
LSP	Lefty Grove Randy Johnson Sandy Koufax	Carl Hubbell Whitey Ford Ron Guidry
RSP	Greg Maddux Walter Johnson Christy Mathewson	Roger Clemens Mordecai Brown Pete Alexander
REL	John Wetteland Hoyt Wilhelm Tom Henke Rich Gossage	Bruce Sutter Doug Jones John Franco Dan Quisenberry

It's interesting to imagine what these teams would be like if they were magically able to take the field. I'm certain there would be plenty of dissension. Everybody on both rosters was an everyday player. Most were accustomed to being the undisputed stars of their teams. Some, like Cobb and Hornsby, were ornery, to employ an inadequate euphemism. Their manager, whoever he might be, would have a thankless job. Arguments about playing time would occur daily.

But there can be no doubt that the on-field performances would be amazing. I have gathered the summit figures for all 52 players, adjusted to 1996–2000 levels and converted to 162-game schedules, of course. The results show what both squads would be like at their very best; they can only be described as extraordinary.

The first team's typical batter, at his peak, launched 53 homers, drove in 138 runs, and batted .348. Leading the way are two Yankee greats. Babe Ruth tops the dream team with 84 homers, while Lou Gehrig has the most runs batted in, 180. Every single player boasts at least 30 homers and 118 RBIs. Ty Cobb and Nap Lajoie both have batting averages above .400, and four others are above .350. The only man to slip below .300 is Mike Schmidt, whose .299 is certainly respectable.

The typical pitcher on the first team worked 223 innings, won 19 games, struck out 247 batters, and registered an ERA of 2.54 in his summit season. The pitching staff includes five 20-game winners and three relievers with at least 30 saves. Everybody has an ERA below 3.00. Christy Mathewson has the most wins, 33. Walter Johnson, with 406 Ks, is the strikeout king. And Greg Maddux and Rich Gossage are tied for the lowest ERA, 2.15.

Here are the summit statistics for all 26 players on the first team:

BATTERS	BATS	HR	RBI	BA	G	AB	R	H	2B	3B	SA
Ty Cobb	L	42	128	.417	153	588	149	245	44	6	.726
Nap Lajoie	R	30	118	.406	144	572	128	232	71	4	.701
Honus Wagner	R	40	128	.388	148	546	137	212	44	4	.703
Ted Williams	L	53	135	.388	141	469	145	182	31	2	.802
Rogers Hornsby	R	53	122	.376	144	542	126	204	31	3	.738
Babe Ruth	L	84	168	.357	158	538	176	192	21	2	.872
Mickey Mantle	B	48	127	.349	145	481	132	168	27	3	.717
Jimmie Foxx	R	70	167	.346	155	581	149	201	25	3	.761
Hank Aaron	R	52	132	.345	144	537	124	185	37	3	.715
Lou Gehrig	L	72	180	.343	162	616	159	211	28	4	.752
Barry Bonds	L	54	123	.323	151	504	131	163	32	3	.720
Bill Dickey	L	37	121	.317	134	495	92	157	23	2	.596
Ernie Banks	R	54	144	.307	162	626	124	192	37	6	.644
Johnny Bench	R	45	146	.304	152	569	111	173	37	2	.613
Eddie Mathews	L	52	134	.304	154	562	125	171	27	5	.648
Mike Schmidt	R	54	142	.299	157	558	128	167	29	3	.652
Average		**53**	**138**	**.348**	**150**	**549**	**134**	**191**	**34**	**3**	**.710**

PITCHERS	THROWS	W	L	SV	ERA	G	IP	ER	H	BB	SO
Greg Maddux	R	21	7	0	2.15	34	260	62	207	45	215
Rich Gossage	R	10	7	30	2.15	60	113	27	80	49	141
Walter Johnson	R	32	14	4	2.17	51	378	91	302	82	406
John Wetteland	R	5	4	38	2.22	66	73	18	54	24	85
Randy Johnson	L	19	6	0	2.50	34	245	68	184	74	343
Hoyt Wilhelm	R	11	6	23	2.62	65	134	39	105	46	120
Sandy Koufax	L	23	8	1	2.71	39	292	88	230	83	338
Christy Mathewson	R	33	11	4	2.78	48	366	113	321	100	382
Lefty Grove	L	28	7	9	2.88	46	297	95	259	85	345
Tom Henke	R	5	3	32	2.92	62	74	24	57	27	90
Average		**19**	**7**	**14**	**2.54**	**51**	**223**	**63**	**180**	**62**	**247**

The second team is marginally inferior. Its collective batting average is 13 points lower than the first team's (.348 to .335), and its ERA is 30 points higher (2.54 to 2.84), but I can't imagine that too many managers would be unhappy with a lineup that included Stan Musial, Joe DiMaggio, Willie Mays, Frank Robinson, Pete Alexander, and Whitey Ford.

Here are the summit numbers for the second team:

BATTERS	BATS	HR	RBI	BA	G	AB	R	H	2B	3B	SA
Stan Musial	L	48	129	.373	162	635	148	237	52	10	.713
Eddie Collins	L	21	90	.368	155	574	140	211	47	7	.584
Larry Walker	L	38	112	.355	140	502	119	178	37	4	.671
Joe DiMaggio	R	55	158	.351	145	570	130	200	30	5	.711
George Brett	L	30	117	.347	138	530	110	184	44	7	.626
Willie Mays	R	55	132	.345	158	594	141	205	34	8	.707
Frank Baker	L	39	131	.343	157	600	119	206	33	4	.607
Frank Robinson	R	45	133	.341	151	546	129	186	44	3	.679
Charlie Gehringer	R	27	112	.335	152	597	133	200	47	4	.563
Arky Vaughan	L	24	92	.331	147	553	115	183	40	6	.555
Willie Stargell	L	48	137	.327	144	511	113	167	40	2	.695
Hank Greenberg	R	66	175	.319	158	601	140	192	34	3	.715
Mickey Cochrane	L	29	93	.318	137	491	109	156	27	2	.558
Yogi Berra	L	34	118	.311	146	556	101	173	31	3	.561
Joe Cronin	R	29	117	.306	152	565	110	173	43	5	.554
Mark McGwire	R	57	127	.290	139	455	109	132	19	0	.708
Average		**40**	**123**	**.335**	**149**	**555**	**123**	**186**	**38**	**5**	**.638**

PITCHERS	THROWS	W	L	SV	ERA	G	IP	ER	H	BB	SO
John Franco	L	7	4	31	2.45	64	77	21	67	29	59
Doug Jones	R	6	7	36	2.48	69	87	24	79	15	76
Bruce Sutter	R	6	6	40	2.57	68	112	32	91	34	117
Roger Clemens	R	21	6	0	2.63	33	253	74	205	76	267
Carl Hubbell	L	24	11	7	2.72	45	311	94	273	56	277
Pete Alexander	R	31	13	4	2.73	50	396	120	351	94	370
Mordecai Brown	R	27	10	10	2.75	48	311	95	279	77	250
Dan Quisenberry	R	8	6	41	3.00	74	132	44	133	18	59
Whitey Ford	L	21	6	2	3.17	38	261	92	235	87	215
Ron Guidry	L	20	7	1	3.26	33	246	89	217	68	235
Average		**17**	**8**	**17**	**2.84**	**52**	**219**	**69**	**193**	**55**	**193**

5 ◎ The Best and Worst Teams

Baseball fans are forever arguing about the great teams of past and present. Who was better, the Yankees of Babe Ruth and Lou Gehrig or the Yankees of Derek Jeter and Bernie Williams? How would the Brooklyn Dodgers of the mid-fifties, the famed Boys of Summer, stack up against Sandy Koufax, Don Drysdale and the Los Angeles Dodgers of the following decade? Do later champions like the 1975 Cincinnati Reds and 1986 New York Mets deserve to be listed among the best teams ever?

We all know, of course, that we will never get a definitive answer to any of these questions. They certainly can't be settled on the field. Babe Ruth will never dig in against David Cone. Nor will Jackie Robinson, Maury Wills, Johnny Bench, or Mookie Wilson ever take the diamond again.

Our only alternative, imperfect though it may be, is to rely on statistical comparisons. That's why I devised a computer program to identify the best teams of baseball's modern era. It evaluates 228 squads that have enjoyed outstanding seasons since 1901.

If you read Chapter 1, you're already familiar with my formula. If you decided to save your eyesight and skip the fine print, let me briefly reiterate what I tried to do. My goal was to single out teams that won often, won easily, defeated tough competitors, and boasted the best combinations of offensive power and defensive skill. I took the following factors into

account, as measured by the statistics in parentheses:

○ Record (winning percentage)
○ Offense (runs scored)
○ Pitching and defense (runs allowed)
○ Ability to win big (margin of victory)
○ Ability to beat tough opponents (statistical competition factor)
○ Best team of the year (World Series and league titles)
○ Best team of the decade (bonus points)
○ Best team of the extended period, either 1901–1961 or 1962–2001 (bonus points)

These statistics have been adjusted to reflect current performance levels and to fit a 162-game schedule. I chose an adjusted winning percentage of .600 as my threshold, giving me the pool of 228 eligible teams mentioned above. If a team couldn't win at least 60 percent of its games, as I said in Chapter 1, I don't see how it could possibly be considered one of the greatest of all time.

One other point is worth noting: My formula emphasizes the regular season. Six months of play tell us much more about a team's ability than any short series could. Baseball's ultimate prize, the World Series, is not always won by the best team in a given year. It's won by the squad that's hot enough in late October (and sometimes early November) to take four games out of seven, a winning percentage of just .571. Some of the greatest teams in history didn't win the World Series, as you'll see. But they all proved their excellence over the long haul, and that's what matters most.

My rankings start below, running for the next couple of pages. The leader is fixed at 100 points, with every other team's score based off of that benchmark. Each team is followed by six adjusted statistics and its actual win–loss record. These are the columns from left to right:

ADJUSTED STATISTICS

W: Wins

L: Losses

W%: Winning percentage

R/G: Runs scored per game

OR/G: Runs allowed per game (also known as: opponents' runs per game)

Diff.: Difference between R/G and OR/G

ACTUAL STATISTICS

W^{Act}: Wins

L^{Act}: Losses

The Best Teams Ever

Here, then, are the 100 greatest teams of the modern era, led by the 1927 New York Yankees:

RANK	TEAM	SCORE	W	L	W%	R/G	OR/G	DIFF.	W^{ACT}	L^{ACT}
1	1927 New York Yankees	100.00	116	46	.716	6.86	4.21	2.65	110	44
2	1998 New York Yankees	93.75	114	48	.704	6.43	4.37	2.06	114	48
3	1902 Pittsburgh Pirates	91.72	120	42	.741	6.33	3.59	2.74	103	36
4	1939 New York Yankees	89.04	114	48	.704	6.81	3.91	2.90	106	45
5	1975 Cincinnati Reds	87.07	108	54	.667	6.33	4.41	1.92	108	54
6	1944 St. Louis Cardinals	84.04	110	52	.679	6.05	3.84	2.21	105	49
7	1969 Baltimore Orioles	83.49	109	53	.673	6.06	4.02	2.04	109	53
8	1910 Philadelphia Athletics	82.06	110	52	.679	5.82	3.81	2.01	102	48
9	1986 New York Mets	80.15	108	54	.667	5.60	4.14	1.46	108	54
10	1906 Chicago Cubs	80.14	124	38	.765	6.46	3.49	2.97	116	36
11	1929 Philadelphia Athletics	76.21	112	50	.691	5.91	4.03	1.88	104	46
12	1936 New York Yankees	73.70	108	54	.667	6.87	4.72	2.15	102	51
13	1953 Brooklyn Dodgers	73.56	110	52	.679	6.96	5.03	1.93	105	49
14	1919 Cincinnati Reds	72.03	111	51	.685	5.44	3.78	1.66	96	44
15	1976 Cincinnati Reds	70.60	102	60	.630	6.83	5.04	1.79	102	60
16	1995 Cleveland Indians	68.40	112	50	.691	6.18	4.47	1.71	100	44
17	1942 St. Louis Cardinals	68.08	112	50	.691	6.10	3.89	2.21	106	48
18	1984 Detroit Tigers	67.20	104	58	.642	6.19	4.80	1.39	104	58
19	1970 Baltimore Orioles	66.62	108	54	.667	5.77	4.18	1.59	108	54
20	1909 Pittsburgh Pirates	65.96	117	45	.722	6.58	4.21	2.37	110	42
21	1968 Detroit Tigers	65.63	103	59	.636	6.18	4.53	1.65	103	59
22	1912 Boston Red Sox	63.50	112	50	.691	5.86	3.99	1.87	105	47
23	1907 Chicago Cubs	61.02	114	48	.704	5.37	3.65	1.72	107	45
24	1954 Cleveland Indians	59.68	117	45	.722	5.60	3.78	1.82	111	43
25	1932 New York Yankees	57.48	113	49	.698	6.81	4.92	1.89	107	47
26	1942 New York Yankees	55.71	108	54	.667	6.55	4.15	2.40	103	51
27	2001 Seattle Mariners	53.96	116	46	.716	6.18	4.18	2.00	116	46

(The Best Teams Ever, continued)

RANK	TEAM	SCORE	W	L	W%	R/G	OR/G	DIFF.	WACT	LACT
28	1961 New York Yankees	53.12	109	53	.673	5.74	4.25	1.49	109	53
29	1905 New York Giants	52.20	111	51	.685	6.65	4.30	2.35	105	48
30	1971 Baltimore Orioles	51.97	104	58	.642	6.20	4.43	1.77	101	57
31	1911 Philadelphia Athletics	51.47	108	54	.667	6.46	4.51	1.95	101	50
32	1988 Oakland Athletics	50.69	104	58	.642	6.12	4.75	1.37	104	58
33	1943 St. Louis Cardinals	47.21	111	51	.685	5.66	3.96	1.70	105	49
34	1974 Los Angeles Dodgers	45.36	102	60	.630	6.16	4.33	1.83	102	60
35	1995 Atlanta Braves	45.32	101	61	.623	4.70	3.94	0.76	90	54
36	1937 New York Yankees	44.62	107	55	.660	6.61	4.53	2.08	102	52
37	1953 New York Yankees	44.24	106	56	.654	5.89	4.02	1.87	99	52
38	1940 Cincinnati Reds	43.41	106	56	.654	4.97	3.72	1.25	100	53
39	1928 New York Yankees	41.68	106	56	.654	6.32	4.85	1.47	101	53
40	1967 St. Louis Cardinals	40.77	102	60	.630	5.91	4.74	1.17	101	60
41	1921 New York Yankees	37.14	104	58	.642	6.63	4.95	1.68	98	55
42	1955 Brooklyn Dodgers	37.09	104	58	.642	6.40	4.86	1.54	98	55
43	1963 New York Yankees	36.65	105	57	.648	5.76	4.42	1.34	104	57
44	1979 Baltimore Orioles	36.23	104	58	.642	5.48	4.21	1.27	102	57
45	1913 Philadelphia Athletics	35.84	102	60	.630	6.64	4.95	1.69	96	57
46	1904 New York Giants	34.04	112	50	.691	6.50	4.16	2.34	106	47
47	1989 Oakland Athletics	33.99	99	63	.611	5.45	4.41	1.04	99	63
48	1931 Philadelphia Athletics	33.17	114	48	.704	6.00	4.38	1.62	107	45
49	1966 Baltimore Orioles	32.69	98	64	.605	6.09	4.84	1.25	97	63
50	1956 New York Yankees	32.63	102	60	.630	6.45	4.75	1.70	97	57
51	1946 Boston Red Sox	32.59	109	53	.673	6.55	4.91	1.64	104	50
52	1923 New York Yankees	32.03	104	58	.642	5.80	4.38	1.42	98	54
53	1914 Philadelphia Athletics	30.86	105	57	.648	6.54	4.62	1.92	99	53
54	1972 Cincinnati Reds	30.43	100	62	.617	6.43	5.06	1.37	95	59
55	1903 Boston Red Sox	30.20	107	55	.660	5.82	4.15	1.67	91	47
56	1983 Baltimore Orioles	30.05	98	64	.605	5.92	4.83	1.09	98	64
57	1977 Los Angeles Dodgers	29.52	98	64	.605	5.46	4.13	1.33	98	64
58	1917 Chicago White Sox	28.88	105	57	.648	6.01	4.26	1.75	100	54
59	1965 Minnesota Twins	28.82	102	60	.630	6.35	4.59	1.76	93	58
60	1935 Detroit Tigers	28.69	100	62	.617	6.03	4.08	1.95	96	58
61	1948 Cleveland Indians	28.59	101	61	.623	6.62	4.96	1.66	98	56
62	1920 Cleveland Indians	28.56	103	59	.636	6.12	4.65	1.47	101	53
63	1941 New York Yankees	28.54	106	56	.654	5.66	4.27	1.39	101	53
64	1931 St. Louis Cardinals	28.40	106	56	.654	6.19	4.34	1.85	104	50
65	1910 Chicago Cubs	28.28	109	53	.673	6.05	4.32	1.73	97	57
66	1947 New York Yankees	28.17	102	60	.630	6.52	4.80	1.72	99	53
67	1938 New York Yankees	28.08	106	56	.654	5.46	3.84	1.62	106	56
68	1998 Atlanta Braves	27.82	106	56	.654	5.56	4.18	1.38	97	57
69	1954 New York Giants	27.50	102	60	.630	5.74	4.53	1.21	102	52
70	1930 Philadelphia Athletics	27.30	107	55	.660	6.09	4.23	1.86	103	48
71	1912 New York Giants	26.94	110	52	.679	5.10	4.39	0.71	99	63
72	1963 Los Angeles Dodgers	26.25	99	63	.611	5.81	4.45	1.36	95	59
73	1952 New York Yankees	26.15	100	62	.617	5.96	4.67	1.29	95	58
74	1925 Pittsburgh Pirates	26.13	101	61	.623	5.82	4.41	1.41	94	59
75	1921 New York Giants	26.09	99	63	.611	5.65	4.58	1.07	98	56
76	1943 New York Yankees	26.01	103	59	.636	5.55	3.97	1.58	99	54
77	1911 New York Giants	26.00	105	57	.648	5.55	3.97	1.58	99	54

(The Best Teams Ever, continued)

RANK	TEAM	SCORE	W	L	W%	R/G	OR/G	DIFF.	W^{ACT}	L^{ACT}
78	1934 Detroit Tigers	25.81	106	56	.654	6.59	4.87	1.72	101	53
79	1957 Milwaukee Braves	25.75	100	62	.617	5.97	4.75	1.22	95	59
80	1960 Pittsburgh Pirates	25.41	100	62	.617	5.63	4.55	1.08	95	59
81	1979 Pittsburgh Pirates	25.29	98	64	.605	5.47	4.53	0.94	98	64
82	1922 New York Giants	25.19	98	64	.605	5.79	4.47	1.32	93	61
83	1951 New York Yankees	25.14	103	59	.636	5.86	4.56	1.30	98	56
84	1946 St. Louis Cardinals	24.93	101	61	.623	5.84	4.47	1.37	96	58
85	1914 Boston Braves	24.86	99	63	.611	5.70	4.75	0.95	94	59
86	1915 Boston Red Sox	24.78	108	54	.667	5.83	4.35	1.48	101	50
87	1920 Brooklyn Dodgers	24.26	98	64	.605	4.98	3.99	0.99	93	61
88	1999 Atlanta Braves	24.09	103	59	.636	5.23	4.12	1.11	103	59
89	1999 New York Yankees	24.04	98	64	.605	5.61	4.56	1.05	98	64
90	1934 St. Louis Cardinals	23.96	101	61	.623	5.40	4.43	0.97	95	58
91	1909 Chicago Cubs	23.56	110	52	.679	5.90	3.63	2.27	104	49
92	1902 Philadelphia Athletics	23.13	99	63	.611	6.62	5.43	1.19	83	53
93	1913 New York Giants	23.10	108	54	.667	5.57	4.19	1.38	101	51
94	1950 New York Yankees	22.90	103	59	.636	6.25	4.72	1.53	98	56
95	1929 Chicago Cubs	22.75	105	57	.648	6.29	4.86	1.43	98	54
96	1957 New York Yankees	22.70	103	59	.636	5.58	4.12	1.46	98	56
97	1985 St. Louis Cardinals	22.66	101	61	.623	5.44	4.17	1.27	101	61
98	1907 Detroit Tigers	22.65	99	63	.611	6.67	5.11	1.56	92	58
98	1969 New York Mets	22.65	100	62	.617	4.91	4.21	0.70	100	62
100	1933 Washington Senators	22.60	106	56	.654	6.44	5.04	1.40	99	53

The Yankees, to no one's surprise, dominate the rankings. They hold first, second, and fourth places. And they own nearly a quarter of the top 100 slots – 23, to be precise. No other team has more than eight.

Two of the three runners-up, the New York Giants and Philadelphia Athletics, no longer exist. Both headed west during baseball's peripatetic decade, the 1950s. That makes the St. Louis Cardinals the only existing franchise with eight entries. A total of 22 franchises are represented in the top 100:

	TOP 100 TEAMS	
1	New York Yankees	23
2	New York Giants	8
2	Philadelphia Athletics	8
2	St. Louis Cardinals	8
5	Baltimore Orioles	6
6	Chicago Cubs	5
6	Cincinnati Reds	5
6	Detroit Tigers	5
6	Pittsburgh Pirates	5
10	Boston Red Sox	4
10	Cleveland Indians	4
12	Atlanta Braves	3
12	Brooklyn Dodgers	3
12	Los Angeles Dodgers	3
15	New York Mets	2
15	Oakland Athletics	2
17	Boston Braves	1
17	Chicago White Sox	1
17	Milwaukee Braves	1
17	Minnesota Twins	1
17	Seattle Mariners	1
17	Washington Senators	1

The rankings of the modern era's 100 best teams can be sliced and diced into smaller lists for all ten decades. (The first and last of those decades – 1901–1909 and 1990–2001 – weren't ten years long, but you get the idea.) The result is a list of the best teams for any period.

Each league has been on top for five decades.

The American League boasted the best team of the 1910s ('10 Philadelphia A's), twenties ('27 Yankees), thirties ('39 Yanks), sixties ('69 Orioles), and nineties ('98 Yankees). The National League was supreme in the 1900s ('02 Pirates), forties ('44 Cardinals), fifties ('53 Dodgers), seventies ('75 Reds), and eighties ('86 Mets):

DECADE	AL BEST (OVERALL RANK)	NL BEST (OVERALL RANK)
1901–1909	1903 Boston Red Sox (55)	1902 Pittsburgh Pirates (3)
1910–1919	1910 Philadelphia Athletics (8)	1919 Cincinnati Reds (14)
1920–1929	1927 New York Yankees (1)	1925 Pittsburgh Pirates (74)
1930–1939	1939 New York Yankees (4)	1931 St. Louis Cardinals (64)
1940–1949	1942 New York Yankees (26)	1944 St. Louis Cardinals (6)
1950–1959	1954 Cleveland Indians (24)	1953 Brooklyn Dodgers (13)
1960–1969	1969 Baltimore Orioles (7)	1967 St. Louis Cardinals (40)
1970–1979	1970 Baltimore Orioles (19)	1975 Cincinnati Reds (5)
1980–1989	1984 Detroit Tigers (18)	1986 New York Mets (9)
1990–2001	1998 New York Yankees (2)	1995 Atlanta Braves (35)

Excellence is a rare commodity. That's why most seasons have placed only one team in the top 100 – or none at all. But there were 25 instances of two teams sharing the spotlight. The first came in 1902, when the Pirates (3rd in the rankings) and Athletics (92nd) both made the list. The most-recent occurrence was in 1999, when the Braves (88th) and Yankees (89th) both qualified.

Seasons blessed with two juggernauts usually ended with a monumental World Series. Top-100 teams have squared off 22 times in postseason play since 1901. The team with the higher rating won nine of these matchups; the lower-rated team took thirteen, attesting to the unpredictability of a short series:

YEAR	FIRST TEAM (OVERALL RANK)	SECOND TEAM (OVERALL RANK)	WORLD SERIES
1902	Pittsburgh Pirates (3)	Philadelphia Athletics (92)	(no series)
1907	Chicago Cubs (23)	Detroit Tigers (98)	Cubs 4, Tigers 0
1909	Pittsburgh Pirates (20)	Chicago Cubs (91)	Pirates 4, Detroit Tigers 3*
1910	Philadelphia Athletics (8)	Chicago Cubs (65)	Athletics 4, Cubs 1
1911	Philadelphia Athletics (31)	New York Giants (77)	Athletics 4, Giants 2
1912	Boston Red Sox (22)	New York Giants (71)	Red Sox 4, Giants 3
1913	Philadelphia Athletics (45)	New York Giants (93)	Athletics 4, Giants 1
1914	Philadelphia Athletics (53)	Boston Braves (85)	Braves 4, Athletics 0
1920	Cleveland Indians (62)	Brooklyn Dodgers (87)	Indians 5, Dodgers 2
1921	New York Yankees (41)	New York Giants (75)	Giants 5, Yankees 3
1929	Philadelphia Athletics (11)	Chicago Cubs (95)	Athletics 4, Cubs 1
1931	Philadelphia Athletics (48)	St. Louis Cardinals (64)	Cardinals 4, Athletics 3

(continued)

YEAR	FIRST TEAM (OVERALL RANK)	SECOND TEAM (OVERALL RANK)	WORLD SERIES
1934	Detroit Tigers (78)	St. Louis Cardinals (90)	Cardinals 4, Tigers 3
1942	St. Louis Cardinals (17)	New York Yankees (26)	Cardinals 4, Yankees 1
1943	St. Louis Cardinals (33)	New York Yankees (76)	Yankees 4, Cardinals 1
1946	Boston Red Sox (51)	St. Louis Cardinals (84)	Cardinals 4, Red Sox 3
1953	Brooklyn Dodgers (13)	New York Yankees (37)	Yankees 4, Dodgers 2
1954	Cleveland Indians (24)	New York Giants (69)	Giants 4, Indians 0
1957	Milwaukee Braves (79)	New York Yankees (96)	Braves 4, Yankees 3
1963	New York Yankees (43)	Los Angeles Dodgers (72)	Dodgers 4, Yankees 0
1969	Baltimore Orioles (7)	New York Mets (98)	Mets 4, Orioles 1
1979	Baltimore Orioles (44)	Pittsburgh Pirates (81)	Pirates 4, Orioles 3
1995	Cleveland Indians (16)	Atlanta Braves (35)	Braves 4, Indians 2
1998	New York Yankees (2)	Atlanta Braves (68)	Yankees 4, San Diego Padres 0**
1999	Atlanta Braves (88)	New York Yankees (89)	Yankees 4, Braves 0

* Cubs were second in the National League in 1909.
** Braves lost NLCS to San Diego in 1998.

Coming next are brief profiles of the 20 best teams of the modern era. All of the player statistics mentioned in the text are adjusted, unless otherwise noted. (Team standings and playoff results are a different matter. Any reference to a divisional title means an actual division, not one I created in Chapter 2. If I say a team finished X games ahead of the runner-up, that's X actual games. And World Series results cited here are real, not simulated.) Each profile concludes with adjusted statistics for every batter with at least 200 adjusted at bats and every pitcher who worked at least 50 adjusted innings. (Keys to the abbreviations used in the batting and pitching charts can be found near the beginning of Chapters 2, 6, and 7.)

1. 1927 NEW YORK YANKEES

The greatest team of the modern era was nicknamed Murderers Row, and for good reason. It killed opposing pitchers. The Yankees hit nearly three times as many home runs as any other American League team in 1927. Right fielder Babe Ruth smashed 89 homers and drove in 179 runs. He was followed in the batting order by first baseman Lou Gehrig, the AL's Most Valuable Player, who drilled 83 homers and 191 RBIs. No other team in baseball history has packed such a powerful one-two punch. Left fielder Bob Meusel and second baseman Tony Lazzeri each contributed more than 100 RBIs. Gehrig, Ruth, Meusel, and center fielder Earle Combs all batted over .300.

The pitching staff boasted three 20-game winners: Waite Hoyt, Herb Pennock, and Wilcy Moore. (Urban Shocker came close with nineteen wins.) Moore also chipped in 21 saves and led the American League in earned run average, earning the hypothetical Cy Young Award for 1927.

The Yanks won regularly; their adjusted record was 116-46. And they won with ease, scoring 2.65 runs per game more than their opponents. They cruised to the American League title by nineteen games over the runner-up Philadelphia Athletics, then swept the Pittsburgh Pirates in the World Series.

BATTERS	HR	RBI	BA	G	AB	R	H	2B	3B	SA
Lou Gehrig	83	191	.354	162	610	162	216	32	4	.828
Earle Combs	23	69	.339	159	678	149	230	52	13	.556
Babe Ruth	89	179	.338	158	565	173	191	15	1	.841
Bob Meusel	23	112	.319	141	539	81	172	50	4	.555
Tony Lazzeri	37	111	.294	160	596	100	175	21	2	.522
Mark Koenig	12	67	.270	129	552	108	149	30	7	.415
Johnny Grabowski	0	27	.261	73	203	31	53	6	6	.350
Pat Collins	14	39	.260	96	262	41	68	7	1	.454
Joe Dugan	7	47	.255	117	404	48	103	32	1	.391
Ray Morehart	4	22	.241	76	203	49	49	10	1	.360

PITCHERS	W	L	SV	ERA	G	IP	ER	H	BB	SO
Wilcy Moore	20	7	21	2.59	52	222	64	183	73	180
Waite Hoyt	23	7	3	2.99	38	271	90	244	67	211
Urban Shocker	19	6	0	3.23	32	206	74	203	50	90
Herb Pennock	20	8	5	3.41	36	222	84	227	60	131
Dutch Ruether	13	6	0	3.82	28	191	81	200	64	113
George Pipgras	10	3	0	4.66	30	172	89	146	95	181
Myles Thomas	7	4	0	5.52	22	93	57	111	54	63

The 1927 New York Yankees (aka Murderers Row). The greatest team of the modern era.

2. 1998 NEW YORK YANKEES

The Yankees regained their swagger during the latter half of the 1990s. Their 1996 world championship was their first in eighteen years. They did even better two years later, winning 114 games during the 1998 regular season (clinching the American League East title by 22 games over second-place Boston), then taking 11 of 13 postseason contests for their second title in three years. The World Series itself was never in doubt, as the Yanks swept the San Diego Padres.

Power was evenly distributed throughout the Yankee lineup, though the 1998 team couldn't match its 1927 counterpart in slugging. Eight batters hit at least 18 home runs, led by first baseman Tino Martinez with 29. Four racked up at least 100 RBIs, again led by Martinez with 128. Center fielder Bernie Williams topped the AL with a .343 batting average.

The Yanks' pitching staff registered an actual ERA of 3.82, by far the lowest in the American League. No other team was below 4.18. The two aces were David Cone (whose 20 wins were the most in the league) and David Wells (who posted a nifty 18–4 record). Closer Mariano Rivera had 35 saves.

BATTERS	HR	RBI	BA	G	AB	R	H	2B	3B	SA
Bernie Williams	27	101	.343	128	499	105	171	30	5	.585
Derek Jeter	20	87	.327	149	626	132	205	25	8	.489
Paul O'Neill	25	120	.321	152	602	98	193	40	2	.518
Scott Brosius	20	102	.304	152	530	89	161	34	0	.481
Tim Raines	5	49	.293	109	321	55	94	13	1	.386
Tino Martinez	29	128	.284	142	531	95	151	33	1	.514
Joe Girardi	3	32	.280	78	254	32	71	11	4	.390
Jorge Posada	18	65	.271	111	358	58	97	23	0	.486
Chuck Knoblauch	18	66	.269	150	603	121	162	25	4	.413
Darryl Strawberry	25	59	.251	101	295	46	74	11	2	.556
Chad Curtis	10	58	.246	151	456	82	112	22	1	.364

PITCHERS	W	L	SV	ERA	G	IP	ER	H	BB	SO
Mariano Rivera	3	0	35	1.92	54	61	13	48	18	36
Orlando Hernandez	12	4	0	3.26	21	141	51	114	55	130
Ramiro Mendoza	10	2	0	3.32	41	130	48	132	32	55
Darren Holmes	0	3	1	3.53	34	51	20	53	15	31
David Wells	18	4	0	3.62	30	214	86	197	30	161
David Cone	20	7	0	3.68	31	208	85	189	62	208
Hideki Irabu	13	9	0	4.21	29	173	81	150	80	125
Andy Pettitte	16	11	0	4.38	33	216	105	229	92	145
Mike Stanton	4	1	5	5.70	67	79	50	72	27	68

3. 1902 PITTSBURGH PIRATES

Baseball was a much different game a century ago, but the 1902 Pirates shared one essential trait with the great teams of later years. They knew how to win.

Pittsburgh's adjusted record was 120–42, resulting in a winning percentage of .741, second-best in the modern era. The Pirates took the National League title by 27½ games over the runner-up Brooklyn Dodgers, and then they went home. The World Series wouldn't debut until the following season. (The Pirates would qualify for the inaugural series in 1903, but lose to the Red Sox.)

Pittsburgh led the National League in almost every individual batting category in 1902. Right fielder/shortstop Honus Wagner, the league's Most Valuable Player, ranked first in runs scored (134), runs batted in (116), slugging average (.573), and stolen bases (27). Center fielder Ginger Beaumont topped the league in batting average (.360), hits (222), and doubles (83). And third baseman Tommy Leach hit the most home runs (37).

Pittsburgh's pitching staff and defense held opponents to just 3.59 adjusted runs per game. Jack Chesbro, who would later star for the Yankees, anchored the Pirates' rotation with a 32–7 record and 318 strikeouts. Deacon Phillippe and Jesse Tannehill added 23 wins each.

BATTERS	HR	RBI	BA	G	AB	R	H	2B	3B	SA
Ginger Beaumont	0	85	.360	148	616	127	222	83	7	.518
Honus Wagner	25	116	.333	155	609	134	203	53	9	.573
Fred Clarke	19	67	.319	129	524	131	167	51	8	.555
Kitty Bransfield	0	87	.309	116	470	62	145	69	8	.489
Jimmy Burke	0	33	.300	68	230	30	69	34	2	.465
Lefty Davis	0	25	.281	67	263	66	74	30	3	.418
Tommy Leach	37	108	.280	154	586	123	164	17	9	.529
Claude Ritchey	13	70	.280	131	461	68	129	19	0	.406
Wid Conroy	10	60	.245	113	417	70	102	21	4	.386
Harry Smith	0	15	.190	57	211	18	40	18	0	.275

PITCHERS	W	L	SV	ERA	G	IP	ER	H	BB	SO
Jesse Tannehill	23	7	0	2.80	30	267	83	236	42	241
Deacon Phillippe	23	10	0	2.93	35	307	100	301	42	285
Jack Chesbro	32	7	1	3.11	40	327	113	277	102	318
Sam Leever	18	8	5	3.44	32	254	97	233	51	208
Ed Doheny	18	5	0	3.66	25	214	87	184	101	205

4. 1939 NEW YORK YANKEES

The Yankees suffered an unexpected blow early in the 1939 season, one that could have derailed their entire season. First baseman Lou Gehrig, the future Hall of Famer who had played in every game since June 1925, voluntarily benched himself in early May. It was revealed a month later that he had been stricken with amyotrophic lateral sclerosis. He would never play again.

The Yanks kept rolling despite the loss of Gehrig, winning the American League title by seventeen games and sweeping Cincinnati in the World Series. Center fielder Joe DiMaggio filled the void with 46 homers, 139 RBIs, and a league-leading .373 batting average. He was named Most Valuable Player. Second baseman Joe Gordon added 43 home runs, catcher Bill Dickey 36, and left fielder George Selkirk 32. All four men drove in at least 100 runs. Third baseman Red Rolfe led the AL in hits (222) and doubles (52).

Yankee pitchers were the stingiest in the majors in 1939, yielding just 8.1 actual hits per game. No other American League team was lower than 9.2. Red Ruffing, with a 23–7 record and a 3.13 ERA, was the ace of the staff. Reliever Johnny Murphy topped the league with 28 saves.

BATTERS	HR	RBI	BA	G	AB	R	H	2B	3B	SA
Joe DiMaggio	46	139	.373	128	493	119	184	28	2	.718
Charlie Keller	21	91	.326	118	423	96	138	22	3	.541
Red Rolfe	27	88	.321	162	691	153	222	52	6	.531
George Selkirk	32	111	.300	136	444	113	133	15	2	.559
Bill Dickey	36	115	.296	136	510	108	151	20	2	.555
Joe Gordon	43	122	.278	161	605	101	168	28	2	.544
Tommy Henrich	16	63	.272	106	372	71	101	19	2	.462
Babe Dahlgren	26	98	.230	153	564	78	130	17	3	.410
Frank Crosetti	19	61	.227	162	699	120	159	27	3	.356

PITCHERS	W	L	SV	ERA	G	IP	ER	H	BB	SO
Marius Russo	8	3	5	2.58	22	122	35	88	44	105
Steve Sundra	12	1	0	2.95	26	131	43	116	63	58
Red Ruffing	23	7	0	3.13	30	250	87	219	83	189
Bump Hadley	13	6	5	3.20	28	166	59	138	95	130
Oral Hildebrand	10	4	5	3.25	22	133	48	104	44	98
Lefty Gomez	13	9	0	3.63	28	213	86	180	93	198
Atley Donald	14	3	3	3.96	26	166	73	151	67	112
Johnny Murphy	3	6	28	4.77	41	66	35	59	31	58
Monte Pearson	13	5	0	4.82	23	153	82	153	75	143

5. 1975 CINCINNATI REDS

The Big Red Machine made a mockery of the National League West in 1975, wrapping up the divisional title on September 7, the earliest clinching date in league history. The Reds finished 20 games ahead of second-place Los Angeles. They swept Pittsburgh in the NL playoffs, then took the world championship with a nail-biting win over the Boston Red Sox in the seventh game of one of the most thrilling World Series ever.

Second baseman Joe Morgan was foremost among Cincinnati's stars, batting .341 and driving in 110 runs to win Most Valuable Player honors.

Third baseman Pete Rose led the NL in runs (131) and doubles (65), while catcher Johnny Bench led the Reds in home runs (38) and RBIs (128). Other sluggers of note were first baseman Tony Perez with 127 RBIs, and left fielder George Foster with 32 homers.

Cincinnati's pitching staff was surprisingly nondescript. Don Gullett turned in the best performance, 15–4 with a 2.98 ERA. Gary Nolan and Jack Billingham also won fifteen. The only Reds pitcher to top the league in an individual category was reliever Rawly Eastwick with 30 saves.

BATTERS	HR	RBI	BA	G	AB	R	H	2B	3B	SA
Joe Morgan	25	110	.341	146	498	125	170	33	5	.578
Pete Rose	12	86	.331	162	662	131	219	65	3	.492
Ken Griffey Sr.	7	54	.317	132	463	111	147	24	10	.458
George Foster	32	91	.313	134	463	83	145	27	3	.592
Johnny Bench	38	128	.296	142	530	97	157	42	1	.594
Dan Driessen	10	44	.295	88	210	44	62	9	1	.490
Tony Perez	29	127	.294	137	511	86	150	32	2	.534
Dave Concepcion	9	57	.286	140	507	72	145	31	1	.404
Cesar Geronimo	10	62	.269	148	501	80	135	34	4	.413

PITCHERS	W	L	SV	ERA	G	IP	ER	H	BB	SO
Don Gullett	15	4	0	2.98	22	160	53	135	58	128
Will McEnaney	5	2	23	3.07	70	91	31	98	24	63
Clay Carroll	7	5	11	3.19	56	96	34	99	33	58
Rawly Eastwick	5	3	30	3.20	67	125	51	154	22	40
Pedro Borbon	9	5	8	3.67	67	125	51	215	30	100
Gary Nolan	15	9	0	3.92	32	211	92	215	30	62
Pat Darcy	11	5	1	4.40	27	131	64	143	61	62
Fred Norman	12	4	0	4.60	34	188	96	173	87	155
Jack Billingham	15	10	0	5.11	33	208	118	236	79	105
Clay Kirby	10	6	0	5.84	26	111	72	121	56	64

6. 1944 ST. LOUIS CARDINALS

Yes, it was wartime, and yes, the quality of baseball was diluted. But the 1944 Cardinals would have been an excellent team in any decade. Just look at what the Cards did after World War II had ended. They won the 1946 World Series with many of the same players, then finished second in the National League the following three seasons.

How dominant were the 1944 Cardinals? They entered September with a 20-game lead over the rest of the league, inexplicably lost 15 of their next 20 outings, yet finished with an adjusted record of 110–52. Their margin over second-place Pittsburgh at season's end was

14½ games. The capper was an all-St. Louis World Series, with the Cards triumphing over the Browns.

Right fielder Stan Musial, just 23 years old, slapped the most hits (211) and doubles (62) in the NL, and registered the highest slugging average in either league (.659). He also hit 32 homers, putting him among six Cardinals with 28 or more. Smooth-fielding shortstop Marty Marion was named the league's MVP.

St. Louis's actual ERA of 2.67 was the lowest in the majors and nearly a full point below the National League average. Mort Cooper, with 23 wins, was the ace of the staff.

BATTERS	HR	RBI	BA	G	AB	R	H	2B	3B	SA
Stan Musial	32	116	.359	151	587	139	211	62	9	.659
Johnny Hopp	28	88	.347	143	542	131	188	41	6	.600
Walker Cooper	28	89	.328	116	411	69	135	25	2	.603
Ray Sanders	30	126	.304	159	621	107	189	39	5	.528
Whitey Kurowski	40	108	.279	154	574	118	160	23	3	.538
Marty Marion	16	78	.275	149	524	62	144	33	1	.433
Danny Litwhiler	31	101	.273	144	506	65	138	23	2	.510
Emil Verban	0	53	.266	151	515	63	137	39	2	.350
Ken O'Dea	13	46	.255	88	274	43	70	11	1	.445

PITCHERS	W	L	SV	ERA	G	IP	ER	H	BB	SO
Red Munger	12	3	4	1.70	22	127	24	100	48	111
Blix Donnelly	2	1	7	2.73	28	79	24	66	40	86
Mort Cooper	23	7	2	3.18	35	260	92	243	69	197
Harry Gumbert	4	2	2	3.25	10	61	22	62	21	33
Ted Wilks	17	4	0	3.42	37	213	81	184	56	145
Max Lanier	18	12	0	3.43	34	231	88	205	82	264
Harry Brecheen	17	5	0	3.72	31	196	81	187	53	174
Freddy Schmidt	7	3	14	4.08	38	117	53	100	67	112
Al Jurisich	7	9	4	4.43	31	134	66	109	76	107

7. 1969 BALTIMORE ORIOLES

It appeared that no one could stop the Orioles in 1969. Not their opponents in the American League East; Baltimore breezed to the division title by nineteen games. And certainly not the best team in the AL West; the Orioles easily swept Minnesota in the inaugural American League Championship Series.

That left only the New York Mets. The "Miracle Mets" had stunned the baseball world by not only posting their first above-.500 season, but also winning their first National League crown. The Orioles were prohibitive favorites in the World Series, but the Mets breezed to victory in five games. (My computer says that if the two teams had met in 100 series, the Orioles would have won 65 times.)

The 1969 Orioles nonetheless are remembered as one of the greatest teams in history. Six regulars batted over .300, led by right fielder Frank Robinson at .334. Robinson and first baseman Boog Powell were a potent combination in the heart of the order, with 87 homers and 265 RBIs between them.

Baltimore's pitchers yielded the fewest runs and hits of any big-league staff in 1969. Mike Cuellar tied for the Cy Young Award, winning 23 games and striking out 206. Dave McNally was also a 20-game winner.

BATTERS	HR	RBI	BA	G	AB	R	H	2B	3B	SA
Frank Robinson	41	120	.334	148	539	133	180	26	4	.625
Boog Powell	46	145	.330	152	533	99	176	32	0	.649
Don Buford	15	76	.316	144	554	119	175	43	3	.486
Mark Belanger	4	60	.311	150	530	91	165	29	4	.404
Paul Blair	34	91	.309	150	625	122	193	43	4	.554
Dave Johnson	9	68	.303	142	511	62	155	48	1	.454
Andy Etchebarren	4	31	.272	73	217	35	59	13	2	.406
Ellie Hendricks	15	45	.264	105	295	43	78	7	0	.441
Brooks Robinson	29	100	.254	156	598	87	152	28	3	.457

PITCHERS	W	L	SV	ERA	G	IP	ER	H	BB	SO
Eddie Watt	5	2	21	2.03	56	71	16	54	27	52
Dick Hall	5	2	8	2.45	39	66	18	55	9	35
Pete Richert	7	4	16	2.84	44	57	18	46	14	60
Jim Palmer	16	4	0	2.98	26	181	60	145	66	139
Mike Cuellar	23	11	0	3.03	39	291	98	237	82	206
Dave Leonhard	7	4	1	3.16	37	94	33	87	39	43
Dave McNally	20	7	0	4.08	41	269	122	258	87	188
Tom Phoebus	14	7	0	4.46	35	202	100	200	90	132
Jim Hardin	6	7	1	4.57	30	138	70	143	45	73
Marcelino Lopez	5	3	0	5.61	27	69	43	72	35	63

8. 1910 PHILADELPHIA ATHLETICS

The 1910 Athletics could swing the bat, no doubt about that. They were first in the American League in hits, doubles, triples, batting average, and slugging average. But it was their outstanding pitching that secured them a place on the modern era's honor roll.

Philadelphia's staff registered an actual earned run average of 1.79, to this day the lowest team ERA in AL history. Four starters picked up at least seventeen adjusted wins; three had adjusted ERAs below 2.70. Jack Coombs earned the hypothetical Most Valuable Player and Cy Young Awards with a 32–9 record, 2.12 ERA, and 376 strikeouts. Chief Bender (24–5) and

Eddie Plank (17–11 with seven saves) polished the credentials that would eventually land them in Cooperstown.

Another future Hall of Famer, second baseman Eddie Collins, was the spark plug of the batting order. He hit .350, drove in 104 runs, and led the league with 43 stolen bases. Three other regulars topped .300.

The A's, who finished with an adjusted record of 110–52, were 14½ games ahead of the runner-up Yankees. They continued their winning ways in the World Series, trouncing the Cubs, four games to one.

BATTERS	HR	RBI	BA	G	AB	R	H	2B	3B	SA
Eddie Collins	26	104	.350	160	608	104	213	28	7	.548
Rube Oldring	27	73	.332	140	570	101	189	39	5	.560
Danny Murphy	29	82	.324	158	586	90	190	43	7	.570
Frank Baker	19	95	.306	153	588	107	180	50	8	.515
Bris Lord	10	26	.302	73	291	68	88	28	7	.550
Jack Barry	18	77	.280	152	511	83	143	24	2	.440
Harry Davis	9	52	.267	145	513	78	137	39	3	.407
Jack Lapp	0	22	.255	74	200	23	51	18	3	.375
Topsy Hartsel	0	28	.238	94	298	58	71	33	2	.362

PITCHERS	W	L	SV	ERA	G	IP	ER	H	BB	SO
Jack Coombs	32	9	4	2.12	47	369	87	295	145	376
Cy Morgan	19	13	0	2.55	38	307	87	258	149	236
Chief Bender	24	5	0	2.62	31	258	75	214	58	257
Eddie Plank	17	11	7	3.31	40	264	97	262	70	215
Jimmy Dygert	4	4	0	4.20	20	105	49	98	63	101
Tommy Atkins	3	2	7	4.43	16	61	30	65	30	51
Harry Krause	6	6	0	4.76	17	119	63	120	54	104

9. 1986 NEW YORK METS

The Mets came tantalizingly close to winning the National League East in 1984 and 1985, falling just 6½ games off the pace the first season, inching within 3 games the next. They finished in second place both years.

Revenge was theirs in 1986, when they blew away the competition with a record of 108–54, for a winning percentage of .667. The closest team in their division, Philadelphia, was 21½ games back. The going got harder in the playoffs, but the Mets persevered. They ousted Houston from the NL Championship Series in six games, then battled back (with a little help from Bill Buckner)

to best the Red Sox in a World Series that went the full seven.

New York was a well-balanced team in 1986, scoring the most runs in the National League and giving up the fewest earned runs. Spearheading the offense were right fielder Darryl Strawberry (31 homers), catcher Gary Carter (117 RBIs), and first baseman Keith Hernandez (.325 batting average).

The Mets' staff boasted five pitchers with at least fourteen wins. The ace was Bobby Ojeda, who went 18–5 with a 2.94 ERA. Relievers Roger McDowell and Jesse Orosco combined for 45 saves.

BATTERS	HR	RBI	BA	G	AB	R	H	2B	3B	SA
Wally Backman	1	30	.333	124	387	75	129	24	2	.413
Keith Hernandez	16	92	.325	149	551	105	179	38	1	.485
Ray Knight	13	85	.311	137	486	57	151	28	2	.457
Lenny Dykstra	10	50	.309	147	431	86	133	31	7	.483
Mookie Wilson	11	50	.302	123	381	68	115	19	5	.465
Kevin Mitchell	14	48	.290	108	328	57	95	25	2	.506
Darryl Strawberry	31	104	.269	136	475	85	128	30	5	.549
Gary Carter	28	117	.265	132	490	90	130	15	2	.476
Tim Teufel	5	35	.258	93	279	39	72	23	1	.401
Howard Johnson	12	43	.255	88	220	33	56	15	0	.486
George Foster	15	42	.236	72	233	31	55	7	1	.468
Rafael Santana	1	31	.228	139	394	42	90	15	0	.274

PITCHERS	W	L	SV	ERA	G	IP	ER	H	BB	SO
Jesse Orosco	8	6	22	2.67	58	81	24	68	37	69
Bobby Ojeda	18	5	0	2.94	32	217	71	196	55	164
Rick Anderson	2	1	1	3.06	15	50	17	48	12	23
Ron Darling	15	6	0	3.23	34	237	85	215	86	204
Dwight Gooden	17	6	0	3.28	33	250	91	209	85	221
Roger McDowell	14	9	23	3.52	75	128	50	113	44	73
Doug Sisk	4	2	1	3.55	41	71	28	82	33	35
Sid Fernandez	16	6	1	4.06	32	204	92	170	96	219
Rick Aguilera	10	7	0	4.50	28	142	71	154	38	115

10. 1906 CHICAGO CUBS

No team in baseball history was better at winning (in the regular season, anyway) than the 1906 Cubs. Their adjusted record remains the best of the entire modern era: 124 wins against 38 losses, yielding a winning percentage of .765. They were especially impressive on the road, where they won 80 percent of the time, another mark never equaled.

The Cubs mounted a relentless attack. Eight batters smashed at least ten homers; five scored at least 100 runs. Manager-first baseman Frank Chance was the National League's Most Valuable Player, batting .347 and leading the league in runs (141) and stolen bases (32). Third baseman Harry Steinfeldt topped the NL with 201 hits.

Pitcher Mordecai "Three Finger" Brown, destined for the Hall of Fame, earned 1906's hypothetical Cy Young Award with a 27–6 record and a 1.78 ERA, the latter the best in the majors. Jack Pfiester and Ed Reulbach won 21 and 20 games, respectively.

The only blemish on the Cubs' seemingly spotless record came in the World Series, which they inexplicably lost in six games to a White Sox squad known as the "Hitless Wonders." My computer says if the series were replayed 100 times, the Cubs would win 94, which makes the Sox's victory the greatest upset in World Series history.

BATTERS	HR	RBI	BA	G	AB	R	H	2B	3B	SA
Harry Steinfeldt	27	113	.356	158	564	110	201	39	4	.583
Frank Chance	25	97	.347	142	495	141	172	34	4	.584
Johnny Kling	18	63	.340	112	359	61	122	22	4	.574
Frank Schulte	38	82	.307	153	590	105	181	16	3	.537
Jimmy Sheckard	13	61	.287	156	575	123	165	59	7	.482
Solly Hofman	10	27	.279	67	204	41	57	2	1	.446
Johnny Evers	13	69	.278	161	557	88	155	37	4	.429
Pat Moran	0	48	.275	73	236	30	65	37	0	.432
Jimmy Slagle	0	45	.261	133	522	97	136	43	10	.381
Joe Tinker	12	87	.254	155	548	102	139	36	2	.392

PITCHERS	W	L	SV	ERA	G	IP	ER	H	BB	SO
Mordecai Brown	27	6	4	1.78	38	293	58	238	90	258
Jack Pfiester	21	8	0	2.57	32	259	74	203	91	262
Ed Reulbach	20	4	8	2.84	34	225	71	151	134	168
Jack Taylor	13	3	0	3.17	18	156	55	140	58	66
Orval Overall	13	3	2	3.20	19	152	54	140	76	162
Carl Lundgren	18	6	3	3.81	28	215	91	189	130	182
Fred Beebe	8	1	4	4.68	15	75	39	68	48	93
Bob Wicker	3	5	0	5.13	10	72	41	80	27	44

11. 1929 PHILADELPHIA ATHLETICS

Few teams could have prevented the relentless Yankees from grabbing their fourth consecutive American League pennant in 1929, but the Athletics were more than equal to the task. They finished with 112 adjusted wins, leaving New York eighteen games behind, then breezed through the Cubs in a five-game World Series.

The Yanks may have had Ruth and Gehrig, but the A's boasted two Hall-of-Fame sluggers of their own. Left fielder Al Simmons blasted 54 homers, first baseman Jimmie Foxx, 50. They drove in 286 runs between them.

The Athletics were blessed with two outstanding pitchers. George Earnshaw topped the majors with 26 wins, and the incomparable Lefty Grove had the lowest ERA (2.87) and the most strikeouts (365) in the big leagues.

BATTERS	HR	RBI	BA	G	AB	R	H	2B	3B	SA
Al Simmons	54	163	.339	153	622	118	211	32	3	.661
Jimmie Foxx	50	123	.330	160	555	128	183	17	3	.641
Bing Miller	20	97	.311	158	598	87	186	40	8	.505
Mickey Cochrane	16	99	.308	145	552	117	170	42	4	.486
Jimmy Dykes	24	82	.304	128	431	79	131	31	3	.557
Mule Haas	30	85	.292	149	620	119	181	38	3	.508
Sammy Hale	3	41	.257	108	405	53	104	24	2	.348
Joe Boley	5	49	.233	98	326	37	76	23	4	.374
Max Bishop	8	37	.215	138	508	105	109	25	4	.327

PITCHERS	W	L	SV	ERA	G	IP	ER	H	BB	SO
Lefty Grove	21	6	10	2.87	45	295	94	274	94	365
Eddie Rommel	13	2	10	2.90	34	121	39	132	39	63
Howard Ehmke	8	2	0	3.30	12	60	22	48	18	49
George Earnshaw	26	9	3	3.34	47	272	101	229	146	322
Rube Walberg	19	12	8	3.66	43	288	117	253	116	226
Bill Shores	12	6	16	3.68	42	164	67	148	69	119
Jack Quinn	12	10	6	4.06	38	175	79	182	46	104

12. 1936 NEW YORK YANKEES

The 1936 Yankees were a blend of two teams that rank higher on this list. Slugging first baseman Lou Gehrig (70 homers, 157 RBIs) and second baseman Tony Lazzeri (113 RBIs) were holdovers from the 1927 Yanks, the greatest team ever. Rookie left fielder Joe DiMaggio (50 homers, 129 RBIs) and catcher Bill Dickey (.344 batting average) would become mainstays of the 1939 team, fourth in the all-time standings.

New York won two-thirds of its games in 1936, producing an adjusted record of 108–54. Second-place Detroit was 19½ games back. The Yanks defeated the crosstown Giants in the World Series, four games to two.

The pitching staff did its part, fashioning the lowest ERA in the American League. Red Ruffing posted 21 wins, Monte Pearson 20.

BATTERS	HR	RBI	BA	G	AB	R	H	2B	3B	SA
Bill Dickey	36	110	.344	117	442	102	152	21	3	.649
Lou Gehrig	70	157	.336	162	605	173	203	26	3	.736
Joe DiMaggio	50	129	.307	144	665	136	204	38	6	.608
Red Rolfe	23	72	.302	141	593	120	179	45	9	.524
George Selkirk	32	110	.293	143	515	96	151	24	4	.542
Jake Powell	13	49	.286	91	343	64	98	12	2	.446
Frank Crosetti	29	80	.272	158	661	142	180	33	4	.466
Tony Lazzeri	26	113	.272	157	562	85	153	27	3	.470

PITCHERS	W	L	SV	ERA	G	IP	ER	H	BB	SO
Johnny Murphy	9	3	11	3.36	28	91	34	86	39	68
Monte Pearson	20	7	3	3.76	34	230	96	181	147	226
Pat Malone	13	4	15	3.87	37	142	61	140	66	140
Red Ruffing	21	12	0	3.87	34	279	120	259	97	205
Johnny Broaca	13	7	8	4.27	39	217	103	228	73	171
Bump Hadley	14	4	3	4.37	32	179	87	184	96	146
Lefty Gomez	13	7	0	4.43	32	195	96	175	133	199
Jumbo Brown	1	4	4	5.91	21	67	44	90	32	40

13. 1953 BROOKLYN DODGERS

Brooklyn won its only world championship in 1955, but the Dodgers had been better two years earlier. They piled up 110 adjusted wins and finished thirteen games ahead of the rest of the National League, before letting the World Series slip away to the Yankees in six.

The famed Boys of Summer were an offensive machine, leading the majors in runs, homers, batting average, and slugging percentage in 1953. Five Brooklyn regulars batted over .300

and drove in more than 100 runs. Catcher Roy Campanella, the NL's Most Valuable Player, set the pace with 50 homers and 161 RBIs. Center fielder Duke Snider topped the majors in slugging (.676).

Dodgers pitchers, though not overpowering like the hitters, were good enough to win a pennant. The best was Carl Erskine, with 21 wins and an ERA of 3.89.

BATTERS	HR	RBI	BA	G	AB	R	H	2B	3B	SA
Carl Furillo	28	104	.351	138	501	92	176	47	4	.629
Duke Snider	52	142	.342	160	617	149	211	44	3	.676
Jackie Robinson	16	107	.335	142	505	123	169	45	5	.539
Roy Campanella	50	161	.318	151	544	116	173	30	2	.656
Gil Hodges	39	137	.308	147	542	113	167	26	5	.590
Billy Cox	13	50	.294	105	343	50	101	21	1	.475
Jim Gilliam	9	71	.283	158	633	141	179	47	14	.444
Pee Wee Reese	18	68	.277	146	546	121	151	32	5	.452
Bobby Morgan	10	37	.263	72	205	39	54	8	1	.459

PITCHERS	W	L	SV	ERA	G	IP	ER	H	BB	SO
Clem Labine	12	6	11	3.03	39	116	39	98	32	74
Bob Milliken	8	4	5	3.70	39	124	51	101	45	106
Jim Hughes	4	3	18	3.84	50	89	38	85	43	78
Carl Erskine	21	6	6	3.89	41	259	112	227	101	291
Ben Wade	7	5	7	4.16	33	93	43	83	34	99
Johnny Podres	9	4	0	4.65	34	118	61	132	67	126
Preacher Roe	11	3	0	4.80	26	163	87	181	42	136
Billy Loes	14	8	0	5.04	33	168	94	173	55	122
Russ Meyer	16	5	0	5.05	36	203	114	217	68	173
Joe Black	6	3	10	5.84	36	77	50	80	29	68

14. 1919 CINCINNATI REDS

History tells us that the Reds were sadly overmatched in the 1919 World Series, which they won only because the White/Black Sox threw several games. History is wrong.

Cincinnati's adjusted record of 111–51 in 1919 was nine games ahead of the Sox. It remains the best in team history, surpassing even the powerful Reds squads of the mid-seventies. Chicago had better hitters, to be sure, but Cincinnati was superior on the mound and in the field. The Reds gave up roughly one less run per game than the Sox did during the regular season, and they committed 25 fewer errors over the entire year.

Center fielder Edd Roush, batting .329 and driving in 103 runs, was named the National League's Most Valuable Player. Pitchers Slim Sallee, Hod Eller, and Dutch Ruether had 25, 23, and 22 wins.

BATTERS	HR	RBI	BA	G	AB	R	H	2B	3B	SA
Edd Roush	25	103	.329	154	584	105	192	29	6	.527
Heinie Groh	26	91	.319	141	518	114	165	22	4	.527
Jake Daubert	18	63	.282	162	621	114	175	22	9	.433
Ivey Wingo	0	39	.278	88	284	43	79	38	6	.454
Larry Kopf	0	83	.277	156	581	73	161	63	4	.399
Morrie Rath	9	42	.271	160	623	111	169	31	0	.364
Greasy Neale	11	78	.247	161	579	82	143	27	11	.389
Bill Rariden	7	35	.221	86	253	23	56	10	1	.352

PITCHERS	W	L	SV	ERA	G	IP	ER	H	BB	SO
Dutch Ruether	22	7	0	2.71	38	279	84	238	129	194
Slim Sallee	25	8	0	3.07	34	267	91	276	31	67
Ray Fisher	16	6	5	3.22	30	201	72	173	59	106
Jimmy Ring	12	10	11	3.35	37	212	79	185	79	151
Hod Eller	23	10	8	3.56	44	288	114	266	78	314
Dolf Luque	12	4	13	3.92	35	124	54	111	57	98

15. 1976 CINCINNATI REDS

Big Red Machine, take two. Cincinnati, whose 1975 squad ranks fifth on this list, came back nearly as strong in 1976. The Reds ended up with 102 wins, six fewer than the previous year, but good enough to clinch the National League West by ten games. The playoffs were easier than in 1975, as the Reds swept a total of seven games from the Phillies and Yankees for the league and world championships.

The cast of characters was familiar. Second baseman Joe Morgan repeated as NL Most Valuable Player, batting .337 with 42 home runs. Third baseman Pete Rose led the league in runs (160) and hits (227), while left fielder George Foster was first in RBIs (149).

The pitching staff, once again, was serviceable. Gary Nolan's 15 wins topped the group. Reliever Rawly Eastwick posted a league-leading 34 saves.

BATTERS	HR	RBI	BA	G	AB	R	H	2B	3B	SA
Ken Griffey Sr.	13	91	.354	148	562	136	199	44	8	.530
Pete Rose	20	77	.341	162	665	160	227	57	5	.532
Joe Morgan	42	136	.337	141	472	139	159	32	3	.684
Cesar Geronimo	6	60	.323	149	486	72	157	43	11	.494
George Foster	46	149	.322	144	562	105	181	23	6	.630
Doug Flynn	3	24	.297	93	219	24	65	9	3	.406
Dave Concepcion	18	85	.297	152	576	91	171	39	5	.476
Tony Perez	31	112	.273	139	527	94	144	36	4	.533
Dan Driessen	11	54	.260	98	219	39	57	12	1	.475
Johnny Bench	25	91	.247	135	465	76	115	26	1	.469

PITCHERS	W	L	SV	ERA	G	IP	ER	H	BB	SO
Rawly Eastwick	11	5	34	2.75	71	108	33	101	30	94
Pat Zachry	14	7	0	3.57	38	204	81	183	94	190
Don Gullett	11	3	1	3.93	23	126	55	128	54	87
Fred Norman	12	7	0	4.05	33	180	81	165	79	167
Pedro Borbon	4	3	12	4.39	69	121	59	146	35	73
Gary Nolan	15	9	0	4.52	34	239	120	250	30	155
Jack Billingham	12	10	1	5.64	34	177	111	205	70	105
Santo Alcala	11	4	0	6.14	30	132	90	141	76	91
Will McEnaney	2	6	11	6.38	55	72	51	104	26	39

16. 1995 CLEVELAND INDIANS

The young Indians suddenly came of age in 1995, claiming Cleveland's first American League title in 41 years. And they did it in dominant fashion, racking up 100 actual wins in a strike-shortened 144-game season, the same as an adjusted record of 112–50. The only black mark on Cleveland's ledger was its six-game loss to Atlanta in the World Series.

The Indians' offensive firepower was unmatched. They led both leagues in runs, hits, homers, batting average, and slugging average. Six regulars batted above .310, led by designated hitter Eddie Murray at .327. Left fielder Albert Belle had 59 homers, the most in the majors.

Pitcher Orel Hershiser, in his first year in Cleveland, won eighteen games, as did Charles Nagy. Reliever Jose Mesa picked up 52 saves, tops in the big leagues.

BATTERS	HR	RBI	BA	G	AB	R	H	2B	3B	SA
Eddie Murray	25	94	.327	127	490	78	160	23	0	.527
Albert Belle	59	145	.320	161	615	140	197	59	1	.707
Carlos Baerga	18	104	.317	152	627	100	199	33	2	.463
Jim Thome	30	84	.317	154	508	106	161	34	3	.573
Kenny Lofton	9	61	.312	133	542	107	169	27	14	.463
Manny Ramirez	37	123	.311	154	544	98	169	29	1	.572
Sandy Alomar Jr.	12	40	.303	74	228	37	69	7	0	.491
Omar Vizquel	7	64	.267	153	610	100	163	35	0	.359
Tony Pena	6	32	.264	102	295	29	78	17	0	.383
Paul Sorrento	29	91	.237	117	363	57	86	16	0	.521
Wayne Kirby	1	16	.208	114	212	33	44	13	2	.302

PITCHERS	W	L	SV	ERA	G	IP	ER	H	BB	SO
Jose Mesa	3	0	52	1.13	70	72	9	56	19	67
Julian Tavarez	11	2	0	2.46	64	95	26	86	24	78
Eric Plunk	7	2	1	2.75	63	72	22	55	31	82
Chad Ogea	9	3	0	3.10	23	122	42	110	34	67
Dennis Martinez	14	6	0	3.15	32	214	75	201	53	117
Jim Poole	3	3	0	3.86	47	56	24	45	19	47
Orel Hershiser	18	7	0	3.99	29	187	83	171	58	128
Ken Hill	5	1	0	4.14	14	87	40	91	38	58
Charles Nagy	18	7	0	4.70	33	203	106	224	70	164
Mark Clark	10	8	0	5.45	25	142	86	165	48	80
Bud Black	4	2	0	7.10	12	52	41	70	18	39

17. 1942 ST. LOUIS CARDINALS

The Cardinals were the class of the National League throughout the 1940s, hauling in four pennants and finishing no lower than third place. They also won three World Series, the first coming over the Yankees in 1942. That five-game triumph capped a regular season that featured 112 adjusted wins and a winning percentage of .691.

Two young players ticketed for Cooperstown, right fielder Enos Slaughter and left fielder Stan Musial, powered the Cardinal attack. Both batted over .330, combining for 58 home runs and 213 RBIs.

But pitching was St. Louis's real strength. Mort Cooper led the league in wins (23) and ERA (2.33), capturing both the Most Valuable Player and Cy Young Awards, the latter hypothetical. Johnny Beazley was a step behind with 22 wins.

BATTERS	HR	RBI	BA	G	AB	R	H	2B	3B	SA
Enos Slaughter	33	123	.339	158	614	126	208	39	12	.603
Stan Musial	25	90	.335	145	484	109	162	40	7	.601
Terry Moore	16	61	.307	135	508	101	156	35	2	.478
Walker Cooper	18	82	.298	130	456	73	136	42	5	.531
Marty Marion	0	68	.293	153	505	83	148	74	4	.455
Johnny Hopp	9	47	.275	99	327	52	90	24	6	.468
Jimmy Brown	4	89	.273	151	631	94	172	53	4	.388
Whitey Kurowski	19	53	.269	119	379	64	102	18	2	.478
Ray Sanders	12	49	.269	99	294	47	79	20	1	.466
Creepy Crespi	0	44	.259	97	305	42	79	16	3	.331

PITCHERS	W	L	SV	ERA	G	IP	ER	H	BB	SO
Mort Cooper	23	7	0	2.33	38	286	74	228	73	284
Johnny Beazley	22	6	9	2.80	45	225	70	203	80	180
Howie Krist	13	3	4	3.32	35	122	45	114	46	92
Ernie White	7	5	6	3.32	27	133	49	126	44	127
Howie Pollet	7	5	0	3.74	28	113	47	113	42	83
Murry Dickson	6	3	8	3.85	37	124	53	100	66	123
Max Lanier	13	8	6	3.90	35	166	72	152	65	173
Harry Gumbert	9	5	14	4.26	39	167	79	172	63	104
Lon Warneke	6	4	0	4.28	12	82	39	82	16	59

18. 1984 DETROIT TIGERS

The Tigers won their first nine games in 1984, and 35 of their first 40. They became the second team in American League history to occupy first place every day of a season. (The 1927 Yankees were the first.) Detroit finished with a mark of 104–58, swept Kansas City in the AL Championship Series, and dispatched San Diego in five games in the World Series.

The Tigers walloped the most homers and scored the most runs in the majors. Their chief power sources were catcher Lance Parrish (41 homers, 114 RBIs) and right fielder Kirk Gibson (36 homers, 106 RBIs).

The team's pitching ace wasn't a starter. He was reliever Willie Hernandez, who went 9–3 with 34 saves, capturing Most Valuable Player and Cy Young honors. Jack Morris paced Detroit's starters with nineteen wins.

BATTERS	HR	RBI	BA	G	AB	R	H	2B	3B	SA
Alan Trammell	20	80	.324	139	555	99	180	41	4	.521
Lou Whitaker	18	65	.299	143	558	104	167	30	1	.453
Barbaro Garbey	7	60	.297	110	327	52	97	21	1	.431
Chet Lemon	27	88	.297	141	509	89	151	39	5	.552
Ruppert Jones	15	43	.293	79	215	30	63	13	1	.572
Kirk Gibson	36	106	.292	149	531	107	155	26	8	.574
Larry Herndon	10	50	.290	125	407	60	118	23	4	.440
Dave Bergman	10	51	.284	120	271	49	77	10	4	.461
Howard Johnson	16	58	.256	116	355	50	91	16	1	.442
Tom Brookens	7	30	.254	113	224	37	57	14	3	.438
Lance Parrish	41	114	.246	147	578	87	142	16	2	.493
Darrell Evans	21	73	.239	131	401	70	96	12	1	.431

PITCHERS	W	L	SV	ERA	G	IP	ER	H	BB	SO
Willie Hernandez	9	3	34	2.31	80	140	36	100	41	134
Aurelio Lopez	10	1	15	3.52	71	138	54	114	59	114
Dan Petry	18	8	0	3.90	35	233	101	241	75	175
Juan Berenguer	11	10	0	4.18	31	168	78	152	89	143
Jack Morris	19	11	0	4.31	35	240	115	231	98	180
Dave Rozema	7	6	0	4.46	29	101	50	115	20	60
Doug Bair	5	3	4	4.50	47	94	47	86	41	70
Milt Wilcox	17	8	0	4.82	33	194	104	192	75	146

19. 1970 BALTIMORE ORIOLES

The 1970 Orioles weren't quite as good as the previous year's version, which ranks seventh on this list. The '69 team won 109 games; the '70 squad won 108. The 1969 Orioles had a higher batting average, lower ERA, and fewer errors.

Yet there was one area where the 1970 squad was superior. Baltimore cruised through the postseason, sweeping Minnesota for the league title, then trouncing Cincinnati in the World Series. It was a sharp turnaround from the Orioles' upset loss to the Mets the year before.

Right fielder Frank Robinson (.325 batting average) and first baseman Boog Powell (129 RBIs) starred at the plate. Powell was the league's MVP. But it was pitching that carried Baltimore to the title. The Orioles had three 20-game winners: Dave McNally (24), Mike Cuellar (24), and Jim Palmer (20).

BATTERS	HR	RBI	BA	G	AB	R	H	2B	3B	SA
Merv Rettenmund	21	66	.343	106	338	68	116	21	2	.604
Frank Robinson	29	88	.325	132	471	100	153	30	1	.577
Boog Powell	40	129	.314	154	526	93	165	35	0	.608
Dave Johnson	12	60	.298	149	530	77	158	35	1	.436
Brooks Robinson	22	106	.293	158	608	95	178	41	3	.479
Don Buford	21	75	.288	144	504	112	145	20	2	.460
Paul Blair	21	73	.283	133	480	89	136	31	2	.488
Ellie Hendricks	14	46	.258	106	322	36	83	11	0	.422
Andy Etchebarren	5	32	.257	78	230	21	59	13	1	.387
Mark Belanger	1	41	.231	145	459	60	106	11	5	.283

PITCHERS	W	L	SV	ERA	G	IP	ER	H	BB	SO
Pete Richert	7	2	15	2.29	50	55	14	39	25	73
Marcelino Lopez	1	1	0	2.51	25	61	17	51	38	55
Jim Palmer	20	10	0	3.19	39	305	108	283	101	226
Tom Phoebus	5	5	0	3.60	27	135	54	114	63	82
Dick Hall	10	5	3	3.69	32	61	25	55	6	34
Eddie Watt	7	7	13	3.76	53	55	23	47	29	37
Dave McNally	24	9	0	3.80	40	296	125	299	79	210
Mike Cuellar	24	8	0	4.11	40	298	136	295	70	216
Jim Hardin	6	5	1	4.16	36	145	67	161	26	89

20. 1909 PITTSBURGH PIRATES

A pair of Hall of Famers anchored Pittsburgh's two great teams in the modern era's first decade. Fred Clarke managed and played left field for the 1902 squad, 3rd in the all-time standings, and the 1909 team, which ranks 20th. And shortstop Honus Wagner took National League Most Valuable Player honors both times.

The Pirates fended off a tough competitor for the 1909 NL pennant. Their adjusted record of 117–45 put them just 6½ games ahead of the Cubs, themselves 91st on the list of greatest teams. Pittsburgh then edged Detroit in a seven-game World Series.

None of it could have been accomplished without Wagner, who led the league in batting average (.375), RBIs (140), and slugging average (.671). Three Pittsburgh pitchers were 20-game winners, led by Howie Camnitz with 26.

BATTERS	HR	RBI	BA	G	AB	R	H	2B	3B	SA
Honus Wagner	35	140	.375	144	520	128	195	43	3	.671
Fred Clarke	27	95	.318	160	579	135	184	23	4	.511
Dots Miller	28	121	.307	159	590	99	181	46	5	.544
Chief Wilson	31	82	.301	162	599	89	180	27	4	.514
George Gibson	20	72	.292	158	537	58	157	41	4	.495
Tommy Leach	35	60	.288	159	618	177	178	26	2	.506
Bill Abstein	14	97	.286	144	538	71	154	45	7	.474
Jap Barbeau	0	35	.244	96	369	84	90	50	2	.390

PITCHERS	W	L	SV	ERA	G	IP	ER	H	BB	SO
Babe Adams	12	3	7	2.00	26	135	30	107	33	114
Howie Camnitz	26	6	8	2.91	43	297	96	254	97	239
Nick Maddox	14	9	0	4.00	33	216	96	215	56	107
Vic Willis	23	12	4	4.04	41	305	137	300	119	177
Deacon Phillippe	8	3	0	4.17	23	138	64	149	20	72
Lefty Leifield	20	9	0	4.29	34	214	102	214	78	84
Sam Leever	8	1	7	5.11	20	74	42	92	20	43

The Worst Teams Ever

Now it's time for an unusual twist – a separate list of the worst teams of all time, led (if that's the right word) by the 1916 Philadelphia Athletics.

I simply reversed the formula that I used to identify the best teams. All 241 franchises with single-season adjusted winning percentages below .400 were eligible. I gave the highest scores to the worst performers in each category, like the team with the lowest winning percentage or the fewest runs scored per game. The very worst squad was given exactly 100 points, with every other team's score based off that benchmark. Each team is listed with six adjusted statistics and its actual win–loss record, using the abbreviations explained at the beginning of this chapter:

RANK	TEAM	SCORE	W	L	W%	R/G	OR/G	DIFF.	W^{ACT}	L^{ACT}
1	1916 Philadelphia Athletics	100.00	38	124	.235	4.21	7.31	-3.10	36	117
2	1962 New York Mets	95.24	40	122	.247	4.45	6.83	-2.38	40	120
3	1909 Washington Senators	89.79	45	117	.278	3.51	6.06	-2.55	42	110
4	1919 Philadelphia Athletics	87.42	42	120	.259	4.37	7.10	-2.73	36	104
5	1904 Washington Senators	86.11	41	121	.253	3.84	6.53	-2.69	38	113
6	1942 Philadelphia Phillies	85.54	45	117	.278	3.26	5.85	-2.59	42	109
7	1996 Detroit Tigers	85.04	53	109	.327	4.98	7.01	-2.03	53	109
8	1945 Philadelphia Phillies	79.74	48	114	.296	4.42	6.97	-2.55	46	108
9	1965 New York Mets	79.47	50	112	.309	3.90	5.91	-2.01	50	112
10	1928 Philadelphia Phillies	79.42	46	116	.284	4.78	6.93	-2.15	43	109
11	1952 Pittsburgh Pirates	76.47	44	118	.272	4.08	6.29	-2.21	42	112
12	1963 New York Mets	75.47	51	111	.315	4.02	6.21	-2.19	51	111
13	1941 Philadelphia Phillies	75.02	45	117	.278	3.68	5.83	-2.15	43	111
14	1911 Boston Braves	72.17	47	115	.290	5.20	7.59	-2.39	44	107
15	1988 Baltimore Orioles	71.74	54	108	.333	4.24	6.07	-1.83	54	107
16	1935 Boston Braves	71.06	40	122	.247	3.95	5.85	-1.90	38	115
16	1979 Toronto Blue Jays	71.06	53	109	.327	4.35	6.12	-1.77	53	109
18	1969 San Diego Padres	70.71	52	110	.321	3.64	5.80	-2.16	52	110
19	1981 Toronto Blue Jays	66.53	57	105	.352	3.97	5.62	-1.65	37	69
20	1932 Boston Red Sox	65.90	45	117	.278	3.82	6.18	-2.36	43	111
21	1915 Philadelphia Athletics	65.46	46	116	.284	4.88	7.95	-3.07	43	109
22	1974 San Diego Padres	65.26	60	102	.370	4.17	6.41	-2.24	60	102
23	1998 Florida Marlins	62.88	54	108	.333	4.41	6.10	-1.69	54	108
24	1939 St. Louis Browns	60.32	45	117	.278	5.08	7.17	-2.09	43	111
25	1910 St. Louis Browns	60.01	49	113	.302	3.82	6.30	-2.48	47	107
26	1926 Boston Red Sox	59.03	49	113	.302	4.05	6.02	-1.97	46	107
27	1903 Washington Senators	57.84	51	111	.315	3.59	5.68	-2.09	43	94
28	1937 St. Louis Browns	55.89	49	113	.302	4.90	7.02	-2.12	46	108
29	1973 Texas Rangers	53.08	57	105	.352	4.66	6.36	-1.70	57	105
30	1923 Philadelphia Phillies	50.67	53	109	.327	5.21	7.03	-1.82	50	104
31	1954 Philadelphia Athletics	50.38	54	108	.333	4.10	6.62	-2.52	51	103
32	1991 Cleveland Indians	49.64	57	105	.352	4.23	5.57	-1.34	57	105
33	1978 Seattle Mariners	49.00	57	105	.352	4.84	6.57	-1.73	56	104
34	1905 Brooklyn Dodgers	48.61	51	111	.315	4.34	6.92	-2.58	48	104
35	1969 Montreal Expos	48.45	52	110	.321	4.52	6.15	-1.63	52	110
36	1938 Philadelphia Phillies	47.93	49	113	.302	3.83	5.84	-2.01	45	105
37	1940 Philadelphia Phillies	46.88	53	109	.327	3.52	5.35	-1.83	50	103
38	1989 Detroit Tigers	46.47	59	103	.364	4.76	6.30	-1.54	59	103
39	1995 Minnesota Twins	45.69	63	99	.389	5.22	6.60	-1.38	56	88
40	1953 Pittsburgh Pirates	43.36	53	109	.327	4.53	6.45	-1.92	50	104
41	1906 Boston Red Sox	42.83	51	111	.315	4.27	6.52	-2.25	49	105
42	1987 Cleveland Indians	42.74	61	101	.377	4.99	6.44	-1.45	61	101
43	1920 Philadelphia Athletics	41.79	51	111	.315	4.22	6.31	-2.09	48	106
44	1964 New York Mets	41.41	53	109	.327	4.47	6.09	-1.62	53	109
45	1976 Montreal Expos	40.98	55	107	.340	4.23	5.85	-1.62	55	107
46	1985 Pittsburgh Pirates	38.61	57	105	.352	4.16	5.19	-1.03	57	104
47	1963 Washington Senators	38.54	56	106	.346	4.67	6.57	-1.90	56	106
48	1951 St. Louis Browns	38.31	55	107	.340	4.53	6.53	-2.00	52	102
49	1925 Boston Red Sox	38.29	50	112	.309	4.20	6.07	-1.87	47	105
50	1908 New York Yankees	37.20	54	108	.333	4.53	7.04	-2.51	51	103

No wonder Philadelphia fans are so quick to heckle and boo their own teams. They've suffered more than anyone else in the modern era. The Phillies occupy 7 slots in the bottom 50, the most of any franchise, while the late, unlamented Philadelphia A's are second with 5. That means Philly fans have had to endure nearly one-quarter of baseball's worst teams – 12 out of 50.

The two leagues attained parity in ineptitude. Each has been saddled with the worst team in five of the modern era's ten decades. The American League was at the bottom during the first couple ('09 Senators and '16 Athletics) and the three most-recent decades ('79 Blue Jays, '88 Orioles, '96 Tigers). The National League filled the gap by rattling off five in a row: '28 Phillies, '35 Braves, '42 Phillies, '52 Pirates, and, of course, the infamous '62 Mets:

	BOTTOM 50 TEAMS	
1	Philadelphia Phillies	7
2	Philadelphia Athletics	5
3	Boston Red Sox	4
3	New York Mets	4
3	St. Louis Browns	4
3	Washington Senators	4
7	Pittsburgh Pirates	3
8	Boston Braves	2
8	Cleveland Indians	2
8	Detroit Tigers	2
8	Montreal Expos	2
8	San Diego Padres	2
8	Toronto Blue Jays	2
14	Baltimore Orioles	1
14	Brooklyn Dodgers	1
14	Florida Marlins	1
14	Minnesota Twins	1
14	New York Yankees	1
14	Seattle Mariners	1
14	Texas Rangers	1

DECADE	AL WORST (OVERALL RANK)	NL WORST (OVERALL RANK)
1901–1909	1909 Washington Senators (3)	1905 Brooklyn Dodgers (34)
1910–1919	1916 Philadelphia Athletics (1)	1911 Boston Braves (14)
1920–1929	1926 Boston Red Sox (26)	1928 Philadelphia Phillies (10)
1930–1939	1932 Boston Red Sox (20)	1935 Boston Braves (16)
1940–1949	1943 Philadelphia Athletics (56)	1942 Philadelphia Phillies (6)
1950–1959	1954 Philadelphia Athletics (31)	1952 Pittsburgh Pirates (11)
1960–1969	1963 Washington Senators (47)	1962 New York Mets (2)
1970–1979	1979 Toronto Blue Jays (16)	1974 San Diego Padres (22)
1980–1989	1988 Baltimore Orioles (15)	1985 Pittsburgh Pirates (46)
1990–2001	1996 Detroit Tigers (7)	1998 Florida Marlins (23)

Let's finish with a quick look at the five worst teams of all time, using the same format for the 20 best teams profiled earlier. All individual statistics cited in the text are adjusted, unless otherwise noted, while league standings and playoff results are real, not simulated. Adjusted statistics are shown for all batters with 200 or more adjusted at bats and all pitchers with 50 or more adjusted innings.

1. 1916 PHILADELPHIA ATHLETICS

Bring up the subject of baseball incompetence, and most fans immediately think of the 1962 New York Mets. But the 1916 Athletics, believe it or not, were even worse. They had the lowest adjusted winning percentage in the modern era, .235, based on 38 wins and 124 losses.

It was bad enough that the A's landed an unbelievable 54½ games behind the first-place Boston Red Sox, but it was even worse that they finished 40 games out of seventh place in the eight-team American League. Philadelphia was consistently terrible in every phase of the game. Its team batting average, ERA, and fielding percentage were the AL's worst.

Center fielder Amos Strunk bucked the trend, putting up the best numbers of his seventeen-year career. He batted .344 with 22 homers and 100 runs scored. But he got little help. Only one of his teammates topped .290. None scored more than 89 runs.

Three of the Athletics' starters lost at least 21 games, with Joe Bush's 25 leading the league. Jack Nabors's record was an atrocious 1–21, though his 5.85 ERA was second-best on the club. Compounding these pitching woes was a porous infield. Shortstop Whitey Witt committed 78 actual errors, third baseman Charlie Pick, 42.

BATTERS	HR	RBI	BA	G	AB	R	H	2B	3B	SA
Amos Strunk	22	69	.344	158	573	100	197	45	4	.551
Stuffy McInnis	9	84	.322	147	538	59	173	51	1	.470
Wally Schang	26	53	.289	116	356	57	103	12	2	.553
Nap Lajoie	13	49	.267	119	449	46	120	20	2	.408
Whitey Witt	19	50	.266	150	591	89	157	32	8	.443
Charlie Pick	0	28	.261	127	418	40	109	40	3	.371
Jimmy Walsh	9	38	.253	120	411	59	104	26	4	.401

PITCHERS	W	L	SV	ERA	G	IP	ER	H	BB	SO
Joe Bush	16	25	0	4.34	42	301	145	268	175	275
Jack Nabors	1	21	5	5.85	42	223	145	249	127	136
Elmer Myers	15	24	3	6.18	46	329	226	337	225	315
Tom Sheehan	1	17	0	6.23	40	198	137	239	127	102
Jing Johnson	2	9	0	6.33	13	91	64	112	54	48
Marsh Williams	0	7	0	13.34	11	56	83	89	43	33

2. 1962 NEW YORK METS

They were lovable. They were trendy. They were just plain awful. The 1962 Mets captured New York's heart and shocked the baseball world with their bumbling inefficiency. They yielded 2.38 more runs than they scored per game, resulting in an adjusted winning percentage of .247 (40 wins, 122 losses). They nestled deep into last place in the National League, 60½ games off the pace.

"They've shown me ways to lose that I never knew existed," moaned manager Casey Stengel. There was truth behind his humor. The Mets gave up more runs and hits than any other big-league team in 1962, and they also committed the most

errors. Their batting average was by far the lowest in either league.

Right fielder Richie Ashburn, destined for the Hall of Fame, wrapped up his fifteen-year career by hitting a respectable .319. Left fielder Frank Thomas blasted 39 homers and drove in 105 runs. But the rest of the offense was anemic.

The pitching staff was equally disappointing. Veteran Roger Craig topped the Mets with ten wins. The problem was that he also led the National League with 24 losses. Starters Al Jackson and Jay Hook suffered 20 and 19 defeats, respectively.

BATTERS	HR	RBI	BA	G	AB	R	H	2B	3B	SA
Richie Ashburn	9	31	.319	136	392	67	125	10	2	.423
Felix Mantilla	13	66	.286	142	469	60	134	24	3	.433
Frank Thomas	39	105	.278	157	575	77	160	30	2	.541
Charlie Neal	14	65	.271	137	512	66	139	20	7	.420
Rod Kanehl	5	30	.260	134	354	58	92	14	1	.347
Jim Hickman	15	51	.256	141	395	60	101	24	1	.435
Marv Throneberry	19	55	.256	117	360	32	92	15	2	.467
Joe Christopher	7	36	.253	120	273	40	69	14	1	.388
Elio Chacon	2	30	.248	119	371	55	92	16	2	.318

The lovable, and lousy, 1962 New York Mets. The computer couldn't save these guys.

PITCHERS	W	L	SV	ERA	G	IP	ER	H	BB	SO
Al Jackson	8	20	0	5.10	36	231	131	257	83	143
Roger Craig	10	24	4	5.21	42	233	135	275	74	143
Bob Moorhead	0	2	0	5.23	38	105	61	124	44	76
Jay Hook	8	19	0	5.59	37	214	133	243	75	137
Bob Miller	1	12	0	5.69	33	144	91	154	66	110
Ken MacKenzie	5	4	1	5.74	42	80	51	92	36	61
Craig Anderson	3	17	5	6.18	50	131	90	158	67	75
Willard Hunter	1	6	0	6.43	27	63	45	71	36	48
Ray Daviault	1	5	0	7.22	36	81	65	97	51	61

3. 1909 WASHINGTON SENATORS

If you scan the roster of the 1909 Senators, one name leaps out: Walter Johnson. The Big Train, then just 21 years old, offered a glimpse of the Hall of Famer he was to become, striking out 288 batters and fashioning a respectable 3.99 ERA. But he was unable to counteract the ineptitude of his teammates, who saddled him with 26 losses, the most in any of his 21 seasons.

The Senators, as a whole, suffered 117 adjusted defeats for a winning percentage of .278. They finished last in the American League, 56 games out of first and 20 games behind next-to-last St. Louis.

Washington's offense was virtually nonexistent, churning out just 3.51 runs per game. No one on the roster scored more than 60 runs or drove in more than 56. Left fielder Jack Lelivelt had the best batting average on the team, .322, but he didn't hit a single home run and could manage only 33 RBIs.

The surprise was that Johnson, at 14–26, didn't have the most losses on the pitching staff. Bob Groom did him one better, topping the American League with 27 defeats. He also dealt a league-leading 151 walks in 273 innings.

BATTERS	HR	RBI	BA	G	AB	R	H	2B	3B	SA
Jack Lelivelt	0	33	.322	95	332	34	107	38	9	.491
George Browne	12	22	.301	107	408	55	123	30	2	.473
Bob Unglaub	24	56	.291	135	498	59	145	18	3	.484
Wid Conroy	12	27	.269	144	506	60	136	26	2	.399
Jiggs Donahue	0	38	.263	87	293	18	77	38	0	.392
George McBride	0	47	.258	162	523	52	135	56	0	.365
Jim Delahanty	10	29	.244	93	312	25	76	21	2	.420
Gabby Street	0	40	.232	142	422	34	98	45	0	.339
Clyde Milan	10	20	.219	135	415	49	91	21	2	.352

PITCHERS	W	L	SV	ERA	G	IP	ER	H	BB	SO
Walter Johnson	14	26	1	3.99	42	311	138	304	120	288
Doc Reisling	2	4	0	4.43	10	67	33	83	23	39
Tom Hughes	4	7	6	4.86	23	126	68	139	47	132
Bob Groom	7	27	0	5.18	46	273	157	268	151	233
Charlie Smith	3	13	0	5.92	24	152	100	171	53	127
Dolly Gray	5	20	0	6.51	37	224	162	253	108	155
Roy Witherup	1	5	0	7.68	12	68	58	93	27	45

4. 1919 PHILADELPHIA ATHLETICS

The 1916 Athletics, as we have seen, were the worst team in the modern era. Philadelphia improved slightly the following two seasons – climbing above 50 victories both times – but remained in last place in the American League. That set the stage for another steep dive in 1919, when the A's plummeted to an adjusted 42-120, just four games better than 1916.

A couple of familiar faces were still around. Whitey Witt, who batted .274, was better with the glove since changing positions. The error-prone shortstop now played second base and the outfield. Right fielder Amos Strunk, back in Philly after a sojourn with the Red Sox, batted a miserable .215.

But the bulk of the blame fell on newcomers. Rookie pitcher Rollie Naylor lost 21 games. Scott Perry, in his second full season, lost 20. Left fielder Merlin Kopp and third baseman Fred Thomas, with 156 games of prior big-league experience between them, batted .231 and .216 respectively.

Two of the A's did have solid years. First baseman George Burns and center fielder Tilly Walker both flirted with .300 and ripped at least 30 homers. Burns would be traded the following year to Cleveland, where he became the AL's Most Valuable Player in 1926.

BATTERS	HR	RBI	BA	G	AB	R	H	2B	3B	SA
Braggo Roth	20	42	.329	56	228	48	75	13	3	.675
George Burns	33	82	.303	146	545	91	165	30	3	.550
Tilly Walker	35	93	.299	145	529	68	158	26	2	.554
Joe Dugan	8	43	.277	120	447	36	124	33	1	.409
Whitey Witt	0	47	.274	141	532	81	146	53	7	.400
Dick Burrus	0	11	.263	81	224	24	59	15	6	.384
Cy Perkins	13	42	.258	117	353	32	91	19	3	.439
Merlin Kopp	7	17	.231	87	273	49	63	4	2	.337
Fred Thomas	14	33	.216	143	522	60	113	20	6	.358
Amos Strunk	0	19	.215	69	223	21	48	21	5	.354

PITCHERS	W	L	SV	ERA	G	IP	ER	H	BB	SO
Rollie Naylor	6	21	0	4.99	36	238	132	260	100	170
Scott Perry	5	20	3	5.37	29	213	127	238	113	100
Jing Johnson	10	17	0	5.39	39	232	139	272	96	165
Walt Kinney	10	17	12	5.45	50	236	143	246	143	229
Tom Rogers	5	14	0	6.42	27	164	117	190	95	96
Socks Seibold	2	3	0	7.96	16	52	46	70	40	45
Win Noyes	1	6	0	8.54	12	59	56	85	24	50

5. 1904 WASHINGTON SENATORS

You've surely heard the vaudeville joke about Washington: "First in war, first in peace, and last in the American League." It obscured the Senators' moments of glory (which included three league pennants) while overstating the frequency of their cellar-dwelling. The Senators actually finished eighth in the eight-team AL just ten times in their 60-year history.

What sustained the joke was the miserable quality of the Washington teams that did finish last, with 1904 a perfect example. That year's Senators weren't just bad; they were abysmally bad, with an adjusted winning percentage of .253. They finished 55½ games behind the AL champion Red Sox. They hit the fewest home runs, had the lowest batting average, and allowed the most earned runs in the major leagues that year.

No everyday player for Washington batted higher than first baseman Jake Stahl's .284 or drove in more runs than Stahl's 66. Shortstop Joe Cassidy was the only other Senator with more than 400 at bats to hit above .250.

None of the team's starting pitchers kept his ERA below 5.00. Three lost at least 24 games, led by the misnamed Happy Townsend, who suffered 27 defeats, the most in the majors.

BATTERS	HR	RBI	BA	G	AB	R	H	2B	3B	SA
Bill Coughlin	0	22	.300	67	273	37	82	42	4	.484
Jake Stahl	23	66	.284	147	538	71	153	42	5	.509
Frank Huelsman	12	40	.271	87	314	28	85	23	2	.471
Bill O'Neill	9	21	.265	98	377	44	100	17	0	.382
Malachi Kittridge	0	32	.262	84	275	15	72	26	0	.356
Joe Cassidy	15	43	.262	157	600	83	157	35	15	.445
Patsy Donovan	0	25	.249	129	450	40	112	34	0	.324
Charles Moran	0	9	.243	64	251	36	61	27	0	.351
Barry McCormick	0	52	.237	117	418	48	99	40	0	.333
Boileryard Clarke	0	22	.228	88	285	30	65	29	0	.330
Hunter Hill	0	22	.215	79	298	24	64	25	0	.299

PITCHERS	W	L	SV	ERA	G	IP	ER	H	BB	SO
Case Patten	14	24	7	5.29	46	366	215	422	127	264
Bill Wolfe	6	10	0	5.64	18	134	84	155	37	82
Tom Hughes	2	14	1	6.00	17	132	88	158	57	89
Beany Jacobson	6	24	0	6.10	34	261	177	319	92	137
Happy Townsend	5	27	0	6.17	37	299	205	368	163	248
Al Orth	3	4	0	8.15	10	74	67	99	24	41
Davey Dunkle	2	9	0	8.51	12	74	70	106	36	40

6 ⚾ The Batter Register

The rest of Leveling the Field is an encyclopedia of adjusted statistics for more than 400 of the greatest players in baseball history. This chapter concentrates on hitters; the final chapter covers pitchers.

You'll find season-by-season batting statistics here for 254 great hitters. I have included every position player who met any of these criteria (using actual, not adjusted, career totals):

- ⚪ Member of the Hall of Fame
- ⚪ Most Valuable Player in any season since 1901
- ⚪ 2,500 games played
- ⚪ 2,500 hits
- ⚪ 400 home runs
- ⚪ .320 career batting average in 1,000 games or more

There's also a fudge factor. I've added about two dozen players who went oh-for-six on the checklist above, but were stars nonetheless. Players like Bob Boone, Walker Cooper, Gil Hodges, Minnie Minoso, Tony Oliva, Ron Santo, and Alan Trammell didn't meet any of the basic criteria, but they still made *Total Baseball*'s list of the 400 greatest players ever, and they deserve to be included here, as well.

The records in this chapter are arranged alphabetically from Hank Aaron to Robin Yount. Each season's numbers have been adjusted to a 162-game schedule and 1996–2000 performance levels.

A player's entry contains eleven adjusted figures for each big-league season, followed by his actual number of home runs and runs batted in, and his actual batting average for that year. These are the columns from left to right:

BASIC INFORMATION

Year

Team, followed by **league abbreviation:** American Association (AA), American League (A), Federal League (F), National League (N), Players League (P), and Union Association (U)

ADJUSTED STATISTICS

HR: Home runs

RBI: Runs batted in

BA: Batting average

G: Games played

AB: At bats

R: Runs scored

H: Hits

2B: Doubles

3B: Triples

SA: Slugging average

Pay: Estimated value of hitter's performance (in millions of Year 2001 dollars)

ACTUAL STATISTICS

HR: Home runs

RBI: Runs batted in

BA: Batting average

Each player's entry ends with three lines in bold type. The first line has career totals for all adjusted and actual statistics. The second row provides career averages, calculated by dividing career totals by the player's number of seasons. The third line has "summit" figures, the average statistics for a hitter's five best seasons, showing what he was like at his peak. (I added the adjusted batting and slugging averages for each season in which a hitter had at least 324 adjusted at bats, the equivalent of two ABs per game in a 162-game season. The five years with the highest combined batting-slugging averages were defined as a player's summit years.)

HANK AARON

YEAR	TEAM	HR	RBI	BA	G	AB	R	H	2B	3B	SA	PAY	HR	RBI	BA
						ADJUSTED REGULAR SEASON								ACTUAL RESULTS		
1954	Milwaukee (N)	19	81	.289	128	491	68	142	35	4	.493	$7.5	13	69	.280
1955	Milwaukee (N)	34	122	.327	161	633	121	207	51	6	.588	$15.1	27	106	.314
1956	Milwaukee (N)	32	106	.342	160	637	122	218	48	10	.600	$18.4	26	92	.328
1957	Milwaukee (N)	54	160	.337	158	644	143	217	35	4	.655	$25.8	44	132	.322
1958	Milwaukee (N)	36	114	.340	161	632	131	215	44	3	.590	$25.7	30	95	.326
1959	Milwaukee (N)	46	143	.373	159	649	135	242	58	6	.693	$26.6	39	123	.355
1960	Milwaukee (N)	51	151	.308	161	621	122	191	26	8	.622	$26.1	40	126	.292
1961	Milwaukee (N)	40	136	.341	162	630	130	215	51	8	.638	$25.9	34	120	.327
1962	Milwaukee (N)	51	142	.338	156	592	141	200	36	4	.671	$25.7	45	128	.323
1963	Milwaukee (N)	54	161	.348	160	627	150	218	38	3	.676	$28.6	44	130	.319
1964	Milwaukee (N)	29	116	.353	145	570	125	201	39	2	.581	$16.8	24	95	.328
1965	Milwaukee (N)	39	109	.347	150	570	134	198	51	1	.646	$16.7	32	89	.318
1966	Atlanta (N)	52	155	.302	157	599	143	181	29	1	.614	$20.4	44	127	.279
1967	Atlanta (N)	53	141	.340	155	600	146	204	46	2	.688	$19.9	39	109	.307
1968	Atlanta (N)	44	121	.327	159	602	118	197	42	3	.626	$19.4	29	86	.287
1969	Atlanta (N)	54	116	.325	147	547	120	178	39	3	.704	$13.5	44	97	.300
1970	Atlanta (N)	44	134	.316	150	516	117	163	32	1	.638	$9.6	38	118	.298
1971	Atlanta (N)	60	148	.354	139	495	119	175	26	3	.782	$9.4	47	118	.327
1972	Atlanta (N)	47	106	.291	135	470	103	137	13	0	.619	$9.0	34	77	.265
1973	Atlanta (N)	48	112	.316	120	392	98	124	14	1	.724	$6.6	40	96	.301
1974	Atlanta (N)	27	81	.279	111	337	55	94	18	0	.573	$3.5	20	69	.268
1975	Milwaukee (A)	18	70	.245	137	465	52	114	18	2	.409	$3.5	12	60	.234
1976	Milwaukee (A)	15	43	.241	86	274	27	66	9	0	.438	$2.0	10	35	.229
	Career	**947**	**2,768**	**.325**	**3,357**	**12,593**	**2,620**	**4,097**	**798**	**75**	**.626**	**$375.7**	**755**	**2,297**	**.305**
	Average season	**41**	**120**	**.325**	**146**	**548**	**114**	**178**	**35**	**3**	**.626**	**$16.3**	**33**	**100**	**.305**
	Summit season	**52**	**132**	**.345**	**144**	**537**	**124**	**185**	**37**	**3**	**.715**	**$15.2**	**42**	**109**	**.320**

DICK ALLEN

		ADJUSTED REGULAR SEASON											ACTUAL RESULTS		
YEAR	TEAM	HR	RBI	BA	G	AB	R	H	2B	3B	SA	PAY	HR	RBI	BA
1963	Philadelphia (N)	0	2	.333	10	24	7	8	3	1	.542	$0.0	0	2	.292
1964	Philadelphia (N)	37	111	.342	162	632	152	216	50	11	.631	$11.7	29	91	.318
1965	Philadelphia (N)	27	104	.331	161	619	114	205	43	11	.567	$15.1	20	85	.302
1966	Philadelphia (N)	49	135	.344	141	524	138	180	34	8	.719	$14.8	40	110	.317
1967	Philadelphia (N)	33	100	.341	122	463	115	158	41	8	.678	$14.8	23	77	.307
1968	Philadelphia (N)	50	127	.299	152	521	123	156	21	7	.655	$15.6	33	90	.263
1969	Philadelphia (N)	39	107	.313	118	438	95	137	30	3	.662	$12.0	32	89	.288
1970	St. Louis (N)	40	114	.296	122	459	100	136	21	4	.621	$12.1	34	101	.279
1971	Los Angeles (N)	31	113	.319	155	549	103	175	31	1	.548	$12.6	23	90	.295
1972	Chicago (A)	54	157	.340	156	533	125	181	36	4	.726	$16.0	37	113	.308
1973	Chicago (A)	20	48	.332	72	250	46	83	24	3	.692	$4.8	16	41	.316
1974	Chicago (A)	43	104	.314	127	458	99	144	25	1	.655	$6.9	32	88	.301
1975	Philadelphia (N)	18	72	.243	119	416	63	101	25	2	.442	$3.9	12	62	.233
1976	Philadelphia (N)	22	60	.282	85	298	64	84	17	1	.567	$2.6	15	49	.268
1977	Oakland (A)	6	34	.246	54	171	21	42	5	0	.380	$1.9	5	31	.240
	Career	469	1,388	.316	1,756	6,355	1,365	2,006	406	65	.621	$144.8	351	1,119	.292
	Average season	31	93	.316	117	424	91	134	27	4	.621	$9.7	23	75	.292
	Summit season	42	122	.336	140	518	125	174	38	7	.680	$13.9	32	96	.309

CAP ANSON

		ADJUSTED REGULAR SEASON											ACTUAL RESULTS		
YEAR	TEAM	HR	RBI	BA	G	AB	R	H	2B	3B	SA	PAY	HR	RBI	BA
1876	Chicago (N)	48	138	.363	162	758	147	275	22	7	.600	$51.2	2	59	.356
1877	Chicago (N)	0	83	.336	159	687	136	231	131	2	.533	$32.6	0	32	.337
1878	Chicago (N)	0	110	.355	159	692	152	246	112	7	.538	$39.1	0	40	.341
1879	Chicago (N)	0	68	.335	100	445	80	149	87	2	.539	$11.4	0	34	.317
1880	Chicago (N)	23	155	.373	162	671	112	250	56	1	.562	$26.5	1	74	.337
1881	Chicago (N)	25	164	.417	162	662	134	276	60	8	.645	$28.8	1	82	.399
1882	Chicago (N)	17	141	.393	141	598	117	235	88	7	.649	$16.9	1	83	.362
1883	Chicago (N)	0	104	.322	162	683	107	220	124	5	.518	$23.3	0	68	.308
1884	Chicago (N)	68	138	.370	161	683	147	253	27	1	.712	$25.8	21	102	.335
1885	Chicago (N)	40	152	.343	161	667	141	229	49	3	.606	$25.3	7	108	.310
1886	Chicago (N)	48	174	.407	161	649	138	264	41	3	.701	$25.6	10	147	.371
1887	Chicago (N)	31	105	.346	156	604	110	209	47	4	.591	$19.7	7	102	.347
1888	Chicago (N)	46	103	.389	160	615	124	239	26	4	.668	$19.0	12	84	.344
1889	Chicago (N)	27	119	.318	160	619	102	197	44	3	.530	$18.8	7	117	.311
1890	Chicago (N)	26	105	.322	162	587	93	189	16	1	.486	$12.9	7	107	.312
1891	Chicago (N)	30	126	.308	161	639	85	197	33	2	.507	$12.9	8	120	.291
1892	Chicago (N)	7	80	.299	161	616	67	184	67	6	.461	$9.0	1	74	.272
1893	Chicago (N)	0	92	.303	130	502	70	152	62	2	.434	$4.6	0	91	.314
1894	Chicago (N)	15	85	.339	100	410	70	139	31	1	.529	$3.4	5	99	.388
1895	Chicago (N)	12	87	.304	149	579	83	176	45	3	.454	$6.5	2	91	.335
1896	Chicago (N)	11	93	.307	133	495	74	152	31	1	.440	$4.4	2	90	.331
1897	Chicago (N)	15	76	.263	134	498	67	131	22	1	.402	$4.3	3	75	.285
	Career	489	2,498	.344	3,296	13,359	2,356	4,593	1,221	74	.556	$422.0	97	1,879	.329
	Average season	22	114	.344	150	607	107	209	56	3	.556	$19.2	4	85	.329
	Summit season	41	144	.395	157	641	132	253	48	5	.677	$23.2	9	100	.360

LUIS APARICIO

		ADJUSTED REGULAR SEASON											ACTUAL RESULTS		
YEAR	TEAM	HR	RBI	BA	G	AB	R	H	2B	3B	SA	PAY	HR	RBI	BA
1956	Chicago (A)	4	65	.278	160	561	80	156	28	4	.364	$8.9	3	56	.266
1957	Chicago (A)	5	49	.269	149	599	98	161	34	5	.367	$11.2	3	41	.257
1958	Chicago (A)	2	48	.277	152	584	91	162	33	8	.372	$9.1	2	40	.266
1959	Chicago (A)	8	59	.269	158	636	114	171	27	4	.362	$12.3	6	51	.257
1960	Chicago (A)	4	73	.292	161	631	103	184	32	6	.380	$12.4	2	61	.277
1961	Chicago (A)	7	48	.283	155	621	97	176	31	3	.377	$11.5	6	45	.272
1962	Chicago (A)	8	44	.251	153	581	80	146	32	4	.361	$9.0	7	40	.241
1963	Baltimore (A)	7	56	.273	146	601	91	164	29	7	.379	$7.3	5	45	.250
1964	Baltimore (A)	13	45	.286	145	574	112	164	28	2	.409	$7.1	10	37	.266
1965	Baltimore (A)	11	49	.246	144	564	82	139	30	9	.390	$6.7	8	40	.225
1966	Baltimore (A)	9	51	.299	153	668	121	200	38	7	.418	$9.3	6	41	.276
1967	Baltimore (A)	7	40	.258	135	550	71	142	35	5	.378	$3.8	4	31	.233
1968	Chicago (A)	8	51	.299	155	622	78	186	42	4	.418	$4.9	4	36	.264
1969	Chicago (A)	8	61	.304	156	599	92	182	37	4	.419	$6.8	5	51	.280
1970	Chicago (A)	6	48	.332	146	552	97	183	41	2	.446	$4.2	5	43	.313
1971	Boston (A)	6	56	.251	125	491	70	123	33	0	.354	$3.3	4	45	.232
1972	Boston (A)	5	54	.283	115	456	65	129	41	3	.419	$2.7	3	39	.257
1973	Boston (A)	0	57	.283	132	499	65	141	30	1	.347	$2.7	0	49	.271
	Career	118	954	.280	2,640	10,389	1,607	2,909	601	78	.387	$133.2	83	791	.262
	Average season	7	53	.280	147	577	89	162	33	4	.387	$7.4	5	44	.262
	Summit season	7	53	.304	145	579	91	176	40	4	.423	$5.6	5	42	.279

LUKE APPLING

		ADJUSTED REGULAR SEASON											ACTUAL RESULTS		
YEAR	TEAM	HR	RBI	BA	G	AB	R	H	2B	3B	SA	PAY	HR	RBI	BA
1930	Chicago (A)	0	2	.269	6	26	2	7	3	0	.385	$0.0	0	2	.308
1931	Chicago (A)	4	31	.227	100	309	39	70	19	3	.346	$2.0	1	28	.232
1932	Chicago (A)	9	70	.267	148	521	73	139	28	7	.399	$5.3	3	63	.274
1933	Chicago (A)	19	102	.321	162	657	108	211	52	6	.505	$11.9	6	85	.322
1934	Chicago (A)	6	67	.292	125	479	82	140	44	4	.438	$7.9	2	61	.303
1935	Chicago (A)	3	78	.297	162	556	103	165	49	5	.419	$15.1	1	71	.307
1936	Chicago (A)	15	134	.369	146	556	116	205	39	5	.538	$12.6	6	128	.388
1937	Chicago (A)	10	83	.308	162	604	106	186	58	5	.470	$12.8	4	77	.317
1938	Chicago (A)	0	49	.298	88	319	46	95	26	0	.379	$5.2	0	44	.303
1939	Chicago (A)	0	60	.307	155	540	89	166	36	6	.396	$7.2	0	56	.314
1940	Chicago (A)	0	89	.351	157	592	108	208	53	12	.481	$9.3	0	79	.348
1941	Chicago (A)	3	66	.322	160	615	107	198	50	8	.444	$9.3	1	57	.314
1942	Chicago (A)	10	70	.278	155	593	103	165	45	4	.418	$9.3	3	53	.262
1943	Chicago (A)	12	105	.349	162	611	83	213	58	1	.506	$9.4	3	80	.328
1945	Chicago (A)	3	12	.383	19	60	15	23	3	1	.617	$1.4	1	10	.368
1946	Chicago (A)	3	70	.325	156	609	75	198	56	5	.448	$4.6	1	55	.309
1947	Chicago (A)	14	57	.316	145	525	79	166	37	0	.467	$3.3	8	49	.306
1948	Chicago (A)	0	53	.320	146	522	71	167	36	2	.397	$2.7	0	47	.314
1949	Chicago (A)	9	65	.308	149	516	92	159	32	4	.438	$4.6	5	58	.301
1950	Chicago (A)	0	14	.241	52	133	12	32	7	3	.338	$1.2	0	13	.234
	Career	120	1,277	.312	2,555	9,343	1,509	2,913	731	81	.446	$135.1	45	1,116	.310
	Average season	6	64	.312	128	467	75	146	37	4	.446	$6.8	2	56	.310
	Summit season	12	97	.342	154	588	99	201	48	5	.502	$9.3	5	84	.338

RICHIE ASHBURN

		ADJUSTED REGULAR SEASON											ACTUAL RESULTS		
YEAR	TEAM	HR	RBI	BA	G	AB	R	H	2B	3B	SA	PAY	HR	RBI	BA
1948	Philadelphia (N)	6	45	.340	122	483	88	164	30	3	.451	$7.4	2	40	.333
1949	Philadelphia (N)	3	41	.290	162	696	94	202	37	11	.388	$12.0	1	37	.284
1950	Philadelphia (N)	4	43	.306	156	614	88	188	40	12	.430	$9.2	2	41	.303
1951	Philadelphia (N)	7	72	.355	162	676	105	240	49	4	.470	$14.5	4	63	.344
1952	Philadelphia (N)	3	52	.301	162	645	115	194	54	5	.414	$14.4	1	42	.282
1953	Philadelphia (N)	4	63	.336	162	646	123	217	40	8	.441	$14.9	2	57	.330
1954	Philadelphia (N)	2	48	.323	161	588	131	190	32	8	.415	$15.2	1	41	.313
1955	Philadelphia (N)	4	48	.352	147	560	104	197	49	7	.486	$12.1	3	42	.338
1956	Philadelphia (N)	4	58	.316	162	661	109	209	40	6	.413	$12.7	3	50	.303
1957	Philadelphia (N)	0	39	.311	162	650	111	202	42	7	.397	$12.3	0	33	.297
1958	Philadelphia (N)	2	40	.365	160	647	118	236	41	12	.474	$12.2	2	33	.350
1959	Philadelphia (N)	1	23	.278	160	590	101	164	25	2	.332	$5.0	1	20	.266
1960	Chicago (N)	0	47	.306	157	569	117	174	27	5	.371	$7.1	0	40	.291
1961	Chicago (N)	0	21	.267	113	318	55	85	12	4	.330	$2.4	0	19	.257
1962	New York (N)	9	31	.319	136	392	67	125	10	2	.423	$2.6	7	28	.306
	Career	49	671	.319	2,284	8,735	1,526	2,787	528	96	.418	$154.0	29	586	.308
	Average season	3	45	.319	152	582	102	186	35	6	.418	$10.3	2	39	.308
	Summit season	5	54	.350	151	602	108	211	42	7	.468	$12.2	3	47	.339

EARL AVERILL

		ADJUSTED REGULAR SEASON											ACTUAL RESULTS		
YEAR	TEAM	HR	RBI	BA	G	AB	R	H	2B	3B	SA	PAY	HR	RBI	BA
1929	Cleveland (A)	34	99	.309	161	637	113	197	41	5	.549	$19.3	18	96	.332
1930	Cleveland (A)	30	114	.308	146	561	98	173	28	3	.529	$14.8	19	119	.339
1931	Cleveland (A)	57	158	.324	162	655	154	212	24	3	.631	$23.9	32	143	.333
1932	Cleveland (A)	54	137	.305	162	668	128	204	30	5	.608	$28.0	32	124	.314
1933	Cleveland (A)	30	111	.300	162	643	100	193	47	9	.541	$17.0	11	92	.301
1934	Cleveland (A)	50	123	.302	162	629	140	190	40	2	.610	$24.9	31	113	.313
1935	Cleveland (A)	35	85	.278	145	583	117	162	32	6	.533	$13.2	19	79	.288
1936	Cleveland (A)	49	128	.360	157	634	139	228	33	7	.666	$19.6	28	126	.378
1937	Cleveland (A)	36	98	.291	162	632	129	184	31	5	.527	$19.8	21	92	.299
1938	Cleveland (A)	27	101	.325	142	511	110	166	31	8	.575	$9.1	14	93	.330
1939	Cle.-Det. (A)	20	70	.258	116	380	71	98	28	3	.505	$4.5	11	65	.264
1940	Detroit (A)	3	23	.282	67	124	11	35	4	1	.403	$1.7	2	20	.280
1941	Boston (N)	0	2	.118	8	17	2	2	0	0	.118	$0.8	0	2	.118
	Career	425	1,249	.306	1,752	6,674	1,312	2,044	369	57	.570	$196.6	238	1,164	.318
	Average season	33	96	.306	135	513	101	157	28	4	.570	$15.1	18	90	.318
	Summit season	47	129	.323	157	619	134	200	32	5	.619	$21.1	27	120	.334

JEFF BAGWELL

		ADJUSTED REGULAR SEASON											ACTUAL RESULTS		
YEAR	TEAM	HR	RBI	BA	G	AB	R	H	2B	3B	SA	PAY	HR	RBI	BA
1991	Houston (N)	20	93	.310	156	554	90	172	30	4	.487	$12.2	15	82	.294
1992	Houston (N)	26	114	.287	162	586	104	168	38	6	.505	$15.2	18	96	.273
1993	Houston (N)	24	94	.325	142	535	81	174	40	4	.550	$11.8	20	88	.320
1994	Houston (N)	57	166	.367	155	564	149	207	44	2	.755	$19.4	39	116	.368
1995	Houston (N)	25	100	.292	128	503	101	147	33	0	.507	$14.4	21	87	.290
1996	Houston (N)	31	119	.313	162	568	110	178	49	2	.570	$19.5	31	120	.315
1997	Houston (N)	45	141	.288	162	566	113	163	40	2	.604	$22.2	43	135	.286
1998	Houston (N)	35	115	.307	147	540	129	166	32	1	.565	$16.1	34	111	.304
1999	Houston (N)	41	123	.302	162	562	140	170	35	0	.584	$22.8	42	126	.304
2000	Houston (N)	45	128	.308	159	590	147	182	37	1	.603	$19.9	47	132	.310
2001	Houston (N)	38	135	.293	161	600	131	176	42	4	.567	$20.4	39	130	.288
	Career	387	1,328	.309	1,696	6,168	1,295	1,903	420	26	.573	$193.9	349	1,223	.303
	Average season	35	121	.309	154	561	118	173	38	2	.573	$17.6	32	111	.303
	Summit season	44	135	.316	160	570	132	180	41	1	.623	$20.8	40	126	.313

HAROLD BAINES

		ADJUSTED REGULAR SEASON											ACTUAL RESULTS		
YEAR	TEAM	HR	RBI	BA	G	AB	R	H	2B	3B	SA	PAY	HR	RBI	BA
1980	Chicago (A)	19	56	.259	141	491	63	127	26	5	.448	$5.9	13	49	.255
1981	Chicago (A)	25	77	.300	125	427	78	128	20	8	.560	$6.3	10	41	.286
1982	Chicago (A)	32	121	.280	161	608	102	170	32	7	.513	$14.2	25	105	.271
1983	Chicago (A)	26	113	.289	156	596	87	172	36	2	.487	$12.3	20	99	.280
1984	Chicago (A)	39	109	.315	147	569	83	179	32	8	.605	$12.2	29	94	.304
1985	Chicago (A)	27	127	.324	159	636	97	206	32	2	.508	$15.5	22	113	.309
1986	Chicago (A)	25	98	.309	145	570	80	176	33	2	.505	$11.9	21	88	.296
1987	Chicago (A)	21	97	.299	132	505	62	151	28	4	.495	$9.1	20	93	.293
1988	Chicago (A)	19	97	.294	159	603	65	177	45	1	.466	$9.6	13	81	.277
1989	Chi.-Tex. (A)	23	85	.327	146	505	86	165	32	1	.531	$7.2	16	72	.309
1990	Tex.-Oak. (A)	21	75	.296	135	415	60	123	16	1	.492	$5.4	16	65	.284
1991	Oakland (A)	25	103	.311	141	488	87	152	27	1	.525	$5.0	20	90	.295
1992	Oakland (A)	22	90	.266	140	478	69	127	18	0	.441	$4.7	16	76	.253
1993	Baltimore (A)	23	84	.317	118	416	69	132	23	0	.538	$3.7	20	78	.313
1994	Baltimore (A)	24	79	.294	136	472	64	139	17	1	.487	$3.8	16	54	.294
1995	Baltimore (A)	29	73	.302	143	434	69	131	22	1	.558	$3.3	24	63	.299
1996	Chicago (A)	22	94	.311	143	495	79	154	30	0	.505	$4.3	22	95	.311
1997	Chi.-Balt. (A)	17	70	.303	137	452	57	137	23	0	.467	$3.2	16	67	.301
1998	Baltimore (A)	9	59	.304	104	293	41	89	18	0	.457	$2.1	9	57	.300
1999	Balt.-Cle. (A)	24	101	.309	135	430	61	133	18	1	.523	$3.1	25	103	.312
2000	Balt.-Chi. (A)	10	38	.254	96	283	25	72	13	0	.406	$1.7	11	39	.254
2001	Chicago (A)	0	6	.131	32	84	3	11	1	0	.143	$0.8	0	6	.131
	Career	482	1,852	.298	2,931	10,250	1,487	3,051	542	45	.500	$145.3	384	1,628	.289
	Average season	22	84	.298	133	466	68	139	25	2	.500	$6.6	17	74	.289
	Summit season	28	86	.313	136	470	77	147	26	4	.564	$6.5	20	70	.303

FRANK BAKER

		ADJUSTED REGULAR SEASON											ACTUAL RESULTS		
YEAR	TEAM	HR	RBI	BA	G	AB	R	H	2B	3B	SA	PAY	HR	RBI	BA
1908	Philadelphia (A)	0	3	.323	9	31	7	10	7	0	.548	$0.0	0	2	.290
1909	Philadelphia (A)	35	120	.336	157	574	103	193	38	8	.613	$7.0	4	85	.305
1910	Philadelphia (A)	19	95	.306	153	588	107	180	50	8	.515	$11.4	2	74	.283
1911	Philadelphia (A)	41	131	.339	158	632	109	214	40	3	.606	$14.9	11	115	.334
1912	Philadelphia (A)	44	147	.348	158	612	131	213	38	6	.645	$19.6	10	130	.347
1913	Philadelphia (A)	41	147	.351	158	598	145	210	29	2	.612	$25.5	12	117	.337
1914	Philadelphia (A)	34	111	.338	154	585	105	198	22	3	.561	$18.8	9	89	.319
1916	New York (A)	29	72	.291	104	374	64	109	14	0	.561	$7.0	10	52	.269
1917	New York (A)	27	99	.305	153	580	79	177	20	1	.483	$11.8	6	71	.282
1918	New York (A)	37	105	.324	162	648	110	210	24	2	.539	$10.1	6	62	.306
1919	New York (A)	32	119	.300	162	651	100	195	18	0	.475	$13.0	10	83	.293
1921	New York (A)	18	78	.271	100	351	50	95	12	1	.464	$3.6	9	71	.294
1922	New York (A)	14	39	.258	73	248	32	64	10	1	.476	$2.1	7	36	.278
	Career	371	1,266	.320	1,701	6,472	1,142	2,068	322	35	.552	$144.8	96	987	.307
	Average season	29	97	.320	131	498	88	159	25	3	.552	$11.1	7	76	.307
	Summit season	39	131	.343	157	600	119	206	33	4	.607	$17.2	9	107	.329

DAVE BANCROFT

		ADJUSTED REGULAR SEASON											ACTUAL RESULTS		
YEAR	TEAM	HR	RBI	BA	G	AB	R	H	2B	3B	SA	PAY	HR	RBI	BA
1915	Philadelphia (N)	25	39	.273	162	596	111	163	15	1	.428	$11.6	7	30	.254
1916	Philadelphia (N)	14	46	.230	149	501	74	115	10	0	.333	$7.8	3	33	.212
1917	Philadelphia (N)	22	60	.262	134	504	78	132	23	1	.442	$7.7	4	43	.243
1918	Philadelphia (N)	0	44	.280	162	647	118	181	82	4	.419	$12.4	0	26	.265
1919	Philadelphia (N)	0	36	.277	108	393	66	109	47	7	.433	$5.8	0	25	.272
1920	Phi.-N.Y. (N)	0	42	.290	157	642	121	186	85	7	.444	$9.4	0	36	.299
1921	New York (N)	21	73	.294	162	642	132	189	36	7	.470	$12.7	6	67	.318
1922	New York (N)	13	63	.299	162	676	124	202	56	2	.445	$16.1	4	60	.321
1923	New York (N)	4	34	.288	113	469	88	135	55	1	.435	$4.7	1	31	.304
1924	Boston (N)	7	23	.263	83	335	54	88	14	0	.367	$2.6	2	21	.279
1925	Boston (N)	7	51	.295	136	509	78	150	46	4	.442	$3.8	2	49	.319
1926	Boston (N)	5	49	.299	134	478	78	143	34	5	.423	$3.0	1	44	.311
1927	Boston (N)	5	34	.230	116	392	48	90	21	3	.337	$1.9	1	31	.243
1928	Brooklyn (N)	0	56	.236	156	539	51	127	41	4	.327	$2.6	0	51	.247
1929	Brooklyn (N)	3	45	.256	110	379	36	97	19	2	.340	$1.9	1	44	.277
1930	New York (N)	0	0	.053	11	19	0	1	1	0	.105	$0.5	0	0	.059
	Career	126	695	.273	2,055	7,721	1,257	2,108	585	48	.410	$104.5	32	591	.279
	Average season	8	43	.273	128	483	79	132	37	3	.410	$6.5	2	37	.279
	Summit season	9	53	.293	146	588	109	172	56	4	.447	$9.3	3	49	.313

ERNIE BANKS

		ADJUSTED REGULAR SEASON											ACTUAL RESULTS		
YEAR	TEAM	HR	RBI	BA	G	AB	R	H	2B	3B	SA	PAY	HR	RBI	BA
1953	Chicago (N)	3	6	.314	10	35	3	11	1	1	.657	$0.0	2	6	.314
1954	Chicago (N)	28	93	.284	162	624	82	177	25	4	.471	$6.4	19	79	.275
1955	Chicago (N)	54	135	.308	162	627	113	193	39	6	.648	$12.1	44	117	.295
1956	Chicago (N)	34	96	.309	143	553	93	171	34	5	.573	$11.2	28	85	.297
1957	Chicago (N)	52	122	.297	162	617	136	183	44	4	.634	$19.5	43	102	.285
1958	Chicago (N)	58	156	.327	162	649	144	212	30	8	.666	$26.4	47	129	.313
1959	Chicago (N)	54	169	.318	162	616	114	196	32	5	.649	$25.5	45	143	.304
1960	Chicago (N)	51	139	.285	162	620	111	177	40	5	.613	$22.7	41	117	.271
1961	Chicago (N)	33	90	.289	143	530	84	153	29	3	.542	$12.0	29	80	.278
1962	Chicago (N)	43	115	.280	154	610	96	171	26	4	.548	$12.5	37	104	.269
1963	Chicago (N)	22	79	.248	130	432	51	107	26	1	.465	$3.9	18	64	.227
1964	Chicago (N)	28	116	.284	157	591	81	168	38	5	.508	$7.1	23	95	.264
1965	Chicago (N)	34	128	.290	161	604	95	175	32	2	.518	$9.6	28	106	.265
1966	Chicago (N)	19	92	.294	141	511	64	150	33	5	.489	$4.7	15	75	.272
1967	Chicago (N)	33	123	.305	151	573	88	175	34	3	.548	$6.7	23	95	.276
1968	Chicago (N)	46	117	.279	149	548	100	153	32	0	.589	$6.8	32	83	.246
1969	Chicago (N)	29	126	.275	154	561	71	154	25	2	.481	$6.5	23	106	.253
1970	Chicago (N)	14	50	.266	72	222	28	59	8	2	.509	$2.2	12	44	.252
1971	Chicago (N)	4	7	.205	39	83	5	17	3	0	.386	$1.3	3	6	.193
	Career	639	1,959	.292	2,576	9,606	1,559	2,802	531	65	.560	$197.1	512	1,636	.274
	Average season	34	103	.292	136	506	82	147	28	3	.560	$10.4	27	86	.274
	Summit season	54	144	.307	162	626	124	192	37	6	.644	$21.2	44	122	.294

DON BAYLOR

		ADJUSTED REGULAR SEASON											ACTUAL RESULTS		
YEAR	TEAM	HR	RBI	BA	G	AB	R	H	2B	3B	SA	PAY	HR	RBI	BA
1970	Baltimore (A)	0	5	.235	8	17	5	4	0	0	.235	$0.0	0	4	.235
1971	Baltimore (A)	0	1	.000	1	2	0	0	0	0	.000	$0.0	0	1	.000
1972	Baltimore (A)	17	52	.280	107	336	46	94	18	3	.503	$2.7	11	38	.253
1973	Baltimore (A)	15	59	.299	118	405	75	121	26	4	.494	$4.3	11	51	.286
1974	Baltimore (A)	16	70	.284	137	489	79	139	28	1	.444	$5.9	10	59	.272
1975	Baltimore (A)	36	90	.295	148	535	94	158	24	4	.557	$9.3	25	76	.282
1976	Oakland (A)	25	84	.260	158	599	105	156	29	1	.437	$14.3	15	68	.247
1977	California (A)	29	83	.255	154	561	96	143	28	0	.460	$12.0	25	75	.251
1978	California (A)	44	117	.266	158	591	122	157	26	0	.533	$12.6	34	99	.255
1979	California (A)	44	154	.299	162	628	132	188	35	2	.572	$22.3	36	139	.296
1980	California (A)	8	59	.253	91	344	45	87	14	2	.375	$5.7	5	51	.250
1981	California (A)	35	119	.252	152	556	94	140	27	1	.493	$9.4	17	66	.239
1982	California (A)	30	107	.271	157	608	92	165	26	1	.465	$9.7	24	93	.263
1983	New York (A)	28	97	.313	144	534	94	167	36	2	.545	$6.9	21	85	.303
1984	New York (A)	34	103	.270	134	493	97	133	31	1	.544	$6.9	27	89	.262
1985	New York (A)	27	104	.242	143	480	80	116	26	1	.469	$6.3	23	91	.231
1986	Boston (A)	35	105	.248	161	589	104	146	26	1	.474	$9.1	31	94	.238
1987	Bos-Minn. (A)	16	66	.250	128	388	70	97	10	0	.399	$3.6	16	63	.245
1988	Oakland (A)	10	40	.231	92	264	33	61	8	0	.375	$2.1	7	34	.220
	Career	449	1,515	.270	2,353	8,419	1,463	2,272	418	24	.485	$143.1	338	1,276	.260
	Average season	24	80	.270	124	443	77	120	22	1	.485	$7.5	18	67	.260
	Summit season	37	112	.290	149	556	108	161	30	2	.550	$11.6	29	98	.280

JAKE BECKLEY

		ADJUSTED REGULAR SEASON											ACTUAL RESULTS		
YEAR	TEAM	HR	RBI	BA	G	AB	R	H	2B	3B	SA	PAY	HR	RBI	BA
1888	Pittsburgh (N)	0	32	.387	83	331	42	128	53	2	.559	$3.3	0	27	.343
1889	Pittsburgh (N)	32	100	.309	149	632	94	195	31	4	.522	$9.0	9	97	.301
1890	Pittsburgh (P)	45	128	.334	153	652	116	218	57	8	.653	$15.3	9	120	.324
1891	Pittsburgh (N)	25	76	.310	157	654	98	203	45	10	.524	$14.9	4	73	.292
1892	Pittsburgh (N)	39	99	.260	158	642	105	167	27	5	.500	$15.4	10	96	.236
1893	Pittsburgh (N)	26	104	.291	162	670	106	195	59	8	.519	$19.5	5	106	.303
1894	Pittsburgh (N)	25	104	.299	161	655	105	196	49	6	.507	$18.8	7	120	.343
1895	Pittsburgh (N)	25	104	.298	156	641	98	191	51	8	.520	$15.3	5	110	.328
1896	Pit.-N.Y. (N)	29	72	.255	128	486	83	124	14	2	.471	$7.3	9	70	.276
1897	N.Y.-Cin. (N)	31	88	.304	135	513	85	156	19	3	.534	$7.4	8	87	.330
1898	Cincinnati (N)	23	74	.293	122	475	88	139	27	4	.512	$7.0	4	72	.294
1899	Cincinnati (N)	20	97	.318	139	532	85	169	47	7	.545	$6.8	3	99	.333
1900	Cincinnati (N)	15	101	.329	159	629	105	207	57	5	.507	$9.8	2	94	.341
1901	Cincinnati (N)	20	91	.303	160	663	90	201	64	6	.508	$9.9	3	79	.307
1902	Cincinnati (N)	29	88	.333	148	609	105	203	28	2	.529	$9.6	5	69	.330
1903	Cincinnati (N)	19	103	.335	138	528	108	177	50	5	.557	$6.9	2	81	.327
1904	St. Louis (N)	12	89	.355	148	574	96	204	54	6	.533	$7.0	1	67	.325
1905	St. Louis (N)	12	73	.311	141	541	62	168	48	6	.488	$4.7	1	57	.286
1906	St. Louis (N)	0	61	.269	92	338	40	91	51	6	.456	$2.4	0	44	.247
1907	St. Louis (N)	0	10	.227	33	119	8	27	12	0	.328	$1.2	0	7	.209
	Career	427	1,694	.309	2,722	10,884	1,719	3,359	843	103	.523	$191.5	87	1,575	.308
	Average season	21	85	.309	136	544	86	168	42	5	.523	$9.6	4	79	.308
	Summit season	19	90	.342	132	523	89	179	52	6	.574	$7.9	3	79	.329

BUDDY BELL

		ADJUSTED REGULAR SEASON											ACTUAL RESULTS		
YEAR	TEAM	HR	RBI	BA	G	AB	R	H	2B	3B	SA	PAY	HR	RBI	BA
1972	Cleveland (A)	15	49	.281	137	484	67	136	30	1	.440	$5.9	9	36	.255
1973	Cleveland (A)	19	69	.281	156	631	100	177	31	7	.442	$11.5	14	59	.268
1974	Cleveland (A)	11	55	.274	116	423	61	116	21	1	.407	$6.1	7	46	.262
1975	Cleveland (A)	16	70	.284	156	564	78	160	27	3	.427	$8.9	10	59	.271
1976	Cleveland (A)	14	75	.296	162	615	94	182	38	2	.433	$11.9	7	60	.281
1977	Cleveland (A)	14	71	.298	130	483	71	144	27	3	.453	$7.6	11	64	.292
1978	Cleveland (A)	11	75	.294	145	568	86	167	39	7	.445	$9.6	6	62	.282
1979	Texas (A)	23	111	.303	162	670	98	203	48	2	.484	$15.1	18	101	.299
1980	Texas (A)	24	95	.333	128	486	87	162	27	3	.549	$7.2	17	83	.329
1981	Texas (A)	24	121	.311	150	557	83	173	28	1	.494	$9.8	10	64	.294
1982	Texas (A)	17	77	.305	148	537	71	164	31	2	.466	$9.2	13	67	.296
1983	Texas (A)	19	75	.285	155	614	85	175	41	2	.451	$7.4	14	66	.277
1984	Texas (A)	16	97	.325	149	557	103	181	45	4	.506	$7.3	11	83	.315
1985	Tex. (A)-Cin. (N)	13	77	.239	151	560	69	134	33	4	.382	$6.8	10	68	.229
1986	Cincinnati (N)	23	84	.290	155	568	99	165	32	3	.479	$7.3	20	75	.278
1987	Cincinnati (N)	17	73	.289	143	522	77	151	21	2	.435	$6.3	17	70	.284
1988	Cin.-Hou. (N)	10	47	.254	95	323	32	82	12	1	.390	$2.1	7	40	.241
1989	Texas (A)	0	4	.195	34	82	5	16	6	0	.268	$1.0	0	3	.183
	Career	286	1,325	.291	2,472	9,244	1,366	2,688	537	48	.452	$141.0	201	1,106	.279
	Average season	16	74	.291	137	514	76	149	30	3	.452	$7.8	11	61	.279
	Summit season	21	100	.316	147	561	88	177	36	2	.499	$9.7	14	80	.307

GEORGE BELL

		ADJUSTED REGULAR SEASON											ACTUAL RESULTS		
YEAR	TEAM	HR	RBI	BA	G	AB	R	H	2B	3B	SA	PAY	HR	RBI	BA
1981	Toronto (A)	12	22	.244	92	250	36	61	4	1	.412	$2.4	5	12	.233
1983	Toronto (A)	3	19	.277	39	112	6	31	7	3	.473	$1.3	2	17	.268
1984	Toronto (A)	34	100	.302	158	602	98	182	44	3	.555	$7.3	26	87	.292
1985	Toronto (A)	34	108	.288	158	611	99	176	31	5	.522	$11.2	28	95	.275
1986	Toronto (A)	36	120	.322	158	637	112	205	42	6	.576	$14.8	31	108	.309
1987	Toronto (A)	49	140	.315	156	610	116	192	35	4	.626	$18.5	47	134	.308
1988	Toronto (A)	32	115	.285	156	614	92	175	29	5	.505	$12.6	24	97	.269
1989	Toronto (A)	26	123	.315	153	613	104	193	46	2	.524	$12.8	18	104	.297
1990	Toronto (A)	27	99	.276	142	562	77	155	26	0	.466	$9.7	21	86	.265
1991	Chicago (N)	32	99	.299	151	565	73	169	29	0	.520	$7.0	25	86	.285
1992	Chicago (A)	34	133	.268	155	627	88	168	28	0	.475	$9.6	25	112	.255
1993	Chicago (A)	16	69	.220	102	410	39	90	17	2	.388	$2.9	13	64	.217
	Career	335	1,147	.289	1,620	6,213	940	1,797	338	31	.515	$110.1	265	1,002	.278
	Average season	28	96	.289	135	518	78	150	28	3	.515	$9.2	22	84	.278
	Summit season	35	116	.311	155	605	101	188	39	3	.559	$12.1	29	104	.299

ALBERT BELLE

		ADJUSTED REGULAR SEASON											ACTUAL RESULTS		
YEAR	TEAM	HR	RBI	BA	G	AB	R	H	2B	3B	SA	PAY	HR	RBI	BA
1989	Cleveland (A)	10	44	.239	62	218	26	52	9	4	.454	$2.9	7	37	.225
1990	Cleveland (A)	1	3	.174	9	23	1	4	0	0	.304	$0.9	1	3	.174
1991	Cleveland (A)	34	108	.297	123	461	68	137	33	2	.599	$5.5	28	95	.282
1992	Cleveland (A)	44	133	.274	153	585	96	160	22	1	.540	$9.1	34	112	.260
1993	Cleveland (A)	44	139	.295	159	594	100	175	36	3	.588	$14.3	38	129	.290
1994	Cleveland (A)	53	147	.355	152	591	131	210	49	3	.717	$19.4	36	101	.357
1995	Cleveland (A)	59	145	.320	161	615	140	197	59	1	.707	$22.9	50	126	.317
1996	Cleveland (A)	48	148	.310	159	606	124	188	39	3	.622	$23.2	48	148	.311
1997	Chicago (A)	32	121	.276	162	638	94	176	46	1	.502	$16.9	30	116	.274
1998	Chicago (A)	50	157	.332	162	605	116	201	47	2	.664	$19.5	49	152	.328
1999	Baltimore (A)	36	114	.295	161	610	106	180	36	1	.534	$13.9	37	117	.297
2000	Baltimore (A)	22	100	.279	141	559	69	156	36	1	.465	$7.3	23	103	.281
	Career	433	1,359	.301	1,604	6,105	1,071	1,836	412	22	.588	$155.8	381	1,239	.295
	Average season	36	113	.301	134	509	89	153	34	2	.588	$13.0	32	103	.295
	Summit season	49	141	.325	151	576	116	187	45	2	.665	$18.1	42	124	.318

JOHNNY BENCH

		ADJUSTED REGULAR SEASON											ACTUAL RESULTS		
YEAR	TEAM	HR	RBI	BA	G	AB	R	H	2B	3B	SA	PAY	HR	RBI	BA
1967	Cincinnati (N)	2	8	.186	26	86	9	16	3	1	.314	$0.3	1	6	.163
1968	Cincinnati (N)	24	115	.313	153	560	94	175	54	2	.545	$6.4	15	82	.275
1969	Cincinnati (N)	33	107	.318	147	528	99	168	30	1	.566	$9.0	26	90	.293
1970	Cincinnati (N)	53	168	.311	158	605	110	188	43	3	.655	$14.9	45	148	.293
1971	Cincinnati (N)	36	76	.256	149	562	100	144	24	2	.498	$14.3	27	61	.238

(Johnny Bench, continued)

		ADJUSTED REGULAR SEASON											ACTUAL RESULTS		
YEAR	TEAM	HR	RBI	BA	G	AB	R	H	2B	3B	SA	PAY	HR	RBI	BA
1972	Cincinnati (N)	57	174	.298	155	567	121	169	27	2	.654	$19.9	40	125	.270
1973	Cincinnati (N)	32	122	.266	152	557	97	148	21	3	.487	$15.5	25	104	.253
1974	Cincinnati (N)	45	153	.293	159	617	128	181	43	2	.588	$25.5	33	129	.280
1975	Cincinnati (N)	38	128	.296	142	530	97	157	42	1	.594	$15.1	28	110	.283
1976	Cincinnati (N)	25	91	.247	135	465	76	115	26	1	.469	$9.4	16	74	.234
1977	Cincinnati (N)	36	121	.279	142	494	74	138	37	1	.577	$9.4	31	109	.275
1978	Cincinnati (N)	30	87	.270	121	396	62	107	17	1	.545	$5.7	23	73	.260
1979	Cincinnati (N)	27	89	.280	131	468	81	131	20	0	.496	$4.8	22	80	.276
1980	Cincinnati (N)	29	78	.255	113	357	59	91	11	0	.529	$3.0	24	68	.250
1981	Cincinnati (N)	17	46	.326	78	267	26	87	13	0	.566	$2.2	8	25	.309
1982	Cincinnati (N)	17	44	.266	119	399	51	106	18	0	.439	$2.5	13	38	.258
1983	Cincinnati (N)	16	62	.261	110	310	36	81	16	2	.481	$1.8	12	54	.255
	Career	517	1,669	.283	2,190	7,768	1,320	2,202	445	22	.546	$159.7	389	1,376	.267
	Average season	30	98	.283	129	457	78	130	26	1	.546	$9.4	23	81	.267
	Summit season	45	146	.304	152	569	111	173	37	2	.613	$16.9	34	120	.284

YOGI BERRA

		ADJUSTED REGULAR SEASON											ACTUAL RESULTS		
YEAR	TEAM	HR	RBI	BA	G	AB	R	H	2B	3B	SA	PAY	HR	RBI	BA
1946	New York (A)	3	5	.364	7	22	4	8	1	0	.818	$0.0	2	4	.364
1947	New York (A)	17	64	.290	87	307	48	89	17	2	.524	$2.8	11	54	.280
1948	New York (A)	25	111	.311	131	492	79	153	30	6	.549	$6.3	14	98	.305
1949	New York (A)	28	101	.284	121	433	66	123	22	1	.533	$6.1	20	91	.277
1950	New York (A)	36	133	.326	158	625	124	204	35	4	.568	$15.2	28	124	.322
1951	New York (A)	37	101	.303	148	574	105	174	23	3	.547	$14.2	27	88	.294
1952	New York (A)	42	121	.291	149	560	120	163	19	1	.554	$15.1	30	98	.273
1953	New York (A)	36	125	.302	147	540	92	163	28	3	.565	$14.6	27	108	.296
1954	New York (A)	30	147	.316	158	611	103	193	35	4	.534	$15.9	22	125	.307
1955	New York (A)	33	124	.282	155	570	97	161	27	2	.511	$12.4	27	108	.272
1956	New York (A)	35	121	.311	147	547	107	170	38	1	.576	$12.2	30	105	.298
1957	New York (A)	30	100	.262	141	507	90	133	18	1	.479	$7.3	24	82	.251
1958	New York (A)	27	108	.278	128	454	72	126	22	2	.513	$5.0	22	90	.266
1959	New York (A)	23	81	.298	137	494	75	147	31	1	.504	$5.0	19	69	.284
1960	New York (A)	18	74	.291	125	374	54	109	18	1	.489	$3.0	15	62	.276
1961	New York (A)	24	66	.283	118	392	67	111	13	0	.500	$2.6	22	61	.271
1962	New York (A)	11	39	.233	86	232	28	54	10	0	.418	$1.7	10	35	.224
1963	New York (A)	10	35	.320	64	147	25	47	8	0	.578	$1.3	8	28	.293
1965	New York (N)	0	0	.222	4	9	1	2	0	0	.222	$0.4	0	0	.222
	Career	465	1,656	.295	2,211	7,890	1,357	2,330	395	32	.530	$141.1	358	1,430	.285
	Average season	24	87	.295	116	415	71	123	21	2	.530	$7.4	19	75	.285
	Summit season	34	118	.311	146	556	101	173	31	3	.561	$12.5	25	105	.303

WADE BOGGS

		ADJUSTED REGULAR SEASON											ACTUAL RESULTS		
YEAR	TEAM	HR	RBI	BA	G	AB	R	H	2B	3B	SA	PAY	HR	RBI	BA
1982	Boston (A)	7	51	.361	104	338	59	122	18	1	.482	$4.9	5	44	.349
1983	Boston (A)	8	84	.373	153	582	114	217	58	6	.534	$12.1	5	74	.361
1984	Boston (A)	9	64	.336	158	625	126	210	43	4	.461	$15.3	6	55	.325
1985	Boston (A)	11	88	.385	160	649	121	250	53	2	.524	$19.4	8	78	.368
1986	Boston (A)	10	80	.373	150	584	120	218	55	2	.526	$18.8	8	71	.357
1987	Boston (A)	25	93	.372	147	551	113	205	44	5	.606	$12.7	24	89	.363
1988	Boston (A)	8	69	.389	155	584	152	227	59	7	.555	$22.3	5	58	.366
1989	Boston (A)	5	64	.349	156	621	134	217	72	7	.512	$17.0	3	54	.330
1990	Boston (A)	9	72	.315	155	619	102	195	55	5	.464	$13.2	6	63	.302
1991	Boston (A)	11	58	.350	144	546	106	191	50	2	.509	$7.4	8	51	.332
1992	Boston (A)	11	59	.272	143	514	74	140	27	4	.405	$5.0	7	50	.259
1993	New York (A)	2	63	.307	143	560	89	172	34	1	.382	$6.8	2	59	.302
1994	New York (A)	17	80	.342	139	524	88	179	27	1	.494	$6.3	11	55	.342
1995	New York (A)	6	72	.326	141	515	87	168	27	4	.429	$4.6	5	63	.324
1996	New York (A)	2	41	.311	132	501	79	156	29	2	.389	$3.6	2	41	.311
1997	New York (A)	4	29	.295	103	353	57	104	24	1	.402	$2.2	4	28	.292
1998	Tampa Bay (A)	7	54	.283	123	435	53	123	24	4	.405	$2.3	7	52	.280
1999	Tampa Bay (A)	2	28	.298	90	292	39	87	14	1	.373	$1.5	2	29	.301
	Career	154	1,149	.339	2,496	9,393	1,713	3,181	713	59	.476	$175.4	118	1,014	.328
	Average season	9	64	.339	139	522	95	177	40	3	.476	$9.7	7	56	.328
	Summit season	12	83	.378	153	590	124	223	54	4	.544	$17.1	10	74	.363

BARRY BONDS

		ADJUSTED REGULAR SEASON											ACTUAL RESULTS		
YEAR	TEAM	HR	RBI	BA	G	AB	R	H	2B	3B	SA	PAY	HR	RBI	BA
1986	Pittsburgh (N)	18	53	.232	113	413	80	96	29	3	.448	$7.0	16	48	.223
1987	Pittsburgh (N)	26	62	.267	150	551	104	147	38	8	.506	$9.2	25	59	.261
1988	Pittsburgh (N)	33	70	.299	146	545	117	163	33	5	.560	$11.7	24	58	.283
1989	Pittsburgh (N)	27	68	.264	157	573	112	151	38	5	.489	$14.3	19	58	.248
1990	Pittsburgh (N)	41	131	.314	151	519	120	163	34	3	.628	$14.9	33	114	.301
1991	Pittsburgh (N)	32	132	.308	153	510	108	157	30	4	.571	$15.1	25	116	.292
1992	Pittsburgh (N)	45	123	.328	140	473	130	155	36	4	.706	$15.5	34	103	.311
1993	San Francisco (N)	53	132	.341	159	539	139	184	38	4	.722	$22.2	46	123	.336
1994	San Francisco (N)	54	116	.312	158	552	127	172	24	1	.652	$16.6	37	81	.312
1995	San Francisco (N)	40	120	.297	162	569	126	169	35	7	.594	$22.8	33	104	.294
1996	San Francisco (N)	42	128	.308	158	517	121	159	28	3	.617	$13.9	42	129	.308
1997	San Francisco (N)	42	105	.293	159	532	128	156	25	5	.596	$13.8	40	101	.291
1998	San Francisco (N)	38	126	.307	155	548	124	168	43	7	.619	$14.0	37	122	.303
1999	San Francisco (N)	33	81	.259	102	355	89	92	20	2	.606	$5.1	34	83	.262
2000	San Francisco (N)	47	103	.304	143	480	125	146	28	4	.673	$9.1	49	106	.306
2001	San Francisco (N)	72	142	.334	153	476	134	159	32	2	.863	$13.1	73	137	.328
	Career	643	1,692	.299	2,359	8,152	1,884	2,437	511	67	.615	$218.3	567	1,542	.292
	Average season	40	106	.299	147	510	118	152	32	4	.615	$13.6	35	96	.292
	Summit season	54	123	.323	151	504	131	163	32	3	.720	$15.3	48	110	.319

BOBBY BONDS

		ADJUSTED REGULAR SEASON											ACTUAL RESULTS		
YEAR	TEAM	HR	RBI	BA	G	AB	R	H	2B	3B	SA	PAY	HR	RBI	BA
1968	San Francisco (N)	15	49	.290	81	307	78	89	14	4	.508	$5.6	9	35	.254
1969	San Francisco (N)	41	108	.280	158	622	144	174	34	5	.548	$18.5	32	90	.259
1970	San Francisco (N)	32	88	.320	157	663	152	212	47	8	.560	$25.7	26	78	.302
1971	San Francisco (N)	44	128	.310	155	619	138	192	40	4	.601	$19.9	33	102	.288
1972	San Francisco (N)	39	110	.285	160	655	163	187	38	5	.537	$31.5	26	80	.259
1973	San Francisco (N)	48	112	.297	160	643	153	191	41	4	.597	$31.7	39	96	.283
1974	San Francisco (N)	31	84	.268	150	567	116	152	27	7	.504	$19.5	21	71	.256
1975	New York (A)	43	100	.282	147	536	110	151	28	3	.586	$12.8	32	85	.270
1976	California (A)	17	66	.278	99	378	59	105	12	2	.455	$6.7	10	54	.265
1977	California (A)	44	127	.269	158	592	114	159	25	6	.554	$12.8	37	115	.264
1978	Chi.-Tex. (A)	41	107	.278	156	565	110	157	20	3	.542	$9.7	31	90	.267
1979	Cleveland (A)	30	94	.279	147	542	103	151	26	1	.496	$7.4	25	85	.275
1980	St. Louis (N)	7	28	.208	86	231	43	48	6	2	.342	$2.7	5	24	.203
1981	Chicago (N)	14	36	.224	69	250	49	56	11	1	.444	$2.3	6	19	.215
	Career	446	1,237	.282	1,883	7,170	1,532	2,024	369	55	.536	$206.8	332	1,024	.268
	Average season	32	88	.282	135	512	109	145	26	4	.536	$14.8	24	73	.268
	Summit season	42	107	.298	155	617	139	184	38	5	.580	$21.7	32	90	.281

BOB BOONE

		ADJUSTED REGULAR SEASON											ACTUAL RESULTS		
YEAR	TEAM	HR	RBI	BA	G	AB	R	H	2B	3B	SA	PAY	HR	RBI	BA
1972	Philadelphia (N)	2	6	.296	17	54	6	16	1	0	.426	$0.0	1	4	.275
1973	Philadelphia (N)	14	71	.273	145	521	49	142	26	2	.411	$4.5	10	61	.261
1974	Philadelphia (N)	5	62	.254	146	488	49	124	35	3	.369	$5.1	3	52	.242
1975	Philadelphia (N)	3	23	.256	97	289	33	74	20	2	.370	$3.1	2	20	.246
1976	Philadelphia (N)	8	66	.285	121	361	49	103	26	2	.435	$3.6	4	54	.271
1977	Philadelphia (N)	14	73	.289	132	440	61	127	30	3	.466	$4.1	11	66	.284
1978	Philadelphia (N)	18	73	.294	132	435	57	128	21	3	.480	$4.2	12	62	.283
1979	Philadelphia (N)	12	63	.291	118	395	41	115	24	2	.453	$2.6	9	58	.286
1980	Philadelphia (N)	13	63	.233	141	480	39	112	27	1	.375	$2.8	9	55	.229
1981	Philadelphia (N)	10	44	.222	115	343	35	76	12	0	.344	$2.1	4	24	.211
1982	California (A)	10	67	.265	143	472	48	125	21	0	.373	$2.6	7	58	.256
1983	California (A)	12	59	.265	142	468	52	124	21	0	.387	$2.2	9	52	.256
1984	California (A)	4	37	.209	139	450	38	94	21	1	.287	$1.9	3	32	.202
1985	California (A)	6	62	.259	150	460	42	119	21	0	.343	$2.2	5	55	.248
1986	California (A)	8	55	.231	144	442	53	102	15	2	.328	$2.2	7	49	.222
1987	California (A)	3	34	.247	128	389	44	96	20	0	.321	$1.8	3	33	.242
1988	California (A)	7	46	.313	122	352	45	110	21	0	.432	$1.8	5	39	.295
1989	Kansas City (A)	1	51	.289	131	405	39	117	22	3	.365	$1.9	1	43	.274
1990	Kansas City (A)	0	10	.248	40	117	13	29	5	0	.291	$0.8	0	9	.239
	Career	150	965	.263	2,303	7,361	793	1,933	389	24	.383	$49.5	105	826	.254
	Average season	8	51	.263	121	387	42	102	20	1	.383	$2.6	6	43	.254
	Summit season	12	64	.295	125	397	51	117	24	2	.456	$3.3	8	56	.284

JIM BOTTOMLEY

		ADJUSTED REGULAR SEASON											ACTUAL RESULTS		
YEAR	TEAM	HR	RBI	BA	G	AB	R	H	2B	3B	SA	PAY	HR	RBI	BA
1922	St. Louis (N)	11	38	.302	39	159	31	48	8	2	.585	$2.6	5	35	.325
1923	St. Louis (N)	24	103	.353	141	550	86	194	43	6	.584	$7.5	8	94	.371
1924	St. Louis (N)	34	122	.297	144	555	95	165	26	4	.542	$9.6	14	111	.316
1925	St. Louis (N)	42	133	.339	162	655	95	222	39	4	.603	$15.3	21	128	.367
1926	St. Louis (N)	43	132	.286	160	626	108	179	31	4	.554	$18.9	19	120	.299
1927	St. Louis (N)	42	137	.288	161	608	105	175	25	5	.553	$19.4	19	124	.303
1928	St. Louis (N)	59	151	.311	157	607	136	189	33	6	.677	$25.5	31	136	.325
1929	St. Louis (N)	47	140	.293	154	591	110	173	24	4	.585	$16.6	29	137	.314
1930	St. Louis (N)	24	93	.277	138	513	89	142	29	3	.485	$9.9	15	97	.304
1931	St. Louis (N)	22	83	.337	114	403	81	136	31	2	.588	$7.2	9	75	.348
1932	St. Louis (N)	19	52	.289	95	325	49	94	13	1	.511	$2.9	11	48	.296
1933	Cincinnati (N)	29	99	.249	154	583	68	145	22	4	.449	$5.0	13	83	.250
1934	Cincinnati (N)	24	86	.274	151	591	79	162	34	6	.474	$5.0	11	78	.284
1935	Cincinnati (N)	3	54	.249	113	421	48	105	31	1	.349	$2.7	1	49	.258
1936	St. Louis (A)	25	98	.282	146	567	74	160	40	6	.506	$4.4	12	95	.298
1937	St. Louis (A)	2	13	.228	68	114	12	26	8	0	.351	$1.3	1	12	.239
	Career	450	1,534	.294	2,097	7,868	1,266	2,315	437	58	.536	$153.8	219	1,422	.310
	Average season	28	96	.294	131	492	79	145	27	4	.536	$9.6	14	89	.310
	Summit season	39	122	.326	146	561	102	183	34	4	.610	$14.4	20	114	.345

LOU BOUDREAU

		ADJUSTED REGULAR SEASON											ACTUAL RESULTS		
YEAR	TEAM	HR	RBI	BA	G	AB	R	H	2B	3B	SA	PAY	HR	RBI	BA
1938	Cleveland (A)	0	0	.000	1	1	0	0	0	0	.000	$0.0	0	0	.000
1939	Cleveland (A)	0	21	.252	56	238	46	60	26	3	.387	$1.5	0	19	.258
1940	Cleveland (A)	18	113	.296	162	655	109	194	58	6	.485	$9.6	9	101	.295
1941	Cleveland (A)	21	65	.264	155	606	110	160	53	5	.472	$11.4	10	56	.257
1942	Cleveland (A)	8	73	.300	153	527	72	158	35	11	.454	$9.2	2	58	.283
1943	Cleveland (A)	12	90	.303	161	571	92	173	55	6	.483	$14.6	3	67	.286
1944	Cleveland (A)	10	84	.339	157	611	114	207	74	4	.522	$15.3	3	67	.327
1945	Cleveland (A)	10	63	.318	107	381	65	121	35	1	.493	$7.4	3	48	.307
1946	Cleveland (A)	15	78	.310	145	533	64	165	41	4	.486	$7.0	6	62	.293
1947	Cleveland (A)	8	78	.317	155	556	92	176	64	2	.482	$9.2	4	67	.307
1948	Cleveland (A)	30	119	.364	158	582	130	212	39	4	.600	$12.5	18	106	.355
1949	Cleveland (A)	8	67	.292	141	500	59	146	29	2	.406	$4.8	4	60	.284
1950	Cleveland (A)	1	31	.271	85	273	25	74	20	1	.363	$2.3	1	29	.269
1951	Boston (A)	8	54	.276	86	286	42	79	22	1	.444	$2.3	5	47	.267
1952	Boston (A)	0	2	.000	4	2	1	0	0	0	.000	$0.5	0	2	.000
	Career	149	938	.304	1,726	6,322	1,021	1,925	551	50	.478	$107.6	68	789	.295
	Average season	10	63	.304	115	421	68	128	37	3	.478	$7.2	5	53	.295
	Summit season	15	84	.330	144	533	93	176	51	3	.522	$10.3	7	70	.319

KEN BOYER

		ADJUSTED REGULAR SEASON											ACTUAL RESULTS		
YEAR	TEAM	HR	RBI	BA	G	AB	R	H	2B	3B	SA	PAY	HR	RBI	BA
1955	St. Louis (N)	22	71	.275	155	559	90	154	36	1	.462	$9.6	18	62	.264
1956	St. Louis (N)	30	112	.318	156	619	104	197	39	1	.530	$14.6	26	98	.306
1957	St. Louis (N)	24	75	.277	149	571	96	158	24	2	.452	$12.0	19	62	.265
1958	St. Louis (N)	29	109	.320	158	600	122	192	28	7	.535	$15.2	23	90	.307
1959	St. Louis (N)	35	111	.324	157	593	102	192	24	4	.555	$15.4	28	94	.309
1960	St. Louis (N)	41	116	.322	158	578	113	186	34	8	.621	$12.5	32	97	.304
1961	St. Louis (N)	29	108	.344	160	616	124	212	36	8	.570	$16.5	24	95	.329
1962	St. Louis (N)	27	108	.305	159	607	101	185	35	4	.509	$15.9	24	98	.291
1963	St. Louis (N)	30	138	.311	159	617	107	192	37	2	.524	$13.7	24	111	.285
1964	St. Louis (N)	31	145	.317	162	628	122	199	40	8	.554	$19.4	24	119	.295
1965	St. Louis (N)	17	92	.284	144	535	87	152	24	2	.432	$7.5	13	75	.260
1966	New York (N)	17	76	.288	138	503	77	145	37	2	.471	$6.8	14	61	.266
1967	N.Y. (N)-Chi. (A)	11	44	.275	113	346	44	95	17	2	.431	$2.6	7	34	.249
1968	Chi. (A)-L.A. (N)	10	58	.294	93	245	28	72	10	2	.473	$1.9	6	41	.257
1969	Los Angeles (N)	0	5	.235	25	34	0	8	2	0	.294	$0.7	0	4	.206
	Career	353	1,368	.306	2,086	7,651	1,317	2,339	423	53	.513	$164.3	282	1,141	.287
	Average season	24	91	.306	139	510	88	156	28	4	.513	$11.0	19	76	.287
	Summit season	33	118	.325	159	603	117	196	32	7	.566	$15.8	26	99	.309

ROGER BRESNAHAN

		ADJUSTED REGULAR SEASON											ACTUAL RESULTS		
YEAR	TEAM	HR	RBI	BA	G	AB	R	H	2B	3B	SA	PAY	HR	RBI	BA
1897	Washington (N)	0	3	.368	7	19	1	7	0	0	.368	$0.0	0	3	.375
1900	Chicago (N)	0	0	.000	2	2	0	0	0	0	.000	$0.0	0	0	.000
1901	Baltimore (A)	9	38	.266	103	353	48	94	22	6	.439	$2.5	1	32	.268
1902	Balt. (A)-N.Y. (N)	26	71	.281	133	474	59	133	18	3	.496	$4.8	5	56	.278
1903	New York (N)	26	69	.359	129	463	110	166	35	2	.611	$7.2	4	55	.350
1904	New York (N)	25	43	.310	112	413	107	128	20	2	.550	$7.5	5	33	.284
1905	New York (N)	0	59	.329	109	347	75	114	54	2	.496	$7.1	0	46	.302
1906	New York (N)	0	59	.306	131	428	95	131	69	4	.486	$8.8	0	43	.281
1907	New York (N)	22	53	.277	115	343	80	95	8	1	.499	$7.0	4	38	.253
1908	New York (N)	11	77	.318	144	462	100	147	49	1	.500	$7.2	1	54	.283
1909	St. Louis (N)	0	32	.267	76	247	38	66	25	0	.368	$3.4	0	23	.244
1910	St. Louis (N)	0	35	.300	93	247	45	74	42	2	.486	$3.1	0	27	.278
1911	St. Louis (N)	13	45	.279	83	233	24	65	19	3	.554	$1.8	3	41	.278
1912	St. Louis (N)	5	17	.330	51	115	9	38	8	1	.548	$0.8	1	15	.333
1913	Chicago (N)	5	26	.237	72	169	25	40	6	1	.373	$1.0	1	21	.228
1914	Chicago (N)	0	30	.295	105	258	53	76	30	4	.442	$1.4	0	24	.278
1915	Chicago (N)	6	24	.217	80	230	24	50	11	0	.343	$0.9	1	19	.204
	Career	148	681	.296	1,545	4,803	893	1,424	416	32	.489	$64.5	26	530	.279
	Average season	9	40	.296	91	283	53	84	24	2	.489	$3.8	2	31	.279
	Summit season	12	61	.324	125	423	97	137	45	2	.525	$7.6	2	46	.300

GEORGE BRETT

		ADJUSTED REGULAR SEASON											ACTUAL RESULTS		
YEAR	TEAM	HR	RBI	BA	G	AB	R	H	2B	3B	SA	PAY	HR	RBI	BA
1973	Kansas City (A)	0	0	.125	13	40	2	5	3	0	.200	$0.0	0	0	.125
1974	Kansas City (A)	4	56	.295	133	457	58	135	36	5	.422	$3.5	2	47	.282
1975	Kansas City (A)	18	104	.322	159	634	98	204	48	12	.521	$8.9	11	89	.308
1976	Kansas City (A)	15	82	.352	159	645	115	227	53	13	.544	$12.2	7	67	.333
1977	Kansas City (A)	28	97	.317	139	564	116	179	37	9	.564	$12.4	22	88	.312
1978	Kansas City (A)	15	73	.306	128	510	94	156	56	6	.527	$11.6	9	62	.294
1979	Kansas City (A)	31	118	.333	154	645	131	215	51	16	.606	$19.5	23	107	.329
1980	Kansas City (A)	34	136	.396	117	449	100	178	36	7	.735	$12.1	24	118	.390
1981	Kansas City (A)	17	83	.332	140	546	81	181	55	10	.562	$11.9	6	43	.314
1982	Kansas City (A)	28	94	.310	144	552	116	171	36	8	.556	$12.3	21	82	.301
1983	Kansas City (A)	31	105	.320	122	460	102	147	40	2	.617	$9.4	25	93	.310
1984	Kansas City (A)	18	80	.294	104	377	49	111	24	2	.512	$5.5	13	69	.284
1985	Kansas City (A)	36	127	.351	155	550	123	193	42	4	.638	$10.0	30	112	.335
1986	Kansas City (A)	19	81	.304	124	441	78	134	32	4	.524	$5.0	16	73	.290
1987	Kansas City (A)	23	82	.297	115	427	74	127	20	2	.515	$4.7	22	78	.290
1988	Kansas City (A)	33	123	.324	158	593	107	192	46	3	.578	$10.1	24	103	.306
1989	Kansas City (A)	17	95	.300	124	457	79	137	30	3	.490	$4.5	12	80	.282
1990	Kansas City (A)	19	101	.343	143	548	95	188	53	7	.569	$6.7	14	87	.329
1991	Kansas City (A)	13	69	.269	131	505	88	136	46	2	.446	$6.4	10	61	.255
1992	Kansas City (A)	11	72	.301	152	592	65	178	44	6	.451	$4.7	7	61	.285
1993	Kansas City (A)	23	80	.270	145	560	74	151	33	3	.463	$4.6	19	75	.266
	Career	433	1,858	.317	2,759	10,552	1,845	3,345	821	124	.541	$176.0	317	1,595	.305
	Average season	21	88	.317	131	502	88	159	39	6	.541	$8.4	15	76	.305
	Summit season	30	117	.347	138	530	110	184	44	7	.626	$11.5	23	103	.337

LOU BROCK

		ADJUSTED REGULAR SEASON											ACTUAL RESULTS		
YEAR	TEAM	HR	RBI	BA	G	AB	R	H	2B	3B	SA	PAY	HR	RBI	BA
1961	Chicago (N)	0	0	.091	4	11	1	1	0	0	.091	$0.0	0	0	.091
1962	Chicago (N)	11	39	.274	123	434	81	119	32	5	.447	$3.4	9	35	.263
1963	Chicago (N)	13	46	.282	148	547	98	154	29	10	.442	$5.7	9	37	.258
1964	Chi.-St.L. (N)	19	70	.339	155	634	135	215	42	9	.524	$11.6	14	58	.315
1965	St. Louis (N)	21	84	.315	155	631	131	199	48	6	.510	$15.1	16	69	.288
1966	St. Louis (N)	20	56	.308	156	643	115	198	35	10	.487	$14.7	15	46	.285
1967	St. Louis (N)	33	99	.332	160	693	147	230	46	9	.567	$25.6	21	76	.299
1968	St. Louis (N)	11	72	.317	159	660	130	209	77	14	.526	$16.8	6	51	.279
1969	St. Louis (N)	17	56	.324	157	655	116	212	49	9	.504	$15.7	12	47	.298
1970	St. Louis (N)	17	64	.322	155	664	129	214	39	4	.470	$16.5	13	57	.304
1971	St. Louis (N)	11	76	.338	156	636	157	215	56	7	.500	$14.0	7	61	.313
1972	St. Louis (N)	6	57	.343	159	645	111	221	47	10	.474	$9.9	3	42	.311
1973	St. Louis (N)	10	73	.311	160	650	129	202	42	9	.449	$13.6	7	63	.297
1974	St. Louis (N)	6	57	.321	154	639	126	205	42	8	.440	$13.0	3	48	.306
1975	St. Louis (N)	6	54	.323	135	524	90	169	41	6	.458	$4.5	3	47	.309
1976	St. Louis (N)	9	82	.317	133	498	90	158	38	5	.468	$4.7	4	67	.301
1977	St. Louis (N)	3	51	.276	141	489	76	135	30	5	.376	$3.5	2	46	.272

(Lou Brock, continued)

YEAR	TEAM	ADJUSTED REGULAR SEASON											ACTUAL RESULTS		
		HR	RBI	BA	G	AB	R	H	2B	3B	SA	PAY	HR	RBI	BA
1978	St. Louis (N)	0	14	.232	92	298	37	69	16	0	.285	$1.7	0	12	.221
1979	St. Louis (N)	8	41	.308	119	402	61	124	19	3	.430	$2.1	5	38	.304
	Career	221	1,091	.314	2,621	10,353	1,960	3,249	728	129	.473	$192.1	149	900	.293
	Average season	12	57	.314	138	545	103	171	38	7	.473	$10.1	8	47	.293
	Summit season	18	75	.329	157	656	137	216	54	10	.524	$16.7	12	59	.300

DAN BROUTHERS

YEAR	TEAM	ADJUSTED REGULAR SEASON											ACTUAL RESULTS		
		HR	RBI	BA	G	AB	R	H	2B	3B	SA	PAY	HR	RBI	BA
1879	Troy (N)	29	36	.289	82	353	36	102	8	0	.558	$3.4	4	17	.274
1880	Troy (N)	0	2	.167	6	24	0	4	0	0	.167	$0.8	0	1	.167
1881	Buffalo (N)	56	91	.330	127	528	121	174	13	3	.684	$7.4	8	45	.319
1882	Buffalo (N)	54	120	.400	162	677	135	271	37	5	.709	$19.5	6	63	.368
1883	Buffalo (N)	39	148	.393	162	703	130	276	85	10	.708	$25.8	3	97	.374
1884	Buffalo (N)	58	105	.361	132	559	109	202	25	5	.735	$19.0	14	79	.327
1885	Buffalo (N)	44	83	.397	142	590	123	234	48	4	.715	$19.4	7	59	.359
1886	Detroit (N)	53	85	.405	156	630	165	255	48	5	.749	$27.1	11	72	.370
1887	Detroit (N)	46	104	.337	157	638	158	215	44	6	.641	$28.0	12	101	.338
1888	Detroit (N)	39	82	.345	156	631	147	218	49	4	.621	$28.2	9	66	.307
1889	Boston (N)	29	122	.382	153	589	109	225	39	4	.610	$16.8	7	118	.373
1890	Boston (P)	8	102	.343	153	572	123	196	85	5	.551	$14.0	1	97	.330
1891	Boston (AA)	27	113	.371	152	568	122	211	52	9	.637	$13.5	5	109	.350
1892	Brooklyn (N)	28	125	.370	156	603	122	223	57	8	.630	$13.9	5	124	.335
1893	Brooklyn (N)	12	59	.324	96	352	57	114	43	5	.577	$4.6	2	59	.337
1894	Baltimore (N)	33	113	.301	154	657	121	198	52	7	.553	$18.5	9	128	.347
1895	Balt.-Lou. (N)	7	19	.269	35	145	14	39	13	0	.503	$1.8	2	20	.300
1896	Philadelphia (N)	6	43	.320	71	272	44	87	26	1	.489	$1.9	1	41	.344
1904	New York (N)	0	0	.000	2	5	0	0	0	0	.000	$0.6	0	0	.000
	Career	568	1,552	.357	2,254	9,096	1,836	3,244	724	81	.641	$264.2	106	1,296	.342
	Average season	30	82	.357	119	479	97	171	38	4	.641	$13.9	6	68	.342
	Summit season	50	108	.392	151	632	132	248	49	6	.726	$22.2	8	74	.360

PETE BROWNING

YEAR	TEAM	ADJUSTED REGULAR SEASON											ACTUAL RESULTS		
		HR	RBI	BA	G	AB	R	H	2B	3B	SA	PAY	HR	RBI	BA
1882	Louisville (AA)	40	—	.411	140	584	134	240	24	1	.661	$9.4	5	—	.378
1883	Louisville (AA)	35	—	.355	139	592	145	210	20	3	.576	$9.0	4	—	.338
1884	Louisville (AA)	29	65	.371	152	660	141	245	66	5	.618	$14.3	4	47	.336
1885	Louisville (AA)	51	103	.401	162	696	139	279	46	3	.695	$25.4	9	73	.362
1886	Louisville (AA)	15	73	.372	131	546	92	203	56	2	.564	$11.9	2	68	.340
1887	Louisville (AA)	22	111	.400	156	637	129	255	63	7	.625	$25.2	4	118	.402
1888	Louisville (AA)	17	86	.353	115	445	69	157	43	4	.582	$9.6	3	72	.313
1889	Louisville (AA)	9	31	.261	96	375	38	98	33	2	.432	$5.7	2	32	.256
1890	Cleveland (P)	26	97	.387	146	610	117	236	64	3	.630	$12.6	5	93	.373

(Pete Browning, continued)

		ADJUSTED REGULAR SEASON												ACTUAL RESULTS		
YEAR	TEAM	HR	RBI	BA	G	AB	R	H	2B	3B	SA	PAY	HR	RBI	BA
1891	Pit.-Cin. (N)	17	63	.336	123	491	66	165	37	2	.523	$5.5	4	61	.317
1892	Lou.-Cin. (N)	14	58	.321	109	402	59	129	26	2	.500	$4.3	3	56	.292
1893	Louisville (N)	6	38	.340	73	282	39	96	24	1	.496	$2.3	1	37	.355
1894	St.L.-Bkn. (N)	0	2	.250	4	12	2	3	0	0	.250	$0.7	0	2	.333
	Career	281	727	.366	1,546	6,332	1,170	2,316	502	35	.589	$135.9	46	659	.341
	Average season	22	56	.366	119	487	90	178	39	3	.589	$10.5	4	51	.341
	Summit season	34	75	.394	151	637	132	251	53	4	.650	$17.4	5	66	.371

BILL BUCKNER

		ADJUSTED REGULAR SEASON												ACTUAL RESULTS		
YEAR	TEAM	HR	RBI	BA	G	AB	R	H	2B	3B	SA	PAY	HR	RBI	BA
1969	Los Angeles (N)	0	0	.000	1	1	0	0	0	0	.000	$0.0	0	0	.000
1970	Los Angeles (N)	0	5	.206	28	68	7	14	4	1	.294	$0.0	0	4	.191
1971	Los Angeles (N)	7	51	.299	108	358	46	107	22	1	.425	$2.7	5	41	.277
1972	Los Angeles (N)	9	51	.352	110	401	65	141	23	3	.491	$3.8	5	37	.319
1973	Los Angeles (N)	12	54	.287	140	575	79	165	28	0	.398	$5.9	8	46	.275
1974	Los Angeles (N)	12	69	.329	145	580	99	191	43	3	.476	$9.0	7	58	.314
1975	Los Angeles (N)	9	36	.253	92	288	35	73	14	2	.410	$4.3	6	31	.243
1976	Los Angeles (N)	15	73	.316	154	642	93	203	42	3	.461	$11.5	7	60	.301
1977	Chicago (N)	13	66	.289	122	426	44	123	30	0	.451	$5.7	11	60	.284
1978	Chicago (N)	9	88	.336	117	446	56	150	33	1	.475	$4.5	5	74	.323
1979	Chicago (N)	19	73	.288	149	591	79	170	40	5	.469	$6.9	14	66	.284
1980	Chicago (N)	15	78	.329	145	578	79	190	51	2	.502	$6.7	10	68	.324
1981	Chicago (N)	25	140	.328	162	643	84	211	64	4	.557	$9.4	10	75	.311
1982	Chicago (N)	21	121	.315	161	657	107	207	41	4	.486	$10.1	15	105	.306
1983	Chicago (N)	22	75	.288	153	626	90	180	44	5	.479	$9.2	16	66	.280
1984	Chi. (N)-Bos. (A)	15	80	.282	135	482	63	136	25	2	.436	$4.8	11	69	.272
1985	Boston (A)	20	124	.312	161	669	100	209	53	2	.487	$9.5	16	110	.299
1986	Boston (A)	22	114	.278	154	633	82	176	44	2	.458	$8.9	18	102	.267
1987	Bos.-Cal. (A)	5	77	.292	132	469	41	137	20	2	.375	$3.2	5	74	.286
1988	Cal.-K.C. (A)	4	51	.263	108	285	22	75	18	0	.368	$2.1	3	43	.249
1989	Kansas City (A)	1	19	.227	79	176	8	40	7	1	.295	$1.3	1	16	.216
1990	Boston (A)	1	3	.186	22	43	5	8	0	0	.256	$0.4	1	3	.186
	Career	256	1,448	.302	2,578	9,637	1,284	2,906	646	43	.457	$119.9	174	1,208	.289
	Average season	12	66	.302	117	438	58	132	29	2	.457	$5.5	8	55	.289
	Summit season	14	85	.334	136	530	77	177	43	3	.506	$6.7	7	62	.318

JESSE BURKETT

		ADJUSTED REGULAR SEASON												ACTUAL RESULTS		
YEAR	TEAM	HR	RBI	BA	G	AB	R	H	2B	3B	SA	PAY	HR	RBI	BA
1890	New York (N)	23	61	.319	121	480	68	153	39	5	.565	$6.4	4	60	.309
1891	Cleveland (N)	0	13	.286	46	192	30	55	23	4	.448	$3.3	0	13	.269
1892	Cleveland (N)	29	69	.302	154	646	125	195	25	5	.491	$12.0	6	66	.275
1893	Cleveland (N)	29	82	.335	157	642	146	215	41	6	.553	$18.9	6	82	.348

(Jesse Burkett, continued)

ADJUSTED REGULAR SEASON   **ACTUAL RESULTS**

YEAR	TEAM	HR	RBI	BA	G	AB	R	H	2B	3B	SA	PAY	HR	RBI	BA
1894	Cleveland (N)	27	83	.311	156	653	122	203	35	4	.501	$19.2	8	94	.358
1895	Cleveland (N)	26	80	.372	162	680	148	253	38	6	.560	$31.2	5	83	.409
1896	Cleveland (N)	32	72	.382	160	705	163	269	44	6	.597	$31.6	6	72	.410
1897	Cleveland (N)	15	63	.354	156	635	136	225	56	4	.526	$22.8	2	60	.383
1898	Cleveland (N)	0	43	.341	156	649	118	221	77	11	.493	$16.3	0	42	.341
1899	St. Louis (N)	31	69	.378	147	582	114	220	24	2	.586	$12.5	7	71	.396
1900	St. Louis (N)	34	74	.351	161	638	96	224	16	5	.552	$10.1	7	68	.363
1901	St. Louis (N)	43	86	.373	162	686	164	256	21	4	.603	$20.4	10	75	.376
1902	St. Louis (A)	31	67	.309	160	641	125	198	36	4	.523	$19.2	5	52	.306
1903	St. Louis (A)	22	51	.301	154	601	94	181	27	3	.466	$9.5	3	40	.293
1904	St. Louis (A)	19	36	.296	153	598	96	177	28	5	.455	$9.1	2	27	.271
1905	Boston (A)	27	61	.278	157	608	102	169	16	5	.454	$8.8	4	47	.257
	Career	388	1,010	.334	2,362	9,636	1,847	3,214	546	79	.527	$251.3	75	952	.338
	Average season	24	63	.334	148	602	115	201	34	5	.527	$15.7	5	60	.338
	Summit season	33	76	.371	158	658	137	244	29	5	.581	$21.2	7	74	.391

GEORGE BURNS

ADJUSTED REGULAR SEASON   **ACTUAL RESULTS**

YEAR	TEAM	HR	RBI	BA	G	AB	R	H	2B	3B	SA	PAY	HR	RBI	BA
1914	Detroit (A)	21	71	.309	141	492	69	152	24	2	.494	$7.3	5	57	.291
1915	Detroit (A)	19	64	.270	109	407	63	110	16	1	.455	$6.0	5	50	.253
1916	Detroit (A)	22	102	.310	141	500	83	155	25	2	.500	$8.7	4	73	.286
1917	Detroit (A)	11	56	.245	125	428	58	105	30	5	.416	$6.0	1	40	.226
1918	Philadelphia (A)	40	115	.375	162	629	100	236	24	3	.614	$12.4	6	70	.352
1919	Philadelphia (A)	33	82	.303	146	545	91	165	30	3	.550	$11.2	8	57	.296
1920	Phi.-Cle. (A)	4	24	.240	69	121	9	29	9	0	.413	$3.6	1	20	.250
1921	Cleveland (A)	0	53	.332	88	256	56	85	42	2	.512	$4.9	0	49	.361
1922	Boston (A)	26	79	.286	155	588	76	168	30	2	.476	$5.6	12	73	.306
1923	Boston (A)	20	90	.312	154	581	100	181	55	2	.516	$7.0	7	82	.328
1924	Cleveland (A)	14	75	.291	137	491	71	143	45	2	.477	$5.9	4	68	.310
1925	Cleveland (A)	15	81	.311	133	511	71	159	44	2	.493	$4.7	6	79	.336
1926	Cleveland (A)	15	127	.343	159	635	108	218	81	1	.545	$9.7	4	114	.358
1927	Cleveland (A)	10	86	.302	148	580	92	175	66	1	.471	$7.2	3	78	.319
1928	Cle.-N.Y. (A)	10	33	.242	90	223	33	54	10	0	.422	$2.3	5	30	.254
1929	N.Y.-Phi. (A)	2	11	.213	40	61	5	13	4	0	.377	$1.2	1	11	.224
	Career	262	1,149	.305	1,997	7,048	1,085	2,148	535	28	.500	$103.7	72	951	.307
	Average season	16	72	.305	125	441	68	134	33	2	.500	$6.5	5	59	.307
	Summit season	26	103	.330	152	578	96	191	43	2	.547	$9.8	6	79	.326

JEFF BURROUGHS

		ADJUSTED REGULAR SEASON											ACTUAL RESULTS		
YEAR	TEAM	HR	RBI	BA	G	AB	R	H	2B	3B	SA	PAY	HR	RBI	BA
1970	Washington (A)	0	1	.167	6	12	1	2	0	0	.167	$0.0	0	1	.167
1971	Washington (A)	7	32	.250	60	184	25	46	12	0	.429	$1.2	5	25	.232
1972	Texas (A)	2	4	.206	23	68	5	14	1	0	.309	$0.3	1	3	.185
1973	Texas (A)	38	99	.293	151	526	83	154	20	1	.551	$6.0	30	85	.279
1974	Texas (A)	36	142	.315	153	558	101	176	39	2	.586	$9.6	25	118	.301
1975	Texas (A)	38	110	.236	152	585	94	138	21	0	.467	$12.2	29	94	.226
1976	Texas (A)	29	105	.248	158	604	87	150	24	2	.439	$15.1	18	86	.237
1977	Atlanta (N)	47	126	.276	154	579	101	160	20	1	.558	$15.6	41	114	.271
1978	Atlanta (N)	32	91	.314	153	488	85	153	33	5	.598	$12.1	23	77	.301
1979	Atlanta (N)	14	52	.228	117	400	54	91	15	1	.375	$7.5	11	47	.224
1980	Atlanta (N)	17	59	.267	100	281	41	75	14	0	.498	$4.0	13	51	.263
1981	Seattle (A)	22	74	.266	131	470	58	125	21	1	.455	$5.2	10	41	.254
1982	Oakland (A)	20	55	.284	113	285	48	81	14	2	.558	$3.4	16	48	.277
1983	Oakland (A)	14	64	.277	121	401	49	111	17	1	.429	$2.5	10	56	.269
1984	Oakland (A)	3	9	.225	58	71	6	16	1	0	.366	$1.0	2	8	.211
1985	Toronto (A)	8	32	.269	87	193	22	52	10	3	.477	$1.2	6	28	.257
	Career	327	1,055	.271	1,737	5,705	860	1,544	262	19	.495	$96.9	240	882	.261
	Average season	20	66	.271	109	357	54	97	16	1	.495	$6.1	15	55	.261
	Summit season	35	106	.294	148	524	86	154	27	2	.553	$9.7	26	87	.283

DOLPH CAMILLI

		ADJUSTED REGULAR SEASON											ACTUAL RESULTS		
YEAR	TEAM	HR	RBI	BA	G	AB	R	H	2B	3B	SA	PAY	HR	RBI	BA
1933	Chicago (N)	4	8	.226	17	62	10	14	1	1	.468	$0.2	2	7	.224
1934	Chi.-Phi. (N)	28	96	.258	143	531	76	137	24	2	.469	$5.8	16	87	.267
1935	Philadelphia (N)	39	89	.251	162	625	95	157	18	2	.474	$11.3	25	83	.261
1936	Philadelphia (N)	46	106	.299	159	558	110	167	24	5	.608	$11.9	28	102	.315
1937	Philadelphia (N)	41	86	.330	137	497	109	164	19	3	.628	$9.7	27	80	.339
1938	Brooklyn (N)	39	110	.247	157	547	117	135	24	5	.523	$15.8	24	100	.251
1939	Brooklyn (N)	42	111	.283	162	583	112	165	27	5	.563	$13.5	26	104	.290
1940	Brooklyn (N)	37	107	.289	147	530	102	153	29	6	.575	$9.6	23	96	.287
1941	Brooklyn (N)	53	138	.293	154	547	106	160	24	2	.634	$13.0	34	120	.285
1942	Brooklyn (N)	47	138	.268	157	548	113	147	20	3	.573	$13.1	26	109	.252
1943	Brooklyn (N)	17	58	.261	101	375	75	98	18	4	.467	$4.4	6	43	.246
1945	Boston (A)	6	23	.221	65	204	29	45	7	1	.353	$2.1	2	19	.212
	Career	399	1,070	.275	1,561	5,607	1,054	1,542	235	39	.544	$110.4	239	950	.277
	Average season	33	89	.275	130	467	88	129	20	3	.544	$9.2	20	79	.277
	Summit season	44	110	.298	152	543	108	162	25	4	.602	$11.5	28	100	.303

KEN CAMINITI

		ADJUSTED REGULAR SEASON											ACTUAL RESULTS		
YEAR	TEAM	HR	RBI	BA	G	AB	R	H	2B	3B	SA	PAY	HR	RBI	BA
1987	Houston (N)	3	24	.251	63	203	10	51	8	1	.345	$1.4	3	23	.246
1988	Houston (N)	1	8	.193	30	83	6	16	3	0	.265	$0.5	1	7	.181
1989	Houston (N)	15	85	.270	161	585	84	158	37	3	.421	$6.2	10	72	.255
1990	Houston (N)	6	59	.253	153	541	60	137	27	2	.344	$5.7	4	51	.242
1991	Houston (N)	17	91	.265	152	574	74	152	34	3	.423	$7.7	13	80	.253
1992	Houston (N)	19	74	.310	135	506	81	157	35	2	.500	$6.8	13	62	.294
1993	Houston (N)	16	80	.265	143	543	80	144	33	0	.414	$7.0	13	75	.262
1994	Houston (N)	27	107	.282	156	571	90	161	40	2	.501	$9.5	18	75	.283
1995	San Diego (N)	31	108	.304	161	592	85	180	38	0	.525	$9.3	26	94	.302
1996	San Diego (N)	40	129	.324	146	546	108	177	38	2	.621	$9.4	40	130	.326
1997	San Diego (N)	27	94	.292	137	486	96	142	27	0	.514	$7.1	26	90	.290
1998	San Diego (N)	30	85	.254	131	452	90	115	28	0	.515	$6.8	29	82	.252
1999	Houston (N)	13	55	.282	78	273	44	77	11	1	.473	$2.5	13	56	.286
2000	Houston (N)	14	44	.303	59	208	41	63	13	0	.567	$1.9	15	45	.303
2001	Tex. (A)-Atl. (N)	15	42	.233	118	356	37	83	16	1	.410	$2.0	15	41	.228
	Career	274	1,085	.278	1,823	6,519	986	1,813	388	17	.469	$83.8	239	983	.272
	Average season	18	72	.278	122	435	66	121	26	1	.469	$5.6	16	66	.272
	Summit season	29	102	.302	147	540	92	163	36	1	.533	$8.4	25	90	.300

ROY CAMPANELLA

		ADJUSTED REGULAR SEASON											ACTUAL RESULTS		
YEAR	TEAM	HR	RBI	BA	G	AB	R	H	2B	3B	SA	PAY	HR	RBI	BA
1948	Brooklyn (N)	14	51	.264	87	292	36	77	13	2	.466	$3.9	9	45	.258
1949	Brooklyn (N)	31	91	.294	135	453	72	133	24	1	.556	$6.2	22	82	.287
1950	Brooklyn (N)	38	95	.284	132	458	75	130	21	2	.587	$5.4	31	89	.281
1951	Brooklyn (N)	43	121	.335	147	519	101	174	36	1	.657	$9.0	33	108	.325
1952	Brooklyn (N)	31	120	.286	134	490	90	140	20	1	.520	$9.2	22	97	.269
1953	Brooklyn (N)	50	161	.318	151	544	116	173	30	2	.656	$9.8	41	142	.312
1954	Brooklyn (N)	25	60	.213	117	418	51	89	17	2	.443	$4.0	19	51	.207
1955	Brooklyn (N)	38	123	.331	129	468	93	155	26	1	.635	$6.9	32	107	.318
1956	Brooklyn (N)	23	84	.229	130	407	45	93	8	1	.423	$3.6	20	73	.219
1957	Brooklyn (N)	16	75	.254	108	346	37	88	11	0	.425	$2.3	13	62	.242
	Career	309	981	.285	1,270	4,395	716	1,252	206	13	.549	$60.3	242	856	.276
	Average season	31	98	.285	127	440	72	125	21	1	.549	$6.0	24	86	.276
	Summit season	40	118	.314	139	488	91	153	27	1	.619	$7.5	32	106	.306

JOSÉ CANSECO

		ADJUSTED REGULAR SEASON											ACTUAL RESULTS		
YEAR	TEAM	HR	RBI	BA	G	AB	R	H	2B	3B	SA	PAY	HR	RBI	BA
1985	Oakland (A)	6	15	.313	29	96	18	30	3	0	.531	$0.9	5	13	.302
1986	Oakland (A)	38	131	.250	157	600	95	150	31	1	.495	$8.8	33	117	.240
1987	Oakland (A)	32	118	.263	159	630	85	166	38	3	.486	$11.8	31	113	.257
1988	Oakland (A)	53	147	.325	158	610	142	198	35	0	.643	$19.1	42	124	.307
1989	Oakland (A)	21	68	.286	65	227	47	65	9	1	.612	$6.5	17	57	.269
1990	Oakland (A)	45	116	.287	131	481	96	138	14	2	.605	$11.9	37	101	.274
1991	Oakland (A)	53	139	.280	154	572	131	160	33	1	.619	$18.8	44	122	.266
1992	Oak.-Tex. (A)	33	104	.257	119	439	88	113	14	0	.515	$9.6	26	87	.244
1993	Texas (A)	12	49	.260	60	231	32	60	15	1	.489	$4.2	10	46	.255
1994	Texas (A)	45	130	.282	158	611	127	172	26	3	.555	$16.4	31	90	.282
1995	Boston (A)	29	93	.307	115	446	74	137	29	1	.572	$6.7	24	81	.306
1996	Boston (A)	28	81	.289	96	360	67	104	23	1	.592	$3.6	28	82	.289
1997	Oakland (A)	24	77	.237	108	388	58	92	18	0	.469	$3.7	23	74	.235
1998	Toronto (A)	47	110	.238	150	579	101	138	26	0	.527	$7.3	46	107	.237
1999	Tampa Bay (A)	33	93	.277	113	430	73	119	18	1	.553	$3.9	34	95	.279
2000	T.B.-N.Y. (A)	14	48	.250	99	332	46	83	18	0	.431	$2.4	15	49	.252
2001	Chicago (A)	16	51	.262	76	256	48	67	8	0	.480	$2.1	16	49	.258
	Career	529	1,570	.273	1,947	7,288	1,328	1,992	358	15	.544	$137.7	462	1,407	.266
	Average season	31	92	.273	115	429	78	117	21	1	.544	$8.1	27	83	.266
	Summit season	42	115	.298	131	494	102	147	27	1	.611	$12.0	35	102	.288

ROD CAREW

		ADJUSTED REGULAR SEASON											ACTUAL RESULTS		
YEAR	TEAM	HR	RBI	BA	G	AB	R	H	2B	3B	SA	PAY	HR	RBI	BA
1967	Minnesota (A)	13	65	.324	135	506	84	164	33	6	.490	$8.7	8	51	.292
1968	Minnesota (A)	2	59	.310	127	461	65	143	47	2	.434	$7.1	1	42	.273
1969	Minnesota (A)	11	67	.360	123	458	95	165	43	3	.539	$7.8	8	56	.332
1970	Minnesota (A)	5	32	.387	51	191	31	74	17	2	.576	$3.9	4	28	.366
1971	Minnesota (A)	4	61	.332	149	585	112	194	30	12	.444	$9.3	2	48	.307
1972	Minnesota (A)	0	70	.351	149	561	84	197	43	8	.456	$9.0	0	51	.318
1973	Minnesota (A)	9	72	.367	149	580	114	213	45	11	.529	$11.6	6	62	.350
1974	Minnesota (A)	6	65	.382	152	595	102	227	51	5	.514	$11.7	3	55	.364
1975	Minnesota (A)	22	95	.375	146	546	106	205	32	3	.566	$9.7	14	80	.359
1976	Minnesota (A)	19	110	.349	156	605	119	211	43	10	.547	$15.7	9	90	.331
1977	Minnesota (A)	20	111	.395	156	620	143	245	49	12	.610	$13.8	14	100	.388
1978	Minnesota (A)	10	83	.348	152	564	101	196	37	10	.502	$9.8	5	70	.333
1979	California (A)	5	48	.323	110	409	86	132	21	2	.421	$5.0	3	44	.318
1980	California (A)	6	69	.338	146	548	87	185	49	6	.482	$7.1	3	59	.331
1981	California (A)	6	38	.321	137	536	103	172	39	1	.431	$4.5	2	21	.305
1982	California (A)	5	50	.329	138	523	101	172	36	5	.446	$4.4	3	44	.319
1983	California (A)	4	50	.350	129	472	75	165	33	2	.453	$3.4	2	44	.339
1984	California (A)	5	36	.304	93	329	49	100	12	1	.392	$2.0	3	31	.295
1985	California (A)	3	44	.293	127	443	78	130	22	2	.372	$2.6	2	39	.280
	Career	155	1,225	.345	2,525	9,532	1,735	3,290	682	103	.487	$147.1	92	1,015	.328
	Average season	8	64	.345	133	502	91	173	36	5	.487	$7.7	5	53	.328
	Summit season	16	91	.370	146	562	115	208	42	8	.559	$11.7	10	78	.353

MAX CAREY

		ADJUSTED REGULAR SEASON											ACTUAL RESULTS		
YEAR	TEAM	HR	RBI	BA	G	AB	R	H	2B	3B	SA	PAY	HR	RBI	BA
1910	Pittsburgh (N)	0	2	.500	2	6	2	3	0	0	.500	$0.0	0	2	.500
1911	Pittsburgh (N)	21	48	.260	135	447	86	116	16	3	.450	$3.9	5	43	.258
1912	Pittsburgh (N)	25	75	.302	160	626	129	189	24	2	.466	$11.5	5	66	.302
1913	Pittsburgh (N)	25	60	.289	161	648	122	187	29	3	.458	$12.2	5	49	.277
1914	Pittsburgh (N)	10	39	.257	160	608	95	156	58	12	.441	$11.8	1	31	.243
1915	Pittsburgh (N)	18	34	.272	145	584	97	159	35	2	.432	$9.6	3	27	.254
1916	Pittsburgh (N)	32	57	.286	159	618	124	177	22	3	.487	$14.2	7	42	.264
1917	Pittsburgh (N)	13	70	.321	160	607	112	195	52	8	.498	$12.4	1	51	.296
1918	Pittsburgh (N)	26	81	.291	162	602	119	175	20	2	.460	$15.3	3	48	.274
1919	Pittsburgh (N)	0	13	.316	77	285	60	90	34	2	.449	$4.1	0	9	.307
1920	Pittsburgh (N)	6	41	.280	136	507	87	142	36	3	.398	$6.6	1	35	.289
1921	Pittsburgh (N)	19	60	.285	147	547	92	156	36	1	.459	$7.1	7	56	.309
1922	Pittsburgh (N)	26	75	.307	162	657	150	202	32	5	.490	$13.0	10	70	.329
1923	Pittsburgh (N)	21	69	.291	161	642	131	187	47	10	.494	$13.1	6	63	.308
1924	Pittsburgh (N)	24	61	.279	158	635	125	177	31	4	.454	$13.0	8	55	.297
1925	Pittsburgh (N)	15	46	.317	141	575	113	182	53	7	.511	$9.3	5	44	.343
1926	Pit.-Bkn. (N)	0	38	.221	117	439	70	97	36	6	.330	$3.3	0	35	.231
1927	Brooklyn (N)	5	59	.252	151	564	76	142	54	7	.399	$4.6	1	54	.266
1928	Brooklyn (N)	5	21	.235	113	310	45	73	13	0	.326	$1.8	2	19	.247
1929	Brooklyn (N)	0	1	.292	20	24	2	7	0	0	.292	$0.6	0	1	.304
	Career	291	950	.283	2,627	9,931	1,837	2,812	628	80	.450	$167.4	70	800	.285
	Average season	15	48	.283	131	497	92	141	31	4	.450	$8.4	4	40	.285
	Summit season	21	63	.305	157	620	126	189	41	7	.495	$12.4	6	54	.308

GARY CARTER

		ADJUSTED REGULAR SEASON											ACTUAL RESULTS		
YEAR	TEAM	HR	RBI	BA	G	AB	R	H	2B	3B	SA	PAY	HR	RBI	BA
1974	Montreal (N)	2	7	.444	9	27	6	12	0	1	.741	$0.0	1	6	.407
1975	Montreal (N)	24	79	.282	144	503	68	142	23	1	.475	$5.0	17	68	.270
1976	Montreal (N)	10	47	.232	91	311	38	72	9	1	.363	$3.8	6	38	.219
1977	Montreal (N)	36	93	.289	154	522	95	151	31	1	.559	$7.5	31	84	.284
1978	Montreal (N)	27	85	.266	157	533	90	142	28	1	.475	$9.4	20	72	.255
1979	Montreal (N)	28	84	.287	143	512	83	147	29	4	.523	$9.1	22	75	.283
1980	Montreal (N)	38	117	.268	154	549	88	147	26	4	.537	$12.0	29	101	.264
1981	Montreal (N)	35	125	.264	150	561	88	148	32	2	.515	$12.2	16	68	.251
1982	Montreal (N)	36	112	.302	154	557	105	168	34	1	.560	$14.7	29	97	.293
1983	Montreal (N)	22	89	.277	144	537	71	149	42	2	.486	$9.3	17	79	.270
1984	Montreal (N)	35	124	.303	160	600	87	182	36	1	.542	$12.3	27	106	.294
1985	New York (N)	38	114	.294	149	555	94	163	18	1	.535	$11.7	32	100	.281
1986	New York (N)	28	117	.265	132	490	90	130	15	2	.476	$7.0	24	105	.255
1987	New York (N)	21	87	.241	139	523	57	126	20	2	.407	$4.9	20	83	.235
1988	New York (N)	16	55	.255	132	462	47	118	18	2	.407	$3.6	11	46	.242
1989	New York (N)	3	18	.196	50	153	17	30	9	0	.314	$1.6	2	15	.183
1990	San Francisco (N)	11	31	.266	92	244	28	65	11	0	.447	$1.3	9	27	.254
1991	Los Angeles (N)	8	30	.258	101	248	25	64	16	0	.419	$1.1	6	26	.246
1992	Montreal (N)	7	34	.228	95	285	29	65	21	1	.382	$1.1	5	29	.218
	Career	425	1,448	.272	2,350	8,172	1,206	2,221	418	27	.486	$127.6	324	1,225	.262
	Average season	22	76	.272	124	430	63	117	22	1	.486	$6.7	17	64	.262
	Summit season	35	105	.295	152	549	93	162	30	2	.548	$11.1	28	92	.287

NORM CASH

		ADJUSTED REGULAR SEASON											ACTUAL RESULTS		
YEAR	TEAM	HR	RBI	BA	G	AB	R	H	2B	3B	SA	PAY	HR	RBI	BA
1958	Chicago (A)	0	0	.222	14	9	3	2	0	0	.222	$0.0	0	0	.250
1959	Chicago (A)	5	19	.250	60	108	19	27	0	1	.407	$0.5	4	16	.240
1960	Detroit (A)	23	75	.302	127	371	77	112	20	2	.553	$4.4	18	63	.286
1961	Detroit (A)	46	143	.376	158	532	128	200	27	6	.709	$12.1	41	132	.361
1962	Detroit (A)	44	99	.253	149	510	105	129	21	1	.557	$11.9	39	89	.243
1963	Detroit (A)	32	98	.294	147	493	83	145	25	1	.544	$9.6	26	79	.270
1964	Detroit (A)	28	100	.275	143	476	76	131	20	4	.511	$9.3	23	83	.257
1965	Detroit (A)	36	101	.291	142	467	97	136	29	1	.589	$9.3	30	82	.266
1966	Detroit (A)	39	114	.302	160	603	120	182	24	2	.542	$12.9	32	93	.279
1967	Detroit (A)	31	92	.268	151	485	82	130	20	4	.518	$7.0	22	72	.242
1968	Detroit (A)	36	88	.299	125	405	70	121	18	1	.615	$4.7	25	63	.263
1969	Detroit (A)	29	89	.302	142	483	97	146	20	3	.536	$6.9	22	74	.280
1970	Detroit (A)	17	60	.276	130	370	66	102	23	2	.486	$3.3	15	53	.259
1971	Detroit (A)	42	114	.305	135	452	90	138	12	3	.624	$4.5	32	91	.283
1972	Detroit (A)	32	83	.285	142	456	69	130	20	0	.539	$4.2	22	61	.259
1973	Detroit (A)	24	47	.273	121	363	60	99	23	0	.534	$2.5	19	40	.262
1974	Detroit (A)	10	14	.242	53	149	20	36	3	2	.490	$1.5	7	12	.228
	Career	474	1,336	.292	2,099	6,732	1,262	1,966	305	33	.558	$104.6	377	1,103	.271
	Average season	28	79	.292	123	396	74	116	18	2	.558	$6.2	22	65	.271
	Summit season	37	104	.317	137	445	92	141	21	3	.627	$7.0	29	86	.295

PHIL CAVARRETTA

		ADJUSTED REGULAR SEASON											ACTUAL RESULTS		
YEAR	TEAM	HR	RBI	BA	G	AB	R	H	2B	3B	SA	PAY	HR	RBI	BA
1934	Chicago (N)	1	6	.381	7	21	5	8	0	1	.619	$0.0	1	6	.381
1935	Chicago (N)	19	90	.266	154	621	93	165	35	7	.436	$6.5	8	82	.275
1936	Chicago (N)	16	58	.258	130	480	57	124	16	1	.396	$5.4	9	56	.273
1937	Chicago (N)	11	61	.279	112	348	47	97	22	4	.460	$4.8	5	56	.286
1938	Chicago (N)	3	30	.233	97	283	31	66	18	3	.350	$4.1	1	28	.239
1939	Chicago (N)	0	0	.259	23	58	4	15	5	2	.414	$1.4	0	0	.273
1940	Chicago (N)	5	25	.282	68	202	38	57	15	2	.450	$2.4	2	22	.280
1941	Chicago (N)	13	46	.293	112	362	53	106	21	2	.470	$3.6	6	40	.286
1942	Chicago (N)	9	68	.286	142	503	74	144	44	4	.443	$5.7	3	54	.270
1943	Chicago (N)	24	97	.309	150	556	123	172	35	6	.523	$11.7	8	73	.291
1944	Chicago (N)	18	101	.331	157	634	131	210	56	11	.539	$18.6	5	82	.321
1945	Chicago (N)	19	121	.369	138	521	117	192	50	8	.605	$12.2	6	97	.355
1946	Chicago (N)	19	100	.310	145	532	114	165	39	6	.513	$12.5	8	78	.294
1947	Chicago (N)	5	74	.324	133	481	66	156	37	4	.449	$9.0	2	63	.314
1948	Chicago (N)	6	45	.284	116	349	46	99	25	4	.430	$2.9	3	40	.278
1949	Chicago (N)	13	55	.302	110	377	51	114	28	3	.496	$2.7	8	49	.294
1950	Chicago (N)	12	33	.276	86	268	52	74	12	1	.463	$1.9	10	31	.273
1951	Chicago (N)	9	32	.321	93	215	27	69	9	1	.498	$1.4	6	28	.311
1952	Chicago (N)	2	10	.258	43	66	9	17	1	1	.394	$0.6	1	8	.238
1953	Chicago (N)	0	3	.273	28	22	3	6	4	0	.455	$0.2	0	3	.286
1954	Chicago (A)	4	28	.327	74	165	25	54	8	0	.448	$0.6	3	24	.316
1955	Chicago (A)	0	0	.000	6	4	1	0	0	0	.000	$0.0	0	0	.000
	Career	208	1,083	.299	2,124	7,068	1,167	2,110	480	71	.475	$108.2	95	920	.293
	Average season	9	49	.299	97	321	53	96	22	3	.475	$4.9	4	42	.293
	Summit season	19	95	.326	140	524	107	171	42	7	.542	$11.5	7	76	.312

CESAR CEDENO

		ADJUSTED REGULAR SEASON											ACTUAL RESULTS		
YEAR	TEAM	HR	RBI	BA	G	AB	R	H	2B	3B	SA	PAY	HR	RBI	BA
1970	Houston (N)	9	47	.330	90	355	52	117	28	3	.501	$4.5	7	42	.310
1971	Houston (N)	14	101	.285	161	611	106	174	57	5	.463	$11.3	10	81	.264
1972	Houston (N)	35	114	.354	147	591	144	209	55	8	.651	$15.3	22	82	.320
1973	Houston (N)	32	82	.335	139	525	100	176	43	2	.608	$11.7	25	70	.320
1974	Houston (N)	37	122	.282	160	610	113	172	35	4	.534	$19.0	26	102	.269
1975	Houston (N)	20	73	.300	131	500	108	150	38	2	.504	$12.3	13	63	.288
1976	Houston (N)	30	102	.313	150	575	109	180	30	4	.536	$14.8	18	83	.297
1977	Houston (N)	18	78	.285	141	530	102	151	42	6	.489	$12.1	14	71	.279
1978	Houston (N)	10	27	.292	50	192	37	56	9	2	.516	$4.9	7	23	.281
1979	Houston (N)	8	59	.266	132	470	63	125	33	3	.400	$7.4	6	54	.262
1980	Houston (N)	16	83	.313	136	495	81	155	39	6	.513	$5.9	10	73	.309
1981	Houston (N)	12	61	.285	121	452	76	129	35	0	.442	$4.5	5	34	.271
1982	Cincinnati (N)	11	65	.297	138	492	60	146	42	1	.453	$5.3	8	57	.289
1983	Cincinnati (N)	12	44	.238	98	332	46	79	18	0	.401	$2.4	9	39	.232
1984	Cincinnati (N)	13	54	.287	110	380	68	109	28	2	.474	$2.5	10	47	.276
1985	Cin.-St.L. (N)	11	56	.304	111	296	43	90	19	1	.486	$2.1	9	49	.291
1986	Los Angeles (N)	0	7	.244	37	78	6	19	2	1	.295	$0.8	0	6	.231
	Career	**288**	**1,175**	**.299**	**2,052**	**7,484**	**1,314**	**2,237**	**553**	**50**	**.502**	**$136.8**	**199**	**976**	**.285**
	Average season	**17**	**69**	**.299**	**121**	**440**	**77**	**132**	**33**	**3**	**.502**	**$8.0**	**12**	**57**	**.285**
	Summit season	**24**	**86**	**.329**	**132**	**508**	**97**	**167**	**39**	**5**	**.567**	**$10.4**	**16**	**70**	**.311**

ORLANDO CEPEDA

		ADJUSTED REGULAR SEASON											ACTUAL RESULTS		
YEAR	TEAM	HR	RBI	BA	G	AB	R	H	2B	3B	SA	PAY	HR	RBI	BA
1958	San Francisco (N)	30	116	.325	156	636	106	207	49	3	.553	$18.5	25	96	.312
1959	San Francisco (N)	33	124	.333	159	637	109	212	46	3	.570	$18.8	27	105	.317
1960	San Francisco (N)	30	114	.314	157	592	96	186	46	2	.551	$14.8	24	96	.297
1961	San Francisco (N)	53	162	.324	159	612	119	198	36	3	.652	$19.0	46	142	.311
1962	San Francisco (N)	39	124	.320	159	613	114	196	32	1	.566	$18.7	35	114	.306
1963	San Francisco (N)	42	121	.345	156	579	124	200	44	3	.649	$15.6	34	97	.316
1964	San Francisco (N)	37	118	.327	142	529	91	173	34	2	.609	$14.6	31	97	.304
1965	San Francisco (N)	1	6	.206	33	34	1	7	1	0	.324	$3.9	1	5	.176
1966	S.F.-St.L. (N)	24	89	.327	142	501	86	164	34	0	.539	$7.0	20	73	.301
1967	St. Louis (N)	35	145	.362	152	567	119	205	47	0	.630	$11.8	25	111	.325
1968	St. Louis (N)	26	103	.282	157	600	100	169	35	2	.477	$9.8	16	73	.248
1969	Atlanta (N)	28	105	.277	154	573	88	159	37	2	.496	$9.3	22	88	.257
1970	Atlanta (N)	39	126	.323	148	567	98	183	40	0	.600	$9.5	34	111	.305
1971	Atlanta (N)	18	55	.296	71	250	39	74	13	1	.572	$2.7	14	44	.276
1972	Atl. (N)-Oak. (A)	6	12	.322	32	90	8	29	4	0	.567	$1.6	4	9	.287
1973	Boston (A)	26	100	.302	142	550	59	166	32	0	.502	$3.4	20	86	.289
1974	Kansas City (A)	2	21	.224	33	107	4	24	6	0	.336	$0.8	1	18	.215
	Career	**469**	**1,641**	**.318**	**2,152**	**8,037**	**1,361**	**2,552**	**536**	**22**	**.565**	**$179.8**	**379**	**1,365**	**.297**
	Average season	**28**	**97**	**.318**	**127**	**473**	**80**	**150**	**32**	**1**	**.565**	**$10.6**	**22**	**80**	**.297**
	Summit season	**41**	**134**	**.336**	**151**	**571**	**110**	**192**	**40**	**2**	**.629**	**$14.1**	**34**	**112**	**.312**

FRANK CHANCE

		ADJUSTED REGULAR SEASON											ACTUAL RESULTS		
YEAR	TEAM	HR	RBI	BA	G	AB	R	H	2B	3B	SA	PAY	HR	RBI	BA
1898	Chicago (N)	6	15	.277	56	155	33	43	6	1	.445	$1.6	1	14	.279
1899	Chicago (N)	6	22	.275	68	204	37	56	9	1	.417	$2.1	1	22	.286
1900	Chicago (N)	0	14	.285	62	165	27	47	26	2	.467	$1.7	0	13	.295
1901	Chicago (N)	0	42	.276	80	279	44	77	35	4	.430	$3.0	0	36	.278
1902	Chicago (N)	9	39	.291	86	275	50	80	16	2	.462	$3.3	1	31	.288
1903	Chicago (N)	19	104	.336	146	515	107	173	41	5	.546	$9.2	2	81	.327
1904	Chicago (N)	30	65	.339	129	469	119	159	15	2	.571	$8.8	6	49	.310
1905	Chicago (N)	18	90	.342	123	409	118	140	29	6	.575	$11.4	2	70	.316
1906	Chicago (N)	25	97	.347	142	495	141	172	34	4	.584	$12.4	3	71	.319
1907	Chicago (N)	11	68	.321	116	399	81	128	35	1	.496	$7.1	1	49	.293
1908	Chicago (N)	17	78	.307	132	463	92	142	39	2	.510	$9.0	2	55	.272
1909	Chicago (N)	0	63	.299	97	338	73	101	52	4	.476	$3.8	0	46	.272
1910	Chicago (N)	0	47	.321	93	312	70	100	46	7	.513	$2.7	0	36	.298
1911	Chicago (N)	5	19	.242	32	91	25	22	7	1	.505	$1.5	1	17	.239
1912	Chicago (N)	0	0	.200	2	5	2	1	0	0	.200	$0.6	0	0	.200
1913	New York (A)	0	8	.231	13	26	4	6	0	0	.231	$0.3	0	6	.208
1914	New York (A)	0	0	.000	1	0	0	0	0	0	.000	$0.0	0	0	.000
	Career	146	771	.315	1,378	4,600	1,023	1,447	390	42	.513	$78.5	20	596	.296
	Average season	9	45	.315	81	271	60	85	23	2	.513	$4.6	1	35	.296
	Summit season	21	85	.337	131	457	113	154	31	4	.560	$9.8	3	64	.314

FRED CLARKE

		ADJUSTED REGULAR SEASON											ACTUAL RESULTS		
YEAR	TEAM	HR	RBI	BA	G	AB	R	H	2B	3B	SA	PAY	HR	RBI	BA
1894	Louisville (N)	18	42	.232	93	384	47	89	11	1	.406	$4.3	7	48	.268
1895	Louisville (N)	19	78	.316	161	671	91	212	32	2	.455	$9.5	4	82	.347
1896	Louisville (N)	37	80	.301	158	624	97	188	18	5	.524	$12.1	9	79	.325
1897	Louisville (N)	32	69	.360	155	627	125	226	40	4	.590	$14.7	6	67	.390
1898	Louisville (N)	22	49	.306	157	631	121	193	41	5	.491	$14.8	3	47	.307
1899	Louisville (N)	26	69	.327	155	630	120	206	31	3	.510	$15.4	5	70	.342
1900	Pittsburgh (N)	18	35	.266	123	463	93	123	26	5	.460	$8.8	3	32	.276
1901	Pittsburgh (N)	32	70	.322	149	609	138	196	32	5	.548	$12.6	6	60	.324
1902	Pittsburgh (N)	19	67	.319	129	524	131	167	51	8	.555	$9.7	2	53	.316
1903	Pittsburgh (N)	32	88	.362	119	489	111	177	38	5	.656	$9.5	5	70	.351
1904	Pittsburgh (N)	0	33	.334	75	290	68	97	32	15	.548	$3.0	0	25	.306
1905	Pittsburgh (N)	21	65	.325	147	547	122	178	36	8	.536	$7.2	2	51	.299
1906	Pittsburgh (N)	15	53	.338	124	438	95	148	35	9	.562	$4.0	1	39	.309
1907	Pittsburgh (N)	23	81	.319	153	518	134	165	33	6	.539	$7.2	2	59	.289
1908	Pittsburgh (N)	23	77	.298	158	577	121	172	36	8	.508	$9.4	2	53	.265
1909	Pittsburgh (N)	27	95	.318	160	579	135	184	23	4	.511	$12.8	3	68	.287
1910	Pittsburgh (N)	15	81	.284	129	450	73	128	38	4	.487	$6.3	2	63	.263
1911	Pittsburgh (N)	23	54	.327	115	410	81	134	29	4	.585	$4.2	5	49	.324
1913	Pittsburgh (N)	0	0	.077	9	13	0	1	1	0	.154	$1.1	0	0	.077
1914	Pittsburgh (N)	0	0	.000	2	2	0	0	0	0	.000	$0.5	0	0	.000
1915	Pittsburgh (N)	0	0	.500	1	2	0	1	0	0	.500	$0.1	0	0	.500
	Career	402	1,186	.315	2,472	9,478	1,903	2,985	583	101	.525	$167.2	67	1,015	.312
	Average season	19	56	.315	118	451	91	142	28	5	.525	$8.0	3	48	.312
	Summit season	24	66	.341	128	498	109	170	39	6	.588	$8.4	4	56	.340

ROBERTO CLEMENTE

YEAR	TEAM	ADJUSTED REGULAR SEASON HR	RBI	BA	G	AB	R	H	2B	3B	SA	PAY	ACTUAL RESULTS HR	RBI	BA
1955	Pittsburgh (N)	7	54	.266	130	497	55	132	36	9	.416	$5.6	5	47	.255
1956	Pittsburgh (N)	8	68	.324	152	561	75	182	43	5	.462	$7.0	7	60	.311
1957	Pittsburgh (N)	6	36	.263	116	471	50	124	26	6	.382	$5.4	4	30	.253
1958	Pittsburgh (N)	8	60	.301	147	545	83	164	36	9	.444	$7.3	6	50	.289
1959	Pittsburgh (N)	5	59	.311	110	453	71	141	25	7	.430	$6.0	4	50	.296
1960	Pittsburgh (N)	21	112	.331	151	598	106	198	30	5	.503	$11.9	16	94	.314
1961	Pittsburgh (N)	28	102	.367	154	603	114	221	41	8	.600	$14.3	23	89	.351
1962	Pittsburgh (N)	12	82	.327	145	542	106	177	39	7	.491	$11.9	10	74	.312
1963	Pittsburgh (N)	23	94	.350	152	600	96	210	33	6	.540	$12.0	17	76	.320
1964	Pittsburgh (N)	15	106	.365	155	622	116	227	55	6	.545	$15.8	12	87	.339
1965	Pittsburgh (N)	15	79	.361	151	585	111	211	32	12	.533	$12.0	10	65	.329
1966	Pittsburgh (N)	37	146	.343	154	638	129	219	43	8	.610	$13.8	29	119	.317
1967	Pittsburgh (N)	34	142	.398	146	581	132	231	35	8	.661	$13.2	23	110	.357
1968	Pittsburgh (N)	30	80	.331	131	498	104	165	25	11	.606	$9.2	18	57	.291
1969	Pittsburgh (N)	26	109	.375	138	507	104	190	29	11	.629	$9.4	19	91	.345
1970	Pittsburgh (N)	18	68	.374	108	412	73	154	30	8	.617	$4.4	14	60	.352
1971	Pittsburgh (N)	20	108	.368	132	522	103	192	41	7	.588	$6.5	13	86	.341
1972	Pittsburgh (N)	16	83	.345	107	397	94	137	29	7	.574	$4.4	10	60	.312
	Career	329	1,588	.340	2,479	9,632	1,722	3,275	628	140	.537	$170.1	240	1,305	.317
	Average season	18	88	.340	138	535	96	182	35	8	.537	$9.5	13	73	.317
	Summit season	25	106	.377	136	525	105	198	35	8	.617	$9.6	18	87	.349

TY COBB

YEAR	TEAM	ADJUSTED REGULAR SEASON HR	RBI	BA	G	AB	R	H	2B	3B	SA	PAY	ACTUAL RESULTS HR	RBI	BA
1905	Detroit (A)	5	19	.261	43	157	24	41	6	0	.395	$1.5	1	15	.240
1906	Detroit (A)	12	47	.344	105	384	63	132	32	2	.531	$3.8	1	34	.316
1907	Detroit (A)	41	169	.385	159	641	137	247	36	5	.649	$14.8	5	119	.350
1908	Detroit (A)	37	158	.364	158	612	129	223	57	9	.668	$15.5	4	108	.324
1909	Detroit (A)	47	146	.417	160	588	158	245	27	2	.709	$25.1	9	107	.377
1910	Detroit (A)	40	117	.415	146	528	137	219	36	3	.722	$19.5	8	91	.383
1911	Detroit (A)	40	143	.425	154	623	166	265	61	8	.742	$31.2	8	127	.420
1912	Detroit (A)	39	93	.411	147	581	134	239	35	7	.697	$19.6	7	83	.409
1913	Detroit (A)	25	84	.406	129	453	87	184	28	7	.664	$12.2	4	67	.390
1914	Detroit (A)	14	72	.390	101	356	87	139	40	5	.649	$9.4	2	57	.368
1915	Detroit (A)	23	127	.398	162	585	186	233	54	6	.629	$23.6	3	99	.369
1916	Detroit (A)	30	95	.405	152	568	158	230	39	3	.643	$16.7	5	68	.371
1917	Detroit (A)	44	143	.415	160	619	150	257	60	9	.754	$23.6	6	102	.383
1918	Detroit (A)	32	106	.407	140	531	138	216	33	7	.676	$13.6	3	64	.382
1919	Detroit (A)	10	101	.394	143	573	133	226	89	10	.637	$13.5	1	70	.384
1920	Detroit (A)	11	74	.324	117	447	102	145	45	4	.517	$7.4	2	63	.334
1921	Detroit (A)	32	110	.361	135	535	135	193	38	5	.630	$10.1	12	101	.389
1922	Detroit (A)	14	106	.375	143	549	106	206	66	8	.601	$9.1	4	99	.401
1923	Detroit (A)	18	96	.322	152	583	112	188	51	3	.513	$9.5	6	88	.340
1924	Detroit (A)	15	84	.317	161	649	125	206	55	5	.487	$19.0	4	78	.338
1925	Detroit (A)	26	104	.350	126	432	99	151	30	5	.623	$6.6	12	102	.378

(Ty Cobb, continued)

YEAR	TEAM	ADJUSTED REGULAR SEASON HR	RBI	BA	G	AB	R	H	2B	3B	SA	PAY	ACTUAL RESULTS HR	RBI	BA
1926	Detroit (A)	12	68	.326	82	242	53	79	18	2	.566	$3.2	4	62	.339
1927	Philadelphia (A)	16	101	.340	140	512	113	174	39	3	.521	$6.8	5	93	.357
1928	Philadelphia (A)	4	44	.309	101	375	60	116	40	3	.464	$2.6	1	40	.323
	Career	587	2,407	.376	3,216	12,123	2,792	4,554	1,015	121	.625	$317.9	117	1,937	.366
	Average season	24	100	.376	134	505	116	190	42	5	.625	$13.2	5	81	.366
	Summit season	42	128	.417	153	588	149	245	44	6	.726	$23.8	8	102	.395

MICKEY COCHRANE

YEAR	TEAM	ADJUSTED REGULAR SEASON HR	RBI	BA	G	AB	R	H	2B	3B	SA	PAY	ACTUAL RESULTS HR	RBI	BA
1925	Philadelphia (A)	15	57	.306	142	445	72	136	23	2	.467	$6.3	6	55	.331
1926	Philadelphia (A)	21	54	.262	130	401	57	105	7	3	.451	$5.7	8	47	.273
1927	Philadelphia (A)	26	87	.320	132	453	87	145	16	2	.536	$7.7	12	80	.338
1928	Philadelphia (A)	24	63	.280	139	497	102	139	27	5	.499	$9.2	10	57	.293
1929	Philadelphia (A)	16	99	.308	145	552	117	170	42	4	.486	$12.4	7	95	.331
1930	Philadelphia (A)	18	82	.326	137	513	106	167	40	2	.517	$11.9	10	85	.357
1931	Philadelphia (A)	34	99	.338	129	485	97	164	24	2	.606	$11.8	17	89	.349
1932	Philadelphia (A)	37	123	.285	146	544	129	155	27	1	.542	$16.1	23	112	.293
1933	Philadelphia (A)	31	72	.320	139	459	125	147	27	1	.586	$11.9	15	60	.322
1934	Detroit (A)	5	83	.308	136	461	81	142	45	1	.443	$9.3	2	76	.320
1935	Detroit (A)	12	52	.307	123	440	104	135	39	2	.486	$6.9	5	47	.319
1936	Detroit (A)	4	18	.258	46	132	25	34	8	0	.409	$1.8	2	17	.270
1937	Detroit (A)	4	13	.294	28	102	29	30	10	1	.529	$1.3	2	12	.306
	Career	247	902	.304	1,572	5,484	1,131	1,669	335	26	.510	$112.3	119	832	.320
	Average season	19	69	.304	121	422	87	128	26	2	.510	$8.6	9	64	.320
	Summit season	29	93	.318	137	491	109	156	27	2	.558	$11.9	15	85	.331

ROCKY COLAVITO

YEAR	TEAM	ADJUSTED REGULAR SEASON HR	RBI	BA	G	AB	R	H	2B	3B	SA	PAY	ACTUAL RESULTS HR	RBI	BA
1955	Cleveland (A)	0	0	.444	5	9	3	4	3	0	.778	$0.0	0	0	.444
1956	Cleveland (A)	25	75	.287	106	338	63	97	15	3	.571	$3.6	21	65	.276
1957	Cleveland (A)	30	103	.262	142	489	81	128	33	0	.513	$7.1	25	84	.252
1958	Cleveland (A)	49	137	.316	151	516	97	163	33	2	.672	$9.4	41	113	.303
1959	Cleveland (A)	50	131	.270	162	619	106	167	30	0	.561	$18.5	42	111	.257
1960	Detroit (A)	43	105	.263	153	586	80	154	22	1	.524	$14.4	35	87	.249
1961	Detroit (A)	49	151	.302	162	579	139	175	36	1	.622	$25.3	45	140	.290
1962	Detroit (A)	42	125	.284	162	605	100	172	38	1	.559	$16.6	37	112	.273
1963	Detroit (A)	27	113	.296	160	597	113	177	39	2	.504	$16.5	22	91	.271
1964	Kansas City (A)	40	123	.295	159	584	108	172	39	2	.574	$16.5	34	102	.274
1965	Cleveland (A)	32	132	.314	162	592	113	186	32	2	.537	$13.7	26	108	.287
1966	Cleveland (A)	36	88	.257	151	533	83	137	17	0	.492	$9.3	30	72	.238
1967	Cle.-Chi. (A)	12	65	.257	123	381	39	98	17	1	.402	$3.6	8	50	.231
1968	L.A. (N)-N.Y. (A)	12	33	.239	78	201	29	48	6	2	.468	$2.1	8	24	.211
	Career	447	1,381	.283	1,876	6,629	1,154	1,878	360	17	.545	$156.6	374	1,159	.266
	Average season	32	99	.283	134	474	82	134	26	1	.545	$11.2	27	83	.266
	Summit season	39	124	.305	148	522	104	159	31	2	.596	$13.7	33	106	.286

EDDIE COLLINS

		ADJUSTED REGULAR SEASON											ACTUAL RESULTS		
YEAR	TEAM	HR	RBI	BA	G	AB	R	H	2B	3B	SA	PAY	HR	RBI	BA
1906	Philadelphia (A)	0	0	.222	7	18	3	4	0	0	.222	$0.0	0	0	.200
1907	Philadelphia (A)	0	3	.400	15	25	0	10	0	3	.640	$0.0	0	2	.348
1908	Philadelphia (A)	11	57	.306	105	340	56	104	35	3	.524	$2.9	1	40	.273
1909	Philadelphia (A)	29	78	.383	162	605	146	232	46	5	.620	$9.6	3	56	.347
1910	Philadelphia (A)	26	104	.350	160	608	104	213	28	7	.548	$12.1	3	81	.324
1911	Philadelphia (A)	20	83	.370	141	527	105	195	38	6	.579	$12.0	3	73	.365
1912	Philadelphia (A)	0	72	.350	162	575	155	201	78	9	.517	$19.7	0	64	.348
1913	Philadelphia (A)	21	91	.359	157	566	157	203	40	6	.562	$19.5	3	73	.345
1914	Philadelphia (A)	16	106	.365	156	540	153	197	48	9	.576	$19.7	2	85	.344
1915	Chicago (A)	24	100	.358	162	545	153	195	30	4	.560	$26.1	4	77	.332
1916	Chicago (A)	0	72	.335	162	570	121	191	63	21	.519	$16.6	0	52	.308
1917	Chicago (A)	0	92	.312	162	586	126	183	71	13	.478	$17.0	0	67	.289
1918	Chicago (A)	16	52	.292	127	432	88	126	11	1	.433	$9.2	2	30	.276
1919	Chicago (A)	23	115	.327	162	599	126	196	27	3	.497	$13.5	4	80	.319
1920	Chicago (A)	17	90	.363	161	633	139	230	64	7	.567	$14.0	3	76	.372
1921	Chicago (A)	9	63	.312	146	552	85	172	36	6	.447	$7.4	2	58	.337
1922	Chicago (A)	6	74	.302	161	625	98	189	44	9	.430	$13.1	1	69	.324
1923	Chicago (A)	16	72	.342	151	526	96	180	29	2	.496	$6.8	5	67	.360
1924	Chicago (A)	20	94	.328	160	585	119	192	32	3	.496	$9.5	6	86	.349
1925	Chicago (A)	9	82	.320	124	447	82	143	34	1	.461	$4.7	3	80	.346
1926	Chicago (A)	4	69	.331	111	393	73	130	50	3	.504	$4.2	1	62	.344
1927	Philadelphia (A)	4	16	.318	99	236	54	75	18	0	.445	$2.1	1	15	.336
1928	Philadelphia (A)	0	8	.286	38	35	3	10	5	0	.429	$0.8	0	7	.303
1929	Philadelphia (A)	0	0	.000	10	8	0	0	0	0	.000	$0.3	0	0	.000
1930	Philadelphia (A)	0	0	.500	3	2	1	1	0	0	.500	$0.0	0	0	.500
	Career	271	1,593	.338	3,004	10,578	2,243	3,572	827	121	.516	$240.8	47	1,300	.333
	Average season	11	64	.338	120	423	90	143	33	5	.516	$9.6	2	52	.333
	Summit season	21	90	.368	155	574	140	211	47	7	.584	$15.0	3	73	.355

JIMMY COLLINS

		ADJUSTED REGULAR SEASON											ACTUAL RESULTS		
YEAR	TEAM	HR	RBI	BA	G	AB	R	H	2B	3B	SA	PAY	HR	RBI	BA
1895	Bos.-Lou. (N)	22	54	.246	130	499	71	123	20	1	.423	$7.0	7	57	.273
1896	Boston (N)	8	47	.273	103	373	49	102	27	5	.437	$5.1	1	46	.296
1897	Boston (N)	31	137	.319	161	636	106	203	36	4	.535	$14.7	6	132	.346
1898	Boston (N)	47	117	.327	162	636	113	208	25	1	.591	$15.2	15	111	.328
1899	Boston (N)	25	91	.265	160	635	98	168	37	3	.450	$12.5	5	92	.277
1900	Boston (N)	26	103	.293	162	669	113	196	31	2	.462	$16.6	6	95	.304
1901	Boston (A)	33	111	.329	162	662	128	218	59	6	.586	$17.0	6	94	.332
1902	Boston (A)	31	80	.325	127	504	93	164	23	3	.567	$7.0	6	61	.322
1903	Boston (A)	34	91	.304	149	619	111	188	41	6	.554	$9.9	5	72	.296
1904	Boston (A)	25	88	.295	161	651	112	192	52	5	.505	$13.1	3	67	.271
1905	Boston (A)	24	85	.299	139	539	86	161	29	1	.490	$7.1	4	65	.276
1906	Boston (A)	8	22	.300	39	150	23	45	11	2	.560	$1.8	1	16	.275
1907	Bos.-Phi. (A)	0	62	.305	146	544	71	166	85	0	.461	$3.5	0	45	.278
1908	Philadelphia (A)	0	43	.243	119	448	49	109	52	2	.368	$2.2	0	30	.217
	Career	314	1,131	.296	1,920	7,565	1,223	2,243	528	41	.502	$132.7	65	983	.294
	Average season	22	81	.296	137	540	87	160	38	3	.502	$9.5	5	70	.294
	Summit season	35	107	.321	152	611	110	196	37	4	.566	$12.8	8	94	.325

EARLE COMBS

		ADJUSTED REGULAR SEASON											ACTUAL RESULTS		
YEAR	TEAM	HR	RBI	BA	G	AB	R	H	2B	3B	SA	PAY	HR	RBI	BA
1924	New York (A)	0	2	.389	25	36	11	14	7	0	.583	$0.0	0	2	.400
1925	New York (A)	10	62	.316	156	617	119	195	54	9	.481	$7.0	3	61	.342
1926	New York (A)	25	61	.287	152	635	125	182	33	5	.472	$11.4	8	55	.299
1927	New York (A)	23	69	.339	159	678	149	230	52	13	.556	$18.4	6	64	.356
1928	New York (A)	22	62	.297	157	660	131	196	44	11	.497	$16.7	7	56	.310
1929	New York (A)	9	66	.320	149	615	121	197	52	9	.478	$15.7	3	65	.345
1930	New York (A)	17	79	.313	144	559	124	175	39	12	.517	$12.6	7	82	.344
1931	New York (A)	16	63	.308	144	587	132	181	41	8	.487	$9.9	5	58	.318
1932	New York (A)	20	70	.313	150	616	156	193	35	5	.484	$13.9	9	65	.321
1933	New York (A)	17	76	.300	130	444	103	133	31	10	.529	$6.9	5	64	.300
1934	New York (A)	5	27	.308	66	263	51	81	18	4	.464	$2.7	2	25	.319
1935	New York (A)	8	40	.271	97	325	53	88	9	2	.385	$2.4	3	35	.282
	Career	172	677	.309	1,529	6,035	1,275	1,865	415	88	.492	$117.6	58	632	.325
	Average season	14	56	.309	127	503	106	155	35	7	.492	$9.8	5	53	.325
	Summit season	15	70	.319	148	583	123	186	46	11	.513	$12.1	5	67	.340

DAVE CONCEPCION

		ADJUSTED REGULAR SEASON											ACTUAL RESULTS		
YEAR	TEAM	HR	RBI	BA	G	AB	R	H	2B	3B	SA	PAY	HR	RBI	BA
1970	Cincinnati (N)	1	21	.275	101	265	43	73	11	3	.351	$2.6	1	19	.260
1971	Cincinnati (N)	1	25	.220	130	327	30	72	9	6	.294	$2.8	1	20	.205
1972	Cincinnati (N)	4	40	.229	125	397	55	91	23	2	.327	$3.9	2	29	.209
1973	Cincinnati (N)	11	54	.299	89	328	45	98	24	3	.491	$3.8	8	46	.287
1974	Cincinnati (N)	21	97	.295	159	590	83	174	32	1	.459	$7.8	14	82	.281
1975	Cincinnati (N)	9	57	.286	140	507	72	145	31	1	.404	$6.5	5	49	.274
1976	Cincinnati (N)	18	85	.297	152	576	91	171	39	5	.476	$11.3	9	69	.281
1977	Cincinnati (N)	10	71	.276	156	572	65	158	31	2	.390	$7.0	8	64	.271
1978	Cincinnati (N)	10	80	.315	154	569	89	179	44	3	.455	$9.1	6	67	.301
1979	Cincinnati (N)	21	93	.285	150	594	101	169	29	2	.446	$11.8	16	84	.281
1980	Cincinnati (N)	8	88	.265	155	618	82	164	42	7	.395	$7.3	5	77	.260
1981	Cincinnati (N)	14	123	.323	159	632	105	204	55	0	.476	$10.1	5	67	.306
1982	Cincinnati (N)	8	61	.295	147	572	55	169	34	3	.407	$5.0	5	53	.287
1983	Cincinnati (N)	1	54	.241	143	528	62	127	32	0	.307	$4.0	1	47	.233
1984	Cincinnati (N)	6	67	.252	154	531	53	134	33	1	.352	$3.4	4	58	.245
1985	Cincinnati (N)	9	54	.263	155	560	67	147	23	2	.359	$3.2	7	48	.252
1986	Cincinnati (N)	4	33	.273	90	311	47	85	15	2	.373	$1.8	3	30	.260
1987	Cincinnati (N)	1	35	.326	104	279	33	91	16	0	.394	$1.5	1	33	.319
1988	Cincinnati (N)	0	10	.211	85	199	13	42	13	0	.276	$0.9	0	8	.198
	Career	157	1,148	.278	2,548	8,955	1,191	2,493	536	43	.400	$103.8	101	950	.267
	Average season	8	60	.278	134	471	63	131	28	2	.400	$5.5	5	50	.267
	Summit season	15	88	.306	143	539	83	165	39	2	.469	$8.4	8	66	.291

ROGER CONNOR

		ADJUSTED REGULAR SEASON											ACTUAL RESULTS		
YEAR	TEAM	HR	RBI	BA	G	AB	R	H	2B	3B	SA	PAY	HR	RBI	BA
1880	Troy (N)	43	101	.367	162	664	114	244	26	4	.613	$25.4	3	47	.332
1881	Troy (N)	31	60	.302	162	699	108	211	31	4	.491	$19.9	2	31	.292
1882	Troy (N)	49	79	.358	154	664	122	238	48	11	.685	$19.4	4	42	.330
1883	New York (N)	20	76	.374	162	676	122	253	85	14	.630	$25.7	1	50	.357
1884	New York (N)	25	108	.350	162	666	129	233	51	2	.545	$26.6	4	82	.317
1885	New York (N)	15	92	.410	159	658	144	270	85	14	.650	$31.4	1	65	.371
1886	New York (N)	44	85	.389	154	633	126	246	46	8	.695	$16.8	7	71	.355
1887	New York (N)	54	105	.283	159	590	114	167	26	5	.619	$16.9	17	104	.285
1888	New York (N)	49	85	.328	157	564	118	185	18	5	.638	$16.6	14	71	.291
1889	New York (N)	45	137	.325	162	613	123	199	40	6	.630	$19.7	13	130	.317
1890	New York (P)	50	107	.362	151	594	138	215	25	4	.670	$19.2	14	103	.349
1891	New York (N)	30	100	.308	154	572	119	176	45	4	.558	$13.4	7	94	.290
1892	Philadelphia (N)	40	75	.324	162	589	127	191	42	3	.610	$19.2	12	73	.294
1893	New York (N)	33	100	.294	161	609	105	179	26	2	.506	$13.1	11	105	.305
1894	N.Y.-St.L. (N)	29	78	.275	143	546	78	150	46	7	.544	$6.8	8	93	.316
1895	St. Louis (N)	27	72	.299	124	479	73	143	32	2	.543	$4.6	8	77	.329
1896	St. Louis (N)	35	75	.263	156	598	74	157	20	2	.478	$6.8	11	72	.284
1897	St. Louis (N)	4	13	.216	27	102	14	22	3	0	.363	$1.3	1	12	.229
	Career	623	1,548	.331	2,671	10,516	1,948	3,479	695	97	.593	$302.8	138	1,322	.317
	Average season	35	86	.331	148	584	108	193	39	5	.593	$16.8	8	73	.317
	Summit season	36	88	.378	156	645	130	244	58	10	.667	$22.5	5	66	.353

WALKER COOPER

		ADJUSTED REGULAR SEASON											ACTUAL RESULTS		
YEAR	TEAM	HR	RBI	BA	G	AB	R	H	2B	3B	SA	PAY	HR	RBI	BA
1940	St. Louis (N)	0	2	.316	6	19	3	6	2	0	.421	$0.0	0	2	.316
1941	St. Louis (N)	2	23	.249	71	209	22	52	13	1	.349	$1.1	1	20	.245
1942	St. Louis (N)	18	82	.298	130	456	73	136	42	5	.531	$4.8	7	65	.281
1943	St. Louis (N)	24	108	.339	129	475	69	161	35	3	.577	$6.0	9	81	.318
1944	St. Louis (N)	28	89	.328	116	411	69	135	25	2	.603	$4.6	13	72	.317
1945	St. Louis (N)	0	1	.389	4	18	4	7	0	0	.389	$2.0	0	1	.389
1946	New York (N)	15	60	.280	92	296	37	83	10	1	.473	$3.3	8	46	.268
1947	New York (N)	52	144	.315	146	537	93	169	25	4	.667	$3.9	35	122	.305
1948	New York (N)	22	61	.271	95	303	45	82	11	0	.525	$2.2	16	54	.266
1949	N.Y.-Cin. (N)	29	92	.263	129	472	53	124	14	3	.489	$3.5	20	83	.258
1950	Cin.-Bos. (N)	18	68	.315	122	400	58	126	26	2	.525	$2.9	14	64	.313
1951	Boston (N)	24	67	.324	114	358	48	116	15	1	.573	$2.2	18	59	.313
1952	Boston (N)	15	68	.249	107	366	41	91	14	1	.415	$2.2	10	55	.235
1953	Milwaukee (N)	4	18	.225	55	142	13	32	7	0	.359	$1.1	3	16	.219
1954	Pit.-Chi. (N)	10	39	.311	75	183	25	57	15	1	.568	$1.2	7	33	.301
1955	Chicago (N)	8	17	.291	57	117	13	34	10	1	.598	$0.7	7	15	.279
1956	St. Louis (N)	2	16	.282	42	71	6	20	7	1	.493	$0.3	2	14	.265
1957	St. Louis (N)	4	12	.284	50	81	8	23	6	1	.531	$0.3	3	10	.269
	Career	275	967	.296	1,540	4,914	680	1,454	277	27	.531	$42.3	173	812	.285
	Average season	15	54	.296	86	273	38	81	15	2	.531	$2.4	10	45	.285
	Summit season	29	95	.323	125	436	67	141	25	2	.589	$3.9	18	80	.313

DOC CRAMER

		ADJUSTED REGULAR SEASON											ACTUAL RESULTS		
YEAR	TEAM	HR	RBI	BA	G	AB	R	H	2B	3B	SA	PAY	HR	RBI	BA
1929	Philadelphia (A)	0	0	.000	2	6	0	0	0	0	.000	$0.0	0	0	.000
1930	Philadelphia (A)	0	6	.207	32	87	12	18	5	0	.264	$0.0	0	6	.232
1931	Philadelphia (A)	6	22	.253	69	237	41	60	9	1	.376	$1.5	2	20	.260
1932	Philadelphia (A)	8	50	.326	97	405	80	132	36	4	.494	$3.9	3	46	.336
1933	Philadelphia (A)	23	89	.294	162	704	130	207	33	4	.450	$14.4	8	75	.295
1934	Philadelphia (A)	16	50	.300	162	687	108	206	39	6	.444	$11.7	6	46	.311
1935	Philadelphia (A)	9	79	.321	162	700	108	225	56	3	.449	$16.0	3	70	.332
1936	Boston (A)	0	42	.277	161	672	102	186	57	7	.382	$12.3	0	41	.292
1937	Boston (A)	0	55	.297	140	589	97	175	45	11	.411	$6.7	0	51	.305
1938	Boston (A)	0	78	.297	160	711	129	210	69	6	.409	$13.7	0	71	.301
1939	Boston (A)	0	61	.304	146	628	121	191	57	5	.411	$9.3	0	56	.311
1940	Boston (A)	3	57	.305	158	696	106	212	48	11	.418	$10.0	1	51	.303
1941	Washington (A)	6	76	.280	160	686	107	192	45	5	.386	$12.5	2	66	.273
1942	Detroit (A)	0	54	.281	157	655	89	184	59	5	.386	$7.0	0	43	.263
1943	Detroit (A)	5	56	.320	146	632	104	202	44	5	.429	$6.7	1	43	.300
1944	Detroit (A)	8	52	.302	149	602	86	182	40	10	.442	$4.7	2	42	.292
1945	Detroit (A)	18	72	.285	147	564	77	161	31	5	.454	$4.5	6	58	.275
1946	Detroit (A)	3	33	.310	71	213	33	66	15	2	.441	$1.7	1	26	.294
1947	Detroit (A)	4	35	.273	75	161	24	44	3	1	.379	$1.4	2	30	.268
1948	Detroit (A)	0	1	.000	4	4	1	0	0	0	.000	$0.5	0	1	.000
	Career	109	968	.296	2,360	9,639	1,555	2,853	691	91	.420	$138.5	37	842	.296
	Average season	5	48	.296	118	482	78	143	35	5	.420	$6.9	2	42	.296
	Summit season	11	65	.312	143	609	102	190	42	5	.452	$9.1	3	55	.309

SAM CRAWFORD

		ADJUSTED REGULAR SEASON											ACTUAL RESULTS		
YEAR	TEAM	HR	RBI	BA	G	AB	R	H	2B	3B	SA	PAY	HR	RBI	BA
1899	Cincinnati (N)	7	19	.290	32	131	24	38	6	3	.542	$1.4	1	20	.307
1900	Cincinnati (N)	28	63	.251	114	439	73	110	17	4	.499	$4.7	7	59	.260
1901	Cincinnati (N)	50	119	.328	149	586	104	192	15	3	.619	$11.4	16	104	.330
1902	Cincinnati (N)	29	100	.337	161	638	118	215	36	14	.574	$15.3	3	78	.333
1903	Detroit (A)	36	116	.345	162	650	115	224	37	12	.605	$18.7	4	89	.335
1904	Detroit (A)	20	93	.278	150	562	63	156	41	7	.482	$12.2	2	73	.254
1905	Detroit (A)	34	97	.322	162	605	94	195	42	3	.570	$15.1	6	75	.297
1906	Detroit (A)	24	101	.322	156	606	91	195	50	9	.553	$14.6	2	72	.295
1907	Detroit (A)	36	114	.355	152	614	144	218	50	7	.635	$18.5	4	81	.323
1908	Detroit (A)	45	117	.350	160	622	149	218	36	5	.641	$19.7	7	80	.311
1909	Detroit (A)	40	132	.348	160	604	113	210	37	5	.624	$16.4	6	97	.314
1910	Detroit (A)	33	155	.312	161	615	107	192	36	7	.554	$16.7	5	120	.289
1911	Detroit (A)	33	129	.383	154	605	122	232	43	4	.631	$16.9	7	115	.378
1912	Detroit (A)	27	122	.327	157	612	91	200	44	9	.560	$13.0	4	109	.325
1913	Detroit (A)	42	103	.330	162	645	97	213	37	7	.605	$13.5	9	83	.317
1914	Detroit (A)	41	131	.333	162	601	93	200	27	10	.616	$13.0	8	104	.314
1915	Detroit (A)	27	144	.322	162	636	104	205	49	9	.555	$13.6	4	112	.299
1916	Detroit (A)	0	59	.311	105	338	57	105	42	16	.530	$3.4	0	42	.286
1917	Detroit (A)	6	17	.183	64	109	8	20	2	0	.367	$1.6	2	12	.173
	Career	558	1,931	.327	2,685	10,218	1,767	3,338	647	134	.580	$239.7	97	1,525	.309
	Average season	29	102	.327	141	538	93	176	34	7	.580	$12.6	5	80	.309
	Summit season	38	122	.355	158	619	129	220	41	7	.628	$18.0	6	92	.332

JOE CRONIN

		ADJUSTED REGULAR SEASON											ACTUAL RESULTS		
YEAR	TEAM	HR	RBI	BA	G	AB	R	H	2B	3B	SA	PAY	HR	RBI	BA
1926	Pittsburgh (N)	0	12	.259	39	85	10	22	5	2	.365	$0.5	0	11	.265
1927	Pittsburgh (N)	0	3	.227	12	22	2	5	2	0	.318	$0.0	0	3	.227
1928	Washington (A)	0	27	.231	66	238	25	55	20	4	.349	$1.5	0	25	.242
1929	Washington (A)	17	62	.261	154	525	74	137	32	3	.430	$5.4	8	61	.281
1930	Washington (A)	23	121	.314	162	617	122	194	40	4	.504	$12.4	13	126	.346
1931	Washington (A)	30	138	.296	162	635	113	188	43	6	.524	$18.9	12	126	.306
1932	Washington (A)	16	127	.310	150	584	104	181	56	11	.526	$15.6	6	116	.318
1933	Washington (A)	16	140	.309	161	638	106	197	65	7	.508	$26.1	5	118	.309
1934	Washington (A)	16	110	.273	133	528	74	144	36	5	.451	$12.3	7	101	.284
1935	Boston (A)	21	103	.285	151	583	76	166	44	7	.492	$12.0	9	95	.295
1936	Boston (A)	5	44	.268	85	310	37	83	30	2	.426	$4.2	2	43	.281
1937	Boston (A)	30	119	.300	156	601	111	180	38	2	.519	$12.4	18	110	.307
1938	Boston (A)	30	104	.319	154	571	108	182	54	3	.581	$9.5	17	94	.325
1939	Boston (A)	31	118	.300	152	553	107	166	31	2	.532	$9.5	19	107	.308
1940	Boston (A)	37	126	.286	157	577	118	165	34	3	.548	$13.3	24	111	.285
1941	Boston (A)	30	110	.319	149	540	114	172	40	4	.574	$9.9	16	95	.311
1942	Boston (A)	7	31	.321	48	84	9	27	3	0	.607	$2.0	4	24	.304
1943	Boston (A)	9	39	.333	62	81	11	27	3	0	.704	$1.6	5	29	.312
1944	Boston (A)	10	35	.246	79	199	30	49	6	0	.427	$1.4	5	28	.241
1945	Boston (A)	0	1	.375	3	8	1	3	0	0	.375	$0.2	0	1	.375
	Career	328	1,570	.294	2,235	7,979	1,352	2,343	582	65	.506	$168.7	170	1,424	.301
	Average season	16	79	.294	112	399	68	117	29	3	.506	$8.4	9	71	.301
	Summit season	29	117	.306	152	565	110	173	43	5	.554	$11.6	16	105	.309

LAVE CROSS

		ADJUSTED REGULAR SEASON											ACTUAL RESULTS		
YEAR	TEAM	HR	RBI	BA	G	AB	R	H	2B	3B	SA	PAY	HR	RBI	BA
1887	Louisville (AA)	0	24	.266	63	237	30	63	24	2	.384	$2.2	0	26	.266
1888	Louisville (AA)	0	18	.255	55	212	24	54	15	0	.325	$1.9	0	15	.227
1889	Philadelphia (AA)	0	23	.226	65	235	22	53	22	2	.336	$2.0	0	23	.221
1890	Philadelphia (P)	16	48	.308	77	299	43	92	11	3	.525	$3.1	3	47	.298
1891	Philadelphia (AA)	24	52	.319	125	457	66	146	34	5	.573	$4.8	5	52	.301
1892	Philadelphia (N)	20	71	.303	146	564	86	171	27	4	.472	$7.1	4	69	.275
1893	Philadelphia (N)	18	76	.287	117	506	79	145	26	2	.453	$7.4	4	78	.299
1894	Philadelphia (N)	23	111	.337	149	662	109	223	43	3	.515	$15.1	7	125	.386
1895	Philadelphia (N)	12	96	.246	152	651	90	160	51	4	.392	$12.4	2	101	.271
1896	Philadelphia (N)	6	76	.237	132	506	66	120	49	3	.381	$7.0	1	73	.256
1897	Philadelphia (N)	14	53	.239	106	414	38	99	21	2	.401	$4.5	3	51	.259
1898	St. Louis (N)	21	82	.315	159	634	74	200	47	3	.498	$5.1	3	79	.317
1899	Cle.-St.L. (N)	22	82	.284	147	581	74	165	22	1	.439	$4.6	5	84	.298
1900	St.L.-Bkn. (N)	21	79	.283	152	597	86	169	22	2	.432	$5.0	4	73	.293
1901	Philadelphia (A)	16	87	.324	118	500	97	162	55	6	.554	$5.0	2	73	.328
1902	Philadelphia (A)	0	143	.345	162	661	119	228	119	7	.546	$12.8	0	108	.342
1903	Philadelphia (A)	18	117	.300	162	661	78	198	35	2	.440	$9.2	2	90	.292
1904	Philadelphia (A)	12	95	.317	162	634	98	201	72	6	.506	$9.1	1	71	.290
1905	Philadelphia (A)	0	101	.289	157	627	90	181	87	4	.440	$9.2	0	77	.266

(Lave Cross, continued)

		ADJUSTED REGULAR SEASON											ACTUAL RESULTS		
YEAR	TEAM	HR	RBI	BA	G	AB	R	H	2B	3B	SA	PAY	HR	RBI	BA
1906	Washington (A)	13	64	.288	139	528	76	152	32	4	.438	$4.6	1	46	.263
1907	Washington (A)	0	14	.219	43	169	18	37	21	0	.343	$1.6	0	10	.199
	Career	256	1,512	.292	2,588	10,335	1,463	3,019	835	65	.460	$133.7	47	1,371	.292
	Average season	12	72	.292	123	492	70	144	40	3	.460	$6.4	2	65	.292
	Summit season	15	98	.329	143	583	98	192	65	5	.535	$9.4	3	86	.330

KIKI CUYLER

		ADJUSTED REGULAR SEASON											ACTUAL RESULTS		
YEAR	TEAM	HR	RBI	BA	G	AB	R	H	2B	3B	SA	PAY	HR	RBI	BA
1921	Pittsburgh (N)	0	0	.000	1	3	0	0	0	0	.000	$0.0	0	0	.000
1922	Pittsburgh (N)	0	0	.000	1	0	0	0	0	0	.000	$0.0	0	0	.000
1923	Pittsburgh (N)	0	2	.227	12	44	5	10	6	0	.364	$0.0	0	2	.250
1924	Pittsburgh (N)	27	94	.332	124	494	104	164	29	7	.583	$5.4	9	85	.354
1925	Pittsburgh (N)	42	106	.329	162	653	150	215	44	10	.620	$14.8	18	102	.357
1926	Pittsburgh (N)	26	100	.308	162	634	124	195	34	6	.503	$15.4	8	92	.321
1927	Pittsburgh (N)	10	33	.292	88	295	65	86	16	3	.468	$5.5	3	31	.309
1928	Chicago (N)	33	87	.272	140	525	101	143	20	3	.510	$9.7	17	79	.285
1929	Chicago (N)	27	102	.334	144	527	111	176	26	3	.548	$9.8	15	102	.360
1930	Chicago (N)	25	127	.324	162	667	147	216	52	7	.535	$19.7	13	134	.355
1931	Chicago (N)	24	96	.320	160	637	120	204	40	6	.515	$14.0	9	88	.330
1932	Chicago (N)	21	84	.283	116	470	63	133	19	4	.474	$5.1	10	77	.291
1933	Chicago (N)	12	41	.318	74	277	44	88	14	2	.513	$2.9	5	35	.317
1934	Chicago (N)	15	76	.327	151	594	88	194	53	6	.512	$6.4	6	69	.338
1935	Chi.-Cin. (N)	13	44	.249	113	401	64	100	14	2	.392	$2.3	6	40	.258
1936	Cincinnati (N)	17	76	.309	151	595	99	184	36	7	.479	$4.7	7	74	.326
1937	Cincinnati (N)	0	34	.262	122	423	51	111	26	4	.343	$2.3	0	32	.271
1938	Brooklyn (N)	6	25	.268	88	272	50	73	17	6	.441	$1.6	2	23	.273
	Career	298	1,127	.305	1,971	7,511	1,386	2,292	446	76	.504	$119.6	128	1,065	.321
	Average season	17	63	.305	110	417	77	127	25	4	.504	$6.6	7	59	.321
	Summit season	27	101	.329	149	587	120	193	41	7	.560	$11.2	12	98	.353

JAKE DAUBERT

		ADJUSTED REGULAR SEASON											ACTUAL RESULTS		
YEAR	TEAM	HR	RBI	BA	G	AB	R	H	2B	3B	SA	PAY	HR	RBI	BA
1910	Brooklyn (N)	36	64	.285	150	575	86	164	14	4	.511	$9.5	8	50	.264
1911	Brooklyn (N)	24	50	.310	157	604	100	187	20	3	.472	$11.5	5	45	.307
1912	Brooklyn (N)	22	74	.308	154	594	91	183	30	7	.493	$11.7	3	66	.308
1913	Brooklyn (N)	16	65	.364	148	541	95	197	32	4	.527	$7.2	2	52	.350
1914	Brooklyn (N)	26	58	.348	133	500	115	174	18	2	.548	$7.0	6	45	.329
1915	Brooklyn (N)	16	61	.325	158	573	81	186	39	4	.490	$9.1	2	47	.301
1916	Brooklyn (N)	20	46	.344	132	497	104	171	23	3	.523	$4.7	3	33	.316
1917	Brooklyn (N)	15	41	.281	130	487	81	137	6	2	.394	$3.8	2	30	.261
1918	Brooklyn (N)	26	80	.327	139	510	85	167	25	9	.565	$4.7	2	47	.308
1919	Cincinnati (N)	18	63	.282	162	621	114	175	22	9	.433	$7.2	2	44	.276

(Jake Daubert, continued)

	ADJUSTED REGULAR SEASON												ACTUAL RESULTS		
YEAR	TEAM	HR	RBI	BA	G	AB	R	H	2B	3B	SA	PAY	HR	RBI	BA
1920	Cincinnati (N)	20	57	.295	149	580	115	171	40	6	.488	$6.5	4	48	.304
1921	Cincinnati (N)	10	70	.284	144	546	75	155	34	6	.423	$4.5	2	64	.306
1922	Cincinnati (N)	33	70	.313	162	633	121	198	17	9	.524	$9.3	12	66	.336
1923	Cincinnati (N)	9	59	.277	131	524	68	145	46	6	.439	$4.3	2	54	.292
1924	Cincinnati (N)	5	34	.263	108	429	52	113	28	7	.396	$2.4	1	31	.281
	Career	296	892	.307	2,157	8,214	1,383	2,523	394	81	.483	$103.4	56	722	.303
	Average season	20	59	.307	144	548	92	168	26	5	.483	$6.9	4	48	.303
	Summit season	24	64	.338	143	536	104	181	23	5	.534	$6.6	5	49	.329

GEORGE DAVIS

	ADJUSTED REGULAR SEASON												ACTUAL RESULTS		
YEAR	TEAM	HR	RBI	BA	G	AB	R	H	2B	3B	SA	PAY	HR	RBI	BA
1890	Cleveland (N)	27	73	.273	162	627	99	171	29	3	.458	$14.7	6	73	.264
1891	Cleveland (N)	16	90	.307	156	654	117	201	72	6	.509	$18.7	3	89	.289
1892	Cleveland (N)	24	85	.265	152	630	99	167	43	4	.460	$15.4	5	82	.241
1893	New York (N)	45	113	.342	158	652	106	223	31	9	.624	$18.7	11	119	.355
1894	New York (N)	27	76	.307	144	563	100	173	33	6	.531	$14.5	8	91	.352
1895	New York (N)	21	97	.309	135	528	104	163	50	4	.538	$12.3	5	101	.340
1896	New York (N)	25	101	.296	151	602	100	178	37	5	.498	$15.2	5	99	.320
1897	New York (N)	37	139	.325	154	615	114	200	30	3	.564	$18.7	10	136	.353
1898	New York (N)	15	88	.305	125	502	82	153	34	2	.470	$11.5	2	86	.307
1899	New York (N)	8	57	.321	115	443	68	142	45	3	.490	$6.8	1	57	.337
1900	New York (N)	16	67	.308	131	490	76	151	31	2	.478	$7.1	3	61	.319
1901	New York (N)	29	75	.298	149	563	80	168	27	2	.508	$7.3	7	65	.301
1902	Chicago (A)	22	122	.302	155	570	99	172	41	4	.504	$9.5	3	93	.299
1903	New York (N)	0	1	.263	5	19	3	5	0	0	.263	$1.3	0	1	.267
1904	Chicago (A)	12	92	.275	158	585	100	161	64	9	.477	$7.1	1	69	.252
1905	Chicago (A)	10	69	.303	155	565	93	171	54	0	.451	$6.8	1	55	.278
1906	Chicago (A)	0	110	.303	140	509	86	154	81	6	.485	$4.4	0	80	.277
1907	Chicago (A)	12	71	.260	136	480	81	125	29	1	.400	$4.6	1	52	.238
1908	Chicago (A)	0	37	.244	133	435	59	106	49	0	.356	$2.7	0	26	.217
1909	Chicago (A)	0	3	.143	29	70	7	10	4	0	.200	$1.1	0	2	.132
	Career	346	1,566	.296	2,643	10,102	1,673	2,994	784	69	.490	$198.4	72	1,437	.295
	Average season	17	78	.296	132	505	84	150	39	3	.490	$9.9	4	72	.295
	Summit season	29	103	.319	149	602	108	192	43	6	.555	$16.6	7	107	.337

WILLIE DAVIS

	ADJUSTED REGULAR SEASON												ACTUAL RESULTS		
YEAR	TEAM	HR	RBI	BA	G	AB	R	H	2B	3B	SA	PAY	HR	RBI	BA
1960	Los Angeles (N)	3	12	.337	23	92	14	31	7	1	.533	$0.6	2	10	.318
1961	Los Angeles (N)	14	51	.265	135	358	64	95	26	5	.483	$3.5	12	45	.254
1962	Los Angeles (N)	25	92	.297	154	589	112	175	25	7	.491	$8.9	21	85	.285
1963	Los Angeles (N)	13	74	.268	155	512	74	137	27	6	.420	$7.1	9	60	.245
1964	Los Angeles (N)	16	92	.316	155	605	109	191	32	6	.468	$12.1	12	77	.294

(Willie Davis, continued)

		ADJUSTED REGULAR SEASON											ACTUAL RESULTS		
YEAR	TEAM	HR	RBI	BA	G	AB	R	H	2B	3B	SA	PAY	HR	RBI	BA
1965	Los Angeles (N)	13	70	.262	142	558	64	146	33	2	.398	$9.3	10	57	.238
1966	Los Angeles (N)	14	75	.308	153	624	91	192	44	4	.458	$11.9	11	61	.284
1967	Los Angeles (N)	10	53	.285	143	569	84	162	42	8	.439	$9.3	6	41	.257
1968	Los Angeles (N)	14	44	.285	160	643	122	183	40	10	.443	$12.0	7	31	.250
1969	Los Angeles (N)	16	71	.337	129	498	79	168	34	7	.530	$6.7	11	59	.311
1970	Los Angeles (N)	11	106	.323	147	597	105	193	34	15	.486	$9.7	8	93	.305
1971	Los Angeles (N)	15	92	.334	158	641	105	214	50	10	.513	$12.2	10	74	.309
1972	Los Angeles (N)	31	109	.320	156	644	112	206	32	7	.536	$10.0	19	79	.289
1973	Los Angeles (N)	22	90	.299	152	599	96	179	38	9	.503	$9.3	16	77	.285
1974	Montreal (N)	20	107	.309	154	615	103	190	38	8	.494	$9.6	12	89	.295
1975	Tex. (A)-St.L. (N)	17	77	.289	139	515	66	149	35	7	.483	$5.0	11	67	.277
1976	San Diego (N)	11	56	.282	141	493	75	139	29	10	.448	$4.3	5	46	.268
1979	California (A)	0	2	.250	43	56	10	14	3	1	.339	$1.2	0	2	.250
	Career	265	1,273	.300	2,439	9,208	1,485	2,764	569	123	.475	$142.7	182	1,053	.279
	Average season	15	71	.300	136	512	83	154	32	7	.475	$7.9	10	59	.279
	Summit season	19	97	.324	149	599	101	194	38	9	.513	$9.6	12	79	.302

ANDRE DAWSON

		ADJUSTED REGULAR SEASON											ACTUAL RESULTS		
YEAR	TEAM	HR	RBI	BA	G	AB	R	H	2B	3B	SA	PAY	HR	RBI	BA
1976	Montreal (N)	0	9	.247	24	85	11	21	7	1	.353	$0.4	0	7	.235
1977	Montreal (N)	24	72	.288	139	525	71	151	30	6	.505	$5.0	19	65	.282
1978	Montreal (N)	35	85	.264	157	609	100	161	27	6	.501	$8.7	25	72	.253
1979	Montreal (N)	33	103	.280	157	647	100	181	27	9	.502	$12.1	25	92	.275
1980	Montreal (N)	25	100	.314	151	577	111	181	48	5	.544	$14.2	17	87	.308
1981	Montreal (N)	51	118	.317	155	593	131	188	32	3	.639	$18.4	24	64	.302
1982	Montreal (N)	30	95	.311	148	608	123	189	42	6	.548	$15.5	23	83	.301
1983	Montreal (N)	42	128	.308	158	629	118	194	39	8	.596	$16.4	32	113	.299
1984	Montreal (N)	23	100	.257	139	537	85	138	27	5	.454	$10.0	17	86	.248
1985	Montreal (N)	28	104	.266	140	533	74	142	30	2	.488	$9.4	23	91	.255
1986	Montreal (N)	24	88	.296	131	500	73	148	36	2	.520	$5.1	20	78	.284
1987	Chicago (N)	51	145	.293	154	625	95	183	27	2	.587	$9.6	49	137	.287
1988	Chicago (N)	32	93	.320	156	587	92	188	34	8	.569	$7.3	24	79	.303
1989	Chicago (N)	28	91	.267	118	416	73	111	19	5	.538	$4.7	21	77	.252
1990	Chicago (N)	35	115	.323	147	529	83	171	30	5	.597	$6.5	27	100	.310
1991	Chicago (N)	39	120	.285	151	571	80	163	22	4	.543	$6.5	31	104	.272
1992	Chicago (N)	30	107	.292	143	542	71	158	28	2	.517	$4.6	22	90	.277
1993	Boston (A)	16	72	.278	121	461	47	128	31	1	.453	$3.2	13	67	.273
1994	Boston (A)	23	69	.240	106	413	49	99	25	0	.467	$2.5	16	48	.240
1995	Florida (N)	10	43	.259	89	255	35	66	12	3	.447	$1.8	8	37	.257
1996	Florida (N)	2	14	.276	42	58	6	16	2	0	.414	$0.8	2	14	.276
	Career	581	1,871	.289	2,726	10,300	1,628	2,977	575	83	.530	$162.7	438	1,591	.279
	Average season	28	89	.289	130	490	78	142	27	4	.530	$7.7	21	76	.279
	Summit season	42	120	.312	154	593	104	185	32	5	.595	$11.6	31	99	.299

ED DELAHANTY

YEAR	TEAM	ADJUSTED REGULAR SEASON HR	RBI	BA	G	AB	R	H	2B	3B	SA	PAY	ACTUAL RESULTS HR	RBI	BA
1888	Philadelphia (N)	7	39	.258	91	357	50	92	26	1	.395	$4.1	1	31	.228
1889	Philadelphia (N)	0	29	.299	70	308	39	92	41	2	.445	$3.4	0	27	.293
1890	Cleveland (P)	20	67	.306	142	638	112	195	54	6	.503	$9.1	3	64	.296
1891	Philadelphia (N)	22	89	.258	150	636	96	164	30	4	.421	$11.7	5	86	.243
1892	Philadelphia (N)	30	94	.336	129	500	81	168	51	8	.650	$9.1	6	91	.306
1893	Philadelphia (N)	58	142	.355	161	726	141	258	36	4	.656	$26.9	19	146	.368
1894	Philadelphia (N)	18	116	.356	143	613	131	218	65	7	.573	$19.5	4	131	.407
1895	Philadelphia (N)	37	100	.369	141	583	142	215	54	3	.662	$25.4	11	106	.404
1896	Philadelphia (N)	48	132	.369	153	621	137	229	50	5	.697	$23.6	13	126	.397
1897	Philadelphia (N)	29	100	.349	156	641	113	224	60	6	.598	$22.7	5	96	.377
1898	Philadelphia (N)	25	99	.333	156	594	124	198	53	3	.559	$17.0	4	92	.334
1899	Philadelphia (N)	38	136	.392	154	613	134	240	60	2	.682	$19.4	9	137	.410
1900	Philadelphia (N)	14	120	.312	151	621	90	194	66	5	.502	$13.2	2	109	.323
1901	Philadelphia (N)	38	126	.352	161	628	124	221	47	5	.624	$19.9	8	108	.354
1902	Washington (A)	48	122	.381	144	554	135	211	42	4	.731	$13.7	10	93	.376
1903	Washington (A)	7	27	.341	49	182	28	62	15	0	.538	$2.3	1	21	.333
	Career	439	1,538	.338	2,151	8,815	1,677	2,981	750	65	.587	$241.0	101	1,464	.346
	Average season	27	96	.338	134	551	105	186	47	4	.587	$15.1	6	92	.346
	Summit season	46	126	.373	151	619	138	231	48	4	.687	$21.8	12	122	.391

BILL DICKEY

YEAR	TEAM	ADJUSTED REGULAR SEASON HR	RBI	BA	G	AB	R	H	2B	3B	SA	PAY	ACTUAL RESULTS HR	RBI	BA
1928	New York (A)	0	2	.176	11	17	1	3	3	0	.353	$0.0	0	2	.200
1929	New York (A)	19	66	.301	137	471	61	142	29	3	.497	$3.8	10	65	.324
1930	New York (A)	10	63	.308	115	386	53	119	28	3	.474	$4.5	5	65	.339
1931	New York (A)	18	86	.317	136	499	71	158	20	5	.485	$6.3	6	78	.327
1932	New York (A)	25	91	.301	112	439	71	132	16	2	.517	$7.1	15	84	.310
1933	New York (A)	31	116	.317	139	511	69	162	24	3	.558	$8.6	14	97	.318
1934	New York (A)	22	78	.309	109	414	61	128	22	2	.531	$7.0	12	72	.322
1935	New York (A)	26	91	.270	130	485	61	131	25	2	.491	$7.5	14	81	.279
1936	New York (A)	36	110	.344	117	442	102	152	21	3	.649	$7.1	22	107	.362
1937	New York (A)	43	141	.323	144	545	92	176	28	1	.615	$9.8	29	133	.332
1938	New York (A)	39	122	.308	136	468	89	144	23	1	.611	$9.3	27	115	.313
1939	New York (A)	36	115	.296	136	510	108	151	20	2	.555	$9.4	24	105	.302
1940	New York (A)	14	61	.249	111	390	51	97	11	1	.390	$3.8	9	54	.247
1941	New York (A)	14	82	.291	113	361	40	105	17	3	.471	$2.9	7	71	.284
1942	New York (A)	6	47	.313	86	281	35	88	20	1	.456	$2.3	2	37	.295
1943	New York (A)	12	44	.372	89	253	38	94	23	1	.613	$1.7	4	33	.351
1946	New York (A)	4	13	.277	57	141	13	39	9	0	.426	$0.9	2	10	.261
	Career	355	1,328	.306	1,878	6,613	1,016	2,021	339	33	.528	$92.0	202	1,209	.313
	Average season	21	78	.306	110	389	60	119	20	2	.528	$5.4	12	71	.313
	Summit season	37	121	.317	134	495	92	157	23	2	.596	$8.8	23	111	.325

JOE DIMAGGIO

		ADJUSTED REGULAR SEASON											ACTUAL RESULTS		
YEAR	TEAM	HR	RBI	BA	G	AB	R	H	2B	3B	SA	PAY	HR	RBI	BA
1936	New York (A)	50	129	.307	144	665	136	204	38	6	.608	$26.2	29	125	.323
1937	New York (A)	69	179	.338	156	642	161	217	28	6	.723	$32.4	46	167	.346
1938	New York (A)	50	149	.318	150	620	137	197	29	6	.626	$27.1	32	140	.324
1939	New York (A)	46	139	.373	128	493	119	184	28	2	.718	$18.7	30	126	.381
1940	New York (A)	47	150	.354	138	531	105	188	26	4	.684	$19.0	31	133	.352
1941	New York (A)	52	144	.366	144	560	141	205	41	5	.736	$19.9	30	125	.357
1942	New York (A)	46	146	.324	162	642	157	208	31	7	.609	$31.4	21	114	.305
1946	New York (A)	44	123	.306	139	530	105	162	19	4	.606	$10.1	25	95	.290
1947	New York (A)	33	114	.325	147	557	114	181	37	6	.591	$13.1	20	97	.315
1948	New York (A)	59	177	.326	161	625	125	204	27	6	.672	$19.9	39	155	.320
1949	New York (A)	21	74	.353	79	283	64	100	17	4	.664	$3.9	14	67	.346
1950	New York (A)	41	130	.305	145	548	122	167	39	6	.622	$9.4	32	122	.301
1951	New York (A)	17	81	.271	122	436	83	118	28	3	.466	$4.7	12	71	.263
	Career	575	1,735	.327	1,815	7,132	1,569	2,335	388	65	.642	$235.8	361	1,537	.325
	Average season	44	133	.327	140	549	121	180	30	5	.642	$18.1	28	118	.325
	Summit season	55	158	.351	145	570	130	200	30	5	.711	$22.0	35	141	.350

LARRY DOBY

		ADJUSTED REGULAR SEASON											ACTUAL RESULTS		
YEAR	TEAM	HR	RBI	BA	G	AB	R	H	2B	3B	SA	PAY	HR	RBI	BA
1947	Cleveland (A)	0	2	.152	30	33	3	5	2	0	.212	$0.0	0	2	.156
1948	Cleveland (A)	24	74	.306	126	457	93	140	28	5	.547	$4.7	14	66	.301
1949	Cleveland (A)	35	96	.286	155	577	119	165	28	2	.523	$11.6	24	85	.280
1950	Cleveland (A)	32	109	.330	148	524	117	173	29	3	.580	$11.8	25	102	.326
1951	Cleveland (A)	28	79	.304	140	467	96	142	32	3	.565	$11.8	20	69	.295
1952	Cleveland (A)	46	128	.294	146	541	128	159	30	5	.623	$12.8	32	104	.276
1953	Cleveland (A)	37	115	.268	156	537	104	144	21	3	.525	$12.5	29	102	.263
1954	Cleveland (A)	42	147	.280	159	600	110	168	22	2	.533	$16.4	32	126	.272
1955	Cleveland (A)	32	86	.304	138	517	105	157	23	4	.549	$9.3	26	75	.291
1956	Chicago (A)	28	118	.280	147	529	103	148	29	2	.501	$9.8	24	102	.268
1957	Chicago (A)	17	95	.303	124	433	68	131	35	1	.506	$5.0	14	79	.288
1958	Cleveland (A)	15	54	.295	94	261	50	77	14	1	.529	$2.8	13	45	.283
1959	Det.-Chi. (A)	0	15	.244	41	119	7	29	6	2	.328	$1.4	0	13	.230
	Career	336	1,118	.293	1,604	5,595	1,103	1,638	299	33	.538	$109.9	253	970	.283
	Average season	26	86	.293	123	430	85	126	23	3	.538	$8.5	19	75	.283
	Summit season	32	95	.307	140	501	108	154	28	4	.571	$10.1	23	83	.298

BOBBY DOERR

		ADJUSTED REGULAR SEASON											**ACTUAL RESULTS**		
YEAR	**TEAM**	**HR**	**RBI**	**BA**	**G**	**AB**	**R**	**H**	**2B**	**3B**	**SA**	**PAY**	**HR**	**RBI**	**BA**
1937	Boston (A)	4	15	.219	58	155	24	34	5	1	.342	$1.4	2	14	.224
1938	Boston (A)	12	89	.283	157	551	78	156	36	5	.432	$6.1	5	80	.289
1939	Boston (A)	22	80	.312	135	558	82	174	29	1	.486	$7.5	12	73	.318
1940	Boston (A)	37	119	.292	159	627	98	183	38	4	.542	$14.3	22	105	.291
1941	Boston (A)	29	108	.289	138	523	86	151	27	2	.514	$11.5	16	93	.282
1942	Boston (A)	33	131	.309	153	579	91	179	39	2	.554	$14.7	15	102	.290
1943	Boston (A)	36	99	.287	162	631	103	181	31	1	.510	$18.5	16	75	.270
1944	Boston (A)	34	101	.337	130	487	118	164	31	5	.630	$12.2	15	81	.325
1946	Boston (A)	35	148	.285	157	606	121	173	37	5	.536	$19.3	18	116	.271
1947	Boston (A)	29	111	.267	151	580	92	155	28	6	.486	$12.3	17	95	.258
1948	Boston (A)	40	125	.291	146	550	106	160	24	3	.564	$12.6	27	111	.285
1949	Boston (A)	29	121	.316	145	564	101	178	36	6	.555	$12.5	18	109	.309
1950	Boston (A)	36	129	.297	157	617	111	183	35	7	.551	$13.2	27	120	.294
1951	Boston (A)	19	84	.296	112	425	69	126	26	1	.496	$5.0	13	73	.289
	Career	395	1,460	.295	1,960	7,453	1,280	2,197	422	49	.524	$161.1	223	1,247	.288
	Average season	28	104	.295	140	532	91	157	30	4	.524	$11.5	16	89	.288
	Summit season	34	121	.309	146	559	105	173	33	5	.569	$13.0	20	105	.300

MIKE DONLIN

		ADJUSTED REGULAR SEASON											**ACTUAL RESULTS**		
YEAR	**TEAM**	**HR**	**RBI**	**BA**	**G**	**AB**	**R**	**H**	**2B**	**3B**	**SA**	**PAY**	**HR**	**RBI**	**BA**
1899	St. Louis (N)	19	26	.309	69	278	48	86	7	1	.547	$3.0	6	27	.323
1900	St. Louis (N)	27	52	.314	89	315	43	99	6	1	.597	$3.7	10	48	.326
1901	Baltimore (A)	29	81	.337	145	570	129	192	34	4	.563	$11.4	5	67	.340
1902	Cincinnati (N)	0	11	.287	39	164	38	47	20	5	.470	$3.1	0	9	.287
1903	Cincinnati (N)	41	85	.361	145	571	140	206	25	5	.637	$14.2	7	67	.351
1904	Cin.-N.Y. (N)	21	69	.359	105	379	78	136	24	3	.604	$7.5	3	52	.329
1905	New York (N)	41	103	.388	157	634	160	246	35	5	.653	$19.4	7	80	.356
1906	New York (N)	7	19	.344	39	128	21	44	5	0	.547	$4.7	1	14	.314
1908	New York (N)	40	152	.377	160	612	101	231	30	4	.636	$12.0	6	106	.334
1911	N.Y.-Bos. (N)	11	39	.320	71	244	40	78	15	0	.516	$2.4	3	35	.316
1912	Pittsburgh (N)	13	40	.315	82	260	31	82	12	3	.535	$1.9	2	35	.316
1914	New York (N)	3	4	.156	36	32	1	5	0	0	.438	$0.9	1	3	.161
	Career	252	681	.347	1,137	4,187	830	1,452	213	31	.593	$84.2	51	543	.333
	Average season	21	57	.347	95	349	69	121	18	3	.593	$7.0	4	45	.333
	Summit season	34	98	.365	142	553	122	202	30	4	.618	$12.9	6	74	.343

LARRY DOYLE

		ADJUSTED REGULAR SEASON											ACTUAL RESULTS		
YEAR	TEAM	HR	RBI	BA	G	AB	R	H	2B	3B	SA	PAY	HR	RBI	BA
1907	New York (N)	0	22	.287	72	237	22	68	22	0	.380	$1.9	0	16	.260
1908	New York (N)	0	47	.348	107	388	93	135	63	9	.557	$4.3	0	33	.308
1909	New York (N)	37	66	.333	151	586	117	195	26	3	.577	$9.1	6	49	.302
1910	New York (N)	38	89	.307	158	602	125	185	20	4	.543	$14.4	8	69	.285
1911	New York (N)	47	86	.313	150	552	114	173	22	6	.630	$14.5	13	77	.310
1912	New York (N)	36	100	.330	150	585	109	193	25	2	.564	$15.1	10	90	.330
1913	New York (N)	22	89	.292	137	500	82	146	27	1	.482	$11.8	5	73	.280
1914	New York (N)	23	80	.275	151	561	110	154	22	2	.444	$14.3	5	63	.260
1915	New York (N)	25	91	.344	157	619	111	213	57	4	.570	$12.3	4	70	.320
1916	N.Y.-Chi. (N)	20	75	.303	127	499	85	151	42	5	.527	$7.3	3	54	.278
1917	Chicago (N)	25	83	.276	139	490	65	135	15	1	.463	$7.2	6	61	.254
1918	New York (N)	18	62	.277	98	336	65	93	7	1	.464	$3.5	3	36	.261
1919	New York (N)	28	75	.296	131	442	88	131	14	3	.532	$3.9	7	52	.289
1920	New York (N)	15	59	.276	143	492	57	136	23	1	.419	$3.5	4	50	.285
	Career	334	1,024	.306	1,871	6,889	1,243	2,108	385	42	.520	$123.1	74	793	.290
	Average season	24	73	.306	134	492	89	151	28	3	.520	$8.8	5	57	.290
	Summit season	29	78	.333	143	546	109	182	39	5	.582	$11.1	7	64	.314

HUGH DUFFY

		ADJUSTED REGULAR SEASON											ACTUAL RESULTS		
YEAR	TEAM	HR	RBI	BA	G	AB	R	H	2B	3B	SA	PAY	HR	RBI	BA
1888	Chicago (N)	23	50	.317	85	357	74	113	11	1	.546	$5.5	7	41	.282
1889	Chicago (N)	37	90	.302	162	696	146	210	23	2	.500	$19.1	12	89	.295
1890	Chicago (P)	35	81	.331	162	700	160	232	54	5	.573	$26.4	7	82	.320
1891	Boston (AA)	33	114	.357	148	625	139	223	26	2	.563	$19.9	9	110	.336
1892	Boston (N)	25	85	.332	157	654	132	217	48	5	.535	$26.0	5	81	.301
1893	Boston (N)	26	116	.349	162	693	145	242	34	3	.519	$31.4	6	118	.363
1894	Boston (N)	46	125	.385	152	655	138	252	49	4	.682	$27.0	18	145	.440
1895	Boston (N)	31	96	.320	160	654	106	209	33	1	.515	$22.7	9	100	.352
1896	Boston (N)	24	117	.278	161	648	100	180	23	3	.434	$22.2	5	113	.300
1897	Boston (N)	39	133	.313	161	661	134	207	23	2	.531	$23.3	11	129	.340
1898	Boston (N)	29	114	.296	162	605	102	179	11	1	.461	$13.2	8	108	.298
1899	Boston (N)	23	102	.266	156	624	103	166	35	2	.439	$13.1	5	102	.279
1900	Boston (N)	9	34	.295	63	207	29	61	7	2	.478	$2.6	2	31	.304
1901	Milwaukee (A)	14	53	.298	92	332	47	99	25	4	.524	$2.6	2	45	.302
1904	Philadelphia (N)	0	7	.306	19	49	14	15	8	0	.469	$0.9	0	5	.283
1905	Philadelphia (N)	0	4	.326	16	43	9	14	9	0	.535	$0.4	0	3	.300
1906	Philadelphia (N)	0	0	.000	1	1	0	0	0	0	.000	$0.1	0	0	.000
	Career	394	1,321	.319	2,019	8,204	1,578	2,619	419	37	.523	$256.4	106	1,302	.324
	Average season	23	78	.319	119	483	93	154	25	2	.523	$15.1	6	77	.324
	Summit season	33	104	.350	156	665	143	233	42	4	.574	$26.1	9	107	.350

BOB ELLIOTT

		ADJUSTED REGULAR SEASON											ACTUAL RESULTS		
YEAR	TEAM	HR	RBI	BA	G	AB	R	H	2B	3B	SA	PAY	HR	RBI	BA
1939	Pittsburgh (N)	6	21	.328	34	137	20	45	11	2	.569	$1.4	3	19	.333
1940	Pittsburgh (N)	11	71	.293	154	573	98	168	48	7	.459	$6.2	5	64	.292
1941	Pittsburgh (N)	8	87	.280	146	546	85	153	39	8	.425	$8.6	3	76	.273
1942	Pittsburgh (N)	24	115	.316	153	599	97	189	35	5	.511	$12.1	9	89	.296
1943	Pittsburgh (N)	23	132	.335	161	600	107	201	43	9	.552	$15.2	7	101	.315
1944	Pittsburgh (N)	27	133	.307	147	553	105	170	35	10	.553	$15.1	10	108	.297
1945	Pittsburgh (N)	21	135	.300	151	567	99	170	47	4	.508	$12.6	8	108	.290
1946	Pittsburgh (N)	12	87	.278	146	507	64	141	35	2	.426	$9.3	5	68	.263
1947	Boston (N)	35	135	.328	158	585	111	192	40	3	.586	$15.7	22	113	.317
1948	Boston (N)	35	114	.290	159	569	112	165	25	3	.529	$13.2	23	100	.283
1949	Boston (N)	26	83	.286	143	496	85	142	34	3	.524	$7.0	17	76	.280
1950	Boston (N)	31	113	.309	147	550	99	170	32	3	.547	$9.4	24	107	.305
1951	Boston (N)	21	80	.293	142	501	83	147	35	1	.493	$6.9	15	70	.285
1952	New York (N)	15	43	.241	103	286	41	69	7	1	.430	$2.2	10	35	.228
1953	St.L.-Chi. (A)	12	68	.260	119	381	48	99	23	1	.420	$2.5	9	61	.255
	Career	307	1,417	.298	2,063	7,450	1,254	2,221	489	62	.504	$137.4	170	1,195	.289
	Average season	20	94	.298	138	497	84	148	33	4	.504	$9.2	11	80	.289
	Summit season	28	126	.319	153	577	104	184	37	6	.549	$13.5	14	104	.306

DARRELL EVANS

		ADJUSTED REGULAR SEASON											ACTUAL RESULTS		
YEAR	TEAM	HR	RBI	BA	G	AB	R	H	2B	3B	SA	PAY	HR	RBI	BA
1969	Atlanta (N)	0	1	.269	12	26	4	7	0	0	.269	$0.0	0	1	.231
1970	Atlanta (N)	0	10	.341	12	44	5	15	1	1	.409	$0.0	0	9	.318
1971	Atlanta (N)	16	48	.262	89	260	53	68	14	1	.508	$2.5	12	38	.242
1972	Atlanta (N)	28	98	.281	131	438	92	123	16	0	.509	$6.0	19	71	.254
1973	Atlanta (N)	51	122	.294	161	595	133	175	30	7	.625	$15.5	41	104	.281
1974	Atlanta (N)	35	93	.250	159	567	117	142	24	3	.489	$18.4	25	79	.240
1975	Atlanta (N)	30	86	.254	157	571	96	145	25	2	.462	$15.4	22	73	.243
1976	Atl.-S.F. (N)	17	56	.215	136	396	65	85	10	1	.374	$6.8	11	46	.205
1977	San Francisco (N)	20	80	.258	144	461	71	119	20	2	.440	$7.0	17	72	.254
1978	San Francisco (N)	27	92	.254	159	547	97	139	25	2	.455	$9.8	20	78	.243
1979	San Francisco (N)	22	77	.256	160	562	75	144	26	1	.423	$6.9	17	70	.253
1980	San Francisco (N)	27	91	.268	155	560	80	150	24	0	.455	$7.2	20	78	.264
1981	San Francisco (N)	27	86	.270	149	522	91	141	21	5	.485	$7.0	12	48	.258
1982	San Francisco (N)	21	70	.265	141	465	74	123	23	3	.462	$4.8	16	61	.256
1983	San Francisco (N)	38	94	.287	142	523	107	150	30	2	.570	$6.7	30	82	.277
1984	Detroit (A)	21	73	.239	131	401	70	96	12	1	.431	$4.2	16	63	.232
1985	Detroit (A)	46	107	.260	152	508	92	132	18	0	.567	$6.5	40	94	.248
1986	Detroit (A)	33	95	.250	151	507	87	127	16	0	.477	$6.5	29	85	.241
1987	Detroit (A)	35	104	.263	150	499	94	131	22	0	.517	$6.6	34	99	.257
1988	Detroit (A)	28	76	.220	144	437	57	96	9	0	.432	$4.2	22	64	.208
1989	Atlanta (N)	15	47	.219	108	279	37	61	6	1	.409	$2.2	11	39	.207
	Career	537	1,606	.258	2,743	9,168	1,597	2,369	372	32	.482	$144.2	414	1,354	.248
	Average season	26	76	.258	131	437	76	113	18	2	.482	$6.9	20	64	.248
	Summit season	40	105	.277	147	513	104	142	23	2	.563	$8.3	33	90	.264

DWIGHT EVANS

		ADJUSTED REGULAR SEASON												ACTUAL RESULTS		
YEAR	TEAM	HR	RBI	BA	G	AB	R	H	2B	3B	SA	PAY	HR	RBI	BA
1972	Boston (A)	2	8	.283	19	60	3	17	4	1	.483	$0.0	1	6	.263
1973	Boston (A)	13	37	.234	119	282	54	66	16	1	.436	$2.4	10	32	.223
1974	Boston (A)	17	83	.294	133	463	71	136	26	7	.490	$5.4	10	70	.281
1975	Boston (A)	19	66	.287	130	418	72	120	30	5	.519	$5.4	13	56	.274
1976	Boston (A)	28	76	.253	146	501	75	127	39	3	.511	$7.6	17	62	.242
1977	Boston (A)	17	40	.291	73	230	43	67	9	1	.561	$4.6	14	36	.287
1978	Boston (A)	32	74	.257	146	494	88	127	25	2	.510	$7.9	24	63	.247
1979	Boston (A)	26	65	.277	154	495	77	137	26	1	.491	$7.6	21	58	.274
1980	Boston (A)	25	70	.271	150	469	84	127	41	4	.535	$5.8	18	60	.266
1981	Boston (A)	48	131	.312	162	618	155	193	30	4	.607	$22.8	22	71	.296
1982	Boston (A)	41	113	.300	162	609	140	183	41	6	.589	$22.5	32	98	.292
1983	Boston (A)	28	66	.245	126	470	84	115	20	3	.479	$7.0	22	58	.238
1984	Boston (A)	42	121	.306	162	630	140	193	42	6	.592	$20.3	32	104	.295
1985	Boston (A)	35	88	.274	158	613	124	168	31	1	.499	$19.3	29	78	.263
1986	Boston (A)	30	109	.271	153	532	96	144	37	2	.517	$9.6	26	97	.259
1987	Boston (A)	35	129	.312	154	541	114	169	40	2	.588	$12.6	34	123	.305
1988	Boston (A)	29	132	.311	149	559	114	174	34	7	.553	$12.4	21	111	.293
1989	Boston (A)	28	119	.302	146	520	97	157	29	3	.531	$9.2	20	100	.285
1990	Boston (A)	17	72	.261	123	445	76	116	20	3	.434	$4.7	13	63	.249
1991	Baltimore (A)	8	43	.285	101	270	40	77	10	1	.419	$2.4	6	38	.270
	Career	520	1,642	.283	2,666	9,219	1,747	2,613	550	63	.526	$189.5	385	1,384	.272
	Average season	26	82	.283	133	461	87	131	28	3	.526	$9.5	19	69	.272
	Summit season	39	125	.308	158	591	133	182	37	5	.585	$18.1	28	101	.296

JOHNNY EVERS

		ADJUSTED REGULAR SEASON												ACTUAL RESULTS		
YEAR	TEAM	HR	RBI	BA	G	AB	R	H	2B	3B	SA	PAY	HR	RBI	BA
1902	Chicago (N)	0	3	.221	30	104	9	23	0	0	.221	$0.1	0	2	.222
1903	Chicago (N)	0	67	.300	145	543	90	163	81	6	.471	$5.0	0	52	.293
1904	Chicago (N)	0	62	.289	158	553	65	160	58	8	.423	$6.1	0	47	.265
1905	Chicago (N)	9	47	.299	103	354	56	106	19	1	.435	$4.6	1	37	.276
1906	Chicago (N)	13	69	.278	161	557	88	155	37	4	.429	$8.9	1	51	.255
1907	Chicago (N)	18	71	.274	158	532	92	146	26	2	.432	$8.9	2	51	.250
1908	Chicago (N)	0	52	.338	129	426	118	144	67	6	.523	$8.7	0	37	.300
1909	Chicago (N)	12	33	.291	133	485	122	141	39	4	.462	$9.2	1	24	.263
1910	Chicago (N)	0	36	.284	131	454	112	129	46	8	.421	$6.9	0	28	.263
1911	Chicago (N)	0	8	.228	47	158	31	36	13	3	.348	$2.6	0	7	.226
1912	Chicago (N)	10	71	.343	152	508	82	174	50	7	.528	$5.9	1	63	.341
1913	Chicago (N)	16	60	.296	142	466	100	138	27	2	.466	$3.7	3	49	.285
1914	Boston (N)	8	50	.295	143	505	102	149	39	1	.424	$4.6	1	40	.279
1915	Boston (N)	7	28	.281	86	288	49	81	7	0	.378	$2.3	1	22	.263
1916	Boston (N)	0	21	.234	73	248	45	58	20	0	.315	$1.8	0	15	.216
1917	Bos.-Phi. (N)	7	16	.232	83	276	34	64	7	0	.333	$1.3	1	12	.214
1922	Chicago (A)	0	1	.000	1	3	0	0	0	0	.000	$0.2	0	1	.000
1929	Boston (N)	0	0	.000	1	0	0	0	0	0	.000	$0.0	0	0	.000
	Career	100	695	.289	1,876	6,460	1,195	1,867	536	52	.435	$80.8	12	538	.270
	Average season	6	39	.289	104	359	66	104	30	3	.435	$4.5	1	30	.270
	Summit season	8	57	.313	140	486	102	152	53	5	.492	$6.5	1	45	.297

BUCK EWING

		ADJUSTED REGULAR SEASON											ACTUAL RESULTS		
YEAR	TEAM	HR	RBI	BA	G	AB	R	H	2B	3B	SA	PAY	HR	RBI	BA
1880	Troy (N)	0	11	.195	25	87	2	17	6	0	.264	$0.1	0	5	.178
1881	Troy (N)	0	49	.258	128	520	79	134	71	13	.444	$4.4	0	25	.250
1882	Troy (N)	29	54	.294	141	625	126	184	42	8	.526	$9.0	2	29	.271
1883	New York (N)	53	62	.318	145	620	137	197	9	3	.598	$12.2	10	41	.303
1884	New York (N)	27	54	.306	131	532	118	163	38	14	.583	$11.6	3	41	.277
1885	New York (N)	37	89	.336	117	494	114	166	22	4	.621	$11.8	6	63	.304
1886	New York (N)	21	37	.338	95	358	70	121	15	2	.567	$7.1	4	31	.309
1887	New York (N)	25	45	.304	97	401	84	122	22	4	.566	$7.3	6	44	.305
1888	New York (N)	30	70	.346	121	488	100	169	31	6	.619	$6.9	6	58	.306
1889	New York (N)	21	91	.335	122	502	96	168	43	7	.574	$7.1	4	87	.327
1890	New York (P)	34	75	.349	102	433	102	151	24	4	.658	$6.9	8	72	.338
1891	New York (N)	0	20	.367	17	60	9	22	10	0	.533	$1.6	0	18	.347
1892	New York (N)	31	79	.342	111	415	60	142	13	4	.617	$2.9	8	76	.310
1893	Cleveland (N)	29	123	.331	146	629	117	208	46	6	.561	$9.4	6	122	.344
1894	Cleveland (N)	7	34	.217	66	263	28	57	16	1	.365	$1.9	2	39	.251
1895	Cincinnati (N)	23	90	.289	129	533	86	154	35	5	.503	$4.5	5	94	.318
1896	Cincinnati (N)	7	40	.256	87	332	43	85	27	2	.413	$2.2	1	38	.278
1897	Cincinnati (N)	0	0	.000	1	1	0	0	0	0	.000	$0.5	0	0	.000
	Career	374	1,023	.310	1,781	7,293	1,371	2,260	470	83	.551	$107.4	71	883	.303
	Average season	21	57	.310	99	405	76	126	26	5	.551	$6.0	4	49	.303
	Summit season	37	75	.337	119	490	103	165	20	4	.620	$8.1	8	62	.312

RICK FERRELL

		ADJUSTED REGULAR SEASON											ACTUAL RESULTS		
YEAR	TEAM	HR	RBI	BA	G	AB	R	H	2B	3B	SA	PAY	HR	RBI	BA
1929	St. Louis (A)	0	20	.212	67	151	21	32	12	0	.291	$1.5	0	20	.229
1930	St. Louis (A)	3	39	.242	106	330	41	80	24	3	.361	$3.1	1	41	.268
1931	St. Louis (A)	9	63	.296	123	406	52	120	37	2	.463	$4.7	3	57	.306
1932	St. Louis (A)	6	71	.307	133	462	73	142	43	3	.452	$6.0	2	65	.315
1933	St.L.-Bos. (A)	12	91	.290	148	521	69	151	28	2	.420	$7.7	4	77	.290
1934	Boston (A)	3	52	.287	139	460	54	132	46	3	.420	$4.6	1	48	.297
1935	Boston (A)	8	67	.290	140	482	59	140	45	2	.442	$5.4	3	61	.301
1936	Boston (A)	16	56	.295	126	427	60	126	28	3	.487	$4.4	8	55	.312
1937	Bos.-Wash. (A)	5	38	.237	107	354	41	84	10	0	.308	$2.2	2	36	.244
1938	Washington (A)	3	63	.288	144	438	60	126	38	4	.413	$2.7	1	58	.292
1939	Washington (A)	0	34	.276	92	290	35	80	22	1	.359	$1.8	0	31	.281
1940	Washington (A)	0	31	.275	108	342	39	94	30	1	.368	$1.8	0	28	.273
1941	Wash.-St.L. (A)	5	41	.263	125	400	44	105	28	3	.385	$1.9	2	36	.256
1942	St. Louis (A)	0	34	.236	106	292	26	69	17	2	.308	$1.3	0	26	.223
1943	St. Louis (A)	0	27	.255	78	220	16	56	19	0	.341	$1.0	0	20	.239
1944	Washington (A)	0	31	.287	104	356	18	102	28	2	.376	$1.3	0	25	.277
1945	Washington (A)	4	47	.274	95	299	41	82	21	1	.391	$1.4	1	38	.266
1947	Washington (A)	0	14	.317	39	104	12	33	16	0	.471	$0.6	0	12	.303
	Career	74	819	.277	1,980	6,334	761	1,754	492	32	.400	$53.4	28	734	.281
	Average season	4	46	.277	110	352	42	97	27	2	.400	$3.0	2	41	.281
	Summit season	10	70	.296	134	460	63	136	36	2	.448	$5.6	4	63	.304

CARLTON FISK

		ADJUSTED REGULAR SEASON											ACTUAL RESULTS		
YEAR	TEAM	HR	RBI	BA	G	AB	R	H	2B	3B	SA	PAY	HR	RBI	BA
1969	Boston (A)	0	0	.000	2	5	0	0	0	0	.000	$0.0	0	0	.000
1971	Boston (A)	3	7	.333	14	48	9	16	3	1	.625	$0.0	2	6	.313
1972	Boston (A)	34	84	.324	137	478	102	155	38	8	.651	$5.3	22	61	.293
1973	Boston (A)	32	83	.258	135	508	76	131	26	0	.498	$6.0	26	71	.246
1974	Boston (A)	15	31	.316	52	187	43	59	13	1	.636	$3.7	11	26	.299
1975	Boston (A)	15	61	.346	80	266	55	92	17	3	.602	$5.1	10	52	.331
1976	Boston (A)	28	71	.269	134	487	93	131	19	3	.493	$5.8	17	58	.255
1977	Boston (A)	31	114	.320	153	540	118	173	29	2	.554	$9.5	26	102	.315
1978	Boston (A)	28	104	.296	156	567	111	168	43	4	.534	$11.9	20	88	.284
1979	Boston (A)	13	47	.275	92	324	55	89	26	2	.488	$3.5	10	42	.272
1980	Boston (A)	25	72	.293	133	485	85	142	28	2	.513	$5.0	18	62	.289
1981	Chicago (A)	17	84	.276	147	518	82	143	22	0	.417	$5.1	7	45	.263
1982	Chicago (A)	18	75	.275	135	476	76	131	19	3	.441	$3.9	14	65	.267
1983	Chicago (A)	33	98	.297	138	488	97	145	28	3	.570	$4.6	26	86	.289
1984	Chicago (A)	26	50	.240	102	359	63	86	21	1	.521	$2.6	21	43	.231
1985	Chicago (A)	43	121	.249	152	539	96	134	24	1	.536	$6.5	37	107	.238
1986	Chicago (A)	16	70	.230	125	457	47	105	13	0	.363	$3.2	14	63	.221
1987	Chicago (A)	24	74	.262	135	454	71	119	24	1	.478	$3.3	23	71	.256
1988	Chicago (A)	24	59	.292	76	253	44	74	8	1	.617	$2.2	19	50	.277
1989	Chicago (A)	18	81	.311	104	379	56	118	29	2	.541	$2.4	13	68	.293
1990	Chicago (A)	23	75	.299	137	452	75	135	22	0	.500	$3.2	18	65	.285
1991	Chicago (A)	22	84	.254	134	460	48	117	27	0	.457	$2.6	18	74	.241
1992	Chicago (A)	4	25	.239	62	188	14	45	5	1	.340	$1.5	3	21	.229
1993	Chicago (A)	1	4	.189	25	53	2	10	0	0	.245	$0.7	1	4	.189
	Career	493	1,574	.281	2,560	8,971	1,518	2,518	484	39	.508	$97.6	376	1,330	.269
	Average season	21	66	.281	107	374	63	105	20	2	.508	$4.1	16	55	.269
	Summit season	29	96	.310	138	490	97	152	33	4	.571	$6.7	21	81	.295

ELMER FLICK

		ADJUSTED REGULAR SEASON											ACTUAL RESULTS		
YEAR	TEAM	HR	RBI	BA	G	AB	R	H	2B	3B	SA	PAY	HR	RBI	BA
1898	Philadelphia (N)	34	87	.300	145	490	90	147	15	3	.551	$11.7	8	81	.302
1899	Philadelphia (N)	15	97	.326	134	512	97	167	44	5	.520	$11.6	2	98	.342
1900	Philadelphia (N)	44	121	.355	159	628	117	223	36	5	.639	$19.2	11	110	.367
1901	Philadelphia (N)	39	103	.331	160	626	131	207	39	5	.596	$19.6	8	88	.333
1902	Phi.-Cle. (A)	19	84	.299	143	545	112	163	42	7	.506	$15.0	2	64	.297
1903	Cleveland (A)	21	65	.304	162	605	103	184	43	9	.509	$18.4	2	51	.296
1904	Cleveland (A)	38	75	.333	158	610	131	203	37	5	.597	$18.9	6	56	.306
1905	Cleveland (A)	30	82	.335	138	523	92	175	42	7	.614	$9.6	4	64	.308
1906	Cleveland (A)	16	83	.340	162	644	132	219	89	16	.602	$16.4	1	62	.311
1907	Cleveland (A)	31	79	.332	151	564	110	187	25	9	.573	$12.4	3	58	.302
1908	Cleveland (A)	0	3	.257	9	35	6	9	6	0	.429	$1.5	0	2	.229
1909	Cleveland (A)	0	21	.280	69	246	39	69	34	2	.435	$1.8	0	15	.255
1910	Cleveland (A)	4	9	.279	24	68	6	19	2	0	.485	$0.7	1	7	.265
	Career	291	909	.323	1,614	6,096	1,166	1,972	454	73	.565	$156.8	48	756	.313
	Average season	22	70	.323	124	469	90	152	35	6	.565	$12.1	4	58	.313
	Summit season	33	93	.338	155	606	121	205	49	8	.609	$16.7	6	76	.325

CURT FLOOD

		ADJUSTED REGULAR SEASON											ACTUAL RESULTS		
YEAR	TEAM	HR	RBI	BA	G	AB	R	H	2B	3B	SA	PAY	HR	RBI	BA
1956	Cincinnati (N)	0	0	.000	5	1	0	0	0	0	.000	$0.0	0	0	.000
1957	Cincinnati (N)	1	1	.333	3	3	2	1	0	0	1.333	$0.0	1	1	.333
1958	St. Louis (N)	12	49	.271	127	443	60	120	23	2	.413	$3.4	10	41	.261
1959	St. Louis (N)	9	31	.266	127	218	28	58	9	3	.459	$1.9	7	26	.255
1960	St. Louis (N)	10	45	.249	146	413	44	103	27	1	.392	$3.9	8	38	.237
1961	St. Louis (N)	2	24	.337	138	350	60	118	22	4	.440	$3.9	2	21	.322
1962	St. Louis (N)	14	77	.309	150	631	109	195	40	4	.452	$9.3	12	70	.296
1963	St. Louis (N)	7	78	.331	158	662	139	219	53	8	.467	$14.8	5	63	.302
1964	St. Louis (N)	7	56	.334	162	679	118	227	38	2	.427	$15.1	5	46	.311
1965	St. Louis (N)	14	102	.339	156	617	110	209	42	2	.481	$15.6	11	83	.310
1966	St. Louis (N)	13	96	.289	160	626	78	181	30	4	.412	$14.6	10	78	.267
1967	St. Louis (N)	9	65	.373	135	518	89	193	36	1	.498	$9.0	5	50	.335
1968	St. Louis (N)	11	85	.343	150	618	100	212	31	4	.460	$11.9	5	60	.301
1969	St. Louis (N)	5	68	.310	153	606	96	188	47	3	.422	$9.8	4	57	.285
1971	Washington (A)	0	2	.229	13	35	5	8	0	0	.229	$1.2	0	2	.200
	Career	114	779	.317	1,783	6,420	1,038	2,032	398	38	.444	$114.4	85	636	.293
	Average season	8	52	.317	119	428	69	135	27	3	.444	$7.6	6	42	.293
	Summit season	9	71	.344	147	553	100	190	37	4	.474	$11.0	6	55	.312

LEW FONSECA

		ADJUSTED REGULAR SEASON											ACTUAL RESULTS		
YEAR	TEAM	HR	RBI	BA	G	AB	R	H	2B	3B	SA	PAY	HR	RBI	BA
1921	Cincinnati (N)	4	45	.254	87	315	42	80	18	1	.356	$3.8	1	41	.276
1922	Cincinnati (N)	11	48	.338	84	302	58	102	22	1	.526	$4.1	4	45	.361
1923	Cincinnati (N)	9	30	.262	68	248	36	65	13	2	.440	$3.3	3	28	.278
1924	Cincinnati (N)	0	10	.217	21	60	5	13	6	0	.317	$1.5	0	9	.228
1925	Philadelphia (N)	17	62	.294	133	493	81	145	32	2	.471	$5.4	7	60	.319
1927	Cleveland (A)	8	44	.295	119	455	66	134	32	4	.435	$4.6	2	40	.311
1928	Cleveland (A)	8	39	.314	78	274	41	86	22	2	.496	$2.6	3	36	.327
1929	Cleveland (A)	16	106	.344	158	604	100	208	57	8	.545	$9.6	6	103	.369
1930	Cleveland (A)	0	16	.252	42	135	19	34	14	2	.385	$2.2	0	17	.279
1931	Cle.-Chi. (A)	10	93	.304	153	596	94	181	47	4	.446	$5.0	3	85	.312
1932	Chicago (A)	0	7	.128	19	39	0	5	2	0	.179	$1.1	0	6	.135
1933	Chicago (A)	4	18	.203	25	64	10	13	1	0	.406	$0.7	2	15	.203
	Career	87	518	.297	987	3,585	552	1,066	266	26	.459	$43.9	31	485	.316
	Average season	7	43	.297	82	299	46	89	22	2	.459	$3.7	3	40	.316
	Summit season	13	76	.311	141	537	85	167	42	5	.480	$6.2	5	72	.329

GEORGE FOSTER

		ADJUSTED REGULAR SEASON											ACTUAL RESULTS		
YEAR	TEAM	HR	RBI	BA	G	AB	R	H	2B	3B	SA	PAY	HR	RBI	BA
1969	San Francisco (N)	0	1	.400	9	5	1	2	0	0	.400	$0.0	0	1	.400
1970	San Francisco (N)	1	5	.316	9	19	2	6	1	1	.632	$0.0	1	4	.316
1971	S.F.-Cin. (N)	18	73	.260	140	473	62	123	31	4	.457	$4.1	13	58	.241
1972	Cincinnati (N)	3	17	.224	62	152	21	34	6	1	.336	$1.5	2	12	.200
1973	Cincinnati (N)	5	10	.308	17	39	7	12	4	0	.795	$0.9	4	9	.282
1974	Cincinnati (N)	10	48	.278	105	273	36	76	22	0	.469	$3.3	7	41	.264
1975	Cincinnati (N)	32	91	.313	134	463	83	145	27	3	.592	$5.6	23	78	.300
1976	Cincinnati (N)	46	149	.322	144	562	105	181	23	6	.630	$9.5	29	121	.306
1977	Cincinnati (N)	59	165	.327	158	615	137	201	32	1	.670	$16.3	52	149	.320
1978	Cincinnati (N)	53	143	.294	159	608	116	179	27	4	.613	$16.8	40	120	.281
1979	Cincinnati (N)	36	109	.306	122	444	76	136	19	2	.601	$9.6	30	98	.302
1980	Cincinnati (N)	33	107	.277	143	524	90	145	22	4	.523	$9.5	25	93	.273
1981	Cincinnati (N)	47	166	.311	162	621	118	193	36	2	.602	$14.0	22	90	.295
1982	New York (N)	17	80	.255	151	550	73	140	26	2	.402	$7.1	13	70	.247
1983	New York (N)	35	103	.248	157	601	84	149	20	2	.463	$9.3	28	90	.241
1984	New York (N)	31	100	.278	146	553	78	154	24	1	.494	$6.6	24	86	.269
1985	New York (N)	25	87	.274	129	452	65	124	26	1	.502	$3.5	21	77	.263
1986	N.Y. (N)-Chi. (A)	16	47	.236	87	284	33	67	7	3	.451	$2.1	14	42	.225
	Career	467	1,501	.286	2,034	7,238	1,187	2,067	353	37	.538	$119.7	348	1,239	.274
	Average season	26	83	.286	113	402	66	115	20	2	.538	$6.7	19	69	.274
	Summit season	48	146	.312	149	570	110	178	27	3	.623	$13.2	35	116	.301

BOB FOTHERGILL

		ADJUSTED REGULAR SEASON											ACTUAL RESULTS		
YEAR	TEAM	HR	RBI	BA	G	AB	R	H	2B	3B	SA	PAY	HR	RBI	BA
1922	Detroit (A)	0	31	.302	44	159	21	48	23	3	.484	$1.9	0	29	.322
1923	Detroit (A)	4	53	.300	106	253	37	76	26	1	.458	$3.0	1	49	.315
1924	Detroit (A)	0	16	.285	56	172	30	49	19	2	.419	$2.2	0	15	.301
1925	Detroit (A)	5	29	.324	74	213	39	69	15	0	.465	$2.5	2	28	.353
1926	Detroit (A)	12	80	.352	114	401	69	141	40	4	.561	$3.8	3	73	.367
1927	Detroit (A)	25	124	.341	149	549	101	187	39	4	.563	$7.0	9	114	.359
1928	Detroit (A)	10	70	.303	117	366	54	111	39	5	.519	$4.3	3	63	.317
1929	Detroit (A)	13	62	.329	120	289	42	95	26	4	.581	$2.5	6	62	.354
1930	Det.-Chi. (A)	5	37	.252	113	294	23	74	21	1	.381	$2.1	2	38	.277
1931	Chicago (A)	9	61	.275	112	324	27	89	10	2	.401	$2.0	3	56	.282
1932	Chicago (A)	14	56	.286	124	370	40	106	23	0	.462	$2.1	7	50	.295
1933	Boston (A)	0	6	.353	30	34	1	12	2	0	.412	$0.5	0	5	.344
	Career	97	625	.309	1,159	3,424	484	1,057	283	26	.492	$33.9	36	582	.325
	Average season	8	52	.309	97	285	40	88	24	2	.492	$2.8	3	49	.325
	Summit season	14	78	.316	123	402	58	127	30	3	.510	$3.8	5	71	.329

NELLIE FOX

		ADJUSTED REGULAR SEASON											ACTUAL RESULTS		
YEAR	TEAM	HR	RBI	BA	G	AB	R	H	2B	3B	SA	PAY	HR	RBI	BA
1947	Philadelphia (A)	0	0	.000	7	3	2	0	0	0	.000	$0.0	0	0	.000
1948	Philadelphia (A)	0	0	.154	3	13	0	2	0	0	.154	$0.0	0	0	.154
1949	Philadelphia (A)	0	24	.261	93	261	47	68	14	2	.330	$1.6	0	21	.255
1950	Chicago (A)	0	32	.251	135	475	48	119	23	6	.324	$3.4	0	30	.247
1951	Chicago (A)	7	63	.322	154	633	106	204	52	10	.469	$7.4	4	55	.313
1952	Chicago (A)	0	47	.316	158	674	93	213	51	11	.424	$9.3	0	39	.296
1953	Chicago (A)	5	80	.290	160	648	103	188	48	6	.406	$12.4	3	72	.285
1954	Chicago (A)	4	55	.329	162	659	130	217	41	6	.428	$15.0	2	47	.319
1955	Chicago (A)	8	67	.325	161	665	114	216	43	5	.441	$15.0	6	59	.311
1956	Chicago (A)	6	60	.309	162	683	126	211	32	8	.406	$15.9	4	52	.296
1957	Chicago (A)	9	73	.331	162	647	133	214	40	7	.456	$16.4	6	61	.317
1958	Chicago (A)	0	58	.313	162	651	98	204	33	6	.382	$12.3	0	49	.300
1959	Chicago (A)	2	81	.321	162	648	98	208	49	5	.421	$13.0	2	70	.306
1960	Chicago (A)	4	71	.305	158	637	102	194	38	9	.411	$9.7	2	59	.289
1961	Chicago (A)	2	55	.261	158	602	72	157	17	5	.316	$6.9	2	51	.251
1962	Chicago (A)	2	60	.279	157	621	87	173	41	6	.374	$7.0	2	54	.267
1963	Chicago (A)	3	52	.284	137	539	67	153	27	0	.351	$3.4	2	42	.260
1964	Houston (N)	0	34	.285	133	442	55	126	21	6	.360	$2.2	0	28	.265
1965	Houston (N)	0	1	.293	21	41	4	12	3	0	.366	$0.7	0	1	.268
	Career	52	913	.302	2,445	9,542	1,485	2,879	573	98	.399	$151.6	35	790	.288
	Average season	3	48	.302	129	502	78	152	30	5	.399	$8.0	2	42	.288
	Summit season	6	68	.326	160	650	116	212	45	7	.445	$13.4	4	58	.313

JIMMIE FOXX

		ADJUSTED REGULAR SEASON											ACTUAL RESULTS		
YEAR	TEAM	HR	RBI	BA	G	AB	R	H	2B	3B	SA	PAY	HR	RBI	BA
1925	Philadelphia (A)	0	0	.600	11	10	2	6	2	0	.800	$0.0	0	0	.667
1926	Philadelphia (A)	0	6	.294	28	34	9	10	6	0	.471	$0.0	0	5	.313
1927	Philadelphia (A)	8	22	.309	64	136	25	42	6	2	.559	$0.9	3	20	.323
1928	Philadelphia (A)	28	88	.314	125	424	95	133	26	3	.587	$5.3	13	79	.328
1929	Philadelphia (A)	50	123	.330	160	555	128	183	17	3	.641	$14.2	33	118	.354
1930	Philadelphia (A)	53	150	.305	161	591	122	180	25	4	.629	$15.5	30	120	.291
1931	Philadelphia (A)	52	134	.283	147	545	104	154	21	3	.618	$38.6	58	169	.364
1932	Philadelphia (A)	82	186	.354	162	615	166	218	22	3	.800	$38.6	58	169	.364
1933	Philadelphia (A)	79	196	.357	159	611	150	218	26	3	.797	$33.3	48	163	.356
1934	Philadelphia (A)	64	143	.322	159	571	132	184	21	2	.702	$31.4	44	130	.334
1935	Philadelphia (A)	57	130	.335	160	582	134	195	26	3	.684	$32.2	36	115	.346
1936	Boston (A)	61	148	.321	162	611	134	196	23	3	.668	$28.6	41	143	.338
1937	Boston (A)	52	138	.277	158	599	120	166	19	2	.576	$23.2	36	127	.285
1938	Boston (A)	73	196	.342	161	611	155	209	28	4	.759	$29.8	50	175	.349
1939	Boston (A)	54	116	.352	132	497	143	175	26	5	.751	$13.7	35	105	.360
1940	Boston (A)	51	134	.298	151	540	120	161	26	2	.637	$19.2	36	119	.297
1941	Boston (A)	34	122	.306	141	509	101	156	27	4	.576	$13.0	19	105	.300
1942	Bos. (A)-Chi. (N)	15	42	.241	105	320	55	77	12	0	.419	$3.8	8	33	.226
1944	Chicago (N)	0	2	.050	15	20	0	1	1	0	.100	$1.3	0	2	.050
1945	Philadelphia (N)	14	48	.278	94	237	38	66	10	1	.506	$1.6	7	38	.268
	Career	827	2,124	.317	2,455	8,618	1,933	2,730	370	47	.659	$324.6	534	1,922	.325
	Average season	41	106	.317	123	431	97	137	19	2	.659	$16.2	27	96	.325
	Summit season	70	167	.346	155	581	149	201	25	3	.761	$29.4	47	148	.353

BILL FREEHAN

				ADJUSTED REGULAR SEASON										ACTUAL RESULTS		
YEAR	TEAM	HR	RBI	BA	G	AB	R	H	2B	3B	SA	PAY	HR	RBI	BA
1961	Detroit (A)	0	4	.400	4	10	1	4	0	0	.400	$0.0	0	4	.400
1963	Detroit (A)	11	45	.267	100	300	46	80	16	2	.443	$2.4	9	36	.243
1964	Detroit (A)	24	97	.322	143	516	83	166	20	6	.523	$6.1	18	80	.300
1965	Detroit (A)	13	53	.258	130	431	55	111	19	0	.392	$5.1	10	43	.234
1966	Detroit (A)	15	56	.252	136	492	58	124	29	0	.402	$6.2	12	46	.234
1967	Detroit (A)	28	95	.313	154	514	85	161	29	1	.537	$9.2	20	74	.282
1968	Detroit (A)	37	117	.298	153	533	102	159	30	2	.570	$11.6	25	84	.263
1969	Detroit (A)	21	59	.284	143	489	73	139	23	3	.472	$8.7	16	49	.262
1970	Detroit (A)	19	59	.256	117	395	50	101	21	2	.463	$4.7	16	52	.241
1971	Detroit (A)	29	89	.298	148	516	71	154	33	4	.547	$6.8	21	71	.277
1972	Detroit (A)	15	76	.289	115	387	69	112	25	2	.481	$4.6	10	56	.262
1973	Detroit (A)	8	34	.245	110	380	38	93	14	1	.350	$2.3	6	29	.234
1974	Detroit (A)	27	71	.310	130	445	69	138	20	4	.555	$2.9	18	60	.297
1975	Detroit (A)	20	56	.256	122	434	50	111	20	3	.454	$2.5	14	47	.246
1976	Detroit (A)	9	33	.283	71	237	27	67	13	1	.460	$1.6	5	27	.270
	Career	276	944	.283	1,776	6,079	877	1,720	312	31	.481	$74.7	200	758	.262
	Average season	18	63	.283	118	405	58	115	21	2	.481	$5.0	13	51	.262
	Summit season	29	94	.309	146	505	82	156	26	3	.545	$7.3	20	74	.283

FRANKIE FRISCH

				ADJUSTED REGULAR SEASON										ACTUAL RESULTS		
YEAR	TEAM	HR	RBI	BA	G	AB	R	H	2B	3B	SA	PAY	HR	RBI	BA
1919	New York (N)	8	34	.229	62	218	30	50	3	1	.362	$2.5	2	24	.226
1920	New York (N)	18	91	.272	115	460	67	125	13	4	.435	$5.6	4	77	.280
1921	New York (N)	26	109	.317	162	654	132	207	39	6	.514	$15.1	8	100	.341
1922	New York (N)	17	54	.304	137	533	107	162	24	6	.467	$9.4	5	51	.327
1923	New York (N)	32	122	.330	160	679	128	224	34	4	.533	$20.0	12	111	.348
1924	New York (N)	24	76	.308	153	636	134	196	42	7	.509	$19.6	7	69	.328
1925	New York (N)	23	50	.305	128	535	93	163	24	3	.490	$11.4	11	48	.331
1926	New York (N)	17	50	.301	145	585	85	176	33	2	.451	$11.7	5	44	.314
1927	St. Louis (N)	28	86	.320	162	653	123	209	32	5	.513	$15.6	10	78	.337
1928	St. Louis (N)	24	95	.287	148	574	118	165	29	4	.477	$12.1	10	86	.300
1929	St. Louis (N)	13	75	.310	145	554	94	172	51	6	.495	$9.6	5	74	.334
1930	St. Louis (N)	19	110	.315	140	568	116	179	46	4	.511	$9.8	10	114	.346
1931	St. Louis (N)	13	91	.302	138	546	107	165	29	2	.434	$7.5	4	82	.311
1932	St. Louis (N)	7	64	.284	119	503	63	143	33	1	.396	$4.9	3	60	.292
1933	St. Louis (N)	13	78	.301	155	617	87	186	46	4	.452	$9.4	4	66	.303
1934	St. Louis (N)	8	81	.294	147	578	80	170	45	4	.427	$6.5	3	75	.305
1935	St. Louis (N)	3	60	.283	108	371	57	105	27	1	.385	$2.4	1	55	.294
1936	St. Louis (N)	3	27	.259	97	316	41	82	16	0	.339	$1.9	1	26	.274
1937	St. Louis (N)	0	4	.206	18	34	3	7	3	0	.294	$0.7	0	4	.219
	Career	296	1,357	.300	2,439	9,614	1,665	2,886	569	64	.465	$175.7	105	1,244	.316
	Average season	16	71	.300	128	506	88	152	30	3	.465	$9.2	6	65	.316
	Summit season	26	101	.318	155	638	127	203	39	5	.517	$16.0	9	94	.340

GARY GAETTI

		ADJUSTED REGULAR SEASON											ACTUAL RESULTS		
YEAR	TEAM	HR	RBI	BA	G	AB	R	H	2B	3B	SA	PAY	HR	RBI	BA
1981	Minnesota (A)	4	5	.211	13	38	7	8	0	0	.526	$0.0	2	3	.192
1982	Minnesota (A)	31	97	.236	145	508	68	120	28	3	.486	$5.3	25	84	.230
1983	Minnesota (A)	27	89	.252	157	584	92	147	33	2	.454	$8.6	21	78	.245
1984	Minnesota (A)	8	75	.270	162	588	64	159	39	3	.388	$7.7	5	65	.262
1985	Minnesota (A)	24	71	.257	160	560	80	144	35	0	.448	$9.3	20	63	.246
1986	Minnesota (A)	39	120	.300	157	596	101	179	37	1	.562	$14.3	34	108	.287
1987	Minnesota (A)	32	114	.262	154	584	99	153	40	2	.502	$9.7	31	109	.257
1988	Minnesota (A)	36	104	.318	133	468	78	149	31	2	.624	$7.2	28	88	.301
1989	Minnesota (A)	26	89	.265	130	498	75	132	12	4	.462	$7.2	19	75	.251
1990	Minnesota (A)	21	98	.239	154	577	70	138	30	5	.418	$6.8	16	85	.229
1991	California (A)	23	75	.258	152	586	66	151	24	1	.420	$4.9	18	66	.246
1992	California (A)	17	57	.237	130	456	49	108	14	2	.388	$2.9	12	48	.226
1993	Cal.-K.C. (A)	16	54	.248	102	331	43	82	21	1	.462	$2.4	14	50	.245
1994	Kansas City (A)	18	81	.286	127	461	76	132	21	4	.466	$2.6	12	57	.287
1995	Kansas City (A)	41	111	.263	154	578	87	152	31	0	.529	$4.6	35	96	.261
1996	St. Louis (N)	23	79	.272	141	522	70	142	28	4	.473	$3.5	23	80	.274
1997	St. Louis (N)	18	72	.253	148	502	65	127	24	1	.412	$3.5	17	69	.251
1998	St.L.-Chi. (N)	20	72	.283	127	431	62	122	34	1	.506	$3.2	19	70	.281
1999	Chicago (N)	9	45	.200	113	280	21	56	9	1	.336	$1.8	9	46	.204
2000	Boston (A)	0	1	.000	5	10	0	0	0	0	.000	$0.6	0	1	.000
	Career	433	1,509	.262	2,564	9,158	1,273	2,401	491	37	.466	$106.1	360	1,341	.255
	Average season	22	75	.262	128	458	64	120	25	2	.466	$5.3	18	67	.255
	Summit season	34	104	.284	145	531	85	151	35	1	.546	$7.8	29	94	.277

STEVE GARVEY

		ADJUSTED REGULAR SEASON											ACTUAL RESULTS		
YEAR	TEAM	HR	RBI	BA	G	AB	R	H	2B	3B	SA	PAY	HR	RBI	BA
1969	Los Angeles (N)	0	0	.333	3	3	0	1	0	0	.333	$0.0	0	0	.333
1970	Los Angeles (N)	1	7	.280	34	93	9	26	7	0	.387	$0.0	1	6	.269
1971	Los Angeles (N)	9	32	.244	81	225	34	55	16	1	.444	$1.6	7	26	.227
1972	Los Angeles (N)	14	41	.297	100	306	49	91	19	2	.510	$2.7	9	30	.269
1973	Los Angeles (N)	11	58	.318	114	349	43	111	22	3	.493	$3.7	8	50	.304
1974	Los Angeles (N)	31	132	.327	156	642	113	210	40	3	.544	$12.1	21	111	.312
1975	Los Angeles (N)	27	111	.334	160	659	99	220	47	5	.543	$14.7	18	95	.319
1976	Los Angeles (N)	24	98	.334	162	631	104	211	48	3	.534	$15.2	13	80	.317
1977	Los Angeles (N)	39	127	.303	162	646	101	196	27	2	.533	$16.0	33	115	.297
1978	Los Angeles (N)	31	134	.330	162	639	105	211	42	7	.563	$16.0	21	113	.316
1979	Los Angeles (N)	34	121	.319	162	648	101	207	34	1	.532	$16.0	28	110	.315
1980	Los Angeles (N)	35	122	.309	162	654	89	202	29	1	.517	$13.1	26	106	.304
1981	Los Angeles (N)	24	115	.298	162	635	114	189	40	1	.477	$13.1	10	64	.283
1982	Los Angeles (N)	21	99	.290	162	625	76	181	41	1	.459	$9.3	16	86	.282
1983	San Diego (N)	18	67	.302	99	384	86	116	24	0	.505	$4.7	14	59	.294
1984	San Diego (N)	12	100	.293	161	617	83	181	35	2	.415	$6.9	8	86	.284
1985	San Diego (N)	21	92	.295	162	654	91	193	40	5	.468	$9.0	17	81	.281
1986	San Diego (N)	24	90	.266	155	557	65	148	24	0	.438	$4.5	21	81	.255
1987	San Diego (N)	1	9	.211	27	76	5	16	2	0	.276	$1.3	1	9	.211
	Career	377	1,555	.306	2,386	9,043	1,367	2,765	537	37	.498	$159.9	272	1,308	.294
	Average season	20	82	.306	126	476	72	146	28	2	.498	$8.4	14	69	.294
	Summit season	29	119	.329	160	644	104	212	42	4	.542	$14.8	20	102	.316

LOU GEHRIG

		ADJUSTED REGULAR SEASON											ACTUAL RESULTS		
YEAR	TEAM	HR	RBI	BA	G	AB	R	H	2B	3B	SA	PAY	HR	RBI	BA
1923	New York (A)	3	10	.393	14	28	7	11	4	0	.857	$0.1	1	9	.423
1924	New York (A)	0	6	.462	11	13	2	6	2	0	.615	$0.0	0	5	.500
1925	New York (A)	35	69	.273	131	454	74	124	18	3	.557	$4.5	20	68	.295
1926	New York (A)	42	124	.299	162	598	150	179	42	7	.604	$15.0	16	112	.313
1927	New York (A)	83	191	.354	162	610	162	216	32	4	.828	$26.5	47	175	.373
1928	New York (A)	51	157	.359	162	591	154	212	38	4	.695	$31.2	27	142	.374
1929	New York (A)	53	128	.278	162	582	129	162	23	3	.601	$31.9	35	126	.300
1930	New York (A)	60	168	.345	162	611	138	211	33	5	.710	$33.0	41	174	.379
1931	New York (A)	76	204	.331	162	647	180	214	19	4	.725	$48.3	46	184	.341
1932	New York (A)	54	164	.339	162	619	150	210	32	3	.662	$35.6	34	151	.349
1933	New York (A)	61	167	.334	162	632	166	211	33	4	.688	$36.6	32	139	.334
1934	New York (A)	72	181	.350	162	609	140	213	29	2	.759	$36.0	49	165	.363
1935	New York (A)	50	135	.318	162	582	142	185	22	4	.627	$26.4	30	119	.329
1936	New York (A)	70	157	.336	162	605	173	203	26	3	.736	$32.6	49	152	.354
1937	New York (A)	56	170	.342	162	587	147	201	31	3	.692	$26.3	37	159	.351
1938	New York (A)	44	121	.290	162	594	122	172	28	2	.566	$20.6	29	114	.295
1939	New York (A)	0	1	.125	9	32	2	4	0	0	.125	$2.2	0	1	.143
	Career	810	2,153	.326	2,271	8,394	2,038	2,734	412	51	.676	$406.8	493	1,995	.340
	Average season	48	127	.326	134	494	120	161	24	3	.676	$23.9	29	117	.340
	Summit season	72	180	.343	162	616	159	211	28	4	.752	$35.3	46	170	.362

CHARLIE GEHRINGER

		ADJUSTED REGULAR SEASON											ACTUAL RESULTS		
YEAR	TEAM	HR	RBI	BA	G	AB	R	H	2B	3B	SA	PAY	HR	RBI	BA
1924	Detroit (A)	0	1	.462	5	13	2	6	0	0	.462	$0.0	0	1	.462
1925	Detroit (A)	0	0	.167	8	18	3	3	0	0	.167	$0.0	0	0	.167
1926	Detroit (A)	6	52	.266	127	474	68	126	39	13	.441	$3.7	1	48	.277
1927	Detroit (A)	15	66	.300	138	527	119	158	39	6	.482	$6.3	4	61	.317
1928	Detroit (A)	19	81	.306	162	634	119	194	40	9	.487	$12.4	6	74	.320
1929	Detroit (A)	29	107	.315	162	663	133	209	50	8	.546	$19.8	13	106	.339
1930	Detroit (A)	29	94	.301	162	642	139	193	46	6	.526	$25.5	16	98	.330
1931	Detroit (A)	12	58	.301	106	402	74	121	28	2	.470	$9.0	4	53	.311
1932	Detroit (A)	36	118	.290	161	655	124	190	41	4	.530	$22.5	19	107	.298
1933	Detroit (A)	29	123	.325	162	656	121	213	45	3	.535	$22.5	12	105	.325
1934	Detroit (A)	24	138	.343	162	632	146	217	55	4	.557	$23.6	11	127	.356
1935	Detroit (A)	36	120	.318	160	651	137	207	31	3	.541	$24.7	19	108	.330
1936	Detroit (A)	31	120	.337	162	674	150	227	63	6	.586	$25.7	15	116	.354
1937	Detroit (A)	25	104	.360	151	591	144	213	40	1	.558	$20.0	14	96	.371
1938	Detroit (A)	32	115	.301	159	594	143	179	31	2	.522	$20.4	20	107	.306
1939	Detroit (A)	27	93	.317	123	423	93	134	28	3	.589	$6.8	16	86	.325
1940	Detroit (A)	17	91	.315	145	537	121	169	37	2	.486	$12.5	10	81	.313
1941	Detroit (A)	7	53	.225	133	457	76	103	28	2	.341	$6.3	3	46	.220
1942	Detroit (A)	2	9	.277	47	47	8	13	0	0	.404	$1.3	1	7	.267
	Career	376	1,543	.309	2,435	9,290	1,920	2,875	641	74	.516	$263.0	184	1,427	.320
	Average season	20	81	.309	128	489	101	151	34	4	.516	$13.8	10	75	.320
	Summit season	27	112	.335	152	597	133	200	47	4	.563	$19.2	14	106	.350

JASON GIAMBI

		ADJUSTED REGULAR SEASON											ACTUAL RESULTS		
YEAR	TEAM	HR	RBI	BA	G	AB	R	H	2B	3B	SA	PAY	HR	RBI	BA
1995	Oakland (A)	7	29	.256	61	199	31	51	8	0	.402	$2.4	6	25	.256
1996	Oakland (A)	20	78	.289	140	536	83	155	41	1	.481	$6.2	20	79	.291
1997	Oakland (A)	21	84	.295	142	519	69	153	42	2	.505	$7.3	20	81	.293
1998	Oakland (A)	28	114	.299	153	562	95	168	28	0	.498	$11.7	27	110	.295
1999	Oakland (A)	32	120	.313	158	575	112	180	36	1	.546	$15.2	33	123	.315
2000	Oakland (A)	41	134	.331	153	513	105	170	29	1	.632	$12.4	43	137	.333
2001	Oakland (A)	37	124	.350	154	520	113	182	46	2	.660	$15.9	38	120	.342
	Career	186	683	.309	961	3,424	608	1,059	230	7	.544	$71.1	187	675	.308
	Average season	27	98	.309	137	489	87	151	33	1	.544	$10.2	27	96	.308
	Summit season	32	115	.318	152	538	99	171	36	1	.567	$12.5	32	114	.315

KIRK GIBSON

		ADJUSTED REGULAR SEASON											ACTUAL RESULTS		
YEAR	TEAM	HR	RBI	BA	G	AB	R	H	2B	3B	SA	PAY	HR	RBI	BA
1979	Detroit (A)	1	4	.237	12	38	3	9	4	0	.421	$0.0	1	4	.237
1980	Detroit (A)	11	18	.269	51	175	27	47	2	1	.480	$0.9	9	16	.263
1981	Detroit (A)	21	73	.344	123	430	74	148	19	4	.553	$4.5	9	40	.328
1982	Detroit (A)	11	40	.286	69	266	39	76	18	2	.492	$3.1	8	35	.278
1983	Detroit (A)	20	58	.234	128	401	68	94	14	7	.454	$5.3	15	51	.227
1984	Detroit (A)	36	106	.292	149	531	107	155	26	8	.574	$11.3	27	91	.282
1985	Detroit (A)	35	111	.301	155	585	110	176	41	4	.564	$14.3	29	97	.287
1986	Detroit (A)	32	96	.279	119	441	94	123	12	2	.533	$7.4	28	86	.268
1987	Detroit (A)	25	83	.283	128	487	99	138	28	3	.507	$9.5	24	79	.277
1988	Los Angeles (N)	33	90	.306	150	542	126	166	30	1	.548	$12.2	25	76	.290
1989	Los Angeles (N)	12	34	.226	72	257	42	58	9	2	.416	$2.6	9	28	.213
1990	Los Angeles (N)	11	44	.273	89	315	68	86	22	0	.448	$2.8	8	38	.260
1991	Kansas City (A)	21	63	.249	132	462	92	115	18	5	.446	$3.9	16	55	.236
1992	Pittsburgh (N)	2	6	.214	16	56	7	12	0	0	.321	$0.9	2	5	.196
1993	Detroit (A)	16	66	.266	116	403	66	107	19	6	.462	$2.2	13	62	.261
1994	Detroit (A)	34	103	.275	138	465	101	128	23	2	.553	$4.2	23	72	.276
1995	Detroit (A)	11	40	.262	79	256	43	67	14	2	.461	$1.7	9	35	.260
	Career	332	1,035	.279	1,726	6,110	1,166	1,705	299	49	.507	$86.8	255	870	.268
	Average season	20	61	.279	102	359	69	100	18	3	.507	$5.1	15	51	.268
	Summit season	32	97	.303	143	511	104	155	28	4	.562	$9.3	23	75	.290

JUAN GONZALEZ

		ADJUSTED REGULAR SEASON											ACTUAL RESULTS		
YEAR	TEAM	HR	RBI	BA	G	AB	R	H	2B	3B	SA	PAY	HR	RBI	BA
1989	Texas (A)	1	8	.167	24	60	7	10	4	0	.283	$0.1	1	7	.150
1990	Texas (A)	5	14	.300	25	90	13	27	8	1	.578	$0.4	4	12	.289
1991	Texas (A)	34	116	.277	142	545	89	151	36	1	.534	$6.4	27	102	.264
1992	Texas (A)	55	130	.274	155	584	92	160	23	2	.603	$8.8	43	109	.260
1993	Texas (A)	52	127	.315	140	536	113	169	33	1	.672	$11.7	46	118	.310
1994	Texas (A)	29	122	.274	152	599	82	164	26	5	.479	$14.7	19	85	.275

(Juan Gonzalez, continued)

YEAR	TEAM	ADJUSTED REGULAR SEASON											ACTUAL RESULTS		
		HR	RBI	BA	G	AB	R	H	2B	3B	SA	PAY	HR	RBI	BA
1995	Texas (A)	32	94	.299	101	395	65	118	22	2	.608	$8.7	27	82	.295
1996	Texas (A)	47	142	.313	133	537	88	168	34	2	.646	$12.1	47	144	.314
1997	Texas (A)	44	136	.298	133	533	90	159	23	3	.600	$11.9	42	131	.296
1998	Texas (A)	47	163	.322	154	606	114	195	50	2	.644	$15.7	45	157	.318
1999	Texas (A)	38	125	.324	144	562	111	182	36	1	.594	$12.4	39	128	.326
2000	Detroit (A)	21	65	.286	115	461	67	132	29	2	.495	$7.1	22	67	.289
2001	Cleveland (A)	34	145	.331	140	532	100	176	33	1	.588	$9.3	35	140	.325
	Career	439	1,387	.300	1,558	6,040	1,031	1,811	357	23	.585	$119.3	397	1,282	.297
	Average season	34	107	.300	120	465	79	139	27	2	.585	$9.2	31	99	.297
	Summit season	44	140	.321	142	555	105	178	37	1	.629	$12.2	42	137	.319

JOE GORDON

YEAR	TEAM	ADJUSTED REGULAR SEASON											ACTUAL RESULTS		
		HR	RBI	BA	G	AB	R	H	2B	3B	SA	PAY	HR	RBI	BA
1938	New York (A)	37	103	.250	131	472	88	118	21	3	.542	$11.2	25	97	.255
1939	New York (A)	43	122	.278	161	605	101	168	28	2	.544	$15.5	28	111	.284
1940	New York (A)	46	116	.283	162	644	126	182	31	4	.557	$19.3	30	103	.281
1941	New York (A)	40	100	.283	162	611	120	173	24	3	.529	$19.0	24	87	.276
1942	New York (A)	37	132	.342	155	567	112	194	30	2	.598	$18.7	18	103	.322
1943	New York (A)	37	91	.264	159	568	108	150	26	2	.512	$18.7	17	69	.249
1946	New York (A)	19	61	.220	118	396	45	87	14	0	.399	$5.8	11	47	.210
1947	Cleveland (A)	43	108	.281	160	580	104	163	28	3	.562	$9.4	29	93	.272
1948	Cleveland (A)	46	140	.286	150	573	108	164	21	2	.571	$9.6	32	124	.280
1949	Cleveland (A)	29	94	.258	156	570	83	147	20	2	.453	$7.3	20	84	.251
1950	Cleveland (A)	23	60	.240	124	383	63	92	13	1	.460	$3.9	19	57	.236
	Career	400	1,127	.274	1,638	5,969	1,058	1,638	256	24	.526	$138.4	253	975	.268
	Average season	36	102	.274	149	543	96	149	23	2	.526	$12.6	23	89	.268
	Summit season	43	124	.293	158	594	110	174	28	3	.567	$14.5	27	107	.287

GOOSE GOSLIN

YEAR	TEAM	ADJUSTED REGULAR SEASON											ACTUAL RESULTS		
		HR	RBI	BA	G	AB	R	H	2B	3B	SA	PAY	HR	RBI	BA
1921	Washington (A)	3	7	.241	15	54	9	13	1	0	.426	$0.1	1	6	.260
1922	Washington (A)	9	57	.303	106	376	47	114	27	4	.468	$3.2	3	53	.324
1923	Washington (A)	27	108	.283	157	628	93	178	35	8	.494	$8.9	9	99	.300
1924	Washington (A)	33	140	.324	160	602	109	195	30	6	.558	$14.4	12	129	.344
1925	Washington (A)	39	118	.309	160	641	121	198	32	8	.566	$18.9	18	113	.334
1926	Washington (A)	41	122	.339	157	607	119	206	21	5	.593	$19.3	17	108	.354
1927	Washington (A)	34	129	.316	153	601	103	190	36	5	.562	$18.8	13	120	.334
1928	Washington (A)	35	112	.363	141	476	88	173	31	3	.662	$12.0	17	102	.379
1929	Washington (A)	31	93	.267	154	587	84	157	23	2	.472	$12.3	18	91	.288
1930	Wash.-St.L. (A)	52	133	.281	156	616	111	173	27	4	.591	$16.2	37	138	.308
1931	St. Louis (A)	47	116	.318	159	622	126	198	31	4	.608	$16.8	24	105	.328

(Goose Goslin, continued)

ADJUSTED REGULAR SEASON **ACTUAL RESULTS**

YEAR	TEAM	HR	RBI	BA	G	AB	R	H	2B	3B	SA	PAY	HR	RBI	BA
1932	St. Louis (A)	32	114	.290	158	603	96	175	25	3	.501	$13.5	17	104	.299
1933	Washington (A)	26	76	.297	140	582	115	173	40	5	.517	$9.8	10	64	.297
1934	Detroit (A)	26	109	.294	159	647	116	190	39	4	.487	$13.9	13	100	.305
1935	Detroit (A)	20	121	.281	157	630	98	177	38	3	.446	$13.2	9	109	.292
1936	Detroit (A)	40	130	.299	155	603	127	180	28	3	.554	$13.3	24	125	.315
1937	Detroit (A)	7	38	.232	83	190	32	44	10	1	.405	$2.4	4	35	.238
1938	Washington (A)	3	9	.161	41	62	7	10	3	0	.355	$1.4	2	8	.158
	Career	505	1,732	.301	2,411	9,127	1,601	2,744	477	68	.534	$208.4	248	1,609	.316
	Average season	28	96	.301	134	507	89	152	27	4	.534	$11.6	14	89	.316
	Summit season	38	124	.330	154	582	109	192	30	5	.595	$16.3	17	113	.346

HANK GREENBERG

ADJUSTED REGULAR SEASON **ACTUAL RESULTS**

YEAR	TEAM	HR	RBI	BA	G	AB	R	H	2B	3B	SA	PAY	HR	RBI	BA
1930	Detroit (A)	0	0	.000	1	1	0	0	0	0	.000	$0.0	0	0	.000
1933	Detroit (A)	25	102	.299	122	468	69	140	31	2	.534	$5.0	12	87	.301
1934	Detroit (A)	46	152	.327	161	624	129	204	56	3	.647	$14.9	26	139	.339
1935	Detroit (A)	62	189	.317	162	660	134	209	40	6	.677	$26.1	36	170	.328
1936	Detroit (A)	2	17	.320	13	50	11	16	8	1	.640	$4.7	1	16	.348
1937	Detroit (A)	63	198	.329	161	621	148	204	42	5	.717	$27.2	40	183	.337
1938	Detroit (A)	76	157	.310	162	581	155	180	17	1	.735	$26.5	58	146	.315
1939	Detroit (A)	50	121	.305	144	522	121	159	36	3	.672	$15.3	33	112	.312
1940	Detroit (A)	60	170	.343	155	600	146	206	46	3	.730	$28.8	41	150	.340
1941	Detroit (A)	3	14	.282	20	71	14	20	5	1	.507	$4.1	2	12	.269
1945	Detroit (A)	25	75	.320	82	284	59	91	18	1	.655	$3.5	13	60	.311
1946	Detroit (A)	68	163	.292	148	545	116	159	24	2	.717	$9.5	44	127	.277
1947	Pittsburgh (N)	35	87	.256	130	418	83	107	13	1	.543	$3.6	25	74	.249
	Career	515	1,445	.311	1,461	5,445	1,185	1,695	336	29	.667	$169.2	331	1,276	.313
	Average season	40	111	.311	112	419	91	130	26	2	.667	$13.0	25	98	.313
	Summit season	66	175	.319	158	601	140	192	34	3	.715	$23.6	44	155	.320

BOBBY GRICH

ADJUSTED REGULAR SEASON **ACTUAL RESULTS**

YEAR	TEAM	HR	RBI	BA	G	AB	R	H	2B	3B	SA	PAY	HR	RBI	BA
1970	Baltimore (A)	0	9	.221	30	95	12	21	2	4	.326	$0.4	0	8	.211
1971	Baltimore (A)	1	7	.333	7	30	9	10	0	0	.433	$0.1	1	6	.300
1972	Baltimore (A)	19	69	.308	140	484	91	149	30	3	.500	$5.1	12	50	.278
1973	Baltimore (A)	16	58	.263	162	581	96	153	38	7	.435	$7.6	12	50	.251
1974	Baltimore (A)	28	98	.275	160	582	110	160	36	5	.498	$12.2	19	82	.263
1975	Baltimore (A)	20	68	.272	153	534	96	145	32	3	.455	$12.1	13	57	.260
1976	Baltimore (A)	22	66	.280	144	518	114	145	38	3	.492	$11.9	13	54	.266
1977	California (A)	8	25	.249	52	181	27	45	6	0	.414	$4.5	7	23	.243
1978	California (A)	10	50	.261	144	487	81	127	20	2	.372	$5.7	6	42	.251
1979	California (A)	37	111	.298	153	534	86	159	32	4	.581	$7.3	30	101	.294

(Bobby Grich, continued)

		ADJUSTED REGULAR SEASON												ACTUAL RESULTS		
YEAR	TEAM	HR	RBI	BA	G	AB	R	H	2B	3B	SA	PAY	HR	RBI	BA
1980	California (A)	20	72	.275	152	505	70	139	25	2	.451	$5.7	14	62	.271
1981	California (A)	45	110	.319	147	517	101	165	21	2	.629	$7.0	22	61	.304
1982	California (A)	25	75	.269	145	506	85	136	32	4	.496	$6.8	19	65	.261
1983	California (A)	20	71	.302	120	387	74	117	18	0	.504	$3.9	16	62	.292
1984	California (A)	23	67	.264	116	363	70	96	16	1	.504	$3.7	18	58	.256
1985	California (A)	16	60	.253	144	479	84	121	21	2	.405	$4.3	13	53	.242
1986	California (A)	11	33	.281	98	313	47	88	20	0	.450	$2.0	9	30	.268
	Career	321	1,049	.278	2,067	7,096	1,253	1,976	387	42	.481	$100.3	224	864	.266
	Average season	19	62	.278	122	417	74	116	23	2	.481	$5.9	13	51	.266
	Summit season	30	92	.299	144	501	92	150	27	3	.545	$7.1	20	71	.284

KEN GRIFFEY JR.

		ADJUSTED REGULAR SEASON												ACTUAL RESULTS		
YEAR	TEAM	HR	RBI	BA	G	AB	R	H	2B	3B	SA	PAY	HR	RBI	BA
1989	Seattle (A)	22	72	.279	127	455	72	127	25	0	.479	$7.4	16	61	.264
1990	Seattle (A)	30	92	.313	155	597	105	187	31	6	.536	$12.4	22	80	.300
1991	Seattle (A)	28	114	.343	154	548	87	188	45	1	.582	$12.0	22	100	.327
1992	Seattle (A)	37	123	.324	142	565	99	183	40	4	.605	$12.3	27	103	.308
1993	Seattle (A)	51	117	.314	156	582	121	183	38	3	.653	$18.9	45	109	.309
1994	Seattle (A)	60	132	.323	161	628	138	203	34	5	.680	$25.5	40	90	.323
1995	Seattle (A)	20	48	.260	80	289	59	75	8	0	.495	$7.7	17	42	.258
1996	Seattle (A)	49	140	.302	141	549	125	166	27	2	.627	$15.5	49	140	.303
1997	Seattle (A)	58	153	.308	157	608	130	187	33	3	.658	$19.9	56	147	.304
1998	Seattle (A)	58	152	.287	162	637	125	183	32	3	.620	$22.6	56	146	.284
1999	Seattle (A)	46	131	.284	160	606	120	172	26	3	.564	$22.7	48	134	.285
2000	Cincinnati (N)	38	113	.269	144	516	96	139	22	3	.545	$12.5	40	118	.271
2001	Cincinnati (N)	21	67	.291	111	364	59	106	20	2	.530	$4.7	22	65	.286
	Career	518	1,454	.302	1,850	6,944	1,336	2,099	381	35	.591	$194.1	460	1,335	.296
	Average season	40	112	.302	142	534	103	161	29	3	.591	$14.9	35	103	.296
	Summit season	51	133	.314	151	586	123	184	34	3	.643	$18.4	43	118	.309

DICK GROAT

		ADJUSTED REGULAR SEASON												ACTUAL RESULTS		
YEAR	TEAM	HR	RBI	BA	G	AB	R	H	2B	3B	SA	PAY	HR	RBI	BA
1952	Pittsburgh (N)	3	35	.303	99	400	46	121	12	1	.360	$4.0	1	29	.284
1955	Pittsburgh (N)	5	58	.277	159	549	52	152	40	1	.381	$5.7	4	51	.267
1956	Pittsburgh (N)	0	42	.284	147	538	45	153	29	2	.346	$5.4	0	37	.273
1957	Pittsburgh (N)	9	65	.330	131	525	70	173	42	4	.476	$6.1	7	54	.315
1958	Pittsburgh (N)	4	79	.312	159	615	81	192	52	7	.439	$8.6	3	66	.300
1959	Pittsburgh (N)	7	60	.288	154	621	87	179	32	7	.396	$7.1	5	51	.275
1960	Pittsburgh (N)	3	59	.343	144	598	101	205	38	3	.431	$9.1	2	50	.325
1961	Pittsburgh (N)	7	63	.287	156	628	81	180	35	5	.392	$9.3	6	55	.275
1962	Pittsburgh (N)	2	68	.306	162	682	84	209	48	2	.391	$7.4	2	61	.294

(Dick Groat, continued)

		ADJUSTED REGULAR SEASON											ACTUAL RESULTS		
YEAR	TEAM	HR	RBI	BA	G	AB	R	H	2B	3B	SA	PAY	HR	RBI	BA
1963	St. Louis (N)	8	91	.349	158	631	105	220	63	9	.515	$9.7	6	73	.319
1964	St. Louis (N)	1	85	.314	161	636	85	200	52	6	.420	$9.4	1	70	.292
1965	St. Louis (N)	0	64	.278	153	587	67	163	40	5	.363	$6.8	0	52	.254
1966	Philadelphia (N)	3	65	.281	155	584	71	164	32	3	.361	$4.6	2	53	.260
1967	Phi.-S.F. (N)	0	6	.177	44	96	9	17	2	2	.240	$1.1	0	5	.156
	Career	52	840	.303	1,982	7,690	984	2,328	517	57	.405	$94.3	39	707	.286
	Average season	4	60	.303	142	549	70	166	37	4	.405	$6.7	3	51	.286
	Summit season	5	76	.329	151	601	88	198	49	6	.456	$8.6	4	63	.310

TONY GWYNN

		ADJUSTED REGULAR SEASON											ACTUAL RESULTS		
YEAR	TEAM	HR	RBI	BA	G	AB	R	H	2B	3B	SA	PAY	HR	RBI	BA
1982	San Diego (N)	1	20	.300	54	190	38	57	16	2	.421	$2.1	1	17	.289
1983	San Diego (N)	1	42	.320	85	300	38	96	18	3	.410	$3.1	1	37	.309
1984	San Diego (N)	9	82	.365	158	606	102	221	31	10	.493	$8.8	5	71	.351
1985	San Diego (N)	9	52	.331	154	622	102	206	37	4	.447	$9.3	6	46	.317
1986	San Diego (N)	17	66	.343	160	642	119	220	39	7	.505	$14.3	14	59	.329
1987	San Diego (N)	7	56	.379	157	589	125	223	41	12	.525	$14.5	7	54	.370
1988	San Diego (N)	11	84	.331	134	525	76	174	29	5	.469	$11.2	7	70	.313
1989	San Diego (N)	7	73	.356	158	604	97	215	40	7	.480	$11.8	4	62	.336
1990	San Diego (N)	6	83	.323	141	573	91	185	40	11	.462	$9.5	4	72	.309
1991	San Diego (N)	6	71	.334	134	530	79	177	36	12	.481	$7.2	4	62	.317
1992	San Diego (N)	10	49	.335	128	520	92	174	34	3	.469	$4.8	6	41	.317
1993	San Diego (N)	9	63	.364	122	489	75	178	46	3	.526	$3.9	7	59	.358
1994	San Diego (N)	18	89	.394	152	579	110	228	48	1	.573	$7.3	12	64	.394
1995	San Diego (N)	11	104	.372	152	602	94	224	39	1	.495	$7.4	9	90	.368
1996	San Diego (N)	3	50	.353	116	451	66	159	27	2	.441	$3.4	3	50	.353
1997	San Diego (N)	18	124	.375	149	592	101	222	50	2	.557	$8.8	17	119	.372
1998	San Diego (N)	17	71	.325	127	461	67	150	35	0	.512	$3.6	16	69	.321
1999	San Diego (N)	10	61	.336	111	411	58	138	26	0	.472	$2.6	10	62	.338
2000	San Diego (N)	1	16	.323	36	127	16	41	11	0	.433	$1.5	1	17	.323
2001	San Diego (N)	1	18	.333	71	102	5	34	8	1	.461	$0.8	1	17	.324
	Career	172	1,274	.349	2,499	9,515	1,551	3,322	651	86	.490	$135.9	135	1,138	.338
	Average season	9	64	.349	125	476	78	166	33	4	.490	$6.8	7	57	.338
	Summit season	13	87	.377	146	570	101	215	45	4	.539	$8.4	10	77	.372

CHICK HAFEY

		ADJUSTED REGULAR SEASON											ACTUAL RESULTS		
YEAR	TEAM	HR	RBI	BA	G	AB	R	H	2B	3B	SA	PAY	HR	RBI	BA
1924	St. Louis (N)	5	24	.242	25	95	11	23	5	1	.474	$1.0	2	22	.253
1925	St. Louis (N)	11	59	.279	98	377	37	105	26	1	.440	$3.4	5	57	.302
1926	St. Louis (N)	10	42	.261	81	234	33	61	17	1	.470	$3.0	4	38	.271
1927	St. Louis (N)	34	69	.311	109	366	68	114	17	1	.642	$4.9	18	63	.329
1928	St. Louis (N)	47	122	.322	145	546	111	176	34	2	.650	$9.5	27	111	.337

(Chick Hafey, continued)

		ADJUSTED REGULAR SEASON											ACTUAL RESULTS		
YEAR	TEAM	HR	RBI	BA	G	AB	R	H	2B	3B	SA	PAY	HR	RBI	BA
1929	St. Louis (N)	46	127	.314	141	544	103	171	37	3	.647	$11.8	29	125	.338
1930	St. Louis (N)	39	103	.306	126	468	104	143	31	4	.639	$11.6	26	107	.336
1931	St. Louis (N)	33	105	.339	128	472	104	160	28	3	.621	$11.9	16	95	.349
1932	Cincinnati (N)	5	39	.336	87	265	37	89	25	1	.494	$4.3	2	36	.344
1933	Cincinnati (N)	19	73	.302	152	600	91	181	42	3	.477	$9.6	7	62	.303
1934	Cincinnati (N)	32	74	.283	149	569	82	161	26	2	.504	$9.0	18	67	.293
1935	Cincinnati (N)	2	10	.333	16	63	11	21	7	1	.571	$1.1	1	9	.339
1937	Cincinnati (N)	15	44	.253	93	269	42	68	10	3	.480	$1.9	9	41	.261
	Career	298	891	.303	1,350	4,868	834	1,473	305	26	.560	$83.0	164	833	.317
	Average season	23	69	.303	104	374	64	113	23	2	.560	$6.4	13	64	.317
	Summit season	40	105	.319	130	479	98	153	29	3	.643	$9.9	23	100	.338

BILLY HAMILTON

		ADJUSTED REGULAR SEASON											ACTUAL RESULTS		
YEAR	TEAM	HR	RBI	BA	G	AB	R	H	2B	3B	SA	PAY	HR	RBI	BA
1888	Kansas City (AA)	0	14	.297	43	158	26	47	19	5	.481	$1.4	0	11	.264
1889	Kansas City (AA)	17	76	.309	160	624	144	193	34	8	.471	$11.6	3	77	.301
1890	Philadelphia (N)	17	50	.336	150	605	137	203	30	6	.489	$12.4	2	49	.325
1891	Philadelphia (N)	13	62	.361	156	618	147	223	55	4	.526	$18.5	2	60	.340
1892	Philadelphia (N)	17	54	.363	145	578	136	210	41	3	.533	$15.3	3	53	.330
1893	Philadelphia (N)	20	43	.367	100	433	107	159	31	3	.591	$9.1	5	44	.380
1894	Philadelphia (N)	19	77	.353	162	683	171	241	43	6	.517	$32.7	4	87	.404
1895	Philadelphia (N)	27	70	.354	150	630	159	223	27	2	.532	$23.1	7	74	.389
1896	Boston (N)	19	57	.340	161	644	159	219	47	5	.517	$27.9	3	55	.366
1897	Boston (N)	18	62	.316	152	607	157	192	27	2	.456	$23.8	3	61	.343
1898	Boston (N)	19	53	.367	117	444	117	163	24	2	.559	$7.2	3	50	.369
1899	Boston (N)	7	33	.295	89	315	63	93	14	0	.406	$3.5	1	33	.310
1900	Boston (N)	9	51	.322	155	593	112	191	49	3	.460	$9.9	1	47	.333
1901	Boston (N)	14	44	.285	118	403	83	115	12	1	.424	$3.6	3	38	.287
	Career	216	746	.337	1,858	7,335	1,718	2,472	453	50	.501	$200.0	40	739	.344
	Average season	15	53	.337	133	524	123	177	32	4	.501	$14.3	3	53	.344
	Summit season	19	56	.362	134	541	133	196	36	3	.545	$14.6	4	56	.359

MIKE HARGROVE

		ADJUSTED REGULAR SEASON											ACTUAL RESULTS		
YEAR	TEAM	HR	RBI	BA	G	AB	R	H	2B	3B	SA	PAY	HR	RBI	BA
1974	Texas (A)	7	79	.337	132	418	68	141	30	6	.488	$7.1	4	66	.323
1975	Texas (A)	17	72	.316	145	519	96	164	28	2	.476	$9.5	11	62	.303
1976	Texas (A)	13	71	.301	151	541	98	163	40	1	.451	$11.9	7	58	.287
1977	Texas (A)	22	76	.310	153	525	108	163	32	3	.509	$12.1	18	69	.305
1978	Texas (A)	11	47	.261	146	494	75	129	29	1	.391	$7.0	7	40	.251
1979	S.D. (N)-Cle. (A)	13	71	.294	153	466	83	137	31	3	.457	$7.0	10	64	.289
1980	Cleveland (A)	17	99	.309	162	596	100	184	26	2	.445	$12.7	11	85	.304
1981	Cleveland (A)	6	94	.333	148	507	83	169	49	0	.465	$6.9	2	49	.317

(Mike Hargrove, continued)

		ADJUSTED REGULAR SEASON											ACTUAL RESULTS		
YEAR	TEAM	HR	RBI	BA	G	AB	R	H	2B	3B	SA	PAY	HR	RBI	BA
1982	Cleveland (A)	6	75	.279	160	591	77	165	35	1	.372	$9.5	4	65	.271
1983	Cleveland (A)	5	65	.294	134	469	65	138	29	4	.405	$4.7	3	57	.286
1984	Cleveland (A)	3	51	.275	132	349	51	96	19	2	.367	$2.6	2	44	.267
1985	Cleveland (A)	1	31	.299	107	284	35	85	19	1	.384	$1.7	1	27	.285
	Career	121	831	.301	1,723	5,759	939	1,734	367	26	.437	$92.7	80	686	.290
	Average season	10	69	.301	144	480	78	145	31	2	.437	$7.7	7	57	.290
	Summit season	14	84	.320	148	513	91	164	33	3	.478	$9.7	9	66	.309

GABBY HARTNETT

		ADJUSTED REGULAR SEASON											ACTUAL RESULTS		
YEAR	TEAM	HR	RBI	BA	G	AB	R	H	2B	3B	SA	PAY	HR	RBI	BA
1922	Chicago (N)	0	4	.176	32	74	4	13	6	0	.257	$0.0	0	4	.194
1923	Chicago (N)	15	42	.252	89	242	30	61	9	1	.483	$1.8	8	39	.268
1924	Chicago (N)	31	74	.282	117	373	62	105	11	2	.571	$4.5	16	67	.299
1925	Chicago (N)	37	69	.266	123	418	63	111	18	1	.579	$5.1	24	67	.289
1926	Chicago (N)	18	45	.264	97	296	39	78	19	1	.517	$4.3	8	41	.275
1927	Chicago (N)	24	88	.278	134	474	61	132	28	2	.498	$7.0	10	80	.294
1928	Chicago (N)	28	63	.287	126	407	67	117	22	3	.563	$6.0	14	57	.302
1929	Chicago (N)	2	9	.261	26	23	2	6	2	0	.609	$1.4	1	9	.273
1930	Chicago (N)	47	116	.308	146	526	79	162	21	1	.620	$5.8	37	122	.339
1931	Chicago (N)	17	76	.272	120	393	58	107	27	0	.471	$4.2	8	70	.282
1932	Chicago (N)	21	57	.263	127	426	57	112	21	1	.465	$2.6	12	52	.271
1933	Chicago (N)	30	104	.276	147	515	65	142	18	1	.489	$3.9	16	88	.276
1934	Chicago (N)	34	100	.288	139	468	64	135	16	1	.545	$3.6	22	90	.299
1935	Chicago (N)	25	99	.332	122	434	73	144	32	3	.592	$3.7	13	91	.344
1936	Chicago (N)	15	66	.290	127	445	51	129	28	3	.467	$2.7	7	64	.307
1937	Chicago (N)	21	89	.344	116	375	51	129	21	3	.584	$2.5	12	82	.354
1938	Chicago (N)	16	64	.269	93	316	43	85	18	1	.484	$2.2	10	59	.274
1939	Chicago (N)	19	64	.273	101	319	39	87	16	1	.508	$2.1	12	59	.278
1940	Chicago (N)	2	13	.269	39	67	3	18	3	0	.403	$0.9	1	12	.266
1941	New York (N)	8	30	.310	66	155	23	48	4	0	.490	$1.0	5	26	.300
	Career	410	1,272	.285	2,087	6,746	934	1,921	340	25	.525	$65.3	236	1,179	.297
	Average season	21	64	.285	104	337	47	96	17	1	.525	$3.3	12	59	.297
	Summit season	30	88	.310	125	423	66	131	21	2	.582	$4.5	18	84	.328

HARRY HEILMANN

		ADJUSTED REGULAR SEASON											ACTUAL RESULTS		
YEAR	TEAM	HR	RBI	BA	G	AB	R	H	2B	3B	SA	PAY	HR	RBI	BA
1914	Detroit (A)	7	23	.241	71	187	31	45	7	0	.390	$2.1	2	18	.225
1916	Detroit (A)	16	102	.306	142	471	79	144	51	6	.541	$6.0	2	73	.282
1917	Detroit (A)	30	120	.304	158	586	79	178	25	4	.514	$9.2	5	86	.281
1918	Detroit (A)	26	65	.293	100	362	57	106	8	1	.536	$5.9	5	39	.276
1919	Detroit (A)	38	134	.329	162	621	107	204	35	5	.585	$15.1	8	93	.320
1920	Detroit (A)	27	105	.301	152	569	78	171	25	1	.490	$11.8	9	89	.309

(Harry Heilmann, continued)

		ADJUSTED REGULAR SEASON											ACTUAL RESULTS		
YEAR	TEAM	HR	RBI	BA	G	AB	R	H	2B	3B	SA	PAY	HR	RBI	BA
1921	Detroit (A)	44	152	.364	157	634	124	231	38	4	.645	$19.3	19	139	.394
1922	Detroit (A)	39	98	.331	123	474	98	157	22	3	.637	$12.1	21	92	.356
1923	Detroit (A)	41	125	.383	151	549	132	210	40	4	.694	$15.8	18	115	.403
1924	Detroit (A)	30	124	.324	159	592	116	192	49	7	.583	$16.8	10	114	.346
1925	Detroit (A)	29	137	.362	156	596	99	216	39	5	.591	$16.1	13	134	.393
1926	Detroit (A)	25	112	.353	145	516	98	182	39	3	.585	$9.5	9	103	.367
1927	Detroit (A)	34	130	.379	146	523	114	198	44	3	.669	$9.8	14	120	.398
1928	Detroit (A)	31	118	.315	159	588	92	185	36	3	.544	$9.9	14	107	.328
1929	Detroit (A)	27	122	.320	131	475	87	152	37	3	.581	$7.1	15	120	.344
1930	Cincinnati (N)	29	87	.303	149	482	76	146	36	2	.566	$6.4	19	91	.333
1932	Cincinnati (N)	0	7	.242	16	33	3	8	3	0	.333	$1.4	0	6	.258
	Career	473	1,761	.330	2,277	8,258	1,470	2,725	534	54	.580	$174.3	183	1,539	.342
	Average season	28	104	.330	134	486	86	160	31	3	.580	$10.3	11	91	.342
	Summit season	37	128	.364	147	555	113	202	37	4	.645	$14.6	17	120	.390

RICKEY HENDERSON

		ADJUSTED REGULAR SEASON											ACTUAL RESULTS		
YEAR	TEAM	HR	RBI	BA	G	AB	R	H	2B	3B	SA	PAY	HR	RBI	BA
1979	Oakland (A)	1	29	.276	89	351	54	97	20	3	.359	$3.8	1	26	.274
1980	Oakland (A)	14	61	.308	158	591	128	182	28	3	.437	$11.7	9	53	.303
1981	Oakland (A)	17	64	.336	161	631	163	212	38	9	.506	$18.6	6	35	.319
1982	Oakland (A)	14	59	.274	149	536	137	147	29	3	.418	$14.5	10	51	.267
1983	Oakland (A)	13	55	.302	145	513	120	155	32	5	.460	$12.4	9	48	.292
1984	Oakland (A)	22	67	.303	142	502	131	152	32	3	.510	$14.3	16	58	.293
1985	New York (A)	30	82	.328	144	551	167	181	32	4	.564	$19.1	24	72	.314
1986	New York (A)	33	82	.275	153	608	145	167	34	5	.510	$19.9	28	74	.263
1987	New York (A)	17	39	.296	95	358	82	106	19	3	.508	$6.7	17	37	.291
1988	New York (A)	10	60	.323	141	558	141	180	38	2	.452	$12.5	6	50	.305
1989	N.Y.-Oak. (A)	18	67	.290	150	541	134	157	30	3	.457	$12.6	12	57	.274
1990	Oakland (A)	36	70	.339	136	489	137	166	35	3	.644	$7.3	28	61	.325
1991	Oakland (A)	23	65	.283	134	470	120	133	18	1	.472	$7.3	18	57	.268
1992	Oakland (A)	21	55	.298	117	396	92	118	19	3	.520	$4.9	15	46	.283
1993	Oak.-Tor. (A)	25	63	.293	134	481	122	141	23	2	.505	$7.2	21	59	.289
1994	Oakland (A)	9	29	.258	124	422	95	109	19	0	.367	$3.5	6	20	.260
1995	Oakland (A)	11	62	.301	126	458	77	138	36	1	.456	$3.6	9	54	.300
1996	San Diego (N)	9	29	.241	148	465	109	112	17	2	.344	$4.2	9	29	.241
1997	S.D. (N)-Ana. (A)	9	35	.251	120	403	87	101	14	0	.352	$2.6	8	34	.248
1998	Oakland (A)	15	59	.238	152	542	105	129	16	1	.354	$6.4	14	57	.236
1999	New York (N)	11	41	.313	120	434	86	136	30	0	.459	$3.2	12	42	.315
2000	N.Y. (N)-Sea. (A)	4	31	.231	123	420	73	97	13	2	.300	$2.5	4	32	.233
2001	San Diego (N)	8	43	.232	123	379	72	88	16	3	.354	$2.5	8	42	.227
	Career	370	1,247	.289	3,084	11,099	2,577	3,204	588	61	.453	$201.3	290	1,094	.280
	Average season	16	54	.289	134	483	112	139	26	3	.453	$8.8	13	48	.280
	Summit season	25	68	.323	140	514	138	166	31	4	.545	$12.8	18	54	.308

BABE HERMAN

		ADJUSTED REGULAR SEASON											ACTUAL RESULTS		
YEAR	TEAM	HR	RBI	BA	G	AB	R	H	2B	3B	SA	PAY	HR	RBI	BA
1926	Brooklyn (N)	29	89	.305	143	518	71	158	31	4	.548	$8.8	11	81	.319
1927	Brooklyn (N)	30	80	.258	137	434	71	112	20	3	.525	$7.5	14	73	.272
1928	Brooklyn (N)	26	100	.325	140	508	70	165	33	3	.555	$8.7	12	91	.340
1929	Brooklyn (N)	39	116	.356	155	604	108	215	38	5	.629	$14.6	21	113	.381
1930	Brooklyn (N)	52	125	.358	161	646	138	231	38	3	.667	$19.9	35	130	.393
1931	Brooklyn (N)	41	108	.303	160	646	104	196	38	7	.574	$19.1	18	97	.313
1932	Cincinnati (N)	33	95	.318	155	604	95	192	39	9	.576	$15.7	16	87	.326
1933	Chicago (N)	35	110	.288	144	534	91	154	35	5	.569	$11.8	16	93	.289
1934	Chicago (N)	26	93	.294	133	497	71	146	33	3	.529	$7.3	14	84	.304
1935	Pit.-Cin. (N)	20	71	.305	124	452	57	138	32	3	.522	$3.8	10	65	.316
1936	Cincinnati (N)	22	73	.263	125	399	61	105	21	1	.486	$3.0	13	71	.279
1937	Detroit (A)	0	3	.286	18	21	2	6	4	0	.476	$1.1	0	3	.300
1945	Brooklyn (N)	2	11	.278	39	36	8	10	1	0	.472	$0.6	1	9	.265
	Career	355	1,074	.310	1,634	5,899	947	1,828	363	46	.568	$121.9	181	997	.324
	Average season	27	83	.310	126	454	73	141	28	4	.568	$9.4	14	77	.324
	Summit season	38	109	.332	154	602	103	200	37	5	.600	$15.6	20	104	.351

BILLY HERMAN

		ADJUSTED REGULAR SEASON											ACTUAL RESULTS		
YEAR	TEAM	HR	RBI	BA	G	AB	R	H	2B	3B	SA	PAY	HR	RBI	BA
1931	Chicago (N)	0	18	.314	26	102	15	32	12	0	.431	$1.0	0	16	.327
1932	Chicago (N)	3	56	.306	162	690	112	211	68	5	.432	$7.8	1	51	.314
1933	Chicago (N)	0	52	.280	161	651	97	182	68	2	.390	$9.4	0	44	.279
1934	Chicago (N)	8	46	.291	120	484	87	141	32	4	.424	$7.0	3	42	.303
1935	Chicago (N)	17	91	.330	162	701	124	231	71	3	.512	$19.1	7	83	.341
1936	Chicago (N)	13	96	.317	161	665	105	211	72	5	.499	$18.8	5	93	.334
1937	Chicago (N)	18	70	.327	145	593	115	194	43	7	.514	$14.6	8	65	.335
1938	Chicago (N)	3	60	.272	160	657	93	179	56	6	.390	$12.8	1	56	.277
1939	Chicago (N)	17	75	.300	162	647	119	194	46	12	.487	$15.9	7	70	.307
1940	Chicago (N)	10	64	.295	142	587	87	173	32	2	.407	$9.4	5	57	.292
1941	Chi.-Bkn. (N)	8	47	.292	149	592	93	173	46	4	.424	$6.9	3	41	.285
1942	Brooklyn (N)	7	82	.271	162	597	96	162	59	1	.409	$9.3	2	65	.256
1943	Brooklyn (N)	8	134	.351	162	619	101	217	76	1	.515	$10.0	2	100	.330
1946	Bkn.-Bos. (N)	8	63	.313	126	450	71	141	47	4	.489	$4.4	3	50	.298
1947	Pittsburgh (N)	0	7	.220	16	50	4	11	6	0	.340	$1.3	0	6	.213
	Career	120	961	.303	2,016	8,085	1,319	2,452	734	56	.452	$147.7	47	839	.304
	Average season	8	64	.303	134	539	88	163	49	4	.452	$9.8	3	56	.304
	Summit season	13	91	.328	151	606	103	199	62	4	.508	$13.4	5	78	.330

KEITH HERNANDEZ

		ADJUSTED REGULAR SEASON											ACTUAL RESULTS		
YEAR	TEAM	HR	RBI	BA	G	AB	R	H	2B	3B	SA	PAY	HR	RBI	BA
1974	St. Louis (N)	0	2	.294	14	34	4	10	1	3	.500	$0.0	0	2	.294
1975	St. Louis (N)	5	23	.261	64	188	23	49	10	2	.415	$1.0	3	20	.250
1976	St. Louis (N)	13	56	.305	129	374	66	114	28	4	.505	$3.8	7	46	.289
1977	St. Louis (N)	18	101	.296	161	560	100	166	47	3	.488	$7.9	15	91	.291
1978	St. Louis (N)	17	76	.266	159	542	107	144	38	3	.441	$9.6	11	64	.255
1979	St. Louis (N)	15	115	.350	160	606	127	212	60	9	.553	$18.6	11	105	.344
1980	St. Louis (N)	24	114	.326	159	595	128	194	46	6	.545	$19.5	16	99	.321
1981	St. Louis (N)	21	92	.321	162	591	125	190	53	5	.535	$19.5	8	48	.306
1982	St. Louis (N)	10	108	.307	160	579	91	178	44	6	.456	$16.1	7	94	.299
1983	St.L.-N.Y. (N)	18	72	.307	150	538	88	165	28	5	.478	$11.8	12	63	.297
1984	New York (N)	20	109	.322	154	550	96	177	36	0	.496	$12.3	15	94	.311
1985	New York (N)	13	103	.324	158	593	99	192	41	3	.469	$9.7	10	91	.309
1986	New York (N)	16	92	.325	149	551	105	179	38	1	.485	$9.5	13	83	.310
1987	New York (N)	19	93	.296	154	587	91	174	30	2	.451	$9.7	18	89	.290
1988	New York (N)	15	66	.293	96	352	51	103	18	0	.472	$3.6	11	55	.276
1989	New York (N)	6	22	.247	75	215	21	53	9	0	.372	$1.7	4	19	.233
1990	Cleveland (A)	1	9	.208	43	130	8	27	3	0	.254	$1.0	1	8	.200
	Career	231	1,253	.307	2,147	7,585	1,330	2,327	530	52	.482	$155.3	162	1,071	.296
	Average season	14	74	.307	126	446	78	137	31	3	.482	$9.1	10	63	.296
	Summit season	19	97	.326	153	543	108	177	45	5	.532	$14.7	11	78	.317

GIL HODGES

		ADJUSTED REGULAR SEASON											ACTUAL RESULTS		
YEAR	TEAM	HR	RBI	BA	G	AB	R	H	2B	3B	SA	PAY	HR	RBI	BA
1943	Brooklyn (N)	0	0	.000	1	2	0	0	0	0	.000	$0.0	0	0	.000
1947	Brooklyn (N)	2	8	.163	29	80	11	13	4	1	.313	$0.0	1	7	.156
1948	Brooklyn (N)	19	79	.254	140	503	54	128	21	3	.421	$4.5	11	70	.249
1949	Brooklyn (N)	33	128	.292	162	619	104	181	26	3	.504	$9.4	23	115	.285
1950	Brooklyn (N)	40	121	.286	160	587	105	168	29	1	.543	$12.2	32	113	.283
1951	Brooklyn (N)	51	115	.276	162	597	132	165	27	2	.585	$19.0	40	103	.268
1952	Brooklyn (N)	44	126	.271	160	531	107	144	30	1	.580	$15.6	32	102	.254
1953	Brooklyn (N)	39	137	.308	147	542	113	167	26	5	.590	$12.8	31	122	.302
1954	Brooklyn (N)	54	154	.314	162	609	125	191	27	3	.634	$22.3	42	130	.304
1955	Brooklyn (N)	33	117	.301	158	575	86	173	33	4	.544	$12.8	27	102	.289
1956	Brooklyn (N)	37	101	.276	161	579	99	160	38	3	.544	$10.0	32	87	.265
1957	Brooklyn (N)	34	119	.313	158	610	114	191	37	5	.557	$13.4	27	98	.299
1958	Los Angeles (N)	26	77	.271	148	499	82	135	19	1	.469	$6.9	22	64	.259
1959	Los Angeles (N)	30	94	.288	129	430	67	124	24	2	.563	$4.9	25	80	.276
1960	Los Angeles (N)	10	36	.208	106	207	26	43	10	1	.411	$2.0	8	30	.198
1961	Los Angeles (N)	10	35	.251	115	227	29	57	5	0	.405	$1.6	8	31	.242
1962	New York (N)	10	19	.260	54	127	17	33	1	0	.504	$1.0	9	17	.252
1963	New York (N)	0	4	.227	11	22	2	5	0	0	.227	$0.2	0	3	.227
	Career	472	1,470	.283	2,163	7,346	1,273	2,078	357	35	.534	$148.6	370	1,274	.273
	Average season	26	82	.283	120	408	71	115	20	2	.534	$8.3	21	71	.273
	Summit season	44	130	.298	158	578	118	172	29	3	.587	$16.6	34	111	.286

HARRY HOOPER

		ADJUSTED REGULAR SEASON											ACTUAL RESULTS		
YEAR	TEAM	HR	RBI	BA	G	AB	R	H	2B	3B	SA	PAY	HR	RBI	BA
1909	Boston (A)	0	17	.310	86	271	41	84	21	8	.446	$2.4	0	12	.282
1910	Boston (A)	19	34	.289	159	599	102	173	18	5	.431	$6.4	2	27	.267
1911	Boston (A)	20	51	.315	138	556	105	175	25	2	.475	$7.8	4	45	.311
1912	Boston (A)	15	59	.243	155	622	110	151	35	5	.387	$11.6	2	53	.242
1913	Boston (A)	24	50	.300	159	630	127	189	42	5	.497	$14.4	4	40	.288
1914	Boston (A)	10	51	.274	145	541	106	148	53	10	.464	$9.6	1	41	.258
1915	Boston (A)	17	66	.253	156	593	117	150	37	6	.422	$14.9	2	51	.235
1916	Boston (A)	11	51	.294	157	598	104	176	48	8	.457	$11.8	1	37	.271
1917	Boston (A)	22	61	.277	156	578	122	160	30	5	.460	$12.0	3	45	.256
1918	Boston (A)	16	74	.307	162	609	137	187	69	10	.532	$16.3	1	44	.289
1919	Boston (A)	18	71	.273	150	575	111	157	37	3	.442	$9.9	3	49	.267
1920	Boston (A)	28	63	.304	146	563	108	171	35	6	.536	$9.7	7	53	.312
1921	Chicago (A)	19	63	.303	114	442	81	134	25	2	.498	$4.9	8	58	.327
1922	Chicago (A)	26	85	.284	159	630	119	179	36	3	.475	$13.0	11	80	.304
1923	Chicago (A)	24	70	.273	151	600	94	164	31	2	.452	$8.8	10	65	.288
1924	Chicago (A)	26	68	.309	137	502	118	155	25	2	.522	$6.5	10	62	.328
1925	Chicago (A)	14	57	.245	134	466	64	114	24	2	.395	$4.3	6	55	.265
	Career	309	991	.284	2,464	9,375	1,766	2,667	591	84	.464	$164.3	75	817	.281
	Average season	18	58	.284	145	551	104	157	35	5	.464	$9.7	4	48	.281
	Summit season	23	64	.304	144	549	114	167	39	5	.519	$10.4	6	51	.308

ROGERS HORNSBY

		ADJUSTED REGULAR SEASON											ACTUAL RESULTS		
YEAR	TEAM	HR	RBI	BA	G	AB	R	H	2B	3B	SA	PAY	HR	RBI	BA
1915	St. Louis (N)	0	5	.267	19	60	7	16	6	0	.367	$0.0	0	4	.246
1916	St. Louis (N)	33	91	.340	147	523	89	178	19	4	.581	$5.6	6	65	.313
1917	St. Louis (N)	42	92	.355	153	552	121	196	23	4	.639	$9.5	8	66	.327
1918	St. Louis (N)	33	98	.298	142	514	83	153	21	4	.547	$9.2	5	60	.281
1919	St. Louis (N)	34	104	.326	162	601	99	196	15	3	.531	$15.1	8	71	.318
1920	St. Louis (N)	36	111	.361	156	617	114	223	51	7	.642	$18.9	9	94	.370
1921	St. Louis (N)	48	137	.368	162	623	143	229	39	5	.677	$25.2	21	126	.397
1922	St. Louis (N)	72	164	.376	162	655	152	246	34	4	.769	$31.7	42	152	.401
1923	St. Louis (N)	37	91	.364	113	448	98	163	28	3	.688	$12.4	17	83	.384
1924	St. Louis (N)	53	103	.399	150	562	133	224	32	4	.753	$20.0	25	94	.424
1925	St. Louis (N)	63	149	.371	146	533	138	198	28	3	.790	$16.7	39	143	.403
1926	St. Louis (N)	27	102	.303	139	547	105	166	28	2	.510	$12.3	11	93	.317
1927	New York (N)	49	136	.343	162	594	145	204	22	2	.635	$23.1	26	125	.361
1928	Boston (N)	40	104	.372	148	514	110	191	34	2	.679	$13.1	21	94	.387
1929	Chicago (N)	58	150	.355	162	625	157	222	34	2	.694	$24.7	39	149	.380
1930	Chicago (N)	4	17	.284	44	109	14	31	5	0	.440	$2.6	2	18	.308
1931	Chicago (N)	29	99	.321	104	371	70	119	26	0	.625	$4.6	16	90	.331
1932	Chicago (N)	2	8	.213	20	61	11	13	2	0	.344	$1.3	1	7	.224
1933	St.L. (N)-St.L. (A)	6	27	.330	60	97	13	32	6	0	.577	$0.8	3	23	.326
1934	St. Louis (A)	2	12	.292	25	24	2	7	2	0	.625	$0.5	1	11	.304
1935	St. Louis (A)	0	3	.208	10	24	1	5	4	0	.375	$0.0	0	3	.208

(Rogers Hornsby, continued)

	ADJUSTED REGULAR SEASON												**ACTUAL RESULTS**		
YEAR	**TEAM**	**HR**	**RBI**	**BA**	**G**	**AB**	**R**	**H**	**2B**	**3B**	**SA**	**PAY**	**HR**	**RBI**	**BA**
1936	St. Louis (A)	0	2	.400	2	5	1	2	0	0	.400	$0.0	0	2	.400
1937	St. Louis (A)	2	12	.305	21	59	8	18	3	0	.458	$0.0	1	11	.321
	Career	670	1,817	.348	2,409	8,718	1,814	3,032	462	49	.643	$247.3	301	1,584	.358
	Average season	29	79	.348	105	379	79	132	20	2	.643	$10.8	13	69	.358
	Summit season	53	122	.376	144	542	126	204	31	3	.738	$18.8	29	113	.401

ELSTON HOWARD

	ADJUSTED REGULAR SEASON												**ACTUAL RESULTS**		
YEAR	**TEAM**	**HR**	**RBI**	**BA**	**G**	**AB**	**R**	**H**	**2B**	**3B**	**SA**	**PAY**	**HR**	**RBI**	**BA**
1955	New York (A)	14	49	.304	102	293	38	89	11	5	.519	$3.8	10	43	.290
1956	New York (A)	7	39	.272	103	305	40	83	12	2	.393	$3.7	5	34	.262
1957	New York (A)	10	53	.264	116	375	40	99	19	3	.411	$4.3	8	44	.253
1958	New York (A)	14	79	.327	108	394	54	129	26	4	.520	$3.8	11	66	.314
1959	New York (A)	22	86	.287	131	464	69	133	31	5	.517	$4.5	18	73	.273
1960	New York (A)	8	46	.257	112	338	34	87	16	2	.388	$3.4	6	39	.245
1961	New York (A)	24	83	.363	128	443	69	161	21	4	.591	$3.0	21	77	.348
1962	New York (A)	24	101	.291	136	494	70	144	30	4	.514	$3.7	21	91	.279
1963	New York (A)	35	106	.314	136	491	94	154	29	5	.607	$4.7	28	85	.287
1964	New York (A)	19	101	.337	148	543	76	183	36	2	.516	$5.1	15	84	.313
1965	New York (A)	11	55	.256	110	391	46	100	19	1	.394	$2.6	9	45	.233
1966	New York (A)	8	44	.278	128	417	47	116	26	2	.408	$2.4	6	35	.256
1967	N.Y.-Bos. (A)	6	36	.199	107	312	28	62	12	0	.295	$1.7	4	28	.178
1968	Boston (A)	8	25	.276	71	203	31	56	5	0	.419	$1.2	5	18	.241
	Career	210	903	.292	1,636	5,463	736	1,596	293	39	.475	$47.9	167	762	.274
	Average season	15	65	.292	117	390	53	114	21	3	.475	$3.4	12	54	.274
	Summit season	23	94	.326	131	473	73	154	28	4	.548	$4.1	19	81	.307

FRANK HOWARD

	ADJUSTED REGULAR SEASON												**ACTUAL RESULTS**		
YEAR	**TEAM**	**HR**	**RBI**	**BA**	**G**	**AB**	**R**	**H**	**2B**	**3B**	**SA**	**PAY**	**HR**	**RBI**	**BA**
1958	Los Angeles (N)	1	2	.241	8	29	3	7	1	0	.379	$0.0	1	2	.241
1959	Los Angeles (N)	1	7	.143	9	21	2	3	0	1	.381	$0.0	1	6	.143
1960	Los Angeles (N)	29	92	.282	123	471	65	133	19	1	.512	$4.7	23	77	.268
1961	Los Angeles (N)	18	51	.309	97	282	41	87	13	2	.560	$3.3	15	45	.296
1962	Los Angeles (N)	35	129	.308	138	483	87	149	32	4	.609	$7.4	31	119	.296
1963	Los Angeles (N)	33	79	.300	122	414	71	124	20	1	.592	$7.1	28	64	.273
1964	Los Angeles (N)	28	83	.244	132	427	72	104	16	2	.487	$7.4	24	69	.226
1965	Washington (A)	27	103	.316	149	516	65	163	30	5	.550	$6.9	21	84	.289
1966	Washington (A)	23	89	.300	149	503	65	151	27	3	.503	$5.9	18	71	.278
1967	Washington (A)	48	116	.284	150	522	92	148	24	2	.613	$9.2	36	89	.256
1968	Washington (A)	64	151	.312	159	602	112	188	34	2	.694	$10.0	44	106	.274
1969	Washington (A)	59	133	.321	161	592	133	190	22	2	.664	$13.7	48	111	.296
1970	Washington (A)	51	143	.300	161	566	102	170	19	1	.608	$13.8	44	126	.283

(Frank Howard, continued)

		ADJUSTED REGULAR SEASON											ACTUAL RESULTS		
YEAR	TEAM	HR	RBI	BA	G	AB	R	H	2B	3B	SA	PAY	HR	RBI	BA
1971	Washington (A)	36	106	.300	156	560	76	168	32	2	.557	$9.7	26	83	.279
1972	Tex.-Det. (A)	15	52	.268	113	332	40	89	13	0	.443	$3.2	10	38	.244
1973	Detroit (A)	15	34	.269	85	227	30	61	11	1	.524	$1.9	12	29	.256
	Career	483	1,370	.296	1,912	6,547	1,056	1,935	313	29	.574	$104.2	382	1,119	.273
	Average season	30	86	.296	120	409	66	121	20	2	.574	$6.5	24	70	.273
	Summit season	51	134	.306	154	553	105	169	26	2	.637	$10.8	41	110	.281

MONTE IRVIN

		ADJUSTED REGULAR SEASON											ACTUAL RESULTS		
YEAR	TEAM	HR	RBI	BA	G	AB	R	H	2B	3B	SA	PAY	HR	RBI	BA
1949	New York (N)	0	8	.231	37	78	8	18	6	2	.359	$0.2	0	7	.224
1950	New York (N)	20	71	.302	116	394	66	119	23	3	.528	$3.0	15	66	.299
1951	New York (N)	35	137	.321	156	576	106	185	23	8	.571	$6.9	24	121	.312
1952	New York (N)	6	26	.328	48	131	12	43	3	1	.504	$1.5	4	21	.310
1953	New York (N)	28	109	.335	130	465	81	156	26	3	.585	$3.9	21	97	.329
1954	New York (N)	26	75	.269	142	454	73	122	16	2	.485	$3.8	19	64	.262
1955	New York (N)	1	20	.264	54	159	18	42	10	1	.358	$1.3	1	17	.253
1956	Chicago (N)	18	57	.282	115	351	50	99	18	2	.499	$2.2	15	50	.271
	Career	134	503	.301	798	2,608	414	784	125	22	.520	$22.8	99	443	.293
	Average season	17	63	.301	100	326	52	98	16	3	.520	$2.9	12	55	.293
	Summit season	25	90	.304	132	448	75	136	21	4	.536	$4.0	19	80	.297

JOE JACKSON

		ADJUSTED REGULAR SEASON											ACTUAL RESULTS		
YEAR	TEAM	HR	RBI	BA	G	AB	R	H	2B	3B	SA	PAY	HR	RBI	BA
1908	Philadelphia (A)	0	4	.130	5	23	0	3	0	0	.130	$0.0	0	3	.130
1909	Philadelphia (A)	0	4	.176	5	17	4	3	0	0	.176	$0.0	0	3	.176
1910	Cleveland (A)	7	14	.413	20	75	18	31	3	2	.787	$0.3	1	11	.387
1911	Cleveland (A)	34	92	.414	153	594	140	246	58	7	.707	$8.6	7	83	.408
1912	Cleveland (A)	24	100	.396	161	598	135	237	79	12	.689	$12.0	3	90	.395
1913	Cleveland (A)	35	88	.389	155	553	135	215	48	5	.684	$15.0	7	71	.373
1914	Cleveland (A)	20	67	.359	126	468	77	168	36	6	.590	$11.4	3	53	.338
1915	Cle.-Chi. (A)	27	105	.331	134	483	82	160	25	5	.571	$11.6	5	81	.308
1916	Chicago (A)	26	109	.372	162	619	127	230	73	11	.651	$18.5	3	78	.341
1917	Chicago (A)	33	103	.327	152	560	126	183	25	6	.570	$14.9	5	75	.301
1918	Chicago (A)	6	34	.381	22	84	15	32	2	1	.643	$3.4	1	20	.354
1919	Chicago (A)	35	139	.360	161	598	114	215	39	6	.620	$15.8	7	96	.351
1920	Chicago (A)	43	145	.373	154	601	125	224	43	6	.679	$15.9	12	121	.382
	Career	290	1,004	.369	1,410	5,273	1,098	1,947	431	67	.641	$127.4	54	785	.356
	Average season	22	77	.369	108	406	84	150	33	5	.641	$9.8	4	60	.356
	Summit season	32	107	.388	157	593	132	230	60	8	.678	$14.0	6	89	.380

REGGIE JACKSON

					ADJUSTED REGULAR SEASON								ACTUAL RESULTS		
YEAR	TEAM	HR	RBI	BA	G	AB	R	H	2B	3B	SA	PAY	HR	RBI	BA
1967	Kansas City (A)	2	8	.195	35	118	17	23	7	3	.356	$0.7	1	6	.178
1968	Oakland (A)	44	104	.284	153	549	115	156	17	4	.570	$7.1	29	74	.250
1969	Oakland (A)	57	142	.299	152	549	148	164	46	3	.705	$15.3	47	118	.275
1970	Oakland (A)	26	75	.251	149	426	64	107	26	2	.505	$8.7	23	66	.237
1971	Oakland (A)	42	101	.299	151	571	110	171	36	3	.594	$15.1	32	80	.277
1972	Oakland (A)	36	103	.292	141	521	99	152	33	2	.570	$12.4	25	75	.265
1973	Oakland (A)	40	137	.306	151	539	116	165	34	2	.599	$14.7	32	117	.293
1974	Oakland (A)	39	111	.302	148	506	107	153	28	1	.593	$14.6	29	93	.289
1975	Oakland (A)	48	121	.265	157	593	106	157	42	2	.585	$15.7	36	104	.253
1976	Baltimore (A)	40	112	.291	134	498	103	145	28	2	.596	$11.7	27	91	.277
1977	New York (A)	37	122	.291	146	525	103	153	42	1	.587	$12.1	32	110	.286
1978	New York (A)	36	114	.286	138	507	96	145	13	4	.540	$7.4	27	97	.274
1979	New York (A)	35	100	.301	133	472	87	142	25	2	.585	$7.0	29	89	.297
1980	New York (A)	51	128	.305	143	514	108	157	22	3	.658	$9.5	41	111	.300
1981	New York (A)	32	100	.250	142	505	61	126	27	1	.497	$6.8	15	54	.237
1982	California (A)	47	116	.283	153	530	106	150	18	1	.587	$8.9	39	101	.275
1983	California (A)	18	56	.199	116	397	49	79	15	1	.378	$3.3	14	49	.194
1984	California (A)	31	94	.230	143	525	78	121	18	2	.450	$4.5	25	81	.223
1985	California (A)	32	96	.263	143	460	73	121	29	0	.535	$4.4	27	85	.252
1986	California (A)	21	65	.251	132	419	72	105	13	2	.442	$3.3	18	58	.241
1987	Oakland (A)	15	45	.226	115	336	44	76	15	1	.411	$2.2	15	43	.220
	Career	729	2,050	.275	2,875	10,060	1,862	2,768	534	42	.554	$185.4	563	1,702	.262
	Average season	35	98	.275	137	479	89	132	25	2	.554	$8.8	27	81	.262
	Summit season	46	124	.302	149	536	118	162	33	2	.629	$13.8	36	104	.286

TRAVIS JACKSON

					ADJUSTED REGULAR SEASON								ACTUAL RESULTS		
YEAR	TEAM	HR	RBI	BA	G	AB	R	H	2B	3B	SA	PAY	HR	RBI	BA
1922	New York (N)	0	0	.000	3	8	1	0	0	0	.000	$0.0	0	0	.000
1923	New York (N)	13	41	.259	102	347	49	90	15	3	.432	$2.5	4	37	.275
1924	New York (N)	28	83	.283	159	628	89	178	24	2	.462	$7.2	11	76	.302
1925	New York (N)	17	61	.263	119	437	53	115	12	1	.412	$5.1	9	59	.285
1926	New York (N)	22	58	.315	119	413	73	130	22	2	.538	$5.9	8	51	.327
1927	New York (N)	29	107	.301	133	491	73	148	22	1	.527	$7.9	14	98	.318
1928	New York (N)	28	84	.258	157	562	80	145	30	2	.468	$9.3	14	77	.270
1929	New York (N)	36	97	.274	159	588	95	161	18	4	.502	$12.4	21	94	.294
1930	New York (N)	22	79	.309	122	453	67	140	25	3	.523	$7.8	13	82	.339
1931	New York (N)	16	79	.301	154	589	72	177	33	6	.458	$9.6	5	71	.310
1932	New York (N)	8	42	.248	55	206	25	51	16	0	.442	$3.3	4	38	.256
1933	New York (N)	0	14	.244	55	127	13	31	10	0	.323	$2.0	0	12	.246
1934	New York (N)	29	111	.258	145	554	82	143	24	3	.469	$5.7	16	101	.268
1935	New York (N)	20	86	.292	133	531	80	155	23	6	.471	$3.6	9	80	.301
1936	New York (N)	13	55	.218	133	491	43	107	8	1	.318	$2.7	7	53	.230
	Career	281	997	.276	1,748	6,425	895	1,771	282	34	.461	$85.0	135	929	.291
	Average season	19	66	.276	117	428	60	118	19	2	.461	$5.7	9	62	.291
	Summit season	26	85	.297	133	495	78	147	22	3	.511	$7.5	13	81	.314

HUGHIE JENNINGS

		ADJUSTED REGULAR SEASON											ACTUAL RESULTS		
YEAR	TEAM	HR	RBI	BA	G	AB	R	H	2B	3B	SA	PAY	HR	RBI	BA
1891	Louisville (AA)	8	59	.308	103	412	54	127	30	5	.464	$5.3	1	58	.292
1892	Louisville (N)	12	63	.243	160	625	67	152	33	1	.357	$7.7	2	61	.222
1893	Lou.-Balt. (N)	4	15	.172	49	180	12	31	4	0	.261	$2.8	1	15	.182
1894	Baltimore (N)	18	97	.292	161	630	119	184	46	6	.470	$11.9	4	109	.335
1895	Baltimore (N)	19	120	.351	161	650	153	228	65	3	.548	$15.6	4	125	.386
1896	Baltimore (N)	0	125	.373	160	641	130	239	94	6	.538	$18.4	0	121	.401
1897	Baltimore (N)	14	81	.328	139	522	136	171	47	5	.517	$15.3	2	79	.355
1898	Baltimore (N)	10	90	.327	150	560	141	183	61	7	.514	$16.8	1	87	.328
1899	Balt.-Bkn. (N)	0	42	.283	74	240	44	68	17	17	.496	$4.8	0	42	.299
1900	Brooklyn (N)	8	75	.263	131	502	66	132	41	3	.404	$7.0	1	69	.272
1901	Philadelphia (N)	6	45	.260	95	350	44	91	35	1	.417	$2.5	1	39	.262
1902	Philadelphia (N)	9	42	.275	92	342	42	94	25	2	.439	$2.0	1	32	.272
1903	Brooklyn (N)	0	1	.250	7	20	3	5	0	0	.250	$0.7	0	1	.235
1907	Detroit (A)	0	0	.250	1	4	0	1	1	0	.500	$0.2	0	0	.250
1909	Detroit (A)	0	3	.500	2	4	1	2	0	0	.500	$0.0	0	2	.500
1912	Detroit (A)	0	0	.000	1	1	0	0	0	0	.000	$0.0	0	0	.000
1918	Detroit (A)	0	0	.000	1	0	0	0	0	0	.000	$0.0	0	0	.000
	Career	108	858	.301	1,487	5,683	1,012	1,708	499	56	.465	$111.0	18	840	.311
	Average season	6	50	.301	87	334	60	100	29	3	.465	$6.5	1	49	.311
	Summit season	10	95	.341	143	557	123	190	59	5	.519	$14.3	2	94	.356

JACKIE JENSEN

		ADJUSTED REGULAR SEASON											ACTUAL RESULTS		
YEAR	TEAM	HR	RBI	BA	G	AB	R	H	2B	3B	SA	PAY	HR	RBI	BA
1950	New York (A)	1	5	.178	47	73	14	13	3	1	.288	$0.3	1	5	.171
1951	New York (A)	11	29	.305	59	177	34	54	9	1	.554	$1.5	8	25	.298
1952	N.Y.-Wash. (A)	17	100	.299	156	609	101	182	42	4	.465	$8.6	10	82	.280
1953	Washington (A)	15	96	.271	157	590	100	160	44	5	.439	$11.2	10	84	.266
1954	Boston (A)	34	137	.284	158	603	107	171	31	4	.517	$15.1	25	117	.276
1955	Boston (A)	32	133	.286	160	604	109	173	37	4	.520	$19.2	26	116	.275
1956	Boston (A)	25	112	.329	158	605	92	199	33	8	.534	$15.9	20	97	.315
1957	Boston (A)	28	126	.294	153	574	100	169	38	1	.510	$12.8	23	103	.281
1958	Boston (A)	41	147	.298	161	573	99	171	39	0	.581	$16.1	35	122	.286
1959	Boston (A)	33	133	.291	156	564	120	164	39	0	.535	$13.2	28	112	.277
1961	Boston (A)	15	71	.273	136	494	69	135	26	1	.421	$6.9	13	66	.263
	Career	252	1,089	.291	1,501	5,466	945	1,591	341	29	.502	$120.8	199	929	.279
	Average season	23	99	.291	136	497	86	145	31	3	.502	$11.0	18	84	.279
	Summit season	32	130	.300	158	584	104	175	37	3	.538	$15.4	26	110	.287

CHIPPER JONES

YEAR	TEAM	ADJUSTED REGULAR SEASON											ACTUAL RESULTS		
		HR	RBI	BA	G	AB	R	H	2B	3B	SA	PAY	HR	RBI	BA
1993	Atlanta (N)	0	0	.667	8	3	2	2	1	0	1.000	$0.0	0	0	.667
1995	Atlanta (N)	28	99	.267	158	591	100	158	26	3	.464	$7.2	23	86	.265
1996	Atlanta (N)	30	109	.308	157	598	113	184	33	5	.530	$12.4	30	110	.309
1997	Atlanta (N)	22	115	.296	157	597	104	177	42	3	.487	$14.5	21	111	.295
1998	Atlanta (N)	35	111	.316	160	601	128	190	29	5	.556	$19.6	34	107	.313
1999	Atlanta (N)	43	108	.317	157	567	113	180	41	1	.621	$19.2	45	110	.319
2000	Atlanta (N)	34	107	.309	156	579	114	179	37	1	.553	$18.8	36	111	.311
2001	Atlanta (N)	37	106	.337	159	572	117	193	32	5	.605	$16.2	38	102	.330
	Career	229	755	.307	1,112	4,108	791	1,263	241	23	.545	$107.9	227	737	.307
	Average season	29	94	.307	139	514	99	158	30	3	.545	$13.5	28	92	.307
	Summit season	36	108	.317	158	583	117	185	34	3	.571	$17.2	37	108	.316

AL KALINE

YEAR	TEAM	ADJUSTED REGULAR SEASON											ACTUAL RESULTS		
		HR	RBI	BA	G	AB	R	H	2B	3B	SA	PAY	HR	RBI	BA
1953	Detroit (A)	1	2	.241	31	29	10	7	0	0	.345	$0.0	1	2	.250
1954	Detroit (A)	7	50	.285	144	526	49	150	26	2	.382	$3.8	4	43	.276
1955	Detroit (A)	34	117	.354	160	619	139	219	34	6	.593	$14.2	27	102	.340
1956	Detroit (A)	33	147	.329	160	645	110	212	44	7	.572	$15.5	27	128	.314
1957	Detroit (A)	29	109	.308	157	608	101	187	38	3	.523	$15.0	23	90	.295
1958	Detroit (A)	20	103	.326	154	573	102	187	47	5	.531	$15.2	16	85	.313
1959	Detroit (A)	33	111	.343	143	537	101	184	24	2	.579	$14.6	27	94	.327
1960	Detroit (A)	20	81	.293	155	581	92	170	38	3	.472	$14.5	15	68	.278
1961	Detroit (A)	21	88	.338	152	582	125	197	52	5	.553	$15.1	19	82	.324
1962	Detroit (A)	34	105	.318	101	402	87	128	21	4	.644	$9.3	29	94	.304
1963	Detroit (A)	34	126	.341	145	551	111	188	33	2	.593	$12.0	27	101	.312
1964	Detroit (A)	21	82	.315	145	521	93	164	42	4	.532	$9.8	17	68	.293
1965	Detroit (A)	22	88	.308	125	399	88	123	24	2	.544	$7.1	18	72	.281
1966	Detroit (A)	34	108	.311	142	479	104	149	37	1	.605	$7.3	29	88	.288
1967	Detroit (A)	34	100	.343	130	455	121	156	34	2	.651	$7.2	25	78	.308
1968	Detroit (A)	16	74	.327	101	324	69	106	19	1	.540	$3.9	10	53	.287
1969	Detroit (A)	26	83	.294	131	456	89	134	23	0	.515	$5.1	21	69	.272
1970	Detroit (A)	19	80	.296	131	467	72	138	31	3	.497	$4.5	16	71	.278
1971	Detroit (A)	21	68	.316	133	405	86	128	25	2	.543	$4.2	15	54	.294
1972	Detroit (A)	16	44	.344	110	288	63	99	16	2	.580	$2.3	10	32	.313
1973	Detroit (A)	13	53	.268	91	310	47	83	16	0	.445	$2.1	10	45	.255
1974	Detroit (A)	20	76	.274	147	558	84	153	35	2	.452	$4.4	13	64	.262
	Career	508	1,895	.316	2,888	10,315	1,943	3,262	659	58	.539	$187.1	399	1,583	.297
	Average season	23	86	.316	131	469	88	148	30	3	.539	$8.5	18	72	.297
	Summit season	34	112	.341	136	513	112	175	29	3	.608	$11.5	27	94	.320

WILLIE KEELER

			ADJUSTED REGULAR SEASON										ACTUAL RESULTS		
YEAR	TEAM	HR	RBI	BA	G	AB	R	H	2B	3B	SA	PAY	HR	RBI	BA
1892	New York (N)	0	6	.351	15	57	7	20	8	0	.491	$0.0	0	6	.321
1893	N.Y.-Bkn. (N)	6	15	.309	32	123	18	38	3	1	.496	$0.7	2	16	.317
1894	Baltimore (N)	23	83	.324	162	741	147	240	48	9	.506	$12.4	5	94	.371
1895	Baltimore (N)	23	74	.343	161	694	156	238	45	8	.530	$15.0	4	78	.377
1896	Baltimore (N)	25	85	.359	155	669	159	240	41	6	.550	$19.6	4	82	.386
1897	Baltimore (N)	0	76	.392	154	673	149	264	99	19	.596	$26.4	0	74	.424
1898	Baltimore (N)	15	46	.384	136	591	132	227	23	2	.506	$15.0	1	44	.385
1899	Brooklyn (N)	13	61	.362	152	614	142	222	41	11	.528	$18.6	1	61	.379
1900	Brooklyn (N)	25	74	.350	155	642	115	225	24	6	.523	$18.4	4	68	.362
1901	Brooklyn (N)	19	51	.337	161	704	147	237	42	7	.497	$16.4	2	43	.339
1902	Brooklyn (N)	0	48	.336	153	643	110	216	82	5	.479	$12.0	0	38	.333
1903	New York (A)	0	42	.320	157	609	125	195	64	9	.455	$9.9	0	32	.313
1904	New York (A)	21	53	.375	149	566	104	212	27	4	.548	$6.8	2	40	.343
1905	New York (A)	24	50	.328	159	598	106	196	16	1	.478	$7.0	4	38	.302
1906	New York (A)	21	45	.333	159	619	131	206	14	1	.460	$7.3	2	33	.304
1907	New York (A)	0	24	.257	114	451	71	116	35	4	.353	$2.9	0	17	.234
1908	New York (A)	10	20	.297	95	337	55	100	5	0	.401	$2.0	1	14	.263
1909	New York (A)	12	45	.291	105	382	62	111	15	2	.435	$2.1	1	32	.264
1910	New York (N)	0	0	.364	20	11	7	4	0	0	.364	$0.5	0	0	.300
	Career	237	898	.340	2,394	9,724	1,943	3,307	632	95	.498	$193.0	33	810	.341
	Average season	12	47	.340	126	512	102	174	33	5	.498	$10.2	2	43	.341
	Summit season	15	64	.374	149	623	137	233	46	8	.546	$17.3	2	60	.384

GEORGE KELL

			ADJUSTED REGULAR SEASON										ACTUAL RESULTS		
YEAR	TEAM	HR	RBI	BA	G	AB	R	H	2B	3B	SA	PAY	HR	RBI	BA
1943	Philadelphia (A)	0	1	.200	1	5	1	1	0	1	.600	$0.0	0	1	.200
1944	Philadelphia (A)	0	55	.278	145	536	63	149	40	4	.368	$4.1	0	44	.268
1945	Philadelphia (A)	13	70	.281	156	602	63	169	46	2	.429	$6.1	4	56	.272
1946	Phi.-Det. (A)	12	66	.339	137	545	90	185	43	8	.514	$6.5	4	52	.322
1947	Detroit (A)	11	108	.330	156	603	87	199	44	4	.471	$12.0	5	93	.320
1948	Detroit (A)	5	50	.312	97	388	53	121	35	2	.451	$5.9	2	44	.304
1949	Detroit (A)	6	66	.352	140	545	108	192	59	7	.519	$11.3	3	59	.343
1950	Detroit (A)	11	106	.345	162	661	120	228	70	4	.513	$18.6	8	101	.340
1951	Detroit (A)	4	68	.330	155	631	106	208	56	2	.444	$12.1	2	59	.319
1952	Det.-Bos. (A)	12	69	.332	118	443	63	147	33	1	.492	$6.7	7	57	.311
1953	Boston (A)	16	83	.312	142	487	77	152	51	1	.520	$7.2	12	73	.307
1954	Bos.-Chi. (A)	7	68	.283	101	339	47	96	17	0	.395	$2.7	5	58	.276
1955	Chicago (A)	10	93	.325	134	449	50	146	32	1	.468	$3.0	8	81	.312
1956	Chi.-Balt. (A)	11	55	.283	129	446	60	126	29	1	.426	$2.8	9	48	.271
1957	Baltimore (A)	12	53	.310	104	326	34	101	12	0	.457	$2.2	9	44	.297
	Career	130	1,011	.317	1,877	7,006	1,022	2,220	567	38	.464	$101.2	78	870	.306
	Average season	9	67	.317	125	467	68	148	38	3	.464	$6.7	5	58	.306
	Summit season	11	78	.338	140	536	92	181	51	4	.509	$10.1	7	68	.326

JOE KELLEY

		ADJUSTED REGULAR SEASON												ACTUAL RESULTS		
YEAR	TEAM	HR	RBI	BA	G	AB	R	H	2B	3B	SA	PAY	HR	RBI	BA
1891	Boston (N)	0	3	.264	14	53	7	14	7	0	.396	$0.0	0	3	.244
1892	Pit.-Balt. (N)	0	33	.257	69	249	30	64	28	7	.426	$1.6	0	32	.235
1893	Baltimore (N)	35	75	.294	156	626	119	184	36	5	.535	$8.9	9	76	.305
1894	Baltimore (N)	24	99	.342	162	637	147	218	73	7	.592	$18.8	6	111	.393
1895	Baltimore (N)	38	129	.331	161	637	142	211	32	7	.582	$25.6	10	134	.365
1896	Baltimore (N)	37	103	.339	161	638	154	216	44	6	.600	$32.0	8	100	.364
1897	Baltimore (N)	25	121	.334	156	601	116	201	41	4	.541	$25.8	5	118	.362
1898	Baltimore (N)	18	115	.319	130	486	74	155	38	8	.541	$14.2	2	110	.321
1899	Brooklyn (N)	30	94	.311	154	579	109	180	27	4	.527	$18.7	6	93	.325
1900	Brooklyn (N)	29	99	.309	138	518	98	160	33	6	.564	$9.9	6	91	.319
1901	Brooklyn (N)	24	77	.304	142	582	92	177	34	5	.503	$11.7	4	65	.307
1902	Balt. (A)-Cin. (N)	17	59	.317	115	435	95	138	44	5	.559	$7.2	2	46	.315
1903	Cincinnati (N)	19	57	.324	121	441	108	143	25	2	.519	$5.0	3	45	.316
1904	Cincinnati (N)	0	83	.306	127	464	99	142	74	11	.513	$5.1	0	63	.281
1905	Cincinnati (N)	10	47	.301	94	335	55	101	14	4	.457	$2.8	1	37	.277
1906	Cincinnati (N)	13	72	.248	135	487	59	121	41	6	.437	$3.8	1	53	.228
1908	Boston (N)	11	24	.291	76	237	36	69	8	1	.473	$1.7	2	17	.259
	Career	330	1,290	.312	2,111	8,005	1,540	2,494	599	88	.532	$192.8	65	1,194	.317
	Average season	19	76	.312	124	471	91	147	35	5	.532	$11.3	4	70	.317
	Summit season	28	102	.334	151	590	131	197	47	6	.576	$21.9	6	102	.362

GEORGE KELLY

		ADJUSTED REGULAR SEASON												ACTUAL RESULTS		
YEAR	TEAM	HR	RBI	BA	G	AB	R	H	2B	3B	SA	PAY	HR	RBI	BA
1915	New York (N)	2	5	.175	18	40	3	7	0	0	.325	$0.0	1	4	.158
1916	New York (N)	0	4	.177	51	79	6	14	8	0	.278	$0.0	0	3	.158
1917	N.Y.-Pit. (N)	0	0	.067	19	30	3	2	0	0	.067	$0.0	0	0	.067
1919	New York (N)	5	20	.298	37	124	17	37	8	1	.500	$0.6	1	14	.290
1920	New York (N)	33	111	.259	162	617	81	160	19	3	.460	$7.4	11	94	.266
1921	New York (N)	45	134	.285	158	622	104	177	32	2	.559	$11.4	23	122	.308
1922	New York (N)	35	114	.305	157	616	102	188	29	2	.529	$12.4	17	107	.328
1923	New York (N)	33	114	.291	154	595	90	173	19	1	.492	$14.9	16	103	.307
1924	New York (N)	44	150	.304	151	599	100	182	27	3	.579	$12.7	21	136	.324
1925	New York (N)	35	104	.284	157	626	91	178	22	1	.490	$12.5	20	99	.309
1926	New York (N)	29	91	.291	146	536	79	156	18	1	.491	$9.3	13	80	.303
1927	Cincinnati (N)	12	23	.257	65	237	30	61	14	2	.485	$2.3	5	21	.270
1928	Cincinnati (N)	9	64	.284	123	426	51	121	43	4	.467	$2.8	3	58	.296
1929	Cincinnati (N)	12	104	.272	154	604	74	164	56	5	.440	$4.8	5	103	.293
1930	Cin.-Chi. (N)	13	51	.281	93	366	38	103	13	1	.429	$2.2	8	54	.308
1932	Brooklyn (N)	8	24	.237	67	211	25	50	8	0	.389	$1.5	4	22	.243
	Career	315	1,113	.280	1,712	6,328	894	1,773	316	26	.488	$94.8	148	1,020	.297
	Average season	20	70	.280	107	396	56	111	20	2	.488	$5.9	9	64	.297
	Summit season	37	121	.295	153	594	95	175	25	2	.530	$12.1	18	110	.314

KING KELLY

		ADJUSTED REGULAR SEASON											ACTUAL RESULTS		
YEAR	TEAM	HR	RBI	BA	G	AB	R	H	2B	3B	SA	PAY	HR	RBI	BA
1878	Cincinnati (N)	0	74	.293	159	628	79	184	75	6	.432	$12.2	0	27	.283
1879	Cincinnati (N)	43	96	.368	154	690	161	254	42	8	.639	$25.7	2	47	.348
1880	Chicago (N)	26	125	.320	158	647	150	207	46	8	.536	$26.2	1	60	.291
1881	Chicago (N)	31	109	.335	158	680	168	228	48	2	.549	$31.9	2	55	.323
1882	Chicago (N)	16	105	.331	162	727	155	241	111	3	.558	$33.3	1	55	.305
1883	Chicago (N)	32	93	.267	162	708	141	189	47	5	.483	$32.5	3	61	.255
1884	Chicago (N)	52	129	.391	155	649	163	254	31	2	.686	$39.5	13	95	.354
1885	Chicago (N)	43	105	.318	153	626	174	199	27	2	.573	$32.9	9	75	.288
1886	Chicago (N)	28	93	.425	152	581	184	247	58	5	.687	$29.2	4	79	.388
1887	Boston (N)	32	65	.320	148	618	123	198	44	3	.557	$22.9	8	63	.322
1888	Boston (N)	36	86	.360	127	522	104	188	31	4	.642	$12.3	9	71	.318
1889	Boston (N)	31	81	.301	152	617	124	186	50	2	.540	$13.7	9	78	.294
1890	Boston (P)	20	69	.337	111	424	87	143	26	2	.550	$4.9	4	66	.326
1891	Bos. (N)-Cin.-Bos. (AA)														
		11	64	.304	118	405	67	123	32	3	.479	$3.9	2	62	.286
1892	Boston (N)	7	43	.207	83	299	42	62	9	0	.308	$2.4	2	41	.189
1893	New York (N)	0	14	.263	24	80	9	21	5	0	.325	$1.0	0	15	.269
	Career	408	1,351	.329	2,176	8,901	1,931	2,924	682	55	.555	$324.5	69	950	.308
	Average season	26	84	.329	136	556	121	183	43	3	.555	$20.3	4	59	.308
	Summit season	40	102	.371	148	614	157	228	38	4	.642	$27.9	7	73	.339

JEFF KENT

		ADJUSTED REGULAR SEASON											ACTUAL RESULTS		
YEAR	TEAM	HR	RBI	BA	G	AB	R	H	2B	3B	SA	PAY	HR	RBI	BA
1992	Tor. (A)-N.Y. (N)	15	59	.252	102	305	62	77	23	2	.489	$5.0	11	50	.239
1993	New York (N)	25	86	.274	140	496	70	136	25	0	.476	$7.2	21	80	.270
1994	New York (N)	22	98	.290	153	593	76	172	35	6	.481	$9.2	14	68	.292
1995	New York (N)	24	75	.280	141	532	75	149	26	3	.476	$8.6	20	65	.278
1996	N.Y. (N)-Cle. (A)	12	54	.284	128	437	60	124	28	1	.435	$6.3	12	55	.284
1997	San Francisco (N)	31	126	.252	155	580	93	146	38	2	.484	$9.5	29	121	.250
1998	San Francisco (N)	32	132	.299	136	522	97	156	37	3	.565	$9.3	31	128	.297
1999	San Francisco (N)	22	99	.288	138	511	84	147	40	2	.503	$9.1	23	101	.290
2000	San Francisco (N)	31	121	.332	159	587	110	195	40	7	.583	$12.9	33	125	.334
2001	San Francisco (N)	21	110	.303	159	607	87	184	48	6	.506	$9.9	22	106	.298
	Career	235	960	.287	1,411	5,170	814	1,486	340	32	.502	$87.0	216	899	.285
	Average season	24	96	.287	141	517	81	149	34	3	.502	$8.7	22	90	.285
	Summit season	26	112	.303	149	564	91	171	40	5	.530	$10.1	25	106	.303

HARMON KILLEBREW

		ADJUSTED REGULAR SEASON											ACTUAL RESULTS		
YEAR	TEAM	HR	RBI	BA	G	AB	R	H	2B	3B	SA	PAY	HR	RBI	BA
1954	Washington (A)	0	3	.308	9	13	1	4	1	0	.385	$0.0	0	3	.308
1955	Washington (A)	5	8	.202	40	84	14	17	1	0	.393	$0.1	4	7	.200
1956	Washington (A)	6	15	.231	46	104	12	24	3	0	.433	$0.4	5	13	.222
1957	Washington (A)	2	6	.290	9	31	5	9	3	0	.581	$0.0	2	5	.290
1958	Washington (A)	0	2	.212	14	33	2	7	0	0	.212	$0.0	0	2	.194
1959	Washington (A)	50	124	.254	161	575	116	146	25	2	.565	$8.8	42	105	.242
1960	Washington (A)	38	95	.292	130	463	100	135	23	1	.592	$7.5	31	80	.276
1961	Minnesota (A)	52	133	.301	151	545	103	164	25	5	.651	$14.4	46	122	.288
1962	Minnesota (A)	53	139	.254	154	548	93	139	26	1	.595	$15.5	48	126	.243
1963	Minnesota (A)	54	120	.281	143	519	110	146	23	0	.638	$14.7	45	96	.258
1964	Minnesota (A)	58	134	.290	157	573	115	166	14	1	.621	$19.3	49	111	.270
1965	Minnesota (A)	30	92	.294	113	401	96	118	20	1	.574	$9.2	25	75	.269
1966	Minnesota (A)	46	135	.304	162	569	109	173	34	1	.610	$16.5	39	110	.281
1967	Minnesota (A)	57	145	.298	161	540	134	161	28	1	.670	$22.3	44	113	.269
1968	Minnesota (A)	25	56	.237	100	295	56	70	8	2	.532	$3.9	17	40	.210
1969	Minnesota (A)	60	168	.299	162	555	127	166	26	2	.677	$19.3	49	140	.276
1970	Minnesota (A)	47	128	.287	157	527	109	151	24	1	.603	$13.0	41	113	.271
1971	Minnesota (A)	37	151	.274	149	507	77	139	24	1	.544	$9.5	28	119	.254
1972	Minnesota (A)	37	102	.255	146	455	73	116	16	2	.543	$6.7	26	74	.231
1973	Minnesota (A)	7	37	.254	69	248	34	63	12	1	.395	$2.3	5	32	.242
1974	Minnesota (A)	18	64	.233	121	330	33	77	8	0	.421	$2.3	13	54	.222
1975	Kansas City (A)	18	51	.208	106	312	29	65	13	0	.423	$1.9	14	44	.199
	Career	700	1,908	.274	2,460	8,227	1,548	2,256	357	22	.578	$187.6	573	1,584	.256
	Average season	32	87	.274	112	374	70	103	16	1	.578	$8.5	26	72	.256
	Summit season	54	140	.297	156	546	117	162	27	2	.650	$17.4	45	116	.275

RALPH KINER

		ADJUSTED REGULAR SEASON											ACTUAL RESULTS		
YEAR	TEAM	HR	RBI	BA	G	AB	R	H	2B	3B	SA	PAY	HR	RBI	BA
1946	Pittsburgh (N)	38	104	.260	151	526	81	137	15	1	.510	$11.6	23	81	.247
1947	Pittsburgh (N)	70	149	.324	158	587	139	190	22	2	.726	$19.3	51	127	.313
1948	Pittsburgh (N)	55	138	.271	162	576	116	156	17	2	.594	$19.5	40	123	.265
1949	Pittsburgh (N)	72	143	.317	160	578	131	183	19	2	.730	$25.3	54	127	.310
1950	Pittsburgh (N)	57	127	.276	158	576	121	159	23	4	.627	$25.6	47	118	.272
1951	Pittsburgh (N)	56	125	.318	158	556	142	177	34	3	.692	$22.9	42	109	.309
1952	Pittsburgh (N)	51	107	.259	156	540	111	140	19	1	.581	$16.2	37	87	.244
1953	Pit.-Chi. (N)	43	131	.284	165	587	112	167	23	2	.550	$16.9	35	116	.279
1954	Chicago (N)	30	86	.295	155	587	104	173	45	3	.535	$12.9	22	73	.285
1955	Cleveland (A)	21	62	.251	119	338	64	85	17	0	.488	$3.9	18	54	.243
	Career	493	1,172	.287	1,542	5,451	1,121	1,567	234	20	.609	$174.1	369	1,015	.279
	Average season	49	117	.287	154	545	112	157	23	2	.609	$17.4	37	102	.279
	Summit season	62	136	.301	159	575	130	173	23	3	.675	$22.5	47	121	.294

DAVE KINGMAN

		ADJUSTED REGULAR SEASON											ACTUAL RESULTS		
YEAR	TEAM	HR	RBI	BA	G	AB	R	H	2B	3B	SA	PAY	HR	RBI	BA
1971	San Francisco (N)	8	30	.304	41	115	21	35	12	2	.652	$1.7	6	24	.278
1972	San Francisco (N)	42	114	.247	141	493	89	122	22	3	.560	$7.0	29	83	.225
1973	San Francisco (N)	29	64	.213	112	305	63	65	11	1	.541	$5.4	24	55	.203
1974	San Francisco (N)	24	65	.234	121	350	49	82	20	2	.509	$5.4	18	55	.223
1975	New York (N)	46	103	.241	134	502	76	121	23	1	.566	$8.6	36	88	.231
1976	New York (N)	50	106	.251	123	474	86	119	13	1	.599	$7.9	37	86	.238
1977	N.Y.-S.D. (N)-Cal.- N.Y. (A)	29	86	.226	132	439	52	99	21	0	.472	$4.8	26	78	.221
1978	Chicago (N)	37	94	.276	119	395	77	109	17	3	.615	$5.7	28	79	.266
1979	Chicago (N)	57	127	.291	145	532	107	155	19	4	.664	$9.5	48	115	.288
1980	Chicago (N)	22	66	.282	81	255	36	72	7	0	.569	$2.5	18	57	.278
1981	New York (N)	46	111	.232	154	544	75	126	17	3	.528	$6.9	22	59	.221
1982	New York (N)	44	114	.209	149	535	92	112	9	1	.477	$7.0	37	99	.204
1983	New York (N)	16	33	.202	100	248	28	50	7	0	.423	$2.1	13	29	.198
1984	Oakland (A)	43	137	.277	147	549	79	152	25	1	.561	$4.6	35	118	.268
1985	Oakland (A)	35	103	.248	158	592	75	147	18	0	.456	$6.4	30	91	.238
1986	Oakland (A)	39	105	.219	144	561	78	123	21	0	.465	$4.4	35	94	.210
	Career	567	1,458	.245	2,001	6,889	1,083	1,689	262	22	.537	$89.9	442	1,210	.236
	Average season	35	91	.245	125	431	68	106	16	1	.537	$5.6	28	76	.236
	Summit season	46	116	.268	135	489	88	131	19	2	.597	$6.9	35	96	.258

CHUCK KLEIN

		ADJUSTED REGULAR SEASON											ACTUAL RESULTS		
YEAR	TEAM	HR	RBI	BA	G	AB	R	H	2B	3B	SA	PAY	HR	RBI	BA
1928	Philadelphia (N)	20	38	.346	68	269	46	93	11	1	.617	$3.5	11	34	.360
1929	Philadelphia (N)	62	148	.331	157	649	128	215	31	2	.672	$15.1	43	145	.356
1930	Philadelphia (N)	57	162	.352	162	673	150	237	44	2	.678	$26.3	40	170	.386
1931	Philadelphia (N)	55	134	.326	155	622	134	203	23	3	.638	$20.0	31	121	.337
1932	Philadelphia (N)	63	150	.339	162	684	167	232	40	5	.689	$38.9	38	137	.348
1933	Philadelphia (N)	54	144	.368	162	646	121	238	37	3	.686	$28.1	28	120	.368
1934	Chicago (N)	32	88	.290	123	465	86	135	22	1	.548	$9.9	20	80	.301
1935	Chicago (N)	32	80	.283	125	456	77	129	11	1	.522	$9.2	21	73	.293
1936	Chi.-Phi. (N)	42	108	.290	154	634	106	184	29	3	.544	$10.1	25	104	.306
1937	Philadelphia (N)	24	61	.316	120	424	80	134	18	1	.533	$4.6	15	57	.325
1938	Philadelphia (N)	15	67	.243	138	490	58	119	24	1	.388	$3.9	8	61	.247
1939	Phi.-Pit. (N)	20	61	.278	116	334	49	93	17	3	.527	$2.7	12	56	.284
1940	Philadelphia (N)	12	42	.218	122	372	44	81	17	1	.366	$2.1	7	37	.218
1941	Philadelphia (N)	1	3	.132	52	76	7	10	0	0	.171	$0.8	1	3	.123
1942	Philadelphia (N)	0	0	.067	15	15	0	1	0	0	.067	$0.3	0	0	.071
1943	Philadelphia (N)	0	4	.100	12	20	0	2	0	0	.100	$0.0	0	3	.100
1944	Philadelphia (N)	0	0	.143	4	7	1	1	0	0	.143	$0.0	0	0	.143
	Career	489	1,290	.308	1,847	6,836	1,254	2,107	324	27	.578	$175.5	300	1,201	.320
	Average season	29	76	.308	109	402	74	124	19	2	.578	$10.3	18	71	.320
	Summit season	58	148	.344	160	655	140	225	35	3	.672	$25.7	36	139	.359

NAP LAJOIE

		ADJUSTED REGULAR SEASON											ACTUAL RESULTS		
YEAR	TEAM	HR	RBI	BA	G	AB	R	H	2B	3B	SA	PAY	HR	RBI	BA
1896	Philadelphia (N)	16	44	.300	49	220	38	66	14	2	.600	$3.3	4	42	.326
1897	Philadelphia (N)	44	132	.334	154	661	111	221	50	7	.631	$12.0	9	127	.361
1898	Philadelphia (N)	33	137	.322	159	658	121	212	55	4	.568	$15.6	6	127	.324
1899	Philadelphia (N)	24	69	.360	81	328	69	118	20	2	.652	$7.3	6	70	.378
1900	Philadelphia (N)	30	101	.325	117	517	104	168	41	4	.594	$11.9	7	92	.337
1901	Philadelphia (A)	55	149	.424	155	644	174	273	47	4	.766	$25.9	14	125	.426
1902	Phi.-Cle. (A)	32	86	.381	103	417	107	159	33	2	.700	$11.3	7	65	.378
1903	Cleveland (A)	38	119	.353	145	563	115	199	40	3	.638	$12.7	7	93	.344
1904	Cleveland (A)	36	138	.411	147	581	124	239	66	5	.728	$16.1	5	102	.376
1905	Cleveland (A)	12	53	.358	68	260	37	93	14	1	.558	$4.6	2	41	.329
1906	Cleveland (A)	0	123	.389	157	622	119	242	138	7	.633	$10.1	0	91	.355
1907	Cleveland (A)	20	86	.327	140	520	72	170	48	3	.546	$5.1	2	63	.299
1908	Cleveland (A)	20	106	.327	162	600	110	196	54	3	.527	$9.6	2	74	.289
1909	Cleveland (A)	13	65	.358	134	491	78	176	69	4	.595	$5.1	1	47	.324
1910	Cleveland (A)	26	94	.415	160	595	117	247	70	3	.674	$9.1	4	76	.384
1911	Cleveland (A)	10	66	.368	93	326	40	120	26	0	.540	$2.6	2	60	.365
1912	Cleveland (A)	0	100	.370	122	467	73	173	80	2	.550	$3.6	0	90	.368
1913	Cleveland (A)	8	84	.348	143	485	81	169	47	1	.499	$4.4	1	68	.335
1914	Cleveland (A)	0	63	.273	125	433	47	118	45	2	.386	$2.5	0	50	.258
1915	Philadelphia (A)	9	80	.300	136	517	52	155	50	3	.460	$3.2	1	61	.280
1916	Philadelphia (A)	13	49	.267	119	449	46	120	20	2	.408	$2.3	2	35	.246
	Career	439	1,944	.351	2,669	10,354	1,835	3,634	1,027	64	.590	$178.3	82	1,599	.338
	Average season	21	93	.351	127	493	87	173	49	3	.590	$8.5	4	76	.338
	Summit season	30	118	.406	144	572	128	232	71	4	.701	$14.5	6	92	.384

BARRY LARKIN

		ADJUSTED REGULAR SEASON											ACTUAL RESULTS		
YEAR	TEAM	HR	RBI	BA	G	AB	R	H	2B	3B	SA	PAY	HR	RBI	BA
1986	Cincinnati (N)	4	21	.296	41	159	30	47	5	3	.440	$1.8	3	19	.283
1987	Cincinnati (N)	12	45	.248	125	439	67	109	18	2	.380	$4.3	12	43	.244
1988	Cincinnati (N)	18	67	.313	152	592	109	185	39	5	.486	$8.7	12	56	.296
1989	Cincinnati (N)	7	43	.363	97	325	56	118	19	4	.511	$4.5	4	36	.342
1990	Cincinnati (N)	11	77	.314	158	614	98	193	31	7	.441	$11.7	7	67	.301
1991	Cincinnati (N)	26	79	.317	123	464	100	147	29	4	.565	$9.1	20	69	.302
1992	Cincinnati (N)	18	93	.319	140	533	90	170	37	6	.512	$11.4	12	78	.304
1993	Cincinnati (N)	10	55	.320	100	384	61	123	22	3	.471	$5.5	8	51	.315
1994	Cincinnati (N)	14	74	.277	155	602	111	167	34	6	.424	$12.2	9	52	.279
1995	Cincinnati (N)	18	76	.321	147	557	113	179	35	6	.503	$9.6	15	66	.319
1996	Cincinnati (N)	33	88	.298	152	517	116	154	33	4	.569	$7.3	33	89	.298
1997	Cincinnati (N)	4	21	.321	73	224	35	72	18	3	.482	$2.4	4	20	.317
1998	Cincinnati (N)	18	75	.312	145	538	96	168	34	10	.513	$6.8	17	72	.309
1999	Cincinnati (N)	11	73	.290	160	579	105	168	30	4	.413	$7.3	12	75	.293
2000	Cincinnati (N)	10	39	.311	101	392	68	122	25	5	.477	$2.4	11	41	.313
2001	Cincinnati (N)	2	18	.263	45	156	30	41	11	0	.372	$1.5	2	17	.256
	Career	216	944	.306	1,914	7,075	1,285	2,163	420	72	.477	$106.5	181	851	.299
	Average season	14	59	.306	120	442	80	135	26	5	.477	$6.7	11	53	.299
	Summit season	20	76	.318	131	475	92	151	30	6	.533	$7.8	17	69	.308

TONY LAZZERI

		ADJUSTED REGULAR SEASON											ACTUAL RESULTS		
YEAR	TEAM	HR	RBI	BA	G	AB	R	H	2B	3B	SA	PAY	HR	RBI	BA
1926	New York (A)	40	126	.263	162	616	87	162	21	4	.505	$15.3	18	114	.275
1927	New York (A)	37	111	.294	160	596	100	175	21	2	.522	$15.5	18	102	.309
1928	New York (A)	24	90	.318	122	425	68	135	30	5	.581	$9.0	10	82	.332
1929	New York (A)	33	108	.330	155	575	103	190	34	4	.576	$14.8	18	106	.354
1930	New York (A)	19	116	.275	150	599	104	165	38	7	.457	$15.3	9	121	.303
1931	New York (A)	20	91	.259	141	506	74	131	25	3	.439	$11.6	8	83	.267
1932	New York (A)	30	122	.292	147	528	85	154	27	7	.540	$11.7	15	113	.300
1933	New York (A)	38	124	.294	148	557	112	164	20	5	.553	$12.5	18	104	.294
1934	New York (A)	25	73	.257	129	459	64	118	22	3	.481	$7.0	14	67	.267
1935	New York (A)	24	93	.263	141	517	81	136	18	3	.449	$7.0	13	83	.273
1936	New York (A)	26	113	.272	157	562	85	153	27	3	.470	$9.5	14	109	.287
1937	New York (A)	23	74	.237	130	460	59	109	18	1	.430	$3.8	14	70	.244
1938	Chicago (N)	7	25	.260	57	127	23	33	4	0	.457	$1.9	5	23	.267
1939	Bkn.-N.Y. (N)	6	15	.279	28	86	14	24	1	0	.500	$1.1	4	14	.289
	Career	352	1,281	.280	1,827	6,613	1,059	1,849	306	47	.500	$136.0	178	1,191	.292
	Average season	25	92	.280	131	472	76	132	22	3	.500	$9.7	13	85	.292
	Summit season	32	111	.306	146	536	94	164	26	5	.552	$12.7	16	101	.317

FREDDIE LINDSTROM

		ADJUSTED REGULAR SEASON											ACTUAL RESULTS		
YEAR	TEAM	HR	RBI	BA	G	AB	R	H	2B	3B	SA	PAY	HR	RBI	BA
1924	New York (N)	0	4	.238	55	84	21	20	9	0	.345	$0.5	0	4	.253
1925	New York (N)	12	34	.263	111	380	45	100	20	6	.442	$2.8	4	33	.287
1926	New York (N)	25	86	.290	150	582	102	169	18	3	.460	$7.4	9	76	.302
1927	New York (N)	21	63	.290	144	586	116	170	40	3	.476	$9.0	7	58	.306
1928	New York (N)	32	117	.343	160	676	109	232	38	4	.553	$15.4	14	107	.358
1929	New York (N)	27	94	.296	139	587	102	174	20	3	.479	$14.3	15	91	.319
1930	New York (N)	35	102	.346	156	642	122	222	33	3	.570	$19.2	22	106	.379
1931	New York (N)	13	40	.292	83	322	42	94	12	3	.469	$6.4	5	36	.300
1932	New York (N)	27	100	.263	151	624	90	164	23	2	.436	$12.4	15	92	.271
1933	Pittsburgh (N)	15	65	.310	145	565	82	175	55	6	.508	$9.5	5	55	.310
1934	Pittsburgh (N)	10	54	.280	104	411	65	115	30	2	.436	$4.3	4	49	.290
1935	Chicago (N)	8	68	.266	95	361	54	96	28	2	.421	$4.3	3	62	.275
1936	Brooklyn (N)	0	10	.255	27	110	12	28	7	0	.318	$1.9	0	10	.264
	Career	225	837	.297	1,520	5,930	962	1,759	333	37	.479	$107.4	103	779	.311
	Average season	17	64	.297	117	456	74	135	26	3	.479	$8.3	8	60	.311
	Summit season	26	88	.319	149	611	106	195	37	4	.520	$13.5	13	83	.336

SHERM LOLLAR

		ADJUSTED REGULAR SEASON											ACTUAL RESULTS		
YEAR	TEAM	HR	RBI	BA	G	AB	R	H	2B	3B	SA	PAY	HR	RBI	BA
1946	Cleveland (A)	2	11	.250	29	64	9	16	8	0	.469	$0.3	1	9	.242
1947	New York (A)	2	7	.219	11	32	5	7	0	1	.469	$0.0	1	6	.219
1948	New York (A)	0	5	.225	23	40	0	9	0	0	.225	$0.0	0	4	.211
1949	St. Louis (A)	12	55	.266	114	297	31	79	10	1	.428	$2.4	8	49	.261
1950	St. Louis (A)	17	70	.282	133	418	59	118	27	2	.478	$4.5	13	65	.280
1951	St. Louis (A)	11	50	.261	103	326	50	85	25	0	.439	$4.1	8	44	.252
1952	Chicago (A)	19	61	.254	137	389	43	99	18	0	.447	$5.1	13	50	.240
1953	Chicago (A)	10	60	.292	117	346	51	101	23	0	.445	$3.7	8	54	.287
1954	Chicago (A)	9	40	.251	112	331	36	83	16	0	.381	$3.1	7	34	.244
1955	Chicago (A)	19	69	.272	144	445	76	121	17	1	.443	$4.4	16	61	.261
1956	Chicago (A)	13	87	.307	143	473	63	145	38	1	.474	$3.0	11	75	.293
1957	Chicago (A)	14	85	.269	106	368	40	99	15	1	.429	$2.6	11	70	.256
1958	Chicago (A)	24	101	.286	133	441	63	126	21	0	.497	$3.6	20	84	.273
1959	Chicago (A)	27	98	.277	145	523	73	145	29	2	.495	$4.6	22	84	.265
1960	Chicago (A)	9	55	.266	136	444	52	118	30	0	.394	$2.6	7	46	.252
1961	Chicago (A)	8	44	.293	115	334	41	98	13	1	.410	$2.1	7	41	.282
1962	Chicago (A)	2	29	.282	84	220	19	62	16	0	.382	$1.4	2	26	.268
1963	Chicago (A)	0	7	.260	35	73	5	19	5	0	.329	$0.6	0	6	.233
	Career	198	934	.275	1,820	5,564	716	1,530	311	10	.441	$48.1	155	808	.264
	Average season	11	52	.275	101	309	40	85	17	1	.441	$2.7	9	45	.264
	Summit season	18	83	.289	134	440	62	127	28	1	.480	$3.9	15	72	.279

ERNIE LOMBARDI

		ADJUSTED REGULAR SEASON											ACTUAL RESULTS		
YEAR	TEAM	HR	RBI	BA	G	AB	R	H	2B	3B	SA	PAY	HR	RBI	BA
1931	Brooklyn (N)	9	25	.286	77	192	22	55	6	0	.458	$1.8	4	23	.297
1932	Cincinnati (N)	22	74	.295	123	431	47	127	21	4	.515	$4.7	11	68	.303
1933	Cincinnati (N)	10	56	.281	113	370	35	104	24	1	.432	$4.3	4	47	.283
1934	Cincinnati (N)	18	68	.294	141	445	46	131	19	2	.467	$5.1	9	62	.305
1935	Cincinnati (N)	21	70	.332	126	349	39	116	21	2	.585	$4.9	12	64	.343
1936	Cincinnati (N)	21	70	.315	127	406	43	128	20	1	.525	$5.2	12	68	.333
1937	Cincinnati (N)	16	63	.326	125	383	44	125	21	1	.512	$3.7	9	59	.334
1938	Cincinnati (N)	30	104	.337	138	523	66	176	28	1	.566	$5.5	19	95	.342
1939	Cincinnati (N)	30	91	.281	135	467	46	131	22	1	.525	$4.6	20	85	.287
1940	Cincinnati (N)	21	83	.321	114	393	56	126	20	0	.532	$2.8	14	74	.319
1941	Cincinnati (N)	17	70	.270	123	418	38	113	11	1	.423	$2.8	10	60	.264
1942	Boston (N)	22	60	.351	113	333	42	117	14	0	.592	$2.4	11	46	.330
1943	New York (N)	20	67	.324	108	306	25	99	6	0	.539	$2.1	10	51	.305
1944	New York (N)	19	72	.262	122	389	46	102	12	0	.440	$2.2	10	58	.255
1945	New York (N)	32	87	.318	121	387	57	123	5	1	.584	$2.4	19	70	.307
1946	New York (N)	19	51	.306	93	252	25	77	3	1	.552	$1.7	12	39	.290
1947	New York (N)	6	25	.287	50	115	9	33	5	0	.487	$1.1	4	21	.282
	Career	333	1,136	.306	1,949	6,159	686	1,883	258	16	.515	$57.3	190	990	.306
	Average season	20	67	.306	115	362	40	111	15	1	.515	$3.4	11	58	.306
	Summit season	25	81	.332	122	397	52	132	18	1	.572	$3.6	15	70	.329

FRED LYNN

		ADJUSTED REGULAR SEASON											ACTUAL RESULTS		
YEAR	TEAM	HR	RBI	BA	G	AB	R	H	2B	3B	SA	PAY	HR	RBI	BA
1974	Boston (A)	3	12	.442	15	43	6	19	3	2	.814	$0.2	2	10	.419
1975	Boston (A)	31	124	.346	147	535	122	185	57	6	.649	$7.5	21	105	.331
1976	Boston (A)	19	80	.331	132	507	93	168	43	6	.552	$9.0	10	65	.314
1977	Boston (A)	23	85	.263	130	501	90	132	33	3	.479	$9.3	18	76	.260
1978	Boston (A)	30	96	.311	149	537	88	167	36	2	.553	$12.2	22	82	.298
1979	Boston (A)	47	136	.338	149	538	130	182	44	1	.686	$15.1	39	122	.333
1980	Boston (A)	18	71	.305	111	419	78	128	37	2	.532	$9.1	12	61	.301
1981	California (A)	12	56	.231	112	377	50	87	14	1	.369	$5.5	5	31	.219
1982	California (A)	27	99	.307	138	472	102	145	41	1	.570	$9.1	21	86	.299
1983	California (A)	28	84	.281	117	437	64	123	21	2	.531	$5.6	22	74	.272
1984	California (A)	30	92	.280	142	517	97	145	32	3	.528	$6.9	23	79	.271
1985	Baltimore (A)	27	78	.277	125	452	67	125	13	1	.489	$4.6	23	68	.263
1986	Baltimore (A)	26	75	.300	112	397	75	119	14	1	.537	$3.8	23	67	.287
1987	Baltimore (A)	23	63	.258	111	396	51	102	26	0	.497	$2.9	23	60	.253
1988	Balt.-Det. (A)	31	66	.261	114	391	54	102	14	1	.540	$2.4	25	56	.246
1989	Detroit (A)	15	54	.255	117	353	52	90	12	1	.422	$2.2	11	46	.241
1990	San Diego (N)	8	26	.250	90	196	21	49	3	1	.398	$1.3	6	23	.240
	Career	398	1,297	.293	2,011	7,068	1,240	2,068	443	34	.534	$106.7	306	1,111	.283
	Average season	23	76	.293	118	416	73	122	26	2	.534	$6.3	18	65	.283
	Summit season	31	107	.326	143	518	107	169	44	3	.602	$10.6	23	92	.315

SHERRY MAGEE

		ADJUSTED REGULAR SEASON											ACTUAL RESULTS		
YEAR	TEAM	HR	RBI	BA	G	AB	R	H	2B	3B	SA	PAY	HR	RBI	BA
1904	Philadelphia (N)	21	76	.303	99	379	68	115	20	4	.544	$6.2	3	57	.277
1905	Philadelphia (N)	34	126	.324	162	630	128	204	31	6	.554	$15.5	5	98	.299
1906	Philadelphia (N)	35	92	.309	162	592	105	183	34	2	.551	$15.1	6	67	.282
1907	Philadelphia (N)	33	123	.361	152	546	109	197	38	4	.626	$14.8	4	85	.328
1908	Philadelphia (N)	22	82	.319	149	529	114	169	57	9	.586	$14.6	2	57	.283
1909	Philadelphia (N)	22	92	.297	150	548	83	163	57	7	.547	$12.1	2	66	.270
1910	Philadelphia (N)	35	157	.358	159	536	140	192	48	5	.662	$19.1	6	123	.331
1911	Philadelphia (N)	38	106	.291	128	471	89	137	20	1	.580	$11.8	15	94	.288
1912	Philadelphia (N)	26	75	.306	141	496	90	152	24	2	.520	$11.7	6	66	.306
1913	Philadelphia (N)	34	84	.319	141	480	111	153	28	1	.594	$9.5	11	70	.306
1914	Philadelphia (N)	48	133	.333	154	574	124	191	31	3	.648	$12.6	15	103	.314
1915	Boston (N)	16	111	.301	161	589	92	177	60	6	.504	$12.3	2	87	.280
1916	Boston (N)	16	74	.261	125	429	60	112	20	2	.429	$4.8	3	54	.241
1917	Bos.-Cin. (N)	11	71	.303	121	396	56	120	33	4	.490	$3.7	1	52	.279
1918	Cincinnati (N)	24	126	.315	144	501	76	158	29	7	.545	$4.9	2	76	.298
1919	Cincinnati (N)	0	30	.222	65	189	16	42	19	0	.323	$1.9	0	21	.215
	Career	415	1,558	.313	2,213	7,885	1,461	2,465	549	63	.556	$170.6	83	1,176	.291
	Average season	26	97	.313	138	493	91	154	34	4	.556	$10.7	5	74	.291
	Summit season	34	116	.338	151	533	120	180	40	4	.619	$14.1	8	88	.313

MICKEY MANTLE

YEAR	TEAM	ADJUSTED REGULAR SEASON											ACTUAL RESULTS		
		HR	RBI	BA	G	AB	R	H	2B	3B	SA	PAY	HR	RBI	BA
1951	New York (A)	19	75	.276	101	359	70	99	13	4	.493	$6.3	13	65	.267
1952	New York (A)	35	107	.332	149	576	116	191	46	5	.611	$14.3	23	87	.311
1953	New York (A)	27	106	.300	136	494	121	148	30	2	.532	$12.3	21	92	.295
1954	New York (A)	38	120	.309	153	569	152	176	22	8	.576	$19.4	27	102	.300
1955	New York (A)	46	114	.317	155	545	140	173	34	8	.662	$19.7	37	99	.306
1956	New York (A)	62	151	.369	158	561	153	207	28	3	.761	$26.4	52	130	.353
1957	New York (A)	42	114	.382	151	497	147	190	37	4	.726	$25.9	34	94	.365
1958	New York (A)	49	116	.319	157	543	153	173	26	1	.641	$26.7	42	97	.304
1959	New York (A)	38	88	.298	151	567	123	169	29	3	.561	$19.9	31	75	.285
1960	New York (A)	50	112	.290	160	551	142	160	22	4	.617	$22.3	40	94	.275
1961	New York (A)	60	138	.331	152	511	143	169	19	4	.736	$16.9	54	128	.317
1962	New York (A)	34	99	.334	123	377	106	126	19	1	.660	$9.9	30	89	.321
1963	New York (A)	18	43	.343	65	172	50	59	10	0	.715	$3.5	15	35	.314
1964	New York (A)	41	133	.325	141	458	110	149	31	2	.670	$9.2	35	111	.303
1965	New York (A)	23	56	.280	122	361	54	101	15	1	.518	$3.5	19	46	.255
1966	New York (A)	28	69	.313	109	336	49	105	16	1	.616	$2.7	23	56	.288
1967	New York (A)	29	71	.272	143	437	81	119	21	0	.519	$4.3	22	55	.245
1968	New York (A)	27	75	.268	142	429	79	115	17	1	.501	$3.4	18	54	.237
	Career	666	1,787	.315	2,468	8,343	1,989	2,629	435	52	.619	$246.6	536	1,509	.298
	Average season	37	99	.315	137	464	111	146	24	3	.619	$13.7	30	84	.298
	Summit season	48	127	.349	145	481	132	168	27	3	.717	$17.7	41	110	.333

HEINIE MANUSH

YEAR	TEAM	ADJUSTED REGULAR SEASON											ACTUAL RESULTS		
		HR	RBI	BA	G	AB	R	H	2B	3B	SA	PAY	HR	RBI	BA
1923	Detroit (A)	12	59	.317	114	322	64	102	24	2	.516	$5.2	4	54	.334
1924	Detroit (A)	23	74	.270	125	440	90	119	22	2	.486	$7.3	9	68	.289
1925	Detroit (A)	11	48	.280	103	289	47	81	13	1	.446	$4.9	5	47	.302
1926	Detroit (A)	33	94	.363	140	513	104	186	28	2	.618	$9.3	14	86	.378
1927	Detroit (A)	21	97	.284	157	617	110	175	40	9	.480	$14.6	6	90	.298
1928	St. Louis (A)	34	119	.362	162	671	115	243	52	9	.618	$18.8	13	108	.378
1929	St. Louis (A)	15	82	.331	149	602	86	199	55	5	.513	$14.5	6	81	.355
1930	St.L.-Wash. (A)	18	90	.320	144	582	96	186	53	5	.521	$9.9	9	94	.350
1931	Washington (A)	18	76	.298	152	641	121	191	49	6	.477	$12.8	6	70	.307
1932	Washington (A)	30	127	.334	157	659	133	220	43	7	.557	$16.6	14	116	.342
1933	Washington (A)	18	113	.336	162	697	137	234	52	12	.522	$19.9	5	95	.336
1934	Washington (A)	24	96	.336	143	580	95	195	48	6	.564	$9.6	11	89	.349
1935	Washington (A)	11	61	.264	125	503	74	133	34	6	.421	$6.9	4	56	.273
1936	Boston (A)	0	46	.274	86	328	44	90	28	5	.390	$2.8	0	45	.291
1937	Brooklyn (N)	10	78	.324	138	487	61	158	34	5	.476	$3.2	4	73	.333
1938	Bkn.-Pit. (N)	0	11	.250	34	68	12	17	8	2	.426	$1.0	0	10	.250
1939	Pittsburgh (N)	0	1	.000	11	13	0	0	0	0	.000	$0.4	0	1	.000
	Career	278	1,272	.316	2,102	8,012	1,389	2,529	583	84	.513	$157.7	110	1,183	.330
	Average season	16	75	.316	124	471	82	149	34	5	.513	$9.3	6	70	.330
	Summit season	28	110	.346	153	624	117	216	45	7	.575	$14.8	11	99	.356

RABBIT MARANVILLE

	ADJUSTED REGULAR SEASON											ACTUAL RESULTS		
YEAR	TEAM	HR	RBI	BA	G	AB	R	H	2B	3B	SA	PAY	HR	RBI	BA
1912	Boston (N)	0	9	.213	27	89	9	19	6	0	.281	$0.3	0	8	.209
1913	Boston (N)	15	59	.257	150	599	84	154	23	4	.384	$6.0	2	48	.247
1914	Boston (N)	20	97	.260	160	601	92	156	29	2	.414	$8.9	4	78	.246
1915	Boston (N)	14	55	.262	154	526	65	138	35	2	.416	$6.4	2	43	.244
1916	Boston (N)	25	52	.255	159	620	108	158	21	5	.426	$12.0	4	38	.235
1917	Boston (N)	24	59	.282	147	581	95	164	29	5	.473	$11.3	3	43	.260
1918	Boston (N)	0	5	.333	14	48	5	16	0	4	.500	$2.3	0	3	.316
1919	Boston (N)	25	62	.273	152	557	63	152	23	4	.463	$6.5	5	43	.267
1920	Boston (N)	7	51	.259	142	522	57	135	44	11	.425	$4.2	1	43	.266
1921	Pittsburgh (N)	5	76	.272	161	644	98	175	53	7	.399	$7.2	1	70	.294
1922	Pittsburgh (N)	0	67	.275	162	702	123	193	65	13	.405	$15.9	0	63	.295
1923	Pittsburgh (N)	5	44	.262	148	610	85	160	41	7	.377	$5.1	1	41	.277
1924	Pittsburgh (N)	9	78	.250	161	629	68	157	59	14	.431	$7.2	2	71	.266
1925	Chicago (N)	0	24	.214	79	280	38	60	21	2	.304	$2.1	0	23	.233
1926	Brooklyn (N)	0	27	.224	82	246	36	55	20	5	.346	$1.7	0	24	.235
1927	St. Louis (N)	0	0	.219	10	32	0	7	3	0	.313	$0.5	0	0	.241
1928	St. Louis (N)	5	37	.231	118	386	44	89	25	7	.370	$1.4	1	34	.240
1929	Boston (N)	0	56	.264	154	591	89	156	51	8	.377	$2.5	0	55	.284
1930	Boston (N)	6	41	.256	149	586	81	150	37	4	.363	$2.5	2	43	.281
1931	Boston (N)	0	36	.251	151	585	75	147	47	4	.345	$3.3	0	33	.260
1932	Boston (N)	0	40	.227	156	598	73	136	38	4	.304	$3.5	0	37	.235
1933	Boston (N)	0	44	.217	149	498	54	108	35	4	.303	$2.3	0	38	.218
1935	Boston (N)	0	5	.143	24	70	3	10	3	0	.186	$0.7	0	5	.149
	Career	160	1,024	.254	2,809	10,600	1,445	2,695	708	116	.388	$113.8	28	884	.258
	Average season	7	45	.254	122	461	63	117	31	5	.388	$4.9	1	38	.258
	Summit season	18	60	.263	152	582	78	153	35	8	.443	$8.2	3	48	.258

MARTY MARION

	ADJUSTED REGULAR SEASON											ACTUAL RESULTS		
YEAR	TEAM	HR	RBI	BA	G	AB	R	H	2B	3B	SA	PAY	HR	RBI	BA
1940	St. Louis (N)	6	51	.279	130	452	49	126	24	1	.376	$5.1	3	46	.278
1941	St. Louis (N)	8	67	.259	162	572	58	148	33	3	.369	$6.5	3	58	.252
1942	St. Louis (N)	0	68	.293	153	505	83	148	74	4	.455	$7.2	0	54	.276
1943	St. Louis (N)	5	70	.297	137	444	51	132	33	3	.419	$5.9	1	52	.280
1944	St. Louis (N)	16	78	.275	149	524	62	144	33	1	.433	$7.4	6	63	.267
1945	St. Louis (N)	4	73	.286	129	451	78	129	51	4	.443	$7.3	1	59	.277
1946	St. Louis (N)	8	58	.245	152	518	65	127	42	3	.384	$5.4	3	46	.233
1947	St. Louis (N)	9	87	.281	155	562	67	158	30	5	.400	$6.7	4	74	.272
1948	St. Louis (N)	8	48	.257	151	595	79	153	39	2	.370	$6.7	4	43	.252
1949	St. Louis (N)	9	77	.279	138	530	67	148	42	1	.413	$3.8	5	70	.272
1950	St. Louis (N)	6	43	.249	112	393	39	98	15	1	.338	$2.5	4	40	.247
1952	St. Louis (A)	3	23	.263	70	194	20	51	16	0	.392	$1.5	2	19	.247
1953	St. Louis (A)	0	0	.000	3	7	0	0	0	0	.000	$0.4	0	0	.000
	Career	82	743	.272	1,641	5,747	718	1,562	432	28	.400	$66.4	36	624	.263
	Average season	6	57	.272	126	442	55	120	33	2	.400	$5.1	3	48	.263
	Summit season	7	73	.285	141	491	68	140	47	3	.436	$6.3	3	60	.274

ROGER MARIS

		ADJUSTED REGULAR SEASON											ACTUAL RESULTS		
YEAR	TEAM	HR	RBI	BA	G	AB	R	H	2B	3B	SA	PAY	HR	RBI	BA
1957	Cleveland (A)	18	62	.245	123	380	75	93	12	4	.439	$6.4	14	51	.235
1958	Cle.-K.C. (A)	34	95	.251	156	606	104	152	24	3	.469	$12.2	28	80	.240
1959	Kansas City (A)	20	85	.286	128	454	81	130	28	6	.507	$9.1	16	72	.273
1960	New York (A)	49	134	.298	142	521	117	155	23	5	.643	$14.2	39	112	.283
1961	New York (A)	67	153	.280	160	586	142	164	19	3	.666	$19.8	61	142	.269
1962	New York (A)	36	111	.268	157	590	102	158	43	1	.527	$18.9	33	100	.256
1963	New York (A)	28	66	.295	91	315	66	93	18	1	.625	$6.6	23	53	.269
1964	New York (A)	31	85	.302	139	506	103	153	15	2	.524	$9.7	26	71	.281
1965	New York (A)	9	33	.265	46	155	27	41	9	0	.497	$3.3	8	27	.239
1966	New York (A)	16	53	.251	120	351	46	88	12	2	.433	$2.4	13	43	.233
1967	St. Louis (N)	15	72	.291	126	413	83	120	26	5	.487	$3.0	9	55	.261
1968	St. Louis (N)	9	64	.290	100	310	35	90	25	2	.471	$2.1	5	45	.255
	Career	332	1,013	.277	1,488	5,187	981	1,437	254	34	.531	$107.7	275	851	.260
	Average season	28	84	.277	124	432	82	120	21	3	.531	$9.0	23	71	.260
	Summit season	41	114	.286	145	531	109	152	26	3	.578	$14.3	35	99	.272

BILLY MARTIN

		ADJUSTED REGULAR SEASON											ACTUAL RESULTS		
YEAR	TEAM	HR	RBI	BA	G	AB	R	H	2B	3B	SA	PAY	HR	RBI	BA
1950	New York (A)	1	9	.263	36	38	11	10	1	0	.368	$0.2	1	8	.250
1951	New York (A)	0	2	.262	54	61	11	16	2	2	.361	$0.1	0	2	.259
1952	New York (A)	6	41	.285	115	383	40	109	21	2	.397	$2.7	3	33	.267
1953	New York (A)	21	86	.262	160	630	83	165	32	4	.425	$7.3	15	75	.257
1955	New York (A)	1	10	.311	21	74	9	23	3	0	.392	$1.6	1	9	.300
1956	New York (A)	11	56	.274	127	481	88	132	34	3	.426	$5.8	9	49	.264
1957	N.Y.-K.C. (A)	13	47	.262	122	431	54	113	19	4	.415	$3.7	10	39	.251
1958	Detroit (A)	9	51	.267	138	525	67	140	25	1	.370	$4.0	7	42	.255
1959	Cleveland (A)	11	28	.275	77	255	44	70	9	0	.439	$2.8	9	24	.260
1960	Cincinnati (N)	4	19	.258	107	329	40	85	22	1	.368	$1.6	3	16	.246
1961	Mil. (N)-Minn. (A)	7	39	.251	115	383	49	96	20	4	.379	$1.9	6	36	.242
	Career	84	388	.267	1,072	3,590	496	959	188	21	.401	$31.7	64	333	.257
	Average season	8	35	.267	97	326	45	87	17	2	.401	$2.9	6	30	.257
	Summit season	12	56	.269	132	490	66	132	26	3	.408	$4.7	9	48	.259

EDDIE MATHEWS

		ADJUSTED REGULAR SEASON											ACTUAL RESULTS		
YEAR	TEAM	HR	RBI	BA	G	AB	R	H	2B	3B	SA	PAY	HR	RBI	BA
1952	Boston (N)	36	71	.259	152	553	99	143	27	3	.514	$11.6	25	58	.242
1953	Milwaukee (N)	58	150	.308	162	597	122	184	35	5	.675	$19.3	47	135	.302
1954	Milwaukee (N)	51	122	.298	145	500	113	149	24	3	.664	$15.0	40	103	.290
1955	Milwaukee (N)	49	116	.300	148	524	124	157	30	4	.653	$15.6	41	101	.289
1956	Milwaukee (N)	43	109	.284	158	578	119	164	28	1	.559	$19.2	37	95	.272
1957	Milwaukee (N)	40	114	.306	155	599	132	183	37	7	.591	$25.2	32	94	.292

(Eddie Mathews, continued)

		\<ADJUSTED REGULAR SEASON\>											\<ACTUAL RESULTS\>		
YEAR	TEAM	HR	RBI	BA	G	AB	R	H	2B	3B	SA	PAY	HR	RBI	BA
1958	Milwaukee (N)	37	93	.261	157	575	117	150	23	1	.497	$19.0	31	77	.251
1959	Milwaukee (N)	55	133	.321	153	614	137	197	20	7	.645	$25.7	46	114	.306
1960	Milwaukee (N)	49	149	.293	161	577	130	169	24	5	.607	$22.9	39	124	.277
1961	Milwaukee (N)	37	103	.319	159	598	117	191	30	5	.572	$16.9	32	91	.306
1962	Milwaukee (N)	34	100	.276	152	536	117	148	33	4	.543	$15.9	29	90	.265
1963	Milwaukee (N)	28	104	.287	157	544	101	156	36	3	.518	$13.4	23	84	.263
1964	Milwaukee (N)	27	90	.251	141	502	101	126	24	1	.464	$9.2	23	74	.233
1965	Milwaukee (N)	39	116	.275	156	546	94	150	28	0	.540	$9.4	32	95	.251
1966	Atlanta (N)	20	64	.269	133	449	88	121	29	3	.481	$5.1	16	53	.250
1967	Hou. (N)-Det. (A)	22	73	.261	136	433	68	113	20	2	.469	$4.3	16	57	.236
1968	Detroit (A)	4	11	.231	31	52	6	12	0	0	.462	$1.3	3	8	.212
	Career	629	1,718	.286	2,456	8,777	1,785	2,513	448	54	.565	$249.0	512	1,453	.271
	Average season	37	101	.286	144	516	105	148	26	3	.565	$14.6	30	85	.271
	Summit season	52	134	.304	154	562	125	171	27	5	.648	$19.7	43	115	.293

DON MATTINGLY

		\<ADJUSTED REGULAR SEASON\>											\<ACTUAL RESULTS\>		
YEAR	TEAM	HR	RBI	BA	G	AB	R	H	2B	3B	SA	PAY	HR	RBI	BA
1982	New York (A)	0	1	.167	7	12	0	2	0	0	.167	$0.0	0	1	.167
1983	New York (A)	6	36	.290	91	279	39	81	18	3	.441	$1.8	4	32	.283
1984	New York (A)	30	128	.355	153	603	105	214	50	2	.594	$8.7	23	110	.343
1985	New York (A)	42	166	.338	160	656	122	222	52	3	.619	$15.5	35	145	.324
1986	New York (A)	36	126	.368	162	677	130	249	59	2	.620	$20.0	31	113	.352
1987	New York (A)	31	120	.334	141	569	97	190	42	2	.578	$15.3	30	115	.327
1988	New York (A)	25	105	.328	145	603	112	198	42	0	.522	$18.6	18	88	.311
1989	New York (A)	32	135	.321	159	635	94	204	41	2	.543	$19.1	23	113	.303
1990	New York (A)	7	48	.266	102	394	46	105	19	0	.368	$5.5	5	42	.256
1991	New York (A)	12	77	.303	152	587	73	178	41	0	.434	$9.2	9	68	.288
1992	New York (A)	21	102	.303	157	640	106	194	45	0	.472	$12.1	14	86	.288
1993	New York (A)	21	92	.294	134	530	84	156	28	2	.474	$5.1	17	86	.291
1994	New York (A)	9	74	.302	139	533	90	161	30	1	.413	$7.0	6	51	.304
1995	New York (A)	8	56	.291	143	512	67	149	39	2	.422	$4.8	7	49	.288
	Career	280	1,266	.319	1,845	7,230	1,165	2,303	506	19	.510	$142.7	222	1,099	.307
	Average season	20	90	.319	132	516	83	165	36	1	.510	$10.2	16	79	.307
	Summit season	34	135	.344	155	628	110	216	49	2	.591	$15.7	28	119	.330

WILLIE MAYS

		\<ADJUSTED REGULAR SEASON\>											\<ACTUAL RESULTS\>		
YEAR	TEAM	HR	RBI	BA	G	AB	R	H	2B	3B	SA	PAY	HR	RBI	BA
1951	New York (N)	28	77	.282	125	479	66	135	26	3	.524	$7.4	20	68	.274
1952	New York (N)	7	29	.254	36	134	21	34	3	3	.478	$3.6	4	23	.236
1954	New York (N)	56	130	.356	159	595	141	212	41	7	.731	$14.4	41	110	.345
1955	New York (N)	64	146	.332	160	611	142	203	25	9	.717	$19.0	51	127	.319
1956	New York (N)	43	97	.309	160	608	117	188	37	5	.599	$15.6	36	84	.296

(Willie Mays, continued)

		ADJUSTED REGULAR SEASON											ACTUAL RESULTS		
YEAR	TEAM	HR	RBI	BA	G	AB	R	H	2B	3B	SA	PAY	HR	RBI	BA
1957	New York (N)	47	118	.349	160	616	136	215	36	15	.685	$26.1	35	97	.333
1958	San Francisco (N)	37	116	.362	160	632	146	229	45	8	.634	$26.7	29	96	.347
1959	San Francisco (N)	41	123	.329	159	605	148	199	55	4	.636	$25.7	34	104	.313
1960	San Francisco (N)	38	122	.337	159	618	127	208	38	9	.612	$22.6	29	103	.319
1961	San Francisco (N)	46	140	.321	161	598	147	192	41	2	.627	$23.3	40	123	.308
1962	San Francisco (N)	54	154	.318	159	610	142	194	45	4	.670	$23.6	49	141	.304
1963	San Francisco (N)	47	128	.342	157	596	143	204	43	5	.668	$19.9	38	103	.314
1964	San Francisco (N)	58	135	.318	157	578	148	184	27	7	.690	$20.3	47	111	.296
1965	San Francisco (N)	63	137	.348	156	554	144	193	26	2	.744	$19.5	52	112	.317
1966	San Francisco (N)	45	127	.311	153	556	122	173	38	3	.633	$13.8	37	103	.288
1967	San Francisco (N)	30	90	.292	141	486	107	142	28	2	.543	$9.0	22	70	.263
1968	San Francisco (N)	36	111	.329	147	495	118	163	26	4	.616	$9.2	23	79	.289
1969	San Francisco (N)	17	69	.308	117	403	77	124	24	3	.509	$4.5	13	58	.283
1970	San Francisco (N)	33	94	.308	139	478	106	147	19	2	.563	$6.6	28	83	.291
1971	San Francisco (N)	24	76	.293	136	417	103	122	31	5	.564	$6.4	18	61	.271
1972	S.F.-N.Y. (N)	12	30	.274	91	252	48	69	15	1	.484	$2.2	8	22	.250
1973	New York (N)	8	29	.220	66	209	28	46	12	0	.392	$1.7	6	25	.211
	Career	834	2,278	.321	3,058	11,130	2,477	3,576	681	103	.626	$321.1	660	1,903	.302
	Average season	38	104	.321	139	506	113	163	31	5	.626	$14.6	30	87	.302
	Summit season	55	132	.345	158	594	141	205	34	8	.707	$19.8	43	110	.326

BILL MAZEROSKI

		ADJUSTED REGULAR SEASON											ACTUAL RESULTS		
YEAR	TEAM	HR	RBI	BA	G	AB	R	H	2B	3B	SA	PAY	HR	RBI	BA
1956	Pittsburgh (N)	4	16	.254	84	264	34	67	10	1	.345	$2.1	3	14	.243
1957	Pittsburgh (N)	11	65	.296	155	551	71	163	39	5	.445	$5.5	8	54	.283
1958	Pittsburgh (N)	24	82	.286	160	597	83	171	33	5	.479	$7.6	19	68	.275
1959	Pittsburgh (N)	10	69	.252	141	515	58	130	21	5	.371	$6.3	7	59	.241
1960	Pittsburgh (N)	15	76	.288	158	563	69	162	29	4	.433	$8.7	11	64	.273
1961	Pittsburgh (N)	15	67	.276	160	587	81	162	28	2	.407	$9.1	13	59	.265
1962	Pittsburgh (N)	17	90	.283	160	576	61	163	33	7	.453	$8.6	14	81	.271
1963	Pittsburgh (N)	10	64	.268	142	534	53	143	32	2	.391	$7.3	8	52	.245
1964	Pittsburgh (N)	13	78	.288	162	601	80	173	31	7	.428	$9.3	10	64	.268
1965	Pittsburgh (N)	8	65	.298	129	490	63	146	23	1	.398	$4.8	6	54	.271
1966	Pittsburgh (N)	21	100	.283	162	621	68	176	32	5	.452	$7.2	16	82	.262
1967	Pittsburgh (N)	14	99	.290	162	635	79	184	38	2	.422	$9.5	9	77	.261
1968	Pittsburgh (N)	6	59	.285	142	502	50	143	31	2	.390	$3.6	3	42	.251
1969	Pittsburgh (N)	4	30	.247	67	227	16	56	10	1	.352	$1.9	3	25	.229
1970	Pittsburgh (N)	9	44	.243	112	367	33	89	17	0	.362	$2.1	7	39	.229
1971	Pittsburgh (N)	2	20	.275	70	193	21	53	6	2	.358	$1.1	1	16	.254
1972	Pittsburgh (N)	0	4	.206	36	68	4	14	7	0	.309	$0.3	0	3	.188
	Career	183	1,028	.278	2,202	7,891	924	2,195	420	51	.414	$95.0	138	853	.260
	Average season	11	60	.278	130	464	54	129	25	3	.414	$5.6	8	50	.260
	Summit season	18	83	.287	159	582	70	167	33	5	.454	$7.5	14	70	.273

TOMMY McCARTHY

		ADJUSTED REGULAR SEASON											ACTUAL RESULTS		
YEAR	TEAM	HR	RBI	BA	G	AB	R	H	2B	3B	SA	PAY	HR	RBI	BA
1884	Boston (U)	0	0	.237	77	304	51	72	17	4	.319	$2.2	0	0	.215
1885	Boston (N)	0	15	.199	57	211	22	42	12	0	.256	$1.7	0	11	.182
1886	Philadelphia (N)	0	4	.189	11	37	8	7	7	0	.378	$0.5	0	3	.185
1887	Philadelphia (N)	0	6	.180	23	89	7	16	9	0	.281	$0.5	0	6	.186
1888	St. Louis (AA)	7	82	.309	155	605	130	187	56	1	.440	$7.8	1	68	.274
1889	St. Louis (AA)	12	61	.298	161	695	133	207	52	4	.436	$12.2	2	63	.291
1890	St. Louis (AA)	28	68	.363	155	639	135	232	40	3	.567	$15.0	6	69	.350
1891	St. Louis (AA)	29	97	.329	156	663	129	218	28	2	.508	$20.0	8	95	.310
1892	Boston (N)	19	66	.266	162	643	125	171	30	2	.407	$17.0	4	63	.242
1893	Boston (N)	21	109	.333	143	570	105	190	42	2	.525	$12.6	5	111	.346
1894	Boston (N)	32	109	.304	155	658	102	200	19	1	.482	$16.7	13	126	.349
1895	Boston (N)	10	70	.263	144	556	86	146	23	1	.362	$9.4	2	73	.290
1896	Brooklyn (N)	13	48	.230	127	460	63	106	11	2	.348	$4.0	3	47	.249
	Career	171	735	.293	1,526	6,130	1,096	1,794	346	22	.440	$119.6	44	735	.292
	Average season	13	57	.293	117	472	84	138	27	2	.440	$9.2	3	57	.292
	Summit season	23	93	.327	153	627	120	205	37	2	.502	$14.4	7	94	.326

FRANK McCORMICK

		ADJUSTED REGULAR SEASON											ACTUAL RESULTS		
YEAR	TEAM	HR	RBI	BA	G	AB	R	H	2B	3B	SA	PAY	HR	RBI	BA
1934	Cincinnati (N)	0	5	.294	13	17	1	5	3	1	.588	$0.0	0	5	.313
1937	Cincinnati (N)	0	10	.314	25	86	5	27	9	0	.419	$0.0	0	9	.325
1938	Cincinnati (N)	12	117	.320	162	687	98	220	55	2	.459	$8.7	5	106	.327
1939	Cincinnati (N)	31	138	.324	162	654	106	212	41	2	.535	$11.8	18	128	.332
1940	Cincinnati (N)	31	143	.311	162	646	104	201	44	2	.529	$12.8	19	127	.309
1941	Cincinnati (N)	31	113	.276	162	634	90	175	31	3	.481	$12.8	17	97	.269
1942	Cincinnati (N)	27	114	.294	153	595	74	175	26	0	.474	$12.0	13	89	.277
1943	Cincinnati (N)	21	74	.322	132	494	74	159	31	0	.512	$5.0	8	56	.303
1944	Cincinnati (N)	40	128	.316	160	608	106	192	34	1	.572	$9.9	20	102	.305
1945	Cincinnati (N)	24	101	.285	160	611	85	174	37	0	.463	$9.5	10	81	.276
1946	Philadelphia (N)	22	84	.298	141	526	59	157	23	1	.471	$4.8	11	66	.284
1947	Phi.-Bos. (N)	6	60	.346	100	263	36	91	29	1	.532	$2.3	3	51	.333
1948	Boston (N)	7	39	.253	79	190	16	48	11	1	.432	$1.6	4	34	.250
	Career	252	1,126	.305	1,611	6,011	854	1,836	374	14	.498	$91.2	128	951	.299
	Average season	19	87	.305	124	462	66	141	29	1	.498	$7.0	10	73	.299
	Summit season	27	120	.319	156	618	98	197	41	1	.519	$9.6	14	104	.316

WILLIE McCOVEY

ADJUSTED REGULAR SEASON

YEAR	TEAM	HR	RBI	BA	G	AB	R	H	2B	3B	SA	PAY	ACTUAL RESULTS HR	RBI	BA
1959	San Francisco (N)	17	45	.369	55	203	38	75	12	4	.719	$3.3	13	38	.354
1960	San Francisco (N)	16	60	.252	105	270	44	68	19	2	.515	$4.1	13	51	.238
1961	San Francisco (N)	21	57	.283	111	343	67	97	16	2	.525	$4.9	18	50	.271
1962	San Francisco (N)	22	58	.304	89	224	44	68	8	1	.643	$4.2	20	54	.293
1963	San Francisco (N)	54	127	.307	152	564	128	173	25	4	.652	$12.0	44	102	.280
1964	San Francisco (N)	21	66	.236	130	364	67	86	18	1	.464	$7.1	18	54	.220
1965	San Francisco (N)	48	112	.302	159	537	113	162	22	3	.622	$14.3	39	92	.276
1966	San Francisco (N)	44	119	.319	151	505	105	161	34	5	.667	$14.4	36	96	.295
1967	San Francisco (N)	42	118	.307	135	456	94	140	21	3	.643	$9.4	31	91	.276
1968	San Francisco (N)	53	148	.333	147	519	114	173	19	3	.688	$12.5	36	105	.293
1969	San Francisco (N)	55	151	.346	149	491	121	170	34	2	.760	$12.9	45	126	.320
1970	San Francisco (N)	44	143	.307	152	495	111	152	47	2	.677	$13.0	39	126	.289
1971	San Francisco (N)	24	88	.298	105	329	56	98	16	0	.565	$4.8	18	70	.277
1972	San Francisco (N)	20	48	.236	85	276	41	65	10	0	.489	$2.8	14	35	.213
1973	San Francisco (N)	36	88	.279	130	383	61	107	16	3	.619	$3.6	29	75	.266
1974	San Diego (N)	29	75	.265	128	344	63	91	21	1	.584	$2.5	22	63	.253
1975	San Diego (N)	30	79	.264	122	413	50	109	18	0	.525	$2.5	23	68	.252
1976	S.D. (N)-Oak. (A)	11	44	.212	82	226	24	48	10	0	.403	$1.7	7	36	.204
1977	San Francisco (N)	32	95	.285	141	478	60	136	22	0	.531	$3.2	28	86	.280
1978	San Francisco (N)	16	76	.236	108	351	38	83	21	2	.444	$2.2	12	64	.228
1979	San Francisco (N)	18	63	.252	117	353	37	89	9	0	.431	$2.0	15	57	.249
1980	San Francisco (N)	1	18	.204	48	113	9	23	11	0	.327	$1.1	1	16	.204
	Career	654	1,878	.288	2,601	8,237	1,485	2,374	429	38	.588	$138.5	521	1,555	.270
	Average season	30	85	.288	118	374	68	108	20	2	.588	$6.3	24	71	.270
	Summit season	50	138	.322	150	515	116	166	32	3	.687	$13.0	40	111	.295

WILLIE McGEE

ADJUSTED REGULAR SEASON

YEAR	TEAM	HR	RBI	BA	G	AB	R	H	2B	3B	SA	PAY	ACTUAL RESULTS HR	RBI	BA
1982	St. Louis (N)	6	64	.306	123	422	49	129	17	9	.431	$5.4	4	56	.296
1983	St. Louis (N)	8	85	.295	146	597	85	176	30	7	.409	$8.7	5	75	.286
1984	St. Louis (N)	10	58	.301	145	571	95	172	28	11	.441	$9.1	6	50	.291
1985	St. Louis (N)	15	93	.369	152	612	129	226	34	17	.554	$14.4	10	82	.353
1986	St. Louis (N)	8	54	.267	125	501	73	134	26	7	.395	$8.8	7	48	.256
1987	St. Louis (N)	11	110	.292	153	620	79	181	42	10	.445	$9.8	11	105	.285
1988	St. Louis (N)	5	59	.310	137	562	86	174	34	7	.422	$7.4	3	50	.292
1989	St. Louis (N)	4	20	.250	57	196	27	49	13	2	.398	$2.8	3	17	.236
1990	St.L. (N)-Oak. (A)	5	89	.339	154	614	114	208	49	7	.466	$7.4	3	77	.324
1991	San Francisco (N)	6	49	.328	131	497	76	163	38	3	.453	$3.6	4	43	.312
1992	San Francisco (N)	1	43	.312	138	474	67	148	32	3	.399	$2.8	1	36	.297
1993	San Francisco (N)	5	49	.305	130	475	57	145	33	1	.411	$2.9	4	46	.301
1994	San Francisco (N)	7	32	.280	63	218	27	61	4	0	.394	$1.4	5	23	.282
1995	Boston (A)	2	17	.286	75	224	37	64	14	3	.402	$1.2	2	15	.285
1996	St. Louis (N)	5	41	.307	123	309	52	95	15	2	.417	$1.5	5	41	.307
1997	St. Louis (N)	3	39	.303	122	300	30	91	20	4	.427	$1.3	3	38	.300

(Willie McGee, continued)

		ADJUSTED REGULAR SEASON											ACTUAL RESULTS		
YEAR	TEAM	HR	RBI	BA	G	AB	R	H	2B	3B	SA	PAY	HR	RBI	BA
1998	St. Louis (N)	3	35	.255	119	267	28	68	10	1	.333	$1.2	3	34	.253
1999	St. Louis (N)	0	20	.249	133	273	25	68	6	0	.271	$1.1	0	20	.251
	Career	104	957	.304	2,226	7,732	1,136	2,352	445	94	.426	$90.8	79	856	.295
	Average season	6	53	.304	124	430	63	131	25	5	.426	$5.0	4	48	.295
	Summit season	9	80	.326	147	583	99	190	38	10	.472	$8.9	7	71	.313

JOHN McGRAW

		ADJUSTED REGULAR SEASON											ACTUAL RESULTS		
YEAR	TEAM	HR	RBI	BA	G	AB	R	H	2B	3B	SA	PAY	HR	RBI	BA
1891	Baltimore (AA)	0	14	.288	38	132	17	38	14	6	.485	$1.0	0	14	.270
1892	Baltimore (N)	6	27	.296	84	304	43	90	26	1	.447	$2.5	1	26	.269
1893	Baltimore (N)	24	63	.308	158	597	122	184	14	4	.466	$9.1	5	64	.321
1894	Baltimore (N)	8	82	.297	156	644	139	191	47	8	.432	$15.2	1	92	.340
1895	Baltimore (N)	12	46	.335	118	477	106	160	27	3	.480	$9.0	2	48	.369
1896	Baltimore (N)	0	14	.298	28	94	21	28	8	3	.447	$3.9	0	14	.325
1897	Baltimore (N)	0	49	.299	126	465	92	139	52	2	.419	$8.7	0	48	.325
1898	Baltimore (N)	0	55	.341	150	540	150	184	49	15	.487	$12.1	0	53	.342
1899	Baltimore (N)	9	33	.373	125	426	141	159	32	2	.521	$8.8	1	33	.391
1900	St. Louis (N)	12	36	.333	113	381	92	127	18	2	.486	$7.6	2	33	.344
1901	Baltimore (A)	0	34	.346	88	280	86	97	48	8	.575	$6.2	0	28	.349
1902	Balt. (A)-N.Y. (N)	7	10	.256	63	195	34	50	4	1	.395	$2.6	1	8	.253
1903	New York (N)	0	1	.308	14	13	3	4	0	0	.308	$0.9	0	1	.273
1904	New York (N)	0	0	.333	5	12	0	4	0	0	.333	$0.3	0	0	.333
1905	New York (N)	0	0	.000	3	0	0	0	0	0	.000	$0.0	0	0	.000
1906	New York (N)	0	0	.000	4	2	0	0	0	0	.000	$0.0	0	0	.000
	Career	78	464	.319	1,273	4,562	1,046	1,455	339	55	.469	$87.9	13	462	.334
	Average season	5	29	.319	80	285	65	91	21	3	.469	$5.5	1	29	.334
	Summit season	11	47	.337	133	484	122	163	28	5	.483	$9.3	2	46	.352

FRED McGRIFF

		ADJUSTED REGULAR SEASON											ACTUAL RESULTS		
YEAR	TEAM	HR	RBI	BA	G	AB	R	H	2B	3B	SA	PAY	HR	RBI	BA
1986	Toronto (A)	0	0	.200	3	5	1	1	0	0	.200	$0.0	0	0	.200
1987	Toronto (A)	20	45	.254	107	295	61	75	17	0	.515	$2.7	20	43	.247
1988	Toronto (A)	44	97	.299	154	536	119	160	37	4	.629	$8.7	34	82	.282
1989	Toronto (A)	46	109	.285	161	551	116	157	28	3	.597	$14.3	36	92	.269
1990	Toronto (A)	43	101	.312	153	557	105	174	22	1	.587	$14.8	35	88	.300
1991	San Diego (N)	38	121	.294	153	528	96	155	20	1	.551	$15.1	31	106	.278
1992	San Diego (N)	46	124	.301	152	531	94	160	30	3	.629	$12.2	35	104	.286
1993	S.D.-Atl. (N)	43	108	.294	151	557	119	164	29	2	.585	$12.5	37	101	.291
1994	Atlanta (N)	50	136	.318	161	604	117	192	35	1	.627	$16.3	34	94	.318
1995	Atlanta (N)	32	107	.283	162	594	98	168	31	1	.500	$10.1	27	93	.280
1996	Atlanta (N)	28	106	.293	159	617	80	181	38	1	.494	$10.1	28	107	.295

(Fred McGriff, continued)

ADJUSTED REGULAR SEASON | | | | | | | | | | | | ACTUAL RESULTS

YEAR	TEAM	HR	RBI	BA	G	AB	R	H	2B	3B	SA	PAY	HR	RBI	BA
1997	Atlanta (N)	23	101	.278	152	564	80	157	25	1	.449	$7.5	22	97	.277
1998	Tampa Bay (A)	20	84	.287	151	564	76	162	33	0	.452	$7.2	19	81	.284
1999	Tampa Bay (A)	31	102	.308	144	529	73	163	30	1	.544	$6.3	32	104	.310
2000	Tampa Bay (A)	26	103	.275	159	570	80	157	18	0	.444	$6.7	27	106	.277
2001	T.B. (A)-Chi. (N)	30	106	.312	146	513	69	160	25	2	.544	$4.5	31	102	.306
	Career	520	1,550	.294	2,268	8,115	1,384	2,386	418	21	.543	$149.0	448	1,400	.287
	Average season	33	97	.294	142	507	87	149	26	1	.543	$9.3	28	88	.287
	Summit season	46	113	.304	156	556	110	169	30	2	.613	$13.3	35	92	.290

MARK McGWIRE

ADJUSTED REGULAR SEASON | | | | | | | | | | | | ACTUAL RESULTS

YEAR	TEAM	HR	RBI	BA	G	AB	R	H	2B	3B	SA	PAY	HR	RBI	BA
1986	Oakland (A)	4	10	.189	18	53	11	10	1	0	.434	$0.3	3	9	.189
1987	Oakland (A)	50	124	.296	151	557	102	165	31	4	.636	$7.5	49	118	.289
1988	Oakland (A)	41	117	.275	155	550	103	151	23	1	.544	$11.7	32	99	.260
1989	Oakland (A)	41	113	.245	143	490	88	120	17	0	.531	$11.2	33	95	.231
1990	Oakland (A)	47	124	.245	156	523	100	128	16	0	.545	$15.0	39	108	.235
1991	Oakland (A)	27	85	.211	154	483	71	102	22	0	.424	$11.5	22	75	.201
1992	Oakland (A)	53	124	.281	139	467	104	131	21	0	.666	$9.7	42	104	.268
1993	Oakland (A)	10	26	.333	27	84	17	28	6	0	.762	$3.2	9	24	.333
1994	Oakland (A)	13	36	.250	67	192	37	48	4	0	.474	$3.1	9	25	.252
1995	Oakland (A)	46	104	.277	117	357	87	99	14	0	.703	$3.6	39	90	.274
1996	Oakland (A)	52	112	.312	130	423	103	132	21	0	.730	$4.7	52	113	.312
1997	Oak. (A)-St.L. (N)	60	128	.276	156	540	89	149	26	0	.657	$7.4	58	123	.274
1998	St. Louis (N)	71	152	.302	154	506	134	153	20	0	.763	$13.7	70	147	.299
1999	St. Louis (N)	64	145	.277	154	524	116	145	21	1	.687	$12.8	65	147	.278
2000	St. Louis (N)	31	71	.305	89	236	58	72	8	0	.733	$3.4	32	73	.305
2001	St. Louis (N)	29	66	.191	97	299	50	57	4	0	.495	$3.3	29	64	.187
	Career	639	1,537	.269	1,907	6,284	1,270	1,690	255	6	.616	$122.1	583	1,414	.263
	Average season	40	96	.269	119	393	79	106	16	0	.616	$7.6	36	88	.263
	Summit season	57	127	.290	139	455	109	132	19	0	.708	$8.9	54	120	.287

BID McPHEE

ADJUSTED REGULAR SEASON | | | | | | | | | | | | ACTUAL RESULTS

YEAR	TEAM	HR	RBI	BA	G	AB	R	H	2B	3B	SA	PAY	HR	RBI	BA
1882	Cincinnati (AA)	19	62	.248	158	630	86	156	27	6	.400	$11.9	1	31	.228
1883	Cincinnati (AA)	24	64	.257	159	608	93	156	19	6	.426	$12.0	2	42	.245
1884	Cincinnati (AA)	29	87	.307	162	651	146	200	13	3	.470	$19.5	5	64	.278
1885	Cincinnati (AA)	0	65	.292	159	623	110	182	63	5	.409	$14.6	0	46	.265
1886	Cincinnati (AA)	36	73	.292	161	644	147	188	26	3	.509	$20.0	8	70	.268
1887	Cincinnati (AA)	15	83	.287	154	645	132	185	49	11	.467	$25.3	2	87	.289
1888	Cincinnati (AA)	22	62	.270	131	541	107	146	22	5	.451	$9.9	4	51	.240
1889	Cincinnati (AA)	20	55	.274	155	620	106	170	37	3	.440	$12.5	5	57	.269
1890	Cincinnati (N)	23	40	.264	160	640	128	169	37	12	.467	$12.8	3	39	.256

(Bid McPhee, continued)

YEAR	TEAM	ADJUSTED REGULAR SEASON HR	RBI	BA	G	AB	R	H	2B	3B	SA	PAY	ACTUAL RESULTS HR	RBI	BA
1891	Cincinnati (N)	30	39	.271	162	660	111	179	25	6	.464	$9.6	6	38	.256
1892	Cincinnati (N)	22	62	.301	151	601	115	181	36	4	.484	$9.4	4	60	.274
1893	Cincinnati (N)	18	67	.270	157	607	100	164	33	5	.430	$9.6	3	68	.281
1894	Cincinnati (N)	17	76	.264	155	583	93	154	27	3	.408	$9.4	5	88	.304
1895	Cincinnati (N)	8	72	.272	141	530	103	144	54	8	.449	$6.7	1	75	.299
1896	Cincinnati (N)	9	93	.283	148	548	86	155	44	4	.427	$6.7	1	87	.305
1897	Cincinnati (N)	8	40	.279	98	341	47	95	27	4	.452	$2.4	1	39	.301
1898	Cincinnati (N)	9	61	.248	137	501	74	124	53	5	.427	$4.2	1	60	.249
1899	Cincinnati (N)	8	63	.264	115	386	58	102	34	4	.435	$2.4	1	65	.279
	Career	317	1,164	.275	2,663	10,359	1,842	2,850	626	97	.446	$198.9	53	1,067	.271
	Average season	18	65	.275	148	576	102	158	35	5	.446	$11.1	3	59	.271
	Summit season	26	69	.292	158	640	130	187	30	5	.477	$16.8	5	64	.273

JOE MEDWICK

YEAR	TEAM	ADJUSTED REGULAR SEASON HR	RBI	BA	G	AB	R	H	2B	3B	SA	PAY	ACTUAL RESULTS HR	RBI	BA
1932	St. Louis (N)	4	13	.336	27	110	14	37	13	0	.564	$0.7	2	12	.349
1933	St. Louis (N)	39	116	.306	156	627	109	192	38	4	.566	$7.9	18	98	.306
1934	St. Louis (N)	37	116	.308	157	653	120	201	42	9	.570	$14.6	18	106	.319
1935	St. Louis (N)	43	138	.342	162	667	145	228	43	6	.618	$19.4	23	126	.353
1936	St. Louis (N)	36	143	.332	162	665	119	221	64	6	.609	$26.1	18	138	.351
1937	St. Louis (N)	51	164	.364	161	653	118	238	51	4	.689	$26.1	31	154	.374
1938	St. Louis (N)	35	131	.316	152	614	107	194	48	4	.578	$19.5	21	122	.322
1939	St. Louis (N)	26	127	.325	157	634	106	206	53	4	.544	$19.5	14	117	.332
1940	St.L.-Bkn. (N)	30	96	.302	149	605	93	183	33	7	.529	$12.4	17	86	.301
1941	Brooklyn (N)	34	101	.327	137	554	115	181	34	5	.590	$12.0	18	88	.318
1942	Brooklyn (N)	12	121	.319	148	576	87	184	57	4	.495	$11.7	4	96	.300
1943	Bkn.-N.Y. (N)	16	92	.294	131	517	71	152	41	2	.474	$5.1	5	70	.278
1944	New York (N)	19	107	.349	134	513	80	179	31	2	.528	$6.9	7	85	.337
1945	N.Y.-Bos. (N)	8	46	.300	97	327	39	98	24	0	.446	$2.6	3	37	.290
1946	Brooklyn (N)	4	23	.329	42	79	9	26	4	0	.532	$1.4	2	18	.312
1947	St. Louis (N)	7	33	.314	78	156	22	49	14	0	.538	$1.2	4	28	.307
1948	St. Louis (N)	0	2	.200	21	20	0	4	0	0	.200	$0.2	0	2	.211
	Career	401	1,569	.323	2,071	7,970	1,354	2,573	590	57	.562	$186.9	205	1,383	.324
	Average season	24	92	.323	122	469	80	151	35	3	.562	$11.0	12	81	.324
	Summit season	40	135	.336	155	631	121	212	48	5	.618	$20.5	22	126	.345

MINNIE MINOSO

		ADJUSTED REGULAR SEASON											ACTUAL RESULTS		
YEAR	TEAM	HR	RBI	BA	G	AB	R	H	2B	3B	SA	PAY	HR	RBI	BA
1949	Cleveland (A)	1	1	.188	9	16	2	3	0	0	.375	$0.0	1	1	.188
1951	Cle.-Chi. (A)	17	87	.337	153	555	128	187	49	11	.557	$4.6	10	76	.326
1952	Chicago (A)	22	74	.299	153	592	118	177	33	7	.490	$9.3	13	61	.281
1953	Chicago (A)	21	116	.318	157	578	116	184	33	5	.502	$11.9	15	104	.313
1954	Chicago (A)	29	136	.330	160	594	140	196	41	12	.586	$13.8	19	116	.320
1955	Chicago (A)	13	80	.301	145	539	90	162	38	5	.462	$9.3	10	70	.288
1956	Chicago (A)	26	102	.329	159	574	123	189	40	8	.563	$13.1	21	88	.316
1957	Chicago (A)	15	124	.323	160	594	116	192	49	4	.495	$13.5	12	103	.310
1958	Cleveland (A)	29	97	.315	158	590	114	186	33	2	.525	$9.5	24	80	.302
1959	Cleveland (A)	25	109	.316	156	601	109	190	41	0	.509	$12.4	21	92	.302
1960	Chicago (A)	26	126	.328	162	622	107	204	43	3	.532	$12.7	20	105	.311
1961	Chicago (A)	16	88	.291	151	536	98	156	34	2	.451	$7.0	14	82	.280
1962	St. Louis (N)	1	11	.206	39	97	15	20	7	0	.309	$1.7	1	10	.196
1963	Washington (A)	5	37	.251	109	315	47	79	17	2	.365	$2.1	4	30	.229
1964	Chicago (A)	1	6	.258	30	31	5	8	0	0	.355	$0.6	1	5	.226
1976	Chicago (A)	0	0	.125	3	8	0	1	0	0	.125	$0.0	0	0	.125
1980	Chicago (A)	0	0	.000	2	2	0	0	0	0	.000	$0.0	0	0	.000
	Career	247	1,194	.312	1,906	6,844	1,328	2,134	458	61	.505	$121.5	186	1,023	.298
	Average season	15	70	.312	112	403	78	126	27	4	.505	$7.1	11	60	.298
	Summit season	25	110	.327	158	587	122	192	41	7	.549	$10.7	19	93	.315

KEVIN MITCHELL

		ADJUSTED REGULAR SEASON											ACTUAL RESULTS		
YEAR	TEAM	HR	RBI	BA	G	AB	R	H	2B	3B	SA	PAY	HR	RBI	BA
1984	New York (N)	0	1	.214	7	14	0	3	0	0	.214	$0.0	0	1	.214
1986	New York (N)	14	48	.290	108	328	57	95	25	2	.506	$2.7	12	43	.277
1987	S.D.-S.F. (N)	23	73	.287	131	464	71	133	22	2	.491	$5.3	22	70	.280
1988	San Francisco (N)	26	95	.265	148	505	71	134	28	7	.503	$6.5	19	80	.251
1989	San Francisco (N)	60	149	.308	154	543	119	167	35	5	.722	$14.5	47	125	.291
1990	San Francisco (N)	43	107	.303	140	524	104	159	24	2	.603	$12.1	35	93	.290
1991	San Francisco (N)	32	79	.270	113	371	59	100	13	1	.569	$5.9	27	69	.256
1992	Seattle (A)	13	80	.300	99	360	57	108	27	0	.483	$5.6	9	67	.286
1993	Cincinnati (N)	22	69	.347	93	323	60	112	22	3	.638	$4.4	19	64	.341
1994	Cincinnati (N)	44	110	.325	134	437	81	142	24	1	.686	$3.9	30	77	.326
1996	Bos. (A)-Cin. (N)	8	39	.316	64	206	27	65	15	0	.505	$2.0	8	39	.316
1997	Cleveland (A)	4	11	.153	20	59	7	9	1	0	.373	$1.1	4	11	.153
1998	Oakland (A)	2	22	.228	51	127	14	29	7	1	.346	$0.9	2	21	.228
	Career	291	883	.295	1,262	4,261	727	1,256	243	24	.568	$64.9	234	760	.284
	Average season	22	68	.295	97	328	56	97	19	2	.568	$5.0	18	58	.284
	Summit season	39	99	.302	130	441	84	133	24	2	.630	$7.8	30	81	.288

JOHNNY MIZE

		ADJUSTED REGULAR SEASON											ACTUAL RESULTS		
YEAR	TEAM	HR	RBI	BA	G	AB	R	H	2B	3B	SA	PAY	HR	RBI	BA
1936	St. Louis (N)	33	96	.311	132	434	79	135	26	3	.613	$8.8	19	93	.329
1937	St. Louis (N)	41	120	.356	150	579	110	206	36	2	.637	$14.5	25	113	.364
1938	St. Louis (N)	45	109	.332	155	552	91	183	33	8	.665	$14.3	27	102	.337
1939	St. Louis (N)	47	117	.342	160	590	112	202	42	7	.676	$18.7	28	108	.349
1940	St. Louis (N)	63	153	.316	161	601	124	190	28	6	.697	$19.9	43	137	.314
1941	St. Louis (N)	31	117	.325	132	496	78	161	40	4	.609	$12.2	16	100	.317
1942	New York (N)	49	140	.324	149	568	124	184	23	4	.637	$15.8	26	110	.305
1946	New York (N)	37	90	.356	106	396	90	141	16	1	.682	$6.8	22	70	.337
1947	New York (N)	70	163	.312	161	613	162	191	25	1	.698	$19.8	51	138	.302
1948	New York (N)	56	141	.295	159	586	124	173	24	2	.630	$19.2	40	125	.289
1949	N.Y. (N)-N.Y. (A)	26	71	.269	124	428	70	115	17	0	.491	$4.7	19	64	.263
1950	New York (A)	29	77	.280	94	286	46	80	13	0	.629	$3.4	25	72	.277
1951	New York (A)	14	56	.266	119	350	42	93	17	1	.440	$2.4	10	49	.259
1952	New York (A)	6	36	.278	82	144	11	40	11	0	.479	$1.3	4	29	.263
1953	New York (A)	5	31	.250	87	112	7	28	4	0	.420	$1.0	4	27	.250
	Career	552	1,517	.315	1,971	6,735	1,270	2,122	355	39	.625	$162.8	359	1,337	.312
	Average season	37	101	.315	131	449	85	141	24	3	.625	$10.9	24	89	.312
	Summit season	52	126	.329	149	550	116	181	29	5	.684	$15.9	34	111	.327

PAUL MOLITOR

		ADJUSTED REGULAR SEASON											ACTUAL RESULTS		
YEAR	TEAM	HR	RBI	BA	G	AB	R	H	2B	3B	SA	PAY	HR	RBI	BA
1978	Milwaukee (A)	10	53	.284	125	521	86	148	34	3	.418	$7.7	6	45	.273
1979	Milwaukee (A)	14	69	.327	141	588	98	192	37	14	.509	$11.3	9	62	.322
1980	Milwaukee (A)	14	43	.309	111	450	93	139	35	1	.484	$7.6	9	37	.304
1981	Milwaukee (A)	6	34	.282	95	373	82	105	23	0	.391	$6.1	2	19	.267
1982	Milwaukee (A)	26	81	.311	159	662	156	206	31	7	.497	$19.1	19	71	.302
1983	Milwaukee (A)	21	53	.278	152	608	108	169	32	5	.451	$12.1	15	47	.270
1984	Milwaukee (A)	0	7	.217	13	46	3	10	2	0	.261	$2.7	0	6	.217
1985	Milwaukee (A)	13	55	.310	141	580	106	180	33	3	.445	$7.3	10	48	.297
1986	Milwaukee (A)	11	62	.295	106	441	70	130	28	6	.460	$4.3	9	55	.281
1987	Milwaukee (A)	16	78	.361	118	465	120	168	45	5	.583	$6.6	16	75	.353
1988	Milwaukee (A)	19	71	.330	154	609	136	201	40	6	.509	$9.9	13	60	.312
1989	Milwaukee (A)	17	66	.335	155	615	100	206	43	4	.501	$9.5	11	56	.315
1990	Milwaukee (A)	16	52	.297	103	418	74	124	31	6	.514	$3.9	12	45	.285
1991	Milwaukee (A)	24	85	.341	158	665	152	227	38	12	.543	$19.2	17	75	.325
1992	Milwaukee (A)	19	106	.337	158	609	106	205	43	7	.524	$9.5	12	89	.320
1993	Toronto (A)	27	119	.336	160	636	130	214	40	5	.542	$13.3	22	111	.332
1994	Toronto (A)	21	107	.341	162	640	123	218	43	5	.522	$18.8	14	75	.341
1995	Toronto (A)	18	69	.273	146	590	72	161	36	2	.432	$8.9	15	60	.270
1996	Minnesota (A)	9	112	.339	161	660	98	224	42	8	.468	$12.8	9	113	.341
1997	Minnesota (A)	11	92	.307	135	538	65	165	32	4	.442	$6.3	10	89	.305
1998	Minnesota (A)	4	71	.283	126	502	78	142	30	5	.386	$4.4	4	69	.281
	Career	316	1,485	.315	2,779	11,216	2,056	3,534	718	108	.483	$201.3	234	1,307	.306
	Average season	15	71	.315	132	534	98	168	34	5	.483	$9.6	11	62	.306
	Summit season	21	99	.342	151	603	126	206	42	7	.539	$13.5	16	85	.333

JOE MORGAN

		ADJUSTED REGULAR SEASON											ACTUAL RESULTS		
YEAR	TEAM	HR	RBI	BA	G	AB	R	H	2B	3B	SA	PAY	HR	RBI	BA
1963	Houston (N)	0	4	.280	8	25	6	7	0	1	.360	$0.0	0	3	.240
1964	Houston (N)	0	0	.216	10	37	5	8	0	0	.216	$0.0	0	0	.189
1965	Houston (N)	19	49	.298	157	601	123	179	32	10	.479	$6.5	14	40	.271
1966	Houston (N)	7	51	.308	121	422	73	130	22	7	.443	$5.0	5	42	.285
1967	Houston (N)	10	54	.306	133	494	94	151	42	10	.492	$7.4	6	42	.275
1968	Houston (N)	0	0	.300	10	20	8	6	0	1	.400	$2.2	0	0	.250
1969	Houston (N)	20	51	.254	147	535	113	136	25	4	.428	$8.7	15	43	.236
1970	Houston (N)	10	59	.285	144	548	115	156	39	7	.436	$9.2	8	52	.268
1971	Houston (N)	19	70	.276	160	583	109	161	38	10	.473	$11.6	13	56	.256
1972	Cincinnati (N)	26	101	.321	157	582	170	187	34	4	.527	$22.5	16	73	.292
1973	Cincinnati (N)	33	96	.304	157	576	136	175	43	2	.557	$16.7	26	82	.290
1974	Cincinnati (N)	31	79	.306	148	509	127	156	36	3	.572	$12.9	22	67	.293
1975	Cincinnati (N)	25	110	.341	146	498	125	170	33	5	.578	$13.2	17	94	.327
1976	Cincinnati (N)	42	136	.337	141	472	139	159	32	3	.684	$13.1	27	111	.320
1977	Cincinnati (N)	27	86	.294	153	521	125	153	23	4	.509	$13.1	22	78	.288
1978	Cincinnati (N)	18	90	.245	133	444	81	109	29	0	.432	$7.1	13	75	.236
1979	Cincinnati (N)	12	35	.253	128	439	78	111	29	1	.405	$4.6	9	32	.250
1980	Houston (N)	16	56	.247	140	458	76	113	20	4	.413	$4.3	11	49	.243
1981	San Francisco (N)	18	55	.252	131	448	84	113	26	1	.435	$3.5	8	31	.240
1982	San Francisco (N)	19	70	.298	134	463	78	138	23	3	.484	$3.5	14	61	.289
1983	Philadelphia (N)	20	67	.237	122	401	82	95	21	1	.444	$3.4	16	59	.230
1984	Oakland (A)	8	50	.252	116	365	58	92	26	0	.389	$2.4	6	43	.244
	Career	380	1,369	.287	2,696	9,441	2,005	2,705	573	81	.485	$170.9	268	1,133	.271
	Average season	17	62	.287	123	429	91	123	26	4	.485	$7.8	12	52	.271
	Summit season	31	104	.321	150	527	139	169	36	3	.577	$15.7	22	85	.303

THURMAN MUNSON

		ADJUSTED REGULAR SEASON											ACTUAL RESULTS		
YEAR	TEAM	HR	RBI	BA	G	AB	R	H	2B	3B	SA	PAY	HR	RBI	BA
1969	New York (A)	1	11	.279	26	86	7	24	1	3	.395	$0.3	1	9	.256
1970	New York (A)	7	59	.320	131	450	66	144	35	3	.458	$4.2	6	53	.302
1971	New York (A)	15	52	.271	125	451	89	122	21	4	.435	$5.4	10	42	.251
1972	New York (A)	12	63	.310	146	533	74	165	26	3	.437	$6.3	7	46	.280
1973	New York (A)	26	86	.314	147	519	93	163	37	4	.551	$9.2	20	74	.301
1974	New York (A)	20	71	.273	144	517	76	141	24	2	.443	$8.9	13	60	.261
1975	New York (A)	19	121	.332	159	605	98	201	32	3	.489	$14.3	12	102	.318
1976	New York (A)	29	131	.318	155	628	99	200	32	1	.511	$12.3	17	105	.302
1977	New York (A)	23	111	.313	149	595	94	186	33	3	.494	$11.9	18	100	.308
1978	New York (A)	10	84	.310	153	613	86	190	36	1	.421	$11.9	6	71	.297
1979	New York (A)	5	43	.293	98	386	47	113	24	2	.404	$3.0	3	39	.288
	Career	167	832	.306	1,433	5,383	829	1,649	301	29	.466	$87.7	113	701	.292
	Average season	15	76	.306	130	489	75	150	27	3	.466	$8.0	10	64	.292
	Summit season	21	102	.320	148	559	90	179	34	3	.504	$10.4	15	87	.306

DALE MURPHY

YEAR	TEAM	ADJUSTED REGULAR SEASON HR	RBI	BA	G	AB	R	H	2B	3B	SA	PAY	ACTUAL RESULTS HR	RBI	BA
1976	Atlanta (N)	0	11	.277	19	65	4	18	9	0	.415	$0.1	0	9	.262
1977	Atlanta (N)	3	15	.316	18	76	6	24	8	1	.566	$0.3	2	14	.316
1978	Atlanta (N)	31	94	.236	151	530	78	125	15	2	.447	$5.7	23	79	.226
1979	Atlanta (N)	26	63	.278	105	388	59	108	7	2	.508	$4.8	21	57	.276
1980	Atlanta (N)	42	103	.286	157	573	114	164	27	2	.560	$11.6	33	89	.281
1981	Atlanta (N)	29	92	.259	157	557	79	144	19	1	.452	$11.7	13	50	.247
1982	Atlanta (N)	44	125	.289	162	598	130	173	24	2	.557	$19.0	36	109	.281
1983	Atlanta (N)	45	138	.312	162	589	150	184	25	3	.594	$25.4	36	121	.302
1984	Atlanta (N)	46	116	.300	162	607	109	182	35	6	.605	$19.5	36	100	.290
1985	Atlanta (N)	44	126	.315	162	616	134	194	34	2	.591	$23.2	37	111	.300
1986	Atlanta (N)	34	93	.277	161	618	100	171	32	7	.516	$16.5	29	83	.265
1987	Atlanta (N)	46	111	.302	160	570	121	172	30	1	.600	$16.5	44	105	.295
1988	Atlanta (N)	32	92	.240	158	600	92	144	38	4	.477	$12.9	24	77	.226
1989	Atlanta (N)	27	100	.242	155	578	71	140	17	0	.412	$7.5	20	84	.228
1990	Atl.-Phi. (N)	30	95	.256	154	563	69	144	24	1	.462	$7.1	24	83	.245
1991	Philadelphia (N)	23	92	.265	153	544	75	144	36	1	.461	$5.0	18	81	.252
1992	Philadelphia (N)	2	8	.177	18	62	6	11	1	0	.290	$1.3	2	7	.161
1993	Colorado (N)	0	8	.143	26	42	1	6	1	0	.167	$0.8	0	7	.143
	Career	504	1,482	.275	2,240	8,176	1,398	2,248	382	35	.515	$188.9	398	1,266	.265
	Average season	28	82	.275	124	454	78	125	21	2	.515	$10.5	22	70	.265
	Summit season	45	119	.303	161	591	126	179	30	3	.592	$19.2	37	105	.294

EDDIE MURRAY

YEAR	TEAM	ADJUSTED REGULAR SEASON HR	RBI	BA	G	AB	R	H	2B	3B	SA	PAY	ACTUAL RESULTS HR	RBI	BA
1977	Baltimore (A)	32	98	.288	161	615	90	177	32	1	.499	$14.6	27	88	.283
1978	Baltimore (A)	37	113	.298	162	614	101	183	34	2	.541	$15.4	27	95	.285
1979	Baltimore (A)	31	111	.300	162	617	101	185	32	2	.509	$18.4	25	99	.295
1980	Baltimore (A)	42	134	.304	158	621	115	189	38	1	.572	$18.9	32	116	.300
1981	Baltimore (A)	48	148	.308	153	584	108	180	33	2	.618	$18.6	22	78	.294
1982	Baltimore (A)	39	126	.326	150	546	99	178	32	1	.603	$15.1	32	110	.316
1983	Baltimore (A)	42	127	.316	156	582	131	184	32	2	.595	$19.7	33	111	.306
1984	Baltimore (A)	38	128	.316	162	588	112	186	29	2	.566	$20.0	29	110	.306
1985	Baltimore (A)	37	142	.310	157	587	127	182	40	1	.571	$17.0	31	124	.297
1986	Baltimore (A)	20	94	.319	137	495	68	158	29	1	.503	$9.7	17	84	.305
1987	Baltimore (A)	31	95	.283	160	618	93	175	31	3	.494	$15.6	30	91	.277
1988	Baltimore (A)	37	100	.300	162	607	89	182	29	2	.537	$9.9	28	84	.284
1989	Los Angeles (N)	28	106	.261	162	601	79	157	32	1	.458	$9.6	20	88	.247
1990	Los Angeles (N)	34	109	.344	155	558	111	192	23	3	.579	$9.6	26	95	.330
1991	Los Angeles (N)	24	109	.274	153	576	79	158	24	1	.444	$7.4	19	96	.260
1992	New York (N)	23	111	.274	156	551	76	151	40	2	.479	$6.7	16	93	.261
1993	New York (N)	32	107	.290	154	610	83	177	29	1	.498	$8.8	27	100	.285
1994	Cleveland (A)	26	110	.253	155	621	83	157	30	1	.430	$8.9	17	76	.254
1995	Cleveland (A)	25	94	.327	127	490	78	160	23	0	.527	$4.5	21	82	.323
1996	Cle.-Balt. (A)	22	78	.258	151	562	68	145	21	1	.416	$4.7	22	79	.260
1997	Ana. (A)-L.A. (N)	3	19	.222	55	167	13	37	7	0	.317	$1.6	3	18	.222
	Career	651	2,259	.296	3,148	11,810	1,904	3,493	620	30	.519	$254.7	504	1,917	.287
	Average season	31	108	.296	150	562	91	166	30	1	.519	$12.1	24	91	.287
	Summit season	40	128	.322	155	572	112	184	30	2	.591	$16.6	28	101	.311

STAN MUSIAL

		ADJUSTED REGULAR SEASON											ACTUAL RESULTS		
YEAR	TEAM	HR	RBI	BA	G	AB	R	H	2B	3B	SA	PAY	HR	RBI	BA
1941	St. Louis (N)	2	8	.431	13	51	10	22	5	0	.647	$0.2	1	7	.426
1942	St. Louis (N)	25	90	.335	145	484	109	162	40	7	.601	$5.8	10	72	.315
1943	St. Louis (N)	40	108	.379	166	652	144	247	63	14	.702	$18.6	13	81	.357
1944	St. Louis (N)	32	116	.359	151	587	139	211	62	9	.659	$18.7	12	94	.347
1946	St. Louis (N)	37	131	.386	162	648	158	250	64	13	.696	$27.2	16	103	.365
1947	St. Louis (N)	33	111	.322	155	611	133	197	38	8	.573	$25.9	19	95	.312
1948	St. Louis (N)	62	148	.385	162	639	153	246	50	10	.786	$31.7	39	131	.376
1949	St. Louis (N)	53	136	.347	162	631	141	219	47	7	.696	$28.5	36	123	.338
1950	St. Louis (N)	37	118	.350	155	589	114	206	49	4	.635	$16.9	28	109	.346
1951	St. Louis (N)	46	123	.367	159	605	142	222	37	8	.683	$23.5	32	108	.355
1952	St. Louis (N)	33	113	.359	162	608	130	218	54	4	.623	$19.8	21	91	.336
1953	St. Louis (N)	39	126	.343	162	612	141	210	64	6	.658	$20.3	30	113	.337
1954	St. Louis (N)	47	149	.341	161	622	142	212	50	6	.667	$24.9	35	126	.330
1955	St. Louis (N)	40	124	.332	162	591	111	196	40	4	.616	$13.9	33	108	.319
1956	St. Louis (N)	32	125	.323	162	617	99	199	44	4	.562	$13.3	27	109	.310
1957	St. Louis (N)	36	124	.367	141	528	100	194	49	2	.672	$9.2	29	102	.351
1958	St. Louis (N)	20	75	.351	142	496	77	174	46	2	.573	$6.5	17	62	.337
1959	St. Louis (N)	17	52	.267	121	359	44	96	16	2	.465	$2.7	14	44	.255
1960	St. Louis (N)	20	75	.290	121	345	58	100	21	1	.530	$2.5	17	63	.275
1961	St. Louis (N)	18	80	.300	129	390	52	117	28	3	.526	$2.5	15	70	.288
1962	St. Louis (N)	21	90	.344	134	430	63	148	23	1	.549	$2.7	19	82	.330
1963	St. Louis (N)	15	72	.279	124	337	42	94	13	2	.463	$2.3	12	58	.255
	Career	705	2,294	.345	3,151	11,432	2,302	3,940	903	117	.629	$317.6	475	1,951	.331
	Average season	32	104	.345	143	520	105	179	41	5	.629	$14.4	22	89	.331
	Summit season	48	129	.373	162	635	148	237	52	10	.713	$25.9	27	109	.358

GRAIG NETTLES

		ADJUSTED REGULAR SEASON											ACTUAL RESULTS		
YEAR	TEAM	HR	RBI	BA	G	AB	R	H	2B	3B	SA	PAY	HR	RBI	BA
1967	Minnesota (A)	0	0	.333	3	3	0	1	1	0	.667	$0.0	0	0	.333
1968	Minnesota (A)	7	11	.250	22	76	18	19	2	1	.579	$0.1	5	8	.224
1969	Minnesota (A)	9	31	.240	96	225	32	54	13	2	.436	$1.7	7	26	.222
1970	Cleveland (A)	30	70	.250	157	549	92	137	16	1	.446	$5.9	26	62	.235
1971	Cleveland (A)	37	108	.281	158	598	98	168	23	1	.508	$11.5	28	86	.261
1972	Cleveland (A)	26	96	.280	156	579	89	162	37	0	.478	$11.8	17	70	.253
1973	New York (A)	28	95	.245	160	552	76	135	22	0	.437	$9.6	22	81	.234
1974	New York (A)	31	89	.256	155	566	88	145	25	1	.468	$9.6	22	75	.246
1975	New York (A)	30	107	.279	159	588	84	164	28	3	.490	$9.7	21	91	.267
1976	New York (A)	47	116	.268	161	594	110	159	30	2	.562	$9.7	32	93	.254
1977	New York (A)	43	118	.260	158	589	110	153	25	3	.531	$9.9	37	107	.255
1978	New York (A)	36	110	.288	158	583	95	168	24	2	.521	$9.6	27	93	.276
1979	New York (A)	25	81	.256	147	528	79	135	17	1	.434	$7.1	20	73	.253
1980	New York (A)	20	52	.247	89	324	60	80	14	0	.475	$3.2	16	45	.244
1981	New York (A)	32	85	.255	156	529	85	135	11	1	.461	$6.3	15	46	.244
1982	New York (A)	22	63	.240	122	405	54	97	12	2	.442	$2.5	18	55	.232
1983	New York (A)	26	86	.275	129	462	64	127	18	2	.491	$3.2	20	75	.266

(Graig Nettles, continued)

YEAR	TEAM	HR	RBI	BA	G	AB	R	H	2B	3B	SA	PAY	HR	RBI	BA
		ADJUSTED REGULAR SEASON											ACTUAL RESULTS		
1984	San Diego (N)	25	75	.235	124	395	65	93	12	1	.461	$2.7	20	65	.228
1985	San Diego (N)	18	69	.273	137	440	75	120	26	1	.459	$3.2	15	61	.261
1986	San Diego (N)	18	61	.226	126	354	40	80	10	0	.407	$2.3	16	55	.218
1987	Atlanta (N)	5	35	.212	113	179	17	38	9	1	.358	$1.5	5	33	.209
1988	Montreal (N)	1	17	.183	80	93	6	17	6	0	.280	$0.8	1	14	.172
	Career	516	1,575	.259	2,766	9,211	1,437	2,387	381	25	.474	$121.9	390	1,314	.248
	Average season	23	72	.259	126	419	65	109	17	1	.474	$5.5	18	60	.248
	Summit season	39	112	.275	159	590	99	162	26	2	.524	$10.1	29	94	.262

BOB O'FARRELL

YEAR	TEAM	HR	RBI	BA	G	AB	R	H	2B	3B	SA	PAY	HR	RBI	BA
		ADJUSTED REGULAR SEASON											ACTUAL RESULTS		
1915	Chicago (N)	0	0	.333	2	3	0	1	0	0	.333	$0.0	0	0	.333
1916	Chicago (N)	0	0	.000	1	0	0	0	0	0	.000	$0.0	0	0	.000
1917	Chicago (N)	0	1	.375	3	8	1	3	3	0	.750	$0.0	0	1	.375
1918	Chicago (N)	8	23	.302	64	139	15	42	9	1	.554	$0.6	1	14	.283
1919	Chicago (N)	0	13	.221	57	145	16	32	13	2	.338	$0.7	0	9	.216
1920	Chicago (N)	10	23	.243	99	284	34	69	11	2	.401	$2.0	3	19	.248
1921	Chicago (N)	11	35	.232	102	276	35	64	13	3	.420	$2.4	4	32	.250
1922	Chicago (N)	13	64	.302	133	407	72	123	24	3	.472	$5.0	4	60	.324
1923	Chicago (N)	25	92	.303	138	476	80	144	22	1	.511	$7.1	12	84	.319
1924	Chicago (N)	7	31	.228	75	193	27	44	5	1	.373	$3.7	3	28	.240
1925	Chi.-St.L. (N)	8	36	.249	117	357	40	89	16	1	.367	$3.5	3	35	.271
1926	St. Louis (N)	21	75	.281	153	512	69	144	30	4	.479	$5.3	7	68	.293
1927	St. Louis (N)	0	20	.253	65	190	21	48	20	0	.358	$1.9	0	18	.264
1928	St.L.-N.Y. (N)	4	26	.192	95	193	32	37	7	0	.290	$1.4	2	24	.200
1929	New York (N)	9	43	.284	97	264	36	75	15	1	.451	$1.6	4	42	.306
1930	New York (N)	7	52	.275	99	262	36	72	17	2	.435	$1.5	4	54	.301
1931	New York (N)	4	21	.217	90	184	12	40	10	1	.348	$1.0	1	19	.224
1932	New York (N)	0	9	.225	53	71	8	16	6	0	.310	$0.5	0	8	.239
1933	St. Louis (N)	5	24	.238	58	172	19	41	5	1	.366	$0.7	2	20	.239
1934	Cin.-Chi. (N)	3	15	.228	70	202	14	46	15	3	.376	$0.5	1	14	.237
1935	St. Louis (N)	0	0	.000	15	11	0	0	0	0	.000	$0.0	0	0	.000
	Career	135	603	.260	1,586	4,349	567	1,130	241	26	.420	$39.4	51	549	.273
	Average season	6	29	.260	76	207	27	54	11	1	.420	$1.9	2	26	.273
	Summit season	17	67	.285	135	438	65	125	23	2	.463	$5.2	7	62	.303

TONY OLIVA

		ADJUSTED REGULAR SEASON											ACTUAL RESULTS		
YEAR	TEAM	HR	RBI	BA	G	AB	R	H	2B	3B	SA	PAY	HR	RBI	BA
1962	Minnesota (A)	0	3	.444	9	9	3	4	1	0	.556	$0.0	0	3	.444
1963	Minnesota (A)	0	1	.429	7	7	0	3	0	0	.429	$0.0	0	1	.429
1964	Minnesota (A)	40	114	.347	160	668	132	232	56	7	.632	$9.1	32	94	.323
1965	Minnesota (A)	20	120	.352	149	576	131	203	53	4	.563	$11.9	16	98	.321
1966	Minnesota (A)	32	107	.333	159	622	121	207	43	5	.572	$15.2	25	87	.307
1967	Minnesota (A)	24	106	.321	144	549	97	176	46	5	.554	$14.8	17	83	.289
1968	Minnesota (A)	29	96	.330	128	470	76	155	33	4	.602	$11.5	18	68	.289
1969	Minnesota (A)	31	121	.336	153	637	116	214	53	3	.575	$15.9	24	101	.309
1970	Minnesota (A)	28	121	.344	157	628	109	216	47	6	.572	$12.8	23	107	.325
1971	Minnesota (A)	31	103	.364	128	495	93	180	39	3	.642	$9.3	22	81	.337
1972	Minnesota (A)	0	1	.355	11	31	1	11	2	0	.419	$1.7	0	1	.321
1973	Minnesota (A)	22	107	.305	146	571	73	174	25	0	.464	$4.9	16	92	.291
1974	Minnesota (A)	19	67	.299	126	455	51	136	20	2	.477	$2.8	13	57	.285
1975	Minnesota (A)	19	69	.281	133	462	54	130	12	0	.431	$2.7	13	58	.270
1976	Minnesota (A)	2	20	.220	67	123	4	27	4	0	.301	$1.3	1	16	.211
	Career	297	1,156	.328	1,677	6,303	1,061	2,068	434	39	.551	$113.9	220	947	.304
	Average season	20	77	.328	112	420	71	138	29	3	.551	$7.6	15	63	.304
	Summit season	30	111	.347	144	567	108	197	46	5	.605	$10.9	22	90	.320

AL OLIVER

		ADJUSTED REGULAR SEASON											ACTUAL RESULTS		
YEAR	TEAM	HR	RBI	BA	G	AB	R	H	2B	3B	SA	PAY	HR	RBI	BA
1968	Pittsburgh (N)	0	0	.125	4	8	1	1	0	0	.125	$0.0	0	0	.125
1969	Pittsburgh (N)	22	84	.309	129	463	66	143	26	2	.516	$4.3	17	70	.285
1970	Pittsburgh (N)	15	94	.287	151	551	71	158	43	4	.461	$7.0	12	83	.270
1971	Pittsburgh (N)	20	80	.304	143	529	86	161	43	6	.522	$7.3	14	64	.282
1972	Pittsburgh (N)	20	122	.345	146	589	121	203	39	4	.526	$14.3	12	89	.312
1973	Pittsburgh (N)	26	116	.306	158	654	105	200	49	7	.521	$15.3	20	99	.292
1974	Pittsburgh (N)	18	101	.337	147	617	114	208	53	12	.549	$15.3	11	85	.321
1975	Pittsburgh (N)	27	98	.293	156	632	106	185	48	7	.519	$12.7	18	84	.280
1976	Pittsburgh (N)	21	75	.341	121	443	76	151	27	4	.562	$7.0	12	61	.323
1977	Pittsburgh (N)	24	91	.313	154	568	83	178	34	4	.514	$9.5	19	82	.308
1978	Texas (A)	21	106	.337	133	525	77	177	42	4	.552	$5.1	14	89	.324
1979	Texas (A)	16	84	.327	136	492	76	161	33	3	.504	$4.7	12	76	.323
1980	Texas (A)	27	134	.324	162	652	110	211	49	2	.529	$12.9	19	117	.319
1981	Texas (A)	11	104	.326	157	648	100	211	62	1	.475	$9.9	4	55	.309
1982	Montreal (N)	29	125	.340	160	617	103	210	49	2	.567	$12.4	22	109	.331
1983	Montreal (N)	12	95	.310	156	610	79	189	47	2	.452	$9.0	8	84	.300
1984	S.F.-Phi. (N)	0	56	.313	119	432	42	135	38	2	.410	$3.2	0	48	.301
1985	L.A. (N)-Tor. (A)	6	35	.263	96	266	24	70	13	1	.387	$1.9	5	31	.252
	Career	315	1,600	.318	2,428	9,296	1,440	2,952	695	67	.508	$151.8	219	1,326	.303
	Average season	18	89	.318	135	516	80	164	39	4	.508	$8.4	12	74	.303
	Summit season	22	106	.341	141	558	98	190	42	5	.552	$10.8	14	87	.322

TIP O'NEILL

		ADJUSTED REGULAR SEASON											ACTUAL RESULTS		
YEAR	TEAM	HR	RBI	BA	G	AB	R	H	2B	3B	SA	PAY	HR	RBI	BA
1883	New York (N)	0	8	.206	38	126	12	26	11	0	.294	$0.5	0	5	.197
1884	St. Louis (AA)	23	75	.306	115	438	68	134	28	6	.555	$4.4	3	54	.276
1885	St. Louis (AA)	18	53	.387	75	297	62	115	10	1	.609	$4.2	3	38	.350
1886	St. Louis (AA)	24	114	.359	161	676	113	243	55	7	.568	$15.2	3	107	.328
1887	St. Louis (AA)	49	117	.433	146	609	159	264	58	5	.787	$16.2	14	123	.435
1888	St. Louis (AA)	27	119	.378	154	627	117	237	46	5	.596	$16.7	5	98	.335
1889	St. Louis (AA)	31	108	.344	154	614	120	211	41	3	.572	$22.2	9	110	.335
1890	Chicago (P)	22	74	.311	161	678	111	211	43	8	.496	$19.6	3	75	.302
1891	St. Louis (AA)	32	97	.339	148	598	114	203	32	1	.557	$13.0	10	95	.321
1892	Cincinnati (N)	11	53	.276	114	438	65	121	27	2	.422	$4.7	2	52	.251
	Career	237	818	.346	1,266	5,101	941	1,765	351	38	.569	$116.7	52	757	.326
	Average season	24	82	.346	127	510	94	177	35	4	.569	$11.7	5	76	.326
	Summit season	33	111	.371	153	625	125	232	46	4	.616	$16.7	8	107	.350

JIM O'ROURKE

		ADJUSTED REGULAR SEASON											ACTUAL RESULTS		
YEAR	TEAM	HR	RBI	BA	G	AB	R	H	2B	3B	SA	PAY	HR	RBI	BA
1876	Boston (N)	41	94	.332	162	722	134	240	35	2	.557	$47.8	2	43	.327
1877	Boston (N)	0	59	.362	162	704	177	255	125	8	.563	$48.6	0	23	.362
1878	Boston (N)	38	81	.289	162	689	123	199	51	8	.552	$26.0	1	29	.278
1879	Providence (N)	29	89	.368	154	688	135	253	55	8	.597	$28.8	1	46	.348
1880	Boston (N)	57	93	.303	162	684	148	207	18	3	.588	$29.5	6	45	.275
1881	Buffalo (N)	0	60	.312	162	679	143	212	107	13	.508	$28.2	0	30	.302
1882	Buffalo (N)	27	70	.305	162	714	118	218	36	4	.480	$20.1	2	37	.281
1883	Buffalo (N)	17	58	.344	155	719	156	247	78	7	.542	$20.3	1	38	.328
1884	Buffalo (N)	32	83	.384	152	657	158	252	58	4	.630	$20.6	5	63	.347
1885	New York (N)	39	59	.330	162	690	169	228	39	8	.580	$25.1	5	42	.300
1886	New York (N)	10	40	.338	137	574	127	194	66	4	.519	$9.1	1	34	.309
1887	New York (N)	18	89	.284	129	497	73	141	28	6	.473	$6.6	3	88	.285
1888	New York (N)	20	60	.309	126	482	60	149	27	3	.502	$4.2	4	50	.274
1889	New York (N)	15	85	.329	158	620	93	204	69	3	.523	$6.9	3	81	.321
1890	New York (P)	35	119	.372	136	586	116	218	42	1	.626	$6.9	9	115	.360
1891	New York (N)	23	100	.313	162	661	97	207	47	3	.498	$9.2	5	95	.295
1892	New York (N)	0	58	.335	122	475	65	159	76	3	.507	$4.4	0	56	.304
1893	Washington (N)	12	94	.277	161	683	74	189	44	2	.400	$9.5	2	95	.287
1904	New York (N)	0	0	.250	1	4	1	1	0	0	.250	$1.0	0	0	.250
	Career	413	1,391	.327	2,727	11,528	2,167	3,773	1,001	90	.537	$352.8	50	1,010	.310
	Average season	22	73	.327	144	607	114	199	53	5	.537	$18.6	3	53	.310
	Summit season	27	82	.362	153	665	151	241	64	6	.598	$26.0	4	58	.341

MEL OTT

		ADJUSTED REGULAR SEASON											ACTUAL RESULTS		
YEAR	TEAM	HR	RBI	BA	G	AB	R	H	2B	3B	SA	PAY	HR	RBI	BA
1926	New York (N)	0	5	.369	38	65	8	24	6	0	.462	$0.0	0	4	.383
1927	New York (N)	4	21	.269	86	171	25	46	10	1	.409	$1.1	1	19	.282
1928	New York (N)	32	85	.309	130	456	76	141	19	1	.566	$5.2	18	77	.322
1929	New York (N)	58	156	.306	160	581	143	178	25	1	.652	$15.4	42	151	.328
1930	New York (N)	36	115	.319	156	549	118	175	26	2	.570	$15.3	25	119	.349
1931	New York (N)	48	128	.283	146	526	116	149	14	2	.591	$15.4	29	115	.292
1932	New York (N)	57	135	.309	162	595	130	184	21	3	.642	$26.6	38	123	.318
1933	New York (N)	40	120	.282	158	603	114	170	27	1	.529	$19.9	23	103	.283
1934	New York (N)	55	148	.315	162	616	131	194	23	4	.633	$26.5	35	135	.326
1935	New York (N)	49	123	.312	158	616	122	192	26	2	.599	$26.0	31	114	.322
1936	New York (N)	50	140	.311	158	562	125	175	21	2	.623	$25.5	33	135	.328
1937	New York (N)	44	101	.286	156	563	105	161	22	1	.563	$19.2	31	95	.294
1938	New York (N)	53	127	.306	160	562	127	172	20	2	.632	$17.0	36	116	.311
1939	New York (N)	39	89	.301	134	425	94	128	19	1	.626	$9.7	27	80	.308
1940	New York (N)	30	90	.291	161	571	102	166	26	2	.501	$12.8	19	79	.289
1941	New York (N)	41	104	.293	154	546	103	160	24	0	.562	$9.8	27	90	.286
1942	New York (N)	50	119	.315	160	578	151	182	18	0	.606	$13.9	30	93	.295
1943	New York (N)	32	62	.248	130	395	85	98	9	1	.519	$5.1	18	47	.234
1944	New York (N)	44	102	.298	125	416	114	124	12	1	.649	$7.2	26	82	.288
1945	New York (N)	38	99	.319	142	474	91	151	19	0	.599	$6.7	21	79	.308
1946	New York (N)	2	5	.083	33	72	3	6	1	0	.181	$1.3	1	4	.074
1947	New York (N)	0	0	.000	4	4	0	0	0	0	.000	$0.8	0	0	.000
	Career	802	2,074	.299	2,873	9,946	2,083	2,976	388	27	.586	$280.4	511	1,860	.304
	Average season	36	94	.299	131	452	95	135	18	1	.586	$12.7	23	85	.304
	Summit season	53	134	.307	154	554	129	170	20	2	.637	$18.5	35	121	.316

RAFAEL PALMEIRO

		ADJUSTED REGULAR SEASON											ACTUAL RESULTS		
YEAR	TEAM	HR	RBI	BA	G	AB	R	H	2B	3B	SA	PAY	HR	RBI	BA
1986	Chicago (N)	3	13	.260	22	73	10	19	4	0	.438	$0.4	3	12	.247
1987	Chicago (N)	15	32	.281	85	224	34	63	17	1	.567	$1.9	14	30	.276
1988	Chicago (N)	12	62	.325	151	576	88	187	51	5	.493	$5.8	8	53	.307
1989	Texas (A)	13	76	.292	156	559	90	163	29	4	.428	$7.4	8	64	.275
1990	Texas (A)	19	102	.333	154	598	83	199	41	6	.517	$11.3	14	89	.319
1991	Texas (A)	33	100	.339	159	631	131	214	53	3	.590	$18.7	26	88	.322
1992	Texas (A)	31	101	.281	159	608	100	171	29	4	.495	$15.4	22	85	.268
1993	Texas (A)	42	113	.300	160	597	133	179	41	2	.586	$16.2	37	105	.295
1994	Baltimore (A)	34	111	.318	161	632	120	201	46	0	.552	$17.0	23	76	.319
1995	Baltimore (A)	47	120	.313	161	624	103	195	34	2	.599	$16.3	39	104	.310
1996	Baltimore (A)	39	140	.288	161	622	108	179	41	2	.548	$19.2	39	142	.289
1997	Baltimore (A)	40	114	.256	158	614	99	157	23	2	.495	$13.2	38	110	.254
1998	Baltimore (A)	44	125	.299	162	619	101	185	36	1	.574	$13.5	43	121	.296
1999	Texas (A)	45	145	.322	158	565	94	182	30	1	.618	$10.1	47	148	.324
2000	Texas (A)	37	116	.287	158	565	99	162	28	3	.543	$9.5	39	120	.288
2001	Texas (A)	46	127	.278	160	600	101	167	32	0	.562	$13.0	47	123	.273
	Career	500	1,597	.301	2,325	8,707	1,494	2,623	535	36	.543	$188.9	447	1,470	.294
	Average season	31	100	.301	145	544	93	164	33	2	.543	$11.8	28	92	.294
	Summit season	42	121	.315	160	607	112	191	39	2	.593	$15.0	38	113	.309

DAVE PARKER

		ADJUSTED REGULAR SEASON											ACTUAL RESULTS		
YEAR	TEAM	HR	RBI	BA	G	AB	R	H	2B	3B	SA	PAY	HR	RBI	BA
1973	Pittsburgh (N)	5	16	.302	54	139	20	42	12	1	.511	$1.1	4	14	.288
1974	Pittsburgh (N)	6	34	.295	73	220	32	65	14	3	.468	$2.0	4	29	.282
1975	Pittsburgh (N)	37	119	.322	149	562	88	181	41	8	.621	$7.4	25	101	.308
1976	Pittsburgh (N)	24	110	.330	138	537	101	177	37	8	.562	$8.9	13	90	.313
1977	Pittsburgh (N)	26	97	.344	159	637	118	219	51	6	.565	$15.3	21	88	.338
1978	Pittsburgh (N)	43	140	.349	149	585	122	204	36	8	.658	$18.5	30	117	.334
1979	Pittsburgh (N)	32	103	.314	157	618	119	194	50	5	.566	$19.3	25	94	.310
1980	Pittsburgh (N)	23	91	.301	139	518	82	156	34	1	.504	$9.5	17	79	.295
1981	Pittsburgh (N)	21	92	.271	105	376	56	102	24	4	.524	$5.9	9	48	.258
1982	Pittsburgh (N)	8	33	.279	73	244	47	68	23	3	.496	$3.7	6	29	.270
1983	Pittsburgh (N)	17	79	.288	144	552	78	159	34	3	.453	$4.6	12	69	.279
1984	Cincinnati (N)	21	109	.295	156	607	85	179	33	0	.453	$6.8	16	94	.285
1985	Cincinnati (N)	41	142	.326	160	635	100	207	47	3	.603	$9.7	34	125	.312
1986	Cincinnati (N)	36	129	.286	162	637	99	182	35	3	.520	$12.9	31	116	.273
1987	Cincinnati (N)	27	102	.258	153	589	81	152	31	0	.448	$8.8	26	97	.253
1988	Oakland (A)	16	65	.273	101	377	51	103	20	1	.459	$3.3	12	55	.257
1989	Oakland (A)	30	115	.280	144	553	66	155	29	0	.495	$4.6	22	97	.264
1990	Milwaukee (A)	28	106	.302	157	610	82	184	33	3	.503	$6.5	21	92	.289
1991	Cal.-Tor. (A)	15	67	.251	132	502	53	126	29	2	.406	$3.3	11	59	.239
	Career	456	1,749	.301	2,505	9,498	1,480	2,855	613	62	.522	$152.1	339	1,493	.290
	Average season	24	92	.301	132	500	78	150	32	3	.522	$8.0	18	79	.290
	Summit season	34	122	.335	151	591	106	198	42	7	.602	$12.0	25	104	.321

ROGER PECKINPAUGH

		ADJUSTED REGULAR SEASON											ACTUAL RESULTS		
YEAR	TEAM	HR	RBI	BA	G	AB	R	H	2B	3B	SA	PAY	HR	RBI	BA
1910	Cleveland (A)	0	7	.222	15	45	1	10	0	0	.222	$0.0	0	6	.200
1912	Cleveland (A)	6	24	.211	72	246	20	52	5	0	.305	$1.2	1	22	.212
1913	Cle.-N.Y. (A)	9	39	.277	100	354	44	98	20	4	.432	$2.8	1	32	.268
1914	New York (A)	17	64	.236	162	588	69	139	19	2	.362	$6.0	3	51	.223
1915	New York (A)	23	57	.236	149	567	87	134	18	2	.397	$7.0	5	44	.220
1916	New York (A)	23	80	.278	152	575	90	160	27	2	.452	$9.5	4	58	.255
1917	New York (A)	0	57	.281	155	569	87	160	76	6	.436	$11.2	0	41	.260
1918	New York (A)	0	73	.244	157	574	100	140	61	4	.364	$11.7	0	43	.231
1919	New York (A)	26	47	.312	140	520	128	162	18	1	.500	$11.4	7	33	.305
1920	New York (A)	25	64	.262	146	561	130	147	23	1	.440	$11.9	8	54	.270
1921	New York (A)	21	78	.266	158	612	140	163	26	3	.422	$16.6	8	71	.288
1922	Washington (A)	7	52	.237	155	548	67	130	24	3	.330	$7.3	2	48	.254
1923	Washington (A)	8	67	.249	161	594	79	148	29	3	.348	$7.3	2	62	.264
1924	Washington (A)	8	79	.254	161	543	78	138	31	3	.366	$6.9	2	73	.272
1925	Washington (A)	11	67	.272	134	449	70	122	18	2	.394	$3.6	4	64	.294
1926	Washington (A)	4	16	.229	61	157	21	36	5	0	.338	$1.6	1	14	.238
1927	Chicago (A)	0	25	.278	72	230	25	64	18	3	.383	$1.4	0	23	.295
	Career	188	896	.259	2,150	7,732	1,236	2,003	418	39	.396	$117.4	48	739	.259
	Average season	11	53	.259	126	455	73	118	25	2	.396	$6.9	3	43	.259
	Summit season	17	57	.281	139	516	96	145	33	3	.455	$9.4	4	44	.270

TERRY PENDLETON

		ADJUSTED REGULAR SEASON											ACTUAL RESULTS		
YEAR	TEAM	HR	RBI	BA	G	AB	R	H	2B	3B	SA	PAY	HR	RBI	BA
1984	St. Louis (N)	1	38	.336	67	262	43	88	25	3	.466	$3.3	1	33	.324
1985	St. Louis (N)	7	78	.250	149	559	63	140	22	2	.335	$6.3	5	69	.240
1986	St. Louis (N)	1	66	.249	160	582	63	145	33	6	.332	$7.2	1	59	.239
1987	St. Louis (N)	12	100	.293	159	583	86	171	32	4	.424	$9.5	12	96	.286
1988	St. Louis (N)	9	63	.269	110	391	52	105	23	2	.407	$5.9	6	53	.253
1989	St. Louis (N)	19	86	.279	160	605	97	169	33	5	.445	$9.5	13	74	.264
1990	St. Louis (N)	8	67	.239	121	447	53	107	24	2	.356	$4.8	6	58	.230
1991	Atlanta (N)	29	98	.336	153	586	107	197	38	7	.573	$9.5	22	86	.319
1992	Atlanta (N)	30	125	.327	160	640	117	209	43	1	.538	$10.0	21	105	.311
1993	Atlanta (N)	21	90	.275	161	633	87	174	36	1	.434	$9.4	17	84	.272
1994	Atlanta (N)	10	43	.252	109	437	36	110	27	4	.400	$3.5	7	30	.252
1995	Florida (N)	17	91	.292	151	582	81	170	38	1	.448	$7.0	14	78	.290
1996	Fla.-Atl. (N)	11	74	.236	153	568	50	134	27	1	.345	$3.4	11	75	.238
1997	Cincinnati (N)	1	18	.248	50	113	11	28	10	0	.363	$1.1	1	17	.248
1998	Kansas City (A)	3	30	.262	79	237	18	62	10	0	.342	$1.4	3	29	.257
	Career	179	1,067	.278	1,942	7,225	964	2,009	421	39	.421	$91.8	140	946	.270
	Average season	12	71	.278	129	482	64	134	28	3	.421	$6.1	9	63	.270
	Summit season	21	100	.306	157	599	98	183	37	4	.486	$9.1	16	88	.294

TONY PEREZ

		ADJUSTED REGULAR SEASON											ACTUAL RESULTS		
YEAR	TEAM	HR	RBI	BA	G	AB	R	H	2B	3B	SA	PAY	HR	RBI	BA
1964	Cincinnati (N)	0	1	.080	12	25	1	2	1	0	.120	$0.0	0	1	.080
1965	Cincinnati (N)	15	58	.285	104	281	49	80	18	3	.530	$2.5	12	47	.260
1966	Cincinnati (N)	6	48	.285	100	260	31	74	15	3	.435	$2.9	4	39	.265
1967	Cincinnati (N)	38	132	.322	156	600	101	193	37	5	.590	$8.9	26	102	.290
1968	Cincinnati (N)	30	129	.320	159	621	131	199	35	6	.541	$15.3	18	92	.282
1969	Cincinnati (N)	46	145	.318	159	625	123	199	40	2	.610	$19.0	37	122	.294
1970	Cincinnati (N)	47	146	.336	158	587	121	197	36	5	.654	$19.9	40	129	.317
1971	Cincinnati (N)	34	114	.291	158	609	90	177	28	3	.514	$16.0	25	91	.269
1972	Cincinnati (N)	32	125	.314	143	542	89	170	45	6	.596	$12.1	21	90	.283
1973	Cincinnati (N)	35	118	.328	151	564	85	185	41	3	.598	$12.2	27	101	.314
1974	Cincinnati (N)	39	120	.277	157	592	96	164	32	2	.535	$9.7	28	101	.265
1975	Cincinnati (N)	29	127	.294	137	511	86	150	32	2	.534	$7.2	20	109	.282
1976	Cincinnati (N)	31	112	.273	139	527	94	144	36	4	.533	$7.3	19	91	.260
1977	Montreal (N)	24	101	.288	154	559	78	161	36	4	.496	$7.3	19	91	.283
1978	Montreal (N)	21	92	.303	148	544	75	165	44	2	.507	$6.4	14	78	.290
1979	Montreal (N)	17	82	.274	134	496	65	136	34	3	.458	$4.3	13	73	.270
1980	Boston (A)	34	123	.280	153	593	85	166	33	2	.514	$6.7	25	105	.275
1981	Boston (A)	21	72	.264	126	459	64	121	18	4	.458	$3.4	9	39	.252
1982	Boston (A)	8	36	.270	69	196	21	53	16	2	.495	$1.8	6	31	.260
1983	Philadelphia (N)	8	48	.248	90	250	20	62	13	2	.412	$1.8	6	43	.241
1984	Cincinnati (N)	3	17	.248	71	137	10	34	7	1	.380	$0.9	2	15	.241
1985	Cincinnati (N)	8	37	.344	72	183	28	63	8	0	.519	$0.9	6	33	.328
1986	Cincinnati (N)	2	32	.265	77	200	16	53	15	1	.380	$0.9	2	29	.255
	Career	528	2,015	.296	2,827	9,961	1,559	2,948	620	65	.530	$167.4	379	1,652	.279
	Average season	23	88	.296	123	433	68	128	27	3	.530	$7.3	16	72	.279
	Summit season	40	133	.324	153	584	104	189	40	4	.611	$14.4	30	109	.300

MIKE PIAZZA

		ADJUSTED REGULAR SEASON											ACTUAL RESULTS		
YEAR	TEAM	HR	RBI	BA	G	AB	R	H	2B	3B	SA	PAY	HR	RBI	BA
1992	Los Angeles (N)	1	8	.246	21	69	6	17	4	0	.348	$0.1	1	7	.232
1993	Los Angeles (N)	40	120	.324	149	547	87	177	24	2	.594	$6.3	35	112	.318
1994	Los Angeles (N)	35	132	.318	152	575	92	183	25	0	.544	$9.2	24	92	.319
1995	Los Angeles (N)	38	107	.348	126	488	94	170	19	0	.621	$9.1	32	93	.346
1996	Los Angeles (N)	36	104	.335	148	547	86	183	16	0	.561	$12.4	36	105	.336
1997	Los Angeles (N)	42	129	.365	152	556	108	203	31	1	.651	$12.2	40	124	.362
1998	L.A.-Fla.-N.Y. (N)	33	115	.332	151	561	91	186	37	1	.578	$11.8	32	111	.328
1999	New York (N)	38	120	.302	140	530	97	160	25	0	.564	$9.8	40	124	.303
2000	New York (N)	36	109	.322	136	482	87	155	25	0	.598	$7.0	38	113	.324
2001	New York (N)	35	97	.306	141	503	84	154	29	0	.573	$7.0	36	94	.300
	Career	334	1,041	.327	1,316	4,858	832	1,588	235	4	.583	$84.9	314	975	.325
	Average season	33	104	.327	132	486	83	159	24	0	.583	$8.5	31	98	.325
	Summit season	38	116	.338	143	527	93	178	27	1	.609	$9.3	35	111	.335

VADA PINSON

		ADJUSTED REGULAR SEASON											ACTUAL RESULTS		
YEAR	TEAM	HR	RBI	BA	G	AB	R	H	2B	3B	SA	PAY	HR	RBI	BA
1958	Cincinnati (N)	1	10	.280	28	100	24	28	10	0	.410	$0.9	1	8	.271
1959	Cincinnati (N)	25	99	.331	162	682	155	226	62	8	.556	$14.3	20	84	.316
1960	Cincinnati (N)	26	72	.303	160	677	127	205	50	9	.518	$15.3	20	61	.287
1961	Cincinnati (N)	19	99	.357	162	639	115	228	47	6	.538	$15.3	16	87	.343
1962	Cincinnati (N)	27	111	.305	155	619	118	189	42	5	.520	$19.0	23	100	.292
1963	Cincinnati (N)	29	132	.342	162	652	119	223	53	11	.590	$19.7	22	106	.313
1964	Cincinnati (N)	29	101	.285	155	621	120	177	31	9	.504	$19.0	23	84	.266
1965	Cincinnati (N)	29	115	.335	159	669	119	224	46	8	.558	$25.3	22	94	.305
1966	Cincinnati (N)	21	94	.312	158	626	87	195	48	5	.505	$15.3	16	76	.288
1967	Cincinnati (N)	28	85	.320	158	650	116	208	40	10	.542	$15.7	18	66	.288
1968	Cincinnati (N)	10	67	.307	129	495	84	152	46	5	.481	$7.4	5	48	.271
1969	St. Louis (N)	14	84	.277	132	495	69	137	32	5	.446	$7.0	10	70	.255
1970	Cleveland (A)	29	93	.303	148	574	84	174	37	5	.537	$6.9	24	82	.286
1971	Cleveland (A)	16	44	.284	146	566	75	161	32	4	.440	$4.6	11	35	.263
1972	California (A)	12	67	.303	142	505	77	153	37	2	.455	$3.9	7	49	.275
1973	California (A)	12	66	.273	124	466	65	127	19	6	.416	$3.5	8	57	.260
1974	Kansas City (A)	10	49	.288	115	406	55	117	24	2	.431	$2.2	6	41	.276
1975	Kansas City (A)	7	26	.232	103	319	44	74	20	4	.386	$1.7	4	22	.223
	Career	344	1,414	.307	2,498	9,761	1,653	2,998	676	104	.503	$197.0	256	1,170	.286
	Average season	19	79	.307	139	542	92	167	38	6	.503	$10.9	14	65	.286
	Summit season	26	106	.337	161	658	125	222	50	9	.559	$18.1	20	87	.312

BOOG POWELL

YEAR	TEAM	ADJUSTED REGULAR SEASON HR	RBI	BA	G	AB	R	H	2B	3B	SA	PAY	ACTUAL RESULTS HR	RBI	BA
1961	Baltimore (A)	0	1	.077	4	13	0	1	0	0	.077	$0.0	0	1	.077
1962	Baltimore (A)	18	59	.253	124	400	49	101	17	1	.435	$3.2	15	53	.243
1963	Baltimore (A)	30	102	.289	140	491	83	142	29	2	.540	$6.3	25	82	.265
1964	Baltimore (A)	46	120	.311	133	421	89	131	21	0	.689	$7.4	39	99	.290
1965	Baltimore (A)	21	88	.271	144	472	66	128	26	2	.468	$8.6	17	72	.248
1966	Baltimore (A)	41	136	.311	142	498	97	155	23	0	.604	$12.0	34	109	.287
1967	Baltimore (A)	18	72	.258	126	418	69	108	18	1	.435	$8.6	13	55	.234
1968	Baltimore (A)	33	120	.284	154	550	85	156	27	1	.516	$12.2	22	85	.249
1969	Baltimore (A)	46	145	.330	152	533	99	176	32	0	.649	$14.2	37	121	.304
1970	Baltimore (A)	40	129	.314	154	526	93	165	35	0	.608	$11.8	35	114	.297
1971	Baltimore (A)	29	118	.276	131	428	76	118	24	0	.535	$9.1	22	92	.256
1972	Baltimore (A)	31	112	.277	147	488	73	135	26	1	.525	$9.3	21	81	.252
1973	Baltimore (A)	14	63	.278	114	370	61	103	16	1	.441	$3.7	11	54	.265
1974	Baltimore (A)	17	54	.276	110	344	44	95	16	1	.477	$2.7	12	45	.265
1975	Cleveland (A)	36	103	.310	137	445	76	138	19	0	.596	$3.8	27	86	.297
1976	Cleveland (A)	14	41	.227	97	299	36	68	10	0	.401	$2.2	9	33	.215
1977	Los Angeles (N)	0	6	.244	50	41	0	10	0	0	.244	$0.8	0	5	.244
	Career	434	1,469	.286	2,059	6,737	1,096	1,930	339	10	.533	$115.9	339	1,187	.266
	Average season	26	86	.286	121	396	64	114	20	1	.533	$6.8	20	70	.266
	Summit season	42	127	.315	144	485	91	153	26	0	.629	$9.8	34	106	.295

KIRBY PUCKETT

YEAR	TEAM	ADJUSTED REGULAR SEASON HR	RBI	BA	G	AB	R	H	2B	3B	SA	PAY	ACTUAL RESULTS HR	RBI	BA
1984	Minnesota (A)	0	36	.307	128	557	73	171	23	7	.373	$6.0	0	31	.296
1985	Minnesota (A)	6	84	.301	161	691	91	208	40	13	.423	$12.3	4	74	.288
1986	Minnesota (A)	36	107	.343	161	680	133	233	41	6	.579	$18.7	31	96	.328
1987	Minnesota (A)	29	104	.340	157	624	100	212	35	5	.551	$14.7	28	99	.332
1988	Minnesota (A)	33	144	.377	158	657	129	248	48	5	.616	$19.6	24	121	.356
1989	Minnesota (A)	14	101	.359	159	635	89	228	58	4	.529	$18.5	9	85	.339
1990	Minnesota (A)	16	92	.310	146	551	94	171	47	3	.494	$11.7	12	80	.298
1991	Minnesota (A)	21	101	.336	152	611	105	205	34	5	.511	$12.4	15	89	.319
1992	Minnesota (A)	28	131	.346	160	639	124	221	43	4	.557	$16.2	19	110	.329
1993	Minnesota (A)	26	95	.301	156	622	95	187	41	3	.502	$9.9	22	89	.296
1994	Minnesota (A)	30	163	.316	155	630	115	199	45	4	.543	$13.6	20	112	.317
1995	Minnesota (A)	27	114	.317	154	605	95	192	45	0	.526	$12.9	23	99	.314
	Career	266	1,272	.330	1,847	7,502	1,243	2,475	500	59	.519	$166.5	207	1,085	.318
	Average season	22	106	.330	154	625	104	206	42	5	.519	$13.9	17	90	.318
	Summit season	28	117	.352	159	647	115	228	45	5	.567	$17.5	22	102	.337

TIM RAINES

		ADJUSTED REGULAR SEASON											ACTUAL RESULTS		
YEAR	TEAM	HR	RBI	BA	G	AB	R	H	2B	3B	SA	PAY	HR	RBI	BA
1979	Montreal (N)	0	0	.000	6	0	3	0	0	0	.000	$0.0	0	0	.000
1980	Montreal (N)	0	0	.050	15	20	6	1	0	0	.050	$0.0	0	0	.050
1981	Montreal (N)	14	68	.319	132	470	112	150	26	10	.506	$5.0	5	37	.304
1982	Montreal (N)	6	49	.284	156	647	103	184	44	8	.405	$8.7	4	43	.277
1983	Montreal (N)	16	80	.308	155	611	151	188	39	6	.470	$15.1	11	71	.298
1984	Montreal (N)	12	70	.319	161	626	124	200	51	8	.484	$19.0	8	60	.309
1985	Montreal (N)	15	47	.335	151	579	132	194	38	12	.520	$14.8	11	41	.320
1986	Montreal (N)	11	69	.349	152	584	102	204	42	10	.512	$14.8	9	62	.334
1987	Montreal (N)	19	71	.338	139	530	129	179	38	7	.543	$14.3	18	68	.330
1988	Montreal (N)	17	56	.287	108	425	77	122	22	7	.492	$5.9	12	48	.270
1989	Montreal (N)	14	71	.304	145	517	90	157	36	6	.478	$9.1	9	60	.286
1990	Montreal (N)	13	71	.300	130	457	75	137	14	5	.438	$6.8	9	62	.287
1991	Chicago (A)	8	57	.281	155	609	116	171	27	6	.384	$9.2	5	50	.268
1992	Chicago (A)	11	64	.309	144	551	122	170	28	10	.456	$7.2	7	54	.294
1993	Chicago (A)	19	58	.311	115	415	80	129	16	4	.506	$3.9	16	54	.306
1994	Chicago (A)	15	75	.265	145	551	116	146	23	6	.410	$7.4	10	52	.266
1995	Chicago (A)	15	77	.286	149	562	93	161	30	4	.434	$6.8	12	67	.285
1996	New York (A)	9	33	.284	59	201	45	57	10	0	.468	$2.0	9	33	.284
1997	New York (A)	4	39	.325	74	271	58	88	21	2	.461	$2.1	4	38	.321
1998	New York (A)	5	49	.293	109	321	55	94	13	1	.386	$2.0	5	47	.290
1999	Oakland (A)	4	17	.215	58	135	20	29	5	0	.341	$1.0	4	17	.215
2001	Mon. (N)-Balt. (A)	1	9	.315	51	89	14	28	7	1	.449	$0.7	1	9	.303
	Career	228	1,130	.304	2,509	9,171	1,823	2,789	530	113	.461	$155.8	169	973	.295
	Average season	10	51	.304	114	417	83	127	24	5	.461	$7.1	8	44	.295
	Summit season	16	63	.331	138	516	111	171	32	9	.521	$10.6	12	52	.321

WILLIE RANDOLPH

		ADJUSTED REGULAR SEASON											ACTUAL RESULTS		
YEAR	TEAM	HR	RBI	BA	G	AB	R	H	2B	3B	SA	PAY	HR	RBI	BA
1975	Pittsburgh (N)	0	3	.164	30	61	10	10	3	0	.213	$0.0	0	3	.164
1976	New York (A)	3	50	.281	127	437	73	123	29	4	.387	$3.9	1	40	.267
1977	New York (A)	6	44	.279	147	551	101	154	38	9	.414	$6.1	4	40	.274
1978	New York (A)	6	49	.291	133	495	102	144	25	6	.402	$7.3	3	42	.279
1979	New York (A)	8	68	.273	155	582	110	159	22	12	.393	$12.2	5	61	.270
1980	New York (A)	11	53	.300	138	513	114	154	31	6	.448	$11.7	7	46	.294
1981	New York (A)	6	44	.244	141	541	110	132	31	5	.353	$11.3	2	24	.232
1982	New York (A)	5	41	.289	144	553	98	160	30	4	.385	$9.5	3	36	.280
1983	New York (A)	3	43	.288	104	420	83	121	27	1	.379	$5.3	2	38	.279
1984	New York (A)	4	36	.298	142	564	100	168	34	2	.387	$7.0	2	31	.287
1985	New York (A)	6	46	.288	144	500	86	144	27	2	.386	$5.8	5	40	.276
1986	New York (A)	6	56	.289	141	492	85	142	18	2	.370	$3.9	5	50	.276
1987	New York (A)	7	70	.312	120	449	101	140	27	2	.428	$4.7	7	67	.305
1988	New York (A)	3	41	.243	111	408	51	99	27	1	.336	$2.7	2	34	.230
1989	Los Angeles (N)	4	43	.298	147	557	74	166	29	0	.372	$3.9	2	36	.282
1990	L.A. (N)-Oak. (A)	4	34	.271	119	388	60	105	18	4	.369	$2.1	2	30	.260

(Willie Randolph, continued)

		ADJUSTED REGULAR SEASON											ACTUAL RESULTS		
YEAR	TEAM	HR	RBI	BA	G	AB	R	H	2B	3B	SA	PAY	HR	RBI	BA
1991	Milwaukee (A)	0	61	.343	124	431	68	148	23	4	.415	$2.4	0	54	.327
1992	New York (N)	4	18	.266	90	286	34	76	14	1	.364	$1.5	2	15	.252
	Career	86	800	.285	2,257	8,228	1,460	2,345	453	65	.387	$101.3	54	687	.276
	Average season	5	44	.285	125	457	81	130	25	4	.387	$5.6	3	38	.276
	Summit season	6	55	.303	132	488	97	148	29	5	.420	$6.4	4	50	.294

PEE WEE REESE

		ADJUSTED REGULAR SEASON											ACTUAL RESULTS		
YEAR	TEAM	HR	RBI	BA	G	AB	R	H	2B	3B	SA	PAY	HR	RBI	BA
1940	Brooklyn (N)	10	31	.272	87	323	65	88	10	2	.409	$4.1	5	28	.272
1941	Brooklyn (N)	6	53	.234	157	615	87	144	37	4	.337	$8.7	2	46	.229
1942	Brooklyn (N)	10	67	.271	158	590	110	160	41	4	.405	$11.6	3	53	.255
1946	Brooklyn (N)	14	76	.300	157	560	100	168	26	8	.450	$11.6	5	60	.284
1947	Brooklyn (N)	20	86	.292	148	496	95	145	30	2	.482	$9.3	12	73	.284
1948	Brooklyn (N)	16	84	.280	158	592	108	166	40	2	.436	$12.2	9	75	.274
1949	Brooklyn (N)	25	81	.285	161	641	147	183	32	2	.459	$22.3	16	73	.279
1950	Brooklyn (N)	15	55	.264	147	554	103	146	26	3	.403	$7.4	11	52	.260
1951	Brooklyn (N)	17	94	.294	158	632	105	186	28	6	.438	$13.2	10	84	.286
1952	Brooklyn (N)	12	71	.289	156	585	116	169	28	7	.422	$9.9	6	58	.272
1953	Brooklyn (N)	18	68	.277	146	546	121	151	32	5	.452	$9.3	13	61	.271
1954	Brooklyn (N)	15	81	.318	148	582	115	185	50	5	.498	$9.4	10	69	.309
1955	Brooklyn (N)	13	70	.293	153	584	114	171	40	3	.438	$9.2	10	61	.282
1956	Brooklyn (N)	11	53	.267	155	603	98	161	27	1	.370	$6.9	9	46	.257
1957	Brooklyn (N)	1	35	.234	108	346	40	81	6	1	.266	$2.4	1	29	.224
1958	Los Angeles (N)	5	20	.234	62	154	25	36	9	2	.416	$1.3	4	17	.224
	Career	208	1,025	.278	2,259	8,403	1,549	2,340	462	57	.421	$148.8	126	885	.269
	Average season	13	64	.278	141	525	97	146	29	4	.421	$9.3	8	55	.269
	Summit season	18	84	.297	154	582	112	173	33	5	.464	$13.2	11	72	.288

JIM RICE

		ADJUSTED REGULAR SEASON											ACTUAL RESULTS		
YEAR	TEAM	HR	RBI	BA	G	AB	R	H	2B	3B	SA	PAY	HR	RBI	BA
1974	Boston (A)	2	15	.284	24	67	7	19	3	1	.448	$0.4	1	13	.269
1975	Boston (A)	32	121	.322	146	572	109	184	34	3	.559	$7.3	22	102	.309
1976	Boston (A)	40	104	.298	153	581	92	173	28	5	.570	$9.3	25	85	.282
1977	Boston (A)	49	127	.326	161	648	116	211	33	10	.634	$15.5	39	114	.320
1978	Boston (A)	62	164	.328	162	673	143	221	27	11	.678	$26.9	46	139	.315
1979	Boston (A)	48	145	.329	160	627	131	206	42	5	.641	$25.6	39	130	.325
1980	Boston (A)	33	101	.299	126	512	95	153	24	5	.559	$14.5	24	86	.294
1981	Boston (A)	38	114	.298	162	677	94	202	29	1	.513	$25.3	17	62	.284
1982	Boston (A)	31	112	.318	145	573	99	182	28	4	.543	$12.3	24	97	.309
1983	Boston (A)	48	144	.315	155	626	103	197	35	1	.604	$15.9	39	126	.305
1984	Boston (A)	37	142	.289	159	657	114	190	28	6	.519	$16.8	28	122	.280
1985	Boston (A)	33	116	.304	139	542	96	165	22	2	.535	$9.4	27	103	.291

(Jim Rice, continued)

ADJUSTED REGULAR SEASON | | | | | | | | | | | | **ACTUAL RESULTS**

YEAR	TEAM	HR	RBI	BA	G	AB	R	H	2B	3B	SA	PAY	HR	RBI	BA
1986	Boston (A)	24	123	.338	158	622	110	210	45	2	.532	$13.5	20	110	.324
1987	Boston (A)	13	65	.285	108	404	69	115	15	0	.418	$4.8	13	62	.277
1988	Boston (A)	20	85	.278	135	485	67	135	20	3	.456	$4.9	15	72	.264
1989	Boston (A)	4	33	.249	56	209	26	52	13	2	.388	$1.9	3	28	.234
	Career	514	1,711	.309	2,149	8,475	1,471	2,615	426	61	.555	$204.3	382	1,451	.298
	Average season	32	107	.309	134	530	92	163	27	4	.555	$12.8	24	91	.298
	Summit season	48	140	.324	157	629	120	204	34	6	.626	$18.2	37	122	.315

SAM RICE

ADJUSTED REGULAR SEASON | | | | | | | | | | | | **ACTUAL RESULTS**

YEAR	TEAM	HR	RBI	BA	G	AB	R	H	2B	3B	SA	PAY	HR	RBI	BA
1915	Washington (A)	0	0	.375	4	8	0	3	0	0	.375	$0.0	0	0	.375
1916	Washington (A)	7	23	.325	59	200	35	65	12	1	.500	$1.2	1	17	.299
1917	Washington (A)	0	94	.327	160	605	105	198	83	7	.488	$7.6	0	69	.302
1918	Washington (A)	0	5	.367	9	30	5	11	4	0	.500	$1.2	0	3	.348
1919	Washington (A)	21	101	.329	161	636	114	209	40	5	.506	$9.8	3	71	.321
1920	Washington (A)	17	96	.330	162	661	99	218	47	5	.493	$12.3	3	80	.338
1921	Washington (A)	15	85	.304	150	588	90	179	56	6	.497	$9.2	4	79	.330
1922	Washington (A)	18	74	.275	162	666	98	183	51	6	.450	$13.0	6	69	.295
1923	Washington (A)	13	81	.300	155	623	127	187	59	11	.493	$12.9	3	75	.316
1924	Washington (A)	5	82	.314	160	671	115	211	75	10	.478	$13.3	1	76	.334
1925	Washington (A)	4	91	.324	162	692	116	224	62	11	.462	$13.7	1	87	.350
1926	Washington (A)	14	85	.324	162	683	110	221	52	9	.488	$13.1	3	76	.337
1927	Washington (A)	9	70	.282	147	624	105	176	55	9	.442	$9.2	2	65	.297
1928	Washington (A)	8	60	.315	155	645	104	203	55	11	.471	$9.3	2	55	.328
1929	Washington (A)	3	63	.300	159	653	122	196	65	6	.432	$9.5	1	62	.323
1930	Washington (A)	3	70	.318	155	625	117	199	57	8	.450	$9.3	1	73	.349
1931	Washington (A)	0	46	.300	125	430	89	129	43	8	.437	$3.5	0	42	.310
1932	Washington (A)	3	37	.316	112	304	64	96	27	5	.467	$2.4	1	34	.323
1933	Washington (A)	3	14	.289	77	90	23	26	5	2	.489	$1.2	1	12	.294
1934	Cleveland (A)	3	36	.281	102	352	52	99	28	1	.392	$1.7	1	33	.293
	Career	146	1,213	.310	2,538	9,786	1,690	3,033	876	121	.469	$153.4	34	1,078	.322
	Average season	7	61	.310	127	489	85	152	44	6	.469	$7.7	2	54	.322
	Summit season	13	92	.323	159	635	104	205	56	6	.491	$10.4	3	75	.326

CAL RIPKEN JR.

ADJUSTED REGULAR SEASON | | | | | | | | | | | | **ACTUAL RESULTS**

YEAR	TEAM	HR	RBI	BA	G	AB	R	H	2B	3B	SA	PAY	HR	RBI	BA
1981	Baltimore (A)	0	0	.136	35	59	2	8	0	0	.136	$0.0	0	0	.128
1982	Baltimore (A)	35	106	.273	159	594	103	162	35	4	.522	$7.0	28	93	.264
1983	Baltimore (A)	35	116	.329	162	663	138	218	51	2	.570	$15.6	27	102	.318
1984	Baltimore (A)	36	100	.315	162	641	119	202	42	6	.568	$18.5	27	86	.304
1985	Baltimore (A)	32	126	.296	162	646	133	191	36	4	.512	$25.9	26	110	.282
1986	Baltimore (A)	29	90	.295	162	627	109	185	39	1	.499	$19.5	25	81	.282

(Cal Ripken, Jr., continued)

		ADJUSTED REGULAR SEASON											ACTUAL RESULTS		
YEAR	TEAM	HR	RBI	BA	G	AB	R	H	2B	3B	SA	PAY	HR	RBI	BA
1987	Baltimore (A)	28	103	.258	162	624	101	161	31	3	.452	$19.2	27	98	.252
1988	Baltimore (A)	31	97	.280	162	579	104	162	27	1	.491	$18.8	23	81	.264
1989	Baltimore (A)	29	110	.272	162	646	95	176	33	0	.458	$15.9	21	93	.257
1990	Baltimore (A)	28	97	.260	162	604	90	157	31	4	.464	$12.6	21	84	.250
1991	Baltimore (A)	43	130	.340	162	650	113	221	50	4	.628	$16.3	34	114	.323
1992	Baltimore (A)	21	86	.264	162	637	87	168	32	1	.416	$10.0	14	72	.251
1993	Baltimore (A)	28	96	.261	162	641	93	167	27	3	.443	$10.1	24	90	.257
1994	Baltimore (A)	20	110	.315	162	642	104	202	28	4	.464	$12.9	13	75	.315
1995	Baltimore (A)	21	101	.263	162	619	82	163	39	2	.435	$9.5	17	88	.262
1996	Baltimore (A)	26	100	.277	162	636	93	176	41	1	.467	$9.4	26	102	.278
1997	Baltimore (A)	18	87	.272	162	615	82	167	30	0	.408	$8.9	17	84	.270
1998	Baltimore (A)	15	63	.275	161	601	67	165	27	1	.398	$6.4	14	61	.271
1999	Baltimore (A)	17	56	.337	86	332	50	112	27	0	.572	$2.3	18	57	.340
2000	Baltimore (A)	14	54	.256	83	309	42	79	16	0	.443	$2.0	15	56	.256
2001	Baltimore (A)	14	70	.243	128	477	44	116	16	0	.365	$2.4	14	68	.239
	Career	520	1,898	.284	3,082	11,842	1,851	3,358	658	41	.478	$243.2	431	1,695	.276
	Average season	25	90	.284	147	564	88	160	31	2	.478	$11.6	21	81	.276
	Summit season	33	106	.323	147	586	111	189	41	3	.572	$15.7	26	94	.311

PHIL RIZZUTO

		ADJUSTED REGULAR SEASON											ACTUAL RESULTS		
YEAR	TEAM	HR	RBI	BA	G	AB	R	H	2B	3B	SA	PAY	HR	RBI	BA
1941	New York (A)	9	53	.315	138	534	75	168	34	7	.455	$7.3	3	46	.307
1942	New York (A)	12	86	.302	151	580	100	175	40	6	.453	$11.3	4	68	.284
1946	New York (A)	6	49	.270	133	497	68	134	28	1	.366	$5.6	2	38	.257
1947	New York (A)	5	71	.282	160	574	92	162	44	8	.413	$9.0	2	60	.273
1948	New York (A)	12	57	.258	135	489	74	126	17	1	.370	$5.9	6	50	.252
1949	New York (A)	10	72	.282	160	642	123	181	34	6	.400	$9.6	5	65	.275
1950	New York (A)	10	70	.329	162	645	134	212	50	4	.465	$13.1	7	66	.324
1951	New York (A)	4	49	.283	151	566	99	160	35	5	.383	$6.8	2	43	.274
1952	New York (A)	4	53	.271	160	608	110	165	44	9	.393	$9.3	2	43	.254
1953	New York (A)	3	62	.277	144	444	62	123	31	2	.376	$3.5	2	54	.271
1954	New York (A)	3	18	.202	133	322	55	65	15	0	.276	$2.0	2	15	.195
1955	New York (A)	1	10	.267	85	150	22	40	7	1	.347	$1.1	1	9	.259
1956	New York (A)	0	7	.236	33	55	7	13	0	0	.236	$0.5	0	6	.231
	Career	79	657	.282	1,745	6,106	1,021	1,724	379	50	.400	$85.0	38	563	.273
	Average season	6	51	.282	134	470	79	133	29	4	.400	$6.5	3	43	.273
	Summit season	9	70	.303	154	595	105	180	40	6	.435	$10.1	4	61	.293

BROOKS ROBINSON

		ADJUSTED REGULAR SEASON											ACTUAL RESULTS		
YEAR	TEAM	HR	RBI	BA	G	AB	R	H	2B	3B	SA	PAY	HR	RBI	BA
1955	Baltimore (A)	0	1	.091	6	22	0	2	0	0	.091	$0.0	0	1	.091
1956	Baltimore (A)	1	1	.234	16	47	6	11	6	0	.426	$0.0	1	1	.227
1957	Baltimore (A)	3	17	.250	53	124	16	31	7	1	.395	$0.5	2	14	.239
1958	Baltimore (A)	4	39	.247	153	489	37	121	24	2	.329	$3.3	3	32	.238
1959	Baltimore (A)	5	28	.297	92	327	34	97	20	2	.416	$2.5	4	24	.284
1960	Baltimore (A)	19	105	.310	160	626	88	194	38	7	.484	$8.6	14	88	.294
1961	Baltimore (A)	8	65	.300	162	664	96	199	49	5	.425	$11.5	7	61	.287
1962	Baltimore (A)	27	95	.317	162	634	85	201	39	7	.528	$12.1	23	86	.303
1963	Baltimore (A)	14	83	.275	161	589	83	162	36	3	.418	$12.0	11	67	.251
1964	Baltimore (A)	34	143	.340	162	608	99	207	45	2	.589	$15.1	28	118	.317
1965	Baltimore (A)	22	98	.326	144	559	99	182	33	2	.510	$12.2	18	80	.297
1966	Baltimore (A)	28	124	.291	159	628	113	183	46	2	.505	$16.1	23	100	.269
1967	Baltimore (A)	32	100	.298	159	614	115	183	33	4	.521	$15.9	22	77	.269
1968	Baltimore (A)	28	106	.288	162	608	92	175	50	5	.525	$12.5	17	75	.253
1969	Baltimore (A)	29	100	.254	156	598	87	152	28	3	.457	$9.6	23	84	.234
1970	Baltimore (A)	22	106	.293	158	608	95	178	41	3	.479	$9.7	18	94	.276
1971	Baltimore (A)	28	118	.293	160	604	86	177	28	1	.482	$9.7	20	92	.272
1972	Baltimore (A)	14	89	.275	161	585	66	161	36	2	.415	$7.0	8	64	.250
1973	Baltimore (A)	13	84	.270	155	549	62	148	23	2	.390	$4.5	9	72	.257
1974	Baltimore (A)	12	70	.302	153	553	55	167	38	0	.436	$4.2	7	59	.288
1975	Baltimore (A)	10	63	.209	147	492	59	103	20	1	.315	$3.2	6	53	.201
1976	Baltimore (A)	6	13	.220	71	218	20	48	10	2	.367	$1.4	3	11	.211
1977	Baltimore (A)	1	4	.149	24	47	3	7	2	0	.255	$0.6	1	4	.149
	Career	360	1,652	.286	2,936	10,793	1,496	3,089	652	56	.457	$172.2	268	1,357	.267
	Average season	16	72	.286	128	469	65	134	28	2	.457	$7.5	12	59	.267
	Summit season	29	108	.314	158	605	98	190	40	4	.537	$13.6	22	87	.288

FRANK ROBINSON

		ADJUSTED REGULAR SEASON											ACTUAL RESULTS		
YEAR	TEAM	HR	RBI	BA	G	AB	R	H	2B	3B	SA	PAY	HR	RBI	BA
1956	Cincinnati (N)	45	95	.303	159	598	141	181	35	4	.600	$19.6	38	83	.290
1957	Cincinnati (N)	36	91	.337	158	644	118	217	38	4	.576	$19.7	29	75	.322
1958	Cincinnati (N)	38	100	.281	156	584	109	164	33	5	.550	$15.6	31	83	.269
1959	Cincinnati (N)	44	149	.326	154	570	126	186	39	3	.637	$19.1	36	125	.311
1960	Cincinnati (N)	39	98	.314	144	481	102	151	41	4	.659	$14.3	31	83	.297
1961	Cincinnati (N)	43	142	.337	161	573	134	193	42	5	.653	$19.3	37	124	.323
1962	Cincinnati (N)	43	151	.356	162	609	149	217	65	1	.678	$26.4	39	136	.342
1963	Cincinnati (N)	26	113	.284	140	482	98	137	26	2	.508	$14.8	21	91	.259
1964	Cincinnati (N)	35	116	.330	155	564	125	186	48	5	.619	$16.6	29	96	.306
1965	Cincinnati (N)	41	139	.325	156	582	134	189	43	4	.624	$17.0	33	113	.296
1966	Baltimore (A)	58	152	.343	157	583	152	200	44	2	.724	$23.2	49	122	.316
1967	Baltimore (A)	42	123	.346	130	483	108	167	30	5	.689	$9.9	30	94	.311
1968	Baltimore (A)	23	73	.304	130	421	98	128	36	1	.558	$7.3	15	52	.268
1969	Baltimore (A)	41	120	.334	148	539	133	180	26	4	.625	$13.1	32	100	.308
1970	Baltimore (A)	29	88	.325	132	471	100	153	30	1	.577	$7.2	25	78	.306
1971	Baltimore (A)	38	127	.303	136	465	105	141	21	2	.602	$6.9	28	99	.281

(Frank Robinson, continued)

YEAR	TEAM	ADJUSTED REGULAR SEASON HR	RBI	BA	G	AB	R	H	2B	3B	SA	PAY	ACTUAL RESULTS HR	RBI	BA
1972	Los Angeles (N)	27	82	.279	108	359	57	100	8	1	.532	$4.3	19	59	.251
1973	California (A)	37	113	.279	147	534	99	149	34	0	.551	$6.9	30	97	.266
1974	Cal.-Cle. (A)	30	80	.257	143	474	96	122	31	3	.525	$6.4	22	68	.245
1975	Cleveland (A)	12	28	.250	50	120	23	30	5	0	.592	$1.7	9	24	.237
1976	Cleveland (A)	4	13	.232	37	69	6	16	0	0	.406	$1.1	3	10	.224
	Career	731	2,193	.314	2,863	10,205	2,213	3,207	675	56	.606	$270.4	586	1,812	.294
	Average season	35	104	.314	136	486	105	153	32	3	.606	$12.9	28	86	.294
	Summit season	45	133	.341	151	546	129	186	44	3	.679	$18.6	37	112	.319

JACKIE ROBINSON

YEAR	TEAM	ADJUSTED REGULAR SEASON HR	RBI	BA	G	AB	R	H	2B	3B	SA	PAY	ACTUAL RESULTS HR	RBI	BA
1947	Brooklyn (N)	22	56	.306	158	617	148	189	39	3	.486	$18.8	12	48	.297
1948	Brooklyn (N)	22	96	.303	154	601	122	182	47	5	.507	$15.8	12	85	.296
1949	Brooklyn (N)	27	138	.351	162	616	136	216	49	8	.588	$22.5	16	124	.342
1950	Brooklyn (N)	18	87	.331	151	543	106	180	48	3	.530	$12.3	14	81	.328
1951	Brooklyn (N)	27	98	.349	157	562	119	196	41	5	.584	$10.1	19	88	.338
1952	Brooklyn (N)	29	92	.328	156	534	128	175	21	2	.537	$13.0	19	75	.308
1953	Brooklyn (N)	16	107	.335	142	505	123	169	45	5	.539	$9.5	12	95	.329
1954	Brooklyn (N)	21	69	.321	130	405	73	130	27	3	.558	$4.9	15	59	.311
1955	Brooklyn (N)	11	41	.265	110	332	58	88	9	1	.398	$3.2	8	36	.256
1956	Brooklyn (N)	12	50	.285	123	375	70	107	21	1	.443	$2.7	10	43	.275
	Career	205	834	.321	1,443	5,090	1,083	1,632	347	36	.524	$112.8	137	734	.311
	Average season	21	83	.321	144	509	108	163	35	4	.524	$11.3	14	73	.311
	Summit season	24	101	.338	149	524	116	177	37	5	.565	$12.0	16	88	.327

IVAN RODRIGUEZ

YEAR	TEAM	ADJUSTED REGULAR SEASON HR	RBI	BA	G	AB	R	H	2B	3B	SA	PAY	ACTUAL RESULTS HR	RBI	BA
1991	Texas (A)	4	31	.279	88	280	27	78	19	0	.389	$2.5	3	27	.264
1992	Texas (A)	12	44	.274	123	420	46	115	18	1	.407	$4.0	8	37	.260
1993	Texas (A)	12	71	.277	137	473	60	131	31	4	.436	$5.4	10	66	.273
1994	Texas (A)	24	82	.296	141	517	81	153	27	1	.491	$7.0	16	57	.298
1995	Texas (A)	15	77	.306	146	553	64	169	37	2	.461	$7.3	12	67	.303
1996	Texas (A)	19	85	.299	152	635	114	190	48	3	.474	$14.3	19	86	.300
1997	Texas (A)	21	80	.317	150	597	102	189	34	4	.492	$12.1	20	77	.313
1998	Texas (A)	22	94	.325	145	579	91	188	40	4	.522	$11.8	21	91	.321
1999	Texas (A)	34	110	.328	144	600	113	197	29	1	.550	$14.6	35	113	.332
2000	Texas (A)	26	80	.344	91	363	64	125	27	4	.656	$5.8	27	83	.347
2001	Texas (A)	24	67	.314	111	442	72	139	24	2	.541	$6.6	25	65	.308
	Career	205	834	.321	1,443	5,090	1,083	1,632	347	36	.524	$112.8	137	734	.311
	Average season	21	83	.321	144	509	108	163	35	4	.524	$11.3	14	73	.311
	Summit season	24	101	.338	149	524	116	177	37	5	.565	$12.0	16	88	.327

PETE ROSE

		ADJUSTED REGULAR SEASON											ACTUAL RESULTS		
YEAR	TEAM	HR	RBI	BA	G	AB	R	H	2B	3B	SA	PAY	HR	RBI	BA
1963	Cincinnati (N)	9	51	.299	157	623	126	186	38	8	.429	$14.7	6	41	.273
1964	Cincinnati (N)	6	41	.289	135	512	77	148	19	2	.369	$7.9	4	34	.269
1965	Cincinnati (N)	15	99	.342	162	670	144	229	51	10	.515	$19.8	11	81	.312
1966	Cincinnati (N)	21	87	.340	158	662	120	225	52	4	.526	$18.8	16	70	.313
1967	Cincinnati (N)	19	98	.335	148	585	111	196	47	6	.533	$15.0	12	76	.301
1968	Cincinnati (N)	18	69	.383	148	622	132	238	65	5	.590	$19.2	10	49	.335
1969	Cincinnati (N)	22	97	.377	155	623	143	235	48	10	.592	$25.2	16	82	.348
1970	Cincinnati (N)	19	59	.334	159	649	136	217	51	7	.522	$16.8	15	52	.316
1971	Cincinnati (N)	19	55	.328	160	632	108	207	38	4	.491	$12.9	13	44	.304
1972	Cincinnati (N)	11	79	.339	162	679	148	230	53	13	.504	$23.3	6	57	.307
1973	Cincinnati (N)	8	75	.354	160	680	134	241	53	9	.494	$19.2	5	64	.338
1974	Cincinnati (N)	6	60	.298	162	648	130	193	67	7	.451	$14.0	3	51	.284
1975	Cincinnati (N)	12	86	.331	162	662	131	219	65	3	.492	$19.8	7	74	.317
1976	Cincinnati (N)	20	77	.341	162	665	160	227	57	5	.532	$20.4	10	63	.323
1977	Cincinnati (N)	12	71	.318	162	655	105	208	47	5	.460	$13.0	9	64	.311
1978	Cincinnati (N)	12	62	.316	160	659	123	208	65	2	.475	$13.0	7	52	.302
1979	Philadelphia (N)	6	64	.337	162	624	99	210	53	5	.466	$12.4	4	59	.331
1980	Philadelphia (N)	1	74	.287	162	655	110	188	61	1	.388	$12.4	1	64	.282
1981	Philadelphia (N)	0	61	.342	162	653	136	223	53	9	.450	$12.6	0	33	.325
1982	Philadelphia (N)	5	62	.279	162	634	92	177	37	4	.374	$9.1	3	54	.271
1983	Philadelphia (N)	0	51	.253	150	490	59	124	24	3	.314	$3.6	0	45	.245
1984	Mon.-Cin. (N)	0	39	.297	121	374	50	111	24	3	.377	$2.3	0	34	.286
1985	Cincinnati (N)	3	52	.277	119	405	68	112	15	2	.346	$2.4	2	46	.264
1986	Cincinnati (N)	0	28	.228	72	237	17	54	11	2	.291	$1.3	0	25	.219
	Career	244	1,597	.322	3,622	14,298	2,659	4,606	1,094	129	.468	$329.1	160	1,314	.303
	Average season	10	67	.322	151	596	111	192	46	5	.468	$13.7	7	55	.303
	Summit season	20	86	.355	154	631	133	224	54	6	.555	$19.7	13	68	.324

AL ROSEN

		ADJUSTED REGULAR SEASON											ACTUAL RESULTS		
YEAR	TEAM	HR	RBI	BA	G	AB	R	H	2B	3B	SA	PAY	HR	RBI	BA
1947	Cleveland (A)	0	0	.111	7	9	1	1	0	0	.111	$0.0	0	0	.111
1948	Cleveland (A)	0	0	.200	5	5	0	1	0	0	.200	$0.0	0	0	.200
1949	Cleveland (A)	0	6	.152	24	46	3	7	3	0	.217	$0.0	0	5	.159
1950	Cleveland (A)	45	124	.290	162	579	107	168	26	3	.579	$7.8	37	116	.287
1951	Cleveland (A)	32	116	.274	161	599	93	164	34	1	.494	$9.5	24	102	.265
1952	Cleveland (A)	41	130	.322	155	594	125	191	38	3	.603	$15.1	28	105	.302
1953	Cleveland (A)	54	164	.342	162	626	129	214	32	3	.661	$23.1	43	145	.336
1954	Cleveland (A)	31	119	.311	142	483	88	150	23	1	.555	$11.8	24	102	.300
1955	Cleveland (A)	25	93	.253	146	517	70	131	17	1	.435	$9.9	21	81	.244
1956	Cleveland (A)	18	70	.277	126	433	73	120	25	1	.464	$4.9	15	61	.267
	Career	246	822	.295	1,090	3,891	689	1,147	198	13	.542	$82.1	192	717	.285
	Average season	25	82	.295	109	389	69	115	20	1	.542	$8.2	19	72	.285
	Summit season	41	131	.307	156	576	108	177	31	2	.582	$13.5	31	114	.298

EDD ROUSH

		ADJUSTED REGULAR SEASON											ACTUAL RESULTS		
YEAR	TEAM	HR	RBI	BA	G	AB	R	H	2B	3B	SA	PAY	HR	RBI	BA
1913	Chicago (A)	0	0	.091	10	11	3	1	0	0	.091	$0.0	0	0	.100
1914	Indianapolis (F)	7	37	.347	76	170	32	59	12	2	.565	$1.3	1	30	.325
1915	Newark (F)	21	78	.320	152	578	95	185	32	4	.498	$6.2	3	60	.298
1916	N.Y.-Cin. (N)	0	28	.289	113	357	53	103	33	20	.493	$3.7	0	20	.267
1917	Cincinnati (N)	29	91	.371	140	537	112	199	26	5	.600	$9.2	4	67	.341
1918	Cincinnati (N)	35	103	.355	142	547	101	194	21	3	.596	$11.5	5	62	.333
1919	Cincinnati (N)	25	103	.329	154	584	105	192	29	6	.527	$14.3	4	71	.321
1920	Cincinnati (N)	22	107	.330	157	610	96	201	35	7	.518	$15.1	4	90	.339
1921	Cincinnati (N)	15	78	.324	119	444	74	144	39	5	.536	$9.1	4	71	.352
1922	Cincinnati (N)	4	26	.326	51	172	31	56	11	3	.494	$3.3	1	24	.352
1923	Cincinnati (N)	20	96	.332	145	554	96	184	58	9	.578	$9.1	6	88	.351
1924	Cincinnati (N)	15	79	.327	128	511	74	167	39	13	.542	$5.7	3	72	.348
1925	Cincinnati (N)	22	86	.313	142	572	94	179	33	8	.514	$6.7	8	83	.339
1926	Cincinnati (N)	22	86	.310	149	583	104	181	40	4	.506	$7.3	7	79	.323
1927	New York (N)	19	63	.288	146	594	90	171	27	2	.436	$6.9	7	58	.304
1928	New York (N)	5	14	.241	48	170	22	41	5	1	.371	$1.8	2	13	.252
1929	New York (N)	17	54	.301	123	481	78	145	20	3	.462	$3.2	8	52	.324
1931	Cincinnati (N)	5	45	.263	106	395	51	104	21	3	.370	$1.9	1	41	.271
	Career	283	1,174	.318	2,101	7,870	1,311	2,506	481	98	.512	$116.3	68	981	.323
	Average season	16	65	.318	117	437	73	139	27	5	.512	$6.5	4	55	.323
	Summit season	23	89	.343	135	519	91	178	37	7	.574	$8.9	4	72	.345

BABE RUTH

		ADJUSTED REGULAR SEASON											ACTUAL RESULTS		
YEAR	TEAM	HR	RBI	BA	G	AB	R	H	2B	3B	SA	PAY	HR	RBI	BA
1914	Boston (A)	0	2	.200	5	10	1	2	2	0	.400	$0.0	0	2	.200
1915	Boston (A)	11	27	.344	44	96	21	33	6	0	.750	$0.7	4	21	.315
1916	Boston (A)	11	21	.296	70	142	25	42	4	1	.570	$1.2	3	15	.272
1917	Boston (A)	9	17	.352	54	128	19	45	5	1	.617	$1.1	2	12	.325
1918	Boston (A)	48	112	.317	122	407	85	129	18	2	.725	$5.9	11	66	.300
1919	Boston (A)	73	168	.329	153	508	152	167	20	2	.807	$15.1	29	114	.322
1920	New York (A)	91	164	.366	149	481	189	176	16	1	.971	$26.1	54	137	.376
1921	New York (A)	94	188	.350	161	572	195	200	25	3	.897	$47.9	59	171	.378
1922	New York (A)	54	107	.294	116	428	101	126	16	2	.720	$18.8	35	99	.315
1923	New York (A)	73	145	.372	162	556	168	207	32	3	.835	$40.3	41	131	.393
1924	New York (A)	75	134	.355	162	560	159	199	22	1	.800	$29.9	46	121	.378
1925	New York (A)	34	67	.267	102	374	62	100	7	1	.564	$7.2	25	66	.290
1926	New York (A)	73	163	.357	159	518	155	185	15	1	.813	$23.6	47	146	.372
1927	New York (A)	89	179	.338	158	565	173	191	15	1	.841	$26.1	60	164	.356
1928	New York (A)	78	157	.309	162	564	181	174	17	2	.761	$26.3	54	142	.323
1929	New York (A)	62	157	.320	142	525	123	168	17	2	.714	$19.7	46	154	.345
1930	New York (A)	64	148	.327	153	547	145	179	19	3	.724	$26.0	49	153	.359
1931	New York (A)	69	181	.363	152	560	165	203	18	1	.768	$30.9	46	163	.373
1932	New York (A)	55	148	.333	138	474	130	158	8	1	.703	$18.9	41	137	.341
1933	New York (A)	53	123	.301	146	489	116	147	14	1	.658	$13.2	34	103	.301

(Babe Ruth, continued)

		ADJUSTED REGULAR SEASON											ACTUAL RESULTS		
YEAR	TEAM	HR	RBI	BA	G	AB	R	H	2B	3B	SA	PAY	HR	RBI	BA
1934	New York (A)	33	91	.277	131	383	85	106	13	1	.574	$6.9	22	84	.288
1935	Boston (N)	8	13	.169	30	77	14	13	0	0	.481	$1.9	6	12	.181
	Career	1,157	2,512	.329	2,671	8,964	2,464	2,950	309	30	.757	$387.7	714	2,213	.342
	Average season	53	114	.329	121	407	112	134	14	1	.757	$17.6	32	101	.342
	Summit season	84	168	.357	158	538	176	192	21	2	.872	$32.8	52	150	.375

JIMMY RYAN

		ADJUSTED REGULAR SEASON											ACTUAL RESULTS		
YEAR	TEAM	HR	RBI	BA	G	AB	R	H	2B	3B	SA	PAY	HR	RBI	BA
1885	Chicago (N)	0	3	.529	4	17	3	9	3	0	.706	$0.0	0	2	.462
1886	Chicago (N)	22	62	.333	108	420	68	140	23	2	.555	$3.7	4	53	.306
1887	Chicago (N)	36	76	.284	161	649	120	184	24	3	.496	$11.8	11	74	.285
1888	Chicago (N)	54	78	.374	154	655	141	245	38	3	.689	$14.9	16	64	.332
1889	Chicago (N)	50	73	.314	161	687	142	216	33	5	.595	$25.8	17	72	.307
1890	Chicago (P)	26	88	.351	139	572	98	201	41	2	.566	$14.9	6	89	.340
1891	Chicago (N)	36	69	.294	140	599	116	176	32	5	.544	$15.3	9	66	.277
1892	Chicago (N)	36	70	.322	141	556	114	179	25	3	.572	$11.8	10	65	.293
1893	Chicago (N)	14	30	.288	105	431	83	124	35	3	.480	$5.8	3	30	.299
1894	Chicago (N)	11	53	.313	130	571	113	179	56	2	.476	$9.2	3	62	.361
1895	Chicago (N)	23	46	.288	132	535	79	154	28	3	.480	$4.7	6	49	.317
1896	Chicago (N)	18	89	.282	157	600	85	169	43	4	.457	$7.1	3	86	.305
1897	Chicago (N)	27	86	.276	160	612	104	169	47	7	.508	$9.5	5	85	.300
1898	Chicago (N)	26	83	.322	153	608	129	196	50	5	.549	$12.9	4	79	.323
1899	Chicago (N)	19	68	.286	133	559	91	160	33	4	.462	$6.7	3	68	.301
1900	Chicago (N)	19	62	.266	117	462	70	123	28	1	.455	$4.3	5	59	.277
1902	Washington (A)	31	57	.323	141	569	121	184	35	2	.555	$6.8	6	44	.320
1903	Washington (A)	28	59	.255	132	506	53	129	18	1	.460	$3.3	7	46	.249
	Career	476	1,152	.306	2,368	9,608	1,730	2,937	592	55	.527	$168.5	118	1,093	.306
	Average season	26	64	.306	132	534	96	163	33	3	.527	$9.4	7	61	.306
	Summit season	38	74	.339	141	578	113	196	32	3	.602	$14.2	11	69	.316

RYNE SANDBERG

		ADJUSTED REGULAR SEASON											ACTUAL RESULTS		
YEAR	TEAM	HR	RBI	BA	G	AB	R	H	2B	3B	SA	PAY	HR	RBI	BA
1981	Philadelphia (N)	0	0	.222	20	9	4	2	0	0	.222	$0.0	0	0	.167
1982	Chicago (N)	10	62	.279	156	635	118	177	44	4	.408	$6.2	7	54	.271
1983	Chicago (N)	12	55	.269	158	633	107	170	32	3	.385	$9.2	8	48	.261
1984	Chicago (N)	28	98	.325	157	640	133	208	45	16	.577	$14.9	19	84	.314
1985	Chicago (N)	32	94	.320	153	609	128	195	35	5	.552	$18.6	26	83	.305
1986	Chicago (N)	17	86	.296	156	635	77	188	33	5	.444	$15.0	14	76	.284
1987	Chicago (N)	17	62	.302	133	527	85	159	27	2	.457	$11.7	16	59	.294
1988	Chicago (N)	26	81	.279	154	614	91	171	26	8	.474	$12.0	19	69	.264
1989	Chicago (N)	40	90	.307	157	606	123	186	27	5	.566	$12.3	30	76	.290
1990	Chicago (N)	50	115	.319	155	615	134	196	31	3	.623	$15.7	40	100	.306

(Ryne Sandberg, continued)

		ADJUSTED REGULAR SEASON											ACTUAL RESULTS		
YEAR	TEAM	HR	RBI	BA	G	AB	R	H	2B	3B	SA	PAY	HR	RBI	BA
1991	Chicago (N)	33	115	.306	160	592	120	181	35	2	.539	$13.4	26	100	.291
1992	Chicago (N)	36	104	.320	158	612	119	196	34	7	.575	$13.6	26	87	.304
1993	Chicago (N)	11	48	.314	116	452	71	142	22	0	.436	$5.0	9	45	.309
1994	Chicago (N)	8	35	.237	82	321	52	76	13	6	.389	$2.9	5	24	.238
1996	Chicago (N)	25	91	.242	150	554	84	134	29	4	.444	$4.7	25	92	.244
1997	Chicago (N)	13	66	.266	135	447	56	119	26	0	.412	$2.4	12	64	.264
	Career	358	1,202	.294	2,200	8,501	1,502	2,500	459	70	.491	$157.6	282	1,061	.285
	Average season	22	75	.294	138	531	94	156	29	4	.491	$9.9	18	66	.285
	Summit season	37	100	.318	156	616	127	196	34	7	.576	$15.0	28	86	.304

RON SANTO

		ADJUSTED REGULAR SEASON											ACTUAL RESULTS		
YEAR	TEAM	HR	RBI	BA	G	AB	R	H	2B	3B	SA	PAY	HR	RBI	BA
1960	Chicago (N)	12	52	.265	99	362	52	96	31	1	.456	$4.8	9	44	.251
1961	Chicago (N)	26	93	.296	160	601	95	178	41	5	.511	$11.4	23	83	.284
1962	Chicago (N)	20	92	.237	162	604	48	143	27	3	.391	$9.2	17	83	.227
1963	Chicago (N)	31	123	.324	162	630	98	204	40	5	.551	$14.5	25	99	.297
1964	Chicago (N)	37	139	.336	161	592	114	199	44	11	.635	$18.7	30	114	.313
1965	Chicago (N)	41	122	.311	162	601	107	187	38	3	.589	$18.8	33	101	.285
1966	Chicago (N)	38	115	.339	155	561	114	190	29	6	.615	$19.0	30	94	.312
1967	Chicago (N)	43	127	.334	161	586	139	196	29	3	.614	$25.5	31	98	.300
1968	Chicago (N)	39	138	.279	161	573	121	160	22	3	.532	$25.2	26	98	.246
1969	Chicago (N)	37	146	.313	159	571	115	179	24	3	.560	$16.8	29	123	.289
1970	Chicago (N)	31	129	.283	154	555	94	157	38	3	.530	$15.9	26	114	.267
1971	Chicago (N)	29	110	.288	154	555	96	160	28	1	.499	$12.6	21	88	.267
1972	Chicago (N)	26	101	.333	138	481	93	160	34	5	.586	$7.2	17	74	.302
1973	Chicago (N)	25	91	.280	150	540	76	151	37	2	.494	$7.1	20	77	.267
1974	Chicago (A)	8	48	.231	116	372	34	86	16	1	.344	$2.8	5	41	.221
	Career	443	1,626	.299	2,254	8,184	1,396	2,446	478	55	.533	$209.5	342	1,331	.277
	Average season	30	108	.299	150	546	93	163	32	4	.533	$14.0	23	89	.277
	Summit season	37	121	.330	155	564	113	186	35	6	.610	$17.8	28	96	.302

HANK SAUER

		ADJUSTED REGULAR SEASON											ACTUAL RESULTS		
YEAR	TEAM	HR	RBI	BA	G	AB	R	H	2B	3B	SA	PAY	HR	RBI	BA
1941	Cincinnati (N)	0	6	.303	9	33	4	10	6	0	.485	$0.0	0	5	.303
1942	Cincinnati (N)	3	5	.250	7	20	5	5	0	0	.700	$0.0	2	4	.250
1945	Cincinnati (N)	9	25	.301	33	123	23	37	1	0	.528	$0.8	5	20	.293
1948	Cincinnati (N)	48	111	.266	154	563	89	150	21	1	.563	$4.8	35	97	.260
1949	Cin.-Chi. (N)	41	110	.281	143	527	89	148	24	1	.564	$3.8	31	99	.275
1950	Chicago (N)	40	111	.277	153	570	91	158	36	1	.554	$7.0	32	103	.274
1951	Chicago (N)	40	101	.271	147	547	87	148	21	3	.539	$7.1	30	89	.263
1952	Chicago (N)	52	149	.287	158	593	109	170	35	2	.616	$13.0	37	121	.270
1953	Chicago (N)	25	67	.269	113	413	69	111	20	3	.513	$4.3	19	60	.263

(Hank Sauer, continued)

		ADJUSTED REGULAR SEASON											ACTUAL RESULTS		
YEAR	TEAM	HR	RBI	BA	G	AB	R	H	2B	3B	SA	PAY	HR	RBI	BA
1954	Chicago (N)	51	121	.297	149	546	115	162	20	1	.617	$8.9	41	103	.288
1955	Chicago (N)	14	32	.219	83	274	33	60	10	1	.416	$2.2	12	28	.211
1956	St. Louis (N)	6	27	.312	78	157	13	49	5	0	.459	$1.5	5	24	.298
1957	New York (N)	31	93	.271	134	399	56	108	18	1	.554	$2.5	26	76	.259
1958	San Francisco (N)	14	56	.261	93	249	33	65	10	0	.470	$1.6	12	46	.250
1959	San Francisco (N)	1	1	.063	14	16	1	1	0	0	.250	$0.5	1	1	.067
	Career	375	1,015	.275	1,468	5,030	817	1,382	227	14	.549	$58.0	288	876	.266
	Average season	25	68	.275	98	335	54	92	15	1	.549	$3.9	19	58	.266
	Summit season	46	120	.282	151	560	99	158	27	1	.580	$7.5	35	105	.273

RAY SCHALK

		ADJUSTED REGULAR SEASON											ACTUAL RESULTS		
YEAR	TEAM	HR	RBI	BA	G	AB	R	H	2B	3B	SA	PAY	HR	RBI	BA
1912	Chicago (A)	0	9	.288	24	66	8	19	6	0	.379	$0.2	0	8	.286
1913	Chicago (A)	8	47	.254	137	426	47	108	29	3	.392	$3.3	1	38	.244
1914	Chicago (A)	0	45	.287	140	404	38	116	40	2	.396	$3.8	0	36	.270
1915	Chicago (A)	8	70	.285	141	431	59	123	28	3	.420	$5.2	1	54	.266
1916	Chicago (A)	0	57	.252	135	429	50	108	44	10	.401	$5.3	0	41	.232
1917	Chicago (A)	14	70	.246	145	439	66	108	16	2	.387	$6.1	2	51	.226
1918	Chicago (A)	0	38	.232	141	435	60	101	34	6	.338	$5.5	0	22	.219
1919	Chicago (A)	0	49	.289	152	457	82	132	42	3	.394	$6.3	0	34	.282
1920	Chicago (A)	6	73	.262	159	511	76	134	47	3	.401	$7.8	1	61	.270
1921	Chicago (A)	0	51	.232	135	439	35	102	48	2	.351	$4.0	0	47	.252
1922	Chicago (A)	11	64	.262	148	461	61	121	26	1	.395	$4.7	4	60	.281
1923	Chicago (A)	4	47	.216	128	398	45	86	19	1	.299	$3.8	1	44	.228
1924	Chicago (A)	3	12	.186	60	161	16	30	5	1	.286	$1.1	1	11	.196
1925	Chicago (A)	0	53	.253	131	359	45	91	33	0	.345	$2.1	0	52	.274
1926	Chicago (A)	0	35	.253	86	237	29	60	22	0	.346	$1.3	0	32	.265
1927	Chicago (A)	0	2	.214	17	28	2	6	3	0	.321	$0.3	0	2	.231
1928	Chicago (A)	0	1	1.000	2	1	0	1	0	0	1.000	$0.2	0	1	1.000
1929	New York (N)	0	0	.000	5	2	0	0	0	0	.000	$0.0	0	0	.000
	Career	54	723	.254	1,886	5,684	719	1,446	442	37	.374	$61.0	11	594	.253
	Average season	3	40	.254	105	316	40	80	25	2	.374	$3.4	1	33	.253
	Summit season	5	60	.276	148	453	63	125	37	2	.400	$5.6	1	49	.274

MIKE SCHMIDT

		ADJUSTED REGULAR SEASON											ACTUAL RESULTS		
YEAR	TEAM	HR	RBI	BA	G	AB	R	H	2B	3B	SA	PAY	HR	RBI	BA
1972	Philadelphia (N)	2	4	.216	14	37	3	8	0	0	.378	$0.0	1	3	.206
1973	Philadelphia (N)	22	61	.204	132	367	50	75	14	0	.422	$3.3	18	52	.196
1974	Philadelphia (N)	50	138	.296	162	568	129	168	32	5	.634	$12.1	36	116	.282
1975	Philadelphia (N)	50	111	.260	158	562	108	146	36	2	.598	$12.3	38	95	.249
1976	Philadelphia (N)	55	131	.276	160	584	138	161	31	2	.618	$19.6	38	107	.262
1977	Philadelphia (N)	45	112	.279	154	544	126	152	29	8	.610	$19.3	38	101	.274

(Mike Schmidt, continued)

		ADJUSTED REGULAR SEASON												ACTUAL RESULTS		
YEAR	TEAM	HR	RBI	BA	G	AB	R	H	2B	3B	SA	PAY	HR	RBI	BA
1978	Philadelphia (N)	29	92	.261	145	513	110	134	29	2	.495	$12.4	21	78	.251
1979	Philadelphia (N)	53	125	.257	159	538	120	138	25	3	.610	$16.4	45	114	.253
1980	Philadelphia (N)	60	140	.292	150	548	120	160	25	5	.684	$16.1	48	121	.286
1981	Philadelphia (N)	63	169	.333	154	534	144	178	28	2	.747	$19.3	31	91	.316
1982	Philadelphia (N)	43	100	.288	148	514	124	148	28	3	.605	$13.3	35	87	.280
1983	Philadelphia (N)	49	124	.262	153	531	118	139	16	3	.580	$13.9	40	109	.255
1984	Philadelphia (N)	45	123	.286	151	528	108	151	25	2	.597	$13.0	36	106	.277
1985	Philadelphia (N)	40	106	.290	158	549	101	159	34	4	.585	$9.4	33	93	.277
1986	Philadelphia (N)	43	134	.303	161	555	109	168	31	1	.595	$12.4	37	119	.290
1987	Philadelphia (N)	36	118	.301	147	522	92	157	31	0	.567	$8.9	35	113	.293
1988	Philadelphia (N)	16	73	.264	108	390	62	103	23	2	.456	$4.3	12	62	.249
1989	Philadelphia (N)	8	33	.216	42	148	22	32	7	0	.426	$1.9	6	28	.203
	Career	709	1,894	.279	2,456	8,532	1,784	2,377	444	44	.590	$207.9	548	1,595	.267
	Average season	39	105	.279	136	474	99	132	25	2	.590	$11.6	30	89	.267
	Summit season	54	142	.299	157	558	128	167	29	3	.652	$15.9	38	111	.285

RED SCHOENDIENST

		ADJUSTED REGULAR SEASON												ACTUAL RESULTS		
YEAR	TEAM	HR	RBI	BA	G	AB	R	H	2B	3B	SA	PAY	HR	RBI	BA
1945	St. Louis (N)	5	58	.286	143	590	110	169	47	6	.412	$11.4	1	47	.278
1946	St. Louis (N)	0	43	.295	147	627	119	185	60	5	.407	$12.1	0	34	.281
1947	St. Louis (N)	7	56	.261	157	685	107	179	43	8	.378	$14.9	3	48	.253
1948	St. Louis (N)	8	40	.278	124	425	72	118	30	2	.414	$6.5	4	36	.272
1949	St. Louis (N)	6	59	.304	156	661	112	201	39	1	.393	$14.2	3	54	.297
1950	St. Louis (N)	11	68	.279	162	680	87	190	57	6	.429	$12.3	7	63	.276
1951	St. Louis (N)	10	61	.299	141	578	100	173	45	6	.450	$9.3	6	54	.289
1952	St. Louis (N)	13	83	.323	160	653	113	211	59	5	.489	$12.5	7	67	.303
1953	St. Louis (N)	20	88	.348	151	583	119	203	45	3	.539	$12.1	15	79	.342
1954	St. Louis (N)	8	93	.325	156	643	116	209	58	6	.471	$15.9	5	79	.315
1955	St. Louis (N)	14	59	.279	153	584	78	163	30	2	.409	$7.2	11	51	.268
1956	St.L.-N.Y. (N)	2	33	.315	137	505	69	159	31	2	.396	$3.9	2	29	.302
1957	N.Y.-Mil. (N)	20	78	.323	157	678	110	219	44	6	.494	$9.7	15	65	.309
1958	Milwaukee (N)	1	29	.273	112	451	57	123	32	1	.355	$2.6	1	24	.262
1959	Milwaukee (N)	0	0	.000	5	3	0	0	0	0	.000	$0.7	0	0	.000
1960	Milwaukee (N)	1	23	.272	72	239	25	65	13	1	.347	$1.1	1	19	.257
1961	St. Louis (N)	1	14	.312	75	125	10	39	12	0	.432	$0.5	1	12	.300
1962	St. Louis (N)	2	13	.317	97	142	23	45	6	0	.401	$0.4	2	12	.301
1963	St. Louis (N)	0	0	.000	6	5	0	0	0	0	.000	$0.0	0	0	.000
	Career	129	898	.299	2,311	8,857	1,427	2,651	651	60	.430	$147.3	84	773	.289
	Average season	7	47	.299	122	466	75	140	34	3	.430	$7.8	4	41	.289
	Summit season	14	81	.324	153	627	112	203	50	5	.486	$11.9	10	69	.312

FRANK SCHULTE

		ADJUSTED REGULAR SEASON											ACTUAL RESULTS		
YEAR	TEAM	HR	RBI	BA	G	AB	R	H	2B	3B	SA	PAY	HR	RBI	BA
1904	Chicago (N)	8	17	.307	21	88	21	27	3	0	.614	$1.0	2	13	.286
1905	Chicago (N)	13	60	.298	129	517	86	154	38	10	.485	$5.3	1	47	.274
1906	Chicago (N)	38	82	.307	153	590	105	181	16	3	.537	$9.1	7	60	.281
1907	Chicago (N)	18	44	.315	101	356	61	112	20	2	.534	$5.1	2	32	.287
1908	Chicago (N)	10	61	.264	105	397	60	105	34	1	.431	$6.2	1	43	.236
1909	Chicago (N)	29	83	.291	146	561	79	163	18	3	.488	$9.0	4	60	.264
1910	Chicago (N)	44	88	.324	159	589	121	191	26	3	.603	$12.0	10	68	.301
1911	Chicago (N)	57	118	.304	159	596	116	181	21	4	.639	$12.6	21	107	.300
1912	Chicago (N)	38	72	.265	148	589	102	156	18	2	.496	$12.0	12	64	.264
1913	Chicago (N)	30	84	.288	138	520	105	150	23	1	.510	$9.7	9	68	.278
1914	Chicago (N)	21	77	.255	142	482	68	123	23	2	.442	$5.0	5	61	.241
1915	Chicago (N)	36	80	.267	157	572	85	153	13	1	.483	$7.0	12	62	.249
1916	Chi.-Pit. (N)	21	56	.302	131	420	59	127	14	1	.490	$3.5	5	41	.278
1917	Pit.-Phi. (N)	7	30	.231	97	260	44	60	20	0	.388	$2.1	1	22	.214
1918	Washington (A)	0	72	.306	116	333	57	102	49	4	.477	$2.3	0	44	.288
	Career	370	1,024	.289	1,902	6,870	1,169	1,985	336	37	.510	$101.9	92	792	.270
	Average season	25	68	.289	127	458	78	132	22	2	.510	$6.8	6	53	.270
	Summit season	37	83	.308	142	530	102	163	21	3	.568	$9.7	10	67	.290

JOE SEWELL

		ADJUSTED REGULAR SEASON											ACTUAL RESULTS		
YEAR	TEAM	HR	RBI	BA	G	AB	R	H	2B	3B	SA	PAY	HR	RBI	BA
1920	Cleveland (A)	0	14	.315	23	73	16	23	12	0	.479	$0.7	0	12	.329
1921	Cleveland (A)	15	101	.294	162	602	110	177	52	5	.472	$9.0	4	93	.318
1922	Cleveland (A)	7	89	.279	160	584	86	163	47	4	.409	$11.5	2	83	.299
1923	Cleveland (A)	12	120	.334	162	586	108	196	65	5	.524	$15.2	3	109	.353
1924	Cleveland (A)	14	117	.297	162	629	109	187	58	2	.463	$19.2	4	106	.316
1925	Cleveland (A)	3	100	.310	162	635	80	197	64	5	.441	$15.5	1	98	.336
1926	Cleveland (A)	15	95	.311	162	608	101	189	52	2	.477	$15.5	4	85	.324
1927	Cleveland (A)	4	101	.301	162	602	91	181	78	3	.460	$12.2	1	92	.316
1928	Cleveland (A)	11	77	.309	162	615	86	190	50	1	.447	$12.0	4	70	.323
1929	Cleveland (A)	15	75	.292	162	616	93	180	41	1	.435	$11.9	7	73	.315
1930	Cleveland (A)	0	46	.263	115	372	42	98	31	4	.368	$2.7	0	48	.289
1931	New York (A)	15	70	.292	136	506	112	148	22	0	.425	$5.0	6	64	.302
1932	New York (A)	20	73	.266	130	523	103	139	19	1	.421	$5.1	11	68	.272
1933	New York (A)	7	64	.272	144	559	104	152	30	1	.367	$7.0	2	54	.273
	Career	138	1,142	.296	2,004	7,510	1,241	2,220	621	34	.442	$142.5	49	1,055	.312
	Average season	10	82	.296	143	536	89	159	44	2	.442	$10.2	4	75	.312
	Summit season	12	107	.307	162	605	104	186	61	3	.478	$14.2	3	97	.325

AL SIMMONS

		ADJUSTED REGULAR SEASON											ACTUAL RESULTS		
YEAR	TEAM	HR	RBI	BA	G	AB	R	H	2B	3B	SA	PAY	HR	RBI	BA
1924	Philadelphia (A)	24	114	.289	162	633	77	183	33	4	.468	$14.2	8	102	.308
1925	Philadelphia (A)	46	134	.358	162	692	127	248	36	4	.621	$19.8	24	129	.387
1926	Philadelphia (A)	45	125	.328	159	631	103	207	43	3	.620	$19.0	19	109	.341
1927	Philadelphia (A)	34	118	.372	111	425	94	158	30	4	.701	$11.4	15	108	.392
1928	Philadelphia (A)	31	119	.336	126	491	86	165	29	3	.597	$11.9	15	107	.351
1929	Philadelphia (A)	54	163	.339	153	622	118	211	32	3	.661	$18.9	34	157	.365
1930	Philadelphia (A)	54	159	.347	145	582	146	202	33	5	.699	$19.3	36	165	.381
1931	Philadelphia (A)	46	144	.378	136	545	118	206	29	5	.703	$15.8	22	128	.390
1932	Philadelphia (A)	55	166	.313	162	705	158	221	21	3	.586	$35.2	35	151	.322
1933	Chicago (A)	34	144	.330	157	651	102	215	30	4	.545	$23.0	14	119	.331
1934	Chicago (A)	33	114	.332	146	590	112	196	34	3	.568	$13.5	18	104	.344
1935	Chicago (A)	29	87	.258	136	558	75	144	20	3	.461	$9.3	16	79	.267
1936	Detroit (A)	26	116	.310	150	596	99	185	38	3	.515	$9.8	13	112	.327
1937	Washington (A)	16	89	.271	106	431	63	117	24	5	.462	$4.6	8	84	.279
1938	Washington (A)	34	104	.296	133	500	86	148	22	2	.552	$4.7	21	95	.302
1939	Bos.-Cin. (N)	13	47	.266	106	365	42	97	18	3	.438	$2.4	7	44	.274
1940	Philadelphia (A)	2	21	.306	39	85	8	26	5	0	.435	$1.3	1	19	.309
1941	Philadelphia (A)	0	1	.125	9	24	1	3	2	0	.208	$0.6	0	1	.125
1943	Boston (A)	3	16	.214	42	140	12	30	7	0	.329	$0.5	1	12	.203
1944	Philadelphia (A)	0	2	.500	4	6	1	3	0	0	.500	$0.0	0	2	.500
	Career	579	1,983	.320	2,344	9,272	1,628	2,965	486	57	.572	$235.2	307	1,827	.334
	Average season	29	99	.320	117	464	81	148	24	3	.572	$11.8	15	91	.334
	Summit season	47	144	.358	141	573	121	205	32	4	.674	$17.0	26	137	.382

TED SIMMONS

		ADJUSTED REGULAR SEASON											ACTUAL RESULTS		
YEAR	TEAM	HR	RBI	BA	G	AB	R	H	2B	3B	SA	PAY	HR	RBI	BA
1968	St. Louis (N)	0	0	.333	2	3	0	1	0	0	.333	$0.0	0	0	.333
1969	St. Louis (N)	0	4	.214	5	14	0	3	0	1	.357	$0.0	0	3	.214
1970	St. Louis (N)	4	27	.257	82	284	33	73	11	2	.352	$1.7	3	24	.243
1971	St. Louis (N)	10	96	.328	132	506	79	166	46	4	.494	$5.5	7	77	.304
1972	St. Louis (N)	26	131	.334	158	617	96	206	51	6	.562	$9.3	16	96	.303
1973	St. Louis (N)	18	106	.325	161	619	72	201	47	2	.494	$11.8	13	91	.310
1974	St. Louis (N)	30	124	.285	153	603	79	172	41	5	.519	$14.4	20	103	.272
1975	St. Louis (N)	27	116	.347	156	577	93	200	39	2	.562	$14.4	18	100	.332
1976	St. Louis (N)	10	92	.306	150	546	73	167	52	2	.463	$11.6	5	75	.291
1977	St. Louis (N)	25	105	.324	150	516	91	167	28	2	.531	$11.9	21	95	.318
1978	St. Louis (N)	31	95	.298	152	516	84	154	44	4	.579	$9.3	22	80	.287
1979	St. Louis (N)	31	95	.288	122	444	74	128	23	0	.550	$6.8	26	87	.283
1980	St. Louis (N)	28	113	.309	145	495	97	153	36	1	.556	$9.3	21	98	.303
1981	Milwaukee (A)	30	111	.226	149	566	82	128	21	3	.433	$7.1	14	61	.216
1982	Milwaukee (A)	29	111	.277	136	535	83	148	31	0	.497	$6.9	23	97	.269
1983	Milwaukee (A)	18	123	.318	153	600	87	191	46	2	.492	$9.4	13	108	.308
1984	Milwaukee (A)	6	61	.230	133	501	51	115	29	2	.331	$3.8	4	52	.221
1985	Milwaukee (A)	15	87	.286	144	532	68	152	33	2	.440	$4.4	12	76	.273
1986	Atlanta (N)	5	28	.260	76	127	16	33	6	0	.425	$1.5	4	25	.252

(Ted Simmons, continued)

		ADJUSTED REGULAR SEASON											ACTUAL RESULTS		
YEAR	TEAM	HR	RBI	BA	G	AB	R	H	2B	3B	SA	PAY	HR	RBI	BA
1987	Atlanta (N)	4	31	.282	73	177	21	50	9	0	.401	$1.3	4	30	.277
1988	Atlanta (N)	3	13	.204	79	108	7	22	7	0	.352	$0.7	2	11	.196
	Career	350	1,669	.296	2,511	8,886	1,286	2,630	600	40	.491	$141.1	248	1,389	.285
	Average season	17	79	.296	120	423	61	125	29	2	.491	$6.7	12	66	.285
	Summit season	27	112	.324	152	544	92	176	40	3	.557	$10.8	20	94	.309

GEORGE SISLER

		ADJUSTED REGULAR SEASON											ACTUAL RESULTS		
YEAR	TEAM	HR	RBI	BA	G	AB	R	H	2B	3B	SA	PAY	HR	RBI	BA
1915	St. Louis (A)	12	37	.306	83	281	35	86	9	1	.473	$3.1	3	29	.285
1916	St. Louis (A)	26	104	.333	155	595	114	198	28	5	.528	$9.4	4	76	.305
1917	St. Louis (A)	19	72	.382	141	563	83	215	55	5	.599	$9.2	2	52	.353
1918	St. Louis (A)	25	71	.361	150	595	120	215	44	5	.578	$12.3	2	41	.341
1919	St. Louis (A)	43	120	.361	153	592	139	214	33	5	.652	$15.4	10	83	.352
1920	St. Louis (A)	56	145	.398	162	664	164	264	41	5	.727	$26.8	19	122	.407
1921	St. Louis (A)	33	113	.343	145	612	136	210	41	6	.592	$19.9	12	104	.371
1922	St. Louis (A)	25	113	.392	149	615	144	241	57	8	.633	$23.0	8	105	.420
1924	St. Louis (A)	26	82	.286	160	674	104	193	28	4	.455	$22.2	9	74	.305
1925	St. Louis (A)	29	108	.319	158	684	103	218	23	6	.497	$13.8	12	105	.345
1926	St. Louis (A)	23	78	.279	157	642	86	179	23	5	.438	$9.8	7	71	.290
1927	St. Louis (A)	17	106	.311	156	643	95	200	42	3	.465	$9.7	5	97	.327
1928	Wash. (A)-Bos. (N)	12	76	.318	144	563	79	179	35	2	.451	$6.9	4	70	.331
1929	Boston (N)	6	80	.304	162	662	68	201	61	4	.435	$6.9	2	79	.326
1930	Boston (N)	8	64	.280	122	453	52	127	19	4	.393	$3.1	3	67	.309
	Career	360	1,369	.333	2,197	8,838	1,522	2,940	539	68	.531	$191.5	102	1,175	.340
	Average season	24	91	.333	146	589	101	196	36	5	.531	$12.8	7	78	.340
	Summit season	34	104	.380	151	606	130	230	46	6	.644	$17.3	8	81	.378

ENOS SLAUGHTER

		ADJUSTED REGULAR SEASON											ACTUAL RESULTS		
YEAR	TEAM	HR	RBI	BA	G	AB	R	H	2B	3B	SA	PAY	HR	RBI	BA
1938	St. Louis (N)	16	62	.271	116	409	63	111	24	5	.472	$5.7	8	58	.276
1939	St. Louis (N)	23	93	.312	156	632	103	197	57	3	.521	$12.3	12	86	.320
1940	St. Louis (N)	30	81	.309	145	534	107	165	27	7	.554	$11.6	17	73	.306
1941	St. Louis (N)	26	88	.318	118	444	82	141	24	5	.570	$9.0	13	76	.311
1942	St. Louis (N)	33	123	.339	158	614	126	208	39	12	.603	$19.3	13	98	.318
1946	St. Louis (N)	36	166	.316	162	632	127	200	33	4	.552	$22.2	18	130	.300
1947	St. Louis (N)	20	101	.304	153	573	117	174	44	9	.517	$12.6	10	86	.294
1948	St. Louis (N)	21	102	.327	153	575	103	188	36	7	.523	$13.0	11	90	.321
1949	St. Louis (N)	23	106	.344	156	587	101	202	47	9	.572	$10.1	13	96	.336
1950	St. Louis (N)	15	109	.293	157	590	89	173	35	4	.442	$9.6	10	101	.290
1951	St. Louis (N)	7	73	.289	129	429	55	124	26	7	.431	$4.0	4	64	.281
1952	St. Louis (N)	20	125	.319	147	536	90	171	25	10	.515	$6.7	11	101	.300
1953	St. Louis (N)	9	99	.297	148	509	71	151	47	6	.466	$4.6	6	89	.291

(Enos Slaughter, continued)

		ADJUSTED REGULAR SEASON											ACTUAL RESULTS		
YEAR	TEAM	HR	RBI	BA	G	AB	R	H	2B	3B	SA	PAY	HR	RBI	BA
1954	New York (A)	1	22	.254	72	130	22	33	7	1	.346	$1.7	1	19	.248
1955	N.Y.-K.C. (A)	6	40	.326	123	288	57	94	18	3	.472	$2.1	5	35	.315
1956	K.C.-N.Y. (A)	2	31	.292	121	322	60	94	28	3	.416	$1.8	2	27	.281
1957	New York (A)	6	41	.264	101	220	29	58	10	1	.400	$1.3	5	34	.254
1958	New York (A)	5	23	.315	80	143	25	45	5	1	.469	$1.0	4	19	.304
1959	N.Y. (A)-Mil. (N)	7	26	.182	88	121	12	22	3	0	.380	$0.8	6	22	.171
	Career	306	1,511	.308	2,483	8,288	1,439	2,551	535	97	.507	$149.4	169	1,304	.300
	Average season	16	80	.308	131	436	76	134	28	5	.507	$7.9	9	69	.300
	Summit season	30	113	.326	148	562	109	183	34	7	.571	$14.4	15	95	.315

OZZIE SMITH

		ADJUSTED REGULAR SEASON											ACTUAL RESULTS		
YEAR	TEAM	HR	RBI	BA	G	AB	R	H	2B	3B	SA	PAY	HR	RBI	BA
1978	San Diego (N)	3	54	.268	159	590	82	158	28	7	.354	$9.1	1	46	.258
1979	San Diego (N)	0	30	.213	157	591	85	126	28	7	.284	$7.8	0	27	.211
1980	San Diego (N)	0	40	.233	157	605	77	141	31	6	.304	$8.9	0	35	.230
1981	San Diego (N)	0	38	.234	162	663	95	155	35	3	.296	$11.4	0	21	.222
1982	St. Louis (N)	3	49	.256	140	488	67	125	31	1	.342	$6.4	2	43	.248
1983	St. Louis (N)	5	57	.250	158	549	78	137	40	6	.372	$5.9	3	50	.243
1984	St. Louis (N)	1	51	.267	124	412	61	110	30	5	.371	$4.3	1	44	.257
1985	St. Louis (N)	8	61	.289	158	537	79	155	27	2	.391	$5.8	6	54	.276
1986	St. Louis (N)	0	60	.292	154	517	75	151	26	5	.362	$3.8	0	54	.280
1987	St. Louis (N)	0	78	.310	158	600	109	186	43	4	.395	$7.4	0	75	.303
1988	St. Louis (N)	5	60	.285	153	575	95	164	38	1	.381	$7.0	3	51	.270
1989	St. Louis (N)	4	58	.289	153	585	96	169	43	9	.414	$6.9	2	50	.273
1990	St. Louis (N)	1	57	.266	143	512	70	136	31	1	.336	$4.3	1	50	.254
1991	St. Louis (N)	5	57	.300	150	550	109	165	39	3	.409	$6.3	3	50	.285
1992	St. Louis (N)	0	37	.311	132	518	87	161	34	3	.388	$3.5	0	31	.295
1993	St. Louis (N)	1	57	.292	141	545	80	159	29	7	.376	$4.2	1	53	.288
1994	St. Louis (N)	4	43	.261	138	537	73	140	27	4	.348	$3.5	3	30	.262
1995	St. Louis (N)	0	13	.198	50	177	19	35	7	1	.249	$1.2	0	11	.199
1996	St. Louis (N)	2	18	.282	82	227	36	64	10	2	.370	$1.2	2	18	.282
	Career	42	918	.270	2,669	9,778	1,473	2,637	577	77	.357	$108.9	28	793	.262
	Average season	2	48	.270	140	515	78	139	30	4	.357	$5.7	1	42	.262
	Summit season	3	58	.299	150	558	96	167	37	4	.396	$6.0	2	52	.287

REGGIE SMITH

		ADJUSTED REGULAR SEASON											ACTUAL RESULTS		
YEAR	TEAM	HR	RBI	BA	G	AB	R	H	2B	3B	SA	PAY	HR	RBI	BA
1966	Boston (A)	0	0	.154	6	26	1	4	2	0	.231	$0.0	0	0	.154
1967	Boston (A)	22	79	.273	158	565	101	154	32	5	.464	$5.8	15	61	.246
1968	Boston (A)	25	97	.301	155	558	110	168	52	4	.543	$9.6	15	69	.265
1969	Boston (A)	33	111	.335	143	543	104	182	40	6	.613	$11.5	25	93	.309
1970	Boston (A)	27	84	.322	147	580	123	187	41	6	.553	$14.8	22	74	.303

(Reggie Smith, continued)

		ADJUSTED REGULAR SEASON											ACTUAL RESULTS		
YEAR	TEAM	HR	RBI	BA	G	AB	R	H	2B	3B	SA	PAY	HR	RBI	BA
1971	Boston (A)	40	120	.306	159	618	106	189	42	2	.574	$18.8	30	96	.283
1972	Boston (A)	31	102	.297	137	488	103	145	33	4	.572	$12.3	21	74	.270
1973	Boston (A)	27	81	.317	115	423	92	134	28	2	.584	$9.6	21	69	.303
1974	St. Louis (N)	34	120	.324	144	521	95	169	32	7	.608	$9.9	23	100	.309
1975	St. Louis (N)	27	88	.315	134	473	77	149	30	2	.558	$7.3	19	76	.302
1976	St.L.-L.A. (N)	28	60	.266	112	395	67	105	16	3	.534	$5.6	18	49	.253
1977	Los Angeles (N)	37	96	.314	148	488	115	153	29	3	.613	$7.2	32	87	.307
1978	Los Angeles (N)	38	110	.309	128	447	97	138	27	2	.633	$5.1	29	93	.295
1979	Los Angeles (N)	12	35	.278	68	234	45	65	14	1	.500	$2.4	10	32	.274
1980	Los Angeles (N)	19	63	.328	91	308	54	101	13	0	.555	$2.8	15	55	.322
1981	Los Angeles (N)	2	14	.216	60	51	9	11	2	0	.373	$1.1	1	8	.200
1982	San Francisco (N)	22	64	.292	106	349	59	102	12	0	.516	$1.9	18	56	.284
	Career	424	1,324	.305	2,011	7,067	1,358	2,156	445	47	.561	$125.7	314	1,092	.287
	Average season	25	78	.305	118	416	80	127	26	3	.561	$7.4	18	64	.287
	Summit season	34	104	.320	136	484	101	155	31	4	.612	$8.7	26	88	.305

DUKE SNIDER

		ADJUSTED REGULAR SEASON											ACTUAL RESULTS		
YEAR	TEAM	HR	RBI	BA	G	AB	R	H	2B	3B	SA	PAY	HR	RBI	BA
1947	Brooklyn (N)	0	6	.253	42	87	7	22	5	1	.333	$0.1	0	5	.241
1948	Brooklyn (N)	9	23	.247	55	166	25	41	7	4	.500	$1.1	5	21	.244
1949	Brooklyn (N)	34	102	.299	152	575	111	172	32	4	.546	$7.3	23	92	.292
1950	Brooklyn (N)	41	114	.325	159	649	116	211	37	6	.590	$14.4	31	107	.321
1951	Brooklyn (N)	39	113	.286	154	622	107	178	30	4	.535	$15.1	29	101	.277
1952	Brooklyn (N)	33	114	.323	151	560	99	181	32	5	.575	$14.7	21	92	.303
1953	Brooklyn (N)	52	142	.342	160	617	149	211	44	3	.676	$25.9	42	126	.336
1954	Brooklyn (N)	54	154	.351	157	615	142	216	48	5	.709	$26.3	40	130	.341
1955	Brooklyn (N)	51	157	.321	156	567	145	182	45	4	.684	$23.2	42	136	.309
1956	Brooklyn (N)	50	117	.303	159	571	130	173	43	1	.644	$22.8	43	101	.292
1957	Brooklyn (N)	49	112	.287	146	534	110	153	32	5	.640	$15.9	40	92	.274
1958	Los Angeles (N)	19	70	.327	112	346	54	113	16	2	.549	$4.7	15	58	.312
1959	Los Angeles (N)	28	103	.322	131	385	69	124	13	2	.584	$4.8	23	88	.308
1960	Los Angeles (N)	18	43	.255	106	247	45	63	16	4	.571	$2.4	14	36	.243
1961	Los Angeles (N)	19	64	.307	89	244	40	75	11	2	.602	$2.2	16	56	.296
1962	Los Angeles (N)	6	33	.288	79	156	31	45	15	2	.526	$1.5	5	30	.278
1963	New York (N)	18	56	.266	129	354	55	94	11	2	.460	$2.0	14	45	.243
1964	San Francisco (N)	5	21	.228	91	167	19	38	9	0	.371	$1.1	4	17	.210
	Career	525	1,544	.307	2,228	7,462	1,454	2,292	446	56	.593	$185.5	407	1,333	.295
	Average season	29	86	.307	124	415	81	127	25	3	.593	$10.3	23	74	.295
	Summit season	51	136	.322	156	581	135	187	42	4	.671	$22.8	41	117	.311

SAMMY SOSA

		ADJUSTED REGULAR SEASON											ACTUAL RESULTS		
YEAR	TEAM	HR	RBI	BA	G	AB	R	H	2B	3B	SA	PAY	HR	RBI	BA
1989	Tex.-Chi. (A)	6	15	.273	58	183	32	50	9	0	.421	$1.7	4	13	.257
1990	Chicago (A)	21	80	.242	153	532	83	129	30	9	.451	$5.8	15	70	.233
1991	Chicago (A)	13	38	.212	116	316	44	67	11	1	.377	$4.0	10	33	.203
1992	Chicago (N)	11	30	.275	67	262	49	72	7	2	.443	$3.5	8	25	.260
1993	Chicago (N)	38	99	.264	158	594	98	157	26	5	.517	$9.6	33	93	.261
1994	Chicago (N)	37	102	.300	151	613	86	184	25	8	.548	$11.3	25	70	.300
1995	Chicago (N)	43	137	.269	162	635	103	171	20	3	.513	$15.4	36	119	.268
1996	Chicago (N)	40	99	.273	124	498	83	136	21	2	.564	$11.3	40	100	.273
1997	Chicago (N)	38	124	.252	162	642	93	162	31	4	.491	$12.8	36	119	.251
1998	Chicago (N)	67	163	.311	158	639	138	199	20	0	.657	$22.8	66	158	.308
1999	Chicago (N)	61	138	.286	162	625	111	179	24	2	.624	$16.8	63	141	.288
2000	Chicago (N)	48	134	.318	156	604	103	192	38	1	.623	$13.8	50	138	.320
2001	Chicago (N)	63	166	.334	160	577	151	193	33	5	.737	$24.6	64	160	.328
	Career	486	1,325	.281	1,787	6,720	1,174	1,891	295	42	.555	$153.4	450	1,239	.277
	Average season	37	102	.281	137	517	90	145	23	3	.555	$11.8	35	95	.277
	Summit season	55	141	.309	157	612	118	189	28	3	.634	$17.9	54	133	.309

TRIS SPEAKER

		ADJUSTED REGULAR SEASON											ACTUAL RESULTS		
YEAR	TEAM	HR	RBI	BA	G	AB	R	H	2B	3B	SA	PAY	HR	RBI	BA
1907	Boston (A)	0	1	.158	7	19	0	3	0	0	.158	$0.0	0	1	.158
1908	Boston (A)	0	13	.250	32	120	17	30	10	3	.383	$0.3	0	9	.224
1909	Boston (A)	41	108	.341	152	578	103	197	24	3	.606	$7.1	7	77	.309
1910	Boston (A)	36	82	.367	145	553	117	203	21	4	.615	$8.8	7	65	.340
1911	Boston (A)	32	79	.337	149	528	99	178	35	4	.600	$9.6	8	70	.334
1912	Boston (A)	42	101	.384	161	610	153	234	48	3	.679	$20.0	10	90	.383
1913	Boston (A)	23	90	.379	151	557	119	211	66	11	.661	$15.2	3	71	.363
1914	Boston (A)	25	112	.359	161	582	126	209	73	8	.641	$19.1	4	90	.338
1915	Boston (A)	0	89	.346	157	573	140	198	83	11	.529	$19.5	0	69	.322
1916	Cleveland (A)	17	109	.422	156	564	141	238	75	4	.660	$19.6	2	79	.386
1917	Cleveland (A)	18	82	.383	147	541	124	207	73	6	.640	$12.8	2	60	.352
1918	Cleveland (A)	0	101	.337	159	590	121	199	116	11	.571	$16.6	0	61	.318
1919	Cleveland (A)	15	91	.303	156	575	121	174	73	7	.532	$16.4	2	63	.296
1920	Cleveland (A)	31	128	.379	158	581	164	220	55	3	.644	$20.2	8	107	.388
1921	Cleveland (A)	11	81	.334	139	533	116	178	79	6	.567	$9.9	3	75	.362
1922	Cleveland (A)	26	76	.352	137	446	91	157	49	3	.650	$7.2	11	71	.378
1923	Cleveland (A)	40	143	.360	159	608	147	219	57	4	.664	$20.3	17	130	.380
1924	Cleveland (A)	25	72	.322	143	515	104	166	36	3	.550	$8.7	9	65	.344
1925	Cleveland (A)	24	89	.360	122	447	81	161	32	2	.602	$6.4	12	87	.389
1926	Cleveland (A)	22	96	.292	158	568	107	166	55	3	.516	$12.4	7	86	.304
1927	Washington (A)	8	78	.310	145	538	76	167	61	4	.483	$6.4	2	73	.327
1928	Philadelphia (A)	7	33	.256	68	203	31	52	22	1	.478	$1.9	3	30	.267
	Career	443	1,854	.348	2,962	10,829	2,298	3,767	1,143	104	.595	$258.4	117	1,529	.345
	Average season	20	84	.348	135	492	104	171	52	5	.595	$11.7	5	70	.345
	Summit season	31	114	.384	157	584	145	224	60	5	.663	$19.1	8	95	.380

WILLIE STARGELL

		ADJUSTED REGULAR SEASON											ACTUAL RESULTS		
YEAR	TEAM	HR	RBI	BA	G	AB	R	H	2B	3B	SA	PAY	HR	RBI	BA
1962	Pittsburgh (N)	0	4	.290	10	31	1	9	4	1	.484	$0.0	0	4	.290
1963	Pittsburgh (N)	14	58	.266	108	304	42	81	15	5	.487	$2.5	11	47	.243
1964	Pittsburgh (N)	26	95	.292	117	421	64	123	25	6	.565	$5.2	21	78	.273
1965	Pittsburgh (N)	34	130	.299	143	529	83	158	33	6	.577	$7.7	27	107	.272
1966	Pittsburgh (N)	39	125	.342	140	485	103	166	39	0	.664	$11.3	33	102	.315
1967	Pittsburgh (N)	28	94	.301	133	459	69	138	24	5	.558	$9.1	20	73	.271
1968	Pittsburgh (N)	35	94	.269	127	432	80	116	18	1	.558	$9.2	24	67	.237
1969	Pittsburgh (N)	37	110	.333	145	522	107	174	42	5	.646	$9.7	29	92	.307
1970	Pittsburgh (N)	37	96	.278	136	474	79	132	23	2	.570	$7.1	31	85	.264
1971	Pittsburgh (N)	61	157	.319	141	511	130	163	31	0	.738	$12.4	48	125	.295
1972	Pittsburgh (N)	47	154	.323	144	517	103	167	36	2	.673	$9.7	33	112	.293
1973	Pittsburgh (N)	54	139	.312	148	522	124	163	51	3	.732	$10.1	44	119	.299
1974	Pittsburgh (N)	35	114	.315	140	508	107	160	43	4	.622	$9.9	25	96	.301
1975	Pittsburgh (N)	31	106	.308	125	465	83	143	36	2	.594	$7.1	22	90	.295
1976	Pittsburgh (N)	31	80	.271	117	428	66	116	21	2	.547	$4.5	20	65	.257
1977	Pittsburgh (N)	15	39	.280	63	186	32	52	13	0	.591	$2.0	13	35	.274
1978	Pittsburgh (N)	36	116	.308	123	393	72	121	19	2	.641	$3.2	28	97	.295
1979	Pittsburgh (N)	37	90	.285	125	421	66	120	19	0	.594	$2.7	32	82	.281
1980	Pittsburgh (N)	14	44	.267	67	202	32	54	10	1	.535	$1.8	11	38	.262
1981	Pittsburgh (N)	0	17	.295	60	95	4	28	11	0	.411	$1.2	0	9	.283
1982	Pittsburgh (N)	4	20	.247	74	73	7	18	4	0	.466	$0.7	3	17	.233
	Career	615	1,882	.301	2,386	7,978	1,454	2,402	517	47	.609	$127.1	475	1,540	.282
	Average season	29	90	.301	114	380	69	114	25	2	.609	$6.1	23	73	.282
	Summit season	48	137	.327	144	511	113	167	40	2	.695	$10.6	37	110	.302

RUSTY STAUB

		ADJUSTED REGULAR SEASON											ACTUAL RESULTS		
YEAR	TEAM	HR	RBI	BA	G	AB	R	H	2B	3B	SA	PAY	HR	RBI	BA
1963	Houston (N)	8	56	.246	150	513	53	126	25	3	.353	$6.1	6	45	.224
1964	Houston (N)	10	43	.233	89	292	32	68	13	2	.394	$4.1	8	35	.216
1965	Houston (N)	17	77	.280	131	410	53	115	26	1	.473	$5.5	14	63	.256
1966	Houston (N)	16	99	.304	152	550	73	167	39	2	.469	$7.9	13	81	.280
1967	Houston (N)	15	96	.370	149	546	92	202	61	1	.568	$9.1	10	74	.333
1968	Houston (N)	11	102	.332	161	591	76	196	58	1	.489	$12.0	6	72	.291
1969	Montreal (N)	37	95	.328	158	549	107	180	35	4	.608	$14.6	29	79	.302
1970	Montreal (N)	36	106	.290	160	569	111	165	29	6	.552	$15.4	30	94	.274
1971	Montreal (N)	27	121	.336	162	599	118	201	46	5	.564	$18.7	19	97	.311
1972	New York (N)	14	52	.324	69	250	44	81	15	0	.552	$6.4	9	38	.293
1973	New York (N)	20	89	.292	153	589	90	172	46	1	.475	$11.9	15	76	.279
1974	New York (N)	27	93	.271	151	561	77	152	26	2	.469	$9.5	19	78	.258
1975	New York (N)	28	123	.294	155	574	108	169	35	3	.512	$11.8	19	105	.282
1976	Detroit (A)	26	119	.315	162	593	90	187	35	2	.513	$9.9	15	96	.299
1977	Detroit (A)	27	112	.283	158	623	93	176	38	2	.480	$9.9	22	101	.278
1978	Detroit (A)	33	144	.285	162	642	89	183	32	1	.492	$13.6	24	121	.273
1979	Det. (A)-Mon. (N)	15	60	.248	107	335	46	83	17	1	.439	$3.0	12	54	.244
1980	Texas (A)	13	63	.306	108	337	48	103	27	1	.507	$2.5	9	55	.300

(Rusty Staub, continued)

		ADJUSTED REGULAR SEASON											ACTUAL RESULTS		
YEAR	TEAM	HR	RBI	BA	G	AB	R	H	2B	3B	SA	PAY	HR	RBI	BA
1981	New York (N)	12	40	.335	108	248	17	83	15	0	.540	$1.8	5	21	.317
1982	New York (N)	4	31	.251	112	219	13	55	11	0	.356	$1.2	3	27	.242
1983	New York (N)	4	32	.304	104	115	6	35	7	0	.470	$0.8	3	28	.296
1984	New York (N)	1	21	.278	78	72	2	20	6	0	.403	$0.4	1	18	.264
1985	New York (N)	1	9	.289	54	45	2	13	3	0	.422	$0.2	1	8	.267
	Career	402	1,783	.299	2,993	9,822	1,440	2,932	645	38	.495	$176.3	292	1,466	.279
	Average season	17	78	.299	130	427	63	127	28	2	.495	$7.7	13	64	.279
	Summit season	28	107	.327	158	571	104	187	41	4	.560	$13.5	21	88	.304

RIGGS STEPHENSON

		ADJUSTED REGULAR SEASON											ACTUAL RESULTS		
YEAR	TEAM	HR	RBI	BA	G	AB	R	H	2B	3B	SA	PAY	HR	RBI	BA
1921	Cleveland (A)	6	37	.306	68	216	49	66	20	1	.491	$3.4	2	34	.330
1922	Cleveland (A)	6	34	.316	90	244	50	77	33	2	.541	$3.5	2	32	.339
1923	Cleveland (A)	14	71	.302	96	318	53	96	22	3	.522	$4.5	5	65	.319
1924	Cleveland (A)	10	49	.350	75	254	36	89	19	0	.543	$3.8	4	44	.371
1925	Cleveland (A)	2	9	.281	20	57	8	16	3	0	.439	$1.7	1	9	.296
1926	Chicago (N)	10	49	.325	86	295	44	96	20	1	.502	$3.8	3	44	.338
1927	Chicago (N)	22	90	.326	161	613	111	200	53	4	.533	$7.2	7	82	.344
1928	Chicago (N)	21	99	.310	144	538	83	167	39	4	.515	$6.7	8	90	.324
1929	Chicago (N)	29	110	.337	141	513	91	173	30	2	.573	$9.2	17	110	.362
1930	Chicago (N)	9	64	.333	113	354	53	118	21	0	.469	$3.6	5	68	.367
1931	Chicago (N)	4	57	.311	83	273	37	85	21	3	.454	$2.5	1	52	.319
1932	Chicago (N)	11	93	.315	155	615	94	194	60	2	.473	$7.3	4	85	.324
1933	Chicago (N)	12	60	.330	102	364	53	120	21	2	.497	$2.6	4	51	.329
1934	Chicago (N)	0	8	.213	41	80	6	17	0	0	.213	$1.0	0	7	.216
	Career	156	830	.320	1,375	4,734	768	1,514	362	24	.505	$60.8	63	773	.336
	Average season	11	59	.320	98	338	55	108	26	2	.505	$4.3	5	55	.336
	Summit season	19	85	.328	132	476	78	156	33	2	.525	$5.9	8	80	.344

ICHIRO SUZUKI

		ADJUSTED REGULAR SEASON											ACTUAL RESULTS		
YEAR	TEAM	HR	RBI	BA	G	AB	R	H	2B	3B	SA	PAY	HR	RBI	BA
2001	Seattle (A)	8	71	.357	157	692	131	247	31	8	.460	$19.6	8	69	.350
	Career	8	71	.357	157	692	131	247	31	8	.460	$19.6	8	69	.350
	Average season	8	71	.357	157	692	131	247	31	8	.460	$19.6	8	69	.350
	Summit season	8	71	.357	157	692	131	247	31	8	.460	$19.6	8	69	.350

GENE TENACE

		ADJUSTED REGULAR SEASON											ACTUAL RESULTS		
YEAR	TEAM	HR	RBI	BA	G	AB	R	H	2B	3B	SA	PAY	HR	RBI	BA
1969	Oakland (A)	1	2	.184	16	38	1	7	0	0	.263	$0.0	1	2	.158
1970	Oakland (A)	8	23	.324	38	105	21	34	7	0	.619	$0.7	7	20	.305
1971	Oakland (A)	9	31	.296	65	179	33	53	9	0	.497	$1.7	7	25	.274
1972	Oakland (A)	8	44	.248	86	238	30	59	7	3	.403	$2.3	5	32	.225
1973	Oakland (A)	30	98	.271	160	510	97	138	22	2	.498	$7.4	24	84	.259
1974	Oakland (A)	35	87	.221	158	484	85	107	18	1	.479	$7.9	26	73	.211
1975	Oakland (A)	38	101	.267	158	498	97	133	18	0	.532	$9.2	29	87	.255
1976	Oakland (A)	32	82	.262	129	420	79	110	19	1	.540	$7.0	22	66	.249
1977	San Diego (N)	18	67	.238	147	437	73	104	27	3	.437	$7.1	15	61	.233
1978	San Diego (N)	22	72	.234	142	401	71	94	19	3	.461	$4.0	16	61	.224
1979	San Diego (N)	25	74	.266	152	466	68	124	18	3	.479	$4.0	20	67	.263
1980	San Diego (N)	21	57	.226	132	314	53	71	11	1	.468	$2.6	17	50	.222
1981	St. Louis (N)	11	42	.243	91	202	50	49	11	0	.460	$2.1	5	22	.233
1982	St. Louis (N)	9	21	.266	66	124	21	33	9	0	.556	$1.2	7	18	.258
1983	Pittsburgh (N)	0	7	.177	53	62	8	11	7	0	.290	$0.6	0	6	.177
	Career	267	808	.252	1,593	4,478	787	1,127	202	17	.483	$57.8	201	674	.241
	Average season	18	54	.252	106	299	52	75	13	1	.483	$3.9	13	45	.241
	Summit season	32	88	.256	151	476	85	122	19	1	.502	$7.1	24	75	.247

BILL TERRY

		ADJUSTED REGULAR SEASON											ACTUAL RESULTS		
YEAR	TEAM	HR	RBI	BA	G	AB	R	H	2B	3B	SA	PAY	HR	RBI	BA
1923	New York (N)	0	0	.143	3	7	1	1	0	0	.143	$0.0	0	0	.143
1924	New York (N)	10	26	.222	81	171	28	38	5	1	.439	$1.0	5	24	.239
1925	New York (N)	23	73	.295	142	522	78	154	29	3	.494	$5.3	11	70	.319
1926	New York (N)	13	49	.278	105	241	29	67	11	2	.502	$3.1	5	43	.289
1927	New York (N)	43	132	.310	157	607	110	188	25	4	.577	$9.6	20	121	.326
1928	New York (N)	35	111	.313	156	595	110	186	31	4	.555	$12.1	17	101	.326
1929	New York (N)	27	121	.346	160	647	106	224	37	2	.535	$15.7	14	117	.372
1930	New York (N)	39	124	.366	162	666	134	244	35	5	.610	$19.9	23	129	.401
1931	New York (N)	28	125	.338	162	647	135	219	51	11	.581	$19.5	9	112	.349
1932	New York (N)	48	128	.342	162	676	136	231	35	4	.618	$20.1	28	117	.350
1933	New York (N)	16	67	.322	128	494	79	159	23	3	.478	$7.2	6	58	.322
1934	New York (N)	19	91	.342	162	637	119	218	37	3	.499	$13.1	8	83	.354
1935	New York (N)	15	69	.330	151	621	98	205	41	5	.485	$9.2	6	64	.341
1936	New York (N)	5	40	.295	83	241	37	71	14	4	.448	$2.0	2	39	.310
	Career	321	1,156	.326	1,814	6,772	1,200	2,205	374	51	.538	$137.8	154	1,078	.341
	Average season	23	83	.326	130	484	86	158	27	4	.538	$9.8	11	77	.341
	Summit season	37	126	.341	161	649	124	221	37	5	.584	$17.0	19	119	.360

FRANK THOMAS

YEAR	TEAM	ADJUSTED REGULAR SEASON											ACTUAL RESULTS		
		HR	RBI	BA	G	AB	R	H	2B	3B	SA	PAY	HR	RBI	BA
1990	Chicago (A)	9	36	.346	60	191	45	66	12	3	.581	$3.2	7	31	.330
1991	Chicago (A)	40	124	.335	158	559	119	187	33	2	.615	$14.5	32	109	.318
1992	Chicago (A)	34	137	.340	160	573	129	195	49	2	.611	$19.1	24	115	.323
1993	Chicago (A)	47	138	.322	153	549	114	177	36	0	.645	$18.5	41	128	.317
1994	Chicago (A)	56	147	.353	162	572	154	202	48	1	.734	$31.6	38	101	.353
1995	Chicago (A)	47	127	.310	162	551	117	171	30	0	.621	$25.9	40	111	.308
1996	Chicago (A)	40	133	.349	141	527	109	184	27	0	.628	$19.0	40	134	.349
1997	Chicago (A)	37	131	.350	147	534	115	187	35	0	.624	$16.4	35	125	.347
1998	Chicago (A)	30	112	.269	159	581	112	156	35	2	.491	$16.6	29	109	.265
1999	Chicago (A)	14	75	.302	135	486	72	147	36	0	.463	$9.3	15	77	.305
2000	Chicago (A)	41	139	.326	159	582	111	190	44	0	.613	$13.3	43	143	.328
2001	Chicago (A)	4	10	.221	20	68	8	15	3	0	.441	$1.8	4	10	.221
	Career	399	1,309	.325	1,616	5,773	1,205	1,877	388	10	.603	$189.2	348	1,193	.319
	Average season	33	109	.325	135	481	100	156	32	1	.603	$15.8	29	99	.319
	Summit season	43	137	.343	153	551	124	189	39	1	.652	$20.9	36	121	.337

SAM THOMPSON

YEAR	TEAM	ADJUSTED REGULAR SEASON											ACTUAL RESULTS		
		HR	RBI	BA	G	AB	R	H	2B	3B	SA	PAY	HR	RBI	BA
1885	Detroit (N)	35	65	.334	95	383	85	128	13	3	.658	$7.4	7	44	.303
1886	Detroit (N)	40	105	.338	157	647	119	219	23	4	.572	$15.6	8	89	.310
1887	Detroit (N)	44	171	.371	162	695	121	258	42	8	.645	$26.0	10	166	.372
1888	Detroit (N)	23	50	.318	68	289	64	92	13	3	.623	$7.4	6	40	.282
1889	Philadelphia (N)	52	118	.303	160	666	109	202	33	1	.590	$16.4	20	111	.296
1890	Philadelphia (N)	22	105	.324	161	670	120	217	69	4	.537	$16.6	4	102	.313
1891	Philadelphia (N)	29	94	.312	156	650	112	203	35	3	.509	$15.9	7	90	.294
1892	Philadelphia (N)	34	107	.336	160	637	112	214	37	3	.564	$13.5	9	104	.305
1893	Philadelphia (N)	41	123	.357	160	733	127	262	46	4	.599	$24.7	11	126	.370
1894	Philadelphia (N)	42	125	.355	124	547	96	194	35	8	.678	$9.5	13	141	.407
1895	Philadelphia (N)	56	158	.357	145	656	125	234	45	5	.697	$19.4	18	165	.392
1896	Philadelphia (N)	37	104	.275	148	643	108	177	26	2	.495	$12.9	12	100	.298
1897	Philadelphia (N)	0	3	.235	4	17	2	4	0	0	.235	$1.6	0	3	.231
1898	Philadelphia (N)	5	16	.353	15	68	15	24	6	1	.691	$1.4	1	15	.349
1906	Detroit (A)	0	4	.257	9	35	6	9	0	2	.371	$0.5	0	3	.226
	Career	460	1,348	.332	1,724	7,336	1,321	2,437	423	51	.592	$188.8	126	1,299	.331
	Average season	31	90	.332	115	489	88	162	28	3	.592	$12.6	8	87	.331
	Summit season	44	128	.357	137	603	111	215	36	6	.655	$17.4	12	128	.375

JOE TINKER

		ADJUSTED REGULAR SEASON											ACTUAL RESULTS		
YEAR	TEAM	HR	RBI	BA	G	AB	R	H	2B	3B	SA	PAY	HR	RBI	BA
1902	Chicago (N)	16	69	.264	151	569	70	150	32	2	.411	$7.9	2	54	.261
1903	Chicago (N)	17	90	.299	145	538	86	161	33	3	.467	$9.4	2	70	.291
1904	Chicago (N)	22	54	.242	146	505	73	122	17	4	.422	$7.8	3	41	.221
1905	Chicago (N)	17	85	.267	156	573	90	153	31	3	.421	$11.4	2	66	.247
1906	Chicago (N)	12	87	.254	155	548	102	139	36	2	.392	$11.7	1	64	.233
1907	Chicago (N)	11	50	.243	122	419	50	102	19	1	.372	$6.1	1	36	.221
1908	Chicago (N)	36	97	.301	161	562	95	169	23	4	.548	$11.6	6	68	.266
1909	Chicago (N)	29	79	.283	149	538	77	152	30	3	.511	$7.0	4	57	.256
1910	Chicago (N)	20	89	.311	141	498	62	155	36	4	.520	$5.7	3	69	.288
1911	Chicago (N)	21	76	.281	149	555	67	156	33	4	.468	$6.9	4	69	.278
1912	Chicago (N)	0	85	.282	151	585	90	165	67	6	.417	$6.8	0	75	.282
1913	Cincinnati (N)	9	70	.328	114	396	57	130	45	8	.551	$2.9	1	57	.317
1914	Chicago (F)	12	58	.270	130	452	63	122	34	3	.438	$3.0	2	46	.256
1915	Chicago (F)	0	11	.290	32	69	9	20	9	0	.420	$1.3	0	9	.269
1916	Chicago (N)	0	1	.100	7	10	0	1	0	0	.100	$0.4	0	1	.100
	Career	222	1,001	.278	1,909	6,817	991	1,897	445	47	.455	$99.9	31	782	.262
	Average season	15	67	.278	127	454	66	126	30	3	.455	$6.7	2	52	.262
	Summit season	22	85	.302	142	506	75	153	33	4	.514	$7.3	3	64	.281

JOE TORRE

		ADJUSTED REGULAR SEASON											ACTUAL RESULTS		
YEAR	TEAM	HR	RBI	BA	G	AB	R	H	2B	3B	SA	PAY	HR	RBI	BA
1960	Milwaukee (N)	0	0	.500	2	2	0	1	0	0	.500	$0.0	0	0	.500
1961	Milwaukee (N)	12	47	.290	118	424	45	123	28	3	.455	$2.9	10	42	.278
1962	Milwaukee (N)	6	29	.295	80	220	25	65	10	1	.432	$2.1	5	26	.282
1963	Milwaukee (N)	18	87	.320	141	497	70	159	26	3	.493	$5.7	14	71	.293
1964	Milwaukee (N)	25	133	.346	154	601	106	208	48	4	.564	$11.6	20	109	.321
1965	Milwaukee (N)	33	98	.319	148	523	83	167	27	1	.564	$9.3	27	80	.291
1966	Atlanta (N)	44	123	.341	147	542	101	185	26	2	.640	$14.2	36	101	.315
1967	Atlanta (N)	27	88	.308	135	477	87	147	23	1	.530	$11.4	20	68	.277
1968	Atlanta (N)	17	77	.307	114	420	63	129	16	2	.476	$7.8	10	55	.271
1969	St. Louis (N)	24	121	.314	159	602	86	189	41	5	.518	$12.1	18	101	.289
1970	St. Louis (N)	26	113	.345	161	624	101	215	37	7	.551	$12.5	21	100	.325
1971	St. Louis (N)	34	171	.392	160	630	121	247	46	7	.649	$16.5	24	137	.363
1972	St. Louis (N)	18	111	.318	155	566	97	180	39	6	.504	$9.6	11	81	.289
1973	St. Louis (N)	18	81	.301	141	519	78	156	22	2	.455	$7.2	13	69	.287
1974	St. Louis (N)	18	84	.295	148	533	71	157	36	1	.467	$7.1	11	70	.282
1975	New York (N)	10	41	.258	114	361	38	93	21	2	.410	$2.6	6	35	.247
1976	New York (N)	10	38	.323	114	310	44	100	14	2	.477	$1.9	5	31	.306
1977	New York (N)	1	10	.176	26	51	2	9	3	0	.294	$0.7	1	9	.176
	Career	341	1,452	.320	2,217	7,902	1,218	2,530	463	49	.521	$135.2	252	1,185	.297
	Average season	19	81	.320	123	439	68	141	26	3	.521	$7.5	14	66	.297
	Summit season	32	128	.349	154	584	102	204	37	4	.591	$12.8	26	105	.324

ALAN TRAMMELL

		ADJUSTED REGULAR SEASON											ACTUAL RESULTS		
YEAR	TEAM	HR	RBI	BA	G	AB	R	H	2B	3B	SA	PAY	HR	RBI	BA
1977	Detroit (A)	0	0	.186	19	43	7	8	0	0	.186	$0.0	0	0	.186
1978	Detroit (A)	4	40	.279	139	448	58	125	22	6	.382	$3.3	2	34	.268
1979	Detroit (A)	9	55	.279	143	463	75	129	15	3	.382	$4.9	6	50	.276
1980	Detroit (A)	14	74	.306	145	556	123	170	27	4	.444	$9.0	9	65	.300
1981	Detroit (A)	6	56	.271	156	582	94	158	34	5	.378	$11.3	2	31	.258
1982	Detroit (A)	12	65	.266	157	489	76	130	41	3	.436	$8.7	9	57	.258
1983	Detroit (A)	19	75	.329	142	505	95	166	35	2	.519	$9.5	14	66	.319
1984	Detroit (A)	20	80	.324	139	555	99	180	41	4	.521	$11.6	14	69	.314
1985	Detroit (A)	17	65	.269	150	609	90	164	25	6	.414	$11.9	13	57	.258
1986	Detroit (A)	25	84	.289	151	574	119	166	38	7	.510	$14.3	21	75	.277
1987	Detroit (A)	29	110	.352	151	597	114	210	37	3	.570	$12.5	28	105	.343
1988	Detroit (A)	21	82	.328	128	466	86	153	28	1	.528	$7.3	15	69	.311
1989	Detroit (A)	8	51	.256	121	449	64	115	26	3	.381	$6.6	5	43	.243
1990	Detroit (A)	19	102	.317	146	559	82	177	42	1	.497	$7.1	14	89	.304
1991	Detroit (A)	12	63	.261	101	375	65	98	22	0	.416	$3.0	9	55	.248
1992	Detroit (A)	1	13	.284	29	102	13	29	10	1	.431	$1.4	1	11	.275
1993	Detroit (A)	15	64	.334	112	401	77	134	27	3	.529	$2.7	12	60	.329
1994	Detroit (A)	12	40	.265	107	411	54	109	24	1	.416	$1.9	8	28	.267
1995	Detroit (A)	2	26	.272	83	250	32	68	15	0	.356	$1.2	2	23	.269
1996	Detroit (A)	1	16	.233	66	193	16	45	2	0	.259	$1.0	1	16	.233
	Career	246	1,161	.294	2,385	8,627	1,439	2,534	511	53	.451	$129.2	185	1,003	.285
	Average season	12	58	.294	119	431	72	127	26	3	.451	$6.5	9	50	.285
	Summit season	21	82	.335	134	505	94	169	34	3	.539	$8.7	17	74	.324

PIE TRAYNOR

		ADJUSTED REGULAR SEASON											ACTUAL RESULTS		
YEAR	TEAM	HR	RBI	BA	G	AB	R	H	2B	3B	SA	PAY	HR	RBI	BA
1920	Pittsburgh (N)	0	2	.200	18	55	7	11	8	0	.345	$0.0	0	2	.212
1921	Pittsburgh (N)	0	2	.263	7	19	0	5	0	0	.263	$0.0	0	2	.263
1922	Pittsburgh (N)	14	86	.262	148	595	95	156	26	6	.397	$5.9	4	81	.282
1923	Pittsburgh (N)	34	110	.319	161	648	118	207	22	8	.535	$11.6	12	101	.338
1924	Pittsburgh (N)	18	90	.276	150	576	95	159	34	7	.453	$11.4	5	82	.294
1925	Pittsburgh (N)	18	110	.296	159	626	118	185	50	7	.484	$18.8	6	106	.320
1926	Pittsburgh (N)	15	101	.304	157	593	91	180	40	10	.481	$14.6	3	92	.317
1927	Pittsburgh (N)	17	115	.326	155	596	100	194	40	5	.495	$14.5	5	106	.342
1928	Pittsburgh (N)	11	139	.324	153	605	101	196	58	7	.498	$12.5	3	124	.337
1929	Pittsburgh (N)	11	110	.330	137	569	96	188	39	7	.482	$11.7	4	108	.356
1930	Pittsburgh (N)	18	115	.334	137	524	87	175	24	4	.498	$9.8	9	119	.366
1931	Pittsburgh (N)	8	113	.288	162	643	89	185	62	11	.456	$13.1	2	103	.298
1932	Pittsburgh (N)	6	74	.320	142	540	81	173	43	8	.463	$6.8	2	68	.329
1933	Pittsburgh (N)	5	97	.305	162	656	100	200	53	5	.424	$9.9	1	82	.304
1934	Pittsburgh (N)	3	68	.297	128	478	69	142	40	10	.441	$4.7	1	61	.309
1935	Pittsburgh (N)	3	39	.270	60	215	26	58	15	3	.409	$1.8	1	36	.279
1937	Pittsburgh (N)	0	0	.167	5	12	3	2	0	0	.167	$0.8	0	0	.167
	Career	181	1,371	.304	2,041	7,950	1,276	2,416	554	98	.467	$147.9	58	1,273	.320
	Average season	11	81	.304	120	468	75	142	33	6	.467	$8.7	3	75	.320
	Summit season	18	118	.327	149	588	100	192	37	6	.502	$12.0	7	112	.347

GEORGE VAN HALTREN

		ADJUSTED REGULAR SEASON											ACTUAL RESULTS		
YEAR	TEAM	HR	RBI	BA	G	AB	R	H	2B	3B	SA	PAY	HR	RBI	BA
1887	Chicago (N)	8	17	.202	57	218	31	44	3	0	.326	$1.9	3	17	.203
1888	Chicago (N)	23	41	.318	96	377	56	120	18	7	.586	$3.6	4	34	.283
1889	Chicago (N)	32	82	.316	160	648	128	205	26	4	.517	$14.4	9	81	.309
1890	Brooklyn (P)	24	55	.347	112	458	86	159	11	3	.541	$7.1	5	54	.335
1891	Baltimore (AA)	37	86	.338	162	660	141	223	21	5	.553	$19.3	9	83	.318
1892	Balt.-Pit. (N)	31	64	.322	155	640	119	206	33	4	.531	$18.9	7	62	.293
1893	Pittsburgh (N)	19	77	.326	153	653	127	213	30	5	.475	$19.6	3	79	.338
1894	New York (N)	19	87	.288	162	614	91	177	23	1	.422	$15.3	7	104	.331
1895	New York (N)	33	99	.309	161	640	108	198	32	7	.536	$16.2	8	103	.340
1896	New York (N)	31	76	.326	162	685	140	223	33	9	.536	$22.7	5	74	.351
1897	New York (N)	19	65	.305	153	669	119	204	38	5	.462	$16.3	3	64	.330
1898	New York (N)	19	69	.311	161	675	132	210	61	8	.510	$19.3	2	68	.312
1899	New York (N)	14	58	.287	161	644	117	185	38	1	.415	$13.5	2	58	.301
1900	New York (N)	9	55	.305	162	656	125	200	70	4	.465	$13.1	1	51	.315
1901	New York (N)	10	54	.332	155	623	95	207	57	3	.482	$9.5	1	47	.335
1902	New York (N)	0	9	.262	28	103	18	27	7	3	.388	$1.3	0	7	.261
1903	New York (N)	0	35	.263	96	320	53	84	29	0	.353	$1.8	0	28	.257
	Career	328	1,029	.311	2,296	9,283	1,686	2,885	530	69	.489	$213.8	69	1,014	.316
	Average season	19	61	.311	135	546	99	170	31	4	.489	$12.6	4	60	.316
	Summit season	29	64	.330	137	564	108	186	23	6	.546	$14.3	6	61	.317

ARKY VAUGHAN

		ADJUSTED REGULAR SEASON											ACTUAL RESULTS		
YEAR	TEAM	HR	RBI	BA	G	AB	R	H	2B	3B	SA	PAY	HR	RBI	BA
1932	Pittsburgh (N)	12	67	.309	136	524	78	162	21	6	.441	$8.7	4	61	.318
1933	Pittsburgh (N)	26	115	.313	160	603	100	189	37	11	.541	$14.7	9	97	.314
1934	Pittsburgh (N)	26	104	.322	160	599	128	193	46	6	.549	$19.1	12	94	.333
1935	Pittsburgh (N)	36	109	.373	145	528	119	197	32	4	.653	$15.2	19	99	.385
1936	Pittsburgh (N)	20	80	.317	162	590	125	187	35	6	.498	$19.8	9	78	.335
1937	Pittsburgh (N)	14	78	.313	133	495	77	155	26	12	.499	$11.7	5	72	.322
1938	Pittsburgh (N)	15	74	.317	158	578	96	183	43	3	.479	$15.2	7	68	.322
1939	Pittsburgh (N)	15	68	.298	161	630	103	188	41	7	.457	$15.1	6	62	.306
1940	Pittsburgh (N)	15	106	.301	162	617	126	186	54	9	.491	$18.9	7	95	.300
1941	Pittsburgh (N)	14	44	.325	110	388	80	126	25	4	.518	$5.7	6	38	.316
1942	Brooklyn (N)	7	62	.295	134	518	104	153	33	4	.415	$9.0	2	49	.277
1943	Brooklyn (N)	18	88	.325	158	647	150	210	59	4	.512	$16.6	5	66	.305
1947	Brooklyn (N)	4	29	.333	67	132	28	44	7	1	.492	$2.0	2	25	.325
1948	Brooklyn (N)	5	25	.248	68	129	21	32	4	0	.395	$1.5	3	22	.244
	Career	227	1,049	.316	1,914	6,978	1,335	2,205	463	77	.502	$173.2	96	926	.318
	Average season	16	75	.316	137	498	95	158	33	6	.502	$12.4	7	66	.318
	Summit season	24	92	.331	147	553	115	183	40	6	.555	$14.3	10	79	.330

MO VAUGHN

		ADJUSTED REGULAR SEASON											ACTUAL RESULTS		
YEAR	TEAM	HR	RBI	BA	G	AB	R	H	2B	3B	SA	PAY	HR	RBI	BA
1991	Boston (A)	5	36	.274	74	219	24	60	14	0	.406	$2.5	4	32	.260
1992	Boston (A)	18	68	.245	113	355	50	87	17	2	.456	$4.4	13	57	.234
1993	Boston (A)	34	108	.301	152	539	92	162	35	1	.558	$8.7	29	101	.297
1994	Boston (A)	38	117	.309	156	554	92	171	34	1	.579	$11.3	26	82	.310
1995	Boston (A)	47	146	.303	158	621	113	188	32	3	.591	$18.7	39	126	.300
1996	Boston (A)	44	142	.324	161	635	117	206	30	1	.583	$22.5	44	143	.326
1997	Boston (A)	37	100	.317	141	527	95	167	24	0	.573	$12.0	35	96	.315
1998	Boston (A)	42	119	.340	154	609	111	207	31	2	.604	$16.1	40	115	.337
1999	Anaheim (A)	32	106	.279	139	524	62	146	20	0	.500	$7.0	33	108	.281
2000	Anaheim (A)	34	113	.270	161	614	90	166	30	0	.485	$9.9	36	117	.272
	Career	331	1,055	.300	1,409	5,197	846	1,560	267	10	.546	$113.1	299	977	.298
	Average season	33	106	.300	141	520	85	156	27	1	.546	$11.3	30	98	.298
	Summit season	42	125	.319	154	589	106	188	30	1	.587	$16.1	37	112	.319

ZOILO VERSALLES

		ADJUSTED REGULAR SEASON											ACTUAL RESULTS		
YEAR	TEAM	HR	RBI	BA	G	AB	R	H	2B	3B	SA	PAY	HR	RBI	BA
1959	Washington (A)	1	1	.159	31	63	5	10	0	0	.206	$0.0	1	1	.153
1960	Washington (A)	0	5	.146	16	48	2	7	3	2	.292	$0.0	0	4	.133
1961	Minnesota (A)	8	58	.292	130	514	71	150	32	4	.416	$4.2	7	53	.280
1962	Minnesota (A)	20	73	.252	159	564	76	142	24	2	.408	$5.8	17	67	.241
1963	Minnesota (A)	14	67	.285	160	625	92	178	47	11	.462	$8.7	10	54	.261
1964	Minnesota (A)	25	77	.279	159	655	114	183	44	8	.485	$14.8	20	64	.259
1965	Minnesota (A)	25	94	.299	160	666	155	199	62	9	.532	$19.5	19	77	.273
1966	Minnesota (A)	10	44	.269	137	543	89	146	30	4	.394	$11.2	7	36	.249
1967	Minnesota (A)	10	64	.221	158	574	80	127	25	6	.338	$11.5	6	50	.200
1968	Los Angeles (N)	4	34	.223	122	403	41	90	27	4	.340	$4.4	2	24	.196
1969	Cle.-Wash. (A)	1	23	.257	103	292	36	75	20	2	.349	$2.7	1	19	.236
1971	Atlanta (N)	7	27	.206	66	194	26	40	14	0	.387	$1.3	5	22	.191
	Career	125	567	.262	1,401	5,141	787	1,347	328	52	.419	$84.1	95	471	.242
	Average season	10	47	.262	117	428	66	112	27	4	.419	$7.0	8	39	.242
	Summit season	16	68	.285	149	601	104	171	43	7	.459	$11.7	13	57	.264

HONUS WAGNER

		ADJUSTED REGULAR SEASON											ACTUAL RESULTS		
YEAR	TEAM	HR	RBI	BA	G	AB	R	H	2B	3B	SA	PAY	HR	RBI	BA
1897	Louisville (N)	11	41	.313	74	288	39	90	23	2	.521	$3.5	2	39	.338
1898	Louisville (N)	35	110	.297	159	619	83	184	23	0	.504	$9.0	10	105	.299
1899	Louisville (N)	32	111	.321	154	598	96	192	51	4	.580	$11.9	7	113	.336
1900	Pittsburgh (N)	26	110	.369	156	609	118	225	85	10	.670	$14.9	4	100	.381
1901	Pittsburgh (N)	32	147	.350	162	635	118	222	49	3	.587	$25.3	6	126	.353
1902	Pittsburgh (N)	25	116	.333	155	609	134	203	53	9	.573	$19.6	3	91	.330
1903	Pittsburgh (N)	36	128	.366	148	587	123	215	39	7	.641	$16.5	5	101	.355
1904	Pittsburgh (N)	29	100	.381	137	509	129	194	61	5	.692	$12.8	4	75	.349

(Honus Wagner, continued)

ADJUSTED REGULAR SEASON | | | | | | | | | | | | ACTUAL RESULTS

YEAR	TEAM	HR	RBI	BA	G	AB	R	H	2B	3B	SA	PAY	HR	RBI	BA
1905	Pittsburgh (N)	37	130	.395	154	574	147	227	37	4	.667	$17.0	6	101	.363
1906	Pittsburgh (N)	21	97	.372	149	541	141	201	66	4	.625	$13.3	2	71	.339
1907	Pittsburgh (N)	41	113	.385	147	533	136	205	42	4	.709	$13.1	6	82	.350
1908	Pittsburgh (N)	56	158	.399	158	594	145	237	37	5	.761	$20.1	10	109	.354
1909	Pittsburgh (N)	35	140	.375	144	520	128	195	43	3	.671	$13.4	5	100	.339
1910	Pittsburgh (N)	26	105	.346	158	586	117	203	46	3	.568	$13.1	4	81	.320
1911	Pittsburgh (N)	34	99	.337	136	495	97	167	22	4	.604	$9.0	9	89	.334
1912	Pittsburgh (N)	36	116	.326	155	596	103	194	39	6	.592	$12.4	7	102	.324
1913	Pittsburgh (N)	15	69	.313	119	431	63	135	23	1	.476	$4.3	3	56	.300
1914	Pittsburgh (N)	10	62	.266	154	567	75	151	34	7	.404	$6.4	1	50	.252
1915	Pittsburgh (N)	32	100	.294	162	588	87	173	39	6	.544	$6.7	6	78	.274
1916	Pittsburgh (N)	11	54	.312	127	446	62	139	33	6	.487	$2.6	1	39	.287
1917	Pittsburgh (N)	0	33	.288	76	236	20	68	27	0	.403	$1.7	0	24	.265
	Career	580	2,139	.342	2,984	11,161	2,161	3,820	872	93	.593	$246.6	101	1,732	.327
	Average season	28	102	.342	142	531	103	182	42	4	.593	$11.7	5	82	.327
	Summit season	40	128	.388	148	546	137	212	44	4	.703	$15.3	6	93	.351

LARRY WALKER

ADJUSTED REGULAR SEASON | | | | | | | | | | | | ACTUAL RESULTS

YEAR	TEAM	HR	RBI	BA	G	AB	R	H	2B	3B	SA	PAY	HR	RBI	BA
1989	Montreal (N)	0	5	.170	20	47	5	8	0	0	.170	$0.0	0	4	.170
1990	Montreal (N)	24	59	.251	133	419	68	105	19	3	.482	$3.8	19	51	.241
1991	Montreal (N)	21	73	.305	138	491	68	150	33	2	.509	$5.7	16	64	.290
1992	Montreal (N)	32	111	.316	143	528	101	167	32	4	.574	$8.8	23	93	.301
1993	Montreal (N)	26	92	.270	137	486	90	131	25	5	.502	$9.6	22	86	.265
1994	Montreal (N)	29	123	.321	146	560	109	180	62	2	.595	$14.4	19	86	.322
1995	Colorado (N)	43	116	.309	147	554	110	171	35	5	.623	$12.0	36	101	.306
1996	Colorado (N)	18	58	.276	83	272	58	75	18	4	.570	$5.3	18	58	.276
1997	Colorado (N)	51	135	.370	153	568	149	210	46	4	.734	$16.0	49	130	.366
1998	Colorado (N)	24	69	.368	130	454	117	167	46	3	.641	$7.0	23	67	.363
1999	Colorado (N)	36	113	.377	127	438	106	165	26	4	.701	$6.9	37	115	.379
2000	Colorado (N)	8	49	.306	87	314	62	96	21	7	.494	$3.8	9	51	.309
2001	Colorado (N)	37	127	.356	142	497	111	177	34	3	.660	$7.4	38	123	.350
	Career	349	1,130	.320	1,586	5,628	1,154	1,802	397	46	.593	$100.7	309	1,029	.315
	Average season	27	87	.320	122	433	89	139	31	4	.593	$7.7	24	79	.315
	Summit season	38	112	.355	140	502	119	178	37	4	.671	$9.9	37	107	.353

BOBBY WALLACE

ADJUSTED REGULAR SEASON | | | | | | | | | | | | ACTUAL RESULTS

YEAR	TEAM	HR	RBI	BA	G	AB	R	H	2B	3B	SA	PAY	HR	RBI	BA
1894	Cleveland (N)	0	1	.125	5	16	0	2	2	0	.250	$0.0	0	1	.154
1895	Cleveland (N)	0	10	.198	37	121	15	24	9	3	.322	$0.3	0	10	.214
1896	Cleveland (N)	5	17	.218	54	179	19	39	10	1	.369	$0.9	1	17	.235
1897	Cleveland (N)	27	118	.309	160	635	105	196	58	10	.559	$9.0	4	112	.335
1898	Cleveland (N)	21	102	.268	160	616	83	165	42	5	.455	$9.6	3	99	.270

(Bobby Wallace, continued)

		ADJUSTED REGULAR SEASON											ACTUAL RESULTS		
YEAR	TEAM	HR	RBI	BA	G	AB	R	H	2B	3B	SA	PAY	HR	RBI	BA
1899	St. Louis (N)	40	106	.281	158	604	89	170	24	3	.530	$12.3	12	108	.295
1900	St. Louis (N)	20	76	.258	144	554	76	143	37	4	.448	$11.6	4	70	.268
1901	St. Louis (N)	16	105	.320	153	628	79	201	71	8	.535	$12.4	2	91	.324
1902	St. Louis (A)	11	81	.288	154	572	91	165	69	7	.491	$9.7	1	63	.285
1903	St. Louis (A)	11	69	.273	157	594	81	162	46	4	.419	$9.3	1	54	.266
1904	St. Louis (A)	16	91	.300	144	560	75	168	45	2	.473	$9.1	2	69	.275
1905	St. Louis (A)	12	75	.293	162	610	85	179	56	6	.464	$7.4	1	59	.271
1906	St. Louis (A)	19	92	.282	146	500	88	141	33	3	.474	$5.1	2	67	.258
1907	St. Louis (A)	0	98	.282	154	564	78	159	78	6	.441	$7.1	0	70	.257
1908	St. Louis (A)	11	87	.283	143	508	85	144	48	2	.451	$6.8	1	60	.253
1909	St. Louis (A)	0	49	.262	122	424	50	111	46	2	.380	$2.6	0	35	.238
1910	St. Louis (A)	0	46	.277	141	519	59	144	63	6	.422	$3.2	0	37	.258
1911	St. Louis (A)	0	35	.234	133	436	40	102	35	2	.323	$2.1	0	31	.232
1912	St. Louis (A)	0	34	.240	103	333	43	80	37	4	.375	$1.6	0	31	.241
1913	St. Louis (A)	0	26	.217	57	152	13	33	13	0	.303	$0.9	0	21	.211
1914	St. Louis (A)	0	6	.233	26	73	4	17	8	0	.342	$0.4	0	5	.219
1915	St. Louis (A)	0	5	.231	9	13	1	3	0	0	.231	$0.1	0	4	.231
1916	St. Louis (A)	0	1	.278	14	18	0	5	0	0	.278	$0.0	0	1	.278
1917	St. Louis (N)	0	3	.100	8	10	0	1	0	0	.100	$0.0	0	2	.100
1918	St. Louis (N)	0	7	.163	40	123	5	20	6	0	.211	$0.0	0	4	.153
	Career	209	1,340	.275	2,584	9,362	1,264	2,574	836	78	.448	$121.5	34	1,121	.268
	Average season	8	54	.275	103	374	51	103	33	3	.448	$4.9	1	45	.268
	Summit season	22	100	.300	154	600	88	180	53	6	.518	$10.5	4	89	.303

LLOYD WANER

		ADJUSTED REGULAR SEASON											ACTUAL RESULTS		
YEAR	TEAM	HR	RBI	BA	G	AB	R	H	2B	3B	SA	PAY	HR	RBI	BA
1927	Pittsburgh (N)	10	29	.336	156	654	144	220	32	5	.446	$12.4	2	27	.355
1928	Pittsburgh (N)	18	68	.322	162	702	135	226	33	8	.469	$19.1	5	61	.335
1929	Pittsburgh (N)	16	75	.329	159	697	136	229	41	13	.494	$19.7	5	74	.353
1930	Pittsburgh (N)	3	35	.327	72	275	31	90	13	2	.422	$5.5	1	36	.362
1931	Pittsburgh (N)	15	62	.305	161	712	99	217	37	8	.442	$15.4	4	57	.314
1932	Pittsburgh (N)	6	41	.324	141	595	99	193	45	8	.457	$9.2	2	38	.333
1933	Pittsburgh (N)	0	30	.276	127	525	69	145	36	6	.368	$5.9	0	26	.276
1934	Pittsburgh (N)	3	53	.273	150	655	105	179	47	6	.377	$11.8	1	48	.283
1935	Pittsburgh (N)	0	50	.299	129	568	91	170	49	14	.435	$5.9	0	46	.309
1936	Pittsburgh (N)	4	32	.305	110	430	69	131	25	7	.423	$4.2	1	31	.321
1937	Pittsburgh (N)	3	49	.322	136	566	87	182	41	3	.420	$5.9	1	45	.330
1938	Pittsburgh (N)	12	62	.309	157	661	86	204	36	5	.433	$6.8	5	57	.313
1939	Pittsburgh (N)	0	26	.278	119	403	54	112	29	3	.365	$2.2	0	24	.285
1940	Pittsburgh (N)	0	3	.260	75	173	34	45	7	0	.301	$1.3	0	3	.259
1941	Pit.-Bos.-Cin. (N)	0	13	.298	80	228	30	68	12	2	.368	$1.2	0	11	.292
1942	Philadelphia (N)	0	13	.277	108	307	30	85	21	5	.378	$0.9	0	10	.261
1944	Bkn.-Pit. (N)	0	4	.345	35	29	6	10	0	0	.345	$0.2	0	3	.321
1945	Pittsburgh (N)	0	1	.250	24	20	6	5	0	0	.250	$0.0	0	1	.263
	Career	90	646	.306	2,101	8,200	1,311	2,511	504	95	.424	$127.6	27	598	.316
	Average season	5	36	.306	117	456	73	140	28	5	.424	$7.1	2	33	.316
	Summit season	13	55	.323	156	672	123	217	38	8	.461	$15.2	4	51	.338

PAUL WANER

		ADJUSTED REGULAR SEASON											ACTUAL RESULTS		
YEAR	TEAM	HR	RBI	BA	G	AB	R	H	2B	3B	SA	PAY	HR	RBI	BA
1926	Pittsburgh (N)	28	86	.323	149	555	111	179	41	10	.584	$14.6	8	79	.336
1927	Pittsburgh (N)	29	142	.362	161	647	123	234	49	9	.600	$25.2	9	131	.380
1928	Pittsburgh (N)	20	96	.355	162	642	159	228	69	11	.590	$26.7	6	86	.370
1929	Pittsburgh (N)	31	102	.312	159	628	134	196	43	6	.548	$26.2	15	100	.336
1930	Pittsburgh (N)	19	74	.335	153	621	113	208	40	9	.520	$19.4	8	77	.368
1931	Pittsburgh (N)	18	77	.313	157	585	97	183	42	6	.497	$15.6	6	70	.322
1932	Pittsburgh (N)	19	90	.332	162	663	117	220	73	6	.546	$16.7	8	82	.341
1933	Pittsburgh (N)	22	82	.309	162	650	119	201	52	9	.518	$16.3	7	70	.309
1934	Pittsburgh (N)	31	100	.349	157	644	136	225	36	9	.578	$17.0	14	90	.362
1935	Pittsburgh (N)	25	86	.310	147	581	108	180	33	6	.516	$9.9	11	78	.321
1936	Pittsburgh (N)	13	96	.355	154	609	110	216	68	6	.550	$13.2	5	94	.373
1937	Pittsburgh (N)	6	80	.344	162	651	102	224	51	7	.472	$13.3	2	74	.354
1938	Pittsburgh (N)	14	75	.274	158	667	84	183	41	3	.408	$10.0	6	69	.280
1939	Pittsburgh (N)	8	49	.320	132	487	68	156	43	4	.474	$4.2	3	45	.328
1940	Pittsburgh (N)	2	35	.293	92	246	35	72	20	1	.407	$1.8	1	32	.290
1941	Bkn.-Bos. (N)	5	57	.275	109	338	51	93	15	1	.370	$2.1	2	50	.267
1942	Boston (N)	4	51	.276	123	359	56	99	29	1	.396	$2.0	1	39	.258
1943	Brooklyn (N)	4	35	.331	87	239	39	79	27	0	.494	$1.4	1	26	.311
1944	Bkn. (N)-N.Y. (A)	0	21	.289	96	149	21	43	10	2	.383	$1.1	0	17	.280
1945	New York (A)	0	0	.000	1	0	0	0	0	0	.000	$0.3	0	0	.000
	Career	298	1,434	.323	2,683	9,961	1,783	3,219	782	106	.513	$237.0	113	1,309	.333
	Average season	15	72	.323	134	498	89	161	39	5	.513	$11.9	6	65	.333
	Summit season	24	104	.349	157	619	128	216	53	9	.580	$19.3	8	96	.365

JOHN WARD

		ADJUSTED REGULAR SEASON											ACTUAL RESULTS		
YEAR	TEAM	HR	RBI	BA	G	AB	R	H	2B	3B	SA	PAY	HR	RBI	BA
1878	Providence (N)	22	41	.202	97	362	38	73	8	3	.423	$3.8	1	15	.196
1879	Providence (N)	30	80	.302	158	693	139	209	13	2	.456	$14.9	2	41	.286
1880	Providence (N)	0	55	.249	160	662	109	165	66	5	.364	$12.3	0	27	.228
1881	Providence (N)	0	104	.251	162	680	110	171	89	11	.415	$15.4	0	53	.244
1882	Providence (N)	16	74	.266	160	684	110	182	30	2	.386	$19.7	1	39	.245
1883	New York (N)	40	82	.267	145	626	116	167	16	2	.490	$15.1	7	54	.255
1884	New York (N)	18	67	.280	158	674	129	189	29	5	.418	$25.4	2	51	.253
1885	New York (N)	0	52	.249	161	647	102	161	51	15	.374	$14.7	0	37	.226
1886	New York (N)	17	97	.298	159	640	98	191	35	2	.439	$15.1	2	81	.273
1887	New York (N)	9	53	.336	162	684	115	230	43	3	.447	$15.5	1	53	.338
1888	New York (N)	14	59	.283	143	598	84	169	32	2	.413	$9.6	2	49	.251
1889	New York (N)	7	70	.306	141	592	91	181	38	4	.419	$9.3	1	67	.299
1890	Brooklyn (P)	26	62	.346	156	684	138	237	29	6	.520	$15.9	4	60	.335
1891	Brooklyn (N)	0	41	.294	124	521	89	153	52	4	.409	$6.7	0	39	.277
1892	Brooklyn (N)	8	47	.292	152	631	110	184	36	2	.393	$9.4	1	47	.265
1893	New York (N)	12	73	.317	161	701	123	222	61	4	.466	$13.3	2	77	.328
1894	New York (N)	0	64	.230	161	639	83	147	40	3	.302	$7.2	0	77	.265
	Career	219	1,121	.283	2,560	10,718	1,784	3,031	668	75	.420	$223.3	26	867	.275
	Average season	13	66	.283	151	630	105	178	39	4	.420	$13.1	2	51	.275
	Summit season	23	70	.314	156	678	126	213	32	3	.472	$14.9	3	57	.314

ZACK WHEAT

		ADJUSTED REGULAR SEASON											ACTUAL RESULTS		
YEAR	TEAM	HR	RBI	BA	G	AB	R	H	2B	3B	SA	PAY	HR	RBI	BA
1909	Brooklyn (N)	0	5	.340	27	106	21	36	23	2	.594	$0.6	0	4	.304
1910	Brooklyn (N)	18	70	.307	162	629	100	193	70	7	.526	$7.0	2	55	.284
1911	Brooklyn (N)	24	85	.289	147	561	61	162	33	5	.494	$7.1	5	76	.287
1912	Brooklyn (N)	29	73	.305	130	479	79	146	22	2	.541	$7.1	8	65	.305
1913	Brooklyn (N)	30	73	.312	147	570	80	178	30	3	.533	$9.4	7	58	.301
1914	Brooklyn (N)	34	114	.338	153	562	85	190	25	3	.575	$11.4	9	89	.319
1915	Brooklyn (N)	26	86	.276	154	557	83	154	18	4	.463	$11.5	5	66	.258
1916	Brooklyn (N)	40	101	.338	155	591	105	200	30	3	.602	$14.3	9	73	.312
1917	Brooklyn (N)	12	56	.339	113	375	52	127	33	7	.560	$5.2	1	41	.312
1918	Brooklyn (N)	0	86	.356	135	526	66	187	70	5	.508	$6.7	0	51	.335
1919	Brooklyn (N)	27	88	.305	157	614	100	187	31	4	.500	$9.9	5	62	.297
1920	Brooklyn (N)	32	86	.319	155	611	105	195	26	4	.532	$9.3	9	73	.328
1921	Brooklyn (N)	33	93	.297	158	606	100	180	27	3	.515	$9.5	14	85	.320
1922	Brooklyn (N)	35	120	.312	159	628	98	196	28	4	.537	$10.1	16	112	.335
1923	Brooklyn (N)	19	70	.355	102	363	68	129	13	2	.559	$3.9	8	65	.375
1924	Brooklyn (N)	35	106	.352	148	594	101	209	36	2	.596	$9.0	14	97	.375
1925	Brooklyn (N)	33	107	.331	159	653	130	216	43	6	.567	$12.9	14	103	.359
1926	Brooklyn (N)	14	39	.277	116	430	75	119	30	1	.449	$3.5	5	35	.290
1927	Philadelphia (A)	4	41	.306	92	258	37	79	18	0	.422	$2.2	1	38	.324
	Career	445	1,499	.317	2,569	9,713	1,546	3,083	606	67	.531	$150.6	132	1,248	.317
	Average season	23	79	.317	135	511	81	162	32	4	.531	$7.9	7	66	.317
	Summit season	28	89	.344	134	497	82	171	27	3	.579	$8.8	8	73	.338

BILLY WILLIAMS

		ADJUSTED REGULAR SEASON											ACTUAL RESULTS		
YEAR	TEAM	HR	RBI	BA	G	AB	R	H	2B	3B	SA	PAY	HR	RBI	BA
1959	Chicago (N)	0	2	.171	19	35	0	6	0	1	.229	$0.0	0	2	.152
1960	Chicago (N)	3	8	.298	12	47	5	14	0	1	.532	$0.0	2	7	.277
1961	Chicago (N)	30	97	.289	152	551	85	159	26	5	.517	$5.8	25	86	.278
1962	Chicago (N)	26	101	.311	159	618	104	192	30	6	.505	$9.3	22	91	.298
1963	Chicago (N)	32	118	.312	161	612	108	191	50	7	.574	$14.7	25	95	.286
1964	Chicago (N)	39	119	.335	162	645	122	216	50	2	.600	$19.6	33	98	.312
1965	Chicago (N)	42	131	.345	162	637	139	220	50	5	.637	$25.7	34	108	.315
1966	Chicago (N)	36	112	.299	162	648	123	194	31	4	.526	$26.0	29	91	.276
1967	Chicago (N)	42	109	.308	162	634	119	195	28	9	.579	$22.5	28	84	.278
1968	Chicago (N)	47	138	.328	162	638	128	209	39	6	.629	$22.7	30	98	.288
1969	Chicago (N)	28	113	.318	162	638	123	203	46	9	.550	$17.0	21	95	.293
1970	Chicago (N)	49	146	.341	161	636	155	217	43	3	.649	$20.5	42	129	.322
1971	Chicago (N)	38	116	.325	157	594	108	193	34	5	.591	$13.8	28	93	.301
1972	Chicago (N)	54	167	.367	156	597	130	219	44	5	.729	$19.5	37	122	.333
1973	Chicago (N)	26	101	.302	157	580	85	175	28	2	.491	$13.0	20	86	.288
1974	Chicago (N)	23	81	.292	117	404	65	118	26	0	.527	$4.5	16	68	.280
1975	Oakland (A)	31	94	.256	155	520	79	133	21	1	.479	$6.6	23	81	.244
1976	Oakland (A)	17	51	.223	121	354	44	79	13	0	.404	$2.4	11	41	.211
	Career	563	1,804	.312	2,499	9,388	1,722	2,933	559	71	.567	$243.6	426	1,475	.290
	Average season	31	100	.312	139	522	96	163	31	4	.567	$13.5	24	82	.290
	Summit season	46	140	.342	161	631	135	216	45	4	.645	$21.6	35	111	.313

TED WILLIAMS

				ADJUSTED REGULAR SEASON									ACTUAL RESULTS		
YEAR	TEAM	HR	RBI	BA	G	AB	R	H	2B	3B	SA	PAY	HR	RBI	BA
1939	Boston (A)	51	160	.320	159	603	145	193	40	5	.657	$32.6	31	145	.327
1940	Boston (A)	39	127	.347	151	588	151	204	45	7	.646	$31.5	23	113	.344
1941	Boston (A)	57	139	.417	149	475	157	198	27	1	.838	$26.0	37	120	.406
1942	Boston (A)	65	178	.381	160	557	183	212	30	2	.792	$39.2	36	137	.356
1946	Boston (A)	64	158	.361	156	535	182	193	33	4	.796	$38.7	38	123	.342
1947	Boston (A)	49	133	.354	161	545	146	193	44	4	.719	$29.3	32	114	.343
1948	Boston (A)	38	143	.379	143	531	140	201	47	2	.689	$23.8	25	127	.369
1949	Boston (A)	59	179	.351	162	592	168	208	41	2	.726	$36.0	43	159	.343
1950	Boston (A)	34	105	.320	94	353	89	113	26	1	.688	$7.3	28	97	.317
1951	Boston (A)	41	145	.329	156	560	126	184	33	3	.618	$20.2	30	126	.318
1952	Boston (A)	2	4	.400	6	10	2	4	0	1	1.200	$2.1	1	3	.400
1953	Boston (A)	15	39	.417	39	96	19	40	7	0	.958	$1.8	13	34	.407
1954	Boston (A)	36	104	.356	122	402	109	143	26	1	.694	$4.4	29	89	.345
1955	Boston (A)	33	95	.372	103	336	88	125	28	2	.762	$2.5	28	83	.356
1956	Boston (A)	28	94	.359	142	418	82	150	37	1	.653	$4.3	24	82	.345
1957	Boston (A)	45	106	.407	139	442	117	180	35	1	.796	$6.9	38	87	.388
1958	Boston (A)	31	102	.342	135	430	97	147	29	1	.630	$6.5	26	85	.328
1959	Boston (A)	12	51	.267	108	285	38	76	19	0	.460	$2.5	10	43	.254
1960	Boston (A)	35	86	.334	119	326	67	109	18	0	.712	$3.3	29	72	.316
	Career	734	2,148	.355	2,404	8,084	2,106	2,873	565	38	.707	$318.9	521	1,839	.344
	Average season	39	113	.355	127	425	111	151	30	2	.707	$16.8	27	97	.344
	Summit season	53	135	.388	141	469	145	182	31	2	.802	$22.7	35	110	.369

MAURY WILLS

				ADJUSTED REGULAR SEASON									ACTUAL RESULTS		
YEAR	TEAM	HR	RBI	BA	G	AB	R	H	2B	3B	SA	PAY	HR	RBI	BA
1959	Los Angeles (N)	0	8	.271	86	251	31	68	9	2	.323	$1.6	0	7	.260
1960	Los Angeles (N)	0	32	.311	156	544	90	169	24	2	.362	$4.8	0	27	.295
1961	Los Angeles (N)	1	35	.294	156	646	120	190	20	10	.361	$6.8	1	31	.282
1962	Los Angeles (N)	9	52	.312	162	682	141	213	21	9	.409	$9.8	6	48	.299
1963	Los Angeles (N)	0	42	.329	133	523	102	172	33	3	.403	$6.7	0	34	.302
1964	Los Angeles (N)	3	41	.294	156	622	97	183	26	5	.367	$6.8	2	34	.275
1965	Los Angeles (N)	0	40	.314	158	650	113	204	27	7	.377	$7.2	0	33	.286
1966	Los Angeles (N)	1	48	.295	143	594	73	175	26	1	.347	$4.7	1	39	.273
1967	Pittsburgh (N)	6	58	.335	148	612	118	205	25	10	.438	$6.9	3	45	.302
1968	Pittsburgh (N)	0	43	.316	152	623	107	197	32	9	.396	$6.5	0	31	.278
1969	Mon.-L.A. (N)	7	56	.297	151	623	96	185	18	9	.388	$6.6	4	47	.274
1970	Los Angeles (N)	0	39	.285	133	526	88	150	31	2	.352	$4.2	0	34	.270
1971	Los Angeles (N)	5	55	.303	149	601	91	182	25	4	.383	$4.6	3	44	.281
1972	Los Angeles (N)	0	5	.145	74	138	22	20	5	1	.196	$1.2	0	4	.129
	Career	32	554	.303	1,957	7,635	1,289	2,313	322	74	.377	$78.4	20	458	.281
	Average season	2	40	.303	140	545	92	165	23	5	.377	$5.6	1	33	.281
	Summit season	3	47	.320	151	618	116	198	28	8	.406	$7.4	2	38	.293

HACK WILSON

YEAR	TEAM	ADJUSTED REGULAR SEASON HR	RBI	BA	G	AB	R	H	2B	3B	SA	PAY	ACTUAL RESULTS HR	RBI	BA
1923	New York (N)	0	0	.200	3	10	0	2	0	0	.200	$0.0	0	0	.200
1924	New York (N)	25	63	.277	113	404	68	112	17	4	.525	$3.7	10	57	.295
1925	New York (N)	11	31	.219	66	192	29	42	6	1	.432	$2.5	6	30	.239
1926	Chicago (N)	43	120	.309	148	551	107	170	25	2	.595	$9.0	21	109	.321
1927	Chicago (N)	56	143	.301	155	585	132	176	20	3	.632	$15.3	30	129	.318
1928	Chicago (N)	52	133	.301	153	549	98	165	22	3	.636	$14.7	31	120	.313
1929	Chicago (N)	54	160	.322	156	597	136	192	20	1	.630	$22.7	39	159	.345
1930	Chicago (N)	70	181	.324	161	608	139	197	23	1	.711	$28.8	56	190	.356
1931	Chicago (N)	24	66	.252	116	409	72	103	16	1	.472	$9.1	13	61	.261
1932	Brooklyn (N)	38	135	.289	142	506	84	146	29	2	.579	$9.4	23	123	.297
1933	Brooklyn (N)	18	63	.266	121	372	47	99	11	1	.446	$3.8	9	54	.267
1934	Bkn.-Phi. (N)	9	33	.238	78	202	26	48	4	0	.391	$2.0	6	30	.245
	Career	400	1,128	.291	1,412	4,985	938	1,452	193	19	.578	$121.0	244	1,062	.307
	Average season	33	94	.291	118	415	78	121	16	2	.578	$10.1	20	89	.307
	Summit season	55	147	.311	155	578	122	180	22	2	.642	$18.1	35	141	.331

DAVE WINFIELD

YEAR	TEAM	ADJUSTED REGULAR SEASON HR	RBI	BA	G	AB	R	H	2B	3B	SA	PAY	ACTUAL RESULTS HR	RBI	BA
1973	San Diego (N)	4	14	.291	56	141	10	41	5	1	.426	$0.7	3	12	.277
1974	San Diego (N)	29	89	.277	145	498	68	138	22	4	.512	$5.3	20	75	.265
1975	San Diego (N)	22	89	.279	143	509	86	142	24	2	.464	$7.4	15	76	.267
1976	San Diego (N)	23	85	.297	137	492	99	146	32	3	.514	$8.9	13	69	.283
1977	San Diego (N)	30	102	.280	157	615	115	172	33	5	.496	$15.1	25	92	.275
1978	San Diego (N)	34	115	.322	158	587	104	189	33	4	.566	$14.9	24	97	.308
1979	San Diego (N)	43	131	.313	160	601	108	188	30	7	.601	$19.1	34	118	.308
1980	San Diego (N)	28	100	.281	161	555	102	156	27	4	.495	$12.4	20	87	.276
1981	New York (A)	30	126	.310	159	588	96	182	43	1	.539	$12.7	13	68	.294
1982	New York (A)	46	122	.288	140	539	97	155	26	6	.614	$11.8	37	106	.280
1983	New York (A)	41	133	.291	152	598	113	174	28	6	.564	$13.0	32	116	.283
1984	New York (A)	26	116	.353	141	567	123	200	40	3	.571	$10.0	19	100	.340
1985	New York (A)	32	130	.287	156	637	120	183	39	5	.515	$13.9	26	114	.275
1986	New York (A)	28	116	.273	154	565	100	154	35	5	.501	$10.1	24	104	.262
1987	New York (A)	28	102	.282	156	575	87	162	24	1	.473	$9.3	27	97	.275
1988	New York (A)	34	128	.341	150	563	115	192	40	2	.600	$9.5	25	107	.322
1990	N.Y.-Cal. (A)	27	90	.278	132	475	81	132	22	2	.503	$6.4	21	78	.267
1991	California (A)	35	98	.276	150	568	85	157	29	4	.526	$6.8	28	86	.262
1992	Toronto (A)	36	129	.305	156	583	110	178	34	3	.559	$9.6	26	108	.290
1993	Minnesota (A)	25	81	.274	143	547	77	150	28	2	.470	$6.4	21	76	.271
1994	Minnesota (A)	15	62	.250	110	420	50	105	22	4	.429	$3.3	10	43	.252
1995	Cleveland (A)	2	5	.192	52	130	13	25	7	0	.292	$1.4	2	4	.191
	Career	618	2,163	.293	3,068	11,353	1,959	3,321	623	74	.524	$208.0	465	1,833	.283
	Average season	28	98	.293	139	516	89	151	28	3	.524	$9.5	21	83	.283
	Summit season	37	122	.324	150	571	109	185	34	4	.592	$13.1	28	106	.312

JIM WYNN

		ADJUSTED REGULAR SEASON											ACTUAL RESULTS		
YEAR	TEAM	HR	RBI	BA	G	AB	R	H	2B	3B	SA	PAY	HR	RBI	BA
1963	Houston (N)	5	33	.268	70	250	38	67	15	4	.420	$3.0	4	27	.244
1964	Houston (N)	6	22	.242	67	219	23	53	9	0	.365	$2.4	5	18	.224
1965	Houston (N)	28	89	.301	157	564	110	170	40	5	.539	$8.7	22	73	.275
1966	Houston (N)	21	75	.278	104	414	75	115	27	1	.500	$5.9	18	62	.256
1967	Houston (N)	50	139	.276	158	594	132	164	35	2	.594	$15.4	37	107	.249
1968	Houston (N)	40	95	.306	156	542	120	166	30	4	.598	$15.3	26	67	.269
1969	Houston (N)	41	104	.291	149	495	136	144	22	1	.588	$18.6	33	87	.269
1970	Houston (N)	31	100	.298	157	554	93	165	40	2	.545	$15.6	27	88	.282
1971	Houston (N)	10	56	.218	123	404	47	88	22	0	.347	$6.0	7	45	.203
1972	Houston (N)	36	126	.302	154	576	164	174	39	3	.568	$17.0	24	90	.273
1973	Houston (N)	26	64	.231	139	481	105	111	17	5	.449	$9.4	20	55	.220
1974	Los Angeles (N)	43	129	.284	150	535	124	152	19	3	.572	$10.1	32	108	.271
1975	Los Angeles (N)	24	68	.257	130	412	93	106	17	0	.473	$7.1	18	58	.248
1976	Atlanta (N)	25	81	.218	148	449	92	98	20	1	.434	$7.1	17	66	.207
1977	N.Y.-Mil. (A)	1	14	.180	66	194	19	35	8	1	.247	$2.0	1	13	.175
	Career	387	1,195	.271	1,928	6,683	1,371	1,808	360	32	.508	$143.6	291	964	.250
	Average season	26	80	.271	129	446	91	121	24	2	.508	$9.6	19	64	.250
	Summit season	42	119	.292	153	548	135	160	29	3	.586	$15.3	30	92	.266

CARL YASTRZEMSKI

		ADJUSTED REGULAR SEASON											ACTUAL RESULTS		
YEAR	TEAM	HR	RBI	BA	G	AB	R	H	2B	3B	SA	PAY	HR	RBI	BA
1961	Boston (A)	12	86	.276	147	579	76	160	40	4	.421	$9.6	11	80	.266
1962	Boston (A)	22	105	.309	162	654	111	202	57	4	.509	$18.5	19	94	.296
1963	Boston (A)	18	85	.352	152	574	114	202	55	2	.549	$15.4	14	68	.321
1964	Boston (A)	20	81	.310	151	567	94	176	40	7	.511	$14.4	15	67	.289
1965	Boston (A)	24	88	.342	133	494	96	169	58	2	.613	$11.8	20	72	.312
1966	Boston (A)	19	98	.301	160	594	99	179	52	1	.488	$15.4	16	80	.278
1967	Boston (A)	59	157	.363	161	579	145	210	38	3	.744	$19.8	44	121	.326
1968	Boston (A)	35	105	.341	157	539	127	184	42	2	.622	$16.5	23	74	.301
1969	Boston (A)	49	133	.277	162	603	115	167	36	2	.587	$22.3	40	111	.255
1970	Boston (A)	46	115	.348	161	566	142	197	36	0	.655	$22.9	40	102	.329
1971	Boston (A)	21	88	.274	148	508	94	139	28	2	.461	$9.6	15	70	.254
1972	Boston (A)	19	94	.291	131	477	97	139	25	2	.472	$7.3	12	68	.264
1973	Boston (A)	25	111	.311	152	540	96	168	32	4	.524	$9.8	19	95	.296
1974	Boston (A)	23	94	.315	148	515	111	162	31	2	.517	$9.3	15	79	.301
1975	Boston (A)	21	71	.280	151	550	107	154	36	1	.464	$8.8	14	60	.269
1976	Boston (A)	33	125	.282	155	546	87	154	24	2	.515	$8.9	21	102	.267
1977	Boston (A)	33	114	.301	151	562	110	169	30	2	.537	$9.2	28	102	.296
1978	Boston (A)	24	95	.289	143	519	82	150	23	2	.480	$6.7	17	81	.277
1979	Boston (A)	26	97	.274	149	525	77	144	31	1	.486	$6.6	21	87	.270
1980	Boston (A)	20	58	.278	106	367	57	102	22	1	.507	$3.2	15	50	.275
1981	Boston (A)	17	98	.257	137	509	66	131	25	1	.411	$4.3	7	53	.246
1982	Boston (A)	20	83	.283	131	459	61	130	24	1	.471	$3.3	16	72	.275
1983	Boston (A)	13	64	.274	119	380	43	104	27	0	.447	$2.4	10	56	.266
	Career	599	2,245	.302	3,367	12,206	2,207	3,692	812	48	.524	$256.0	452	1,844	.285
	Average season	26	98	.302	146	531	96	161	35	2	.524	$11.1	20	80	.285
	Summit season	36	110	.349	153	550	125	192	46	2	.636	$17.3	28	87	.318

ROSS YOUNGS

		ADJUSTED REGULAR SEASON											ACTUAL RESULTS		
YEAR	TEAM	HR	RBI	BA	G	AB	R	H	2B	3B	SA	PAY	HR	RBI	BA
1917	New York (N)	0	1	.385	7	26	7	10	7	2	.808	$0.0	0	1	.346
1918	New York (N)	17	43	.320	158	619	121	198	46	6	.496	$6.0	1	25	.302
1919	New York (N)	14	62	.319	150	564	105	180	57	4	.509	$8.0	2	43	.311
1920	New York (N)	27	92	.342	160	608	109	208	34	5	.548	$14.3	6	78	.351
1921	New York (N)	13	111	.302	149	533	98	161	40	9	.484	$14.3	3	102	.327
1922	New York (N)	20	91	.309	155	582	112	180	41	4	.497	$14.9	7	86	.331
1923	New York (N)	12	95	.319	161	631	133	201	55	7	.485	$19.8	3	87	.336
1924	New York (N)	28	81	.334	140	554	123	185	34	4	.561	$15.4	10	74	.356
1925	New York (N)	15	55	.243	139	535	86	130	26	3	.387	$11.9	6	53	.264
1926	New York (N)	13	49	.293	102	399	70	117	14	2	.436	$5.7	4	43	.306
	Career	159	680	.311	1,321	5,051	964	1,570	354	46	.494	$110.3	42	592	.322
	Average season	16	68	.311	132	505	96	157	35	5	.494	$11.0	4	59	.322
	Summit season	21	74	.325	153	585	114	190	42	5	.521	$11.7	5	61	.331

ROBIN YOUNT

		ADJUSTED REGULAR SEASON											ACTUAL RESULTS		
YEAR	TEAM	HR	RBI	BA	G	AB	R	H	2B	3B	SA	PAY	HR	RBI	BA
1974	Milwaukee (A)	6	31	.262	107	344	57	90	22	5	.407	$3.8	3	26	.250
1975	Milwaukee (A)	12	60	.280	147	558	78	156	36	2	.416	$6.3	8	52	.267
1976	Milwaukee (A)	6	66	.266	162	642	73	171	35	3	.358	$8.9	2	54	.252
1977	Milwaukee (A)	5	54	.293	154	605	73	177	43	3	.398	$7.8	4	49	.288
1978	Milwaukee (A)	15	84	.305	127	502	78	153	29	8	.484	$7.8	9	71	.293
1979	Milwaukee (A)	12	56	.270	150	581	80	157	32	4	.401	$8.8	8	51	.267
1980	Milwaukee (A)	32	100	.298	143	611	140	182	55	8	.571	$14.6	23	87	.293
1981	Milwaukee (A)	24	89	.288	143	562	91	162	27	6	.486	$11.8	10	49	.273
1982	Milwaukee (A)	38	130	.341	155	631	148	215	53	10	.637	$19.7	29	114	.331
1983	Milwaukee (A)	24	91	.318	149	578	116	184	48	8	.554	$18.6	17	80	.308
1984	Milwaukee (A)	23	93	.309	161	628	123	194	33	6	.490	$16.6	16	80	.298
1985	Milwaukee (A)	19	78	.289	123	470	87	136	29	3	.485	$9.4	15	68	.277
1986	Milwaukee (A)	11	52	.327	141	526	92	172	37	7	.487	$9.1	9	46	.312
1987	Milwaukee (A)	22	108	.320	158	635	104	203	28	8	.493	$13.0	21	103	.312
1988	Milwaukee (A)	19	108	.324	162	621	109	201	45	11	.523	$10.0	13	91	.306
1989	Milwaukee (A)	30	122	.337	160	614	120	207	44	8	.581	$13.2	21	103	.318
1990	Milwaukee (A)	23	89	.257	158	587	113	151	19	5	.424	$12.9	17	77	.247
1991	Milwaukee (A)	13	88	.274	130	503	75	138	24	4	.416	$6.5	10	77	.260
1992	Milwaukee (A)	13	92	.278	150	557	84	155	47	3	.443	$6.7	8	77	.264
1993	Milwaukee (A)	10	55	.262	127	454	66	119	27	3	.401	$3.5	8	51	.258
	Career	357	1,646	.296	2,907	11,209	1,907	3,323	713	115	.476	$209.0	251	1,406	.285
	Average season	18	82	.296	145	560	95	166	36	6	.476	$10.5	13	70	.285
	Summit season	29	110	.324	154	611	127	198	49	9	.576	$15.2	21	95	.311

7 ○ The Pitcher Register

Now it's the pitchers' turn. This chapter provides season-by-season statistics for 177 great pitchers. I have included everyone who met any of these criteria (using actual, not adjusted, career totals):

○ Member of the Hall of Fame
○ Most Valuable Player in any season since 1901
○ Cy Young Award–winner in any season since 1901
○ 1,000 games pitched
○ 600 games started
○ 250 wins
○ 300 saves

I have also made room for a few special cases, just as I did in the previous chapter. Pitchers like Lew Burdette, Elroy Face, Jerry Koosman, Dick Radatz, and Luis Tiant qualified for *Total Baseball*'s list of the 400 greatest players ever, so they're included here, too, even though they didn't meet my basic criteria.

The records in this chapter are arranged alphabetically from Rick Aguilera to Cy Young. Each season's numbers have been adjusted to reflect 1996–2000 performance levels over a 162-game schedule.

A pitcher's entry contains eleven adjusted figures for each big-league season, followed by his actual number of wins, losses, and saves, and his actual earned run average for that year. These are the columns from left to right:

BASIC INFORMATION

Year

Team, followed by **league abbreviation**: American Association (AA), American League (A), Federal League (F), National League (N), Players League (P), and Union Association (U)

ADJUSTED STATISTICS

W: Wins

L: Losses

SV: Saves

ERA: Earned run average

G: Games pitched

IP: Innings pitched

ER: Earned runs allowed

H: Hits allowed

BB: Walks

SO: Strikeouts

Pay: Estimated value of pitcher's performance (in millions of Year 2001 dollars)

ACTUAL STATISTICS

W: Wins

L: Losses

SV: Saves

ERA: Earned run average

Each pitcher's entry begins with three lines in bold type. The first row provides career totals for all adjusted and actual statistics. The second line has career averages, determined by dividing career totals by the pitcher's number of seasons. The third line has "summit" figures, the average statistics for his five best seasons, showing what he was like at his peak. (I developed a point system that took into account a pitcher's adjusted wins, saves, and ERA in each season when he had at least 54 adjusted innings pitched, the equivalent of one-third of an inning per game in a 162-game season. The five years with the highest point totals were defined as a pitcher's summit years.)

RICK AGUILERA

YEAR	TEAM	ADJUSTED REGULAR SEASON W	L	SV	ERA	G	IP	ER	H	BB	SO	PAY	ACTUAL RESULTS W	L	SV	ERA
1985	New York (N)	10	7	0	3.84	21	122	52	125	40	90	$5.4	10	7	0	3.24
1986	New York (N)	10	7	0	4.50	28	142	71	154	38	115	$5.7	10	7	0	3.88
1987	New York (N)	11	3	0	3.83	18	115	49	128	34	84	$5.4	11	3	0	3.60
1988	New York (N)	0	4	0	8.64	11	25	24	32	12	19	$1.2	0	4	0	6.93
1989	N.Y. (N)-Minn. (A)	9	11	7	3.48	47	145	56	140	42	156	$5.9	9	11	7	2.79
1990	Minnesota (A)	5	3	31	3.32	56	65	24	58	20	69	$4.5	5	3	32	2.76
1991	Minnesota (A)	4	5	40	2.74	63	69	21	47	32	68	$4.8	4	5	42	2.35
1992	Minnesota (A)	2	6	40	3.49	64	67	26	65	19	60	$4.9	2	6	41	2.84
1993	Minnesota (A)	4	3	32	3.38	65	72	27	61	15	65	$4.4	4	3	34	3.11
1994	Minnesota (A)	1	6	34	3.66	63	64	26	81	15	69	$4.1	1	4	23	3.63
1995	Minn.-Bos. (A)	3	3	37	2.71	59	63	19	53	15	61	$4.0	3	3	32	2.60
1996	Minnesota (A)	8	6	0	5.35	19	111	66	123	27	83	$4.5	8	6	0	5.42
1997	Minnesota (A)	5	4	26	3.97	61	68	30	65	23	67	$3.2	5	4	26	3.82
1998	Minnesota (A)	4	9	37	4.38	68	74	36	76	16	56	$3.2	4	9	38	4.24
1999	Minn. (A)-Chi. (N)	9	4	13	2.91	61	68	22	54	12	46	$2.7	9	4	14	2.93
2000	Chicago (N)	1	2	29	4.69	54	48	25	47	17	38	$2.3	1	2	29	4.91
	Career	86	83	326	3.92	758	1,318	574	1,309	377	1,146	$66.2	86	81	318	3.57
	Average season	5	5	20	3.92	47	82	36	82	24	72	$4.1	5	5	20	3.57
	Summit season	5	4	32	3.00	61	66	22	55	20	61	$4.2	5	4	32	2.69

PETE ALEXANDER

YEAR	TEAM	ADJUSTED REGULAR SEASON W	L	SV	ERA	G	IP	ER	H	BB	SO	PAY	ACTUAL RESULTS W	L	SV	ERA
1911	Philadelphia (N)	30	14	6	3.48	51	390	151	315	154	378	$60.0	28	13	3	2.57
1912	Philadelphia (N)	20	18	8	3.81	49	331	140	317	127	326	$52.3	19	17	3	2.81
1913	Philadelphia (N)	22	8	8	4.17	48	313	145	321	93	274	$42.1	22	8	2	2.79
1914	Philadelphia (N)	28	16	2	3.75	48	370	154	381	95	351	$55.3	27	15	1	2.38
1915	Philadelphia (N)	33	11	6	1.92	52	399	85	304	81	415	$60.1	31	10	3	1.22
1916	Philadelphia (N)	34	13	3	2.60	50	405	117	387	66	299	$59.7	33	12	3	1.55
1917	Philadelphia (N)	31	14	0	3.11	47	405	140	401	75	380	$61.0	30	13	0	1.83
1918	Chicago (N)	3	1	0	2.83	4	35	11	29	5	41	$4.3	2	1	0	1.73
1919	Chicago (N)	19	13	2	2.56	35	274	78	223	59	282	$30.6	16	11	1	1.72
1920	Chicago (N)	28	15	5	2.49	48	379	105	346	93	378	$51.6	27	14	5	1.91
1921	Chicago (N)	16	14	2	3.83	33	268	114	280	45	189	$18.4	15	13	1	3.39
1922	Chicago (N)	16	13	3	4.09	34	253	115	272	42	121	$18.1	16	13	1	3.63
1923	Chicago (N)	23	13	4	3.64	41	321	130	306	36	180	$30.2	22	12	2	3.19

(Pete Alexander, continued)

		ADJUSTED REGULAR SEASON											ACTUAL RESULTS			
YEAR	TEAM	W	L	SV	ERA	G	IP	ER	H	BB	SO	PAY	W	L	SV	ERA
1924	Chicago (N)	13	5	0	3.41	22	177	67	179	31	88	$7.0	12	5	0	3.03
1925	Chicago (N)	16	12	0	3.59	34	251	100	261	35	162	$16.3	15	11	0	3.39
1926	Chi.-St.L. (N)	12	10	5	3.57	31	207	82	191	36	118	$7.5	12	10	2	3.05
1927	St. Louis (N)	22	11	5	2.84	39	282	89	262	47	126	$17.3	21	10	3	2.52
1928	St. Louis (N)	17	10	4	3.84	36	258	110	267	45	146	$16.7	16	9	2	3.36
1929	St. Louis (N)	9	8	0	3.98	23	138	61	143	26	81	$5.6	9	8	0	3.89
1930	Philadelphia (N)	0	3	0	8.59	9	22	21	36	7	12	$1.3	0	3	0	9.14
	Career	392	222	63	3.31	734	5,478	2,015	5,221	1,198	4,347	$615.4	373	208	32	2.56
	Average season	20	11	3	3.31	37	274	101	261	60	217	$30.8	19	10	2	2.56
	Summit season	31	13	4	2.73	50	396	120	351	94	370	$58.5	30	12	3	1.81

JOHNNY ANTONELLI

		ADJUSTED REGULAR SEASON											ACTUAL RESULTS			
YEAR	TEAM	W	L	SV	ERA	G	IP	ER	H	BB	SO	PAY	W	L	SV	ERA
1948	Boston (N)	0	0	2	2.25	4	4	1	2	3	0	$0.0	0	0	1	2.25
1949	Boston (N)	3	7	0	3.96	23	100	44	106	38	87	$3.1	3	7	0	3.56
1950	Boston (N)	2	3	0	6.20	21	61	42	87	21	56	$1.7	2	3	0	5.93
1953	Milwaukee (N)	12	12	2	3.53	32	181	71	175	74	200	$5.9	12	12	1	3.18
1954	New York (N)	22	7	4	2.68	41	272	81	230	97	246	$19.7	21	7	2	2.30
1955	New York (N)	15	17	2	3.81	40	248	105	229	84	219	$16.2	14	16	1	3.33
1956	New York (N)	21	14	2	3.29	43	271	99	250	77	212	$25.9	20	13	1	2.86
1957	New York (N)	13	19	0	4.48	42	223	111	254	77	163	$15.8	12	18	0	3.77
1958	San Francisco (N)	17	14	5	3.88	43	253	109	239	99	196	$19.7	16	13	3	3.28
1959	San Francisco (N)	20	11	2	3.62	42	296	119	274	86	221	$26.9	19	10	1	3.10
1960	San Francisco (N)	6	7	16	4.50	43	118	59	120	52	76	$6.0	6	7	11	3.77
1961	Cle. (A)-Mil. (N)	1	4	0	7.63	20	59	50	89	22	39	$3.0	1	4	0	6.75
	Career	132	115	35	3.84	394	2,086	891	2,055	730	1,715	$143.9	126	110	21	3.34
	Average season	11	10	3	3.84	33	174	74	171	61	143	$12.0	11	9	2	3.34
	Summit season	19	13	3	3.46	42	268	103	244	89	219	$21.7	18	12	2	2.96

JIM BAGBY

		ADJUSTED REGULAR SEASON											ACTUAL RESULTS			
YEAR	TEAM	W	L	SV	ERA	G	IP	ER	H	BB	SO	PAY	W	L	SV	ERA
1912	Cincinnati (N)	2	1	0	4.24	5	17	8	17	10	15	$0.1	2	1	0	3.12
1916	Cleveland (A)	17	18	11	4.40	50	284	139	304	89	162	$15.7	16	17	5	2.61
1917	Cleveland (A)	24	14	11	3.34	51	334	124	330	99	169	$32.5	23	13	7	1.96
1918	Cleveland (A)	22	20	13	4.50	57	344	172	389	126	172	$34.0	17	16	6	2.72
1919	Cleveland (A)	20	13	6	4.17	41	283	131	322	69	159	$27.5	17	11	3	2.80
1920	Cleveland (A)	32	13	0	3.81	50	354	150	349	107	177	$52.0	31	12	0	2.89
1921	Cleveland (A)	15	13	10	5.33	42	201	119	230	59	95	$14.7	14	12	4	4.70
1922	Cleveland (A)	4	5	5	7.15	26	102	81	130	49	62	$4.8	4	5	1	6.32
1923	Pittsburgh (N)	3	2	10	6.00	22	72	48	94	31	40	$3.3	3	2	3	5.24
	Career	139	99	66	4.39	344	1,991	972	2,165	639	1,051	$184.6	127	89	29	3.11
	Average season	15	11	7	4.39	38	221	108	241	71	117	$20.5	14	10	3	3.11
	Summit season	23	16	8	4.02	50	320	143	339	98	168	$32.3	21	14	4	2.58

RED BARRETT

		ADJUSTED REGULAR SEASON											ACTUAL RESULTS			
YEAR	TEAM	W	L	SV	ERA	G	IP	ER	H	BB	SO	PAY	W	L	SV	ERA
1937	Cincinnati (N)	0	0	0	1.50	1	6	1	5	2	2	$0.0	0	0	0	1.42
1938	Cincinnati (N)	2	0	0	3.41	6	29	11	27	15	11	$0.0	2	0	0	3.14
1939	Cincinnati (N)	0	0	0	1.80	2	5	1	5	1	2	$0.0	0	0	0	1.69
1940	Cincinnati (N)	1	0	0	9.00	3	3	3	6	1	0	$0.0	1	0	0	6.75
1943	Boston (N)	13	19	0	4.33	40	268	129	273	71	134	$8.3	12	18	0	3.18
1944	Boston (N)	9	17	6	5.30	44	241	142	280	74	118	$8.0	9	16	2	4.06
1945	Bos.-St.L. (N)	24	13	5	3.82	47	297	126	311	59	163	$20.5	23	12	2	3.00
1946	St. Louis (N)	3	2	7	5.40	24	70	42	84	25	39	$3.6	3	2	2	4.03
1947	Boston (N)	12	13	2	4.18	38	222	103	219	53	103	$8.3	11	12	1	3.55
1948	Boston (N)	7	8	0	4.04	36	136	61	143	25	77	$4.6	7	8	0	3.65
1949	Boston (N)	1	1	0	6.26	24	46	32	62	9	32	$1.3	1	1	0	5.68
	Career	72	73	20	4.43	265	1,323	651	1,415	335	681	$54.6	69	69	7	3.53
	Average season	7	7	2	4.43	24	120	59	129	30	62	$5.0	6	6	1	3.53
	Summit season	13	14	3	4.33	41	233	112	245	56	119	$9.9	12	13	1	3.44

STEVE BEDROSIAN

		ADJUSTED REGULAR SEASON											ACTUAL RESULTS			
YEAR	TEAM	W	L	SV	ERA	G	IP	ER	H	BB	SO	PAY	W	L	SV	ERA
1981	Atlanta (N)	2	3	0	5.59	23	37	23	25	26	20	$0.5	1	2	0	4.44
1982	Atlanta (N)	8	6	13	2.87	64	138	44	107	65	154	$5.4	8	6	11	2.42
1983	Atlanta (N)	9	10	21	4.28	70	120	57	105	57	139	$7.8	9	10	19	3.60
1984	Atlanta (N)	9	6	12	2.89	40	84	27	68	38	96	$5.4	9	6	11	2.37
1985	Atlanta (N)	7	15	0	4.52	37	207	104	211	121	163	$8.4	7	15	0	3.83
1986	Philadelphia (N)	8	6	30	3.90	68	90	39	83	36	90	$7.6	8	6	29	3.39
1987	Philadelphia (N)	5	3	41	3.03	65	89	30	81	29	80	$7.6	5	3	40	2.83
1988	Philadelphia (N)	6	6	28	4.62	57	74	38	81	31	70	$5.3	6	6	28	3.75
1989	Phi.-S.F. (N)	3	7	22	3.60	68	85	34	61	44	68	$4.6	3	7	23	2.87
1990	San Francisco (N)	9	9	15	5.01	68	79	44	76	48	49	$3.9	9	9	17	4.20
1991	Minnesota (A)	5	3	5	5.14	56	77	44	75	38	49	$3.3	5	3	6	4.42
1993	Atlanta (N)	5	2	0	1.80	49	50	10	35	15	37	$1.7	5	2	0	1.63
1994	Atlanta (N)	0	3	0	3.32	65	65	24	58	26	64	$1.8	0	2	0	3.33
1995	Atlanta (N)	1	2	0	6.19	33	32	22	46	14	26	$0.4	1	2	0	6.11
	Career	77	81	187	3.96	763	1,227	540	1,112	588	1,105	$63.7	76	79	184	3.38
	Average season	6	6	13	3.96	55	88	39	79	42	79	$4.6	5	6	13	3.38
	Summit season	8	6	23	3.38	61	104	39	89	45	112	$6.8	8	6	22	2.92

CHIEF BENDER

		ADJUSTED REGULAR SEASON											ACTUAL RESULTS			
YEAR	TEAM	W	L	SV	ERA	G	IP	ER	H	BB	SO	PAY	W	L	SV	ERA
1903	Philadelphia (A)	20	17	0	4.51	43	323	162	294	114	268	$33.5	17	14	0	3.07
1904	Philadelphia (A)	10	11	0	4.95	30	211	116	194	96	246	$15.6	10	11	0	2.87
1905	Philadelphia (A)	19	12	0	4.57	37	242	123	229	136	240	$19.5	18	11	0	2.83
1906	Philadelphia (A)	16	11	9	4.36	39	258	125	257	73	281	$25.4	15	10	3	2.53

(Chief Bender, continued)

		ADJUSTED REGULAR SEASON											ACTUAL RESULTS			
YEAR	TEAM	W	L	SV	ERA	G	IP	ER	H	BB	SO	PAY	W	L	SV	ERA
1907	Philadelphia (A)	17	9	8	3.77	36	239	100	232	53	216	$19.6	16	8	3	2.05
1908	Philadelphia (A)	8	10	1	3.39	19	146	55	153	34	151	$8.5	8	9	1	1.75
1909	Philadelphia (A)	19	8	5	2.99	36	265	88	243	65	279	$26.0	18	8	1	1.66
1910	Philadelphia (A)	24	5	0	2.62	31	258	75	214	58	257	$26.2	23	5	0	1.58
1911	Philadelphia (A)	18	5	7	2.93	33	230	75	220	69	193	$19.5	17	5	3	2.16
1912	Philadelphia (A)	14	9	5	3.72	29	184	76	187	40	155	$15.5	13	8	2	2.74
1913	Philadelphia (A)	22	11	17	3.26	51	251	91	240	76	239	$27.5	21	10	13	2.21
1914	Philadelphia (A)	18	3	5	3.55	29	185	73	184	68	174	$16.2	17	3	2	2.26
1915	Baltimore (F)	4	17	3	6.28	27	185	129	233	46	155	$9.4	4	16	1	3.99
1916	Philadelphia (N)	7	7	9	6.31	28	127	89	164	45	78	$4.9	7	7	3	3.74
1917	Philadelphia (N)	8	2	6	2.87	21	119	38	101	36	86	$4.5	8	2	2	1.67
1925	Chicago (A)	0	0	0	18.00	1	1	2	1	1	0	$0.1	0	0	0	18.00
	Career	224	137	75	3.96	490	3,224	1,417	3,146	1,010	3,018	$271.9	212	127	34	2.46
	Average season	14	9	5	3.96	31	202	89	197	63	189	$17.0	13	8	2	2.46
	Summit season	20	6	7	3.03	36	238	80	220	67	228	$23.1	19	6	4	1.95

EWELL BLACKWELL

		ADJUSTED REGULAR SEASON											ACTUAL RESULTS			
YEAR	TEAM	W	L	SV	ERA	G	IP	ER	H	BB	SO	PAY	W	L	SV	ERA
1942	Cincinnati (N)	0	0	0	9.00	2	3	3	3	3	2	$0.0	0	0	0	6.00
1946	Cincinnati (N)	9	13	0	3.24	34	200	72	175	82	168	$5.1	9	13	0	2.45
1947	Cincinnati (N)	23	8	0	2.89	35	290	93	250	96	333	$25.5	22	8	0	2.47
1948	Cincinnati (N)	7	9	2	5.03	23	145	81	143	49	189	$7.7	7	9	1	4.54
1949	Cincinnati (N)	5	5	4	4.67	31	79	41	85	31	93	$4.8	5	5	1	4.23
1950	Cincinnati (N)	18	16	6	3.09	42	274	94	215	104	309	$25.8	17	15	4	2.97
1951	Cincinnati (N)	17	16	4	3.89	40	245	106	223	98	213	$16.2	16	15	2	3.44
1952	Cin. (N)-N.Y. (A)	4	12	2	5.83	29	122	79	133	76	88	$5.3	4	12	1	4.73
1953	New York (A)	2	0	2	4.09	9	22	10	19	15	19	$2.1	2	0	1	3.66
1955	Kansas City (A)	0	1	0	6.75	2	4	3	3	5	3	$0.3	0	1	0	6.75
	Career	85	80	20	3.78	247	1,384	582	1,249	559	1,417	$92.8	82	78	10	3.30
	Average season	9	8	2	3.78	25	138	58	125	56	142	$9.3	8	8	1	3.30
	Summit season	15	12	2	3.47	35	231	89	201	86	242	$16.1	14	12	1	3.05

VIDA BLUE

		ADJUSTED REGULAR SEASON											ACTUAL RESULTS			
YEAR	TEAM	W	L	SV	ERA	G	IP	ER	H	BB	SO	PAY	W	L	SV	ERA
1969	Oakland (A)	1	1	1	8.36	12	42	39	54	19	27	$0.5	1	1	1	6.64
1970	Oakland (A)	2	0	0	2.54	6	39	11	22	12	39	$0.8	2	0	0	2.09
1971	Oakland (A)	24	8	0	2.39	39	312	83	231	97	354	$26.2	24	8	0	1.82
1972	Oakland (A)	6	10	0	3.96	26	157	69	139	57	135	$5.6	6	10	0	2.80
1973	Oakland (A)	20	9	0	3.99	37	264	117	228	112	197	$19.2	20	9	0	3.28
1974	Oakland (A)	17	15	0	4.12	40	282	129	258	103	244	$20.6	17	15	0	3.25
1975	Oakland (A)	22	11	1	3.72	39	278	115	258	103	244	$26.1	22	11	1	3.01
1976	Oakland (A)	18	13	0	3.05	37	298	101	289	71	224	$26.9	18	13	0	2.35

(Vida Blue, continued)

YEAR	TEAM	ADJUSTED REGULAR SEASON											ACTUAL RESULTS			
		W	L	SV	ERA	G	IP	ER	H	BB	SO	PAY	W	L	SV	ERA
1977	Oakland (A)	14	19	0	4.40	38	280	137	293	94	199	$20.2	14	19	0	3.83
1978	San Francisco (N)	18	10	0	3.45	35	258	99	248	77	229	$20.3	18	10	0	2.79
1979	San Francisco (N)	14	14	0	5.77	34	237	152	252	123	187	$15.9	14	14	0	5.01
1980	San Francisco (N)	14	10	0	3.54	31	224	88	208	70	175	$15.3	14	10	0	2.97
1981	San Francisco (N)	12	9	0	3.15	26	180	63	151	88	126	$8.1	8	6	0	2.45
1982	Kansas City (A)	13	12	0	4.48	31	181	90	170	91	134	$8.1	13	12	0	3.78
1983	Kansas City (A)	0	5	0	7.09	19	85	67	100	39	67	$3.3	0	5	0	6.01
1985	San Francisco (N)	8	8	0	5.22	33	131	76	122	87	124	$3.6	8	8	0	4.47
1986	San Francisco (N)	10	10	0	3.78	28	157	66	145	82	111	$3.7	10	10	0	3.27
	Career	213	164	2	3.97	511	3,405	1,502	3,172	1,327	2,797	$224.4	209	161	2	3.27
	Average season	13	10	0	3.97	30	200	88	187	78	165	$13.2	12	9	0	3.27
	Summit season	20	10	0	3.29	37	282	103	251	92	250	$23.7	20	10	0	2.62

BERT BLYLEVEN

YEAR	TEAM	ADJUSTED REGULAR SEASON											ACTUAL RESULTS			
		W	L	SV	ERA	G	IP	ER	H	BB	SO	PAY	W	L	SV	ERA
1970	Minnesota (A)	10	9	0	3.73	27	164	68	154	48	151	$7.8	10	9	0	3.18
1971	Minnesota (A)	16	15	0	3.72	38	278	115	296	65	266	$19.5	16	15	0	2.81
1972	Minnesota (A)	18	18	0	3.81	41	302	128	296	82	279	$26.2	17	17	0	2.73
1973	Minnesota (A)	20	17	0	3.07	40	325	111	315	71	316	$32.8	20	17	0	2.52
1974	Minnesota (A)	17	17	0	3.36	37	281	105	260	83	314	$26.7	17	17	0	2.66
1975	Minnesota (A)	15	10	0	3.71	36	284	117	240	90	305	$26.2	15	10	0	3.00
1976	Minn.-Tex. (A)	13	16	0	3.74	36	298	124	306	91	290	$26.0	13	16	0	2.87
1977	Texas (A)	14	12	0	3.10	30	235	81	186	76	226	$16.0	14	12	0	2.72
1978	Pittsburgh (N)	14	10	0	3.76	34	244	102	231	73	241	$16.1	14	10	0	3.03
1979	Pittsburgh (N)	12	5	0	4.14	37	237	109	244	101	228	$15.5	12	5	0	3.60
1980	Pittsburgh (N)	8	13	0	4.56	34	217	110	226	68	222	$9.7	8	13	0	3.82
1981	Cleveland (A)	17	11	0	3.68	31	247	101	242	70	224	$16.2	11	7	0	2.88
1982	Cleveland (A)	2	2	0	5.85	4	20	13	16	12	23	$1.8	2	2	0	4.87
1983	Cleveland (A)	7	10	0	4.62	24	156	80	167	49	152	$4.8	7	10	0	3.91
1984	Cleveland (A)	19	7	0	3.45	33	245	94	213	84	206	$14.6	19	7	0	2.87
1985	Cle.-Minn. (A)	17	16	0	3.70	37	294	121	281	82	250	$18.5	17	16	0	3.16
1986	Minnesota (A)	17	14	0	4.63	36	272	140	278	61	238	$18.5	17	14	0	4.01
1987	Minnesota (A)	15	12	0	4.28	37	267	127	256	105	213	$17.0	15	12	0	4.01
1988	Minnesota (A)	10	17	0	6.65	33	207	153	259	59	169	$7.4	10	17	0	5.43
1989	California (A)	17	5	0	3.36	33	241	90	243	49	153	$13.2	17	5	0	2.73
1990	California (A)	8	7	0	6.25	23	134	93	173	27	80	$3.7	8	7	0	5.24
1992	California (A)	8	12	0	5.82	25	133	86	161	32	83	$3.6	8	12	0	4.74
	Career	294	255	0	4.02	706	5,081	2,268	5,043	1,478	4,629	$341.8	287	250	0	3.31
	Average season	13	12	0	4.02	32	231	103	229	67	210	$15.5	13	11	0	3.31
	Summit season	18	13	0	3.42	37	279	106	265	74	254	$22.7	18	13	0	2.69

ED BRANDT

		ADJUSTED REGULAR SEASON											ACTUAL RESULTS			
YEAR	TEAM	W	L	SV	ERA	G	IP	ER	H	BB	SO	PAY	W	L	SV	ERA
1928	Boston (N)	9	22	0	5.81	40	237	153	237	132	195	$9.4	9	21	0	5.07
1929	Boston (N)	8	14	0	5.64	27	174	109	187	94	118	$5.7	8	13	0	5.53
1930	Boston (N)	4	12	4	4.76	43	155	82	157	71	133	$5.3	4	11	1	5.01
1931	Boston (N)	19	11	3	3.21	34	258	92	223	91	227	$16.3	18	11	2	2.92
1932	Boston (N)	17	17	2	4.35	37	269	130	273	71	174	$16.4	16	16	1	3.97
1933	Boston (N)	19	15	7	3.10	43	302	104	265	96	233	$26.7	18	14	4	2.60
1934	Boston (N)	17	15	9	3.78	43	274	115	251	98	212	$26.3	16	14	5	3.53
1935	Boston (N)	5	20	0	5.39	31	187	112	227	79	131	$8.4	5	19	0	5.00
1936	Brooklyn (N)	11	13	5	3.53	39	240	94	232	70	204	$15.7	11	13	2	3.50
1937	Pittsburgh (N)	12	11	6	3.32	35	187	69	179	74	139	$8.3	11	10	2	3.11
1938	Pittsburgh (N)	5	4	0	3.72	26	104	43	97	38	78	$3.9	5	4	0	3.46
	Career	126	154	36	4.16	398	2,387	1,103	2,328	914	1,844	$142.4	121	146	17	3.86
	Average season	11	14	3	4.16	36	217	100	212	83	168	$12.9	11	13	2	3.86
	Summit season	17	14	5	3.56	38	258	102	238	86	197	$18.8	16	13	3	3.22

TOMMY BRIDGES

		ADJUSTED REGULAR SEASON											ACTUAL RESULTS			
YEAR	TEAM	W	L	SV	ERA	G	IP	ER	H	BB	SO	PAY	W	L	SV	ERA
1930	Detroit (A)	3	2	0	3.79	8	38	16	25	26	33	$1.0	3	2	0	4.06
1931	Detroit (A)	8	17	0	5.56	37	183	113	183	132	206	$5.4	8	16	0	4.99
1932	Detroit (A)	15	13	3	3.68	36	213	87	175	149	219	$9.6	14	12	1	3.36
1933	Detroit (A)	14	12	5	3.71	34	240	99	195	136	248	$15.6	14	12	2	3.09
1934	Detroit (A)	23	12	2	3.91	38	290	126	246	121	284	$27.0	22	11	1	3.67
1935	Detroit (A)	22	11	2	3.79	38	290	122	276	134	318	$33.0	21	10	1	3.51
1936	Detroit (A)	24	12	0	3.63	41	310	125	279	127	335	$40.7	23	11	0	3.60
1937	Detroit (A)	16	13	0	4.36	36	260	126	271	100	249	$26.0	15	12	0	4.07
1938	Detroit (A)	14	9	2	4.93	26	157	86	172	60	182	$13.8	13	9	1	4.59
1939	Detroit (A)	18	7	3	3.73	30	205	85	186	65	230	$17.5	17	7	2	3.50
1940	Detroit (A)	12	9	0	3.75	30	204	85	175	97	227	$13.8	12	9	0	3.37
1941	Detroit (A)	9	12	0	4.03	26	154	69	136	73	161	$7.2	9	12	0	3.41
1942	Detroit (A)	9	7	3	3.61	24	182	73	185	67	184	$7.0	9	7	1	2.74
1943	Detroit (A)	12	7	0	3.26	26	199	72	179	68	226	$7.2	12	7	0	2.39
1945	Detroit (A)	1	0	0	4.09	4	11	5	15	2	11	$0.6	1	0	0	3.27
1946	Detroit (A)	1	1	3	7.71	9	21	18	25	8	26	$0.8	1	1	1	5.91
	Career	201	144	23	3.98	443	2,957	1,307	2,723	1,365	3,139	$226.2	194	138	10	3.57
	Average season	13	9	1	3.98	28	185	82	170	85	196	$14.1	12	9	1	3.57
	Summit season	20	11	2	3.74	37	262	109	232	119	277	$25.6	19	10	1	3.54

MORDECAI BROWN

		ADJUSTED REGULAR SEASON											ACTUAL RESULTS			
YEAR	TEAM	W	L	SV	ERA	G	IP	ER	H	BB	SO	PAY	W	L	SV	ERA
1903	St. Louis (N)	10	15	0	3.80	30	232	98	275	100	172	$9.5	9	13	0	2.60
1904	Chicago (N)	16	10	1	3.19	27	220	78	180	82	146	$9.9	15	10	1	1.86
1905	Chicago (N)	19	12	0	3.50	31	257	100	254	64	156	$16.4	18	12	0	2.17
1906	Chicago (N)	27	6	4	1.78	38	293	58	238	90	258	$32.9	26	6	3	1.04
1907	Chicago (N)	21	6	7	2.51	36	247	69	219	60	204	$26.2	20	6	3	1.39
1908	Chicago (N)	30	9	5	2.82	45	319	100	262	76	225	$40.8	29	9	5	1.47
1909	Chicago (N)	28	9	13	2.35	52	356	93	299	75	303	$53.2	27	9	7	1.31
1910	Chicago (N)	26	15	7	3.07	48	308	105	305	80	248	$41.1	25	14	7	1.86
1911	Chicago (N)	22	11	20	3.79	55	280	118	289	64	215	$39.9	21	11	13	2.80
1912	Chicago (N)	5	6	0	3.60	16	95	38	102	24	60	$5.6	5	6	0	2.64
1913	Cincinnati (N)	12	13	12	4.35	41	182	88	199	56	78	$7.3	11	12	6	2.91
1914	St.L.-Bkn. (F)	14	11	0	5.57	36	239	148	270	75	188	$13.3	14	11	0	3.52
1915	Chicago (F)	18	8	8	3.31	37	250	92	227	81	173	$16.2	17	8	4	2.09
1916	Chicago (N)	2	3	0	6.56	12	48	35	59	11	36	$1.9	2	3	0	3.91
	Career	250	134	77	3.30	504	3,326	1,220	3,178	938	2,462	$314.2	239	130	49	2.06
	Average season	18	10	6	3.30	36	238	87	227	67	176	$22.4	17	9	4	2.06
	Summit season	27	10	10	2.75	48	311	95	279	77	250	$41.6	26	10	7	1.67

JIM BUNNING

		ADJUSTED REGULAR SEASON											ACTUAL RESULTS			
YEAR	TEAM	W	L	SV	ERA	G	IP	ER	H	BB	SO	PAY	W	L	SV	ERA
1955	Detroit (A)	3	5	2	7.33	16	54	44	66	33	56	$2.1	3	5	1	6.35
1956	Detroit (A)	5	1	2	4.26	16	57	27	62	29	50	$2.1	5	1	1	3.71
1957	Detroit (A)	21	8	2	3.19	47	279	99	236	82	254	$19.5	20	8	1	2.69
1958	Detroit (A)	15	13	0	4.19	37	232	108	210	91	239	$15.4	14	12	0	3.52
1959	Detroit (A)	18	14	2	4.57	42	262	133	244	85	264	$20.1	17	13	1	3.89
1960	Detroit (A)	12	15	0	3.32	38	266	98	246	71	262	$19.9	11	14	0	2.79
1961	Detroit (A)	17	11	1	3.63	38	268	108	244	73	238	$20.1	17	11	1	3.19
1962	Detroit (A)	19	10	7	4.15	41	258	119	277	78	220	$20.4	19	10	6	3.59
1963	Detroit (A)	12	13	1	5.12	39	248	141	273	84	219	$14.9	12	13	1	3.88
1964	Philadelphia (N)	19	8	2	3.36	41	284	106	271	55	241	$24.7	19	8	2	2.63
1965	Philadelphia (N)	19	9	0	3.37	39	291	109	284	72	293	$25.5	19	9	0	2.60
1966	Philadelphia (N)	19	14	1	3.12	43	314	109	288	68	282	$30.8	19	14	1	2.41
1967	Philadelphia (N)	17	15	0	3.16	40	302	106	275	88	275	$24.1	17	15	0	2.29
1968	Pittsburgh (N)	4	14	0	5.96	27	160	106	198	61	106	$5.6	4	14	0	3.88
1969	Pit.-L.A. (N)	13	10	0	4.67	34	212	110	235	61	176	$7.5	13	10	0	3.69
1970	Philadelphia (N)	10	15	0	4.85	34	219	118	251	57	167	$7.1	10	15	0	4.11
1971	Philadelphia (N)	5	12	1	7.28	29	110	89	140	41	70	$3.0	5	12	1	5.48
	Career	228	187	21	4.08	601	3,816	1,730	3,800	1,129	3,412	$262.8	224	184	16	3.27
	Average season	13	11	1	4.08	35	224	102	224	66	201	$15.5	13	11	1	3.27
	Summit season	19	10	2	3.41	42	285	108	271	71	258	$24.2	19	10	2	2.76

LEW BURDETTE

		ADJUSTED REGULAR SEASON											ACTUAL RESULTS			
YEAR	TEAM	W	L	SV	ERA	G	IP	ER	H	BB	SO	PAY	W	L	SV	ERA
1950	New York (A)	0	0	0	9.00	2	1	1	2	0	0	$0.0	0	0	0	6.75
1951	Boston (N)	0	0	0	6.75	3	4	3	6	4	2	$0.0	0	0	0	6.23
1952	Boston (N)	6	11	15	4.47	47	143	71	156	50	78	$4.3	6	11	7	3.61
1953	Milwaukee (N)	15	5	14	3.57	47	179	71	184	58	96	$7.8	15	5	8	3.24
1954	Milwaukee (N)	16	15	0	3.23	40	251	90	247	64	135	$15.1	15	14	0	2.76
1955	Milwaukee (N)	14	8	0	4.59	44	241	123	281	74	112	$10.2	13	8	0	4.03
1956	Milwaukee (N)	20	11	2	3.11	41	269	93	260	53	163	$20.3	19	10	1	2.70
1957	Milwaukee (N)	18	9	0	4.42	39	271	133	291	68	115	$19.1	17	9	0	3.72
1958	Milwaukee (N)	21	11	0	3.43	42	289	110	310	57	158	$24.4	20	10	0	2.91
1959	Milwaukee (N)	22	15	2	4.76	42	297	157	340	42	140	$25.3	21	15	1	4.07
1960	Milwaukee (N)	20	14	6	4.03	47	288	129	311	38	112	$24.3	19	13	4	3.36
1961	Milwaukee (N)	19	12	0	4.53	42	286	144	327	35	122	$24.1	18	11	0	4.00
1962	Milwaukee (N)	10	9	3	5.69	37	144	91	182	24	72	$5.9	10	9	2	4.89
1963	Mil.-St.L. (N)	9	13	3	4.90	36	182	99	198	48	83	$5.9	9	13	2	3.71
1964	St.L.-Chi. (N)	10	9	0	5.94	36	141	93	177	27	48	$3.3	10	9	0	4.66
1965	Chi.-Phi. (N)	3	5	0	7.12	26	91	72	136	24	31	$2.1	3	5	0	5.44
1966	California (A)	7	2	6	4.39	54	80	39	89	15	31	$2.2	7	2	5	3.39
1967	California (A)	1	0	1	7.00	19	18	14	18	0	9	$0.4	1	0	1	4.91
	Career	211	149	52	4.35	644	3,175	1,533	3,515	681	1,507	$194.7	203	144	31	3.66
	Average season	12	8	3	4.35	36	176	85	195	38	84	$10.8	11	8	2	3.66
	Summit season	20	11	5	3.82	44	264	112	281	50	134	$20.4	19	11	3	3.28

STEVE CARLTON

		ADJUSTED REGULAR SEASON											ACTUAL RESULTS			
YEAR	TEAM	W	L	SV	ERA	G	IP	ER	H	BB	SO	PAY	W	L	SV	ERA
1965	St. Louis (N)	0	0	0	3.24	15	25	9	30	9	23	$0.0	0	0	0	2.52
1966	St. Louis (N)	3	3	0	3.98	9	52	23	62	22	28	$0.7	3	3	0	3.12
1967	St. Louis (N)	14	9	1	4.15	30	193	89	198	75	182	$7.7	14	9	1	2.98
1968	St. Louis (N)	13	11	0	4.58	34	232	118	253	78	180	$9.3	13	11	0	2.99
1969	St. Louis (N)	17	11	0	2.75	31	236	72	205	97	235	$15.8	17	11	0	2.17
1970	St. Louis (N)	10	19	0	4.39	34	254	124	258	111	218	$15.7	10	19	0	3.73
1971	St. Louis (N)	20	9	0	4.68	37	273	142	305	109	207	$20.1	20	9	0	3.56
1972	Philadelphia (N)	28	10	0	2.75	43	363	111	307	104	376	$51.4	27	10	0	1.97
1973	Philadelphia (N)	13	20	0	4.76	40	293	155	312	120	274	$26.1	13	20	0	3.90
1974	Philadelphia (N)	16	13	0	4.05	39	291	131	266	147	305	$27.2	16	13	0	3.22
1975	Philadelphia (N)	15	14	0	4.41	37	255	125	230	108	246	$20.0	15	14	0	3.56
1976	Philadelphia (N)	20	7	0	4.09	35	253	115	242	81	257	$18.7	20	7	0	3.13
1977	Philadelphia (N)	23	10	0	3.02	36	283	95	235	69	215	$25.4	23	10	0	2.64
1978	Philadelphia (N)	16	13	0	3.53	34	247	97	243	98	278	$18.3	16	13	0	2.84
1979	Philadelphia (N)	18	11	0	4.16	35	251	116	207	98	278	$24.2	18	11	0	3.62
1980	Philadelphia (N)	24	9	0	2.78	38	304	94	250	103	370	$37.0	24	9	0	2.34
1981	Philadelphia (N)	20	6	0	3.06	36	285	97	245	105	350	$29.4	13	4	0	2.42
1982	Philadelphia (N)	23	11	0	3.68	38	296	121	264	98	356	$31.0	23	11	0	3.10
1983	Philadelphia (N)	15	16	0	3.68	37	284	116	290	94	335	$24.2	15	16	0	3.11
1984	Philadelphia (N)	13	7	0	4.28	33	229	109	224	89	197	$13.4	13	7	0	3.58
1985	Philadelphia (N)	1	8	0	3.91	16	92	40	89	58	59	$3.0	1	8	0	3.33

(Steve Carlton, continued)

YEAR	TEAM	W	L	SV	ERA	G	IP	ER	H	BB	SO	PAY	W	L	SV	ERA
				ADJUSTED REGULAR SEASON									ACTUAL RESULTS			
1986	Phi.-S.F. (N)-Chi. (A)	9	14	0	5.88	32	176	115	208	91	133	$5.6	9	14	0	5.10
1987	Cle.-Minn. (A)	6	14	1	6.16	32	152	104	170	90	99	$3.3	6	14	1	5.74
1988	Minnesota (A)	0	1	0	20.70	4	10	23	22	6	6	$0.0	0	1	0	16.76
	Career	337	246	2	3.95	755	5,329	2,341	5,115	2,060	5,177	$427.5	329	244	2	3.22
	Average season	14	10	0	3.95	31	222	98	213	86	216	$17.8	14	10	0	3.22
	Summit season	24	9	0	3.06	38	306	104	260	102	340	$34.8	22	9	0	2.48

DEAN CHANCE

YEAR	TEAM	W	L	SV	ERA	G	IP	ER	H	BB	SO	PAY	W	L	SV	ERA
				ADJUSTED REGULAR SEASON									ACTUAL RESULTS			
1961	Los Angeles (A)	0	2	0	8.00	5	18	16	34	5	13	$0.0	0	2	0	6.87
1962	Los Angeles (A)	14	10	11	3.43	50	207	79	206	70	153	$8.0	14	10	8	2.96
1963	Los Angeles (A)	13	18	4	4.21	45	248	116	256	109	189	$15.1	13	18	3	3.19
1964	Los Angeles (A)	20	9	5	2.10	46	278	65	211	104	228	$20.3	20	9	4	1.65
1965	California (A)	15	10	0	4.10	36	226	103	222	118	180	$15.9	15	10	0	3.15
1966	California (A)	12	17	1	4.02	41	260	116	228	143	202	$18.9	12	17	1	3.08
1967	Minnesota (A)	20	14	1	3.77	41	284	119	279	82	241	$26.3	20	14	1	2.73
1968	Minnesota (A)	16	16	1	3.85	43	292	125	264	80	259	$25.7	16	16	1	2.53
1969	Minnesota (A)	5	4	0	3.78	20	88	37	84	36	56	$4.7	5	4	0	2.95
1970	Cle. (A)-N.Y. (N)	9	9	6	5.16	48	157	90	189	62	123	$8.1	9	9	5	4.36
1971	Detroit (A)	4	6	0	4.60	31	90	46	101	56	77	$4.4	4	6	0	3.51
	Career	128	115	29	3.82	406	2,148	912	2,074	865	1,721	$147.4	128	115	23	2.92
	Average season	12	10	3	3.82	37	195	83	189	79	156	$13.4	12	10	2	2.92
	Summit season	17	12	4	3.43	43	257	98	236	91	212	$19.2	17	12	3	2.56

SPUD CHANDLER

YEAR	TEAM	W	L	SV	ERA	G	IP	ER	H	BB	SO	PAY	W	L	SV	ERA
				ADJUSTED REGULAR SEASON									ACTUAL RESULTS			
1937	New York (A)	7	4	0	3.07	12	82	28	75	21	55	$3.6	7	4	0	2.84
1938	New York (A)	15	5	0	4.32	24	179	86	184	49	75	$5.8	14	5	0	4.03
1939	New York (A)	3	0	0	3.00	12	21	7	28	10	9	$1.2	3	0	0	2.84
1940	New York (A)	8	7	0	5.11	28	178	101	189	66	106	$4.6	8	7	0	4.60
1941	New York (A)	10	4	10	3.76	29	170	71	155	62	115	$6.7	10	4	4	3.19
1942	New York (A)	17	5	0	3.10	25	209	72	197	81	148	$8.4	16	5	0	2.38
1943	New York (A)	21	4	0	2.24	31	261	65	220	59	252	$17.3	20	4	0	1.64
1944	New York (A)	0	0	0	6.00	1	6	4	6	1	2	$1.0	0	0	0	4.50
1945	New York (A)	2	1	0	5.81	4	31	20	31	7	24	$1.3	2	1	0	4.65
1946	New York (A)	21	8	4	2.78	36	272	84	225	96	237	$16.9	20	8	2	2.10
1947	New York (A)	10	5	0	2.91	18	136	44	110	42	123	$3.7	9	5	0	2.46
	Career	114	43	14	3.39	220	1,545	582	1,420	494	1,146	$70.5	109	43	6	2.84
	Average season	10	4	1	3.39	20	140	53	129	45	104	$6.4	10	4	1	2.84
	Summit season	17	5	3	3.14	29	218	76	196	69	165	$11.0	16	5	1	2.53

JACK CHESBRO

		ADJUSTED REGULAR SEASON											ACTUAL RESULTS			
YEAR	TEAM	W	L	SV	ERA	G	IP	ER	H	BB	SO	PAY	W	L	SV	ERA
1899	Pittsburgh (N)	6	9	0	4.87	20	157	85	161	79	92	$4.6	6	9	0	4.11
1900	Pittsburgh (N)	17	15	4	4.55	37	249	126	239	120	174	$15.2	15	13	1	3.67
1901	Pittsburgh (N)	25	12	4	3.11	42	336	116	294	86	298	$34.1	21	10	1	2.38
1902	Pittsburgh (N)	32	7	1	3.11	40	327	113	277	102	318	$42.7	28	6	1	2.17
1903	New York (A)	25	18	0	4.06	48	390	176	371	130	313	$54.2	21	15	0	2.77
1904	New York (A)	42	12	0	3.11	57	471	163	391	143	417	$67.7	41	12	0	1.82
1905	New York (A)	20	16	0	3.56	44	326	129	316	108	275	$50.6	19	15	0	2.20
1906	New York (A)	24	18	6	5.11	51	338	192	373	109	271	$50.1	23	17	1	2.96
1907	New York (A)	11	11	0	4.62	32	220	113	236	70	153	$17.9	10	10	0	2.53
1908	New York (A)	15	21	5	5.68	47	301	190	346	106	229	$25.0	14	20	1	2.93
1909	N.Y.-Bos. (A)	0	6	0	11.21	11	61	76	99	25	39	$2.5	0	5	0	6.14
	Career	217	145	20	4.19	429	3,176	1,479	3,103	1,078	2,579	$364.6	198	132	5	2.68
	Average season	20	13	2	4.19	39	289	134	282	98	234	$33.1	18	12	0	2.68
	Summit season	30	13	2	3.68	48	372	152	341	114	323	$49.8	27	12	1	2.38

EDDIE CICOTTE

		ADJUSTED REGULAR SEASON											ACTUAL RESULTS			
YEAR	TEAM	W	L	SV	ERA	G	IP	ER	H	BB	SO	PAY	W	L	SV	ERA
1905	Detroit (A)	1	1	0	5.50	3	18	11	28	7	10	$0.0	1	1	0	3.50
1908	Boston (A)	12	13	9	4.71	41	218	114	250	95	175	$8.1	11	12	2	2.43
1909	Boston (A)	15	5	5	3.52	29	174	68	147	82	149	$8.5	14	5	1	1.94
1910	Boston (A)	15	11	0	4.52	37	257	129	250	107	181	$15.7	15	11	0	2.74
1911	Boston (A)	12	16	0	3.82	37	233	99	261	87	181	$15.3	11	15	0	2.82
1912	Bos.-Chi. (A)	10	10	0	4.74	30	205	108	232	61	152	$9.5	10	10	0	3.50
1913	Chicago (A)	19	12	4	2.34	43	281	73	255	93	218	$20.3	18	11	1	1.58
1914	Chicago (A)	11	16	10	3.21	46	275	98	251	88	203	$19.3	11	16	3	2.04
1915	Chicago (A)	14	13	8	4.75	41	235	124	258	60	188	$16.0	13	12	3	3.02
1916	Chicago (A)	16	7	14	2.98	46	196	65	166	93	161	$14.5	15	7	5	1.78
1917	Chicago (A)	29	12	8	2.59	51	361	104	292	94	291	$49.5	28	12	4	1.53
1918	Chicago (A)	16	25	6	4.60	50	350	179	405	67	300	$39.4	12	19	2	2.77
1919	Chicago (A)	33	8	3	2.70	46	353	106	313	75	269	$51.6	29	7	1	1.82
1920	Chicago (A)	22	11	4	4.30	39	320	153	331	102	208	$37.6	21	10	2	3.26
	Career	225	160	71	3.71	539	3,476	1,431	3,439	1,111	2,686	$305.3	209	148	24	2.38
	Average season	16	11	5	3.71	39	248	102	246	79	192	$21.8	15	11	2	2.38
	Summit season	24	10	7	2.98	45	302	100	271	91	229	$34.7	22	9	3	2.01

JOHN CLARKSON

		ADJUSTED REGULAR SEASON											ACTUAL RESULTS			
YEAR	TEAM	W	L	SV	ERA	G	IP	ER	H	BB	SO	PAY	W	L	SV	ERA
1882	Worcester (N)	2	4	0	7.31	6	48	39	100	10	14	$0.5	1	2	0	4.50
1884	Chicago (N)	14	4	0	3.14	20	169	59	141	78	186	$6.0	10	3	0	2.14
1885	Chicago (N)	76	23	0	2.75	100	890	272	751	244	741	$103.4	53	16	0	1.85
1886	Chicago (N)	46	22	0	3.24	71	602	217	569	145	584	$80.8	36	17	0	2.41
1887	Chicago (N)	49	27	0	3.35	77	671	250	618	141	656	$92.5	38	21	0	3.08
1888	Boston (N)	39	24	0	4.27	64	573	272	590	230	448	$83.4	33	20	0	2.76
1889	Boston (N)	60	23	5	3.14	89	756	264	703	256	618	$101.1	49	19	1	2.73
1890	Boston (N)	31	22	0	3.85	53	461	197	441	162	318	$69.0	26	18	0	3.27
1891	Boston (N)	38	22	4	3.61	64	536	215	517	173	311	$74.3	33	19	3	2.79
1892	Bos.-Cle. (N)	27	17	3	3.43	48	415	158	399	146	293	$62.8	25	16	1	2.48
1893	Cleveland (N)	20	21	0	4.37	45	369	179	405	107	239	$50.4	16	17	0	4.45
1894	Cleveland (N)	10	12	0	3.79	27	185	78	171	53	108	$13.8	8	10	0	4.42
	Career	412	221	12	3.49	664	5,675	2,200	5,405	1,745	4,516	$738.0	328	178	5	2.81
	Average season	34	18	1	3.49	55	473	183	450	145	376	$61.5	27	15	0	2.81
	Summit season	54	23	2	3.18	80	691	244	632	192	582	$90.4	42	18	1	2.55

ROGER CLEMENS

		ADJUSTED REGULAR SEASON											ACTUAL RESULTS			
YEAR	TEAM	W	L	SV	ERA	G	IP	ER	H	BB	SO	PAY	W	L	SV	ERA
1984	Boston (A)	9	4	0	5.21	21	133	77	153	33	149	$5.8	9	4	0	4.32
1985	Boston (A)	7	5	0	3.86	15	98	42	88	40	89	$4.8	7	5	0	3.29
1986	Boston (A)	24	4	0	2.87	33	254	81	189	71	262	$19.8	24	4	0	2.48
1987	Boston (A)	20	9	0	3.16	36	282	99	255	87	277	$25.9	20	9	0	2.97
1988	Boston (A)	18	12	0	3.58	35	264	105	234	72	331	$26.2	18	12	0	2.93
1989	Boston (A)	17	11	0	3.88	35	253	109	231	104	263	$25.6	17	11	0	3.13
1990	Boston (A)	21	6	0	2.29	31	228	58	204	58	236	$20.0	21	6	0	1.93
1991	Boston (A)	18	10	0	3.06	35	271	92	234	70	268	$26.1	18	10	0	2.62
1992	Boston (A)	18	11	0	2.95	32	247	81	218	69	240	$20.2	18	11	0	2.41
1993	Boston (A)	11	14	0	4.88	29	192	104	179	72	178	$10.0	11	14	0	4.46
1994	Boston (A)	13	10	0	2.90	34	242	78	175	103	250	$14.9	9	7	0	2.85
1995	Boston (A)	11	6	0	4.27	26	158	75	161	69	153	$7.3	10	5	0	4.18
1996	Boston (A)	10	13	0	3.59	34	243	97	215	107	260	$14.0	10	13	0	3.63
1997	Toronto (A)	21	7	0	2.11	34	264	62	206	70	289	$18.9	21	7	0	2.05
1998	Toronto (A)	20	6	0	2.72	33	235	71	171	93	270	$16.8	20	6	0	2.65
1999	New York (A)	14	10	0	4.50	30	188	94	183	87	165	$7.6	14	10	0	4.60
2000	New York (A)	13	8	0	3.57	32	204	81	182	79	189	$12.6	13	8	0	3.70
2001	New York (A)	20	3	0	3.64	33	220	89	209	79	208	$16.2	20	3	0	3.51
	Career	285	149	0	3.38	558	3,976	1,495	3,487	1,363	4,077	$292.7	280	145	0	3.10
	Average season	16	8	0	3.38	31	221	83	194	76	227	$16.3	16	8	0	3.10
	Summit season	21	6	0	2.63	33	253	74	205	76	267	$20.3	21	6	0	2.43

DAVID CONE

		ADJUSTED REGULAR SEASON											ACTUAL RESULTS			
YEAR	TEAM	W	L	SV	ERA	G	IP	ER	H	BB	SO	PAY	W	L	SV	ERA
1986	Kansas City (A)	0	0	0	6.26	11	23	16	31	14	24	$0.0	0	0	0	5.56
1987	New York (N)	5	6	1	4.00	21	99	44	89	46	74	$3.2	5	6	1	3.71
1988	New York (N)	20	3	0	2.73	35	231	70	191	93	245	$14.9	20	3	0	2.22
1989	New York (N)	14	8	0	4.38	34	220	107	198	83	218	$9.9	14	8	0	3.52
1990	New York (N)	14	10	0	3.82	31	212	90	188	71	261	$15.3	14	10	0	3.23
1991	New York (N)	14	14	0	3.86	34	233	100	219	79	267	$16.4	14	14	0	3.29
1992	N.Y. (N)-Tor. (A)	17	10	0	3.42	35	250	95	216	123	298	$19.8	17	10	0	2.81
1993	Kansas City (A)	11	14	0	3.65	34	254	103	209	122	213	$15.9	11	14	0	3.33
1994	Kansas City (A)	22	7	0	2.97	32	239	79	180	77	193	$19.4	16	5	0	2.94
1995	Tor.-N.Y. (A)	20	9	0	3.67	34	260	106	223	101	223	$18.9	18	8	0	3.57
1996	New York (A)	7	2	0	2.88	11	72	23	50	34	72	$4.1	7	2	0	2.88
1997	New York (A)	12	6	0	2.95	29	195	64	157	89	219	$8.9	12	6	0	2.82
1998	New York (A)	20	7	0	3.68	31	208	85	189	62	208	$14.4	20	7	0	3.55
1999	New York (A)	12	9	0	3.36	31	193	72	162	87	179	$7.2	12	9	0	3.44
2000	New York (A)	4	14	0	6.68	30	155	115	191	78	121	$3.8	4	14	0	6.91
2001	Boston (A)	9	7	0	4.50	25	136	68	152	63	112	$3.9	9	7	0	4.31
	Career	201	126	1	3.74	458	2,980	1,237	2,645	1,222	2,927	$176.0	193	123	1	3.44
	Average season	13	8	0	3.74	29	186	77	165	76	183	$11.0	12	8	0	3.44
	Summit season	20	7	0	3.29	33	238	87	200	91	233	$17.5	18	7	0	3.01

JACK COOMBS

		ADJUSTED REGULAR SEASON											ACTUAL RESULTS			
YEAR	TEAM	W	L	SV	ERA	G	IP	ER	H	BB	SO	PAY	W	L	SV	ERA
1906	Philadelphia (A)	11	11	0	4.31	25	188	90	178	104	165	$8.4	10	10	0	2.50
1907	Philadelphia (A)	7	10	6	5.69	25	144	91	136	100	138	$7.6	6	9	2	3.12
1908	Philadelphia (A)	7	5	0	3.85	27	159	68	162	102	144	$5.9	7	5	0	2.00
1909	Philadelphia (A)	13	12	4	4.19	32	219	102	194	106	176	$9.7	12	11	1	2.32
1910	Philadelphia (A)	32	9	4	2.12	47	369	87	295	145	376	$51.5	31	9	1	1.30
1911	Philadelphia (A)	30	13	5	4.80	50	358	191	400	142	312	$52.0	28	12	2	3.53
1912	Philadelphia (A)	22	11	6	4.48	42	275	137	245	112	205	$33.3	21	10	2	3.29
1913	Philadelphia (A)	0	0	0	14.40	2	5	8	5	7	0	$2.6	0	0	0	10.13
1914	Philadelphia (A)	0	1	0	6.75	2	8	6	9	4	2	$1.4	0	1	0	4.50
1915	Brooklyn (N)	16	11	0	4.05	31	209	94	201	117	106	$7.2	15	10	0	2.58
1916	Brooklyn (N)	13	8	0	4.47	28	165	82	162	58	87	$4.6	13	8	0	2.66
1917	Brooklyn (N)	7	11	0	6.78	32	146	110	174	66	69	$4.2	7	11	0	3.96
1918	Brooklyn (N)	10	18	0	6.32	35	245	172	277	81	135	$7.4	8	14	0	3.81
1920	Detroit (A)	0	0	0	4.50	2	6	3	7	3	2	$0.3	0	0	0	3.18
	Career	168	120	25	4.47	380	2,496	1,241	2,445	1,147	1,917	$196.1	158	110	8	2.78
	Average season	12	9	2	4.47	27	178	89	175	82	137	$14.0	11	8	1	2.78
	Summit season	23	11	4	3.84	40	286	122	267	124	235	$30.7	21	10	1	2.58

MORT COOPER

YEAR	TEAM	ADJUSTED REGULAR SEASON											ACTUAL RESULTS			
		W	L	SV	ERA	G	IP	ER	H	BB	SO	PAY	W	L	SV	ERA
1938	St. Louis (N)	2	1	1	3.38	4	24	9	17	12	20	$0.4	2	1	1	3.04
1939	St. Louis (N)	13	6	11	3.48	47	220	85	210	104	237	$9.5	12	6	4	3.25
1940	St. Louis (N)	11	12	8	4.03	39	237	106	230	94	173	$10.0	11	12	3	3.63
1941	St. Louis (N)	13	9	0	4.62	30	193	99	185	71	208	$9.6	13	9	0	3.91
1942	St. Louis (N)	23	7	0	2.33	38	286	74	228	73	284	$27.0	22	7	0	1.78
1943	St. Louis (N)	22	8	6	3.15	39	289	101	260	89	272	$32.2	21	8	3	2.30
1944	St. Louis (N)	23	7	2	3.18	35	260	92	243	69	197	$26.5	22	7	1	2.46
1945	St.L.-Bos. (N)	9	4	4	3.74	25	106	44	105	38	114	$7.3	9	4	1	2.92
1946	Boston (N)	13	11	3	4.11	29	206	94	200	40	144	$13.9	13	11	1	3.12
1947	Bos.-N.Y. (N)	3	11	0	6.34	19	88	62	109	26	51	$3.6	3	10	0	5.40
1949	Chicago (N)	0	0	0	—	1	0	3	2	1	0	$0.0	0	0	0	—
	Career	132	76	35	3.63	306	1,909	769	1,789	617	1,700	$140.0	128	75	14	2.97
	Average season	12	7	3	3.63	28	174	70	163	56	155	$12.7	12	7	1	2.97
	Summit season	19	8	4	3.18	38	252	89	228	75	227	$21.8	18	8	2	2.51

WILBUR COOPER

YEAR	TEAM	ADJUSTED REGULAR SEASON											ACTUAL RESULTS			
		W	L	SV	ERA	G	IP	ER	H	BB	SO	PAY	W	L	SV	ERA
1912	Pittsburgh (N)	3	0	0	2.13	6	38	9	33	17	45	$1.2	3	0	0	1.66
1913	Pittsburgh (N)	5	3	0	4.88	31	96	52	110	56	70	$3.5	5	3	0	3.29
1914	Pittsburgh (N)	16	15	0	3.33	41	273	101	281	97	173	$15.0	16	15	0	2.13
1915	Pittsburgh (N)	5	16	12	5.18	39	191	110	210	64	127	$5.9	5	16	4	3.30
1916	Pittsburgh (N)	12	11	8	3.14	43	252	88	223	96	194	$15.4	12	11	2	1.87
1917	Pittsburgh (N)	17	11	5	4.01	41	305	136	324	72	195	$25.5	17	11	1	2.36
1918	Pittsburgh (N)	25	18	5	3.48	49	352	136	314	107	325	$41.5	19	14	3	2.11
1919	Pittsburgh (N)	22	15	3	3.96	41	336	148	285	116	263	$40.5	19	13	1	2.67
1920	Pittsburgh (N)	25	16	4	3.16	46	342	120	318	70	263	$42.6	24	15	2	2.39
1921	Pittsburgh (N)	23	15	0	3.66	40	344	140	330	107	312	$50.7	22	14	0	3.25
1922	Pittsburgh (N)	24	15	0	3.55	43	309	122	322	78	297	$41.0	23	14	0	3.18
1923	Pittsburgh (N)	18	20	0	4.09	41	310	141	330	87	190	$32.6	17	19	0	3.57
1924	Pittsburgh (N)	21	15	2	3.69	40	283	116	293	50	162	$25.2	20	14	1	3.28
1925	Chicago (N)	13	15	0	4.54	34	226	114	241	73	110	$13.9	12	14	0	4.28
1926	Chi. (N)-Det. (A)	2	5	0	6.78	17	73	55	95	36	50	$3.1	2	5	0	5.77
	Career	231	190	39	3.83	552	3,730	1,588	3,709	1,126	2,776	$357.6	216	178	14	2.89
	Average season	15	13	3	3.83	37	249	106	247	75	185	$23.8	14	12	1	2.89
	Summit season	24	16	2	3.55	44	337	133	314	96	292	$43.3	21	14	1	2.73

STAN COVELESKI

YEAR	TEAM	ADJUSTED REGULAR SEASON											ACTUAL RESULTS			
---	---	W	L	SV	ERA	G	IP	ER	H	BB	SO	PAY	W	L	SV	ERA
1912	Philadelphia (A)	2	1	0	4.71	5	21	11	19	5	15	$0.2	2	1	0	3.43
1916	Cleveland (A)	15	13	10	5.77	46	237	152	291	75	137	$9.4	15	13	3	3.41
1917	Cleveland (A)	20	15	9	3.09	47	312	107	241	128	258	$26.8	19	14	4	1.81
1918	Cleveland (A)	28	16	3	3.00	48	393	131	368	122	253	$50.8	22	13	1	1.82
1919	Cleveland (A)	28	14	7	3.89	50	333	144	354	94	286	$51.5	24	12	4	2.61
1920	Cleveland (A)	25	15	2	3.27	43	330	120	295	88	298	$51.3	24	14	2	2.49
1921	Cleveland (A)	24	14	4	3.82	45	330	140	329	112	239	$41.1	23	13	2	3.37
1922	Cleveland (A)	18	15	3	3.73	37	292	121	287	82	235	$31.6	17	14	2	3.32
1923	Cleveland (A)	14	15	4	3.16	35	242	85	252	52	136	$18.0	13	14	2	2.76
1924	Cleveland (A)	16	17	0	4.55	39	253	128	283	92	151	$18.0	15	16	0	4.04
1925	Washington (A)	21	5	0	2.99	34	256	85	222	87	151	$17.0	20	5	0	2.84
1926	Washington (A)	15	12	3	3.61	38	259	104	278	97	130	$13.6	14	11	1	3.12
1927	Washington (A)	2	1	0	3.86	5	14	6	12	9	7	$1.3	2	1	0	3.14
1928	New York (A)	5	1	0	6.57	13	63	46	75	25	14	$1.7	5	1	0	5.74
	Career	233	154	45	3.72	485	3,335	1,380	3,306	1,068	2,310	$332.3	215	142	21	2.89
	Average season	17	11	3	3.72	35	238	99	236	76	165	$23.7	15	10	2	2.89
	Summit season	25	15	5	3.39	47	340	128	317	109	267	$44.3	22	13	3	2.43

MIKE CUELLAR

YEAR	TEAM	ADJUSTED REGULAR SEASON											ACTUAL RESULTS			
---	---	W	L	SV	ERA	G	IP	ER	H	BB	SO	PAY	W	L	SV	ERA
1959	Cincinnati (N)	0	0	0	18.00	2	4	8	7	4	6	$0.0	0	0	0	15.75
1964	St. Louis (N)	5	5	5	5.75	32	72	46	87	40	62	$2.6	5	5	4	4.50
1965	Houston (N)	1	4	2	4.66	25	56	29	62	24	51	$1.6	1	4	2	3.54
1966	Houston (N)	12	10	2	2.85	38	227	72	213	64	196	$8.2	12	10	2	2.22
1967	Houston (N)	16	11	1	4.21	36	246	115	266	76	221	$15.3	16	11	1	3.03
1968	Houston (N)	8	11	1	4.21	28	171	80	180	58	147	$7.7	8	11	1	2.74
1969	Baltimore (A)	23	11	0	3.03	39	291	98	237	82	206	$24.3	23	11	0	2.38
1970	Baltimore (A)	24	8	0	4.11	40	298	136	295	70	216	$25.6	24	8	0	3.48
1971	Baltimore (A)	21	9	0	4.05	39	300	135	284	89	155	$24.9	20	9	0	3.08
1972	Baltimore (A)	19	13	0	3.59	37	263	105	238	86	165	$24.3	18	12	0	2.57
1973	Baltimore (A)	18	13	0	4.01	38	267	119	282	89	176	$22.5	18	13	0	3.27
1974	Baltimore (A)	22	10	0	3.91	38	269	117	270	92	141	$22.6	22	10	0	3.11
1975	Baltimore (A)	14	12	0	4.52	37	263	132	250	89	144	$16.5	14	12	0	3.66
1976	Baltimore (A)	4	13	1	6.48	26	107	77	139	56	45	$3.0	4	13	1	4.96
1977	California (A)	0	1	0	21.00	2	3	7	8	3	3	$0.6	0	1	0	18.90
	Career	187	131	12	4.05	457	2,837	1,276	2,818	922	1,934	$199.7	185	130	11	3.14
	Average season	12	9	1	4.05	30	189	85	188	61	129	$13.3	12	9	1	3.14
	Summit season	22	10	0	3.74	39	284	118	265	84	177	$24.3	21	10	0	2.93

MARK DAVIS

		ADJUSTED REGULAR SEASON											ACTUAL RESULTS			
YEAR	TEAM	W	L	SV	ERA	G	IP	ER	H	BB	SO	PAY	W	L	SV	ERA
1980	Philadelphia (N)	0	0	0	2.57	2	7	2	4	6	7	$0.0	0	0	0	2.57
1981	Philadelphia (N)	2	6	0	9.94	14	67	74	82	42	61	$1.8	1	4	0	7.74
1983	San Francisco (N)	6	4	0	4.14	20	111	51	97	56	103	$3.8	6	4	0	3.49
1984	San Francisco (N)	5	17	0	6.48	46	175	126	211	61	150	$4.7	5	17	0	5.36
1985	San Francisco (N)	5	12	8	4.18	77	114	53	94	44	152	$4.9	5	12	7	3.54
1986	San Francisco (N)	5	7	4	3.43	67	84	32	66	36	98	$4.2	5	7	4	2.99
1987	S.F.-S.D. (N)	9	8	2	4.26	63	133	63	127	62	107	$5.2	9	8	2	3.99
1988	San Diego (N)	5	10	28	2.48	62	98	27	75	49	116	$5.7	5	10	28	2.01
1989	San Diego (N)	4	3	44	2.32	70	93	24	71	35	104	$7.7	4	3	44	1.85
1990	Kansas City (A)	2	7	5	6.13	53	69	47	76	57	82	$4.2	2	7	6	5.11
1991	Kansas City (A)	6	3	0	5.29	29	63	37	59	42	53	$3.5	6	3	1	4.45
1992	K.C. (A)-Atl. (N)	2	3	0	8.66	27	53	51	69	45	40	$1.7	2	3	0	7.13
1993	Phi.-S.D. (N)	1	5	3	4.63	60	70	36	81	47	78	$2.2	1	5	4	4.26
1994	San Diego (N)	0	1	0	9.00	28	23	23	28	19	22	$0.2	0	1	0	8.82
1997	Milwaukee (A)	0	0	0	5.63	19	16	10	21	5	13	$0.0	0	0	0	5.51
	Career	52	86	94	5.02	637	1,176	656	1,161	606	1,186	$49.8	51	84	96	4.17
	Average season	3	6	6	5.02	42	78	44	77	40	79	$3.3	3	6	6	4.17
	Summit season	6	8	17	3.46	68	104	40	87	45	115	$5.5	6	8	17	2.98

DIZZY DEAN

		ADJUSTED REGULAR SEASON											ACTUAL RESULTS			
YEAR	TEAM	W	L	SV	ERA	G	IP	ER	H	BB	SO	PAY	W	L	SV	ERA
1930	St. Louis (N)	1	0	0	1.00	1	9	1	3	3	9	$0.0	1	0	0	1.00
1932	St. Louis (N)	19	16	6	3.59	48	298	119	278	125	365	$20.2	18	15	2	3.30
1933	St. Louis (N)	21	19	7	3.63	50	305	123	287	79	392	$33.0	20	18	4	3.04
1934	St. Louis (N)	32	7	11	2.84	53	330	104	286	87	361	$51.5	30	7	7	2.66
1935	St. Louis (N)	30	13	8	3.26	53	345	125	324	91	373	$55.6	28	12	5	3.04
1936	St. Louis (N)	25	14	13	3.19	53	327	116	296	57	365	$54.6	24	13	11	3.17
1937	St. Louis (N)	13	10	3	2.90	28	205	66	199	35	209	$20.4	13	10	1	2.69
1938	Chicago (N)	8	1	0	1.91	14	80	17	65	9	46	$5.0	7	1	0	1.81
1939	Chicago (N)	6	4	0	3.56	20	101	40	100	18	55	$5.0	6	4	0	3.36
1940	Chicago (N)	3	3	0	5.80	11	59	38	74	23	36	$2.2	3	3	0	5.17
1941	Chicago (N)	0	0	0	18.00	1	1	2	3	0	2	$0.0	0	0	0	18.00
1947	St. Louis (A)	0	0	0	0.00	1	4	0	3	1	0	$0.0	0	0	0	0.00
	Career	158	87	48	3.27	333	2,064	751	1,918	528	2,213	$247.5	150	83	30	3.02
	Average season	13	7	4	3.27	28	172	63	160	44	184	$20.6	13	7	3	3.02
	Summit season	25	14	9	3.28	51	321	117	294	88	371	$43.0	24	13	6	3.04

JOHN DENNY

		ADJUSTED REGULAR SEASON											ACTUAL RESULTS			
YEAR	TEAM	W	L	SV	ERA	G	IP	ER	H	BB	SO	PAY	W	L	SV	ERA
1974	St. Louis (N)	0	0	0	0.00	2	2	0	3	0	1	$0.0	0	0	0	0.00
1975	St. Louis (N)	10	7	0	4.90	25	136	74	159	53	94	$4.2	10	7	0	3.97
1976	St. Louis (N)	11	9	0	3.26	30	207	75	204	83	103	$5.7	11	9	0	2.52
1977	St. Louis (N)	8	8	0	5.16	26	150	86	170	68	78	$5.0	8	8	0	4.51
1978	St. Louis (N)	14	11	0	3.69	33	234	96	213	82	142	$9.9	14	11	0	2.96
1979	St. Louis (N)	8	11	0	5.55	31	206	127	211	110	136	$8.1	8	11	0	4.85
1980	Cleveland (A)	8	6	0	5.28	16	109	64	120	54	81	$5.0	8	6	0	4.39
1981	Cleveland (A)	16	9	0	4.03	30	230	103	237	118	201	$15.1	10	6	0	3.15
1982	Cle. (A)-Phi. (N)	6	13	0	5.81	25	161	104	151	95	145	$5.8	6	13	0	4.87
1983	Philadelphia (N)	19	6	0	2.81	36	243	76	240	59	176	$15.8	19	6	0	2.37
1984	Philadelphia (N)	7	7	0	2.92	22	154	50	127	33	115	$4.9	7	7	0	2.45
1985	Philadelphia (N)	11	14	0	4.48	33	231	115	268	90	151	$8.4	11	14	0	3.82
1986	Cincinnati (N)	11	10	0	4.84	27	171	92	189	59	128	$7.0	11	10	0	4.20
	Career	129	111	0	4.28	336	2,234	1,062	2,292	904	1,551	$94.9	123	108	0	3.59
	Average season	10	9	0	4.28	26	172	82	176	70	119	$7.3	9	8	0	3.59
	Summit season	13	8	0	3.36	30	214	80	204	75	147	$10.3	12	8	0	2.67

DICK DONOVAN

		ADJUSTED REGULAR SEASON											ACTUAL RESULTS			
YEAR	TEAM	W	L	SV	ERA	G	IP	ER	H	BB	SO	PAY	W	L	SV	ERA
1950	Boston (N)	0	2	0	8.70	10	30	29	29	30	16	$0.0	0	2	0	8.19
1951	Boston (N)	0	0	0	5.79	8	14	9	18	11	7	$0.0	0	0	0	5.27
1952	Boston (N)	0	2	2	6.92	7	13	10	20	12	9	$0.0	0	2	1	5.54
1954	Detroit (A)	0	0	0	12.00	2	6	8	9	5	3	$0.0	0	0	0	10.50
1955	Chicago (A)	16	9	0	3.78	30	193	81	203	48	135	$5.9	15	9	0	3.32
1956	Chicago (A)	13	11	0	4.21	36	248	116	237	61	177	$9.6	12	10	0	3.64
1957	Chicago (A)	17	6	0	3.30	29	229	84	223	51	127	$9.9	16	6	0	2.77
1958	Chicago (A)	16	15	0	3.56	36	263	104	269	61	178	$19.1	15	14	0	3.01
1959	Chicago (A)	9	10	0	4.28	32	185	88	187	64	95	$6.9	9	10	0	3.66
1960	Chicago (A)	6	1	5	6.51	35	83	60	99	28	41	$3.4	6	1	3	5.38
1961	Washington (A)	10	10	0	2.72	23	169	51	146	36	79	$4.7	10	10	0	2.40
1962	Cleveland (A)	20	10	0	4.16	34	251	116	270	50	115	$13.9	20	10	0	3.59
1963	Cleveland (A)	11	13	0	5.59	30	206	128	236	34	96	$5.9	11	13	0	4.24
1964	Cleveland (A)	7	9	1	5.81	30	158	102	198	35	92	$3.8	7	9	1	4.55
1965	Cleveland (A)	1	3	0	7.83	12	23	20	37	7	13	$1.0	1	3	0	5.96
	Career	126	101	8	4.37	354	2,071	1,006	2,181	533	1,183	$84.1	122	99	5	3.67
	Average season	8	7	1	4.37	24	138	67	145	36	79	$5.6	8	7	0	3.67
	Summit season	16	10	0	3.54	30	221	87	222	49	127	$10.7	15	10	0	3.06

DOUG DRABEK

		ADJUSTED REGULAR SEASON											ACTUAL RESULTS			
YEAR	TEAM	W	L	SV	ERA	G	IP	ER	H	BB	SO	PAY	W	L	SV	ERA
1986	New York (A)	7	8	0	4.70	27	132	69	134	53	85	$4.7	7	8	0	4.10
1987	Pittsburgh (N)	11	12	0	4.14	29	176	81	169	48	131	$5.9	11	12	0	3.88
1988	Pittsburgh (N)	15	7	0	3.78	33	219	92	209	58	149	$9.6	15	7	0	3.08
1989	Pittsburgh (N)	14	12	0	3.47	35	244	94	231	77	143	$10.2	14	12	0	2.80
1990	Pittsburgh (N)	22	6	0	3.27	33	231	84	201	61	151	$16.2	22	6	0	2.76
1991	Pittsburgh (N)	15	14	0	3.60	35	235	94	263	67	160	$15.9	15	14	0	3.07
1992	Pittsburgh (N)	15	11	0	3.40	34	257	97	234	60	207	$19.3	15	11	0	2.77
1993	Houston (N)	9	18	0	4.16	34	238	110	248	64	176	$15.2	9	18	0	3.79
1994	Houston (N)	17	8	0	2.87	32	229	73	183	64	177	$14.2	12	6	0	2.84
1995	Houston (N)	11	10	0	4.91	35	209	114	234	62	167	$8.5	10	9	0	4.77
1996	Houston (N)	7	9	0	4.53	30	175	88	207	60	138	$6.7	7	9	0	4.57
1997	Chicago (A)	12	11	0	6.02	31	169	113	172	71	83	$6.6	12	11	0	5.74
1998	Baltimore (A)	6	11	0	7.51	23	109	91	140	31	55	$2.9	6	11	0	7.29
	Career	161	137	0	4.12	411	2,623	1,200	2,625	776	1,822	$135.9	155	134	0	3.73
	Average season	12	11	0	4.12	32	202	92	202	60	140	$10.5	12	10	0	3.73
	Summit season	17	9	0	3.38	33	234	88	218	62	169	$15.0	16	9	0	2.90

DON DRYSDALE

		ADJUSTED REGULAR SEASON											ACTUAL RESULTS			
YEAR	TEAM	W	L	SV	ERA	G	IP	ER	H	BB	SO	PAY	W	L	SV	ERA
1956	Brooklyn (N)	5	5	0	3.06	26	103	35	105	32	79	$3.9	5	5	0	2.64
1957	Brooklyn (N)	18	10	0	3.19	36	234	83	221	70	210	$10.2	17	9	0	2.69
1958	Los Angeles (N)	13	14	0	4.93	46	221	121	237	82	178	$9.9	12	13	0	4.17
1959	Los Angeles (N)	18	14	3	4.04	46	283	127	262	105	313	$25.9	17	13	2	3.46
1960	Los Angeles (N)	16	15	3	3.41	43	282	107	241	80	316	$26.4	15	14	2	2.84
1961	Los Angeles (N)	14	11	0	4.18	42	256	119	261	89	233	$19.3	13	10	0	3.69
1962	Los Angeles (N)	24	9	1	3.25	42	307	111	280	80	270	$33.2	25	9	1	2.83
1963	Los Angeles (N)	19	17	0	3.46	42	315	121	320	69	282	$32.6	19	17	0	2.63
1964	Los Angeles (N)	18	16	0	2.78	40	321	99	264	82	261	$32.6	18	16	0	2.18
1965	Los Angeles (N)	23	12	1	3.62	44	308	124	303	76	231	$33.4	23	12	1	2.77
1966	Los Angeles (N)	13	16	0	4.43	40	274	135	310	56	199	$20.0	13	16	0	3.42
1967	Los Angeles (N)	13	16	0	3.80	38	282	119	308	72	215	$20.1	13	16	0	2.74
1968	Los Angeles (N)	14	12	0	3.28	31	239	87	237	71	172	$14.5	14	12	0	2.15
1969	Los Angeles (N)	5	4	0	5.71	12	63	40	79	14	27	$2.4	5	4	0	4.45
	Career	213	171	8	3.68	528	3,488	1,428	3,428	978	2,986	$284.4	209	166	6	2.95
	Average season	15	12	1	3.68	38	249	102	245	70	213	$20.3	15	12	0	2.95
	Summit season	20	13	0	3.27	41	297	108	278	75	251	$28.4	20	13	0	2.61

DENNIS ECKERSLEY

YEAR	TEAM	ADJUSTED REGULAR SEASON W	L	SV	ERA	G	IP	ER	H	BB	SO	PAY	ACTUAL RESULTS W	L	SV	ERA
1975	Cleveland (A)	13	7	3	3.23	35	192	69	161	96	199	$7.5	13	7	2	2.60
1976	Cleveland (A)	13	12	1	4.48	37	205	102	172	90	263	$12.6	13	12	1	3.43
1977	Cleveland (A)	14	13	0	4.04	33	247	111	220	59	237	$13.5	14	13	0	3.53
1978	Boston (A)	20	8	0	3.73	35	268	111	275	78	219	$17.2	20	8	0	2.99
1979	Boston (A)	17	10	0	3.43	33	247	94	240	65	203	$16.4	17	10	0	2.99
1980	Boston (A)	12	14	0	5.14	30	198	113	194	50	164	$7.5	12	14	0	4.28
1981	Boston (A)	14	12	0	5.46	35	234	142	262	60	166	$13.1	9	8	0	4.27
1982	Boston (A)	13	13	0	4.42	33	224	110	238	49	165	$7.7	13	13	0	3.73
1983	Boston (A)	9	13	0	6.65	28	176	130	233	43	98	$5.6	9	13	0	5.61
1984	Bos. (A)-Chi. (N)	14	12	0	4.32	33	225	108	233	55	140	$7.5	14	12	0	3.60
1985	Chicago (N)	11	7	0	3.62	25	169	68	154	21	142	$6.1	11	7	0	3.08
1986	Chicago (N)	6	11	0	5.28	33	201	118	240	45	152	$5.8	6	11	0	4.57
1987	Oakland (A)	6	8	18	3.26	54	116	42	102	18	123	$3.9	6	8	16	3.03
1988	Oakland (A)	4	2	45	2.84	60	73	23	56	13	81	$3.5	4	2	45	2.35
1989	Oakland (A)	4	0	33	1.86	51	58	12	35	3	63	$3.1	4	0	33	1.56
1990	Oakland (A)	4	2	46	0.74	63	73	6	43	4	81	$3.8	4	2	48	0.61
1991	Oakland (A)	5	4	41	3.43	67	76	29	64	10	95	$5.7	5	4	43	2.96
1992	Oakland (A)	7	1	50	2.36	69	80	21	67	12	105	$7.0	7	1	51	1.91
1993	Oakland (A)	2	4	35	4.57	64	67	34	69	14	87	$3.7	2	4	36	4.16
1994	Oakland (A)	7	6	27	4.29	64	63	30	69	19	70	$3.6	5	4	19	4.26
1995	Oakland (A)	5	7	32	4.89	59	57	31	61	13	47	$3.0	4	6	29	4.83
1996	St. Louis (N)	0	6	30	3.30	63	60	22	65	6	49	$2.7	0	6	30	3.30
1997	St. Louis (N)	1	5	36	4.08	57	53	24	50	8	44	$2.5	1	5	36	3.91
1998	Boston (A)	4	1	0	4.95	50	40	22	47	9	22	$1.5	4	1	1	4.76
	Career	205	178	397	4.16	1,111	3,402	1,572	3,350	840	3,015	$164.5	197	171	390	3.50
	Average season	9	7	17	4.16	46	142	66	140	35	126	$6.9	8	7	16	3.50
	Summit season	8	3	35	2.86	56	110	35	95	22	110	$6.9	8	3	35	2.28

CHUCK ESTRADA

YEAR	TEAM	ADJUSTED REGULAR SEASON W	L	SV	ERA	G	IP	ER	H	BB	SO	PAY	ACTUAL RESULTS W	L	SV	ERA
1960	Baltimore (A)	19	12	3	4.30	38	220	105	183	113	190	$19.5	18	11	2	3.58
1961	Baltimore (A)	15	9	0	4.20	33	212	99	167	136	196	$16.1	15	9	0	3.69
1962	Baltimore (A)	9	17	0	4.44	34	223	110	210	129	196	$15.0	9	17	0	3.83
1963	Baltimore (A)	3	2	0	6.10	8	31	21	29	23	18	$2.2	3	2	0	4.60
1964	Baltimore (A)	3	2	0	6.71	17	55	41	68	26	36	$2.1	3	2	0	5.27
1966	Chicago (N)	1	1	0	9.75	9	12	13	17	6	3	$0.1	1	1	0	7.30
1967	New York (N)	1	2	0	13.09	9	22	32	32	21	16	$0.1	1	2	0	9.41
	Career	51	45	3	4.89	148	775	421	706	454	655	$55.1	50	44	2	4.07
	Average season	7	6	0	4.89	21	111	60	101	65	94	$7.9	7	6	0	4.07
	Summit season	12	10	1	4.50	31	178	89	157	101	155	$13.2	11	10	1	3.83

RED FABER

		ADJUSTED REGULAR SEASON											ACTUAL RESULTS			
YEAR	TEAM	W	L	SV	ERA	G	IP	ER	H	BB	SO	PAY	W	L	SV	ERA
1914	Chicago (A)	10	9	13	4.21	41	186	87	176	79	146	$9.7	10	9	4	2.68
1915	Chicago (A)	25	15	6	4.01	52	312	139	312	124	310	$33.9	24	14	2	2.55
1916	Chicago (A)	18	10	4	3.40	37	217	82	203	82	158	$19.1	17	9	1	2.02
1917	Chicago (A)	17	14	8	3.29	43	260	95	269	116	169	$20.5	16	13	3	1.92
1918	Chicago (A)	5	1	4	2.01	14	103	23	100	38	75	$5.8	4	1	1	1.23
1919	Chicago (A)	13	10	0	5.74	29	188	120	228	70	114	$9.2	11	9	0	3.83
1920	Chicago (A)	24	14	2	3.95	42	335	147	346	120	251	$31.6	23	13	1	2.99
1921	Chicago (A)	26	16	2	2.78	45	346	107	281	116	291	$39.1	25	15	1	2.48
1922	Chicago (A)	22	18	4	3.15	45	368	129	324	105	342	$49.4	21	17	2	2.81
1923	Chicago (A)	14	11	0	3.90	33	240	104	228	74	208	$18.6	14	11	0	3.41
1924	Chicago (A)	9	12	0	4.37	22	169	82	170	73	119	$7.1	9	11	0	3.85
1925	Chicago (A)	13	12	0	4.00	36	252	112	256	70	180	$13.3	12	11	0	3.78
1926	Chicago (A)	16	9	0	4.17	28	192	89	204	67	155	$7.3	15	9	0	3.56
1927	Chicago (A)	4	7	0	5.15	19	117	67	132	51	95	$3.4	4	7	0	4.55
1928	Chicago (A)	13	9	0	4.26	28	209	99	223	81	105	$6.1	13	9	0	3.75
1929	Chicago (A)	14	14	0	3.98	33	249	110	236	71	166	$12.7	13	13	0	3.88
1930	Chicago (A)	9	14	3	3.98	31	181	80	178	60	133	$5.8	8	13	1	4.21
1931	Chicago (A)	10	15	4	4.22	46	192	90	208	68	107	$6.0	10	14	1	3.82
1932	Chicago (A)	2	12	18	4.11	45	114	52	126	48	60	$3.3	2	11	6	3.74
1933	Chicago (A)	3	4	15	4.12	39	94	43	99	36	45	$2.6	3	4	5	3.44
	Career	267	226	83	3.87	708	4,324	1,857	4,299	1,549	3,229	$304.5	254	213	28	3.15
	Average season	13	11	4	3.87	35	216	93	215	77	161	$15.2	13	11	1	3.15
	Summit season	23	15	4	3.42	45	324	123	306	116	273	$34.9	22	14	2	2.58

ELROY FACE

		ADJUSTED REGULAR SEASON											ACTUAL RESULTS			
YEAR	TEAM	W	L	SV	ERA	G	IP	ER	H	BB	SO	PAY	W	L	SV	ERA
1953	Pittsburgh (N)	6	8	0	7.27	43	125	101	155	32	92	$4.4	6	8	0	6.58
1955	Pittsburgh (N)	5	7	10	4.09	44	132	60	142	41	127	$5.2	5	7	5	3.58
1956	Pittsburgh (N)	12	13	13	4.08	70	139	63	142	42	134	$7.9	12	13	6	3.52
1957	Pittsburgh (N)	4	6	18	3.67	62	98	40	108	27	75	$5.1	4	6	10	3.07
1958	Pittsburgh (N)	5	2	30	3.38	60	88	33	85	25	65	$5.4	5	2	20	2.89
1959	Pittsburgh (N)	19	1	18	3.12	60	98	34	101	28	91	$9.2	18	1	10	2.70
1960	Pittsburgh (N)	10	8	33	3.45	71	120	46	105	32	94	$8.2	10	8	24	2.90
1961	Pittsburgh (N)	6	13	24	4.31	65	96	46	103	11	71	$6.8	6	12	17	3.82
1962	Pittsburgh (N)	8	7	33	2.18	63	91	22	78	19	55	$6.8	8	7	28	1.88
1963	Pittsburgh (N)	3	9	22	4.24	56	70	33	84	23	47	$3.6	3	9	16	3.23
1964	Pittsburgh (N)	3	3	5	6.64	55	80	59	90	33	70	$3.1	3	3	4	5.20
1965	Pittsburgh (N)	5	2	0	3.60	16	20	8	22	8	21	$1.3	5	2	0	2.66
1966	Pittsburgh (N)	6	6	21	3.47	54	70	27	75	30	74	$2.9	6	6	18	2.70
1967	Pittsburgh (N)	7	5	22	3.41	61	74	28	71	26	45	$2.6	7	5	17	2.42
1968	Pit. (N)-Det. (A)	2	4	18	3.98	44	52	23	56	10	38	$2.0	2	4	13	2.55
1969	Montreal (N)	4	2	7	5.03	44	59	33	69	15	38	$2.0	4	2	5	3.94
	Career	105	96	274	4.18	868	1,412	656	1,486	402	1,137	$76.5	104	95	193	3.48
	Average season	7	6	17	4.18	54	88	41	93	25	71	$4.8	7	6	12	3.48
	Summit season	10	5	27	3.16	63	94	33	88	26	70	$6.4	10	5	20	2.58

BOB FELLER

YEAR	TEAM	ADJUSTED REGULAR SEASON											ACTUAL RESULTS			
		W	L	SV	ERA	G	IP	ER	H	BB	SO	PAY	W	L	SV	ERA
1936	Cleveland (A)	5	3	3	3.34	14	62	23	48	49	114	$3.6	5	3	1	3.34
1937	Cleveland (A)	9	7	3	3.62	27	154	62	115	115	235	$7.7	9	7	1	3.39
1938	Cleveland (A)	18	12	3	4.35	41	292	141	228	222	414	$26.5	17	11	1	4.08
1939	Cleveland (A)	25	9	3	3.03	41	312	105	230	154	426	$40.2	24	9	1	2.85
1940	Cleveland (A)	28	12	4	2.90	45	335	108	254	131	436	$52.2	27	11	4	2.61
1941	Cleveland (A)	26	14	4	3.69	46	359	147	303	204	451	$55.3	25	13	2	3.15
1945	Cleveland (A)	6	3	0	3.15	10	80	28	58	41	112	$7.8	5	3	0	2.50
1946	Cleveland (A)	27	16	6	2.86	50	387	123	307	161	541	$57.9	26	15	4	2.18
1947	Cleveland (A)	20	11	7	3.15	43	306	107	244	124	330	$34.4	20	11	3	2.68
1948	Cleveland (A)	20	16	5	3.96	46	293	129	272	110	290	$32.6	19	15	3	3.56
1949	Cleveland (A)	16	15	0	4.16	38	223	103	216	78	198	$19.8	15	14	0	3.75
1950	Cleveland (A)	17	12	0	3.59	37	261	104	245	96	208	$18.9	16	11	0	3.43
1951	Cleveland (A)	23	8	0	3.96	34	257	113	255	94	197	$24.3	22	8	0	3.50
1952	Cleveland (A)	9	13	0	5.86	31	198	129	246	87	131	$8.4	9	13	0	4.74
1953	Cleveland (A)	10	7	0	3.98	26	183	81	173	63	101	$7.1	10	7	0	3.59
1954	Cleveland (A)	14	3	0	3.61	20	147	59	140	40	99	$5.9	13	3	0	3.09
1955	Cleveland (A)	4	4	0	3.98	26	86	38	78	31	40	$2.3	4	4	0	3.47
1956	Cleveland (A)	0	4	2	5.75	20	61	39	70	24	27	$1.1	0	4	1	4.97
	Career	277	169	40	3.69	595	3,996	1,639	3,482	1,824	4,350	$406.0	266	162	21	3.25
	Average season	15	9	2	3.69	33	222	91	193	101	242	$22.6	15	9	1	3.25
	Summit season	25	12	5	3.12	45	340	118	268	155	437	$48.0	24	12	3	2.68

WES FERRELL

YEAR	TEAM	ADJUSTED REGULAR SEASON											ACTUAL RESULTS			
		W	L	SV	ERA	G	IP	ER	H	BB	SO	PAY	W	L	SV	ERA
1927	Cleveland (A)	0	0	0	27.00	1	1	3	3	2	0	$0.0	0	0	0	27.00
1928	Cleveland (A)	0	2	0	2.81	2	16	5	14	6	9	$0.0	0	2	0	2.25
1929	Cleveland (A)	22	11	9	3.67	46	260	106	252	128	233	$16.1	21	10	5	3.60
1930	Cleveland (A)	26	14	4	3.14	45	310	108	276	126	288	$32.2	25	13	3	3.31
1931	Cleveland (A)	23	13	5	4.16	42	290	134	275	157	254	$32.4	22	12	3	3.75
1932	Cleveland (A)	24	14	1	4.01	40	303	135	300	129	225	$40.2	23	13	1	3.66
1933	Cleveland (A)	12	13	0	5.07	30	215	121	238	89	100	$15.2	11	12	0	4.21
1934	Boston (A)	15	5	3	3.88	27	188	81	200	56	132	$15.2	14	5	1	3.63
1935	Boston (A)	26	15	0	3.78	43	338	142	332	126	231	$34.5	25	14	0	3.52
1936	Boston (A)	21	16	0	4.22	41	316	148	319	131	219	$32.4	20	15	0	4.19
1937	Bos.-Wash. (A)	14	20	0	5.26	38	289	169	320	130	223	$25.9	14	19	0	4.90
1938	Wash.-N.Y. (A)	16	10	0	6.76	29	185	139	245	89	88	$9.8	15	10	0	6.28
1939	New York (A)	1	2	0	5.21	3	19	11	13	17	11	$1.9	1	2	0	4.66
1940	Brooklyn (N)	0	0	0	6.75	1	4	3	4	4	6	$0.5	0	0	0	6.75
1941	Boston (N)	2	1	0	5.79	4	14	9	13	9	16	$0.5	2	1	0	5.14
	Career	202	136	22	4.30	392	2,748	1,314	2,804	1,199	2,035	$256.8	193	128	13	4.04
	Average season	13	9	1	4.30	26	183	88	187	80	136	$17.1	13	9	1	4.04
	Summit season	24	13	4	3.75	43	300	125	287	133	246	$31.1	23	12	2	3.56

ROLLIE FINGERS

		ADJUSTED REGULAR SEASON											ACTUAL RESULTS			
YEAR	TEAM	W	L	SV	ERA	G	IP	ER	H	BB	SO	PAY	W	L	SV	ERA
1968	Oakland (A)	0	0	0	45.00	1	1	5	4	1	0	$0.0	0	0	0	27.00
1969	Oakland (A)	6	7	16	4.69	60	119	62	129	43	70	$4.1	6	7	12	3.71
1970	Oakland (A)	7	9	2	4.32	45	148	71	148	49	90	$4.8	7	9	2	3.65
1971	Oakland (A)	4	6	22	3.98	48	129	57	104	33	116	$5.5	4	6	17	2.99
1972	Oakland (A)	12	9	26	3.49	68	116	45	101	38	135	$8.4	11	9	21	2.51
1973	Oakland (A)	7	8	25	2.34	62	127	33	114	42	134	$8.3	7	8	22	1.92
1974	Oakland (A)	9	5	33	3.33	76	119	44	111	31	120	$9.5	9	5	18	2.65
1975	Oakland (A)	10	6	33	3.69	75	127	52	101	34	145	$15.1	10	6	24	2.98
1976	Oakland (A)	13	11	27	3.20	70	135	48	128	45	147	$15.3	13	11	20	2.47
1977	San Diego (N)	8	9	40	3.41	78	132	50	126	39	139	$15.5	8	9	35	2.99
1978	San Diego (N)	6	13	40	3.11	67	107	37	89	32	96	$8.4	6	13	37	2.52
1979	San Diego (N)	9	9	16	5.14	54	84	48	94	41	86	$6.8	9	9	13	4.52
1980	San Diego (N)	11	9	26	3.32	66	103	38	104	37	92	$8.1	11	9	23	2.80
1981	Milwaukee (A)	9	4	45	1.32	70	116	17	88	22	120	$8.9	6	3	28	1.04
1982	Milwaukee (A)	5	6	30	3.04	50	80	27	66	23	89	$5.7	5	6	29	2.60
1984	Milwaukee (A)	1	2	23	2.35	33	46	12	40	15	48	$2.6	1	2	23	1.96
1985	Milwaukee (A)	1	6	18	5.89	47	55	36	62	21	30	$2.2	1	6	17	5.04
	Career	118	119	422	3.52	970	1,744	682	1,609	546	1,657	$129.2	114	118	341	2.90
	Average season	7	7	25	3.52	57	103	40	95	32	97	$7.6	7	7	20	2.90
	Summit season	10	9	36	2.90	71	121	39	106	35	127	$11.3	9	9	28	2.41

EDDIE FISHER

		ADJUSTED REGULAR SEASON											ACTUAL RESULTS			
YEAR	TEAM	W	L	SV	ERA	G	IP	ER	H	BB	SO	PAY	W	L	SV	ERA
1959	San Francisco (N)	2	6	2	9.21	18	42	43	63	9	20	$0.7	2	6	1	7.88
1960	San Francisco (N)	1	0	0	4.15	3	13	6	12	2	9	$0.0	1	0	0	3.55
1961	San Francisco (N)	0	2	2	6.00	16	36	24	41	10	21	$0.3	0	2	1	5.35
1962	Chicago (A)	9	5	7	3.59	57	183	73	179	48	107	$5.1	9	5	5	3.10
1963	Chicago (A)	9	8	0	5.21	33	121	70	128	34	76	$4.4	9	8	0	3.95
1964	Chicago (A)	6	3	11	3.89	59	125	54	94	39	82	$5.0	6	3	9	3.02
1965	Chicago (A)	15	7	29	3.11	82	165	57	132	50	99	$9.5	15	7	24	2.40
1966	Chi.-Balt. (A)	6	6	23	3.28	67	107	39	96	45	64	$5.7	6	6	19	2.52
1967	Baltimore (A)	4	3	1	5.00	46	90	50	94	32	58	$4.7	4	3	1	3.61
1968	Cleveland (A)	4	2	6	4.36	54	95	46	103	22	48	$3.6	4	2	4	2.85
1969	California (A)	3	2	3	4.64	52	97	50	112	29	54	$3.0	3	2	2	3.63
1970	California (A)	4	4	9	3.60	67	130	52	126	35	84	$3.6	4	4	8	3.04
1971	California (A)	10	8	4	3.55	57	119	47	102	55	98	$4.3	10	8	3	2.72
1972	Cal.-Chi. (A)	4	6	5	5.50	51	108	66	124	48	52	$2.5	4	6	4	3.91
1973	Chi. (A)-St.L. (N)	8	8	0	5.72	32	118	75	147	42	74	$3.2	8	8	0	4.67
	Career	85	70	102	4.37	694	1,549	752	1,553	500	946	$55.6	85	70	81	3.41
	Average season	6	5	7	4.37	46	103	50	104	33	63	$3.7	6	5	5	3.41
	Summit season	9	6	15	3.47	64	140	54	121	47	90	$5.9	9	6	12	2.77

MIKE FLANAGAN

		ADJUSTED REGULAR SEASON											ACTUAL RESULTS			
YEAR	TEAM	W	L	SV	ERA	G	IP	ER	H	BB	SO	PAY	W	L	SV	ERA
1975	Baltimore (A)	0	1	0	3.60	2	10	4	10	6	10	$0.0	0	1	0	2.79
1976	Baltimore (A)	3	5	0	5.40	20	85	51	90	37	75	$2.7	3	5	0	4.13
1977	Baltimore (A)	15	10	1	4.17	36	235	109	242	77	188	$8.5	15	10	1	3.64
1978	Baltimore (A)	19	15	0	5.03	40	281	157	288	96	225	$19.1	19	15	0	4.03
1979	Baltimore (A)	24	9	0	3.54	40	272	107	257	79	259	$26.0	23	9	0	3.08
1980	Baltimore (A)	16	13	0	4.91	37	251	137	286	81	175	$19.5	16	13	0	4.12
1981	Baltimore (A)	14	9	0	5.35	31	180	107	181	65	152	$10.2	9	6	0	4.19
1982	Baltimore (A)	15	11	0	4.73	36	236	124	243	86	136	$15.9	15	11	0	3.97
1983	Baltimore (A)	12	4	0	3.89	20	125	54	141	34	64	$4.8	12	4	0	3.30
1984	Baltimore (A)	13	13	0	4.24	34	227	107	223	92	141	$8.8	13	13	0	3.53
1985	Baltimore (A)	4	5	0	6.07	15	86	58	107	30	52	$3.4	4	5	0	5.13
1986	Baltimore (A)	7	11	0	4.87	29	172	93	190	70	107	$4.6	7	11	0	4.24
1987	Balt.-Tor. (A)	6	8	0	4.31	23	144	69	152	53	101	$3.3	6	8	0	4.06
1988	Toronto (A)	13	13	0	5.12	34	211	120	237	93	117	$5.8	13	13	0	4.18
1989	Toronto (A)	8	10	0	4.87	30	172	93	201	52	56	$3.2	8	10	0	3.93
1990	Toronto (A)	2	2	0	6.30	5	20	14	29	9	6	$0.6	2	2	0	5.31
1991	Baltimore (A)	2	7	2	2.76	64	98	30	90	27	62	$2.5	2	7	3	2.38
1992	Baltimore (A)	0	0	0	9.77	42	35	38	54	26	20	$0.3	0	0	0	8.05
	Career	173	146	3	4.66	538	2,840	1,472	3,021	1,013	1,946	$139.2	167	143	4	3.90
	Average season	10	8	0	4.66	30	158	82	168	56	108	$7.7	9	8	0	3.90
	Summit season	18	12	0	4.48	38	255	127	263	84	197	$17.8	18	12	0	3.76

WHITEY FORD

		ADJUSTED REGULAR SEASON											ACTUAL RESULTS			
YEAR	TEAM	W	L	SV	ERA	G	IP	ER	H	BB	SO	PAY	W	L	SV	ERA
1950	New York (A)	9	1	2	2.97	21	118	39	93	48	102	$5.4	9	1	1	2.81
1953	New York (A)	19	6	0	3.31	34	220	81	202	119	181	$15.1	18	6	0	3.00
1954	New York (A)	17	8	2	3.31	36	223	82	188	105	203	$15.9	16	8	1	2.82
1955	New York (A)	19	7	4	3.00	41	267	89	209	116	212	$20.4	18	7	2	2.63
1956	New York (A)	20	6	2	2.85	33	240	76	210	88	207	$20.3	19	6	1	2.47
1957	New York (A)	11	5	0	3.07	25	135	46	126	61	117	$8.4	11	5	0	2.57
1958	New York (A)	14	7	2	2.38	31	227	60	190	69	194	$15.9	14	7	1	2.01
1959	New York (A)	17	11	2	3.54	37	216	85	218	102	154	$15.5	16	10	1	3.04
1960	New York (A)	12	9	0	3.71	34	199	82	186	71	113	$7.4	12	9	0	3.08
1961	New York (A)	25	4	0	3.66	39	283	115	255	94	256	$25.5	25	4	0	3.21
1962	New York (A)	17	8	0	3.35	38	258	96	257	73	193	$18.4	17	8	0	2.90
1963	New York (A)	24	7	1	3.61	38	269	108	268	68	212	$25.1	24	7	1	2.74
1964	New York (A)	17	6	1	2.72	39	245	74	232	69	190	$17.2	17	6	1	2.13
1965	New York (A)	16	13	1	4.24	37	244	115	271	58	178	$16.6	16	13	1	3.24
1966	New York (A)	2	5	0	3.21	22	73	26	88	30	48	$2.6	2	5	0	2.47
1967	New York (A)	2	4	0	2.25	7	44	11	46	11	23	$1.3	2	4	0	1.64
	Career	241	107	17	3.27	512	3,261	1,185	3,039	1,182	2,583	$231.0	236	106	10	2.75
	Average season	15	7	1	3.27	32	204	74	190	74	161	$14.4	15	7	1	2.75
	Summit season	21	6	2	3.17	38	261	92	235	87	215	$21.7	21	6	1	2.66

JOHN FRANCO

		ADJUSTED REGULAR SEASON											ACTUAL RESULTS			
YEAR	TEAM	W	L	SV	ERA	G	IP	ER	H	BB	SO	PAY	W	L	SV	ERA
1984	Cincinnati (N)	6	2	4	3.19	54	79	28	77	41	66	$4.0	6	2	4	2.61
1985	Cincinnati (N)	12	3	13	2.55	67	99	28	88	44	75	$5.5	12	3	12	2.18
1986	Cincinnati (N)	6	6	30	3.39	74	101	38	95	47	92	$5.9	6	6	29	2.94
1987	Cincinnati (N)	8	5	33	2.74	68	82	25	78	28	67	$5.7	8	5	32	2.52
1988	Cincinnati (N)	6	6	39	1.88	70	86	18	65	31	54	$5.7	6	6	39	1.57
1989	Cincinnati (N)	4	8	32	3.89	60	81	35	83	40	69	$5.7	4	8	32	3.12
1990	New York (N)	5	3	32	3.04	55	68	23	70	23	64	$5.3	5	3	33	2.53
1991	New York (N)	5	9	28	3.44	52	55	21	65	19	50	$4.4	5	9	30	2.93
1992	New York (N)	6	2	14	1.91	31	33	7	26	12	23	$2.5	6	2	15	1.64
1993	New York (N)	4	3	9	5.75	35	36	23	47	20	32	$2.3	4	3	10	5.20
1994	New York (N)	1	6	43	2.79	67	71	22	67	28	63	$4.1	1	4	30	2.70
1995	New York (N)	6	3	33	2.48	54	58	16	54	19	48	$3.4	5	3	29	2.44
1996	New York (N)	4	3	28	1.83	51	54	11	54	21	48	$2.6	4	3	28	1.83
1997	New York (N)	5	3	36	2.70	59	60	18	50	21	52	$3.1	5	3	36	2.55
1998	New York (N)	0	8	37	3.74	61	65	27	67	31	59	$3.1	0	8	38	3.62
1999	New York (N)	0	2	19	2.85	46	41	13	40	18	42	$2.1	0	2	19	2.88
2000	New York (N)	5	4	4	3.21	62	56	20	46	25	57	$2.4	5	4	4	3.40
2001	New York (N)	6	2	1	4.25	58	53	25	56	21	48	$1.8	6	2	2	4.05
	Career	89	78	435	3.04	1,024	1,178	398	1,128	489	1,009	$69.6	88	76	422	2.75
	Average season	5	4	24	3.04	57	65	22	63	27	56	$3.9	5	4	23	2.75
	Summit season	7	4	31	2.45	64	77	21	67	29	59	$4.7	7	4	30	2.21

JIM GALVIN

		ADJUSTED REGULAR SEASON											ACTUAL RESULTS			
YEAR	TEAM	W	L	SV	ERA	G	IP	ER	H	BB	SO	PAY	W	L	SV	ERA
1879	Buffalo (N)	76	55	0	4.13	135	1,213	556	1,157	277	647	$144.7	37	27	0	2.28
1880	Buffalo (N)	38	67	0	5.29	111	878	516	1,079	193	546	$109.6	20	35	0	2.71
1881	Buffalo (N)	55	47	0	3.87	109	923	397	1,050	200	649	$113.5	28	24	0	2.37
1882	Buffalo (N)	54	44	0	5.20	100	856	495	935	193	681	$109.6	28	23	0	3.17
1883	Buffalo (N)	76	48	0	3.83	126	1,088	463	1,086	192	874	$132.0	46	29	0	2.72
1884	Buffalo (N)	65	31	0	2.91	101	893	289	833	190	683	$117.4	46	22	0	1.99
1885	Buff. (N)-Pit. (AA)	23	38	2	6.06	64	542	365	707	113	305	$76.4	16	26	1	3.99
1886	Pittsburgh (AA)	34	24	0	3.61	58	504	202	560	113	130	$70.7	29	21	0	2.67
1887	Pittsburgh (N)	37	27	0	3.58	64	576	229	604	105	240	$73.6	28	21	0	3.29
1888	Pittsburgh (N)	27	29	0	4.08	58	507	230	575	99	220	$60.0	23	25	0	2.63
1889	Pittsburgh (N)	28	20	0	4.87	50	416	225	470	98	178	$54.7	23	16	0	4.17
1890	Pittsburgh (P)	15	17	0	5.14	33	275	157	346	59	91	$24.0	12	13	0	4.35
1891	Pittsburgh (N)	18	17	0	3.73	39	292	121	310	71	107	$24.0	15	14	0	2.88
1892	Pit.-St. L. (N)	10	13	0	4.09	25	196	89	230	59	118	$7.3	10	12	0	2.92
	Career	556	477	2	4.26	1,073	9,159	4,334	9,942	1,962	5,469	$1,117.5	361	308	1	2.87
	Average season	40	34	0	4.26	77	654	310	710	140	391	$79.8	26	22	0	2.87
	Summit season	65	45	0	3.98	114	995	440	1,012	210	707	$123.4	37	25	0	2.47

NED GARVER

		ADJUSTED REGULAR SEASON												ACTUAL RESULTS			
YEAR	TEAM	W	L	SV	ERA	G	IP	ER	H	BB	SO	PAY	W	L	SV	ERA
1948	St. Louis (A)	7	12	10	3.76	40	208	87	215	91	140	$8.3	7	11	5	3.41
1949	St. Louis (A)	13	18	6	4.40	43	235	115	266	94	136	$10.0	12	17	3	3.98
1950	St. Louis (A)	14	19	0	3.55	39	274	108	281	100	153	$16.0	13	18	0	3.39
1951	St. Louis (A)	21	13	0	4.21	35	261	122	261	98	158	$19.4	20	12	0	3.73
1952	St.L.-Det. (A)	8	10	0	4.47	23	165	82	158	61	104	$7.9	8	10	0	3.60
1953	Detroit (A)	11	11	2	4.92	31	205	112	240	69	115	$9.2	11	11	1	4.45
1954	Detroit (A)	15	12	2	3.29	37	260	95	239	64	158	$16.1	14	11	1	2.81
1955	Detroit (A)	13	17	0	4.56	35	245	124	282	69	133	$10.0	12	16	0	3.98
1956	Detroit (A)	0	2	0	4.50	6	18	9	16	13	9	$1.3	0	2	0	4.08
1957	Kansas City (A)	6	14	0	4.59	25	151	77	132	62	88	$4.2	6	13	0	3.84
1958	Kansas City (A)	12	11	2	4.78	32	207	110	209	74	100	$6.6	12	11	1	4.03
1959	Kansas City (A)	11	14	2	4.33	34	214	103	241	48	85	$4.9	10	13	1	3.71
1960	Kansas City (A)	4	9	0	4.61	29	127	65	123	38	66	$3.7	4	9	0	3.83
1961	Los Angeles (A)	0	3	0	6.21	12	29	20	42	16	11	$0.6	0	3	0	5.59
	Career	135	165	24	4.26	421	2,599	1,229	2,705	897	1,456	$118.2	129	157	12	3.73
	Average season	10	12	2	4.26	30	186	88	193	64	104	$8.4	9	11	1	3.73
	Summit season	15	16	2	3.99	38	255	113	266	85	148	$14.3	14	15	1	3.57

BOB GIBSON

		ADJUSTED REGULAR SEASON												ACTUAL RESULTS			
YEAR	TEAM	W	L	SV	ERA	G	IP	ER	H	BB	SO	PAY	W	L	SV	ERA
1959	St. Louis (N)	3	5	0	3.89	14	81	35	87	45	65	$2.8	3	5	0	3.33
1960	St. Louis (N)	3	6	0	6.70	28	90	67	108	53	89	$3.3	3	6	0	5.61
1961	St. Louis (N)	14	13	2	3.67	37	223	91	207	130	214	$9.3	13	12	1	3.24
1962	St. Louis (N)	15	13	1	3.31	32	234	86	184	101	245	$10.2	15	13	1	2.85
1963	St. Louis (N)	18	9	0	4.48	36	255	127	250	117	229	$19.0	18	9	0	3.39
1964	St. Louis (N)	19	12	1	3.83	40	287	122	273	104	269	$26.4	19	12	1	3.01
1965	St. Louis (N)	20	12	1	4.00	38	299	133	273	120	296	$32.3	20	12	1	3.07
1966	St. Louis (N)	21	12	0	3.15	35	280	98	232	97	251	$27.0	21	12	0	2.44
1967	St. Louis (N)	13	7	0	4.11	24	175	80	172	48	160	$8.9	13	7	0	2.98
1968	St. Louis (N)	22	9	0	1.71	34	305	58	233	79	296	$31.4	22	9	0	1.12
1969	St. Louis (N)	20	13	0	2.75	35	314	96	279	99	301	$31.5	20	13	0	2.18
1970	St. Louis (N)	23	7	0	3.67	34	294	120	282	89	307	$31.4	23	7	0	3.12
1971	St. Louis (N)	16	13	0	4.02	31	246	110	239	84	221	$17.3	16	13	0	3.04
1972	St. Louis (N)	20	11	0	3.46	35	286	110	265	103	250	$24.0	19	11	0	2.46
1973	St. Louis (N)	12	10	0	3.37	25	195	73	169	61	175	$12.5	12	10	0	2.77
1974	St. Louis (N)	11	13	0	4.84	33	240	129	252	112	168	$12.8	11	13	0	3.83
1975	St. Louis (N)	3	10	3	6.28	22	109	76	128	64	79	$3.4	3	10	2	5.04
	Career	253	175	8	3.71	533	3,913	1,611	3,633	1,506	3,615	$303.5	251	174	6	2.91
	Average season	15	10	0	3.71	31	230	95	214	89	213	$17.9	15	10	0	2.91
	Summit season	21	10	0	2.92	35	296	96	258	93	281	$29.1	21	10	0	2.25

TOM GLAVINE

YEAR	TEAM	ADJUSTED REGULAR SEASON											ACTUAL RESULTS			
		W	L	SV	ERA	G	IP	ER	H	BB	SO	PAY	W	L	SV	ERA
1987	Atlanta (N)	2	4	0	5.94	9	50	33	56	34	22	$0.7	2	4	0	5.54
1988	Atlanta (N)	7	17	0	5.58	34	195	121	217	73	99	$4.6	7	17	0	4.56
1989	Atlanta (N)	14	8	0	4.55	29	186	94	185	45	105	$5.8	14	8	0	3.68
1990	Atlanta (N)	10	12	0	5.09	33	214	121	245	84	148	$8.1	10	12	0	4.28
1991	Atlanta (N)	20	11	0	2.99	34	247	82	216	75	216	$16.4	20	11	0	2.55
1992	Atlanta (N)	20	8	0	3.36	33	225	84	212	77	151	$15.9	20	8	0	2.76
1993	Atlanta (N)	22	6	0	3.50	36	239	93	241	96	135	$19.3	22	6	0	3.20
1994	Atlanta (N)	19	13	0	4.05	36	238	107	248	104	212	$20.2	13	9	0	3.97
1995	Atlanta (N)	18	8	0	3.15	33	226	79	209	76	149	$19.1	16	7	0	3.08
1996	Atlanta (N)	15	10	0	2.95	36	235	77	220	86	182	$18.9	15	10	0	2.98
1997	Atlanta (N)	14	7	0	3.08	33	240	82	199	82	149	$15.8	14	7	0	2.96
1998	Atlanta (N)	20	6	0	2.55	33	229	65	204	78	155	$14.9	20	6	0	2.47
1999	Atlanta (N)	14	11	0	4.00	35	234	104	256	80	139	$14.2	14	11	0	4.12
2000	Atlanta (N)	21	9	0	3.25	35	241	87	220	61	153	$17.9	21	9	0	3.40
2001	Atlanta (N)	16	7	0	3.70	35	219	90	218	106	113	$13.9	16	7	0	3.57
	Career	232	137	0	3.69	484	3,218	1,319	3,146	1,157	2,128	$205.7	224	132	0	3.40
	Average season	15	9	0	3.69	32	215	88	210	77	142	$13.7	15	9	0	3.40
	Summit season	21	8	0	3.13	34	236	82	219	77	162	$16.9	21	8	0	2.886

LEFTY GOMEZ

YEAR	TEAM	ADJUSTED REGULAR SEASON											ACTUAL RESULTS			
		W	L	SV	ERA	G	IP	ER	H	BB	SO	PAY	W	L	SV	ERA
1930	New York (A)	2	5	3	5.34	16	64	38	62	34	47	$1.7	2	5	1	5.55
1931	New York (A)	22	9	7	2.89	42	255	82	205	102	291	$19.2	21	9	3	2.63
1932	New York (A)	25	7	3	4.62	38	273	140	260	127	333	$32.2	24	7	1	4.21
1933	New York (A)	17	11	4	3.81	37	248	105	228	134	323	$25.7	16	10	2	3.18
1934	New York (A)	27	5	3	2.46	40	296	81	220	111	296	$41.1	26	5	1	2.33
1935	New York (A)	13	16	3	3.43	37	268	102	229	105	280	$26.4	12	15	1	3.18
1936	New York (A)	13	7	0	4.43	32	195	96	175	133	199	$15.4	13	7	0	4.39
1937	New York (A)	22	11	0	2.48	35	287	79	229	99	329	$32.9	21	11	0	2.33
1938	New York (A)	19	12	0	3.59	33	246	98	237	102	239	$19.9	18	12	0	3.35
1939	New York (A)	13	9	0	3.63	28	213	86	180	93	198	$15.5	12	8	0	3.41
1940	New York (A)	3	3	0	7.33	9	27	22	36	19	24	$2.2	3	3	0	6.59
1941	New York (A)	16	5	0	4.42	24	163	80	161	108	141	$8.2	15	5	0	3.74
1942	New York (A)	6	4	0	5.65	14	86	54	77	73	81	$3.8	6	4	0	4.28
1943	Washington (A)	0	1	0	7.20	1	5	4	5	6	0	$0.2	0	1	0	5.79
	Career	198	105	23	3.66	386	2,626	1,067	2,304	1,246	2,781	$244.4	189	102	9	3.34
	Average season	14	8	2	3.66	28	188	76	165	89	199	$17.5	14	7	1	3.34
	Summit season	23	9	3	3.19	38	271	96	230	108	298	$29.1	22	9	1	2.95

DWIGHT GOODEN

		ADJUSTED REGULAR SEASON											ACTUAL RESULTS			
YEAR	TEAM	W	L	SV	ERA	G	IP	ER	H	BB	SO	PAY	W	L	SV	ERA
1984	New York (N)	17	9	0	3.14	31	218	76	168	83	319	$19.5	17	9	0	2.60
1985	New York (N)	24	4	0	1.79	35	277	55	210	75	318	$32.5	24	4	0	1.53
1986	New York (N)	17	6	0	3.28	33	250	91	209	85	221	$20.2	17	6	0	2.84
1987	New York (N)	15	7	0	3.40	25	180	68	167	55	161	$15.1	15	7	0	3.21
1988	New York (N)	18	9	0	3.92	34	248	108	261	66	204	$19.9	18	9	0	3.19
1989	New York (N)	9	4	1	3.58	19	118	47	100	52	115	$7.8	9	4	1	2.89
1990	New York (N)	19	7	0	4.56	34	233	118	243	76	252	$19.3	19	7	0	3.83
1991	New York (N)	13	7	0	4.22	27	190	89	198	60	168	$9.8	13	7	0	3.60
1992	New York (N)	10	13	0	4.50	31	206	103	212	77	169	$9.5	10	13	0	3.67
1993	New York (N)	12	15	0	3.79	29	209	88	193	65	166	$9.8	12	15	0	3.45
1994	New York (N)	4	6	0	6.41	10	59	42	66	22	60	$3.5	3	4	0	6.31
1996	New York (A)	11	7	0	5.00	29	171	95	168	89	127	$6.7	11	7	0	5.01
1997	New York (A)	9	5	0	5.09	20	106	60	117	55	65	$4.0	9	5	0	4.91
1998	Cleveland (A)	8	6	0	3.90	23	134	58	137	54	82	$4.2	8	6	0	3.76
1999	Cleveland (A)	3	4	0	6.10	26	115	78	126	65	89	$3.7	3	4	0	6.26
2000	Hou. (N)-T.B.-N.Y. (A)	6	5	2	4.54	27	105	53	118	42	55	$2.6	6	5	2	4.71
	Career	195	114	3	3.92	433	2,819	1,229	2,693	1,021	2,571	$188.1	194	112	3	3.51
	Average season	12	7	0	3.92	27	176	77	168	64	161	$11.8	12	7	0	3.51
	Summit season	19	7	0	3.31	33	245	90	218	77	263	$22.3	19	7	0	2.76

RICH GOSSAGE

		ADJUSTED REGULAR SEASON											ACTUAL RESULTS			
YEAR	TEAM	W	L	SV	ERA	G	IP	ER	H	BB	SO	PAY	W	L	SV	ERA
1972	Chicago (A)	7	1	3	6.00	38	84	56	86	53	70	$4.4	7	1	2	4.28
1973	Chicago (A)	0	4	0	9.18	20	50	51	61	40	41	$1.6	0	4	0	7.43
1974	Chicago (A)	4	6	2	5.26	39	89	52	98	51	81	$3.6	4	6	1	4.13
1975	Chicago (A)	9	8	32	2.28	62	142	36	105	73	163	$8.2	9	8	26	1.84
1976	Chicago (A)	9	17	1	5.14	31	224	128	231	102	181	$8.4	9	17	1	3.94
1977	Pittsburgh (N)	11	9	31	1.83	72	133	27	80	54	181	$9.8	11	9	26	1.62
1978	New York (A)	10	11	31	2.49	63	134	37	92	65	157	$10.1	10	11	27	2.01
1979	New York (A)	5	3	20	2.95	36	58	19	49	21	54	$4.4	5	3	18	2.62
1980	New York (A)	6	2	37	2.73	64	99	30	76	42	131	$9.5	6	2	33	2.27
1981	New York (A)	5	3	31	1.03	48	70	8	36	24	93	$5.6	3	2	20	0.77
1982	New York (A)	4	5	32	2.61	56	93	27	66	32	125	$8.1	4	5	30	2.23
1983	New York (A)	13	5	23	2.69	57	87	26	85	28	109	$7.3	13	5	22	2.27
1984	San Diego (N)	10	6	26	3.53	62	102	40	78	41	100	$7.3	10	6	25	2.90
1985	San Diego (N)	5	3	27	2.16	50	79	19	68	18	63	$4.6	5	3	26	1.82
1986	San Diego (N)	5	7	21	5.12	45	65	37	74	21	69	$4.2	5	7	21	4.45
1987	San Diego (N)	5	4	12	3.29	40	52	19	48	20	48	$2.5	5	4	11	3.12
1988	Chicago (N)	4	4	13	5.32	46	44	26	54	18	36	$2.0	4	4	13	4.33
1989	S.F. (N)-N.Y. (A)	3	1	4	3.57	42	58	23	50	33	35	$1.6	3	1	5	2.95
1991	Texas (A)	4	2	0	4.28	44	40	19	35	17	31	$1.1	4	2	1	3.57
1992	Oakland (A)	0	2	0	3.55	30	38	15	34	21	30	$0.6	0	2	0	2.84
1993	Oakland (A)	4	5	0	4.88	39	48	26	50	28	45	$1.0	4	5	1	4.53
1994	Seattle (A)	4	0	1	4.24	52	68	32	63	22	44	$1.2	3	0	1	4.18
	Career	127	108	347	3.65	1,036	1,857	753	1,619	824	1,887	$107.1	124	107	310	3.01
	Average season	6	5	16	3.65	47	84	34	74	37	86	$4.9	6	5	14	3.01
	Summit season	10	7	30	2.15	60	113	27	80	49	141	$8.2	9	7	24	1.81

BURLEIGH GRIMES

		ADJUSTED REGULAR SEASON											ACTUAL RESULTS			
YEAR	TEAM	W	L	SV	ERA	G	IP	ER	H	BB	SO	PAY	W	L	SV	ERA
1916	Pittsburgh (N)	2	3	0	3.91	6	46	20	46	13	35	$0.9	2	3	0	2.36
1917	Pittsburgh (N)	3	16	0	6.02	38	199	133	219	94	140	$4.5	3	16	0	3.53
1918	Brooklyn (N)	24	11	6	3.53	51	344	135	299	124	312	$32.1	19	9	1	2.14
1919	Brooklyn (N)	12	13	0	5.19	29	210	121	221	94	194	$9.6	10	11	0	3.47
1920	Brooklyn (N)	24	12	4	2.93	42	319	104	282	91	294	$33.5	23	11	2	2.22
1921	Brooklyn (N)	23	14	0	3.19	39	319	113	304	102	311	$40.6	22	13	0	2.83
1922	Brooklyn (N)	18	15	3	5.37	38	273	163	319	108	234	$26.3	17	14	1	4.76
1923	Brooklyn (N)	22	19	0	4.11	41	344	157	354	122	281	$41.6	21	18	0	3.58
1924	Brooklyn (N)	23	14	2	4.32	40	327	157	347	114	321	$41.5	22	13	1	3.82
1925	Brooklyn (N)	13	20	0	5.32	35	262	155	295	122	186	$18.3	12	19	0	5.04
1926	Brooklyn (N)	12	13	0	4.33	31	233	112	238	104	157	$14.4	12	13	0	3.71
1927	New York (N)	20	8	7	4.02	41	273	122	275	108	242	$24.7	19	8	2	3.54
1928	Pittsburgh (N)	27	15	6	3.41	51	351	133	317	93	234	$39.4	25	14	3	2.99
1929	Pittsburgh (N)	18	7	5	3.21	35	247	88	239	81	152	$17.2	17	7	2	3.13
1930	Bos.-St.L. (N)	17	12	0	3.87	35	214	92	232	79	156	$16.3	16	11	0	4.07
1931	St. Louis (N)	18	10	0	4.04	31	227	102	244	72	148	$16.5	17	9	0	3.65
1932	Chicago (N)	6	12	3	5.25	32	151	88	177	63	81	$4.0	6	11	1	4.78
1933	Chi.-St.L. (N)	3	7	9	4.55	22	87	44	89	46	38	$2.6	3	7	4	3.78
1934	St.L.-Pit. (N)-N.Y. (A)	4	5	3	6.55	23	55	40	61	30	30	$1.7	4	5	1	6.11
	Career	289	226	48	4.18	660	4,481	2,079	4,558	1,660	3,546	$385.7	270	212	18	3.53
	Average season	15	12	3	4.18	35	236	109	240	87	187	$20.3	14	11	1	3.53
	Summit season	24	13	4	3.47	45	332	128	310	105	294	$37.4	22	12	1	2.82

LEFTY GROVE

		ADJUSTED REGULAR SEASON											ACTUAL RESULTS			
YEAR	TEAM	W	L	SV	ERA	G	IP	ER	H	BB	SO	PAY	W	L	SV	ERA
1925	Philadelphia (A)	11	13	5	5.01	48	210	117	201	159	258	$14.9	10	12	1	4.75
1926	Philadelphia (A)	14	14	15	2.91	49	281	91	239	125	409	$27.0	13	13	6	2.51
1927	Philadelphia (A)	21	14	15	3.63	53	273	110	249	97	364	$33.1	20	13	9	3.19
1928	Philadelphia (A)	25	8	6	2.91	41	275	89	230	77	371	$34.3	24	8	4	2.58
1929	Philadelphia (A)	21	6	10	2.87	45	295	94	274	94	365	$41.5	20	6	4	2.81
1930	Philadelphia (A)	30	5	15	2.40	53	308	82	255	72	394	$54.3	28	5	9	2.54
1931	Philadelphia (A)	33	4	5	2.26	43	303	76	247	74	342	$54.0	31	4	5	2.06
1932	Philadelphia (A)	26	10	9	3.10	46	305	105	267	97	363	$51.5	25	10	7	2.84
1933	Philadelphia (A)	26	9	10	3.83	48	294	125	296	105	254	$49.5	24	8	6	3.20
1934	Boston (A)	8	8	0	6.95	23	114	88	146	37	84	$8.2	8	8	0	6.50
1935	Boston (A)	21	13	2	2.90	37	289	93	268	77	249	$31.1	20	12	1	2.70
1936	Boston (A)	18	13	4	2.82	37	268	84	230	72	257	$23.3	17	12	2	2.81
1937	Boston (A)	18	10	0	3.24	34	278	100	273	91	275	$22.9	17	9	0	3.02
1938	Boston (A)	15	4	3	3.31	26	177	65	176	56	189	$12.9	14	4	1	3.08
1939	Boston (A)	16	4	0	2.73	25	208	63	190	65	163	$12.9	15	4	0	2.54
1940	Boston (A)	7	6	0	4.44	23	160	79	165	56	115	$5.8	7	6	0	3.99
1941	Boston (A)	7	7	0	5.14	22	140	80	166	44	103	$3.7	7	7	0	4.37
	Career	317	148	99	3.32	653	4,178	1,541	3,872	1,398	4,555	$480.9	300	141	55	3.06
	Average season	19	9	6	3.32	38	246	91	228	82	268	$28.3	18	8	3	3.06
	Summit season	28	7	9	2.88	46	297	95	259	85	345	$48.7	26	7	6	2.64

RON GUIDRY

YEAR	TEAM	ADJUSTED REGULAR SEASON											ACTUAL RESULTS			
		W	L	SV	ERA	G	IP	ER	H	BB	SO	PAY	W	L	SV	ERA
1975	New York (A)	0	1	0	4.50	10	16	8	16	10	19	$0.0	0	1	0	3.45
1976	New York (A)	0	0	0	7.31	7	16	13	22	5	16	$0.0	0	0	0	5.63
1977	New York (A)	16	7	1	3.24	31	211	76	179	71	217	$8.2	16	7	1	2.82
1978	New York (A)	25	3	0	2.17	35	274	66	199	80	322	$25.5	25	3	0	1.74
1979	New York (A)	18	8	3	3.17	33	236	83	208	78	262	$19.3	18	8	2	2.78
1980	New York (A)	17	10	1	4.25	37	220	104	222	92	220	$19.3	17	10	1	3.56
1981	New York (A)	17	8	0	3.54	35	193	76	164	45	209	$16.1	11	5	0	2.76
1982	New York (A)	14	8	0	4.54	34	222	112	225	79	207	$14.6	14	8	0	3.81
1983	New York (A)	21	9	0	4.03	31	250	112	242	67	196	$18.5	21	9	0	3.42
1984	New York (A)	10	11	0	5.42	29	196	118	234	50	154	$8.5	10	11	0	4.51
1985	New York (A)	22	6	0	3.82	34	259	110	258	46	176	$18.6	22	6	0	3.27
1986	New York (A)	9	12	0	4.59	30	192	98	214	40	154	$7.2	9	12	0	3.98
1987	New York (A)	5	8	0	3.89	22	118	51	115	40	104	$3.6	5	8	0	3.67
1988	New York (A)	2	3	0	5.14	12	56	32	61	17	38	$1.6	2	3	0	4.18
	Career	176	94	5	3.88	380	2,459	1,059	2,359	720	2,294	$161.0	170	91	4	3.29
	Average season	13	7	0	3.88	27	176	76	169	51	164	$11.5	12	7	0	3.29
	Summit season	20	7	1	3.26	33	246	89	217	68	235	$18.0	20	7	1	2.79

NOODLES HAHN

YEAR	TEAM	ADJUSTED REGULAR SEASON											ACTUAL RESULTS			
		W	L	SV	ERA	G	IP	ER	H	BB	SO	PAY	W	L	SV	ERA
1899	Cincinnati (N)	24	8	0	3.15	39	317	111	266	88	388	$42.8	23	8	0	2.68
1900	Cincinnati (N)	18	23	0	4.03	44	351	157	324	131	369	$42.5	16	20	0	3.27
1901	Cincinnati (N)	25	22	0	3.55	48	429	169	409	112	507	$58.4	22	19	0	2.71
1902	Cincinnati (N)	26	14	0	2.53	41	366	103	323	95	336	$52.5	23	12	0	1.77
1903	Cincinnati (N)	25	14	0	3.71	39	340	140	352	78	260	$42.0	22	12	0	2.52
1904	Cincinnati (N)	16	19	0	3.53	36	306	120	297	56	178	$27.4	16	18	0	2.06
1905	Cincinnati (N)	5	3	0	4.55	14	83	42	103	14	33	$4.3	5	3	0	2.81
1906	New York (A)	3	2	0	6.64	6	42	31	43	8	30	$2.7	3	2	0	3.86
	Career	142	105	0	3.52	267	2,234	873	2,117	582	2,101	$272.6	130	94	0	2.55
	Average season	18	13	0	3.52	33	279	109	265	73	263	$34.1	16	12	0	2.55
	Summit season	24	16	0	3.39	42	361	136	335	101	372	$47.6	21	14	0	2.59

JESSE HAINES

YEAR	TEAM	ADJUSTED REGULAR SEASON											ACTUAL RESULTS			
		W	L	SV	ERA	G	IP	ER	H	BB	SO	PAY	W	L	SV	ERA
1918	Cincinnati (N)	0	0	0	3.60	1	5	2	6	1	5	$0.0	0	0	0	1.80
1920	St. Louis (N)	14	21	7	3.94	49	315	138	314	109	271	$16.2	13	20	2	2.98
1921	St. Louis (N)	19	13	0	3.98	39	258	114	254	75	201	$16.1	18	12	0	3.50
1922	St. Louis (N)	12	10	0	4.32	31	196	94	207	59	152	$9.3	11	9	0	3.84
1923	St. Louis (N)	21	14	0	3.57	39	280	111	282	92	180	$25.4	20	13	0	3.11
1924	St. Louis (N)	8	20	0	4.98	37	235	130	273	83	174	$14.9	8	19	0	4.41
1925	St. Louis (N)	14	15	0	4.81	31	221	118	227	62	160	$8.9	13	14	0	4.57

(Jesse Haines, continued)

		ADJUSTED REGULAR SEASON											ACTUAL RESULTS			
YEAR	TEAM	W	L	SV	ERA	G	IP	ER	H	BB	SO	PAY	W	L	SV	ERA
1926	St. Louis (N)	13	4	4	3.76	34	189	79	186	56	114	$8.2	13	4	1	3.25
1927	St. Louis (N)	25	11	2	3.08	40	316	108	273	96	221	$25.9	24	10	1	2.72
1928	St. Louis (N)	21	8	0	3.64	35	255	103	243	87	184	$18.9	20	8	0	3.18
1929	St. Louis (N)	13	10	0	5.85	29	186	121	219	82	138	$7.6	13	10	0	5.71
1930	St. Louis (N)	14	9	3	4.11	31	195	89	204	66	146	$12.6	13	8	1	4.30
1931	St. Louis (N)	13	3	0	3.35	20	129	48	134	34	61	$3.9	12	3	0	3.02
1932	St. Louis (N)	3	5	0	5.20	21	90	52	117	20	59	$2.9	3	5	0	4.75
1933	St. Louis (N)	10	6	4	3.00	34	123	41	119	47	86	$3.7	9	6	1	2.50
1934	St. Louis (N)	4	4	4	3.69	39	95	39	85	22	36	$2.3	4	4	1	3.50
1935	St. Louis (N)	6	5	7	3.88	32	123	53	111	33	54	$2.8	6	5	2	3.59
1936	St. Louis (N)	7	5	3	3.93	26	103	45	105	23	41	$2.6	7	5	1	3.90
1937	St. Louis (N)	3	3	0	4.89	17	70	38	83	25	36	$1.4	3	3	0	4.52
	Career	220	166	34	4.05	585	3,384	1,523	3,442	1,072	2,319	$183.6	210	158	10	3.64
	Average season	12	9	2	4.05	31	178	80	181	56	122	$9.7	11	8	1	3.64
	Summit season	20	13	2	3.63	40	285	115	273	92	211	$20.5	19	13	1	3.08

TOM HENKE

		ADJUSTED REGULAR SEASON											ACTUAL RESULTS			
YEAR	TEAM	W	L	SV	ERA	G	IP	ER	H	BB	SO	PAY	W	L	SV	ERA
1982	Texas (A)	1	0	0	1.13	8	16	2	15	9	12	$0.0	1	0	0	1.15
1983	Texas (A)	1	0	1	3.94	8	16	7	17	4	21	$0.0	1	0	1	3.38
1984	Texas (A)	1	1	2	7.71	25	28	24	37	22	29	$0.3	1	1	2	6.35
1985	Toronto (A)	3	3	14	2.48	28	40	11	31	9	49	$1.9	3	3	13	2.03
1986	Toronto (A)	9	5	28	3.86	63	91	39	66	34	127	$5.7	9	5	27	3.35
1987	Toronto (A)	0	6	36	2.68	72	94	28	64	26	136	$5.8	0	6	34	2.49
1988	Toronto (A)	4	4	25	3.57	52	68	27	65	28	76	$4.8	4	4	25	2.91
1989	Toronto (A)	8	3	19	2.33	64	89	23	71	28	129	$6.9	8	3	20	1.92
1990	Toronto (A)	2	4	30	2.52	61	75	21	62	21	85	$4.2	2	4	32	2.17
1991	Toronto (A)	0	2	30	2.70	49	50	15	35	12	58	$3.3	0	2	32	2.32
1992	Toronto (A)	3	2	33	2.73	57	56	17	43	24	53	$3.5	3	2	34	2.26
1993	Texas (A)	5	5	39	3.16	66	74	26	56	29	86	$3.7	5	5	40	2.91
1994	Texas (A)	4	9	22	3.83	53	54	23	47	18	58	$2.8	3	6	15	3.79
1995	St. Louis (N)	1	1	41	1.89	59	62	13	48	21	57	$3.1	1	1	36	1.82
	Career	42	45	320	3.06	665	813	276	657	285	976	$46.0	41	42	311	2.67
	Average season	3	3	23	3.06	48	58	20	47	20	70	$3.3	3	3	22	2.67
	Summit season	5	3	32	2.92	62	74	24	57	27	90	$4.6	5	3	31	2.52

PAT HENTGEN

YEAR	TEAM	ADJUSTED REGULAR SEASON											ACTUAL RESULTS			
		W	L	SV	ERA	G	IP	ER	H	BB	SO	PAY	W	L	SV	ERA
1991	Toronto (A)	0	0	0	2.57	3	7	2	5	3	3	$0.0	0	0	0	2.45
1992	Toronto (A)	5	2	0	6.66	28	50	37	52	35	45	$1.3	5	2	0	5.36
1993	Toronto (A)	19	9	0	4.25	34	216	102	220	79	137	$8.5	19	9	0	3.87
1994	Toronto (A)	18	11	0	3.46	34	247	95	223	86	218	$15.7	13	8	0	3.40
1995	Toronto (A)	11	16	0	5.27	34	227	133	270	103	158	$10.0	10	14	0	5.11
1996	Toronto (A)	20	10	0	3.18	35	266	94	237	95	179	$20.1	20	10	0	3.22
1997	Toronto (A)	15	10	0	3.85	35	264	113	256	73	157	$19.0	15	10	0	3.68
1998	Toronto (A)	12	11	0	5.36	29	178	106	211	73	93	$8.1	12	11	0	5.17
1999	Toronto (A)	11	12	0	4.66	34	199	103	223	63	119	$9.2	11	12	0	4.79
2000	St. Louis (N)	15	12	0	4.55	33	194	98	200	84	118	$8.2	15	12	0	4.72
2001	Baltimore (A)	2	3	0	3.63	9	62	25	52	21	32	$2.1	2	3	0	3.47
	Career	128	96	0	4.28	308	1,910	908	1,949	715	1,259	$102.2	122	91	0	4.18
	Average season	12	9	0	4.28	28	174	83	177	65	114	$9.3	11	8	0	4.18
	Summit season	17	10	0	3.80	34	237	100	227	83	162	$14.3	16	10	0	3.75

WILLIE HERNANDEZ

YEAR	TEAM	ADJUSTED REGULAR SEASON											ACTUAL RESULTS			
		W	L	SV	ERA	G	IP	ER	H	BB	SO	PAY	W	L	SV	ERA
1977	Chicago (N)	8	7	5	3.44	67	110	42	97	31	98	$5.3	8	7	4	3.03
1978	Chicago (N)	8	2	4	4.65	54	60	31	61	39	51	$3.5	8	2	3	3.77
1979	Chicago (N)	4	4	0	5.70	51	79	50	87	43	71	$3.8	4	4	0	5.01
1980	Chicago (N)	1	9	0	5.25	53	108	63	118	52	100	$3.9	1	9	0	4.40
1981	Chicago (N)	0	0	3	5.14	18	21	12	23	14	26	$0.6	0	0	2	3.95
1982	Chicago (N)	4	6	11	3.60	75	75	30	77	27	69	$3.2	4	6	10	3.00
1983	Chi.-Phi. (N)	9	4	9	3.91	74	115	50	114	36	115	$5.1	9	4	8	3.28
1984	Detroit (A)	9	3	34	2.31	80	140	36	100	41	134	$8.3	9	3	32	1.92
1985	Detroit (A)	8	10	32	3.20	74	107	38	87	15	92	$8.0	8	10	31	2.70
1986	Detroit (A)	8	7	25	4.15	64	89	41	93	22	85	$6.8	8	7	24	3.55
1987	Detroit (A)	3	4	9	3.86	45	49	21	55	21	33	$2.8	3	4	8	3.67
1988	Detroit (A)	6	5	9	3.71	63	68	28	54	36	69	$3.8	6	5	10	3.06
1989	Detroit (A)	2	2	15	6.97	32	31	24	38	18	33	$2.0	2	2	15	5.74
	Career	70	63	156	3.99	750	1,052	466	1,004	395	976	$57.1	70	63	147	3.38
	Average season	5	5	12	3.99	58	81	36	77	30	75	$4.4	5	5	11	3.38
	Summit season	8	6	21	3.29	72	112	41	98	29	105	$6.7	8	6	20	2.82

OREL HERSHISER

YEAR	TEAM	ADJUSTED REGULAR SEASON											ACTUAL RESULTS			
		W	L	SV	ERA	G	IP	ER	H	BB	SO	PAY	W	L	SV	ERA
1983	Los Angeles (N)	0	0	1	4.50	8	8	4	7	7	6	$0.0	0	0	1	3.38
1984	Los Angeles (N)	11	8	2	3.17	45	190	67	168	57	181	$5.5	11	8	2	2.66
1985	Los Angeles (N)	19	3	0	2.36	36	240	63	190	74	191	$15.2	19	3	0	2.03
1986	Los Angeles (N)	14	14	0	4.44	35	231	114	225	91	170	$10.0	14	14	0	3.85
1987	Los Angeles (N)	16	16	1	3.26	37	265	96	254	77	207	$19.5	16	16	1	3.06
1988	Los Angeles (N)	23	8	1	2.76	35	267	82	224	85	208	$26.0	23	8	1	2.26

(Orel Hershiser, continued)

YEAR	TEAM	ADJUSTED REGULAR SEASON W	L	SV	ERA	G	IP	ER	H	BB	SO	PAY	ACTUAL RESULTS W	L	SV	ERA
1989	Los Angeles (N)	15	15	0	2.87	35	257	82	244	86	206	$19.5	15	15	0	2.31
1990	Los Angeles (N)	1	1	0	5.04	4	25	14	27	4	18	$1.9	1	1	0	4.26
1991	Los Angeles (N)	7	2	0	4.02	21	112	50	120	35	82	$4.4	7	2	0	3.46
1992	Los Angeles (N)	10	15	0	4.48	33	211	105	225	76	152	$7.0	10	15	0	3.67
1993	Los Angeles (N)	12	14	0	3.92	33	216	94	206	77	158	$7.1	12	14	0	3.59
1994	Los Angeles (N)	9	9	0	3.87	30	193	83	208	61	108	$3.9	6	6	0	3.79
1995	Cleveland (A)	18	7	0	3.99	29	187	83	171	58	128	$7.2	16	6	0	3.87
1996	Cleveland (A)	15	9	0	4.19	33	206	96	237	58	126	$7.3	15	9	0	4.24
1997	Cleveland (A)	14	6	0	4.66	32	195	101	201	71	105	$6.3	14	6	0	4.47
1998	San Francisco (N)	11	10	0	4.54	34	202	102	203	90	125	$7.1	11	10	0	4.41
1999	New York (N)	13	12	0	4.47	32	179	89	173	74	90	$5.9	13	12	0	4.58
2000	Los Angeles (N)	1	5	0	12.60	10	25	35	42	13	13	$1.0	1	5	0	13.14
	Career	209	154	5	3.81	522	3,209	1,360	3,125	1,094	2,274	$154.8	204	150	5	3.48
	Average season	12	9	0	3.81	29	178	76	174	61	126	$8.6	11	8	0	3.48
	Summit season	18	10	0	3.00	34	243	81	217	76	188	$17.5	18	10	0	2.63

TREVOR HOFFMAN

YEAR	TEAM	ADJUSTED REGULAR SEASON W	L	SV	ERA	G	IP	ER	H	BB	SO	PAY	ACTUAL RESULTS W	L	SV	ERA
1993	Fla.-S.D. (N)	4	6	4	4.30	67	90	43	82	42	88	$3.9	4	6	5	3.90
1994	San Diego (N)	6	6	27	2.57	65	77	22	53	28	98	$4.9	4	4	20	2.57
1995	San Diego (N)	8	5	34	4.05	62	60	27	55	16	60	$4.7	7	4	31	3.88
1996	San Diego (N)	9	5	42	2.25	70	88	22	50	31	112	$8.4	9	5	42	2.25
1997	San Diego (N)	6	4	37	2.78	70	81	25	59	25	109	$8.2	6	4	37	2.66
1998	San Diego (N)	4	2	52	1.48	66	73	12	42	22	85	$8.0	4	2	53	1.48
1999	San Diego (N)	2	3	40	2.01	64	67	15	47	14	74	$4.7	2	3	40	2.14
2000	San Diego (N)	4	7	43	2.88	70	72	23	60	10	85	$4.9	4	7	43	2.99
2001	San Diego (N)	3	4	43	3.60	62	60	24	49	23	61	$4.4	3	4	43	3.43
	Career	46	42	322	2.87	596	668	213	497	211	772	$52.1	43	39	314	2.79
	Average season	5	5	36	2.87	66	74	24	55	23	86	$5.8	5	4	35	2.79
	Summit season	5	4	43	2.25	68	76	19	52	20	93	$6.8	5	4	43	2.31

LAMARR HOYT

YEAR	TEAM	ADJUSTED REGULAR SEASON W	L	SV	ERA	G	IP	ER	H	BB	SO	PAY	ACTUAL RESULTS W	L	SV	ERA
1979	Chicago (A)	0	0	0	0.00	2	3	0	2	0	0	$0.0	0	0	0	0.00
1980	Chicago (A)	9	3	0	5.46	24	112	68	126	47	75	$3.8	9	3	0	4.57
1981	Chicago (A)	14	5	18	4.53	66	139	70	132	49	124	$7.9	9	3	10	3.57
1982	Chicago (A)	19	15	0	4.20	39	240	112	259	55	162	$15.5	19	15	0	3.53
1983	Chicago (A)	24	10	0	4.34	36	261	126	247	34	188	$25.5	24	10	0	3.66
1984	Chicago (A)	13	18	0	5.38	34	236	141	256	49	155	$16.2	13	18	0	4.47
1985	San Diego (N)	16	8	0	4.07	31	210	95	223	22	103	$10.1	16	8	0	3.47
1986	San Diego (N)	8	11	0	5.94	35	159	105	180	72	95	$7.9	8	11	0	5.15
	Career	103	70	18	4.74	267	1,360	717	1,425	328	902	$86.9	98	68	10	3.99
	Average season	13	9	2	4.74	33	170	90	178	41	113	$10.9	12	9	1	3.99
	Summit season	17	11	4	4.52	41	217	109	223	42	146	$15.0	16	11	2	3.77

WAITE HOYT

		ADJUSTED REGULAR SEASON											ACTUAL RESULTS			
YEAR	TEAM	W	L	SV	ERA	G	IP	ER	H	BB	SO	PAY	W	L	SV	ERA
1918	New York (N)	0	0	0	0.00	1	1	0	0	0	3	$0.0	0	0	0	0.00
1919	Boston (A)	5	7	0	4.87	15	122	66	122	34	71	$3.3	4	6	0	3.25
1920	Boston (A)	6	6	5	5.81	23	127	82	128	64	103	$4.3	6	6	1	4.38
1921	New York (A)	20	14	8	3.49	46	302	117	296	111	247	$20.1	19	13	3	3.09
1922	New York (A)	20	13	0	3.84	39	279	119	265	97	227	$20.2	19	12	0	3.43
1923	New York (A)	18	9	4	3.46	39	252	97	226	81	150	$19.4	17	9	1	3.02
1924	New York (A)	19	14	10	4.28	49	263	125	295	96	183	$26.3	18	13	4	3.79
1925	New York (A)	11	15	15	4.22	48	254	119	269	92	209	$20.1	11	14	6	4.00
1926	New York (A)	17	13	8	4.48	42	229	114	228	74	190	$19.5	16	12	4	3.85
1927	New York (A)	23	7	3	2.99	38	271	90	244	67	211	$26.9	22	7	1	2.63
1928	New York (A)	24	7	11	3.84	44	286	122	281	72	163	$32.4	23	7	8	3.36
1929	New York (A)	11	10	3	4.31	32	215	103	215	80	140	$15.8	10	9	1	4.24
1930	N.Y.-Det. (A)	12	11	8	4.50	36	194	97	225	68	79	$9.7	11	10	4	4.71
1931	Det.-Phi. (A)	14	14	0	5.54	34	216	133	257	84	92	$8.6	13	13	0	4.97
1932	Bkn.-N.Y. (N)	6	10	3	4.74	27	129	68	140	45	78	$4.5	6	10	1	4.35
1933	Pittsburgh (N)	5	7	12	3.48	38	124	48	124	24	98	$4.6	5	7	4	2.92
1934	Pittsburgh (N)	16	6	14	3.10	51	203	70	184	50	200	$13.9	15	6	5	2.93
1935	Pittsburgh (N)	7	12	14	3.66	41	172	70	185	32	131	$6.1	7	11	6	3.40
1936	Pittsburgh (N)	7	5	3	2.73	23	122	37	111	22	77	$3.6	7	5	1	2.70
1937	Pit.-Bkn. (N)	8	9	7	3.64	40	205	83	212	39	124	$6.2	8	9	2	3.42
1938	Brooklyn (N)	0	3	0	5.06	6	16	9	23	5	6	$0.5	0	3	0	4.96
	Career	249	192	128	4.00	712	3,982	1,769	4,030	1,237	2,782	$266.0	237	182	52	3.59
	Average season	12	9	6	4.00	34	190	84	192	59	132	$12.7	11	9	2	3.59
	Summit season	20	10	9	3.57	46	265	105	260	79	201	$23.9	19	9	4	3.17

CARL HUBBELL

		ADJUSTED REGULAR SEASON											ACTUAL RESULTS			
YEAR	TEAM	W	L	SV	ERA	G	IP	ER	H	BB	SO	PAY	W	L	SV	ERA
1928	New York (N)	11	6	2	3.25	21	130	47	118	25	88	$5.7	10	6	1	2.83
1929	New York (N)	19	12	3	3.77	42	289	121	271	78	250	$25.5	18	11	1	3.69
1930	New York (N)	18	13	4	3.67	39	255	104	246	70	238	$20.2	17	12	2	3.87
1931	New York (N)	15	13	7	2.92	38	262	85	211	81	302	$25.7	14	12	3	2.65
1932	New York (N)	19	12	5	2.72	42	298	90	259	49	281	$32.4	18	11	2	2.50
1933	New York (N)	24	13	8	1.98	47	322	71	263	58	328	$41.6	23	12	5	1.66
1934	New York (N)	22	13	13	2.44	52	332	90	285	43	236	$41.3	21	12	8	2.30
1935	New York (N)	24	13	0	3.52	44	317	124	310	57	299	$39.8	23	12	0	3.27
1936	New York (N)	27	6	6	2.32	44	318	82	254	62	248	$40.9	26	6	3	2.31
1937	New York (N)	23	8	7	3.43	40	268	102	255	58	274	$32.5	22	8	4	3.20
1938	New York (N)	14	11	1	3.25	26	194	70	179	36	201	$17.6	13	10	1	3.07
1939	New York (N)	12	10	4	2.95	31	165	54	156	26	124	$7.5	11	9	2	2.75
1940	New York (N)	12	13	0	4.07	33	228	103	233	67	162	$12.8	11	12	0	3.65
1941	New York (N)	11	9	3	4.18	27	170	79	179	55	140	$6.2	11	9	1	3.57
1942	New York (N)	11	8	0	5.21	25	164	95	177	37	122	$5.9	11	8	0	3.95
1943	New York (N)	4	4	0	6.68	12	66	49	94	26	57	$2.4	4	4	0	4.91
	Career	266	164	63	3.25	563	3,778	1,366	3,490	828	3,350	$358.0	253	154	33	2.98
	Average season	17	10	4	3.25	35	236	85	218	52	209	$22.4	16	10	2	2.98
	Summit season	24	11	7	2.72	45	311	94	273	56	277	$39.2	23	10	4	2.52

TEX HUGHSON

YEAR	TEAM	ADJUSTED REGULAR SEASON											ACTUAL RESULTS			
		W	L	SV	ERA	G	IP	ER	H	BB	SO	PAY	W	L	SV	ERA
1941	Boston (A)	5	3	0	4.91	13	66	36	77	14	44	$2.1	5	3	0	4.13
1942	Boston (A)	24	6	8	3.39	41	303	114	299	84	232	$25.8	22	6	4	2.59
1943	Boston (A)	13	16	4	3.62	37	281	113	277	82	226	$19.9	12	15	2	2.64
1944	Boston (A)	19	5	5	2.94	29	211	69	185	48	217	$16.3	18	5	5	2.26
1946	Boston (A)	21	12	6	3.64	41	292	118	282	54	288	$33.3	20	11	3	2.75
1947	Boston (A)	12	11	0	3.90	30	196	85	186	70	204	$15.1	12	11	0	3.33
1948	Boston (A)	3	1	0	5.57	16	21	13	23	7	12	$1.9	3	1	0	5.12
1949	Boston (A)	4	2	9	5.96	30	80	53	87	37	64	$3.8	4	2	3	5.33
	Career	101	56	32	3.73	237	1,450	601	1,416	396	1,287	$118.2	96	54	17	2.94
	Average season	13	7	4	3.73	30	181	75	177	50	161	$14.8	12	7	2	2.94
	Summit season	18	10	5	3.50	36	257	100	246	68	233	$22.1	17	10	3	2.70

CATFISH HUNTER

YEAR	TEAM	ADJUSTED REGULAR SEASON											ACTUAL RESULTS			
		W	L	SV	ERA	G	IP	ER	H	BB	SO	PAY	W	L	SV	ERA
1965	Kansas City (A)	8	8	0	5.55	32	133	82	139	53	90	$5.1	8	8	0	4.26
1966	Kansas City (A)	9	11	0	5.24	30	177	103	175	80	116	$5.7	9	11	0	4.02
1967	Kansas City (A)	13	17	0	3.88	35	260	112	239	102	214	$15.2	13	17	0	2.81
1968	Oakland (A)	13	13	1	5.12	36	234	133	248	88	191	$10.1	13	13	1	3.35
1969	Oakland (A)	12	15	0	4.26	38	247	117	233	88	170	$15.0	12	15	0	3.35
1970	Oakland (A)	18	14	0	4.50	40	262	131	272	75	201	$19.2	18	14	0	3.81
1971	Oakland (A)	21	11	0	3.91	37	274	119	249	89	218	$20.6	21	11	0	2.96
1972	Oakland (A)	22	7	0	2.86	40	311	99	240	84	236	$32.4	21	7	0	2.04
1973	Oakland (A)	21	5	0	4.08	36	256	116	236	73	156	$20.5	21	5	0	3.34
1974	Oakland (A)	25	12	0	3.14	41	318	111	285	49	189	$33.9	25	12	0	2.49
1975	New York (A)	23	14	0	3.18	39	328	116	263	86	232	$40.4	23	14	0	2.58
1976	New York (A)	17	15	0	4.60	37	307	157	297	79	240	$32.4	17	15	0	3.53
1977	New York (A)	9	9	0	5.41	22	143	86	141	51	68	$7.9	9	9	0	4.71
1978	New York (A)	12	6	0	4.50	21	118	59	104	39	77	$5.0	12	6	0	3.58
1979	New York (A)	2	9	0	6.09	19	105	71	131	37	48	$3.1	2	9	0	5.31
	Career	225	166	1	4.18	503	3,473	1,612	3,252	1,073	2,446	$266.5	224	166	1	3.26
	Average season	15	11	0	4.18	34	232	107	217	72	163	$17.8	15	11	0	3.26
	Summit season	22	10	0	3.39	39	297	112	255	76	206	$29.6	22	10	0	2.65

LARRY JACKSON

YEAR	TEAM	ADJUSTED REGULAR SEASON											ACTUAL RESULTS			
		W	L	SV	ERA	G	IP	ER	H	BB	SO	PAY	W	L	SV	ERA
1955	St. Louis (N)	9	15	4	4.96	39	187	103	211	74	137	$8.0	9	14	2	4.31
1956	St. Louis (N)	2	2	17	4.75	53	89	47	83	46	72	$4.8	2	2	9	4.11
1957	St. Louis (N)	16	9	2	4.11	43	221	101	218	65	139	$9.8	15	9	1	3.47
1958	St. Louis (N)	14	14	12	4.37	52	210	102	237	59	171	$10.2	13	13	8	3.68
1959	St. Louis (N)	15	14	0	3.85	42	269	115	302	72	195	$19.1	14	13	0	3.30

(Larry Jackson, continued)

		ADJUSTED REGULAR SEASON											ACTUAL RESULTS			
YEAR	TEAM	W	L	SV	ERA	G	IP	ER	H	BB	SO	PAY	W	L	SV	ERA
1960	St. Louis (N)	19	14	0	4.18	45	295	137	312	77	225	$26.2	18	13	0	3.48
1961	St. Louis (N)	14	11	0	4.27	34	217	103	220	59	145	$15.2	14	11	0	3.75
1962	St. Louis (N)	16	11	0	4.32	36	252	121	282	68	136	$16.1	16	11	0	3.75
1963	Chicago (N)	14	18	0	3.37	37	275	103	286	65	174	$18.0	14	18	0	2.55
1964	Chicago (N)	24	11	0	4.02	40	298	133	290	70	164	$24.8	24	11	0	3.14
1965	Chicago (N)	14	21	0	5.04	39	257	144	301	66	145	$15.0	14	21	0	3.85
1966	Chi.-Phi. (N)	15	15	0	4.31	38	255	122	285	77	127	$14.7	15	15	0	3.32
1967	Philadelphia (N)	13	15	0	4.29	40	262	125	277	65	153	$13.6	13	15	0	3.10
1968	Philadelphia (N)	13	17	0	4.24	34	244	115	271	77	142	$12.7	13	17	0	2.77
	Career	198	187	35	4.24	572	3,331	1,571	3,575	940	2,125	$208.2	194	183	20	3.40
	Average season	14	13	3	4.24	41	238	112	255	67	152	$14.9	14	13	1	3.40
	Summit season	17	13	3	3.98	43	260	115	269	67	175	$17.8	17	13	2	3.23

BILL JAMES

		ADJUSTED REGULAR SEASON											ACTUAL RESULTS			
YEAR	TEAM	W	L	SV	ERA	G	IP	ER	H	BB	SO	PAY	W	L	SV	ERA
1913	Boston (N)	6	10	0	4.15	25	141	65	152	72	127	$4.9	6	10	0	2.79
1914	Boston (N)	27	7	8	2.99	47	340	113	298	145	259	$33.1	26	7	3	1.90
1915	Boston (N)	5	4	0	4.76	13	68	36	77	26	40	$3.6	5	4	0	3.03
1919	Boston (N)	0	0	0	5.40	1	5	3	6	3	2	$1.0	0	0	0	3.38
	Career	38	21	8	3.53	86	554	217	533	246	428	$42.6	37	21	3	2.28
	Average season	10	5	2	3.53	22	139	54	133	62	107	$10.7	9	5	1	2.28
	Summit season	13	7	3	3.49	28	183	71	176	81	142	$13.9	12	7	1	2.27

FERGIE JENKINS

		ADJUSTED REGULAR SEASON											ACTUAL RESULTS			
YEAR	TEAM	W	L	SV	ERA	G	IP	ER	H	BB	SO	PAY	W	L	SV	ERA
1965	Philadelphia (N)	2	1	1	3.00	7	12	4	8	2	11	$0.0	2	1	1	2.19
1966	Phi.-Chi. (N)	6	8	6	4.30	61	184	88	166	65	167	$5.2	6	8	5	3.32
1967	Chicago (N)	20	13	0	3.86	38	289	124	263	100	257	$19.6	20	13	0	2.80
1968	Chicago (N)	20	15	0	4.03	40	308	138	301	83	287	$26.2	20	15	0	2.63
1969	Chicago (N)	21	15	1	4.08	43	311	141	315	73	305	$32.8	21	15	1	3.21
1970	Chicago (N)	22	16	0	4.00	40	313	139	285	61	308	$34.3	22	16	0	3.39
1971	Chicago (N)	24	13	0	3.66	39	325	132	337	41	313	$41.3	24	13	0	2.77
1972	Chicago (N)	21	12	0	4.52	37	297	149	296	72	222	$32.6	20	12	0	3.20
1973	Chicago (N)	14	16	0	4.75	38	271	143	284	60	211	$25.4	14	16	0	3.89
1974	Texas (A)	25	12	0	3.57	41	328	130	305	48	289	$40.9	25	12	0	2.82
1975	Texas (A)	17	18	0	4.87	37	270	146	278	58	205	$24.0	17	18	0	3.93
1976	Boston (A)	12	11	0	4.26	30	209	99	217	48	189	$13.9	12	11	0	3.27
1977	Boston (A)	10	10	0	4.24	28	193	91	196	39	133	$8.4	10	10	0	3.68
1978	Texas (A)	18	8	0	3.80	34	249	105	243	45	211	$17.6	18	8	0	3.04
1979	Texas (A)	16	14	0	4.66	37	259	134	258	89	221	$16.3	16	14	0	4.07
1980	Texas (A)	12	12	0	4.50	29	198	99	196	60	173	$7.3	12	12	0	3.77

(Fergie Jenkins, continued)

		ADJUSTED REGULAR SEASON											ACTUAL RESULTS			
YEAR	TEAM	W	L	SV	ERA	G	IP	ER	H	BB	SO	PAY	W	L	SV	ERA
1981	Texas (A)	8	12	0	5.78	29	162	104	201	69	132	$5.9	5	8	0	4.50
1982	Chicago (N)	14	15	0	3.73	34	217	90	230	77	173	$7.5	14	15	0	3.15
1983	Chicago (N)	6	9	0	5.12	33	167	95	184	51	121	$3.8	6	9	0	4.30
	Career	288	230	8	4.24	675	4,562	2,151	4,563	1,141	3,928	$363.0	284	226	7	3.34
	Average season	15	12	0	4.24	36	240	113	240	60	207	$19.1	15	12	0	3.34
	Summit season	22	14	0	3.82	40	313	133	301	65	294	$33.8	22	14	0	3.00

TOMMY JOHN

		ADJUSTED REGULAR SEASON											ACTUAL RESULTS			
YEAR	TEAM	W	L	SV	ERA	G	IP	ER	H	BB	SO	PAY	W	L	SV	ERA
1963	Cleveland (A)	0	2	0	3.15	6	20	7	25	7	10	$0.0	0	2	0	2.21
1964	Cleveland (A)	2	9	0	4.98	25	94	52	106	42	72	$2.7	2	9	0	3.91
1965	Chicago (A)	14	7	4	4.01	39	184	82	182	68	139	$5.9	14	7	3	3.09
1966	Chicago (A)	14	11	0	3.39	34	223	84	216	71	155	$9.2	14	11	0	2.62
1967	Chicago (A)	10	13	0	3.44	31	178	68	163	57	120	$7.7	10	13	0	2.47
1968	Chicago (A)	10	5	0	3.05	25	177	60	159	62	130	$8.2	10	5	0	1.98
1969	Chicago (A)	9	11	0	4.11	33	232	106	255	93	145	$9.4	9	11	0	3.25
1970	Chicago (A)	12	17	0	3.85	37	269	115	272	102	157	$15.1	12	17	0	3.27
1971	Chicago (A)	13	16	0	4.76	38	229	121	270	64	158	$9.8	13	16	0	3.61
1972	Los Angeles (N)	11	5	0	4.06	30	193	87	203	47	142	$8.4	11	5	0	2.89
1973	Los Angeles (N)	16	7	0	3.80	36	218	92	215	53	146	$10.0	16	7	0	3.10
1974	Los Angeles (N)	13	3	0	3.29	22	153	56	142	45	103	$8.0	13	3	0	2.59
1976	Los Angeles (N)	10	10	0	4.00	31	207	92	223	69	125	$7.3	10	10	0	3.09
1977	Los Angeles (N)	20	7	0	3.19	31	220	78	231	55	155	$14.3	20	7	0	2.78
1978	Los Angeles (N)	17	10	1	4.10	33	213	97	245	58	168	$14.1	17	10	1	3.30
1979	New York (A)	21	9	0	3.39	37	276	104	275	71	154	$17.3	21	9	0	2.96
1980	New York (A)	22	9	0	4.08	36	265	120	278	64	110	$17.1	22	9	0	3.43
1981	New York (A)	14	12	0	3.34	30	210	78	218	66	106	$7.6	9	8	0	2.63
1982	N.Y.-Cal. (A)	14	12	0	4.38	37	222	108	250	44	91	$7.5	14	12	0	3.69
1983	California (A)	11	13	0	5.13	34	235	134	301	55	85	$7.2	11	13	0	4.33
1984	California (A)	7	13	0	5.42	32	181	109	233	63	59	$3.6	7	13	0	4.52
1985	Cal.-Oak. (A)	4	10	0	6.49	23	86	62	124	30	31	$2.1	4	10	0	5.53
1986	New York (A)	5	3	0	3.42	13	71	27	78	16	31	$1.6	5	3	0	2.93
1987	New York (A)	13	6	0	4.31	33	188	90	219	49	70	$3.7	13	6	0	4.03
1988	New York (A)	9	8	0	5.52	35	176	108	238	53	96	$3.6	9	8	0	4.49
1989	New York (A)	2	7	0	7.17	10	64	51	94	25	21	$1.2	2	7	0	5.80
	Career	293	235	5	4.12	771	4,784	2,188	5,215	1,429	2,779	$202.6	288	231	4	3.34
	Average season	11	9	0	4.12	30	184	84	201	55	107	$7.8	11	9	0	3.34
	Summit season	19	8	0	3.71	35	238	98	249	60	147	$14.6	19	8	0	3.12

RANDY JOHNSON

		ADJUSTED REGULAR SEASON											ACTUAL RESULTS			
YEAR	TEAM	W	L	SV	ERA	G	IP	ER	H	BB	SO	PAY	W	L	SV	ERA
1988	Montreal (N)	3	0	0	3.12	4	26	9	25	8	28	$0.7	3	0	0	2.42
1989	Mon. (N)-Sea. (A)	7	13	0	5.98	29	161	107	159	108	150	$4.9	7	13	0	4.82
1990	Seattle (A)	14	11	0	4.34	33	220	106	184	131	220	$9.4	14	11	0	3.65
1991	Seattle (A)	13	10	0	4.66	33	201	104	161	165	251	$9.5	13	10	0	3.98
1992	Seattle (A)	12	14	0	4.63	31	210	108	165	160	272	$10.1	12	14	0	3.77
1993	Seattle (A)	19	8	1	3.53	35	255	100	189	106	337	$20.6	19	8	1	3.24
1994	Seattle (A)	19	9	0	3.24	33	247	89	189	106	306	$20.3	13	6	0	3.19
1995	Seattle (A)	20	2	0	2.56	34	243	69	182	74	342	$24.3	18	2	0	2.48
1996	Seattle (A)	5	0	1	3.69	14	61	25	47	25	85	$3.9	5	0	1	3.67
1997	Seattle (A)	20	4	0	2.37	30	213	56	149	79	289	$17.8	20	4	0	2.28
1998	Sea. (A)-Hou. (N)	19	11	0	3.39	34	244	92	205	91	327	$18.9	19	11	0	3.28
1999	Arizona (N)	17	9	0	2.42	35	272	73	205	68	369	$23.1	17	9	0	2.48
2000	Arizona (N)	19	7	0	2.53	35	249	70	200	72	350	$23.3	19	7	0	2.64
2001	Arizona (N)	21	6	0	2.56	35	250	71	185	78	367	$23.8	21	6	0	2.49
	Career	208	104	2	3.40	415	2,852	1,079	2,245	1,271	3,693	$210.6	200	101	2	3.13
	Average season	15	7	0	3.40	30	204	77	160	91	264	$15.0	14	7	0	3.13
	Summit season	19	6	0	2.50	34	245	68	184	74	343	$22.5	19	6	0	2.48

WALTER JOHNSON

		ADJUSTED REGULAR SEASON											ACTUAL RESULTS			
YEAR	TEAM	W	L	SV	ERA	G	IP	ER	H	BB	SO	PAY	W	L	SV	ERA
1907	Washington (A)	5	10	0	3.43	15	118	45	123	31	129	$4.4	5	9	0	1.88
1908	Washington (A)	15	15	4	3.19	38	271	96	246	85	285	$16.1	14	14	1	1.65
1909	Washington (A)	14	26	1	3.99	42	311	138	304	120	288	$20.5	13	25	1	2.22
1910	Washington (A)	26	17	2	2.24	46	378	94	305	93	489	$52.5	25	17	1	1.36
1911	Washington (A)	26	14	1	2.56	42	338	96	319	82	338	$42.3	25	13	1	1.90
1912	Washington (A)	35	13	4	1.86	53	391	81	281	91	484	$60.1	33	12	2	1.39
1913	Washington (A)	38	7	4	1.70	50	360	68	262	47	409	$60.7	36	7	2	1.14
1914	Washington (A)	29	18	3	2.71	52	379	114	326	90	361	$59.1	28	18	1	1.72
1915	Washington (A)	28	14	6	2.44	49	351	95	305	70	347	$57.6	27	13	4	1.55
1916	Washington (A)	26	20	2	3.18	49	377	133	340	106	382	$57.9	25	20	1	1.90
1917	Washington (A)	23	16	7	3.76	48	333	139	289	90	342	$52.5	23	16	3	2.21
1918	Washington (A)	29	16	4	2.09	49	410	95	337	112	428	$60.0	23	13	3	1.27
1919	Washington (A)	23	16	4	2.20	44	328	80	282	77	334	$49.4	20	14	2	1.49
1920	Washington (A)	8	10	4	4.11	22	151	69	141	37	166	$13.7	8	10	3	3.13
1921	Washington (A)	18	15	2	3.97	37	279	123	258	125	316	$30.6	17	14	1	3.51
1922	Washington (A)	16	17	8	3.37	43	294	110	276	127	248	$25.0	15	16	4	2.99
1923	Washington (A)	18	13	9	3.99	44	273	121	260	89	288	$23.3	17	12	4	3.48
1924	Washington (A)	24	7	0	3.06	39	285	97	224	94	344	$30.3	23	7	0	2.72
1925	Washington (A)	21	7	0	3.25	32	244	88	210	94	254	$23.0	20	7	0	3.07
1926	Washington (A)	16	17	0	4.24	35	276	130	265	88	287	$23.6	15	16	0	3.63
1927	Washington (A)	5	6	0	5.84	19	114	74	114	33	112	$5.6	5	6	0	5.10
	Career	443	294	65	3.00	848	6,261	2,086	5,467	1,781	6,631	$768.2	417	279	34	2.17
	Average season	21	14	3	3.00	40	298	99	260	85	316	$36.6	20	13	2	2.17
	Summit season	32	14	4	2.17	51	378	91	302	82	406	$59.5	29	13	2	1.42

DOUG JONES

YEAR	TEAM	ADJUSTED REGULAR SEASON											ACTUAL RESULTS			
		W	L	SV	ERA	G	IP	ER	H	BB	SO	PAY	W	L	SV	ERA
1982	Milwaukee (A)	0	0	0	12.00	4	3	4	6	1	1	$0.0	0	0	0	10.13
1986	Cleveland (A)	1	0	1	3.00	11	18	6	19	6	13	$0.0	1	0	1	2.50
1987	Cleveland (A)	6	5	9	3.36	49	91	34	104	25	94	$3.9	6	5	8	3.15
1988	Cleveland (A)	3	4	37	2.82	51	83	26	74	18	83	$4.7	3	4	37	2.27
1989	Cleveland (A)	7	10	32	2.89	59	81	26	82	15	75	$4.4	7	10	32	2.34
1990	Cleveland (A)	5	5	41	3.00	66	84	28	70	24	63	$4.8	5	5	43	2.56
1991	Cleveland (A)	4	8	6	6.57	36	63	46	93	18	54	$3.4	4	8	7	5.54
1992	Houston (N)	11	8	34	2.25	80	112	28	103	19	107	$8.2	11	8	36	1.85
1993	Houston (N)	4	10	24	4.98	71	85	47	104	22	73	$3.7	4	10	26	4.54
1994	Philadelphia (N)	3	6	38	2.25	66	76	19	77	9	56	$3.3	2	4	27	2.17
1995	Baltimore (A)	0	5	24	5.09	59	53	30	63	18	49	$2.6	0	4	22	5.01
1996	Chi. (N)-Mil. (A)	7	2	3	4.22	52	64	30	72	20	61	$2.7	7	2	3	4.22
1997	Milwaukee (A)	6	6	36	2.14	75	80	19	62	9	80	$3.7	6	6	36	2.02
1998	Mil. (N)-Cle. (A)	4	6	12	4.66	69	85	44	100	18	70	$3.2	4	6	13	4.54
1999	Oakland (A)	5	5	9	3.46	70	104	40	105	23	64	$3.3	5	5	10	3.55
2000	Oakland (A)	4	2	2	3.82	54	73	31	85	17	54	$2.4	4	2	2	3.93
	Career	70	82	308	3.57	872	1,155	458	1,219	262	997	$54.3	69	79	303	3.30
	Average season	4	5	19	3.57	55	72	29	76	16	62	$3.4	4	5	19	3.30
	Summit season	6	7	36	2.48	69	87	24	79	15	76	$4.9	6	7	35	2.17

RANDY JONES

YEAR	TEAM	ADJUSTED REGULAR SEASON											ACTUAL RESULTS			
		W	L	SV	ERA	G	IP	ER	H	BB	SO	PAY	W	L	SV	ERA
1973	San Diego (N)	7	6	0	3.86	20	140	60	138	39	96	$4.9	7	6	0	3.16
1974	San Diego (N)	8	22	4	5.63	40	208	130	231	84	161	$7.9	8	22	2	4.45
1975	San Diego (N)	20	12	0	2.78	37	285	88	257	58	138	$16.4	20	12	0	2.24
1976	San Diego (N)	22	14	0	3.57	40	315	125	295	56	131	$25.4	22	14	0	2.74
1977	San Diego (N)	6	12	0	5.27	27	147	86	178	39	57	$5.4	6	12	0	4.58
1978	San Diego (N)	13	14	0	3.59	37	253	101	280	71	100	$15.0	13	14	0	2.88
1979	San Diego (N)	11	12	0	4.14	39	263	121	264	70	155	$15.4	11	12	0	3.63
1980	San Diego (N)	5	13	0	4.68	24	154	80	170	33	74	$4.9	5	13	0	3.91
1981	New York (N)	2	12	0	6.23	20	91	63	108	66	31	$2.9	1	8	0	4.85
1982	New York (N)	7	10	0	5.50	28	108	66	136	58	58	$3.3	7	10	0	4.60
	Career	101	127	4	4.22	312	1,964	920	2,057	574	1,001	$101.5	100	123	2	3.42
	Average season	10	13	0	4.22	31	196	92	206	57	100	$10.2	10	12	0	3.42
	Summit season	15	12	0	3.55	35	251	99	247	59	124	$15.4	15	12	0	2.89

SAM JONES

		ADJUSTED REGULAR SEASON											ACTUAL RESULTS			
YEAR	TEAM	W	L	SV	ERA	G	IP	ER	H	BB	SO	PAY	W	L	SV	ERA
1951	Cleveland (A)	0	1	0	2.00	2	9	2	4	5	7	$0.0	0	1	0	2.08
1952	Cleveland (A)	2	3	2	9.00	15	39	39	45	41	44	$0.8	2	3	1	7.25
1955	Chicago (N)	15	21	0	4.69	38	255	133	195	192	293	$10.1	14	20	0	4.10
1956	Chicago (N)	9	14	0	4.50	34	194	97	169	117	239	$7.8	9	14	0	3.91
1957	St. Louis (N)	12	9	0	4.29	29	189	90	180	80	208	$7.3	12	9	0	3.60
1958	St. Louis (N)	15	14	0	3.41	37	264	100	·228	123	300	$18.2	14	13	0	2.88
1959	San Francisco (N)	22	16	7	3.29	53	287	105	260	125	278	$25.2	21	15	4	2.83
1960	San Francisco (N)	19	15	0	3.80	41	246	104	226	101	247	$18.6	18	14	0	3.19
1961	San Francisco (N)	8	8	2	5.13	39	135	77	149	62	134	$6.1	8	8	1	4.49
1962	Detroit (A)	2	4	1	4.22	30	81	38	81	37	86	$3.2	2	4	1	3.65
1963	St. Louis (N)	2	0	3	12.27	11	11	15	17	6	9	$0.8	2	0	2	9.00
1964	Baltimore (A)	0	0	0	3.60	7	10	4	5	6	6	$0.0	0	0	0	2.61
	Career	106	105	15	4.21	336	1,720	804	1,559	895	1,851	$98.1	102	101	9	3.59
	Average season	9	9	1	4.21	28	143	67	130	75	154	$8.2	9	8	1	3.59
	Summit season	17	15	1	3.85	40	248	106	218	124	265	$15.9	16	14	1	3.29

ADDIE JOSS

		ADJUSTED REGULAR SEASON											ACTUAL RESULTS			
YEAR	TEAM	W	L	SV	ERA	G	IP	ER	H	BB	SO	PAY	W	L	SV	ERA
1902	Cleveland (A)	20	15	0	3.99	38	320	142	268	129	266	$33.3	17	13	0	2.77
1903	Cleveland (A)	21	15	0	3.21	37	328	117	276	62	248	$33.8	18	13	0	2.19
1904	Cleveland (A)	15	10	0	2.70	26	200	60	186	49	149	$15.4	14	10	0	1.59
1905	Cleveland (A)	21	12	0	3.26	34	295	107	285	67	226	$27.2	20	12	0	2.01
1906	Cleveland (A)	22	9	3	2.95	35	290	95	258	62	191	$27.1	21	9	1	1.72
1907	Cleveland (A)	28	11	3	3.35	43	347	129	328	79	240	$42.3	27	11	2	1.83
1908	Cleveland (A)	25	11	5	2.22	43	333	82	285	46	238	$42.3	24	11	2	1.16
1909	Cleveland (A)	14	13	0	3.06	34	250	85	239	43	124	$19.6	14	13	0	1.71
1910	Cleveland (A)	5	5	0	3.70	13	107	44	109	22	81	$5.9	5	5	0	2.26
	Career	171	101	11	3.14	303	2,470	861	2,234	559	1,763	$246.9	160	97	5	1.89
	Average season	19	11	1	3.14	34	274	96	248	62	196	$27.4	18	11	1	1.89
	Summit season	23	12	2	2.99	38	319	106	286	63	229	$34.5	22	11	1	1.77

JIM KAAT

		ADJUSTED REGULAR SEASON											ACTUAL RESULTS			
YEAR	TEAM	W	L	SV	ERA	G	IP	ER	H	BB	SO	PAY	W	L	SV	ERA
1959	Washington (A)	0	2	0	14.40	3	5	8	7	4	3	$0.0	0	2	0	12.60
1960	Washington (A)	1	5	0	6.67	14	54	40	56	36	34	$0.6	1	5	0	5.58
1961	Minnesota (A)	9	17	0	4.43	36	201	99	198	85	151	$5.1	9	17	0	3.90
1962	Minnesota (A)	18	14	1	3.65	39	269	109	256	79	207	$15.5	18	14	1	3.14
1963	Minnesota (A)	10	10	1	5.56	31	178	110	218	46	118	$7.6	10	10	1	4.19
1964	Minnesota (A)	17	11	1	4.11	36	243	111	252	73	189	$16.0	17	11	1	3.22
1965	Minnesota (A)	18	11	2	3.68	45	264	108	300	73	170	$19.6	18	11	2	2.83

(Jim Kaat, continued)

YEAR	TEAM	ADJUSTED REGULAR SEASON											ACTUAL RESULTS			
		W	L	SV	ERA	G	IP	ER	H	BB	SO	PAY	W	L	SV	ERA
1966	Minnesota (A)	25	13	0	3.57	41	305	121	300	68	231	$32.4	25	13	0	2.75
1967	Minnesota (A)	16	13	0	4.20	41	257	120	301	49	225	$20.3	16	13	0	3.04
1968	Minnesota (A)	14	12	0	4.50	30	208	104	227	51	145	$15.3	14	12	0	2.94
1969	Minnesota (A)	14	13	1	4.43	40	242	119	280	78	158	$16.1	14	13	1	3.49
1970	Minnesota (A)	14	10	0	4.19	45	230	107	263	59	137	$13.7	14	10	0	3.56
1971	Minnesota (A)	13	14	0	4.40	39	260	127	305	52	166	$14.5	13	14	0	3.32
1972	Minnesota (A)	11	2	0	2.90	16	121	39	114	24	80	$4.8	10	2	0	2.06
1973	Minn.-Chi. (A)	15	13	0	5.34	36	224	133	266	46	137	$8.8	15	13	0	4.37
1974	Chicago (A)	21	13	0	3.67	42	277	113	280	68	186	$17.2	21	13	0	2.92
1975	Chicago (A)	20	14	0	3.85	43	304	130	342	80	188	$23.2	20	14	0	3.11
1976	Philadelphia (N)	12	14	0	4.54	38	228	115	261	36	116	$7.7	12	14	0	3.48
1977	Philadelphia (N)	6	11	0	6.19	35	160	110	217	44	71	$3.9	6	11	0	5.39
1978	Philadelphia (N)	8	5	0	5.14	26	140	80	160	35	67	$3.6	8	5	0	4.10
1979	Phi. (N)-N.Y. (A)	3	3	3	4.43	43	67	33	75	21	35	$1.6	3	3	2	3.92
1980	N.Y. (A)-St.L. (N)	8	8	5	4.73	53	135	71	153	43	53	$2.9	8	8	4	3.94
1981	St. Louis (N)	9	9	7	4.34	64	83	40	101	30	18	$2.2	6	6	4	3.40
1982	St. Louis (N)	5	3	2	4.80	62	75	40	82	26	46	$2.0	5	3	2	4.08
1983	St. Louis (N)	0	0	0	4.63	24	35	18	51	11	24	$0.8	0	0	0	3.89
	Career	287	240	23	4.35	922	4,565	2,205	5,065	1,217	2,955	$255.4	283	237	18	3.45
	Average season	11	10	1	4.35	37	183	88	203	49	118	$10.2	11	9	1	3.45
	Summit season	20	13	1	3.68	42	284	116	296	74	196	$21.6	20	13	1	2.95

TIM KEEFE

YEAR	TEAM	ADJUSTED REGULAR SEASON											ACTUAL RESULTS			
		W	L	SV	ERA	G	IP	ER	H	BB	SO	PAY	W	L	SV	ERA
1880	Troy (N)	12	12	0	1.66	24	201	37	136	100	162	$9.4	6	6	0	0.86
1881	Troy (N)	34	52	0	5.43	86	768	463	830	363	487	$78.3	18	27	0	3.25
1882	Troy (N)	32	50	0	4.05	82	715	322	714	400	493	$78.5	17	26	0	2.50
1883	New York (AA)	69	45	0	3.39	114	1,038	391	785	432	1,095	$122.5	41	27	0	2.41
1884	New York (AA)	54	25	0	3.30	84	700	257	577	223	631	$95.4	37	17	0	2.25
1885	New York (N)	47	19	0	2.35	67	583	152	463	266	547	$86.7	32	13	0	1.58
1886	New York (N)	55	26	0	3.45	84	702	269	662	174	573	$98.9	42	20	0	2.56
1887	New York (N)	44	24	0	3.40	70	596	225	502	163	520	$86.0	35	19	0	3.12
1888	New York (N)	41	14	0	2.68	60	511	152	412	172	622	$80.7	35	12	0	1.74
1889	New York (N)	35	16	6	3.85	58	449	192	385	194	474	$69.6	28	13	1	3.31
1890	New York (P)	21	14	0	3.99	37	282	125	275	105	208	$40.6	17	11	0	3.38
1891	N.Y.-Phi. (N)	6	13	2	5.79	22	154	99	180	64	133	$14.0	5	11	1	4.46
1892	Philadelphia (N)	20	17	0	3.26	41	329	119	296	109	260	$32.3	19	16	0	2.36
1893	Philadelphia (N)	12	9	0	4.33	27	218	105	224	88	197	$12.6	10	7	0	4.40
	Career	482	336	8	3.61	856	7,246	2,908	6,441	2,853	6,402	$905.5	342	225	2	2.62
	Average season	34	24	1	3.61	61	518	208	460	204	457	$64.7	24	16	0	2.62
	Summit season	54	28	0	3.22	84	724	259	598	252	673	$97.9	37	19	0	2.41

JIM KONSTANTY

YEAR	TEAM	ADJUSTED REGULAR SEASON											ACTUAL RESULTS			
		W	L	SV	ERA	G	IP	ER	H	BB	SO	PAY	W	L	SV	ERA
1944	Cincinnati (N)	6	4	0	3.66	21	118	48	123	39	42	$3.3	6	4	0	2.80
1946	Boston (N)	0	1	0	6.88	11	17	13	20	8	16	$0.4	0	1	0	5.28
1948	Philadelphia (N)	1	0	3	0.90	6	10	1	7	2	12	$0.1	1	0	2	0.93
1949	Philadelphia (N)	10	5	19	3.62	56	102	41	106	27	80	$4.2	9	5	7	3.25
1950	Philadelphia (N)	16	7	38	2.77	76	156	48	112	45	98	$8.3	16	7	22	2.66
1951	Philadelphia (N)	4	12	22	4.57	61	122	62	139	31	52	$4.4	4	11	9	4.05
1952	Philadelphia (N)	5	3	14	4.82	44	84	45	99	22	28	$3.7	5	3	6	3.94
1953	Philadelphia (N)	15	10	9	4.90	50	178	97	210	44	76	$7.1	14	10	5	4.43
1954	Phi. (N)-N.Y. (A)	3	4	10	3.50	44	72	28	80	18	24	$2.1	3	4	5	3.01
1955	New York (A)	7	2	20	2.69	47	77	23	75	24	30	$2.6	7	2	11	2.32
1956	N.Y. (A)-St.L. (N)	1	1	13	5.37	36	52	31	67	12	20	$1.7	1	1	7	4.65
	Career	68	49	148	3.98	452	988	437	1,038	272	478	$37.9	66	48	74	3.46
	Average season	6	4	13	3.98	41	90	40	94	25	43	$3.4	6	4	7	3.46
	Summit season	10	7	22	3.83	58	127	54	128	34	67	$5.3	10	7	11	3.47

JERRY KOOSMAN

YEAR	TEAM	ADJUSTED REGULAR SEASON											ACTUAL RESULTS			
		W	L	SV	ERA	G	IP	ER	H	BB	SO	PAY	W	L	SV	ERA
1967	New York (N)	0	2	0	8.18	9	22	20	25	23	12	$0.0	0	2	0	6.04
1968	New York (N)	19	12	0	3.17	35	264	93	261	88	198	$10.1	19	12	0	2.08
1969	New York (N)	17	9	0	2.88	32	241	77	208	71	203	$15.5	17	9	0	2.28
1970	New York (N)	12	7	0	3.69	30	212	87	204	72	135	$9.4	12	7	0	3.14
1971	New York (N)	6	11	0	4.01	26	166	74	178	57	116	$7.7	6	11	0	3.04
1972	New York (N)	11	12	1	5.84	35	168	109	182	61	175	$8.4	11	12	1	4.14
1973	New York (N)	14	15	0	3.46	35	263	101	249	81	195	$15.6	14	15	0	2.84
1974	New York (N)	15	11	0	4.25	35	265	125	275	92	241	$14.9	15	11	0	3.36
1975	New York (N)	14	13	3	4.24	36	240	113	249	102	223	$14.6	14	13	2	3.42
1976	New York (N)	21	10	0	3.50	34	247	96	221	74	261	$18.8	21	10	0	2.69
1977	New York (N)	8	20	0	4.00	32	227	101	201	89	237	$14.0	8	20	0	3.49
1978	New York (N)	3	15	3	4.67	38	235	122	235	93	213	$7.2	3	15	2	3.75
1979	Minnesota (A)	20	13	0	3.85	37	264	113	275	91	212	$16.7	20	13	0	3.38
1980	Minnesota (A)	16	13	2	4.81	38	243	130	259	79	201	$13.1	16	13	2	4.03
1981	Minn.-Chi. (A)	6	19	8	5.10	40	180	102	200	69	154	$6.1	4	13	5	4.01
1982	Chicago (A)	11	7	3	4.58	42	173	88	202	43	115	$6.2	11	7	3	3.84
1983	Chicago (A)	11	7	2	5.66	37	170	107	185	59	115	$5.9	11	7	2	4.77
1984	Philadelphia (N)	14	15	0	3.90	36	224	97	243	68	167	$7.5	14	15	0	3.25
1985	Philadelphia (N)	6	4	0	5.45	19	99	60	113	37	73	$3.3	6	4	0	4.62
	Career	224	215	22	4.19	626	3,903	1,815	3,965	1,349	3,246	$195.0	222	209	17	3.36
	Average season	12	11	1	4.19	33	205	96	209	71	171	$10.3	12	11	1	3.36
	Summit season	18	12	0	3.38	35	256	96	243	81	214	$15.3	18	12	0	2.66

SANDY KOUFAX

		ADJUSTED REGULAR SEASON											ACTUAL RESULTS			
YEAR	TEAM	W	L	SV	ERA	G	IP	ER	H	BB	SO	PAY	W	L	SV	ERA
1955	Brooklyn (N)	2	2	0	3.40	13	45	17	38	29	46	$1.1	2	2	0	3.02
1956	Brooklyn (N)	2	4	0	5.66	17	62	39	74	30	44	$1.3	2	4	0	4.91
1957	Brooklyn (N)	5	4	0	4.66	36	110	57	93	59	161	$4.2	5	4	0	3.88
1958	Los Angeles (N)	12	12	2	5.34	42	167	99	147	121	176	$5.9	11	11	1	4.48
1959	Los Angeles (N)	8	6	3	4.73	36	158	83	148	103	215	$5.9	8	6	2	4.05
1960	Los Angeles (N)	8	14	2	4.70	39	184	96	150	112	248	$8.2	8	13	1	3.91
1961	Los Angeles (N)	19	14	1	4.00	44	268	119	234	103	336	$20.4	18	13	1	3.52
1962	Los Angeles (N)	14	7	1	2.93	27	178	58	136	58	240	$9.9	14	7	1	2.54
1963	Los Angeles (N)	25	5	0	2.49	40	311	86	238	70	341	$33.8	25	5	0	1.88
1964	Los Angeles (N)	19	5	1	2.22	29	223	55	168	64	243	$19.8	19	5	1	1.74
1965	Los Angeles (N)	26	8	2	2.65	43	336	99	242	82	416	$51.2	26	8	2	2.04
1966	Los Angeles (N)	27	9	0	2.23	41	323	80	266	96	352	$50.9	27	9	0	1.73
	Career	167	90	12	3.38	407	2,365	888	1,934	927	2,818	$212.6	165	87	9	2.76
	Average season	14	8	1	3.38	34	197	74	161	77	235	$17.7	14	7	1	2.76
	Summit season	23	8	1	2.71	39	292	88	230	83	338	$35.2	23	8	1	2.15

RAY KREMER

		ADJUSTED REGULAR SEASON											ACTUAL RESULTS			
YEAR	TEAM	W	L	SV	ERA	G	IP	ER	H	BB	SO	PAY	W	L	SV	ERA
1924	Pittsburgh (N)	19	10	5	3.61	43	272	109	258	64	166	$26.0	18	10	1	3.19
1925	Pittsburgh (N)	18	8	7	3.88	42	225	97	221	55	156	$18.1	17	8	2	3.69
1926	Pittsburgh (N)	21	6	8	3.03	38	238	80	220	59	177	$23.9	20	6	5	2.61
1927	Pittsburgh (N)	20	8	5	2.79	36	232	72	200	64	154	$18.7	19	8	2	2.47
1928	Pittsburgh (N)	16	14	0	5.31	36	232	137	258	82	148	$17.7	15	13	0	4.64
1929	Pittsburgh (N)	19	11	0	4.37	36	235	114	220	69	160	$16.7	18	10	0	4.26
1930	Pittsburgh (N)	21	13	0	4.78	41	290	154	341	75	130	$22.8	20	12	0	5.02
1931	Pittsburgh (N)	11	16	0	3.67	31	238	97	242	77	126	$12.7	11	15	0	3.33
1932	Pittsburgh (N)	4	3	0	4.65	12	62	32	64	21	14	$1.9	4	3	0	4.29
1933	Pittsburgh (N)	1	0	0	12.60	7	20	28	36	11	9	$0.9	1	0	0	10.35
	Career	150	89	25	4.05	322	2,044	920	2,060	577	1,240	$159.4	143	85	10	3.76
	Average season	15	9	3	4.05	32	204	92	206	58	124	$15.9	14	9	1	3.76
	Summit season	20	9	5	3.66	40	251	102	248	63	157	$21.9	19	9	2	3.45

VERN LAW

		ADJUSTED REGULAR SEASON											ACTUAL RESULTS			
YEAR	TEAM	W	L	SV	ERA	G	IP	ER	H	BB	SO	PAY	W	L	SV	ERA
1950	Pittsburgh (N)	7	9	0	5.14	28	133	76	144	45	99	$4.8	7	9	0	4.92
1951	Pittsburgh (N)	6	9	5	5.11	29	118	67	117	51	74	$4.6	6	9	2	4.50
1954	Pittsburgh (N)	9	14	6	6.51	41	170	123	222	58	96	$5.6	9	13	3	5.51
1955	Pittsburgh (N)	10	10	2	4.37	45	210	102	245	62	129	$8.0	10	10	1	3.81
1956	Pittsburgh (N)	8	16	3	5.01	40	201	112	237	49	89	$5.8	8	16	2	4.32
1957	Pittsburgh (N)	10	8	2	3.39	32	178	67	188	36	80	$5.7	10	8	1	2.87
1958	Pittsburgh (N)	15	13	4	4.71	37	214	112	264	45	80	$8.3	14	12	3	3.96

(Vern Law, continued)

YEAR	TEAM	ADJUSTED REGULAR SEASON											ACTUAL RESULTS			
		W	L	SV	ERA	G	IP	ER	H	BB	SO	PAY	W	L	SV	ERA
1959	Pittsburgh (N)	19	10	2	3.48	36	282	109	275	60	151	$19.6	18	9	1	2.98
1960	Pittsburgh (N)	21	10	0	3.70	37	287	118	302	44	162	$25.5	20	9	0	3.08
1961	Pittsburgh (N)	3	4	0	5.40	12	65	39	83	20	28	$3.3	3	4	0	4.70
1962	Pittsburgh (N)	10	7	0	4.53	23	139	70	164	29	94	$5.0	10	7	0	3.94
1963	Pittsburgh (N)	4	5	0	6.55	18	77	56	102	16	35	$2.6	4	5	0	4.93
1964	Pittsburgh (N)	12	13	0	4.59	35	192	98	222	39	104	$4.8	12	13	0	3.61
1965	Pittsburgh (N)	17	9	0	2.82	29	217	68	204	40	112	$8.2	17	9	0	2.15
1966	Pittsburgh (N)	12	8	0	5.26	31	178	104	226	30	100	$5.8	12	8	0	4.05
1967	Pittsburgh (N)	2	6	0	5.75	25	97	62	140	22	47	$2.6	2	6	0	4.18
	Career	165	151	24	4.51	498	2,758	1,383	3,135	646	1,480	$120.2	162	147	13	3.77
	Average season	10	9	2	4.51	31	172	86	196	40	93	$7.5	10	9	1	3.77
	Summit season	16	10	2	3.62	34	236	95	247	45	117	$13.5	16	9	1	3.00

BILL LEE

YEAR	TEAM	ADJUSTED REGULAR SEASON											ACTUAL RESULTS			
		W	L	SV	ERA	G	IP	ER	H	BB	SO	PAY	W	L	SV	ERA
1934	Chicago (N)	14	15	3	3.61	37	227	91	217	87	201	$15.7	13	14	1	3.40
1935	Chicago (N)	21	6	3	3.19	41	265	94	239	99	207	$20.5	20	6	1	2.96
1936	Chicago (N)	19	12	3	3.32	45	271	100	229	102	207	$25.8	18	11	1	3.31
1937	Chicago (N)	15	16	7	3.79	44	285	120	289	79	201	$25.8	14	15	3	3.54
1938	Chicago (N)	23	9	6	2.84	46	304	96	283	77	237	$33.5	22	9	2	2.66
1939	Chicago (N)	20	15	0	3.69	38	290	119	294	90	202	$26.9	19	15	0	3.44
1940	Chicago (N)	9	18	0	5.61	39	223	139	259	79	134	$15.0	9	17	0	5.03
1941	Chicago (N)	8	15	3	4.42	29	173	85	189	44	118	$7.3	8	14	1	3.76
1942	Chicago (N)	13	13	0	5.07	33	227	128	246	72	151	$8.8	13	13	0	3.85
1943	Chi.-Phi. (N)	4	12	6	5.50	27	144	88	172	53	72	$4.2	4	12	3	4.01
1944	Philadelphia (N)	11	12	3	4.09	33	222	101	220	68	111	$7.2	10	11	1	3.15
1945	Phi.-Bos. (N)	10	10	0	4.59	31	196	100	243	75	58	$3.6	9	9	0	3.58
1946	Boston (N)	10	9	0	5.55	26	146	90	165	47	58	$3.3	10	9	0	4.18
1947	Chicago (N)	0	2	0	5.19	15	26	15	29	15	17	$0.8	0	2	0	4.50
	Career	177	164	34	4.10	484	2,999	1,366	3,074	987	1,974	$198.4	169	157	13	3.54
	Average season	13	12	2	4.10	35	214	98	220	71	141	$14.2	12	11	1	3.54
	Summit season	20	12	4	3.37	43	283	106	267	89	211	$26.5	19	11	1	3.18

BOB LEMON

YEAR	TEAM	ADJUSTED REGULAR SEASON											ACTUAL RESULTS			
		W	L	SV	ERA	G	IP	ER	H	BB	SO	PAY	W	L	SV	ERA
1946	Cleveland (A)	4	5	4	3.25	33	97	35	85	71	67	$3.8	4	5	1	2.49
1947	Cleveland (A)	11	5	8	4.03	38	172	77	160	96	118	$5.9	11	5	3	3.44
1948	Cleveland (A)	21	15	4	3.11	45	307	106	246	123	266	$26.4	20	14	2	2.82
1949	Cleveland (A)	23	11	2	3.33	39	295	109	229	127	255	$27.0	22	10	1	2.99
1950	Cleveland (A)	24	12	5	4.04	46	301	135	297	135	287	$34.1	23	11	3	3.84
1951	Cleveland (A)	18	15	5	3.98	44	276	122	265	125	235	$27.4	17	14	2	3.52
1952	Cleveland (A)	23	12	6	3.08	44	324	111	267	111	215	$38.8	22	11	4	2.50

(Bob Lemon, continued)

				ADJUSTED REGULAR SEASON									ACTUAL RESULTS			
YEAR	TEAM	W	L	SV	ERA	G	IP	ER	H	BB	SO	PAY	W	L	SV	ERA
1953	Cleveland (A)	22	16	2	3.71	43	301	124	302	117	166	$31.1	21	15	1	3.36
1954	Cleveland (A)	24	7	0	3.18	37	266	94	246	93	180	$25.5	23	7	0	2.72
1955	Cleveland (A)	19	11	3	4.44	37	223	110	243	76	157	$18.5	18	10	2	3.88
1956	Cleveland (A)	21	15	4	3.49	41	268	104	255	92	141	$23.2	20	14	3	3.03
1957	Cleveland (A)	6	12	0	5.49	22	123	75	144	74	65	$3.9	6	11	0	4.60
1958	Cleveland (A)	0	1	0	6.43	12	28	20	48	19	12	$1.2	0	1	0	5.33
	Career	216	137	43	3.69	481	2,981	1,222	2,787	1,259	2,164	$266.8	207	128	22	3.23
	Average season	17	11	3	3.69	37	229	94	214	97	166	$20.5	16	10	2	3.23
	Summit season	23	11	3	3.34	42	299	111	257	118	241	$30.4	22	11	2	2.97

JIM LONBORG

				ADJUSTED REGULAR SEASON									ACTUAL RESULTS			
YEAR	TEAM	W	L	SV	ERA	G	IP	ER	H	BB	SO	PAY	W	L	SV	ERA
1965	Boston (A)	9	17	0	5.84	32	185	120	217	75	124	$5.9	9	17	0	4.47
1966	Boston (A)	10	10	2	4.99	45	182	101	192	69	147	$8.0	10	10	2	3.86
1967	Boston (A)	22	9	0	4.38	39	273	133	260	100	267	$20.4	22	9	0	3.16
1968	Boston (A)	6	10	0	6.61	23	113	83	105	75	81	$5.2	6	10	0	4.29
1969	Boston (A)	7	11	0	5.75	29	144	92	165	68	113	$5.7	7	11	0	4.51
1970	Boston (A)	4	1	0	3.71	9	34	14	36	9	24	$2.2	4	1	0	3.18
1971	Boston (A)	10	7	0	5.46	27	168	102	186	74	121	$5.6	10	7	0	4.13
1972	Milwaukee (A)	14	12	1	3.95	34	230	101	232	89	173	$9.6	14	12	1	2.83
1973	Philadelphia (N)	13	16	0	5.97	38	199	132	232	85	133	$8.3	13	16	0	4.88
1974	Philadelphia (N)	17	13	0	4.07	39	283	128	299	75	161	$17.8	17	13	0	3.21
1975	Philadelphia (N)	8	6	0	5.09	27	159	90	171	46	95	$4.9	8	6	0	4.12
1976	Philadelphia (N)	18	10	1	4.01	33	222	99	227	56	160	$14.1	18	10	1	3.08
1977	Philadelphia (N)	11	4	0	4.73	25	158	83	162	55	97	$6.8	11	4	0	4.11
1978	Philadelphia (N)	8	10	0	6.55	22	114	83	141	50	67	$3.4	8	10	0	5.23
1979	Philadelphia (N)	0	1	0	12.86	4	7	10	14	4	9	$0.7	0	1	0	11.05
	Career	157	137	4	4.99	426	2,471	1,371	2,639	930	1,772	$118.6	157	137	4	3.86
	Average season	10	9	0	4.99	28	165	91	176	62	118	$7.9	10	9	0	3.86
	Summit season	16	10	0	4.21	34	233	109	236	75	172	$13.7	16	10	0	3.22

DOLF LUQUE

				ADJUSTED REGULAR SEASON									ACTUAL RESULTS			
YEAR	TEAM	W	L	SV	ERA	G	IP	ER	H	BB	SO	PAY	W	L	SV	ERA
1914	Boston (N)	0	1	0	7.00	2	9	7	6	5	2	$0.0	0	1	0	4.15
1915	Boston (N)	0	0	0	5.40	2	5	3	7	5	5	$0.0	0	0	0	3.60
1918	Cincinnati (N)	8	4	0	6.32	15	104	73	118	51	74	$3.6	6	3	0	3.80
1919	Cincinnati (N)	12	4	13	3.92	35	124	54	111	57	98	$5.4	10	3	3	2.63
1920	Cincinnati (N)	14	9	6	3.33	39	219	81	175	82	167	$9.7	13	9	1	2.51
1921	Cincinnati (N)	18	20	4	3.81	43	319	135	307	86	245	$26.7	17	19	3	3.38
1922	Cincinnati (N)	14	24	0	3.71	41	274	113	260	92	193	$18.2	13	23	0	3.31
1923	Cincinnati (N)	28	8	5	2.21	43	338	83	276	107	340	$40.7	27	8	2	1.93
1924	Cincinnati (N)	11	16	0	3.55	33	233	92	228	67	210	$14.9	10	15	0	3.16

(Dolf Luque, continued)

		ADJUSTED REGULAR SEASON											ACTUAL RESULTS			
YEAR	TEAM	W	L	SV	ERA	G	IP	ER	H	BB	SO	PAY	W	L	SV	ERA
1925	Cincinnati (N)	17	19	0	2.76	38	307	94	252	92	324	$30.7	16	18	0	2.63
1926	Cincinnati (N)	13	16	0	4.00	35	241	107	230	90	197	$13.6	13	16	0	3.43
1927	Cincinnati (N)	14	13	0	3.64	31	247	100	229	71	189	$13.2	13	12	0	3.20
1928	Cincinnati (N)	12	11	3	4.05	35	249	112	260	102	173	$13.1	11	10	1	3.57
1929	Cincinnati (N)	5	17	0	4.60	33	182	93	203	63	104	$3.9	5	16	0	4.50
1930	Brooklyn (N)	15	9	4	4.08	33	212	96	209	70	135	$7.4	14	8	2	4.30
1931	Brooklyn (N)	7	6	0	5.08	20	108	61	122	33	56	$3.1	7	6	0	4.56
1932	New York (N)	6	7	15	4.42	40	116	57	129	40	71	$3.5	6	7	5	4.01
1933	New York (N)	8	2	12	3.25	36	83	30	77	23	52	$3.0	8	2	4	2.69
1934	New York (N)	4	3	15	4.11	28	46	21	55	20	25	$1.8	4	3	7	3.83
1935	New York (N)	1	0	0	0.00	2	4	0	1	1	4	$0.5	1	0	0	0.00
	Career	207	189	77	3.72	584	3,420	1,412	3,255	1,157	2,664	$213.0	194	179	28	3.24
	Average season	10	9	4	3.72	29	171	71	163	58	133	$10.7	10	9	1	3.24
	Summit season	18	12	6	3.07	40	261	89	224	85	235	$22.6	17	11	2	2.61

SPARKY LYLE

		ADJUSTED REGULAR SEASON											ACTUAL RESULTS			
YEAR	TEAM	W	L	SV	ERA	G	IP	ER	H	BB	SO	PAY	W	L	SV	ERA
1967	Boston (A)	1	2	6	3.14	27	43	15	37	17	45	$1.3	1	2	5	2.28
1968	Boston (A)	6	1	15	4.23	49	66	31	79	18	58	$3.3	6	1	11	2.74
1969	Boston (A)	8	3	23	3.23	71	103	37	101	50	104	$5.6	8	3	17	2.54
1970	Boston (A)	1	7	22	4.57	63	67	34	67	34	57	$3.8	1	7	20	3.88
1971	Boston (A)	6	4	21	3.63	50	52	21	45	25	44	$3.6	6	4	16	2.75
1972	New York (A)	9	5	40	2.71	62	113	34	101	35	92	$8.3	9	5	35	1.92
1973	New York (A)	5	9	29	3.07	51	82	28	70	19	77	$5.6	5	9	27	2.51
1974	New York (A)	9	3	27	2.05	66	114	26	99	46	113	$9.2	9	3	15	1.66
1975	New York (A)	5	7	10	3.86	50	91	39	102	38	85	$5.7	5	7	6	3.12
1976	New York (A)	7	8	30	2.91	65	105	34	90	48	83	$6.7	7	8	23	2.26
1977	New York (A)	13	5	31	2.50	72	137	38	135	36	87	$8.3	13	5	26	2.17
1978	New York (A)	9	3	13	4.34	59	112	54	124	37	47	$4.3	9	3	9	3.47
1979	Texas (A)	5	8	16	3.60	67	95	38	80	31	65	$4.7	5	8	13	3.13
1980	Tex. (A)-Phi. (N)	3	2	12	5.12	59	95	54	112	39	67	$3.5	3	2	10	4.28
1981	Philadelphia (N)	14	9	4	5.68	73	114	72	139	57	62	$3.7	9	6	2	4.44
1982	Phi. (N)-Chi. (A)	3	3	3	5.51	45	49	30	64	22	25	$1.5	3	3	3	4.62
	Career	104	79	302	3.66	929	1,438	585	1,445	552	1,111	$79.1	99	76	238	2.88
	Average season	7	5	19	3.66	58	90	37	90	35	69	$4.9	6	5	15	2.88
	Summit season	9	5	30	2.68	67	114	34	105	43	96	$7.6	9	5	23	2.10

TED LYONS

		ADJUSTED REGULAR SEASON											ACTUAL RESULTS			
YEAR	TEAM	W	L	SV	ERA	G	IP	ER	H	BB	SO	PAY	W	L	SV	ERA
1923	Chicago (A)	2	1	0	7.43	9	23	19	29	18	14	$0.2	2	1	0	6.35
1924	Chicago (A)	13	12	9	5.51	43	227	139	275	90	135	$8.2	12	11	3	4.87
1925	Chicago (A)	22	12	7	3.44	45	275	105	261	98	120	$19.1	21	11	3	3.26
1926	Chicago (A)	19	17	3	3.50	41	298	116	272	127	134	$20.2	18	16	2	3.01
1927	Chicago (A)	23	15	2	3.20	41	323	115	291	83	181	$33.4	22	14	2	2.84
1928	Chicago (A)	16	15	8	4.54	41	252	127	279	82	146	$20.3	15	14	6	3.98
1929	Chicago (A)	15	21	2	4.19	39	273	127	267	87	142	$20.1	14	20	2	4.10
1930	Chicago (A)	23	16	2	3.58	44	312	124	307	68	152	$32.3	22	15	1	3.78
1931	Chicago (A)	4	6	0	4.42	23	106	52	117	40	37	$4.4	4	6	0	4.01
1932	Chicago (A)	11	16	5	3.56	35	245	97	246	88	131	$13.8	10	15	2	3.28
1933	Chicago (A)	11	23	2	5.28	39	247	145	279	96	173	$14.0	10	21	1	4.38
1934	Chicago (A)	12	14	3	5.22	32	219	127	250	78	111	$7.3	11	13	1	4.87
1935	Chicago (A)	16	8	0	3.26	24	199	72	191	65	116	$8.3	15	8	0	3.02
1936	Chicago (A)	11	14	0	5.19	28	196	113	225	51	105	$6.0	10	13	0	5.14
1937	Chicago (A)	13	7	0	4.42	23	177	87	182	49	87	$5.9	12	7	0	4.15
1938	Chicago (A)	10	12	0	3.95	25	212	93	250	57	115	$6.2	9	11	0	3.70
1939	Chicago (A)	15	6	0	2.93	22	181	59	164	28	128	$7.0	14	6	0	2.76
1940	Chicago (A)	13	8	0	3.60	23	195	78	196	41	135	$7.1	12	8	0	3.24
1941	Chicago (A)	13	10	0	4.36	23	196	95	213	38	123	$7.0	12	10	0	3.70
1942	Chicago (A)	15	7	0	2.73	22	198	60	197	30	109	$7.0	14	6	0	2.10
1946	Chicago (A)	1	4	0	3.14	5	43	15	41	9	18	$1.3	1	4	0	2.32
	Career	278	244	43	4.02	627	4,397	1,965	4,532	1,323	2,412	$249.1	260	230	23	3.67
	Average season	13	12	2	4.02	30	209	94	216	63	115	$11.9	12	11	1	3.67
	Summit season	20	13	3	3.33	39	281	104	266	81	139	$22.4	19	12	2	3.07

GREG MADDUX

		ADJUSTED REGULAR SEASON											ACTUAL RESULTS			
YEAR	TEAM	W	L	SV	ERA	G	IP	ER	H	BB	SO	PAY	W	L	SV	ERA
1986	Chicago (N)	2	4	0	6.39	6	31	22	47	12	22	$0.4	2	4	0	5.52
1987	Chicago (N)	6	14	0	6.00	30	156	104	187	78	110	$4.3	6	14	0	5.61
1988	Chicago (N)	18	8	0	3.90	34	249	108	248	94	165	$10.0	18	8	0	3.18
1989	Chicago (N)	19	12	0	3.63	35	238	96	239	91	157	$15.3	19	12	0	2.95
1990	Chicago (N)	15	15	0	4.10	35	237	108	256	77	165	$15.5	15	15	0	3.46
1991	Chicago (N)	15	11	0	3.94	37	263	115	249	71	223	$19.8	15	11	0	3.35
1992	Chicago (N)	20	11	0	2.65	35	268	79	216	77	231	$25.5	20	11	0	2.18
1993	Atlanta (N)	20	10	0	2.56	36	267	76	233	56	220	$20.6	20	10	0	2.36
1994	Atlanta (N)	23	9	0	1.58	36	291	51	215	46	236	$27.5	16	6	0	1.56
1995	Atlanta (N)	22	2	0	1.69	32	240	45	170	27	213	$25.8	19	2	0	1.63
1996	Atlanta (N)	15	11	0	2.68	35	245	73	224	28	173	$19.5	15	11	0	2.72
1997	Atlanta (N)	19	4	0	2.28	33	233	59	203	21	174	$19.6	19	4	0	2.20
1998	Atlanta (N)	18	9	0	2.29	34	251	64	203	47	202	$18.5	18	9	0	2.22
1999	Atlanta (N)	19	9	0	3.45	33	219	84	255	36	137	$14.6	19	9	0	3.57
2000	Atlanta (N)	19	9	0	2.86	35	249	79	223	40	191	$18.6	19	9	0	3.00
2001	Atlanta (N)	17	11	0	3.17	34	233	82	225	29	168	$17.6	17	11	0	3.05
	Career	267	149	0	3.05	520	3,670	1,245	3,393	830	2,787	$273.1	257	146	0	2.84
	Average season	17	9	0	3.05	33	229	78	212	52	174	$17.1	16	9	0	2.84
	Summit season	21	7	0	2.15	34	260	62	207	45	215	$23.8	19	7	0	2.02

SAL MAGLIE

		ADJUSTED REGULAR SEASON											ACTUAL RESULTS			
YEAR	TEAM	W	L	SV	ERA	G	IP	ER	H	BB	SO	PAY	W	L	SV	ERA
1945	New York (N)	5	4	0	2.97	14	91	30	81	25	68	$3.7	5	4	0	2.35
1950	New York (N)	19	4	2	2.85	49	215	68	178	79	167	$8.6	18	4	1	2.71
1951	New York (N)	24	6	7	3.30	43	305	112	269	84	254	$30.6	23	6	4	2.93
1952	New York (N)	19	8	2	3.59	37	228	91	227	80	182	$17.7	18	8	1	2.92
1953	New York (N)	8	9	0	4.59	28	151	77	167	49	128	$7.0	8	9	0	4.15
1954	New York (N)	15	6	4	3.82	36	231	98	246	72	193	$13.7	14	6	2	3.26
1955	N.Y. (N)-Cle. (A)	10	7	4	4.31	35	165	79	189	57	128	$6.1	9	7	2	3.77
1956	Cle. (A)-Bkn. (N)	13	5	0	3.33	31	203	75	175	55	158	$7.2	13	5	0	2.89
1957	Bkn. (N)-N.Y. (A)	8	6	7	3.20	26	132	47	127	37	84	$3.8	8	6	4	2.69
1958	N.Y. (A)-St.L. (N)	3	7	0	5.56	18	81	50	82	39	40	$2.1	3	7	0	4.72
	Career	124	62	26	3.63	317	1,802	727	1,741	577	1,402	$100.5	119	62	14	3.15
	Average season	12	6	3	3.63	32	180	73	174	58	140	$10.1	12	6	1	3.15
	Summit season	18	6	3	3.39	39	236	89	219	74	191	$15.6	17	6	2	2.94

PAT MALONE

		ADJUSTED REGULAR SEASON											ACTUAL RESULTS			
YEAR	TEAM	W	L	SV	ERA	G	IP	ER	H	BB	SO	PAY	W	L	SV	ERA
1928	Chicago (N)	19	14	5	3.22	44	263	94	220	119	324	$27.4	18	13	2	2.84
1929	Chicago (N)	23	11	4	3.63	42	280	113	273	117	348	$34.0	22	10	2	3.57
1930	Chicago (N)	21	9	10	3.74	47	284	118	268	114	282	$33.7	20	9	4	3.94
1931	Chicago (N)	16	9	0	4.33	37	235	113	224	104	223	$20.1	16	9	0	3.90
1932	Chicago (N)	16	18	0	3.71	39	250	103	223	96	245	$20.4	15	17	0	3.38
1933	Chicago (N)	11	15	0	4.68	33	198	103	195	75	161	$10.0	10	14	0	3.91
1934	Chicago (N)	15	7	0	3.79	36	202	85	199	64	207	$13.7	14	7	0	3.53
1935	New York (A)	3	6	10	5.81	32	62	40	55	41	53	$3.1	3	5	3	5.43
1936	New York (A)	13	4	15	3.87	37	142	61	140	66	140	$8.1	12	4	9	3.81
1937	New York (A)	4	4	14	5.87	29	95	62	108	38	87	$4.5	4	4	6	5.48
	Career	141	97	58	3.99	376	2,011	892	1,905	834	2,070	$175.0	134	92	26	3.74
	Average season	14	10	6	3.99	38	201	89	191	83	207	$17.5	13	9	3	3.74
	Summit season	18	11	7	3.61	42	244	98	225	102	268	$24.7	17	11	3	3.49

JUAN MARICHAL

		ADJUSTED REGULAR SEASON											ACTUAL RESULTS			
YEAR	TEAM	W	L	SV	ERA	G	IP	ER	H	BB	SO	PAY	W	L	SV	ERA
1960	San Francisco (N)	6	2	0	3.22	11	81	29	63	30	72	$3.7	6	2	0	2.66
1961	San Francisco (N)	13	10	0	4.43	30	191	94	199	51	158	$8.0	13	10	0	3.89
1962	San Francisco (N)	18	11	1	3.87	36	256	110	239	93	179	$16.0	18	11	1	3.36
1963	San Francisco (N)	25	8	0	3.17	41	321	113	289	74	278	$32.9	21	8	0	2.41
1964	San Francisco (N)	21	8	0	3.14	33	269	94	263	63	227	$26.3	21	8	0	2.48
1965	San Francisco (N)	22	13	1	2.78	39	295	91	251	53	263	$33.2	22	13	1	2.13
1966	San Francisco (N)	25	6	0	2.87	37	307	98	252	44	249	$40.2	25	6	0	2.23
1967	San Francisco (N)	14	10	0	3.83	26	202	86	223	51	181	$15.9	14	10	0	2.76
1968	San Francisco (N)	26	9	0	3.73	38	326	135	348	58	243	$40.7	26	9	0	2.43
1969	San Francisco (N)	21	11	0	2.67	37	300	89	271	56	231	$31.0	21	11	0	2.10

(Juan Marichal, continued)

		ADJUSTED REGULAR SEASON											ACTUAL RESULTS			
YEAR	TEAM	W	L	SV	ERA	G	IP	ER	H	BB	SO	PAY	W	L	SV	ERA
1970	San Francisco (N)	12	10	0	4.85	34	243	131	291	49	141	$14.7	12	10	0	4.12
1971	San Francisco (N)	18	11	0	3.87	37	279	120	270	62	192	$24.3	18	11	0	2.94
1972	San Francisco (N)	6	17	0	5.23	26	172	100	209	55	89	$6.6	6	16	0	3.71
1973	San Francisco (N)	11	15	0	4.65	34	207	107	246	39	110	$6.1	11	15	0	3.82
1974	Boston (A)	5	1	0	6.16	11	57	39	65	15	28	$1.8	5	1	0	4.87
1975	Los Angeles (N)	0	1	0	16.50	2	6	11	12	5	1	$0.1	0	1	0	13.50
	Career	243	143	2	3.71	472	3,512	1,447	3,491	798	2,642	$301.5	243	142	2	2.89
	Average season	15	9	0	3.71	30	220	90	218	50	165	$18.8	15	9	0	2.89
	Summit season	24	9	0	3.05	38	310	105	282	57	253	$35.6	24	9	0	2.27

RUBE MARQUARD

		ADJUSTED REGULAR SEASON											ACTUAL RESULTS			
YEAR	TEAM	W	L	SV	ERA	G	IP	ER	H	BB	SO	PAY	W	L	SV	ERA
1908	New York (N)	0	1	0	7.20	1	5	4	7	3	4	$0.0	0	1	0	3.60
1909	New York (N)	5	13	6	4.73	30	179	94	188	103	185	$4.8	5	13	1	2.60
1910	New York (N)	4	4	0	7.34	14	76	62	80	52	87	$3.1	4	4	0	4.46
1911	New York (N)	25	7	10	3.38	47	290	109	240	125	369	$26.9	24	7	3	2.50
1912	New York (N)	27	12	3	3.48	45	308	119	308	95	288	$33.4	26	11	1	2.57
1913	New York (N)	24	10	7	3.73	44	302	125	283	62	267	$34.3	23	10	3	2.50
1914	New York (N)	13	23	4	4.82	41	282	151	307	59	162	$26.5	12	22	2	3.06
1915	N.Y.-Bkn. (N)	11	10	9	6.39	34	200	142	243	47	161	$15.7	11	10	3	4.04
1916	Brooklyn (N)	13	6	12	2.64	37	211	62	200	50	185	$15.9	13	6	5	1.58
1917	Brooklyn (N)	20	12	0	4.37	38	239	116	235	80	219	$19.5	19	12	0	2.55
1918	Brooklyn (N)	12	23	0	4.37	44	309	150	334	97	255	$24.2	9	18	0	2.64
1919	Brooklyn (N)	3	3	0	3.41	9	66	25	64	15	65	$3.4	3	3	0	2.29
1920	Brooklyn (N)	10	7	0	4.27	29	196	93	186	47	193	$8.1	10	7	0	3.23
1921	Cincinnati (N)	18	15	0	3.84	41	279	119	281	67	211	$17.7	17	14	0	3.39
1922	Boston (N)	12	16	4	5.75	41	208	133	250	84	141	$7.1	11	15	1	5.09
1923	Boston (N)	12	15	0	4.29	40	252	120	264	80	188	$13.0	11	14	0	3.73
1924	Boston (N)	1	2	0	3.50	6	36	14	31	16	24	$1.4	1	2	0	3.00
1925	Boston (N)	2	9	0	6.12	28	78	53	104	33	50	$1.9	2	8	0	5.75
	Career	212	188	55	4.33	569	3,516	1,691	3,605	1,115	3,054	$256.9	201	177	19	3.08
	Average season	12	10	3	4.33	32	195	94	200	62	170	$14.3	11	10	1	3.08
	Summit season	22	9	6	3.53	42	270	106	253	82	266	$26.0	21	9	2	2.38

MIKE MARSHALL

		ADJUSTED REGULAR SEASON											ACTUAL RESULTS			
YEAR	TEAM	W	L	SV	ERA	G	IP	ER	H	BB	SO	PAY	W	L	SV	ERA
1967	Detroit (A)	1	3	13	2.75	37	59	18	58	24	45	$2.1	1	3	10	1.98
1969	Seattle (A)	3	10	0	6.55	20	88	64	111	37	53	$3.0	3	10	0	5.13
1970	Hou.-Mon. (N)	3	8	3	4.50	28	70	35	69	34	49	$2.2	3	8	3	3.86
1971	Montreal (N)	5	8	31	5.68	66	111	70	111	55	101	$5.3	5	8	23	4.28
1972	Montreal (N)	15	8	23	2.53	68	121	34	97	56	115	$8.2	14	8	18	1.78
1973	Montreal (N)	14	11	36	3.27	92	179	65	173	80	153	$15.8	14	11	31	2.66

(Mike Marshall, continued)

		ADJUSTED REGULAR SEASON											ACTUAL RESULTS			
YEAR	TEAM	W	L	SV	ERA	G	IP	ER	H	BB	SO	PAY	W	L	SV	ERA
1974	Los Angeles (N)	15	12	39	3.07	106	208	71	204	60	184	$25.5	15	12	21	2.42
1975	Los Angeles (N)	9	14	18	4.05	57	109	49	104	40	83	$8.3	9	14	13	3.29
1976	L.A.-Atl. (N)	6	4	20	5.18	54	99	57	106	44	76	$7.0	6	4	14	3.99
1977	Atl. (N)-Tex. (A)	3	2	1	5.36	16	42	25	56	17	31	$2.5	3	2	1	4.75
1978	Minnesota (A)	10	12	24	3.09	54	99	34	85	41	76	$4.9	10	12	21	2.45
1979	Minnesota (A)	10	15	38	3.02	90	143	48	136	53	110	$7.1	10	15	32	2.65
1980	Minnesota (A)	1	3	1	7.31	18	32	26	43	14	18	$1.4	1	3	1	6.12
1981	New York (N)	5	3	0	3.38	31	48	18	43	14	18	$1.7	3	2	0	2.61
	Career	100	113	247	3.92	737	1,408	614	1,396	569	1,112	$95.0	97	112	188	3.14
	Average season	7	8	18	3.92	53	101	44	100	41	79	$6.8	7	8	13	3.14
	Summit season	13	12	32	3.00	82	150	50	139	58	128	$12.3	13	12	25	2.43

PEDRO MARTINEZ

		ADJUSTED REGULAR SEASON											ACTUAL RESULTS			
YEAR	TEAM	W	L	SV	ERA	G	IP	ER	H	BB	SO	PAY	W	L	SV	ERA
1992	Los Angeles (N)	0	1	0	2.25	2	8	2	6	1	9	$0.0	0	1	0	2.25
1993	Los Angeles (N)	10	5	1	2.86	65	107	34	78	61	131	$4.5	10	5	2	2.61
1994	Montreal (N)	16	7	1	3.47	34	205	79	162	65	211	$9.4	11	5	1	3.42
1995	Montreal (N)	16	11	0	3.62	34	221	89	181	76	203	$10.0	14	10	0	3.51
1996	Montreal (N)	13	10	0	3.69	33	217	89	188	71	225	$15.2	13	10	0	3.70
1997	Montreal (N)	17	8	0	1.98	31	241	53	159	69	302	$19.7	17	8	0	1.90
1998	Boston (A)	19	7	0	2.96	33	234	77	191	71	250	$19.5	19	7	0	2.89
1999	Boston (A)	23	4	0	1.99	31	213	47	158	36	316	$20.3	23	4	0	2.07
2000	Boston (A)	18	6	0	1.66	29	217	40	127	30	286	$19.9	18	6	0	1.74
2001	Boston (A)	7	3	0	2.46	18	117	32	86	27	160	$8.3	7	3	0	2.39
	Career	139	62	2	2.74	310	1,780	542	1,336	507	2,093	$126.8	132	59	3	2.66
	Average season	14	6	0	2.74	31	178	54	134	51	209	$12.7	13	6	0	2.66
	Summit season	19	6	0	2.39	32	222	59	159	54	273	$17.8	18	6	0	2.33

CHRISTY MATHEWSON

		ADJUSTED REGULAR SEASON											ACTUAL RESULTS			
YEAR	TEAM	W	L	SV	ERA	G	IP	ER	H	BB	SO	PAY	W	L	SV	ERA
1900	New York (N)	0	4	0	6.23	7	39	27	40	30	42	$0.4	0	3	0	5.08
1901	New York (N)	23	20	0	3.15	46	386	135	319	159	468	$40.2	20	17	0	2.41
1902	New York (N)	16	20	0	3.05	40	325	110	284	124	368	$27.2	14	17	0	2.11
1903	New York (N)	34	15	2	3.30	51	415	152	374	166	500	$58.1	30	13	2	2.26
1904	New York (N)	34	12	2	3.48	49	375	145	349	125	359	$57.2	33	12	1	2.03
1905	New York (N)	32	9	4	2.06	45	354	81	295	95	347	$56.6	31	9	3	1.28
1906	New York (N)	23	13	3	5.12	40	281	160	315	114	231	$41.6	22	12	1	2.97
1907	New York (N)	25	13	4	3.65	43	330	134	301	79	325	$53.2	24	12	2	2.00
1908	New York (N)	38	11	8	2.73	58	405	123	354	66	448	$63.8	37	11	5	1.43
1909	New York (N)	26	6	5	2.07	38	283	65	231	50	257	$42.1	25	6	2	1.14
1910	New York (N)	28	9	0	3.12	40	335	116	351	76	315	$54.0	27	9	0	1.89
1911	New York (N)	27	14	5	2.69	47	321	96	331	44	239	$52.3	26	13	3	1.99

(Christy Mathewson, continued)

YEAR	TEAM	ADJUSTED REGULAR SEASON											ACTUAL RESULTS			
		W	L	SV	ERA	G	IP	ER	H	BB	SO	PAY	W	L	SV	ERA
1912	New York (N)	24	13	7	2.86	45	324	103	335	40	229	$40.9	23	12	4	2.12
1913	New York (N)	26	12	3	3.06	42	321	109	333	26	174	$39.9	25	11	2	2.06
1914	New York (N)	25	14	3	4.73	43	327	172	368	29	143	$39.4	24	13	2	3.00
1915	New York (N)	8	15	0	5.64	28	193	121	235	25	104	$8.6	8	14	0	3.58
1916	N.Y.-Cin. (N)	4	4	4	5.06	14	80	45	91	11	37	$2.8	4	4	2	3.01
	Career	393	204	50	3.35	676	5,094	1,894	4,906	1,259	4,586	$678.3	373	188	29	2.13
	Average season	23	12	3	3.35	40	300	111	289	74	270	$39.9	22	11	2	2.13
	Summit season	33	11	4	2.78	48	366	113	321	100	382	$55.6	31	10	3	1.66

JIM McCORMICK

YEAR	TEAM	ADJUSTED REGULAR SEASON											ACTUAL RESULTS			
		W	L	SV	ERA	G	IP	ER	H	BB	SO	PAY	W	L	SV	ERA
1878	Indianapolis (N)	13	21	0	3.35	36	301	112	321	142	209	$19.6	5	8	0	1.69
1879	Cleveland (N)	39	79	0	4.42	122	1,075	528	1,117	704	881	$105.8	20	40	0	2.42
1880	Cleveland (N)	86	53	0	3.48	141	1,253	484	1,159	462	1,082	$140.9	45	28	0	1.85
1881	Cleveland (N)	49	57	0	3.99	112	999	443	890	367	817	$115.2	26	30	0	2.45
1882	Cleveland (N)	69	58	0	3.83	131	1,148	489	1,074	510	851	$135.9	36	30	0	2.37
1883	Cleveland (N)	46	20	3	2.59	70	557	160	498	253	445	$89.1	28	12	1	1.84
1884	Cle. (N)-Cin. (U)	58	36	0	3.47	95	819	316	767	278	650	$107.7	40	25	0	2.37
1885	Prov.-Chi. (N)	30	10	0	3.65	40	360	146	336	153	236	$64.1	21	7	0	2.43
1886	Chicago (N)	40	14	0	3.83	54	447	190	463	169	328	$70.0	31	11	0	2.82
1887	Pittsburgh (N)	17	30	0	4.72	47	421	221	465	133	236	$57.9	13	23	0	4.30
	Career	447	378	3	3.77	848	7,380	3,089	7,090	3,171	5,735	$906.2	265	214	1	2.43
	Average season	45	38	0	3.77	85	738	309	709	317	574	$90.6	27	21	0	2.43
	Summit season	62	45	1	3.56	110	955	378	878	374	769	$117.8	35	25	0	2.19

MIKE McCORMICK

YEAR	TEAM	ADJUSTED REGULAR SEASON											ACTUAL RESULTS			
		W	L	SV	ERA	G	IP	ER	H	BB	SO	PAY	W	L	SV	ERA
1956	New York (N)	0	1	0	10.29	3	7	8	8	10	6	$0.0	0	1	0	9.45
1957	New York (N)	3	1	0	4.85	25	78	42	88	37	70	$2.4	3	1	0	4.10
1958	San Francisco (N)	12	8	2	5.44	44	187	113	213	68	114	$5.4	11	8	1	4.59
1959	San Francisco (N)	13	17	7	4.67	49	235	122	235	97	199	$9.8	12	16	4	3.99
1960	San Francisco (N)	16	13	5	3.21	42	266	95	258	72	203	$16.4	15	12	3	2.70
1961	San Francisco (N)	14	17	0	3.63	42	263	106	260	81	212	$19.1	13	16	0	3.20
1962	San Francisco (N)	5	5	0	6.25	27	95	66	114	46	50	$4.4	5	5	0	5.38
1963	Baltimore (A)	6	8	0	5.69	25	136	86	147	80	85	$5.2	6	8	0	4.30
1964	Baltimore (A)	0	2	0	6.88	4	17	13	23	10	14	$0.7	0	2	0	5.19
1965	Washington (A)	8	8	1	4.39	44	158	77	178	42	97	$4.7	8	8	1	3.36
1966	Washington (A)	11	14	0	4.48	42	221	110	219	65	117	$7.7	11	14	0	3.46
1967	San Francisco (N)	22	10	0	3.95	40	262	115	251	98	165	$16.1	22	10	0	2.85
1968	San Francisco (N)	12	14	1	5.50	38	198	121	231	62	134	$9.4	12	14	1	3.58
1969	San Francisco (N)	11	9	0	4.25	32	197	93	195	80	87	$8.1	11	9	0	3.34

(Mike McCormick, continued)

		ADJUSTED REGULAR SEASON											ACTUAL RESULTS			
YEAR	TEAM	W	L	SV	ERA	G	IP	ER	H	BB	SO	PAY	W	L	SV	ERA
1970	S.F. (N)-N.Y. (A)	5	4	2	7.27	32	99	80	114	50	56	$3.9	5	4	2	6.18
1971	Kansas City (A)	0	0	0	12.60	4	10	14	16	6	2	$0.5	0	0	0	9.31
	Career	138	131	18	4.67	493	2,429	1,261	2,550	904	1,611	$113.8	134	128	12	3.73
	Average season	9	8	1	4.67	31	152	79	159	57	101	$7.1	8	8	1	3.73
	Summit season	15	13	2	3.89	41	245	106	240	86	173	$13.9	15	13	1	3.19

JACK McDOWELL

		ADJUSTED REGULAR SEASON											ACTUAL RESULTS			
YEAR	TEAM	W	L	SV	ERA	G	IP	ER	H	BB	SO	PAY	W	L	SV	ERA
1987	Chicago (A)	3	0	0	1.93	4	28	6	16	6	16	$0.5	3	0	0	1.93
1988	Chicago (A)	5	10	0	4.87	26	159	86	159	79	100	$4.2	5	10	0	3.97
1990	Chicago (A)	14	9	0	4.52	33	205	103	200	84	188	$8.2	14	9	0	3.82
1991	Chicago (A)	17	10	0	4.00	35	254	113	227	89	215	$15.7	17	10	0	3.41
1992	Chicago (A)	20	10	0	3.90	34	261	113	266	83	208	$19.5	20	10	0	3.18
1993	Chicago (A)	22	10	0	3.68	34	257	105	267	74	177	$20.4	22	10	0	3.37
1994	Chicago (A)	14	13	0	3.79	36	261	110	268	62	193	$19.7	10	9	0	3.73
1995	New York (A)	17	11	0	4.04	34	247	111	242	90	184	$19.5	15	10	0	3.93
1996	Cleveland (A)	13	9	0	5.06	30	192	108	213	67	142	$9.9	13	9	0	5.11
1997	Cleveland (A)	3	3	0	5.27	8	41	24	45	19	38	$2.7	3	3	0	5.09
1998	Anaheim (A)	5	3	0	5.21	14	76	44	97	20	45	$2.8	5	3	0	5.09
1999	Anaheim (A)	0	4	0	8.05	4	19	17	31	5	12	$0.4	0	4	0	8.05
	Career	133	92	0	4.23	292	2,000	940	2,031	678	1,518	$123.5	127	87	0	3.85
	Average season	11	8	0	4.23	24	167	78	169	57	127	$10.3	11	7	0	3.85
	Summit season	18	11	0	3.87	35	256	110	254	80	195	$19.0	17	10	0	3.49

JOE McGINNITY

		ADJUSTED REGULAR SEASON											ACTUAL RESULTS			
YEAR	TEAM	W	L	SV	ERA	G	IP	ER	H	BB	SO	PAY	W	L	SV	ERA
1899	Baltimore (N)	30	17	3	3.17	51	389	137	352	125	241	$56.8	28	16	2	2.68
1900	Brooklyn (N)	32	9	0	3.62	50	390	157	374	168	283	$58.1	28	8	0	2.94
1901	Baltimore (A)	31	24	2	4.68	58	462	240	482	166	195	$60.8	26	20	1	3.56
1902	Balt. (A)-N.Y. (N)	24	21	0	4.08	51	408	185	398	131	269	$56.1	21	18	0	2.84
1903	New York (N)	36	23	3	3.55	63	497	196	460	182	352	$64.2	31	20	2	2.43
1904	New York (N)	36	8	7	2.75	52	416	127	350	138	257	$59.0	35	8	5	1.61
1905	New York (N)	22	16	9	4.66	48	334	173	339	105	221	$49.9	21	15	3	2.87
1906	New York (N)	29	13	5	3.88	48	362	156	384	106	200	$53.1	27	12	2	2.25
1907	New York (N)	19	19	9	5.81	49	324	209	385	86	230	$38.7	18	18	4	3.16
1908	New York (N)	11	7	15	4.38	38	191	93	237	58	104	$12.9	11	7	5	2.27
	Career	270	157	53	3.99	508	3,773	1,673	3,761	1,265	2,352	$509.6	246	142	24	2.66
	Average season	27	16	5	3.99	51	377	167	376	127	235	$51.0	25	14	2	2.66
	Summit season	33	14	4	3.39	53	411	155	384	144	267	$58.2	30	13	2	2.36

DENNY McLAIN

		ADJUSTED REGULAR SEASON											ACTUAL RESULTS			
YEAR	TEAM	W	L	SV	ERA	G	IP	ER	H	BB	SO	PAY	W	L	SV	ERA
1963	Detroit (A)	2	1	0	5.57	3	21	13	22	19	24	$0.3	2	1	0	4.29
1964	Detroit (A)	4	5	0	5.13	19	100	57	92	45	77	$3.3	4	5	0	4.05
1965	Detroit (A)	16	6	1	3.40	33	220	83	195	72	210	$9.4	16	6	1	2.61
1966	Detroit (A)	20	14	0	5.08	38	264	149	226	130	215	$16.3	20	14	0	3.92
1967	Detroit (A)	17	16	0	5.25	37	235	137	239	88	176	$15.8	17	16	0	3.79
1968	Detroit (A)	31	6	0	2.97	41	336	111	284	80	309	$42.8	31	6	0	1.96
1969	Detroit (A)	24	9	0	3.54	42	325	128	320	69	205	$34.5	24	9	0	2.80
1970	Detroit (A)	3	5	0	5.44	14	91	55	107	28	59	$5.4	3	5	0	4.63
1971	Washington (A)	10	23	0	5.65	34	223	140	266	82	129	$10.1	10	22	0	4.28
1972	Oak. (A)-Atl. (N)	4	7	1	9.00	21	80	80	110	31	37	$3.4	4	7	1	6.37
	Career	131	92	2	4.53	282	1,895	953	1,861	644	1,441	$141.3	131	91	2	3.39
	Average season	13	9	0	4.53	28	190	95	186	64	144	$14.1	13	9	0	3.39
	Summit season	22	10	0	3.98	38	276	122	253	88	223	$23.8	22	10	0	2.95

ANDY MESSERSMITH

		ADJUSTED REGULAR SEASON											ACTUAL RESULTS			
YEAR	TEAM	W	L	SV	ERA	G	IP	ER	H	BB	SO	PAY	W	L	SV	ERA
1968	California (A)	4	2	5	3.44	28	81	31	52	45	81	$3.7	4	2	4	2.21
1969	California (A)	16	11	3	3.20	40	250	89	187	104	236	$15.4	16	11	2	2.52
1970	California (A)	11	10	6	3.55	37	195	77	155	79	182	$9.5	11	10	5	3.01
1971	California (A)	20	13	0	3.93	38	277	121	248	135	216	$20.0	20	13	0	2.99
1972	California (A)	8	11	3	3.94	26	176	77	148	81	171	$9.4	8	11	2	2.81
1973	Los Angeles (N)	14	10	0	3.31	33	250	92	209	82	219	$16.1	14	10	0	2.70
1974	Los Angeles (N)	20	6	0	3.27	39	292	106	242	101	282	$26.6	20	6	0	2.59
1975	Los Angeles (N)	19	14	1	2.82	42	322	101	259	99	276	$27.5	19	14	1	2.29
1976	Atlanta (N)	11	11	1	3.96	29	207	91	179	83	180	$10.2	11	11	1	3.04
1977	Atlanta (N)	5	4	0	5.03	16	102	57	104	43	86	$4.5	5	4	0	4.40
1978	New York (A)	0	3	0	6.95	6	22	17	25	16	21	$1.1	0	3	0	5.64
1979	Los Angeles (N)	2	4	0	5.66	11	62	39	56	37	36	$1.3	2	4	0	4.91
	Career	130	99	19	3.61	345	2,236	898	1,864	905	1,986	$145.3	130	99	15	2.86
	Average season	11	8	2	3.61	29	186	75	155	75	166	$12.1	11	8	1	2.86
	Summit season	18	11	1	3.30	38	278	102	229	104	246	$21.1	18	11	1	2.61

JEFF MONTGOMERY

		ADJUSTED REGULAR SEASON											ACTUAL RESULTS			
YEAR	TEAM	W	L	SV	ERA	G	IP	ER	H	BB	SO	PAY	W	L	SV	ERA
1987	Cincinnati (N)	2	2	0	7.11	14	19	15	25	9	14	$0.1	2	2	0	6.52
1988	Kansas City (A)	7	2	0	4.29	45	63	30	59	35	55	$2.4	7	2	1	3.45
1989	Kansas City (A)	7	3	17	1.66	63	92	17	71	28	106	$5.1	7	3	18	1.37
1990	Kansas City (A)	6	5	22	2.87	73	94	30	85	37	105	$5.4	6	5	24	2.39
1991	Kansas City (A)	4	4	30	3.40	67	90	34	89	30	86	$5.6	4	4	33	2.90
1992	Kansas City (A)	1	6	38	2.71	65	83	25	66	30	80	$5.5	1	6	39	2.18
1993	Kansas City (A)	7	5	44	2.48	69	87	24	66	25	73	$7.8	7	5	45	2.27
1994	Kansas City (A)	3	4	38	4.14	59	63	29	68	22	73	$4.3	2	3	27	4.03
1995	Kansas City (A)	2	3	36	3.53	61	74	29	68	29	57	$4.3	2	3	31	3.43

(Jeff Montgomery, continued)

	ADJUSTED REGULAR SEASON											ACTUAL RESULTS			
YEAR	TEAM	W	L	SV	ERA	G	IP	ER	H	BB	SO	PAY	W	L	SV	ERA
1996	Kansas City (A)	4	6	24	4.29	48	63	30	58	19	45	$3.5	4	6	24	4.26
1997	Kansas City (A)	1	4	13	3.66	55	59	24	53	18	47	$2.8	1	4	14	3.49
1998	Kansas City (A)	2	5	35	5.14	56	56	32	59	23	54	$2.7	2	5	36	4.98
1999	Kansas City (A)	1	4	12	6.71	49	51	38	71	20	27	$1.6	1	4	12	6.84
	Career	47	53	309	3.59	724	894	357	838	325	822	$51.1	46	52	304	3.27
	Average season	4	4	24	3.59	56	69	27	64	25	63	$3.9	4	4	23	3.27
	Summit season	5	5	30	2.63	67	89	26	75	30	90	$5.9	5	5	32	2.22

WILCY MOORE

	ADJUSTED REGULAR SEASON											ACTUAL RESULTS			
YEAR	TEAM	W	L	SV	ERA	G	IP	ER	H	BB	SO	PAY	W	L	SV	ERA
1927	New York (A)	20	7	21	2.59	52	222	64	183	73	180	$27.0	19	7	13	2.28
1928	New York (A)	4	4	7	4.78	37	64	34	72	38	43	$4.4	4	4	2	4.18
1929	New York (A)	6	4	20	4.22	43	64	30	62	22	49	$3.6	6	4	8	4.13
1931	Boston (A)	12	14	22	4.32	56	196	94	196	67	84	$8.4	11	13	10	3.88
1932	Bos.-N.Y. (A)	6	10	22	5.05	49	114	64	124	59	78	$4.8	6	10	8	4.61
1933	New York (A)	5	6	18	6.68	37	66	49	97	25	40	$2.6	5	6	8	5.52
	Career	53	45	110	4.15	274	726	335	734	284	474	$50.8	51	44	49	3.70
	Average season	9	8	18	4.15	46	121	56	122	47	79	$8.5	9	7	8	3.70
	Summit season	10	8	18	3.89	47	132	57	127	52	87	$9.6	9	8	8	3.52

JACK MORRIS

	ADJUSTED REGULAR SEASON											ACTUAL RESULTS			
YEAR	TEAM	W	L	SV	ERA	G	IP	ER	H	BB	SO	PAY	W	L	SV	ERA
1977	Detroit (A)	1	1	0	4.30	7	46	22	39	25	36	$0.6	1	1	0	3.74
1978	Detroit (A)	3	5	0	5.43	28	106	64	114	54	66	$3.0	3	5	0	4.33
1979	Detroit (A)	17	7	0	3.77	27	198	83	184	65	153	$8.1	17	7	0	3.28
1980	Detroit (A)	16	15	0	5.00	36	250	139	260	100	155	$10.2	16	15	0	4.18
1981	Detroit (A)	21	10	0	3.87	37	293	126	244	131	199	$20.6	14	7	0	3.05
1982	Detroit (A)	17	16	0	4.80	37	266	142	257	109	176	$19.9	17	16	0	4.06
1983	Detroit (A)	20	13	0	3.95	37	294	129	269	93	288	$27.5	20	13	0	3.34
1984	Detroit (A)	19	11	0	4.31	35	240	115	231	98	180	$19.8	19	11	0	3.60
1985	Detroit (A)	16	11	0	3.92	35	257	112	225	120	231	$20.0	16	11	0	3.33
1986	Detroit (A)	21	8	0	3.78	35	267	112	243	87	246	$26.3	21	8	0	3.27
1987	Detroit (A)	18	11	0	3.62	34	266	107	233	97	226	$19.1	18	11	0	3.38
1988	Detroit (A)	15	13	0	4.83	34	235	126	243	96	197	$15.0	15	13	0	3.94
1989	Detroit (A)	6	14	0	6.04	24	170	114	204	66	133	$7.1	6	14	0	4.86
1990	Detroit (A)	15	18	0	5.36	36	250	149	245	105	186	$14.5	15	18	0	4.51
1991	Minnesota (A)	18	12	0	4.01	35	247	110	243	100	184	$13.4	18	12	0	3.43
1992	Toronto (A)	21	6	0	4.93	34	241	132	239	89	156	$13.6	21	6	0	4.04
1993	Toronto (A)	7	12	0	6.76	27	153	115	194	70	116	$5.9	7	12	0	6.19
1994	Cleveland (A)	14	9	0	5.72	33	203	129	234	99	151	$7.5	10	6	0	5.60
	Career	265	192	0	4.58	571	3,982	2,026	3,901	1,604	3,079	$252.1	254	186	0	3.90
	Average season	15	11	0	4.58	32	221	113	217	89	171	$14.0	14	10	0	3.90
	Summit season	20	10	0	4.00	35	272	121	246	99	223	$21.4	19	9	0	3.42

TONY MULLANE

		ADJUSTED REGULAR SEASON											ACTUAL RESULTS			
YEAR	TEAM	W	L	SV	ERA	G	IP	ER	H	BB	SO	PAY	W	L	SV	ERA
1881	Detroit (N)	2	8	0	8.18	10	88	80	108	80	37	$1.9	1	4	0	4.91
1882	Louisville (AA)	61	48	0	3.01	111	929	311	855	404	749	$98.6	30	24	0	1.88
1883	St. Louis (AA)	58	25	4	3.07	88	765	261	595	292	600	$95.7	35	15	1	2.19
1884	Toledo (AA)	53	38	0	3.69	99	838	344	745	286	634	$101.8	36	26	0	2.52
1886	Cincinnati (AA)	38	31	0	5.04	72	605	339	603	250	425	$84.9	33	27	0	3.70
1887	Cincinnati (AA)	37	20	0	3.53	57	494	194	462	174	271	$72.5	31	17	0	3.24
1888	Cincinnati (AA)	31	19	1	4.41	52	449	220	447	144	369	$66.9	26	16	1	2.84
1889	Cincinnati (AA)	13	10	14	3.45	38	253	97	246	106	226	$33.3	11	9	5	2.99
1890	Cincinnati (N)	14	12	3	2.62	30	251	73	208	111	203	$26.2	12	10	1	2.24
1891	Cincinnati (N)	27	31	0	4.18	60	502	233	469	213	278	$57.4	23	26	0	3.23
1892	Cincinnati (N)	22	14	2	3.59	39	311	124	249	140	226	$31.4	21	13	1	2.59
1893	Cin.-Balt. (N)	22	27	10	4.35	61	457	221	458	213	353	$55.4	18	22	2	4.44
1894	Balt.-Cle. (N)	9	14	7	5.69	31	193	122	201	118	166	$14.3	7	11	4	6.59
	Career	387	297	41	3.84	748	6,135	2,619	5,646	2,531	4,537	$740.3	284	220	15	3.05
	Average season	30	23	3	3.84	58	472	201	434	195	349	$56.9	22	17	1	3.05
	Summit season	49	32	1	3.60	85	726	290	652	281	536	$90.7	33	22	0	2.72

RANDY MYERS

		ADJUSTED REGULAR SEASON											ACTUAL RESULTS			
YEAR	TEAM	W	L	SV	ERA	G	IP	ER	H	BB	SO	PAY	W	L	SV	ERA
1985	New York (N)	0	0	0	0.00	1	2	0	0	1	2	$0.0	0	0	0	0.00
1986	New York (N)	0	0	0	4.91	10	11	6	12	10	15	$0.0	0	0	0	4.22
1987	New York (N)	3	6	7	4.20	54	75	35	63	31	98	$2.9	3	6	6	3.96
1988	New York (N)	7	3	27	2.09	56	69	16	49	20	80	$4.2	7	3	26	1.72
1989	New York (N)	7	4	23	2.89	65	84	27	67	44	99	$5.3	7	4	24	2.35
1990	Cincinnati (N)	4	6	29	2.48	66	87	24	63	41	110	$5.8	4	6	31	2.08
1991	Cincinnati (N)	6	13	5	4.16	58	132	61	124	87	121	$7.6	6	13	6	3.55
1992	San Diego (N)	3	6	37	5.29	66	80	47	91	38	77	$5.4	3	6	38	4.29
1993	Chicago (N)	2	4	52	3.36	73	75	28	66	28	94	$5.7	2	4	53	3.11
1994	Chicago (N)	1	7	31	3.79	54	57	24	56	23	48	$3.2	1	5	21	3.79
1995	Chicago (N)	1	2	43	4.00	64	63	28	56	32	69	$4.2	1	2	38	3.88
1996	Baltimore (A)	4	4	31	3.51	62	59	23	60	29	75	$4.2	4	4	31	3.53
1997	Baltimore (A)	2	3	45	1.50	61	60	10	48	23	55	$3.9	2	3	45	1.51
1998	Tor. (A)-S.D. (N)	4	7	27	5.05	62	57	32	60	28	41	$2.6	4	7	28	4.92
	Career	44	65	357	3.57	752	911	361	815	435	984	$55.0	44	63	347	3.19
	Average season	3	5	26	3.57	54	65	26	58	31	70	$3.9	3	5	25	3.19
	Summit season	4	4	35	2.52	64	75	21	59	31	88	$5.0	4	4	36	2.19

RAY NARLESKI

		ADJUSTED REGULAR SEASON											ACTUAL RESULTS			
YEAR	TEAM	W	L	SV	ERA	G	IP	ER	H	BB	SO	PAY	W	L	SV	ERA
1954	Cleveland (A)	3	3	22	2.61	44	93	27	65	45	84	$5.2	3	3	13	2.22
1955	Cleveland (A)	9	1	32	4.23	63	117	55	101	53	137	$8.4	9	1	19	3.71
1956	Cleveland (A)	3	2	8	1.77	33	61	12	39	19	58	$3.9	3	2	4	1.52
1957	Cleveland (A)	12	5	22	3.68	49	164	67	153	81	134	$9.6	11	5	16	3.09
1958	Cleveland (A)	14	11	2	4.82	47	196	105	203	106	143	$9.8	13	10	1	4.07
1959	Detroit (A)	4	13	9	6.77	44	109	82	116	67	94	$5.3	4	12	5	5.78
	Career	45	35	95	4.23	280	740	348	677	371	650	$42.2	43	33	58	3.60
	Average season	8	6	16	4.23	47	123	58	113	62	108	$7.0	7	6	10	3.60
	Summit season	8	4	17	3.79	47	126	53	112	61	111	$7.4	8	4	11	3.22

DON NEWCOMBE

		ADJUSTED REGULAR SEASON											ACTUAL RESULTS			
YEAR	TEAM	W	L	SV	ERA	G	IP	ER	H	BB	SO	PAY	W	L	SV	ERA
1949	Brooklyn (N)	17	8	3	3.51	39	251	98	236	66	259	$20.4	17	8	1	3.17
1950	Brooklyn (N)	20	12	5	3.88	42	281	121	274	69	226	$26.7	19	11	3	3.70
1951	Brooklyn (N)	21	9	0	3.71	41	279	115	250	89	278	$27.4	20	9	0	3.28
1954	Brooklyn (N)	10	9	0	5.38	31	154	92	177	51	135	$9.4	9	8	0	4.55
1955	Brooklyn (N)	21	5	0	3.64	36	247	100	248	39	219	$20.3	20	5	0	3.20
1956	Brooklyn (N)	28	7	0	3.51	40	282	110	244	47	205	$32.2	27	7	0	3.06
1957	Brooklyn (N)	11	12	0	4.15	29	206	95	219	37	128	$9.9	11	12	0	3.49
1958	L.A.-Cin. (N)	7	14	2	5.56	33	178	110	239	41	98	$7.2	7	13	1	4.67
1959	Cincinnati (N)	14	9	2	3.68	32	237	97	244	31	138	$14.1	13	8	1	3.16
1960	Cin. (N)-Cle. (A)	6	10	2	5.38	38	144	86	181	24	85	$4.4	6	9	1	4.48
	Career	155	95	14	4.08	361	2,259	1,024	2,312	494	1,771	$172.0	149	90	7	3.56
	Average season	16	10	1	4.08	36	226	102	231	49	177	$17.2	15	9	1	3.56
	Summit season	21	8	2	3.66	40	268	109	250	62	237	$25.4	21	8	1	3.28

HAL NEWHOUSER

		ADJUSTED REGULAR SEASON											ACTUAL RESULTS			
YEAR	TEAM	W	L	SV	ERA	G	IP	ER	H	BB	SO	PAY	W	L	SV	ERA
1939	Detroit (A)	0	1	0	5.40	1	5	3	3	4	6	$0.0	0	1	0	5.40
1940	Detroit (A)	9	9	0	5.41	29	138	83	153	84	152	$4.7	9	9	0	4.86
1941	Detroit (A)	9	11	0	5.66	34	178	112	175	142	187	$5.6	9	11	0	4.79
1942	Detroit (A)	8	14	11	3.19	39	189	67	151	123	192	$8.0	8	14	5	2.45
1943	Detroit (A)	8	18	3	4.15	39	206	95	186	126	259	$9.3	8	17	1	3.04
1944	Detroit (A)	30	9	6	2.87	49	326	104	286	120	359	$41.0	29	9	2	2.22
1945	Detroit (A)	26	9	4	2.30	42	329	84	260	122	400	$42.6	25	9	2	1.81
1946	Detroit (A)	27	9	2	2.54	39	308	87	240	104	430	$51.4	26	9	1	1.94
1947	Detroit (A)	17	17	4	3.36	41	292	109	285	108	300	$34.4	17	17	2	2.87
1948	Detroit (A)	22	13	2	3.34	41	286	106	267	94	258	$33.6	21	12	1	3.01
1949	Detroit (A)	19	12	3	3.72	40	307	127	300	102	265	$33.4	18	11	1	3.36
1950	Detroit (A)	15	13	5	4.54	36	220	111	242	73	151	$16.2	15	13	3	4.34
1951	Detroit (A)	6	6	0	4.46	16	103	51	109	19	69	$5.6	6	6	0	3.92

(Hal Newhouser, continued)

	ADJUSTED REGULAR SEASON											ACTUAL RESULTS			
YEAR	TEAM	W	L	SV	ERA	G	IP	ER	H	BB	SO	PAY	W	L	SV	ERA
1952	Detroit (A)	9	9	0	4.61	26	160	82	167	49	94	$7.6	9	9	0	3.74
1953	Detroit (A)	0	1	2	7.77	7	22	19	32	8	10	$0.9	0	1	1	7.06
1954	Cleveland (A)	7	2	11	3.00	27	48	16	37	18	40	$2.2	7	2	7	2.51
1955	Cleveland (A)	0	0	0	0.00	2	2	0	1	3	1	$0.0	0	0	0	0.00
	Career	212	153	53	3.62	508	3,119	1,256	2,894	1,299	3,173	$296.5	207	150	26	3.06
	Average season	12	9	3	3.62	30	183	74	170	76	187	$17.4	12	9	2	3.06
	Summit season	25	10	3	2.95	42	311	102	271	108	342	$40.4	24	10	1	2.45

KID NICHOLS

	ADJUSTED REGULAR SEASON											ACTUAL RESULTS			
YEAR	TEAM	W	L	SV	ERA	G	IP	ER	H	BB	SO	PAY	W	L	SV	ERA
1890	Boston (N)	33	23	0	2.62	58	512	149	447	129	487	$70.0	27	19	0	2.23
1891	Boston (N)	35	20	4	3.08	60	491	168	488	114	489	$69.9	30	17	3	2.39
1892	Boston (N)	37	17	0	3.95	56	479	210	456	132	393	$68.4	35	16	0	2.84
1893	Boston (N)	42	17	4	3.42	64	523	199	472	130	354	$72.7	34	14	1	3.52
1894	Boston (N)	39	16	0	4.07	61	497	225	480	138	408	$71.8	32	13	0	4.75
1895	Boston (N)	32	20	5	3.24	58	469	169	437	113	454	$69.4	26	16	3	3.41
1896	Boston (N)	37	17	5	2.94	60	456	149	418	139	352	$68.2	30	14	1	2.83
1897	Boston (N)	37	13	4	2.78	55	440	136	379	95	398	$67.3	31	11	3	2.64
1898	Boston (N)	33	13	6	2.69	53	411	123	325	112	381	$64.1	31	12	4	2.13
1899	Boston (N)	22	20	1	3.53	44	360	141	316	109	324	$55.9	21	19	1	2.99
1900	Boston (N)	15	18	0	3.80	33	263	111	229	107	165	$26.8	13	16	0	3.07
1901	Boston (N)	22	19	0	4.23	44	372	175	343	149	328	$49.9	19	16	0	3.22
1904	St. Louis (N)	22	14	1	3.44	38	335	128	317	83	244	$32.5	21	13	1	2.02
1905	St.L.-Phi. (N)	11	11	0	5.05	25	198	111	226	68	118	$7.3	11	11	0	3.12
1906	Philadelphia (N)	0	1	0	17.18	4	11	21	19	18	2	$1.1	0	1	0	9.82
	Career	417	239	30	3.43	713	5,817	2,215	5,352	1,636	4,897	$795.3	361	208	17	2.95
	Average season	28	16	2	3.43	48	388	148	357	109	326	$53.0	24	14	1	2.95
	Summit season	37	16	5	3.01	58	464	155	416	118	395	$68.4	31	14	2	2.71

PHIL NIEKRO

	ADJUSTED REGULAR SEASON											ACTUAL RESULTS			
YEAR	TEAM	W	L	SV	ERA	G	IP	ER	H	BB	SO	PAY	W	L	SV	ERA
1964	Milwaukee (N)	0	0	0	6.00	10	15	10	16	8	9	$0.0	0	0	0	4.80
1965	Milwaukee (N)	2	3	7	3.72	41	75	31	82	30	54	$2.1	2	3	6	2.89
1966	Atlanta (N)	4	3	2	5.40	28	50	30	53	28	19	$1.0	4	3	2	4.11
1967	Atlanta (N)	11	9	11	2.57	46	207	59	188	66	141	$8.0	11	9	9	1.87
1968	Atlanta (N)	14	12	3	3.96	37	257	113	269	57	157	$10.2	14	12	2	2.59
1969	Atlanta (N)	23	13	1	3.23	40	284	102	261	59	217	$25.5	23	13	1	2.56
1970	Atlanta (N)	12	18	0	5.05	34	230	129	240	69	190	$15.7	12	18	0	4.27
1971	Atlanta (N)	15	14	3	3.95	42	269	118	275	78	208	$18.4	15	14	2	2.98
1972	Atlanta (N)	17	13	0	4.30	40	297	142	305	63	203	$24.2	16	12	0	3.06
1973	Atlanta (N)	13	10	5	4.04	42	245	110	228	95	164	$14.5	13	10	4	3.31
1974	Atlanta (N)	20	13	2	3.01	41	302	101	265	95	252	$25.5	20	13	1	2.38

(Phil Niekro, continued)

YEAR	TEAM	ADJUSTED REGULAR SEASON W	L	SV	ERA	G	IP	ER	H	BB	SO	PAY	ACTUAL RESULTS W	L	SV	ERA
1975	Atlanta (N)	15	15	0	3.95	39	276	121	304	74	190	$17.0	15	15	0	3.20
1976	Atlanta (N)	17	11	0	4.28	38	271	129	269	114	232	$17.4	17	11	0	3.29
1977	Atlanta (N)	16	20	0	4.64	44	330	170	324	180	324	$29.5	16	20	0	4.03
1978	Atlanta (N)	19	18	1	3.58	44	334	133	314	112	329	$30.2	19	18	1	2.88
1979	Atlanta (N)	21	20	0	3.88	45	350	151	326	127	287	$36.7	21	20	0	3.39
1980	Atlanta (N)	15	18	1	4.35	40	275	133	264	97	236	$17.5	15	18	1	3.63
1981	Atlanta (N)	11	11	0	3.96	33	209	92	194	95	130	$7.4	7	7	0	3.10
1982	Atlanta (N)	17	4	0	4.27	35	234	111	235	83	186	$13.5	17	4	0	3.61
1983	Atlanta (N)	11	10	0	4.72	34	202	106	222	118	161	$7.2	11	10	0	3.97
1984	New York (A)	16	8	0	3.71	32	216	89	230	86	165	$12.5	16	8	0	3.09
1985	New York (A)	16	12	0	4.83	33	220	118	216	131	181	$12.9	16	12	0	4.09
1986	Cleveland (A)	11	11	0	4.97	34	210	116	255	101	91	$6.1	11	11	0	4.32
1987	Cle.-Tor. (A)-Atl. (N)	7	13	0	6.73	26	139	104	168	69	71	$3.6	7	13	0	6.30
	Career	323	279	36	4.12	878	5,497	2,518	5,503	2,035	4,197	$356.6	318	274	29	3.35
	Average season	13	12	2	4.12	37	229	105	229	85	175	$14.9	13	11	1	3.35
	Summit season	19	15	3	3.33	43	295	109	271	92	245	$25.2	19	15	2	2.69

JESSE OROSCO

YEAR	TEAM	ADJUSTED REGULAR SEASON W	L	SV	ERA	G	IP	ER	H	BB	SO	PAY	ACTUAL RESULTS W	L	SV	ERA
1979	New York (N)	1	2	0	5.66	18	35	22	34	24	30	$0.4	1	2	0	4.89
1981	New York (N)	0	2	2	2.08	12	26	6	21	10	35	$0.3	0	1	1	1.59
1982	New York (N)	4	10	5	3.22	54	109	39	96	45	112	$3.8	4	10	4	2.72
1983	New York (N)	13	7	18	1.72	62	110	21	79	42	104	$5.6	13	7	17	1.47
1984	New York (N)	10	6	32	3.10	60	87	30	61	38	101	$6.0	10	6	31	2.59
1985	New York (N)	8	6	18	3.19	54	79	28	70	37	81	$5.5	8	6	17	2.73
1986	New York (N)	8	6	22	2.67	58	81	24	68	37	69	$5.8	8	6	21	2.33
1987	New York (N)	3	9	18	4.79	58	77	41	80	32	84	$5.2	3	9	16	4.44
1988	Los Angeles (N)	3	2	8	3.40	55	53	20	44	35	50	$3.3	3	2	9	2.72
1989	Cleveland (A)	3	4	2	2.54	69	78	22	58	29	90	$3.4	3	4	3	2.08
1990	Cleveland (A)	5	4	1	4.57	55	65	33	62	41	62	$2.5	5	4	2	3.90
1991	Cleveland (A)	2	0	0	4.30	47	46	22	56	16	41	$1.1	2	0	0	3.74
1992	Milwaukee (A)	3	1	0	3.92	59	39	17	35	14	45	$1.1	3	1	1	3.23
1993	Milwaukee (A)	3	5	7	3.47	57	57	22	48	18	74	$1.8	3	5	8	3.18
1994	Milwaukee (A)	4	1	0	5.24	56	55	32	45	38	54	$1.3	3	1	0	5.08
1995	Baltimore (A)	2	4	2	3.38	73	56	21	32	31	67	$1.6	2	4	3	3.26
1996	Baltimore (A)	3	1	0	3.38	66	56	21	42	28	53	$1.3	3	1	0	3.40
1997	Baltimore (A)	6	3	0	2.34	71	50	13	29	31	45	$1.2	6	3	0	2.32
1998	Baltimore (A)	4	1	6	3.32	69	57	21	47	30	50	$1.5	4	1	7	3.18
1999	Baltimore (A)	0	2	0	5.06	65	32	18	28	19	35	$0.6	0	2	1	5.34
2000	St. Louis (N)	0	0	0	4.50	6	2	1	3	2	3	$0.0	0	0	0	3.86
2001	Los Angeles (N)	0	1	0	3.94	35	16	7	17	8	20	$0.0	0	1	0	3.94
	Career	85	77	141	3.42	1,159	1,266	481	1,055	605	1,305	$53.3	84	76	141	3.04
	Average season	4	4	6	3.42	53	58	22	48	28	59	$2.4	4	3	6	3.04
	Summit season	8	6	18	2.59	61	87	25	67	37	89	$5.3	8	6	18	2.19

AL ORTH

		ADJUSTED REGULAR SEASON											ACTUAL RESULTS			
YEAR	TEAM	W	L	SV	ERA	G	IP	ER	H	BB	SO	PAY	W	L	SV	ERA
1895	Philadelphia (N)	9	1	2	3.72	13	104	43	104	28	81	$5.1	8	1	1	3.89
1896	Philadelphia (N)	19	12	0	4.63	31	243	125	268	64	89	$9.8	15	10	0	4.41
1897	Philadelphia (N)	17	23	0	4.90	44	345	188	375	118	219	$27.1	14	19	0	4.62
1898	Philadelphia (N)	16	14	0	3.82	35	273	116	310	72	161	$19.3	15	13	0	3.02
1899	Philadelphia (N)	15	3	3	2.96	22	152	50	145	25	110	$9.4	14	3	1	2.49
1900	Philadelphia (N)	16	16	5	4.68	38	302	157	328	90	212	$26.0	14	14	1	3.78
1901	Philadelphia (N)	23	14	3	2.97	41	330	109	283	53	223	$33.4	20	12	1	2.27
1902	Washington (A)	23	21	0	5.77	45	384	246	438	68	203	$41.6	19	18	0	3.97
1903	Washington (A)	12	26	3	6.43	42	326	233	393	105	189	$26.8	10	22	2	4.34
1904	Wash.-N.Y. (A)	14	10	0	5.86	31	218	142	243	55	127	$14.0	14	10	0	3.41
1905	New York (A)	19	17	0	4.64	43	328	169	329	93	219	$25.9	18	16	0	2.86
1906	New York (A)	28	18	0	4.02	47	354	158	378	97	243	$39.3	27	17	0	2.34
1907	New York (A)	15	22	0	4.77	38	262	139	296	80	154	$18.2	14	21	0	2.61
1908	New York (A)	2	14	0	6.66	22	146	108	169	48	44	$3.2	2	13	0	3.42
1909	New York (A)	0	0	0	21.00	1	3	7	7	1	2	$0.8	0	0	0	12.00
	Career	228	211	16	4.75	493	3,770	1,990	4,066	997	2,276	$299.9	204	189	6	3.37
	Average season	15	14	1	4.75	33	251	133	271	66	152	$20.0	14	13	0	3.37
	Summit season	22	14	1	4.24	37	293	138	302	61	174	$26.7	19	12	0	3.07

JOE PAGE

		ADJUSTED REGULAR SEASON											ACTUAL RESULTS			
YEAR	TEAM	W	L	SV	ERA	G	IP	ER	H	BB	SO	PAY	W	L	SV	ERA
1944	New York (A)	5	7	0	5.92	20	108	71	109	62	121	$4.3	5	7	0	4.56
1945	New York (A)	6	3	0	3.62	21	107	43	103	51	100	$4.3	6	3	0	2.82
1946	New York (A)	10	9	7	4.72	33	145	76	143	77	132	$5.7	9	8	3	3.57
1947	New York (A)	15	8	27	2.90	59	149	48	115	73	193	$9.9	14	8	17	2.48
1948	New York (A)	7	8	28	4.74	58	114	60	126	64	133	$8.4	7	8	16	4.26
1949	New York (A)	14	8	37	2.85	63	142	45	111	69	170	$14.8	13	8	27	2.59
1950	New York (A)	3	7	21	5.28	39	58	34	70	29	56	$4.0	3	7	13	5.04
1954	Pittsburgh (N)	0	0	0	13.50	7	10	15	17	7	7	$1.1	0	0	0	11.17
	Career	60	50	120	4.24	300	833	392	794	432	912	$52.5	57	49	76	3.53
	Average season	8	6	15	4.24	38	104	49	99	54	114	$6.6	7	6	10	3.53
	Summit season	10	7	20	3.71	47	131	54	120	67	146	$8.6	10	7	13	3.11

SATCHEL PAIGE

		ADJUSTED REGULAR SEASON											ACTUAL RESULTS			
YEAR	TEAM	W	L	SV	ERA	G	IP	ER	H	BB	SO	PAY	W	L	SV	ERA
1948	Cleveland (A)	6	1	2	2.72	22	76	23	65	21	76	$2.5	6	1	1	2.48
1949	Cleveland (A)	4	7	12	3.38	33	88	33	77	31	96	$3.0	4	7	5	3.04
1951	St. Louis (A)	3	4	10	5.40	24	65	39	73	29	79	$2.4	3	4	5	4.79
1952	St. Louis (A)	13	10	17	3.81	48	144	61	131	60	142	$6.1	12	10	10	3.07
1953	St. Louis (A)	3	9	21	3.92	60	124	54	123	42	85	$3.6	3	9	11	3.53
1965	Kansas City (A)	0	0	0	0.00	1	3	0	1	0	1	$0.5	0	0	0	0.00
	Career	29	31	62	3.78	188	500	210	470	183	479	$18.1	28	31	32	3.29
	Average season	5	5	10	3.78	31	83	35	78	31	80	$3.0	5	5	5	3.29
	Summit season	6	6	12	3.82	37	99	42	94	37	96	$3.5	6	6	6	3.31

JIM PALMER

		ADJUSTED REGULAR SEASON											ACTUAL RESULTS			
YEAR	TEAM	W	L	SV	ERA	G	IP	ER	H	BB	SO	PAY	W	L	SV	ERA
1965	Baltimore (A)	5	4	1	4.89	27	92	50	84	65	82	$3.9	5	4	1	3.72
1966	Baltimore (A)	15	10	0	4.50	30	208	104	195	113	164	$8.4	15	10	0	3.46
1967	Baltimore (A)	3	1	0	4.04	9	49	22	39	24	25	$2.0	3	1	0	2.94
1969	Baltimore (A)	16	4	0	2.98	26	181	60	145	66	139	$8.4	16	4	0	2.34
1970	Baltimore (A)	20	10	0	3.19	39	305	108	283	101	226	$25.7	20	10	0	2.71
1971	Baltimore (A)	21	9	0	3.54	38	290	114	263	121	228	$25.7	20	9	0	2.68
1972	Baltimore (A)	22	11	0	2.89	38	290	93	264	84	228	$27.4	21	10	0	2.07
1973	Baltimore (A)	22	9	1	2.92	38	296	96	239	120	198	$32.2	22	9	1	2.40
1974	Baltimore (A)	7	12	0	4.12	26	179	82	188	75	111	$8.5	7	12	0	3.27
1975	Baltimore (A)	24	11	1	2.58	40	331	95	275	85	258	$34.1	23	11	1	2.09
1976	Baltimore (A)	22	13	0	3.26	40	315	114	275	94	217	$32.5	22	13	0	2.51
1977	Baltimore (A)	20	11	0	3.33	39	319	118	270	108	243	$30.8	20	11	0	2.91
1978	Baltimore (A)	21	12	0	3.07	38	296	101	262	107	190	$30.5	21	12	0	2.46
1979	Baltimore (A)	10	6	0	3.75	23	156	65	148	47	93	$7.2	10	6	0	3.30
1980	Baltimore (A)	16	10	0	4.74	34	224	118	245	85	150	$14.4	16	10	0	3.98
1981	Baltimore (A)	11	12	0	4.80	34	197	105	195	81	78	$5.9	7	8	0	3.75
1982	Baltimore (A)	15	5	1	3.73	36	227	94	203	72	136	$7.6	15	5	1	3.13
1983	Baltimore (A)	5	4	0	5.03	14	77	43	90	21	44	$2.4	5	4	0	4.23
1984	Baltimore (A)	0	3	0	11.00	5	18	22	23	20	5	$0.5	0	3	0	9.17
	Career	275	157	4	3.56	574	4,050	1,604	3,686	1,489	2,815	$308.1	268	152	4	2.86
	Average season	14	8	0	3.56	30	213	84	194	78	148	$16.2	14	8	0	2.86
	Summit season	22	11	0	2.94	39	306	100	263	98	218	$31.3	22	11	0	2.31

MEL PARNELL

		ADJUSTED REGULAR SEASON											ACTUAL RESULTS			
YEAR	TEAM	W	L	SV	ERA	G	IP	ER	H	BB	SO	PAY	W	L	SV	ERA
1947	Boston (A)	2	3	0	7.59	15	51	43	63	26	40	$1.0	2	3	0	6.39
1948	Boston (A)	16	8	0	3.50	37	224	87	222	87	146	$8.3	15	8	0	3.14
1949	Boston (A)	26	7	5	3.08	41	310	106	279	124	230	$27.1	25	7	2	2.77
1950	Boston (A)	19	11	6	3.79	42	261	110	258	98	166	$19.8	18	10	3	3.61
1951	Boston (A)	19	12	4	3.67	38	233	95	251	78	143	$19.8	18	11	2	3.26
1952	Boston (A)	13	13	4	4.48	35	227	113	238	96	176	$19.1	12	12	2	3.62
1953	Boston (A)	22	8	0	3.37	40	254	95	233	124	221	$25.8	21	8	0	3.06
1954	Boston (A)	3	7	0	4.36	20	97	47	115	36	64	$4.3	3	7	0	3.70
1955	Boston (A)	2	3	2	9.00	14	50	50	71	26	30	$2.1	2	3	1	7.83
1956	Boston (A)	7	6	0	4.37	22	138	67	144	61	62	$4.0	7	6	0	3.77
	Career	129	78	21	3.97	304	1,845	813	1,874	756	1,278	$131.3	123	75	10	3.50
	Average season	13	8	2	3.97	30	185	81	187	76	128	$13.1	12	8	1	3.50
	Summit season	20	9	3	3.48	40	256	99	249	102	181	$20.2	19	9	1	3.15

HERB PENNOCK

		ADJUSTED REGULAR SEASON											ACTUAL RESULTS			
YEAR	TEAM	W	L	SV	ERA	G	IP	ER	H	BB	SO	PAY	W	L	SV	ERA
1912	Philadelphia (A)	1	2	8	6.11	18	53	36	52	36	61	$2.3	1	2	2	4.50
1913	Philadelphia (A)	2	1	0	7.75	15	36	31	35	29	31	$0.9	2	1	0	5.13
1914	Philadelphia (A)	11	4	9	4.41	29	157	77	157	81	147	$5.8	11	4	3	2.79
1915	Phi.-Bos. (A)	3	6	4	10.02	17	62	69	84	50	55	$2.6	3	6	1	6.36
1916	Boston (A)	0	2	3	5.00	9	27	15	27	10	21	$0.9	0	2	1	3.04
1917	Boston (A)	5	5	5	5.66	25	105	66	108	31	70	$4.3	5	5	1	3.31
1919	Boston (A)	19	10	0	4.05	38	260	117	282	76	180	$15.3	16	8	0	2.71
1920	Boston (A)	17	14	5	4.87	39	255	138	255	84	163	$15.7	16	13	2	3.68
1921	Boston (A)	14	15	0	4.59	34	237	121	263	80	214	$15.8	13	14	0	4.04
1922	Boston (A)	11	18	3	4.86	34	215	116	228	96	147	$10.1	10	17	1	4.32
1923	New York (A)	20	6	8	3.61	37	252	101	235	84	218	$20.2	19	6	3	3.13
1924	New York (A)	22	9	8	3.17	42	301	106	298	80	249	$32.5	21	9	3	2.83
1925	New York (A)	17	18	7	3.11	49	289	100	253	83	217	$26.8	16	17	2	2.96
1926	New York (A)	24	12	4	4.21	42	280	131	299	51	194	$30.9	23	11	2	3.62
1927	New York (A)	20	8	5	3.41	36	222	84	227	60	131	$18.3	19	8	2	3.00
1928	New York (A)	18	6	4	2.92	29	219	71	215	47	127	$17.6	17	6	3	2.56
1929	New York (A)	9	11	5	5.02	28	163	91	196	32	115	$8.3	9	11	2	4.92
1930	New York (A)	11	7	0	4.09	26	163	74	179	24	99	$6.0	11	7	0	4.32
1931	New York (A)	11	6	0	4.75	26	197	104	244	36	138	$7.0	11	6	0	4.28
1932	New York (A)	9	5	0	5.06	23	153	86	190	46	115	$3.9	9	5	0	4.60
1933	New York (A)	8	4	9	6.72	25	71	53	104	27	52	$2.7	7	4	4	5.54
1934	Boston (A)	2	0	4	3.27	32	66	24	68	19	34	$1.7	2	0	1	3.05
	Career	254	169	91	4.31	653	3,783	1,811	3,999	1,162	2,778	$249.6	241	162	33	3.60
	Average season	12	8	4	4.31	30	172	82	182	53	126	$11.3	11	7	2	3.60
	Summit season	21	8	6	3.49	37	255	99	255	64	184	$23.9	20	8	3	3.05

GAYLORD PERRY

		ADJUSTED REGULAR SEASON											ACTUAL RESULTS			
YEAR	TEAM	W	L	SV	ERA	G	IP	ER	H	BB	SO	PAY	W	L	SV	ERA
1962	San Francisco (N)	3	1	0	6.07	13	43	29	57	15	24	$0.9	3	1	0	5.23
1963	San Francisco (N)	1	6	3	5.33	31	76	45	94	35	59	$2.4	1	6	2	4.03
1964	San Francisco (N)	12	11	6	3.50	44	206	80	195	52	170	$7.9	12	11	5	2.75
1965	San Francisco (N)	8	12	1	5.46	47	196	119	218	82	186	$6.0	8	12	1	4.19
1966	San Francisco (N)	21	8	0	3.87	36	256	110	268	50	225	$19.0	21	8	0	2.99
1967	San Francisco (N)	15	17	1	3.59	39	293	117	264	101	251	$20.5	15	17	1	2.61
1968	San Francisco (N)	16	15	1	3.74	39	291	121	283	75	193	$20.1	16	15	1	2.44
1969	San Francisco (N)	19	14	0	3.16	40	325	114	322	94	263	$32.7	19	14	0	2.49
1970	San Francisco (N)	23	13	0	3.78	41	329	138	315	85	243	$31.7	23	13	0	3.20
1971	San Francisco (N)	16	12	0	3.63	37	280	113	283	74	192	$19.0	16	12	0	2.76
1972	Cleveland (A)	25	17	1	2.68	43	359	107	302	98	287	$40.6	24	16	1	1.92
1973	Cleveland (A)	19	19	0	4.13	41	344	158	335	122	295	$38.8	19	19	0	3.38
1974	Cleveland (A)	21	13	0	3.16	37	322	113	245	106	278	$30.5	21	13	0	2.51
1975	Cle.-Tex. (A)	18	17	0	4.00	37	306	136	295	72	299	$29.8	18	17	0	3.24
1976	Texas (A)	15	14	0	4.21	32	250	117	250	58	193	$16.7	15	14	0	3.24
1977	Texas (A)	15	12	0	3.86	34	238	102	246	61	220	$16.4	15	12	0	3.37
1978	San Diego (N)	21	6	0	3.38	37	261	98	257	73	208	$17.5	21	6	0	2.73

(Gaylord Perry, continued)

YEAR	TEAM	ADJUSTED REGULAR SEASON											ACTUAL RESULTS			
		W	L	SV	ERA	G	IP	ER	H	BB	SO	PAY	W	L	SV	ERA
1979	San Diego (N)	12	11	0	3.52	32	233	91	231	74	189	$13.0	12	11	0	3.06
1980	Tex.-N.Y. (A)	10	13	0	4.37	34	206	100	231	74	181	$7.4	10	13	0	3.68
1981	Atlanta (N)	12	14	0	5.03	35	229	128	299	41	128	$7.5	8	9	0	3.94
1982	Seattle (A)	10	12	0	5.23	32	217	126	256	61	151	$7.0	10	12	0	4.40
1983	Sea.-K.C. (A)	7	14	0	5.52	30	186	114	224	55	106	$3.8	7	14	0	4.64
	Career	319	271	13	3.93	791	5,446	2,376	5,470	1,558	4,341	$389.2	314	265	11	3.11
	Average season	15	12	1	3.93	36	248	108	249	71	197	$17.7	14	12	1	3.11
	Summit season	22	13	0	3.22	40	319	114	288	91	256	$30.6	22	12	0	2.56

JIM PERRY

YEAR	TEAM	ADJUSTED REGULAR SEASON											ACTUAL RESULTS			
		W	L	SV	ERA	G	IP	ER	H	BB	SO	PAY	W	L	SV	ERA
1959	Cleveland (A)	13	10	7	3.09	46	160	55	135	62	106	$8.5	12	10	4	2.65
1960	Cleveland (A)	19	10	2	4.34	43	274	132	290	101	160	$20.0	18	10	1	3.62
1961	Cleveland (A)	10	17	0	5.34	35	224	133	251	90	113	$9.7	10	17	0	4.71
1962	Cleveland (A)	12	12	0	4.78	35	194	103	225	63	91	$8.2	12	12	0	4.14
1963	Cle.-Minn. (A)	9	9	1	5.08	40	179	101	200	72	82	$7.6	9	9	1	3.83
1964	Minnesota (A)	6	3	2	4.43	42	65	32	66	28	60	$3.8	6	3	2	3.44
1965	Minnesota (A)	12	7	0	3.43	36	168	64	160	55	98	$5.9	12	7	0	2.63
1966	Minnesota (A)	11	7	0	3.28	33	184	67	165	66	137	$8.0	11	7	0	2.54
1967	Minnesota (A)	8	7	0	4.19	37	131	61	141	61	103	$4.5	8	7	0	3.03
1968	Minnesota (A)	8	6	1	3.50	32	139	54	133	33	78	$4.4	8	6	1	2.27
1969	Minnesota (A)	20	6	0	3.57	46	262	104	272	68	174	$14.9	20	6	0	2.82
1970	Minnesota (A)	24	12	0	3.58	40	279	111	278	58	191	$19.1	24	12	0	3.04
1971	Minnesota (A)	17	17	1	5.59	41	277	172	299	116	158	$17.1	17	17	1	4.23
1972	Minnesota (A)	14	17	0	4.70	37	230	120	230	72	107	$12.8	13	16	0	3.35
1973	Detroit (A)	14	13	0	4.92	35	203	111	240	58	84	$7.2	14	13	0	4.03
1974	Cleveland (A)	17	12	0	3.75	36	252	105	258	69	95	$12.7	17	12	0	2.96
1975	Cle.-Oak. (A)	4	10	0	6.69	23	105	78	114	45	58	$3.1	4	10	0	5.38
	Career	218	175	14	4.34	637	3,326	1,603	3,457	1,117	1,895	$167.5	215	174	10	3.45
	Average season	13	10	1	4.34	37	196	94	203	66	111	$9.9	13	10	1	3.45
	Summit season	19	10	2	3.71	42	245	101	247	72	145	$15.0	18	10	1	3.05

BILLY PIERCE

YEAR	TEAM	ADJUSTED REGULAR SEASON											ACTUAL RESULTS			
		W	L	SV	ERA	G	IP	ER	H	BB	SO	PAY	W	L	SV	ERA
1945	Detroit (A)	0	0	0	2.70	5	10	3	6	11	16	$0.0	0	0	0	1.80
1948	Detroit (A)	3	0	0	6.98	23	58	45	50	49	62	$1.8	3	0	0	6.34
1949	Chicago (A)	7	16	0	4.30	34	182	87	158	105	173	$4.9	7	15	0	3.88
1950	Chicago (A)	12	16	2	4.18	34	226	105	197	125	198	$8.3	12	16	1	3.98
1951	Chicago (A)	16	15	4	3.42	39	253	96	259	74	203	$15.5	15	14	2	3.03
1952	Chicago (A)	15	12	2	3.18	34	263	93	238	82	226	$19.0	15	12	1	2.57
1953	Chicago (A)	19	13	5	3.00	42	285	95	230	109	294	$26.7	18	12	3	2.72
1954	Chicago (A)	10	11	6	4.07	38	199	90	198	89	231	$15.2	9	10	3	3.48

(Billy Pierce, continued)

		ADJUSTED REGULAR SEASON											ACTUAL RESULTS			
YEAR	TEAM	W	L	SV	ERA	G	IP	ER	H	BB	SO	PAY	W	L	SV	ERA
1955	Chicago (A)	15	10	2	2.25	34	212	53	176	64	229	$15.8	15	10	1	1.97
1956	Chicago (A)	21	10	2	3.82	37	292	124	292	104	277	$27.3	20	9	1	3.32
1957	Chicago (A)	21	13	3	3.89	39	271	117	255	82	241	$26.2	20	12	2	3.26
1958	Chicago (A)	18	12	3	3.16	37	259	91	228	75	199	$20.5	17	11	2	2.68
1959	Chicago (A)	14	15	0	4.25	35	231	109	237	69	151	$14.8	14	15	0	3.62
1960	Chicago (A)	15	7	0	4.35	34	209	101	230	52	145	$14.0	14	7	0	3.62
1961	Chicago (A)	10	9	4	4.30	39	180	86	200	55	131	$8.2	10	9	3	3.80
1962	San Francisco (N)	15	6	1	4.01	29	157	70	150	36	89	$7.0	16	6	1	3.49
1963	San Francisco (N)	3	11	11	5.64	38	99	62	118	24	59	$3.2	3	11	8	4.27
1964	San Francisco (N)	3	0	5	2.76	34	49	15	44	12	32	$1.7	3	0	4	2.20
	Career	217	176	50	3.78	605	3,435	1,442	3,266	1,217	2,956	$230.1	211	169	32	3.27
	Average season	12	10	3	3.78	34	191	80	181	68	164	$12.8	12	9	2	3.27
	Summit season	19	12	3	3.27	38	264	96	236	87	248	$23.3	18	11	2	2.83

EDDIE PLANK

		ADJUSTED REGULAR SEASON											ACTUAL RESULTS			
YEAR	TEAM	W	L	SV	ERA	G	IP	ER	H	BB	SO	PAY	W	L	SV	ERA
1901	Philadelphia (A)	20	15	0	4.35	39	308	149	290	115	218	$32.2	17	13	0	3.31
1902	Philadelphia (A)	24	18	0	4.78	43	358	190	383	105	274	$42.0	20	15	0	3.30
1903	Philadelphia (A)	27	19	0	3.50	51	399	155	388	112	364	$55.2	23	16	0	2.38
1904	Philadelphia (A)	27	18	0	3.71	46	374	154	365	142	350	$53.9	26	17	0	2.17
1905	Philadelphia (A)	26	13	0	3.65	44	372	151	346	114	363	$54.5	24	12	0	2.26
1906	Philadelphia (A)	20	6	0	3.87	28	228	98	212	77	198	$25.9	19	6	0	2.25
1907	Philadelphia (A)	26	17	0	4.01	46	368	164	347	130	345	$51.5	24	16	0	2.20
1908	Philadelphia (A)	14	16	3	4.18	35	252	117	250	72	239	$24.1	14	16	1	2.17
1909	Philadelphia (A)	20	11	0	3.17	36	281	99	267	89	237	$25.4	19	10	0	1.76
1910	Philadelphia (A)	17	11	7	3.31	40	264	97	262	70	215	$24.4	16	10	2	2.01
1911	Philadelphia (A)	25	9	7	2.84	43	276	87	266	93	253	$29.3	23	8	4	2.10
1912	Philadelphia (A)	27	6	5	2.99	39	274	91	254	100	190	$29.7	26	6	2	2.22
1913	Philadelphia (A)	19	10	10	3.88	43	255	110	241	72	261	$29.0	18	10	4	2.60
1914	Philadelphia (A)	15	7	9	4.52	35	191	96	205	52	178	$16.5	15	7	3	2.87
1915	St. Louis (F)	22	11	7	3.27	43	275	100	246	66	250	$29.7	21	11	3	2.08
1916	St. Louis (A)	16	15	5	3.90	38	242	105	240	87	157	$16.9	16	15	3	2.33
1917	St. Louis (A)	5	6	4	3.07	21	138	47	127	52	55	$3.7	5	6	1	1.79
	Career	350	208	57	3.73	670	4,855	2,010	4,689	1,548	4,147	$543.9	326	194	23	2.35
	Average season	21	12	3	3.73	39	286	118	276	91	244	$32.0	19	11	1	2.35
	Summit season	26	13	2	3.40	45	339	128	324	112	304	$44.5	24	12	1	2.23

HOWIE POLLET

		ADJUSTED REGULAR SEASON											ACTUAL RESULTS			
YEAR	TEAM	W	L	SV	ERA	G	IP	ER	H	BB	SO	PAY	W	L	SV	ERA
1941	St. Louis (N)	5	2	0	2.31	9	70	18	56	27	65	$3.0	5	2	0	1.93
1942	St. Louis (N)	7	5	0	3.74	28	113	47	113	42	83	$4.2	7	5	0	2.88
1943	St. Louis (N)	9	4	0	2.36	17	126	33	96	36	118	$5.2	8	4	0	1.75
1946	St. Louis (N)	22	11	7	2.77	42	279	86	255	91	188	$19.7	21	10	5	2.10
1947	St. Louis (N)	9	11	5	5.12	38	181	103	208	85	131	$8.3	9	11	2	4.34

(Howie Polett, continued)

YEAR	TEAM	ADJUSTED REGULAR SEASON W	L	SV	ERA	G	IP	ER	H	BB	SO	PAY	ACTUAL RESULTS W	L	SV	ERA
1948	St. Louis (N)	14	8	0	5.03	38	197	110	234	64	149	$9.8	13	8	0	4.54
1949	St. Louis (N)	21	9	3	3.08	40	237	81	242	53	195	$19.8	20	9	1	2.77
1950	St. Louis (N)	15	14	4	3.45	39	245	94	243	63	203	$18.9	14	13	2	3.29
1951	St.L.-Pit. (N)	6	13	2	5.67	28	146	92	171	59	102	$7.6	6	13	1	4.98
1952	Pittsburgh (N)	7	17	0	5.09	32	221	125	243	74	146	$9.4	7	16	0	4.12
1953	Pit.-Chi. (N)	6	7	2	5.27	31	128	75	155	52	87	$4.2	6	7	1	4.79
1954	Chicago (N)	8	11	0	4.20	21	135	63	144	56	96	$4.1	8	10	0	3.58
1955	Chicago (N)	4	3	9	6.47	25	64	46	69	28	42	$2.2	4	3	5	5.61
1956	Chi. (A)-Pit. (N)	3	5	6	4.24	31	51	24	49	19	34	$1.7	3	5	3	3.62
	Career	136	120	38	4.09	419	2,193	997	2,278	749	1,639	$118.1	131	116	20	3.51
	Average season	10	9	3	4.09	30	157	71	163	54	117	$8.4	9	8	1	3.51
	Summit season	16	9	3	3.36	35	217	81	214	61	171	$14.7	15	9	2	2.92

DAN QUISENBERRY

YEAR	TEAM	ADJUSTED REGULAR SEASON W	L	SV	ERA	G	IP	ER	H	BB	SO	PAY	ACTUAL RESULTS W	L	SV	ERA
1979	Kansas City (A)	3	2	6	3.60	32	40	16	43	8	18	$1.3	3	2	5	3.15
1980	Kansas City (A)	12	7	37	3.66	75	128	52	133	31	52	$5.5	12	7	33	3.09
1981	Kansas City (A)	2	6	31	2.20	63	98	24	100	27	45	$4.8	1	4	18	1.73
1982	Kansas City (A)	9	7	37	3.02	72	137	46	132	14	62	$8.1	9	7	35	2.57
1983	Kansas City (A)	5	3	46	2.27	69	139	35	123	12	62	$9.3	5	3	45	1.94
1984	Kansas City (A)	6	3	45	3.21	72	129	46	126	14	51	$7.9	6	3	44	2.64
1985	Kansas City (A)	8	9	39	2.79	84	129	40	151	17	67	$8.4	8	9	37	2.37
1986	Kansas City (A)	3	7	13	3.22	62	81	29	97	25	40	$3.7	3	7	12	2.77
1987	Kansas City (A)	4	1	9	2.94	47	49	16	60	10	19	$2.5	4	1	8	2.76
1988	K.C. (A)-St.L. (N)	2	1	0	6.29	53	63	44	92	13	33	$2.0	2	1	1	5.12
1989	St. Louis (N)	3	1	5	3.27	62	77	28	83	15	43	$1.6	3	1	6	2.64
1990	San Francisco (N)	0	1	0	15.43	5	7	12	14	3	2	$0.0	0	1	0	13.50
	Career	57	48	268	3.24	696	1,077	388	1,154	189	494	$55.1	56	46	244	2.76
	Average season	5	4	22	3.24	58	90	32	96	16	41	$4.6	5	4	20	2.76
	Summit season	8	6	41	3.00	74	132	44	133	18	59	$7.8	8	6	39	2.51

DICK RADATZ

YEAR	TEAM	ADJUSTED REGULAR SEASON W	L	SV	ERA	G	IP	ER	H	BB	SO	PAY	ACTUAL RESULTS W	L	SV	ERA
1962	Boston (A)	9	6	30	2.55	63	127	36	102	43	169	$15.0	9	6	24	2.24
1963	Boston (A)	15	6	30	2.59	66	132	38	105	62	177	$16.0	15	6	25	1.97
1964	Boston (A)	16	9	34	2.92	79	157	51	112	70	196	$19.9	16	9	29	2.29
1965	Boston (A)	9	11	25	5.08	63	124	70	117	62	131	$15.0	9	11	22	3.91
1966	Bos.-Cle. (A)	0	5	17	6.04	55	76	51	81	56	76	$5.3	0	5	14	4.64
1967	Cle. (A)-Chi. (N)	1	0	6	9.00	23	26	26	19	31	21	$2.4	1	0	5	6.49
1969	Det. (A)-Mon. (N)	2	6	4	6.28	33	53	37	51	24	55	$2.2	2	6	3	4.89
	Career	52	43	146	4.00	382	695	309	587	348	825	$75.8	52	43	122	3.13
	Average season	7	6	21	4.00	55	99	44	84	50	118	$10.8	7	6	17	3.13
	Summit season	10	7	27	3.59	65	123	49	103	59	150	$14.2	10	7	23	2.83

CHARLEY RADBOURN

YEAR	TEAM	ADJUSTED REGULAR SEASON											ACTUAL RESULTS			
		W	L	SV	ERA	G	IP	ER	H	BB	SO	PAY	W	L	SV	ERA
1881	Providence (N)	48	21	0	4.00	78	619	275	573	285	532	$87.6	25	11	0	2.43
1882	Providence (N)	64	39	0	3.37	106	914	342	839	247	831	$116.2	33	20	0	2.09
1883	Providence (N)	80	41	4	2.86	126	1,048	333	899	216	969	$135.5	48	25	1	2.05
1884	Providence (N)	84	17	5	2.00	107	968	215	788	303	825	$132.6	59	12	1	1.38
1885	Providence (N)	41	31	0	3.30	72	655	240	662	216	393	$95.0	28	21	0	2.20
1886	Boston (N)	37	43	0	4.07	80	703	318	760	200	451	$91.4	27	31	0	3.00
1887	Boston (N)	31	29	0	5.00	64	544	302	610	206	266	$71.9	24	23	0	4.55
1888	Boston (N)	8	19	0	4.46	28	242	120	243	86	131	$18.9	7	16	0	2.87
1889	Boston (N)	24	13	0	4.26	40	336	159	336	90	220	$39.8	20	11	0	3.67
1890	Boston (P)	34	15	0	3.90	51	427	185	435	119	198	$51.8	27	12	0	3.31
1891	Cincinnati (N)	13	16	0	5.54	31	260	160	288	71	125	$16.3	11	13	0	4.25
	Career	464	284	9	3.55	783	6,716	2,649	6,433	2,039	4,941	$857.0	309	195	2	2.67
	Average season	42	26	1	3.55	71	611	241	585	185	449	$77.9	28	18	0	2.67
	Summit season	63	30	2	3.01	98	841	281	752	253	710	$113.4	39	18	0	1.95

JEFF REARDON

YEAR	TEAM	ADJUSTED REGULAR SEASON											ACTUAL RESULTS			
		W	L	SV	ERA	G	IP	ER	H	BB	SO	PAY	W	L	SV	ERA
1979	New York (N)	1	2	3	2.14	18	21	5	13	10	14	$0.1	1	2	2	1.74
1980	New York (N)	8	7	7	3.11	61	110	38	99	54	130	$4.8	8	7	6	2.61
1981	N.Y.-Mon. (N)	5	0	14	2.80	65	106	33	78	36	99	$5.0	3	0	8	2.18
1982	Montreal (N)	7	4	29	2.48	75	109	30	91	41	109	$5.8	7	4	26	2.06
1983	Montreal (N)	7	9	23	3.62	66	92	37	91	49	96	$5.8	7	9	21	3.03
1984	Montreal (N)	7	7	24	3.52	68	87	34	73	42	94	$5.8	7	7	23	2.90
1985	Montreal (N)	2	8	42	3.78	63	88	37	72	28	81	$6.0	2	8	41	3.18
1986	Montreal (N)	7	9	35	4.55	62	89	45	88	28	74	$7.8	7	9	35	3.94
1987	Minnesota (A)	8	8	32	4.84	63	80	43	72	29	89	$6.7	8	8	31	4.48
1988	Minnesota (A)	2	4	42	3.08	63	73	25	73	17	65	$4.6	2	4	42	2.47
1989	Minnesota (A)	5	4	30	5.05	65	73	41	73	13	53	$4.2	5	4	31	4.07
1990	Boston (A)	5	3	20	3.71	47	51	21	41	20	38	$3.1	5	3	21	3.16
1991	Boston (A)	1	4	38	3.51	57	59	23	58	17	49	$2.8	1	4	40	3.03
1992	Bos. (A)-Atl. (N)	5	2	28	4.19	60	58	27	72	10	46	$2.7	5	2	30	3.41
1993	Cincinnati (N)	4	6	7	4.50	58	62	31	68	11	39	$2.1	4	6	8	4.09
1994	New York (A)	1	0	3	8.36	16	14	13	25	4	6	$0.8	1	0	2	8.38
	Career	75	77	377	3.71	907	1,172	483	1,087	409	1,082	$68.1	73	77	367	3.16
	Average season	5	5	24	3.71	57	73	30	68	26	68	$4.3	5	5	23	3.16
	Summit season	5	6	34	3.44	66	89	34	79	31	85	$6.0	5	6	33	2.89

EPPA RIXEY

YEAR	TEAM	ADJUSTED REGULAR SEASON											ACTUAL RESULTS			
		W	L	SV	ERA	G	IP	ER	H	BB	SO	PAY	W	L	SV	ERA
1912	Philadelphia (N)	11	11	0	3.38	25	176	66	164	67	106	$7.7	10	10	0	2.50
1913	Philadelphia (N)	9	5	9	4.67	36	160	83	166	70	132	$8.1	9	5	2	3.12
1914	Philadelphia (N)	2	11	0	6.90	25	107	82	144	56	71	$4.3	2	11	0	4.37

(Eppa Rixey, continued)

		ADJUSTED REGULAR SEASON											ACTUAL RESULTS			
YEAR	TEAM	W	L	SV	ERA	G	IP	ER	H	BB	SO	PAY	W	L	SV	ERA
1915	Philadelphia (N)	12	13	3	3.76	31	189	79	198	82	158	$8.3	11	12	1	2.39
1916	Philadelphia (N)	23	11	0	3.10	40	302	104	289	99	240	$25.9	22	10	0	1.85
1917	Philadelphia (N)	17	22	1	3.86	41	296	127	300	92	237	$20.5	16	21	1	2.27
1919	Philadelphia (N)	7	14	0	5.97	27	181	120	200	79	154	$9.2	6	12	0	3.97
1920	Philadelphia (N)	12	23	5	4.62	43	298	153	299	94	248	$20.5	11	22	2	3.48
1921	Cincinnati (N)	20	19	2	3.13	42	316	110	313	88	189	$26.1	19	18	1	2.78
1922	Cincinnati (N)	26	14	0	3.97	42	329	145	329	57	200	$32.9	25	13	0	3.53
1923	Cincinnati (N)	21	16	3	3.19	44	324	115	331	79	233	$31.9	20	15	1	2.80
1924	Cincinnati (N)	16	15	3	3.11	37	252	87	217	59	149	$18.6	15	14	1	2.76
1925	Cincinnati (N)	22	12	3	3.04	41	302	102	288	55	178	$30.9	21	11	1	2.88
1926	Cincinnati (N)	14	8	0	3.95	38	239	105	229	67	150	$14.9	14	8	0	3.40
1927	Cincinnati (N)	13	11	3	3.94	36	233	102	243	54	111	$12.6	12	10	1	3.48
1928	Cincinnati (N)	20	19	4	3.89	46	312	135	327	82	148	$23.6	19	18	2	3.43
1929	Cincinnati (N)	11	14	3	4.25	37	212	100	228	69	94	$7.1	10	13	1	4.16
1930	Cincinnati (N)	10	14	0	4.86	34	174	94	195	57	83	$5.8	9	13	0	5.10
1931	Cincinnati (N)	4	7	0	4.36	23	132	64	142	36	50	$3.0	4	7	0	3.91
1932	Cincinnati (N)	5	5	0	2.87	26	116	37	107	19	33	$2.3	5	5	0	2.66
1933	Cincinnati (N)	6	3	0	3.78	17	100	42	124	15	26	$2.0	6	3	0	3.15
	Career	281	267	39	3.89	731	4,750	2,052	4,833	1,376	2,990	$316.2	266	251	14	3.15
	Average season	13	13	2	3.89	35	226	98	230	66	142	$15.1	13	12	1	3.15
	Summit season	22	14	2	3.29	42	315	115	310	76	208	$29.5	21	13	1	2.78

ROBIN ROBERTS

		ADJUSTED REGULAR SEASON											ACTUAL RESULTS			
YEAR	TEAM	W	L	SV	ERA	G	IP	ER	H	BB	SO	PAY	W	L	SV	ERA
1948	Philadelphia (N)	7	9	0	3.56	21	154	61	159	58	149	$5.4	7	9	0	3.19
1949	Philadelphia (N)	16	16	8	4.10	45	237	108	247	69	177	$15.1	15	15	4	3.69
1950	Philadelphia (N)	21	11	2	3.14	41	312	109	292	69	248	$26.9	20	11	1	3.02
1951	Philadelphia (N)	22	16	4	3.42	46	329	125	308	64	231	$33.1	21	15	2	3.03
1952	Philadelphia (N)	29	7	4	3.19	41	347	123	332	47	243	$50.6	28	7	2	2.59
1953	Philadelphia (N)	24	17	3	3.03	46	362	122	344	64	318	$52.4	23	16	2	2.75
1954	Philadelphia (N)	24	16	5	3.48	47	352	136	316	57	300	$52.2	23	15	4	2.97
1955	Philadelphia (N)	24	15	3	3.74	43	320	133	324	54	247	$42.0	23	14	3	3.28
1956	Philadelphia (N)	20	19	4	5.15	45	311	178	364	41	230	$34.2	19	18	3	4.45
1957	Philadelphia (N)	11	23	3	4.88	41	262	142	274	49	183	$20.0	10	22	2	4.07
1958	Philadelphia (N)	18	15	0	3.82	37	285	121	302	58	182	$24.3	17	14	0	3.24
1959	Philadelphia (N)	16	18	0	5.00	37	272	151	299	40	186	$18.4	15	17	0	4.27
1960	Philadelphia (N)	13	17	2	4.84	37	251	135	291	38	164	$14.6	12	16	1	4.02
1961	Philadelphia (N)	1	10	0	6.64	27	122	90	169	25	71	$4.0	1	10	0	5.85
1962	Baltimore (A)	10	9	0	3.20	27	191	68	185	43	123	$5.7	10	9	0	2.78
1963	Baltimore (A)	14	13	0	4.41	35	251	123	257	48	141	$7.5	14	13	0	3.33
1964	Baltimore (A)	13	7	0	3.71	31	204	84	222	63	121	$6.0	13	7	0	2.91
1965	Balt. (A)-Hou. (N)	10	9	0	3.63	30	191	77	192	35	108	$5.9	10	9	0	2.78
1966	Hou.-Chi. (N)	5	8	1	6.27	24	112	78	156	26	62	$3.2	5	8	1	4.82
	Career	298	255	39	4.00	701	4,865	2,164	5,033	948	3,484	$421.5	286	245	25	3.41
	Average season	16	13	2	4.00	37	256	114	265	50	183	$22.2	15	13	1	3.41
	Summit season	25	14	4	3.37	45	342	128	325	57	268	$46.1	24	13	3	2.91

EDDIE ROMMEL

YEAR	TEAM	ADJUSTED REGULAR SEASON W	L	SV	ERA	G	IP	ER	H	BB	SO	PAY	ACTUAL RESULTS W	L	SV	ERA
1920	Philadelphia (A)	7	7	5	3.77	34	179	75	169	58	102	$5.6	7	7	1	2.85
1921	Philadelphia (A)	17	24	5	4.47	48	298	148	300	116	176	$19.5	16	23	3	3.94
1922	Philadelphia (A)	28	14	6	3.68	53	306	125	285	80	138	$27.5	27	13	2	3.28
1923	Philadelphia (A)	19	20	13	3.73	59	314	130	305	133	189	$32.7	18	19	5	3.27
1924	Philadelphia (A)	19	16	4	4.45	46	297	147	303	120	188	$32.5	18	15	1	3.95
1925	Philadelphia (A)	22	11	11	3.88	55	276	119	274	113	172	$32.7	21	10	3	3.69
1926	Philadelphia (A)	12	12	0	3.61	40	237	95	235	66	136	$16.2	11	11	0	3.08
1927	Philadelphia (A)	11	3	4	4.97	31	152	84	164	59	84	$8.3	11	3	1	4.36
1928	Philadelphia (A)	14	5	12	3.48	46	186	72	182	32	94	$9.6	13	5	4	3.06
1929	Philadelphia (A)	13	2	10	2.90	34	121	39	132	39	63	$6.6	12	2	4	2.85
1930	Philadelphia (A)	10	4	9	4.04	37	138	62	133	33	77	$6.7	9	4	3	4.28
1931	Philadelphia (A)	7	5	0	3.29	26	123	45	135	32	41	$3.8	7	5	0	2.97
1932	Philadelphia (A)	1	2	7	6.00	18	69	46	85	22	37	$2.4	1	2	2	5.51
	Career	180	125	86	3.96	527	2,696	1,187	2,702	903	1,497	$204.1	171	119	29	3.54
	Average season	14	10	7	3.96	41	207	91	208	69	115	$15.7	13	9	2	3.54
	Summit season	19	10	10	3.62	49	241	97	236	79	131	$21.8	18	10	4	3.29

CHARLIE ROOT

YEAR	TEAM	ADJUSTED REGULAR SEASON W	L	SV	ERA	G	IP	ER	H	BB	SO	PAY	ACTUAL RESULTS W	L	SV	ERA
1923	St. Louis (A)	0	4	0	6.53	28	62	45	66	22	60	$1.4	0	4	0	5.70
1926	Chicago (N)	19	18	4	3.26	44	284	103	270	73	290	$16.3	18	17	2	2.82
1927	Chicago (N)	28	16	4	4.25	51	328	155	299	147	337	$34.5	26	15	2	3.76
1928	Chicago (N)	15	19	4	4.05	42	249	112	216	88	266	$19.8	14	18	2	3.57
1929	Chicago (N)	20	6	12	3.54	45	285	112	276	95	277	$33.5	19	6	5	3.47
1930	Chicago (N)	16	14	6	4.10	38	226	103	224	74	238	$20.3	16	14	3	4.33
1931	Chicago (N)	18	15	5	3.85	41	264	113	239	85	264	$24.8	17	14	2	3.48
1932	Chicago (N)	16	11	8	3.93	41	227	99	211	68	199	$18.2	15	10	3	3.58
1933	Chicago (N)	16	11	0	3.13	37	256	89	242	77	194	$18.2	15	10	0	2.60
1934	Chicago (N)	4	7	0	4.61	36	125	64	141	62	92	$4.7	4	7	0	4.28
1935	Chicago (N)	16	8	6	3.31	40	212	78	191	55	190	$12.7	15	8	2	3.08
1936	Chicago (N)	3	6	4	4.15	35	78	36	79	22	65	$2.9	3	6	1	4.15
1937	Chicago (N)	14	5	13	3.61	45	187	75	173	35	137	$7.1	13	5	5	3.37
1938	Chicago (N)	8	7	20	3.05	46	168	57	164	31	137	$7.1	8	7	8	2.86
1939	Chicago (N)	8	8	10	4.34	36	172	83	188	36	125	$6.0	8	8	4	4.03
1940	Chicago (N)	2	4	4	4.27	38	118	56	124	37	92	$3.4	2	4	1	3.86
1941	Chicago (N)	8	7	0	6.35	20	112	79	143	39	87	$3.4	8	7	0	5.40
	Career	211	166	100	3.92	663	3,353	1,459	3,246	1,046	3,050	$234.3	201	160	40	3.59
	Average season	12	10	6	3.92	39	197	86	191	62	179	$13.8	12	9	2	3.59
	Summit season	20	13	6	3.67	44	275	112	255	91	272	$24.4	19	12	3	3.35

RED RUFFING

		ADJUSTED REGULAR SEASON											ACTUAL RESULTS			
YEAR	TEAM	W	L	SV	ERA	G	IP	ER	H	BB	SO	PAY	W	L	SV	ERA
1924	Boston (A)	0	0	0	7.43	8	23	19	27	11	22	$0.0	0	0	0	6.65
1925	Boston (A)	9	19	4	5.31	39	229	135	243	89	161	$5.7	9	18	1	5.01
1926	Boston (A)	6	16	7	5.14	39	175	100	172	82	140	$5.4	6	15	2	4.39
1927	Boston (A)	5	14	5	5.32	27	164	97	158	107	173	$5.4	5	13	2	4.66
1928	Boston (A)	10	26	5	4.43	44	303	149	305	115	268	$19.0	10	25	2	3.89
1929	Boston (A)	10	23	2	4.99	37	258	143	272	136	246	$15.0	9	22	1	4.86
1930	Bos.-N.Y. (A)	16	8	4	4.17	40	233	108	216	81	255	$15.8	15	8	1	4.38
1931	New York (A)	17	15	4	4.90	39	250	136	240	105	263	$19.5	16	14	2	4.41
1932	New York (A)	19	7	5	3.38	36	266	100	214	139	350	$26.7	18	7	2	3.09
1933	New York (A)	10	15	7	4.68	37	248	129	240	117	258	$19.4	9	14	3	3.91
1934	New York (A)	20	12	0	4.18	38	271	126	230	122	279	$26.3	19	11	0	3.93
1935	New York (A)	18	12	0	3.36	33	244	91	208	93	177	$19.4	16	11	0	3.12
1936	New York (A)	21	12	0	3.87	34	279	120	259	97	205	$24.4	20	12	0	3.85
1937	New York (A)	21	7	0	3.19	32	265	94	239	73	234	$24.8	20	7	0	2.98
1938	New York (A)	22	7	0	3.53	32	255	100	245	85	238	$24.8	21	7	0	3.31
1939	New York (A)	23	7	0	3.13	30	250	87	219	83	189	$24.6	21	7	0	2.93
1940	New York (A)	16	12	0	3.77	31	234	98	224	84	177	$16.6	15	12	0	3.38
1941	New York (A)	16	6	0	4.18	24	194	90	189	56	118	$12.5	15	6	0	3.54
1942	New York (A)	15	7	0	4.19	25	202	94	205	45	158	$12.6	14	7	0	3.21
1945	New York (A)	8	3	0	3.69	12	95	39	96	23	54	$3.3	7	3	0	2.89
1946	New York (A)	5	1	0	2.36	8	61	16	39	23	33	$1.9	5	1	0	1.77
1947	Chicago (A)	3	5	0	7.13	9	53	42	66	15	20	$1.2	3	5	0	6.11
	Career	290	234	43	4.18	654	4,552	2,113	4,306	1,781	4,018	$324.3	273	225	16	3.80
	Average season	13	11	2	4.18	30	207	96	196	81	183	$14.7	12	10	1	3.80
	Summit season	21	8	1	3.42	33	263	100	235	95	243	$25.1	20	8	0	3.25

AMOS RUSIE

		ADJUSTED REGULAR SEASON											ACTUAL RESULTS			
YEAR	TEAM	W	L	SV	ERA	G	IP	ER	H	BB	SO	PAY	W	L	SV	ERA
1889	Indianapolis (N)	15	12	0	6.23	40	273	189	293	147	234	$19.7	12	10	0	5.32
1890	New York (N)	35	41	3	3.00	80	655	218	514	333	721	$77.6	29	34	1	2.56
1891	New York (N)	39	24	7	3.29	73	599	219	477	306	693	$79.1	33	20	1	2.55
1892	New York (N)	34	33	0	3.95	69	574	252	462	302	601	$75.2	32	31	0	2.84
1893	New York (N)	39	25	2	3.14	67	577	201	485	236	673	$80.9	33	21	1	3.23
1894	New York (N)	43	15	5	2.34	64	526	137	404	225	622	$79.3	36	13	1	2.78
1895	New York (N)	28	28	0	3.55	60	482	190	398	211	600	$70.7	23	23	0	3.73
1897	New York (N)	33	12	0	2.66	45	382	113	326	122	403	$62.3	28	10	0	2.54
1898	New York (N)	21	11	5	3.83	38	308	131	288	133	301	$51.7	20	11	1	3.03
1901	Cincinnati (N)	0	1	0	11.45	3	22	28	42	4	12	$2.9	0	1	0	8.59
	Career	287	202	22	3.43	539	4,398	1,678	3,689	2,019	4,860	$599.4	246	174	5	3.07
	Average season	29	20	2	3.43	54	440	168	369	202	486	$59.9	25	17	1	3.07
	Summit season	38	23	3	2.92	66	548	178	441	244	622	$75.8	32	20	1	2.74

BABE RUTH

YEAR	TEAM	ADJUSTED REGULAR SEASON											ACTUAL RESULTS			
		W	L	SV	ERA	G	IP	ER	H	BB	SO	PAY	W	L	SV	ERA
1914	Boston (A)	2	1	0	6.26	4	23	16	23	8	5	$0.0	2	1	0	3.91
1915	Boston (A)	19	8	0	3.86	33	224	96	194	105	193	$9.6	18	8	0	2.44
1916	Boston (A)	24	13	4	2.93	46	338	110	276	157	297	$33.5	23	12	1	1.75
1917	Boston (A)	25	13	3	3.42	42	334	127	285	144	247	$34.0	24	13	2	2.01
1918	Boston (A)	17	9	0	3.67	26	216	88	181	81	122	$16.2	13	7	0	2.22
1919	Boston (A)	11	6	2	4.41	20	157	77	186	92	79	$8.5	9	5	1	2.97
1920	New York (A)	1	0	0	6.75	1	4	3	3	3	0	$1.6	1	0	0	4.50
1921	New York (A)	2	0	0	10.00	2	9	10	13	12	5	$0.9	2	0	0	9.00
1930	New York (A)	1	0	0	3.00	1	9	3	10	2	6	$0.1	1	0	0	3.00
1933	New York (A)	1	0	0	6.00	1	9	6	12	4	0	$0.0	1	0	0	5.00
	Career	103	50	9	3.65	176	1,323	536	1,183	608	954	$104.4	94	46	4	2.28
	Average season	10	5	1	3.65	18	132	54	118	61	95	$10.4	9	5	0	2.28
	Summit season	19	10	2	3.54	33	254	100	224	116	188	$20.4	17	9	1	2.16

NOLAN RYAN

YEAR	TEAM	ADJUSTED REGULAR SEASON											ACTUAL RESULTS			
		W	L	SV	ERA	G	IP	ER	H	BB	SO	PAY	W	L	SV	ERA
1966	New York (N)	0	1	0	18.00	2	3	6	6	4	6	$0.0	0	1	0	15.00
1968	New York (N)	6	9	0	4.77	21	134	71	110	96	146	$4.2	6	9	0	3.09
1969	New York (N)	6	3	1	4.45	25	89	44	66	55	102	$3.9	6	3	1	3.53
1970	New York (N)	7	11	1	4.02	27	132	59	93	99	140	$4.8	7	11	1	3.42
1971	New York (N)	10	14	0	5.27	30	152	89	138	129	162	$5.8	10	14	0	3.97
1972	California (A)	20	17	0	3.19	41	299	106	199	189	394	$26.6	19	16	0	2.28
1973	California (A)	21	16	1	3.51	41	326	127	253	173	454	$34.5	21	16	1	2.87
1974	California (A)	22	16	0	3.65	42	333	135	235	219	452	$42.0	22	16	0	2.89
1975	California (A)	14	12	0	4.27	28	198	94	162	137	233	$16.0	14	12	0	3.45
1976	California (A)	17	18	0	4.37	39	284	138	207	207	409	$32.6	17	18	0	3.36
1977	California (A)	19	16	0	3.16	37	299	105	203	225	409	$33.4	19	16	0	2.77
1978	California (A)	10	13	0	4.63	31	235	121	195	165	329	$16.4	10	13	0	3.72
1979	California (A)	16	14	0	4.12	34	223	102	173	126	286	$17.5	16	14	0	3.60
1980	Houston (N)	11	10	0	4.00	35	234	104	211	113	261	$14.4	11	10	0	3.35
1981	Houston (N)	16	7	0	2.17	31	220	53	157	114	269	$14.5	11	5	0	1.69
1982	Houston (N)	16	12	0	3.74	35	250	104	204	124	304	$18.3	16	12	0	3.16
1983	Houston (N)	14	9	0	3.54	29	196	77	140	113	223	$7.7	14	9	0	2.98
1984	Houston (N)	12	11	0	3.67	30	184	75	150	78	232	$7.5	12	11	0	3.04
1985	Houston (N)	10	12	0	4.46	35	232	115	218	103	249	$12.7	10	12	0	3.80
1986	Houston (N)	12	8	0	3.84	30	178	76	126	87	212	$7.1	12	8	0	3.34
1987	Houston (N)	8	16	0	2.93	34	212	69	158	91	289	$7.3	8	16	0	2.76
1988	Houston (N)	12	11	0	4.30	33	220	105	200	101	261	$7.6	12	11	0	3.52
1989	Texas (A)	16	10	0	3.95	32	239	105	174	109	336	$16.3	16	10	0	3.20
1990	Texas (A)	13	9	0	4.10	30	204	93	145	80	259	$7.6	13	9	0	3.44
1991	Texas (A)	12	6	0	3.43	27	173	66	109	78	223	$7.3	12	6	0	2.91
1992	Texas (A)	5	9	0	4.53	27	157	79	148	76	179	$5.7	5	9	0	3.72
1993	Texas (A)	5	5	0	5.32	13	66	39	55	43	51	$2.1	5	5	0	4.88
	Career	330	295	3	3.88	819	5,472	2,357	4,235	3,134	6,870	$373.8	324	292	3	3.19
	Average season	12	11	0	3.88	30	203	87	157	116	254	$13.8	12	11	0	3.19
	Summit season	20	14	0	3.20	38	295	105	209	184	396	$30.2	18	14	0	2.61

BRET SABERHAGEN

		ADJUSTED REGULAR SEASON											ACTUAL RESULTS			
YEAR	TEAM	W	L	SV	ERA	G	IP	ER	H	BB	SO	PAY	W	L	SV	ERA
1984	Kansas City (A)	10	11	1	4.16	38	158	73	145	41	90	$5.7	10	11	1	3.48
1985	Kansas City (A)	20	6	0	3.37	32	235	88	224	41	192	$15.9	20	6	0	2.87
1986	Kansas City (A)	7	12	0	4.79	30	156	83	175	31	124	$7.8	7	12	0	4.15
1987	Kansas City (A)	18	10	0	3.57	33	257	102	253	55	178	$16.4	18	10	0	3.36
1988	Kansas City (A)	14	16	0	4.66	35	261	135	293	68	200	$18.9	14	16	0	3.80
1989	Kansas City (A)	23	6	0	2.68	36	262	78	225	48	222	$20.3	23	6	0	2.16
1990	Kansas City (A)	5	9	0	3.87	20	135	58	155	30	100	$5.9	5	9	0	3.27
1991	Kansas City (A)	13	8	0	3.58	28	196	78	176	48	153	$9.6	13	8	0	3.07
1992	New York (N)	3	5	0	4.32	17	98	47	91	30	94	$4.9	3	5	0	3.50
1993	New York (N)	7	7	0	3.63	19	139	56	134	18	104	$4.9	7	7	0	3.29
1994	New York (N)	20	6	0	2.76	34	251	77	238	19	212	$16.1	14	4	0	2.74
1995	N.Y.-Col. (N)	8	7	0	4.32	28	171	82	187	37	115	$5.7	7	6	0	4.18
1997	Boston (A)	0	1	0	6.92	6	26	20	30	10	14	$1.1	0	1	0	6.58
1998	Boston (A)	15	8	0	4.11	31	175	80	183	31	99	$6.9	15	8	0	3.96
1999	Boston (A)	10	6	0	2.87	22	119	38	121	11	82	$4.2	10	6	0	2.95
2001	Boston (A)	1	2	0	6.00	3	15	10	19	0	10	$0.5	1	2	0	6.00
	Career	174	120	1	3.75	412	2,654	1,105	2,649	518	1,989	$144.8	167	117	1	3.34
	Average season	11	8	0	3.75	26	166	69	166	32	124	$9.1	10	7	0	3.34
	Summit season	19	7	0	3.24	33	236	85	225	39	181	$15.1	18	7	0	2.97

JOHNNY SAIN

		ADJUSTED REGULAR SEASON											ACTUAL RESULTS			
YEAR	TEAM	W	L	SV	ERA	G	IP	ER	H	BB	SO	PAY	W	L	SV	ERA
1942	Boston (N)	4	8	17	5.11	43	104	59	91	71	126	$5.5	4	7	6	3.90
1946	Boston (N)	21	15	2	2.90	39	279	90	252	92	223	$20.0	20	14	2	2.21
1947	Boston (N)	22	13	2	4.15	40	280	129	290	79	238	$26.5	21	12	1	3.52
1948	Boston (N)	25	16	2	2.86	44	330	105	319	79	252	$40.2	24	15	1	2.60
1949	Boston (N)	10	17	0	5.36	38	250	149	303	68	139	$14.9	10	17	0	4.81
1950	Boston (N)	21	13	0	4.12	38	286	131	305	63	169	$24.8	20	13	0	3.94
1951	Bos. (N)-N.Y. (A)	7	14	5	4.74	34	203	107	253	52	150	$8.5	7	14	2	4.20
1952	New York (A)	12	6	12	4.30	37	157	75	171	41	96	$7.1	11	6	7	3.46
1953	New York (A)	15	8	14	3.33	43	203	75	207	49	142	$12.7	14	7	9	3.00
1954	New York (A)	6	6	29	3.71	47	80	33	72	15	54	$3.4	6	6	22	3.16
1955	N.Y.-K.C. (A)	2	5	2	6.40	29	52	37	66	11	27	$1.9	2	5	1	5.58
	Career	145	121	85	4.01	432	2,224	990	2,329	620	1,616	$165.5	139	116	51	3.49
	Average season	13	11	8	4.01	39	202	90	212	56	147	$15.0	13	11	5	3.49
	Summit season	21	13	4	3.46	41	276	106	275	72	205	$24.8	20	12	3	3.05

MIKE SCOTT

		ADJUSTED REGULAR SEASON											ACTUAL RESULTS			
YEAR	TEAM	W	L	SV	ERA	G	IP	ER	H	BB	SO	PAY	W	L	SV	ERA
1979	New York (N)	1	3	0	6.06	18	52	35	60	22	29	$0.6	1	3	0	5.33
1980	New York (N)	1	1	0	5.28	6	29	17	41	9	18	$0.1	1	1	0	4.30
1981	New York (N)	8	15	0	5.00	35	207	115	213	58	115	$4.9	5	10	0	3.90
1982	New York (N)	7	13	3	6.12	37	147	100	193	68	83	$4.4	7	13	3	5.14
1983	Houston (N)	10	6	0	4.41	24	145	71	150	51	93	$5.2	10	6	0	3.72
1984	Houston (N)	5	11	0	5.61	31	154	96	188	49	102	$5.0	5	11	0	4.68
1985	Houston (N)	18	8	0	3.85	36	222	95	206	87	167	$10.0	18	8	0	3.29
1986	Houston (N)	18	10	0	2.55	37	275	78	192	76	333	$20.6	18	10	0	2.22
1987	Houston (N)	16	13	0	3.45	36	248	95	205	83	252	$17.7	16	13	0	3.23
1988	Houston (N)	14	8	0	3.58	32	219	87	175	61	220	$14.5	14	8	0	2.92
1989	Houston (N)	20	10	0	3.85	33	229	98	194	69	198	$17.7	20	10	0	3.10
1990	Houston (N)	9	13	0	4.50	32	206	103	206	72	139	$8.4	9	13	0	3.81
1991	Houston (N)	0	2	0	15.43	2	7	12	12	4	3	$0.8	0	2	0	12.86
	Career	127	113	3	4.21	359	2,140	1,002	2,035	709	1,752	$109.9	124	108	3	3.54
	Average season	10	9	0	4.21	28	165	77	157	55	135	$8.5	10	8	0	3.54
	Summit season	17	10	0	3.43	35	239	91	194	75	234	$16.1	17	10	0	2.93

TOM SEAVER

		ADJUSTED REGULAR SEASON											ACTUAL RESULTS			
YEAR	TEAM	W	L	SV	ERA	G	IP	ER	H	BB	SO	PAY	W	L	SV	ERA
1967	New York (N)	16	13	0	3.80	35	251	106	256	94	186	$19.0	16	13	0	2.76
1968	New York (N)	16	12	1	3.37	36	278	104	264	61	228	$20.3	16	12	1	2.20
1969	New York (N)	25	7	0	2.80	36	273	85	224	85	234	$26.8	25	7	0	2.21
1970	New York (N)	18	12	0	3.31	37	291	107	248	84	317	$27.5	18	12	0	2.82
1971	New York (N)	20	10	0	2.33	36	286	74	232	67	338	$32.8	20	10	0	1.76
1972	New York (N)	22	12	0	4.12	36	269	123	252	90	294	$32.3	21	12	0	2.92
1973	New York (N)	19	10	0	2.54	36	290	82	233	68	306	$32.4	19	10	0	2.08
1974	New York (N)	11	11	0	4.04	32	236	106	212	81	254	$19.0	11	11	0	3.20
1975	New York (N)	22	9	0	2.93	36	280	91	230	91	308	$27.4	22	9	0	2.38
1976	New York (N)	14	11	0	3.35	35	271	101	227	87	305	$19.1	14	11	0	2.59
1977	N.Y.-Cin. (N)	21	6	0	2.97	33	261	86	204	72	243	$19.1	21	6	0	2.58
1978	Cincinnati (N)	16	14	0	3.57	36	260	103	232	98	294	$24.1	16	14	0	2.88
1979	Cincinnati (N)	16	6	0	3.60	32	215	86	192	67	177	$14.4	16	6	0	3.14
1980	Cincinnati (N)	10	8	0	4.34	26	168	81	144	68	137	$7.1	10	8	0	3.64
1981	Cincinnati (N)	21	3	0	3.24	35	253	91	196	114	183	$16.8	14	2	0	2.54
1982	Cincinnati (N)	5	13	0	6.57	21	111	81	142	50	80	$3.5	5	13	0	5.50
1983	New York (N)	9	14	0	4.21	34	231	108	210	96	171	$7.3	9	14	0	3.55
1984	Chicago (A)	15	11	0	4.75	34	237	125	226	69	161	$12.6	15	11	0	3.95
1985	Chicago (A)	16	11	0	3.73	35	239	99	237	75	164	$12.6	16	11	0	3.17
1986	Chi.-Bos. (A)	7	13	0	4.65	28	176	91	191	59	114	$5.6	7	13	0	4.03
	Career	319	206	1	3.56	669	4,876	1,930	4,352	1,576	4,494	$379.7	311	205	1	2.86
	Average season	16	10	0	3.56	33	244	97	218	79	225	$19.0	16	10	0	2.86
	Summit season	21	8	0	2.72	35	278	84	225	77	286	$27.7	21	8	0	2.19

BOBBY SHANTZ

		ADJUSTED REGULAR SEASON											ACTUAL RESULTS			
YEAR	TEAM	W	L	SV	ERA	G	IP	ER	H	BB	SO	PAY	W	L	SV	ERA
1949	Philadelphia (A)	6	8	6	3.80	35	135	57	110	69	109	$5.3	6	8	2	3.40
1950	Philadelphia (A)	8	15	0	4.84	38	227	122	269	79	165	$8.2	8	14	0	4.61
1951	Philadelphia (A)	19	11	0	4.46	34	218	108	235	71	143	$9.9	18	10	0	3.94
1952	Philadelphia (A)	25	7	0	3.06	34	288	98	256	65	240	$26.4	24	7	0	2.48
1953	Philadelphia (A)	5	10	0	4.50	17	112	56	115	28	95	$5.6	5	9	0	4.09
1954	Philadelphia (A)	1	0	0	9.00	2	8	8	13	3	5	$1.6	1	0	0	7.88
1955	Kansas City (A)	5	10	0	5.19	24	130	75	136	67	89	$4.9	5	10	0	4.54
1956	Kansas City (A)	2	7	16	5.01	47	106	59	105	38	96	$4.2	2	7	9	4.35
1957	New York (A)	12	5	8	2.92	32	185	60	178	47	107	$4.9	11	5	5	2.45
1958	New York (A)	7	6	0	3.95	34	130	57	139	39	107	$4.3	7	6	0	3.36
1959	New York (A)	7	3	6	2.76	34	98	30	70	37	86	$4.2	7	3	3	2.38
1960	New York (A)	5	4	17	3.30	44	71	26	64	27	70	$3.7	5	4	11	2.79
1961	Pittsburgh (N)	6	3	3	3.77	45	93	39	100	28	78	$3.1	6	3	2	3.32
1962	Hou.-St.L. (N)	6	4	5	2.31	31	78	20	63	26	72	$2.9	6	4	4	1.95
1963	St. Louis (N)	6	4	16	3.42	55	79	30	61	21	78	$3.1	6	4	11	2.61
1964	St.L.-Chi.-Phi. (N)	2	5	1	3.98	50	61	27	57	23	47	$1.6	2	5	1	3.12
	Career	122	102	78	3.89	556	2,019	872	1,971	668	1,587	$93.9	119	99	48	3.38
	Average season	8	6	5	3.89	35	126	55	123	42	99	$5.9	7	6	3	3.38
	Summit season	14	6	6	3.34	37	170	63	159	46	128	$9.4	13	6	4	2.80

FRANK SMITH

		ADJUSTED REGULAR SEASON											ACTUAL RESULTS			
YEAR	TEAM	W	L	SV	ERA	G	IP	ER	H	BB	SO	PAY	W	L	SV	ERA
1904	Chicago (A)	17	9	0	3.60	27	210	84	182	95	186	$15.7	16	9	0	2.09
1905	Chicago (A)	19	13	0	3.43	40	299	114	247	156	283	$27.1	19	13	0	2.13
1906	Chicago (A)	5	5	6	5.84	21	128	83	149	55	96	$6.0	5	5	1	3.39
1907	Chicago (A)	24	10	0	4.50	42	318	159	330	164	257	$32.8	23	10	0	2.47
1908	Chicago (A)	17	18	4	3.89	43	312	135	268	116	239	$27.0	16	17	1	2.03
1909	Chicago (A)	25	17	6	3.24	52	372	134	331	97	307	$43.0	25	17	1	1.80
1910	Chi.-Bos. (A)	5	11	0	4.20	24	163	76	134	64	103	$8.2	5	11	0	2.53
1911	Bos. (A)-Cin. (N)	10	14	5	5.63	36	184	115	220	67	116	$8.1	10	14	1	4.13
1912	Cincinnati (N)	1	1	0	8.61	7	23	22	36	17	8	$1.4	1	1	0	6.35
1914	Baltimore (F)	10	8	8	4.73	39	175	92	202	57	135	$6.6	10	8	2	2.99
1915	Balt.-Bkn. (F)	10	6	0	6.37	34	161	114	214	62	112	$3.8	9	6	0	4.04
	Career	143	112	29	4.33	365	2,345	1,128	2,313	950	1,842	$179.7	139	111	6	2.59
	Average season	13	10	3	4.33	33	213	103	210	86	167	$16.3	13	10	1	2.59
	Summit season	20	13	2	3.73	41	302	125	272	126	254	$29.1	20	13	0	2.09

LEE SMITH

					ADJUSTED REGULAR SEASON								ACTUAL RESULTS			
YEAR	TEAM	W	L	SV	ERA	G	IP	ER	H	BB	SO	PAY	W	L	SV	ERA
1980	Chicago (N)	2	0	0	3.27	18	22	8	22	16	23	$0.3	2	0	0	2.91
1981	Chicago (N)	5	9	2	4.50	61	102	51	94	54	102	$3.8	3	6	1	3.51
1982	Chicago (N)	2	5	19	3.23	72	117	42	110	42	124	$4.7	2	5	17	2.69
1983	Chicago (N)	4	10	30	1.92	66	103	22	73	46	111	$5.4	4	10	29	1.65
1984	Chicago (N)	9	7	34	4.37	69	101	49	103	40	103	$7.9	9	7	33	3.65
1985	Chicago (N)	7	4	34	3.58	65	98	39	93	35	131	$8.4	7	4	33	3.04
1986	Chicago (N)	9	9	32	3.52	67	92	36	74	45	103	$8.5	9	9	31	3.09
1987	Chicago (N)	4	10	37	3.32	62	84	31	87	34	103	$8.1	4	10	36	3.12
1988	Boston (A)	4	5	29	3.43	64	84	32	78	43	109	$7.8	4	5	29	2.80
1989	Boston (A)	6	1	24	4.44	64	71	35	57	37	107	$4.7	6	1	25	3.57
1990	Bos. (A)-St.L. (N)	5	5	29	2.49	64	83	23	75	31	97	$4.8	5	5	31	2.06
1991	St. Louis (N)	6	3	45	2.71	67	73	22	75	14	75	$4.8	6	3	47	2.34
1992	St. Louis (N)	4	9	42	3.84	70	75	32	67	29	69	$4.8	4	9	43	3.12
1993	St.L. (N)-N.Y. (A)	2	4	45	4.19	63	58	27	54	15	66	$3.5	2	4	46	3.88
1994	Baltimore (A)	1	6	48	3.27	59	55	20	49	16	63	$3.5	1	4	33	3.29
1995	California (A)	0	6	41	3.60	58	55	22	47	28	50	$2.9	0	5	37	3.47
1996	Cal. (A)-Cin. (N)	3	4	2	3.76	54	55	23	56	26	41	$2.1	3	4	2	3.74
1997	Montreal (N)	0	1	5	6.14	25	22	15	29	8	15	$1.0	0	1	5	5.82
	Career	73	98	498	3.53	1,068	1,350	529	1,243	559	1,492	$87.0	71	92	478	3.03
	Average season	4	5	28	3.53	59	75	29	69	31	83	$4.8	4	5	27	3.03
	Summit season	6	6	34	2.80	66	90	28	78	34	103	$6.4	6	6	34	2.43

JOHN SMOLTZ

					ADJUSTED REGULAR SEASON								ACTUAL RESULTS			
YEAR	TEAM	W	L	SV	ERA	G	IP	ER	H	BB	SO	PAY	W	L	SV	ERA
1988	Atlanta (N)	2	7	0	6.75	12	64	48	80	38	43	$1.3	2	7	0	5.48
1989	Atlanta (N)	12	11	0	3.63	29	208	84	172	80	193	$7.6	12	11	0	2.94
1990	Atlanta (N)	14	11	0	4.56	34	231	117	218	97	194	$9.8	14	11	0	3.85
1991	Atlanta (N)	14	13	0	4.46	36	230	114	221	83	167	$9.9	14	13	0	3.80
1992	Atlanta (N)	15	12	0	3.46	35	247	95	221	89	248	$16.4	15	12	0	2.85
1993	Atlanta (N)	15	11	0	3.95	35	244	107	213	107	231	$16.3	15	11	0	3.62
1994	Atlanta (N)	9	14	0	4.22	30	192	90	171	70	169	$9.3	6	10	0	4.14
1995	Atlanta (N)	14	8	0	3.25	33	219	79	191	83	226	$15.2	12	7	0	3.18
1996	Atlanta (N)	24	8	0	2.91	35	254	82	198	55	279	$25.6	24	8	0	2.94
1997	Atlanta (N)	15	12	0	3.16	35	256	90	237	65	238	$19.4	15	12	0	3.02
1998	Atlanta (N)	17	3	0	3.00	26	168	56	147	47	172	$15.0	17	3	0	2.90
1999	Atlanta (N)	11	8	0	3.10	29	186	64	166	38	158	$8.7	11	8	0	3.19
2001	Atlanta (N)	3	3	10	3.51	36	59	23	54	11	55	$3.2	3	3	10	3.36
	Career	165	121	10	3.69	405	2,558	1,049	2,289	863	2,373	$157.7	160	116	10	3.35
	Average season	13	9	1	3.69	31	197	81	176	66	183	$12.1	12	9	1	3.35
	Summit season	17	9	0	3.14	33	229	80	199	68	233	$18.3	17	8	0	2.97

WARREN SPAHN

		ADJUSTED REGULAR SEASON											ACTUAL RESULTS			
YEAR	TEAM	W	L	SV	ERA	G	IP	ER	H	BB	SO	PAY	W	L	SV	ERA
1942	Boston (N)	0	0	0	7.31	4	16	13	27	12	14	$0.0	0	0	0	5.74
1946	Boston (N)	8	5	4	3.92	25	131	57	119	38	113	$4.3	8	5	1	2.94
1947	Boston (N)	22	11	5	2.72	42	304	92	267	84	226	$20.4	21	10	3	2.33
1948	Boston (N)	16	13	2	4.12	38	271	124	256	74	211	$19.1	15	12	1	3.71
1949	Boston (N)	22	14	0	3.40	39	310	117	299	77	270	$32.6	21	14	0	3.07
1950	Boston (N)	22	18	2	3.31	43	307	113	262	102	318	$34.3	21	17	1	3.16
1951	Boston (N)	23	15	0	3.36	41	327	122	303	110	291	$40.5	22	14	0	2.98
1952	Boston (N)	15	20	4	3.69	42	305	125	299	77	290	$32.7	14	19	3	2.98
1953	Milwaukee (N)	24	7	4	2.31	36	273	70	220	73	234	$30.8	23	7	3	2.10
1954	Milwaukee (N)	22	13	4	3.68	41	298	122	289	88	225	$31.4	21	12	3	3.14
1955	Milwaukee (N)	18	15	2	3.73	41	258	107	277	66	173	$19.1	17	14	1	3.26
1956	Milwaukee (N)	21	12	4	3.19	41	296	105	277	53	190	$30.8	20	11	3	2.78
1957	Milwaukee (N)	22	12	4	3.19	41	285	101	268	89	161	$24.0	21	11	3	2.69
1958	Milwaukee (N)	23	12	2	3.63	40	305	123	286	86	208	$29.9	22	11	1	3.07
1959	Milwaukee (N)	22	15	0	3.46	41	299	115	306	77	189	$29.5	21	15	0	2.96
1960	Milwaukee (N)	22	11	3	4.20	42	281	131	287	82	204	$29.1	21	10	2	3.50
1961	Milwaukee (N)	22	14	0	3.42	40	276	105	261	69	151	$23.6	21	13	0	3.02
1962	Milwaukee (N)	18	14	0	3.51	34	269	105	261	58	143	$22.5	18	14	0	3.04
1963	Milwaukee (N)	23	7	0	3.43	33	260	99	270	59	117	$17.5	23	7	0	2.60
1964	Milwaukee (N)	6	13	5	6.78	38	174	131	224	63	87	$6.0	6	13	4	5.29
1965	N.Y.-S.F. (N)	7	16	0	5.23	36	198	115	237	65	100	$5.9	7	16	0	4.01
	Career	378	257	45	3.62	778	5,443	2,192	5,295	1,502	3,915	$484.0	363	245	29	3.09
	Average season	18	12	2	3.62	37	259	104	252	72	186	$23.0	17	12	1	3.09
	Summit season	22	11	3	2.97	40	297	98	267	82	220	$29.3	21	11	2	2.59

STEVE STONE

		ADJUSTED REGULAR SEASON											ACTUAL RESULTS			
YEAR	TEAM	W	L	SV	ERA	G	IP	ER	H	BB	SO	PAY	W	L	SV	ERA
1971	San Francisco (N)	5	9	0	5.51	24	111	68	122	61	76	$3.9	5	9	0	4.15
1972	San Francisco (N)	6	8	0	4.22	28	128	60	114	58	103	$4.4	6	8	0	2.98
1973	Chicago (A)	6	11	1	5.16	36	176	101	173	69	118	$5.3	6	11	1	4.24
1974	Chicago (N)	8	6	0	5.24	38	170	99	198	69	118	$5.3	8	6	0	4.14
1975	Chicago (N)	12	8	0	4.88	33	214	116	210	83	180	$8.4	12	8	0	3.95
1976	Chicago (N)	3	6	0	5.28	17	75	44	76	24	46	$2.7	3	6	0	4.08
1977	Chicago (A)	15	12	0	5.17	31	207	119	235	88	156	$9.3	15	12	0	4.51
1978	Chicago (A)	12	12	0	5.43	30	212	128	209	93	160	$9.3	12	12	0	4.37
1979	Baltimore (A)	11	7	0	4.31	33	192	92	183	83	135	$7.1	11	7	0	3.77
1980	Baltimore (A)	25	7	0	3.87	37	251	108	231	116	202	$18.7	25	7	0	3.23
1981	Baltimore (A)	6	11	0	5.91	23	96	63	104	47	64	$4.3	4	7	0	4.60
	Career	109	97	1	4.90	330	1,832	998	1,855	809	1,408	$78.7	107	93	1	3.97
	Average season	10	9	0	4.90	30	167	91	169	74	128	$7.2	10	8	0	3.97
	Summit season	15	9	0	4.73	33	215	113	214	93	167	$10.6	15	9	0	3.94

RICK SUTCLIFFE

YEAR	TEAM	ADJUSTED REGULAR SEASON											ACTUAL RESULTS			
		W	L	SV	ERA	G	IP	ER	H	BB	SO	PAY	W	L	SV	ERA
1976	Los Angeles (N)	0	0	0	0.00	1	5	0	2	1	4	$0.0	0	0	0	0.00
1978	Los Angeles (N)	0	0	0	0.00	2	2	0	3	1	0	$0.0	0	0	0	0.00
1979	Los Angeles (N)	17	10	0	3.94	39	242	106	222	107	160	$9.2	17	10	0	3.46
1980	Los Angeles (N)	3	9	6	6.63	42	110	81	126	63	81	$4.0	3	9	5	5.56
1981	Los Angeles (N)	3	3	0	5.20	21	71	41	67	34	34	$2.2	2	2	0	4.02
1982	Cleveland (A)	14	8	1	3.50	34	216	84	181	112	183	$9.6	14	8	1	2.96
1983	Cleveland (A)	17	11	0	5.07	36	243	137	262	114	200	$15.3	17	11	0	4.29
1984	Cle. (A)-Chi. (N)	20	6	0	4.37	35	245	119	245	96	254	$19.3	20	6	0	3.64
1985	Chicago (N)	8	8	0	3.74	20	130	54	126	48	123	$7.9	8	8	0	3.18
1986	Chicago (N)	5	14	0	5.34	28	177	105	176	102	136	$7.8	5	14	0	4.64
1987	Chicago (N)	18	10	0	3.91	34	237	103	229	111	189	$15.7	18	10	0	3.68
1988	Chicago (N)	13	14	0	4.74	32	226	119	250	81	169	$8.6	13	14	0	3.86
1989	Chicago (N)	16	11	0	4.52	35	229	115	218	77	177	$14.0	16	11	0	3.66
1990	Chicago (N)	0	2	0	6.86	5	21	16	26	13	8	$1.4	0	2	0	5.91
1991	Chicago (N)	6	5	0	4.82	19	97	52	103	49	59	$3.7	6	5	0	4.10
1992	Baltimore (A)	16	15	0	5.47	36	237	144	269	82	128	$7.3	16	15	0	4.47
1993	Baltimore (A)	10	10	0	6.29	29	166	116	217	79	91	$3.6	10	10	0	5.75
1994	St. Louis (N)	9	6	0	6.59	23	97	71	133	47	39	$2.7	6	4	0	6.52
	Career	175	142	7	4.79	471	2,751	1,463	2,855	1,217	2,035	$132.3	171	139	6	4.08
	Average season	10	8	0	4.79	26	153	81	159	68	113	$7.4	10	8	0	4.08
	Summit season	17	9	0	4.04	35	234	105	219	101	193	$13.6	17	9	0	3.49

BRUCE SUTTER

YEAR	TEAM	ADJUSTED REGULAR SEASON											ACTUAL RESULTS			
		W	L	SV	ERA	G	IP	ER	H	BB	SO	PAY	W	L	SV	ERA
1976	Chicago (N)	6	3	15	3.47	52	83	32	68	29	94	$5.2	6	3	10	2.70
1977	Chicago (N)	7	3	35	1.51	62	107	18	71	25	153	$8.4	7	3	31	1.34
1978	Chicago (N)	8	10	32	4.00	64	99	44	87	38	134	$9.2	8	10	27	3.18
1979	Chicago (N)	6	6	40	2.58	62	101	29	68	35	139	$9.5	6	6	37	2.22
1980	Chicago (N)	5	8	31	3.18	60	102	36	92	39	100	$8.2	5	8	28	2.64
1981	St. Louis (N)	5	8	42	3.35	75	129	48	108	43	120	$9.7	3	5	25	2.62
1982	St. Louis (N)	9	8	39	3.44	70	102	39	92	39	79	$9.2	9	8	36	2.90
1983	St. Louis (N)	9	10	22	5.06	60	89	50	94	33	80	$8.0	9	10	21	4.23
1984	St. Louis (N)	5	7	46	1.83	71	123	25	114	26	94	$9.6	5	7	45	1.54
1985	Atlanta (N)	7	7	24	5.32	58	88	52	96	31	63	$6.6	7	7	23	4.48
1986	Atlanta (N)	2	0	3	5.21	16	19	11	18	10	18	$1.9	2	0	3	4.34
1988	Atlanta (N)	1	4	14	5.80	38	45	29	52	13	46	$2.5	1	4	14	4.76
	Career	70	74	343	3.42	688	1,087	413	960	361	1,120	$88.0	68	71	300	2.83
	Average season	6	6	29	3.42	57	91	34	80	30	93	$7.3	6	6	25	2.83
	Summit season	6	6	40	2.57	68	112	32	91	34	117	$9.3	6	6	35	2.08

DON SUTTON

YEAR	TEAM	ADJUSTED REGULAR SEASON W	L	SV	ERA	G	IP	ER	H	BB	SO	PAY	ACTUAL RESULTS W	L	SV	ERA
1966	Los Angeles (N)	12	12	0	3.86	37	226	97	213	65	233	$15.0	12	12	0	2.99
1967	Los Angeles (N)	11	15	1	5.48	37	233	142	256	69	185	$10.0	11	15	1	3.95
1968	Los Angeles (N)	11	15	1	3.98	35	208	92	212	75	180	$9.5	11	15	1	2.60
1969	Los Angeles (N)	17	18	0	4.39	41	293	143	299	94	244	$20.2	17	18	0	3.47
1970	Los Angeles (N)	15	13	0	4.81	38	260	139	270	79	226	$16.4	15	13	0	4.08
1971	Los Angeles (N)	17	12	1	3.36	38	265	99	256	61	232	$19.8	17	12	1	2.54
1972	Los Angeles (N)	20	9	0	2.91	34	281	91	218	74	248	$26.2	19	9	0	2.08
1973	Los Angeles (N)	18	10	0	2.95	33	256	84	208	59	245	$20.3	18	10	0	2.42
1974	Los Angeles (N)	19	9	0	4.08	40	276	125	257	86	231	$26.0	19	9	0	3.23
1975	Los Angeles (N)	16	13	0	3.54	35	254	100	214	64	226	$20.0	16	13	0	2.87
1976	Los Angeles (N)	21	10	0	4.00	35	268	119	249	92	217	$25.8	21	10	0	3.06
1977	Los Angeles (N)	14	8	0	3.64	33	240	97	213	75	189	$15.0	14	8	0	3.18
1978	Los Angeles (N)	15	11	0	4.42	34	238	117	243	59	207	$15.0	15	11	0	3.55
1979	Los Angeles (N)	12	15	1	4.38	33	226	110	206	67	196	$14.2	12	15	1	3.82
1980	Los Angeles (N)	13	5	1	2.63	32	212	62	167	54	173	$8.8	13	5	1	2.20
1981	Houston (N)	16	13	0	3.33	34	235	87	211	48	209	$13.2	11	9	0	2.61
1982	Hou. (N)-Mil. (A)	17	9	0	3.64	34	250	101	234	73	224	$16.3	17	9	0	3.06
1983	Milwaukee (A)	8	13	0	4.83	31	220	118	218	60	168	$7.3	8	13	0	4.08
1984	Milwaukee (A)	14	12	0	4.52	33	213	107	235	58	174	$7.6	14	12	0	3.77
1985	Oak.-Cal. (A)	15	10	0	4.54	34	226	114	235	64	132	$7.6	15	10	0	3.86
1986	California (A)	15	11	0	4.30	34	207	99	203	52	130	$7.3	15	11	0	3.74
1987	California (A)	11	11	0	5.02	35	192	107	205	43	109	$6.1	11	11	0	4.70
1988	Los Angeles (N)	3	6	0	4.76	16	87	46	98	35	52	$2.7	3	6	0	3.92
	Career	330	260	5	4.02	786	5,366	2,396	5,120	1,506	4,430	$330.3	324	256	5	3.26
	Average season	14	11	0	4.02	34	233	104	223	65	193	$14.4	14	11	0	3.26
	Summit season	19	10	0	3.48	36	269	104	238	74	235	$23.6	19	10	0	2.67

FRANK TANANA

YEAR	TEAM	ADJUSTED REGULAR SEASON W	L	SV	ERA	G	IP	ER	H	BB	SO	PAY	ACTUAL RESULTS W	L	SV	ERA
1973	California (A)	2	2	0	3.81	4	26	11	21	8	26	$0.4	2	2	0	3.08
1974	California (A)	14	19	0	3.95	39	269	118	280	83	233	$9.9	14	19	0	3.12
1975	California (A)	16	9	0	3.22	34	257	92	224	75	333	$19.1	16	9	0	2.62
1976	California (A)	19	10	0	3.16	34	288	101	228	82	337	$26.0	19	10	0	2.43
1977	California (A)	15	9	0	2.91	31	241	78	206	67	252	$19.1	15	9	0	2.54
1978	California (A)	18	12	0	4.56	33	239	121	255	66	186	$19.1	18	12	0	3.65
1979	California (A)	7	5	0	4.50	18	90	45	95	27	62	$5.3	7	5	0	3.89
1980	California (A)	11	12	0	4.94	32	204	112	230	52	153	$9.5	11	12	0	4.15
1981	Boston (A)	6	15	0	5.14	36	212	121	230	73	161	$8.1	4	10	0	4.01
1982	Texas (A)	7	18	0	5.01	30	194	108	207	62	115	$5.6	7	18	0	4.21
1983	Texas (A)	7	9	0	3.74	29	159	66	150	55	135	$5.6	7	9	0	3.16
1984	Texas (A)	15	15	0	3.91	35	246	107	245	92	172	$10.0	15	15	0	3.25
1985	Tex.-Det. (A)	12	14	0	5.02	33	215	120	234	62	192	$8.4	12	14	0	4.27
1986	Detroit (A)	12	9	0	4.79	32	188	100	207	69	132	$7.2	12	9	0	4.16
1987	Detroit (A)	15	10	0	4.19	34	219	102	223	58	159	$8.9	15	10	0	3.91

(Frank Tanana, continued)

YEAR	TEAM	ADJUSTED REGULAR SEASON											ACTUAL RESULTS			
		W	L	SV	ERA	G	IP	ER	H	BB	SO	PAY	W	L	SV	ERA
1988	Detroit (A)	14	11	0	5.19	32	203	117	230	74	149	$8.5	14	11	0	4.21
1989	Detroit (A)	10	14	0	4.42	33	224	110	245	83	171	$7.4	10	14	0	3.58
1990	Detroit (A)	9	8	0	6.29	34	176	123	201	71	131	$5.9	9	8	1	5.31
1991	Detroit (A)	13	12	0	4.31	33	217	104	232	84	121	$7.0	13	12	0	3.69
1992	Detroit (A)	13	11	0	5.39	32	187	112	202	100	108	$5.9	13	11	0	4.39
1993	N.Y. (N)-N.Y. (A)	7	17	0	4.74	32	203	107	221	59	131	$5.8	7	17	0	4.35
	Career	242	241	0	4.39	650	4,257	2,075	4,366	1,402	3,459	$202.7	240	236	1	3.66
	Average season	12	11	0	4.39	31	203	99	208	67	165	$9.7	11	11	0	3.66
	Summit season	17	11	0	3.54	33	254	100	232	76	256	$18.7	17	11	0	2.88

JACK TAYLOR

YEAR	TEAM	ADJUSTED REGULAR SEASON											ACTUAL RESULTS			
		W	L	SV	ERA	G	IP	ER	H	BB	SO	PAY	W	L	SV	ERA
1898	Chicago (N)	5	0	0	2.85	5	41	13	31	13	30	$1.5	5	0	0	2.20
1899	Chicago (N)	19	23	0	4.46	44	381	189	379	114	223	$26.9	18	21	0	3.76
1900	Chicago (N)	11	19	1	3.15	31	246	86	235	84	171	$10.2	10	17	1	2.55
1901	Chicago (N)	15	22	0	4.40	38	317	155	380	72	166	$19.9	13	19	0	3.36
1902	Chicago (N)	26	13	1	1.90	41	370	78	310	70	211	$40.8	23	11	1	1.33
1903	Chicago (N)	24	16	2	3.60	43	363	145	331	96	180	$40.2	21	14	1	2.45
1904	St. Louis (N)	21	20	1	3.80	43	369	156	349	135	192	$41.1	20	19	1	2.22
1905	St. Louis (N)	16	22	1	5.60	39	326	203	358	127	184	$32.7	15	21	1	3.44
1906	St.L.-Chi. (N)	21	13	0	3.43	36	320	122	300	128	118	$25.4	20	12	0	1.99
1907	Chicago (N)	7	5	0	6.02	19	130	87	154	50	45	$4.2	7	5	0	3.29
	Career	165	153	6	3.88	339	2,863	1,234	2,827	889	1,520	$242.9	152	139	5	2.66
	Average season	17	15	1	3.88	34	286	123	283	89	152	$24.3	15	14	1	2.66
	Summit season	22	17	1	3.44	41	361	138	334	109	185	$34.9	20	15	1	2.38

KENT TEKULVE

YEAR	TEAM	ADJUSTED REGULAR SEASON											ACTUAL RESULTS			
		W	L	SV	ERA	G	IP	ER	H	BB	SO	PAY	W	L	SV	ERA
1974	Pittsburgh (N)	1	1	0	8.00	8	9	8	13	5	8	$0.0	1	1	0	6.00
1975	Pittsburgh (N)	1	2	8	2.73	34	56	17	46	24	37	$1.1	1	2	5	2.25
1976	Pittsburgh (N)	5	3	14	3.23	64	103	37	98	28	91	$4.3	5	3	9	2.45
1977	Pittsburgh (N)	10	1	9	3.50	72	103	40	92	36	75	$4.9	10	1	7	3.06
1978	Pittsburgh (N)	8	7	40	2.91	92	136	44	123	61	105	$8.2	8	7	31	2.33
1979	Pittsburgh (N)	10	8	37	3.11	93	133	46	111	53	101	$8.4	10	8	31	2.75
1980	Pittsburgh (N)	8	12	25	4.06	78	93	42	99	46	64	$6.8	8	12	21	3.39
1981	Pittsburgh (N)	8	8	5	3.15	71	103	36	104	30	74	$4.9	5	5	3	2.49
1982	Pittsburgh (N)	12	8	23	3.42	85	129	49	118	53	86	$7.4	12	8	20	2.87
1983	Pittsburgh (N)	7	5	20	1.91	76	99	21	82	40	66	$3.8	7	5	18	1.64
1984	Pittsburgh (N)	3	9	14	3.17	72	88	31	90	37	45	$2.9	3	9	13	2.66
1985	Pit.-Phi. (N)	4	10	15	4.14	61	76	35	79	33	49	$2.8	4	10	14	3.57
1986	Philadelphia (N)	11	5	4	2.95	73	110	36	105	26	63	$3.5	11	5	4	2.54

(Kent Tekulve, continued)

		ADJUSTED REGULAR SEASON											ACTUAL RESULTS			
YEAR	TEAM	W	L	SV	ERA	G	IP	ER	H	BB	SO	PAY	W	L	SV	ERA
1987	Philadelphia (N)	6	4	3	3.26	90	105	38	99	30	65	$3.1	6	4	3	3.09
1988	Philadelphia (N)	3	7	3	4.39	70	80	39	94	26	51	$2.2	3	7	4	3.60
1989	Cincinnati (N)	0	3	0	6.23	37	52	36	60	26	36	$1.0	0	3	1	5.02
	Career	**97**	**93**	**220**	**3.39**	**1,076**	**1,475**	**555**	**1,413**	**554**	**1,016**	**$65.3**	**94**	**90**	**184**	**2.85**
	Average season	**6**	**6**	**14**	**3.39**	**67**	**92**	**35**	**88**	**35**	**64**	**$4.1**	**6**	**6**	**12**	**2.85**
	Summit season	**9**	**8**	**29**	**3.05**	**85**	**118**	**40**	**107**	**51**	**84**	**$6.9**	**9**	**8**	**24**	**2.59**

LUIS TIANT

		ADJUSTED REGULAR SEASON											ACTUAL RESULTS			
YEAR	TEAM	W	L	SV	ERA	G	IP	ER	H	BB	SO	PAY	W	L	SV	ERA
1964	Cleveland (A)	10	4	1	3.61	19	127	51	103	57	115	$5.7	10	4	1	2.83
1965	Cleveland (A)	11	11	1	4.59	41	196	100	186	77	166	$8.4	11	11	1	3.53
1966	Cleveland (A)	12	11	10	3.60	46	155	62	134	62	161	$8.5	12	11	8	2.79
1967	Cleveland (A)	12	9	3	3.79	33	214	90	203	81	237	$10.2	12	9	2	2.74
1968	Cleveland (A)	21	9	0	2.44	34	258	70	179	93	289	$20.5	21	9	0	1.60
1969	Cleveland (A)	9	20	0	4.72	38	250	131	255	135	177	$15.4	9	20	0	3.71
1970	Minnesota (A)	7	3	0	3.97	18	93	41	91	42	57	$4.8	7	3	0	3.40
1971	Boston (A)	1	7	0	6.38	21	72	51	81	35	70	$3.6	1	7	0	4.85
1972	Boston (A)	16	6	4	2.70	45	187	56	152	77	150	$7.3	15	6	3	1.91
1973	Boston (A)	20	13	0	4.07	35	272	123	231	83	253	$18.2	20	13	0	3.34
1974	Boston (A)	22	13	0	3.68	38	311	127	299	88	230	$25.1	22	13	0	2.92
1975	Boston (A)	18	14	0	4.98	35	260	144	279	74	186	$18.8	18	14	0	4.02
1976	Boston (A)	21	12	0	4.00	38	279	124	296	72	180	$23.3	21	12	0	3.06
1977	Boston (A)	12	8	0	5.19	32	189	109	217	56	156	$7.7	12	8	0	4.53
1978	Boston (A)	13	8	0	4.12	32	212	97	197	63	155	$7.7	13	8	0	3.31
1979	New York (A)	13	8	0	4.50	30	196	98	195	58	142	$7.4	13	8	0	3.91
1980	New York (A)	8	9	0	5.82	25	136	88	143	57	113	$3.8	8	9	0	4.89
1981	Pittsburgh (N)	3	8	0	5.06	14	89	50	90	33	68	$2.9	2	5	0	3.92
1982	California (A)	2	2	0	6.90	6	30	23	41	9	37	$1.0	2	2	0	5.76
	Career	**231**	**175**	**19**	**4.17**	**580**	**3,526**	**1,635**	**3,372**	**1,252**	**2,942**	**$200.3**	**229**	**172**	**15**	**3.30**
	Average season	**12**	**9**	**1**	**4.17**	**31**	**186**	**86**	**177**	**66**	**155**	**$10.5**	**12**	**9**	**1**	**3.30**
	Summit season	**20**	**11**	**1**	**3.45**	**38**	**261**	**100**	**231**	**83**	**220**	**$18.9**	**20**	**11**	**1**	**2.64**

DIZZY TROUT

		ADJUSTED REGULAR SEASON											ACTUAL RESULTS			
YEAR	TEAM	W	L	SV	ERA	G	IP	ER	H	BB	SO	PAY	W	L	SV	ERA
1939	Detroit (A)	9	10	5	3.88	34	167	72	168	79	137	$7.9	9	10	2	3.61
1940	Detroit (A)	3	7	6	4.93	34	104	57	129	60	110	$5.0	3	7	2	4.47
1941	Detroit (A)	9	9	7	4.39	39	160	78	155	89	161	$7.8	9	9	2	3.74
1942	Detroit (A)	12	19	0	4.52	36	229	115	236	96	177	$9.6	12	18	0	3.43
1943	Detroit (A)	21	13	9	3.38	46	258	97	231	113	217	$19.7	20	12	6	2.48
1944	Detroit (A)	28	15	0	2.75	51	367	112	339	97	294	$42.7	27	14	0	2.12
1945	Detroit (A)	19	16	4	4.01	43	258	115	274	88	200	$26.0	18	15	2	3.14
1946	Detroit (A)	18	14	6	3.09	40	291	100	274	103	258	$33.0	17	13	3	2.34

(Dizzy Trout, continued)

		ADJUSTED REGULAR SEASON											ACTUAL RESULTS			
YEAR	TEAM	W	L	SV	ERA	G	IP	ER	H	BB	SO	PAY	W	L	SV	ERA
1947	Detroit (A)	10	11	4	4.08	33	192	87	199	64	135	$8.9	10	11	2	3.48
1948	Detroit (A)	11	15	4	3.78	34	195	82	210	70	167	$8.7	10	14	2	3.43
1949	Detroit (A)	3	6	9	4.87	34	61	33	72	19	36	$2.7	3	6	3	4.40
1950	Detroit (A)	13	5	9	3.93	35	190	83	198	58	150	$8.3	13	5	4	3.75
1951	Detroit (A)	9	15	11	4.57	44	201	102	187	75	160	$7.1	9	14	5	4.04
1952	Det.-Bos. (A)	10	13	4	4.85	37	165	89	181	91	123	$5.8	10	13	2	3.92
1957	Baltimore (A)	0	0	0	—	2	0	3	4	0	0	$0.0	0	0	0	81.00
	Career	175	168	78	3.88	542	2,838	1,225	2,857	1,102	2,325	$193.2	170	161	35	3.23
	Average season	12	11	5	3.88	36	189	82	190	73	155	$12.9	11	11	2	3.23
	Summit season	20	13	6	3.33	43	273	101	263	92	224	$25.9	19	12	3	2.66

BOB TURLEY

		ADJUSTED REGULAR SEASON											ACTUAL RESULTS			
YEAR	TEAM	W	L	SV	ERA	G	IP	ER	H	BB	SO	PAY	W	L	SV	ERA
1951	St. Louis (A)	0	1	0	7.71	1	7	6	11	3	8	$0.0	0	1	0	7.36
1953	St. Louis (A)	2	7	0	3.68	11	66	27	43	49	93	$2.1	2	6	0	3.28
1954	Baltimore (A)	15	16	0	4.07	37	261	118	196	189	291	$10.1	14	15	0	3.46
1955	New York (A)	18	14	2	3.50	38	260	101	187	183	309	$19.1	17	13	1	3.06
1956	New York (A)	8	4	2	5.85	28	137	89	152	106	129	$5.9	8	4	1	5.05
1957	New York (A)	14	6	5	3.22	34	187	67	135	99	210	$10.1	13	6	3	2.71
1958	New York (A)	22	7	2	3.52	34	253	99	194	144	224	$20.3	21	7	1	2.97
1959	New York (A)	8	11	0	5.04	34	159	89	154	93	144	$8.2	8	11	0	4.32
1960	New York (A)	10	3	8	3.91	36	184	80	157	98	117	$9.2	9	3	5	3.27
1961	New York (A)	3	5	0	6.50	15	72	52	78	53	59	$3.9	3	5	0	5.75
1962	New York (A)	3	3	1	5.22	24	69	40	72	50	51	$2.2	3	3	1	4.57
1963	L.A.-Bos. (A)	3	11	0	5.58	30	129	80	127	96	118	$3.6	3	11	0	4.20
	Career	106	88	20	4.28	322	1,784	848	1,506	1,163	1,753	$94.7	101	85	12	3.64
	Average season	9	7	2	4.28	27	149	71	126	97	146	$7.9	8	7	1	3.64
	Summit season	16	9	3	3.66	36	229	93	174	143	230	$13.8	15	9	2	3.11

GEORGE UHLE

		ADJUSTED REGULAR SEASON											ACTUAL RESULTS			
YEAR	TEAM	W	L	SV	ERA	G	IP	ER	H	BB	SO	PAY	W	L	SV	ERA
1919	Cleveland (A)	12	6	0	4.35	30	147	71	159	67	121	$7.9	10	5	0	2.91
1920	Cleveland (A)	4	5	6	6.95	28	88	68	101	39	62	$4.6	4	5	1	5.21
1921	Cleveland (A)	17	14	6	4.54	43	250	126	279	85	156	$15.6	16	13	2	4.01
1922	Cleveland (A)	23	17	8	4.58	52	299	152	318	113	200	$26.7	22	16	3	4.07
1923	Cleveland (A)	27	17	10	4.33	57	378	182	378	125	266	$51.5	26	16	5	3.77
1924	Cleveland (A)	10	16	2	5.40	30	210	126	239	96	147	$15.7	9	15	1	4.77
1925	Cleveland (A)	13	11	0	4.33	30	218	105	205	91	166	$16.0	13	11	0	4.10
1926	Cleveland (A)	28	12	1	3.28	41	335	122	305	141	360	$42.9	27	11	1	2.83
1927	Cleveland (A)	8	9	3	4.92	26	159	87	185	73	157	$9.2	8	9	1	4.34
1928	Cleveland (A)	12	18	1	4.64	32	221	114	250	57	170	$15.2	12	17	1	4.07
1929	Detroit (A)	15	11	0	4.17	33	257	119	269	65	226	$19.4	15	11	0	4.08
1930	Detroit (A)	13	13	6	3.45	35	253	97	224	90	237	$14.9	12	12	3	3.65

(George Uhle, continued)

		ADJUSTED REGULAR SEASON											ACTUAL RESULTS			
YEAR	TEAM	W	L	SV	ERA	G	IP	ER	H	BB	SO	PAY	W	L	SV	ERA
1931	Detroit (A)	12	13	4	3.89	31	206	89	192	60	138	$8.5	11	12	2	3.50
1932	Detroit (A)	6	6	14	4.90	35	156	85	154	52	111	$6.9	6	6	5	4.48
1933	Det.-N.Y. (A)-N.Y. (N)	7	2	0	7.06	20	79	62	84	32	68	$3.8	7	2	0	5.85
1934	New York (A)	2	4	0	10.50	11	18	21	31	9	20	$0.9	2	4	0	9.92
1936	Cleveland (A)	0	1	0	8.31	7	13	12	25	5	10	$0.2	0	1	0	8.53
	Career	209	175	61	4.48	541	3,287	1,638	3,398	1,200	2,615	$259.9	200	166	25	3.99
	Average season	12	10	4	4.48	32	193	96	200	71	154	$15.3	12	10	1	3.99
	Summit season	22	15	6	4.04	46	303	136	301	111	244	$30.3	21	14	3	3.64

FERNANDO VALENZUELA

		ADJUSTED REGULAR SEASON											ACTUAL RESULTS			
YEAR	TEAM	W	L	SV	ERA	G	IP	ER	H	BB	SO	PAY	W	L	SV	ERA
1980	Los Angeles (N)	2	0	1	0.00	10	18	0	8	6	21	$0.3	2	0	1	0.00
1981	Los Angeles (N)	19	10	0	3.16	37	285	100	223	102	348	$19.5	13	7	0	2.48
1982	Los Angeles (N)	19	13	0	3.41	37	285	108	258	94	255	$20.3	19	13	0	2.87
1983	Los Angeles (N)	15	10	0	4.45	35	257	127	256	111	236	$19.0	15	10	0	3.75
1984	Los Angeles (N)	12	17	0	3.66	34	261	106	228	120	285	$19.8	12	17	0	3.03
1985	Los Angeles (N)	17	10	0	2.88	35	272	87	224	110	250	$20.3	17	10	0	2.45
1986	Los Angeles (N)	21	11	0	3.61	34	269	108	239	90	266	$25.8	21	11	0	3.14
1987	Los Angeles (N)	14	14	0	4.23	34	251	118	261	130	206	$18.9	14	14	0	3.98
1988	Los Angeles (N)	5	8	1	5.20	23	142	82	153	88	76	$5.6	5	8	1	4.24
1989	Los Angeles (N)	10	13	0	4.25	31	197	93	200	110	135	$8.4	10	13	0	3.43
1990	Los Angeles (N)	13	13	0	5.47	33	204	124	236	84	133	$8.4	13	13	0	4.59
1991	California (A)	0	2	0	14.14	2	7	11	16	3	6	$0.5	0	2	0	12.15
1993	Baltimore (A)	8	10	0	5.43	32	179	108	183	85	89	$4.5	8	10	0	4.94
1994	Philadelphia (N)	1	3	0	3.05	11	62	21	58	10	28	$1.2	1	2	0	3.00
1995	San Diego (N)	9	3	0	5.16	33	103	59	116	39	67	$3.4	8	3	0	4.98
1996	San Diego (N)	13	8	0	3.61	33	172	69	176	68	96	$3.8	13	8	0	3.62
1997	S.D.-St.L (N)	2	12	0	5.16	18	89	51	107	48	60	$2.3	2	12	0	4.96
	Career	180	157	2	4.04	472	3,053	1,372	2,942	1,298	2,557	$182.0	173	153	2	3.54
	Average season	11	9	0	4.04	28	180	81	173	76	150	$10.7	10	9	0	3.54
	Summit season	18	10	0	3.29	35	257	94	224	93	243	$17.9	17	10	0	2.88

DAZZY VANCE

		ADJUSTED REGULAR SEASON											ACTUAL RESULTS			
YEAR	TEAM	W	L	SV	ERA	G	IP	ER	H	BB	SO	PAY	W	L	SV	ERA
1915	Pit. (N)-N.Y. (A)	0	4	0	6.39	9	31	22	30	25	30	$0.1	0	4	0	4.11
1918	New York (A)	0	0	0	27.00	3	3	9	13	3	0	$0.0	0	0	0	15.43
1922	Brooklyn (N)	19	13	0	4.17	38	259	120	254	121	296	$15.4	18	12	0	3.70
1923	Brooklyn (N)	19	16	0	4.00	39	295	131	261	123	405	$24.5	18	15	0	3.50
1924	Brooklyn (N)	30	6	0	2.43	37	326	88	235	97	525	$49.5	28	6	0	2.16
1925	Brooklyn (N)	23	10	0	3.73	33	282	117	238	79	445	$39.5	22	9	0	3.53
1926	Brooklyn (N)	9	10	3	4.55	25	176	89	173	69	273	$14.5	9	10	1	3.89
1927	Brooklyn (N)	17	16	2	3.05	36	289	98	243	86	390	$29.9	16	15	1	2.70
1928	Brooklyn (N)	23	11	4	2.35	40	295	77	228	87	404	$30.9	22	10	2	2.09

(Dazzy Vance, continued)

YEAR	TEAM	ADJUSTED REGULAR SEASON											ACTUAL RESULTS			
		W	L	SV	ERA	G	IP	ER	H	BB	SO	PAY	W	L	SV	ERA
1929	Brooklyn (N)	15	14	0	3.99	33	246	109	239	54	276	$16.9	14	13	0	3.89
1930	Brooklyn (N)	18	16	0	2.47	37	273	75	225	66	330	$23.8	17	15	0	2.61
1931	Brooklyn (N)	12	14	0	3.75	32	233	97	223	65	289	$16.5	11	13	0	3.37
1932	Brooklyn (N)	12	11	3	4.60	28	182	93	169	69	201	$7.4	12	11	1	4.20
1933	St. Louis (N)	6	2	9	4.28	29	103	49	108	35	131	$4.0	6	2	3	3.55
1934	St.L.-Cin. (N)	1	3	4	4.84	26	80	43	88	29	78	$2.7	1	3	1	4.56
1935	Brooklyn (N)	3	2	6	4.83	21	54	29	55	19	55	$1.9	3	2	2	4.41
	Career	207	148	31	3.59	466	3,127	1,246	2,782	1,027	4,128	$277.5	197	140	11	3.24
	Average season	13	9	2	3.59	29	195	78	174	64	258	$17.3	12	9	1	3.24
	Summit season	22	12	1	2.80	37	293	91	234	83	419	$34.7	21	11	1	2.60

HIPPO VAUGHN

YEAR	TEAM	ADJUSTED REGULAR SEASON											ACTUAL RESULTS			
		W	L	SV	ERA	G	IP	ER	H	BB	SO	PAY	W	L	SV	ERA
1908	New York (A)	0	0	0	9.00	2	2	2	1	5	3	$0.0	0	0	0	3.86
1910	New York (A)	13	11	4	3.03	31	229	77	224	72	184	$8.0	13	11	1	1.83
1911	New York (A)	9	11	0	5.96	28	157	104	178	65	128	$5.6	8	10	0	4.39
1912	N.Y.-Wash. (A)	6	11	0	5.26	28	149	87	150	95	153	$5.4	6	11	0	3.88
1913	Chicago (N)	5	1	0	2.09	7	56	13	40	33	59	$3.3	5	1	0	1.45
1914	Chicago (N)	22	14	4	3.21	44	308	110	276	138	275	$26.1	21	13	1	2.05
1915	Chicago (N)	21	13	4	4.52	43	283	142	286	97	257	$25.8	20	12	1	2.87
1916	Chicago (N)	18	16	4	3.69	46	307	126	324	89	254	$27.1	17	15	1	2.20
1917	Chicago (N)	24	13	0	3.42	42	303	115	299	121	348	$40.9	23	13	0	2.01
1918	Chicago (N)	27	12	0	2.85	43	357	113	296	119	381	$52.8	22	10	0	1.74
1919	Chicago (N)	24	16	3	2.66	44	355	105	324	96	333	$51.8	21	14	1	1.79
1920	Chicago (N)	20	17	0	3.36	42	316	118	313	111	292	$38.7	19	16	0	2.54
1921	Chicago (N)	3	12	0	6.83	18	116	88	150	42	74	$4.8	3	11	0	6.01
	Career	192	147	19	3.68	418	2,938	1,200	2,861	1,083	2,741	$290.3	178	137	5	2.49
	Average season	15	11	1	3.68	32	226	92	220	83	211	$22.3	14	11	0	2.49
	Summit season	23	14	1	3.07	43	328	112	302	117	326	$42.1	21	13	0	2.03

FRANK VIOLA

YEAR	TEAM	ADJUSTED REGULAR SEASON											ACTUAL RESULTS			
		W	L	SV	ERA	G	IP	ER	H	BB	SO	PAY	W	L	SV	ERA
1982	Minnesota (A)	4	10	0	6.21	22	126	87	159	43	108	$4.0	4	10	0	5.21
1983	Minnesota (A)	7	15	0	6.51	35	210	152	253	103	160	$5.5	7	15	0	5.49
1984	Minnesota (A)	18	12	0	3.87	35	258	111	236	83	182	$15.3	18	12	0	3.21
1985	Minnesota (A)	18	14	0	4.80	36	251	134	279	74	166	$15.7	18	14	0	4.09
1986	Minnesota (A)	16	13	0	5.20	37	246	142	273	88	212	$16.4	16	13	0	4.51
1987	Minnesota (A)	17	10	0	3.07	36	252	86	237	69	214	$19.7	17	10	0	2.90
1988	Minnesota (A)	24	7	0	3.25	35	255	92	254	62	225	$26.0	24	7	0	2.64
1989	Minn. (A)-N.Y. (N)	13	17	0	4.52	36	261	131	265	82	243	$19.8	13	17	0	3.66
1990	New York (N)	20	12	0	3.17	35	250	88	241	65	208	$20.2	20	12	0	2.67
1991	New York (N)	13	15	0	4.64	35	231	119	278	58	149	$15.7	13	15	0	3.97
1992	Boston (A)	13	12	0	4.20	35	238	111	230	98	142	$14.0	13	12	0	3.44

(Frank Viola, continued)

		ADJUSTED REGULAR SEASON											ACTUAL RESULTS			
YEAR	TEAM	W	L	SV	ERA	G	IP	ER	H	BB	SO	PAY	W	L	SV	ERA
1993	Boston (A)	11	8	0	3.42	29	184	70	184	77	103	$7.2	11	8	0	3.14
1994	Boston (A)	1	1	0	4.61	8	41	21	45	23	13	$1.4	1	1	0	4.65
1995	Cincinnati (N)	0	1	0	6.43	3	14	10	20	3	4	$0.4	0	1	0	6.28
1996	Toronto (A)	1	3	0	7.80	6	30	26	42	21	18	$0.3	1	3	0	7.71
	Career	176	150	0	4.36	423	2,847	1,380	2,996	949	2,147	$181.6	176	150	0	3.73
	Average season	12	10	0	4.36	28	190	92	200	63	143	$12.1	12	10	0	3.73
	Summit season	19	11	0	3.63	35	253	102	249	71	199	$19.4	19	11	0	3.10

PETE VUCKOVICH

		ADJUSTED REGULAR SEASON											ACTUAL RESULTS			
YEAR	TEAM	W	L	SV	ERA	G	IP	ER	H	BB	SO	PAY	W	L	SV	ERA
1975	Chicago (A)	0	1	0	16.20	4	10	18	18	7	6	$0.0	0	1	0	13.06
1976	Chicago (A)	7	4	0	6.05	33	110	74	131	68	84	$3.6	7	4	0	4.65
1977	Toronto (A)	7	7	10	3.95	53	148	65	147	65	152	$5.4	7	7	8	3.47
1978	St. Louis (N)	12	12	1	3.18	45	198	70	199	65	197	$8.1	12	12	1	2.54
1979	St. Louis (N)	15	10	0	4.13	34	233	107	235	70	195	$15.0	15	10	0	3.59
1980	St. Louis (N)	12	9	1	4.05	32	222	100	209	78	178	$9.9	12	9	1	3.40
1981	Milwaukee (A)	21	6	0	4.52	36	225	113	222	97	173	$16.0	14	4	0	3.55
1982	Milwaukee (A)	18	6	0	3.98	30	224	99	245	117	138	$15.7	18	6	0	3.34
1983	Milwaukee (A)	0	2	0	6.00	3	15	10	16	11	13	$1.8	0	2	0	4.91
1985	Milwaukee (A)	6	10	0	6.45	22	113	81	143	52	68	$4.2	6	10	0	5.51
1986	Milwaukee (A)	2	4	0	3.66	6	32	13	35	12	13	$0.9	2	4	0	3.06
	Career	100	71	12	4.41	298	1,530	750	1,600	642	1,217	$80.6	93	69	10	3.66
	Average season	9	6	1	4.41	27	139	68	145	58	111	$7.3	8	6	1	3.66
	Summit season	16	9	0	4.01	35	220	98	222	85	176	$12.9	14	8	0	3.29

RUBE WADDELL

		ADJUSTED REGULAR SEASON											ACTUAL RESULTS			
YEAR	TEAM	W	L	SV	ERA	G	IP	ER	H	BB	SO	PAY	W	L	SV	ERA
1897	Louisville (N)	0	1	0	3.21	2	14	5	15	7	13	$0.0	0	1	0	3.21
1899	Louisville (N)	7	2	1	3.65	10	79	32	64	18	108	$3.4	7	2	1	3.08
1900	Pittsburgh (N)	9	15	0	2.90	34	245	79	194	84	341	$9.4	8	13	0	2.37
1901	Pit.-Chi. (N)	16	19	0	3.95	36	292	128	280	125	364	$19.8	14	16	0	3.01
1902	Philadelphia (A)	28	8	0	2.94	39	327	107	266	109	459	$41.6	24	7	0	2.05
1903	Philadelphia (A)	25	19	0	3.58	46	382	152	332	147	558	$55.3	21	16	0	2.44
1904	Philadelphia (A)	26	20	0	2.77	48	400	123	359	150	559	$58.7	25	19	0	1.62
1905	Philadelphia (A)	29	11	0	2.39	49	350	93	275	136	463	$56.1	27	10	0	1.48
1906	Philadelphia (A)	16	19	0	3.81	47	298	126	275	142	345	$34.1	15	17	0	2.21
1907	Philadelphia (A)	21	14	0	3.94	48	311	136	294	114	413	$41.9	19	13	0	2.15
1908	St. Louis (A)	20	15	8	3.64	45	299	121	280	144	389	$39.1	19	14	3	1.89
1909	St. Louis (A)	12	15	0	4.29	33	235	112	255	83	246	$17.7	11	14	0	2.37
1910	St. Louis (A)	3	1	3	5.73	10	33	21	35	13	27	$2.4	3	1	1	3.55
	Career	212	159	12	3.40	447	3,265	1,235	2,924	1,272	4,285	$379.5	193	143	5	2.16
	Average season	16	12	1	3.40	34	251	95	225	98	330	$29.2	15	11	0	2.16
	Summit season	26	15	2	3.04	45	352	119	302	137	486	$50.2	23	13	1	1.88

ED WALSH

		ADJUSTED REGULAR SEASON											ACTUAL RESULTS			
YEAR	TEAM	W	L	SV	ERA	G	IP	ER	H	BB	SO	PAY	W	L	SV	ERA
1904	Chicago (A)	6	3	8	4.46	19	117	58	107	53	101	$5.2	6	3	1	2.60
1905	Chicago (A)	8	3	0	3.52	23	143	56	142	43	121	$5.5	8	3	0	2.17
1906	Chicago (A)	18	14	8	3.21	43	292	104	257	85	297	$25.6	17	13	2	1.88
1907	Chicago (A)	25	19	11	2.90	58	437	141	405	128	380	$55.0	24	18	4	1.60
1908	Chicago (A)	42	16	10	2.71	69	485	146	429	88	480	$67.8	40	15	6	1.42
1909	Chicago (A)	15	11	5	2.53	32	238	67	201	70	220	$26.8	15	11	2	1.41
1910	Chicago (A)	19	21	6	2.08	47	386	89	287	76	427	$56.2	18	20	5	1.27
1911	Chicago (A)	28	19	10	2.99	59	388	129	359	85	414	$58.9	27	18	4	2.22
1912	Chicago (A)	28	18	16	2.90	64	406	131	352	110	410	$59.0	27	17	10	2.15
1913	Chicago (A)	9	3	3	3.81	17	104	44	106	50	64	$7.2	8	3	1	2.58
1914	Chicago (A)	2	3	0	4.40	8	45	22	37	24	26	$2.8	2	3	0	2.82
1915	Chicago (A)	3	0	0	2.00	3	27	6	22	8	21	$1.9	3	0	0	1.33
1916	Chicago (A)	0	1	0	6.00	2	3	2	4	3	4	$0.0	0	1	0	2.70
1917	Boston (N)	0	1	0	6.00	4	18	12	25	12	8	$0.0	0	1	0	3.50
	Career	203	132	77	2.93	448	3,089	1,007	2,733	835	2,973	$371.9	195	126	35	1.82
	Average season	15	9	6	2.93	32	221	72	195	60	212	$26.6	14	9	3	1.82
	Summit season	28	19	11	2.72	59	420	127	366	97	422	$59.4	27	18	6	1.72

BUCKY WALTERS

		ADJUSTED REGULAR SEASON											ACTUAL RESULTS			
YEAR	TEAM	W	L	SV	ERA	G	IP	ER	H	BB	SO	PAY	W	L	SV	ERA
1934	Philadelphia (N)	0	0	0	1.29	2	7	1	8	2	11	$0.0	0	0	0	1.29
1935	Philadelphia (N)	9	9	0	4.53	25	157	79	165	79	86	$4.2	9	9	0	4.17
1936	Philadelphia (N)	12	22	0	4.28	42	271	129	274	127	141	$9.6	11	21	0	4.26
1937	Philadelphia (N)	15	16	0	5.09	39	260	147	295	94	166	$15.0	14	15	0	4.75
1938	Phi.-Cin. (N)	16	15	3	4.47	42	270	134	269	117	190	$19.1	15	14	1	4.20
1939	Cincinnati (N)	28	12	0	2.44	41	335	91	253	118	266	$40.3	27	11	0	2.29
1940	Cincinnati (N)	23	11	0	2.74	38	322	98	252	103	217	$33.6	22	10	0	2.48
1941	Cincinnati (N)	20	16	2	3.31	39	318	117	314	92	247	$32.1	19	15	2	2.83
1942	Cincinnati (N)	16	15	0	3.48	36	269	104	254	81	218	$24.6	15	14	0	2.66
1943	Cincinnati (N)	16	16	0	4.86	36	261	141	280	124	164	$18.4	15	15	0	3.54
1944	Cincinnati (N)	24	8	3	3.10	36	302	104	256	104	168	$25.8	23	8	1	2.40
1945	Cincinnati (N)	10	10	0	3.43	23	176	67	181	57	98	$6.2	10	10	0	2.68
1946	Cincinnati (N)	10	7	0	3.36	23	158	59	163	67	105	$6.0	10	7	0	2.56
1947	Cincinnati (N)	8	8	0	6.82	21	128	97	150	49	80	$3.8	8	8	0	5.75
1948	Cincinnati (N)	0	3	0	5.14	7	35	20	43	16	33	$0.9	0	3	0	4.63
1950	Boston (N)	0	0	0	4.50	1	4	2	5	2	0	$0.0	0	0	0	4.50
	Career	207	168	8	3.82	451	3,273	1,390	3,162	1,232	2,190	$239.6	198	160	4	3.30
	Average season	13	11	1	3.82	28	205	87	198	77	137	$15.0	12	10	0	3.30
	Summit season	22	12	1	3.00	38	309	103	266	100	223	$31.3	21	12	1	2.53

LON WARNEKE

YEAR	TEAM	ADJUSTED REGULAR SEASON											ACTUAL RESULTS			
		W	L	SV	ERA	G	IP	ER	H	BB	SO	PAY	W	L	SV	ERA
1930	Chicago (N)	0	0	0	36.00	1	1	4	1	4	0	$0.0	0	0	0	33.75
1931	Chicago (N)	2	4	0	3.57	21	68	27	67	45	57	$1.6	2	4	0	3.22
1932	Chicago (N)	23	6	0	2.58	37	293	84	248	79	227	$19.2	22	6	0	2.37
1933	Chicago (N)	19	14	2	2.41	38	303	81	273	94	287	$25.6	18	13	1	2.00
1934	Chicago (N)	24	11	7	3.43	46	312	119	274	78	278	$33.5	22	10	3	3.21
1935	Chicago (N)	21	14	7	3.28	44	274	100	254	58	242	$32.7	20	13	4	3.06
1936	Chicago (N)	17	14	3	3.46	42	252	97	237	83	224	$25.9	16	13	1	3.45
1937	St. Louis (N)	19	11	0	4.85	37	245	132	275	73	160	$20.2	18	11	0	4.53
1938	St. Louis (N)	13	8	0	4.26	32	203	96	198	66	170	$15.3	13	8	0	3.97
1939	St. Louis (N)	14	7	5	4.03	36	172	77	165	53	118	$9.6	13	7	2	3.78
1940	St. Louis (N)	16	10	0	3.50	34	239	93	241	51	157	$15.9	16	10	0	3.14
1941	St. Louis (N)	18	9	0	3.68	39	259	106	244	86	163	$17.7	17	9	0	3.15
1942	St.L.-Chi. (N)	11	11	4	3.59	28	188	75	193	39	119	$8.2	11	11	2	2.73
1943	Chicago (N)	4	5	0	4.35	22	93	45	93	20	61	$4.0	4	5	0	3.16
1945	Chicago (N)	0	1	0	5.14	9	14	8	17	1	12	$0.7	0	1	0	3.86
	Career	201	125	28	3.53	466	2,916	1,144	2,780	830	2,275	$230.1	192	121	13	3.18
	Average season	13	8	2	3.53	31	194	76	185	55	152	$15.3	13	8	1	3.18
	Summit season	21	12	4	3.01	41	287	96	257	78	252	$27.4	20	11	2	2.80

BOB WELCH

YEAR	TEAM	ADJUSTED REGULAR SEASON											ACTUAL RESULTS			
		W	L	SV	ERA	G	IP	ER	H	BB	SO	PAY	W	L	SV	ERA
1978	Los Angeles (N)	7	4	4	2.51	23	111	31	98	29	89	$5.0	7	4	3	2.02
1979	Los Angeles (N)	5	6	6	4.56	25	81	41	84	35	84	$4.3	5	6	5	3.98
1980	Los Angeles (N)	14	9	0	3.91	32	214	93	196	91	189	$9.5	14	9	0	3.29
1981	Los Angeles (N)	13	7	0	4.39	34	209	102	225	69	177	$9.4	9	5	0	3.44
1982	Los Angeles (N)	16	11	0	4.00	36	236	105	208	92	225	$15.7	16	11	0	3.36
1983	Los Angeles (N)	15	12	0	3.13	31	204	71	171	80	194	$10.2	15	12	0	2.65
1984	Los Angeles (N)	13	13	0	4.53	31	179	90	200	66	153	$9.6	13	13	0	3.78
1985	Los Angeles (N)	14	4	0	2.69	23	167	50	149	38	117	$8.5	14	4	0	2.31
1986	Los Angeles (N)	7	13	0	3.78	33	236	99	241	58	203	$9.9	7	13	0	3.28
1987	Los Angeles (N)	15	9	0	3.43	35	252	96	210	90	213	$15.9	15	9	0	3.22
1988	Oakland (A)	17	9	0	4.48	36	245	122	256	94	186	$14.6	17	9	0	3.64
1989	Oakland (A)	17	8	0	3.73	33	210	87	206	87	159	$8.9	17	8	0	3.00
1990	Oakland (A)	27	6	0	3.48	35	238	92	226	83	147	$18.8	27	6	0	2.95
1991	Oakland (A)	12	13	0	5.36	35	220	131	236	98	115	$9.0	12	13	0	4.58
1992	Oakland (A)	11	7	0	3.99	20	124	55	123	48	56	$3.8	11	7	0	3.27
1993	Oakland (A)	9	11	0	5.82	30	167	108	213	60	72	$5.6	9	11	0	5.29
1994	Oakland (A)	4	9	0	7.18	36	99	79	114	64	67	$2.9	3	6	0	7.08
	Career	216	151	10	4.09	528	3,192	1,452	3,156	1,182	2,446	$161.6	211	146	8	3.47
	Average season	13	9	1	4.09	31	188	85	186	70	144	$9.5	12	9	0	3.47
	Summit season	18	8	0	3.32	31	214	79	192	76	166	$12.5	18	8	0	2.87

MICKEY WELCH

		ADJUSTED REGULAR SEASON											ACTUAL RESULTS			
YEAR	TEAM	W	L	SV	ERA	G	IP	ER	H	BB	SO	PAY	W	L	SV	ERA
1880	Troy (N)	66	59	0	4.94	127	1,122	616	1,185	517	540	$130.4	34	30	0	2.54
1881	Troy (N)	40	34	0	4.39	76	699	341	689	349	485	$95.1	21	18	0	2.67
1882	Troy (N)	27	31	0	5.68	63	536	338	652	306	236	$71.8	14	16	0	3.46
1883	New York (N)	41	38	0	3.86	89	702	301	689	258	458	$87.5	25	23	0	2.73
1884	New York (N)	55	29	0	3.67	91	780	318	776	449	634	$97.5	39	21	0	2.50
1885	New York (N)	64	16	1	2.48	81	712	196	570	340	624	$98.1	44	11	1	1.66
1886	New York (N)	43	29	0	4.04	77	653	293	710	281	523	$89.7	33	22	0	2.99
1887	New York (N)	28	19	0	3.66	50	433	176	399	138	325	$67.9	22	15	0	3.36
1888	New York (N)	30	22	0	2.96	55	498	164	425	206	336	$69.7	26	19	0	1.93
1889	New York (N)	34	15	6	3.51	56	467	182	415	193	286	$65.1	27	12	2	3.02
1890	New York (N)	20	17	0	3.52	44	348	136	316	140	223	$42.9	17	14	0	2.99
1891	New York (N)	6	11	7	5.57	26	189	117	214	111	104	$8.9	5	9	1	4.28
1892	New York (N)	0	0	0	19.80	1	5	11	12	4	2	$1.6	0	0	0	14.40
	Career	454	320	14	4.02	836	7,144	3,189	7,052	3,292	4,776	$926.2	307	210	4	2.71
	Average season	35	25	1	4.02	64	550	245	542	253	367	$71.2	24	16	0	2.71
	Summit season	54	34	0	3.91	93	794	345	786	369	556	$100.6	35	21	0	2.48

JOHN WETTELAND

		ADJUSTED REGULAR SEASON											ACTUAL RESULTS			
YEAR	TEAM	W	L	SV	ERA	G	IP	ER	H	BB	SO	PAY	W	L	SV	ERA
1989	Los Angeles (N)	5	8	1	4.63	31	103	53	88	38	110	$4.2	5	8	1	3.77
1990	Los Angeles (N)	2	4	0	5.65	22	43	27	47	18	41	$1.4	2	4	0	4.81
1991	Los Angeles (N)	1	0	0	0.00	6	9	0	5	3	10	$0.0	1	0	0	0.00
1992	Montreal (N)	4	4	36	3.58	67	83	33	68	40	111	$5.0	4	4	37	2.92
1993	Montreal (N)	9	3	42	1.48	70	85	14	59	30	122	$7.7	9	3	43	1.37
1994	Montreal (N)	6	9	35	2.87	74	91	29	66	31	102	$7.9	4	6	25	2.83
1995	New York (A)	1	6	34	3.04	67	68	23	45	16	76	$5.3	1	5	31	2.93
1996	New York (A)	2	3	43	2.81	62	64	20	54	21	70	$5.4	2	3	43	2.83
1997	Texas (A)	7	2	31	2.08	61	65	15	44	22	62	$5.2	7	2	31	1.94
1998	Texas (A)	3	1	41	2.03	63	62	14	48	15	71	$4.3	3	1	42	2.03
1999	Texas (A)	4	4	43	3.55	62	66	26	66	18	61	$4.5	4	4	43	3.68
2000	Texas (A)	6	5	34	4.05	62	60	27	66	23	53	$4.1	6	5	34	4.20
	Career	50	49	340	3.17	647	799	281	656	275	889	$55.0	48	45	330	2.93
	Average season	4	4	28	3.17	54	67	23	55	23	74	$4.6	4	4	28	2.93
	Summit season	5	4	38	2.22	66	73	18	54	24	85	$6.1	5	3	37	2.15

GUS WEYHING

		ADJUSTED REGULAR SEASON											ACTUAL RESULTS			
YEAR	TEAM	W	L	SV	ERA	G	IP	ER	H	BB	SO	PAY	W	L	SV	ERA
1887	Philadelphia (AA)	31	33	0	4.67	65	551	286	516	240	499	$71.1	26	28	0	4.27
1888	Philadelphia (AA)	33	21	0	3.48	56	481	186	414	216	407	$66.0	28	18	0	2.25
1889	Philadelphia (AA)	35	25	0	3.42	63	524	199	436	259	441	$70.3	30	21	0	2.95
1890	Brooklyn (P)	37	20	0	4.24	60	478	225	510	211	402	$67.8	30	16	0	3.60
1891	Philadelphia (AA)	35	23	0	4.10	59	511	233	497	176	449	$70.6	31	20	0	3.18
1892	Philadelphia (N)	34	22	5	3.70	62	494	203	461	184	411	$69.4	32	21	3	2.66
1893	Philadelphia (N)	28	19	0	4.66	51	419	217	438	159	358	$61.4	23	16	0	4.74
1894	Philadelphia (N)	20	18	7	5.01	48	336	187	372	138	297	$52.3	16	14	1	5.81
1895	Phi.-Pit.-Lou. (N)	10	25	0	5.58	37	276	171	324	108	203	$26.0	8	21	0	5.81
1896	Louisville (N)	2	4	0	7.02	6	50	39	65	20	31	$3.1	2	3	0	6.64
1898	Washington (N)	16	27	0	5.78	47	377	242	438	109	265	$30.9	15	26	0	4.51
1899	Washington (N)	18	22	0	5.43	45	350	211	403	101	293	$25.7	17	21	0	4.54
1900	St.L.-Bkn. (N)	7	7	0	5.55	17	107	66	134	61	46	$3.5	6	6	0	4.47
1901	Cle. (A)-Cin. (N)	0	1	0	7.65	3	20	17	30	10	7	$1.1	0	1	0	5.75
	Career	306	267	12	4.49	619	4,974	2,482	5,038	1,992	4,109	$619.2	264	232	4	3.89
	Average season	22	19	1	4.49	44	355	177	360	142	294	$44.2	19	17	0	3.89
	Summit season	35	22	1	3.78	60	498	209	464	209	422	$68.8	30	19	1	2.92

HOYT WILHELM

		ADJUSTED REGULAR SEASON											ACTUAL RESULTS			
YEAR	TEAM	W	L	SV	ERA	G	IP	ER	H	BB	SO	PAY	W	L	SV	ERA
1952	New York (N)	16	3	24	3.00	75	168	56	145	61	170	$19.6	15	3	11	2.43
1953	New York (N)	7	8	28	3.34	71	151	56	135	81	115	$15.0	7	8	15	3.04
1954	New York (N)	13	4	14	2.46	60	117	32	85	54	103	$9.5	12	4	7	2.10
1955	New York (N)	4	1	0	4.50	62	108	54	115	41	106	$4.8	4	1	0	3.93
1956	New York (N)	4	9	16	4.40	67	94	46	108	44	100	$4.6	4	9	8	3.83
1957	St.L. (N)-Cle. (A)	2	4	19	4.87	44	61	33	60	25	41	$2.6	2	4	12	4.14
1958	Cle.-Balt. (A)	3	11	8	2.74	41	138	42	106	51	125	$4.1	3	10	5	2.34
1959	Baltimore (A)	15	11	0	2.55	33	233	66	194	86	182	$7.5	15	11	0	2.19
1960	Baltimore (A)	12	8	11	3.97	43	154	68	141	43	140	$6.1	11	8	7	3.31
1961	Baltimore (A)	9	7	23	2.62	51	110	32	94	42	106	$5.8	9	7	18	2.30
1962	Baltimore (A)	7	10	19	2.23	52	93	23	67	36	105	$5.7	7	10	15	1.94
1963	Chicago (A)	5	8	26	3.51	55	136	53	118	36	124	$6.1	5	8	21	2.64
1964	Chicago (A)	12	9	32	2.54	73	131	37	102	36	105	$7.2	12	9	27	1.99
1965	Chicago (A)	7	7	24	2.38	66	144	38	99	37	116	$6.9	7	7	20	1.81
1966	Chicago (A)	5	2	7	2.11	46	81	19	55	21	68	$3.4	5	2	6	1.66
1967	Chicago (A)	8	3	15	1.82	49	89	18	66	41	82	$3.8	8	3	12	1.31
1968	Chicago (A)	4	4	18	2.68	72	94	28	82	31	80	$3.5	4	4	12	1.73
1969	Cal. (A)-Atl. (N)	7	7	18	2.77	52	78	24	56	23	75	$3.3	7	7	14	2.19
1970	Atl.-Chi. (N)	6	5	15	4.06	53	82	37	79	43	76	$3.4	6	5	13	3.40
1971	Atl.-L.A. (N)	0	1	4	3.60	12	20	8	13	6	19	$0.9	0	1	3	2.70
1972	Los Angeles (N)	0	1	1	6.33	17	27	19	24	18	11	$0.5	0	1	1	4.62
	Career	146	123	322	3.08	1,094	2,309	789	1,944	856	2,049	$124.3	143	122	227	2.52
	Average season	7	6	15	3.08	52	110	38	93	41	98	$5.9	7	6	11	2.52
	Summit season	11	6	23	2.62	65	134	39	105	46	120	$9.8	11	6	17	2.13

VIC WILLIS

		ADJUSTED REGULAR SEASON											ACTUAL RESULTS			
YEAR	TEAM	W	L	SV	ERA	G	IP	ER	H	BB	SO	PAY	W	L	SV	ERA
1898	Boston (N)	27	14	0	3.58	44	334	133	276	201	411	$53.8	25	13	0	2.84
1899	Boston (N)	28	8	6	2.93	43	359	117	268	157	352	$55.4	27	8	2	2.50
1900	Boston (N)	12	20	0	5.21	37	273	158	281	162	168	$25.9	10	17	0	4.19
1901	Boston (N)	23	20	0	3.08	44	354	121	293	129	306	$42.9	20	17	0	2.36
1902	Boston (N)	31	23	3	3.15	58	466	163	424	166	511	$63.5	27	20	3	2.20
1903	Boston (N)	14	21	0	4.39	38	320	156	303	149	256	$32.4	12	18	0	2.98
1904	Boston (N)	19	26	0	4.92	45	366	200	419	180	342	$42.8	18	25	0	2.85
1905	Boston (N)	13	30	0	5.21	43	359	208	402	160	262	$33.6	12	29	0	3.21
1906	Pittsburgh (N)	24	14	4	2.98	43	338	112	353	112	228	$33.8	23	13	1	1.73
1907	Pittsburgh (N)	22	11	4	4.26	40	300	142	275	101	202	$32.3	21	11	1	2.34
1908	Pittsburgh (N)	24	12	0	3.99	43	320	142	301	110	186	$31.8	23	11	0	2.07
1909	Pittsburgh (N)	23	12	4	4.04	41	305	137	300	119	177	$32.0	22	11	1	2.24
1910	St. Louis (N)	10	13	9	5.56	35	225	139	272	78	123	$14.5	9	12	3	3.35
	Career	270	224	30	4.02	554	4,319	1,928	4,167	1,824	3,524	$494.7	249	205	11	2.63
	Average season	21	17	2	4.02	43	332	148	321	140	271	$38.1	19	16	1	2.63
	Summit season	27	16	3	3.14	46	370	129	323	153	362	$49.9	24	14	1	2.32

JOE WOOD

		ADJUSTED REGULAR SEASON											ACTUAL RESULTS			
YEAR	TEAM	W	L	SV	ERA	G	IP	ER	H	BB	SO	PAY	W	L	SV	ERA
1908	Boston (A)	1	1	0	4.70	6	23	12	17	25	19	$0.0	1	1	0	2.38
1909	Boston (A)	12	8	0	3.93	26	174	76	153	64	159	$5.5	11	7	0	2.18
1910	Boston (A)	12	13	0	2.81	36	202	63	182	69	233	$8.4	12	13	0	1.69
1911	Boston (A)	25	18	3	2.72	47	294	89	251	91	368	$32.2	23	17	3	2.02
1912	Boston (A)	36	5	2	2.58	45	360	103	287	97	413	$55.1	34	5	1	1.91
1913	Boston (A)	12	5	5	3.42	25	158	60	142	80	207	$15.8	11	5	2	2.29
1914	Boston (A)	10	3	0	4.14	18	113	52	105	41	105	$8.5	10	3	0	2.62
1915	Boston (A)	16	5	4	2.36	26	164	43	142	55	113	$10.0	15	5	2	1.49
1917	Cleveland (A)	0	1	2	5.63	5	16	10	20	9	4	$1.4	0	1	1	3.45
1919	Cleveland (A)	0	0	1	0.00	1	1	0	0	0	0	$0.4	0	0	1	0.00
1920	Cleveland (A)	0	0	0	31.50	1	2	7	4	3	2	$0.0	0	0	0	22.50
	Career	124	59	17	3.08	236	1,507	515	1,303	534	1,623	$137.3	117	57	10	2.03
	Average season	11	5	2	3.08	21	137	47	118	49	148	$12.5	11	5	1	2.03
	Summit season	20	9	3	2.75	36	236	72	201	78	267	$24.3	19	9	2	1.89

WHIT WYATT

		ADJUSTED REGULAR SEASON											ACTUAL RESULTS			
YEAR	TEAM	W	L	SV	ERA	G	IP	ER	H	BB	SO	PAY	W	L	SV	ERA
1929	Detroit (A)	0	1	0	6.84	4	25	19	27	19	28	$0.0	0	1	0	6.75
1930	Detroit (A)	4	5	6	3.40	22	90	34	71	42	123	$3.7	4	5	2	3.57
1931	Detroit (A)	0	2	0	9.90	4	20	22	28	14	16	$0.1	0	2	0	8.85
1932	Detroit (A)	10	14	4	5.52	46	220	135	232	128	176	$7.6	9	13	1	5.03
1933	Det.-Chi. (A)	3	5	4	5.48	38	110	67	115	68	88	$4.0	3	5	1	4.56

(Whit Wyatt, continued)

		ADJUSTED REGULAR SEASON											ACTUAL RESULTS			
YEAR	TEAM	W	L	SV	ERA	G	IP	ER	H	BB	SO	PAY	W	L	SV	ERA
1934	Chicago (A)	4	11	5	7.73	24	71	61	82	43	68	$3.2	4	11	2	7.18
1935	Chicago (A)	4	3	14	7.36	32	55	45	65	30	45	$2.9	4	3	5	6.75
1936	Chicago (A)	0	0	2	0.00	3	3	0	3	0	0	$0.0	0	0	1	0.00
1937	Cleveland (A)	2	3	0	4.74	30	76	40	67	43	88	$3.1	2	3	0	4.44
1939	Brooklyn (N)	9	3	0	2.48	17	116	32	91	43	101	$3.8	8	3	0	2.31
1940	Brooklyn (N)	15	14	0	3.84	38	246	105	238	68	220	$8.6	15	14	0	3.46
1941	Brooklyn (N)	23	10	3	2.74	39	296	90	233	84	311	$25.1	22	10	1	2.34
1942	Brooklyn (N)	20	7	0	3.58	32	224	89	205	68	199	$17.6	19	7	0	2.73
1943	Brooklyn (N)	15	5	0	3.42	28	195	74	162	50	161	$12.7	14	5	0	2.49
1944	Brooklyn (N)	2	6	0	9.24	9	38	39	53	18	9	$1.7	2	6	0	7.17
1945	Philadelphia (N)	0	8	0	6.75	11	56	42	82	16	23	$1.3	0	7	0	5.26
	Career	111	97	38	4.37	377	1,841	894	1,754	734	1,656	$95.4	106	95	13	3.79
	Average season	7	6	2	4.37	24	115	56	110	46	104	$6.0	7	6	1	3.79
	Summit season	16	8	1	3.27	31	215	78	186	63	198	$13.6	16	8	0	2.71

EARLY WYNN

		ADJUSTED REGULAR SEASON											ACTUAL RESULTS			
YEAR	TEAM	W	L	SV	ERA	G	IP	ER	H	BB	SO	PAY	W	L	SV	ERA
1939	Washington (A)	0	2	0	6.30	3	20	14	25	10	2	$0.0	0	2	0	5.75
1941	Washington (A)	3	1	0	1.80	5	40	8	36	10	27	$0.6	3	1	0	1.58
1942	Washington (A)	11	17	0	6.74	32	203	152	284	82	122	$5.4	10	16	0	5.12
1943	Washington (A)	19	13	0	3.99	39	271	120	265	94	181	$15.7	18	12	0	2.91
1944	Washington (A)	8	18	5	4.38	35	220	107	243	80	140	$8.5	8	17	2	3.38
1946	Washington (A)	8	5	0	4.14	18	113	52	126	35	65	$5.2	8	5	0	3.11
1947	Washington (A)	18	16	0	4.29	35	262	125	277	91	140	$16.1	17	15	0	3.64
1948	Washington (A)	8	20	0	6.47	35	210	151	257	91	97	$7.7	8	19	0	5.82
1949	Cleveland (A)	11	7	0	4.63	27	171	88	199	52	116	$7.9	11	7	0	4.15
1950	Cleveland (A)	19	8	0	3.35	33	220	82	172	92	233	$15.9	18	8	0	3.20
1951	Cleveland (A)	21	14	2	3.39	39	289	109	248	108	239	$26.0	20	13	1	3.02
1952	Cleveland (A)	24	13	4	3.58	44	299	119	271	140	246	$31.2	23	12	3	2.90
1953	Cleveland (A)	18	13	0	4.33	38	266	128	252	115	225	$24.6	17	12	0	3.93
1954	Cleveland (A)	24	12	3	3.20	42	284	101	247	85	251	$31.6	23	11	2	2.73
1955	Cleveland (A)	18	12	0	3.21	34	244	87	232	82	190	$18.9	17	11	0	2.82
1956	Cleveland (A)	21	9	4	3.14	40	292	102	259	94	231	$29.1	20	9	2	2.72
1957	Cleveland (A)	15	18	2	5.15	42	276	158	301	119	257	$23.2	14	17	1	4.31
1958	Chicago (A)	15	17	3	4.89	42	252	137	238	119	242	$17.1	14	16	2	4.13
1959	Chicago (A)	23	10	0	3.70	38	263	108	220	133	232	$23.3	22	10	0	3.17
1960	Chicago (A)	14	13	2	4.20	38	251	117	250	126	209	$16.5	13	12	1	3.49
1961	Chicago (A)	8	2	0	4.01	17	110	49	92	48	79	$3.8	8	2	0	3.51
1962	Chicago (A)	7	15	0	5.14	27	168	96	181	59	110	$5.7	7	15	0	4.46
1963	Cleveland (A)	1	2	1	2.95	20	55	18	56	18	33	$1.3	1	2	1	2.28
	Career	314	257	26	4.20	723	4,779	2,228	4,731	1,883	3,667	$335.3	300	244	15	3.54
	Average season	14	11	1	4.20	31	208	97	206	82	159	$14.6	13	11	1	3.54
	Summit season	23	12	3	3.41	41	285	108	249	112	240	$28.2	22	11	2	2.90

CY YOUNG

		ADJUSTED REGULAR SEASON											ACTUAL RESULTS			
YEAR	TEAM	W	L	SV	ERA	G	IP	ER	H	BB	SO	PAY	W	L	SV	ERA
1890	Cleveland (N)	11	8	0	4.09	20	174	79	169	34	91	$5.9	9	7	0	3.47
1891	Cleveland (N)	31	25	6	3.67	63	485	198	505	154	316	$57.6	27	22	2	2.85
1892	Cleveland (N)	38	13	0	2.65	56	479	141	408	129	349	$63.4	36	12	0	1.93
1893	Cleveland (N)	43	20	3	3.27	67	534	194	504	116	389	$71.4	34	16	1	3.36
1894	Cleveland (N)	33	26	4	3.36	65	511	191	491	124	403	$70.7	26	21	1	3.94
1895	Cleveland (N)	43	12	0	3.10	58	456	157	379	99	400	$70.6	35	10	0	3.26
1896	Cleveland (N)	33	18	9	3.38	61	496	186	505	83	456	$72.2	28	15	3	3.24
1897	Cleveland (N)	26	23	0	4.01	56	408	182	418	70	293	$59.6	21	19	0	3.79
1898	Cleveland (N)	26	14	0	3.20	48	394	140	394	53	288	$57.7	25	13	0	2.53
1899	St. Louis (N)	27	17	1	3.05	46	386	131	356	58	335	$54.4	26	16	1	2.58
1900	St. Louis (N)	22	22	0	3.69	47	368	151	363	53	337	$50.7	19	19	0	3.00
1901	Boston (A)	38	12	0	2.10	50	432	101	363	61	366	$59.8	33	10	0	1.62
1902	Boston (A)	38	13	0	3.08	53	453	155	414	90	395	$62.8	32	11	0	2.15
1903	Boston (A)	32	10	3	3.05	46	393	133	348	62	353	$56.0	28	9	2	2.08
1904	Boston (A)	27	16	1	3.35	44	389	145	375	46	344	$55.0	26	16	1	1.97
1905	Boston (A)	19	20	0	2.96	40	338	111	293	44	352	$48.4	18	19	0	1.82
1906	Boston (A)	14	22	4	5.51	41	302	185	345	37	251	$29.5	13	21	2	3.19
1907	Boston (A)	22	16	5	3.64	45	359	145	343	76	278	$38.4	21	15	2	1.99
1908	Boston (A)	22	12	3	2.42	38	316	85	292	59	276	$30.5	21	11	2	1.26
1909	Cleveland (A)	20	16	0	4.07	37	312	141	331	85	202	$29.1	19	15	0	2.26
1910	Cleveland (A)	7	10	0	4.20	21	163	76	170	32	99	$6.1	7	10	0	2.53
1911	Cle. (A)-Bos. (N)	7	10	0	5.14	19	133	76	151	33	94	$3.9	7	9	0	3.78
	Career	579	355	39	3.37	1,021	8,281	3,103	7,917	1,598	6,667	$1,053.7	511	316	17	2.63
	Average season	26	16	2	3.37	46	376	141	360	73	303	$47.9	23	14	1	2.63
	Summit season	40	14	1	2.87	57	471	150	414	99	380	$65.6	34	12	0	2.46

Photo Credits

AP/Wide World Photos: pp. 10, 22, 23, 261, 263, 268, 279, 288, 289, 295, 330

Major League Baseball: p.285

Transcendental Graphics: pp. 33, 35, 37, 40, 45, 255, 256, 257, 258, 264, 265, 269, 272, 273, 277, 280, 282, 286, 287, 291, 294, 307